Poetry
Criticism

Guide to Gale Literary Criticism Series

For criticism on	Consult these Gale series
Authors now living or who died after December 31, 1999	*CONTEMPORARY LITERARY CRITICISM (CLC)*
Authors who died between 1900 and 1999	*TWENTIETH-CENTURY LITERARY CRITICISM (TCLC)*
Authors who died between 1800 and 1899	*NINETEENTH-CENTURY LITERATURE CRITICISM (NCLC)*
Authors who died between 1400 and 1799	*LITERATURE CRITICISM FROM 1400 TO 1800 (LC)* *SHAKESPEAREAN CRITICISM (SC)*
Authors who died before 1400	*CLASSICAL AND MEDIEVAL LITERATURE CRITICISM (CMLC)*
Authors of books for children and young adults	*CHILDREN'S LITERATURE REVIEW (CLR)*
Dramatists	*DRAMA CRITICISM (DC)*
Poets	*POETRY CRITICISM (PC)*
Short story writers	*SHORT STORY CRITICISM (SSC)*
Literary topics and movements	*HARLEM RENAISSANCE: A GALE CRITICAL COMPANION (HR)* *THE BEAT GENERATION: A GALE CRITICAL COMPANION (BG)* *FEMINISM IN LITERATURE: A GALE CRITICAL COMPANION (FL)* *GOTHIC LITERATURE: A GALE CRITICAL COMPANION (GL)*
Asian American writers of the last two hundred years	*ASIAN AMERICAN LITERATURE (AAL)*
Black writers of the past two hundred years	*BLACK LITERATURE CRITICISM (BLC-1)* *BLACK LITERATURE CRITICISM SUPPLEMENT (BLCS)* *BLACK LITERATURE CRITICISM: CLASSIC AND EMERGING AUTHORS SINCE 1950 (BLC-2)*
Hispanic writers of the late nineteenth and twentieth centuries	*HISPANIC LITERATURE CRITICISM (HLC)* *HISPANIC LITERATURE CRITICISM SUPPLEMENT (HLCS)*
Native North American writers and orators of the eighteenth, nineteenth, and twentieth centuries	*NATIVE NORTH AMERICAN LITERATURE (NNAL)*
Major authors from the Renaissance to the present	*WORLD LITERATURE CRITICISM, 1500 TO THE PRESENT (WLC)* *WORLD LITERATURE CRITICISM SUPPLEMENT (WLCS)*

ISSN 1052-4851

Poetry Criticism

Excerpts from Criticism of the Works of the Most Significant and Widely Studied Poets of World Literature

Volume 109

Michelle Lee
Project Editor

GALE
CENGAGE Learning·

Detroit • New York • San Francisco • New Haven, Conn • Waterville, Maine • London

GALE
CENGAGE Learning™

Poetry Criticism, Vol. 109

Project Editor: Michelle Lee

Editorial: Dana Barnes, Sara Constantakis, Kathy D. Darrow, Kristen Dorsch, Dana Ferguson, Jeffrey W. Hunter, Michelle Kazensky, Jelena O. Krstović, Marie Toft, Lawrence J. Trudeau

Content Conversion: Katrina D. Coach, Gwen Tucker

Indexing Services: Factiva, Inc.

Rights and Acquisitions: Margaret Chamberlain-Gaston, Jackie Jones, and Barb McNeil

Composition and Electronic Capture: Gary Leach

Manufacturing: Rhonda Dover

Product Manager: Janet Witalec

For product information and technology assistance, contact us at
Gale Customer Support, 1-800-877-4253.
For permission to use material from this text or product,
submit all requests online at **www.cengage.com/permissions.**
Further permissions questions can be emailed to
permissionrequest@cengage.com

Gale
27500 Drake Rd.
Farmington Hills, MI, 48331-3535

LIBRARY OF CONGRESS CATALOG CARD NUMBER 81-640179

ISBN-13: 978-1-4144-5986-8
ISBN-10: 1-4144-5986-6

ISSN 1052-4851

Printed in the United States of America
1 2 3 4 5 6 7 14 13 12 11 10

Contents

Preface

*P*oetry Criticism (*PC*) presents significant criticism of the world's greatest poets and provides supplementary biographical and bibliographical material to guide the interested reader to a greater understanding of the genre and its creators. Although major poets and literary movements are covered in such Gale Literary Criticism series as *Contemporary Literary Criticism (CLC), Twentieth-Century Literary Criticism (TCLC), Nineteenth-Century Literature Criticism (NCLC), Literature Criticism from 1400 to 1800 (LC),* and *Classical and Medieval Literature Criticism (CMLC), PC* offers more focused attention on poetry than is possible in the broader, survey-oriented entries on writers in these Gale series. Students, teachers, librarians, and researchers will find that the generous excerpts and supplementary material provided by *PC* supply them with the vital information needed to write a term paper on poetic technique, to examine a poet's most prominent themes, or to lead a poetry discussion group.

Scope of the Series

PC is designed to serve as an introduction to major poets of all eras and nationalities. Since these authors have inspired a great deal of relevant critical material, *PC* is necessarily selective, and the editors have chosen the most important published criticism to aid readers and students in their research. Each author entry presents a historical survey of the critical response to that author's work. The length of an entry is intended to reflect the amount of critical attention the author has received from critics writing in English and from foreign critics in translation. Every attempt has been made to identify and include the most significant essays on each author's work. In order to provide these important critical pieces, the editors sometimes reprint essays that have appeared elsewhere in Gale's Literary Criticism Series. Such duplication, however, never exceeds twenty percent of a *PC* volume.

Organization of the Book

Each *PC* entry consists of the following elements:

- The **Author Heading** cites the name under which the author most commonly wrote, followed by birth and death dates. Also located here are any name variations under which an author wrote, including transliterated forms for authors whose native languages use nonroman alphabets. If the author wrote consistently under a pseudonym, the pseudonym will be listed in the author heading and the author's actual name given in parenthesis on the first line of the biographical and critical introduction. Uncertain birth or death dates are indicated by question marks. Single-work entries are preceded by the title of the work and its date of publication.

- The **Introduction** contains background information that introduces the reader to the author and the critical debates surrounding his or her work.

- The list of **Principal Works** is ordered chronologically by date of first publication and lists the most important works by the author. The first section comprises poetry collections and book-length poems. The second section gives information on other major works by the author. For foreign authors, the editors have provided original foreign-language publication information and have selected what are considered the best and most complete English-language editions of their works.

- Reprinted **Criticism** is arranged chronologically in each entry to provide a useful perspective on changes in critical evaluation over time. All individual titles of poems and poetry collections by the author featured in the entry are printed in boldface type. The critic's name and the date of composition or publication of the critical work are given at the beginning of each piece of criticism. Unsigned criticism is preceded by the title of the source in which it appeared. Footnotes are reprinted at the end of each essay or excerpt. In the case of excerpted criticism, only those footnotes that pertain to the excerpted texts are included.

- Critical essays are prefaced by brief **Annotations** explicating each piece.

- A complete **Bibliographical Citation** of the original essay or book precedes each piece of criticism.

- An annotated bibliography of **Further Reading** appears at the end of each entry and suggests resources for additional study. In some cases, significant essays for which the editors could not obtain reprint rights are included here. Boxed material following the further reading list provides references to other biographical and critical sources on the author in series published by Gale.

Cumulative Indexes

A **Cumulative Author Index** lists all of the authors that appear in a wide variety of reference sources published by Gale, including *PC*. A complete list of these sources is found facing the first page of the Author Index. The index also includes birth and death dates and cross references between pseudonyms and actual names.

A **Cumulative Nationality Index** lists all authors featured in *PC* by nationality, followed by the number of the *PC* volume in which their entry appears.

A **Cumulative Title Index** lists in alphabetical order all individual poems, book-length poems, and collection titles contained in the *PC* series. Titles of poetry collections and separately published poems are printed in italics, while titles of individual poems are printed in roman type with quotation marks. Each title is followed by the author's last name and corresponding volume and page numbers where commentary on the work is located. English-language translations of original foreign-language titles are cross-referenced to the foreign titles so that all references to discussion of a work are combined in one listing.

Citing *Poetry Criticism*

When citing criticism reprinted in the Literary Criticism Series, students should provide complete bibliographic information so that the cited essay can be located in the original print or electronic source. Students who quote directly from reprinted criticism may use any accepted bibliographic format, such as University of Chicago Press style or Modern Language Association (MLA) style. Both the MLA and the University of Chicago formats are acceptable and recognized as being the current standards for citations. It is important, however, to choose one format for all citations; do not mix the two formats within a list of citations.

The examples below follow recommendations for preparing a bibliography set forth in *The Chicago Manual of Style,* 14th ed. (Chicago: The University of Chicago Press, 1993); the first example pertains to material drawn from periodicals, the second to material reprinted from books:

Linkin, Harriet Kramer. "The Language of Speakers in *Songs of Innocence and of Experience*." *Romanticism Past and Present* 10, no. 2 (summer 1986): 5-24. Reprinted in *Poetry Criticism*. Vol. 63, edited by Michelle Lee, 79-88. Detroit: Thomson Gale, 2005.

Glen, Heather. "Blake's Criticism of Moral Thinking in *Songs of Innocence and of Experience.*" In *Interpreting Blake,* edited by Michael Phillips, 32-69. Cambridge: Cambridge University Press, 1978. Reprinted in *Poetry Criticism*. Vol. 63, edited by Michelle Lee, 34-51. Detroit: Thomson Gale, 2005.

Suggestions are Welcome

Readers who wish to suggest new features, topics, or authors to appear in future volumes, or who have other suggestions or comments are cordially invited to call, write, or fax the Associate Product Manager:

Product Manager, Literary Criticism Series
Gale
27500 Drake Road
Farmington Hills, MI 48331-3535
1-800-347-4253 (GALE)
Fax: 248-699-8054

Acknowledgments

The editors wish to thank the copyright holders of the criticism included in this volume and the permissions managers of many book and magazine publishing companies for assisting us in securing reproduction rights. Following is a list of the copyright holders who have granted us permission to reproduce material in this volume of *PC*. Every effort has been made to trace copyright, but if omissions have been made, please let us know.

COPYRIGHTED MATERIAL IN *PC*, VOLUME 109, WAS REPRODUCED FROM THE FOLLOWING PERIODICALS:

Arizona Quarterly, v. 56, spring, 2000 for "William Carlos Williams and the New World" by Jeff Webb. Copyright © 2000 by Arizona Board of Regents. The University of Arizona, Tucson, AZ 85721-0055. Equal Opportunity/Affirmative Action Employer. Reproduced by permission of the publisher and the author.—*Border Crossings,* v. 26, November, 2007. Reproduced by permission.—*Canadian Literature,* v. 34, autumn, 1967. All reproduced by permission of the author.— *Canadian Poetry,* v. 20, spring/summer, 1987; v. 38, spring/summer, 1996. All reproduced by permission.—*CEA Critic,* v. 61, winter and spring/summer, 1999 for "William Carlos Williams's Babel of Voices in the Long Poem 'The Desert Music'" by Glenn Sheldon. Copyright © 1999 by the College English Association, Inc. Reproduced by permission of the publisher and the author.—*Chicago Review,* v. 46, 2000; v. 53/54, summer, 2008. Copyright © 2000, 2008 by *Chicago Review.* All reproduced by permission.—*Contemporary Literature,* v. 40, autumn, 1999; v. 42, summer, 2001. Copyright © 1999, 2001 by the Board of Regents of the University of Wisconsin System. All reproduced by permission—*Denver Quarterly,* v. 36, spring/summer, 2001 for "Between the Gaps, the Silence and the Rubble: Susan Howe, Rosmarie Waldrop, and (Another) Pound Era" by David Clippinger. Reproduced by permission of the author; v. 40, 2006 for "Love, Like Sentences: An Interview with Rosmarie Waldrop" by Matthew Cooperman. Copyright © 2006 by the University of Denver. All rights reserved. Reproduced by permission of the author.—*differences,* v. 12, 2001, pp. 63-69. Copyright, 2001, Brown University and *differences: A Journal of Feminist Cultural Studies.* All rights reserved. Used by permission of the publisher, Duke University Press.—*Essays on Canadian Writing,* v. 69, winter, 1999. Copyright © 1999 Essays on Canadian Writing Ltd. All reproduced by permission.—*Journal of Modern Literature,* v. 29, fall, 2005; v. 30, fall, 2006; v. 30, spring, 2007. Copyright © 2005, 2006, 2007 Indiana University Press. All reproduced by permission.—*Language and Literature,* v. 14, 2005 for "Painting, Poetry, Parallelism: Ekphrasis, Stylistics and Cognitive Poetics" by Peter Verdonk. Copyright © 2005 by SAGE Publications. Reproduced by permission of the publisher and author.—*Literature and Medicine,* v. 23, fall, 2004. Copyright © 2004 by The Johns Hopkins University Press. Reproduced by permission.— *Literature & Theology,* v. 12, March, 1998 for "'I have seen the future brother: it is murder': Apocalypse Noir in Natural Born Killers and Leonard Cohen's 'The Future'" by Daniel C. Noel. Copyright © 1998 Oxford University Press. Reproduced by permission of the publisher and The Literary Estate of Daniel C. Noel.—*Maclean's,* v. 114, October 15, 2001. Copyright © 2001 by *Maclean's Magazine.* Reproduced by permission.—*Paideuma,* v. 32, spring, fall, and winter, 2003; v. 33, spring, 2004. All reproduced by permission of the author.—*Parnassus,* v. 15, 1989 for "An Ecstasy of Space (Jane Cooper, Rosmarie Waldrop)," pp. 231-239, by Rachel Hadas. Copyright © 1989 by Poetry in Review Foundation. All rights reserved. Reproduced by permission of the author.—*Saturday Night,* v. 111, March, 1996 for "Irving Layton, Leonard Cohen and Other Recurring Nightmares: While the Great Poets Embraced the World, Their Wives, Children and Lovers Kept Slipping Through the Ever-Widening Circle" by David Layton. Copyright © 1996 *Saturday Night.* Reproduced by permission of the author.—*Southern Review,* v. 36, summer, 2000 for "In Search of a Foot" by H. T. Kirby-Smith. Reproduced by permission of the author.—*Textual Practice,* v. 18, 2004 for "'What about all this writing?': Williams and Alternative Poetics" by Alan Golding. Copyright © 2004 Taylor & Francis Group, LLC. Reproduced by permission of Taylor & Francis, Ltd., http://www.tandf.co.uk/journals and the author.—*William Carlos Williams Review,* v. 24, fall, 2004; v. 26, spring, 2006. All reproduced by permission.

COPYRIGHTED MATERIAL IN *PC*, VOLUME 109, WAS REPRODUCED FROM THE FOLLOWING BOOKS:

Callan, Ron. From "William Carlos Williams's An Early Martyr: The Descent Beckons," in *Rebound: The American Poetry Book.* Edited by Michael Hinds and Stephen Matterson. Rodopi, 2004. Copyright © Editions Rodopi B.V., Amsterdam 2004. Reproduced by permission.—Hutcheon, Linda. From *ECW's Biographical Guide to Canadian Poets.* ECW

Gale Literature Product Advisory Board

The members of the Gale Literature Product Advisory Board—reference librarians from public and academic library systems—represent a cross-section of our customer base and offer a variety of informed perspectives on both the presentation and content of our literature products. Advisory board members assess and define such quality issues as the relevance, currency, and usefulness of the author coverage, critical content, and literary topics included in our series; evaluate the layout, presentation, and general quality of our printed volumes; provide feedback on the criteria used for selecting authors and topics covered in our series; provide suggestions for potential enhancements to our series; identify any gaps in our coverage of authors or literary topics, recommending authors or topics for inclusion; analyze the appropriateness of our content and presentation for various user audiences, such as high school students, undergraduates, graduate students, librarians, and educators; and offer feedback on any proposed changes/enhancements to our series. We wish to thank the following advisors for their advice throughout the year.

Leonard Cohen
1934-

Canadian poet, novelist, and songwriter.

INTRODUCTION

A popular poet and performer whose career has spanned more than fifty years, Cohen is known for pessimistic, gloomy lyrics that deal with religion, sexuality, and unhappy relationships. Known more for his music than his poetry, critics have often commented on the impossibility of separating the two facets of Cohen's career, and he himself has noted that the process he employs for writing poetry is identical to the one he uses to compose lyrics.

BIOGRAPHICAL INFORMATION

Cohen was born September 21, 1934, in Montreal, Quebec, into a middle-class Jewish family. His parents were Marsha Klinitsky Cohen, a nurse, and Nathan B. Cohen, the owner of a clothing store. His father died when Cohen was only nine years old, but he provided his son with a trust fund that, although modest, enabled Cohen as a young adult to pursue his literary and artistic ambitions. In his teen years, Cohen played piano, clarinet, and guitar and was part of a country-folk band known as the Buckskin Boys. He attended Herzliah High School and McGill University in Montreal, where he studied poetry. He graduated in 1955, spent one term in law school at McGill, followed by a year of study at Columbia University in 1956-57. During the early 1960s, Cohen spent most of his time on the Greek island of Hydra, although when he needed money, he would return to Canada to give poetry readings and musical performances. In 1965, the National Film Board of Canada produced a documentary on his life, increasing his visibility and provoking interest in his work in both Canada and the United States. Gaining recognition for his music as well as his poetry, Cohen began touring with his band and released his first album, *Songs of Leonard Cohen*, in 1968. He became notorious within the New York folk-rock community for self-destructive behavior involving alcohol and drugs, and for his reputation as a womanizer. His poetry began to suffer and in the late 1970s, Cohen suffered a nervous collapse. He did not recover professionally until the late 1980s with the release of his album *I'm Your Man*. In 1993, he entered a California Buddhist monastery where he remained for five years, apparently healthier both physically and emotionally when he emerged. He has continued to produce poetry and music and is today considered a pop icon, particularly in the world of music. In 2009, at the age of seventy-five, Cohen embarked on an extensive world tour.

MAJOR WORKS

Cohen published his first poetry collection, *Let Us Compare Mythologies,* in 1956 while still an undergraduate at McGill. It was followed by *The Spice-Box of Earth* in 1961. Both deal with the poet's thoughts on mythology and religion—both Christianity and Judaism—and their relationship to sexuality. His work became more political with the publication of *Flowers for Hitler* in 1964. Four years later, Cohen produced the highly acclaimed collection of his music, *Songs of Leonard Cohen.* Another book of poetry, *The Energy of Slaves* (1972), written during the time he was performing as a folk-rock musician, received very poor reviews, which precipitated the poet's emotional decline in the late 1970s. In 1978, he published *Death of a Lady's Man,* which features a dialogue between opposing points of view, described by Bruce Meyer and Brian O'Riordan as "a semi-climax in Cohen's poetic career, a moot-court where the inner tensions of the poet's persona are finally put to rest." Most of Cohen's energies from that point on were channeled into the production of music, and he published several collections of song lyrics over the next several years. The primary exception was the 1984 poetry volume *Book of Mercy,* an apparent attempt to reconcile Jewish and Christian mythologies. In 2006, Cohen published *Book of Longing,* containing poems based on his experience in the Buddhist retreat, and a year later collaborated with composer Philip Glass to set the lyrics of the book to music—also under the title *Book of Longing.*

CRITICAL RECEPTION

Cohen has been lauded for the diversity of his artistic endeavors and is today considered by many to be an iconic figure, particularly as a songwriter and musician. Over the course of his lengthy career—beginning with the publication of his first book in 1956 leading up to his current performance tour—he has attracted what many critics consider a cult following. Brian D. Johnson refers to Cohen as the Canadian answer to Bob Dylan, "a prophetic troubadour with an unlikely voice and a self-made persona." According to Johnson, "like Dylan, Cohen has found a new authority as a sage staring down the white tunnel." Stephen Scobie suggests that this "image of the romantic Leonard Cohen, brooding over his tortured soul with a succession of blonde young women on his arm" has now become inseparable from Cohen's work. Michael Q. Abraham considers Cohen "an enigmatic figure" based on the diversity exhibited in his work, as he moves "determinedly from poetry to prose to music," and achieves "national prominence in all three . . . allowing him to weave various and changing personae around himself."

Many critics have explored the themes related to religion and mythology that run throughout Cohen's poetry and prose. Meyer and O'Riordan contend that his poetry and novels exhibit a "transcendent quality," which Cohen achieves by "[relying] heavily on the tone and language of Judaeo-Christian mythology." Desmond Pacey reports that in Cohen's first volume of poetry, *Let Us Compare Mythologies,* "the quest for a lost or unknown God, mysterious, elusive, but compelling" appears, and it is a theme that repeats in most of Cohen's work. Abraham suggests that "Cohen's enigmatic inheritance" is "an almost genetic attachment to religion coupled with the grim knowledge that recent events [the Holocaust] have crippled its reliability." It is perhaps for this reason that Sandra Djwa finds that Cohen's poetry often concerns itself with a "descent into evil" that is apparently both frightening and exhilarating, but which will result in the creation of art. Djwa, however, contends that Cohen's poetry is "often too derivative to be impressive" and that "his mythologies are clever, often witty, sometimes very moving, yet even at its best, Cohen's favourite game is still Eliot's or Baudelaire's or Sartre's." Cohen has been heavily influenced by Baudelaire, as well as Rimbaud, according to Scobie, and Abraham reports that another critic has associated Cohen with such diverse influences as James Joyce and Mickey Spillane. Abraham, however, has studied the influence of A. M. Klein and Irving Layton on Cohen's work, and makes a case for both, concluding that "it is in Cohen's agonized struggle to fuse the influences of two of his literary mentors [Klein and Layton] that the impetus for much of his early poetry can be found." Norman Ravvin, however, suggests that the direct line of influence from Klein to Layton to Cohen, while popular among critics, "is not borne out by the facts."

The single volume of poetry that has received the most critical attention is *Flowers for Hitler,* considered by most critics to be Cohen's departure from the concerns of his earlier work. Pacey claims that its significance "lies in its strenuous effort to broaden and deepen and

objectify its author's interests and sympathies." Meyer and O'Riordan point out that *Flowers for Hitler* also represents a departure from literary and mythological sources and is much more heavily influenced by pop culture references. Sandra Wynands also notes that "in its stance against conventional aesthetics, *Flowers for Hitler* takes a stand against formally 'good' poems," and she contends that the "lack of form" is effective in driving home the point that Cohen is trying to make. His point, according to Wynands, is "that as a poet he can do nothing to make the ugly reality more bearable or digestible. All he can do is make the facts speak for themselves in a language exceedingly sparse." Laurenz Volkmann has also written about *Flowers for Hitler,* commenting on Cohen's use of black humor, which the critic acknowledges creates poems that "are always positioned on a thin line between the tasteless or inadequate and the shocking and unsettling." Volkmann, however, contends that Cohen's representation of the Holocaust succeeds: "Revelling in the fantastic, macabre, and grotesque, the poems are interlaced with traces of the Holocaust as the ultimate proof of the ubiquity of evil."

PRINCIPAL WORKS

Poetry

Let Us Compare Mythologies 1956
The Spice-Box of Earth 1961
Flowers for Hitler 1964
Parasites of Heaven 1966
Songs of Leonard Cohen (songs) 1968
Selected Poems, 1956-1968 1969
Songs from a Room (songs) 1969
The Energy of Slaves 1972
Songs of Love and Hate (songs) 1973
New Skins for the Old Ceremony (songs) 1974
Death of a Ladies' Man (songs) 1977
Death of a Lady's Man 1978
Recent Songs (songs) 1979
Book of Mercy 1984
Various Positions (songs) 1984
I'm Your Man (songs) 1988
The Future (songs) 1992
Stranger Music: Selected Poems and Essays (poetry, prose, and songs) 1993
Ten New Songs (songs) 2001
Dear Heather (songs) 2004
Book of Longing (poetry, prose, and sketches) 2006
Dance Me to the End of Love [with Henrí Matisse] (poetry and art) 2006

Book of Longing [with Philip Glass] (songs) 2007
The Lyrics of Leonard Cohen 2009

Other Major Works

The Favourite Game (novel) 1963
Beautiful Losers (novel) 1966

CRITICISM

Desmond Pacey (essay date autumn 1967)

SOURCE: Pacey, Desmond. "The Phenomenon of Leonard Cohen." *Canadian Literature* 34 (autumn 1967): 5-23.

[*In the following essay, Pacey demonstrates how careful attention to the themes developed in Cohen's first three volumes of poetry, as well as in the novel* The Favorite Game, *leads to a greater understanding of and appreciation for Cohen's second novel,* Beautiful Loser, *which Pacey believes is Cohen's most impressive single achievement.*]

In naming Leonard Cohen a phenomenon, I am motivated by the quantity, quality and variety of his achievement. Still only thirty-three, Cohen has published four books of verse and two novels, and has made a national if not an international reputation by his poetry reading, folk-singing, and skill with the guitar. The best of his poems have lyrical grace and verbal inevitability; his two novels are as perceptive in content and as sophisticated in technique as any that have appeared in English since the Second World War; and his voice has a magic incantatory quality which hypnotizes his audiences, and especially teenage audiences, into a state of bliss if not of grace.

In this paper I intend to place the major emphasis on his second novel, *Beautiful Losers* (1966), his most impressive single achievement, and in my opinion the most intricate, erudite, and fascinating Canadian novel ever written. But since *Beautiful Losers* is not an isolated achievement, but the culmination of Cohen's career to date, I shall begin by seeing how his other books lead up to and enrich our understanding of it.

The title of Cohen's first book of verse, *Let Us Compare Mythologies* (1956), might have applied almost equally well to his latest novel, which among other things is an exercise in comparative mythology. From the first Cohen has been interested in mythology and magic, in the imaginative means which men at all times and in all places have devised to give interest, order, meaning and direction to their world. In *Let Us Compare Mythologies* he was chiefly concerned with the similarities and differences between the Hebrew mythology of his family and the Christian mythology of his environment, but by the time he wrote *Beautiful Losers* he had become much more ecumenical.

The first poem in *Let Us Compare Mythologies*, "Elegy", exhibits a number of characteristics which recur throughout his work: his almost magical control and modulation of verbal melody, his sensuous particularity, the empathetic reach of his imagination, and his fascination with situations which mingle violence and tenderness to heighten the effect of both. We also see emerge for the first time the theme of the quest—here as usually in Cohen the quest for a lost or unknown God, mysterious, elusive, but compelling. Cohen, like his racial ancestor Spinoza (to whom he frequently alludes), is a man drunk with God.

Almost as prominent in *Let Us Compare Mythologies* as the religious theme is that of sex. Indeed, in Cohen's work, as in more ancient mythologies, religion and sex are closely associated: this association reaches its culmination in *Beautiful Losers,* but it is embryonically present in this first book of verse.

These twin quests for God and for sexual fulfillment are motivated by the recognition of the individual's vulnerability, by an agonized sense of loneliness. Loneliness and the means of escaping it—sometimes tragic, sometimes pathetic, sometimes at least temporarily successful—form one of the basic and recurrent themes in *Beautiful Losers*. It is present in this first book of verse in **"Summer Night"**.

> And the girl in my arms
> broke suddenly away, and shouted for us all,
> Help! Help! I am alone. But then all subtlety was
>   gone
> and it was stupid to be obvious before the field and
>   sky,
> experts in simplicity. So we fled on the highways,
> in our armoured cars, back to air-conditioned homes.

But thus to emphasize the serious and tragic aspects of *Let Us Compare Mythologies* is to ignore the wit and humour which here as in all of Cohen's work add variety and contrast to his vision. *Beautiful Losers* is, in one sense, a comic novel, a modern version of picaresque, and among the early poems are several examples of Cohen's comic gift, perhaps best of all, **"The Fly"**.

> In his black armour
>   the house-fly marched the field
> of Freia's sleeping thighs,
> undisturbed by the soft hand
>   which vaguely moved
> to end his exercise.

And it ruined my day—
      this fly which never planned
to charm her or to please
should walk boldly on that ground
      I tried so hard
to lay my trembling knees.

The Spice-Box of Earth (1961) reinforces the themes of religious and sexual affirmation and their frequent identification in Cohen's work. The love play celebrated with such hypnotic tenderness in **"You Have the Lovers"** is compared to a ritual, and the loss of self-consciousness in the sexual union become a paradigm of a mystical epiphany. For Cohen, the state of sexual fulfillment is virtually synonymous with the state of grace: the fulfilled lover feels himself to be a part of a universal harmony. As he puts it in **"Owning Everything"**:

Because you are close,
everything that men make, observe
or plant is close, is mine:
the gulls slowly writhing, slowly singing
on the spears of wind;
the iron gate above the river;
the bridge holding between stone fingers
her cold bright necklace of pearls.
    . . . . .
With your body and your speaking
you have spoken for everything,
robbed me of my strangerhood,
made me one
with the root and gull and stone, . . .

(Incidentally, the image of the necklace, in line 8 above, becomes one of the thematic symbols of *Beautiful Losers*.)

The identification of religion and sex is also seen in **"The Priest Says Goodbye"**, where the priest is the lover and lust is said to "burn like fire in a holy tree," but its most conspicuous occasion is the poem **"Celebration"**, where the act of fellatio becomes a "ceremony" and is likened to the phallus worship of the ancient Romans, and where the man's semen becomes a "blessing." The clearly affirmative tone of this poem surely gives the lie to those critics of *Beautiful Losers* who profess to find satire and disgust in the sexual scenes. An affirmation of all forms of sexual activity, however "perverse" in conventional terms, provided that they do not involve outright cruelty or murder, is surely an organic part of Cohen's philosophy.

But if tenderness and affirmation are present in *The Spice-Box of Earth,* so also are the darker themes of human vulnerability and loneliness and of violence and cruelty. Cohen is a romantic, but he is not the type of romantic optimist who ignores or denies the existence of evil.

Bitterness at the indignities and false guises imposed upon the Jews dominates **"The Genius",** and the bitterness of a betrayed lover **"The Cuckold's Song."** This latter poem is a good illustration of Cohen's versatility of both matter and manner. It begins in anger and modulates into wit and self-mockery; in style it substitutes, for Cohen's usual melodic grace, harsh colloquial diction and angry speech rhythms.

If this looks like a poem
I might as well warn you at the beginning
that it's not meant to be one.
I don't want to turn anything into poetry.
I know all about her part in it
but I'm not concerned with that right now.
This is between you and me.
Personally I don't give a damn who led who on:
in fact I wonder if I give a damn at all.
But a man's got to say something.
Anyhow you fed her 5 MacKewan Ales,
took her to your room, put the right records on,
and in an hour or two it was done.
    . . . . .
What really makes me sick
is that everything goes on as it went before:
I'm still a sort of friend,
I'm still a sort of lover.
But not for long:
that's why I'm telling this to the two of you.
The fact is I'm turning to gold, turning to gold.
It's a long process, they say,
it happens in stages.
This is to inform you that I've already turned to clay.

A particular premonition of *Beautiful Losers* found in *The Spice-Box of Earth* is the mechanical mistress in **"The Girl Toy"**, which points forward to the Danish Vibrator of the novel. This poem is also one of the first indications of Cohen's fascination with machinery, which becomes a thematic motif in both his novels. In the poem, as in the novels, Cohen's attitude towards the machine is ambivalent: it is at once frightening and alluring. **"The Girl Toy"**, in its allusions to Yeats' "Sailing to Byzantium" ("famous golden birds", "hammered figures"), is also premonitory of the strong Yeatsian influences present in *Beautiful Losers*.

Such premonitions in the early poetry, however, fade into relative insignificance when we examine Cohen's first novel, *The Favourite Game* (1963). It positively bristles with allusions, images and thematic motifs which were to be more fully developed in the second novel. *The Favourite Game,* which at first reading one is apt to dismiss as just another if somewhat superior version of the autobiographical novel of the young artist growing to maturity, in fact becomes a much more richly resonant novel when it is re-read after *Beautiful Losers*. For example, the statement that Martin Stark, the "holy idiot" of *The Favourite Game,* "stuck his index fingers in his ears for no apparent reason, squinting as if he were expecting some drum-splitting explosion" is apt to be passed over on first reading as a mere omen of disaster; in the light of the discussion of the Telephone Dance in *Beautiful Losers* it becomes a powerful symbolic allusion to man's perpetual attempts to find connection with the cosmic rhythms. When we read that Wanda's face "blurred into the face of little Lisa . . . that one dissolved into the face of Bertha" we think of the transposition not merely in terms of nostalgia for Breavman's lost loves, but also in terms of the eternal principle of femininity which in *Beautiful Losers* sees Isis, Catherine, Edith, Mary Voolnd, the Virgin Mary, Marilyn Monroe and the blonde housewife in the car blend into one essential Woman or Universal Mother. A seemingly casual statement that "We all want to be Chinese mystics living in thatched huts, but getting laid frequently" becomes much more meaningful when read in the light of the "go down on a saint" motif in *Beautiful Losers,* and that novel's more fully articulated notion of the desirability of combining spiritual vision with physical ecstasy.

The quest motif, which we have seen adumbrated in the early poems, is more fully developed in *The Favourite Game,* but still remains embryonic in contrast with the much more intricate version that occurs in *Beautiful Losers.* Breavman's prayerful invocation of God in his journal entry (see p. 199) is a first sketch for the narrator's prayers in the second novel, and Breavman's wavering between that quest and greed for secular wealth and success is premonitory of the recurrent pattern of aspiration and rebellion through which the narrator of *Beautiful Losers* passes. Breavman also has a vision of the ultimate unity of all things which prefigures the narrator's visions of cosmic unity in the later novel:

> Mozart came loud over the PA, sewing together everything that Breavman observed. It wove, it married the two figures bending over the records, whatever the music touched, child trapped in London Bridge, mountain-top dissolving in mist, empty swing rocking like a pendulum, the row of glistening red canoes, the players clustered underneath the basket, leaping for the ball like a stroboscopic photo of a splashing drop of water—whatever it touched was frozen in an immense tapestry. He was in it, a figure by a railing.

The idea that many forms of popular culture, and especially the hit tunes of the juke-box and the radio, are pathetic but not contemptible versions of this longing for union, this quest for harmony, is also sketched in *The Favourite Game* (see, for example, pp. 222-3), and then much more fully worked out in such sections as "Gavin Gate and the Goddesses" in *Beautiful Losers.*

A rather similar link between the two novels is their mutual concern with magic and miracles, and their joint acceptance of the movie as a contemporary form of magic. The most pervasive thematic motif in *The*

Favourite Game is Breavman's conception of himself as a sort of magician, miracle-worker, or hypnotist. After Bertha, Breavman's childhood girl-friend, falls from the tree, he says:

> "Krantz, there's something special about my voice."
>
> "No, there isn't."
>
> "There is so. I can make things happen."

And after his father's death, he performs a magic rite:

> The day after the funeral Breavman split open one of his father's formal bow ties and sewed in a message. He buried it in the garden, under the snow beside the fence where in summer the neighbour's lilies-of-the-valley infiltrate.

He also declares that "His father's death gave him a touch of mystery, contact with the unknown. He could speak with extra authority on God and Hell." He studies everything he can about hypnotism, and in one of the funniest scenes in the novel hypnotizes his mother's maid and causes her to make love to him. Breavman sounds very much like F. in *Beautiful Losers* when he tells the girl, Tamara, "I want to touch people like a magician, to change them or hurt them, leave my brand, make them beautiful." Again reminding us of F., and even more of the narrator of *Beautiful Losers,* Breavman longs for a miraculous transfiguration of himself:

> In his room in the World Student House, Breavman leans elbows on the windowsill and watches the sun ignite the Hudson. It is no longer the garbage river, catchall for safes, excrement, industrial poison, the route of strings of ponderous barges.
>
> Can something do that to his body?
>
> There must be something written on the fiery water. An affidavit from God. A detailed destiny chart. The address of his perfect wife. A message choosing him for glory or martyrdom.

When he is enjoying the love-affair with Shell, and writing the love poetry which appeared in *The Spice-Box of Earth,* Breavman feels that he is creative because he is "attached to magic." At the boys' camp, he longs to be "calm and magical," to be "the gentle hero the folk come to love, the man who talks to animals, the Baal Shem Tov who carried children piggyback." But the closest approximation in *The Favourite Game* to the great thematic passage about magic in *Beautiful Losers* comes when Breavman watches the firefly and thinks that it is dying:

> He had given himself to the firefly's crisis. The intervals became longer and longer between the small cold flashes. It was Tinker Bell. Everybody had to believe in magic. Nobody believed in magic. He didn't believe in magic. Magic didn't believe in magic. Please don't die.

It didn't. It flashed long after Wanda left. It flashed when Krantz came to borrow Ed's *Time* magazine. It flashed as he tried to sleep. It flashed as he scribbled his journal in the dark.

The firefly there is obviously a symbol of an ultimate light, a pulsing signal from the eternal rhythm, and its continued life, as time (*Time*) is carried away, bespeaks the persistence of Light. This symbolic method of writing, which only occasionally overrides the literal method in *The Favourite Game,* becomes continuous in *Beautiful Losers,* which is a powerful symbolist novel from beginning to end.

A special form of the magical theme is the emphasis Cohen places on the movies as the chief contemporary expression of the magical process. References to movies occur on almost every page of *Beautiful Losers,* but the emphasis first becomes apparent in *The Favourite Game.* Near the beginning of that first novel, Breavman watches a movie of his family in the course of which "A gardener is led shy and grateful into the sunlight to be preserved with his betters." Here, obviously the magical quality of movies is their capacity to confer a sort of immortality. Later on, Breavman imagines himself and the girl Norma as they would appear in the camera eye:

> The camera takes them from faraway, moves through the forest, catches the glint of a raccoon's eyes, examines the water, reeds, closed water-flowers, involves itself with mist and rocks.
>
> "Lie beside me," Norma's voice, maybe Breavman's.
>
> Sudden close-up of her body part by part, lingering over the mounds of her thighs, which are presented immense and shadowed, the blue denim tight on the flesh. The fan of creases between her thighs. Camera searches her jacket for the shape of breasts. She exhumes a pack of cigarettes. Activity is studied closely. Her fingers move like tentacles. Manipulation of cigarette skilled and suggestive. Fingers are slow, violent, capable of holding anything.

Here what fascinates Cohen, as it will again in *Beautiful Losers,* is the magical capacity of the camera to transfigure reality, to intensify experience, and to suggest symbolic overtones by its searching examination of the details of fact. One source of Breavman's magical insight is that a "slow-motion movie" is "always running somewhere in his mind."

This in turn suggests another way in which *The Favourite Game* illuminates one of the themes of *Beautiful Losers.* In the later novel, F. tells the narrator (and since most of the narrative is in the first person, I shall hereafter speak of the narrator as "I") that "We've got to learn to stop bravely at the surface. We've got to learn to love appearances." On other occasions he directs "I" never to overlook the obvious, to "aim

yourself at the tinkly present", and to "Connect nothing . . . Place things side by side on your arborite table, if you must, but connect nothing." Subsequently, in a passage which out of context is rather obscure, he says:

> Of all the laws which bind us to the past, the names of things are the most severe. . . . Names preserve the dignity of Appearance. . . . Science begins in coarse naming, a willingness to disregard the particular shape and destiny of each red life, and call them all Rose. To a more brutal, more active eye, *all* flowers look alike, like Negroes and Chinamen.

What the slow-motion camera does is to reveal the individuality of things, the sensuous particularity of being. Cohen's belief is that the truly magical view is not attained by looking at the world through a haze of generality, or through the still frames of scientific categories, but by examining as closely as possible the particular streaks on the particular tulip. In this he resembles Wordsworth, who sought by close examination of the familiar to discover the element of wonder in it. (If the juxtaposition of Cohen and Wordsworth seems odd, it might be useful to recall that at least once in *Beautiful Losers* there is an obvious echo of Wordsworth's "Tintern Abbey"—"Five years with the length of five years.") Hence it is that we get such passages as the following in *The Favourite Game,* passages in which the search for sensuous exactitude has been developed into a fine art:

> How many leaves have to scrape together to record the rustle of the wind? He tried to distinguish the sound of acacia from the sound of maple.
>
> "If you tape their [birds'] whistles, Shell, and slow them down, you can hear the most extraordinary things. What the naked ear hears as one note is often in reality two or three notes sung simultaneously. A bird can sing three notes at the same time."

There is another way in which the use of movies in *The Favourite Game* points forward to *Beautiful Losers.* Breavman says to his friend Krantz "we're walking into a European movie", and proceeds to imagine himself as an old army officer in such a film. This exemplifies another magical power of the cinema: its capacity to enlarge our experience, to provide us with vicarious living. To this F. alludes in *Beautiful Losers* when he writes to "I", "You know what pain looks like, that kind of pain, you've been inside newsreel Belsen."

Closely related to magic, and serving as a further link between *The Favourite Game* and *Beautiful Losers,* are the games which figure so prominently in both novels. The game is a kind of ritual which imposes order and pleasure on the minutiae of daily living, and is thus in itself a kind of micro-myth or semi-sacred rite. In *Beautiful Losers,* F. says, "Games are nature's most beautiful creation. All animals play games, and the truly

Messianic vision of the brotherhood of creatures must be based on the idea of the game . . ." When F. buys the factory, he does not exploit it for commercial success, but turns it into a playground. Games play a very large part in *The Favourite Game,* as the title suggests: Breavman plays a game with Bertha which leads to her fall from the apple-tree, he plays "The Soldier and the Whore" with Lisa and wrestles with her in the snow, he visualizes Krantz as "first figure of a follow-the-leader game through the woods", he watches a baseball game at the boys' camp where he works for the summer, and at the very end of the novel he remembers "the favourite game" of his childhood:

> Jesus! I just remembered what Lisa's favourite game was. After a heavy snow we would go into a back yard with a few of our friends. The expanse of snow would be white and unbroken. Bertha was the spinner. You held her hands while she turned on her heels, you circled her until your feet left the ground. Then she let go and you flew over the snow. You remained still in whatever position you landed. When everyone had been flung in this fashion into the fresh snow, the beautiful part of the game began. You stood up carefully, taking great pains not to disturb the impression you had made. Now the comparisons. Of course you would have done your best to land in some crazy position, arms and legs sticking out. Then we walked away, leaving a lovely white field of blossom-like shapes with footprint stems.

The dust-jacket of *The Favourite Game* declares that "the favourite game itself is love". This seems to me a serious misreading of the novel. As I read it, and especially the final paragraph, the favourite game is to leave an impression on the snow, to leave behind one an interesting design, and by extension I take this to include the novel itself, which is Cohen's design of his own early life, and by further extension of all artistic creation. The game is beautiful for Cohen because it is associated with the innocence of childhood and because it is a successful attempt of the human imagination to impose order upon reality. Two of F.'s ideas in *Beautiful Losers* are relevant here. At one point he declares "Prayer is translation. A man translates himself into a child asking for all there is in a language he has barely mastered." At another, we are told that F.'s "allegiance is to the notion that he is not bound to the world as given, that he can escape from the painful arrangement of things as they are." "Escapism", so long a derogatory term in twentieth-century literary circles, is for Cohen a desirable thing: movies, games, radio hit tunes, art and prayer are desirable things because they lift us out of the ruck of routine and above the rubble of time.

There are other ways in which *The Favourite Game* is premonitory of *Beautiful Losers*—the incidental comments on Canada, on Montreal, and on Jewish life and values; the humour; the alternation between tenderness and violence; the wavering between self-glorification and self-doubt; the hostile allusions to scientific

achievement; the many ambivalent references to machinery; the stress on sexual ecstasy and especially upon the oral forms of it and upon masturbation; the contempt for conventional bourgeois behaviour and attitudes; recurrent images which give to the novel a poetic resonance; the emphasis upon loneliness and nostalgia—but rather than take time to develop them I feel I must point out how this first novel *differs* from its successor. It is a much more subjective novel, and a much more self-indulgent one. Whereas *Beautiful Losers* is about a cast of characters none of whom bear much resemblance to Cohen himself or to members of his family and his friends, *The Favourite Game* is quite obviously autobiographical. Like Joyce's *Portrait*, it is a novel in the lyrical mode, whereas *Beautiful Losers* is much closer to the dramatic mode of *Finnegan's Wake*. Much of *The Favourite Game* is taken up with family history—the death of Breavman's father, the neurotic possessiveness and ultimate psychosis of his mother, the pathetic respectability of his uncles. These scenes, and those dealing with the author's own youthful memories, are the strongest part of the book: the author is still at the stage of recording rather than dominating and transforming reality. When, in the Shell-Gordon interlude, he tries to get into the minds of a young New England woman and her husband, most of the life and particularity go out of the style.

Since **The Spice-Box of Earth** was also a very personal book, Cohen seems to have felt that he must break out of the prison of self and attempt a more objective art. The significance of his third book of poems, **Flowers for Hitler** (1964), at any rate in relation to *Beautiful Losers,* lies in its strenuous effort to broaden and deepen and objectify its author's interests and sympathies. In a rather too flamboyant but still basically honest note to the publisher, which is printed on the dust-jacket, Cohen declares of **Flowers for Hitler**:

> This book moves me from the world of the golden-boy poet into the dung pile of the front-line writer. I didn't plan it this way. I loved the tender notices **Spice-Box** got but they embarrassed me a little. **Hitler** won't get the same hospitality from the papers. My sounds are too new, therefore people will say: this is derivative, this is slight, his power has failed. Well, I say that there has never been a book like this, prose or poetry, written in Canada. All I ask is that you put it in the hands of my generation and it will be recognized.

I have not read carefully the reviews of **Flowers for Hitler,** so I cannot say whether Cohen's fears were justified. I do know, however, that the charge of derivativeness has been levelled at *Beautiful Losers,* and that it has been compared (very vaguely, as is the safe way) to the writing of Sartre, Gênet, Burroughs, Thomas Pynchon, John Barth, and Allen Ginsberg. One important object of my present exercise is to show that *Beautiful Losers* can best be seen as the culmination of

Cohen's own artistic development, not as the imitation of someone else.

Flowers for Hitler is not quite as different from its predecessors as Cohen's dust-jacket statement might lead us to believe. As the title suggests, there is still the juxtaposition of beauty and ugliness, tenderness and violence, which we have seen to have been a feature of his work from the beginning; there are still a number of love poems which combine wit, tenderness, and passion; there are still poems of humourous self-mockery and ironic ballads of everyday life. But the new element is there, and it predominates. It takes, largely, two forms: disgust at and revulsion from the greed, hypocrisy, and cruelty of twentieth-century politics, and a newly urgent longing for a religious transfiguration which will rid the poet of his self-absorption.

In the political poems, he expresses the idea that the horrors of our age make those of previous generations seem insignificant; that Canadian political life is sordid and dull; and that History is merely an opiate:

> History is a needle
> for putting men asleep
> anointed with the poison
> of all they want to keep

(This passage, incidentally, turns up again in *Beautiful Losers,* in slightly amended form, as "F.'s Invocation to History in the Middle Style".) Canada is "a dying animal" to which he refuses (adapting a line from Yeats) to "be fastened". Everywhere he looks he sees guilt and corruption, and he feels his own involvement in it and repulsion from it.

This part of *Flowers for Hitler* points forward to F.'s political involvement in *Beautiful Losers*; F. is a French-Canadian nationalist, a Separatist, a Member of Parliament, a revolutionary leader, and his final political gesture is to blow up the statue of Queen Victoria on Sherbrooke Street. But F. himself recognizes that the sense of involvement with other men which leads to his kind of political activity is only a stage on the way to the final break-through which he hopes "I" will achieve. "I"'s final apotheosis transcends politics: it involves transfiguration, not an improvement of time but a leap into eternity.

The final answer of *Beautiful Losers,* the loss of self in the pursuit of sainthood, is also adumbrated in *Flowers for Hitler.* The process begins in confession of guilt; in the very first poem, **"What I'm Doing Here,"** Cohen confesses that he has lied, conspired against love, tortured, and hated, and he ends by calling upon "each one of you to confess." Confession leads to humility, as in **"The Hearth"** where he learns that his lust "was not so rare a masterpiece", and to self-abnegation in which he vows to forget his personal style and surrender to the mysterious silence, become a vessel for renewing grace:

> I will forget my style
> Perhaps a mind will open in this world
> perhaps a heart will catch rain
> Nothing will heal and nothing will freeze
> but perhaps a heart will catch rain. . . .

He longs for purgation and discipline leading to a new life:

> There is a whitewashed hotel waiting for me
> somewhere, in which I will begin my fast and
> my new life.

> Oh to stand in the Ganges wielding a yard of
> intestine.

> Let me renew myself
> in the midst of all the things of the world
> which cannot be connected.

This idea is perhaps best expressed in **"For Anyone Dressed in Marble"**, in a passage which also finds its way into *Beautiful Losers*:

> I see an orphan, lawless and serene,
> standing in a corner of the sky,
> body something like bodies that have been,
> but not the scar of naming in his eye.
> Bred close to the ovens, he's burnt inside.
> Light, wind, cold, dark—they use him like a bride.

The "saint" is a lawless orphan because he has detached himself from the claims of family and society; he stands in a corner of the sky because he has transcended earthly values; he has a body because he is still human, but he has overcome the human fault of missing the particular in the general by the use of "coarse names"; aware of human violence as expressed in the gas ovens of Nazi Germany, he has been purged by his closeness to it and has become a kind of empty vessel into which the eternal powers may pour themselves.

With all this as background and context, *Beautiful Losers* (1966) becomes relatively easy to appreciate and understand. I say *relatively* easy, because it remains a difficult and sometimes baffling book.

First, the title. Beautiful Losers are those who achieve the beauty of "sainthood" (and it is necessary to put that word in quotes because Cohen uses it, as we shall see in a moment, in a special sense) by losing, or rather by voluntarily surrendering, their selves and the ordinary world. In the eyes of the world, they are "losers", for they are victims: Catherine dies in agony of slow starvation and self-torture; Edith is crushed by a descending elevator; Mary Voolnd is mauled by savage police dogs; F. dies in an asylum for the criminally insane; "I" is at the end of the novel a ragged, stinking, "freak of the woods." But *sub specie aeternitatis,* or in the eyes of God, these characters are not losers at all: Catherine deliberately surrenders herself to be the Bride of Christ, is canonized, and becomes a miraculous healer; Edith commits voluntary suicide to teach "I" a lesson which at first he ignores but which ultimately leads him to his apotheosis; Mary Voolnd surrenders herself to the sexual pleasure of F. when he is at his unattractive worst and brings him the good news of his recognition as first president of the republic; F. deliberately casts himself in the subordinate role of teacher and guide of "I" and shows him the way to the Promised Land; "I" achieves final apotheosis and in the last paragraph of the novel is seen playing the role of Mediator between God and Man, or of the Suffering Servant who has gone through agony to achieve compassion:

> Poor men, poor men, such as we, they've gone and fled. I will plead from electrical tower. I will plead from turret of plane. He will uncover His face. He will not leave me alone. I will spread His name in Parliament. I will welcome His silence in pain. I have come through the fire of family and love. I smoke with my darling, I sleep with my friend. We talk of the poor men, broken and fled. Alone with my radio I lift up my hands. Welcome to you who read me today. Welcome to you who put my heart down. Welcome to you, darling and friend, who miss me forever in your trip to the end.

Voluntary loss of self for some higher cause is, then, the main theme of *Beautiful Losers,* but it is developed in great complexity and intricacy against a background of mythological ecumenicity and is supplemented by a variety of secondary themes.

At a climactic moment of the novel, Edith breaks into Greek to declare "I am Isis born, of all things, both what is and what shall be, and no mortal has ever lifted my robe." We may recall here that on the first page of the novel "I" declares that he wants to "know what goes on under that rosy blanket" of Catherine Tekakwitha: so Catherine is also Isis. Indeed all the women of the novel are essentially the same woman, or the same goddess, just as Isis gradually took over all the other goddesses in the ancient world. The greatest significance of the Isis cult, which developed in Egypt in the seventeenth century B.C. and gradually spread throughout the whole Mediterranean world, lay in her role of Universal Mother and her agency in effecting immortality of the soul and renewal of life. She included in herself the virtues of all other goddesses, and she offered to her devotees forgiveness, purgation, communion and regeneration. Her mythological role in piecing together the fragments of her husband Osiris symbolized her miraculous healing power. Once one becomes aware of Edith's role as Isis, many of the jigsaw pieces of the novel fall into significant patterns: it is in her Isis role of Universal Mother that Edith, with her phenomenally large nipples, gives herself to "I" and F., comforts the stranger on the beach at Old Orchard, Maine, and even cradles the "famous head" of the presumably forgiven Hitler against her breasts. By her voluntary suicide in the elevator shaft, Edith effects a restoration of her husband similar to Isis's restoration of Osiris. When we read the description of Edith's coating herself with "deep red greasy stuff" and saying to "I" "Let's be other people", we recall that one of Isis's roles was that of the bringer-forth of the indwelling self, of the agent of miraculous transfiguration. "I" notes that Edith's "kisses were loose, somehow unspecific, as if her mouth couldn't choose where to stay"—and this we can relate to the concept of the mouth of Isis as full of the breath of life, issuing forth to heal the soul and regenerate the dead. We recall also that Mary Voolnd, another Isis figure, is a nurse, and that Edith is several times referred to as a nurse.

The second major mythological framework of *Beautiful Losers* is that of Christianity. This is an apt juxtaposition since the cult of Isis rivalled the cult of Christ in the Mediterranean world, and sometimes blended with it. Isis herself was frequently identified with the Virgin Mary, and this identification is made anew in Cohen's novel. Catherine is the Iroquois Virgin, and models herself upon the Virgin Mary; by renouncing the ownership of her own flesh she achieves a mystic vision:

> And as she thus disclaimed the ownership of her flesh she sensed a minute knowledge of his innocence, a tiny awareness of the beauty of all the faces circled round the crackling fires of the village. Ah, the pain eased, the torn flesh she finally did not own healed in its freedom, and a new description of herself, so brutally earned, forced itself into her heart: she was Virgin.

But since Edith and Catherine are obviously one person in different guises, Edith is also the Virgin Mary: although she is not physically a virgin, she plays the role of intercessor and comforter. So also does Mary Voolnd, although her way of expressing compassionate love may seem the very antithesis of virginity.

The men also are loosely associated with Christian figures. F. refers to himself on various occasions as Moses, who has led his friends within sight of the Promised Land but cannot take them there; at other times he speaks of his role in terms which recall John the Baptist. "I", on the other hand, develops eventually into a Christ-figure. In the final paragraph, as we have seen, he becomes the compassionate mediator, pleading from his tower. (In this connection, it is worth noting that in the poem **"Suzanne"** Cohen speaks of Christ being on his "wooden tower", the Cross.) Previous to that, "I" has stayed for a prolonged period in a treehouse in the woods, paralleling Christ's sojourn in the wilderness. Even the bodybuilder Charles Axis is linked with Christ: "Charles Axis is all compassion, he's our sacrifice!", and his name suggests that he too is an axis or link between God and man.

A number of other mythologies are worked into *Beautiful Losers,* but there is space here only to glance at them. There are, as we might expect since "I" is a folklorist, anthropologist, and student of the North American Indians, many references to and indeed detailed descriptions of Red Indian myths and rites—rainmaking (p. 31), mythical cosmogony (p. 85), the wrestling match between the White one and the Dark one (p. 88), Klooskap (p. 89), the Oscotarach or Head-Piercer's Hut (pp. 114, 133, 184), and the Andacwandet or Fuck-Cure (pp. 128-132). Greek mythology is represented, significantly, by Icarus (p. 212) and Prometheus (p. 237), both of whom fit the novel well since they sought to unite heaven and earth, God and man. There are apt references to Oriental Indian mythology and religious rites: to the mandala (p. 214), yoga (pp. 160, 236), Asoka's Circle, and Tantric love perfectionists. The Jewish Kabala is mentioned, as is the Chinese "holy mountain" and the wisdom of Kung.

These more or less ancient mythologies are supplemented with more recent myths and magical manifestations: the magic of Houdini (p. 38), the mythology of the comic strips and radio programmes, the magic rituals of the Masonic Order (p. 145), the myth of astrology (see, for example, the reference to the Virgo disease, p. 162), the magic of firecrackers and guns and rockets. But the contemporary mythology and magic which are most stressed are those of the movies. There are several references to the goddesses of the silver screen, Marilyn Monroe and Brigitte Bardot, and a host of references to the magic powers of the film to heighten reality, preserve the past, record the present, create imaginary worlds, expand the consciousness, enlarge the awareness, arouse the conscience, stimulate the passions, or excite the imagination. The System Theatre becomes the contemporary temple or cathedral, into which only initiates are allowed to pass after negotiating the barrier of the ticket collector in the outer courtyard or foyer.

All of these references to mythology and magic reach their culmination in the passage which announces the secondary (some might argue that it is the primary) theme of *Beautiful Losers:* that magic and religion *not* science and politics are the real powers in the world. In what F. describes as the "sweet burden of my argument," he proclaims:

> God is alive. Magic is afoot. God is afoot. Magic is alive. Alive is a foot. Magic never died. God never sickened. Many poor men lied. Many sick men lied. Magic never weakened. Magic never hid. Magic always ruled. God is afoot. God never died. God was ruler though his funeral lengthened. Though his mourners thickened Magic never fled. . . . Though laws were carved in marble they could not shelter men. . . . Magic is afoot. . . . But Magic is no instrument. Magic is the end. . . . This I mean my mind to serve till

service is but Magic moving through the world, and mind itself is Magic coursing through the flesh, and flesh itself is Magic dancing on a clock, and time itself the Magic Length of God.

As I have said, there are several subsidiary themes running through *Beautiful Losers.* Perhaps the third most important is that which announces the close association of religion and sex. One of the apparent paradoxes of this novel is that its main characters, all of whom are "heroes" in the sense that they are to some degree at least being held up to our admiration, have such divergent attitudes towards sex. Catherine renounces the flesh altogether and remains a virgin; Edith, on the other hand, is a relatively compliant wife to "I" but without compunction commits adultery with F. on six or seven occasions. F. is completely promiscuous, admits that he has chased women wherever they have led him, glories in his sexual "scores" with both sexes, and even in his dying moments has his hand up the skirt of Mary Voolnd. "I" has had homosexual relations with F., has had a rather frustrating sexual life with Edith (she is not compliant enough for him—he has rather special tastes), and spends a great deal of time in masturbation. All the sexuality in the novel, of course, comes to a climax in the orgy which F. and Edith perform with the so-called Danish Vibrator or Sex Machine. What are we to make of all this? Is Cohen upholding virginity or promiscuity, sexual abstinence or sexual orgies?

The clue to the resolution of the paradox is in Cohen's special conception of sainthood. Recalling F.'s advice to "go down on a saint", "I" speculates:

> What is a saint? A saint is someone who has achieved a remote human possibility. It is impossible to say what that possibility is. I think it has something to do with the energy of love. Contact with this energy results in the exercise of a kind of balance in the chaos of existence.

To "go down on a saint", then, is at second-hand to make contact with the energy of love, as well as to combine physical ecstasy with spiritual vision. Catherine is a saint because she has achieved the remote human possibility of making contact with the energy of love, that is God, through the renunciation of the flesh; Edith is a saint because she has made contact through her maternal role towards all men; F. is a saint because he has made contact with divine energy through sex and because he commits himself to the remote possibility of a revolution in Quebec; "I" becomes a saint at the end of the novel because by exiling himself to the wilderness he has purged himself of pride and selfishness and made of himself an empty vessel into which divine love can pour. A saint, if you like, is an extremist. For Cohen, truth is not in the mean but in the extremes. F. declares "I was never drunk enough, never poor enough, never rich enough." Catherine in the extremity of her flagellations is closer to Edith and F. in the extremity of their orgy with the Danish Vibrator than she is to a member of the bourgeoisie leading a respectable and moderate life. Is it too fanciful to suggest that in referring to the sex machine by its initials, D.V., Cohen is suggesting that the surrender to it is not so very different from the surrender to God's will?

A closely related subsidiary theme is that of what we might call pan-orgasmic sex. F. declares that "all parts of the body are erotogenic. All flesh can come!" and he maintains that almost any contact can lead us into "the nourishing anonymity of the climax." (Here, incidentally, is another of the links between religion and sex—sex leads to anonymity, into that loss of self-consciousness which is the prerequisite of religious response.)

Rather than deal further with the minor themes of the novel, I should like now to say something about its technique. In structure it resembles a symbolic poem: it is divided into the traditional three parts, and its parts are woven together by recurrent thematic motifs and thematic images or symbols. Among the motifs are references to "I"'s constipation (a symbol of the self locked in upon itself) to his masturbation (a symbol of his lonely self-absorption and self-indulgence), to games (symbols of life as free choice), to radio music and radio serials (symbols of attempts to reach contact with some outside force or message), to baptism (symbol of purification and the entry into a new life), and above all to movies, films, cinemas and film-stars (symbols, as we have seen, of contemporary magic and escape from this world). Among the thematic images are the blanket or veil (symbol of mystery and the hoped-for apocalypse), birch and pine trees (symbols of natural growth, beauty, and the fragrance of natural things), rivers, springs and pools (symbols of purification and divine grace), birds (symbols of the ingression of the divine upon the human), altars and temples (symbols or worship, aspiration and sacrifice), stars (associated with Isis and symbols of divine perfection and protection), the elevator (an ambivalent symbol, suggesting both the ascent to heaven and the descent into hell), mountains (symbols of contemplation and detached wisdom), machinery (another ambivalent symbol, suggesting the "eternal machinery" of cosmic process and the destructive machinery of warfare and greed), the necklace (symbol of multiplicity in unity, the many in the one), crystals, snowflakes and the rainbow pictures seen through them (symbolic of divine order, intricacy and vision), soap and especially F.'s "soap collection" (symbols of purification through suffering), rockets, firecrackers, and "fiery journeys" (symbols of the attempt to penetrate the veil of heaven), fishes (symbols of Christ and of divine grace), candy (symbol of pleasure and perhaps of God's mercy), the factory which is converted into a playground (symbol of the

transfiguration of labour into play, as in the last stanza of Yeats' "Among School-children.") Each of these motifs or images recurs frequently, and in each case the symbolic suggestion is intended: the result is a novel more intricately interwoven than any Canadian novel of my experience.

An associated feature of the technique of this novel is its clever manipulation of chronology. We move back and forth from the present to the near-past to the distant-past of Catherine Tekakwitha, the seventeenth-century Iroquois virgin, and yet the transitions, though often abrupt and frequent, are never misleading or confusing. Similarly, although we shuttle back and forth between various points of view, we never get confused between the different characters: each is consistent (if only in inconsistency), distinctive, and credible.

Beautiful Losers, the riches of which I have only touched upon, is the chief accomplishment of Leonard Cohen thus far, and the culmination of all his previous work. But it is not likely to be the end of the phenomenon of Leonard Cohen.

Sandra Djwa (essay date autumn 1967)

SOURCE: Djwa, Sandra. "Leonard Cohen: Black Romantic." *Canadian Literature* 34 (autumn 1967): 32-42.

[*In the following essay, Djwa analyzes the "value of experience" in Cohen's works as well as in his conception of the creation of art, and traces many concordances between Cohen's writing and that of other important post-World War II authors.*]

Writing on "The Problem of a Canadian Literature", E. K. Brown pokes fun at the genteel conservatism that characterizes Canadian writing:

> Imagination boggles at the vista of a Canadian Whitman or a Canadian Dos Passos. The prevailing literary standards demand a high degree of moral and social orthodoxy; and popular writers accept these standards without even . . . rueful complaint.[1]

If Brown considers a Whitman or a Dos Passos improbable, a Canadian Gênet, a Canadian Burroughs, or a Günter Grass is clearly beyond expectation. Yet it is in precisely this tradition, that of the contemporary Black Romantics as we might call them, that Leonard Cohen appears to belong.

Cohen's poetry reads like an index to the history of European romanticism; from the epigraph to *Let Us Compare Mythologies* (1956) through *The Spice-Box of Earth* (1961) to the "lady" of "garbage flowers" in

Flowers for Hitler (1964), his progress is from Keats and Lawrence through Baudelaire to Gênet. In brief, this is a movement from a qualified acceptance of the romantic ideal as it is embodied in art ("For ever wilt thou love and she be fair") to the decadent romanticism of a *fin de siècle* æsthetic in which the ugly replaces the beautiful as the inspiration for art.

Reading through Cohen's work we become aware of an unsatisfied search for an absolute. In his world there are no fixed values, spiritual or sensual, that stand beyond the transitory moment, and the moment itself, experience made myth, blends imperceptibly with other moments and other mythologies, so that in the shifting the values change, leaving only the value of experience made art:

> Those days were just the twilight
> And soon the poems and the songs
> Were only associations
> Edged with bitterness
> Focussed into pain
> By paintings in a minor key
> Remembered on warm nights
> When he made love to strangers
> And he would struggle through old words
> Unable to forget he once created new ones
> And fumble at their breasts with broken hands.

Cohen's dominant theme, the relationship between experience and art, and more specifically the suggestion that the value of experience is to be found in the art or "beauty" distilled from it, is a familiar motif of the late romantics. It first appears in Cohen's work as an epigraph to *Mythologies* taken from "The Bear" by William Faulkner:

> 'She cannot fade though thou hast not had thy bliss',
>
> McCaslin said: 'For ever wilt thou love and she be fair'.
>
> 'He's talking about a girl', he said.
>
> 'He had to talk about something', McCaslin said.

This preface to a poet's first book suggests an amused recognition of a certain attitude to experience; the rationale is that of love for art's sake. But if this attitude is familiar, the irrational neo-gothic world from which the poet takes this stance is not at all familiar, at least in Canadian poetry. Particularly in his two later books, *Flowers for Hitler* and *Beautiful Losers* (1966) Cohen would seem to be closest to the European tradition of Baudelaire, Sartre and Gênet, and to their American affiliates Henry Miller and William Burroughs.

In contrast to the later European tradition from Baudelaire to Gênet, Canadian writers have not wandered very far from first generation romanticism. Strongly influenced by Wordsworthian natural piety and rein-forced by the Calvinist urge towards moral uplift, the native line in English Canadian poetry might be characterized by the straightforward statement and explicit morality of a D. C. Scott, an E. J. Pratt, or an Earle Birney. Despite Lampman's flirtation with the Symbolists and Marjorie Pickthall's coy apprenticeship to Swinburne, imagistic technique was not fully recognized as such in Canadian poetry until the thirties, and the Decadent sensibility with its attendant themes of masochistic death, self-flagellation and religious inversion, is reflected only faintly in Carman's work of the nineties, recurs briefly in the thirties with Leo Kennedy's *The Shrouding,* and does not appear again until just recently in the late fifties. Notably, this Decadent sensibility is most explicit in the works of the younger writers Leonard Cohen, Daryl Hine, and Mordecai Richler, all of whom have come into contact with the European tradition.

Consequently Cohen does have some grounds for asserting, as he does on the back cover of *Flowers for Hitler,* that his "sounds" are new in Canada and possibly subject to critical misinterpretation. Admittedly, he does stress the same religious, sexual and social protest as do Klein, Layton and Dudek, and he does take the same missionary delight in the poetic vocation of the Montreal Group *pour épater le bourgeois.* But Cohen's technique is considerably more complex than that of Layton or Dudek, and the vision and sensibility which he expresses are sufficiently different from those of Klein to suggest that he has moved into a different tradition. In this connection we might compare the world view of Klein's *Hitleriad* (1944) with that of Cohen's *Flowers for Hitler* (1964). Along with the structure and style of Pope's *Dunciad,* Klein's *Hitleriad* is invoking the rational Neo-Classical world where human folly can be effectively chastised by the wit of a righteous indignation:

> Let anger take me in its grasp; let hate,
> Hatred of evil prompt me, and dictate.

Cohen, on the other hand, insists upon the relativity of evil; Hitler is "ordinary", Eichmann, "medium". In this perspective, irrational evil is accepted as a normal part of the human make-up which can even come to have a certain attractiveness:

> It happens to everyone. For those with eyes who know
> in their hearts that terror is mutual, then this hard community has a beauty of its own.

This reference to the strange "beauty" which can spring from a community of evil and suffering invokes Baudelaire's *Fleurs du mal.* And it is Baudelaire's flowers of evil grafted with those of Gênet which Cohen uses to provide the structural myth of *Flowers for Hitler.* In this book, the moments of beauty which the poet attempts to create, like those of his protagonist Kerensky, "when poems grew like butterflies on the garbage of his life", are moments which cannot come into being unless evil is first admitted. Like his mentor, the T. S. Eliot of *The Waste Land,* and for that matter like Klein also, Cohen wants to bring a guilty world into recognition of itself: "I wait / for each one of you to confess." But unlike Klein, and again following Eliot, the confession that Cohen demands is one which accepts personal responsibility for evil as the natural corollary of being human. Having accepted this awareness of evil as does the protagonist of **"The New Leader"**, the individual is then released from the negative virtue of "threading history's crushing daisy-chain with beauty after beauty" and face to face with the ugliness of self:

> Drunk at last, he hugged himself, his stomach clean,
> cold and drunk, the sky clean but only for him, free to
> shiver, free to hate, free to begin.

This would seem to be a basically post World War II position: the romantic voyaging "I", bereft of religious belief and Hegel's cosmic rationalism ("the sky clean") sets out to discover his world. And as in Sartre's *Nausea* or Heller's *Catch-22,* this involves the attempt to come to terms with existence itself. Faced with a world which he sees as irrational, evil and grotesque, an evil and an ugliness which he shares because he is human, with only a momentary hope of vision and that perhaps delusive, the modern anti-hero accepts evil as part of existence and immerses himself within it, both in terms of the external world and through the journey into self.

This immersion in destruction, often accomplished through a combination of alcohol, drugs and sex, would seem to be meta-physical in nature in that it is an attempt to find a new answer to the human predicament by going down instead of up. In this sense it might be considered the modern romantic myth. Where Wordsworth and Coleridge attempt the transcendental leap, Baudelaire, Rimbaud, Huysmans, and the modern Gênet, Sartre and Burroughs all spend a season in hell. Experience is the distinguishing mode of the Byronic hero, the later Victorian Decadents and their twentieth-century descendants, the Black Romantics. For the past twenty years, the subject of the modern romantic has been increasingly the fascination of evil and its relationship to the process of destructive metamorphosis. Cyril Connolly, in a recent attempt to define "modernism" finds its essence in this quatrain by Baudelaire:

> Only when we drink poison are we well—
> We want, this fire so burns our brain tissue,
> To drown in the abyss—heaven or hell
> Who cares? Through the unknown we'll find the new.[2]

As this excerpt makes clear, the value of the abyss is not only the pleasure of new sensation but the possibility of a new revelation beyond the experience itself. The danger inherent in this credo would seem to be the temptation it offers to mistake catalogued sensation for new revelation.

In Cohen's work, this possibility of a new revelation is specifically associated with the myth of descent culminating in the creation of art. In his first book of poetry, **Let Us Compare Mythologies,** the structural myth is that of the death of the poet-god Orpheus and the possibility of his resurrection in art. Like Eliot's *Waste Land* the book moves through cycles of winter death followed by spring re-birth, and the poet-victim as a part of this cycle moves between the extremes of innocent and destructive love. In terms of the controlling Orpheus myth, the figure of the beloved woman suggests Eurydice while the madwoman evokes the Bacchanals. In the poem **"Letter"**, the poet-victim, aware of his impending death, addresses the madwoman directly: "How you murdered your family / means nothing to me / as your mouth moves across my body". The poems of this cycle would seem to make a strong case for submission to a destructive love which, unlike the romantic escapism of such poems as **"On Certain Incredible Nights"**, can lead to a new beauty and a new order. Consequently the poet embraces the "real", sacrifice goes on (**"Hallowe'en Poem"**) and the poet's brain exposed, "the final clever thrill of summer lads all dead with love", becomes a "drum" to be "scratched with poetry by Kafka's machine". The rationale for this disintegrative experience is explicit in the poem **"Story"**. Only by allowing the madwoman full sway is it possible for the poet as victim to find his place in art: "to understand one's part in a legend".

It is this myth of art which seems to provide the basic structure in Cohen's work. In his first book the myth of descent is presented primarily as the desolation of Eliot's *Waste Land.* In **The Spice-Box of Earth** this longing for the old lost ideals is re-worked in terms of a neo-Hassidic myth. No longer able to accept a despotic God, the poet as priest is forced beyond Genesis into a desolation which is "unheroic, unbiblical". Lawrence Breavman, the poet as lover, finds himself in the same position in Cohen's next book, *The Favourite Game.* Breavman's alienation grows throughout the novel until he is finally stricken with panic and loneliness; it is then that he realizes that a new experience awaits:

> He stumbled and collapsed, tasting the ground. He lay
> very still while his clothes soaked. Something very
> important was going to happen in this arena. He was
> very sure of that. Not in gold, not in light, but in this
> mud something necessary and inevitable would take
> place. He had to stay to watch it unfold.

The experience that waits for Breavman is a recognition of the evil and irrationality symbolized by Baudelaire's mud-flowers. In **Flowers for Hitler** this recognition is presented as a disintegrative experience which is both frightening and pleasurable. This descent into evil is savoured in much the same way as the young Breavman enjoys his adolescent satanism ("Fuck God"), yet the very process of daring the abyss is a propulsion into an irrational, frightening world. Similarly, the narrator-historian of *Beautiful Losers* is forced through the motions of Sartre's nausea in a grimy sub-basement room that gradually fills up with his own excrement.

In Cohen, as with Baudelaire and Sartre, the value of this disintegrative process is given as the creation of art. **"Elegy"**, the first poem in **Let Us Compare Mythologies,** expresses this myth of descent in the death of the poet-god Orpheus:

> He is descending through cliffs
> Of slow green water
> And the hovering coloured fish
> Kiss his snow-bruised body
> And build their secret nests
> In his fluttering winding sheet.

From the disintegrating body of the dead god comes art; the "secret nests" of "hovering" fish. In a later poem **"These Heroics"**, the poet explains that it is because he cannot be "fish" or "bird" that he makes dreams and poetry from love. The association of poet and bird is common to Horace, Baudelaire and Rilke, and in each case the bird symbolizes the poet's aspiration. Cohen's addition of a "fish" to this complex with primary associations of disintegration, points up his belief that the creative process is one which moves between aspiration and disintegration. Associated with the poetic, sexual and religious aspiration which forms one pole of Cohen's system is the dove, the beloved and Catherine Tekakwitha; clustered about the other pole, the process of disintegration, is the fish, the Black Mass, the Bacchanals, "F" and Edith. Through art—the "nests" of **"Elegy"**, the "kite" of *Spice-Box,* the "butterflies" of *Flowers for Hitler*—the poet attempts to reconcile the two. For example, the exiled poet-priest of **Spice-Box** finds that neither religious belief nor physical love can fill up the void between "a ruined house of bondage and a holy promised land". This reconciliation of the spirit and the flesh is only to be found in the fairy-tale land of art:

> Out of the land of heaven
> Down comes the warm Sabbath sun
> Into the spice-box of earth

or in the artifact itself; the spice-box, one of the symbols of the Jewish Havdallah service marking the Sabbath's end, becomes a metaphor for the human form divine.

A similar conclusion is reached in Cohen's later books; Breavman learns that although love is a "creation", the favourite game is not love alone but the flesh made art:

> When everyone had been flung . . . into the fresh snow, the beautiful part of the game began. You stood up carefully, taking great care not to disturb the impression you had made. Now the comparisons.

Of course you would have done your best to land in some crazy position, arms and legs sticking out. Then we walked away, leaving a lovely field of blossom-like shapes with footprint stems.

In *Flowers for Hitler,* Cohen takes the blackness of the human capacity for evil and from it attempts to extract the flowers of art. In this perspective, the poet emerges as recorder: "neither / father nor child / but one who spins / on an eternal unimportant loom / patterns of war and grass / which do not last the night". Similarly, all the four main characters of *Beautiful Losers* find themselves to be both artist and pattern. Through the experience of failure, the narrator, his Indian wife Edith, his guide and lover "F" (cf. Pynchon's "V") and the Iroquois saint, Catherine Tekakwitha, are each precipitated on a journey into self which results in the recreation of existence:

> Not the pioneer is the American dream. . . . The dream is to be immigrant sailing into the misty aerials of New York, the dream is to be Jesuit in the cities of the Iriquois, for we do not wish to destroy the past and its baggy failures, we only wish the miracles to demonstrate that the past was joyously prophetic, and that possibility occurs to us most plainly on this cargo deck of wide lapels, our kerchief sacks filled with obsolete machine guns from the last war but which will astound and conquer the Indians.

Because it is Cohen's thesis that the experience of failure is indispensable for the creation of art, the book becomes a case study of the *fleur du mal* "beauty" of such losers. Through a pop-art catalogue of sensation, the narrator proceeds to the superior "magic" represented by Catherine Tekakwitha (1656-1680). Tekakwitha functions primarily as an artist of religion, her name is defined as meaning "she who, advancing, arranges the shadows neatly". As the narrator further explains, a saint is associated with the "energy" of love: "contact with this energy results in a kind of balance in the chaos of existence". Through her influence as it is manifested directly and through the other two characters, the narrator-historian passes through nausea (like his prototype, Sartre's Roquentin) to the point that it is suggested that the novel is produced from his experience.

Despite the contrivance of Cohen's central myth, *Spice-Box* and *The Favourite Game* are impressive well-written early books, and perhaps largely because of the glimpses they offer of realized experience. *Flowers for Hitler* and *Beautiful Losers* are less rewarding, not only because they are more dominantly written to formula, but also because of the increasingly self-conscious attitude of the poet as persona in relation to the codification of his central myth. What I miss in Cohen's later books is the sense that the writer is attempting a subjective re-interpretation of evil or failure as the case might be. Instead, Cohen's successive books offer variations on a theme within other men's myths. This technique has the advantage of structural neatness and there are few Canadian readers who have not expressed delight at Cohen's technical virtuosity, but it also has the serious disadvantage of sacrificing organic growth and original discovery to a pre-determined formula. Little can happen in *Flowers for Hitler* or *Beautiful Losers* because Cohen has already determined what will happen even before the experience takes place. Furthermore, because he is committed to a view of life and art which is essentially that of religious aspiration followed by sexual inversion, Cohen is further limited in his presentation of experience and his delineation of character. Experience and characters can only come from the Yellow Books of the 1880's and 90's. The case study of the young hero and his *saison en enfer,* the division of the romantic *femme fatale* into her opposite but complementary aspects of innocent and destroyer (cf. Catherine and Edith) are familiar features of Decadent literature as is the presentation of the satanic, often homosexual, friend and alter-ego ("F").

The limitations of this vision would seem to be the limitations of Decadent literature in general; it substitutes a narrowed, bizarre area of human experience at the expense of the ordinary human average, and it negates the dignity of ordinary human encounter to a hierarchy of art. Because this vision, although limited, is of primary importance to the author, his characters are subordinated to it. As types, they depend on increasing doses of sensationalism to be effective. In this connection it is possible to trace the increasing sensationalism associated with the figure of the friend as he is presented from *The Favourite Game* to *Beautiful Losers*. Like the mentor of Oscar Wilde's *Portrait of Dorian Gray,* "F" is memorable for his epigrams rather than for a sense of character in depth. Part of the difficulty involved in Cohen's perception of character would seem to be related to the fact that his characters are conceived as part of an internal myth. Cohen, for example, is both poet-writer and persona and the two often merge. This can sometimes be effective as in the poem **"You Have The Lovers"** from *Spice-Box* where the poet-lover and poet-spectator are universalized but more often the trio of two lovers and a spectator leads to sensationalism or the plain voyeurism of the sunbathing sequence in *Beautiful Losers*.

The sensibility which reports the sensationalism of the disintegrative experience is quite different in kind from that which we usually associate with Canadian poetry. Faced with an absurd world, Cohen is no longer able to call on Klein's humane rationalism for the redress of evil. Instead, there is some attempt to exorcise evil by filtering it through the comic mode. This Black Humour is apparent in Cohen's description of Nazi concentration camp atrocities:

Peekaboo Miss Human Soap
Pretend it never happened

. . . . .

I say let sleeping ashes lie.

Here the brutal is introduced as a witty aside and the particular *frisson nouveau* of the poem seems to arise from the juxtaposition of the erotic, infantile world of Bathing Beauties, "peekaboo" and "let's pretend", with the horror of real concentration camps where soap is made from human fat and ashes. At first glance, Cohen appears to be having a nasty laugh at the expense of Jewish suffering. Alfred Purdy, in fact, describes the subject of *Flowers for Hitler* as little more than the after-dinner talk of "a good conversationalist who had to say something".[3] But on closer inspection it might be suggested that this is an attempt to come to terms with a painful experience. Through the medium of Black Humour it is possible to see the selection of a Miss Human Soap as the fun and games of an absurd world. And because Cohen has presented horror as an absurdity, there is a possibility of moving on to a new affirmation in a way that is not open to Klein in his *Hitleriad.* But at the same time (and it is this which makes Purdy's comments relevant) the dichotomy between the epigraph to *Flowers for Hitler,* which is an excerpt from Primo Levi warning against the disintegration of personality, and the sensationalism of the book itself, leads us to question the integrity of Cohen's vision—a question which does not arise in connection with the Black Humour of Selby's *Last Exit to Brooklyn* or Grass's *The Tin Drum.*

Coming to terms with this view of experience is as tricky as the attempt to decide whether or not pop-art is a contradiction in terms. Yet it can be said that the qualities which make Cohen's work fairly easy to describe—myth as literary structure, central persona, a consistent view of life and art—are also those qualities which mitigate against further development in his later work. In general I find Cohen's poetry often too derivative to be impressive, and the mythic technique, once the key has been supplied, too simple to be suggestive in the largest sense. Cohen does play the game very well; his mythologies are clever, often witty, sometimes very moving, yet even at its best, Cohen's favourite game is still Eliot's or Baudelaire's or Sartre's. But Cohen is attempting to write of contemporary themes in a contemporary way. His concern with alienation, eroticism and madness, together with the experimental techniques of *Flowers for Hitler* and *Beautiful Losers,* unlike the dominantly early nineteenth-century romanticism of the Montreal Group, are the concerns of post World War Two writing. For Cohen, as for Heller, Burroughs, Grass and Selby, the old rules of religious rationality and romantic idealism exist to be questioned. The last twenty years has seen the codification of a new group of writers whose focus is on the disintegrative vision and it is in their footsteps that Cohen is following. Because this new vision, like that of the Decadents, is an inversion of traditional romantic "myth" and morality, and because it is often presented with the irreverent wit of the new Black Humourists, we might be justified in calling this attitude to experience, Black Romantic.

Within the world of the contemporary Black Romantic, the disintegrative experience is presented not only through the journey into self but also through the form of the work. Both, in turn, are microcosms of the reductionist cycle of the larger world. The form of *Beautiful Losers* with its disjointed inner monologues interspersed with snippets of history and clippings from comic books is substantially the "cut-up" technique of William Burroughs alternating with one of the stylistic tricks from Sartre's *Nausea* which might be distinguished by the fact that Every Word Begins With A Capital. Both techniques suggest the merging of values which cannot occur without a breakdown in the structure of the world which they represent. In *Beautiful Losers*, as in Céline's *Journey To The End Of Night*, it is the universe itself which is breaking down, proceeding gradually but inevitably through the process of entropy. Cohen illustrates this process and then attempts to reverse it when the once glorious "F" disintegrates into a smelly old man but then escapes from the novel page (and, incidentally, the human predicament) by metamorphosing himself into a movie of Ray Charles. This is a flippant example, but it is another reminder that the Black Romantic justifies his presentation of disintegration by insisting that the breakdown of the old "false" categories leaves the way open for both reader and author to create new order. In Cohen's work, this justification is more impressive in theory than in practice. Techniques such as Cohen's "pure list" or Burrough's "cut-up" are successful only when there is some direction suggested for the movement beyond recorded disintegration, and it is this larger revelation which is most absent from extended passages of *Beautiful Losers*.

For these reasons, I suspect that Leonard Cohen is more important in Canadian writing for the contemporary movement which he represents than for the intrinsic merit of his work to date. The world of the Black Romantic may not be a particularly pleasant one, but its awareness of the darker side of human consciousness is a helpful counterbalance to a literary tradition that professes an ignorance of the human animal as complete as any of the Pollyanna Glad Books. As early as 1928 we can find A. J. M. Smith insisting: "the Canadian writer must put up a fight for freedom in the choice and treatment of his subject". Suggesting that desperate conditions require desperate remedies, he concludes: "our condition will not improve until we have been thoroughly shocked by the appearance in our midst of a work of art that is both successful and obscene."[4] *Beautiful Losers*, as successful pop-art, may just provide

the function Smith has in mind. At the same time, I am sorry to see Cohen join Layton in the role of public educator, because if he does have a future as a serious writer—if he wants one—it is back in the writing of *The Favourite Game* before Cohen, persona, solidified.

Footnotes

1. E. K. Brown, "The Problem of A Canadian Poetry," *Masks of Fiction*. Toronto, 1961.

2. Cyril Connolly, *The Modern Movement*. London, 1966.

3. Alfred Purdy, "Leonard Cohen: A Personal Look," *Canadian Literature* 23 (Winter 1965).

4. A. J. M. Smith, "Wanted, Canadian Criticism," *Canadian Forum* 91 (April 1928).

Bruce Meyer and Brian O'Riordan (essay date 1986)

SOURCE: Meyer, Bruce, and Brian O'Riordan. "Leonard Cohen." In *Profiles in Canadian Literature 6*, edited by Jeffrey M. Heath, pp. 49-56. Toronto: Dundurn Press, 1986.

[*In the following essay, Meyer and O'Riordan discuss Cohen's entire literary output up to his 1984* Book of Mercy, *focusing on Cohen's main themes of mythology, spirituality, and the importance of personal relationships.*]

Leonard Cohen is one of the most diverse talents on today's Canadian literary scene. Few writers have had such a variety of artistic careers in so short a time. Cohen's work has been so prismatic and diverse that he has generally defied any easy classification or categorization. His poems and novels have been anthologized all over the world and translated into ten languages. His songs and records have earned him a large cult following, and a somewhat iconographic reputation as a man of the 1960s—a pop idol and a sensitive "late-romantic".

As a poet and novelist Cohen's vagueness and sly wit translate into a transcendent quality, a spirituality which strives for a level of communication beyond the mundane realm of day-to-day existence. To achieve such a transcendent voice in his writings, Cohen relies heavily on the tone and language of Judaeo-Christian mythology and in his later work, such as the recent ***Book of Mercy,*** attempts a synthesis between the two mythologies.

The framework for such an amalgam of mythologies has been the poetic voice of the suffering lover. Cohen owes a great deal to the troubadour poets of twelfth-century France who began by writing hymns and sacred poems to their perfect lover, the Virgin Mary. Later the troubadours developed into wandering minstrels who sang their neo-religious love poems as secular songs and accompanied themselves on musical instruments. Throughout his career Cohen has shown a marked development in this direction.

In 1978 Leonard Cohen published **Death of a Lady's Man** to mixed reviews. The book takes the form of a dialogue between two contrary but empathetic voices as they struggle to resolve the truth of their relationship from two very divergent and complex points of view. Cohen has called this book a "Jungian dialogue between two halves of the same mind." As Platonic and unifying as this may appear, **Death of a Lady's Man,** written in both poetry and prose, represents a semi-climax in Cohen's poetic career, a moot-court where the inner tensions of the poet's persona are finally put to rest.

If you look at Cohen's work as a complete poem, something most critics are not apt to do, you will notice that the poem speaks of a man's struggles with his religion and his loves in order to attain a transcendence, or at least an acceptance, of the temporal realm. The early books, **Let Us Compare Mythologies** and **The Spice-Box of Earth,** present a somewhat saintly voice based on the mythological past and its influence on the present. Poems from **Let Us Compare Mythologies** such as **"For Wilf and His House"** and **"Exodus"** draw heavily on the Judaeo-Christian mythology, the framework of two contemporary religions, and adopt a distant, pious and ethereal tone that is somewhat removed from the harsh realities of the holocaust and modern relationships that fill the later books such as **Flowers for Hitler** and **Energy of Slaves.** In the process of coming to grips with his reality, Cohen has written a personal hagiography, a saint's life similar to the stories related by such hagiographers as the late-medieval Jacobus de Voragine. The resulting "life" which the poems present is that of a man, a holy man, whose transcendent values eventually come into conflict with the mortal pains and sufferings of the world. These harsh realities eventually tear him apart, almost by the process of martyrdom, until he is a dead reflection of his former self, a pair of voices arguing over how things really happened.

The process of personal hagiography through poetry began for Cohen in 1956 while he was still a student at McGill University in Montreal. There he fell under the influence of the Montreal Movement of Canadian poetry. It was a period in which the intense literary activity in that city heralded the rise to prominence of such major writers as Irving Layton, A. M. Klein, Louis Dudek and F. R. Scott. Although most of these writers are noted for their work during the late forties and fifties, Cohen appears at the end of the Montreal Movement's heyday and in many respects sums up the steps

his predecessors took toward a verse of great accessibility, common mythology and tonal control of lucid everyday experience.

When Louis Dudek selected Cohen's **Let Us Compare Mythologies** for the McGill Chapbook series in 1956, he must have been aware of the obvious connections between Cohen's work and that of Layton and Klein as well as the logical progression that the book represented in Canadian literary development. In fact, the connection with Layton is underlined by the poem **"To I. P. L."** where Cohen praises his teacher Layton for being "more furious than any Canadian poet." Like Klein's *The Rocking Chair and other poems,* **Let Us Compare Mythologies** makes generous use of the Montreal and Quebec landscape but in a more urban sense than Klein had achieved. Poems such as **"Saint Catherine Street"** and **"Satan in Westmount"** are examples of the work of a poet who has been influenced by the elders of his native terrain but who is still searching for his definitive voice and stance.

The majority of the poems in **Let Us Compare Mythologies** are lyrical and lilting and their language flows melodically. Their structural proximity to song enforces the hymn-like quality of such poems as **"Prayer for the Messiah"** while at the same time underscoring the mythological elements with a lyric primitivism that had not been seen in Canadian literature for several decades. For the most part, the poems in **Let Us Compare Mythologies** are simple and straightforward with a somewhat classical elegance inherent in their simplicity, meter and rhyme scheme. Perhaps one of the finest poems Cohen has written is **"Exodus"**, a long narrative poem detailing the passage of the Israelities from Egypt to the Promised Land. In this poem, Cohen describes the forty years in the desert through the use of a free verse narrative technique which allows the images to carry the story line of the poem while at the same time enriching the voice of the work with a clever eye for detail.

Cohen's next book, **The Spice-Box of Earth** (1961) shows that **Let Us Compare Mythologies** is not only a first book of poems but an introduction, a first step in a long and mythically oriented progression. In the first poem in **The Spice-Box of Earth, "A Kite is a Victim"**, Cohen plays heavily on the symbols and associations of the crucifixion while simultaneously maintaining an aloof religious stance. What pervades **"A Kite is a Victim"** is the mental picture the reader has of a kite—a cross with a piece of fabric attached to the four outer points. The associations with the crucifixion are further established through the use of such Christian symbols as the fish. However, Cohen never sets up a metaphor. He never says to the reader of this poem, "This is for that." Ambiguity and evasiveness are exactly the effects for which Cohen strives, and are probably the base for many rich interpretations that can be drawn from this poem.

The Spice-Box of Earth is an important book in the canon of Cohen's work because it represents the height of the poet's lyric purity. Poems such as **"Go By Brooks"** achieve an intimacy and serenity with a minimum of words and lines. The transcendent tone of Cohen's earlier work is still present in this volume and the dependence on the religious tradition aptly represented in such poems as **"Before the Story"** where the epigraph is drawn from the Second Book of Samuel in the Old Testament. However, *The Spice-Box of Earth* is also the point in Cohen's poetic career where the a-temporal voice begins to sputter into a vague and confused tongue and where the temporal world of sex, depression and regret takes its toll on the transcendent and innocent qualities of youth. *The Spice-Box of Earth* marks the point in Cohen's poetic career where his poetic voice enters a distinctly concrete, if not harsh, realm of pain, suffering and isolation.

Poems such as **"The Cuckold's Song"** mark a new voice for Cohen as a poet; the bitterness is less lyrical and, in this case, more personal. Leonard Cohen himself becomes a character in the poem. The voice is immediate. The combination of immediacy and personal presence in the poem can be read as the first step in Cohen's progression toward the identification and blurring of the poet with his poems.

From *The Spice-Box of Earth* the reader can perceive the waning of the earlier influences on Cohen and the gradual development of a new voice that exists in the realm of the here and now, a voice which is masochistic if not thoroughly "late romantic".

It is out of this new voice that *Flowers for Hitler* (1964) emerges as yet a further signpost in Cohen's poetic progression. The book which was originally entitled "Opium for Hitler" (but changed on the insistence of the publisher), is diverse in its themes and forms and includes: a one-act ballet-drama, "The New Step", an identification card, "All There Is To Know About Adolph Eichmann"; cartoon line drawings in **"Millenium"** and prose passages such as "Why Commands Are Obeyed". The book displays an increasing influence from pop culture—the forms and themes draw heavily on contemporary rather than literary resources.

In the poem, **"Style"**, Cohen questions the power of his beliefs to reconcile reality to his ability to write and suggests that beliefs have little meaning in the face of the atrocities and complex horrors which exist in the modern world. In previous volumes, style for Cohen had always been his direct link with a higher form of

existence, a knowledge or wisdom that he equated with beauty and which enabled him to maintain an air of purity, a cool objective distance. Here, however, Cohen abandons his "style" in favour of confronting those harsh realities which confound his transcendent gestures.

The world in *Flowers for Hitler* is a place of suffering, a suffering from which Cohen, the romantic and the martyr, cannot turn away. If Man in this context is truly a hostile animal, all that he can hope for in the future is for the establishment of a balanced equilibrium as described in the poem **"Millenium"**, where dogs and cats (contraries) smile at each other in reconciliation.

The problem with existence, as outlined in *Flowers for Hitler,* is that as long as Man continues to survive he will continue to suffer—a cynical, if not depressing, view. The book's epigraph warns the reader, "Take care not to suffer in your own homes what is inflicted upon us here." The best defence against destruction is to be human and to cheat the black angels of destruction with small, seemingly insignificant acts that contain a wealth and depth of meaning for those who resign themselves to an existence that contains little else. The reader is reminded of the famous line from Shakespeare's *King Lear*: "As flies to wanton boys, are we to the gods." To Cohen, the human race is not only at the mercy of its own misery, but in the grasp of a higher, less compassionate power.

As if in amplification of this view, Cohen entitles his next book **"Parasites of Heaven"** (1966). The insignificance of man suggested by the title of the book is enforced by the fact that the poems are untitled and although many seek to attain the slightly elevated mythic voice and stance of the first two volumes they fail because they are rooted in the temporal realm of human love and human experience. Cohen advises the reader to:

> Unmake me as I'm washed
> far from the fiery mask.
> Gather my pride in the coded pain
> which is also your domain.
>
> (p. 63).

The voice of the soul, the hallmark of Cohen's earlier work is now the voice of the body speaking to the soul. The poem, which was later entitled **"Suzanne"** and which became a popular song recorded by Cohen, is as much a dialogue between the voices of the body and the soul as it is a song about a woman whose Christ-like presence fills him with longing.

Suzanne represents but a single phase in the evolution of the female character in Cohen's poetry. The female figure makes many manifestations throughout the canon.

In some instances she is Marianne, a touchstone for Cohen's sadness. In other poems, she is the ideal woman for whom Cohen is searching, a Beatrice or Madonna Laura who takes the name "Marita" as in the poem "Marita please find me, I am almost thirty." Throughout her many personifications, the woman figure in Cohen's poetry is always something of a Circe, a fulcrum for the poet's contact with reality. In *Parasites of Heaven,* it is Suzanne who reveals the levels of meaning in the temporal world and who accents the poet's transcendent nature by providing a framework for his visions, a window into his own soul. This "persona of accessibility" reaches its culmination in the female voice of *Death of Lady's Man.*

Cohen's infatuation with the female figure forms the backbone of *The Energy of Slaves* (1972). However, the relationships, like all attempts at some form of vision for Cohen, break down in this book. Love becomes violence, passion becomes lust. What *The Energy of Slaves* ultimately proves is the inherent failure in all artistic endeavours. No matter how high the artist may attempt to reach, there is always an element of imperfection in his work. Cohen is faced with the dilemma that each small flaw in life or his life's work becomes magnified into the scar of defeat. It is artistically and aesthetically appropriate that each poem in *The Energy of Slaves* is headed, not by a title, but by a small decoration in the shape of a razorblade.

Failure can be a redeeming quality in a poet. Like martyrdom, failure contains a built-in glory, an implied significance and an air-tight reason for reading the next poem. Cohen must have had this very idea in mind when he rejected the 1968 Governor General's Award for Poetry which he won for his *Selected Poems.* When asked, rather angrily, by Mordecai Richler why he rejected the prize, Cohen could find no reasonable explanation. In fact, Cohen did not need to give one. The answer lies in his poetry and not in his critical defence of it.

For Cohen, the role of the poet has always been one of a modern Orpheus, a strangely lyrical person who is eventually torn apart by the wild ravages of passion whose frenzy he cannot fully fathom. Or, like Saint Sebastian, the poet, in Cohen's view, is a martyr, an innocent who through his need to perceive a realm higher than the temporal world is pierced and scarred by the injustices which he cannot completely embrace in the structure of his language. The vagueness, that elusive quality in Cohen's poetry, points to an underlying desire to form a more perfect expression, even if the price of attaining that utterance is hell itself.

The 1978 publication of *Death of A Lady's Man* brought about Cohen's withdrawal from an active role as a literary man, a withdrawal which lasted until 1982

when he resurfaced by writing the **"Introduction"** to Henry Moscovitch's book of poems. Cohen's introductory poem to the book is written in Spenserian stanzas. The lines flow in perfect meter and project a quiet empathy that has not been found in Cohen's work since *Let Us Compare Mythologies* and *The Spice-Box of Earth.*

The quiet empathy and spirituality continue in *Book of Mercy* (1984). *Book of Mercy* is a collection of reflective prose-poem meditations on the nature of mercy, the spirit, the body, faith, and doubt, and the relationship between the poet and his teacher in the process of coming to wisdom. The transcendent voice is present with perhaps more power than in any of Cohen's previous works. For Cohen, mercy is a state of grace or spiritual assurance that is entered into only through a lengthy process of doubt, reflection, initiation, and purgation. What becomes important is not the soul itself but the power of the soul to recognize and become aware of itself—in short, wisdom itself is secondary to the experience of wisdom.

The most important aspect of *Book of Mercy* is that through its confessional tone and its prayer-like invocations to some higher knowledge, it sums up Cohen's career as a poet, the story of a man who is in search of himself and who discovers the mythologies that articulate his role in the world.

Leonard Cohen has written two novels, *The Favorite Game* (1963) and *Beautiful Losers* (1966). Both were popular and controversial bestsellers, particularly in the case of *Beautiful Losers,* which sold over 400,000 copies. The novels have similar themes and motifs, but are radically different in style. Upon publication of *The Favourite Game,* Cohen immediately insisted that it was not a first novel: "One important thing everyone has missed: *The Favourite Game* IS A THIRD NOVEL DISGUISED AS A FIRST NOVEL."[1] Cohen in fact had written a considerable amount of prose in the period between 1956 and 1962, including a novel, *A Ballet of Lepers,* and some twenty short stories, several of which had been published. He also wrote four drafts of *The Favourite Game.*[2] The short stories and *A Ballet of Lepers* contain several incidents, situations and themes which appear, considerably reworked, in *The Favourite Game.*

The manuscripts of the novels and short stories in the Cohen Papers, housed at the University of Toronto, display the author's painstaking craftsmanship, his ability to revise constantly in order to produce tighter, more incisive and more powerful descriptions, images, and dialogues. He appears able to draw upon the resources of his earlier material (no matter how rough or juvenile) for suitable events, characters, and situations. *The Favourite Game* is at once both the culmination and the amalgam of Cohen's early prose efforts.

As in his poetry, one of Cohen's major themes in the novels is the meaning and importance of relationships—of love, sex, infidelity, and transcendence. It is primarily through his relationships with women that the protagonist of *The Favourite Game,* Lawrence Breavman, develops his artistic credo.

Before he meets Shell (one of the major female characters in the novel), Breavman's relationships with women are ritualistic, controlled and limited. Breavman always remains uncommitted, detached, distant, as he did in childhood and adolescent games of sexual torture and humiliation. With Shell, however, he has to confront, for the first time, such questions as:

> Suppose he went along with her toward living intimacy, toward comforting incessant married talk. Wasn't he abandoning something more austere and ideal, even though he laughed at it, something which could apply her beauty to streets, traffic, mountains, ignite the landscape—which he could master if he were alone?[3]

Breavman fears that his relationship with Shell will destroy his creativity, which he sees as being nurtured and inspired in no small way by his ability to use all of life as grist for his artistic mill. As the omniscient narrator informs us, Breavman wants simultaneously to be both actor and director. He wants to avoid hurting or being hurt; he wants to be both creator and created being.

Breavman, in other words, strives for the position of omniscient narrator. Cohen's use of the omniscient narrator's voice, however, reminds us of Breavman's inability to reach such a plateau. It is in fact impossible for someone so involved in the action to stand apart from it and make objective pronouncements. Like other men, Breavman is limited; he is not God-like.

Though Breavman is seldom absent from the foreground of any scene, the story is not told from his point of view. So, while we are clearly invited to sympathize with him, we are also invited to judge him. The narrative also includes Shell's story, and it is impossible not to sympathize with her and to take her side against Breavman. The use of the omniscient narrative voice, then, serves to undercut our sympathy for Breavman and to provoke in the reader an ambiguous reaction to him.

At the end of the novel, Breavman appears to realize that he has really hurt various people with whom he has come in contact. He has left scars on them, like the scars on Shell's ears which are described in the opening paragraphs of the novel. He cannot wipe away the scars and cannot suspend the passage of time. The scars are visible evidence of Breavman's hurtful contact with others. His art cannot immortalize the subjects of his art or himself, but paradoxically, Cohen suggests, the

artist's role is to defy mortality, to leave his mark and pass on. This is the point of Breavman's recollections at the end of the novel concerning his childhood playmates and how they used their bodies to imprint random shapes on the freshly fallen snow after being whirled away from a central spinner. Like the spinner, the artist creates art by using the life, the bodies, around him. Breavman, in the end, recognizes and accepts this reality and his own isolation and ruthlessness. He decides that maybe someday he will feel guilty for what he has done to others, but in the meantime he has to create.

This is certainly a questionable moral stance, but such is the exuberance and lyricism of Breavman's last reflection, the reader is almost swept away into embracing his stance, which is, in effect, a rationalization for ruthlessness. This is the seductiveness of the romantic vision of the artist, as someone different from and better than his fellow man. The power and beauty of Cohen's prose makes us feel as Breavman feels, and forces us to ponder the age-old question of whether the artist can or should be judged by ordinary human standards.

Beautiful Losers marks a deliberate turning-away from the careful, romantic, lyric writing of *The Favourite Game.* In this respect, it is comparable to **Flowers for Hitler** in its relation to Cohen's earlier poetry.

The dust-jacket of the first edition describes *Beautiful Losers* as:

> . . . a love story, a psalm, a Black Mass, a monument, a satire, a prayer, a shriek, a road map through the wilderness, a joke, a tasteless affront, an hallucination, a bore, an irrelevant display of diseased virtuosity, Jesuitical tract, an Orange sneer, a scatological Lutheran extravagance—in short a disagreeable religious epic of incomparable beauty.

There are more echoes in this work of Burroughs, Pynchon, Kafka and Barth than of Joyce or the earlier Cohen.

As in *The Favourite Game,* Canada, Jewishness, Montreal, religion, and the complexity of relationships are extensively commented upon, but the style of the novel is radically different. It is divided into three books. The first book is narrated by an unnamed, aging History professor, who is an authority on an almost extinct tribe of Canadian Indians, the Abishags. He is fascinated by the Iroquois virgin, the Venerable (now Blessed) Kateri Tekakwitha. His narrative is confused and fragmented, but it is possible to grasp that he is alone and decrepit, mourning the loss of both his Abishag wife, Edith, a suicide at age 24 (the same age Tekakwitha was when she died) and the death of his oldest friend, F., a member of Parliament and a Québec Separatist. It is also established that: Edith was raped when she was thirteen; that F., and the narrator were homosexual lovers; that Edith and F. were lovers; and that F. for many years dominated the lives of both Edith and the narrator.

Book Two is a long letter from F. written to the narrator of Book One. It is being read by the professor after F.'s death. In this letter, written while he is in a hospital for the criminally insane, subsequent to his arrest for terrorist activities, F. states for the narrator of Book One his theme and his purpose in writing the letter: "It is my intention to relieve you of your final burden: the useless History under which you suffer in such confusion"[4]. To this end F. writes in detail about: a weekend which he and Edith spent in Argentina, involving encounters with a Danish vibrator and Adolph Hitler; his view of History; and the last years of Tekakwitha's life and the miracles which occurred after her death. F. writes in a brutally direct, uncompromising style, stripping the narrator of any illusions which he may have had about Tekakwitha and her world and about the extent of his wife's debauchery and infidelity. F. feels that the narrator has been limited, oppressed by his academic passion for History, which has resulted in his withdrawal from everyday reality, in his caring more for a dead Indian virgin than for his own wife.

F.'s judgement that the professor's problem is that he is too rational is believable and credible, in that F. writes, even when describing fantastic, surreal scenes of excess, in a dispassionate, urbane, almost academic style. This style is in marked contrast to the deeply personal, jumbled, frantic, angry, self-pitying outpourings of the professor in Book One. They are not what we would have expected from an academic.

If F.'s point is that the professor should embrace the irrational it would seem, from the evidence in Book One, that he has indeed done so. It would also seem that, given the pitiful state to which the professor has been reduced, we should be asking ourselves if F.'s treatment of his friend through the years was a careful, planned, compassionate program of therapy or whether it was merely sadistic and perverse self-indulgence.

At the end of his long letter, F. writes: "Oh darling, be what I want to be" (*BL* [*Beautiful Losers*], p. 226). This is an admission on F.'s part that he cannot become a saint, cannot become "someone who has achieved a remote human possibility". But he does feel that his friend can achieve a kind of modern sainthood, a transcendence of reality. The necessary preconditions for modern sainthood seem to involve, for Cohen, making a spiritual breakthrough of some kind, freeing oneself from the imprisoning limitations of the flesh, as the couple in his poem **"Lovers"** do, or as Christ did in the Resurrection. F. attempts to do this through sexual excess, but in the process contracts a fatal venereal

disease. F. does not feel guilty about what he has done in his life, but the professor does have a sense of guilt. He cannot accept his own or others' sexuality, so he finds the self-mortifications of Tekakwitha attractive and begins to engage in some of his own. He also, however, feels sexually attracted to Tekakwitha. It is exactly this kind of irrational urge that F. counsels that he should act on—make love to a "saint"—and in the process be transformed.

Book Three has an omniscient narrative voice. The surreal events described are, therefore, given a disturbing edge of verisimilitude. In the brief epilogue, which is Book Three, the professor flees his treehouse prison and has a sexual encounter with a blond-haired woman, who tells him she is the ancient Greek goddess, Isis. This is the necessary prelude to his metamorphosis and resurrection at the end of the novel. The Isis-figure resembles the other female figures in the novel in that, like them, she is named (the leading male figures are not) and is a mediating, redemptive force. The professor, despite the sexual crudity of the scene involving the Isis-figure, finds a kind of love. She cradles his head, as Edith did with one of her rapists and with Hitler. Edith was capable of love; F. was not. The professor may finally be capable of it, and may be able to appreciate its force, its power to transform and to redeem. He, therefore, has a greater potential for destroying, losing his former self, and so achieving modern sainthood.

Beautiful Losers is a complex novel, full of literary, historical, religious and contemporary allusions and symbols. It is also a "pop" novel, with many near-pornographic and occasionally overblown, surrealistic passages. It is impossible at times to sort out the serious from the tongue-in-cheek. It is iconographic and iconoclastic, and cannot be easily dismissed or categorized.

Both *Beautiful Losers* and *The Favourite Game* are remarkable achievements. Though they differ so radically in style, they are both works in which the narrative voice at times both distances and seduces the reader simultaneously. *The Favourite Game* is, on the whole, more accessible and tightly structured than *Beautiful Losers,* but *Beautiful Losers* is a shocking, more powerful and more ambitious work.

Notes

1. *News and Notes of Books and Bookmen* (New York: Viking Press, 1963), p. 1.

2. University of Toronto Thomas Fisher Rare Book Library, Cohen Papers, Boxes 1 and 4.

3. Leonard Cohen, *The Favourite Game* (London: Secker and Warburg, 1963), p. 168.

4. Leonard Cohen, *Beautiful Losers* (Toronto: Mc-Clelland and Stewart, 1966), p. 200. Subsequently cited as *BL*.

Ken Norris (essay date spring/summer 1987)

SOURCE: Norris, Ken. "'Healing Itself the Moment It Is Condemned': Cohen's *Death of a Lady's Man*." *Canadian Poetry* 20 (spring/summer 1987): 51-60.

[*In the following essay, Norris presents an in-depth discussion of Cohen's* Death of a Lady's Man, *focusing in particular on the contradictions and ambiguities presented in the commentaries that follow each entry in the work.*]

"I decided to jump literature ahead a few years,"[1] reads the first sentence in **"I Decided,"** a prose poem one encounters some thirty pages into Leonard Cohen's *Death of a Lady's Man.* This is a somewhat curious assertion, reflecting confidence and a degree of egotism on the author's part. Adopting a tone somewhat reminiscent of Irving Layton in his attacks upon the gentility, propriety and philistinism of the Canadian reader, Cohen continues this piece in a spirit of confrontation:

> Because you are angry, I decided to infuriate you. I am infected with the delirious poison of contempt when I rub my huge nose into your lives and your works. I learned contempt from you. Philistine implies a vigour which you do not have. This paragraph cannot be seized by an iron fist. It is understood immediately. It recoils from your love. It has enjoyed your company. My work is alive.

(p. 42)

The reader has been harangued and insulted; at the same time he has become involved in a degree of textual play. Cohen maintains that this paragraph "cannot be seized" and "recoils from your love." At the same time it is "understood immediately" and has enjoyed the reader's company. Cohen's final statement—"My work is alive"—is perhaps meant to counter a statement made in *The Energy of Slaves,* a book that immediately preceded *Death of a Lady's Man*: "I have no talent left / I can't write a poem anymore."[2]

Whether or not we have understood this paragraph immediately, our engagement with it does not end with our reading of it. Because of the way *Death of A Lady's Man* has been structured, the prose poem **"I Decided"** is followed by an italicized commentary entitled "I Decided" which begins:

> Did he "jump literature ahead a few years"? Certainly this phase of his work constitutes one of the fiercest attacks ever launched against both the "psychological"

and "irrationalist" modes of expression. There is a new freedom here which invites, at the very least, a new scheme of determinism. There is also a willing sense of responsibility and manliness such as we do not find among the current and endless repetitions of stale dadaist re-discovery.

(p. 43)

Having been confronted by the author in the initial piece, the reader now encounters another voice in the commentary. This voice questions whether the author of **"I Decided"** succeeded in his desire of jumping literature ahead, assesses the attack upon the "psychological" and "irrationalist" modes of expression that this phase of Cohen's work is asserted to represent, and praises the "responsibility and manliness" of the author. What is this critic doing in the midst of this text? Pulling his own weight in the hall of mirrors, in the concert of voices that is *Death of a Lady's Man.*

Death of a Lady's Man is a difficult book to classify in terms of genre. It is not really a collection of poetry, although its primary text consists of poems and prose poems. Although the book tells a story (in a somewhat non-linear fashion) it falls outside the designation of being a novel. In its pairing of text with commentary it is stylistically reminiscent of Dante's *La Vita Nuova* and the Chinese *I Ching,* or *Book of Changes*. *Death of a Lady's Man* contains ninety-six poems and prose poems, eighty-three of them accompanied by commentaries. The commentaries respond to the poems or prose poems that immediately precede them. The responses are registered from a variety of standpoints, and alternately criticize, canonize, deconstruct, reconstruct, explicate, obscure or enhance the piece to which they are wedded.

In a number of the commentaries we are referred to an unpublished manuscript entitled *My Life in Art,* "from which many of the pieces of this present volume are excerpted or reworked" (p. 21). In a letter to Stephen Scobie, Cohen explained the relationship between *Death of A Lady's Man, My Life in Art,* and another unpublished work, *The Woman Being Born*: "*Death of a Lady's Man* derives from a longer work, called *My Life in Art,* which I finished . . . and decided not to publish. *The Woman Being Born* was the title of another manuscript and also an alternative working title for both *My Life in Art* and *Death of a Lady's Man.*"[3]

Death of a Lady's Man is haunted by the ghosts of these two unpublished manuscripts. Original passages in *My Life in Art* are constantly referred to in the commentaries, and the phrase "the woman being born" appears more than a half dozen times in the text. There is an interesting interplay between the three titles. The "death" of the lady's man is complemented by the woman "being born," while the "life in Art" exists beyond these births and deaths.

Death of a Lady's Man is also haunted by an earlier version of itself. Originally intended for publication in 1977, Cohen withdrew the manuscript in the eleventh hour, in order to effect major revisions, but not before galleys had been sent out to a number of reviewers. Sam Ajzenstat pointed out in his review of the later, revised version (published in 1978) that the major revision is the inclusion of the commentaries which did not appear in the earlier version of the book.[4] What was a somewhat tentative and mediocre book of poetry has been transformed by a wild display of style and irony embodied in the commentaries that interrogate, elucidate and undermine the original text.

While discussing textual relationships and titles, it is worth pointing out that, in the title *Death of a Lady's Man,* with its implication of the man as a womanizer, the spelling of "lady's" shifts the meaning significantly. This would then be a book about the death of one woman's man. Lest we judge Cohen and his publisher as bad spellers, a record album by Cohen released a year before the book was published, and seeming to have the same title, is entitled *Death of a Ladies' Man.* The variation in spelling is upheld and justified when we come to consider the actual content of the book. The discontinuous, non-linear "story" of this book is the progress of a marriage, and its eventual failure. The outcome is never in doubt for very long. The entire relationship is summarized in the poem **"Death of a Lady's Man"** in eight stanzas; we know by page thirty two of a two hundred and sixteen page book what the outcome of the marriage will be. Following this summary, the book is engaged with detailing the actual demise of the marriage, but it is, by no means, the only "marriage" that is presented for our consideration.

Death of a Lady's Man is adorned on the front and back covers, on the title page and at the termination of the text with a reproduction of a Renaissance woodblock print depicting the spiritual union of the male and female principle. This spiritual union is depicted as a sexual union, bringing into play the axis of sexuality/ spirituality upon which *Death of a Lady's Man* often turns. Cohen himself utilizes a sexual metaphor in writing of the marriage in the poem **"Slowly I Married Her,"** which concludes:

> And slowly I come to her
>   slowly we shed
>   the clothes of our doubting
>   and slowly we wed

(p. 182)

The union of opposites—the male and the female, the self and the other, the sacred and the profane, or what Cohen refers to in one passage as "what is holy and what is common" (p. 14)—is a synthesis that pervades the book.

Marriage is a central metaphor that extends outward to other interrelationships: the poet "married" to his life in art, the poem "married" to its commentary, a possible implied marriage of the reader to the text. In a prose poem entitled **"This Marriage,"** Cohen yokes together a paragraph about petty bickering between himself and his wife with a more "spiritual" paragraph in which the marriage is declared to have "foundations" that are "faultless and secure" (p. 54). In the accompanying commentary, the commentator observes about the poem that "It is a marriage and operates like one, healing itself the moment it is condemned" (p. 55). In my view, this is an apt evaluation of the book itself. Because of the interplay between text and commentary, the book is continually "healing itself" of the defects of its rhetoric or conceptual framework. The book constantly proclaims, and thereby transcends, its own limitations; it is a text that is at war and at peace with itself.

The primary text of *Death of a Lady's Man* ranges over a ten year period, telling the story of Cohen's marriage and his acts of infidelity, while at the same time probing his career as a singer-songwriter, his failure to deliver upon his artistic and political promises, as well as detailing his search for spiritual fulfillment. A number of personas pass before us and speak their piece: Cohen the pop star, Cohen the failed artist, Cohen the revolutionary, Cohen the husband, Cohen the religious seeker. The commentaries in the book are written "years later" as Cohen points out several times in his commentary to **"The Unclean Start."** The original text is being judged and evaluated by a later self who has experienced the failure of the marriage and is now engaged in the rigorous spiritual training of Zen Buddhism. In this confrontation and assessment of selves one is reminded of the brilliant mirror scene in Timothy Findley's novel *Famous Last Words.* Having abdicated the British throne, the Duke of Windsor, in the midst of an assassination plot launched against him in Portugal, drunkenly stumbles up to the Martello Tower of the Villa Cascais to hide. In the room where he hides there are a number of Baroque mirrors, and in them he sees three different images of himself. In one he sees himself as the Prince of Wales, in the second as the Duke of Windsor, in the third as an old man. In his drunkenness, the mirror images begin to speak to him and he carries on a conversation with them. When the threat of assassination becomes imminent, the Duke, in a fit of panic, runs through his own reflection, shattering the mirror and scarring his face for life.[5] In *Death of a Lady's Man* a similar interaction with images of self takes place, but the mirrors are never shattered, or a true self revealed.

In several instances mirrors are employed by Cohen's personas in order to affirm the image of the self. The most engaging appearance of the mirror takes place in the commentary to the prose poem **"My Life in Art,"** in which Cohen, in the midst of his Zen training, finds himself being caught up in "the moronic frivolity and despair of hours in the mirror" (p. 193). In this commentary Cohen also states: "Destroy particular self and absolute appears" (p. 193). In *Death of a Lady's Man* the erosion of particular self only leads to the establishment of particular selves, not to a revelation of the absolute, nor to the concrete establishment of the author's presence. Even in so seemingly personal a book, the author is, as Roland Barthes suggests in *The Pleasure of the Text,* "lost in the midst of [the] text."[6]

Before moving on to a consideration of how text and commentary interact in *Death of a Lady's Man,* I would like to cite Barthes' conception of "texts of pleasure" and "texts of bliss" in attempting to assess just what kind of textual expectations this book fulfills. Given that Cohen's whole body of work is steeped in eroticism and perversity, Barthes' sexual metaphor of textual pleasure, with his sense of textual pleasure as perversion and the text as fetish object, seems an appropriate model.

Barthes defines a text of pleasure as "the text that contents, fills, grants euphoria; the text that comes from culture and does not break with it, is linked to a *comfortable* practice of reading."[7] In contrast, the text of bliss is "the text that imposes a state of loss, the text that discomforts (perhaps to the point of a certain boredom), unsettles the reader's historical, cultural, psychological assumptions, the consistency of his tastes, values, memories, brings to a crisis his relation with language."[8] This contrast can perhaps also be recognized, more simply and in a Canadian light, in a statement made by Robin Blaser in an essay evaluating George Bowering's poetry: "So many are devoted to form as rest. Bowering's work is restless."[9]

So, too, is Cohen's. *Death of a Lady's Man* is a book that is certainly not linked to "a *comfortable* practice of reading." It aggravates, it frustrates, it bores, it perplexes and it offends. Although not as extreme in vision or as anti-climactic as Cohen's novel *Beautiful Losers,* it is often coarse, vulgar, obstinately ambiguous and inconclusive. It does not provide a smooth surface or a contented reading. At times when the poems *do* come to rest, the commentary provokes them into restlessness and ambiguity. Although the commentaries are sometimes amusing, we are also discomforted by them. Too often we are told by the commentary to revise our reading of the piece we have just read; this tends to unsettle our reading assumptions, violating, as it does, the reader's integrity, the reader's right to confer interpretation. The reader struggles to defend his own territory against these encroachments, while, at the same time, often being charmed or taken in by them. This makes, of course, for intriguing reading.

There are a number of poems and prose poems in *Death of a Lady's Man* that, judged individually, come up to the standard of Cohen's most anthologized poems ("**The Change,**" "**The Beetle,**" "**The Rose,**" "**Slowly I Married Her,**" and "**How to Speak Poetry**" are notable examples). Much of the energy and interest in the book, however, are generated by the commentaries and the way they interact with the poems.

An example that occurs early in the book is the case of a prose poem entitled "**Death to This Book.**" Not a very aesthetically successful piece, "**Death to This Book**" vitriolically curses and condemns both the book and the marriage in a coarseness of language and spirit. Having read the piece, we move on to the commentary, which reads in part:

> Does he really wish to negate his life and his work? Although the energy is similar, we get a different picture from the first passage of an unpublished manuscript called My Life in Art, from which many of the pieces of this present volume are excerpted or reworked.
>
> We begin the Final Revision of My Life in Art. There hasn't been a book like this in a long time. Much of the effort of this ultimate version will be expended trying to dignify a worthless piece of junk. The modern reader will be provided a framework of defeat through which he may view without intimidation a triumph of blazing genius. I have the manuscript beside me now. It took me years to write . . . It will become clear that I am the stylist of my era and the only honest man in town.
>
> (p. 21)

At the very least, this is all somewhat unsettling for the reader. An obscenity-laced tirade is followed by a commentator who wonders whether the negation of the tirade was delivered in earnest, then produces a passage from an unpublished manuscript which has a similar energy but gives a different picture. So we begin to read a passage from the "final revision" of *My Life in Art* which is incorporated into the "final revision" of *Death of a Lady's Man.* The assertions that "There hasn't been a book like this in a long time" and that "Much of the effort of this ultimate version will be expended trying to dignify a worthless piece of junk" are supposedly about *My Life in Art*; yet they radiate out to become comments about, or at least thoughts to have about, *Death of a Lady's Man.* Although Cohen asserts in this passage that *My Life in Art* is "worthless junk," he also proclaims that he is "the stylist of [his] era and the only honest man in town." The reader feels that he is being conned at every turn, at every staging. Yet perhaps there is some truth in Cohen's statements about style and honesty. *Death of a Lady's Man* is a book in which style and strategy count for just about everything. That the book is a text in which any assertion is rarely ever allowed to rest or to close off discourse also suggests that we might find a greater degree of honesty in the constant contradictions that crop up in this text than in a text that never calls itself into question.

The questions and contradictions come from every direction, in a proliferation of attitudes and voices. In the piece **"Another Room,"** Cohen congratulates himself for having worked upon his writing rather than disturbing the heart of a girl by taking sexual advantage of her. In the commentary, it is the voice of the girl that contradicts the piece: "But you *have* disturbed my heart . . . I am not protected from your agitation of my heart . . . Your song is cruel and selfish . . . It is futile to contact you in the midst of your training but I've been hoping you might fall on a spear and leave your master and live with me on the servicemen's beach behind the Gad Hotel" (p. 23). Similarly, in the commentary to **"The Lover After All,"** it is the voice of the wife that speaks, declaring that "Even though the purity of your love is affirmed by the unanimous quiver of every feather in the celestial host, I am not going back to the axe of your love, O triumphant husbandman and lassoo king of the gateless horses . . . I will be never again the cup of your need" (p. 67).

Whereas these commentaries confront and contradict the persona of the pieces, other commentaries react to the artistry of the pieces themselves. The love poem **"I Have Taken You,"** is followed by a commentary that tells us

> This poem fails because something has been "withheld" from the reader. There is a lie here, or a deep stinginess with the truth. The poem begins to rot after the third line, maybe after the second . . . What happened between them escapes this poem. Their mutuality requires the most obvious crutches of Victorian syntax, just to limp down the page.
>
> (p. 39)

The poem **"O Wife Unmasked,"** a somewhat spiritualized love poem, ends with the lines: "What sad bureaucracy of luck / to be with you and you alone / muddling through the Day of Judgement," (p. 128) to which the commentary immediately responds: "Claustrophobia! Bullshit! Air! Air! Give us air! Is there an antidote to this mustard gas of domestic spiritism?" (p. 129). Lest we think that all of the evaluative commentaries are condemnatory, there is the commentary made in reference to the prose poem **"The Change":** "I think this qualifies as great religious poetry and also earns itself a place in the annals of complaint" (p. 19).

Death of a Lady's Man contains pieces that wrestle with the questions of political allegiances and spiritual revelation, and it is in these instances that the commentaries are sometimes played mostly for laughs. In the prose poem **"Our Government-In-Exile"** Cohen

earnestly proposes a new world order. He writes: "One day this will be over. The war against the poor . . . I'll live to see a decent society built around this page" (p. 24). The commentary informs us:

> This is the work of a middle-class mind flirting with terrorism—not without a certain charm. A modest effort should be made by all concerned to discredit and neutralize this type of inflammatory expression now that the actual business of running the country is in our hands. His thought did have a certain currency among extremists of every persuasion, and he was a familiar figure in the revolutionary cafes of pre-Independence Montreal with his ouija board and Walther PPK automatic. There was inherent, however, in all his positions, an unattractive frivolity which necessarily disqualified him from the responsibilities of leadership. When asked to clarify his stand on certain important matters, he replied, "How can you concern yourself with these things while Layton and I are alive?"
>
> (p. 25)

Behind the surface humour of this passage there are a few serious implications being made about art and politics. Positing that the running of the country is now in the hands of what was once "our government-in-exile," the revolutionaries are depicted as seeking to "neutralize" and "discredit" inflammatory expression; at the same time, they disqualify the artist from "the responsibilities of leadership." The supposed statement Cohen has made about himself and Layton reflects the artist's egotistical concern which takes precedence over questions of truth and justice.

As we have seen, the forms of the commentaries are diverse. Some refer us back to notebooks ("the Nashville Notebooks of 1969" [p. 187], "the blue-spined Italian Notebook, summer of 1975" [p. 117]) or to the original version or final revision of *My Life in Art* in order to elucidate a text or to show how a poem originated. In the commentaries to the prose poems **"Orion"** and **"I Like The Way You Opposed Me"** we are given line-by-line explications that read like religious commentary or pseudo-New Criticism.

In the prose poem **"To Deal With You"** Cohen states that "It was a crude charlatan's trick, trying to associate the obscurity of your style with the mystery of the godhead" (p. 48); while in the commentary we are told that "This paragraph is, I believe, an invitation for the truly bored to come out of the closet and be baffled one more time, one last time" (p. 49). There is no doubt that, in many respects, ***Death of a Lady's Man*** is "a crude charlatan's trick," a network of truthful and misleading information going nowhere in particular. We are lost in a hall of mirrors, the funhouse of the text. For all of its alchemical combining of the high and the low, the serious and the comic, the male and the female, there is no revelation, no transformation, no "triumph of blazing genius" (p. 21). The act of reading *Death of a Lady's Man,* however, certainly involves the reader in pleasures of the text. We may not wind up with many conclusions, but we do become engaged in an elaborate reading experience.

What about the death we were promised in the title? Is it actual or metaphorical? Does it exist at all in this book? Confronting this question in the commentary to **"She Has Given Me the Bullet,"** Cohen writes:

> There is the bullet but there is no death. There is the mist but there is no death. There is the embrace but there is no death. There is the sunset but there is no death. There is the rotting and the hatred and the ambition but there is no death. There is no death in this book and therefore it is a lie.
>
> (p. 113)

There *are* a few places we can look for this "death." There is the poem **"Death of a Lady's Man."** Perhaps there is a metaphorical or symbolic death in that poem. There is something of one; in the seventh stanza we are told

> The last time that I saw him
>   he was trying hard to get
> a woman's education
>   but he's not a woman yet.
>
> (p. 31)

Could this represent the "death" of the lady's man, while at the same time providing a sharp irony to the concept of "the woman being born"? Maybe.

There are a few suggestions of a spiritual or emotional death littering the text—"You are a dead man / writing me a letter" (p. 137); there is even a commentary that reads like a will—

> I leave my silence to a co-operative of poets
> who have already bruised their mouths against it . . .
>
> I leave to several jealous men a second-rate legend
> of my life.
>
> (p. 187)

Nevertheless, the reader is inclined to agree with the commentator who wrote "There is no death in this book . . ." (p. 113). The book continues being written and re-viewed.

How does this text attempt to resolve itself? The last entry in the book is entitled **"Final Examination,"** and is a five line poem followed by a commentary. The poem reads

> I am almost 90
> Everyone I know has died off
> except Leonard

> He can still be seen
> hobbling with his love.
>
> (p. 212)

This somewhat pathetic poem raises more questions than it answers. For one, who is speaking in this poem, who is the I? In the poem, Cohen is still alive, seen "hobbling with his love." Who or what is his love? The wife who has been present throughout the book, from this future perspective, has left him years ago. Is his love another woman, his spiritual devotion, his life in art?

We turn to the commentary, looking for resolution and answers, and read the following:

> I have examined his death. Although it is unstable, I doubt that we shall find the old goat nibbling again at the lacy hem of the various salvations. I am more vulgar than he was, but I never pretended to a spiritual exercise. Furthermore, his death is sexless and cannot be used in politics. There is a cheap sweet smell in the air for which he bears some responsibility. I swear to the police that I have appeared, and do appear, as one of his voices. I see in the insignificance of these pages a shadow of the coming modesty. His death belongs to the future. I am well read. I am well served. I am satisfied and I give in. Long live the marriage of men and women. Long live the one heart.
>
> (p. 212)

We bring together the facts about the "death" of the lady's man that are presented in this paragraph and, like the pieces from different jigsaw puzzles, they don't fit together. The death is "unstable," "sexless and cannot be used in politics," and is a death that "belongs to the future." We may have a death, but we certainly can't produce a corpse, unless it is the body of the text. It certainly *isn't* the body of the author. Looking to the teachings of Zen Buddhism, we find that enlightenment is often spoken of as a "great death, the step of dying to oneself that is coincident with rebirth in realization."[10] This rebirth would never be termed "unstable." As it is, the voice that speaks, that swears "to the police that I have appeared, and do appear, as one of his voices," states that he doubts that "we shall find the old goat nibbling again at the lacy hem of the various salvations." If there is any "rebirth in realization" it is in the recognition that "I am more vulgar than he was, but I never pretended to a spiritual exercise."

The reader reaches outside of this paragraph to the body of the text to come to some conclusion about this concluding paragraph, in an attempt to make sense, to close off the reading, in order to be finished with the text. We know that the marriage is over; in that sense the "lady's man," the husband, has died. The author, with his multitude of voices, goes on living. It is *his* death that "belongs to the future." The voice that speaks on his behalf claims to be "well read," "well served" and "satisfied." In the face of the failure of Cohen's marriage, marriage is affirmed. In **"The Unclean Start"** Cohen had written "We are married: there is only one heart" (p. 86). It is the one heart of marriage that is affirmed in the book's last line.

An ironic ending? Possibly. Certainly an uncomfortable ending for the reader. On the facing page to the "final examination" there is a reproduction of the male and the female principle embracing in spiritual/sexual union, reiterating the primary dynamic of the book. This reader remembers Cohen having written in the commentary to **"The Good Fight"**: "When will we collaborate again, men and women, to establish a measure for our mighty and different energies . . . We are each other's Mystery. This Mystery will not yield to violence or dissection" (p. 115). There is a principle of rest, of union in this. But then, looking again at the illustration, one notices that the male principle is enjoying the superior position in the depicted union, inviting a discussion of sexual politics, and a scathing feminist critique of a book that is overloaded with male dominant ideology.

Death of a Lady's Man is one of a number of somewhat "eccentric" literary works that have been written in Canada over the past twenty years that suggest a direction for Canadian writing other than the realist novel and the social realist poem (Bowering's *Burning Water,* Ondaatje's *The Collected Works of Billy the Kid* and *Coming Through Slaughter,* bp Nichol's *The Martyrology* and Cohen's own *Beautiful Losers* are some other examples). Rather than take as their *raison d'etre* the mimetic representation of everyday life, these works concern themselves with, in George Bowering's words, "the efficacy of the sentence as the basis of reality."[11] Forcing our attention onto the status of the text, and the attendant pleasures of the text, they are inviting Canadian critics to supplement thematic interpretations and character analysis with a discussion of textual strategies and open-ended readings.

Notes

1. Leonard Cohen, *Death of a Lady's Man* (Markham, Ontario: Penguin Books, 1979), p. 42. All other quotations are cited by page number in the text.

2. Leonard Cohen, *The Energy of Slaves* (Toronto: McClelland and Stewart, 1972), p. 112.

3. Stephen Scobie, *Leonard Cohen* (Vancouver: Douglas and McIntyre, 1978), pp. 156-57.

4. Sam Ajzenstat, "The Play's the Thing," *Books in Canada* (October 1978), p. 10.

5. Timothy Findley, *Famous Last Words* (Markham, Ontario: Penguin Books, 1982), pp. 245-252.

6. Roland Barthes, *The Pleasure of the Text* (New York: Hill and Wang, 1975), p. 27.

7. Barthes, *The Pleasure of the Text,* p. 14.

8. Barthes, *The Pleasure of the Text,* p. 14.

9. Robin Blaser, "George Bowering's Plain Song," *Particular Accidents: Selected Poems of George Bowering* (Vancouver: Talonbooks, 1980), p. 9.

10. Robert Aitken, *Taking the Path of Zen* (San Francisco: North Point, 1982), p. 51.

11. George Bowering, unpublished interview in the author's possession, p. 3.

Stephen Scobie (essay date 1991)

SOURCE: Scobie, Stephen. "Leonard Cohen, Phyllis Webb, and the End(s) of Modernism." In *Canadian Canons: Essays in Literary Value,* edited by Robert Lecker, pp. 57-70. Toronto: University of Toronto Press, 1991.

[*In the following essay, Scobie discusses the place of Cohen and Phyllis Webb in the emerging canon of Canadian modern and postmodern literature, arguing that Cohen's work has been less influential than Webb's.*]

POLEMICAL INTRODUCTION[1]

The process of canon-formation in Canadian literature has largely taken place over the last twenty-five years: during, that is, the period of tremendous expansion both in the publication of Canadian writing and in the complementary practices of criticism and institutional teaching. This period is also, in the wider field of literary history, one of transition and interplay between modernism and postmodernism.

I use these terms with some hesitation: postmodernism especially is now bandied about so widely, and in such loose and imprecise ways, that its value as a distinction within critical discourse may well be questioned. At a later stage in this paper, I outline briefly the commonly understood senses of these terms; but almost every writer on modernism and postmodernism now seems to be devoted as much to blurring the distinction as to sharpening it. The 'post,' we are told, does not really indicate temporal sequence; the two movements are implicated in each other. When I use them in this essay, then, they should be understood as having a Derridean mark of erasure hovering over them: I find them useful, even unavoidable, as rhetorical categories, but I do not ultimately believe in their existence.

Given these qualifications, then, what has been the effect on 'the Canadian canon' of its being formed during the period in which these two movements were in transition and interplay? Since canon-formation is an intrinsically conservative process, the dominant effect has been to enshrine modernism (or, more precisely, the *late* modernism of the 1960s and 1970s) as the canonical mainstream of contemporary Canadian literature. This can more clearly be seen in the canonization (one might even say deification) of Margaret Atwood and Robertson Davies. As the critical process filters down from the exalted heights of academic journals like *Essays on Canadian Writing* to the more mundane levels of the books page in *Maclean's,* one might at times be forgiven for thinking that Atwood and Davies are the only two authors in Canada—though Alice Munro, Mavis Gallant, and the memory of Margaret Laurence are also occasionally mentioned. The fiction of this canon is basically realist, though the realism is often very sophisticated in its handling of narrative technique, and it may veer towards the fantastic; the poetry is metaphorical, dominated by the short lyric; and the criticism is thematic and expository.

At the same time, there is a kind of postmodernist alternative canon, promoted in more esoteric journals such as *Open Letter,* which has made much more limited inroads into the popular view of Canadian literature. The fiction of this canon features either metafictional self-reflexiveness, or else the overt abandonment of plot; the poetry is metonymic, moving towards the open form and the long or continuing poem; and the criticism is formal and theoretical. (It is thus frequently subject to charges of academic elitism.) Major figures here would be bpNichol, Robert Kroetsch, and George Bowering. Much feminist writing, such as that of Daphne Marlatt and Lola Lemire Tostevin, seems more closely allied to the postmodernist canon: but a key aspect of feminist theory has been to question the very idea of canon-formation itself.

This paper is focused on the work of two poets, Leonard Cohen and Phyllis Webb, who occupy equivocal positions in relation to this emerging canon and anti-canon. Cohen seems to be securely placed in the modernist canon: of the forty-four major anthologies surveyed by Margery Fee,[2] he appears in twenty-five. His position in literary history, as a major writer of the 1960s, is unchallenged. He is also, like Atwood and Davies, a figure well known to the popular (non-academic) audience, both in Canada and in Europe. Yet his 'modernist' work is continually contaminated (if that is not too loaded a word) by the gestures of postmodernism.

Webb also appears to come out of a strongly modernist tradition, but her work, especially in recent years, has drawn much more attention and support from critics in the postmodernist tradition. She has never achieved quite so secure a place as Cohen's in the mainstream: she appears, for instance, in only eighteen of Fee's anthologies. In 1974 Frank Davey wrote that she 'stands at the juncture between the modernist and post-modernist sensibilities.'[3] My argument in this essay is that both Webb and Cohen stand at this juncture; but that Cohen may ultimately be seen as a modernist in the trappings of postmodernism, while Webb is a postmodernist in the trappings of modernism. It is for this reason, I would argue, that Cohen has been more easily assimilable into the dominant canon.

Another way of phrasing Davey's point is to say that Cohen and Webb stand at the end(s) of modernism. 'End' is here to be understood both as 'aim' or 'purpose,' and as 'final point in a temporal sequence'— and it is always potentially plural. The 'end' (purpose) of modernism may be to fulfil itself, its own aesthetic; or it may be to provide the opening out of its own mode into that of postmodernism. So modernism may or may not 'end' (finish): it may be seen as being superseded by a subsequent movement, or it may be seen to be living on (in) its own post-.

LEONARD COHEN AND PHYLLIS WEBB

The poetic careers of Leonard Cohen and Phyllis Webb may not at first glance appear very similar. Cohen has always been a poet much in the public eye, ever since, quite literally, he invited an NFB film crew into his bathroom; Webb has led an altogether quieter, more reclusive life. The popular image of Cohen would place him on a concert stage in front of a sold-out audience of adoring fans; Webb would be envisaged sitting alone on the shore of Salt Spring Island.

Beyond these differences in the images they have come to project (or to have projected on them), there is a strange parallelism in the broad outlines of their two careers. Both began writing and publishing poetry in Montreal in the early 1950s and were associated with the small magazines of that time, such as *CIV/n.* Webb's first appearance in book form was as part of *Trio* in 1954, and her first solo volume, *Even Your Right Eye,* appeared in 1956—the same year as Leonard Cohen's **Let Us Compare Mythologies.** At that time, both were seen as young writers of great promise, but their work was known mainly within the narrow circles of the Canadian literary audience, especially in Montreal.

For both Webb and Cohen, the first half of the 1960s was a period of intense creativity, during which they produced the finest work of their early careers; but, while Webb's work continued to reach only a specialized readership, Cohen made a decisive breakthrough to a wider audience. In 1962 Webb published *The Sea Is Also a Garden*; in 1965 she turned from extended philosophical meditation to the clarity and compression of *Naked Poems*, a beautiful book, but published only in a limited edition. Cohen's **The Spice-Box of Earth**

(1961), on the other hand, not only established his reputation as a sensuous and romantic lyricist, but also became the best-selling single volume of Canadian poetry. Darker and more sinister, **Flowers for Hitler** (1964) added to his reputation for flamboyant gestures and outrageous excess. During this period, Cohen also published two novels: *The Favourite Game* in 1963 and *Beautiful Losers* in 1966.

After 1966 both Cohen and Webb entered periods of crisis in their writing, though in Cohen's case this is complicated by his shift of emphasis to the medium of popular song. From his first album, **Songs of Leonard Cohen** (1968), onwards, Cohen has maintained a steady output of recordings and concert appearances: so it cannot really be said that he ever lapsed into silence in quite the way that Phyllis Webb did. But the *written* texts which Cohen published (or, more significantly, did not publish) during the decade of the 1970s are all marked by radical uncertainty and self-questioning. This crisis was first signalled in 1969, when Cohen turned down the Governor General's Award given to his **Selected Poems,** saying that while he himself appreciated the honour, the poems forbade it. The poems continued to demonstrate a similar recalcitrance: in 1972 **The Energy of Slaves** launched a direct attack on the poet's own image and standing:

> I have no talent left
> I can't write a poem anymore
> You can call me Len or Lennie now
> like you always wanted[4]

Death of a Lady's Man (1978) is more indirect in its strategy, using a supplementary layer of commentary to undercut and question the rhetorical efficacy of the poet's language and authority.

Webb's silence during this period was more complete. Between *Naked Poems* in 1965 and *Wilson's Bowl* in 1980, only a handful of poems appeared in print: two new pieces in the 1971 *Selected Poems,* and occasional poems in magazines and anthologies such as *Mountain Moving Day.* Webb was at work on a projected series of poems on the Russian anarchist Kropotkin, but this 'legendary' collection never coalesced, surviving only as fragments in *Wilson's Bowl.* For Webb, as for Cohen, the 1970s was a period of withdrawal, doubt, self-questioning, and minimal publication.

In the 1980s both poets have cautiously re-emerged. Neither has quite regained the confidence or productivity of the early 1960s, but both appear to have broken through the barriers of the previous decade. Webb's reappearance in *Wilson's Bowl* was followed by the justly deserved Governor General's Award for *The Vision Tree* in 1982, by *Water and Light* in 1984, and by *Hanging Fire* in 1990. Cohen's **Book of Mercy** (1984) is a volume of prose poems and prayers in which the vocation of the poet is once again proclaimed rather than doubted; he has gone on to produce two of his finest records, **Various Positions** (1985) and **I'm Your Man** (1988). The latter was a huge popular and critical success (especially in Norway!) and returned him to the forefront of public attention.

In their poetic careers, then, Leonard Cohen and Phyllis Webb offer one possible paradigm for the history of Canadian poetry over the last four decades. Both have their roots in the earlier traditions of Canadian modernism through their contacts in 1950s Montreal: Webb through her friendship with F. R. Scott; Cohen through his close associations with Louis Dudek and Irving Layton. Both took part in the burgeoning of Canadian poetry and publishing during the early 1960s, in the retrenchment of the 1970s, and in the cautious pragmatism of the 1980s.

For both Cohen and Webb (as, indeed, for all successful writers), this history has also presented a problem: they have had to confront the accumulations of their own public images as well as their relationships to new styles and younger generations. The image of the romantic Leonard Cohen, brooding over his tortured soul with a succession of blonde young women on his arm, or the image of the reclusive Phyllis Webb, contemplating silence on her lonely island, may be reductive and clichéd, doing little justice to the subtlety and complexity of their poems, but there is a sense in which such images are now, whether the writers like it or not, *part of their work.* In an age in which so much peripheral attention is devoted to authors—in interviews, magazine articles, television features, academic criticism, publicity campaigns, writers' festivals, etc.—it is harder than ever for a reader to maintain a separation of the writer and the work. The writer becomes as fictional as the text; the writer's public image, whether deliberately created or not, *is* a text, and must be read as such.

In this broader sense, 'text' includes not only the officially published work (poems, novels, essays) and its semi-official margins (interviews, concert appearances, book covers), but also the inscription of the poet's *voice.* The limitations of Cohen's vocal range (which he both observes and exploits in his recordings) are as much a part of his signature as Webb's intensely expressive, beautifully modulated reading voice is of hers. The voice, however, is not a privileged access to the 'presence' of the author: it is that presence dramatized, projected, *staged.*

Cohen's career as a popular singer has of course made him acutely aware of voice, and of the degree to which his public image is part of his work; he has participated in the shaping of that image with wit, irony, and detachment. Even the rejection of the Governor General's

Award, however sincere it may have been, contributed strongly to the canonization of Leonard Cohen in his anti-poet stance. Everything from the plain dark suits he constantly wears to the incongruous banana he holds on the cover of *I'm Your Man* plays with or against the associations of the 'Black Romantic' image: the edge of self-parody allows him to distance himself from the absurdity of the pose while at the same time indulging in it anyway. But Webb's image of aloofness and isolation, if less consciously chosen and manipulated on her part, is no less unavoidable. Refusal to play the publicity game becomes another move in the game.

Even before he began releasing records, Cohen's work was directed to a public audience; the poetry readings of the early 1960s, such as those preserved in the NFB documentary *Ladies and Gentlemen, Mr. Leonard Cohen,* show his considerable skill as a stand-up comedian. In entering the world of popular music and concert touring, Cohen was putting himself on the line, offering his own presence and persona as the focus of his work. The enormous stresses which this produced may be seen in *Bird on the Wire,* a documentary by Tony Palmer, filmed during Cohen's 1972 tour of Europe. The constant pressure of touring—the physical demands of the travel, the need to give interviews at every stop, the demands of fans who can switch in a moment from adoration to hostility, the singer's sense of responsibility to the musicians in his band, to the managers, to the promoters—all of this culminates, in the film, in the moment when Cohen walks off a Jerusalem stage, unable to go on singing. The film closes with a memorable image of Cohen sitting on the floor of the tour bus, huddled close into himself, seeking a privacy which has long since vanished.

Yet in many ways Cohen is very good at playing the role of popular musician. In journalistic interviews, he is constantly able to come out with gnomic statements which simultaneously conform to, and mock, the popular idea of 'the poetic.' For example, in an interview with Pia Southam in a Vancouver magazine called *V,* published in December 1988, he responded to the question 'How has your attitude to love changed over the years?' by saying,

> In those days, when I wrote about love I was touched by those images very much; but I didn't know what the real bondage of love was. I hadn't been wiped out by love. I hadn't taken the wound. I'd seen it, but I had never surrendered. I was moving awfully briskly from flower to flower. I saw the dangers, the pain, the beauty; I saw the essential quality, but I never surrendered until I was a lot older. A song like 'I'm Your Man' is on the other side of that surrender. It's only after having taken the wound that you can write the kind of song which is beyond funny. It's kind of desperate humour. It's only when you're no longer much of a prize that you can offer yourself so generously to somebody else.[5]

This is the kind of copy that journalists dream of. But what is the critic to make of it? Is this a throw-away comment to a casual interviewer, a piece of pretentious condescension, or is this a poem? Is it part of the Leonard Cohen canon?

Given the attractions of writing personality profiles, and of telling us once again about who Suzanne was or wasn't, it is not surprising that there is comparatively little serious critical writing about Leonard Cohen. The 1970s saw two books, by Michael Ondaatje in 1970 and by myself in 1978, as well as important articles by Sandra Djwa, Douglas Barbour, and Linda Hutcheon; but the last few years (with the exception of a fine article on *Death of a Lady's Man* by Ken Norris) have been largely devoid of new considerations. It is surely time for a reassessment of the early work, and especially of *Beautiful Losers,* in the wider historical perspective. And the whole body of Cohen's songs is still scandalously unattended to.

Although Phyllis Webb's public profile has never been as high as Leonard Cohen's, her very reclusiveness has itself become a part of her image. In many ways, this has had a more seriously distorting effect on the reading of her work than Cohen's notoriety has had on his. For, though Webb's poetry is often private and solitary, it has always had also a dimension of public care and political concern. The great weakness of Webb criticism has been to present her as inward-turning and solipsistic, to the exclusion of that political world on which Jacobo Timerman turns his astonished eye in 'Prison Report.'[6] As recently as 1987, George Woodcock could still write that 'for Phyllis Webb, growing maturity as a poet has meant growing withdrawal—a narrowing of contacts with the world paralleling a narrowing of the circle of the creative self,' and that she 'has also practised austerities and simplifications in her life and has sought the reclusion that all good artists, like all saints, find necessary at some time in their careers.'[7] This not only demonstrates a limited appreciation of Webb's work for CBC radio (collected in *Talking*) and her active engagement in the work of Amnesty International; it also represents a drastically reductive reading of her poetry.

Yet this image of Webb as a 'saint' has persisted in the criticism of her work. Nowhere is it more evident than in the bizarre article which John Bentley Mays published in *Open Letter* in 1973. While Mays accuses John Hulcoop (not without some justification) of romanticizing Webb as 'a devotee of the "Priestess of Motion,"'[8] he himself is busy transforming her into *his* Romantic image of the suffering, damned artist in the lineage of Sade, Artaud, or Plath. At the end of this line stands, evidently, John Bentley Mays: Webb's poetry is only the excuse for a somewhat tedious self-examination of how the author's naïve 1960s idealism withered in the 1970s.

Implicit in both Woodcock and Mays is the accusation that Webb's work confines itself to an ivory tower of political naïvety (rather than the painfully transparent and fragile 'glass castle' which is Webb's actual image). This accusation was picked up by Frank Davey in his entry on Webb in *From There To Here* (1974), which describes her poetry as 'vain, private, and inconclusive' (262). While Davey is in most cases a very astute critic, this is one comment which says a good deal more about Frank Davey than it does about Phyllis Webb: and what it says is that Davey in 1974, arguing for the advent of a postmodernist literature in Canada, saw Webb at that time as the epitome and culmination (the end) of the modernist tradition to which he was opposed.

In his introduction to *From There to Here,* Davey lists Webb among the 'older modernist poets' (22) whose work is being replaced by the young writers of the electronic age. But in his entry on Webb, Davey recognizes that the case is not quite so simple. It is there he writes that 'Phyllis Webb's poetry stands at the juncture between the modernist and post-modernist sensibilities' (264). Davey's book was one of the earliest statements in Canadian criticism of what have come to be recognized as the broad outlines of the modernist/postmodernist distinction. He describes the characteristics of modernist poetry as 'rigorously disciplined rhetoric, mythic and historical reference, rigidly sculptural structure, and totally impersonal and unemotional tone' (19). The poem is seen as an aesthetic object whose internal formal organization is more important than its external reference; modernism's ideals were those of control, of organic unity, or ironic distance, and of impersonality. On the other hand, postmodernism is radically open-ended, resisting the closure of modernist form. It denies that a writer can ever be fully in control of her work; but rather than deploring this fragmentation, as modernism would do, it celebrates and exploits it. Whereas modernism used its 'mythic and historical reference' as touchstones of order and stability in which to attempt to ground the flux of the chaotic present, postmodernism uses myth and history as elements of intertextuality which extend the free play of reference, which take the text even further into the open-ended field of dissemination. The impersonality of modernism (the judicious self-effacement of T. S. Eliot, for instance) still implied that there was a unitary self, present but hidden, in the figure of the elided artist; postmodernism foregrounds the presence of the writer (the injudicious self-promotion of George Bowering, for instance) but scatters any sense of unity in that self by making it part of the textual play.

The early lyrics of Leonard Cohen can be seen as exercises in modernism, displaying a high degree of formal unity and elaborate rhetoric. Often using regular stanzas and rhyme-schemes, they are presented as polished artefacts, the 'well-wrought urns' approved by the modernist New Critics. Steeped in religious and mythological imagery, they create their own enclosed world, whose values are aesthetic and self-referential. The figure of the poet is presented, reverentially, as a kind of priest or saint, moving in the sacred world of art. The title of Cohen's first book, *Let Us Compare Mythologies,* is in itself a summary of modernist practice: mythology is assumed to contain a general truth, a grounding of experience, which can be discovered by the comparative process of juxtaposition or collage. 'Let us compare mythologies' is one of the major formal impulses of modernism, from the *Cantos* of Ezra Pound to the structural anthropology of Claude Lévi-Strauss.

This modernist stress on the beautiful object persists through *The Spice-Box of Earth* and Cohen's first novel, *The Favourite Game*; but then he attempted a violent reaction against it. *Flowers for Hitler* is, in its strange and excessive way, the first Canadian gesture towards postmodernism. Rejecting the modernist ideal of the well-made, formally complete poem, Cohen presented poems which were deliberately ugly, unfinished, and jarring in tone, accompanied on the page by revisions, deletions, and crude little drawings. Romantic evocations of mythology were replaced by a nightmare vision of a history slipping into oblivion: 'I believe with a perfect faith in all the history / I remember, but it's getting harder and harder / to remember much history.'[9] A note on the back cover proclaimed that 'this book moves me from the world of the golden-boy poet into the dung pile of the front-line writer'—or, it might be argued, from the well-wrought urns of modernism to the harsh discontinuities of postmodernism. It *might* be argued—for it is equally possible to see the pose of the 'front-line writer' as simply the reverse side of the coin of the 'golden-boy poet,' and to argue that in *Flowers for Hitler* Cohen is still pursuing a modernist rhetoric in its negative form.

The paradoxical nature of Cohen's approach to postmodernism is even more apparent in *Beautiful Losers.* Again we have the trappings of the postmodern: a novel which breaks every rule of traditional form; a wild mixture of tones, topics, and styles; a narrative voice which is radically dispersed and fragmented, putting into question the very possibility of the unitary subject. When F. proclaims, 'Connect nothing. Place things side by side on your arborite table, if you must, but connect nothing!'[10] he could be laying out a prescription for the postmodernist novel. Robert Kroetsch, for instance, has argued that the dominant trope of modernism is metaphor, with its vertical layering of images, while that of postmodernism is metonymy, with its horizontal extensions—side by side, connecting nothing. *Beautiful Losers* is the archetypal postmodernist novel.

And yet—the opposite is also there to be argued. In my 1978 study of *Beautiful Losers,* I wrote that 'in fact the book is highly organized, held tightly together by a network of images and connections. Douglas Barbour has pointed to the paradox of a book which proclaims "Connect nothing" and then insistently offers connections which must be made; a book which "prepares to abandon all systems" in a systematic manner.'" In that study I concentrated in a systematic manner on the imagery of the 'stem' emerging from the broken 'system': an image which Cohen is still pursuing more than twenty years later when he sings, in **'First We Take Manhattan,'** 'They sentenced me to twenty years of boredom / For trying to change the system from within' (*I'm Your Man*). It is the kind of paradox which one encounters repeatedly in Leonard Cohen: the systematic breaking up of systems; the artful proclamation of the anti-art pose. Cohen is trying to become a postmodernist, one might say, but he is going about it in a very modernist manner.

In the same way, Cohen's career as a pop singer has taken him to the heart of the electronic media which Frank Davey saw as the harbingers of postmodernism. Cohen's songs have taken him away from the comparatively narrow and elitist readership of published poetry and towards a mass audience, in Canada and especially in Europe, of a kind that no other Canadian writer has enjoyed. But again one might argue that Cohen has approached this postmodernist medium in a modernist way. Most of the song lyrics return to the tightly controlled and polished forms of his early poetry: regular rhyming stanzas, shining epigrammatic images. The songs again project the Romantic figure of Leonard Cohen as priest or saint; even the gestures of self-parody—'I was born like this, I had no choice / I was born with the gift of a golden voice' (**'Tower of Song,'** from *I'm Your Man*)—serve mainly to reinforce the image that they pre-emptively mock. In live performance, the texts of Cohen's songs remain relatively stable: unlike Bob Dylan, who is constantly shifting both words and music in performance, Cohen makes very few changes. Even the anecdotes he tells to introduce the songs are repeated year after year. The vulnerability of early concert appearances (such as those documented in *Bird on the Wire*) has been replaced by a confident mastery on stage; Leonard Cohen has become a modernist singer.

The degree to which Cohen, for all his (very important) gestures towards postmodernism, has remained fundamentally a modernist writer may also be evident in the very limited *influence* he has had on subsequent Canadian writers. It may be that Cohen's style is too individual, not to say idiosyncratic, to be successfully copied; any attempt would end up as parody or pastiche. Even so, he remains an isolated figure, and his work in the 1970s and 1980s has pursued its course quite separately from the main currents of Canadian poetry during these decades. However one defines these currents—the documentary long poems of Ondaatje and Atwood; the feminism of Marlatt and Mouré; the 'continuing poems' of Nichol and Kroetsch—nothing could be farther removed from them than Leonard Cohen's *Book of Mercy*.

Phyllis Webb, on the other hand, has been highly influential on all these currents. One way of assessing the variety of this influence, and also of appreciating at a glance the tension between modernism and postmodernism in her work, is to look at the back-cover blurbs for her 1980 volume, *Wilson's Bowl*. The writers who here pay tribute to Webb range from Northrop Frye, whose role as the mentor of the 1950s 'mythopoeic' poets places him at the centre of Canadian modernism, to bpNichol, the very epitome of postmodern experimentation and open form. In between are two poets—D. G. Jones and Margaret Atwood—who are more difficult to characterize. They both deal with the fragmentation and uncertainty of the postmodern age but are also drawn towards the tightly controlled, elliptical, and ironic forms of modernist poetry.

Even in the short form of the complimentary blurb, each of these writers approaches Webb's work in terms of his or her recognizable presuppositions. Frye, for all his theoretical doubts about evaluation, is magisterial, authoritative, and highly evaluative. 'This is a very rich and rewarding book,' he tells us: 'a landmark in Canadian poetry.' He points to the theme of 'failure' but sees it, not as the inescapable condition of postmodernist writing, but rather, in modernist terms, as a problem to be dealt with. 'The book finds its way through "failure,"' he proclaims, 'and emerges with some beautifully lucid poems at the end.' What he values, then, is not the question but the answer, not the failure but the lucidity.

Similarly, D. G. Jones, who in his own work often conveys a sense of tight-lipped desperation, sees Webb's poetry as *countering* the postmodern condition: 'In a world that promises ever less in the way of real community or even communication, Webb reminds us of our communion with the dead.' Webb is here evoked as a prophetic figure, in the modernist tradition of Eliot's Tiresias or the Odysseus of Pound's first Canto. Atwood too sees Webb in terms of the mythological pattern of death and rebirth: 'She walks into the sea and returns.' This last comment is surely more typical of Atwood's own surfacing protagonists than it is of Webb's Lilo Berliner, who walks into the sea and does not return. But my point is that both Jones and Atwood choose to praise Webb in modernist terms: for them, Webb's poetry rescues order out of disorder, and it does so by means of a modernist appeal to mythology as a stabilizing and order-giving force. Thus for Jones, Webb is allowed, after her communion with the dead, 'to celebrate spring'; for Atwood, she conducts a 'courageous struggle with an angel who blesses reluctantly but does bless.'

Nichol's blurb is quite different; it appeals rather to the values of the postmodernist alternative canon. It makes no mention at all of content or thematic pattern, but concentrates on the form of the poems. Webb is described as 'a writer whose care to get things right informs every word and every line of her poems, who moves fluidly between a diversity of forms and modes'; and Nichol numbers himself as one of 'those of us who have learned from & followed her work.' This is a finely balanced comment. The 'care to get things right' emphasizes Webb's craft, but at the same time Nichol praises the fluidity of her movement between a diversity of forms and modes, that is, the open-ended and postmodernist aspect of her work. As a poet influenced by Webb, Nichol responds both to the care and to the fluidity; as one who has 'learned from & followed her work,' he sees her (in the same way as he saw Sheila Watson) as a modernist whose writing nevertheless provides an opening into postmodernism.

Working along similar lines, Robert Kroetsch has argued that Webb's *Naked Poems* mark the true beginning of the postmodernist long poem in Canada. In his essay 'For Play and Entrance: The Contemporary Canadian Long Poem,' Kroetsch writes:

> Trace: behind many of the long poems of the 1970s in Canada is the shadow (Jungian?) of another poem, a short long poem.
>
> 1965: Phyllis Webb, *Naked Poems.*[12]

Kroetsch's explanation, both of the nature of that influence and of his paradoxical phrase 'a short long poem,' is cast explicitly in terms of postmodernism (the resistance to lyric closure) and of Derridean poststructuralism (trace, *différance*):

> A kind of hesitation even to write the long poem . . . Webb, insisting on that hesitation. On that delay. On nakedness and lyric and yet on a way out, perhaps a way out of the ending of the lyric too, with its ferocious principles of closure, a being compelled out of lyric by lyric:
>
> The poet, the lover, compelled towards an ending (conclusion, death, orgasm: coming) that must, out of love, be (difference) deferred.[13]

What Kroetsch sees here in Webb's work is the way in which even its most traditional and modernist elements (her mastery of the lyric form, for instance) were breaking down into postmodern indeterminacy. *Naked Poems* begins with the lyric impulse, in its starkest, most minimal form ('naked'), but the very conditions of that minimal lyric force it towards the extended sequence, and towards its final, open-ended question, 'Oh?' 'Compelled *out of* lyric *by* lyric,' the sequence enacts

the way in which the postmodern emerges from the end(s) of modernism. The 'post' of postmodernism does not indicate mere temporal sequence; rather, it is what Derrida would call a deconstruction, or even what Leonard Cohen (ironically) would call a changing of the system *from within.*

It is that openness, I would argue, which explains why Webb's poetry has continued to influence other writers (Nichol, Marlatt, Thesen, Wah . . .) in ways that Cohen's has not. Cohen's work, brilliant as it is, remains at some level closed. Such gestures as **The Energy of Slaves** and **Death of a Lady's Man** are desperate, but not entirely successful, attempts to break out of that closure. It is in this sense that I argued earlier that Cohen is a modernist in the trappings of postmodernism, while Webb is a postmodernist in the trappings of modernism.

Both Cohen and Webb reach to the end(s) of modernism. Cohen, one might argue, is stuck there: like F. in *Beautiful Losers,* he could say of himself, 'I was the Moses of our little exodus. I would never cross. My mountain might be very high but it rises from the desert.'[14] For Webb, the ends are definitely plural. Her work shows that there is no single end or purpose to modernism; by the very intensity of the questioning which her long silence subjected it to, modernism in her poetry breaks through to its complementary pair, its waiting Other.

In the works of both writers, modernism and postmodernism play against and with each other in ways which present, in exemplary form, the issues Canadian poetry has faced in the last three decades. This movement is not yet finished; the compression of contemporary literary history is such that our canonical figures are still alive, still changing, still writing. The emerging canon has been slow to recognize the full challenges of postmodernism: Leonard Cohen, for all his outrageousness, has been easier to assimilate than Phyllis Webb. But the canon *is* an emerging one, and any account of it now has to be provisional. It would certainly be my hope that the breaking down of the modernist/postmodernist distinction, so evident in recent criticism, will also be reflected in the evolution of canon-formation: and in this process, the examples of such writers as Leonard Cohen and Phyllis Webb may well be more useful than those of more easily categorized figures.

Notes

1. This introduction is 'polemical' in the sense that it makes some sweeping generalizations for which this paper does not have the time or space to offer detailed support. I am well aware that, like all generalizations, they admit of many exceptions, nuances, and modifications. However, they are advanced here as a broad framework for the main argument of this essay.

2. Margery Fee, *Canadian Poetry in Selected English-Language Anthologies: An Index and Guide* (Halifax: Dalhousie University School of Library Service 1985)

3. Frank Davey, *From There to Here* (Erin, Ont.: Press Porcépic 1974), 264. All further references to this work appear in the text.

4. Leonard Cohen, *The Energy of Slaves* (Toronto: McClelland and Stewart 1972), 112

5. Pia Southam, 'Hot Lunch,' *V,* Dec. 1988, 110

6. Phyllis Webb, *The Vision Tree: Selected Poems* (Vancouver: Talonbooks 1982), 150

7. George Woodcock, *Northern Spring: The Flowering of Canadian Literature* (Vancouver: Douglas and McIntyre 1987), 258

8. John Bentley Mays, 'Phyllis Webb,' *Open Letter,* 2d ser. no. 6 (Fall 1973), 8-33

9. Leonard Cohen, *Flowers for Hitler* (Toronto: McClelland and Stewart 1961), 72

10. Leonard Cohen, *Beautiful Losers* (Toronto: McClelland and Stewart 1966), 16-17.

11. Stephen Scobie, *Leonard Cohen* (Vancouver: Douglas and McIntyre 1978), 96

12. Robert Kroetsch, 'For Play and Entrance: The Contemporary Canadian Long Poem,' in *The Lovely Treachery of Words* (Toronto: Oxford University Press 1989), 118

13. Ibid.

14. Cohen, *Beautiful Losers,* 167

Linda Hutcheon (essay date 1993)

SOURCE: Hutcheon, Linda. "Leonard Cohen (1934-)." In *ECW's Biographical Guide to Canadian Poets,* pp. 232-35. Toronto: ECW Press, 1993.

[*In the following essay, Hutcheon offers a brief and general overview of Cohen's life and works.*]

In 1967 George Bowering wrote that "Leonard Cohen could become the Jewish Kahlil Gibran."[1] And, certainly, with McClelland and Stewart printing or reprinting a half-dozen of his books in the mid-1960s, Cohen's popular success as a poet of the times seemed assured. His early background was probably appropriate, though perhaps less exotic than these somewhat dubious accolades might have suggested. Born into a comfortable Jewish family, Cohen attended McGill University and later, briefly, Columbia University. His interest and skill in poetry writing were manifest early: McGill awarded him the McNaughton Prize in creative writing, and Louis Dudek published *Let Us Compare Mythologies* as the first book of his McGill Poetry Series in 1956. After graduation from McGill, Cohen edited a New York literary magazine called *The Phoenix,* where, in 1957, many of the poems later published in *The Spice-Box of Earth* (1961) appeared. In his early years, Cohen frequently published individual poems in literary journals—*CIV/n* (1953-54), *Forge* [McGill Univ.] (1954-56), *Prism* [Sir George Williams College] (1958), *The Tamarack Review* (1958), and *Queen's Quarterly* (1959).

Freed by a small inheritance, Cohen left North America for the Greek island of Hydra in the late 1950s. Here he lived with a Norwegian woman named Marianne and her son, and here he wrote the poems of *Flowers for Hitler* (1964) and *Parasites of Heaven* (1966). He also tried his hand at two novels: *The Favorite Game* (1963) and *Beautiful Losers* (1966). The *succès de scandale* of the latter coincided with the beginning of Cohen's career as a popular singer and songwriter. At one point, a *Melody Maker* poll listed Cohen as second only to Bob Dylan in popularity. With the help of Judy Collins and brief appearances at concerts (Newport Folk Festival and Central Park, New York) and on television (CBS's *Camera Three*), Cohen soon became the darling of the pop music promoters. The publication of his *Selected Poems 1956-1968* (1968) coincided with the release of his first album, *Songs of Leonard Cohen* (1968), followed shortly by *Songs from a Room* (1969).

Leaving a quiet life in Hydra with Marianne, Cohen began both a new career and life-style—as a concert performer—and a new relationship. His new companion, Suzanne Elrod, was to be the mother of his two children (Adam Nathan and Lorca Sarah) and the "Lady" celebrated, lost, mourned, and scorned in his later *Death of a Lady's Man* (1978). With Cohen's public career came the press cult of the Cohen personality and the spate of articles on, and interviews of, the various newsworthy personae of the lonely rebel drop-out artist; the ironic, sardonic poet-lover; the vegetarian, mystic seer. As a poet, too, Cohen was at the height of his success in the late 1960s, winning the Quebec Award (1964) and the Governor General's Award for Poetry in English (1968), which he refused with predictable irony, claiming that, while much in him strove for the honour, the poems themselves forbade it absolutely. In 1962 Cohen had announced that he would seek his audience in *Esquire* and *Playboy*—which *people* read—rather than literary magazines that only *poets* read. Nevertheless the poetic and academic establishment did not turn its back on its rebel son. In 1971 Dalhousie University awarded him an honorary Litt. D., and the next year the University of Toronto purchased his papers.

Cohen's energy in these years, however, was primarily devoted to his singing and songwriting. In 1971

Columbia Records released *Songs of Love and Hate*, and Robert Altman used Cohen's music as the score for his film *McCabe and Mrs. Miller.* In 1972 Cohen published his first new book of poems in six years—*The Energy of Slaves*—and perhaps it was the generally unfavourable reviews that confirmed Cohen in his choice of a stage career. In Europe in particular, his concerts were major cultural events, and as a result, his poems were translated into French, German, Spanish, Danish, Swedish, and Dutch. The Royal Winnipeg Ballet took *The Shining People of Leonard Cohen* on its European tour. In the next few years Cohen released three more albums: *Live Songs* (1973), *New Skin for the Old Ceremony* (1974), and *The Best of Leonard Cohen* (1975). The show *Sisters of Mercy* was a hit at the 1973 Shaw Festival in Niagara-on-the-Lake, Ontario.

The later 1970s saw a change in Cohen's life and work. After spending some time at a Zen centre in California, Cohen, now separated from Suzanne Elrod, began to write and record the album *Death of a Ladies' Man* (1977) with the help of Phil Spector (note the plural "Ladies'"; the book title is in the singular). The new sound that was born of this odd professional collaboration was greeted with mixed reactions, as was his publication of the book *Death of a Lady's Man* (1978).

When not on the road or recording in Nashville or New York for his albums *Recent Songs* (1979), *Various Positions* (1984), *I'm Your Man* (1988), and *The Future* (1992), Cohen seems to have spent much of his time either in a Saint Dominique Street flat in Montreal's immigrant district or at his upper duplex near Los Angeles. The publication of *Book of Mercy* (1984), a book of "contemporary psalms," consolidated a renewal of Cohen's interest in devotional traditions dating from his earliest verse and clear in the recent songs, presented here in a prose (and quasi-narrative) form. As both Don Owen in his NFB film *Ladies and Gentlemen . . . Mr. Leonard Cohen* (1965) and, later, Harry Rasky in his CBC film *The Song of Leonard Cohen* (1980) learned, Cohen's power as a performer and personality is strong and easily (and entertainingly) documentable. The *enfant terrible* of Canadian poetry may no longer be an *enfant,* but the old desire to shock, to play, to "con," is still strong and appealing as his first video, *I Am a Hotel* (1984), suggested. His European following seems to have remained faithful, as the figures of his sales attest: as early as 1978, his book sales were already estimated at two million and his records at ten million—not bad for a former member of the Buckskin Boys who began playing the guitar to impress the girls at summer camp.

Note

1. George Bowering, "Inside Leonard Cohen," rev. of *Parasites of Heaven, Canadian Literature,* No. 33 (Summer 1967), p. 71.

David Layton (essay date March 1996)

SOURCE: Layton, David. "Irving Layton, Leonard Cohen and Other Recurring Nightmares: While the Great Poets Embraced the World, Their Wives, Children and Lovers Kept Slipping Through the Ever-Widening Circle." *Saturday Night* 111, no. 2 (March 1996): 34, 36, 38, 40, 42-43.

[*In the following essay, Layton (the son of Cohen's fellow Canadian poet Irving Layton) describes his relationship with his father, his father's relationship with Cohen, and the relationships of both poets to others in the world.*]

There are two observations I need to make about the week I spent in LA: first, it rained every day I was there, and second, it was the Tibetan New Year. Neither event was related to the other, except that together they conspired to prevent me from achieving the purpose of my visit—interviewing my godfather, the poet/songwriter Leonard Cohen. I had some notion of doing an article on the performer's capacity for personal relationships, and I think Leonard knew I also wanted him to talk about my father, though I'd written him only that I wanted him to talk about himself.

"He is up in the mountain," was how my mother put it. I was staying at her house in West Hollywood. The mountain in question was Mount Baldy, one of the many snow-capped peaks that glitter in the California sun. I tried to locate it on a map, tracing the rumpled geographical folds northward towards Washington State and British Columbia. That's where I always imagine the Rocky Mountains to be, rising inland of the Pacific rainforest. Despite my many visits I always forget that pristine mountains hover within reach of the crowded Spanish bungalows and car-choked highways of Los Angeles.

It was around the second or third day into my visit that I first heard about the Tibetan New Year and the possible connection between this event and Leonard's absence. He was up on Mount Baldy, meditating. And the rain, it turned out, was keeping him there. The news was full of stories about swollen rivers, collapsing bridges, and flooded highways. Leonard would not, could not, come back down.

That, at least, was the comfortable answer. Unfortunately, there was a more disturbing possibility—that Leonard was avoiding me. I wasn't here as his godson, to pay him a friendly visit, but as a journalist, to interview him, and it was conceivable that he'd had second thoughts about the whole idea, much as I was now having.

"He's an intensely private man," my mother said. This statement was meant to describe a general trait of Leonard's but it also encompassed his present absence from LA, which in turn hinted at another of the reasons I wished to interview him. I wanted his speaking voice on tape. Despite my childhood memories and more recent conversations with Leonard, I couldn't for the life of me remember more than three consecutive words he'd strung together. Stranger still, my mother had the same problem and she'd known Leonard since he was twenty. She could remember his then plump face and awkward smile, and she could remember, in later years, the endless and constant conversations between my father and Leonard, but not a word or phrase in his own accents could she muster. Talking to Leonard was like listening to a melody that you couldn't capture the next day.

After eight days of watching the rain fall, of damp sheets, and disturbed sleep, I decided to leave for Toronto. My mother, always anxious to dissipate family-induced anxiety, especially if it's being induced in her son, assured me that she would speak to Leonard when he got down from his mountain. I decided to leave it in her hands. When it came to either my godfather or my father, it was often smarter to leave it in her hands.

My father is the poet Irving Layton. He too is a performer although in his case he performs nonstop. His role is the potent genius. He truly believes that he belongs in the pantheon with Socrates and Homer and Dante and Shakespeare, and he never ceases to live up to his status. Besides me, Irving has an older son and daughter by his second wife, and a small daughter by his fourth. Up in the attic, my father enters the pantheon and out come poems about his wives. And his children. "Be gunners in the Israeli airforce," his line goes in a poem titled "For My Sons, Max and David." Or he stands on the podium and says, "This is for my son David." People come up afterwards and say, "Your father must love you very much." But I am not—none of us is—as close to him as Leonard Cohen. My father, who first spotted him doing a reading in a Montreal coffee house, calls him the "golden boy."

They're not at all alike. Leonard requires himself to be considerate and polite in all encounters, even if he has to fake it. That doesn't keep him, too, from taking his private dramas and shaping them into poems and songs for public consumption. Long ago, there was Marianne, who wanted to marry him. He wrote her a song saying So Long. But Leonard's style is gentle, even patrician. My father's is not. Leonard's clothes always fitted beautifully, whereas my father dressed like a Romanian factory worker. "You see this shirt!" he'd say proudly, pinching the polyester cloth with his thumb and forefinger. "It cost me thirty dollars." My earliest recollection of Leonard was being driven around in his brand-new sports car. I must have been about six years old. The first car I remember my father driving was a Datsun with a roof so low that a permanent grease stain marked the spot over his head.

There were other differences, age one of them, since my father was two decades older than Leonard. Their backgrounds were another. My father had been born into terrible poverty, Leonard into the wealth and privilege of Westmount. But for all that they had one great thing in common—they were artists. And if my father's opinion was anything to go by they were much more—they were among the elect. Their poems and music would never die but would, like the severed head of Orpheus, sing for all eternity.

Leonard is also close to my mother. Not only was Leonard the first of his friends my father introduced to her, for months he was the only one. My mother, Aviva, is the third of Irving's five wives, though they never actually got married. They came close once. A few years before my birth my father announced one morning, a morning seemingly no different from any other, that he would marry my mother. They called Leonard and all three marched down to a jewelry shop in old Montreal where, incredibly, all Irving did was purchase a silver clasp for his previous wife and head out of the shop. My mother, the disinherited bride-to-be, stood over the glass counter and found herself unable to breathe.

Leonard, with that winsome smile of his, bought the ring my mother coveted, slipped it over her finger, and said, "Aviva, now you're married." During the twenty-five years that my mother spent with Irving, she never once took that ring off her finger.

You can see from all this why the nature of the artist, and the nature of fame, and the effects of both on human relationships—on the possibility of intimacy—are subjects that interest me. And also why I can never get personal about my father without bringing in Leonard, or personal about my godfather without bringing in Irving.

In our house the personal went something like this: I have homework and my mother pretends not to understand grade-four math, this from a woman who has a PhD in English Literature. "Go ask your father." And up I'd go, to the attic, while my mother, safe in her kitchen, would glow with pride at her little, normal family. I'd knock and wait for the thunderclap. "What!" "I have some math homework," I'd say. Then Zeus would heave himself from his throne and admit me into his lair which stank of words and pipe tobacco. His forced benevolence would soon wear thin. "What's wrong with you, man?" His finger would jab at the open textbook.

What was wrong with me? It was a good question. I, the son of a great poet, would sit in the back of the classroom and be admonished for picking my nose. When not in class, I'd try to shove my hand between the legs of pink-cheeked girls. This last habit landed me a two-day suspension from school and a handsome accolade from my father. "That's my boy!" he'd shout. "Stick your hands up the dark mysteries of life." And then he'd thrust his own hand into the air and wiggle his fingers. "You see that?" he'd say to my mother, "he has the hands of an artist."

But now, as I tucked the unwieldy math book under my arm, and fled towards my mother's comforts, I knew that the approval had been withdrawn and forgotten.

"Did it go all right?" my mother would ask. I'd nod my head and tell her that everything was wonderful. "Dad really helped me," I'd say. But as she leaned over to kiss me, I could tell that she knew the truth.

When my father came down from Mount Olympus it was usually for food and an audience. Any audience would do. As I watched the mounds of meat and peas pass from the plate to his belly, my father would rail against the "Philistines" and "ass-lickers" who populated the literary landscape of Canada. If my mother came to the defence of any given writer, it would be dismissed with a wave of his hand and the words "literary tapeworm.," Then my father would start to laugh, and he'd laugh until he choked.

The more excited my father became, the less food made it down his throat. It would come exploding out of his mouth, along with his invective, until at last the table would be littered with the organic matter that, in my young imagination, was the decayed remains of all those Philistines my father had chewed out.

He was different when we had real guests. Then my father would strain his head forward and listen. Carefully. And he'd wait until the conversation began to meander and then he'd mount a pointed interrogation. "What do you think the role of the artist is, exactly?" Then he'd fold his arms and wait again until it was time for him to become the Great Summarizer. He would gather in all the half-baked, drunken, confused, fragmented ideas that had eddied around him and begin to tell his audience what they had all been saying. It was a tour de force.

My father was eighty-one before I had an insight into his technique. We were sitting in an outdoor cafe, on a summer's evening in Toronto, when an attractive waitress came to our table.

"You're beautiful!" my father exclaimed. "Do you read books?" The woman said she did.

"You like reading, then." My father had a way of making the obvious sound ominous. "What do you read?"

The waitress said something like "things," and became embarrassed.

"Have you studied?"

The waitress said she had received her bachelor's degree in English Literature.

"English Literature! Bravo. Do you read poetry? A. M. Klein, have you read him?"

The waitress looked increasingly uncomfortable as my father rattled off the names of several obscure Canadian poets.

"Irving Layton. Have you read Irving Layton?" Irving Layton asked.

To my extreme discomfort the waitress said she hadn't heard of him. I became nervous, but I didn't yet understand.

My father eyed her suspiciously, then said, "Leonard Cohen, have you heard of him?"

The waitress broke out into a radiant smile. "I love Leonard Cohen," she said.

"Good! Good! He's a wonderful writer." My father ordered another bottle of wine and we watched her walk away. I felt a slap on my arm. It was from my father.

"You see that, my boy, first you pull the rug from under them and then, when you give them a few crumbs, they think it's manna from heaven." My father sighed. "I'm too old for all this beauty."

After I failed grade four, we packed our bags and, with no explanation offered, headed for Asia. At first I thought it was a summer vacation but after six months of travelling I became suspicious. Where the hell were we? A place called India, my mother would tell me. But I kept on asking. "Where are we?" India. The word held no meaning, explained nothing, couldn't possibly make me understand why we'd go off every night to a park in New Delhi and meet my "friend," the one whom I initially mis-took for a dog. We'd call out his name and he'd come running towards us. On all fours. The crippled dog-boy, the one with the magnificent smile, the one we'd feed. Dog-boy and I would run towards the Red Fort and when I'd look back there would be my father, sitting on a bench, writing.

My father wouldn't hear of any "luxuries." This apparently included sheets for our beds, light bulbs, and clean food. I became sick. Every half-hour what felt like a knife would rip through my belly. After several weeks, I was shitting on street corners. There would be my father, with an iron constitution, impatient with child and wife. He'd stride into the crowds, with a book in his armpit, and a sea of humanity would close behind him. In my pocket was a small note that became smudged with perspiration. It said: My name is David Layton. If I'm lost please take me to the Canadian Embassy at—. Attached to the note were a few rupees my mother had added.

Calcutta, Kuala Lumpur, Lahore, Jakarta. Names to be sick by. Names to fear. My father would be there one minute and disappear the next. When I was alone with my mother we would go to Western restaurants and gorge on fruits and vegetables.

We finally came to rest at some beach resort in some country that wasn't India. I spent an entire day building a giant castle with a moat and a pop-drink label for a flag. Towards the end of the day, some dark-skinned, menacing boys with rags for clothes came by and began to kick my walls down. They grabbed stones and swooped by, making artillery sounds as they released their ammunition. My father, sitting farther up the beach, merely watched. With a sense of resignation I walked over towards him as he cleared a space beside himself and patted the spot where I was to sit. Together we watched as a day's worth of labour was destroyed. The sun was setting in front of us and behind the boys who came, one by one, to kick my castle down.

"Look carefully, son, and learn. What you create men will come and destroy."

A year went by before we returned to where our "vacation" had begun: Greece. Our first port of call was Leonard Cohen's house on the island of Hydra. I'd been to Greece before, and had spent time in this very house. I felt safe, and desperately relieved to be back in a country whose name had a meaning that I could understand. Part of my relief was also attached to Leonard himself. He was like a calm sea where my father's boat could rest. With Leonard, my father ceased to be the Great Summarizer. He still made speeches, but he never prefaced those speeches with an interrogation.

As I played with my toys in Leonard's courtyard, I'd watch the two of them, their Greek sailors' hats perched rakishly on their heads, their drinks in hand, their bare chests exposed to the sun. I was just old enough to recognize a strange anomaly in the way they spoke to one another. If, as would sometimes happen, Leonard talked about his latest romantic failure my father would laugh and say, "Leonard, are you sure you're doing the wrong thing?" But right after that the conversation would switch to the third person, for Irving would then launch into a discussion about the poet. He'd speak about the poet as being conflicted. They'd examine the poet as archetype—albeit a vanishing one, along with the priest and the warrior—and about the poet as Lover. The poet, I'd hear my father say, "makes love to the world."

This last concept held a particular significance for me. Whenever my father roared this one out to my mother, I knew there was big trouble brewing. "Goddammit, woman, I'm a poet!" Which meant *ipso facto* that he was a Lover. This, my mother would point out, was precisely the issue: whose scent was on his shirt this time? My father would become infuriated. "I'm not a lover to a woman but a lover of Women," he'd say, as often as not launching into a speech about breasts as mounds of earth, vaginas as forests. He had no time for a petty mind, he'd say, meaning that he had no time for an unpoetical mind. I began at an early age to connect the word "lover" with my father's wrath.

Unlike my father, Leonard was a man who never seemed to raise his voice. He merely . . . disappeared. It was just off this very courtyard in Hydra, my father used to tell me, that Leonard had dropped himself and his typewriter into a pit and refused to come out. Marianne, who was living with him at the time, would implore him to come back inside but he continued to work on his second novel, *Beautiful Losers*. With tears in her eyes Marianne would drop food baskets into his hole. Leonard kept on writing until his fingers seized up. Now Marianne was gone.

For my father, this was as it should be. "Leonard happy?" I can hear him saying. "How can he be happy?" Leonard's destiny was to be more than a poet but a poet first. Let Leonard have everything, be anything: as a poet he wouldn't be able to enjoy it. My father always seemed quite delighted by Leonard's predicament, but his delight was never vindictive. Far from it—in my father's eyes it was the fulfilment of all that Leonard was fated to be.

Thus it only stood to reason that Leonard should lose his interest in sex at the very height of his fame. Women in elevators would throw themselves at him, would arrive at his hotel door with nothing on but a mink coat, but Leonard could give only an affirmative answer to my father's mirthful question, "Leonard, are you sure you're doing the wrong thing?"

It seems it was my father who, one evening in Montreal, hit on a ribald solution to Leonard's predicament. A little healthy competition between two great Lovers would spur Leonard's prick to life. Niema Ash, a woman who dressed only in purple, leapt in and offered to sit between the two men and, with their poetic members in her hand, stir the creative juices. "We need some inspiration," my father commanded. And so my mother, the erotic figurehead, balanced herself on the edge of the couch and thrust her bare breasts into the air.

Leonard won the competition.

It was my father's reported delight in his own defeat that gave me pause. For the first time, when Niema told me the story, it crossed my mind that for Irving to call Leonard "golden boy" was tantamount to calling him "golden son."

After Marianne there had been Suzanne. Actually I remember Suzanne quite well because I had a crush on her. In our house we had a photo of Suzanne and Leonard taken outside in our front yard. If I looked carefully at the picture, and I did, I could see Leonard's fingers inching their way around the hemline of her very short skirt. Leonard, no doubt, had the hands of an artist.

There is another memory I have of Suzanne. One day when we arrived at Leonard's house in Montreal, Suzanne was changing her son's diaper. While bare to the world the child began to pee. I was astonished at the power of his bladder. The yellow liquid shot out of his penis, made a magnificent arc over his head, and landed on Suzanne's cotton blouse. I followed the whole amazing performance with my eyes but, as I looked up at Suzanne's face, I saw what could only have been an expression of acute disgust. My mother hurried over to help her diaper the baby before her disgust turned to rage. As for my father and godfather, if memory serves me, they were huddled in a corner, talking in third-person pronouns.

But where was Suzanne now? Where were Leonard's children? Not here, in his house on Hydra. They had disappeared and while I missed Suzanne I was happy to have the kids out of the way. To my father, who constantly burdened himself with wife, children, and mortgage, Leonard's recurrent solitude, even loneliness, must have seemed both appealing and exotic.

That was the autumn the Yom Kippur war broke out. Now the two of them, my father and godfather, would sit on Leonard's patio listening to the sombre voice of the BBC World Service, swivelling the aerial whenever the short-wave lost its focus. While I had only a vague notion of what was going on, "There were people hurting one another," was how my mother put it, I couldn't help but be impressed by how my father and Leonard discussed the war as if it were a personal matter. As in fact it was. The Israelis commandeered a Hercules transport plane to fly Leonard and his guitar to the front lines.

Not to be outdone, my father marched my mother and me down to the Israeli embassy in Athens and offered his services as a warrior and poet. They politely asked for a monetary donation.

This had less of an effect on my father than one might imagine. In his mind it was their loss, not his. The Israelis believed that they needed Leonard much as my father believed that the Israelis needed him. It somehow amounted to the same thing. As famous men, as poets, no event, no matter how enormous, was outside their personal jurisdiction.

While they stretched out their arms to embrace the world, their wives, children, and lovers kept slipping through the ever-widening circle.

It was in Greece again, four years later, that my mother finally decided to get a "divorce." There was a new man in our life. He had eyes the colour of coal and a moustache whose ends he'd twirl with his fingers. I'd see him in the village, usually with my mother, sitting in a taverna. My mother introduced him as a "friend" and she kept on using this euphemism for three entire months.

The village wrapped itself around the side of a hill and at its top, like a crown, stood the remains of a Byzantine fortress. Those who had money found homes in the lower part of the village, those who didn't found themselves in the shadow of the castle wall. The man with the moustache lived in the shadow. I don't think my mother ever looked better than that summer, what with having to run up the hill every night and run down the hill every morning, always remembering to stop at the bakery for the fresh bread and yogurt that her demanding family expected. That summer my father began to shuffle. He'd shuffle into the kitchen, where my mother would prepare breakfast, and then he'd shuffle back to his room. My mother wanted to pretend that what was happening wasn't really happening, so it was my father who told me, one morning when he'd shuffled into the kitchen and found no breakfast and no wife, only an empty space filled partly by a thirteen-year-old son, that things weren't going well between him and my mother. I had a towel slung over my shoulder and was anxious to meet Dania, the first love of my life, down at the beach. After what I thought an appropriate period of mourning I asked to be excused. As I skipped down the cobblestone streets, my father shuffled back into his room to contemplate his own demise.

My mother thought it right that my father and the man with the moustache, who I later found out was named Leon, have a "meeting." In full view of the artistic cabal that congregated every summer in the village, the two men made their way up the street, arm in arm, to an out-of-the-way taverna. Leon, who was expecting the full fury and pain of a man whose wife had been stolen and family destroyed, waited nervously for the explosion.

My father began to explain about the poet as a conflicted being.

"Poets," said my father, "don't make good husbands." Aviva needed to be set free. She needed a good man and Leon, my father implied, was a good man. Leon moved uneasily in his seat. He knew what he was being told: he might be good enough for Aviva, but he could never make love to Women.

My father moved from a treacherous benevolence—"Take her, she deserves better!"—to a rage that could not find a person but only a concept to attach itself to. "Be careful, Leon, women are castrating bitches. If they see one ounce, one OUNCE, of talent in you they'll rip your balls off."

That summer, my father was left with an audience of one. After the "meeting" he began to barge into my room where, with a fresh page of words in his hand, he'd sit beside my bed and carefully read me his newest poem.

Meanwhile another picture of Suzanne and Leonard came to my attention. I stared at it for hours. There was Suzanne, looking beautiful and slightly cruel—exactly the same look of distaste on her face as when her son had pissed all over her. Only now the look had been transferred to Leonard.

For some reason it made me think of another story my father used to tell: about how Leonard once innocently tried to place a collect long-distance call through a Montreal operator "From Leonard Cohen to Suzanne, please." The operator was clearly stunned. Before she recovered Leonard asked her out on a date. Once lucky, he decided to try again, this time with another operator. Thinking that he was on to a good thing, he kept on with this game, until the night he found himself alone in a room dialling operator after operator, waiting for the breathless recognition he could move in on. It never came.

Now, in the picture, Suzanne was sitting in a beautiful restaurant with high-backed banquettes and long-stemmed wineglasses for the red wine. And there was Leonard, sitting beside her, looking miserable. "I've had," Leonard once told me, "that sense most of my life, that it isn't working." In the picture, he was like a stain on the white table cloth, a reminder that an accident had happened. Above the picture were the words, **"Death of a Lady's Man."** It was the title of his new book and album.

Things, it occurred to me, were falling apart a bit for Leonard. Suzanne had left, and his own music was beginning to be defined as defining an era, something that should be played to remind you of what was and not what is. I hadn't yet learned that performers like Irving and Leonard have nine lives.

At twenty-two I was living alone in a basement apartment in downtown Toronto. My mother and Leon were in Los Angeles. My godfather was just somewhere. Who knew with Leonard? It could have been LA, Paris, or Tahiti, and my father was in Montreal living with a twenty-eight-year-old woman named Anna. I'd see him on television talking about Love and Poetry and wonder if he'd actually been in town and not phoned. Sometimes, a friend would ring to tell me that he'd seen my father walking down the street. "Yes," I'd say, "he's in town for a few days." Which was in fact the case—I did, after all, read the newspaper.

Sometimes my father's face would slip through a crack in the door. He had once received, from an admirer, 1,000 envelopes with his face stamped onto them. His stern, unforgiving face, with hair tousled by the wind, would pop through my mail slot and out would fall a series of press clippings: "Irving Layton, Still Fighting Fire With Fire," "The Passion of Irving Layton." These headlines could denote either a speech made to the honourable members of the University of Chicago or a poetry reading given to the Housewives' Association of Mississauga. If there was a letter, it was always typewritten. "The battle has yet to be won," he'd write, and then, if I owed him fifty dollars, he'd speak of the moral imperative to pay back one's debts. And on the reverse side of the letter I could usually detect the carbon smudge left from the duplicate copy he'd made and then sent to the Irving Layton Collection at Concordia University.

It seemed a normal relationship with my father was impossible. Many years ago, when Leonard had given him two hits of acid, the books in my father's library had come out of their bookcase and bowed to one another. It was a ballet as Baudelaire stepped out and was introduced, by my father, to Ben Jonson and Edgar Allan Poe. "Leonard," he said, "I've been here many, many times." The place he was describing was the pantheon. He was there. With Socrates and Homer. He was breathing that air.

Leonard told me this story. He insisted that it was not something my father was putting on. "These," Leonard added, "are his concerns."

This was what I was afraid of.

Prominently displayed on my father's living-room table, whenever either of his sons came to visit, was an anthology of the writings of Freud. Irving's idea, his myth, of fatherhood was that we had come either to bless him or to kill him. His money was on kill. He was just letting us know. One time, I went there to face him down about it. I watched his fingers start their journey across the table and come to rest upon Freud's stern forehead in the cover photo.

"I hear you've been having some problems," he said.

"I need to talk to you," I answered. His fingers began to massage Freud's bald pate with a rhythmic drumming of his fingers.

I began to tell him that we needed to find some common ground. Perhaps, I suggested, if we told each other what we wanted and expected from each other, some kind of arrangement could be worked out. After sitting for fifteen minutes with arms folded, my father suddenly brought his open hand down on the table.

"What the hell are you talking about? 'Arrangements,' 'contracts.' Don't use these words with me. I'm very sorry for you, my son, but your father is not a lawyer, he's not a dentist. He's a poet! Men are vipers, villains, jackals, hyenas. If I've taught my children this one things and this one thing only, then I have done my duty!"

My father leaned back in his chair. There was no point in trying to outperform the performer. I'd lose. But if I wasn't careful he'd start reading his poems to me.

I told him that for his sake I hoped he was one of the immortals but that I myself only wanted to be on some normal footing with my father. "And," I added, "I have another confession to make. I've never read any of your poems."

My father looked at me.

"You've never read any of my poems?"

"Not one."

He started to laugh. He laughed until he choked. "Bravo!" We spent the rest of the day smoking cigars and drinking port.

I moved out of the basement and into a third-floor loft. I enrolled in university as a mature student and used the Christmas breaks to visit my mother and Leon in LA. If Leonard was in town, I'd go and see him for an hour or two and we'd talk about women, Greece, and the mysteries of good office. I also started making the occasional trip to Montreal to see my father. I'd talk. He'd summarize. On one occasion I told him that a woman had left me. "Son," he said, "the worst thing you can find out about yourself is that you're replaceable." I never failed to come away feeling I'd been party to a historic event.

One day in Toronto I received a call from my half-brother's ex-girlfriend, now a well-known painter, who said that there was a book launch for my father's new Selected, Collected something or other. Would I like to come? she asked. Hell, why not?

"My boy!" my father bellowed. "Look at You!" The reception was in full swing by the time I arrived. I grabbed a drink and began to talk to Anna, my father's new wife. While we talked faces would push themselves into the conversation. "David? Is that you?" and I'd say, "Yes, it's me," and then they'd move on. But I'd been invited. Here was the intimate embrace: the invitation. My father, standing on the podium saying. "This is for my son, David."

Halfway through the evening, an awed silence descended. I turned around and saw him. It was Leonard Cohen, who had come from some corner of the globe to surprise my father.

"Leonard, my boy!" my father bellowed. "Look at you." I stood by the entrance, with a drink in my hand, and waited to say hello to my godfather, and thank you to my father. After thirty minutes the two, linked arm in arm, moved towards me, strode on past, and entered the hotel elevator where I watched them ascend to the heights.

This time I booked my appointment with Leonard through his personal assistant. Leonard had a "window" on Saturday, in the late morning. That was three days away.

When I touched down at LAX there was only a thin strip of ozone where thick storm clouds had been on my last visit. I arrived at my mother's house on Friday evening and I thought about phoning Leonard. But then, why tempt fate? I waited until the hour of my appointment.

Leonard? The door to his house was slightly ajar. Before I'd even managed to pass the threshold, he was there, moving towards me, with that gorgeous smile of his. I couldn't help feeling that his presence was somehow attributable to my delicate magic. David Layton, the conjurer of shy spirits.

Leonard quickly deduced that we were short of certain materials. We jumped into his Nissan Pathfinder and headed for the liquor store. Leonard's clothes weren't as elegant as I remembered them; he wore a pair of grubby jeans. I noticed this fact as he moved down the liquor aisle. He spent an enormous amount of time looking at the tequila rack and peering into aromatic cigar boxes. He took the kind of time that indicates a man's occupation. No-one who has spent a lifetime working nine to five would be able to develop such a luxurious spirit.

There was Leonard, searching for bottles in a deserted liquor store. With his all-fitting pants and studious interest he reminded me of an ageing professor searching for books in an obscure and neglected part of the library. The effect didn't make him appear old, just vulnerable.

Back at his house, Leonard offered me a ginseng-soaked cognac. He also placed a cup of coffee on the kitchen table and handed me a fat, lighted Dominican cigar. Before I'd taken my second puff, Lorca, his daughter with Suzanne, dropped by to see us. I've only known Lorca for a few years but even so I have a strange urge to treat her as my younger sister, which is no doubt partly attributable to my mother's desire to treat her like a long-lost daughter. But our links are tenuous and, as with all things in our family, ill defined.

Time passed. I placed my tape recorder on the table and tried to let it speak for me. I couldn't bring myself to ask Lorca to leave. We were the children of famous men and it was we who were always asked to leave.

Lorca, thankfully, saved me from my predicament by taking the initiative and leaving her father and me to conduct the interview. We were alone.

"I don't have much time," he said.

I pushed the play button.

"The relationship I had with Irving was not personal but it was intimate. We weren't friends in the sense that we knew or cared about each other's lives. We did know and care about each other's lives, but that wasn't what it was about. That's a personal relationship. This relationship was the poet talking to the poet about poetry. It was more intimate than a personal relationship could ever be. That kind of intimacy has sustained me my whole life and anything that is not that has always been troublesome."

On his table is a picture of Roshi, the spiritual leader of Leonard's retreat on Mount Baldy. He looks like an Oriental version of my father; the fleshy face, the truculent expression, and, behind it all, the unmistakable hint of mischief. They have the faces of boxers, of men who know about getting in the ring and beating the immortal shit out of each other without hatred.

I couldn't help thinking the connection was more than a passing coincidence. Leonard invited the comparison. Leonard said, "When I study with Roshi, it's consciousness speaking to consciousness about consciousness." And anything else, I thought, is troublesome. A godson is trouble, children are trouble, and wives are the genesis of all trouble.

Speaking of consciousness, I was losing mine. The ginseng was hallucinogenic and the cigar smoke was making me exceptionally sick. "Leonard," I said, "I don't think I can drive home right now." "I know," Leonard answered. "The ginseng has been soaking in the cognac for six months. It's very potent." Leonard smiled. Then, just sitting across the table from me, he

began to sing. All by itself Leonard's voice began to make my upper lip quiver. I cupped my hand over my mouth and when he had finished singing I excused myself and ran for the bathroom where, like some hormonally flushed teenager, I splashed cold water over my face.

When I returned to the kitchen Leonard was on his way out. He had to go, he said, but I could stay for as long as I liked. He'd given me his intimate embrace: the performance. Now I was stoned and alone in his house. I looked for a picture of my father but couldn't find one. I started laughing, and once I started I couldn't stop. "Leonard!" I shouted. "Leonard, you bastard, you've done it again. You've disappeared."

Michael Q. Abraham (essay date spring/summer 1996)

SOURCE: Abraham, Michael Q. "Neurotic Affiliations: Klein, Layton, Cohen, and the Properties of Influence." *Canadian Poetry* 38 (spring/summer 1996): 88-129.

[*In the following essay, Abraham discusses the influence of A. M. Klein and Irving Layton on Cohen's poetry and Cohen's evolving attempts to liberate himself from that influence, culminating in* Flowers for Hitler.]

> I shouldn't be in Canada at all. Winter is all wrong for me. I belong beside the Mediterranean. My ancestors made a terrible mistake. But I have to keep coming back to Montreal to renew my neurotic affiliations.
>
> —Leonard Cohen, *The Spice-Box of Earth* (cover)

Leonard Cohen is an enigmatic figure in Canadian letters. Through the course of nearly four decades of publishing, his muse has been a transient one, blurring the distinctions of genre, moving determinedly from poetry to prose to music, vaulting Cohen into international prominence in all three and allowing him to weave various and changing personae around himself. In attempting to analyze Cohen and his work, critics have examined a variety of possible influences on his evolving poetic vision. Stephen Scobie has written extensively on the influences of Baudelaire and Rimbaud, Sandra Djwa aligns Cohen with a somewhat twisted form of romanticism, and Michael Ondaatje affiliates him with everyone from James Joyce to Mickey Spillane. As can be seen from the epigraph of this essay, however, some of the strongest influences on Cohen lie much closer to home.

To characterize Leonard Cohen's poetic relationships with A. M. Klein and Irving Layton as mere "neurotic affiliations" may at first seem a spurious imputation. The term itself is enough to conjure up images of cowering weaklings and demented paranoics, characterizations decidedly unsuitable when speaking of Klein's eloquence or Layton's bombast. Nor are such representations adequate to describe Cohen's early poetry, in which he attempts to fuse the influences of Klein and Layton. Nevertheless, in attempting to ascertain precisely how Klein and Layton influenced Cohen—to assess the *properties* of each man's influence—the term "neurotic" is entirely appropriate. Indeed, it is in Cohen's agonized struggle to fuse the influences of two of his literary mentors that the impetus for much of his early poetry can be found. This exploration of Klein and Layton's influence on Cohen's literary genesis and evolution will extend from the publication of *Let Us Compare Mythologies* in 1956 to the publication of *Flowers for Hitler* in 1964. More specifically, the paper will examine *The Spice-Box of Earth* (1961) as a distinctly transitional work in which Cohen acknowledges Klein's influence even as he is preparing to renounce it. A requiem for his fallen teacher, the volume is also a manifesto for poetic transformation, a joyous dance with Layton's self-reliance. In attempting to reconcile the influences of his literary mentors, however, Cohen comes to realize the dangers implicit in such adherence. Fearing the loss of his own voice and expression, Cohen moves towards a more direct engagement with his own world and experience.

From the outset, the influencing agents are of two distinct natures. Klein's poetic development and output show a strong adherence to traditional poetic forms and themes. Intent on discovering the great secrets contained in the Bible, Klein views poetry as the artistic form most capable of attracting other mortals to a similar quest for knowledge. The power of words lies in their catalytic potential, their ability to provide a linking agent between ages and men. Attempting to provide understandable, contemporary versions of ancient messages, Klein's vision of the poet is more as a purveyor of inherited (and ultimately ineffable) wisdoms than a creator of them, more interpreter than prophet. It is through the accepted inheritance of tradition and genealogy that the source and purpose of poetry can be found. Influences, the messages which survive from generation to generation, are positive (Hermerén 42) and attractive forces, providing both a link to the past and a path for the future.

For Layton, however, influence is perhaps the most odious form of inspiration. Ironically, following "the soaring genius of Nietzsche" (*Waiting for the Messiah* 184), Layton is influenced to despise influence, holding that the mere survival of messages from generation to generation is no proof of their validity. On the contrary, mankind's inherent cruelty has seen to it that history's true lessons are forgotten. Influence finds its strongest manifestation in the "ludicrous sexual and linguistic taboos" that are designed to repress poetry's spontaneous and pure source—intuition (*Engagements* x-xiii).

History's only positive lesson is its negative example. As such, mankind's only hope lies in a direct acknowledgement of and engagement with its own beastliness, not in reverence for ancient wisdoms. As Usher Caplan recounts Layton's view of Klein:

> Layton, who in his own career was seeking to cultivate a fearless Nietzschean persona, saw Klein as just the opposite; a man who was basically evading reality and who in his writings therefore "romanticizes the Jew, presents him as quaint and vanishing. The emotions he exploits are the minor ones—sentiment, disappointment, heartache. There is a backward-looking quality in his poetry."
>
> (209)

Thus, poetry is not the unifying force Klein imagined it to be, but rather "the most subversive force in the world . . . Good poetry shakes people up, bloodies their apathetic noses for them, disturbs their complacencies" (*Engagements* 95). For his part, Layton has made a career out of reacting against commonly accepted forms and inspirations, even when such trends purport to be reactions themselves. Attempting to "fight the . . . general cultural shoddiness" (x) surrounding him, Layton is by turns spontaneous visionary and inflammatory cynic, nihilist-prophet and satirist-clown. In a strictly textual sense Cohen appears to move from a reliance on Klein's aestheticism, with its emphasis on poetic formalism and religious imagery, to the more decadent world of Layton. This progression from Klein to Layton to Cohen can be seen as dialectical: Klein's more positive thesis meets Layton's antithesis in Cohen's attempt at synthesis. Within that dialectical progression, however, is an increasingly "positive" influence with regard to Layton, in that Cohen's poetic focus and persona are in certain respects increasingly similar to Layton's, and a proportionate increase in "negative" influence with regard to Klein.

But the relationship of this Montreal trio extends far beyond the lines of their poems. Klein and Layton, though almost complete philosophical opposites, were close friends and admirers of each other's work. In Cohen's case, Klein was an important teacher and mentor. Even though Klein's career had effectively ended by the time Cohen's began, his example embodied the influences affecting the younger poet. As Cohen said in 1986:

> There was a line—there were different lines which I thought I inherited . . . the Jewish one, the Montreal Jewish one, the one that connected A. M. Klein to my grandfather and my own family, McGill University, and this consecrated expression of poetry. In A. M. Klein there were a lot of those lines that converged, so he was a very important figure to me, beyond the actual poem on the page.
>
> (qtd. in Benazon 44)

As for Layton, Cohen described their relationship as one of friendship rather than influence:

> I think I became friends with Irving Layton . . . and if he had exercised that master-student relationship . . . if Irving did in some secret part of his mind feel that he was giving me instruction, he did it in a most subtle and beautiful way. He did it as a friend, he never made me feel that I was sitting at his feet.
>
> (qtd. in Harris 95)

Within that friendship, however, Klein's presence was a strong one. As Cohen puts it: "Layton was [also] influenced by Klein's predicament . . . Layton and I have talked about Klein for hours and hours" (qtd. in Benazon 46).

With such close personal lives, Klein and Layton's biographical personalities were as likely to influence Cohen as their poems. As Jay Clayton describes such relationships: "Influence depends on the lives of authors, and in our accounts of these lives, incident should illustrate character and character determine incident" (14). Klein's aestheticism—his persistent formalism and desire for beauty—found and manifested itself in a strong religious faith. When that faith was shattered by, among other factors, the revelations of the holocaust, Klein's previously noble search for beauty seemed irrelevant, mankind's apparently limitless cruelty having reduced it to an elaborate lie. By 1955, Klein's disillusion and despair had brought on a heavy silence. He ceased writing, indeed nearly ceased to speak, and descended into isolation and madness. Layton, on the other hand, responded to the same revelations with a very Nietzschean self-reliance. As Klein grew silent, Layton's shouts increased in volume. As Klein's faith weakened, Layton's egoism grew stronger. It wasn't beauty that had died in the ovens, Layton claimed, but God. Poetry now voiced the individual's will to power. For Cohen, each man's influence is contagious and incites imitation. In his desire to fashion his own reaction to the philosophical and epistemological vacuum that surrounds him, Cohen attempts to choose between the influences of his two mentors.

In *The Anxiety of Influence,* Harold Bloom asserts that a strong poet is born with the realization that:

> poetry [is] . . . both external and internal to himself . . . [which] begins a process that will end only when he has no more poetry in him, long after he has the power (or desire) to discover it outside himself again . . . the poet is condemned to learn his profoundest yearnings through an awareness of other selves. The poem is within him, yet he experiences the shame and splendour of being found by poems—great poems— outside him.
>
> (26)

Bloom's eloquent appraisal is both corroboration of and counterpoint to the central argument of this paper. From the earliest of his published works, it is clear that Co-hen is painfully aware of the poetry which exists within him and without him. His desire to write is precipitated both by a desire to speak with a unique voice and a desire to imitate ancestral poets. In Cohen's early writings, an anxiety of influence is clearly present as he attempts to come to terms with his artistic and Jewish inheritance. Cohen's anxiety, however, stems from a source that is opposite to the one Bloom describes. Rather than fearing his own voice will be drowned by tendencies toward imitation, Cohen actively seeks the certainty and stability of influence.

Writing out of the desolation that follows the holocaust, Cohen struggles to discover meaning in an environment which has none. In *One Generation After* (1970), Elie Wiesel describes the unique brand of suffering that follows the holocaust. Asked to detail their experiences,

> The survivors were reticent, their answers vague. The subject: taboo. They remained silent . . . they feared being inadequate to the task, betraying a unique experience by burying it in worn-out phrases and images. They were afraid of saying what must not be said, of attempting to communicate with language what eludes language, of falling into the trap of easy half-truths . . . Sooner or later, every one of them was tempted to seal his lips and maintain absolute silence. So as to transmit a vision of the holocaust, in the manner of certain mystics, by withdrawing from words. Had all of them remained mute, their accumulated silences would have become unbearable: the impact would have deafened the world.
>
> (7-8)

Unlike his mentors, Cohen comes to manhood in the generation following the holocaust, a survivor in a world where survival is arbitrary rather than earned, where personality is less assumed than imposed. As his poetic career begins, Cohen does not fear the possible dominance of "other selves" or a potentially overwhelming influence. Rather, he fears the desolation of influence, its tragic obsolescence in a world that is ominously, terrifyingly new. After Auschwitz, Cohen fears an external silence will invade his internal world.

In August 1943, writing in the pages of the influential Montreal literary magazine *First Statement,* Layton refers to the early 'forties as an age in transition, engaged in a movement away from the influences of the poets of the early and middle 'thirties. In a tone that suggests both eulogy and prophecy, Layton characterizes the "urgency and moral fervour that marked an important advance upon the poetry of the previous decade" as "a fusion between psycho-analysis and politics . . . [between] introversion and extroversion; Freud and Marx" (*Engagements* 10). Layton's words— written as World War II drew to a close, before the full and terrifying images of the holocaust had burned themselves into the world's psyche—are particularly striking in that, while remembering a political and poetical movement that has ceased to be relevant, Layton outlines the essential elements of a movement that is just beginning.

In explaining the fundamental aspects of the poetry of the early and middle 'thirties, Layton draws the distinction and the correlation between introversion and extroversion, between silence and voice. Layton's reference to Freud is an interesting and helpful one in this discussion. In *Totem and Taboo,* Freud describes the neurotic link between introversion and extroversion in much the same way as Layton characterizes the attempt at poetic fusion present in the poetry of the 'thirties. Neuroticism, writes Freud, manifests itself both in prohibitive anxiety and in compulsive desire; in self-imposed solitude and obsessive action; in silence and in voice. Moreover, Freud contends that the tension between these two contrary influences, the simultaneous impulse to impose and contravene taboos, "stands at the centre of poetical interest" (24). The catalyst that fuses these two apparently divergent elements together is a strong and shared neuroticism, an anxiety that is alternately prohibitive and impulsive, fearful and joyous. On the one hand, the neurotic may severely restrict all contact with people as a means of avoiding a painful or unpleasant impulse, while on the other, such "obsessive acts serve the impulse more and more and come nearer and nearer to the original and forbidden act" (42). Similarly, the neurotic's severing of contact (silence) or impulsive pursuit of it (voice) simultaneously inspires a strict aversion and an arcane envy in those who observe him:

> An individual who has violated a taboo becomes himself a taboo because he has the dangerous property of tempting others to follow his example. He arouses envy; why should he be allowed to do what is prohibited to others? He is therefore really contagious, in so far as every example incites to imitation.
>
> (45)

The duality inherent in neuroticism is inextricably linked to the concept of influence. Both conscious and unconscious, intentional and unintentional, influence determines our actions and inactions. Ultimately, the decision to act or not to act determines the nature of one's personality. That which is permissible is totem; that which is not is taboo. Unfortunately, although contravention of the taboo is unacceptable, it is never impossible. To paraphrase Freud, that which nobody wishes to do requires no prohibition. The individual must always choose between uncertainties. Neuroticism occupies the realm of indecision, the limbo between action and inaction; it is the anxiety of choice.

For the poet, action is voice, inaction is silence. Just as Wiesel's survivors are forced to choose between inevitably inadequate action (voice) and symbolic inaction (silence), so Cohen faces the problematic choice between the desolation of silence and "attempting to communicate with language what eludes language" (*One Generation After* 8). In Cohen's immediate sphere of influence, Klein and Layton each represent one side of the neuroticism which Freud describes. Klein is increasingly convinced of his own poetic inadequacy and is gradually silenced by revelations of man's audacious cruelty. Layton, for his part, is outraged to the point of a delirious liberation. The commandments, the taboos, have been irrevocably shattered. Now, anything is possible. It is this discrepancy which Cohen vainly attempts to reconcile in his early books.

The tension between silence and voice is a strong theme in Klein's 1944 collection, *Poems,* which begins with the psalm sequence "The Psalter of Avram Haktani." Despite the initial subterfuge of the title-pseudonym— "Avram Haktani" is Hebrew for Abraham Klein (Caplan 90)—the psalter is, from the outset, a frank and intensely personal exploration of both Klein's anxiety and his faith. The first psalm, in which Abraham "hearkened to a voice, and there was none" depicts an ominous silence in the heavens while, on earth, chaos reigns. The sequence ends, however, with the comforting "Psalm XXXVI: A Psalm Touching Genealogy" in which Klein asserts the stabilizing solidity of his ancestry and faith:

> Not sole was I born, but entire genesis:
> For to the fathers that begat me, this
> Body is residence. Corpuscular,
> They dwell in my veins, they eavesdrop at my ear,
> They circle, as with Torahs, round my skull.
> In exit and in entrance all day pull
> The latches of my heart, descend and rise—
> And there look generations through my eyes.
>
> (*Collected Poems* 234)

The main body of the psalter consists of prayers against madness, guilt, faithlessness, and sin, but the final psalm portrays a Jewish inheritance which strengthens and stabilizes. Klein's personality is predetermined by the fathers that begat him, his path is foreordained. Thus, the optimistic vision of endurance which appears in "Psalm XXXVI" is counterbalance both to the bleak vision of "Psalm I" and to the thirty-five in between. Evidence of God and his promises lies in the community that surrounds the poet both presently and historically. Proof of redemption lies in the genealogy of faith, the divine "oneness" of persistently shared belief. It is this belief which promises to overcome the grim landscape threatening to close in upon him.

Klein drew his artistic focus from his influential ancestry and his poetic style from the pages of the Bible, a book he enthusiastically described as one in which all secrets could be uncovered: "History, anecdote, tale, genealogy, poetry, play, epigram—all are to be found in these pages. Well did the members of the Great Synagogue say when they did enjoin: 'Go over it and over it, for everything is in it!'" (*Literary Essays and Reviews* 130) As Gretl Fischer notes in describing this aspect of Klein's work: "Proof of God's existence [is] everywhere . . . [and] Klein embraces ecstatically the idea of the oneness and divinity of all creation" (38). But in "The Gesture of the Bible" (1948), Klein describes the Hebrew affinity for words as a compulsive, rather than divine, impulse:

> the whole vocabulary of the Bible is part of an attempt to escape from the aesthetic suppressions occasioned by the Second Commandment: "Thou shalt not make unto thee any graven image, or any likeness of anything that is in heaven above, or that is in the earth beneath, or that is in the water under the earth" . . . But the soul, it would appear, hungers toward such creativity; where such creativity is impeded, frustration ensues. But frustration always seeks some way out. For the ancient Hebrew the way out of the prohibition of the Second Commandment was—to make images in words.
>
> (*Literary Essays and Reviews* 132)

That making images into words should be a way out of the commandment, a circumvention of the taboo, is a sentiment strikingly reminiscent of Freud. The "frustration" of which Klein speaks is precisely the neurotic limbo that exists between action and inaction. Prohibited from revering actual images, the ancient Hebrews redirected their veneration into description and explanation. Reverence for images was replaced by reverence for language; words permitted freedom from the law of artistic silence. Thus writing, the most tangible form of language, imperfect and inadequate as it may be, is a liberating (and legal) action. It is only through words that a problematic world may be understood and explained. Only poets can bring meaning to events.

It is a bleaker vision, however, that prevails in Klein's final collection, *The Rocking Chair and Other Poems* (1948). In "The Cripples," Klein gazes with admiration and longing at the Catholic invalids attempting to climb the steps of the Oratoire de Saint-Joseph, fairly moaning: "I who in my own faith once had faith like this, / but have not now, am crippled more than they" (*Collected Poems* 298-99). In "Portrait of the Poet as Landscape," the collection's concluding and defining poem, the formerly revered figure of the poet is missing and presumed dead. In "our real society," he "simply does not count," yet "shines / like phosphorus. At the bottom of the sea" (330-35). Still the only figure capable of explaining the world around him, of making images into words, the poet is simply ignored by his fellows. Replete with warnings, he is no longer considered reliable, and no one will listen to him.

Such is Cohen's enigmatic inheritance: an almost genetic attachment to religion is coupled with the grim knowledge that recent events have crippled its reli-

ability. Following the revelations of the holocaust, God's existence is very much in doubt. From the opening of *Let Us Compare Mythologies,* Klein's influence is manifested in elegiac, resigned tones and ominous, though ornate, images of disintegration. But "*beyond the actual poem on the page*" (Benazon 44), it is Klein's personal history, the "incident" of his tragic descent into silence, that influences Cohen. The guiding path of the Jewish inheritance has been reduced to the confines of stereotype and the deliberate and determined disintegration of individual personality.

Yearning for originality but frustrated by the crippling lack of a defining vision, Cohen feels his emancipation can only come through writing, through making images into words. As his poetic career begins, Cohen is actively "seeking a new law that prescribes . . . what words to say and no longer to say" (Wiesel, *Legends of Our Time* 16). In his autobiographical novel *The Favourite Game,* Cohen echoes Klein's sentiment in "The Gesture of the Bible" when he remarks: "writing is an essential part of the Jewish tradition and even the degraded contemporary situation cannot suppress it" (102). Even amidst the meaningless desolation of the holocaust, the simple need to write, to describe and explain the world as he sees it, is the strongest impetus behind Cohen's early writing. Lurking within that desire, however, is the uneasy fear that poetry has ceased to matter, that "Auschwitz, by definition, is beyond [his] vocabulary" (*Legends of Our Time* 19). In the midst of this dilemma, Cohen is determined to develop an artistic personality, an original and authentic poetic voice. In the middle of the chaos, however, he has still not decided what to write about. First and foremost, *Let Us Compare Mythologies* is a comparison of dead certainties, a volume in which Cohen debates whether or not he can improve on silence.

Writing in the inaugural issue of *Contact* in 1952, Louis Dudek bemoaned the apparent absence of young voices on the Canadian poetry scene. After suggesting possible reasons for this absence, Dudek concludes with a palpable incredulity: "The poet has more to say and understand today than he has ever had at any other time in history. Why are the young poets at a loss for words?" ("Où sont les jeunes" in *The Making of Modern Poetry in Canada* 144). After four years *à la recherche des jeunes,* Dudek published *Let Us Compare Mythologies* as the first book in his "McGill Poetry Series," a showcase for young literary talent in and around Montreal. It was perhaps due to the dearth of young voices that Cohen's first volume was so well-received, establishing him as the so-called "golden-boy poet," a title he would do his best to relinquish in the years that followed. But Cohen's first volume is not the concrete "communication of something worth saying" that Dudek exhorted young poets to write. Rather, *Let Us Compare Mythologies* is an extended attempt to provide a spiritual and philosophical answer to Dudek's question: where *are* the young?

Conspicuous in the volume is **"Halloween Poem,"** a casual description of the ritual torture of birds and frogs. The poem was published earlier in *CIV/n*, an influential Montreal literary magazine, bearing the longer title **"An Halloween Poem to Delight My Younger Friends"** and, perhaps more importantly, included Dudek's question as a parenthetic subtitle. Cohen's answer to the question "where are the young?" is a chaotic and unsettling one:

> I don't know where the children got the birds. Certainly, there are few around my house. Oh, there is the occasional sparrow or robin or wren, but these were big birds. There were several turns of parcel twine about each bird to secure its wings and feet. It was that particularly hard variety of twine that can't be pulled apart but requires a knife or scissors to be cut. I was so lost in the ritual that I'm not sure if it was seven or eight they burnt.
>
> (56)

One need not go far to draw a correlation between the enthusiastic cruelty of these children and the genocidal cruelty of some modern adults. Ritual, itself the manifestation of profound influence, takes the form of torture and cremation. The victims are the hitherto timeless images of creative, and thus poetic, freedom. Darker still, their murderers are Dudek's *les jeunes*, following the example set for them in the crematoria of Europe. Hitler's influence, it seems, has made *anything* possible.

The holocaust has proven that inherited values, the "seeds sown by earlier generations," are no longer relevant. Cohen's generation is faced with the bitter realization that it is "possible to . . . begin one day to massacre men, women and children, without hesitation and without guilt . . . One's spiritual legacy provides no screen, ethical concepts offer no protection" (5). No absolutes remain. Nietzsche's cataclysmic statement has come true: God is dead. It is little wonder that Dudek's young people are at a loss for words: no adequate words remain. As Richard L. Rubenstein writes in *After Auschwitz*:

> we live in the time of the death of God . . . the thread uniting God and man, heaven and earth has broken. We stand in a cold, silent, unfeeling cosmos, unaided by any purposeful power beyond our own resources. After Auschwitz, what else can a Jew say about God?
>
> (172)

Cohen himself has identified the holocaust as the "central psychic event in his life," saying he "never recovered" from its "illumination of human behaviour" (qtd. in Dorman 66). In his first volume, Cohen is pain-

fully aware that there are no longer any spiritual laws to live by. While it is true that, as Desmond Pacey writes, Cohen engages in "twin quests for God and sexual fulfillment" ("The Phenomenon of Leonard Cohen" 74), he quickly discovers the gods are dead, the girls are unapproachable or unavailable, and chaos reigns. In such a milieu, Cohen betrays the dark fear that nothing he can say will make any difference, that his poetry no longer matters. And yet, as the epigraph from William Faulkner indicates, Cohen simply has to talk about something:

> "She cannot fade, though thou hast not thy bliss," McCaslin
> said: "Forever wilt thou love, and she be fair."
> "He's talking about a girl," he said.
> "He had to talk about something," McCaslin said.
>
> (*Mythologies* [*Let Us Compare Mythologies*] 7)

In a world of dead gods and frustrated love, it is left to writing to "give interest, order, meaning and direction" (Pacey 74) to Cohen's world. As Sandra Djwa writes:

> Reading through Cohen's work we become aware of an unsatisfied search for an absolute. In his world there are no fixed values, spiritual or sensual, that stand beyond the transitory moment, and the moment itself, experience made myth, blends imperceptibly with other moments and other mythologies, so that in the shifting the values change, leaving only the value of experience made art.
>
> (94)

Despite Stephen Scobie's comment that Cohen's vision is so clear and confident from the outset that *Mythologies* "shows [only] occasional signs of being a first book" (15), the volume's ultimate subject is precisely the poet's *lack* of confidence, the *absence* of a defining vision or influence that is sorely needed. As the title of the volume suggests, Cohen compares mythologies which were once absolutes, questions which were once answers. Deep within the neurotic vacuum that so complicates choice, he struggles to decide between the shattered influences that once defined him.

The same events that threaten to silence the younger generation, however, are perfect grist for Layton's philosophical mill. For Layton, there was no greater evidence of God's death than the holocaust, no better proof of God's former life than His tragic death. A devoted follower of Nietzsche, Layton would have corroborated Rubenstein's later assertion that "the time which Nietzsche's madman said was too far off has come upon us" (172). Like the wild-eyed madman in Nietzsche's *The Gay Science*—who answers the question of "Where has God gone?" with *"We have killed him—you and I. All of us are his murderers"* (95)—Layton, himself "A quiet madman, never far from tears" (*Collected Poems* 121), insisted that man acknowledge his complicity in the world's horrors:

Let us admit it openly: we were accomplices before the crime. We helped to arm Hitler, and Mussolini, and Hirohito, the unholy trinity . . . Directly or indirectly we connived at, encouraged and supported every one of Hitler's aggressions. With a wink and a nod and a final handclasp under the table, we assured Hitler that it was quite safe for him to rob and plunder his neighbours . . . Let us, I say, admit all this openly. For unless we do so, and unless we draw the proper conclusions from the facts, this frightful bloodletting will be a monstrous, unforgivable crime.

(*Engagements* 18)

The passage bears the mark of Nietzsche's *Thus Spoke Zarathustra,* in which God's presence or absence is not so important as man's savagery. With belief in God transformed into the retrospective stuff of myths, Zarathustra preaches the *übermensch,* or "Superman," who will take responsibility for his own actions. The Superman is he who overcomes his own beastliness, who quells the "all-too-human" instinct for cruelty and violence by admitting his affinity for it. As Layton would assert a year later in a review of Klein's *Poems:* "To know God truly, one must also have known Satan" (*Engagements* 152). Layton, like Nietzsche, exhorts humans to realize that they are capable of anything.

Nietzsche's influence on Layton is well-known. Two years before the publication of **Let Us Compare Mythologies,** his seminal poem "The Birth of Tragedy" borrowed its title and its theme of the correlation of life and death from Nietzsche's essay on the origin of art. "Orpheus," published the following year, deals subtly with Greek mythology and Nietzsche's theory of eternal recurrence. As Layton writes:

> God was not Love nor Law,
> God was the blood I saw,
> The ever-flowing blood
>   Staining water and sod

(*Collected Poems* 152)

In examining Layton's "zarathustrian" influence on Cohen, it is significant that Cohen's inaugural book of poems also begins with an elegy for Orpheus. What is more, it is ironic that the birth of Cohen's poetic voice should be marked by an announcement of death. Cohen's inaugural poem is, so to speak, a birth of tragedy. Moreover, **"Elegy"** unites the Hebraic, Biblical romanticism of Klein with the Nietzschean nihilism of Layton—a bleak realization that life goes on though God is dead. As Cohen's first poem for Layton indicates, it is his mentor's "delightful / zarathustrian tales" (**"To I. P. L.,"** in *Mythologies* 54) that fascinate him. While Norman Ravvin acknowledges Cohen's "fascination with a kind of Nietzschean self-realization" (23), he sees it as a distinctive characteristic of Cohen's 1966 novel, *Beautiful Losers.* Such an interest is clearly evident, however, from the first poem of Cohen's career.

Read in this Laytonic/Nietzschean light, Cohen's **"Elegy"** emerges as more than a simple lament or romantic vision. The poem begins with a god that is dead. Unlike Layton, who required the "ever-flowing blood / Staining water and sod" to realize both the past existence and the present absence of God, Cohen quickly asserts the pointlessness of looking into "brittle mountain streams," examining "angry rivers," or turning "the shore stones for his blood," for proof of God's passing: evidence is neither available or necessary (13). Scobie's reminder that Orpheus is "a seasonally dying god . . . who will rise again in the spring" (16) is well taken, but there are indications that a resurrected god will be fundamentally altered. Indeed, the god of the second half of the poem resembles Nietzsche's Superman more than Orpheus:

> In truth, man is a polluted river. One must be a sea, to receive a
> polluted river and not be defiled.
> Behold, I teach you the Superman: he is this sea; in him your
> great contempt can go under [*untergehen*].

(*Thus Spoke Zarathustra* 42)

Like the Superman, Cohen's "rising" god is "in the warm salt ocean / He is descending through cliffs / Of slow green water." He is *untergehen,* or descending into the warmth of the sea. Furthermore, like the sea that receives the polluted stream of man, Cohen's god receives "the hovering coloured fish" who "Kiss his snow-bruised body / And build their secret nests / In his fluttering winding sheet." (13) Compare Cohen's image with the experience of Zarathustra:

> I sighed: then icy mist arose from me. My past broke open its graves, many a pain buried alive awoke: they had only been sleeping, concealed in winding sheets.

(183)

As Zarathustra's "icy mist" awakens pain, so Cohen's Orpheus has a body "bruised" by snow. As Zarathustra's pains are concealed in winding sheets, so Cohen's "coloured fish" conceal themselves. Cohen's god is thus both Layton's Orpheus and Nietzsche's Superman united to create poetry. In these lines, the first that Cohen officially presents to the world, we see the embodiment of Layton's dominant theme, that "the poet's heart / Has nowhere counterpart / Which can celebrate / Love equally with Death / Yet by its pulsing bring / A music into everything" (**Collected Poems** 37).

As the volume continues, images of dead gods, be they actual saviours or deified myths, come thick and fast. In **"For Wilf and his House,"** from which the volume takes its name, Cohen learns the "elaborate lie" of how his fathers killed Jesus and "nailed him / like a bat against a barn" (15). **"Prayer for Messiah,"** rather than the plea for heavenly intervention one would expect from the Kleinian¹ title, is a guilt-ridden lament for a god: "his death on my breast is harder than stone" (18). **"Rites"** shows Cohen's father riddled with disease while spectating uncles promise an impossible recovery. **"Saviours"** is perhaps the bleakest listing of the dead, in which "all the saints and prophets / are nailed to stakes and desert trees" (65). In each poem, resurrection is promised, but seems a fool's game, this cyclical life holding only the promise of endless suffering and death, in which "the Kings and men of ages / with deathless words and singing harps / are exhumed to die again in the wilderness." Like Nietzsche's theory of eternal recurrence, "which postulates that everything that happens happens again and again forever" (Francis 281), the painful futility of repeated resurrection is evident in **"Rededication,"** in which the coming of spring finds mankind "almost too tired to begin again / with miracles and leaves" (*Mythologies* 20). The reconstructed life of April, "like the building of cathedrals between wars," can only lead to October and repeated death. The future, like the past, is a resilient burden. A final and heroic death seems preferable, but is no longer possible:

> if I could ruin my feathers
> in flight before the sun;
> do you think I would remain in this room,
> reciting poems to you,
> and making outrageous dreams
> with the smallest movements of your mouth.
>
> **("These Heroics," 28)**

In the present cycle of events, a pathetic messianic figure is "Blinded and hopelessly lame" (25), ignored by Peel Street passersby, while an elegant Satan thrives in the rich refuge of Westmount (51).

Consistent with the Laytonic/Nietzschean theme of death and eternal recurrence is **"Prayer for Sunset,"** a poem that holds decidedly more than the "extraordinarily overstated images" Scobie attributes to Cohen's ostensibly deliberate "courting [of] the absurdities of excess" (24), and is more complex than Ondaatje allows when he decries its youthful lack of originality (7). As brutal as it is romantic, **"Prayer for Sunset"** manages to couple the simple elegance of sunset with the tragedy of violent death.

The link to Nietzsche lies in the philosopher's playful use of the word *untergehen* in *Thus Spoke Zarathustra*. The word is used most often to represent the process of descending into one's self in order to rise over one's self: to "go under" in order to achieve the Superman. The word *untergehen* itself, however, has three meanings: to go under, to die, and to set (as of the sun). With what Cohen himself calls Layton's "zarathustrian" impulses in mind, it is interesting to note that **"Prayer for Sunset"** combines the three meanings, so important to Nietzsche, into one poem. The sun (a dominant mythological image in both Nietzsche and in Layton) "commit[s] its daily suicide" by setting, perishes by "going under" as "slowly, the sea consumes it" (41). Once again, the complex Nietzschean theme of eternal recurrence, with its possibilities for both boundless joy and prohibitive despair, the reconciliation of aspiration and disintegration (Djwa 99), is evoked in the simplest of images. The poem depicts a tragic death which holds both the promise of rebirth and, "tomorrow night," another death. Cohen's plaintive request for a "Joab" is a wistful reference to the commander of King David's army who, in vengeance for his brother's murder, slew David's nemesis and, ironically, was condemned by his master for it (2 Samuel 3:26-30). In Cohen's vision, the tragedy and necessity of this daily suicide is symbolized by Joab's heroic, but altogether fruitless, vengeance. Despite his futile prayer for a sun's avenger, there is no way to halt this cycle of life and death. With the death of God, it is as relentless as it is meaningless.

Layton's influence is also evident in a visceral urgency that pervades many of the poems and is no doubt, as Allan Donaldson derisively comments, to blame for a supposed "overuse of images of sex and violence" (11). The importance of these influences is particularly evident in **"Poem"** in which, in keeping with Faulkner's epigraph, the poet is talking to and about a girl:

> I heard of a man
> who says words so beautifully
> that if he only speaks their name
> women give themselves to him.
>
> If I am dumb beside your body
> while silence blossoms like tumors on our lips
> it is because I hear a man climb stairs
> and clear his throat outside our door.
>
> (55)

The anxiety of voice is here precipitated by the persuasive talents of another poet. The fearful silence that attends the rival's possible intrusion is coupled with a knowledge that silence is no match for a beautiful voice in the battle for love and happiness. Given the choice between the "tumors" of silence and words said beautifully, the woman is unlikely to choose the former. Throughout the collection, the world after Auschwitz—dominated by a silence exemplified by Klein—is viewed with nervous trepidation. **"Poem"** reveals reactive silence as a dangerous disease, but what is the alternative? To recall Rubenstein: with God dead, what is there for a young Jewish poet to talk about? The anxious silence which Cohen dreads is, as Freud describes it, a "neurotic anxiety . . . [which] corresponds to a libido which has been deflected from its object and has found no employment" (*The Interpretation of Dreams* 236).

Over half of the poems in *Let Us Compare Mythologies* depict encounters with women. In nearly every case, true union is frustrated, love has been deflected from its object and stands unemployed and melancholy. **"The Song of the Hellenist"** reveals a frustrated attempt at union between the poet and his Greek hosts. Steeped in reverence for their mythical gods, the poet feels "small and ugly" beside them, "blemishes on the pedestal" (16). Attempting to please, the poet self-consciously flatters, indulging stereotypes about Jews: "I made them laugh / when the child came in: / 'Come I need you for a Passover Cake.'" Yet, it is not feelings of inferiority, but rather, ingrained feelings of racial superiority which preclude union. Though beautiful and tempting, the Grecian women are taboo. Though desiring union with another culture, the poet painfully experiences the prohibition of his own prejudice, "thinking somehow they are unclean, / as scaleless fish." The realization is incredulous, yet it is irrefutable: "Dark women, soon I will not love you" (16).

The theme of deflected or frustrated love is continued in **"Folk Song,"** in which the highly romantic commissioning of "a bottle / to keep your tears in" (29) is frustrated by a woman who cannot cry. In **"Song,"** the poem that follows it, the woman cries, but unfortunately, her grief is precipitated by the poet's absence. The distance of death having kept him from the naked girl, the poet must be content to live only in her memory, mythically heroic. The turning point of **"Summer Night"** occurs when "the girl in my arms / broke suddenly away" (48), destroying the subtlety of romantic seduction and exposing the characters as "stupid" and "obvious." Even a house fly is closer to sexual fulfillment than is the young poet (60).

Of all the depictions of frustrated love in *Let Us Compare Mythologies,* however, the most poignant and telling is **"Lovers,"** a poem in which the sweet negotiations between love and poetry are first frustrated, then obliterated, by the sheer savagery of the holocaust:

> And at the hot ovens they
> Cunningly managed a brief
> Kiss before the soldier came
> To knock out her golden teeth.
>
> And in the furnace itself
> As the flames flamed higher,
> He tried to kiss her burning breasts
> As she burned in the fire.
>
> Later he often wondered;
> Was their barter completed?
> While men around him plundered
> And knew he had been cheated.
>
> (33)

The bleak finality and almost unbearable sense of waste is particularly reminiscent of Klein's powerful "Psalm VI" in which the aspirations and talents of an entire race are, like Cohen's frustrated lovers, deprived of

their rightful realization. Here, the themes of love and sex transcend the adolescent lust evident in many of the other poems, becoming the vital, and tragically unsuccessful, underpinnings of survival. Cheated out of the love due to him, the spared lover bitterly doubts the value of his "history-full of poems" (33). The true union of life and art now seems impossible.

Though rife with apocalyptic images of death, pain, and madness, it is Klein's influence that has the last word in *Mythologies.* In his 1944 poem "Psalm VI," it is clear that, despite the misery and suffering so pervasive in the contemporary world, God's vengeance is at hand:

> The Lord looked down, and saw the cattle-cars:
> Men ululating to a frozen land.
> He saw a man tear at his flogged scars,
> And saw a babe look for its blown-off hand.
> Scholars, he saw, sniffing their bottled wars,
> And doctors who had geniuses unmanned.
>   . . . . .
> And the good Lord said nothing, but with a nod
> Summoned the angels of Sodom down to earth.
>
> (*Collected Poems* 213-14)

Moreover, the establishment of the state of Israel on May 14, 1948 was a source of great comfort for Klein. Indeed, Israel's independence, with its capital Jerusalem, is the focus of his 1951 novel *The Second Scroll,* and in his foreword to Moishe Dickstein's *From Palestine to Israel* (1951), Klein, with a cautious but nevertheless renewed optimism, attempts to reconcile the suffering of the Jewish race with its resilience:

> "From Palestine to Israel"—one would say that that were no distance at all, seeing that the second is geographically of the first; but what centuries, what eras of anguish and of hope, there lie between! . . . [following] the many who . . . came to a Jerusalem in which they found but ruins and the mourners of Zion . . . [this is] Jerusalem a-building, Zion consoled, and on the anniversary of National Independence its jubilant streets [are] joyous and celebrant! . . . Be praised Who has done these things!
>
> (8)

Just as Klein's "The Psalter of Avram Haktani" cuts an anxious path through threatening territory, so *Let Us Compare Mythologies* emerges as a journey through possibility and probability in a milieu which is increasingly uncertain. And just as Klein, at least momentarily, gleans from Israel's independence a renewed faith in the beliefs of his fathers, Cohen also turns to a painful history for comfort. In **"Exodus,"** Cohen juxtaposes the cruelty and punishment of ancient Egyptian pharaohs with the modern and more telling image of "numbers / burnt on our brothers wrists" and ends with the comforting promise of redemption:

> And let this comfort you:
> though no great fish came

to spit your drowning boys on dry land,
and no pillar of light illumined a road back
through the failing water,
still these uncommitted bodies
dried the swamp towards Jerusalem,
and your widows and sweethearts along the shore
wept a prayer which found our God.

(68)

Though a volume that depicts suffering, anxiety, and guilt, *Let Us Compare Mythologies* concludes with an indisputable admission of faith and optimism. Though God is dead, he shall rise again to punish the wicked and avenge the faithful. In **"Beside the Shepherd,"** the volume's concluding poem, the coming of the messiah is, though long overdue, not met with tremendous surprise: "Well finally it has happened" (70). Although providing few answers to Cohen's spiritual dilemma, his first volume's comparison of mythologies concludes with a vision of optimism and renewed faith. Cohen's anxiety, like that of his mentor Klein, is debilitating but curable, frustrating but temporary. As the concluding poems in *Mythologies* reveal, the inexplicable suffering of the modern world is a test of faith, a purifying experience that will revive God from His death-like slumber. In Cohen's next volume, however, such religious stoicism is undermined by Layton's cynical irony, which posits that "the Messiah will only come to earth when every inch of ground under our feet is red with the blood we have ourselves spilled: a point of last judgment which will already have taken us beyond any Messiah's redemption" (Trehearne, "Introduction" xxvii).

Despite the success of *Let Us Compare Mythologies,* it was five years before *The Spice-Box of Earth* appeared. The reasons for the extended silence are not immediately clear, but *The Favourite Game* provides some strong clues. Reflecting on his first book of poems, Cohen's protagonist, Lawrence Breavman, describes the age in which he lives with a cynical bitterness:

> The world was being hoaxed by a disciplined melancholy. All the sketches made a virtue of longing. All that was necessary to be loved widely was to publish one's anxieties. The whole enterprise of art was a calculated display of suffering.

(102)

From such a description, it seems clear that Cohen was unwilling to engage himself any further in the adolescent angst which characterized his first book. Such displays of suffering, no matter how well-intentioned, had become so popular that they had lost all meaning. In what Michael Ondaatje calls "a more professional and less varied book" (15), Cohen sought to blend the romantic imagery of *Let Us Compare Mythologies* with a more indentifiable vision. As such, *The Spice-Box of Earth* contains some poems reminiscent of what has been, and others eerily prophetic of what is to come, in Cohen's poetic vision.

Despite its hostile undertones, undertones which caused Ondaatje to refer to it as a volume which "is far nastier and far more frightening" (21) than the later *Flowers for Hitler, The Spice-Box of Earth* shows a heightened confidence on the part of its author. The opening poem, **"A Kite is a Victim"** shows the poet enjoying more control than ever before. In contrast to the uncertainty so prevalent in *Let Us Compare Mythologies,* the kite is a clear metaphor for the tension between limitation and freedom. From the first line of the poem, Cohen masterfully fuses images of restriction and liberation: the kite is "a victim you are sure of," a "trained falcon," "a fish you have already caught," and most tellingly, "the last poem you've written." The majestic falcon has had its freedom trained out of it. The fish still swims but only while the fisherman plays him. Although the poet's work is eventually set free, the poet himself is not: "you don't let it go / until someone finds you / something else to do" (*Spice-Box* [*The Spice-Box of Earth*] 1). The creative tension between desired freedom and necessary stricture is even more apparent in the book's concluding poem, **"Lines from My Grandfather's Journal"**:

> The language in which I was trained: spoken in despair
>   of priestliness.
> This is not meant for any pulpit, not for men to chant
> or tell their children. Not beautiful enough.
> But perhaps this can suggest a passion. Perhaps this
> passion could be brought to clarify, make more radiant, the standing Law.
> Let judges secretly despair of justice: their verdicts
> will be more acute. Let generals secretly despair of
> triumph: killing will be defamed. Let priests secretly
> despair of faith: their compassion will be true. *It is the
> tension. . . .*

(90; italics mine)

A gentle manifesto, **"Lines from My Grandfather's Journal"** attempts to explain the necessity of a purifying conflict. Just as the judges, the generals, and the priests, find their most perfect manifestation in the flames of passion and uncertainty, so, it stands to reason, the poet must find his voice amidst the threat of silence. As Cohen characterizes the potential vacuum in which he lives: "Desolation means no angels to wrestle . . . Desolation means no comparisons . . ." (92-93). Though words may be inadequate, "not beautiful enough" for pulpits or chants, their only alternative is a potentially murderous silence. Like the kite that "pulls / gentle enough to call you master, / strong enough to call you fool" (1), the poet's voice must be controlled even as it is set free. Completely unbridled, he risks being incomprehensible; controlled too tightly, he risks not being heard. In either case, silence, or "desolation," is the inevitable result. Once again, if desolation is to be avoided, the threat of silence must be dared: one must struggle with the angel to maintain any hope for redemption. The experience of artistic creativity becomes a compromise between an unattainable ideal and an unacceptable nullity, an essential comparison of, and struggle between, opposite visions. It is the tension between these elements, the link between the silent poet and the liberated and liberating poem, that urges Cohen in a particular direction, "knowing that truth lies neither in the one nor the other but in the ceaseless movement between the two" (Starobinski 13).

An attempt to break the silence of desolation, ***The Spice-Box of Earth*** is, like its predecessor, a book of comparisons. Present again is "the romantic view of the artist as prophet, priest, and magician" (Morley 73), but while *Let Us Compare Mythologies* can be seen as a canvassing of available influences, ***The Spice-Box of Earth*** is a more mature attempt to choose among them, showing a heightened determination to find his own way out of his neurotic limbo. In **"I Have Not Lingered in European Monasteries,"** one of the volume's most anthologized poems, traditionally romantic images of poetic inspiration are rejected even as they are indulged. The poem concludes with an image of insipid happiness, seemingly content but devoid of exhilaration:

> I have not been unhappy for ten thousand years.
> During the day I laugh and during the night I sleep.
> My favourite cooks prepare my meals,
> my body cleans and repairs itself,
> and all my work goes well.

> (23)

Essentially, the poem is a catalogue of renunciation. The speaker describes in eloquent detail everything he has not accomplished. Similarly, each ideal image in ***The Spice-Box of Earth*** is countered with a negative vision: Cohen is mourner and murderer, cuckold and lover, resident and traveller, priest and apostate. Dedicated to the memory of his paternal grandmother and his maternal grandfather, ***The Spice-Box of Earth*** contains numerous poems that bear the elegiac tones of Klein. Indeed, two of the volume's best poems are **"To a Teacher"** and **"Song for Abraham Klein,"** both elegies for Klein's silenced voice. Even as it is a melancholy requiem, however, ***The Spice-Box of Earth*** is also an aggressive manifesto for poetic transformation, a decidedly Laytonic attempt to move in a particular poetic direction. Ironically, the nature of Layton's influence on Cohen is like that of Nietzsche on Layton: the master influences the pupil to reject influence. Attempting to be completely original, to find his own poetic path, Cohen looks to Layton for guidance.

Klein's influence is quickly evident in **"After the Sabbath Prayers."** The poem bemoans the passing of religious miracles, leaving the awestruck speaker "in darkness, / Hands pocketed against the flies and cold" (2). The persona in **"After the Sabbath Prayers"** encounters a theological quandary like the one that pervades ***Mythologies.*** The Baal Shem's butterfly has emerged from its chrysalis to do "its glory in the sun" but, after the prayers have ended, faces a quick and final death. Longing for the stability of faith, the speaker is painfully aware of its inevitable passing.

But while the Hebraic romanticism that pervades **"After the Sabbath Prayers"** shows the mourning melancholy of Klein, the Rabelaisian wit (Morley 73) that flavours **"Inquiry into the Nature of Cruelty"** is strongly reminiscent of Layton. The image of the dying butterfly, the evidence of God's glory, is imbued with a more sinister quality. Renouncing the romanticism that attended the butterfly's death, Cohen downgrades the image of the glorious butterfly to that of an inglorious moth, and the persona from butterfly's mourner to moth's murderer, drowning it in his own urine. The same impassive, yet powerful, acknowledgement of cruelty is evident in such early Layton poems as "Therapy," in which the persona, after murdering a badger with an axe, declares himself "strong enough for God and Man" (*Collected Poems* 43) Once again, the Nietzschean imperative of acknowledging one's own savage power is played out in deterministic action. This determined movement from inactive witness to active murderer is a striking one, characterizing the transition—from Klein's elegiac resignation to Layton's bawdy irreverence—occurring in Cohen's book.

A similar conflict is evident between **"There Are Some Men"** and **"If It Were Spring."** In the former, it is abundantly clear that Cohen, in Klein's tradition, views his role as poet as that of mourning witness. As Freud explains: "mourning loves to preoccupy itself with the deceased, to elaborate his memory, and preserve it for the longest possible time" (*Totem and Taboo* 77). Fearing the void of mortality, Cohen remedies the "mighty," yet ultimately disrespectful, silence of an unnamed friend by naming a mountain after him. Though Cohen resists romanticism by insisting his action is not "a mourning-song / but only a naming of this mountain / on which I walk" (*Spice-Box* 9) the poem provides a subtle requiem in the place of an unjust silence.

But while **"There Are Some Men"** depicts a tender generosity on the part of the poet, that vision is sharply contrasted in **"If It Were Spring,"** a dark depiction of delusional self-aggrandizement. In it, the poet does not remember death through his poetry, but causes death for his poetry. Rather than composing an elegy, he contemplates killing for one:

> If it were Spring
> and I killed a man,
> I would change him to leaves
> and hang him from a tree

> (6)

In many ways, the poem is reminiscent of Layton's "Whatever Else Poetry is Freedom" in which the poet, a buffoon-king, romanticizes the beating he has given his wife:

> And I who gave my Kate a blackened eye
> Did to its vivid changing colours
> Make up an incredible musical scale.

(Collected Poems 36)

For all its exaltation, "Whatever Else Poetry is Freedom" seems to contain an implicit warning against "the rhetoric, the trick of lying / All poets pick up sooner or later." Freedom, the prerequisite to all joy and, according to Layton, the result of poetry, can also be the source of corruption and hypocrisy:

> There is nothing inherently good or bad in power. It is not power that corrupts, but the misuse and misdirection of it . . . Power and health are synonymous. Power is energy, the ability to act, to get things done. In our civilization . . . the healthiest elements . . . can translate power into freedom, a pre-condition it should be recognized of creativity. Their freedom, however, is the enslavement of the rest of us.

("Shaw, Pound and Poetry" in Collins 208-9)

Cohen's poem is "about the poet's power over his material . . . [in which] he creates beauty by bringing something to death" (Scobie 28) but is also a satirical investigation of the hypocrisy therein. There is something obscene about making suffering and death the inspiration for art and beauty. In the guise of creative freedom, the poet contorts savagery into beauty, murder into mercy:

> Everywhere I see
> the world waiting you,
> the pens raised, walls prepared,
> hands hung above the strings and keys.

(6)

Through the guise of art, the hostile murderer is transformed into a tender mourner, ghoulish scavengers become gentle artists. Poetry, being "freedom," voices the individual's unique will to power. As such, it can be used either to reveal the truth or evade it. Just as Layton, again advocating "the steady gaze of Nietzsche whose vision . . . never flinched from reality" (Francis 285), warns against poetry's power to romanticize or obscure that reality (Caplan 285), so Cohen warns not only the reader [*caveat lector*],[2] but also the writer, of the potential deception. Once again, it is the tension between silence and voice, between complete control and unbridled freedom, that emerges as the essence of art.

Cohen addresses the conflict between silence and voice more succinctly in the epigrammatic **"Gift."** In it, Cohen responds directly to Klein's silent, rather than poetic, influence as he writes:

> You tell me that silence
> is nearer to peace than poems
> but if for my gift
> I brought you silence
> (for I know silence)
> you would say
> *This is not silence*
> *this is another poem*
> and you would hand it back to me.

(3)

The gentle wit of the poem reveals a much more mature poet, as Cohen states in nine lines what had troubled him so deeply in *Let Us Compare Mythologies*. While Scobie is correct in his appraisal that "Cohen seems to acknowledge [the] inevitability [of voice] in an ironic way: whatever he says will be accepted as a poem; even silence may be" (29), the poem has more to do with the creation of poetry than the negation of silence. For the poet, life depends on the power of words, on the messages people give to one another. The words may inevitably be imperfect, but are the best (and only) weapon against loneliness and death. As in Klein's 1940 poem of the same name, it is the poet and his words that allow heritage to be remembered, that link people to their communities and their Lord:

> I will stitch it with letters of flame,
> With square characters:
> His name, and his father's name;
> And beneath it some terse
> Scriptural verse
>
> Yea, singing the sweet liturgy,
> He'll snare its gold cord,
> Remembering me, even me,
> In the breath of his word,
> In the sight of the Lord.

(Collected Poems 160)

The magic of words is in their reciprocity: be they spoken or written, words are ultimately the domain of both speaker and listener, writer and reader. More than anything, it is voice, "the breath of the word," which links people to one another and to God. Silence, though quiet, cannot be shared and therefore brings not peace but a suffering isolation. In this sense, Klein's descent into the abyss of madness is a clear and painful example of the nullity that true silence can bring. Indeed, Klein's "Portrait of the Poet as Landscape," with its image of the silenced poet, was originally titled "Portrait of the Poet as a Nobody" (Caplan 181). The silent poet "gives" nothing and therefore is no poet.

Just as the "gift" of silence proves to be an illusion, the apparent peace that exists in the silence of **"Summer Haiku"**—"Silence / and a deeper silence / when the crickets hesitate" (77)—is undercut by the ominous associations of **"To a Teacher."** There is a tender and delightful irony in **"Summer Haiku,"** as the song of the crickets is at first mistaken for silence. It is only when they "hesitate" that the vacuum, or "deeper silence," can be apprehended. The deeper silence, however, holds the promise of nullity in **"To a Teacher,"** as the poet's mentor is shown "Hurt once and for all into silence," the result of "A long pain ending without a song to prove it" (22). While Scobie fails to identify the influential teacher in Cohen's poem, refusing even to commit to whether the teacher is male or female (40), the poem is almost certainly a requiem for Klein. More significantly, it is clear that Klein's influence has inspired an almost unbearable awe in his pupil, causing Cohen to ask:

> Who could stand beside you so close to Eden,
> when you glinted in every eye the held-high razor,
> shivering every ram and son.

> (22)

Similarly, Cohen's poem betrays the anxiety that his teacher's song will suffer the same fate as that of the crickets in **"Summer Haiku."** Ignored by most, the teacher "rests" as the crickets "hesitate," his lesson lost in the "deeper" silence of madness. As such, the teacher's influence is simultaneously threatening and attractive, at once the promise of Eden and the looney-bin. Later in **The Spice-Box of Earth,** the more explicit **"Song for Abraham Klein"** holds the same theme as **"To a Teacher,"** as Klein's silence is the result of the fact that "He sang and nothing changed / Though many heard the song" (74).

Despite its more enigmatic title, however, it is **"To a Teacher"** that is the more personal of Cohen's poems for Klein. The poem's final stanza reveals the tension between fear and determination that epitomizes the poetic struggle between silence and voice. Faced with Klein's terrifying and tragic example, Cohen nonetheless affirms the necessity of voice, taking up the burden his mentor can no longer bear:

> Let me cry Help beside you, Teacher.
> I have entered under this dark roof
> as fearlessly as an honoured son
> enters his father's house.

> (22)

The scene itself is strikingly reminiscent of Klein's 1929 poem "Haunted House," in which the burdens of influence—history, tradition, genealogy—are potentially overwhelming:

> There is nothing here for thought.
> Silence nullifies the sane.
> And dust settles on the brain.
> Here is naught.

> (*Collected Poems* 23)

The "house" that Cohen enters is perhaps one Klein describes in the line "Life is a haunted house, haunted by fictions" (24). As in **Let Us Compare Mythologies,**

Cohen acknowledges the burden of influence, the anxiety of defining beliefs made fictions, but is determined to continue his search for truth armed only with his powerful, yet imperfect, words.

Cohen's search for truth, an odyssey which is attractive but anxiety-ridden, manifests itself in an examination of the conflict between action and inaction, and ultimately between silence and voice. In **"The Priest Says Goodbye"**—"one of the frequent allusions to the name 'Cohen' meaning 'priest'" (Scobie 42)—romantic, but apathetic, inaction has caused passion to become commonplace. In the absence of suffering and uncertainty, art and poetry cease to be vital, tumbling into mediocrity and irrelevance:

> And what of art? When passion dies
> friendship hovers round our flesh like flies,
> and we name beautiful the smells
> that corpses give and immortelles.

> (42)

As in Joyce's *Portrait of the Artist as a Young Man,* the only way to be authentic, to achieve the "originality . . . [that is] the only true sign of an author's genius" (Clayton 5), the poet/priest must "say goodbye" to all he has ever known. In order to achieve his own voice, he must try and separate himself from all influences, must dare the silence and travel on alone:

> Do not come with me. When I stand alone
> my voice sings out as though I did not own
> my throat.

> (42)

It is only when the artist "stands alone" outside the limitations of influence that his voice can truly be his own. As Jean Starobinski writes in *The Living Eye:* "in spite of our desire to drown in the vital depths of the work, we are obliged to stand at a distance if we are to speak at all" (12). In order to speak with a unique voice, the artist must distance himself in order to maintain a tangible proximity from his subject. At the same time, if he is to speak at all, the artist can never entirely detach himself from the influence of his subject without becoming incomprehensible. Indeed, the priest's song is so "original" as to be unfamiliar. As though he does not own his own throat, he fails to recognize what is his own voice, unadulterated by influence. In order to be recognized, to be *understood,* the priest needs *familiarity,* the structure of a defining influence. In short, he needs others to be himself.

In his self-imposed exile, Cohen—the priest whose natural language is prayer[3]—engages the conflict between silence and voice in order to achieve an authentic and original purity, a conflict in which "neither the vertigo of distance nor that of proximity is to be rejected" (Starobinski 13). As he writes in **"Lines from My Grandfather's Journal,"** originality is achieved through the indulgence, not the rejection, of influence: "Prayer makes speech a ceremony. To observe this ritual in the absence of arks, altars, a listening sky: this is a rich discipline" (*Spice-Box* 94). The suitable response to the neurotic world that exists between the contrary influences of silence and voice is thus a determined assertion of his own personality within a milieu which threatens to crush it. It requires a steadfast discipline, the determined adoption of a road that will lead to originality and genius: "At certain crossroads we will win / the harvest of our discipline" (42).

That the road is not an easy one is acknowledged in **"Poem to Detain Me,"** the poem following the priest's epic farewell and, as its title suggests, a poem that should give one pause. While **"The Priest Says Goodbye"** regards the impending departure with little or no trepidation, **"A Poem to Detain Me"** examines the painful possibilities of such a long and challenging journey. Thick with suffering and remorse, the priest seems skeptical not of the success of his enterprise, but of its eventual value. Now that the journey is underway, it is doubtful whether it will ever end:

> I'm heading for another border,
> my scrapbooks stuffed with murder
> & a crazy rumour of glory
> whispering through the wires of my spine.
>
> (44)

The glory which was to be "the harvest of our discipline" has become "a crazy rumour." While originality and genius may be found on the road, contentment and satisfaction cannot be apprehended. Implicit in the poem is the painful realization that art, while capable of satisfying and sustaining its audience, cannot do the same for its creator:

> O you will be listening for music
> while I turn on a spit of song;
> you will increase your love
> while I experiment with pain;
> while others amputate their limbs
> you will master a ballet-step
> away from voluntary gangrene.
>
> (44)

It is only in the tension between a diseased silence and a healthy voice that original inspiration can be achieved. Originality, the stuff of unique personality, necessarily isolates its creator. Before experience can be transformed into art, the artist must dare it alone, separated from the comforting influences that will dull its impact. As such, the artist must "travel," must continue to assert his own originality by moving away from the influences that threaten to categorize him, yet he must remain "close by but beyond possession, perfectly absent" (Starobinski 29).

The persona of the travelling stranger is increasingly evident in Cohen's later works, and **"The Priest Says Goodbye"** and **"A Poem to Detain Me"** emerge as symbiotic poems that capture the dilemma of the creative experience. The themes that they suggest, however, are summed up in the appropriately titled **"Travel,"** in which the decision to leave everything one knows is inevitable and necessary:

> Lost in the fields of your hair I was never lost
> Enough to lose a way I had to take;
> Breathless beside your body I could not exhaust
> The will that forbid me contract, vow,
> Or promise, and often while you slept
> I looked in awe beyond your beauty.
>
> (57)

Struggling to explain his infidelity, he alludes to "a way I had to take," an unending journey that defies explanation. While ultimately purifying, the journey is uncertain and difficult:

> I know why many men have stopped and wept
> Half-way between the loves they leave and seek,
> And wondered if travel leads them anywhere.

It is just such a neurotic limbo, the world "half-way between" repressive guilt and aggressive ambition that pervades Cohen's early work. Anxious that his path may not be the right one, he is nonetheless determined to travel it to the end. Badly shaken by the events that silenced Klein, the stunning cruelty that transformed faith into fiction, Cohen seems determined to follow Layton's lead, and attempt to "make clear for us . . . the utter wickedness of Nazism" (*Engagements* 104), to "estimate [his] distance from the Belsen heap" (*Spice-Box* 93), and dare the silence that threatens individual personality.

The most telling indication of the direction Cohen's journey is about to take comes in the poems that bring *The Spice-Box of Earth* to a close. Read in order, they reveal a distinct movement out of the world of "neurotic affiliations" to one of determined defiance. In **"Last Dance at the Four Penny,"** Cohen dances a traditional Jewish "freilach" with Layton. Celebration is evident, but with a winsome finality. Boisterous in celebration, Layton and Cohen eagerly indulge tradition, resurrecting ancient rabbis and revelling in delicious quarrels about the sound of the Ineffable Name. Alas, the momentary indulgence is merely a prelude to surrender:

> As for the cynical,
> such as we were yesterday,
> let them step with us or rot
> in their logical shrouds.
> We've raised a bright white flag,
> and here's our battered fathers' cup of wine,
> and now is music
> until morning and the morning prayers

lay us down again,
we who dance so beautifully
though we know that freilachs end.

(72)

The end of the freilach marks Cohen's imminent poetic departure. The dance is a traditional one, but is also final. The dancers are no longer Jews destined to rot in the logical shrouds of a decaying tradition. Following **"Last Dance at the Four Penny"** is the resonant **"Song for Abraham Klein"** in which Klein's collapse corresponds with the decay of traditional Jewish symbols. The sabbath and the "Sabbath Bride" have "departed," the candles are "black and cold," God and his commandments have been "abandoned," and the sustaining "bread" of his religious psalms has turned to mould (74). In both poems, reverence for Jewish tradition and personality is paramount, but undercut by the regretful knowledge that they have been battered almost beyond recognition. Still inextricably connected to the Jewish tradition, Cohen dances a final freilach with someone of similar experience. As the freilach ends, Cohen is both advocate and antagonist, priest and apostate.

In **"Out of the Land of Heaven,"** Cohen again indulges the metaphoric richness of Klein, celebrating his religion and identity as one of the chosen people:

Out of the land of heaven
Down comes the warm Sabbath sun
Into the spice-box of earth.
The queen will make every Jew her lover.

(79)

Here, the inheritance of the Hebrew nation is vast and glorious. The powerfully romantic image of the sun exists only for the Sabbath, its sole purpose to link the Jew directly to his rightful place in the land of heaven and his deserving position as the chosen mate of its Queen. Fittingly, the Rabbi provides the marriage ring and performs the ceremony:

Down go his hands
Into the spice-box of earth,
And there he finds the fragrant sun
For a wedding-ring,
And draws her wedding-finger through.

(79)

Rife with the message of hope and celebration, **"Out of the Land of Heaven"** exalts the Jew, through a vision which is self-consciously Jewish, as blessed. As aggressive as it is sensuous, the poem urges a spiritual union of religion and identity through an affirmation of the Jewish tradition (Scobie 41).

The traditional vision of promise and redemption is certainly a consummation devoutly to be wished, but like the disintegrating icons that dominate **"Last Dance

at the Four Penny"** and **"Song for Abraham Klein,"** the sustaining love of the Sabbath Queen is no longer a feasible aspiration. Klein's religious influence, so strong in **"Out of the Land of Heaven,"** is quickly undercut by **"Absurd Prayer,"** a poem that bears Layton's satirical edge:

I disdain God's suffering.
Men command sufficient pain.
I'll keep to my tomb
Though the Messiah come.

(81)

Despite the title, the poem is obviously not a prayer, but an assertion that prayer itself has become absurd. Though comforting in their idealism, persistent invocations to the land of heaven have proved to be fruitless. Indeed, the earthly results of prayer have been the opposite of what they promised. Rather than being the chosen people, filling their mouths with good bread and happy songs, the Jews have become the target of mankind's cruelty, stereotyped as at once aggressively evil and neurotically passive. In **"The Genius,"** a bleak listing of various Jewish stereotypes, Cohen portrays himself as a master-magician; a contortionist able to twist his poetic sensibilities into suitable stereotypes. With bitterness and evident self-loathing, Cohen affirms not only his ability, but his apparent willingness, to engage in such stereotypical role-playing. But it is in such role-playing that individual personality becomes mired, and it is only through the loss of personality that people can be victimized with impunity. The poem culminates with the inevitable result of such systematic destruction of personality:

For you
I will be a Dachau jew
and lie down in lime
with twisted limbs
and bloated pain
no mind can understand.

(87)

Using a tone similar to the poetic bombast of **"If It Were Spring,"** **"The Genius"** appears to be another expression of the poet's power over his material. The final image, however, reveals a much darker moral. Though he is **"The Genius"** capable of being anything he wishes to be, Cohen's adherence to an irrelevant tradition is now reductive. In the painful image that ends the poem, he ceases to be the master of his own work, his ability and genius victimized by preconceived notions of his Jewish identity. The passive acceptance of influence (in the form of stereotype) implicit in the constant repetition of "For you / I will . . ." leads inevitably to the final, desolate image of pain and death. The title now ironic, **"The Genius"** no more, the poet seems more tragic puppet than powerful prophet.

Despite an apparent longing for the strength and stability of the Jewish tradition, Cohen is faced with a desolation which is decidedly unheroic and unbiblical, a desolation no amount of prayer can redeem. Expressing but one portion of the Jewish inheritance, one fragrant corner of the spice-box, **"Out of the Land of Heaven"** leaves the vision incomplete. It is not surprising that the rabbi, upon delving into the spice-box, should select such a positive image. For the generation after the holocaust, however, the rabbi's image derives from a "tradition composed of the exuviae of visions" which must be resisted even as it is revered: "It is like the garbage river through a city. Beautiful by day and beautiful by night, but always unfit for bathing" (*Spice-Box* 94). The spice-box of earth, like the collection that bears its name, contains a darker side. Attempting to eschew the confines of tradition, to abandon the limits of influence, Cohen assumes a defiant anti-poetic stance, moving "from the world of the golden-boy poet into the dung pile of the front-line writer" (*Flowers for Hitler,* cover). Faced with the glorious, but dead, vision of **"Out of the Land of Heaven"** and the darkly threatening, but present, vision of **"The Genius,"** Cohen chooses the dark, exploring Jewish victimization and alienation rather than tradition. As he writes in the final stages of **"Lines from My Grandfather's Journal":**

> It is painful to recall a past intensity, to estimate your
> distance from the Belsen heap, to make your peace
> with
> numbers. Just to get up each morning is to make a
> kind of
> peace . . .
>
> . . . . .
> Let me refuse solutions, refuse to be comforted. . . .
>
> (93)

In refusing solutions, Cohen attempts to renounce the influences of his mentors. Although he adopts a tone similar to Layton's, his affiliations lie more with Layton's vituperative rage than his personal style. Even as he borrows Layton's angry and horrific vision, Cohen attempts to reject his mentor's bombastic persona. Unlike Layton, Cohen is not seeking personal joy and power, but rather a full engagement with a "bloated pain / no mind can understand." Ironically, Cohen's attempt to reject Layton's influence and develop his own voice is itself the result of Layton's influence. For the sake of originality, the salvaging of his own personality, Cohen, like Layton, attempts to reject influence and embrace intuition. Taking Klein's despairing silence as a dire warning, Cohen is determined to become, like Layton, "vigorously a poet of this world and its crude mechanisms of pleasure and pain" (Trehearne, "Introduction" xvii). Just as Layton follows Nietzsche by attempting not to follow him, so Cohen embraces his mentor's influence by attempting to reject it.

Cohen's message as *The Spice-Box of Earth* closes is clearly concerned with the disintegration of individual personality. A Freudian analysis reveals that personality is the result of external influences, of messages that enable the receiver to make decisions that ultimately characterize his or her behaviour. At the same time, influence holds the threat of repression, an overwhelming force that precludes personal action and voice. Thus, influence creates personality even as it threatens to destroy it. Cohen's early poems show a distinctly neurotic indecision whether to retreat into silence or lash out in voice. By the time he writes **"The Genius,"** however, he asserts that stereotyping is an escalating attempt to undermine individual personality and contribute to its decline. Stereotyping, then, is an artificial influence; an attempt to categorize people according to criteria that are necessarily superficial, yet sufficiently aggressive to command submission. The complete marginalization of a people is, in effect, the imposition of an ethnic taboo. The Jews themselves become taboo persons (indeed cease to be persons) through the systematic degradation of their personalities. The negative images persistently attributed to them are an attempt to influence their personalities through an enforced submission to stereotyping. In Cohen's pursuit of this idea, the concentration camps become a powerful and concrete symbol of imposed influence.

Cohen begins *Flowers for Hitler* with an epigraph from Primo Levi's stunning first book *If This Is a Man* (unfortunately retitled *Survival in Auschwitz* for the English translation), which locates the tragedy of the holocaust more in the survivors than in the murdered, more in the saved than the drowned. The quotation that Cohen uses is Levi's explication of that tragedy:

> we have learnt that our personality is fragile, that it is
> much more in danger than our life; and the old wise
> ones, instead of warning us 'remember that you must
> die,' would have done better to remind us of this great
> danger that threatens us. *If from inside the Lager, a
> message could have seeped out to free men, it would
> have been this: take care not to suffer in your own
> homes what is inflicted on us here.*
>
> (Levi 55; italics mine)

It is precisely that "message from inside the Lager" that concerns Cohen as *The Spice-Box of Earth* closes and *Flowers for Hitler* begins. The decline of personality which Levi warns against, and which manifested itself in Klein's submission to silence, is what Cohen, like Layton, so aggressively attempts to avoid.

The publication of *Flowers for Hitler* established Cohen's new direction. As he writes in the preface to the first edition:

> This book moves me from the world of the golden-boy
> poet into the dung pile of the front-line writer . . . I
> loved the tender notices *Spice-Box* got but they embar-

rassed me a little. *Hitler* won't get the same hospitality from the papers. My sounds are too new, therefore people will say: this is derivative, this is slight, his power has failed. Well, I say that there has never been a book like this, prose or poetry, written in Canada. All I ask is that you put it in the hands of my generation and it will be recognized.

(*Flowers* [*Flowers for Hitler*] cover)

Indeed, *Flowers for Hitler* contains little of the fragile eloquence that epitomized the "golden-boy poet." Containing terse and violent anti-poetry, a so-called **"Ballet-Drama in One Act,"** and sporadic drawings by the poet, *Flowers for Hitler* holds a more direct fascination with pain, disease, and death. Suffering and finality are handled with a casualness so disarming as to be satirical. The established monsters of recent Jewish history are minimized: Hitler becomes "normal," Eichmann becomes "medium" (66) and Goebbels actually begins to resemble Cohen. While Cohen's declared intention is to provide a voice for his generation and create a new direction for art, however, it is ironic that, while proclaiming a distinctive movement outward, the focus of his poetry and prose turns persistently inward. A determined attempt to salvage his own personality and artistic voice, Cohen's aggressive defiance in *Flowers for Hitler* is like that of Elie Wiesel's Just Man who, having attempted to warn men of their wickedness, realizes:

> In the beginning, I thought I could change man. Today, I know I cannot. If I still shout today, if I still scream, it is to prevent man from ultimately changing me.

(*One Generation After* 72)

The transition over, the new road begun, Cohen abandons his early fixations with poetic alchemy and magic. No longer willing to be stereotyped as Jewish, as a poet, or as a Jewish-poet, Cohen claims to be attempting to move beyond influence to a more direct engagement, anti-stylistic, with his own world and experience.

For all his claims of originality, however, the tone of Cohen's preface and new volume seems like an imitation of Layton. One year before the publication of *Flowers for Hitler,* Layton described the changing role of the poet in contemporary society:

> What must concern the artist today, above all, is the organized nature of twentieth-century wickedness . . . There is a frightful stink in the souls of all men and women living today . . . with [Auschwitz] man touched the infiniteness of evil—and survived! The stink in his soul is not only that of burning flesh, of decomposing bones. It is also the stink of self-guilt. At last he knows the truth about himself and of what he's capable

(*Engagements* 106-7).

In **"What I'm Doing Here,"** the first poem in *Flowers for Hitler,* Cohen nonetheless appears to make good on his promise to "refuse all solutions . . . refuse to be comforted:"

> I do not know if the world has lied
> I have lied
> I do not know if the world has conspired against love
> I have conspired against love
> the atmosphere of torture is no comfort
> I have tortured
> I refuse the universal alibi
> . . . . .
> I refuse the universal alibi

(13)

Using the same assertive tone of **"If It Were Spring"** and **"The Genius"** to starkly admit his complicity in mankind's apathetic cruelty, to acknowledge "the truth about himself and of what he's capable," Cohen then urges the rest of the world to admit to the stink of self-guilt: "I wait / for each one of you to confess". The message that the Germans attempted to obliterate in the camps, "the evil tidings of what man's presumption made of man in Auschwitz" (Levi 55), is the very message that Cohen here hopes to elicit. In an honest attempt to salvage his own personality, Cohen actively contravenes the limits of Judaism and of art. In **"Style,"** the volume's stand-out poem, Cohen claims to renounce all his influences, promising:

> I will forget the grass of my mother's lawn
> I know I will
> I will forget the old telephone number
> Fitzroy seven eight two oh
> I will forget my style
> I will have no style

(28)

Cohen's rejection of "style" is a conscious attempt to ease the burden of influence. Style is, after all, the *result* of influence. Influence, for its part, carries the threat of repression as "a silence develops for every style" (28). Aggressively imposed influence *convinces*; it silences thought by closing minds. In the midst of an apparently cynical fatalism, Cohen desperately hopes that "Perhaps a mind will open in this world / perhaps a heart will catch rain" (28). The appeal to an apathetic world for sympathy and for action is outwardly modest but couched in urgency.

In attempting to renounce influence and be anti-stylistic, however, Cohen moves, consciously and inevitably—as the similarity of his new voice to that of Layton's foreword indicates—towards another style. An attempt to deny all influence in the name of originality, *Flowers for Hitler* is inevitably tied closely to the influences it is designed to reject, as "the pose of having no style is itself a style" (Scobie 45). While influence threatens original thought, it is a necessary component of understanding. Communication requires a shared structure, a "style" that holds some relation to the world to which it speaks. As such, Cohen's determined rejection of "style" is also a satiric acknowledgement of its necessity. To write in an original fashion, Cohen must forget his style; in order to be understood by others, however, he must adopt a style that is somehow familiar. He must be derivative in order to be original. Feigning a rejection of influence, he adopts a pose made popular by Layton. This is similar to Wynne Francis' appraisal of the (anti) influential relationship between Layton and Nietzsche:

> Nietzsche did not want disciples; he provided no dogma or system which "followers" might lean on. Zarathustra taught the over-coming of the self, the glorification of the moment; the affirmation of life through all eternity. A true Dionysian is on his own: he must assert his joy in his own individual existence with all that that entails of cosmic dialectics, history, heredity, environment and personal attributes. Thus, though much in Layton becomes clearer through an understanding of his Nietzschism, his talent and originality derive from a combination of sources unique to him.
>
> (285-6)

Similarly, in order to engage his own world and experience, Cohen "follows" Layton by pretending to reject him. In order to avoid the abyss of silence that swallowed Klein, Cohen must use his voice, must provide "an answer to the ovens. Any answer" (*Spice-Box* 89). In order to attempt a suitable answer to the holocaust, however, he must affiliate himself with Layton's aggressive rage, an intuitive identification which also threatens the development of his own voice and personality. Aware of the paradox of his new "anti-stylistic" style, Cohen, in *Flowers for Hitler,* commits himself to his new pose, and determinedly transfers his affiliations from a neurotic indecision to a decisive anger.

Notes

1. See Klein, "Messiah." *Collected Poems* 37.

2. See Hutcheon 37: "Cohen has never . . . been totally devoid of the con.'"

3. See *The Spice-Box of Earth* 89: "It is strange that even now prayer is my natural language. . . ."

Works Cited

Benazon, Michael. "Leonard Cohen of Montreal." *Matrix* 23 (Fall, 1986): 43-56.

Bloom, Harold. *The Anxiety of Influence: A Theory of Poetry.* New York: Oxford UP, 1973.

Caplan, Usher. *Like One That Dreamed: A Portrait of A. M. Klein.* Toronto: McGraw-Hill Ryerson, 1982.

Clayton, Jay and Eric Rothstein, ed. *Influence and Intertextuality in Literary History.* The U of Wisconsin P, 1991.

Cohen, Leonard. *Let Us Compare Mythologies.* Toronto: McClelland and Stewart, 1956.

———. *The Spice-Box of Earth.* Toronto: McClelland and Stewart, 1961.

———. *The Favourite Game.* Toronto: McClelland and Stewart, 1963.

———. *Flowers for Hitler.* Toronto: McClelland and Stewart, 1964.

Collins, Aileen, ed. *CIV/n: A Literary Magazine of the 50's.* Montreal: Véhicule P, 1983.

Djwa, Sandra. "Leonard Cohen: Black Romantic." *Canadian Literature* 34 (Autumn 1967): 32-42.

Dorman, L. S. and C. L. Rawlins. *Leonard Cohen: Prophet of the Heart.* London: Omnibus, 1990.

Dudek, Louis. "Où sont les jeunes?" *The Making of Modern Poetry in Canada.* Eds. Louis Dudek and Michael Gnarowski. Toronto: Ryerson, 1967. 142-144.

Fischer, Gretl. "Religious Philosophy in the Writings of A. M. Klein." *The A. M. Klein Symposium.* Ed. Seymour Mayne. Ottawa: U of Ottawa P, 1975. 37-45.

Francis, Wynne. "Layton and Nietzsche." *Irving Layton: The Poet and His Critics.* Ed. Seymour Mayne. Toronto: McGraw-Hill Ryerson, 1978. 272-286.

Freud, Sigmund. *Totem and Taboo: Resemblances Between the Psychic Lives of Savages and Neurotics.* Trans. A. A. Brill. New York: Random House, 1918.

———. *The Basic Writings of Sigmund Freud.* Trans. A. A. Brill. 1938 New York: Modern Library, 1966.

Gnarowski, Michael, ed. *Leonard Cohen: The Poet and his Critics.* Toronto: McGraw-Hill Ryerson, 1976.

Harris, Michael. "An Interview with Leonard Cohen." *Duel* 1 (Winter, 1969): 90-114.

Hermerén, Göran. *Influence in Art and Literature.* Princeton: Princeton UP, 1975.

Hutcheon, Linda. "Caveat Lector: The Early Postmodernism of Leonard Cohen." *The Canadian Postmodern: A Study of Contemporary English-Canadian Fiction.* Toronto: Oxford UP, 1988. 26-44.

Klein, Abraham Moses. *Collected Poems.* Ed. Miriam Waddington. Toronto: McGraw-Hill Ryerson, 1974.

———. Forward. *From Palestine to Israel.* By Moishe Dickstein. Montreal: Eagle Publishing, 1951. 7-8

———. *Literary Essays and Reviews.* Ed. Usher Caplan and M. W. Steinberg. Toronto: U of Toronto P, 1987.

Layton, Irving. *The Collected Poems of Irving Layton.* Toronto: McClelland and Stewart, 1971.

————. *Engagements: The Prose of Irving Layton.* Ed. Seymour Mayne. Toronto: McClelland and Stewart, 1972.

————. *Waiting for the Messiah.* Toronto: McClelland and Stewart, 1985.

Levi, Primo. *Survival in Auschwitz: The Nazi Assault on Humanity.* Trans. Stuart Woolf. New York: Collier, 1986.

Mayne, Seymour. ed. *The A. M. Klein Symposium.* Ottawa: U of Ottawa P, 1975.

Nietzsche, Friedrich. *Thus Spoke Zarathustra.* Trans. R. J. Hollingdale. London: Penguin, 1961.

————. *Beyond Good and Evil.* Trans. R. J. Hollingdale. London: Penguin, 1973.

Ondaatje, Michael. *Leonard Cohen.* Toronto: McClelland and Stewart, 1970.

Ravvin, Norman. "Writing Around the Holocaust: Uncovering the Ethical Centre of *Beautiful Losers.*" *Canadian Poetry: Proceedings of the Leonard Cohen Conference* 33 (Fall/Winter 1993): 22-31.

Rubenstein, Richard L. *After Auschwitz: History, Theology, and Contemporary Judaism.* Baltimore: The John Hopkins UP, 1966, 1992.

Scobie, Stephen. *Leonard Cohen.* Vancouver: Douglas and McIntyre, 1978.

Starobinski, Jean. *The Living Eye.* Trans. Albert Goldhammer. Cambridge: Harvard UP, 1989.

Trehearne, Brian. Introduction. Irving Layton, *Fornalutx: Selected Poems, 1928-1990.* Montreal: McGill-Queen's UP, 1992. xv-xxxvi.

Weisel, Elie. *Legends of Our Time.* New York: Avon, 1968.

————. *One Generation After.* Trans. Lily Edelman. New York: Schocken, 1970.

Daniel C. Noel (essay date March 1998)

SOURCE: Noel, Daniel C. "'I have seen the future brother: it is murder': Apocalypse *Noir* in *Natural Born Killers* and Leonard Cohen's 'The Future.'" *Literature and Theology* 12, no. 1 (March 1998): 39-49.

[*In the following essay, Noel analyzes the lyrics of Cohen's "The Future" and "Waiting for the Miracle" alongside the Oliver Stone film* Natural Born Killers, *in which both songs appear. In particular, the critic examines Cohen's message with respect to pre-millenial and biblical notions of apocalypse and violence.*]

We have very little time left in this waning old millennium with its apocalyptic-seeming urgencies. So let me try to be terse with some initial disclaimers as I begin what will be more a swirl of quizzical speculations than a steady march toward settled conclusions.

Forget film *noir.* Although the pop apocalypse I will track is a dark one, Oliver Stone's *Natural Born Killers* is shot as much in colour as in black and white. It may expose, with Leonard Cohen's lyrics, a very large cultural shadow, but it scarcely traffics in visual shadows to do so (unless the black and white images are meant to shadow those in colour to produce a kind of metaphoric chiaroscuro). 'Apocalypse *noir*', as a filmic reference, is more a pun on Francis Ford Coppola's *Apocalypse Now* than a technical designation of how Stone shot his production.

Forget Oliver Stone the conspiracy-theory extremist of *JFK* and *Nixon.* Recall instead Oliver Stone the left-political ethicist of *Platoon, Born on the Fourth of July, Heaven and Earth, Salvador, Wall Street,* and *Talk Radio.* Remember that he is the *only* Hollywood film-maker addressing critically the conservative drift of American foreign and domestic policies in the decades since the death of John F. Kennedy, the debacle in Vietnam, and the downfall of Richard Nixon. Realize that as a man raised Protestant by a Jewish father and a Catholic mother, someone attracted to counter-cultural spiritualities, he may also have something to say about the biblical inheritance of a media-driven culture of drugs and violence in films like the aforementioned *Talk Radio, The Doors,* and, of course, *Natural Born Killers.*

Forget 1996 US presidential candidate Bob Dole, who decried *Natural Born Killers*' scores of murders while applauding *Independence Day*'s millions.

Forget relying overmuch on Margaret Miles' new book *Seeing and Believing: Religion and Values in the Movies.*[1] Although she has some things to say about the relation of on-screen to off-screen violence which I will touch on below, she does not discuss any of Stone's films. I take my informational bearings instead from two earnest books about Stone's work: Susan Mackey-Kallis's *Oliver Stone's America: 'Dreaming the Myth Outward'* and Norman Kagan's *The Cinema of Oliver Stone.*[2]

Forget Foucault and his French friends, at least for the purposes of this brief article, although two valuable collections of essays on postmodern *apocalypse* theory appeared in 1995 under the editorship of Richard Delamora and Malcolm Bull.[3] Do remember Jean Baudrillard's impressionistic book on America.[4]

Instead of such distractions and in light of my alternative advisories, cut to the 'closing credits' and ask what we believe at the end, about the End, after seeing *Natural Born Killers* and hearing the music of Leonard Cohen that accompanies those credits.

* * *

After the bloody prison break in which serial killer lovebirds Mickey and Mallory Knox escape with Wayne Gale, host of the TV show 'American Maniacs', who had been interviewing them, their final murder of the many in the film is of Wayne himself. With his own camcorder still running, Mickey and Mallory perform this execution as virtually a public service, having denounced him for his hypocritical part in stirring up the sort of violence they have manifested. Once he is killed we cut to the television anchor woman portrayed in the movie who has just seen Wayne's tape, and then to a series of clips from actual TV news stories about well-publicized violence. These lead into the final credits, which reprise images from earlier in the film as well as Mickey and Mallory's happily-ever-after life of domesticity on the American road in their RV, while Cohen's **'The Future'** plays behind them.

'Give me back the Berlin Wall', sings Cohen, 'give me Stalin and St. Paul / I have seen the future, brother: / It is murder'.[5] The lyrics of the song are rife with such despairing visions, including a hint that the biblical legacy has locked in a violent end for us without providing an antidote—or at least that we have remembered the assured apocalyptic denouement to our history while forgetting how we might reverse it. The chorus repeats this problematic forcefully, first announcing that 'Things are going to slide in all directions / Won't be nothing / Nothing you can measure anymore', and that 'The blizzard of the world / has crossed the threshold / and it has overturned / the order of the soul', then finally lamenting that 'when they said repent / I wonder what they meant'.[6] The presentation here is insistent: these last two lines are repeated twice, as is each 'repent' within them, as backup singers echo the word as well. Even more eerily enigmatic is the singer's proclamation, halfway through, that he himself, intoning these dire prophecies, is 'the little jew / who wrote the bible'.[7]

And these are the sombre words Oliver Stone chose to go with his surreal and ambiguous closing images. Certainly together with Stone's images throughout the film, which we shall be discussing, Cohen's lyrics raise their own questions, inviting an intertextual reading.

Is the 'murder' we are to fear *in* the future? Or is the future itself—or futurism, an entanglement with final causes if not Final Solutions—what is murderous in our culture? The speaker at the beginning and end of the song wants to go back to the horrible things of the recent and remote past because they are less murderous than the future. Among these horrible things he seems to include St. Paul—as bad as Stalin—and later indicts Christ—'Give me Christ / or give me Hiroshima'[8]—implying he is as genocidal as the Bomb, unless Christ is offered as a positive alternative to Hiroshima (which seems unlikely).

And yet there is that voice—a second voice?—in the middle of the song, 'the little jew who wrote the bible'. While Cohen is nominally Jewish he does not seem to be referring to himself. Is he referring to the biblical God? Who tells the singer—as the 'little jew' in the same stanza?—the following:

> Your servant here he has been told
> to say it clear, to say it cold:
> it's over, it ain't going
> any further . . . ?[9]

Is the 'servant' here one of the prophets of Israel? Jesus as suffering servant? Or simply, after all, the songwriter / singer as God's messenger? Is this an anti-biblical lyric—or an anti-Christian one—which blames the biblical religious heritage for inscribing a futurism that will one day become murderous (or is already)?

Would that one day be a day like 12/31/99, coming soon, when the past may feel culminated and the future, brought up close, strike us as oppressive? Are there connections to be drawn between the bible's teleological scenarios and a brave new cyberworld—an information apocalypse—in which the past is by definition devalued and only the future informs the present? Is our present being sucked murderously through a telecommunications hole by and into the future? Octavio Paz, in remarks Oliver Stone quotes with approval, says of television that 'the civilization of the spectacle is cruel. The spectators have no memory; because of that they also lack remorse and true conscience . . .'.[10]

Or is this middle section of Cohen's song a more positively biblical message: a God weary with the transgressions of His people—our culture—yet holding out, for one last time, apparently, the saving possibility of love? 'Love's the only engine of survival'[11] says the song in its only hopeful moment. So perhaps Cohen allows us one positive possibility, after all. This would be a fairly standard religious sermon for such a dark song, but if love is now, in a newly dark time and contra Darwin, 'the only engine of survival', the ante on love may have been upped apocalyptically.

In either case the stakes are not only world-historical but pointedly personal: as cause or cure the biblical agenda is connected by other lyrics in **'The Future'** to rapacious sexual behavior and violence toward women, with Charles Manson possibly held out as the ethical norm. In such a negatively nihilistic world, what could repentance possibly mean? At the turn of the millennium there seems to be little or no leverage for a personal turning, a moral *metanoia*. And once more we are led to wonder whether Cohen is indicting the biblical God or a backsliding humankind (Western humankind, at any rate) for our sorry millennial state personally and culturally. The presence of all these troubling words at the close of Oliver Stone's equally troubling film only serves to heighten the effect of each.

* * *

The April 1996 issue of an English religious periodical called *Third Way* contains a column by Mike Riddell entitled 'Read my apocalypse! No new fixes'. Riddell calls Leonard Cohen's **The Future** the 'millennial album of the decade', with *Natural Born Killers* getting his vote for the most millennial film. 'Hands up,' Riddell says, 'those who forgot to laugh at the irony of it', adding sardonically on the film's behalf that 'if my talent is killing, who are you to say I shouldn't find myself through self-expression? Well, really'.[12]

Riddell goes on to talk about the kind of apocalyptic that thrives in our particular troubled time (when our sense of time itself seems troubled): 'I'm not talking about the Hal Lindsay school of Dispensational Disneyland—more the sense of foreboding which accompanies the conviction that things can't go on this way. The inescapable feeling that life is going down the plughole and the plug is nowhere to be found'. And then he asks a question that applies just as much to the 'irony' of *Natural Born Killers*: 'Why do we find ourselves laughing in *Pulp Fiction* when a man has his head blown off by accident? As Quentin Tarantino knows, it's representative. It's so meaningless, so casual, so random, so inconsequential. A metaphor for our own lives, a metaphor for our culture . . .'[13]

Quentin Tarantino, as it happens, wrote the story upon which the *Natural Born Killers* screenplay by David Veloz, Richard Rutowski, and Oliver Stone is based. Even more than the latter version, Tarantino's story emphasizes the media as a player in the plot and the dire issues it raises. Tarantino has Mickey and Mallory Knox as 'real' serial killers who have inspired a hit song by a rock group called Redd Kross and a movie to be made about them called *Thrill Killers*—the actors and director are interviewed by Wayne Gale in Tarantino's version. And in that version Mickey says at his trial that watching TV is his favorite pastime aside from murder. His favorite show is 'Have Gun Will Travel'.[14]

Certainly in and out of the film the relation of murder to media involves the issue of 'numbing'. This is something about which Robert Jay Lifton has written eloquently concerning the threat of nuclear war, psychotherapists have commented on in regard to child abuse, and Margaret Miles weighs in about in connection with movie violence.

In *Seeing and Believing* Miles takes great pains to conclude her argument by underscoring the negative role of films in the process of our desensitization to violence off-screen as well as on. She cites studies that link the latter to the former, also noting sociologist Todd Gitlin's comment that 'over the years of chain saws, sharks, abdomen-ripping aliens, and the like, movie violence has come to require, and train, numbness'.[15] Miles goes on to observe, however, that 'what occurs, or threatens to occur, in people's lives needs to be pictured in order to consider how to cope with it. All screen violence cannot, and probably should not, be eliminated'.[16]

How might this right-minded assessment apply to *Natural Born Killers*? How might we 'cope with' the apocalyptic or futuristic violence it presents?

Partly this is a matter of the aforementioned irony, satire, or surrealism of Stone's film. In his Introduction to the dubious 'novelization' of *Natural Born Killers* by John August and Jane Hamsher, he has said that 'when we set out to make *Natural Born Killers* in late 1992, it was surreal. By the time it was finished in 1994, it had become real. In that warped season of the witch, we saw Bobbit, Menendez, Tonya, O. J., Buttafucco, and several dozen other perverted celebrities grasp our national attention span'.[17] Perhaps by editing TV clips of these real-life 'American maniacs' into the end of his film, just before the final credits, Stone was trying to outstrip reality with his intended surrealism—although at least one critic felt the effect was the opposite: Stone's film was less shocking by comparison.[18]

Would a *successful* surrealism of violence, at any rate, *re*-sensitize us to the shock and pain of violence? There have been alleged 'copy-cat killings' by people who saw *Natural Born Killers*. Can these be laid at Stone's doorstep? Or is our innocent indignation, our moralism, part of the problem, perhaps part of the cause of the murderous apocalypse Stone and Cohen seem to be signalling? Mickey and Mallory assert that 'love beats the demon', and apparently Stone and Cohen agree. But could a kind of innocent love even *be* the demon, or help account for the demonism of killers who are 'natural born'?

* * *

In his recent book *The Soul's Code* post-Jungian psychologist James Hillman has a chapter entitled 'The Bad Seed' which examines issues of nature, nurture, and the daimonic/demonic, using the biography of Hitler as his main case study. Hillman also refers to *Natural Born Killers,* first expressing his displeasure with Tarantino and Stone for reneging on their own title by having Mickey and Mallory portrayed as victims of a child abuse that seems to have nurtured their demonism.

'These irrelevant inserts', says Hillman, 'not only establish the psychopath as a victim himself, but they confuse the film's own important insight. Its main themes give the true reasons for the 'senseless behavior' in a three-way combination of irresistible motives: the isolating, anti-social inflation of American being-in-love; the delusional transcendence of media acclaim; and the inborn Bad Seed that calls to kill'.[19]

It could be claimed, in response to Hillman, that child abuse is so cyclically inherent in childrearing over the centuries as to constitute a Bad Seed in the culture—or an original sin, a sin of our repeated developmental origins. Stone almost says as much in his Introduction to the novelization: 'Violence is depicted as generationally handed down from father/mother to son/daughter and on and on. To the end of time'. Indeed, time may end before violence does, since, according to Stone, 'there will be no end to violence'.[20] The film itself may also preserve the thrust of its title in a crucial scene about what it means to 'be a snake' in comparison with what it signifies to 'be a man'.

We have already noted the role of television—and also films—in the culture of violence, wondering whether one of the latter, in depicting the former, serves as an antidote or an exacerbation. But Hillman's other point about love as a motivation for demonic (or is it demonized?) violence is worth probing further. At the end of his chapter on the Bad Seed, in which he cites Manson and serial killers Jeffrey Dahmer and John Wayne Gacy as well as Hitler, he returns to the topic of love and innocence:

> To wrap ourselves round in the Good—that is the American dream, leaving place for the evil nightmare only in the 'other', where it can be diagnosed, treated, prevented, and sermonized about. A history of this habit of the heart has been exposed by Elaine Pagels . . . as a disastrous, perhaps 'evil' essential, an inherent bad seed, in Western religious denominations, making obligatory as countermeasure their relentless insistence on 'love'.

Conversely, he goes on to say,

> the idea of the Bad Seed, the idea that there is a demonic call, should startle our native intelligence, awakening it from the innocence of our American theories so that as a nation we can see that evil is attracted to, belongs with, innocence. Then we might finally recognize that in America, Natural Born Killers are the secret companions of, are even prompted by, Forrest Gumps.[21]

Hillman does not here indict the biblical tradition in his disturbing diagnosis; the attitudes he denounces seem Protestant as well as American, although his citation of Elaine Pagels' *The Origin of Satan* implies a more sweeping charge. His emphasis in *The Soul's Code* is to

identify and honor the daimon, the determining genius, within the assorted human demons whose lives he recounts—not to endorse their reprehensible actions, but to bring a psychological understanding that might obviate such actions.

* * *

Do we get anything similar from Leonard Cohen or Oliver Stone?

Both champion forms of love Hillman might find too innocent, and not least so in being presented as a force by which to survive the apocalypse and, as the film puts it, 'beat the demon'. Cohen's album contains an epigraph from Genesis 24, the wooing of Rebecca at the well, which may have more to do with the actress Rebecca De Mornay being a co-producer of the album than with it being an allusion to human love in ancient Israel, or YHWH's divine promise to and guidance of Abraham and Isaac as progenitors of His people.

The image of the well recurs in one of the more hopefully apocalyptic songs on Cohen's **'The Future'** album, **'Democracy'**: 'From the wells of disappointment / where the women kneel to pray / for the grace of G-d in the desert here / and the desert far away / Democracy is coming to the USA'.[22] Cohen's spelling of the word 'God' as 'G-d' indicates some attention to Jewish practice, though the reference to the desert far away may reflect the recent Persian Gulf War and not the setting of biblical events like Rebecca's wooing.

Nevertheless, the resonance between the desert of the Middle East and the desert of America—in particular the American Southwest—is suggestive. Both seem to be landscapes of apocalypse, the former looking back to a past that conceived apocalypse to start with and the latter, with its atomic bombs and Baudrillardian spaces, speed, and amnesia, to a future where apocalypse becomes an end.[23] It is in the desert of Arizona or New Mexico—near the apocalyptically-numbered Route 666 from Farmington to Gallup—that our lovers, Mickey and Mallory Knox, lost and out of gas and stoned on drugs, stumble into the hogan of a Navajo medicine man or 'singer' and enact the scene that is the moral center of Stone's film.

'Bad bad bad bad bad bad bad bad', says Mallory to Mickey after, somewhat by accident, he shoots the Navajo: 'You killed *life!*' she screams. No more moralizing language than this can be imagined, and it comes in a film that seems to wallow in *a*moral violence otherwise. What is the context of this untoward lapse into pangs of conscience and a suggestion of repentance?

We know from the rest of the film, including its closing credits, that snakes are a persistent image, an image of demonism that may be biblical in its valuation, but also an image of love that could be just as demonic: the rings with which the lovers marry themselves are decorated with intertwined snakes. Shamans and Native American spirituality, probably in contrast to a personal and cultural biblical inheritance Stone may see as tortured, are markers of healing wisdom and ethical vision. A Native American figure functions this way in Stone's earlier film *The Doors,* and he is an evident fan of Carlos Castaneda's neoshamanism: Stone's production company, Ixtlan Films, takes its name from the title of one of Castaneda's books.[24] The actor who plays the Navajo healer in our excerpt is Russell Means, a leader of the American Indian Movement (AIM).

Means' character sees snakes rather differently than does the Book of Genesis. He accepts them as truly and appropriately 'natural born killers', like the coyotes and raptors whose images Stone also flashes past us during the hogan scene. But he does not find them demonic. It is instead the humans, at least the Anglo heirs of the biblical code, who are the actual demons, made sadly sick by too much of their own invention, TV, lost in a media world of ghostly (ghastly) images. In this scene Mickey, played by Woody Harrelson (the cornfed naif from the TV sitcom *Cheers*), and Mallory, acted by Juliette Lewis (the sneering tough girl from films like *True Romance*), do seem to grasp their culpability as demons, and the murder of the medicine man is indeed the only one they regret.

For his part, the Navajo singer, who seems to have tried to heal them with a ritual chant, has foreseen his death at the hands of these demons twenty years earlier. This could be a reference to Stone's first film, *Seizure,* from 1974, a low-budget horror story that concerns the boundary between dreams and waking reality and that features a female demon figure called 'the Queen of Evil'. Lying on his back, dying, the Navajo healer can see the smoke hole in his hogan roof through which he has gestured that his wife's spirit had arisen to the stars at her death.

* * *

The Navajo healer's vision through the smoke hole is perhaps an echo of the night sky scene earlier in the film when Mickey and Mallory, after their initial killing spree depicted in Stone's wildly juxtaposed cuts, are relieving themselves in the desert and druggily philosophizing. 'The whole world is coming to an end, Mal', says Mickey, looking up to the stars. 'I see angels, Mickey', she replies. 'They're coming down for us from heaven. And I see you riding a big red horse. And you're driving the horses, whipping them. And they're spitting and frothing all on the mouth. And they're coming right at us. And I see the future. And there's no death, because you and I we're angels'.

The reference to Mickey driving the red horse echoes a line in Cohen's song **'The Future'**: 'you feel the devil's

riding crop'.[25] But how can we square Mallory's end-time vision—the future as a heavenly reward of immortality for two natural (or unnatural) born killers—with Cohen's lyrics over the closing credits: 'I have seen the future, brother: it is murder'?

Perhaps heavenly visions of angels and immortality are part of why the earthly future is murderous—and all we in the West can do is wait for a miracle. Another song from Cohen's **'The Future'** album plays over the *opening* credits of *Natural Born Killers*. The song is called **'Waiting for the Miracle',** and it is enigmatic enough to be a diagnosis of, as readily as a prescription for, the dark apocalypse Oliver Stone presents. It is couched in terms of private life and love relationships but in ways that reverberate with millennial ramifications for the culture.

The words that we are able to hear over the opening credits—which also accompany the bizarre rampage in a desert diner, part *Bonnie and Clyde* part Keystone Kops part *Dr. Strangelove* part Manson's helter skelter madness in the Tate-La Bianca killings—are as follows:

> . . . it must have hurt your pride
> to have to stand beneath my window
> with your bugle and your drum
> and me I'm up here waiting for the miracle.[26]

Exactly what the miracle is here is hard to say, although we can grasp that the singer is speaking like a lover to someone who has tried to be with him for years but whom he has kept waiting. Could this singer also be the biblical God—'the little jew who wrote the bible', as **'The Future'** proclaims? Could He be apologizing to His people on the eve of the (bi-)millennium, people who have been playing the bugle and drum of war-like Western religion throughout the centuries of waiting, with God looking down from a heaven he suggests would not be especially angelic and may even be hellish (or at least darkly judgmental) for the sinful likes of us? He says 'I do believe you loved me', but immediately goes on to warn

> you wouldn't like it here
> there ain't no entertainment
> and the judgements are severe[27]

Such a speculative reading of Cohen's lyrics would still not explain what the miracle might be, an apocalyptic resolution to history for which an inattentive God has Himself been waiting. To conjecture even more wildly, though, could the miracle be God's little experiment with the Christ, which was supposed to reconcile the world to Himself? Is this the miracle that has yet to pan out, with a Second Coming and a Kingdom long overdue and time running out on God's love life with his creation?

James Hillman notwithstanding, Stone has said of his film (if not of the world) '. . . I do believe there is love at the end. And I do believe that . . . 'love beats the demon.' Without giving away our ending, I find it ironic that it is Mickey and Mallory who are the ones to escape . . .'.[28] So Stone's belief about the end looks forward to the miracle of love, even if it is an ironic love or an ironic, perhaps perverse, miracle, with Cohen's words about a murderous future as its shadow in the musical background. But none of this is meant, finally, to give away our ending.

In any case it won't be long now. We know from several other images during the opening sequence of *Natural Born Killers* that Stone sees our time as running out. Again television is the medium and no doubt the motivating cause, for the filmmaker, of our millennial distress. On the TV screen in the diner we see, first, a scene from *Leave It to Beaver* in which Beaver's mom says to Beaver and Eddie Haskell, 'You're going to be late again'. Beaver answers 'We're just leaving, Mom'. Then we get a quick glimpse of the title shot of *77 Sunset Strip,* indicating that day is just about done in the west and for the West. Next there is Richard Nixon at the denouement of Watergate saying 'As I leave . . .'. Finally a demon's face fills the small black and white screen.

And that is where I shall leave it—with some last words from Leonard Cohen. For our apocalyptic world of the West is itself 'running late', and may, very soon, failing a miracle, need to leave:

> If you're squeezed for information,
> that's when you've got to play it dumb:
> You just say you're out there waiting
> for the miracle to come.[29]

References

1. See Margaret R. Miles, *Seeing and Believing: Religion and Values in the Movies* (Boston: Beacon Press, 1996).

2. See Susan Mackey-Kallis, *Oliver Stone's America: 'Dreaming the Myth Outward'* (Boulder, Colorado: Westview Press, 1996); and Norman Kagan, *The Cinema of Oliver Stone* (New York Continuum, 1996)

3. See Richard Dellamora, ed., *Postmodern Apocalypse Theory and Cultural Practice at the End* (Philadelphia: U of Pennsylvania P, 1995); and Malcolm Bull, ed., *Apocalypse Theory and the Ends of the World* (Oxford Blackwell, 1995).

4. See Jean Baudrillard, *America,* trans Chris Turner (London and New York Verso, 1986/1989).

5. Leonard Cohen, 'The Future' (album), Leonard Cohen Stranger Music, Inc (BMI), all rights reserved, 1992

6. *Ibid.*

7. *Ibid.*

8. *Ibid.*

9. *Ibid.*

10. Quoted by Stone in John August and Jane Hamsher, *Natural Born Killers: A Novel* (New York: Signet, 1994) p. 7

11. Leonard Cohen, *op. cit.*

12. Mike Riddell, 'Read my apocalypse! No new fixes', *Third Way,* April 1996, p. 35.

13. *Ibid.*

14. Quentin Tarantino, *Natural Born Killers* (London and Boston Faber and Faber, 1995) p. 54.

15. Gitlin quoted in Margaret Miles, *op. cit.,* p. 183.

16. *Ibid.,* p. 184.

17. Stone quoted in John August and Jane Hamsher, *op. cit.,* p. 7.

18. Norman Kagan, *op. cit.,* p. 249.

19. James Hillman, *The Soul's Code: In Search of Character and Calling* (New York: Random House, 1996), pp. 277-8.

20. Stone quoted in John August and Jane Hamsher, *op. cit.,* p. 11.

21. James Hillman, *op. cit.,* 247-8 See also Elaine Pagels, *The Ongin of Satan* (New York Random House, 1995); and Regina M. Schwarz, *The Curse of Cain The Violent Legacy of Monotheism* (Chicago and London: U of Chicago P, 1997).

22. Leonard Cohen, *op. cit.*

23. See Jean Baudrillard, *op. cit.,* pp. 121-8.

24. See Carlos Castaneda, *Journey to Ixtlan* (New York: Simon and Schuster, 1972).

25. Leonard Cohen, *op. cit.*

26. *Ibid.*

27. *Ibid.*

28. Stone in John August and Jane Hamsher, *op. cit.,* p. 12.

29. Leonard Cohen, *op. cit.*

Adrienne Clarkson (essay date winter 1999)

SOURCE: Clarkson, Adrienne. "Counterpoint Leonard Cohen." *Essays on Canadian Writing* 69 (winter 1999): 1-2.

[*In the following essay, Clarkson recounts her own interactions with Cohen.*]

Everything Leonard Cohen says is a sleek embodiment of meaning coming down a corridor at you from the gilded rooms of a glittering palace you only dream about. When he speaks to you, a pattern appears in the shadow on the wall, the floor moulds to your feet. Your head turns but as though you were following it and it were on someone else's neck. Each conversation is one in which he doesn't "dwell on what / has passed away / or what is yet to be," because he knows you can "forget your perfect offering. / There is a crack in everything. That's how the light gets in."

The first time Leonard sang on television was in 1967 on our CBC Television show *Take Thirty,* and his grey flannel suit was the most beautifully cut garment with hand-stitched lapels you could ever hope to see. He then slung his guitar over his shoulder with a rueful smile, without messing up the front of the suit. The guitar slid down the front of the suit—and fitted.

We had wondered why he wanted to sing at all, especially as he had just had a firestorm success with *Beautiful Losers,* from which many of us were already memorizing whole passages. "Something in him so loves the world that he gives himself to the laws of gravity and chance. . . . His house is dangerous and finite, but he is at home in the world. . . . It is good to have among us such men, such balancing monsters of love." The producer, Cynthia Scott, and I had both read his poem "I heard of a man / who says words so beautifully / that if he only speaks their name / women give themselves to him" when we were teenagers so short a time before, and we thought he was that man himself.

Now he wanted to sing on our television show with an ethereal group of blond androgynes called the Stormy Clovers. We were giving in to this whim (none of us had heard him sing a note, and we were terrified of doing so, in the dread that our utter adoration of him would crumble into bathos) in order to do a very serious interview with L. Cohen, POET.

It turned out that the interview was ridiculous and the singing a revelation. It was **"The Stranger Song"** and went on for twenty minutes. After the final dress rehearsal, we cut it, delicately, in hushed tones of profound respect. Leonard said to me softly, and with only the slightest hint of irony, "The time is over, Adrienne, when poets sit on marble steps wearing long black capes." The impact on his callow interviewer was such that I could only stare down at my hands, which were plucking at my woollen skirt in an agitated fashion.

Some years later in Montreal, off the Main, we worked desultorily on selecting poems for a collection and making a film about him. He ate Cheese Whiz with a kind of baleful hunger, chased down with freshly squeezed orange juice from Beauty's, the brunch café of choice. His space heater rattled, and he looked through his poems with a wary perfectionism.

To me, the only American presidential debate of any consequence will always be the one between Carter and Ford, because Leonard and I shared a fancy hamburger at the Windsor Arms Hotel while watching it. We assured each other that the debate, surreal in accent and content, wasn't really happening. I think it was immediately after Leonard had been in, through, and out the other side of something—a religion, a car, some person. Sly laughter didn't fill the space between skin and bone that it normally did.

The world is the space for creatures who can compare mythologies. In Paris, he entered the Café Flore, and before two dazzled French fans could shout LAYonard COHEN! he had glided onto the banquette beside me and continued the conversation we had started six years before about terrorism. We were somewhere between conquering Manhattan and taking Berlin.

Once, Leonard showed me where the Cohens of Montreal are buried, on the side of the mountain outside the gate. It is impossible to think of him as joining them there. But maybe he'll just be in California instead. On a forever basis. As he said in one of his latest interviews, "Living in Los Angeles is like being in the French Foreign Legion; no one here has a last name."

Robert de Young (essay date winter 1999)

SOURCE: de Young, Robert. "'My Black Pages': Reconsidering *Death of a Lady's Man* and *Death of a Ladies' Man.*" *Essays on Canadian Writing* 69 (winter 1999): 125-39.

[*In the following essay, de Young examines the complex interplay between poetry and textual commentary in Cohen's* Death of a Lady's Man, *and argues that the volume, along with the 1977 album* Death of a Ladies' Man, *has been neglected by critics.*]

Stephen Scobie remarked in his keynote address at the 1993 Red Deer conference on Leonard Cohen that *Death of a Lady's Man*—the collection of poems and prose poems published in 1978—had attracted little critical attention from either academics or Cohen fans. There are a number of possible explanations for this neglect. Scobie notes William Ruhlmann's point that, "by the late seventies, 'Cohen's reputation among literary critics and academics had simply evaporated since he had so long been identified as a songwriter and pop star'" ("Counterfeiter" 10). Similarly, Linda Hutcheon has made the point that "Cohen's success as a performer, documented by the near-idolatrous reviews of his European concert tours, has almost eclipsed his career as a poet and novelist" (26).[1] And as Scobie himself has bluntly stated, another "reason for Cohen's neglect is, more straightforwardly, academic snobbery. Many critics still have a great deal of trouble dealing with Leonard Cohen as the writer and performer of popular songs" (11). Because the volume was published after the release of the similarly titled album *Death of a Ladies' Man* in 1977, probably the least favourably received of all of Cohen's albums (and one that initially Cohen himself seemed to reject), the merits of *Death of a Lady's Man* seem largely to have been overshadowed by the puzzled responses to Cohen's collaborative efforts with Phil Spector on the album. And while Cohen is frequently celebrated as a "Black Romantic," it has to be said that, even in the context of the sometimes bleak content of his canon, *Death of a Lady's Man* covers some very difficult and unpleasant emotional terrain: the breakdown of a "marriage" between the narrator and his dark lady, Lilith. Ira Nadel quotes Cohen's own statement on this period: "every relationship I had broke down. *Every single relationship broke down.* There was nothing left standing" (218).

However, this critical neglect is contrary to Cohen's own interest in the genesis of *Death of a Lady's Man.* Scobie quotes Cohen's rather obscure and convoluted description of the history of this work in a letter Cohen sent him in July 1977: "*Death of a Lady's Man* derives from a longer book called *My Life in Art,* which I finished last year and decided not to publish. *The Woman Being Born* was the title of another manuscript and also an alternative title for both *My Life in Art* and *Death of a Lady's Man*" ("Counterfeiter" 8). To further complicate matters, all three works mentioned in Cohen's letter—and myriad other "notebooks" from years earlier—are frequently cited in the text of *Death of a Lady's Man* itself and become part of Cohen's playful and complex textual strategies.

We know from Cohen's own comments in interviews that it is not unusual for him to rework material over long periods of time (for example, his five hundred drafts of **"Take This Waltz,"** which he discusses in the CBC documentary with Adrienne Clarkson), whether he is writing poetry, songs, or novels. But *Death of a Lady's Man* arguably has been accorded an extraordinary level of attention by Cohen. As Nadel documents, the protracted publication history of the volume clearly evinces Cohen's continual reworking and revisiting of the text from at least March 1976 to the date of its publication in the fall of 1978. Notwithstanding the pressure from his publisher, Jack McClelland, and his editor to complete the work, Cohen kept making changes and withholding the text from publication. McClelland was hardly thrilled with Cohen's last-minute decision to add the commentaries: "He says he is writ-

ing a 90-page commentary on the book itself. What ever the hell that means. I fear the worst" (qtd. in Nadel 221). Even as recently as 1993, during preparations for the publication of the anthology entitled *Stranger Music,* Cohen returned yet again to the text. As Nadel observes of *Stranger Music,* "the most widely cited text is *Death of a Lady's Man,* reworked and in some cases reordered from the original book, with new headings for some sections. Cohen himself has said that he is happiest with this version of the work, for he at last made the book 'coherent,' ridding it of a great deal that could not be penetrated in the original text" (265). Moreover, *Stranger Music* does not contain any material from Cohen's first novel, *The Favourite Game,* a work that many critics have seen as being of greater literary worth than *Death of a Lady's Man,* and thus a more obvious text to include in the anthology. It seems clear, then, that Cohen himself regards *Death of a Lady's Man* as an important literary enterprise and one worthy of his—and our—continued attention.

This essay reevaluates *Death of a Lady's Man* alongside *Death of a Ladies' Man* in an attempt to reinstate both of these neglected works as central to an understanding of Cohen's craft and powers as a writer as well as a songwriter and performer.

The album *Death of a Ladies' Man,* cowritten with and produced by Phil ("wall of sound") Spector, also has not been well received. Nadel quotes review headlines such as "Leonard Cohen's doo-wop Nightmare" or "Doyen of Doom meets Teen Tycoon" (217), although reviewer Ken Waxman remarked that "Spector's talents spur Cohen in the way that an exceptional director's skill will sometimes pull unexpectedly fine performances from certain actors" (61). To further complicate attempts to assess the album's merits, Cohen continually distanced himself from both Spector and the production during the promotion following the album's release. As he told Janet Maslin for an article in the *New York Times,*

> I never thought I would give up that much control. I didn't even know when it was being mixed—I never heard the mix and I don't approve of it. The mix is a catastrophe. No air. No breath. No rest. It's like what he [Spector] has become himself. He doesn't know how to let a situation breathe, let alone a song. But it's very hard to fight him—he just disappears. He was in possession of the tapes; his bodyguard took them back to his house every night. I knew he was mad, but I thought his madness would be more adorable, on the ordinary daily level. I love the guy, but he's out of control. Finally, I just said let the thing go. There's nothing I like about it, there are four seconds on the record that I think are music. The music in some places is very powerful, but by and large I think it's too loud, too aggressive. . . . I think it's a classic this record. . . . Like a lot of classics—somehow they're too dense, too boring. But they have some enduring

power, and you know there's something excellent and strong about them. You just don't like them, that's all. (18, 40)

In her review, Maslin herself comments that *Death of a Ladies' Man* "combines Cohen's solemn delivery and thoughtful lyrics with Spector's full-blown, danceable production sound. These elements are so unreconciled, and their net effect is at first so bewildering, that this record may be one of the most bizarre, slowly satisfying hybrids pop music has ever produced" (18). Even the album design is unusual for a Cohen album. On the front cover, he sits, in a somewhat uncharacteristic white suit, between a sombre Suzanne Elrod (the mother of Cohen's two children, Adam and Lorca, and usually deemed the dark woman of *Death of a Lady's Man*) and actor Eva LaPierre. Suzanne's image, this time separated from Cohen and the other woman, is repeated on the back cover. According to the liner notes, the cover photograph is by an "anonymous roving photographer at a forgotten Polynesian restaurant." Cohen in a white suit in a restaurant filled with palm trees seems more than a little incongruous as the cover for this album.

Maslin's remark that the elements of this album are "unreconciled" seems to reflect both the "bizarre" production values (the relationship between Cohen and Spector) and the subject matter—marital breakdown. But why does she, like audiences in general, seem to find the effect "so bewildering"? In many respects, the internal tensions and contradictions on this album are strikingly similar to the strategies Cohen uses in his collection of poems and commentaries published the following year. Moreover, it is clear that Cohen was working on these two projects simultaneously. The names already provide a strong link, with only the spelling distinguishing the two. The album title, declaring the "death" of the "ladies' man," is repeated in the titular poem of the published volume *Death of a Lady's Man*, although the death in the literary text is of one "lady's man." Cohen, the apparent "ladies' man," appears between two women on the cover of the album, while, as noted on the dust jacket, the cover of the published text reproduces a sixteenth-century woodcut of "*coniunctio spirituum,* or the spiritual union of the male and female principle from the alchemical text *Rosararium Philosophorum* (1550)." The most direct link between the two works is provided by the lyrics of the final song on the album, which are subsequently published as the poem **"Death of a Lady's Man."**

But perhaps the most revelatory and complex link between these two seemingly disparate works is precisely their postmodern playfulness with form. Maslin is correct in identifying the bizarre differences between Cohen's voice and lyrics and Spector's overwhelming production. Unlike most of Cohen's other albums, these songs are difficult to reproduce outside of the complex studio environment, and, apart from **"Memories,"** which was performed in concerts throughout the late 1970s and early 1980s, very few of these songs have ever been performed live.[2] In keeping with Maslin, Scobie objects to the album performances of **"Fingerprints"** and **"I Left a Woman Waiting"** because he feels the seriousness of the lyrics—both are adapted from earlier poems—is compromised by the music (*Leonard* 171). But this tension and contradiction is precisely the point. Certainly the collaboration of Spector and Cohen is, superficially, somewhat bizarre, but as a strategy for providing playful commentary it is very effective and perfectly in accord with Cohen's eleventh-hour decision the following year to add an italicized commentary on the facing page of each poem in *Death of a Lady's Man.* Ironically, the commentary[3] to the poem **"O Wife Unmasked"**—*"Claustrophobia! Bullshit! Air! Air! Give us air! Is there an antidote to this mustard gas of domestic spiritism?"* (129)—echoes Cohen's own comments to the *New York Times* on Spector's contribution: "The mix is a catastrophe. No air. No breath. No rest. It's like what he has become himself. He doesn't know how to let a situation breathe, let alone a song" (Maslin 40). What Cohen may be objecting to is his lack of creative control in the final production of the album, but the hybridity produced by his collaboration with Spector is strikingly similar to his own strategies in *Death of a Lady's Man,* especially the last-minute addition of the commentaries.

The album opens with **"True Love Leaves No Traces,"** which, as Scobie has observed (*Leonard* 168-74), is largely based on Cohen's earlier poem **"As the Mist Leaves No Scar"** from the 1961 volume *The Spice-Box of Earth.* A performance of this poem also appears in the 1965 Canadian National Film Board documentary *Ladies and Gentlemen, Mr. Leonard Cohen.* Like the poem, the song lyrically echoes the language and themes of seventeenth-century poet John Donne's "A Valediction: Forbidding Mourning" and "Song (Sweetest Love, I Do Not Go)" and provides a deceptively sweet introduction to the largely abrasive songs that follow. Indeed, the song that follows is **"Iodine,"** which, in spite of its rather jaunty musical accompaniment, sets the darker mood and tone for the album:

> You let me love you
> till I was a failure—
> Your beauty on my bruise like iodine
> I asked you if a man
> could be forgiven
> And though I failed at love
> was this a crime?
> You said, Don't worry,
> don't worry, darling
> There are many ways a man
> can serve his time

These lyrics do not appear in *Death of a Lady's Man* the following year—or in the later collection *Stranger Music,* for that matter—but the language and themes are perfectly in accord with the later poems' various accounts of the dissolution of marriage. In this case, though, the role of the commentary (largely used in the volume to distance and provide irony and humour) is provided by Spector's musical arrangement. As Cohen rasps out "Your saintly kisses reeked of iodine / Your fragrance with fume of iodine," Spector's brass instruments lilt joyfully along.

"Paper Thin Hotel" is possibly the song that gives rise to Scobie's comment on the "sheer incongruity between the fragility of Cohen's voice and the massive 'wall of sound' with which Spector surrounds it" (*Leonard* 169). But again, arguably it is this incongruity that provides a strength to the performance of the song, just as throughout *Death of a Lady's Man,* the frail, often shrill voice of the poet is alternately (de)constructed, (re)constructed, and supported by the voices of the commentaries. Cohen's pained, deadpan voice sounds like it is trapped in a paper-thin echo chamber where the voices, sounds, and emotions of the lovers in the next room continually reverberate. The singer's fantasy

> And I can't wait to tell you
> to your face
> And I can't wait for you
> to take my place

echoes the continual "paper-thin" textual slippage between the male and female voices within the poems and commentaries and the poems and commentaries themselves in *Death of a Lady's Man.*

"Memories," with its classic late 1950s-early 1960s Spector sound, is probably the clearest example of the humorous links between the musical arrangements and Cohen's lyrics:

> Frankie Lane was singing "Jezebel"
> I pinned an Iron Cross to my lapel
> I walked up to the tallest
> and the blondest girl
> I said, Look, you don't know me now
> but very soon you will
> So won't you let me see
> Won't you let me see
> Won't you let me see
> Your naked body

The scene is very reminiscent of the ill-fated attempts by Breavman and Krantz to gate-crash a francophone party in order to score in Cohen's first novel, *The Favourite Game.* The song itself takes the form of a dialogue between the hopeful, swaggering youth and the tall and equally determined blonde concerning the sexual mores of an earlier decade, while Spector's rousing musical arrangement provides a witty allusion to

the musical tastes at the dawn of rock and roll, including his own arrangements for songs such as "To Know Him Is to Love Him" or The Crystals' "And Then He Kissed Me." In 1984 Cohen takes this rather playful sense of the historical past a step further in his video *I Am a Hotel,* where he performs "Memories" dressed entirely in black, detached and aloof from the dance floor, his face an expressionless mask behind sunglasses. The narrator/singer is no longer the hapless youth on the dance floor fumbling with a blouse but has instead been transformed into the successful rock star on the balcony.

The raucous and crude "Don't Go Home with Your Hard-On"—which includes Bob Dylan[4] and Allen Ginsberg on backing vocals, and even Spector himself—sees Cohen giving an impressively gravelly vocal performance that recalls the unpleasant, rasping tones of the chorus in "Diamonds in the Mine" from the 1970 album *Songs of Love and Hate*:

> Here comes your bride
> with her veil on
> Approach her, you wretch,
> if you dare
> Approach her, you ape
> with your tail on
> Once you have her she'll always be there
>   . . . . .
> But don't go home
> with your hard-on
> It will only drive you insane
> You can't shake it (or break it)
> with your Motown
> You can't melt it down in the rain

In spite of the speaker's protestation that sexual desire cannot be quenched with "Motown," the creation and existence of the song itself and its urgent performance seem to contradict this idea. Throughout both this album and the poems of *Death of a Lady's Man,* as in most of Cohen's work, there is a continuing play and dialogue between sexual desire and the craft of writing. As Ken Norris has observed of *Death of a Lady's Man,* "Marriage is a central metaphor that extends outward to other interrelationships: the poet 'married' to his life in art, the poem 'married' to its commentary, a possible implied marriage of the reader to the text" (53). This vexed but close relationship between sexual desire and the drive to write is clearly articulated throughout *Death of a Lady's Man.* For example, in "Another Room" we read:

> I climbed the stairs with my key and my brown leather bag and I entered room eight. I heard Aleece mounting the steps behind me. Room eight. My own room in a warm country. A bed, a table, a chair. Perhaps I could become a poet again. Aleece was making noises in the hall. I could see the ocean in the late afternoon light outside my window. I should look at the ocean but I don't feel like it. The interior voice said, You will only

POETRY CRITICISM, Vol. 109

sing again if you give up lechery. Choose. This is a place where you may begin again. But I want her. Let me have her. Throw yourself upon your stiffness and take up your pen.

(22)

And in the witty commentary to **"Daily Commerce,"** Cohen writes: *"my dark erection unmanifested / except within the pants of poesy"* (175). As Hutcheon has summarized, "The pen and the penis meet once again. . . . As in both novels, the autoerotic and the literary are closely connected" (51). Maybe "Motown" can help the speaker with his hard-on after all.

The final song on the album is **"Death of a Ladies' Man,"** which also appears in the poetry volume the following year. The poem/song is arguably the strongest in the collection/album, and its textual strategies—both as performed on the album and in the book—provide an important creative link between the two works. Unlike much of the work in *Death of a Lady's Man,* this poem does not use the first person but instead uses the third person to distance the narrator from the subject matter:

> The man she wanted all her life
> was hanging by a thread.
> "I never even knew how much
> I wanted you," she said.
> His muscles they were numbered
> and his style was obsolete.
> "O baby, I have come too late."
> She knelt beside his feet.

(30)

Spector's production of the song on the album has been much criticized. Nadel gives the following account of the circumstances of the recording session:

> The recording of the song **"Death of a Ladies' Man"** was indicative of the album's creation. The session began at 7:30 in the evening, but by 2:30 in the morning a complete take had not yet been made. The musicians were on double time after midnight; it escalated to quadruple time at 2:00 a.m. By 3:30 in the morning they had not even played the song all the way through yet. Spector took away the charts and prevented the musicians from playing more than six bars. Cohen sat crosslegged on the floor through most of this until around 4:00 a.m., when Spector clapped his hands and told Cohen to do the vocal. Approaching the microphone, a very tired Cohen sang the song flawlessly. Cohen has since said of the song, "It's direct and confessional. I wanted the lyrics in a tender setting rather than a harsh situation. At times that fusion was achieved. Sometimes the heart must roast on the fire like shish kebab."

(216)

More than on any other song on the album, Spector, in spite of the lateness of the hour, seems to have been able to capture the mood of the lyric very effectively.

After the fashion of **"Paper Thin Hotel,"** Cohen's slightly reverberated voice sounds isolated, desolate, and weary and the regularity of the drum beat heavy and monotonous rather than jaunty. "Motown" does not seem to offer much consolation here. While the third-person narration provides some sense of distance, Cohen sounds truly strained. As in some of the confessional, first-person poems in *Death of a Lady's Man,* there is a mood of genuine anguish. Spector's production of the final verse of the song is especially effective:

> So the great affair is over
> but whoever would have guessed
> it would leave us all so vacant
> and so deeply unimpressed.
> It's like our visit to the moon
> or to that other star:
> I guess you go for nothing
> if you really want to go that far.

The musical wall of sound seems literally to collapse under its own weight as Cohen's lyrics grind to a halt— the final four lines are repeated twice as the song, like the marriage and life of the lady's man, unravels and grows less audible and more distant.

Cohen's commentary to the poem **"Death of a Lady's Man"** is worth quoting:

> Darling, I'm afraid we have to go to the end of love.
> *or*
> O Darling, I'm afraid that we will have to go to the end of love.
> *and many variations, some signed, some unsigned, obviously meant for someone's eyes, written in the margin of this and other pages.*

(33)

In many respects this is typical of the commentaries throughout *Death of a Lady's Man.* At one level, they provide textual variations for the reader's contemplation (and, frequently, amusement), although in this case, these "variations" do not seem to be very substantial or contribute anything new to the existing poem: they simply are evidence of the creative process of what Cohen calls "blackening pages." The final remarks are perhaps more interesting and typical of what Norris has called "a wild display of style and irony embodied in the commentaries that interrogate, elucidate and undermine the original text" (53). Unlike the well-known signature at the end of **"Famous Blue Raincoat"**—"Sincerely L. Cohen" (*Stranger* [*Stranger Music*] 153)—Cohen here simultaneously suggests the transparently personal nature of text and yet casually dismisses it. Furthermore, unlike other instances in the commentaries, where there is an almost obsessive level of detail provided on the manuscript sources for the material quoted (e.g., *"The original version is found in a sturdy Swedish notebook, the Atlanta Radio-Serie /A*

2202-6/120 BL. It was written sometime in 1973 at the Bayshore Inn in Vancouver" [105]), Cohen simply states in a rather throwaway fashion that these, and other variations, are *"written in the / margin of this and other pages."* The text, no matter what its content, is continually subject to the artist's commentary. In spite of the emotionally charged nature of the material, Cohen the writer maintains a degree of distance and playful detachment from his "texts." Indeed, the reader has no way of verifying whether or not these variable "texts" have any existence outside the pages of the present work—they simply unsettle the reader and any conclusive meaning.

It seems entirely appropriate, given the internal contradictions and tensions within the text and Cohen's obsession with examining his craft, that one of the sources for **Death of a Lady's Man** that he cites in his letter to Scobie is called "My Life in Art," apparently completed by 1976 but not published. However, as mentioned above, obscure and deliberately confusing references to this earlier text appear throughout **Death of a Lady's Man.** Given that the notion of the "death" of the lady's (or ladies') man is central, it is worth quoting the earliest references to "My Life in Art," which appears in the poem **"Death to This Book"** and its commentary:

Death to this book or fuck this book and fuck this marriage. Fuck the twenty-six letters of my cowardice. Fuck you for breaking the mirror and throwing the eyebrow tweezers out the window. Your dead bed night after night and nothing warm but baby talk. Fuck marriage and theology and the cold goodnight. Fuck the idolatry of anger and the priests who say so. How dare they. How dare they. Thanks for your judgement on me. Murder and a fast train to Paris and me thin again in my blue raincoat, and Barbara waiting at the Cluny Square Hotel. Fuck her for never turning up.

The violence of this paragraph is somewhat mitigated by the sense of nostalgia and loss in the last two lines. Does he really wish to negate his life and his work? Although the energy is similar, we get a different picture from the first passage of an unpublished manuscript called My Life in Art, from which many of the pieces of this present volume are excerpted or reworked.

We begin the Final Revision of My Life in Art. There hasn't been a book like this in a long time. Much of the effort in this ultimate version will be expended trying to dignify a worthless piece of junk. The modern reader will be provided a framework of defeat through which he may view without intimidation a triumph of blazing genius. I have the manuscript beside me now. It took me ten years to write. During this time you were grinding out your bullshit. It will become clear that I am the stylist of my era and the only honest man in town. I did not quarrel with my voices. I took it down out of the air. This is called work by those who know and should not be confused with an Eastern trance.

(20-21)

This passage is one of many examples throughout the volume where there is a rather vexed relationship between the poem and the commentary. As opposed to the condemnation both of "this marriage" and "this book" in the poem, the commentary provides an emotionally detached critique of the "violence" of the poem and suggests that the unpublished work "My Life in Art" is a more satisfactory literary source and provides a more moderated "energy." However, once the author of the commentary begins to justify his claim and quote from "My Life in Art," the circles within circles appear again immediately: "We begin the Final Revision of My Life in Art." Moreover, the nonitalicized passage that follows the commentary, apparently quoted from "My Life in Art," refers to another "manuscript" that took "years to write." It's becoming hard for the alert reader to believe that the author of these multifaceted and layered texts is "the only honest man in town." And, to add to the confusion, a few pages further on we are told of another text that is entitled the "Final Revision of My Life in Art" (29).

In any case, even assuming that "My Life in Art" is an actual completed manuscript, **Death of a Lady's Man** abounds with references to "the Notebooks" (29, 69, 73, 77) and myriad other sources. In the commentary to **"The Photograph,"** he demands: *"Examine this suppressed passage from the original manuscript of My Life in Art"* (57). Why suppressed? Like the other sources cited, it has never been published. As Norris has argued, "In **Death of a Lady's Man** the erosion of particular self only leads to the establishment of particular selves, not to a revelation of the absolute, nor the concrete establishment of the author's presence" (54). As with Spector's wall-of-sound arrangements for **Death of a Ladies' Man,** the commentaries and their entangled relationships with the poems render it almost impossible to discern a single voice. But no matter how much the writer is undermined, the "honesty" and integrity of the writer's craft remain, as the commentary to **"It's Probably Spring"** makes clear:

I would like to lose my faith in this poet, but I can't. I would like to say that I have discovered in him something glib. I want to disqualify him. He comes too close to betraying me. He comes too close to reeling me in. I want to say that he was too rich. I want to prove that his marriage was happy. I want to say that I only thought he was that good because I misunderstood him. But I am afraid I do not misunderstand him. I understand him. Tonight I understand him perfectly. . . . I read the piece again and again, so pleased that the poet has taken such pains not to touch me. If only I had touched her this lightly, I might not be sitting here now.

(59)

In **The Energy of Slaves,** another collection of poetry published in 1972, Cohen declares in poem after poem that he cannot write, that his poetic gifts have left him.

But in *Death of a Lady's Man,* as elsewhere in his work, writing and word games provide consolation for the death of the lady's/ladies' man. But typically for Cohen, even the death itself is subject to question, as the poem **"Final Examination"** makes clear:

> I am almost 90
> Everyone I know has died off
> except Leonard
> He can still be seen
> hobbling with his love
>
> (212)

And, just in case we missed Cohen's self-irony and humour in both *Death of a Ladies' Man* and *Death of a Lady's Man,* Spector provides his own "commentary" in his contribution to the 1996 collection compiled for Cohen's sixtieth birthday, *Take This Waltz:*

> I would be remiss, if I did not mention at this time, one particular person, poet and artist, who confessed to me that he was extremely influenced by the Partridge Family. And that artist is Leonard Cohen. Underneath that brooding, moody, depressed soul which Leonard possesses, lies an out-and-out Partridge Family freak. He never misses their re-runs on Nickelodeon; belongs to their fan club; and for lack of a more appropriate word, is a Partridge Family "groupie," albeit one who still remains "in the closet" in connection with these feelings. May I suggest you contact him, and I am sure he will provide you with much in-depth information as to how profound was the way in which the Partridge Family influenced every facet of his personal and professional life.
>
> (176)

Notes

1. Hutcheon chooses to discuss *Death of a Lady's Man* in the fiction rather than the poetry series of the ECW Press series Canadian Writers and Their Works because of the similarities she observes with both *The Favourite Game* and *Beautiful Losers.*

2. According to Devlin, Cohen performed "Don't Go Home with Your Hard-On" and an early version of "Iodine" as early as 1975 during his North American tour, and he performed "Iodine" a number of times during the 1979 European tour (30-34).

3. As is the printing practice throughout *Death of a Lady's Man,* the names and text of commentaries to poems are given in italics.

4. As I point out in "Behind the Frames," it is worth noting that Bob Dylan, like Cohen, was going through his marriage breakup during this period and his divorce from Sara Lowndes was finalized some three weeks after these recording sessions.

Works Cited

Cohen, Leonard. *Death of a Ladies' Man.* Columbia, 90436, 1977.

———. *Death of a Lady's Man.* London: Deutsch, 1978.

———. "Famous Blue Raincoat." *Stranger Music: Selected Poems and Songs.* Toronto: McClelland, 1994. 153.

Devlin, Jim. *Is This What You Wanted.* N.p.: n.p., 1997.

de Young, Robert. "Behind the Frames." *Metro* 121/122 (2000): 86-94.

Hutcheon, Linda. "Leonard Cohen and His Works." *Canadian Writers and Their Works.* Fiction Series. Vol. 10. Ed. Robert Lecker, Jack David, and Ellen Quigley. Toronto: ECW, 1989. 23-65. 12 vols. 1981-96.

Maslin, Janet. "There's Nothing I Like about It—But It May Be a Classic." *New York Times* 6 Nov. 1977: 18, 40.

Nadel, Ira B. *Various Positions: A Life of Leonard Cohen.* London: Bloomsbury, 1996.

Norris, Ken. "'Healing Itself the Moment It Is Condemned': Cohen's *Death of a Lady's Man.*" *Canadian Poetry* 20 (1987): 55-61.

Scobie, Stephen. "The Counterfeiter Begs Forgiveness: Leonard Cohen and *Leonard Cohen.*" *Proceedings of the Leonard Cohen Conference.* Spec. issue of *Canadian Poetry: Studies, Documents, Reviews* 33 (1993): 7-21.

———. *Leonard Cohen.* Vancouver: Douglas, 1978.

Spector, Phil. "I Would Be Remiss. . . ." *Take This Waltz: A Celebration of Leonard Cohen.* Ed. Michael Fournier and Ken Norris. Quebec: Muses', 1994. 176.

Waxman, Ken. "Rebirth of a Ladies' Man." *Saturday Night* Mar. 1978: 61-63.

Sandra Wynands (essay date winter 1999)

SOURCE: Wynands, Sandra. "The Representation of the Holocaust in *Flowers for Hitler.*" *Essays on Canadian Writing* 69 (winter 1999): 198-209.

[*In the following essay, Wynands discusses the aesthetics of the 1964 volume* Flowers for Hitler, *seen as Cohen's attempt to answer Theodor Adorno's assertion that "[T]o write a poem after Auschwitz is barbaric."*]

For many members of the post-World War II generations who reached intellectual maturity after the war, awareness of the war and the Third Reich raised, beyond the theoretical difficulties of integrating into one's intellectual makeup a completely unprecedented event, a number of personal issues. A decisive factor in the German student revolt of the 1960s, for instance, was critical detachment from the parental generation. These young people had to come to terms with their parents' potentially dubious pasts as party members, or at least with their inexplicable inactivity in the face of pure inhumanity. The ubiquitous generation gap was in this case further exacerbated—rightly or wrongly—by young Germans who viewed their parents as potential murderers or spineless collaborators. Along the same lines, Leonard Cohen might have asked himself where his life would have taken him had he been born in another place—say, Germany. Cohen's generation, Jewish or not, was the first to have to cope with the knowledge and the consequences of the Holocaust, which was a recent event, even in 1964 when Cohen's collection of poems entitled **Flowers for Hitler** was published. This awareness is reflected in the literature of the period, which was written not only with fresh, undigested moral indignation but, as in Cohen's case, also from a perspective of potential personal involvement: Cohen himself belongs to the primary target group of the Nazis' exterminating crusades.

"Where is the poet who can make clear for us Belsen?" (xviii) Irving Layton asks in his preface to *Balls for a One-Armed Juggler* (1963). Layton calls upon intellectuals to speak up against the silence that brings about forgetfulness and to rise to the challenge of trying to make comprehensible the incomprehensible. Just a year later, as if in response to Layton, Cohen publishes **Flowers for Hitler.**

Both Layton (by demanding that the Holocaust be written about) and Cohen (by actually writing about it) have moved beyond a crucial question that provoked substantial controversy in the immediate postwar period, particularly among writers: can and should the Holocaust be written about at all? Do such horrors as happened during the Third Reich defy representation in language altogether? Related to this, and even more important, is the question of whether writing about it is helpful (insofar as it keeps forgetfulness at bay and thus reduces the risk of a phenomenon like the Holocaust reoccurring[1]) or whether writing about it is an indecency toward the suffering of millions, or presumptuousness on the part of the poet? Most famously, Theodor Adorno polemically voiced his objections: *"Noch das äußerste Bewußtsein vom Verhängnis droht zum Geschwätz zu entarten. Kulturkritik findet sich der letzten Stufe der Dialektik von Kultur und Barbarei gegenüber: nach Auschwitz ein Gedicht zu schreiben, ist barbarisch, und das frißt auch die Erkenntnis an, die ausspricht, warum es unmöglich ward, heute Gedichte zu schreiben"* (Die [Die Dialektik der Aufklärung] 30).[2]

Adorno's well-known criticism in his essay *Kulturkritik und Gesellschaft* relies on a twofold assumption, based on the process of aestheticization and repetition inherent in the production of a work of art: by becoming a subject in art, the Holocaust is deprived of its horrify-ing singularity. The work tries to instill in the reader the emotion evoked by the experience by aesthetically recreating it on a more or less mimetic level. It can therefore be maintained, as did Adorno, that any "re-creation" can, in view of the complete incomprehensibility of the event, only be a simulacrum of the original, a weak copy that can never do justice to the experience, that can only be *"Geschwätz"* ("blather") and as such an offence to the sensibilities of people whose lives were destroyed by the Nazi death machine. Taken to its logical conclusion, the argument would be that such an act of re-creation can even be seen as legitimizing the Holocaust by repeating it in an aesthetic realm.

Implicit in this objection is, of course, a disapproval of the aestheticization of the Holocaust. Human beings derive aesthetic pleasure from experiencing art. Again, the question arises whether any kind of pleasure derived (however indirectly) from the disaster the Holocaust represents is an immorality and an offence to the victims. Lawrence Langer suggests, almost perversely, that the inclusion of an inordinate amount of graphic detail of the atrocities could function as a saving grace insofar as a pleasurable response to these details is out of the question. Such an observation merely defers the problem, though, as even though the poem's content is unlikely to instill feelings of pleasure, its success as a poem might. Similarly, the "infiltration into the work of the grotesque, the senseless, and the unimaginable, to such a degree that the possibility of aesthetic pleasure as Adorno conceives of it [?] is intrinsically eliminated" (3), is a doubtful technique. Such a view segregates responses to art into the legitimate and the illegitimate. No matter whether a feeling of pleasure is derived primarily from a poem's subject matter, its careful construction, or a fusion of both, in the ideal case all of these sentiments find their origin in the same root. Paul Celan's poem "Fugue of Death" is extremely moving and instills the feeling of exhilaration that accompanies all great art *because* it achieves such an inseparable unity between content and form—in other words, because it is a well-made poem about the Holocaust. Does Langer suggest a division of pleasure into a superficial and a metaphysical variety, depending on whether it is brought about by conventional aestheticism or its reversal, thus implying that Adorno's criticism could only have been aimed at the former? This distinction seems exceedingly artificial.

Finally, then, the problem of writing after Auschwitz comes down not to questions of technique (superrealism or surrealism) in order to exclude unwanted responses but to fundamental attitudes toward art and a person's faith or distrust in language. Is it possible to move other human beings so deeply through art that making the Holocaust a topic in art is not a condescension? And if so, what strategies are used in order to achieve this objective and do justice to the Holocaust's uniqueness?

Günther Grass says in *Dog Years*: "for even I—you can tell by my modest literary efforts—lack the vital grip, the quivering flesh of reality; the technique is there but not the substance. I've been unable to capture the this-is-how-it-was, the substantial reality that throws a shadow" (471).

By what strategy should artists attempt to capture the essence of what they would like to convey? Langer moves quickly from Grass's famous quote to Peter Weiss's play—or should one say theatrical experiment?—entitled *The Investigation*, which stages with minimum alteration the testimonies of witnesses at the Nuremberg trials. But if "the quivering flesh of reality" were captured in art by replaying the bare facts of reality in a fictional (artificial?) setting, *The Investigation* should have been a dramatic success, yet Langer finds it "singularly undramatic": "oddly, and certainly unintentionally, the result is not a new aesthetic distance, but an aesthetic *indifference*" (31).

Certainly, one interesting question would be whether this verdict of aesthetic indifference is not entirely Langer's personal response. Does it really matter whether the words are spoken by an actual concentration camp survivor or by an impersonator thereof? In other words, do the same words have different effects depending on whether they make their appearance in "reality" or in "art"? The events and their representation in language remain the same. If the stage event is experienced as mediated, then maybe the experience in the courtroom just feeds on a basic voyeurism that the play no longer satisfies. Or is a completely different aesthetic needed in art in order to achieve the same effect—one that moves historical fact inevitably into the realm of fiction in order to do justice to art's own idiosyncratic mechanisms? This would then be a necessary move away from the unembellished "quivering flesh of reality" and potentially toward inadequate *"Geschwätz."* How do artists, and in this particular case Cohen, try to avoid the pitfalls of inadequacy, once they have decided to raise their voices in response to the Holocaust and thus defy the forces that brought it about?

In *The Investigation* the obvious motivation for Weiss to stage the unembellished historical fact is an acute awareness of the inadequacy of one's own imagination when confronted with the Holocaust as an experience. David Rousset writes, "Normal men do not know that everything is possible. Even if the evidence forces their intelligence to admit it, their muscles do not believe it. The concentrationees do know. . . . They are set apart from the rest of the world by an experience impossible to communicate" (168-69). Action and reaction depend upon context. In a given context—say, middle-class everyday life—only a limited range of situations based on an equally limited range of human behavioural patterns are thought likely. Therefore, for lack of experi-

ence, the ordinary imagination does not know how to cope with a phenomenon such as the Holocaust, since its frame of reference is missing.[3] Out of this evolves the belief that there is nothing the creative imagination could add to the event itself. Anything beyond the statement of pure fact would inevitably result in meaningless babble, because the unimaginable cannot be imagined.

Cohen's approach in his poem **"All There Is to Know about Adolph Eichmann"** is reminiscent of Weiss's, except that Cohen moves exclusively in an artistic realm: all of the words were specifically chosen to serve a purpose in an artistic construct. In passport style, the familiar enumeration of a person's identifying features is given, but it turns out that the investigation yields no spectacular results: Eichmann's fact file of distinguishing characteristics fits the vast majority of the human population; he *has no* distinguishing characteristics. He is of ordinary physical appearance and average intelligence.

Cohen does not turn to flamboyantly poetic language, which would tentatively circle and zoom in on the phenomenon "Adolph Eichmann." Instead, he chooses the head-on assault of a mere statement of facts, as if to say that as a poet he can do nothing to make the ugly reality more bearable or digestible. All he can do is make the facts speak for themselves in a language exceedingly sparse so as not to distract from them—and the facts are all the more effective and incomprehensible for their unremarkable nature. Although Eichmann stands out in history for his atrocious deeds, there is nothing in his physical or intellectual makeup or background that singles him out for such a career. A monster, complete with "talons" and "oversize incisors," or a man stricken with "madness" (66) would have implied the comfort of the utterly extraordinary; a case of one in a million. "Madness" would have offered the certainty of an explanation, but the facts are unable to provide any such certainties. Eichmann was singled out only by the opportunity of circumstance: he happened to be in a particular place at a particular time.

An individual's idiosyncratic fate could have been dramatized or given more elaborate descriptions. True to the genre of biography, the poet could have investigated how the individual became what he or she ended up to be through nature and nurture, or causal relationships could have been established between personal tragedies and their disparate psychological effects. But none of this can be done for Eichmann, as he emerges not as an individual but as Everyman. The reader is left with the sheer incomprehensibility of how average human beings can commit crimes such as Eichmann's.

With this goes the awareness of potential reoccurrence: if neither the protagonists nor the circumstances were extraordinary, the implication is that a disaster similar to the Holocaust can repeat itself at any time in a society structured like Western industrialized society. In his book *Modernity and the Holocaust*, Zygmunt Bauman very convincingly reveals the Holocaust to be a phenomenon deeply rooted in modernity: "The truth is that every 'ingredient' of the Holocaust—all those things that rendered it possible—was normal . . . in the sense of being fully in keeping with everything we know about our civilization, its guiding spirit, its priorities, its immanent vision of the world . . ." (8). Bauman reveals the Holocaust to be not a relapse into barbarism[4] as was commonly believed but an outgrowth of modern culture, if not its continuation (110). The Holocaust took neither madmen nor a degenerate society. In their own ways, both Cohen and Bauman arrive at the realization that in order to come to terms with the Holocaust, the conditions that brought it about have to be accepted as part of everyday life.

In Cohen's poetry, this idea resurfaces in the surreal, disjointed ramblings of **"A Migrating Dialogue."** Disparate figures of contemporary Western culture are listed as collaborators in the Nazi crimes: "Joe Palooka manufactured the whips. / Li'l Abner packed the whips in cases. / The Katzenjammer Kids thought up experiments" (72). No peculiarly German form of authoritarianism or mentality produced the Holocaust but rather Western culture as a whole, including exponents of ostensibly "innocent" popular culture such as children's comics. No culture structured along its principles can claim immunity: "I said WIPE THAT SMIRK including the mouth-foam of superior disgust" (72).

In *Flowers for Hitler* this knowledge of the ubiquity of evil results in a reversal of conventional aesthetics. The poems in the book present a series of disparate, surreal glimpses of scenes that revel in the grotesque, the senseless, the tasteless. Rather than follow a logical progression, the individual pictures seem joined together to create an atmospheric effect designed to take the reader into Cohen's world of aesthetic and moral inversions. Cohen becomes a chronicler of the dark side of life, which is at the creative root of the work: *Flowers for Hitler* draws its creative strength from a celebration of all those elements that in conventional aesthetics stand for decay. The back-cover blurb for the book quotes Cohen as saying, "This book moves me from the world of the golden-boy poet into the dung pile of the frontline writer," and Sandra Djwa concludes that "this is a movement from a qualified acceptance of the romantic ideal as it is embodied in art . . . to the decadent romanticism of a *fin de siècle* aesthetic in which the ugly replaces the beautiful as the inspiration for art" (32). Almost as a parallelism to the literature of the Decadence, Cohen looks for new revelations in the experience of failure. Decadence literature follows the same principle: common Romantic motifs are radically reinterpreted, inverted so as to achieve freedom from

the repressive limitations of Victorian, positivist notions of linear growth and progress.

According to Adorno the ideals of the Enlightenment—the further domination of nature in the name of progress in order to enable humans to make their history as autonomous beings, free from the constraints nature puts on them—inevitably turn against themselves (*"Der Fluch des unaufhaltsamen Fortschritts ist die unaufhaltsame Regression"*[5] [*Die* 53]). As soon as nature is reduced to subservience by human instrumentalism, the drive for domination is taken out on other humans who are then dominated in nature's place. Thus, Adorno sees Enlightenment thinking as inevitably spiralling into fascism. As if to break free of the thought patterns that were seen by Adorno to be directly responsible for fascism and the Holocaust, Cohen turns to the same methods with which his Decadent precursors tried to free themselves from the constraints of positivist thought. Even the title of Cohen's book, as has often been noted, evokes Baudelaire's *Les Fleurs du Mal*.

"A Migrating Dialogue," one of the most effective poems in the collection, combines many of the book's distinguishing characteristics. The poem opens with the image of a Nazi henchman in camouflage, travelling abroad with a companion after the war to flee prosecution by the allied forces. He is wearing "a black moustache" (72) (itself, of course, Hitler's own primary characteristic, prominent in every caricature of the man) and cannot quite conceal his mindset: even in camouflage he and his companion are talking "about the gypsies," presumably as being a "subhuman" "race." Cohen establishes firmly what the reader has to expect: he is not going to count himself among the poets who wallow in their own (ostensible) sensitivity and write a poem about the hardships of the Holocaust refugees. Instead, he undermines the expectations of bourgeois morality by perverting the conventional setting: he is going to write about a Nazi on the run from the forces of righteousness.

In the following lines a clearer picture of the "refugee" emerges. His companion showers him with advice: "Don't bite your nails, I told him. / . . . Be cute. / Don't stay up all night watching parades on the Very Very Very Late Show. / Don't ka-ka in your uniform" (72). The advice is centred on simple behavioural patterns that need to be maintained in "exile," so as to remain inconspicuous. It could just as well be directed at an ill-behaved child. Reminiscences of Stanley Kubrick's *Dr. Strangelove* shoot through the reader's head: suddenly the "refugee" is transformed into a pathetic figure who lapses at times of uncontrollable psychological stress into old, deeply ingrained habits, which society does not sanction any longer (parades now have to be watched in the small hours of the morning, "on the Very Very Very Late Show"), and the poem's farcical character is established.

From here onward any logical, linear progression in the poem breaks down and it no longer communicates through a single or unified narrative voice. Some statements the reader can agree with, such as the one that implicates all of Western culture in the possibility of the Holocaust by denying idiosyncratically German traits as its origin. Others are clearly designed to offend the reader's sensibilities: **"Peekaboo Miss Human Soap"** (73) combines the blunt statement of historical fact with a disrespectful way of presenting it.

As an overall poetic strategy, the overstatement of farce or parody is mixed with ideas that sound overly familiar to the reader. Most of the provocative voices reiterate historical statements from the far right of the political spectrum: "Don't believe everything you see in museums. / . . . / Don't tell me we dropped fire into cribs. / I think you are exaggerating" (73). Cohen drives his point home by topping these historical offences with his own, thus intensifying the points: "I think we should let sleeping ashes lie" (73), he says bluntly, as if to rub the reader's nose in the ignorance and obtuseness one is up against.

Mixed in with these statements are allusions that the reader is guaranteed to pick up on and that strike sensitive notes: "Don't tell me we dropped fire into cribs" refers to any air raid during the war, but more specifically to the firebombing of Dresden, and although the reader is unsure of where the narrative voice is coming from, since neither the Nazi protagonist nor his companion are likely to have been part of that, the image of burning Dresden is evoked for effect, not to make sense in any logical progression in the poem; I believe in gold teeth" (73) evokes the mountains of gold teeth extracted from the victims before they were sent to the gas chambers; "There is sad confetti sprinkling / from the windows of departing trains" (73) is reminiscent of both the celebrations that happened around the trains that sent soldiers to the front in World War I and of the boxcars that took Jews to the Nazi death camps. World War I was the most popular war in history. In the reader's mind this exuberance mixes with the awareness that the young men who were called upon to fight in it, and who proudly did, did so with a high probability of not returning from the front. This image of death is topped by the role of trains in the organized mass murder of the Third Reich. A tight network of allusions is established, which makes its point far more forcefully than a graphic description of atrocities could, as more freedom is left to the reader's imagination and a more sweeping treatment of the entire phenomenon is possible.

The slap in the face of (established bourgeois) morality emerges as a way of coming to terms with the horrors the poem describes. In an almost cathartic fashion, Cohen piles one (implied) atrocity on top of the next,

always with a lighthearted flippancy and without going into detail, but in the multiplicity of voices suddenly a single voice emerges that goes beyond the dominant flippancy and articulates concerns similar to Adorno's: "I don't like the way you go to work every morning. / How come the buses still run? / How come they're still making movies?" (73). In the face of the ultimate human tragedy that is the Holocaust, ordinary, everyday pursuits seem mundane, insignificant, and lacking in legitimacy. Apart from the fact that all of these pursuits shrink in significance, Cohen also expresses his incomprehension of the world's "quick" return to business as usual: the world must somehow function differently after it allowed the Holocaust to happen, and if it does not, it is fake, covering up an irrevocably altered conscience and consciousness, suppressing it instead of confronting it.

What the poem conveys very well, then, is the inability to reconcile normality with the knowledge of horror and at the same time the inability to imagine such horror in the presence of normality—which again is reminiscent of Rousset's statement quoted above. The poem is an attempt at overcoming this speechlessness in ramblings that still convey ineffability in their disorganization.

In its stance against conventional aesthetics, *Flowers for Hitler* also takes a stand against formally "good" poems: under no conventional criteria is **"A Migrating Dialogue"** a "good" poem, yet it makes its point precisely because of this lack of form. Cohen thematizes this programmatic stance of the book in the poem entitled **"Style"**: "I will forget my style / I will have no style" (27), he announces—a statement that, as soon as it is elevated to a stance, becomes in itself a style, of course.

Conventional aesthetics, he suspects, has aided the world in lying, and by participating in it he has become a collaborator in the world's insincerity. "I do not know if the world has lied / I have lied" (13), he says in **"What I Am Doing Here,"** the strategically placed poem that, as the title suggests, introduces the collection. In order to free himself from the tangle of these lies and to be true to himself again and escape the *mauvaise foi* in which he has been implicated, he has to radically question every preconceived idea, emblematically epitomized in style (being a set of ideas society has labelled acceptable without questioning its validity). Having become the "front line writer" who (in Cohen's view) functions as the disseminator of the ugly truths of life, he can then lie back, as it were, and "wait for each one of you to confess" (13).

Just like the members of the literary Decadence at the turn of the nineteenth century, then, Cohen presents a work that is a slap in the face of bourgeois sensibilities (cf. Koppen 66). Within the context of Canadian writing at the time, this is a rather unusual and unconventional development: "its awareness of the darker side of human consciousness is a helpful counterbalance to a literary tradition that professes an ignorance of the human animal as complete as any of the Pollyanna Glad books" (42), Djwa says polemically. But Cohen's acute awareness of taking a stance with the book is part of the problem. Again in the blurb on the book's back cover, he says: "I say that there has never been a book like this, prose or poetry, written in Canada: All I ask is that you put it in the hands of my generation and it will be recognized." Cohen is, of course, among other things, referring to the generational conflict outlined at the very beginning of this paper, but he is also making a personal declaration of his function as a poet that is summarized in the golden-boy poet/front-line writer dichotomy. It is his self-conscious positioning of the artist as persona that detracts from the poems as effective works of art about the Holocaust. His conviction that a descent into the underworld of human consciousness and experience is necessary for artistic creation precedes the work and determines it: "Because it is Cohen's thesis that the experience of failure is indispensable for the creation of art, the book becomes a case study of the *fleurs du mal* beauty of such losers," Djwa says (38).

In a way, Cohen brings his own concept of artistic creation along and imposes it on his treatment of his topic. The book's aesthetic is as such only partly determined by the subject matter. Rather, the subject matter lends itself to such a treatment as Cohen has chosen, but it is at least partly used as a vehicle for Cohen's own self-presentation and his concept of artistic creation. Once again Cohen finds his literary forebears in the Decadents, who also set up their own lives as antitheses to bourgeois sensibilities.

By adopting the whole Decadent stance, Cohen avoids a mimetic approach to the Holocaust and thus the dangers outlined in the first pages of this essay: rather than appeal to the readers' empathy, he deliberately alienates them from the work of art by disfiguring it (Langer 3) and thus removing it from the familiar world. What Langer is apparently driving at by his cryptic remark "aesthetic pleasure as Adorno conceives of it" (3) is pleasure derived from a poem that does not make the conventional reception process an issue: in *Flowers for Hitler* the flow of information in the conventional communication model with sender and receiver at opposite ends is obstructed by a "message" that is experienced as unpleasant or perverse (which is the origin of the initial defensive reaction to Decadent art). Thus, the reader is forced to see her—or himself as a radically separate entity rather than one compliant with and pleasurably immersed in the world of the poem. With the reception process becoming an issue, the work takes on vaguely metafictional characteristics: the readers reflect on their own function and that of the poem, and become active constituents in the process. This obstructive mechanism helps Cohen circumvent a representation of the Holocaust.

Notes

1. Cf. Schnurre's comment: *"Lyrik ist sinnlich. Also meint sie das Leben. Also verteidigt sie es. Und da soll sie, nach einem derart globalen Todessieg, schweigen?"* (14; "Poetry is sensual. Therefore it is about life. Therefore it defends it. And now, after such a global victory of death, poetry is supposed to be silent?" [my translation]).

2. "Even the most extreme awareness of the disaster is in danger of degenerating into blather. Cultural criticism is confronted with the final phase of the dialectic of culture and barbarism: to write a poem after Auschwitz is barbaric, and this also influences the realization that articulates why it became impossible to write poems today" (my translation).

3. In fact, one of the problems the Holocaust poses is that the frame of reference was so familiar: inconceivable atrocities happened in a modern, Western, civilized country. What concentrationees learned was not to trust what were believed to be the certainties of everyday life.

4. "The Holocaust was not an irrational outflow of the not-yet-fully-eradicated residues of pre-modern barbarity. It was a legitimate resident in the house of modernity; indeed, one who would not be at home in any other house" (17).

5. "The curse of irresistible progress is irresistible regression" (*Dialectic* 36).

Works Cited

Adorno, Theodor W. *Gesammelte Schriften: Kulturkritik und Gesellschaft 1.* Vol. 10. Frankfurt: Suhrkamp, 1977.

Adorno, Theodor W., and Max Horkheimer. *Dialectic of Enlightenment.* Trans. John Cummings. New York: Continuum, 1990.

———. *Die Dialektik der Aufklärung.* Frankfurt: Suhrkamp, 1981.

Bauman, Zygmunt. *Modernity and the Holocaust.* Ithaca: Cornell UP, 1989.

Cohen, Leonard. *Flowers for Hitler.* Toronto: McClelland, 1964.

Djwa, Sandra. "Leonard Cohen: Black Romantic." *Canadian Literature* 34 (1967): 32-42.

Grass, Günter. *Dog Years.* New York: Harcourt, 1965.

Koppen, Erwin. *Dekadenter Wagnerismus.* Berlin: de Gruyter, 1973.

Langer, Lawrence L. *The Holocaust and the Literary Imagination.* New Haven: Yale UP, 1975.

Layton, Irving. *Balls for a One-Armed Juggler.* Toronto: McClelland, 1963

Rousset, David. *The Other Kingdom.* New York: Reynal, 1947.

Schnurre, Wolfdietrich. "Dichten nach Auschwitz?" *Schreiben nach Auschwitz.* Ed. Peter Mosler. Köln: Bund, 1989. 11-15

Brian D. Johnson (essay date 15 October 2001)

SOURCE: Johnson, Brian D. "Our Poet of the Apocalypse: In the Wake of September 11, Leonard Cohen Reflects on Love and Death—and the War on America." *Maclean's* 114, no. 42 (15 October 2001): 52-8.

[*In the following essay, Johnson reviews Cohen's 2001 album* Ten New Songs *along with biographical insights and a concise overview of Cohen's entire oeuvre.*]

It was the August heat wave, that mirage of endless summer. We talked in the stillness of his un-air-conditioned house in Montreal, as he smoked cigarettes and I drank his strong coffee. After five years in a Zen monastery on California's Mount Baldy, Leonard Cohen was down from the mountain—"back on Boogie Street," to quote his new album. His clinical depression had mysteriously lifted. And in the immobilizing heat of the afternoon, he was buoyant, almost jaunty, as if still discovering the novelty of happiness.

Now it seems like eons ago, the last innocent August when Canadians could choose to worry about global warming, or bask in it, unaware that before the end of the summer they would be worrying about the end of the world. In the wake of Sept. 11, I e-mailed Cohen to ask where he was when he'd heard the news, and to suggest the need for a fresh interview. His reply floated back from cyberspace in the form of an efficient little stanza:

> *writing this from bombay*
> *connections uncertain*
> *will be back in LA end of week*
> *we should talk*

And we did, in a series of phone conversations from his house in Los Angeles—which Cohen calls home most of the time, although he still maintains the house in Montreal. Our first call coincided with his 67th birthday, on Sept. 21. Cohen had just come back from visiting friends in India, which is where he found himself on

the morning the sky fell in Manhattan. "That afternoon," he says, "I went back to my little hotel in Bombay, and the clerk behind the counter, an Indian man, said, 'I'm sorry, the Empire State Building has been knocked over.'" Cohen went up to his room and, like the rest of us, turned on the television. "It was a shock, but not a surprise," he says. "I've been living in an exploded landscape for a long time. I have a place to situate all of this. Because I've felt that things were going to blow up—it wasn't as specific as the twin towers—but I've felt for some time there was going to be a shaking of the situation."

Leonard Cohen may be best known as a poet of romantic disaster, a troubadour who makes "music to slit your wrists by," as one critic famously jibed—or, to a legion of female admirers, simply the sexiest monk alive. But although he is too modest, or shrewd, to admit it, he could also be considered a prophet of the new world disorder: Our Poet of the Apocalypse.

Cohen's incendiary anthems of the late '80s and early '90s, from **First We Take Manhattan** to **The Future,** went much farther afield than his own exquisitely tortured soul. And to listen to them now is a revelation: they illuminate the current geopolitical landscape with chilling prescience. I'll get to the new album later—**Ten New Songs** is a deeply interior meditation on love and death, a balm for the soul that now feels more essential than ever. But first let's go back to **The Future**—and the title song, which has acquired an eerie relevance nine years after its release.

It's a dire manifesto, a fin-de-siècle *Sympathy for the Devil,* in which Cohen assumes the voice of a sinister oracle: "I've seen the future, brother: / it is murder / Things are going to slide in all directions / Won't be nothing / Nothing you can measure any more / The blizzard of the world / has crossed the threshold / and it has overturned / the order of the soul." Cohen goes on to imagine the conflagration of a culture based on privacy and individual freedom: "There'll be the breaking / of the ancient western code / Your private life will suddenly explode / There'll be phantoms / there'll be fires on the road."

Going further back, to 1988, we find Cohen sounding the psyche of extremism with images that could serve as a profile of a suicide bomber: "I'm guided by a signal in the heavens. I'm guided by the birthmark on my skin. I'm guided by the beauty of our weapons. First we take Manhattan, then we take Berlin."

There's no great satisfaction in being a successful prophet of doom, and Cohen feels awkward discussing it. "You can't rub people's faces in it," he says. And this Zen monk—known as Jikan, the Silent One—believes "we're not running the show," so doesn't take any credit for originality. "You don't originate your own thoughts. As Einstein had the humility to say about his equation, these things come from outside. You respond to stimuli, things arise, and a second or two later you claim them."

Cohen's sense of the inevitable, however, doesn't mean he feels America deserved its tragedy, or that we should talk about it in terms of hubris. In fact, he's reluctant to talk about it at all, but when he does he's surprisingly unequivocal.

"I don't feel comfortable putting America down or putting George Bush down," he says. "I hear people in Canada saying George Bush is stupid. First of all, I very seriously doubt whether it's true. And this is not a time to depend on the clichés of the irresponsible—those who are not going to be called on to make any sacrifice. So yes, I think we should get behind America. Or give up Coca-Cola and Nike shoes and gasoline. It's easy to embrace the idea that Ozymandias—the Great—must fall. But we live in the Great and we benefit from the Great, and we drive our cars and wear our clothes and cherish our freedoms of movement and speech. An attack has been made on these institutions."

"In different circumstances," he continues, "it's OK for Canadians to take a slightly superior attitude to America. But we all exist—even the capacity to criticize—all this exists under the umbrella of America's willingness to defend both itself and its critics. So I don't think it's the appropriate moment to bring out our chronic anti-Americanism and parade it as some kind of insulation against events that could very easily have been directed against us ourselves—and still might be. More than 5,000 people have been wiped out. It's not that we haven't done worse. That's not the point. You can say we deserve what we get because we live fat and they starve to death. But this is not the moment. Private discussion, yes. But there's a clear enemy and public discussion weakens us in their eyes. I think it says in the Bible: 'Do not stand idly by your brother's blood.'"

It's jarring to hear Cohen speak so categorically. This is a man you imagine to be beyond the fray of global politics. I asked if the cataclysm made him want to go back up the mountain. "I've always tried to operate on the front line of my own life," he said. "And as I've been at pains to explain, going up to Mount Baldy is not a retreat." Life in the monastery was an engagement. Coming back down was the retreat.

> I'm wanted at the traffic-jam.
> They're saving me a seat.
> I'm what I am, and what I am,
> Is back on Boogie Street.

Distilled from those years of ruthless meditation, Cohen's new album is the most intimate of his career. Spare, hypnotic and wise, it plays as a psalm of reconciliation. It's an aftermath album, finding beauty in the ruins of a life. And after Sept. 11, Cohen was in no mood to promote it. But his Montreal friend Nancy Southam, a theology student, encouraged him, in the belief that the album's timing is providential. "In a wounded world," she says, "these songs have to get out. They provide a spiritual consolation."

The album's tone is one of luxurious solitude. Like a Zen koan, *In My Secret Life* goes behind the lines of a heart that's "crowded and cold," and tries to warm the soul. *By the Rivers Dark* plays as a slow drip of narcotic confession from the depths of Babylon. And the album's masterpiece is an ancient-mariner elegy on unrealized love called *A Thousand Kisses Deep*—a phrase that describes the seacave timbre of Cohen's voice throughout the record. Sinking through uncharted octaves, like a free-diver setting a new record, he finds a register that is low, even for him, a sepulchral rapture of the deep.

Ten New Songs may not be his swan song, but, like Bob Dylan's *Time Out of Mind*, it would do the job nicely, as a coda for a brilliant career. It reminds us that no one sounds remotely like Leonard Cohen. For 40 years, he's steered his own course, as a nomadic sentry in a no man's land between the sacred and the profane, a scorched domain of Greek islands, vintage hotel rooms and monastery bells. He has published two novels, eight volumes of poetry and recorded 13 albums. His first novel, *The Favourite Game*, is now being filmed in Montreal 38 years after its publication. Still cool after all these years, Cohen is the enduring bohemian. And he's achieved the ideal niche of celebrity, the kind that doesn't get in the way—and lets him wait nine years between albums.

Cohen is Canada's most famous poet. He's also our answer to Dylan, a prophetic troubadour with an unlikely voice and a self-made persona. Their styles are as different as sand and glass, but both launched their careers on the tide of Sixties folk music. Now they're pioneering the curious new genre of "elder pop"—like Dylan, Cohen has found fresh authority as a sage staring down the white tunnel of love and death. When Pierre Trudeau was in the last weeks of his life, the former prime minister found solace in listening to some advance tracks from *Ten New Songs*. Cohen, a friend of Trudeau, was an honorary pallbearer at his funeral. And like Trudeau, he is one of those iconic Canadians who came out of a time when anything seemed possible.

> May everyone live,
> And may everyone die.
> Hello, my love,
> And my love, Goodbye.

I was on vacation at a Laurentian lake when I got the call to interview Cohen in Montreal. I picked up a quart of raspberries at a farmer's stall on the highway, because . . . well, because some kind of offering felt appropriate. Cohen has always prized gentle acts of supplication, like *Suzanne*'s tea and oranges that come all the way from China. And whenever a journalist shows up on his doorstep, Leonard is offering something. Plying our photographer with chopped liver on toast at his house in Los Angeles. Offering a shower to a writer from *Saturday Night*.

His Montreal home is a century-old, three-story row house on a parkette off Blvd. St-Laurent, not far from where the late Mordecai Richler grew up. He bought it for just $7,000 in 1972, and eventually bought the house next door, where he created a small Zen centre, Inside, Cohen's home is plain and unrenovated. Bare white walls, a scattering of oriental rugs. I find him in a tiny courtyard at the back, posing for pictures. In the sweltering heat, he looks unnaturally cool: pinstriped pants, black shirt and matching suede slippers.

Urging coffee on me, Cohen steps into the small kitchen and heaps a Melitta filter to the brim with espresso. Perched on the stove is a little figurine of Catherine Tekakwitha, the 17th-century Mohawk saint from his novel *Beautiful Losers*. When I mention it, Leonard ushers me into an adjoining bathroom, which is bigger than the kitchen, and shows me an old portrait of her above the sink. It's a bathroom you could spend time in, with an old-fashioned tub, a chair and a Persian rug. "It was handy when the kids were growing up," he says, referring to Adam and Lorca, his children with former partner Suzanne Elrod (not the Suzanne of the song)—Adam, 29, is a singer-songwriter and Lorca, 27, owns an antique store; both live in Los Angeles.

In the kitchen, two publicists from his record company compose a fruit plate. I add my raspberries, which Leonard samples with reverence. And he opens up a wicker basket, as if it contains a miracle, and offers bagels—"they're two days old, but they're still good." Then suggesting we talk upstairs "where it's quiet," he nimbly mounts a narrow staircase to his bedroom, coffee and cigarettes in hand. We sit at a large antique pine table by the open window. In the room there's a fold-up writing desk. A glass-fronted bookcase displays some Hebrew torns, and *The Essential Guide to Prescription Drugs*. In the corner, a white bed. Next to it nothing but a small old TV and a box of Kleenex.

I ask Cohen why he came down from the mountain in 1999. "I don't know," he says, lighting a Vantage. "For the same reason I went up, which is also unclear." He laughs, then explains he'd been associated with Mount Baldy's Zen community for 30 years and wanted to "intensify" his relationship with it, and with his Japanese teacher, Kyozan Joshu Sasaki—or Roshi—who's now 94 "and in radiant health." For five years,

Cohen followed a punishing regimen of rising before dawn to meditate for long hours. But he tempered his piety with creative truancy.

"I found the meditation hall an excellent place to work on songs. I was supposed to be calming my mind or directing it to other areas, but I was working on rhymes for *A Thousand Kisses Deep*." One day Cohen—who also served as Roshi's cook, driver and occasional drinking buddy—confessed he wasn't really meditating. In his broken English, Roshi gave him his blessing: "Follow song OK."

Cohen is at a loss to explain where his depression went. "I'd tried everything going," he says, "from self-medication to pharmaceuticals to all the excesses that were available in rock 'n' roll. And nothing seemed to work. But I read that the brain cells associated with anxiety begin to die as you get older. I don't know if they're dead, but they're ailing. The depression has lifted in the past three years, and this record comes out of that graceful event."

While *Ten New Songs* may be Cohen's most ascetic album, it's also his most collaborative. He wrote the words, but his friend Sharon Robinson wrote, arranged, produced and performed virtually all the accompaniment on the record, as well as enveloping his wine-dark voice with layers of her own ethereal vocals.

"My range is very limited," says Cohen. "The four notes I can sing get lower and lower. I like it down there. It's close to speaking." It's a voice that sounds like incense. But aside from one guitar track, the instrumentation is completely electronic—"dinky factory music" is how Cohen has described the sound he feels comfortable with. He doesn't like the notes to compete with the words. Even when he's touring with live musicians, he says, "you've got to keep beating them back."

On the new album, however, there is no band. And it has such a haunting intimacy it sounds like Cohen and his co-writer are singing with one mouth. "I feel it's really Sharon's record in a certain way," he says. "Her presence is very strong." Robinson also co-wrote *Everybody Knows* on his 1988 album, *I'm Your Man*. And they'd been planning to write again together ever since. "Out of the blue," recalls Robinson, "Leonard said, 'I'd like you to work on a record with me and it would just take a couple of weeks.' It took two years."

In Los Angeles, Cohen and Robinson worked out of their home studios, swapping digital tracks back and forth. The third partner in their musical ménage was Cohen's veteran engineer, Leanne Unger. Because Cohen's studio is in his garage, which isn't soundproof, he had to get up very early to record his vocals—before the birds started to sing. "It was the same sort of regimen I led up on the mountain," he says. "I was the cook. Leanne and Sharon would come around noon, and I'd make them lunch. We'd work all day, then I'd often prepare them dinner."

Robinson, who's been married for 15 years, has known Cohen since 1979, when he recruited her to join his tour as a backup singer. He's also the godfather of her 12-year-old son. Asked if she and Leonard were ever involved, she declines comment, then, after a pause, she laughs. "I guess I just answered the question." When she was on tour with Cohen 20 years ago, women were constantly drawn to him, she says. "They would always be trying to get in to see him after the show, and there always seemed to be one—not always, but frequently—who would end up spending the evening with him."

Cohen's mystique among women is legendary. They seem to like the fact that he worships them. I've interviewed the likes of Tom Cruise and Harrison Ford, but no one has elicited as much vicarious interest from my female friends as Leonard. Even my wife still says, wistfully, "If only I'd slept with Leonard Cohen." She wrote him a fan note in the late '60s. He replied from Manhattan's Chelsea Hotel, in purple ink on onionskin paper with one sentence: "Thank you for your most perfect letter."

A friend of mine once spent a night with him in Montreal around the same time. "I went back to his hotel," she says, "a Greek hotel where all the staff spoke Greek and everyone seemed to know him as if he'd lived there for years. In the morning, I awoke to find him already up and sneaking into his jeans as if to escape. With one leg in and one leg out, he caught me watching and hastened to the bed to assure me it had been a great night, but that he had to leave because 'I'm a poet and I have to move on.' Later, in New York I ran into quite a few girls who knew Leonard and claimed to be in constant contact by some sort of cosmic arrangement."

Ellen Seligman, the poet's editor at McClelland & Stewart, says, "Not all men are as good as Leonard is in making women feel that he's completely interested. He's not garrulous in a small-talk way. He always invites other people to talk. That is the sexiest thing of all." Seligman says that, phoning from another time zone, he would leave messages for her in the middle of the night. "You'd hear this incredible, husky voice, saying, 'Darling, I just have one more revision.' I'd play it on the speakerphone, and the women in the office would swoon."

Cohen's last visible romance, with actress Rebecca De Mornay, ended when he found he couldn't commit to settling down and having more children. Asked if he'd prefer to live the rest of his life alone or with someone, he says: "I want to live with everyone. That's Boogie Street."

There is, in fact, an actual Boogie Street, he adds. "It's in Singapore. I don't know if it's still there." He stumbled across it years ago when coming home from an Australian tour. By day, he says, it was a bazaar—he found a box of Leonard Cohen bootleg tapes on sale for a dollar apiece—"and at night it was a scene of intense and alarming sexual exchange. To me, Boogie Street is that street of work and desire, the ordinary life, that is relieved by the embrace of your children or the kiss of your beloved, or the peak experience in which you yourself are dissolved. As my old teacher said, 'Paradise is a good place to visit but you can't live there because there are no toilets or restaurants.'"

For Leonard Norman Cohen, all Boogie Streets lead back to Montreal, where he was born in 1934, one of two children in an affluent Westmount Jewish family. His father, who owned a clothing business, died when Leonard was 9. "Outside of that event, which seemed to be perfectly natural at the time," Cohen dismisses his childhood as "very ordinary." His says his teenage rebellion was limited to the "mild delinquency" of sneaking into movies restricted to those over 16. "We'd dress in suits and ties and put Kleenex in our heels to make us look older." As a 17-year-old student at McGill University, Cohen formed a country-and-western trio called the Buckskin Boys, and began to publish poetry. Winning acclaim for *Let Us Compare Mythologies* (1956) then *The Spice Box of Earth* (1961), he travelled to Europe on a grant and spent seven prolific years on the Greek island of Hydra.

Cohen came from the same generation of Jewish Montreal as Richler, though from its upper crust. And like Richler, he showed a talent as a comic novelist, casting a version of himself as *The Favourite Game* (1963), the portrait of a Jewish poet coming of age in Montreal. From the first love scene—of his hero undressing a girl and experiencing the "kind of surprise when the silver paper comes off the triangle of Gruyère in one piece"— his gift for prose was obvious.

But unlike Richler, he didn't stay put. With the verbal acrobatics of his next and last novel, *Beautiful Losers* (1966), a profane feat of acid-inspired delirium, Cohen catapulted himself out of the literary fold and never looked back. He was recruited by Columbia's legendary John Hammond—who also discovered Dylan and Bruce Springsteen—and *Songs of Leonard Cohen* became the folk-boudoir sound track for 1968. Cohen would earn his place in the CanLit canon, but it could not contain him. As his longtime friend poet Irving Layton once said: "Leonard's always had yearnings for sainthood."

When I raise the notion of sainthood with Cohen, he deadpans without missing a beat: "It's right down the line. There's the Governor General's Award, the Pulitzer, the Fulbright and then sainthood."

Cohen shows me a small bronze bust of Layton, who at age 89, is now afflicted with Parkinson's disease. "I saw him when I was here for Trudeau's funeral. It was one of his good days. But he pretended not to recognize me. I said, 'It's Leonard.' He said, 'Leonard who?' I said, 'Leonard Cohen.' He turned to his nurse and asked, 'Who's Leonard Cohen?' I was completely taken in. Then he laughed—'Leonard!'" Layton then talked about how his sexual desire had diminished with age. Cohen asked when that had begun to happen. "Oh, when I was about 15 or 16," Layton replied. When I ask about his own famous libido, Cohen demurs: "It's a very uneventful landscape, very peaceful."

He doesn't spend much time in Montreal these days. He prefers to be close to his children in Los Angeles. And he is nicely anonymous there, an obscure star in celebrity heaven. In Montreal, he is more easily recognized "But it's not an inconvenience or a menace," he says. "A few days ago, I was walking down St. Lawrence Boulevard and stopped to look in this window. A young man beside me said, 'Thanks, Leonard, have a nice evening.' And much of it is on that level."

To see him in his white room, in the house he bought for a song three decades ago, Leonard looks so completely at home. So I wonder:

"Where would you like to . . . ?"

"Die?"

"That's the word I was looking for."

"In that bed would be nice," he says, pointing to the soft whiteness in the corner of the room.

> *The ponies run, the girls are young,*
> *The odds are there to beat.*
> *You win a while, and then it's done—*
> *Your little winning streak.*
> *And summoned now to deal*
> *With your invincible defeat,*
> *You live your life as if it's real,*
> *A Thousand Kisses Deep.*

At his front door, Cohen steps out and looks around, as if dipping his toe into the city. I want to take some groceries back to the lake, so I ask if he knows a fish store in the neighbourhood. There used to be one up the street, he says, then offers to take me there. As we cross the parkette, he explains it once was Carré Vallières but is now called Parc Portugal. It occurs to me that one day it probably will be Carré Leonard Cohen. We pass a handsome grey-haired woman who smiles hello without breaking stride. Leonard smiles hello back.

"See what I mean?" he says.

"Do you know her?"

"No," he replies, having confirmed his fans are cool enough to leave him in peace.

We find the fish store. Even on ice, the salmon looks wilted from the heat. I deliberate for an awkward moment, wondering how I've ended up shopping for fish with Leonard Cohen. We head back without buying. Leonard talks about his plans: to finish a book of some 250 poems, to record another album of his own music, to tour again—"I like singing and drinking"—and first to spend some time with friends in India. But he is cautious to add, as he has learned to do when looking forward to the Future: "God willing."

Laurenz Volkmann (essay date 2003)

SOURCE: Volkmann, Laurenz. "'Flowers for Hitler': Leonard Cohen's Holocaust Poetry in the Context of Jewish and Jewish-Canadian Literature." In *Refractions of Germany in Canadian Literature and Culture,* edited by Heinz Antor, Sylvia Brown, John Considine and Klaus Stierstorfer, pp. 207-37. Berlin: Walter de Gruyter, 2003.

[*In the following essay, after surveying the philosophical and critical literature concerning the treatment of the Holocaust in art, Volkmann discusses Cohen's representation of the Holocaust in* Flowers for Hitler.]

Pop musician, singer-songwriter, media personality, Canadian with a penchant for melancholic, *ennui*-ridden, songs, including the occasional hit record such as **"Suzanne", "Like a Bird on the Wire"** (1969), or, more recently, **"First We Take Manhattan"** (1988)—born in Montreal in 1934, Leonard Cohen is known to a larger audience as an ageing rock star with the status of fading, albeit persevering celebrity. He remains a cult figure with a following of dedicated *afficionados*. Little do contemporary recipients of popular culture know that he was once, back in the late 1950s and early to mid 1960s, deemed to be the future of Canadian poetry. Having established himself with a string of verse collections—*Let Us Compare Mythologies* (1956), *The Spice-Box of Earth* (1961), *Flowers for Hitler* (1964), and finally *Selected Poems 1956-1968* (1968)—Cohen took up a musical career in the late 1960s. To be exact, his performance at the Newport Folk Festival, Rhode Island / New York, marked the beginning of the long chapter of Cohen as the musician with a plaintive voice and dark lyrics. Since then, he has presented more than 500 concerts, with thirteen albums and eleven books as products of his artistic career. In any case, his former achievements as an author have been superseded by those of the musician. As Ira Nadel remarks in summary, "Today, Cohen is thought of first as a musician and second as a writer, an identity not entirely out of touch with his efforts at self-promotion and management."[1] It is not surprising, therefore, to find only little direct or specific academic writing on Leonard Cohen as a literary figure from the period when he was mainly seen as a singer-songwriter, especially the 1980s and early 1990s. Most critical articles and books were written at the beginning of his literary career, and, then again, as a late appreciation, in the 1990s, when he was less prominent as a popstar. Most publications are biographical, almost without exception rather uncritical when it comes to his art of self-fashioning as the melancholic man of underground pop.[2] In fact, his avid followers in academia have produced a number of highly celebratory biographies and laudatory articles, ranging from Christof Graf's painstakingly encyclopaedic *Leonard Cohen. Partisan der Liebe* ("Partisan of Love"), 1996, to the recent critical volume of *Essays on Canadian Writing* from 1999, dedicated entirely to the author. His two novels, *The Favourite Game* (1970) and prominently *Beautiful Losers* (1966), are still regarded to be among the first and best fictions of Canadian postmodernism, a status owing much to Linda Hutcheon's critical appraisal.[3] Given this abundance of recent critical reassessment, which is mostly focused on Cohen the public and private persona and/or his career as a musician, with his poetic ambitions often interpreted as an early artistic phase which led on to a wider artistic extension, there is a dearth of truly critical readings of Leonard Cohen's early writings, especially his poetry. Some critics have been grappling with the interrelated themes of Cohen's Jewish identity and the theme of his fictional coping with Nazism, including the harrowing Holocaust "experience". However, apart from a few scattered remarks on these issues and a recent thematically focused article on "Cohen and the Holocaust",[4] little has been written on this issue. Yet, as the topic of Jewish poetry and the Holocaust has proven to be one of the major issues of Jewish literature and also of perennial importance to critics from Germany, it would seem to be of special interest to trace and gauge Leonard Cohen's early writing within the multi-facetted context of Jewish and non-Jewish literary responses to Nazi atrocities, particularly the Holocaust.

By first sketching the literary background to Cohen's early writings, this article attempts to present a more complex approach to the author's literary explorations of the issue. It is only within the historical context of other literary texts that Cohen's specific contribution can be weighed adequately. Such an approach will not only be intertextual, but will also place Cohen's writings within the framework of controversial ethical and critical discussions about how literature should deal with the "unspeakable" horrors of Hitler's attempted genocide. By means of constructing this larger interpretative framework, a complex web of interpretative questions can be assessed. First, an essential question would be whether the relative absence of explicit or direct references to the Holocaust or to Nazism in Cohen's writings is to be taken at face value or whether we have to take into consideration a "hidden" subtext of omnipresence of this theme. This question entails a quest for concealed allusions in Cohen's texts. An interrelated question would be whether Cohen's poetry could be best categorised as another version of the post-Holocaust "poetry of guilt". This would include further questions such as how Cohen's specific contribution to this tradition can best be characterised.

Further, more evaluative pivotal questions concern Cohen's technique of presenting the Holocaust in his writings. As I will argue and demonstrate, he either neglects the topic in what I would like to call a gesture of purposeful omission, leaving his readers' expectations thwarted if, for instance, a collection entitled ***Flowers for Hitler*** includes only scattered and seemingly frivolous poetic fragments directly referring to the title's alleged topic. Or Cohen, in the few striking instances in which he directly treats the topic of Nazism or the Holocaust, shoehorns semiotically highly charged *topoi* of the Holocaust into a simulacrum of *fleurs-du-mal* imagery, with this randomness and unconnectedness creating a scandalous and provocative effect.

To approach the topic from a different angle, the dimensions of the problem with which any interpretation of Cohen's poetry with regard to the Holocaust theme is faced can best be illustrated by a closer look at the following excerpt from Loranne S. Dorman and Clive L. Rawlins' biography of the artist:

> Eli Mandel [the eminent Canadian-Jewish poet] once asked him [Leonard Cohen] why the concentration camps—that ultimate symbol of lostness, not merely lost freedom—appeared in all his books. Said Leonard, "Well, because I would like to be free of them." He was thereby claiming that freedom—the freedom of 'a bird on the wire . . . like the drunk in a midnight choir . . . like a worm on a hook.'[5]

Both question and answer are indicative of what is at stake when interpreting Cohen's early poetry and fiction. For although traces of concentration camps crop up in all of Cohen's books, they do so in a seemingly haphazard way, never carrying the main theme, motive, or meaning of the book, often not even of the poem or chapter in a novel. As has been argued and as I will discuss later in this paper, they may be interpreted as appearing in a trivialised, travestied form, treating a serious topic in a "burlesque and ludicrous" manner (as the *OED* defines "travesty"). Simultaneously, Cohen's answer in the interview with Mandel hints at an interrelated problem of Cohen's poetry. As the poet here alludes to his usage of Holocaust metaphors as a means of personal catharsis, related not so much to the burden of his Jewish heritage, that of the "survivors", but rather to anxieties of any sort, his "utilisation" of the Holocaust theme has sometimes been questioned as being either a self-indulgent act of soul searching (the allusion Cohen uses here is to his second single **"Bird on the Wire"**), accompanied by an all-too-predictable sweeping "condemnation [. . .] of those tyrants who set themselves against humanity, of whatever race or creed".[6] Or it could appear as a tasteless toying with the heavily laden imagery of Jewish suffering for the mere sake of creating counter-cultural poetic expressions.

After this lengthy introduction, which should serve as an outline of the main interpretative problems concerning Cohen's early poetry, I would like to present two possible general trajectories for such a critical reading. The stance of "eclectic detachment" as germane to Canadian poetry can be viewed as presenting one interpretative guideline. It can be connected with the broad approach of "imagology", which is the discussion of racial and national stereotypes in literature. After introducing and briefly commenting on these two theoretical models for interpretation, I would like to delineate the topic of Jewish poetry after the Holocaust in general before focusing specifically on Jewish-Canadian responses. Then Leonard Cohen's writing will be placed into this context, first by means of critical categorisations of his poetry as a whole, then with a particular emphasis on the theme of how the Holocaust and Nazism are dealt with in his poems. This will include a short analysis of the theme's impact on his novels. In a final interpretative section, a number of his poems will be interpreted with a view to their tackling of the theme, which will eventually lead to an overall assessment of controversies connected with Cohen's handling of the Holocaust and Nazism.

CANADIAN POETRY'S "ECLECTIC DETACHMENT" AND THE APPROACH OF "IMAGOLOGY"

It has been one of the dearest and most simplistic notions of critics of Canadian literature that the literature of the United States is that of a congealed melting pot, while the texts they study reflect a pluralistic, polyglot ethnic mosaic.[7] Thereby, the latter's "truly" multicultural national concept of diversity is privileged. Whatever the discursive uses of such dichotomies, the self-image of Canadian literature has been shaped to a large degree by both its potential as well as its option to draw freely on diverse cultures and traditions without the risk of succumbing to cultural pressure towards creating a unified, homogeneous "Canadian" literature. This entails the relative "freedom" to select one's influences from a wide range of cultural, specifically literary sources, both Canadian and transnational—i. e. often the writer's ancestral national background(s). This distinctively multicultural quality of Canadian literature was described, for instance, by A. J. M. Smith, editor of

The Oxford Book of Canadian Verse. In his remarks on Canadian poetry he argued:

> But the Canadian poet has one advantage—an advantage that derives from his position of separateness and semi-isolation. He can draw upon French, British, and American sources in language and literary conventions; at the same time he enjoys a measure of detachment that enables him to select and adapt what is relevant and useful.[8]

For this sense of not quite belonging to a homogeneous national literary tradition, Smith coined the phrase "eclectic detachment", which has circulated widely in discussions of Canadian poetry. With reference to it, the Canadian poet may be viewed as creating, in the ancient manner of the poet as myth-maker, the various mythologies of a modern Canada with a desire and even need for national myths. As these new myths in "A Country without Mythologies", as a poem by Douglas LePan from 1948 is entitled, are being created, poets are self-consciously aware of the limitations of their contributions—they can merely contribute one tiny part to the "mytho-discursive" construction of the cultural mosaic which is Canada. This marks their respective national or racial contribution.

In the case of the Jewish contribution, it can be argued that Jewish identity, and with it its literary voice, claims its place in Canadian culture as do those of other nations and races. It introduces another "foreign" note, as has been observed, into the rich plurivocity of Canadian literature. As one critic noted, "the English language was a precious jar into which might be poured the rich wine of the Jewish tradition."[9] And the Jewish-Canadian poet A. M. Klein pondered the question "what it means [. . .] to inherit the wonder and the burden of the Jewish past. This involves a sense of mystery, of customs and references accepted but not fully comprehended."[10] Of these customs and traditions, it must be stressed, the experience of the Holocaust has proven to be seminal. All Jewish writing, and with it all Canadian-Jewish writing, is shaped by the post-Holocaust perspective.[11] Indeed, the artistic exploration of these haunting memories may be the most important contribution of Jewish-Canadian literature to Canadian culture.

If, as I have just argued, Jewish literary contribution to Canada rests on its presentation of the Holocaust, this will by its very nature involve both (historic) images of Jewish identities as victims as well as images of the oppressors, persecutors and perpetrators of genocide, the Germans. Such representations always involve the issue of national and racial stereotypes, clichés, and prejudices. Complex questions abound, for example the question of whether the construction of Germans in literary texts on the persecution of Jews and the Holocaust differentiates between Nazi criminals (for example, SS officers in concentration camps) and the "average" German who, as has been argued, may have been ignorant of Nazi atrocities. In other words, does a text presuppose a communal guilt of all Germans by lumping them together in the discursive description as evil and brutal mass-murderers, or does it come towards a more complex image of Germany and the Germans? Given the lasting preoccupation with the Nazi past among German intellectuals, it is not surprising to note the existence of a fairly influential school of literary criticism dealing with national stereotypes (of course, not only referring to the German as Nazi), their presence, meaning and influence in literary texts.[12] This approach of "Imagologie" ("imagology") has been defined by one of its main scholars as "the study of the images of a foreign nation, of its culture and institutions etc. as they are reflected in literature [. . .] as part of a comprehensive interest in national stereotypes".[13] A major result of studies on representations of Germans in Anglophone literatures by critics like Blaicher, Stanzel, and Zacharasiewicz[14] has been quite sobering for the German reader. Most strikingly, Zacharasiewicz has discovered a fossilisation of traditional stereotypes of Germany in both popular and elitist cultural presentations in the United States.[15] There is a time-honoured tradition of highlighting especially the darker sides of the German past, particularly the Hitler years, and their lasting negative impact on contemporary Germany. In novels such as John Hawkes's *The Cannibal* (1949), Kay Boyle's *Generation without Farewell* (1960), Kurt Vonnegut's *Slaughterhouse-Five* (1969), Thomas Pynchon's *Gravity's Rainbow* (1973), Walter Abish's *How German Is It* (1980) and Walter Percy's *The Thanatos Syndrome* (1987), clichés and prejudices of Germans as former or would-be Nazis prevail. As Zacharasiewicz sums up his findings, "Ever since they started to deal intensely with the Holocaust [in the wake of the American film *Holocaust*], American fictions, films and TV have made the SS officer, the concentration camp fascist and the military type out to be the almost exclusive embodiment of the German."[16]

Therefore, if my discussion is to trace the ways in which Jewish poetry responded to the Holocaust, it will have to analyse and gauge the ways in how such poetry draws on a quasi-monolithic repertoire of "imagological" stereotypes of both the Germans and (as I will delineate) of Jewish suffering during the Nazi period. Against the background of the aforesaid, I will also regard how Jewish poets engage in what can be called the cultural proliferation of a relatively "self-referential" intertextual network of stereotypes—that of presentations of both Germans and the Holocaust.

Jewish Identity and the Holocaust in Jewish and Jewish-Canadian Poetry

W. H. Auden is said to have been the first poet of some repute to mention a concentration camp in verses. One of his "Sonnets from China" includes the following lines:

And maps can really point to places
Where life is evil now.
Nanking. Dachau.[17]

It was with lines written by survivors of the death camps, however, that the poetry of the Holocaust emerged.[18] An anthology of such poems written in the camps or after liberation would include many verses written in Hebrew, which were only partly translated into English. It would feature authors such as Natan Alterman, Yehuda Amichai, Hillel Bavli, Israel Efrat, Uri Tzvi Greenberg, Haya Kadmon, Yehuda Karni, Yitzhak Katzenelson, Abba Kovner, Zalman Schneor, David Shimoni, and Avraham Shlonsky.[19] In England, the first poems on the Holocaust were written by refugee poets such as Karen Gershon, Lotte Kramer, and Michael Hamburger in English. In North America, the tradition of Holocaust poetry began with authors like Jacob Glatstein, Anthony Hecht, and Elie Wiesel, but also William Heyen and Czeslaw Milosz.[20] Among the most prominent poets of the death camps writing in German, Nelly Sachs and markedly Paul Celan deserve mentioning. Particularly, the latter's "Todesfuge" ("Fugue of Death") from 1952 became one of the most anthologized poems in post-war Germany and is still on many school curricula. With its dense, intricate, and referentially dark imagery of the death camps, it may well be one of the most paradigmatic poetic responses to the Holocaust. This exemplary nature is shared by another well-known poem, Yevgeny Yevtushenko's "Babi Yar". Written in 1962, it commemorates the killings of tens of thousands of Jews at Babi Yar, a ravine near Kiev in the Ukraine, in September 1941.

As all poetry, the poetry of the Holocaust is chosen to transform emotions into words. It is about presenting a personal reaction to something which is truly "unrealizable". Whatever lyrical forms and expressions are used by the individual poet, a common question is voiced in all Holocaust poetry, implicitly or explicitly: What was the meaning of the Holocaust? And how does the poet come to grips with the historical burden of both terror and guilt? Against this background, the Jewish-Canadian author Eli Mandel has hinted at a double dilemma any author dealing with the Holocaust is faced with. First, that the Holocaust cannot be viewed as a historical aberration. On the contrary, its horrors transcend all other historical experiences. This can be gleaned from Mandel's remark that the Holocaust is "a crack in creation, a flaw, a blemish".[21] In this statement, Mandel refers to similar observations by George Steiner and Elie Wiesel. Steiner once concluded that the true horror of the Holocaust was that it was intrinsic to German if not Western civilization: "The blackness [. . .] rose from within, and from the core of European civilization."[22] In a second remark, Mandel adds that this demands a special language, "a new form unheard of".[23]

In his remarks, Mandel voices the double dilemma of poets dealing with the Holocaust. The first dilemma is clearly how one deals with the fact of being a survivor. How does one free oneself of a nightmare? How does one lament the dead? How does one cope with the burden of guilt, "the predicament of living *after*".[24] Writing about the Holocaust becomes a moral obligation of the survivors, with poetry serving as a memorial. However, the second dilemma remains. How does one put into words the unaccountable? How can poetry do justice to an unspeakable cruelty of the magnitude of Auschwitz and Bergen-Belsen? Will words simply "crack"? This question of finding appropriate language, to convey what cannot be conveyed, has been at the heart of any discussion of Holocaust poetry. As George Steiner put it, "The world of Auschwitz lies outside speech as it lies outside reason."[25] Most prominently, T. W. Adorno's sweeping statement "No poetry after Auschwitz"—"nach Auschwitz ein Gedicht zu schreiben, ist barbarisch"[26]—defies all human ability to convey the tragic truth.

Most indicative of the high degree of self-reflexivity which is exhibited by authors of the Holocaust is a poem by Chaim Chamiel. Composed on the eve of the twentieth anniversary of Israel's independence, it expresses the following in stanza II:

> Forgive me, Lord
> That I am still incapable
> To praise and write poems:
> For my heart
> Is still as bitter as an olive
> And my words still
> Stammer.[27]

Silence and fragmented language appear as a corollary to the situation. This response of hesitation and self-conscious probing appears typical of European poets—"who felt that language itself had been damaged, possibly beyond creative repair, by the politics of terror and mass-murder."[28] Following Adorno's suggestions, *engagée* poetry emerged as the ideal mode.

A different picture is presented with respect to (North) American Jewish responses to the Holocaust. Here, as has been stated, only an indirect identification was possible. As Dittmar puts it rather bluntly, "Here American Jews living in a land of affluence, there six million deaths."[29] This has been interpreted as a historical antinomy which by its very nature appears irresolvable.

> How were these two elements of Jewish experience to be reconciled? The only honest answer was that they could not be: it was a division which anyone who retained even the faintest sense of Jewish identity would have to live with as best he could.[30]

These irreconcilable differences fostered a stereotypical repertoire of images and motives of death and suffering in the concentration camps. To go beyond this soon-established archive of literary topoi has remained a most difficult task for any North American writer on the topic.[31] In fact, Holocaust imagery has become dislodged from its original context to be used for its highly charged emotional significance in connection with other themes of post World War Two poetry. As Murdoch remarks, "Images deriving from the horrors of the Nazi concentration camps have become commonplace in much modern lyric poetry".[32] A range of central motives has established itself:[33] the death trains and the journey to the camp; music as accompanying the misery; the focus on small things, often on what is left from the crematorium or the gas chambers; the shoes, ashes, and the smoke from the chimneys. Other archetypal motifs such as that of the danse macabre evolved, with the Jews playing at their own funeral. If individuals are mentioned, they, again, are iconic, such as Anne Frank. The Eichmann trial at the beginning of the 1960s, and Hannah Arendt's account of it, published as *Eichmann in Jerusalem,* 1963, ensued a spate of literary reactions to the Holocaust, unprecedented at any time since the war, creating a heightened historical consciousness.

> The trial has been the pivotal point in the development of books on virtually every aspect of the Holocaust. The trial finally forced recognition that the Holocaust was an experience whose influence and meanings touch virtually every significant human concern.[34]

The media attention created by the trial and later by the American TV series *Holocaust* fostered further proliferation of concentration camp imagery. In literature, two modes of presenting the Holocaust established themselves: extreme realism, with the writer probing into the horrors of the past as they render themselves through a mimetic, factual account, or surrealism, by which a nightmarish ambience of horror and sometimes paralysis is evoked.[35] Drastic realism and factual enumerations are featured, for example, in Charles Reznikoff's *Holocaust* (1975), a long poem in which Nazi officials serve as speakers to reveal inhuman, bureaucratic attitudes. Kohn sums up his study of numerous highly emotional and individualistic death-camp poems which capture the horror of inhuman barbarity as poetic eyewitness accounts:

> Thus, the entire gamut of poetry reads like a chronicle of the bloody events perpetrated by the Nazis and their collaborators and the indictment of ethically bankrupt Western Civilization.[36]

In popular culture, arguably as a result of media attention, the Holocaust was not only appropriated by the dominant, non-Jewish American culture; other minorities turned to Auschwitz imagery. A case in point were African-American authors who felt that by liking their ethnic fate to that of the Jews during Hitler's tyranny they could draw from a more provocative set of images than those based on the years of slavery.[37] When James

Baldwin referred to Black militants in terms of the victims of concentration camps and called Angela Davis "a Jewish housewife in a boxcar headed for Dachau",[38] he caused a flurry of angry responses. An even more controversial usage of Holocaust imagery was exhibited by the American poet Sylvia Plath. In her poems "Daddy" and "Lady Lazarus" (from the *Ariel* collection), she intertwined her personal traumas with images of the Holocaust. This raised critical questions of not only congruence, but also taste and ethics. The following lines are from "Lady Lazarus" (1962):

> A sort of walking miracle, my skin
> Bright as a Nazi lampshade,
> My right foot
>
> A paperweight
> My face a featureless, fine
> Jew linen.[39]

Such instances may be regarded as crude or cynical, if not offensive connections with the Auschwitz imagery. The question whether this devalues the suffering of countless victims of Nazi terror, mechanically turning the aspects of horror into literary museum pieces, has been raised. Certainly, this does not lead to poetic identification with the victims, an involvement against anti-Semitism and the forces that gave rise to Nazi atrocities. In any case, Plath's poetry serves as an example of the popularisation and trivialisation of the Holocaust theme in American culture in the 1970s.[40] In Eli Mandel's view, writers indulged in what he called "camp kitsch",[41] thus achieving an emotional pitch. Accordingly, as Dittwar elaborates, authors connected associations to the misery of the "human condition" with the powerful image of a "univers concentrationnaire".[42]

The literature of the Holocaust has become a transnational literary genre. However, it does also, as I have delineated above, have specific national aspects to it. In the case of (North) American Holocaust poetry, it has been shaped by the fast establishment of a repertoire of identificatory signs. Resonating richly with a familiar number of over-determined signifiers, such poetry is in danger of trivialising and belittling the historical experience of suffering and death. How, then, does Canadian-Jewish poetry relate to and interact with the transnational and US-American models which I have outlined above? Notwithstanding the general widespread diffusion of Holocaust images in North America, Canada has seen a true evolvement of a "classical" Jewish poetry in its own right.[43] One of the early seminal writers, Abraham Moses Klein, can be regarded as a great influence on Jewish authors such as Irving Layton, Eli Mandel, Miriam Waddington, Phyllis Gotlieb, and Seymour Mayne (and, of course, Leonard Cohen). Klein, "a prominent but enigmatic figure within the history of Canadian poetry",[44] composed texts such as *The Second Scroll* (1951), *Hath not a Jew . . .* (1940), and *The Hit-*

leriad (1944), an attack on Hitler's anti-semitism (see Axel Stähler's contribution in this volume). Highlighting Jewish customs and ceremonies together with the theme of the Holocaust, the author lived his last years in reclusive silence, starting a tradition of a "poetry of absence".[45] Other authors paid homage to his "cries of silence, blanks and whites",[46] to his "vision of a post-Holocaust void and the need for some form of redemption".[47] His influence can be traced in such collections as Louis Dudek's *East of the City* from 1946, or the compilation *Trio*, 1954, by Eli Mandel, Phyllis Webb and Gael Turnbell. One of the most quoted Canadian-Jewish Holocaust poems—apart from Irving Layton's "At the Belsen Memorial"—is certainly Eli Mandel's "On the 25th Anniversary of the Liberation of Auschwitz: Memorial Services, Toronto, January 25, 1970" (1970), presented as an unstructured, fragmented puzzle of sense impressions.

LEONARD COHEN'S POETRY: VARIATIONS ON THE HOLOCAUST THEME

Irving Layton, whom I mentioned above, wrote in 1963, a year before the publication of Leonard Cohen's *Flowers for Hitler,* "Where is the poet who can make clear to us Belsen?"[48] It is not surprising, therefore, to find among Cohen's admiring biographers the implied suggestion that Cohen's collection met this alleged challenge. However, critical voices galore denigrated Cohen's effort to further establish himself as one of Canada's most promising young poets. Fully employing the repertoire of Holocaust motives which I described above, fusing them with a heavy dose of pop poetry motives, Cohen achieves jarring juxtapositions or interrelations. As Nadel fittingly observes, here the Holocaust is featured "along with sex and drugs".[49] Such shocking connections have been, as I will discuss later in detail, gauged as tending towards the spurious and flippant. Or, worse, they have been castigated as capitalising on the suffering of millions of Jews. At best, they appear disconcerting and question the reader's accepted frame of reception, thus adding the quality of "shock and originality"[50] to time-honoured motives of the Holocaust. In the following part of my paper, I will attempt to cover Cohen's usage of Nazi and Holocaust themes in his writings while assessing critical responses to it. From this broader perspective I will then shift, in the ensuing part, to a critical reading of some of his major poems which directly deal with the topic in question.

A few remarks on Leonard Cohen's Jewish-Canadian background should suffice here.[51] In 1934 in Montreal, the artist was born into a conservative, bourgeois family, whose members worked mainly in the textile industry. Ancestors of Leonard's father Nathan Bernhard Cohen had immigrated from Poland (from a part which is Russian now) to North America; in the 1920s Leonard's mother's family (Masha Klinitsky was born in 1907) had immigrated from Lithuania. His traditional education consisted in his grandfather Rabbi Solomon Klinitsky-Klein teaching him the old testament. At age eleven, Cohen, as he himself points out, encountered the moment his "true education began", when he saw the first pictures of concentration camps. Later Cohen studied at McGill and Columbia Universities. Among his first immediate literary influences, authors such as Garcia Lorca, Ginsberg, Burroughs, and the Beat Generation have been noted. His early success was accompanied by the life of an itinerant who moved back and forth between New York, London and the Greek island Hydra, with the periodical return to Montreal "to renew my neurotic affiliations".[52] As mentioned in my introduction, his relative success as a budding young poet who indulged in a bohemian lifestyle—in the wake of his collections *Let Us Compare Mythologies* (1956), *The Spice-Box of Earth* (1961) and *Flowers for Hitler* (1964)—was superseded by his choice to turn to musical expressions for commercial and artistic reasons.

In 1956, the year which also saw the publication of "Howl" by Ginsberg, Cohen's first collection of poems, *Let Us Compare Mythologies,* was published. In this, as in his subsequent collections of poems, critics have noticed the Jewish-Canadian influence of Klein, Layton and Dudek, but in a more pronounced and broader manner the traces of the so-called "mythopoeic group". Including authors like Gwendolyn MacEwen, Jay MacPherson, and James Reaney, this group was grounded in the work of Northrop Frye (1912-91) and his archetypal criticism. A similar approach to poetry and the role of the poet can be detected in Cohen's early poetry—"using poetry as a form of prayer and the role of the poet as a sacred, if not prophetic voice".[53] The first volume of the McGill Poetry Series, *Let Us Compare Mythologies* included 44 poems and five illustrations by Freda Gutman on 79 pages. Although the first print run consisted only of 400 copies, this volume marked the beginning of Cohen's career as "a great talent in Canadian literature".[54] Both literary and critical success came within a decade. This culminated in the publication of *Parasites of Heaven* (1966), many poems of which had been written in 1957 and 1958, the dedication of the Autumn 1967 issue of *Canadian Literature* to "Views of Leonard Cohen", and finally the resounding success of *Selected Poems, 1956-1968* (1968), 200000 copies of which were sold within the first three months.

Rather conventional in metre and form, employing surreal language and images as in his next volumes, Cohen's first book, as the title suggests, probes the similarities and differences between his own Jewish cultural tradition and a range of others, specifically Greek mythology and the Christian mythology of his environment. However, traditions are intertwined in the poet's "twin quest for God and sexual fulfillment".[55]

Religion and sex emerge as the prominent themes of *Let Us Compare Mythologies.* Accordingly, fulfilled lovers are in a state of grace, of universal harmony, with their egos dissolved in sexual ecstasy. This overriding theme of the loss of the self has been put into historical and intertextual perspective by a number of critics, who have observed Cohen's obsession with a "loosened" or "freed" self.[56] In one reading, Cohen appears as a proponent of decadent romanticism "in which the ugly replaces the beautiful as the inspiration for art".[57] Other critics have linked Cohen's obsession with a "loosened" or "freed" self, his toying with concepts of radical individualism in the sense of radical freedom to choose among "a plethora of alienated selves, free-floating I-systems" with beat movement values. These values are "typified by social attitudes which are best described as shifty saintliness and a terrible mobile sense of the self."[58] With the loss of an old, defined self, the new self becomes a plurality of selves, which in turn has been seen to be grounded in "Cohen's relationship with the Jewish religious tradition and in his ambiguous connectedness with the Montreal Jewish community".[59] However, interpretative positions seeking to establish a connectedness between Cohen's Jewish identity and his overriding themes of melancholy, loss and sexual fulfilment are scarce. Most convincingly, Rodenberg argues in his study of American poetry of the 1960s and 1970s that Cohen's "melancholic escapism into ennui and sexual ecstasy"[60] can best be analysed when taking cultural theories by Herbert Marcuse and Wolf Leppenies into account. What Rodenberg describes as "leftist melancholia" appears to be "the constant refusal of the deprived individual to contribute to late-capitalist society in any other way than by the subversive withdrawal of his own productivity—the inability for action becomes action itself."[61] In sum, Graf's categorisation of Cohen as a proponent of American counter-culture seems quite fitting:

> From the perspective of literary history, Cohen is a proponent of American counter-culture of the late fifties and early sixties. From a sociological angle, his poetry takes up subversive ideas in the tradition of Herbert Marcuse, the philosopher of subversive thought.[62]

Let us now turn to his third volume of poetry, *Flowers for Hitler* from 1964, not without noting once again the curious absence of explicit traces of Jewish identity or the Holocaust theme in Cohen's first collection of poetry, *Let Us Compare Mythologies,* and his second, *Spicebox of Earth.* For the obvious reason that its title upset some of its early readers, *Flowers for Hitler* appears as a pivotal text for a discussion of the Holocaust theme in Cohen's writing. A first categorization was suggested by Milton Wilson, who called Leonard Cohen "potentially the most important writer that Canadian poetry has produced since 1950" and lauded him as not merely the most talented but also "the most professionally committed" poet. Wilson described the book as "a version of the poetry of guilt".[63] Such a view seems confirmed by the book's epigraph, in which Cohen quotes Carlo Levi's lines:

> If from the inside of the Lager, a message could have seeped out to free men, it would have been this: Take care not to suffer in your homes what is inflicted on us here.[64]

However, the presaging hint that *Flowers for Hitler* revolves around some sort of communal guilt feeling is counterbalanced by what is printed on its dust-jacket. Here we find Cohen's note to the publisher:

> This book moves me from the world of the golden-boy poet into the dung pile of the front-line writer. I didn't plan it this way. I loved the tender notices *Spice-Box* got but they embarrassed me a little. *Hitler* won't get the same hospitality from the papers. My sounds are too new, therefore people will say: this is derivative, this is slight, his power has failed. Well, I say that there has never been a book like this, prose or poetry, written in Canada. All I ask is that you put it in the hands of my generation and it will be recognized.[65]

This flamboyant gesture shifts the book's seeming preoccupation with Hitler towards a rather transhistorical meaning. Surely, this is even further corroborated by the author's "Note on the title":

> A while ago this book would have been called SUNSHINE FOR NAPOLEON, and earlier still it would have been called WALLS FOR GENGHIS KHAN.[66]

In congruence with these authorial statements, the overriding themes of the book are not Jewish identity, let alone the Holocaust. Images of Nazi leaders and concentration camps are interwoven with the stuff of popular culture, particularly erotica and drugs; the horrors of the Nazi years stand side by side with those of the present, particularly those encountered in Cuba and those of a sordid and dull bourgeois existence in Montreal. Beauty and ugliness, the holy and the mundane, tenderness and violence are forcefully connected.[67] It has been noted that these images are yoked together through the comic mode, strung together by a "*fleurs du mal* beauty".[68] The effect is rather one of a universal message about the ubiquitous nature of human suffering, pain and capacity for finding momentous relief in physical pleasure. Here the limitations of decadent literature are highlighted, as the book subordinates human suffering to an artful description of "narrowed, bizarre area[s] of human experience".[69] Of the mixed reviews *Flowers for Hitler* produced,[70] Purdy's often-quoted remark on the book seems to epitomise the sense of unease most critics felt when exposed to this all-too-universal levelling-out effect of a book with "Hitler" in its title. Purdy noticed that the book was "lacking thematic consistency": "Hitler and the communal guilt ploy seem to me like the talk of a good conversational-

ist who had to say something, whether it was real or not."[71] Certainly, the book's connecting theme is not an imaginary journey into the death-camps of Bergen-Belsen and Auschwitz, a quest for knowledge about man's darker sides, as recently suggested.[72] The theme of the Holocaust is mainly subordinated to the larger concept of the literature of shock, of drastic and irritating imagery. To prove this point, a simple arithmetical approach reveals that of 95 texts (including a ballet-drama in one act) in *Flowers for Hitler,* merely four deal with the Nazi or Holocaust theme in an obvious manner: **"All there is to Know about Adolph Eichmann"** and **"Hitler",** and two poems with the innocuous titles of **"Folk"** and **"A Migrating Dialogue".** Cohen's strategy of thwarting his readers' expectations in the tradition of Modernist poetry is best illustrated by the strangely surrealist **"Goebbels abandons his novel and joins the party",** which has no obvious references to the real Goebbels in it. But also the strangely ahistoric **"Hitler the Brain-Mole"** remains an enigmatic poem. In a typical fashion, incommensurable fields of experience, those of the death camps and of the feelings between two lovers, are interconnected here:

> Hitler the brain-mole looks out of my eyes
> Goering boils ingots of gold in my bowels
> · · · · ·
>
> Confess! confess!
> is what you demand
> although you believe you're giving me everything

(*FH,* [*Flowers for Hitler*] 43)

The same applies to **"Opium and Hitler",** which actually has a direct reference to the *Führer.* Further allusions to Nazism and the Holocaust are rare. **"Millennium"** has two lines worth quoting in it: "I swung my liberty torch / happy as a gestapo brute" (*FH,* 41); **"The Failure of a Secular Life"** again draws the connection between personal disaster and political catastrophe: "He watched her real-life Dachau, / knew his career was ruined" (*FH,* 53). And the poem **"The Music Crept By Us"** surprises with a line which is thrown at the reader in an almost cynical gesture: "and the band is composed / of former SS monsters" (*FH,* 113). Further possible, if oblique, references can be found in **"The New Leader",** in **"Island Bulletin",** and in passing remarks on Jewish identity in some poems such as **"Winter Bulletin".** All in all, to speak of *Flowers for Hitler* as the poetry "which made clear to the reader Belsen" (to paraphrase Layton's suggestion as stated above) would surely be an overstatement. This also applies to Cohen's subsequently published poetry collections. When Cohen published another collection of poetry in 1972, *The Energy of Slaves,* his reputation was already that of a "rock poet". Even if one does not wish to castigate Cohen as finishing his career as a poet by once again doing "his whine-act" in "the weary tone of the supposedly-failed revolutionary",[73] it can be stated that

Cohen discontinued his direct poetic involvement with the Holocaust theme at the beginning of the 1970s. It is in two novels, though, that the theme re-emerges, *The Favourite Game* and *Beautiful Losers*. Before going into a more detailed analysis of poems on the Holocaust/Nazi theme in Cohen's early poetry, a brief interpretation of thematically related passages in these novels could be fruitful.

Set in the 1960s, *The Favourite Game*, Cohen's semi-autobiographical first novel, appears as a Canadian-Jewish version of the portrait of the artist as a young man growing to maturity. Overtalented and oversexed, the protagonist traces his artistic, spiritual, and sexual initiation from Montreal to New York. For the character Laurence Breavman, these rites of passage are constituted by the transgression of moral as well as racial and national boundaries. His Jewish identity is foregrounded, for instance, when Breavman as a writer of the Montreal Jewish community ("one of the most powerful in the world today", *FG*, [*The Favourite Game*] 11) turns down a scholarship which would allow him to do academic work. This causes him to be "considered a mild traitor who could not be condemned outright" (*FG*, 102). "To the marginalization of the writer by the community, Breavman reacts with inner exile"[74]—which later turns into the self-imposed exile of a young bohemian in New York.

The novel is not without a number of incidental comments on Canada, on Montreal, and on Jewish life, narrated in an ironic mode. The Jewish characters' initial unwillingness to mingle with the gentiles is voiced in the words as "We refuse to pass the circumcision line" (*FG*, 11), or, rather blatantly, "We do not wish to join Christian clubs or weaken our blood through intermarriage" (*FG*, 11). Images of the Holocaust are ubiquitous: when Breavman slaps a girl's face, he does it "like a Gestapo investigator" (*FG*, 54). Yet, Jewish identity is neither foregrounded in an explicit nor in a self-reflexive manner. This is, for example, evident when Breavmen expresses that his Jewishness seems to him an "alien experience" (*FG*, 187), only to conclude, without further elaboration: "He was grateful for that" (*FG*, 187).[75] Images of Germany and the Holocaust appear in the form of hackneyed clichés, as described above in the passages on the trivialisation of the Holocaust in North American literature and the prevalence of national and ethnic stereotypes. In the following passage, young Breavman records the fears of a Montreal child who grows up with these secondary representations of the Holocaust in the mass media:

> The Japs and Germans were beautiful enemies. They had buck teeth or cruel monocles and commanded in crude English with much saliva. They started the war because of their nature.
>
> Red Cross ships must be bombed, all parachutists machine-gunned. Their uniforms were stiff and deco-

> rated with skulls. They kept on eating and laughed at appeals for mercy.
>
> They did nothing warlike without a close-up of perverted glee.
>
> Best of all, they tortured. To get secrets, to make soap, to set examples to towns of heroes. But mostly they tortured for fun, because of their nature.
>
> Comic books, movies, radio programmes centred their entertainment around the fact of torture. Nothing fascinates a child like a tale of torture. With the clearest of consciences, with a patriotic intensity, children dreamed, talked, acted orgies of physical abuse. Imaginations were released to wander on a reconnaissance mission from Calvary to Dachau.
>
> European children starved and watched their parents scheme and die. Here we grow up with toy whips. Early warning against our future leaders, the war babies.
>
> (*FG*, 15f.)

If *The Favourite Game* remains a novel which has gleaned little critical acclaim, *Beautiful Losers* (1966), became an immediate *succès de scandale*. It caused a storm of controversy and achieved considerable critical reputation as one of the most celebrated examples of Canadian postmodernism.[76] Its protagonists are constructed as amalgams of several characters; the plot is minimal, with the narrative basically oscillating between various points of view. How, with regard to our topic, is the theme of Jewish identity and its connection with the harrowing Holocaust experience dealt with in this novel? Facile answers seem to abound. In a sweeping statement, Ravvin claims that "Cohen's novel can be seen as an examination of the role of the Holocaust in contemporary culture".[77] And this is so in spite of the novel's exclusion of virtually all images and themes related to traditional Jewish culture and history, as Ravvin concedes. Again, the argument is that the sense of Jewish suffering, as epitomised in the Holocaust, is all-pervasive in the novel and symbolical of all human suffering and loss, specifically in our (post)modern society. This line of argument becomes apparent in Hutcheon's paradigmatic appraisal of the novel:

> Th[e] vision of Nazi torture also pervades *Beautiful Losers*: meat-eating humans are "dietary Nazis" with their Dachau farmyards. The novel is laced with incidental but constant references to the Jews, often concerning their role as a victimized race. F. [a character in the novel] says that each generation must thank its Jews and its Indians for making progress possible—by their victimization. Canadian literature is full of images of a lonely, desolate wilderness, indifferent to human values. Here we are in an increasingly urban society where man is progressively brutalized by the city, becoming, himself, indifferent to human values.[78]

In the novel, references to gas chambers, Zyklon B, and Nazi medical experiments can be found in abundance. They function as described above in my remarks on

Cohen's poetry. The brutal amalgamation of disparate images creates a shocking effect, which might wear off as one gets used to it. In this, *Beautiful Losers* offers nothing strikingly original. In its most shocking scenes, it can create a surrealism which creates moments of drastic intensity.[79] The novel's most notorious scene is a passage in Book II, which I would like to focus on briefly as it includes a startling cameo appearance by Adolf Hitler in the guise of an Argentine waiter. The passage is described from the point of view of F., who is vacationing in Argentina. In a sex orgy with Edith (the narrator's wife) in a hotel, the Danish Vibrator ("D.V.") is featured, as the lovers fantasize about violence, especially how the Jesuit Brébeuf was tortured and bound on a stake by the Iroquois in the 17th century. This connection of sexuality and violence is historically broadened when the scenario becomes even more surreal. Suddenly the Danish Vibrator moves to the beach and a figure emerges from the palms. It is the waiter who enters; he had been introduced earlier as a man with "the moustache and the raincoat" (*BL* [*Beautiful Losers*], 177).[80] What follows is an outrageous bedroom scene, with a number of references to the Holocaust and Nazis in Argentina.

> We did not even have to open the door. The waiter had a passkey. He was wearing the old raincoat and moustache, but underneath he was perfectly nude. We turned toward him.
>
> —Do you like Argentina? I asked for the sake of civil conversation.
>
> —I miss the newsreels, he said.
>
> —And the parades? I offered.
>
> —And the parades. But I can get anything else here. Ah.
>
> He noticed our reddened organs and began to fondle them with great interest.
>
> —Wonderful! Wonderful! I see you have been well prepared.
>
> What followed was old hat. [. . .] [W]e hardly cared to resist his sordid exciting commands, even when he made us kiss the whip.
>
> —I have a treat for you, he said at last.
>
> —He has a treat for us, Edith.
>
> —Shoot, she replied wearily.
>
> From the pocket of his overcoat he withdraw [sic!] a bar of soap.
>
> —Three in a tub, he said merrily in his heavy accent.
>
> So we splashed around with him. He lathered us from head to toe, proclaiming all the while the special qualities of the soap, which, as you must now understand, was derived from melted human flesh.
>
> That bar is now in your hands. We were baptized by it, your wife and I. [. . .] As he opened the door to go, Edith threw her arms around his neck, pulled him to the dry bed, and cradled his famous head against her breasts.

> —What did you do that for? I demanded of her after the waiter had made his stiff exit, and nothing remained of him but the vague stink of sulphurous flatulence.
>
> —For a second I thought he was an A———.
>
> —Oh, Edith!
>
> (*BL*, 193-195)

What is one to make of these almost cynical, at least flippant usages of the Hitler persona with all the usual references to Auschwitz and Nazi brutalities in the context of an exotic sadomasochistic encounter? Again, Nazi imagery is decontextualized, denaturalized. The combination of sexual release and violence could be viewed as an instance of self-denial and self-mortification, which, in turn, could be interpreted as part of larger projects of dehumanization.[81] However, Linda Hutcheon's claim that this scene serves as an example of "ironic defamiliarization"[82] could be seen as offering an extremely disjointed scenario, which smacks of dancing (or in this case having sex) on the graves of six million Jews.

THE WORLD AS ONE OF VIOLENCE AND SUFFERING—"EVERYDAY DACHAU"[83]

In this last part, I would like to return to Cohen's poetry and present specific examples of his description of Nazi terror as a metaphor for ubiquitous terror and of the Holocaust as a metaphor for universal suffering and loss. As discussed above, black humour, the grotesque, a "fleurs du mal" aesthetics of the ugly, the shocking, and the decadent are featured in them. Cohen's essential artistic technique of connecting the unconnected can be illustrated by means of the small poem **"Folk"**, in which the tranquil scenery of a quaint little village is overshadowed by just two lines, as the poem begins and ends with references to Hitler. Just how, for example, is the quirky image of "doggies making love" connected to Hitler remains enigmatic and up to the puzzled reader to decide.

> flowers for hitler the summer yawned
> flowers all over my new grass
> and here is a little village
> they are painting it for a holiday
> here is a little church
> here is a school
> here are some doggies making love
> the flags are bright as laundry
> flowers for hitler the summer yawned[84]

Black humour is one of Cohen's main devices to come to terms with the death camp atrocities he presents in his poetry. Of course, jarring conceits such as in the following lines are always positioned on a thin line between the tasteless or inadequate and the shocking and unsettling.

> Peekaboo Miss Human Soap.
> It never happened
>
> . . . . .

I think we should let sleeping ashes lie.[85]

Within the context of my discussion of Cohen's poetry, Djwa's remarks on these lines seem worth quoting:

> Here the brutal is introduced as a witty aside and the particular *frisson nouveau* of the poem seems to arise from the juxtaposition of the erotic, infantile world of Bathing Beauties, "peekabo" and "let's pretend", with the horror of real concentration camps where soap is made from human fat and ashes. At first glance, Cohen appears to be having a nasty laugh at the expense of Jewish suffering. [. . .] [O]n closer inspection it might be suggested that this is an attempt to come to terms with a painful experience. Through the medium of Black Humour it is possible to see the selection of a Miss Human Soap as an absurdity.[86]

In a series of unrelated, surreal scenes, *Flowers for Hitler* reverses conventional aesthetics and morals. Revelling in the fantastic, macabre and grotesque, the poems are interlaced with traces of the Holocaust as the ultimate proof of the ubiquity of evil. With this the fallibility and sham pretence of conventional, bourgeois world views and modes of representation are exposed.

The bourgeois Western view of history as a linear, teleological progression towards a more peaceful, rational state of civilization is also questioned. History seems a mere sedative; and any sort of progress is negated as the Holocaust is not presented as a singular historical phenomenon or an aberration of Western history, but rather as one whose traces can be found everywhere, especially where one least expects them (as is reflected in the way it crops up in Cohen's poems). In **"A Migrating Dialogue"**, to use an example, there is a macabre rendition of Nazi sadism as an American phenomenon. Just as Horkheimer and Adorno interpreted American mass culture and Nazism as fundamentally identical in their ideological implications, Cohen interconnects images of Hitler's torturers with U.S. comic book characters.

> Wipe that smirk off your face.
> Captain Marvel signed the whip contract.
> Joe Palooka manufactured whips.
> Li'l Abner packed the whips in cases.
> The Katzenjammer Kids thought up experiments.
> Mere cogs.[87]

Other disturbing images connect the death motive, in this case that of the Auschwitz death chambers, with a particular and grotesquely erotic sensitivity. In the following lines from **"Lovers"** this is related in the form of an intense death-in-life scene of nightmarish dimensions.[88]

> And at the hot ovens they
> Cunningly managed a brief
> Kiss before the soldier came
> To knock out her golden teeth.

> And in the furnace itself
> As the flames flamed higher,
> He tried to kiss her burning breasts
> As she burned in the fire.[89]

Less shocking, but arguably very effective, is Cohen's characterisation of Nazi criminals as normal persons, as already shown in the Hitler-as-waiter passage from *Beautiful Losers* cited above. Of course, this observation was first prominently expressed in Hannah Ahrendt's thesis of "the banality of evil", a direct reference to Nazi criminals such as Eichmann. Similarly, in Cohen's poetry Hitler appears to be "ordinary", Eichmann "medium". Actually, in **"All There Is to Know About Adolph [sic!] Eichmann"** the Nazi is characterised as an average person, quite the contrary to the monstrosity of his deeds. As the poem sums up an enumeration of identifying features of no spectacular particularity:

> DISTINGUISHING FEATURES: . . . .
>   . . . None
>   . . . . .

> What did you expect?[90]

It is not only that Cohen here insists on the relativity of evil or that irrational evil is accepted as a normal part of all humans, as Djwa reads the poem. Or that evil "can even come to have a certain attractiveness."[91] Rather, the lurking omnipresence of evil is stressed once again, with the hint that average human beings are capable of committing crimes of the dimensions the Nazis did. Without exculpating genocide, Cohen alludes to concerns similar to Adorno's: "In the face of the ultimate human tragedy that is the Holocaust, ordinary, everyday pursuits seem mundane, insignificant, and lacking in legitimacy."[92]

This is not to say that the Holocaust as a topic takes precedence over all other themes in Cohen's poems. On the contrary, its traces are of diminishing importance. It may not be quite incidental that the last poem in Cohen's last major poetry collection, *The Energy of Slaves,* reduces the theme of Nazism to a muted remark in one of its stanzas:

> A Nazi war criminal
> visited us last night
> a very old man
> in a silk parachute.[93]

Thus, what were once violent juxtapositions have become subdued intertextual echoes. The question remains, though, how Leonard Cohen's usage of Holocaust and Nazi imagery is to be valued. There is certainly a critical controversy when it comes to this issue. On the one hand, there are critics, namely Wynands, who consider Cohen's poems as "effective works of art about the Holocaust. By adopting the whole Decadent stance, Cohen avoids a mimetic approach to the Holocaust . . . he deliberately alienates them [his readers] from the work of art by disfiguring it."[94] The drift of this argument is that by means of its anti-mimetic, anti-realist, anti-art, anti-bourgeois, unorthodox, and provocative dealing with the thorny issues of Nazism and the Holocaust, Cohen's poetry has the power to question the readers' established attitudes, thus opening new vistas on a topic whose imagery has been frozen by the mass media. On the other hand, a large number of critics contend that Cohen's poetry "reek[s] of the world of radical chic".[95] His macabre obsession with the Holocaust has found a valve in his poetry which he wrote to "give himself some sort of titillative mental thrill".[96] At its worst, as Djwa holds it, Cohen's sensationalism "leads us to question the integrity of Cohen's vision".[97] According to this view, in Cohen's poetry the Holocaust is reduced to function as a "handy metaphor" for all kinds of post-1945 ailments. Ravvin surmises:

> [T]he Holocaust exists not as a particular event to be limned, but simply as a handy metaphor that stands in for numerous other kinds of extremity and human suffering. There is a risk that such figurative use of the Holocaust tells us nothing about the particular event, but instead, obscures and diminishes the character of victimization visited on the Jews of Europe by the Nazis. There can be no doubt that Cohen leaves himself open to this kind of criticism by choosing to allude to the Holocaust almost casually, using a tone that is routinely off-handed and ennui-ridden.[98]

The controversy revealed in these diametrically opposed critical positions offers both a challenge as well as a direction for those readings of Cohen's poetry which focus on his treatment of the Holocaust theme. For Cohen's poems may well be both. They may be products of a tradition of trivialisation and popularisation of the Holocaust theme in a consumer and mass media society, occasionally tasteless and frivolous. But they may also be thought-provoking and irritating and thus lead their readers to raise important questions which are at the very heart of critical discussions about literature after the Holocaust—that is, about the ways poetry and fiction can or should present what can never be adequately put into words.

Notes

1. Ira Nadel, *Leonard Cohen: A Life in Art* (Toronto: ECW Press, 1994), 14.

2. Important publications are listed below in chronological order: A. W. Purdy, "Leonard Cohen: A Personal Look", *Canadian Literature* 23 (Winter 1965), 7-16; Sandra Djwa, "Leonard Cohen: Black Romantic", *Canadian Literature* 34 (Autumn 1967), 32-42; Desmond Pacey, "The Phenomenon of Leonard Cohen", *Canadian Literature* 34 (Autumn 1967), 5-31; Michael Ondaatje, *Leonard Cohen* (Toronto: McClelland and Stewart, 1970); Patricia Morley, *The Immoral Moralists: Hugh MacLennann and Leonard Cohen* (Toronto: Charles Irwin, 1972); Linda Hutcheon, "*Beautiful Losers*: All the Polarities", *Canadian Literature* 59 (Winter 1974), 42-56; Tom Wayman, "Cohen's Women", Rev. of *The Energy of Slaves, Canadian Literature* 60 (Spring 1974), 89-93; Michael Gnarowski (ed.), *Leonard Cohen: The Artist and His Critics* (New York: McGraw Hill, 1976); Eli Mandel, "Cohen's Life as a Slave" in *Another Time* (Erin, ON: Porcépic, 1977), 124-36; Stephen Scobie, *Studies in Canadian Literature. Leonard Cohen* (Vancouver: Douglas and McIntyre, 1978); Ken Norris, "Healing Itself the Moment It Is Condemned: Cohen's Death of a Lady's Man", *Canadian Poetry* 20 (1987), 51-60; Linda Hutcheon, *Leonard Cohen and His Works* (Toronto: ECW, 1989); Loranne S. Dorman, Clive L. Rawlins, *Leonard Cohen: Prophet of the Heart* (London: Omnibus Press, 1990); University of Western Ontario / Department of English (ed.), *The Proceedings of The Leonard Cohen Conference.* Canadian Poetry Series 33 (Ontario: University of Western Ontario, 1993); internet version 22 Aug. 2002 <http://www.arts.uwo.ca/canpoetry/cpjrn/vol33/vol33index.htm>; Nadel, *Leonard Cohen*; Christof Graf, *Leonard Cohen. Partisan der Liebe* (Köln: vgs, 1996); "Leonard Cohen" Special Issue, *Essays on Canadian Writing* 69 (Winter 1999). Also cp. the following websites, 12 Jan. 2003, <http://www.leonardcohenfiles.com>, <http://www.netsonic.fi/˜ja/cohen/1cbook4.html>, <news:alt.music.leonard-cohen>, <http://www.webheights.net/cohenconcordance/index.htm>, <http://www.medialab.chalmers.se/guitar/acoustic.guitar.song.collection.html#Lcohen>, <http://www.musiclub.sonystyle.com/artist.jsp?artistId=65997>

3. Hutcheon, *Leonard Cohen and His Works*, and also *Spitting Images: Contemporary Canadian Ironies* (Toronto: Oxford University Press, 1991).

4. Sandra Wynands, "The Representation of the Holocaust in *Flowers for Hitler*", *Essays on Canadian Writing* 69 (Winter 1999), 198-209.

5. Dorman, Rawlins, *Leonard Cohen: Prophet of the Heart,* 119.

6. Dorman, Rawlins, *Leonard Cohen: Prophet of the Heart,* 119.

7. Cp. Walter Pache, "Literatur Kanadas—Die andere nordamerikanische Literatur" in Hubert Zapf

(ed.), *Amerikanische Literaturgeschichte* (Stuttgart: Metzler, 1996), 520-560.

8. A. J. M. Smith, "Eclectic Detachment. Aspects of Identity in Canadian Poetry", *Canadian Literature* 9 (Summer 1961), 6-14.

9. W. J. Keith, *Canadian Literature in English* (London, New York: Longman, 1985), 67.

10. Quoted in Keith, *Canadian Literature in English,* 68.

11. Cp. Kohn's remark on Jewish poetry after the Holocaust: "Ever since then no authentic Jewish poetry can be written without its roots being deeply grounded in the Holocaust." Murray J. Kohn, *The Voice of My Blood Cries Out: The Holocaust as Reflected in Hebrew Poetry* (New York: Shengold Publishers, 1979), 208.

12. While stereotypes, especially national stereotypes, were once considered to be exclusively negative and discriminating, recent research in social psychology has resulted in this attitude towards stereotypes being reviewed. There has been a reversal to Walter Lippman's (see *Public Opinion* from 1922) original idea of stereotypes as basic tools of human cognition which assist the recognition of similarities between objects and persons, hence enabling people to be able to group and generalise. Cp. Harald Husemann (ed.), "As Others See Us: Anglo-German Perceptions", *Fremdsprachenunterricht* 2 (1996).

13. Franz K. Stanzel, "The Canadianness of Canadian Literature. Summary of a Discussion and a Postscript", in Franz K. Stanzel, Waldemar Zacharasiewicz (eds.), *Encounters and Explorations: Canadian Writers and European Critics* (Würzburg: Königshausen und Neumann, 1986, 139-152), 147. A more elaborate definition of imagological studies with respect to their perspectives, methodologies and aims is expressed in the following exemplary quote by Zacharasiewicz: "Aus der Perspektive neuerer literatur-und kulturwissenschaftlicher Denkmodelle, wie des 'New Historicism', gewinnt die Frage des Auftauchens und der Funktion von Fremdbildern cinen noch wesentlich höheren Stellenwert und ein größeres Erkenntnisinteresse [als bei der reinen Beschränkung auf literarische Werke]. Wenn das Schrifttum nicht nach formalen und wirkungsästhetischen Gesichtspunkten differenziert, sondern als Teil der sozialen Praxis verstanden wird, in dem die Machtinteressen von dominierenden Gruppen und ihr Kräftespiel erhebliche Bedeutung gewinnen, dann erlangen die Facetten literarisch vermittelter Bilder fremder Völker und Länder wegen ihrer unterschiedlichen Funktion eine er-

höhte Aussagekraft. Sie besitzen einen gestiegenen Informationswert und können unter Umständen besondere Einsichten in die Spannungsverhältnisse innerhalb der eigenen Kultur und Gesellschaft ermöglichen." Waldemar Zacharasiewicz, *Das Deutschlandbild in der amerikanischen Literatur* (Darmstadt: Wissenschaftliche Buchgesellschaft, 1998), 2.

14. See for example Günther Blaicher, *Das Deutschlandbild in der englischen Literatur* (Darmstadt: Wissenschaftliche Buchgesellschaft, 1992); Franz K. Stanzel, *Europäer. Ein imagologischer Essay* (Heidelberg: Universitätsverlag C. Winter, 1997); Zacharasiewicz, *Das Deutschlandbild in der amerikanischen Literatur.*

15. Zacharasiewicz, *Das Deutschlandbild in der amerikanischen Literatur,* 226, perceives a "deutliche Beharrungstendenz [. . .] auch Jahrzehnte nach dem Zweiten Weltkrieg".

16. "Seit der intensiven Aufarbeitung des Holocausts sind in Belletristik, Film und Fernsehen in den USA der SS-Mann, der KZ-Scherge und der Militarist die beherrschenden deutschen Figurentypen." (Zacharasiewicz, *Das Deutschlandbild in der amerikanischen* Literatur, 278; translation L. V.)

17. W. H. Auden. *Collected Poems,* ed. Edward Mendelson (London: Faber & Faber, 1976), 154.

18. For a general discussion, see the following studies and research articles on the poetry of the Holocaust: Brian Murdoch, "Transformations of the Holocaust: Auschwitz in Modern Lyric Poetry", *Comparative Literature Studies* 11 (1974), 123-150; Sidra DeKoven Ezrahi, *By Words Alone: The Holocaust in Literature* (Chicago, London: University of Chicago Press, 1980); Alwin Rosenfeld, *A Double Dying: Reflections on Holocaust Literature* (Bloomington: Indiana University Press, 1980); Kurt Dittmar, "Der Holocaust in der jüdisch-amerikanischen Literatur" in Claus Uhlig, Volker Bischoff (eds.), *Die amerikanische Literatur in der Weltliteratur. Themen und Aspekte. Festschrift zum 60. Geburtstag von Rudolf Haas* (Berlin: Erich Schmidt Verlag, 1982), 392-414; Leon Israel Yudkin, *Jewish Writing and Identity in the Twentieth Century* (London, Canberra: Croom Helm, 1982); Eli Mandel, "Auschwitz: Poetry of Alienation", *Canadian Literature* 100 (1984), 213-218; Efraim Sicher, *Beyond Marginality: Anglo-Jewish Literature After the Holocaust* (New York: State University of New York Press, 1985); Paul Goetsch, "Der Holocaust in der englischen und amerikanischen Lyrik" in Franz Link (ed.), *Jewish Life and Suffering as Mirrored in English and American Literature. Jüdisches Leben und Leiden im Spiegel*

der englischen und amerikanischen Literatur (Paderborn: Schöningh, 1987), 165-189; Gloria L. Young, "The Moral Function of Remembering: American Holocaust Poetry", *Studies in American Jewish Literature* 9:1 (Spring 1990): 61-72; Michael Greenstein, "Filling the Absence: Metalepsis and Liminality in Jewish-Canadian Poetry", *Ariel* 23:2 (1992), 25-42.

19. On poetry in Hebrew (partly translated there) see especially Yudkin, *Jewish Writing and Identity in the Twentieth Century.*

20. See Young, "The Moral Function of Remembering".

21. Mandel, "Auschwitz: Poetry of Alienation", 215.

22. Quoted in Mandel, "Auschwitz: Poetry of Alienation", 215.

23. Quoted in Mandel, "Auschwitz: Poetry of Alienation", 215.

24. Sicher, *Beyond Marginality: Anglo-Jewish Literature After the Holocaust,* 164.

25. Quoted in Goetsch, "Der Holocaust in der englischen und amerikanischen Lyrik", 185.

26. Theodor W. Adorno, *Gesammelte Schriften: Kulturkritik und Gesellschaft I,* vol. 10 (Frankfurt/Main: Suhrkamp, 1977), 30.

27. Reprinted in Kohn, *The Voice of My Blood Cries Out: The Holocaust as Reflected in Hebrew Poetry,* 208.

28. Steiner in Murdoch, "Transformations of the Holocaust: Auschwitz in Modern Lyric Poetry", 123.

29. "Hier das amerikanische Wohlstandsjudentum, dort sechs Millionen Tote." (Dittmar, "Der Holocaust in der jüdisch-amerikanischen Literatur", 395; translation L. V.)

30. Quoted in Dittmar, "Der Holocaust in der jüdisch-amerikanischen Literatur", 395.

31. See Goetsch, "Der Holocaust in der englischen und amerikanischen Lyrick", 188.

32. Murdoch, "Transformations of the Holocaust: Auschwitz in Modern Lyric Poetry", 123.

33. See Murdoch, "Transformations of the Holocaust: Auschwitz in Modern Lyric Poetry", 125 ff.

34. Quoted in Goetsch, "Der Holocaust in der englischen und amerikanischen Lyrik", 166.

35. See Goetsch, "Der Holocaust in der englischen und amerikanischen Lyrik", 167.

36. Kohn, *The Voice of My Blood Cries Out: The Holocaust as Reflected in Hebrew Poetry,* 207.

37. See Murdoch, "Transformations of the Holocaust: Auschwitz in Modern Lyric Poetry", 139.

38. Quoted in Dittmer, "Der Holocaust in der jüdisch-amerikanischen Literatur", 410.

39. Sylvia Plath, *Collected Poems,* ed. Ted Hughes (London: Faber & Faber, 1981), 244.

40. See Dittmar, "Der Holocaust in der jüdisch-amerikanischen Literatur", 393.

41. "By the 1970s Susan Sontag was telling us of "fascinating fascism", film and poetry toyed with an awful camp kitsch. I remembered Leonard Cohen's equating of comic book mythology and Nazism. Elie Wiesel scorned the TV series "Holocaust" for trivializing horror." (Mandel, "Auschwitz: Poetry of Alienation", 216)

42. "Dort [Bellow, Malamud] wurden die betreffenden historischen Ereignisse als ganzheitlicher Komplex mit der fundamentalen Qualität zeitgenössischer Daseinserfahrung in Zusammenhang gebracht, in existentieller Hinsicht mit dem Ausgeliefertsein des Menschen an die blinde Macht der Faktizität, in kulturkritischer Hinsicht mit der Deprivation des Individuums in der modernen Massengesellschaft. Hier [Plath, Baldwin] jedoch geht es darum, daß alle möglichen Partialphänomene mit Hilfe einer diffusen Assoziationstechnik sozusagen *ad hoc* an die Vorstellung vom "univers concentrationnaire" als Sinnbild einer äußersten Intensivierung menschlichen Leidens angeschlossen werden. Dieses Verfahren steht stets im Verdacht unseriöser oder neurotisch bestimmter Hyperbolik" (Dittmar, "Der Holocaust in der jüdisch-amerikanischen Literatur", 410).

43. See Greenstein, "Filling the Absence".

44. Keith, *Canadian Literature in English,* 69.

45. Greenstein, "Filling the Absence", 41.

46. Greenstein, "Filling the Absence", 42.

47. Greenstein, "Filling the Absence", 26.

48. Irving Layton, *Balls for a One-Armed Juggler* (Toronto: McClelland and Stewart, 1963), xviii.

49. Nadel, *Leonard Cohen: A Life in Art,* 65.

50. Nadel, *Leonard Cohen: A Life in Art,* 79.

51. For the following biographical details cp. especially Nadel, *Leonard Cohen: A Life in Art,* 16ff.

52. Leonard Cohen, *The Favourite Game* (1963. Toronto: McClelland and Stewart, 1970), 4. Further page references in the text, abbreviated as *FG.*

53. Nadel, *Leonard Cohen: A Life in Art,* 40.

54. Cohen "etablierte sich [. . .] als einer der Hoffnungsträger der kanadischen Literatur" (Graf, *Leonard Cohen: Partisan der Liebe,* 55).

55. Pacey, "The Phenomenon of Leonard Cohen", 6.

56. Djwa, "Leonard Cohen: Black Romantic", 32.

57. Djwa, "Leonard Cohen: Black Romantic", 32.

58. Winfried Siemerling, *Discoveries of the Other: Alterity in the Work of Leonard Cohen, Hubert Aquin, Michael Ondaatje, and Nicole Brossard* (Toronto: University of Toronto Press, 1994), 23.

59. Siemerling, *Discoveries of the Other,* 23.

60. Hans-Peter Rodenberg, *Subversive Phantasie. Untersuchungen zur Lyrik der amerikanischen Gegenkultur 1960-1975* (Giessen: Focus Verlag, 1983), 161, "Melancholische Flucht in Weltschmerz und sexuelle Ekstase".

61. "[. . .] die konstante Weigerung des depravierten Individuums, in der spätkapitalistischen Gesellschaft einen anderen Beitrag zu leisten, als den des subversiven Entzugs der eigenen Produktivität—Handlungshemmung als Handlung selbst." (Rodenberg, *Subversive Phantasie,* 165; translation L. V.)

62. "Literaturwissenschaftlich gesehen ist Cohen [. . .] ein Vertreter der amerikanischen Gegenkultur der späten fünfziger und frühen sechziger Jahre. Sozialwissenschaftlich betrachtet greift seine Lyrik subversive Gedanken im Sinne Herbert Marcuses, dem Theoretiker der Subversivität, auf." (Graf, *Leonard Cohen. Partisan der Liebe,* 75; translation L. V.)

63. All quotations in Dorman & Rawlins, *Leonard Cohen: Prophet of the* Heart, 117.

64. Leonard Cohen, *Flowers for Hitler* (1964. Toronto: McClelland and Stewart, 1975). Further page references in the text, abbreviated as *FH.*

65. Cohen, *Flowers for Hitler.*

66. Cohen, *Flowers for Hitler,* Introduction.

67. See also Pacey, "The Phenomenon of Leonard Cohen", 16.

68. Cp. Djwa, "Leonard Cohen: Black Romantic", 38, 40.

69. Djwa, "Leonard Cohen: Black Romantic", 39, cp. also 38: "In *Flowers for Hitler,* Cohen takes the blackness of human capacity for evil and attempts to extract the flowers of art".

70. Two exemplary reactions reveal the critics' irritation: "Die Rezensenten bemängelten die Wiederholung von bereits Gesagtem und sprachen von der Vergeudung eines bereits anerkannten literarischen Talents. Sie wollten von Figuren wie Hitler, Geobbels und Göring nichts mehr hören, über Sex und Drogen nichts lesen, die Literatur der jungen Gegenkultur Nordamerikas nicht akzeptieren. Sie konnten oder wollten sich auf die Welt, in der sich Cohen bewegte—zwischen Europa und Amerika, Krieg, Marihuana und Orgasmen—nicht einlassen. Sie wollten nicht erkennen, was Cohen meinte, wenn er—wie zuvor schon in seinem Gedicht 'Lovers' [in *Let Us Compare Mythologies*]—erklärte, daß der Holocaust noch immer 'allgegenwärtig' sei" (Graf, *Leonard Cohen. Partisan der Liebe,* 70f.). "In a notorious (later suppressed) statement on the cover of the original edition [. . .] Cohen claimed that the book moved him 'from the world of the golden-boy poet into the dung pile of the front-line writer'. But in fact this new phase, for all its difference in tone, bears striking resemblance to the old. Specific contemporary references (to Cuba, Eichmann, the tensions of Montreal in the early 1960s) take precedence over mythical ones, but much of the decadent-romantic treatment remains. [. . .] Images of the Jewish holocaust are still exploited, fierce juxtapositions of the gently idyllic with the violently horrific still occur. [. . .] What develops is an ambiguous posturing that blurs the line between genuine seriousness and mocking parody [. . .] And in his pop-singer phase he becomes a coarsened parody of his earlier self, the myth-maker self-consciously transformed into a myth." (Keith, *Canadian Literature in English,* 88f.)

71. Purdy, "Leonard Cohen: A Personal Look", 14.

72. Martin Löschnigg, Maria Löschnigg, *Kurze Geschichte der Kanadischen Literatur.* UNI Wissen Anglistik, Amerikanistik (Stuttgart: Klett, 2001).

73. Wayman, "Cohen's Women", 90f.

74. Siemerling, *Discoveries of the Other,* 29.

75. Compare also the following dialogue between Breavman and a Jewish friend:

"Krantz, is it true that we are Jewish?"

"So it has been rumoured, Breavman."

"Do you feel Jewish, Krantz?"

"Thoroughly."

"Do your teeth feel Jewish?"

"Especially my teeth, to say nothing of my left ball."

"We really shouldn't joke, what we were just saying reminds me of pictures from the camps."

"True."

Weren't they supposed to be a holy people consecrated to purity, service, spiritual honesty? Weren't they a nation set apart?

(*FG,* 41)

76. Pacey, "The Phenomenon of Leonard Cohen", 23, calls the novel the "culmination of his [Cohen's] previous work"; Hutcheon, "*Beautiful Losers*: All the Polarities", 42, finds that the novel "may also be the most challenging and perceptive novel about Canada and her people yet written"; Pacey even hails it as "in my opinion the most intricate, erudite, and fascinating Canadian novel ever written" (5).

77. Norman Ravvin, "Writing about the Holocaust: Uncovering the Ethical Centre of Beautiful Losers" in *The Proceedings of The Leonard Cohen Conference*, 1.

78. Hutcheon, "*Beautiful Losers*: All the Polarities", 45.

79. Again, one may question the shock value of descriptions such as the following: "Like a cyanide egg dropped into the gas chamber the D.V. [Danish Vibrator] released a glob of Formula Cream at the top of the muscular cleavage I had laboured so hard to define [the division between his buttocks]" (188f.).

80. Further references in the text, abbreviated as *BL*, are from the following edition: Leonard Cohen, *Beautiful Losers* (Toronto: McClelland and Stewart, 1966).

81. See Ravvin, "Writing about the Holocaust", 5.

82. Hutcheon, *Spitting Images*, 81; Hutcheon also calls this scene an example of "post-modern challenges to humanist universals" (82). A similar argument is brought forth by Ravvin, "Writing about the Holocaust", 7, when he writes about "Cohen's suggestion that the outcome of any eroticized interest in victimization and the abuse of power must inevitably bring about total demoralization and spiritual death."

83. From Leonard Cohen, "Letter" in *Selected Poems 1956-1968* (1969. London: Jonathan Cape, 1971), 16.

84. Leonard Cohen, "Folk" in idem, *Flowers for Hitler*, 81.

85. Cohen, *Flowers for Hitler*, 73.

86. Djwa, "Leonard Cohen: Black Romantic", 40.

87. Leonard Cohen, "A Migrating Dialogue" in *Flowers for Hitler*, 72.

88. Purdy, "Leonard Cohen: A Personal Look", 10, interprets the poem's imagery as follows: it presents "not just disillusion and gamey decadence, but the present fact that all good things in life are done and past."

89. Leonard Cohen, *Let Us Compare Mythologies* (1956. Toronto: McClelland and Stewart, 1966), 33.

90. Leonard Cohen, "All There Is to Know About Adolph Eichmann" in Leonard Cohen, *Flowers for Hitler*, 78.

91. Djwa, "Leonard Cohen: Black Romantic", 34.

92. Wynands, "The Representation of the Holocaust in *Flowers for Hitler*", 206.

93. Leonard Cohen, *The Energy of Slaves* (1972. Toronto: McClelland and Stewart, 1974), 127.

94. Wynands, "The Representation of the Holocaust in *Flowers for Hitler*", 208.

95. Wayman, "Cohen's Women", 92.

96. Wayman, "Cohen's Women", 92.

97. Djwa, "Leonard Cohen: Black Romantic", 41.

98. Ravvin, "Writing about the Holocaust", 6.

Robert Enright and Leonard Cohen (interview date November 2007)

SOURCE: Enright, Robert, and Leonard Cohen. "Interview with Leonard Cohen." *Border Crossings* 26, no. 4 (November 2007): 26-40.

[*In the following interview, Enright and Cohen cover a wide range of topics, including Cohen's latest volume of poetry, spirituality, depression, and love.*]

I think there are certain rhythms and connections that for some odd reason use the vehicle of language to deeply penetrate into your psyche, your feelings, or into life itself.

The Book of Longing, a collection of poetry and prose Leonard Cohen published in 2006, is about wisdom. Composed by a man who has lived much in the world, and who has come to understand what all that living has been about, it also knows enough to take its wisdom with a grain of salt. While his ability to write remains undiminished, what he writes about has undergone some adjustments. As the poet himself laments, he now aches in the places where he used to play, and his candour in addressing those moments of pain is no less compelling than it was when he articulated his moments of passion. Cohen, in his 73rd year to heaven, remains our most satisfying poet on the complications of love and the loving body.

Consider the opening lines of **"The Collapse of Zen,"** an erotic poem that shapes itself around a series of rhetorical questions:

> When I can wedge my face into the place and struggle with my breathing as she brings her eager fingers down to separate herself, to help me use my whole mouth against her hungriness, her most private of hungers— why should I want to be enlightened?

Why indeed, when enlightenment comes with the fleshly territory? I am reminded in reading Cohen's poem of an earlier declaration of desire written by W. B. Yeats, which also figured out the answer to a question it set for itself. In "Politics," written only a year before his death in 1939, Yeats wrestles with the competing tug of the personal and the social. He begins by quoting Thomas Mann's famous declaration that "In our time the destiny of man presents its meaning in political terms," and goes on to ask how is it possible to "fix his attention" on politics in the presence of "that girl standing there." Yeats is only marginally prepared to admit there may be something in the positions taken by men of the world and politicians.

It's clear that the real truth lies in transformative youth and physical passion. Cohen, for his part, won't buy back into time, but he holds resolutely to the passionate body. "My heart is broken as usual," he says near the end of **"The Collapse of Zen,"** "over someone's evanescent beauty."

While the quest for beauty has been at the centre of Cohen's life and art for over 50 years, it has not blinded him to mankind's dangerous tendencies. In this regard he leaves Yeats behind and bivouacs with Thomas Mann. He claims he is too old to "learn the names of the new killers" but he is aware of "their old obsolete atrocity / that has driven out / the heart's warm appetite / and humbled evolution / and made a puke of prayer." Earlier in **"The Collapse of Zen"** he observes that "the tender blooming nipple of mankind / is caught in the pincers / of power and muscle and money." A number of these poems play the same chord as the songs in **The Future,** Cohen's prophetic and brilliant album from 1992. He has seen the future; it works; and it is murder.

Cohen's wisdom is in his ability to bring together the cultures of conscience and love. He writes in **"The Mist of Pornography"** that one of the functions of poetry is "to overthrow vulgarity / and set America straight / with the barbed wire / and the regular beatings / of rhyme." To recall Yeats again, a touch of mocking mockers emerges in the formulation. How effective a punishment is being beaten by lines of poetry; how likely is it that the pincers of power will be replaced by the barbs of rhyme?

Finally, though, Cohen is redeemed by love. In the light impression we make on the skin of the world, "it is in love that we are made; in love we disappear." Making and unmaking, the loved and the lover. In Cohen's wise construction of the world, there is no way to tell the poet dancer from the poetic dance.

The following interview combines two telephone conversations recorded from Los Angeles on May 7 and May 12, 2007.

[*Border Crossings*]: *The drawings by Leonard Cohen were included in an exhibition called "Drawn to Words: Visual works from 40 years," which premiered at the Drabinsky Gallery in Toronto on June 3, 2007.*

[Leonard Cohen]: The proofs were printed by Graham Nash, who has a state-of-the-art printing facility on the beach. I think we printed 56. Quite a few, which are in colour, aren't in the **Book of Longing.** A number of the images in the book were details of larger works in which the colours are very rich and the blacks very black. The medium for the drawings ranges from watercolours to oil pastels, to a number of combinations of those, which are then put in Photoshop. A lot of them were drawn on a Wacom tablet with a free-standing stylus fit right into the computer. So it really runs from doodles on napkins to watercolours, oil pastels, charcoal drawings, right up to digitally created images.

There's a little mirror on my desk and I just draw. Then I look and see what expression is there, what is the guy saying, and I annotate it. It's a very accurate presentation of the moment and nothing more.

So you go from doodles to an image that you consciously sit down to orchestrate. Does that cover the way the work comes to you?

Well, you know, just as play is deadly serious for children, so doodles are deadly serious for me.

My question wasn't about forming a hierarchy as much as the way the Muse comes to you. I'm interested in the relationship that exists in your mind between the drawing and your work as a poet, songwriter and novelist. Do they come from the same source?

I think one is relief from the other. I always drew and when my kids were growing up, a large feature of our family activity was to sit around the kitchen table with a lot of different kinds of material and draw. That's always been what I've done, especially in Greece when there seemed to be a lot of time, or when the kids were growing up in Montreal. Then I got interested in computers. I don't know if you remember, but at a certain point Macintosh gave free computers to Canadian writers, including Margaret Atwood, Irving Layton and Jack McClelland. Not only that, they were kind enough to provide tutors who actually came to my house and helped me set up and showed me how to work it. So I got interested in the Macintosh computer quite early.

When you say you've always drawn, how far back do you mean? I've read that you determined at an early age that you were going to be a poet. Was drawing also always part of your expression?

It was just one of the things that I and a number of my friends did. I grew up with the Montreal sculptor Morton Rosengarten and we always drew together. He, of course, did it professionally but I never remotely thought of it as anything that would be treated professionally. I didn't expect it to have a public face.

Your whole career has been a series of abdications from doing anything that might be regarded as professional. At least that's what you keep saying.

"Career" was a word that didn't really describe what I was doing. Of course, I've had to re-examine that notion very carefully in the past couple of years. I found out I better have a career because I don't have any money left. I guess a career was always a necessity but I never thought of it that way I wanted to be paid for my work but I didn't want to work for pay. I would never have used the word "poet." "Writer" is the word I use because, as I've said elsewhere, I think poetry is a verdict that other people make about your work and it's not appropriate to claim it yourself. It's a description of a very high degree.

So your modesty in not referring to yourself as a poet isn't disingenuous?

I know the league I'm operating in. I don't want to claim modesty, either, because that is another title. But you know there is King David, there's Homer, Shakespeare and Dante. When I read Layton, I see the conviction and dedication to the whole enterprise, so I don't think it's difficult to see what I mean. As I wrote in the preface for the catalogue to these drawings, if my songs were the only songs in the world, they'd be really important, and similarly with my poems. But you get into line and if you have even a passing acquaintance with what the tradition is, I think it's appropriate to recognize that you're not going to be at the head of that line. That's all I mean to say.

When you published your first book, you were surrounded by a cluster of remarkable poets, including A. J. M. Smith, Louis Dudek, Irving Layton and A. M. Klein. Montreal was a pretty hot place for poetry back in those days.

I think it probably still is. But there were a couple of street poets—Henry Moskowitz and Philip Tetrault—who didn't get recognized. There were really good poets in the city but I think Irving had such a compelling public projection because of *Fighting Words*. He brought poetry to a larger audience and he dignified the enterprise in some kind of way, although poets don't need too much encouragement to figure themselves important. When we met, we considered it a kind of summit meeting and that great affairs were being determined.

You've said the poets you were writing to were writers like William Butler Yeats. I assume you could take for granted a tradition that happened to take poetic form in Montreal?

I felt we were part of something. I felt also there was a certain power in the fact that we were provincial, that we weren't American and that we weren't English, that somehow our freedom and our rights were protected. By being in this backwater, we could come into it from a position that was a little fresher, a little less burdened by the tradition, but very much aware of it at the same time.

A. J. M. Smith had a notion he called "eclectic detachment" through which Canadian poets could choose the tradition they wanted. I don't know about the detachment but the eclecticism seemed desirable. You could form your own poetic tradition because you weren't in thrall to either of them.

It's something like that. There was a lot of wiggle room. Also, you weren't being judged by anyone because nobody cared. There were no prizes, there was no Canada Council, there were no women.

You mean you couldn't even get laid by writing a poem? That can't be true.

Pretty much. And there was no money. We were putting out those early publications on mimeograph machines. Nobody felt a chip on their shoulder that they couldn't make it as a writer because nobody expected to make it as a writer. So there was an absence of self-pity about the whole thing and people were in it for the activity itself. When we'd meet and read each other our poems, the criticism was savage but it was our thing. It was La Cosa Nostra. I remember Frank Scott reading a poem—Phyllis Webb was there and Irving and Dudek and Ursula and Bob Currie—and it was torn apart and he started crying. Everybody was in their cups. He was the dean of the Law School at that time and he said, "You're right, it was a weak poem and I've spread myself too thin." That was the atmosphere. It was rigorous and you had to defend every word. I don't know if that goes on any more. I get a considerable amount of mail from young poets and they're mostly interested in getting published and somehow advancing their position in some fictitious world of poetry they think exists.

And not in the rigour that made Emily Dickinson consider every syllable, yet alone every word?

Those were the terms in which we had to defend every word and it did often get ugly. But the general feeling was that we were engaged in an important and noble enterprise and that you gave yourself to this without any hope of anything other than the possible claim that you were part of it, that you deserved to be numbered among the great ones.

So you publish two books of poetry that get well reviewed, as well as a novel, and throughout this entire process you realize you're not going to make a living as a writer. It's as if the residue of Montreal continued to haunt you even after you'd become successful.

I wasn't surprised that I couldn't make a living out of poetry. I thought maybe I could make a living out of the novel, which in my case wasn't that far from poetry. There was a moment when I realized there were bills I couldn't pay, so it wasn't a difficult revelation. In retrospect, I'm not sure what made me think that becoming a musician or a singer was going to address the economic crisis, either.

I've always admired your poem "For E. J. P.," which opens, "I once believed a single line in a Chinese poem." In it you make reference to Ezra Pound's Chinese poetry. The poem is dedicated to E. J. Pratt, it quotes Pound, there is in it a hint of Rilke, even Robert Browning. I read the poem as a compendium of other poets to whom you were paying direct homage.

That's a good insight. I dedicated it to E. J. Pratt because I had met him, not because he influenced my work at all. I just had tremendous respect for what he'd done in Canada and his person was very, very appealing. But those echoes are in the poem, especially the Chinese poets.

Has language always been a repository of its own previous use for you?

I think it was A. E. Housman who said it either makes the hair on the back of your neck stand up or it doesn't. I think there are certain rhythms and connections that for some odd reason use the vehicle of language to deeply penetrate into your psyche, your feelings, or into life itself. I think each writer (in fact, I think everybody) has a few of those rhythms, of what they consider highly charged language. Both the message conveyed and the conveyance itself take on tremendous significance. Because you're standing as a young boy in synagogue and you hear the words from The Memorial Service for the Dead, "Lord, what is man that thou regardest him? or the son of man that Thou takest account of him? Man is like to vanity; his days are as a shadow that passeth away. In the morning he flourisheth and sprouteth afresh; in the evening he is cut down, and withereth. So teach us to number our days that we may get us a heart of wisdom." So both the meaning of what is conveyed and, more importantly, the rhythm of the language imprint themselves. I think that's what one goes for, either to emulate, to resist, or to modify it. I

think there's maybe four or five of those patterns that continually compel you, or invite you to recreate that highly charged moment.

In a song like "If it Be Your Will," are you ploying off rhythms that come out of Judaic culture? On a number of occasions you have deliberately invoked the sound of that tradition.

Yes, because it is a powerful tradition. Just the formulation of "If it Be Your Will" has that quality. There are many prayers that have that refrain. There are a lot of references and echoes to both Christian and Jewish traditions.

So it's no accident that your first book would be called **Let Us Compare Mythologies.** *That would be a description of how your imagination functions?*

I think that's so. Temperamentally, I've always resisted the claim for the unique truth of one particular model, and, growing up in Montreal, one had powerful versions of Catholicism, Protestantism and Judaism. It didn't involve a real stretch to be affected by those traditions. It was natural.

Did you systematically set out to learn the traditions?

At different points in my life I seemed to be involved in a closer study than at other times. For instance, when I was a secretary to my teacher, Roshi, it was at a time when there was a kind of rapprochement between Zen and the Roman Catholic church (through people like Thomas Merton). So my teacher, who was probably the heaviest guy around in North America, was invited to the headquarters of the Trappists in Massachusetts. I would accompany him to a lot of these Catholic monasteries in which I would participate in the setting-up routine while Roshi was leading meditations.

So you lingered in North American monasteries but not in European ones?

That's right. I did linger in a number of them and I would talk to the monks and get a feel for things apart from what I was reading, like Simone Weil. I remember an older monk with whom I became friendly. I said to him one day, "How's it going?" and he said, "I've been here 12 years and every morning when I wake up I have to decide whether or not to stay." It's a rough life.

You stayed a while and then decided that the spiritual life wasn't for you. Did you come down from the mountain somewhat discouraged?

I was privileged to have a friendship with Roshi so I took certain personae for the poems as a way of bringing something across in a rather lighthearted way. I'm reluctant to answer your question, because I've already answered it in a number of the poems at the beginning of the **Book of Longing,** like **"Leaving Mt. Baldy,"** **"My Life in Robes," "His Master's Voice," "When I Drink"** and **"The Lovesick Monk."** So your question hits the nail on the head, it's just that it took a whole book to answer it. But I spent many years with Roshi and the friendship continues. I'm not living there but whenever he comes, I see him. Incidentally, he just turned 100 and we had a great party. We were having a drink a couple of years ago when he was 98—he's a good drinker—and he poured his glass, poked me in the arm and said, "Excuse me for not dying."

You mention the word "persona." How much are we to read the work as a series of masks that can be put on and which we shouldn't take as literal positions you hold? Can they be seen as creations or characters?

I see it more through the prism of a friendship you have with the reader, or with someone you're writing for. It's the kind of disclosure that goes with friendship, that kind of confidentiality. I think the essence of friendship is that you always let the other person off the hook.

It's essentially a generosity?

It is a kind of generosity. It doesn't mean to say you have to buy it and that nothing hangs on it. I tried to put that in a song called **"The Night Comes On,"** which goes: "and here's to the few / who forgive what you do / and the fewer who don't even care."

So are the songs scans of sensibility to which you commit yourself? Is that why you often thank the reader for coming into the room with you?

I do feel that. You don't want to name these things too carefully because that is also one of the characteristics of friendship: you don't name it. You don't want to say to anyone, "You're my best friend." So they are expressions. I do feel the liberties and the mild responsibilities that go with friendship.

In a self-portrait called "Too Tough for Us," you draw yourself with the crazed concentration of a Shunga figure, minus the visible sexual apparatus. The self-portraits nin a fair range, from self-ridicule through to a recognition of aging. I gather that's a deliberate scoring of where you find yourself?

That's exactly it. At certain periods of time, I would do a self-portrait to begin the day. I have hundreds of them. For a year I did one every morning. I'd brew a pot of coffee, light a stick of incense—I don't smoke so it's the closest I can get to it—and then do the drawing. There's a little mirror on my desk and I just draw. Then

I look and see what expression is there, what is the guy saying, and I annotate it. It's a very accurate presentation of the moment and nothing more.

You call them "acceptable decorations" in the piece you wrote for your exhibition at the Drabinsky Gallery in Toronto. There's a kind of generous accuracy and—this may be a word that sticks in your craw—a courage about them.

I don't mind somebody else using it as long as I don't have to. I say in one of the poems in **Book of Longing** that I can't claim anything for this path. There's nothing one can say about it, it's just that sometimes you bend down over your labour and you know it's okay, it's not the greatest thing, it's acceptable. A friend wanted me to call it "transcendent decorations," but I said that was too self-congratulatory. It's acceptable in the sense that it gently refers to a lot of things we know in the pictorial tradition. It doesn't have to participate in the current artistic enterprise, which is involved with originality and some kind of abrasive assertion. I don't pretend to understand what is being asserted so abrasively by so many people in the field; it doesn't participate in that kind of world. I use images that refer to things we've liked in art. That's the way I feel these come off, although that was never my intention. My intention was to make something that was accessible and with which I could decorate my notebooks.

Very often the relationship between the self-portraits and the women reminds me of what Picasso was after. There's almost a dialectical representation in the drawings: beauty is then in its plenitude and you're there in the guise of self-ridicule and self-mockery.

That's a nice way to put it. This attention to the drawings is very recent. People have been asking me about writing for about 50 years, so you get a rap, but because I'm not up on the way people talk about art, I don't know the score. I haven't had that chance and maybe that's good. I was never compelled to come up with an apology or a manifesto. To me, "acceptable decorations" is very close. Not to use decoration in a pejorative way but as a legitimate vehicle of pleasure or delight.

In a drawing like "The Grecian," I'm reminded of what Hockney did in his Celia drawings. In the same way that language has its own history and its own ear, maybe the eye does, too.

Yes, I think so. I don't know the particular series you're talking about but I know his work. I think that everything everyone has ever seen is there, especially if what you've looked at is really good.

One of the lovely refrains you have is "do not decode these cries of mine, / they are the road, and not the sign." I'm interested in the work you've done in all

forms as a process you can decode, which does tell us something about your life and your attitude towards living. I guess what I'm saying is they're not just constructed masks but they're about what you've done and how you felt about the world.

Communication exists on so many levels. Like in the interpretation of the Bible—there's the narrative, then there's the aphoristic, then there's metaphor: it wasn't really about crossing the Red Sea, it was about liberation. Then the mystical, in which these are formulas for meditative exercises that are liberating. So you can get into that kind of thing. But the caution I was trying to present there was that this is also about what really happened. When I say "tumbled up in formless circumstance," I mean that's what happened. I was sitting there and the light came in through the window and it really did happen that way. In that moment I was trying to indicate that a cigar is a cigar.

I like the way your written introduction focuses on what's in the room with you. So the candlesticks and the bowls and the fruit, even the table, become utterly important. Does a lot of your work come out of that engagement with the quotidian, with the vernacular?

I've always had beautiful tables. In Greece I had a really good kitchen table, which somebody gave to me, and I still have three or four good ones in Montreal. I got this feeling of freedom about tables from Michel Gameau, a Quebecois writer who just translated **Book of Longing.** He lives across the street and he brought Rosengarten and me to that neighbourhood. I went into his little house and the whole downstairs was just a rectangle and a table had been built on three sides of the room, permanently, against the wall. He said, "I spend my life at tables, so I might as well have a good one and a big one." I've taken the lead on that and I have some really big tables. The one I'm standing in front of right now is nine feet long and three and a half feet wide. A friend of mine, a Seventh Day Adventist, made it for me. He made me three or four of them.

In **"The Mist of Pornography,"** *you talk about the "impeccable order of objects on a table." It is about the satisfaction that comes from seeing one thing in relation to another.*

What really makes it so sweet is to have the time to absorb those things—the ashtray, the candlestick, some pieces of fruit. It stands for the order we can't acquire in our own psyche.

And in our own emotional lives? Is this what you call refuelling; sitting at a table is a chance to do that?

Yes. It's just a delight. You don't want to make too much out of it because these things come upon you with their own sense of urgency at the appropriate mo-

ments. You don't want to get into some kind of disciplinary action where you've got to see the thing perfectly all the time. The moment arises when they assert their beauty and their unassailable perfection.

Is that recognition something that comes with experience and wisdom? The simple is one of the most difficult things to achieve.

First of all, you have to have something in you that responds to that kind of idea, and then it's activated by the people, the artwork and the expressions you bump into. When I was quite young, I used to love Japanese watercolours and paintings. I don't know what it is that made me respond to that, except that it's glorious. It's also empty.

The beauty of the floating world isn't necessarily something that would come naturally.

It has to resonate with something that's already there. Also, when we were setting up our rooms around Montreal, people like Rosengarten and myself, we'd go to the Salvation Army and find a good table and a good chair and bring it back and somehow it filled the room. It was glorious. You don't want too much else; "I choose the rooms that I live in with care, / the windows are small and the walls almost bare, / there's only one bed and there's only one prayer." That was one of the first songs that I wrote and it was really true. My sense of the voluptuous involved that kind of simplicity. It wasn't simplicity I was after, it was the opposite, the voluptuous feeling of simplicity. I don't want to get too paradoxical but that was what was beautiful.

You don't often hear someone talking as a voluptuous puritan. You've also said you've never had much inspiration. So where does the art come from? If it doesn't come out of that ignition, is it about the careful observation of the world?

There was a tiny poem that I left out of the **Book of Longing.** It had a wry self-portrait and it was called **"My Career"**: "so little to say, so urgent to say it." I don't know why I left it out. Maybe it was too close to the bone.

When you talk about the "mysterious impreciseness" of your art, where is the imprecision?

There are 300 self-portraits and none of them looks like me.

But they all look like you.

Yes, that too. From a certain point of view, that's not what I'm going for. Occasionally they do actually look like me and they satisfy those criteria.

What about the drawing called "Jokan?" To pull a phrase from Rumi, it looks like you're a member of "the caravan of despair." It does cover an aspect of your melancholy.

I think that's the one called "The Mysterious Imprecision". We couldn't get the blacks. That's of course what I'm going for: the picture of the inside.

*Rumi has that lovely notion that it's through the wound that the light gets in. Is that your source for **"Anthem"**?*

I did read Rumi a lot, especially when I was younger.

I guess it's a simple recognition of a process of salvation, that if life is this impossible enterprise, then we have to find a way to salvage something from it. Recognizing that the wound is also a way for illumination to occur is a perfectly sensible way of viewing the world.

You know when Moses came down from the mountain and saw the Children of Israel worshipping the Golden Calf, he threw the tablets to the ground and they broke. Then he went back up and came down with the full set again. Now, the interesting thing—and it's not in the Bible but it is in the oral tradition—is that when they built the tabernacle, they put the broken ones in with the whole ones. They kept the broken ones, as if to say this also is part of the immutable, inflexible human law. We are broken. Many years later, the Hassids would say that "from the broken fragments of my heart I will build an altar to the Lord." That sense of brokenness is impossible to avoid today. It seems to be clearer today than it was when I was young, so I say it over and over again, "there is a crack in everything / that's how the light gets in."

The Future *was an extraordinary album. That cluster of poems seems to stand in the same relation to our epoch that T. S. Eliot's* Wasteland *did to his. Did you have a sense in doing it, or a sense now, of how radical a statement it was?*

I do and I was disappointed that nobody got it because it didn't really do very well. It only sold 60,000 or 70,000 copies in America and those numbers don't compel any serious interest or examination. It sold better in Europe. But when the Berlin Wall came down, there was general rejoicing and I must have been the only person who wasn't rejoicing. I felt it was going to present a tremendous disequilibrium. That's why I say, "give me back the Berlin Wall / give me back Stalin and St. Paul," because this is not the beginning of a period of liberation. As I say in a poem in one of my early books, the victor in the Second World War was freedom, but freedom to do horror. And that's what I felt when the Wall came down, freedom to murder. "I

have seen the future and it is murder." It's only recently, because I get sent things from the Internet, that those poems are being talked about. It's really gratifying because people are recognizing that I had the feeling and I said it. Again, I don't know what it is. As I've said, if I knew where the good songs came from, I'd go there more often. But I knew that was seminal at the time. It goes with the territory, you feel that this is really good.

Do the drawings occupy the same register as the songs? Do they elaborate the same ideas about self and society but just in a different medium?

I guess they do, but not intentionally because I didn't prepare them over the years for display. But of course they participated because they were made by the same guy. I just never imagined them. When I see them now, they look true and like acceptable decorations. They don't ask you to know everything there is to know about the tradition and about what's going on. On the other hand, they don't insult your intelligence if you don't know what's going on. That's what I mean by their acceptability.

I'm interested in your notion that you cut personality away from the work of art. T. S. Eliot said that poetry was an escape from personality and not an indulgence in it. I wonder what role personality has played in your work?

I'd elaborate on what Eliot said, which is that every sense of peacefulness derives from the degree to which the personality is forgotten. I think that peace and personality are mutually exclusive.

So, in a sense, the abdication of self is the way you find the richest aspects of yourself?

I think it's the only time you can relax. Who it is that is relaxing is precisely the unexamined elephant in the room. As soon as you examine who is relaxing, then you're not relaxing. It's exactly as you say. It's the abdication of the effort to maintain the heroic dimension of your life that is personality. When that dissolves, you can lay back for a moment or two. You can't live that way because obviously you need a self, an ego and a personality to interact with all the other selves, personalities and egos. But that dissolves in those blessed moments we call grace.

There is in your work the idea that beauty is the way the world can be judged and understood. The quest for it seems central to what you do.

Nothing arises in me to dispute the idea that the quest for beauty is central to my life. I certainly wouldn't resist it. I sometimes hear it more as gossip than anything I can get behind, but I think that conversation about these matters is completely legitimate.

What's changed over the years?

My life was very painful for no reason that I could discern. Most of the time the background was anguish and almost everything I did, from the pursuit of women, drugs and religion to my monastic life, was to address this problem. The cover story was successful: I had money, I had fame, I had most of the things people want. So I felt ashamed about feeling bad. But honestly, to get from moment to moment was extremely difficult. The sense of anguish was acute. What happened was that the background of suffering totally dissolved. Whether it happened because of the 30 years I spent with my dear and beloved teacher, or whether it was the couple of years I spent subsequently in India with another great teacher, I don't know. I read somewhere that as you get older, certain brain cells associated with anxiety die in some people. In any event, what happened was that I stopped suffering.

Was this an epiphany, or was it gradual?

It happened by imperceptible degrees over two or three weeks. I didn't even know it was happening, I just woke up one day and I said to myself, this must be what people feel like, I don't feel great, I don't feel bad. I know that if something bad happens, I'll be bummed out, but everything is okay, the background has dissolved. It's just an ordinary day, it isn't a struggle, it isn't an ordeal.

So the cloud that hung over everything disappeared?

It dissipated. People ask me—was it the meditation, was it the discipline?—and I can't say. Something in me is deeply grateful and I don't know who to be grateful to. But it doesn't really matter. I just feel this sense of gratitude. That's why when I had lost everything, my friends wondered why I wasn't destroyed. It was pretty dramatic and people around me were waiting for me to fall. But it didn't mean fuck all because I felt good. When it all comes down to it, everything is about mood. I don't ask the Lord to be tested but you can be in extreme circumstances and if your mood is okay, your mood is okay. My mood has been good.

I love your notion that life is designed to overthrow you and that nobody masters it. You seem to be doing pretty well on the mastery level.

But listen, you can't claim it. It can come and go. You can't build a house on it, it's given to you and all you can do is say thank you.

When the black cloud lifted, did it have any effect on your creativity?

On the contrary. It's true that sorrow and suffering are the spur or the thorn that often does invite a response in certain kinds of creative individuals. When I say that

the background of anguish disappeared, I mean that something that was imposed on my nature was removed. My own nature, which responds to suffering, to sorrow and to melancholy, had been freed to respond authentically to whatever emotions arose. So I wrote and produced Anjani's record, I finished **Book of Longing** and I've been at it ever since with a kind of graceful intensity that hasn't abated.

Did it occur to you that there might have been a methodology that would help you get rid of the way you were feeling?

I tried everything. I tried wine, women and song in a really serious experiment. It wasn't all hard work but it didn't work, either. And then at the same time—these experiments were often running concurrently—I tried all the conventional antidepressants. None of them worked. I got to the point where I pulled my medications out of my shaving kit where I kept them and threw everything away. I thought, that's the end of it, I'm not trying anything else, I'm going to face it, I'm just humiliated by the attention I've given to medications that don't work.

Had you resolved yourself to the fact that this anxiety would be a condition you would have to undergo for the rest of your life?

That was the spontaneous thought that arose. I had also been given herbal and organic remedies because people were kind, especially in a monastic situation. They want to be helpful and a lot of them were into New Age solutions, which I'm not. I prefer conventional approaches. But I said, "I've had it, I can't do this thing anymore, so screw it. I'm going to go down with my eyes open." Things got really bad and that's when I said to Roshi, I've got to get out of here; it's too hard now. Because that life is designed to overthrow a 20-year-old. You get up very early, you don't get enough sleep and you're doing physical labour. I've talked to Marines about this and it's like boot camp training. If you're an ordained monk and an officer of Zendo or the administration, the life is vigorous. You get up at 2:30 to prepare the stove, especially if it's the winter, then at 3:00 the chanting begins, then there's two hours in the meditation hall, then breakfast and clean-up before the work bell. Then there's work—shovelling snow, cooking, cleaning, and the carpentry necessary to keep the facility going. There's another couple of hours of meditation in the afternoon, then supper—there may be 20 minutes, rest—then maybe two hours more until about 9:30. That's the regular week. But every four weeks there's a full retreat, which is 16 hours of rigorous sitting. Every half hour or so you walk around and shake out your legs but basically from 3:00 in the morning until 10:00 at night you are in the meditation hall with short breaks for meals and one-hour-long work periods. There's a few things you learn whether or not you achieve enlightenment, which I wasn't going for, I was just trying to feel better. But whatever your thing is, you're going to get into good shape and you're going to stop whining. I mean, there's no point.

So if you were already aching in the places where you used to play, this life would have made things that much more difficult?

Exactly. So I said to Roshi, I'm going to go down and poke around. He's very understanding and he asked, "How long will you be gone?" and I said, "I don't know." One of the monks had given me a book by Ramesh S. Balsekar and his writings had started to intrigue me in my last few weeks on Mount Baldy, which were very difficult. I'd been reading him, he's a former president of a branch of the Bank of India, with a lot of pleasure and I don't know why—I don't know why anybody does anything—but when I came down the mountain, I thought, I'm going to look him up. I found out he was still alive. I went to San Francisco to get a visa for India, and within 48 hours I was sitting with him in Bombay, and then that curious thing happened that I described to you. By imperceptible degrees, this tiling lifted. I felt terrific, I felt, I've got a shot at it. I hadn't been able to establish any relationships. You'd choose somebody you thought could get you out of the fix, and then you weren't out of it and you would blame them in some secret chamber of your heart. I could never enjoy the love and the companionship because I was in it for completely different and selfish and divergent reasons. So nothing worked. I mean, I was skillful socially, so I could put on a decent face and come up with the right excuses. But basically it was because I couldn't penetrate this gloom. Then the gloom lifted and my relationships improved.

Were you ever so full of despair that suicide seemed a possibility?

I'm hard-wired against it, tribally. My thing was more, "Fuck this, I'm just going to go out on heroin," or "I'm going to go to Thailand and fuck myself to death." Suicide is so genetically offensive to my scene. You're not allowed to do it; it's a law. So I thought about giving up by getting lost in the world.

It's not as if you weren't productive throughout this period. Why did you bother?

I was doing good work. I think it's just part of my training. You just have to contribute, you can't go on a free ride, there's work to be done. Don't forget that my life was operating, it's just that sometimes it was very, very rough.

There are, after all, tremendously productive alcoholics.

There are. I've known a number of them and I've always wanted to be one. I was getting close to that. In 1993 on tour, I was drinking three bottles of red wine a day before going on stage. But I paid for it. I was in bad shape and I gained a lot of weight and I had to stop. That was one of the reasons I went up to Mount Baldy, I knew I couldn't go on with that amount of alcohol.

So in that sense it was a place of last resort?

People have very romantic ideas but a monastery is a kind of hospital where people end up because they can't make it in any other circumstances. Roshi was aware of what was going on. I can safely say his genius is to be fully aware of your inner predicament but he doesn't perceive it anecdotally. He perceives it as sculpture. He feels there is something off balance. He's not interested in how you feel about your parents, or your work, or anything else. Still, he's a man who needs friendships like everybody else, and so with his friends he will become aware of your actual situation, the name of the woman and the name of your children and what you're going through. That isn't absent from his character but in his work, his mission, he perceives the shape of your inner predicament and he moves in it and against it and around it on that level. It's a very subtle kind of help. The feeling you have sometimes is that he is moving you just to correct an imbalance. He said something to me that was very beautiful. He doesn't speak English very well but he conveyed the full meaning when he said, "Change religion, okay. Friendship important." I never abandoned Roshi. I mean, I'm a practising Jew, and I always was, but I still felt myself a practising monk. We're complex creatures; unless you're dealing with orthodox people on either side who wouldn't be tolerant. But my orthodoxy is this other thing where you can hold various positions. I've never found any conflicts.

Norman Ravvin (essay date 2007)

SOURCE: Ravvin, Norman. "Imaginary Traditions: Irving Layton, Leonard Cohen and the Rest of the Montreal Poets." In *Language Acts: Anglo-Québec Poetry, 1976 to the 21st Century*, edited by Jason Camlot and Todd Swift, pp. 110-30. Montréal: Véhicule Press, 2007.

[*In the following essay, Ravvin presents an analysis of the place of Cohen and Irving Layton among their fellow Montreal poets and in the annals of Canadian and Jewish literature.*]

Belmont Avenue and St. Elisabeth Street are not more than fifteen minutes apart by car, though they exist as opposite poles in Montreal's mythic twentieth-century

Jewish geography. From his bedroom at the back of his parents' Belmont Avenue home, Leonard Cohen meditated on the green preserve of Westmount's Murray Hill Park. The park is a key lyrical presence in his first novel, *The Favorite Game,* which offers it, unnamed, as a kind of public imaginative space where a young poet's dreams of independence and love incubate:

> The park nourished all the sleepers in the surrounding houses. It was the green heart. It gave the children dangerous bushes and heroic landscapes so they could imagine bravery. . . . It gave the retired brokers vignettes of Scottish lanes where loving couples walked, so they could lean on their canes and imagine poetry.[1]

At the other end of Jewish Montreal, east of the Main, Irving Layton was raised on St. Elisabeth Street, an immigrant street par excellence, not far from where writers as different as Saul Bellow and A. M. Klein confronted themselves, their inheritance, and the babel of languages on Montreal's narrow downtown thoroughfares. (When the children in Cohen's *The Favorite Game* fantasize about danger, they conjure a whore on De Bullion Street, the street where Layton's father took him to synagogue).[2] Montreal's once-Jewish downtown, with its potpourri of walk-ups, frilly mansard roofs, corner *dépanneurs,* and granite rowhouses on more venerable blocks, had its own distinct charm. But for Layton, childhood on St. Elisabeth Street in the late '10s and early '20s included its fair share of pauperized immigrant struggle, a youthful abandonment of his parents' orthodoxy, and low-grade street war with the neighbourhood's non-Jewish kids: "If someone had said the words anti-Semitism to me," he writes in his memoir *Waiting for the Messiah,* "I would not have understood. But it was in the streets and alleyways. It blanketed us like a fog. *Maudits Juifs!*"[3] Both Belmont and St. Elisabeth are interesting places to come from, but they are, in many ways, as distant from one another as two continents. Still, Layton and Cohen became companions and inspired one another. Although Layton's seniority suggests a role as mentor (born in 1912, he is twenty-two years the elder) it becomes clear with further attention to the two poets' progress that their artistic entanglement and friendship cannot be characterized simply as the attention paid by an elder, street-smart mentor to a younger, well-heeled and formally educated protégé. It is worth questioning the commonly held view regarding a line of inheritance shared among Montreal Jewish poets of the 1950s and after. Such a line begins, we are told, with A. M. Klein, who is dubbed, depending on who is doing the dubbing, the father or the grandfather of Canadian Jewish literature. Klein's mantle is said to have passed to Layton, to be taken up by Cohen. In a 1945 review of Layton's first collection, *Here and Now,* Klein's approval is not unqualified, but it is strong:

> *Here and Now* reveals an unmistakable talent, a power of expression which is unique and personal, and social awareness which endows poetic utterance with base and substance. Layton can certainly take his place in the Canadian pleiad, not like a twinkling little star, but as one of unquestioned brightness and constancy.[4]

Still, the time-line behind an orderly inheritance is not borne out by the facts. Klein went entirely silent in the middle 1950s, just as Layton's work and public persona broke into popular view. Cohen's first volume of poetry, **Let Us Compare Mythologies,** appears in 1956, a precocious debut under the sponsorship of Louis Dudek's McGill Poetry Series. Though Layton had been bringing out largely self-published books since 1945, it was his 1956 collection, *The Improved Binoculars,* with its prefatory note by William Carlos Williams, that marked a turning point in his career. The three poets' progress overlap in surprising ways: Layton's early books appear as Klein is still seeking a mainstream audience, and Cohen's breakthrough coincided with Layton's arrival as a controversial figure.

The notion of an orderly line of poetic inheritance is challenged, too, by the poets' own claims. In *Waiting for the Messiah,* Layton depicts Klein as a father figure and as an articulate bearer of polyglot knowledge, but not necessarily as a poetic model. Klein tutored Layton in Latin for school exams; he expounded, over coffee at Murray's restaurant, on Talmud and "events of the day."[5] Still, Layton goes out of his way to deny overt poetic influence: "He had little intellectual influence on me. His Zionism and conventionality left me cold. I couldn't reconcile the passionate poet I knew him to be with the paterfamilias and practising lawyer he had become."[6] Of Klein's visits to the group of young modernist poets associated with *First Statement* magazine, Layton opines, "I'd say it was we who influenced his style of writing rather than the other way around."[7]

In interviews, Cohen is equally willing to abandon Layton as a would-be mentor. In 1969 he told poet and interviewer Michael Harris:

> Well I think I became *friends* with Irving Layton, we became close friends. . . . There were many people who sat at his feet, I wasn't one of them. We very rarely discussed poetry or art. We discussed other things.[8]

We might hear, in each of these denials of influence, the poet's necessary overthrow of a precursor in order to assert the primacy of his own voice, alongside the myth of his own self-creation free of precursors. But there are undeniable differences in orientation, style and persona between these three. The differences include their formation in radically different poetic milieus: Klein in the English tradition of Milton and Shakespeare, along with the Yiddish writers of his youth; Layton among his modernist compatriots of the 1940s and the aggressively nativist writing of Americans such as Robert Creeley and William Carlos Williams; and Cohen's early imagistic writing developed under the tutelage of Dudek, but which then gave way to something more unpredictable, informed as much by American folk songs as Chassidic legend. As early as 1953, alongside his contributions to the poetry journal *CIV/n,* Cohen's biography informed readers that he "compose[d] poetry to the guitar."[9] When Klein, Layton and Cohen are viewed in this light, they comprise no poetic line at all. Rather, they appear as three diverse and, one might add, highly unusual personalities, whose Jewish identity was one component in their make-up as postwar Montreal poets. Klein and Layton shared a neighbourhood and the experience of growing up in an orthodox home, but Cohen is an outsider to such experience.

In the past four decades, however, the mythology of a Montreal Jewish poetic royalty (overseen by a kingpin who pronounces on inheritance) has taken hold. These developments have been furthered by, among other things, the resurgence of interest in A. M. Klein and his role as a strong precursor to later poets. Another defining issue has been the absence, in the rest of Canada, of figures as dynamic as Layton, Cohen and Klein, which has tended to increase the attention paid to their influence. The acceptance of a Montreal line of poetic succession has done much to support the belief in the presence, within Canadian literature, of a fully-formed tradition of Jewish writing. Whether such a belief is reliable or not is beyond the scope of this essay. What is intended here, via a careful exploration of Layton and Cohen's work, as well as through an examination of their life in art, is a portrait of the two poets' impact on English-language poetry in Montreal.

The other essays in this volume point to 1976 as a watershed year in any consideration of Montreal's English-language poetic production. That year was, in fact, an interesting one for both poets. Layton published his then-notorious *For My Brother Jesus,* a collection that combined strident Holocaust-related poems with repeated denunciations of what he called the "anti-sexuality, anti-life bias at the heart of Christianity."[10] He was living in Toronto, having left Montreal in 1969 to accept a teaching post in York University's English Department. Upon departing for what would be a nine-year sojourn, Layton bemoaned the deterioration of Montreal's Jewish downtown, complaining, in an uncharacteristically sentimental tone, that the "Hanukkah candles were going out."[11] In the 1970s, Cohen was far busier with song writing and concert tours than with the pursuit of literary success. His increasing interest in Zen led him to spend time near Los Angeles at the Mount Baldy retreat, under the tutelage of his Zen teacher, Roshi. In an unpublished manuscript from this

period called "The Final Revision of My Life in Art," Cohen cites, among other plans, to undertake his responsibilities as "street father to the young writers in Montreal, using the harsh style."[12]

How did two poets who are most commonly associated with Montreal's Jewish milieu, arrive at such circumstances, ensconced far from the city, thinking rather darkly of its possibilities? And what can we glean from these circumstances that helps us recognize the impact of their work on post-1976 Montreal poetry? To answer these questions (to steal a line from another songwriter steeped in folk poetry) we have to go all the way back to the civil war.[13]

THE POETRY WARS

The postwar Montreal literary scene, though the most important in the country, was small and divided between academics and those who denigrated university-based poetry. Poets tended to gravitate toward coteries, which were prone to infighting. A few senior figures such as F. R. Scott, A. J. M. Smith, Dudek and Klein represented a kind of generational authority and order, but their influence (whether through university posts, editorial power, or, in the case of Klein, his formal and traditional poetic rigour) was never dominant. Small press and little magazine activity presented young writers with independent outlets and a model by which to create new venues for their work. Here Layton asserted himself diligently and took up the role of cultural guide and worker alongside his pursuits as a poet. His early poems appeared in *First Statement,* and his first collections were either self-published or brought out by bare bones outfits like Raymond Souster's Contact Press in Toronto. The revolutionary stance taken up by the young writers who moved in these circles was the abandonment of Canadian (or British) poetic models in favour of American ones. And though Layton would later deny the influence of this milieu and its poetic inclinations, his early work profited from what Eli Mandel calls a "measured pro-American stand."[14] This included publishing in such influential American journals as *Black Mountain Review, Jargon,* and *Origin,* and receiving the enthusiastic embrace of Robert Creeley and William Carlos Williams. The latter famously affirmed Layton's arrival in his preface to the 1956 collection *The Improved Binoculars*: "When I first clapped eyes on the poems of Irving Layton, two years ago, I let out a yell of joy. . . . I believe this poet to be capable, to be capable of anything."[15]

In his excellent study of Layton's work, Eli Mandel notes that the "voice that endeared Layton to William Carlos Williams spoke an authentic North American speech. It was vulgar and therefore poetic."[16] Layton's American reception, according to poet and critic Seymour Mayne, can be contrasted with what Mayne forcefully calls a "perennial distaste" and "hostility" among Canadian reviewers and academics. These detractors, among whom Mayne includes Northrop Frye, rejected Layton's aggressive views regarding a "Canadian sensibility [and] . . . colonial gentility."[17] In addition, Mayne adds, most early reviews of Layton's poetry paid "scant attention" to the role of Jewishness in his work. "It is obvious," Mayne wrote in 1978, that "the American critics did not have the same prejudices toward Layton's work as the Canadians did."[18]

The absence of critical appreciation did not limit Layton's influence and involvement with a broad variety of Canadian poets and critics. Though Layton's poetic preferences may have been different, he maintained energetic dialogues, both private and public, with Louis Dudek, Ralph Gustafson, Desmond Pacey, and in later years, Earle Birney, Al Purdy, Milton Acorn, Barry Callaghan, Rienzi Crusz, Ken Sherman, David Solway, and Mayne himself. Leonard Cohen, however, emerges as the most interesting recipient of Layton's poetic and personal attention.

At the height of his popularity as a poet in the late 1960s, Cohen customarily downplayed his ambition to be "in the world of letters." In his 1969 interview with Harris, Cohen is at once emphatic and ambiguous on this matter. On the subject of poetic mentorship he acknowledges that if Layton had offered instruction, he'd done "it in a most subtle and beautiful way." Louis Dudek and Frank Scott were, he says, good teachers "who set out to teach [him] things in more direct ways" when he attended their classes at McGill.[19] More interesting, however, are Cohen's comments on his literary ambitions: "I wanted very much to be a poet in Montreal. . . . You know, to have to put out my work somehow and have it stand for a certain kind of life in the city of Montreal."[20] This suggests a fierce bond with the city itself, built upon the camaraderie, venues and reception that would follow from a writing life in Montreal. But shortly thereafter, Cohen tells Harris,

> I never sent things out to little magazines, poems, or anything like that. I never wanted to be in a world of letters. I wanted to be in the marketplace on a different level. I suppose I always wanted to be a pop singer.
>
> When I say pop singer I mean somehow that the things I put down would have music and lots of people would sing them.[21]

A sampling of Cohen's early poems can in fact be found in a 1953 number of *CIV/n*, a Montreal-based mimeographed "little magazine" whose editorial advisors included Layton and Dudek. Alongside other young poets based in the city, such as Avi Boxer and Phyllis Webb, Cohen contributed rather sketchy work that offers some presentiment of the kind of lyrical, intimate writing that would appear in *Let Us Compare Mytholo-*

gies and *The Favorite Game*. He reappears in a 1955 number with **"The Sparrows,"** in which there are suggestions of his later more successful lyrics:

> Catching winter in their carved nostrils
> the traitor birds have deserted us,
> leaving only the dullest brown sparrows
> for spring negotiations.
>
> I told you we were fools
> to have them in our games,
> but you replied:
>   They are only wind-up birds
> who strut on scarlet feet
> so hopelessly far
> from our curled fingers.[22]

Writing retrospectively of *CIV/n* in 1965, Dudek acknowledges that "a good deal" of the journal's submissions came "from young poets who were gathering around" himself and Layton.[23] Though it is reasonable to assume that Layton attracted Cohen to the pages of *CIV/n*, there is nothing Laytonesque about Cohen's contributions at this early point in his career. Layton's contributions to the journal are declamatory, lean of line, aggressively proclaiming the stance a poet ought to take while dismissing his lessers ("I'll say nothing about E. J. Pratt: / The rhyme's too easy—blat or flat").[24] Cohen's work, by comparison, is introverted, cryptic and disengaged, offering a private voice where Layton exercises what would become his characteristic prophetic tone.

By the late 1960s, Cohen (the would-be protégé) had developed an international career based on his music, while Layton's success was largely a Canadian phenomenon. The divergence in the two poets' artistic progress can be seen by juxtaposing photographs representing the mid-1950s and the mid-1960s. Included in a volume devoted to *CIV/n* is a set of photos taken at a 1954 gathering at Layton's home (a poets' night out attended by Avi Boxer, Eli Mandel, F. R. Scott and Phyllis Webb, among others). Representing old guard and young, Jewish and not, Montreal-born or just visiting, these photos depict a literary group for which Layton was, in its early stages, a kind of spokesman-provocateur. Cohen's interest in something other than this movement is revealed by a 1958 photo, which appears in Ira Nadel's *Various Positions: A Life of Leonard Cohen*. In it, Cohen is perched on a stool at Dunn's Progressive Jazz Parlour, performing his poetry with midnight jazz accompaniment, as he did repeatedly in 1958. According to Layton's report at the time, "Cohen is really laying them in the aisles. A new development in the Montreal School?"[25] Morley Callaghan, who took in one of these shows, was not alone in recognizing that if this was a new direction in the "Montreal School" it was one guided by the "nightclub poets of San Francisco and Greenwich Village."[26] Another photograph, taken in 1966, confirms Cohen's creative distance from what might be seen as a more traditional "Montreal School." In it, Cohen sits on the floor of a New York City apartment with such American folk luminaries as Dave Van Ronk, Joan Baez and Judy Collins, the youthful inheritors of another poetic line of inheritance, which included Hank Williams, Woody Guthrie and Bob Dylan.

Regardless of Cohen's drift from the Montreal scene, his eclipse of Layton and his increasing focus on songwriting, his reputation as an important poet in the city, as well as the inheritor of Layton's mantle, persisted. The notion of a "Montreal School," or, better, "Montreal Schools," was well entrenched. A characteristic description of the situation from the point of view of an influential outsider appears in George Bowering's "On Not Teaching the Vehicle Poets." Bowering suggests that Montreal's post-1950s poets coalesced around two traditions, or schools: "the Anglo line of Scott, Smith, Kennedy, Jones" whose work was in competition with the "Jewish mob led by Layton, but including Cohen (sort of) and the Laytonettes, Boxer, Hertz, Mayne, etc. Neither crowd was particularly noted for keeping up with what was happening in the U.S. or Canada. The Montreal world, self-inflated, was sufficient to itself."[27] Bowering's views are suggestive for a number of reasons. The need to abbreviate Cohen's role in the "tradition" to a "sort of," and the absence of any obvious inheritor after Cohen, makes one question whether the "Jewish mob" was as influential as is typically thought. Beyond this, Bowering points toward a third line of influence in Canadian poetry (the experimental and locally grounded work of Americans like Charles Olson, the Black Mountain Poets, and the Beats, including Allen Ginsberg and Gregory Corso). Layton's rise was clearly influenced by postwar developments in the United States, including some of those who drew Bowering to an American-based poetics. However, writing at a generation's distance in 1993, thousands of miles away in Vancouver, Bowering downplays the variety and unpredictability of Layton's influences.[28]

Bowering's views come into sharper focus when read alongside the introduction to the 1977 anthology *Montreal: English Poetry of the Seventies*. In their co-written introduction, editors Andre Farkas and Ken Norris sketch what might be viewed as an accepted, though largely revisionist history of poetry production in Montreal since the 1950s. Citing the importance of *First Statement* and *CIV/n,* they characterize the 1950s as notable for the rise of Layton, and for the appearance of Cohen's first collection, **Let Us Compare Mythologies,** which together contributed to a move toward "Jewish romantic lyricism." What followed, they argue, was the failure of "a sustained movement of Montreal poetry" in the 1960s, as young writers were bent on "echoing and pale imitation of Dudek, Layton, and Cohen."[29] The local revival, according to Farkas and Norris, originated:

. . . in 1967 when New Wave Canada made its official entrance into Montreal with George Bowering taking up a writer-in-residence post at Sir George Williams University. Bowering brought with him a new orientation towards poetry based on what he had learned from the Black Mountain poets Charles Olson, Robert Creeley, and Robert Duncan; now, as creative writing instructor, he passed on to his students these teachings. However, his most important contribution to the new generation of Montreal poets was the institution of a series of readings at Sir George which exposed them to the diverse experimentation that was taking place across Canada and the U.S. Although immediate results were not visible, by the time Bowering returned to Vancouver in the spring of 1971, the energies of the current movement were beginning to coalesce; this would result in numerous local readings and the establishment of a number of little magazines and small presses.[30]

Notable alongside this celebration of new developments in Montreal poetry is the list of contributors included in *Montreal: English Poetry of the Seventies.* Cohen and Layton are absent, while many of those included (Stephen Morissey, Artie Gold, Marc Plourde, Tom Konyves, Claudia Lapp, as well as Farkas and Norris) came to be associated with a group dubbed the Vehicle Poets. The anthology's account of this group's coalescence has generated its share of controversy, but what is clear in the editors' strategy is their urge to write against (or even to erase) the influence of Layton, Cohen, and any would-be "Laytonettes." The new Montreal School is depicted as American-informed, Bowering-begotten, and thankfully free of the failed decades-old experiment of "Jewish romantic lyricism."[31]

An alternative view of the key lines of influence in Montreal poetry is offered by Michael Harris. Glasgow-born, and like many Montreal poets, a long-time teacher in the CEGEP system, Harris' career ran parallel to that of many of the Vehicle Poets: with Claudia Lapp he initiated a set of poetry readings in 1973 at the St. Catherine Street Véhicule Gallery. Yet, Harris is dubious about any claim that these gatherings marked a reorientation of poetry in the city. They included poets he felt deserved a hearing (Peter Van Toorn, David Solway and others) and once done, he felt:

. . . we should not do this again for another five years, because there were no other poets in town. I mean there weren't any other real poets in town, you know, who had published well, had interesting stuff, had some kind of profile outside the city. And yet, six months later, all of a sudden, there were the so-called Vehicle poets, who . . . began to draw in crowds of each other . . . audiences of six to eight, ten people max, and I had had a couple of hundred. . . . I mean the whole horror of what has happened to poetry in this country is that it's all being subsidized. The League of Poets is a joke. This is Groucho Marx territory. You know, Cohen never belonged, Layton never belonged, Solway never belonged.[32]

Harris suggests that some of what Farkas and Norris celebrate in *Montreal: English Poetry of the Seventies* was supported by Louis Dudek at a time when "his own star had somewhat fallen";[33] thus, linking a figure who was among Cohen's first editorial supporters with a movement that saw its goal as writing away from the work of Cohen and Layton. (Farkas and Norris begin their introduction with a rather portentous quote from Dudek: "It is the destiny of Montreal to show the country from time to time what poetry is.")[34]

When asked whether the figures associated with the Vehicule school of the mid 1970s and after wielded substantial influence over later generations, Harris is brutally direct: "Zero. No. It was a blip on the radar, collectable by university archives."[35] Cohen and Layton, on the other hand (regardless of their long absences from the city, their tendency to publish with Toronto-based McClelland & Stewart, and the lack of a clear follower in their footsteps) remain, in Harris's view, "indistinguishable from the fabric and spirit of Montreal."[36] For Harris (and here he echoes a view often asserted by others) Layton and Cohen exist as iconic figures:

> [It] was a very peculiar thing to be a poet, very strange, not a vocation that one's father for example could offer approval for. So Cohen himself was iconic . . . here was a man who seemed to do no work, didn't have a day job, I mean, I had no idea of his inheritance. . . . He simply seemed to be somebody who got up and either got laid or wrote poems.[37]

Harris recalls seeing Cohen and a companion on the Main on their way to breakfast, Cohen in a "wonderful black suit," the woman with him in a "white shift," creating a "little parade of perfectly dressed people, seven o'clock in the morning. I thought this was splendid." Of Layton, who taught Harris when he was an undergraduate and graduate student, he adds:

> I thought he was iconic also, in the sense that every time he put pen to paper, he actually created something that looked or felt like a poem. . . . It's the presence of that particular person, as a poet, in town, that was an inspiration. I mean, no poet is going to write well every day. So really, it's the phenomenon of the real thing that is inspirational.[38]

An ongoing discussion, which was propelled in part by Layton himself, centred on who would be the next "real thing." In his letters, Layton muses often about who will inherit his poetic mantle. In letters dating from the late 1970s, Montrealer David Solway is said to be "the real thing, a genuine poet who gets stronger with every step he takes."[39] In a 1985 interview with Michael Benazon, Layton is asked if a "Jewish Montreal tradition of poetry" could be seen to pass from Klein, through himself and Cohen to Solway. A little half-heartedly Layton agrees, adding that he "would also include Seymour Mayne, who is perhaps more Jewish than Solway."[40] In a 1984 letter to Toronto poet Ken Sherman, Layton writes,

> I used to think my mantle would fall on David Solway. Regrettably, he, like Leonard Cohen, is entirely wrapped up in himself and like him too he's a narcissist who doesn't love himself. . . . You can only go from strength to strength, scaling ever more daunting heights with your pinions of beauty and terror. At those heights, may my mantle keep you warm.[41]

While Layton juggled this handful of would-be protégés, he maintained a large number of important relationships with younger poets. Among these, one of the longest-lasting and constructive was with Ken Sherman. Though Sherman remembers first meeting Layton "in a friend's basement," where Layton had agreed to address a Zionist youth group, he came to know him as a writing teacher in the early years of Layton's tenure at York University's English department. Sherman has high praise for Layton's refusal to comfort his students and for his willingness to "shake you up." Sherman catches some of the high comedy and pathos of creative writing taught Layton-style:

> Whenever he came upon an image or turn of phrase that he liked he read it aloud in that marvelous voice that could make a shopping list sound impressive. I don't know what he saw in those pseudo-poems but he invited me to join his writing workshop. . . . Like most writing workshops, it was a strange mix. "Honest Ed" Mirvish's wife was in it (Layton called her, simply, "Mirvish"). A John Lennon look-alike told us that he buried his poems late at night in different parts of the city. A girl who had worked as a prostitute before attending university wrote rhyming couplets about her experience.[42]

Throughout Layton's years at York, Sherman feels that he:

> . . . never took to Toronto. As for York, he found it a cold environment. I was amused to note that in four years he never unpacked the boxes he brought from Montreal to his York office. They remained piled up, as if he were ready to make his escape. All he unpacked were two framed photos: one of D. H. Lawrence and the other of Nietzsche. They were on the wall behind his desk.[43]

And to this, Sherman adds an impression regarding Layton's influence, which is echoed by numerous poets. He was "a daunting mountain peak. The sheer number of poems, their vividness and energy, were imposing."[44]

David Solway presents a similar sense of Layton's dominating influence in his lively essay "Framing Layton." The first poem he "committed *voluntarily* to memory," Solway writes, was Layton's "The Cold Green Element," and he refers to the older poet as a "friend, mentor, benefactor, example, and, at times . . . monumental Bloomian impediment. . . . honesty compels me to acknowledge those disturbing moments when I could wish that Layton's shadow were not quite so long and so encompassing."[45] Then, to complicate things, Solway writes in the same essay, that he "was never a student, a disciple, or a protégé of Layton's, but I benefitted enormously from the mere generosity of his presence."[46] Recently, Solway politely rejected the line of poetic influence that might be seen to run through Layton:

> There's no doubt that Layton is the *magister.* His work was in some way the culmination of Klein's. And after him Leonard Cohen was influential to many of us as a figure, as a charismatic individual on the scene, who wrote one or two extraordinary books of poetry, for instance **The Spice Box of Earth,** but then went off into other fields and became a very mediocre poet. Had he remained a poet he would have become the major poet of this country. But he didn't remain a poet. That's a fact. That's why Layton withdrew the mantle, which he'd conferred on Cohen, and gave it to me, as the next in the succession: Klein, Layton, then was supposed to be Cohen. I rejected it, because I don't see myself as a Jewish poet.[47]

Solway does acknowledge the importance of Greece in his life and work, a country that both Cohen and Layton found hospitable:

> The country has had an enormous impact on Canadian, especially Canadian Jewish writing. Cohen went to Greece in the fifties, and that's one of the ways I got there, through Leonard, or through his woman at the time, Marianne. She offered me her house on Hydra, because she was living in Leonard's house, if I would agree to tutor her son. . . . I went and I never recovered from that experience. The impact of the light, the sun, the Retsina, the Greek language, which changed my life.[48]

One does hear, however, a certain Laytonesque rancour (that familiar urge to outrage and foment a more heightened discussion of the country's literature) in an interview Solway gave in 2003:

> [Some] years ago I made a pact with myself to try to say what I see with as much candour and forthrightness as I could muster, and damn the consequences. You might say that the motto I adopted was: *fork out or fuck off,* which I applied equally to myself as to anyone else. The problem is that I don't have a tolerance organ in my psychical make-up for literary fast-food, for mediocrity, pretentiousness, sloppiness and self-aggrandizement.[49]

Clearly, these are the same goals that Layton set himself throughout his turbulent career, the outcome of which, according to Ken Sherman, "was to be turned into a clown by the media and eventually disregarded by the literati. His literary stock has already plummeted and no one can say if it will rise again."[50] Solway has managed to sidestep such dire outcomes in his pursuit of "candour and forthrightness."

Some of Layton's students, however, found his influence neither benign nor inspirational. Lazer Lederhendler, who enrolled in an M.A. poetry workshop at Con-cordia in 1989, encountered Layton near the end of his teaching career. Though Lederhendler approached his would-be mentor as "the author of some good poems," which he'd "read in undergraduate CanLit courses," his experience of being under Layton's tutelage was one of frustration and aimlessness. Lederhendler doesn't recall anything being said in the workshop relating to the existence of a "Montreal School," to the impact of the city on local writers, nor did the issue of Jewishness figure in workshop discussions. The dominant touchstones, he says, were the modernist canon and the murderous quality of twentieth-century life.[51]

The variety of Layton's friendships, his years spent teaching, the mountains of his correspondence with colleagues and enemies, and his often-reported generosity with younger poets created a long-standing, far-reaching and intimate network. Sherman recalls a time when he and Layton were neighbours in midtown Toronto, and the elder poet found the younger bereft of wine.

> The next day there was a knock at our door. By the time I opened it whoever knocked had vanished; I looked down to find a case with twelve assorted bottles of wine (Italian, Spanish, French) and a note that read, "One of the saddest spectacles is a poet with no bottles of wine." It was signed Irving.[52]

In the same vein, the American poet Steven Osterlund, who lived for a time in Canada, published a pamphlet called *Fumigator: An Outsider's View of Irving Layton* (1975). A good part of it is devoted to describing Layton's willingness to instruct the younger poet in the ways of the artist, as well as to depicting Layton's tendency to drop a cheque in the mail when Osterlund was in tight circumstances.[53]

Cohen's career did not produce the same kind of intimate relationships with younger poets, nor do we have an archival portrait of such things as Layton's collected letters offer. Part of the reason for this is Cohen's movement away from regular publication and fully into a career as a songwriter and performer. This movement is confirmed as a conscious strategy in a 1969 piece on Cohen in *Saturday Night* magazine. Here Cohen explains that he has:

> . . . always felt very different from other poets I've met. . . . I've always felt that somehow they've made a decision against life. I don't want to put any poets down, but most of them have closed a lot of doors. I always felt more at home with musicians.[54]

The middle-sixties, the point at which Cohen threw himself most ambitiously into a musical career, also heralded a twenty-year period in which his published work appeared at roughly six year gaps: **Parasites of Heaven** in 1966, **The Energy of Slaves** in 1972, **Death of a Lady's Man** in 1978, followed by **Book of Mercy** in 1984, which could be considered the endpoint of an active public literary career. Although *Beautiful Losers* retains a critical readership, and the reissue of his selected poems in 1993 introduced his work to a younger audience, it is safe to say that Cohen's artistic longevity and increasing celebrity is based not on his literary accomplishments but on the impact of his music and persona on pop cultural taste and creative trends.[55] Proof of this can be found in two relatively recent books, which aim to take the measure of Cohen's full career. Ira Nadel's *Various Positions: A Life of Leonard Cohen* devotes its early chapters to a discussion of a writer's life, while the back half of the biography is largely a portrait of a songwriter and performer whose musical accomplishments have turned him into a cultural icon. Nadel does not downplay the early literary influences, and a reader interested only in Cohen's music must either put up with or thumb quickly through accounts of the influence of Layton, Dudek, and Scott, among others. There is, however, no detailed account in the later chapters of *Various Positions* regarding Cohen's sense of himself as a Montreal poet, nor is there a sustained discussion of his impact upon a younger generation of writers. The reader must decide whether this reflects a negligible impact or whether poetic influence in Montreal is simply too tame a subject in the shadow of questions associated with pop stardom, the recording industry and Zen. Nadel, in fact, suggests that the tendency of Cohen's music to overshadow his writing was entrenched by 1978, when **Death of a Lady's Man** was entirely ignored by reviewers in the United States, where "he had been identified as a singer and songwriter rather than a poet for too long."[56] In the collection *Intricate Preparations: Writing Leonard Cohen*, edited by West Coast poet and critic Stephen Scobie and based on a 1999 issue of *Essays on Canadian Writing* devoted to Cohen, one gets an even more aggressive sense of Cohen's role as a cultural phenomenon and musical icon above that of a poet. Scobie, who was among the first serious critics of Cohen's writing, informs us in his introduction that Cohen is:

> . . . a poet who hasn't published a new collection for sixteen years, and a novelist who hasn't written a new novel for thirty-four years. Yet he remains a vital presence not only in Canadian literature but also on the international stage constituted by the virtual phenomenon of the Internet. Scarcely a day goes by on alt.music.Leonard-cohen without a plaintive inquiry, from somewhere in the world, about a new book, a new record, a new concert tour. Indeed, Cohen is acquiring a new generation of fans who have never seen him perform live (but who are nonetheless fanatical).[57]

It must be said, then, that the record of Cohen's influence on younger poets has been obscured by the tremendous success of his musical output and the celebrity associated with it. There is no difficulty in following Cohen's influence on generations of songwriters. This can be seen by a cursory look at the high calibre of contributors to the best album dedicated to celebrating Cohen's songs. *I'm Your Fan*, released in 1991, presents artfully reworked cover versions of Cohen's songs by the likes of Lloyd Cole, Nick Cave and the Bad Seeds, John Cale, and the Pixies. In the case, for instance, of Nick Cave's raucous, over-the-top version of **"Tower of Song,"** one can't help but recognize how aspects of Cohen's stance, his voice, his laconic humour and idiosyncratic way with a popular song have influenced the younger musician's output. (On Cave's recent recordings he often puts the best aspects of Cohen's style, musical arrangement, and even the thematic mix of gloom and religion to excellent use.)

It is more difficult to get a clear sense of Cohen's impact on younger poets. But if asked, some will give an accounting. Asa Boxer, a Montreal poet in his early thirties, and a recent winner of the CBC Literary Awards for his long poem "The Workshop," has an uncommon view of Cohen's influence. His father, Avi Boxer, was a part of Layton's poetic generation, though he was not prolific and died young. Not unlike Michael Harris, Asa Boxer speaks of Cohen as proof to the uninitiated that becoming a successful poet in Canada is not an impossibility: "He was very quiet and stuck to his own thing and got bad reviews in the *Montreal Star* for God knows how long."[58] Boxer is as emphatic as Harris about Cohen's unique impact (what he refers to as an almost spiritual influence) on Canadian culture:

> He has poems that I think have actually penetrated the consciousness. There is one very short one ("With Annie gone, whose eyes did compare with the morning sun, not that I did compare, but I do compare, now that she's gone.") I heard that around town. . . . Cohen has several magnificent pieces. They're not just Canadian standards, they seem to be world class, international stuff. . . . He's written folk songs for us. We haven't had folk songs. . . . And that's why I think Cohen, in the end, is going to be the survivor poet for us.[59]

On a more personal note, Boxer credits an afternoon chat with Cohen for helping him refine his notion of the workshop, as it relates to the creative act. His poem "The Workshop" took as its guiding image a farmhouse basement in the Laurentians belonging to a cousin. The hoard of things on hand was inspiring, Boxer says, but Cohen turned the poem in a new direction with the casual remark that the workshop should itself be viewed as "a work of art."[60]

Jason Camlot, another Montreal poet who has, like Boxer, lived away from the city and returned to establish a writing life, offers a different view of the impact of Cohen's work on writers who came of age in the last two decades. For Camlot, Cohen's work (and Klein's before it) framed familiar Jewish material, whether canonical stories or the Holocaust, in striking ways that were not otherwise heard as part of a Jewish Day School education in suburban enclaves. Camlot points, in particular, to Cohen's *Flowers for Hitler,* whose tone, in relation to the Holocaust, was aggressively ironic when such subject matter was "typically dealt with as sacred."[61] He argues that Cohen's "great impact on young poets is through his song writing." And he notes that one of Cohen's early accomplishments was the success with which he brought "to the identity of the poet the allure of the pop singer." Cohen's author photos and book cover copy presented the kind of attraction generally reserved for album notes and artwork. Camlot attributes Cohen's early genius on this front to his attraction to a great variety of poetic models, and to an aggressive willingness to transcend the limitations of the Montreal poetry scene as well as those associated with a Canadian national literature.[62]

LANGUAGE: ENGLISH, FRENCH AND JEWISH

A recent trend in certain literary circles has led critics toward a study of what they call "Jewish languages." By this, quite simply, they mean to highlight literary accomplishments by Jewish writers in Hebrew and Yiddish. In the case of the former, critics draw the reader's attention to developments in Israeli literature, while by focusing on Yiddish they examine a largely moribund eastern European literary tradition that existed for roughly a century and ceased in the mid-twentieth century. The most aggressive use of this frame of reference appears in Ruth Wisse's *The Modern Jewish Canon: A Journey Through Language and Culture,* where the one-time Yiddish lecturer at McGill makes use of the framework of "Jewish languages" to delimit her notion of what is in the modern Jewish canon and what is not. Wisse asserts that "modern Jewish literature tells the stories of the Jewish people in the twentieth century," and that a criticism associated with this literature must "establish criteria for Jewishness in the arts" by taking the measure of how contemporary identity is supported by an ongoing relationship between modern Hebrew and "the beginnings of modern Yiddish literature, although the resemblance has yet to be acknowledged or explored." More directly, Wisse writes:

> [Neither] are there likely to be many great Jewish writers of the next century who are uninformed and uninspired by the spirit of Hebrew. Hebrew today is not only the language of Bible and liturgy, it is now also the language of the Jewish state where an increasing majority of the Jewish people resides. Hence, it is the crucible of the national fate. Individual genius may come wherever it comes and do whatever it does, but the Jew who has no access to the heart of the Jewish polity is ever less likely to generate a valuable literature of Jewish experience.[63]

These terms of reference put specific pressure on Jewish writers working in English, in particular figures like Cohen and Layton for whom neither Hebrew or Yiddish were important formative presences or linguistic frameworks. It should come as no surprise that Cohen and Layton do not receive a mention in Wisse's book, while Klein's novel *The Second Scroll* is examined for its portrait of a nascent Hebrew poetic tradition in Israel,[64] and is described, a little too heatedly, as an "exuberant response to the creation of Israel."[65] One finds in Wisse's approach an example of the dark territory a critic falls into when strictures are applied, however subtly, regarding whether a writer's output can be said to fall within or without a cultural tradition, based on a choice of language or particular stories. In such a case, a writer's oeuvre might be characterized in ways that have nothing to do with his or her stated identification and affiliation.

A related problem obscures our understanding of the role of Irving Layton and Leonard Cohen in the broader trends of English-language Quebec literature. From the earliest stages of their rise to prominence, both proved themselves too big and too singular to be subsumed into any imaginary local tradition. Critics, reviewers and anthologists have looked for ways to sequester their influence, in part by overstating the linkages between their work, and then by setting their contribution apart from the mainstream. This essay has highlighted critical moments at which their poetry has been set aside as *something else* (in the case of Farkas and Norris, the weird conglomeration "Jewish romantic lyricism,"[66] while Bowering looks, however lightheartedly, for the "Jewish mob".[67]) These efforts clearly support the notion of firm lines of influence, and of a recognizable "Montreal School," the existence of which would allow the city's English-language poets to assert themselves as a prominent minority voice in Quebec. Cohen and Layton have simply not proved useful in this ongoing project.

Both Layton and Cohen have remained remarkably distant from discussions related to the language issues and political infighting of post-1976 Quebec. Unlike Mordecai Richler, neither made such issues the focus of their work or public utterances. In a 1979 *Canadian Forum* article, Cohen is quoted in French, speaking unguardedly about the Quebec scene:

> Il y a un côté très messianique à la façon dont les gens gouvernent ici. On pense en fonction de sauver une race, d'ériger une nation. Je trouve cela un peu bizarre. Et puis nous autres, les Juifs, on a vu trop de drapeaux monter et descendre, et quand on sait qu'en fin de compte on se dirige tous vers la même chose, la tombe, on ne peut s'empêcher de trouver ces grandes théories et ces beaux idéaux un peu futiles.[68]

Layton, upon one of his numerous returns to the province, claimed that one of his goals was to reimmerse himself in the French Catholic milieu he had not taken seriously enough in the past.[69] In a quote that was picked up by the Canadian Press, and repeated in a Richler column in *Maclean's* magazine, Layton explains that if the "sad choice" of Quebec's separation comes, "I choose Quebec."[70] But such outbursts are too rare (might we even say too surreal?) to account for a deeper relationship between the Quebec political scene and Layton in late career. It is rare, too, for English-language critics to take account of the relationship between Cohen, Layton and local political and linguistic upheavals. One effort to do so appeared in a late-seventies issue of *Canadian Forum*, where A. D. Person wrote provocatively:

> But now Layton and Cohen have come back to Montreal, for their own good reasons I know. Their physical and spiritual repatriation is important for Quebec and Canada. Sun Life goes west, Layton comes back east. When independence comes will there be a line of poets waiting at the border to cross over into Quebec? I suspect there isn't time for the poets to teach us about the necessity for Canada of the independence of Quebec.[71]

Yet in the same article, whose *raison d'être* is in part a consideration of the anthology *Montreal: English Poetry of the Seventies,* Person neglects to mention the exclusion of Cohen and Layton by the anthology's editors. Farkas and Norris, sheepish themselves, make much in their introduction of these two writers' influence "upon the Montreal poets of the sixties," but they choose not to explain why such influence has become negligible to the point of irrelevance in the seventies.[72]

The absence of Layton and Cohen from an anthology like *Montreal: English Poetry of the Seventies* is on the one hand funny, for every reader will expect to see them, and on the other, bad business for the book publisher, since Layton and Cohen alone commanded a popular market; but more darkly, their absence bespeaks of an urgency by the editors to undertake a kind of utopian project (the engineering, let us say, of human souls) in which the contributions of Cohen and Layton to Montreal poetry are downgraded in favour of an effort to "make things new" or reorder the poetic playing field.

This essay might be seen as the beginning of a larger study toward an uncovering of the entanglement of Jewish, English and French Montreal in the best work of Leonard Cohen and Irving Layton. The imprint of both poets on the culture is a surprising blend of the personal, the local, and a range of traditional material broad enough to escape easy definition. Michael Harris celebrates Cohen's ability to strike an iconic pose on the Main, capable of inspiring poetry in others. Layton's iconic status has been debased, yet when talking with working poets, or surveying the history of Montreal literary life, his imprint is singular and inescapable. Both careers seem in danger of becoming obscured by

myth, but one needs only to return to Belmont Avenue on a summer evening, or to St. Elisabeth Street under a hard snow, to recover a clearer view of the matters at hand.

Notes

1. Leonard Cohen, *The Favorite Game* (New York: Viking, 1963), pp. 68-9.

2. Cohen, *The Favorite Game,* p. 24.

3. Irving Layton, *Waiting for the Messiah: A Memoir* (Toronto: McClelland & Stewart, 1985), p. 21.

4. A. M. Klein, "Review of *Here and Now* by Irving Layton," *Literary Essays and Reviews,* ed. U. Caplan and M. W. Steinberg (Toronto: University of Toronto, 1987), p. 215.

5. Layton, *Waiting for the Messiah,* p. 136.

6. Ibid., p. 160.

7. Ibid., p. 224.

8. Emphasis in original. Michael Harris, "Leonard Cohen: The Poet as Hero—2," *Saturday Night* 84.6 (June 1969): p. 27.

9. Aileen Collins, ed., *CIV/n: A Literary Magazine of the 50's* (Montréal: Véhicule, 1983), p. 126.

10. Layton, *For My Brother Jesus* (Toronto: McClelland & Stewart, 1976), p. xvi.

11. Mordecai Richler, "Be it ever so (increasingly) humble, there's no place like home," *Maclean's Magazine* 91 (1 August 1978): 54.

12. Ira Nadel, *Various Positions: A Life of Leonard Cohen* (Toronto: Random House, 1996), p. 27.

13. Tom Waits, *Big Time* (New York, Island Records, 1990).

14. Eli Mandel, *Irving Layton* (Toronto: Forum House, 1969), p. 16.

15. William Carlos Williams, "A Note on Layton," in Irving Layton, *The Improved Binoculars* (Highlands, North Carolina: J. Williams, 1956), pp. 9-10 [page numbers not marked].

16. Mandel, *Irving Layton,* p. 16.

17. Seymour Mayne, "Introduction," *Irving Layton: The Poet and His Critics* (Toronto: McGraw-Hill Ryerson, 1978), pp. 2-3.

18. Ibid., pp. 5, 10.

19. Harris, "Leonard Cohen: The Poet as Hero—2," pp. 27, 30.

20. Ibid., p. 28.

21. Ibid., p. 30.

22. Collins, *CIV/n: A Literary Magazine of the 50's,* p. 211.

23. Ibid., p. 231.

24. Ibid., p. 185.

25. Nadel, *Various Positions: A Life of Leonard Cohen,* p. 62.

26. Ibid., p. 63.

27. George Bowering, "On Not Teaching the Vehicle Poets," in *Vehicle Days: An Unorthodox History of Montreal's Vehicle Poets,* ed. Ken Norris (Montréal: Nuage, 1993), p. 115.

28. There is an argument to be made for the wide-ranging influence of American poets and novelists on Leonard Cohen. One fruitful but unstudied connection might be between Cohen's pop persona and that of Allen Ginsberg. A Cohenseque confusion of poet and singer/musician appears in Ginsberg's *First Blues: Rags, Ballads & Harmonium Songs 1971-74,* where poems are accompanied by musical notation, including guitar chords, while poems with titles like "Walking Blues" receive rhythmic descriptions: "(andante)." To round out the interplay between American popular music and literature, the frontispiece of *First Blues* is a photograph of Ginsberg and a guitar-strumming Bob Dylan seated before the Massachusetts grave of "'Ti Jean' John Kerouac." Allen Ginsberg, *First Blues: Rags, Ballads & Harmonium Songs 1971-74* (New York: Full Court, 1975), p. 11.

29. Andre Farkas and Ken Norris, eds., *Montreal: English Poetry of the Seventies* (Montréal: Véhicule, 1977), p. x.

30. Ibid., p. xi.

31. Cohen and Layton reappear in the 1982 anthology *Cross/cut: Contemporary English Quebec Poetry,* edited by Peter Van Toorn and Ken Norris. The introduction to this volume is notably attentive to American influence and to political concerns. Klein's "meteoric" career is said to have been interrupted by "twenty years of silence," and there is passing mention of Cohen. But the Anglo-Jewish dichotomy is no longer in play; rather, Jewishness is seen to be subsumed in the "pluralist mosaic of Canadian poetry," whose Quebec version Van Toorn depicts as a kind of wedding banquet of Arab, Italian, Scots, Welsh, Irish, Asian and Jewish offerings, all of which are apparently invited in order to consummate "[c]ontact with French civilization." Peter Van Toorn, "Introduction," *Cross/cut: Contemporary English Quebec Poetry* (Montréal: Véhicule, 1982), pp. 28, 36.

32. Michael Harris, personal interview, 14 August 2005.

33. Ibid.

34. Farkas and Norris, *Montreal: English Poetry of the Seventies,* p. ix. This quote originally from Louis Dudek's *Epigrams* (Montreal: DC Books, 1975), p. 30.

35. Harris, personal interview.

36. Ibid.

37. Ibid.

38. Ibid.

39. Irving Layton, letter to Keith Garebian, 5 Feb. 1978, in *Wild Gooseberries: The Selected Letters of Irving Layton,* ed. Francis Mansbridge (Toronto: Macmillan, 1989), p. 306.

40. Michael Benazon, "Irving Layton and the Montreal Poets," *Matrix* 20 (Spring 1985): 16.

41. Layton, letter to Ken Sherman, 29 Apr. 1984, in *Wild Gooseberries: The Selected Letters of Irving Layton,* ed. Mansbridge, pp. 352-53.

42. Sherman, "Five Pieces for Irving Layton," *Books In Canada* 30 (Sep./Oct. 2001): p. 25.

43. Sherman, email correspondence, 9 Aug. 2005.

44. Ibid.

45. Solway, "Framing Layton," *Random Walk: Essays in Elective Criticism* (Montréal/Kingston: McGill-Queen's University Press, 1997), p. 86.

46. Ibid.

47. Solway, personal interview, 16 Nov. 1999.

48. Ibid.

49. Solway, "*TDR* Interview: David Solway," <http://www.danforthreview.com> (18 Aug. 2005). This characterization of the poet's role comes up again and again in Layton's forewords to his own books, as well as in interviews. From a 1975 interview:

"It was necessary to kick the door in, smash a few windows, and let some fresh air in. . . . I enjoyed having fights with librarians, with school principals, and with booksellers. I enjoyed writing letters to publishers and to newspaper editors, because I felt that what I was doing was a good thing, that it had to be done, and that, eventually, my point of view would prevail." Sara D'Agostino, "The War Goes On: A Conversation with Irving Layton," *Acta Victoriana,* vol. 100, no. 1 (Fall 1975), pp. 9, 13.

50. Sherman, "Five Pieces for Irving Layton," p. 25.

51. Lazer Lederhendler, email correspondence, 1 Dec. 2005.

52. Sherman, "Five Pieces for Irving Layton," p. 25.

53. Osterlund writes: "I had no doubts about Layton—through and through he was a poet. Let him storm and rage, be contradictory or wonderfully ridiculous, a buffoon or a warrior. Critics demanded an objective, cool-headed Layton. . . . I wanted the artist and the man—subjective, sensitive, riddled with holes." Steven Osterlund, "Fumigator: An Outsider's View of Irving Layton," in *Irving Layton: The Poet and His Critics,* ed. Mayne, p. 264.

54. Jack Batten, "Leonard Cohen: The Poet as Hero," *Saturday Night* 84 (June 1969): p. 25.

55. One anecdote in Nadel's biography signals a rare case when Cohen's literary output had a direct impact on the musical scene. The story's background is Cohen's infatuation with the singer Nico, who "made it clear that nothing would happen between her and Cohen." In the meantime, she introduced Cohen to her collaborator, Lou Reed, arguably the most important songwriter of the New York underground of the late 1960s: "Reed had a copy of *Flowers for Hitler,* which he asked Cohen to sign, and was an early reader of *Beautiful Losers.* Cohen confided, 'In those days I guess he [Reed] wasn't getting very many compliments for his work and I certainly wasn't. So we told each other how good we were.'" Nadel, *Various Positions: A Life of Leonard Cohen,* pp. 147-48.

56. Ibid., p. 223.

57. Stephen Scobie, "Introduction," *Essays on Canadian Writing* 69 (Winter 1999): 3.

58. Asa Boxer, personal interview, 22 August 2005.

59. Ibid.

60. Ibid.

61. Jason Camlot, personal interview, 1 Nov. 2005.

62. Ibid.

63. Ruth Wisse, *The Modern Jewish Canon: A Journey Through Language and Culture* (New York: Free Press, 2000), pp. 10, 15, 28-9.

64. Ibid., pp. 26-7.

65. Ibid., p. 260.

66. Farkas and Norris, *Montreal: English Poetry of the Seventies,* p. x.

67. Bowering, "On Not Teaching the Vehicle Poets," p. 115.

68. A. D. Person, "The poets were péquistes when Lévesque was a Liberal," *Canadian Forum* 59 (April 1979): 16. Translation: "There is a very messianic dimension to the way people govern here. One thinks in terms of serving to save a race, of setting up a nation. I find this a bit bizarre. And further, we 'others', the Jews, we have seen too many flags rise and fall, and when one knows that in the end we are all headed towards the same thing, the tomb, one can't help but find these big theories and beautiful ideals a bit futile. [Translation by Jason Camlot]

69. In an article for the *Thursday Report,* Concordia University's faculty newspaper, Layton is said to be "coming home" "to discover the 'ties that bind'; he also is demonstrating for the first time a genuine interest in Catholic humanism and "French-Canadian Catholicism." Beverly Smith, "The Gospel According to Irving Layton," *Thursday Report* 2 (26 Oct. 1978): p. 5.

70. Richler, "Be it ever so (increasingly) humble, there's no place like home," p. 54.

71. Person, "The poets were pequistes when Lévesque was a Liberal," p. 15.

72. Farkas and Norris, *Montreal: English Poetry of the Seventies,* p. x.

FURTHER READING

Criticism

Greenstein, Michael. "Canadian Poetry After Auschwitz." *Canadian Poetry* 20 (spring/summer 1987): 1-16.

Discusses the post-Holocaust poetry of Cohen, Irving Layton, and Eli Mandel.

Wrobel, Ruthanne. "Four Grounds: Ways to Play in Cohen's Garden of Verses." *Essays on Canadian Writing*
69 (winter 1999): 117-24.

Offers suggestions for teaching Cohen's poetry to
high school students.

**Additional coverage of Cohen's life and career is contained in the following sources published by
Gale:** *Contemporary Authors,* **Vols. 21-24R;** *Contemporary Authors New Revision Series,* **Vols. 14,
69;** *Contemporary Literary Criticism,* **Vols. 3, 38, 260;** *Contemporary Novelists,* **Eds. 1, 2, 3, 4, 5, 6;**
Contemporary Poets, **Eds. 1, 2, 3, 4, 5, 6, 7;** *Dictionary of Literary Biography,* **Vol. 53;** *Discovering
Authors: Canadian Edition;* *Discovering Authors Modules: Most-studied Authors;* *Encyclopedia of
World Literature in the 20th Century,* **Ed. 3;** *Literature Resource Center;* **and** *Major 20th-Century
Writers,* **Ed. 1.**

Rosmarie Waldrop
1935-

German-born American poet, novelist, essayist, and translator.

INTRODUCTION

An extremely prolific experimental poet, Waldrop has produced more than thirty volumes of poetry over the course of her career, as well as a number of translations, novels, and essays. She has also served as publisher, along with her husband Keith Waldrop, of the independent press Burning Deck. Her work has generally received greater critical attention in France and Germany than in the United States; however, in recent years, her poems have begun appearing in anthologies and are being studied more and more by American scholars, particularly feminists.

BIOGRAPHICAL INFORMATION

Waldrop was born in Kitzingen-am-Main, Germany on August 24, 1935, to Josef Sebald, a high school teacher, and Friederike Wolgemuth Sebald. During the last years of World War II, Waldrop joined a travelling theatre group, but in 1946, she returned to school to study music and to play in a young people's orchestra. The family's home was in the American occupation zone and in 1954, performing there with the orchestra, Waldrop met her future husband, Keith Waldrop, who had recently been discharged from the U.S. Army. From 1954-56, Waldrop attended the University of Wuerzburg, studying comparative literature, followed by a year at the University of Aix-Marseille (1956-57), and a year at the University of Freiburg (1957-58). She came to America in 1958, and she and Keith both enrolled at the University of Michigan; a year later the couple married. In 1961 they bought a used printing press and together with a number of other Ann Arbor writers, started *Burning Deck Magazine,* which the Waldrops eventually turned into Burning Deck Press. They began publishing the work of American experimental poets as well as English translations of French avant-garde poetry, most of which Waldrop translated herself. In 1962, Waldrop became an American citizen and four years later she received her Ph.D. from the University of Michigan. In 1964 she accepted a position teaching comparative and German literature at Wesleyan University. The couple moved to Durham, Connecticut, and

then to Providence, Rhode Island, where they have lived since 1968. She has also served as visiting professor at Tufts University and Brown University.

Waldrop is the recipient of a number of awards for both poetry and translations, among them the Hopwood Award (1963), a Humboldt Fellowship (1970-71); the Rhode Island Governor's Arts Award (1988), the Foundation for Contemporary Arts Award (2003), and the PEN Award for Poetry in Translation (2008), as well as fellowships from the National Endowment for the Arts in Poetry and Translation (1980 and 1994).

MAJOR WORKS

Waldrop's poetry has always focused on language and she has much in common with the poets of the Language School. She began writing poetry in the late sixties, producing *A Dark Octave* in 1967, and *Change of Address,* a collaboration with her husband, a year later. In *Camp Printing* (1970), Waldrop experimented with arranging text on the page in various ways, sometimes using different fonts—apparently inspired by the work she did setting type by hand for Burning Deck Press. In 1978, she published *The Road Is Everywhere, or Stop This Body,* a sequence of eighty poems based on street signs and also employing experimental arrangements of text and space. Waldrop also created a number of poetic collages, such as *The Relaxed Abalone* (1970), based on the language of psychology textbooks, and *Differences for Four Hands* (1984), which cobbled together parts of the life stories of nineteenth-century German composers Clara and Robert Schumann with that of sixteenth-century Italian madrigal composer Don Carlo Gesualdo. In 1986, Waldrop published *Streets Enough to Welcome Snow,* consisting of poems of very short lines written in a very fragmentary style. She has also written several collections of prose poems, among them *The Aggressive Ways of the Casual Stranger* (1972), containing some poems that have no punctuation or internal capitalization; the highly-acclaimed *The Reproduction of Profiles* (1987); and *Lawn of the Excluded Middle* (1993). Waldrop's 1994 collection *A Key into the Language of America* has also been particularly well regarded. A so-called "procedural text," the work has the same title as the 1643 study of the Rhode Island Narragansett language by Roger Williams, and is, in fact, based on Williams's book; it features identical chapter titles as it navigates the territory between European colonizers and the Native American indigenous population.

CRITICAL RECEPTION

Waldrop's experimental style of poetry and the fragmentary nature of some of her early work have received mixed reviews from literary critics. Fred Muratori (see Further Reading) refers to her style as "severely economical" and to her short lines of poetry as "harshly amputated." Rachel Hadas finds the presence of so many short lines in *Streets Enough to Welcome Snow* to be "wearying" and contends that "at times, Waldrop's mini-lines fragment annoyingly what my ear wants to perceive as a fine iambic line." Hadas has been more receptive to the prose poems of *The Reproduction of Profiles* which display the influence of Ludwig Wittgenstein and have certain affinities with the poetry of John Ashbery. According to Hadas, the volume features "beautifully turned—and turning, writhing—sentences [that] are translations, not from French or German, but from pure thought." Christine Hume suggests that *Reluctant Gravities* (1999) is a continuation of the linguistic project begun in *The Reproduction of Profiles,* and Joan Retallack, who has studied Waldrop's experimental style, claims that the poet "explores patterned currents of discontinuous motility and porousness that are all historical residue." Andrew Mossin has examined Waldrop's poetic theories, maintaining that the poet "seeks to uncover what is already present in language."

Another feature of Waldrop's poetry that has merited critical attention is the use of multiple voices. In her interview with Retallack, Waldrop herself explains the way she views the world: "We come to know anything that has any complexity by glimpses. So it is best to have as many different glimpses from as many different perspectives as possible." According to Hume, in Waldrop's "investigations of the interstices between perception and language—especially in the differences between the ways that men and women understand, interact with, and adopt language—Waldrop follows the model of conversation by shifting between speakers." Lynn Keller reports that in her poetry Waldrop is seeking the "dissolution of the constraints of inherited gender categories and expectations."

Waldrop's source material consists of everything from traffic signs to physics textbooks and her literary influences include Wittgenstein, Ezra Pound, and Ashbery among others. Muratori notes that Waldrop's work from the 1980s and 1990s "nods directly toward Wittgenstein, for whom the single sentence and short paragraph were the preferred units of expression." Keller reports that in *Lawn of the Excluded Middle,* "Waldrop calls virtually no attention . . . to that volume's extensive reliance on prior texts"; however, the intention is not to disguise her use of sources. Rather, according to Keller, "the unidentified source texts . . . function largely as examples of the way in which the language we employ is inevitably a previously used, sedimented medium."

David Clippinger has studied the influence of Pound's use of polyphony and historical sources on Waldrop's work. The critic notes that Waldrop's poetry, "tends to gravitate toward aporias and silences in cultural history . . . rather than the 'major' cultural figures Pound delineates." Hume explains the effect of Waldrop's use of sources: "The electric feedback generated by her synthesis of say, John Ashbery, Robert Musil, Heraclitus, and a physics textbook—all in one section—charges the work with uncanny humor and sudden illumination."

PRINCIPAL WORKS

Poetry

A Dark Octave 1967
Change of Address [with Keith Waldrop] 1968
Body Image [with Nelson Howe] 1970
Camp Printing 1970
The Relaxed Abalone; or, What-You-May-Find 1970
Spring Is a Season and Nothing Else 1970
The Aggressive Ways of the Casual Stranger 1972
Alice ffoster-Fallis: (an outline) [with Keith Waldrop] 1972
Until Volume One [with Keith Waldrop] 1973
Words Worth Less [with Keith Waldrop] 1973
Kind Regards 1975
Since Volume One [with Keith Waldrop] 1975
Acquired Pores 1976
The Road Is Everywhere, or Stop This Body 1978
The Ambition of Ghosts 1979
Psyche & Eros 1980
When They Have Senses 1980
Nothing Has Changed 1981
Differences for Four Hands 1984
Morning's Intelligence 1986
Streets Enough to Welcome Snow 1986
The Reproduction of Profiles 1987
Shorter American Memory 1988
Peculiar Motions 1990
Light Travels [with K. Waldrop] 1992
Fan Poem for Deshika 1993
Lawn of the Excluded Middle 1993
Cornered Stone, Split Infinites 1994
A Key into the Language of America 1994
Another Language: Selected Poems 1997
New and Selected Poems 1997
Reluctant Gravities (prose poems) 1999
Blindsight 2003
Love, Like Pronouns 2003
Flat with No Key 2008

Other Major Works

Against Language?: Dissatisfaction with Languages as Theme and as Impulse towards Experiments in Twentieth Century Poetry (criticism) 1971
A Form / of Taking / It All (novel) 1990
Well Well Reality [with Keith Waldrop] (novel) 1997
The Hanky of Pippin's Daughter (novel) 2001
Dissonance (if you are interested) (essays) 2005

CRITICISM

Rachel Hadas (essay date 1989)

SOURCE: Hadas, Rachel. "An Ecstasy of Space (Jane Cooper, Rosmarie Waldrop)." *Parnassus* 15, no. 1 (1989): 217-39.

[*In the following excerpt, Hadas offers a mixed review of Waldrop's fragmentary style in* Streets Enough to Welcome Snow, *and a highly positive review of the prose poems in Waldrop's* The Reproduction of Profiles.]

. . . Rosmarie Waldrop, in *Streets Enough to Welcome Snow,* is a chatelaine of spaces whose spareness is deceptive. Like a resourceful city dweller, Waldrop hoards images in narrow quarters that manage to seem neither cramped nor chaotic. One of the pleasures her work offers is its dovetailing of disparate items, memories, sensations into almost invisibly small corners:

> Once
> I've got something
> I lie
> down on it
> with my whole body.
> Goethe quotations, warm
> sand, a smell of hay,
> long afternoons.

> (from **"Remembering into Sleep"**)

The verticality these short lines create fosters a nimble rapidity of motion that deftly mimics the mind's associative hoppings. For Waldrop is above all a poet of thought; her lines abound in sensation, but the movement of consciousness underlies and informs remembered scents, crackling combs, puffing pipes. The passage just quoted, for example, is followed by an immediate moving away from simple remembered sensation:

> But it
> would take a road

> would turn, with space,
> in on itself,
> would turn
> occasion into offer.

Author of five previous books of poems, a novel, an unclassifiable collection I'll come to in a minute, and many translations, Waldrop is an accomplished writer who seems comfortable with her own style. The short lines so much in evidence throughout *Streets* [*Streets Enough to Welcome Snow*] can become wearying, but the contents of the poems are less simple and restricted than the look of the pages might suggest. At best, the short lines contain vitality; more often they are used with telegraphic effectiveness:

> Distant boots.
> Black beetles at night. A smell
> of sweat.
> The restaurant,
> yes. You've no idea
> how much my father used to eat.
> Place thick with smoke.
> Cards. Beer foaming over
> on the table.

At times, Waldrop's mini-lines fragment annoyingly what my ear wants to perceive as a fine iambic line. Two examples: "For all her beauty / worshipped / but unloved" and "the burn / and the bandage both / making memory." Is the assumption here that the reader is incapable of processing a paradox—or indeed any kind of complexity—unless the contrasts it embodies are separately packaged by the lineation? An occasional foray into the landscape of long lines would give Waldrop a far greater range of effect.

Nor do these poems always benefit from the fragmentation of their syntax. Try to follow the grammar of **"On Being Forgotten,"** from a sequence called **"Actaeon: Eleven Glosses on an Alibi"**:

> How does it happen
> like thin rain
> a look that
> takes too long to arrive
> endless passage from eye
> to eye
> but what does forgetting precisely
> forgetting is now thin rain
> it gnaws at his skin
> with beginning of fear
> fear of water
> it might
> give to the touch
> a look was drowned
> in a wound
> an eye all pupil all open which bleeds.

Should we say simply that the syntax here imitates the putt-putting looseness, the repetitious stammer of lost memory? I don't like to ascribe simplistic motives to a writer of Waldrop's intelligence; she probably knows what effect she wants, but the style can become a tic all the same, albeit a mildly witty tic:

> once upon
> a time
> once upon the impatient sea
> once
> in the kitchen
> get me out please
> I want
> I want
> the rain the river the morning balks at the cold
>
> (from **"Providence in Winter"**)

At other times, Waldrop achieves not only elegance but a sense of remarkably luxuriant leisure in the narrow confines of the framework she has constructed for herself. I've seldom seen a more economical description of falling asleep (falling *into* sleep? diving?) than:

> Castles in sand.
> Or Spain. Space
> of another language.
>   Sleep
> is a body of water.
> You follow your lips
> into its softness. Far down
> the head finds its level.
>
> (from **"Remembering into Sleep"**)

Robert Peters has written that Waldrop has "taken up residence in the abyss between signified and signifier." Assuredly she is not afraid of silence; but even more eloquent than blankness is what one uses to garnish it. Not surprisingly, Waldrop has a striking description of stifled utterance, indeed of general paralysis:

>   The cat
> can't lift its paw,
> its leg longer and longer
> with effort.
> A crying fit
> is cancelled. An aria jelled
> in the larynx.
> Nothing moves in the cotton
> coma
>
> (from **"Remembering into Sleep"**)

It is entirely characteristic of Waldrop that the larger context of this passage is a consideration of how dreams, memories, language itself baffle: "A dream, like trying / to remember, breaks open words for other, hidden meanings." Perhaps what Peters's stylish-sounding formulation means is that Waldrop is an explorer of those meanings. If so, I'd agree.

Streets Enough to Welcome Snow offers many pleasures, but these pale in comparison with the dense, inscrutable little blocks of text that constitute Waldrop's wonderful collection *The Reproduction of Profiles.* So

far as one can tell from the publication dates, *Streets* and *Profiles* [*The Reproduction of Profiles*] were written at about the same time. If the latter volume came later, it would be interesting to try to apply David Kalstone's template in reverse: Is Waldrop moving toward a kind of formal constraint, buttoning what had previously been unbuttoned? Not that either of Waldrop's books is disheveled or self-indulgent; but *Profiles,* the more uniformly shaped of these works, radiates the confidence of an achieved style. Here, in Stevens's words, Waldrop's anima seems to have found its animal. Underneath the bleakness of some of the profiles' surfaces pulses the exuberance of power, the power of exuberance.

I've never been comfortable with the term "prose poem," since samples of the genre often seem to combine the worst features of both parents. Waldrop's paragraph-long profiles, though, manage to unite the intense suggestiveness, and often the rapid pace, of lyric with what Barbara Guest has called the "unnerving leap of suspended narrative."

Of course shreds of story float in the broth of many poetic sequences: Works like *The Waste Land, Paterson, The Bridge,* and Seferis's *Mythistorema,* which share a discontinuous narrative progress, a halo of suggestiveness, and disappearing and reappearing snippets of character and event, have a vague affinity to *The Reproduction of Profiles.* Closer to Waldrop's particular preserve here, however, are (as she has said) Wittgenstein's anti-metaphysical dicta. I think also of the quasi-scientific, precisely lush aphorisms of Malcolm de Chazal's *Sens Plastique*; of the Ashbery of *Three Poems*; and of the miniature (not minimalist!) stories of Lydia Davis (Davis has translated Maurice Blanchot; Waldrop has translated Edmond Jabès and many Austrian poets).

It's easy, in short, to think of *Profiles* as the sort of literary form that comes more easily to Europeans: are these *petits poèmes en prose* in English? But Waldrop's beautifully turned—and turning; writhing—sentences are translations, not from French or German, but from pure thought; like her poems, but in a more distilled and masterful mode, they delineate the movements of the mind. What Bruce Andrews has called Waldrop's constant retrieval from one plane to another is nowhere more in evidence than in these compactly flexible, subtly pithy paragraphs, each of which does indeed execute some kind of bringing back.

Behind Wittgenstein or Baudelaire, I sense in *Profiles* the master of aphorism whose crabbed and enigmatic utterances retain an astounding modernity in their fragmentary state, a state that some scholars argue was never anything other than fragmentary. The following meager sampling of Heraclitus ought to show both the laconic imagistic elegance of his style, and the bite of a complexity that imagist poems are too simple to achieve:

> The name of the bow is life, its work is death.

> The fairest order in the world is a heap of random
> sweepings.

> Death is all we see awake; all we see asleep is sleep.

> Not comprehending, they hear like the deaf. The say-
> ing
> is their witness: absent while present.

> Eyes and ears are poor witnesses for men if their souls
> do not understand the language.

This tragicomedy of the mind's gymnastics Waldrop dons like a leotard, and proceeds to bemuse us with gestures that keep changing. Paradox now defuses, now signals desire; speculation thickens into argument; denial shucks off its erotic guise and puts on dialectic.

From Heraclitus to Wittgenstein, from Proust to Stevens, philosophical writers have taken language as their medium and mirror. Waldrop is no exception; yet she somehow avoids the solipsistic taint which so often imbues ponderings on language, time, and the self. (The alternative to avoiding solipsism is to soak oneself, like Proust, in the destructive element.) Her narrative force, like bursts of fresh air, intermittently clears away the curling groundfog of *me me me*; in these paragraphs there is nearly always an other—one other, often a lover/other, so that although language is a constant preoccupation, it is demystified by context.

> If I fail to deposit a coin, everyday language produces
> the most fundamental confusions, but what pleasure in
> getting lost if it is unavoidable?

> (from page 20)

> Your face was alternately hot and cold, as if translating
> one language into another—gusts from the storm in
> your heart, the pink ribbon in your pocket. Its actual
> color turned out to be unimportant, but its presence
> disclosed something essential about membranes.

> (from page 26)

> I was afraid we would die before we could make a
> statement, but you said that language presupposed
> meaning, which would be swallowed by the roar of the
> waterfall.

> (from page 28)

A "profile" worth quoting in full uses a narrative strategy to limn both a relationship and a frontal assault on the ungraspable sinuosity of language:

> In order to understand the nature of language you began
> to paint, thinking that the logic of reference would
> become evident once you could settle the quarrels of

point, line, and color. I was distracted from sliding words along the scales of significance by smoke on my margin of breath. I waited for the flame, the passage from eye to world. At dawn, you crawled into bed, exhausted, warning me against drawing inferences across blind canvas. I ventured that a line might represent a tower that would reach the sky, or, on the other hand, rain falling. You replied that the world was already taking up too much space.

> (from page 33)

Observe how stealthily we've crossed the border from a temporal to a spatial sense of language. Looking back, one notices that the larger section from which this profile is taken is entitled **"If Words Are Signs."**

The palpable pleasure Waldrop's elegant constructs bestow is at ironic odds, now and then, with the hesitancy of the voice—a voice always supremely articulate, often suave in a deadpan way, yet sometimes querying if not quite querulous, obsessive, nagging. Not that a voice is the same as a self—should one hazard the weary term persona? Yet it won't do, either, to think of the voice as a disembodied emanation. It issues from a body that can feel sleepy, for example:

> I felt sleepy, no doubt because I have a long past and
> don't speak foreign languages.

> (from page 47)

> In the middle of rainy weather, sleep was pinning me
> down on the bed, lids barnacled shut with adjectives in
> color. Sleep, which cannot be divided from itself or
> into parts of speech, pushing a whole sea at my body
> so unable to swallow its grandiose and monotonous
> splendor.

> (from page 80)

The self has distinctive characteristics and reactions:

> Being late is one of my essential properties. Unthink-
> able that I should not possess it, and not even on vaca-
> tion do I deprive myself of its advantages.

> (from page 37)

> I had always resented how nimble your neck became
> whenever you met a woman, regardless of rain falling
> outside or other calamities.

> (from page 27)

It can even manage—temporarily—the last word:

> You said there was still time, you could still break it
> off, go abroad, make a movie. I said (politely, I thought)
> this wouldn't help you. You'd have to kill yourself.

> (from page 26)

That the mind's and body's lapses and eclipses are finally unimportant—or rather are important but not disabling—is reassuringly demonstrated by the way the tics and contretemps, the interruptions and cul-de-sacs of daily life find their way into, and enhance, the glint-ing fabric of the words. This is the paradoxical consola-tion of *Profiles*. The sleepiness Waldrop evokes is akin to the states of drowsiness or incapability conjured up by two poets who have a similarly rueful mastery at turning their liabilities to assets. Listen to Ashbery in *Three Poems*:

> . . . You see that you cannot do without it, that singular isolated moment that has now already slipped so far into the past that it seems a mere spark. You cannot do without it and you cannot have it. At this point a drowsiness overtakes you as of total fatigue and indif-ference; in this unnatural, dreamy state the objects you have been contemplating take on a life of their own, in and for themselves. It seems to you that you are eavesdropping and can understand their private language. . . .

> (from "The System")

And here is David Lehman in the title poem of his col-lection *An Alternative to Speech*, where a supremely articulate poet gesticulates in an elaborate dumbshow that is both frightening and funny:

> Sudden attack of aphasia, I hold my breath like smoke
> And take credit for the brutal gifts
> The darkness bestows. Do you have a friend
> To lend me? . . .
>   From whom I may learn an alternative
> To speech, recipes for staying hungry,
>   instructions on staying awake,
> If death isn't everything.

These protestations of incapability, drowsiness, and aphasia are both ironic and truthful; being alive and awake is often a sleepy business, shot through with oc-casional gleams of insight and energy. The paradoxical consolation, as I've said, is that these confessions of dumbness are not only close to experience but actually enhance our awareness. Our drowsy thoughts glide gratefully through such stimulating labyrinths as Jane Cooper's scrubbed white rooms and the unsettling nooks and crannies of Waldrop's multi-dimensional profiles. All praise is due to the creators of both.

Joan Retallack and Rosmarie Waldrop (interview date autumn 1999)

SOURCE: Retallack, Joan, and Rosmarie Waldrop. "A Conversation with Rosmarie Waldrop." *Contemporary Literature* 40, no. 3 (autumn 1999): 329-77.

[*In the following interview, Retallack's introduction to Waldrop's work and experimental style is followed by a conversation between the two covering a wide range of topics centered around the critical theory that informs a number of Waldrop's works.*]

Back in a medium of German, my mother's Northern variety, not the softer "Frankisch" I had grown up with, memories flooded. I started a novel, *The Hanky of Pip-pin's Daughter*. It began with portraits of my parents, but quickly became a way of trying to understand, to explore, at least obliquely, the Nazi period, the shadow of the past—and the blurred borders of fact, fabrica-tion, tradition, experience, memory. . . .

> Rosmarie Waldrop, in *Contemporary Authors Autobiographical Series*

I don't even have thoughts, I say, I have methods that make language think, take over and me by the hand. Into sense or offense, syntax stretched across rules, relations of force, fluid the dip of the plumb line, the pull of eyes. What if the mother didn't censor the child's looking? Didn't wipe the slate clean? Would the child know from the start that there are no white pages, that we always write over a text already there? No beginnings. All unrepentant middle.

> Rosmarie Waldrop, *A Form / of Taking / It All*

Rosmarie Waldrop, whose reputation in this country and in Europe is primarily that of poet and translator, has written two novels that are gravely, playfully situ-ated in that "unrepentant middle." They are works of compound attention, permeability and generous hu-mor—the kind of humor that renovates medieval no-tions of temperamental fluidities into piquant conceptual shifts. *The Hanky of Pippin's Daughter* (1986) writes over and through textual contusions, surface tensions, odd autobiographical particulars of a small-town Ger-man family's life during Nazi rule. *A Form / of Taking / It All* (1990) opens the novel's pagescape to topologi-cally redistribute historical figures—political and scientific—in discursive gaps whose space-time coordi-nates yield to the new physics even as they evoke the irredeemable legacy of the European conquest of the Americas. In this book quasi-autobiographical characters and personae enact a quantum comedy of manners with figures and grounds and relativities of historical comple-mentarity.

Waldrop composes the cultural flotsam and jetsam out of which we fabricate memory into shifting mosaics whose energy derives from interactions of textual particles (captions, lists, anecdotal fragments, descrip-tive glimpses—data of various, humorous sorts) and narrative/speculative waves that raise questions about our relation to art, science, politics, history. The moving principle in both her novels is transgeneric, a textual graphics of prose and poetic intersections—cultural invention in intercourse with historical crime. The ef-fect is photoelectric, illuminating a contemporary poet-hics of the formally investigative novel with, given the urgent matters addressed, an improbable lightness of form.

As twentieth-century writers and thinkers we have continued to live in the shadow of a nineteenth-century narrative dictum: affix one unit of prose to the next with the *über*-glue of interpretive transition. That this rule has been so spectacularly transgressed—by Stein, Dorothy Richardson, Woolf, Joyce, Beckett, Calvino, Queneau, Sorrentino, Perec—may mislead us into thinking that novels experimenting with *other* logics—associative, collage, paratactic, recursive, procedural, permutative—are numerous. In fact, the scene of the novel is dominated by hundreds of thousands of securely coupled units (sentences, paragraphs, chapters) hurtling like locomotives toward the meta-engineered marvels that configure the architectonics of Romantic profundity—psychologically and philosophically penetrating tunnels, epiphanic climaxes, mirror-image vanishing points.

Nineteenth-century mechanics, in philosophy and literature as well as science and technology, exploited the power of continuous, contiguous, piston-driven momentum toward the transfer of godlike qualities (overarching wisdom and judgment, omnipotence, omniscience) to "man" as author. Twentieth-century, "feminine," gaps and collisions and sensible uncertainties set off alarms, ruptured the nineteenth-century illusion of controlled historical continuity. The intellectual tragicomedy of the Gödelian aftermath has been staged as a dramatic inventory of cultural logics—theological, historical, aesthetic—whose unmoved movers have been, with heavily theorized ceremony, pronounced dead. All the while poets and theorists of complexity have been cavorting in delight as they engage in newly energized explorations.

Complexity—the network of indeterminacies it spawns—is the condition of our freedom. That freedom, insofar as it is exercised as imaginative agency, thrives in long-term projects, like Waldrop's novels, that reconfigure patterns of thought and imagination. (I wonder if human agency—in contrast to human rights—can at this point in our self-conscious cultural undertakings be usefully modeled by isolated instances of "free choice.") This is why, with all the disruptions and anxieties of an age of uncertainty, we are seeing a renaissance of literary and scientific invention brought about by the peculiar twentieth-century dialogue of questions and forms. Things are much more interesting than warmed-over narratives of decline and fall would have it. Where once we thought exclusively in terms of linear developments, with very few first-class tickets or window seats available for the ride, we now notice proliferating opportunities in fractal surfaces—the extraordinary number of detailed contact points that compose the cultural coastline. Draining the "profound depths" of symbolist metaphysics has presented us with the infinite potential of recombinatory, chance-determined play. On the historical surface, whose geometries are more about topological stretches and folds and global networks than developmental chains, it is not surprising that Waldrop's work with the form of the novel resembles *Tris-*

tram Shandy more than *The Magic Mountain* or *Buddenbrooks*. Most importantly, her novels are imaginative, material inquiries into our contemporary conditions. On this matter of timeliness, Gertrude Stein set, many times over, both the modernist and postmodernist scenes: "The whole business of writing is the question of living [one's] contemporariness. . . . The thing that is important is that nobody knows what the contemporariness is. In other words, they don't know where they are going, but they are on their way" (*How Writing Is Written,* [19; Los Angeles: Black Sparrow, 1974] 151).

If logical systems are, as Kurt Gödel tells us, inherently incomplete; if mass *is* energy, particle *is* wave, space *is* time, and vice versa; if natural and cultural histories are chaotic, if complex surfaces *are* fractal (allowing infinite detail to exist within finite space-time delineations), then the question arises, What is implied about the forms with which we attempt to make meaning out of our experience? The answer has not detached itself from the known literary universe. Waldrop, writing attentively out of her own times, explores patterned currents of discontinuous motility and porousness that are all historical residue. But this fluid topography enacts a refusal to stop the event with descriptive certainty. In her prose-poetic spatial manipulations there is such a vigorous widening of the investigative impulse that single point perspective becomes a reversed current flowing right off the page into the ongoing puzzle of contemporanaeity. **"Facts,"** the opening prose poem in Waldrop's ***The Reproduction of Profiles*** (1987), articulates a reimagining of aesthetic truth patterns:

> I had inferred from pictures that the world was real and therefore paused, for who knows what will happen if we talk truth while climbing the stairs. In fact, I was afraid of following the picture to where it reaches right out into reality, laid against it like a ruler. I thought I would die if my name didn't touch me, or only with its very end, leaving the inside open to so many feelers like chance rain pouring down from the clouds. You laughed and told everybody that I had mistaken the Tower of Babel for Noah in his Drunkenness.

In the perverse annals of recapitulation one could say that childhood has always foreshadowed the way in which we lost our (purported) grip on things in the twentieth century. Childhood, in the calmest of eras, is a scintillating scene of absurd and terrifying disproportions. *Alice in Wonderland* or any random selection of fairy tales can be read as instruction manuals for negotiating the speed and glare of associative light as it obliterates the boundary between stable figure and quaking ground. Does the dangerous passage into the dotted-line equilibrium we call adulthood ever end on a personal or historical level? A major source of the practice of storytelling seems to come from our need, first as children, to hear stories that contain the terror, that seduce us in as night-tourists only to skillfully deliver us into the daylight on the other side of a door clearly marked THE END. (Yes, dear, don't worry, the nightmare does stop. Mommy/Daddy/your author will see to that.) There is as well the crucial impulse to tell one's own story, to exercise for oneself the power to fashion a version of reality that can be exited intact.

Now we think we know that the stories we tell tell us as well. This dialogic rhythm forms whole cultures. The panoptical novel reflects and abets a culture of docile bodies, hierarchical power, politically conscripted detail. The romantic and brutal and precise folk tales collected by the Brothers Grimm cannot be without some connection to the romantic and brutal and precise fantasies that Hitler and his myth-manufacturing cronies visited upon Europe.

Rosmarie Waldrop spent her childhood and adolescence in Nazi and postwar Germany. She was not a designated victim. Her family was not Jewish, Gypsy, Communist. As far as I know, no one close to her circle was homosexual. Nonetheless, as a child growing into a sense of her world, she had to contend with the pervasive effects of rampant paranoia, systematic deceit, unjustifiable certainties, rumor, betrayal that formed the atmosphere of Hitler's Germany, as well as with the logical schisms, absences, and terrors associated with any war zone. Bombing raids on the Bavarian town where she lived, Kitzingen-am-Main, brought one's ultimate vulnerability home. Waldrop is the first to say that amidst the bizarre tensions of a family with its own peculiar psychodramas attempting normal life in the context of a major entry into the catalogue of human-constructed hells, there were consolations: her piano, recordings of her favorite music, books, friendship. Under the Allied occupation, the young girl who was then Rosmarie Sebald met an extraordinarily witty, widely read American soldier, Keith Waldrop, who became her dearest friend, literary collaborator, and, a month after her move to the United States in 1958, her husband.

Waldrop's internationally respected career as poet, publisher of Burning Deck books, translator, novelist has taken place entirely in this country. She is most widely known for her poetry—over thirty volumes (some with Keith Waldrop). Among them are the influential post-Wittgensteinian, postpropositional poetics of *The Reproduction of Profiles,* her marvelously titled investigation of feminine logics, *Lawn of Excluded Middle* (1993), and her very specific, word-centered exploration of European intersections with Native American culture, *A Key into the Language of America* (1994). As a leading translator (into English) of Edmond Jabès, as well as of Jacques Roubaud, Paul Celan, and Emmanuel Hocquard, Waldrop has made award-winning contributions to Franco-American let-

ters. *The Hanky of Pippin's Daughter* was the product of a long-standing "impossible" desire to transmute the disequilibrium of ordinary life patterns and Nazi nightmare into a novel. What this finally meant in practical terms was eight years of struggling to find a form, an agon between the vanishing points of irredeemably nasty memories and the complex necessity for what I can only see as poethical courage—the nerve to resist packaging unruly memories in the nineteenth-century conventions of novel as written by God in possession of a world that makes sense.

Waldrop's own statement about *Hanky* [*The Hanky of Pippin's Daughter*] is revealing: "The drive to know our own story moves us to see through it and touch the violence inherent in the mechanism itself." That violence is, in part, the refusal of the material to conform to the palliative gestures of an existing decorum. The twentieth-century paradox of storytelling is that the disturbance that becomes the "drive to know our own story" must enter the *form itself,* thereby making the desired knowledge impossible. Samuel Beckett is interesting on the story as form:

> What am I doing, talking, having my figments talk, it can only be me. Spells of silence too, when I listen, and hear the local sounds, the world sounds, see what an effort I make, to be reasonable. There's my life, why not, it is one, if you like, if you must, I don't say no, this evening. There has to be one, it seems, once there is speech, no need of a story, a story is not compulsory, just a life, that's the mistake I made, one of the mistakes, to have wanted a story for myself, whereas life alone is enough.
>
> ("Texts for Nothing 4")

Oddly or not, this may constitute a functional either/or—"story *or* life" rather than "story *of* life." If one chooses "story of" over life, one chooses the consolation prize of an understanding that removes one from uncertainties and disruptions of extratextual worlds; one is put at rest. The objective is a kind of "moment of inertia," a parameter useful in describing the rotational motion of rigid (inorganic) bodies. The urgent knowledge that erupts onto the page and into the form sends one into the swerving, turbulent patterns of life principles—the messiness and loveliness of ecological interdependence, synergy, exchange, chance. This is what John Cage meant by art that imitates not nature but her processes—processes that render us cheerfully and tragically inconsolable. I suspect it is precisely Beckett's refusal to be consoled (a rejection of sentimentality) that allowed him to "go on." When Waldrop says she doesn't have thoughts, she has methods that make language think, she is referring to a similar movement away from grammars of inertia. Waldrop turns her own restlessness and anxiety of insufficiency into a navigational project, a poetics of formal choices that throw text into motion as life processes themselves.

This has to do with material energies of language—vocabularies, syntaxes, juxtapositional dynamics, interpretive coordinates.

The conversation that follows came about in order to discuss matters that I call "poethical" in relation to the lived ethos I've been referring to in this introduction, for writer and reader, as it came to be embodied in Rosmarie Waldrop's novels. Since their publication by Station Hill Press, both have more or less fallen off the edge of a generically flat literary world, in which anything venturing outside certain well-defined conventions tends to remain all but invisible. My hope in asking Waldrop to participate in a taped conversation, beginning in her kitchen in Providence, Rhode Island, on July 13, 1991, continuing over a weekend and then (with multiple interruptions) by mail into the end of the decade, was that the record of our conversation would create a conceptual lens to bring these two remarkable works of literature into greater visibility, perhaps even into some kind of useful cultural intelligibility. My immense admiration for Waldrop's achievement, along with my writerly curiosity, stemmed in part from my own failed attempt at a generically similar project.

In his 1958 essay "History of Experimental Music in the United States," John Cage wrote that in the midst of "all those interpenetrations which seem at first glance to be hellish—history, for instance . . . one does not then make just any experiment but does what must be done." Of course, we all must decide for ourselves "what must be done." The urgency of a perceived necessity, even in a universe so brilliantly perforated by chance, is what connects experiment with passion. A passion of working through, transfiguring, the materials of one's times can involve all that the word "passion" implies—"suffering" (undergoing, enduring) but also the way in which the register of emotions, from anguish to dread to humor and joy, turns our intellectual and imaginative inventions into richly suggestive humanist prisms. What distinguishes this from sentimentality is the realism and courage involved in a gamut of feelings that makes us permeable to dire intercourse with our world, with others, in the form of love, anger, desire, lust, competitiveness, friendship, the rushing conceptual tumult of shared humor. (Sentimentality, on the other hand, is protective of a closed-down self, hermetically self-serving, in retreat from real consequences.) It is just this that separates the truly consequential experiments in the arts from pro forma imitations.

Rosmarie Waldrop humorously illuminates the emotionally charged character of experiment in her 1990 essay "Alarms and Excursions" (in *The Politics of Poetic Form: Poetry and Public Policy*, ed. Charles Bernstein [New York: Roof]):

> In the early stages of my writing all the poems were about my mother and my relation to her. Rereading them a bit later, I decided I had to get out of this obses-sion. This is when I started to make collages. I would take a novel and decide to take one or two words from every page. The poems were still about my mother. So I realized that you don't have to worry about the contents: your preoccupations will get into the poem no matter what. Tzara ends his recipe for making a chance poem by cutting out words from the newspapers and tossing them in a hat: "The poem will resemble you."

The remarked coincidence of experimental results with what one most cares about happens only when the active consciousness of the experimenter precipitates a focused urgency of choice, one that cannot help but affect the shape of the indeterminate elements. The moral is that in the hands of the poethically innovative artist we need not fear dissociative or denatured or depersonalized forms. Waldrop begins an autobiographical statement (for the Gale's *Dictionary of Literary Biography*) with a quote from John Cage's *Silence,* "Poetry is having nothing to say and saying it: we possess nothing." This means bringing disparate linguistic units into a patterned synergy that will unavoidably emanate from the writer's being in the world, that has tangible sources but which also honors the active intelligence of the reader precisely in the extent to which it eschews ownership or authority over the way in which it is construed. It is sent out into the world in reciprocal dialogue with its other.

In *Hanky* there is a captioned framing, a paratactic pace that serially interweaves the personal anecdotal, the journalistic documentary, the epistolary, the philosophical, the helplessly humorous with a quest for meaning that is neither pretentious nor falsely modest given Waldrop's acknowledged remove from the worst horrors of Nazism. Waldrop arrives at this strategic nexus, one could say, in order to depart from it not as victim but as composer of a novel that, under the pressure of the grotesqueries of Nazism, transmogrifies into a kind of linguistic comic strip. This book could in fact be fruitfully read together with Art Spiegelman's *Maus*, volume 1 of which was also published in 1986. It does with language some of what Spiegelman does with the visual conventions of cartooning. Both Waldrop and Spiegelman are writing about their parents' relation to Nazism from an intimate remove that, though differently situated, leads each to transgress and exceed the scope of the conventional novel in material engagements with impossible material. Spiegelman's humor erupts out of his relationship with his father, whose irritating quirks may or may not be the result of victimization. A similarly important questioning of the limits of victim status is what makes humor possible in Waldrop's work.

Waldrop's "strip" has features of Möbius as it traces the process (not necessarily progress) of moving from personal narrative to narrative persona. It does this by discarding the self-justifying strategies and sentimentalities of certain kinds of novelistic prose—prose that never undermines the power of the narrator even within the conventions of "unreliability." Waldrop has literally turned the uses of her language inside out and in again to leave us with that paradox of all consciously post-modern fictions—that of the acknowledged lie of acknowledging the lie that is the sinister engine of selectivity in all forms. Spiegelman's *Maus: A Survivor's Tale* begins with the humor of its own title and the problematic of its first caption, "My Father Bleeds History." The first caption in Waldrop's humorously titled *Hanky* is "LAST SEASON'S BESTSELLER WAS GREED." Both novels sort through dubious legacies of parents who are simultaneously trapped/free agents in/of their cultures. Humor is located in conceptual shifts between "trapped/free" playing out in *Hanky* as "Jewish/Aryan" in linked "Franz/Josef" figures of the mother's "Lover/Father."

To Theodor Adorno's despairing sense that after Auschwitz it would no longer be possible to write poetry, Edmond Jabès replied, "I saw that we must write. But we cannot write like before." Waldrop, close friend as well as translator of Jabès, has enacted this realization in her own work. Adorno himself attempted to moderate his poetic pessimism (at one point saying it is only *lyric* poetry that is barbaric after Auschwitz) to the very end of his life. The challenging means to a reinvention of possibility was already apparent in his *Minima Moralia,* written during and immediately after World War II: "There is no longer beauty or consolation except in the gaze falling on horror, withstanding it, and in unalleviated consciousness of negativity, holding fast to the possibility of what is better" ([19; London: Verso, 1985] 25).

This raises—in a manner both stark and energetic—the life-and-death urgency of questions of literary form as we navigate through the range of joys and catastrophes and commonplaces and shades of anomie of our violent times—the unexpurgatable mess of lived history. Imaginative structures orient and initiate our intuitions as we confront the congealed givens that can stop breath and hope. Some forms point toward what is yet fluid, what is possible; others encapsulate the brutality, rendering it somehow palatable. By the last vanishing-point punctum at the end of the last beautifully constructed paragraph of the undeconstructed novel, even the Holocaust can acquire a harmonious aspect. One must question the consequences of conventions that protect the formal dynamics of literary production from the terror. This is the reassuring—market-friendly—production of innocuousness: the misleading solace of work too timid to disturb the logic of the universe in which the violence continues to occur.

We are always writing through the impossibility of *after.* This chronic, dispiriting condition can grind imagination to a halt or send it tooling in nostalgic circles. The

most vital of our new writing addresses our need to stay in motion via the disparate and humorous logics of inventing and reinventing our contemporanaeity. Such a process must always take place in acknowledgment of the fact that the materials of invention are nothing other than historical detritus. All the more reason to affirm a poetics of the improbable—our perennial challenge, the heart of an engaged optimism.

[Retallack]: Rosmarie, the poetics of structure, process, image, idea in your work—prose as well as poetry—foregrounds issues of form for me, the uses and consequences of form. I'm curious about the kinds of distinctions you tend to make, whether intuitively or analytically, between the various genres in which you work—particularly between your poetry and the prose books, The Hanky of Pippin's Daughter *and* A Form / of Taking / It All.

[Waldrop]: Well, I'm tempted to say the prose books are just larger. I don't usually start by thinking, Is this going to be prose or verse? I tend to think in terms of tension, and one tension is usually between the impulse to continue, to have a constant flow, and the impulse toward fragmentation. Sometimes one wins out and sometimes the other. The impulse toward flow, for instance, dominates in the poetic text **The Road Is Everywhere, or Stop This Body.** All the sentences merge. The object of one sentence is always also the subject of the next, so that there is no complete sentence, but each poem as a whole becomes one continuous, strangely shifting, ungrammatical sentence. This rapid flow is stronger than the verse's pull toward pause, but not strong enough to become prose. It needed the obstacles of the line-ends to have a rhythmical shape. On the other hand, in **When They Have Senses,** also poetry, the subject matter conspired with my tendency towards fragmentation. The relation of men and women is so complicated that just getting partial little glimpses seemed all I could do. Of course, both tendencies are always present, it's not a matter of one winning out over the other, but of the emphasis being more on one. For instance, in the novel *The Hanky of Pippin's Daughter,* in a larger structure, I really got going once I had found the form that could accommodate both flow and fragmentation: many short, little chapters that have a certain amount of closure and at the same time don't have any closure at all because a sentence may actually continue across chapter boundaries, title and all. The tension cuts across the difference between verse and prose, though in verse it seems to be located between the line and the single word, as well as between line and sentence, and in prose, more between single word and sentence as well as between sentence and the larger units, paragraph, chapter, et cetera. Even so, obviously, verse is very different from prose, a matter of rhythm.

Does that have anything to do with different formal intentions? For instance, telling a story . . .

Yes. Yes, I don't know quite how it connects, but the novel came out of getting claustrophobic with my shorter and shorter verse lines. They were getting so tight that it seemed hard to say anything. Also, this having the object always topple into the subject of the next sentence really makes for a main-clause highway. It did not allow any roads off to the side. It made for speed, but down the middle of the road, as it were. I began to hanker for subordinate clauses, for excursions, amblings. It seemed exhilarating to go from those very short lines to a novel which, at least theoretically, would have room for anything, which would be spacious, not so tight and pared down. An impulse towards plenitude. And also, well, I realized that anything I wrote about my childhood would have in some way to address Nazi Germany. I was ten when the war was over. So I grew up learning about this horror—the immediate past was this horror! Which seemed impossible to name, talk about. It seemed, if I could write about it at all, it would need space so I could approach it very indirectly, via detours, from various angles, from the margins, as it were.

One of the remarkable things about the book in which you address the Nazi past, The Hanky of Pippin's Daughter, *is how you manage to write with both "lightness" and "multiplicity"—to use Italo Calvino's normative terms, from his Charles Eliot Norton lectures* Six Memos for the Next Millennium. *Or, one could equally characterize that novel as a dynamic equilibrium of humor and complexity. You've accomplished this while in fact dealing with a subject of such enormous gravity and horror that many would assume lightness or humor to be a breach of some fundamental decorum. The very particular way in which you build in that lightness page by page, syntactically and graphically, allows you to explore, to question the persuasive narrative momentum associated with the traditional impulse of the novel, as well as with the propagandistic forms of the Nazi era. Specific devices that you employ with the language, like using the beginnings of sentences in the short sections as—*

Chapter headings.

Yes, as paratactic captions; or the end of a sentence becoming the heading for a new section. It's both a framing device and an interruptive pattern that resists the usual novelistic strategy of paragraphs merging as informational tributaries to tell a unified story, of course via fully achieved authorial transitions. You don't allow the narration, the stylistic self-justification built into continuous-flow narration, it's explanatory force, to become too compelling.

Right. I think it's partly because it is such impossible subject matter. It is impossible to "deal" with.

So you've avoided constructing the kind of narrative that might entirely conceal in its smooth transitions, or even deny, the fact of that impossibility.

That would be a false continuity. And also, yes, there is always the feeling that I never have enough information. The process is not so much "telling" as questioning. This implies interruption. And in the gaps we might get hints of much that has to be left unsaid—but should be thought about.

How did you come to that? You have a very particular balance in that book between trying to say as much as you can, but not too much, not more than you can. Not pretending that—

That I know, that I have answers.

Yes. Yes, that epistemology of incompleteness is something you make available in the content of the narrative when you say things explicitly about the limits of knowing, but it's also very much embedded in the form.

Right. As you said, one of the themes is the novel as an attempt to understand, but, even more, that any attempt to understand is a construction, and a violence. Keeping that in mind, especially when the subject involves something as horrible as the Holocaust, even if you only touch on the fringes, how can one pretend to "understand"? And at the same time, I needed to get at some of the things, to understand, or imagine, how people like my parents lived through that time, to what extent they went along. That is the wound of this book. To know that I have come out of this. Trying to deal with origins in this nasty framework. It took me a very long time to write. I worked on it for about eight years. Not exclusively, true. There were other things that I was writing in between. I kept having to put it aside, getting stuck. If there's lightness, it was come by laboriously.

Well, lightness is an artifice. You worked on Hanky *for eight years to achieve that artifice. I presume that if we were to look at pages from early drafts they would appear, graphically, quite different from the published version.*

Yes.

So, it took you a while to discover the form for this book?

Yes, quite.

What kind of process was that? Was it a process of subtraction?

Of addition and subtraction. The very first things were just character sketches of the parent figures, of Josef and Frederika.

Who are closely related to—

Modeled after my parents. Yes, they are. Then I realized that I couldn't possibly talk about them without
bringing in the Nazi times. I finally thought of giving
the mother a Jewish lover as a way of bringing the
"times" in and yet anchoring it all in the personal. Then
the manuscript got very large—I mean for me. It is still
a mammoth book for me, and it's only 150 pages! But
the manuscript got large because I started, in a state of
exhilaration, to pack in anything—anecdotes friends
had told me, things stolen from other books, just wildly
packed-in material. This was my reaction against the
tightness of the poems that preceded. Of course, later I
had to cut most of it out again.

*Was all that in part, do you think, to submerge the
story? Did you become afraid of the story?*

Very likely. I didn't think about it in those terms, but it
may well have been. Yes. That's a curious idea.

*Thinking about the urge to tell that story, or the need to
tell it, I like this sentence on the jacket of* Hanky: *"The
drive to know our own story moves us to see through it
and touch the violence inherent in the mechanism
itself." What I think is interesting about that statement
is that it refers to the violence of the content of "our
stories," but—*

But also to the violence of the process of telling.

*Exactly. When I asked whether you were bringing things
in to submerge the story, I was thinking more of the
content—though these things of course bleed into each
other, make each other bleed. What about the violence
in the mechanism of storytelling?*

Any telling is a falsification, is doing violence. Even
the "truest" telling is at least the imposition of a
perspective and a radical foreshortening. My title refers
to this: according to legend my hometown was founded
on the spot where a shepherd, Kitz, found a handkerchief
dropped by the daughter of the Merovingian king Pippin the Short. This is around the year 750. Nothing else
is known about this woman, not even her name. A
woman's whole life reduced to one legend—to one little
gesture, dropping her hanky. So the construction itself
is necessarily violent, more so with the weight of being
put on paper and not just thought. At bottom, all
speaking/writing is an exercise of power, is violent.
Even on a very general level, experience is necessarily
"killed" when transformed into writing; it is rendered
absent. Also, on a simpler level, it's a nasty story. And
some of the material is the life of my parents who are
dead, and about the dead you're not supposed to say
anything but good.

You use the word "nasty" in the book. Between reading
Hanky *for the first time and rereading it before coming
for our conversation, I saw the German film* The Nasty
Girl. *Have you seen it?*

Yes.

*I wondered if you had any feelings of connectedness to
that. I don't know what the title is in German.*

It's just *Das Schreckliche Mädchen,* "The Terrible Girl."
It's not quite as good a title as the English, as the
"Nasty."

On page 98 of Hanky *you write, "This particular nastiness actually had a pigment. Brown. A perfectly decent
color. It can't be blamed for the people who put it on."*

That's not the nastiness of telling. That's the Nazi color,
"Hitler brown."

But you also felt nasty telling this story?

Yes, also mixing "truth" and fiction. I used family
structures and stories but went beyond them, bending
them to my purpose—making it much worse. Formally
too, for instance, making the dialogue between the two
sisters a quarrel all through. To get a dramatic tension
going between characters.

*Is the sibling structure in this novel from your family?
Do you have twin sisters?*

Yes. This would have been easy to change. But I liked
having literal twins when there are so many other dou-
blings, "twinnings" of characters, stories, past and
present, facts and fictions, unwanted selves . . .

*So there's the sense that this is a nasty thing to do, and
yet you obviously had to do it.*

I obviously wanted to do it.

Wanted to do it.

Yes. The changes that I made go in the opposite direction from what most people will do in using autobiographical material. I made it worse rather than better. I
made it nastier. I guess that was why I felt odd.

*Well, there isn't the sense that you were prettying up
the story in any way—*

On the contrary.

*But on the other hand, the form makes it more than
tolerable; it makes it an exhilarating experience to read,
because of the lightness, the movement.*

That's great! I'm happy you were feeling it that way. I was hoping it would do that. Form as exorcism.

There's a lot of humor in the form. Of the sort that doesn't have to do with jokes, but has to do with quickly shifting temperaments, perceptions, following an intelligence that is simultaneously in control and on the verge of not being able to cope with "the story," a hop-skipping over danger zones lightly defined by dotted lines.

Exactly.

One of the things that was so exciting about this book for me—and it was immediately exciting to start reading it knowing what it was about, seeing how you were handling it formally—I was exhilarated by the constructive tension I found in relation to many traditional uses of storytelling. Often stories are used to make things seem more intelligible than they actually are, more palatable, smoothing over rough edges, building denatured, seamless word-worlds in which anything can turn out to be O.K. Really, almost anything! Mass atrocity, personal brutality, paranoid violence, rape can become oddly palatable as chaos and ruin turn into well-made sentences. No matter how awful the images that the sentences are evoking, there can be a kind of lozenge-like shape to it all, each unit—sentence to paragraph to chapter—designed for easy swallowing. This use of stories is both understandable and worrisome. With your work on the Nazi era, and on the conquest of the Americas in A Form / of Taking / It All, *the resistance to the paved-over silences of certain novelistic conventions invites one to think about the material terms of the novel and about the organizing intelligence in relation to the chaos of history. Now I'm thinking specifically of terms surrounding the "art" of the novel: "fiction" coming from the Latin* fingere, *"to touch"; "story" from* historia *which originally meant "wisdom"; "narrative" from* narus, *meaning "knowing." Did these things—touching, a search for wisdom, knowing—bear on the process as it unfolded for you?*

Yes, as something to react against! At least the wisdom and knowing part. Because I thought exactly the opposite. Even if you write fiction with a limited perspective, you are still pretending to be omniscient. That's what I didn't want. In the same way, we say it's a fault in a novel if there are loose ends, it's all supposed to be tied up and neat. I thought of this as all loose ends.

Though there is a kind of weaving. The image that comes to mind actually is of a braid that has loose ends sticking out along the way, so while there's continuity of overall pattern, there's no illusion of entirely continuous strands.

I like that image. There has to be connection. Dallas Wiebe called this interweaving Wagnerian, but I hope he is wrong! Not just because I hate Wagner. But my weaving has too much interruption to weave a spell. I think the interruptions are in the service of consciousness, of thinking, against a narrative rhythm that might become mesmerizing.

Did you feel that you had come to know more, did you gain wisdom, did you touch previously untouchable things in writing Hanky?

Well, "wisdom" is a big term. But I think I came to understand some mechanisms, for instance how prejudice operates, racial prejudice. That it takes very little to activate it in somebody who maybe didn't think he was a racist, that it may take just one little action to let all of the stereotypes come flooding in. This is what I do with Josef when he finds out that his wife has been sleeping with his friend. If the friend were not Jewish he would have to deal with it in other terms, but since the friend is a Jew he can use the stereotypes as explanation. That "nothing is sacred" for Jews, et cetera. An available substitute for thinking.

There may have been some sort of modulation of perhaps an initial horror that there could be activations and enactments of this prejudice in your own family, but then also gaining an understanding of how it could happen to anyone within a systemically racist society. Did that change your feelings about the characters? Did you feel you had to see them in new ways as you moved along in order to continue writing?

I suppose. On one level, the book was an attempt to understand my mother, with whom I had always had a very hostile relation. Yes, it's almost paradoxical, but I think I learned something personal, about an actual person, by subjecting her to imagined, fictional situations.

Is that different from what happens to you in the process of writing poetry?

I don't know. There is a mimetic framework in the novel. But there is "thinking through" in both, thinking through form.

I love what you wrote in relation to this in your essay "Alarms and Excursions." At some point you realized everything you had ever written had been about your mother. You decided to experiment with nonnarrative forms in an attempt to free yourself from your preoccupation with your mother. And though it wasn't direct or explicit, you were—

Still writing about my mother, even when making collages!

Your feelings about your mother were inextricably connected to the energy in your need to write.

This was a great discovery of Tzara's. He has this wonderful poem, "How to Make a Dada Poem": Take a newspaper article. Cut it into single words. Put them in a bag. Shake gently. Take them out and copy carefully. And, here comes the punch, *the poem will resemble you.* Even if you seem to abdicate choice, you are still choosing, if at a remove. You don't get away from your preoccupations, your passions.

Yes. It's your consciousness that is making all the decisions, whatever they may be. The order of the elements in the procedure. The experimental framework is designed by you.

Yes, as we have said about Jackson Mac Low and John Cage—who both go very much farther than I do. I use a lot of collage. I like choice at one remove, but I never go to a strict system and keep to it. Yes, one's obsessions will out. There's no getting away from them.

Well, given that fact, if it is in fact a fact, that no matter what you're doing and no matter what your procedures are, you are always shaping the material in the terms of your preoccupations, your obsessions, then what does it matter that you tell it more directly? If it's all about your mother anyway—

Good question.

Why not leave it at that?

I'd be bored.

Well, actually, can we let that hover a bit? As you can see, I'm curious about the very specific consequences of form, of the choices you make about language units, spacing, graphic presences, absences—how, why you find yourself working with one kind of structure rather than another.

When I first started thinking about this material, I thought I would have to do it in a realistic way. Which was strange for me. I wasn't sure I really wanted to do that. And wasn't sure I could! Actually, I found out in trying that I couldn't. I came away with a great respect for plain straightforward narrative. It is incredibly hard to do. I found I couldn't sustain it. So my leaps are really a disguise of my limp. I exaggerate my defects and try to make them an asset.

Hmm, I find that a little suspect!

I now think I felt it was material that maybe shouldn't—couldn't—be monkeyed with. As if "realism" weren't also "monkeying," as much of an artifice as any other form. In any case, the only way I could do it was indeed my usual way, trying both for small, fragmentary glimpses and then weaving or braiding, as you say,

those fragments together in a kind of musical flow, with recurrences for rhythm, et cetera. So it was the forms I had practiced in poetry—not in fiction—that enabled me to write this piece of prose. Not to mention the reliance on metaphors.

As you were talking, I thought about something you say in A Form / of Taking / It All. *You are talking about the importance of images making connections of certain kinds. You say, if we didn't connect the dots, we wouldn't know the dots were there.*

Umm. That sounds better than . . . I think you must have formulated that!

No, you say that.

Here we are with Pound and Charles Olson and Whitehead, et cetera: what matters is not things but what happens between them. Or if you take the linguistic model, it is not the phoneme but the connection of phonemes that makes language, the differences in the sequence. It's always relation.

Yes, a moving, dynamic relation that allows things to glance at or by one another—in both senses of the word "glance"—seeing, recognizing, but also glancing off of and past, moving on. So there isn't a connection in the sense of a static bonding.

This is another function of the interruptions. The gaps keep the relations in question.

That way of working with shorter threads, abbreviated, almost anecdotal stories, juxtaposed perceptions, a motley assortment of narrational and descriptive and linguistic units—things you're choosing to attend to— creates a very different kind of world within the text than what we find in the sustained, internally coherent narrative of the more conventional novel. That form, unless it has moved from its nineteenth-century forward-thrusting track toward the "impossible" impediments and complexities of certain modernist novels, is a fully furnished panopticon, doors and windows sealed shut. The reader is led through from well-marked entrance to well-marked exit by an ever-present, entirely solicitous tour guide. Not much chance to wander and turn up things for yourself.

That's a good image.

Quite distinct from this, The Hanky of Pippin's Daughter *was for me a much more permeable form—not fully furnished, more breathing room for the reader. A textual world more inviting to things that lay outside the author's mind.*

Yes, the movement is not that of guiding—a tour or anything else—but of forays, of exploration. This is made thematic, in fact. The way the two narratives and two generations interact in a way parallels the reading and writing processes. On the one hand, the "narrator" is trying to understand her own story while trying to "read" that of the parents—the way we "glance off" into our own meditations and bring them into the text we are reading, as we always do, except maybe in a novel "you can't put down," which really "holds you captive." On the other hand, the sisters' knowledge is spotty so that there is constant conjecture, doubt, inventing or imagining what went on in the past, often using their own lives as a model to project onto the past. The past is a text alternately read and written.

And yet for me this text has an atmosphere, just because of the very particular world that you're evoking—that particular time, that place—that is contained and exotic. The experience of reading it has a quality of breathing a different kind of air. In that sense there is an enclosed quality, because the prose is holding that air in place. And yet . . . again Calvino comes to mind, his thoughts on how many modes must exist simultaneously to make a really exhilarating novel. He wrote in his Norton lectures about the importance of having it all—lightness, quickness, exactitude, visibility, multiplicity. His sixth lecture would have been about consistency had he not died of a sudden heart attack before completing it. Do you know the collection of these lectures?

No, I've not seen that.

I've had problems with the nineteenth-century form of the novel for some time, after an adolescence of living among its native characters, wanting to become one, and of course its well-made plots—longing for a life with a well-made plot. I felt I had to reject all that in order to live in the real, twentieth-century world. But recently I found myself wanting to reopen the question of the novel as contemporary form—not just holdover from the nineteenth century. I found Calvino's Norton lectures very helpful. He talks about those characteristics I mentioned—which, incidentally, I feel he didn't come as close to achieving in his own novels as you have, except possibly in If on a Winter's Night a Traveler. *In the lecture on "multiplicity" he talks about the encyclopedic novel, but also the novel that presents the reader with a system of systems, so that though you feel the kind of containment that even multiple systems create—*

I felt that in "If on a Winter's Night" the system became obtrusive. The initial exhilaration wore off for me. I didn't quite finish it.

We're all, I think, painfully aware of the fact that we are at this historical moment entirely self-conscious about genres and styles—

Right.

That's why I've been so curious about the particulars of your reluctance to engage in the conventional act of fiction—telling a stylistically "realistic" story.

Well, as I said, it was at least partly inability.

Though I had the feeling, from things you said earlier, that you really were not so sure you wanted to do that kind of straightforward narrative.

Well, it goes a little against the grain.

Yes, that's what I'm curious about. Why?

Discontinuity is the natural state to me. It's how I see the world.

Talking, though, about forms that I confess induce claustrophobia in me—entering into certain internally consistent and "compleat" fictional worlds—I wonder is any of that a negative experience for you?

In writing, yes, but I often enjoy reading those novels. In fact sometimes I really get a craving for a real "solid" . . .

Book! [A book on a nearby shelf falls over.]

I wonder which kind this is!

I can't read the title from here; it's that brown one. Do you know what that is? Ah, what just toppled was Harold Brodkey's Stories in an Almost Classical Mode.

Obviously the vibrations.

Criticizing the conventional novel has consequences!

I don't think it's simply a negative for me. In fact, the idea of closure—"closure" has become a dirty word, which is a bit silly because there has to be *some* closure for a form to be perceptible at all. There has to be some "coming together." But the problem is the degree of closure. It's rather like "aesthetic distance"—a very fine line. You want things to be cold, as cold as possible, as far away from the sentimental as possible. But there is a line beyond which it gets so cold that the reader can't get interested. That fine line is as far away from the "warm pulsing" as possible without tumbling over into freezing temperatures. My feeling about closure is similar. It's a matter of *balance*, the paradox within the term "open form." The question is how little closure we can get away with and still have the text "come together."

Yes, I think about that in terms of permeable and semipermeable membranes—the containment within a membrane, but also its openness to breathing, exchang-

ing air with things outside it. That's what makes life possible, isn't it? A form that's alive somehow has to have permeable boundaries.

This is an interesting complement to the way Charles Bernstein talks about absorption and impermeability in "The Artifice of Absorption." He is more concerned with the reception, the reading process. His "impermeable" is all the formal elements that go against that other artifice that aims at absorbing, captivating the reader. But your image is actually closer to Rilke's image of form in the ninth *Duino* elegy: "Krusten, die willig zerspringen, sobald / innen das Handeln entwächst und sich anders begrenzt." Literally, crusts that willingly split open as soon as the inner action outgrows them and seeks other boundaries. Except that Rilke sees the energy totally "within," whereas your membrane puts it at the intersection of within and without, as Charles Olson's "skin" does. I like that better. And I would perhaps describe my own process as rather in the opposite direction: I always have multiplicity, scatter, and must search for the jelling point, the point of intersection, something fluid, but with cohesion.

Whose forms, whose work do you admire? What do you like to read?

God! So many people.

Maybe those are two different questions: (1) Whose work do you admire? (2) Whose work do you like to read?

Well, I go through times when I read one particular writer very avidly and with great intensity. I've had periods of Stein, Pound, Creeley, Ashbery, for instance—when I was really absorbed in them, and absorbing them. And then comes a long stretch when I hardly read them at all because I'm surfeited. I'm just coming around to reading Ashbery again.

Ah, I think immediately of Flow Chart *because you often use the word "flow" about your own work.*

I've heard him read part of it. It was stunning.

What are your thoughts about the relation of that kind of form—a poem that invites in disparate fragments of a life—in relation to your novels? Again, a question of genre. I wonder if certain things are able to happen in that form, a poem, that couldn't happen, even in the most complex interweavings of a novel, and vice versa. What about writers of fiction, novelists?

I love Djuna Barnes. In fact there are parts, phrases from *Nightwood* in *The Hanky.*

Really!

That was one of the books that got put in, along with friends' anecdotes, in the expansive period.

From Nightwood? *I'm ashamed to say I didn't notice.*

At this point I don't quite know which phrases or sentences were worked out of it again and which are still in there. But it's definitely one source. And I love Robert Musil. He may be at the top of my list. Along with Kafka. Then there is Woolf, Lispector, Svevo, Hawkes, Coover, Harry Mathews, Dallas Wiebe . . .

What about Musil, what do you find in his work?

In Musil? Everything!

Everything?

Well, if we take *The Man without Qualities,* first, the story itself is hilarious: Austria, in 1913, is planning a great celebration to rival the planned celebration of the German emperor's birthday in 1918 when we know both countries will be in the war within another year, and devastated by 1918. This may seem a fairly heavy irony, but it's delightful all the way through and constantly undermines the plot, the very progress of the novel. And there is another irony: whereas the plot is driven largely by the celebration committee's desperate search for an *idea,* which they of course cannot find, the novel is what you would call highly permeable for ideas, reflection, sociopolitical analysis, almost small essays worked in. So there is an openness, a grid structure that allows great complexity, a nonlinear narrative, there is a story that is exhilarating in its irony, and the style, the texture is just incredible. The sentences are so good.

That's interesting. You are describing things that I think you accomplish with Hanky. *But in such a different way.*

Of course Musil also has a mystical dimension, which I don't have at all. Which comes in the later part—where incest is presented as an attempt to cross borders into some original state of unity. This you probably haven't read, because it's part of the posthumous material, which was not part of the translation until the new one that came out just recently.

I wasn't aware that there was anything missing. So what about your Franz Josef in Hanky? *Is there anything like mysticism or incest—crossing borders—with the best friend who is Jewish? "Franz Josef" as "the father" is in itself very suggestive historically, and then the fact of this character sort of copulating with himself . . . There seems to be a thread in this novel that has to do with crossing borders and with genetics, biology. If Musil is moving toward a kind of unitary vision through incest, is there anything like this in* Hanky?

Mysticism, or religion, is only there through Josef's kooky metaphysical and astrological systems, but not in a serious way. That's not an area that's being investigated at all. No, actually, the closeness of Franz and Josef—the reason I wanted to make them literal blood brothers through a transfusion is again that I wanted to approximate on a small, almost microscopic level something that is much too large for me to deal with. If you look at German literature, in fact, German culture, contrary to what the Nazis were saying, it is impossible to excise the Jewish component. There is an article by Gershom Scholem that argues that the German Jews embraced German culture to such an extent that the Germans felt ousted from their own patrimony. It's a curious idea that the very degree of their assimilation was in fact what irritated the Germans. He does not go so far as to say that if the Jews had been less assimilated the Holocaust might not have happened.

In Hanky *one of the characters—or perhaps it's the narrator—talks about a typical Nazi accusation, that the Jews really don't have their roots in Germany; they are using the culture on some level without really being committed to it.*

Yet they "used" it so well that they actually shaped it.

Yes, that's what I want to ask, when you say "assimilated the German culture—"

I mean they *were* part of the mainstream of the culture. When you think of the incredible blossoming of the arts from around the turn of the century until it was cut off by Hitler, you simply cannot take out the Jews.

You write about the blossoming of literary culture just prior to the horrors of Nazi Germany in your essay "Alarms and Excursions." You're referring to the idea that language can save us, that the forms we make of our language can improve the world: "The two decades before Hitler came to power were a period of incredible literary flowering, upheaval, exploration in Germany. All the dadaists and expressionists had been questioning, challenging, exploring, changing the language, limbering up its joints. So the German language should have been in very good condition, yet the Nazis had no trouble putting it to work for their purposes, perverting it to where what was said was light years from what was meant. So, while language thinks for us, there is no guarantee that it will be in a direction we like" [in The Politics of Poetic Form: Poetry and Public Policy, edited by Charles Bernstein]. Are you familiar with Allan Janik's and Stephen Toulmin's historico-philosophical analysis of fin-de-siècle Austrian culture, Wittgenstein's Vienna?

No. Not yet.

There was an enormous, blatant corruption in the use of language, public language at that time. They argue that it was the character of Viennese culture—in which public language was used primarily for denial and lies—that brought on the unprecedented attention to the nature of language in the work of Wittgenstein, Freud, Karl Kraus, and others. And that, of course, could strike one as ironic. In the discourse of intellectual circles all that attention is being given to linguistic hygiene—truth functions, language games, the language of the unconscious; it seems to have no effect whatsoever in the larger culture, on the widespread credulity with which Hitler's rhetoric is received.

But of course I pose as a little more naive in that essay than I really am. I mean, the word implies the lie, the possibility of the lie. The possibility of misuse is always right there. Language has nothing to do with ethics. It can be used for good or evil.

In other words, there is no essential connection between language and ethics.

There's nothing inherently ethical in language, I think.

Well, if they don't essentially or inherently connect, should ethics *and* aesthetics *have something to do with one another?*

It would be nice.

When you are putting together a literary form, do you think that you on some level need to perform an ethical act with your use of language? Do you think of your uses of language as having an ethos? Do you, for instance, feel the need to be "honest" in some way?

Well, "honest" in a formal way. Exactness of language. Listening to the words. But I get bothered when people say, This piece of writing is not sincere. What does it mean when people say that about a work of the imagination? I've been thinking about this in connection with the objectivists. Zukofsky keeps talking about "sincerity." Keith [Waldrop] pointed out what must be the source of his statements, the definition of the ideogram for "sincerity" in Pound's translation of Confucius: "pictorially the sun's lance coming to rest on the precise spot verbally . . . to perfect, bring to focus. . . . The eye looking straight into the heart." That image is beautiful. The combination of light, focus, and location in the heart. A work should shed light rather than obfuscate. And it should not be a mere technical exercise, showing off your virtuosity, but grounded in some way in the core of your being. Your postulation of a "poethics" is more radical, I think. And Cage's "One does not then make just any experiment, but does what must be done" seems to imply a responsibility to history, to the cultural moment. But I don't see this as a matter of ethics. I rather think we can't escape our cultural moment anyway. So for me this is as far as the ethical dimension of literature goes: that the form would have to be "true," in the sense of light, precision, and the heart.

Hmm. "The heart"—a term I have trouble with. "The heart" seems to me problematic. With "light," I think of Descartes—"the light of reason."

True, light we're more comfortable with.

Well, the light of reason gets deflected and refracted. If light—the experience of it, the metaphor—implies anything about knowledge, that what we can see is what we can know, things are already very complicated. What we know and what we invent are closely related.

It also gets complicated because in Western culture the complex light-clarity-knowledge is set up as *the* measure of value. Blanchot speaks of the "imperialism of light"—that light lets see, but is not itself seen. It gives illusion of direct knowledge, immediacy: we see clearly on condition that we do not see the light. This sounds rather like the realistic novels you have been talking about, that pretend to transparency.

I wonder about a possible connection between ethical and formal concerns. I mean, every form has an ethos, doesn't it? For instance one might think of constructing enough syntactic and semantic openness so that a reader's mind is not engulfed by your world, so that she or he still has some autonomy and agency, critical distance—the sorts of things that are said about valuing and supporting the "active" versus the "passive" reader. Is it, for instance, an ethical act as a writer to stun the reader into passivity?

I don't think about it in those terms. You exaggerate the power of the writer.

Well, I do think there are powers of seduction that writers quite consciously use.

The reader is after all free not to pick up the book. But I don't think about the reader at all while writing. I don't go as far as Benjamin, who says in "The Task of the Translator": "Art . . . posits man's physical and spiritual existence, but in none of its works is it concerned with his response. No poem is intended for the reader, no picture for the beholder, no symphony for the listener." But the reader is in the future. Once a poem is done I can think about her or him. While I'm writing all I think about is trying to make as good a structure as I can, that is true to—well, I guess, true to what I feel. It's curious. I have problems with these words too—sincerity, heart, feeling. It may be because we are women, and the literary "domain" of women used to be the emotions, the heart, the sentimental story or poem. We don't want to be defined—limited—this way. Maybe our unease with those terms means that we are still fighting a stereotype—which is still around, for that matter.

Yes, there is that. But also more generally, there can be a sense that if you just feel something intensely enough—and this goes back to the unease with sincerity—that somehow it, ipso facto, has value of some kind, including truth value. There have been in the last decade or so what I think of as more interesting ideas about feminine and masculine (not always corresponding to female and male) modes. Do you know, for instance, Carol Gilligan's In a Different Voice?

No.

Though I'm uneasy with hard and fast categorizations and feel it's important for artists to take it upon themselves to transgress and hop across all the chalk lines and put any kind of puzzle together that we like, I do think certain distinctions at certain historical moments can be helpful. Particularly when they draw our attention to things we haven't noticed in a particularly fuzzy or heavily stereotyped area. Gilligan writes about what she identifies as a "female," and what I would call "feminine" (because persons of any anatomy can have it) preference for a kind of web-structured thinking—being attentive to, concerned about, the complex and multidirectional patterns of connections between people, about informal structures between people within communities. So that, for instance, a moral problem might be thought about in the complex pragmatic terms of those affected by certain choices and actions.

Rather than in terms of categories.

Yes, rather than by the abstract simplifications of linear logics, the hierarchically arranged deductions from first principles. Of course it has been those Occam's razored thought processes that we culturally identify with all the values in "clear, masculine thinking." Remember the compliment "She thinks like a man"? Gilligan wanted to say, It's not that women don't reason as well as men, it's that their experience leads them to have different kinds of concerns, values, awarenesses. That's why they tend to think differently, have a different moral consciousness, about the consequences of actions. So, for instance, given an ethical dilemma, a woman prefers the role of concerned mediator to that of arbiter. Which brings to mind your saying in "Alarms and Excursions" that you are uneasy with the idea of the writer as legislator.

Yes.

It seems to me one implication in what Gilligan is saying is that characteristically feminine writing (often enacted by men, such as James Joyce or Calvino's example, Carlo Emilio Gadda) might in one way or another reflect patterns of weblike connectedness. Things that you care about in very different domains, for instance, being brought together with equal weight and value—a horizontal, commodious, generously attentive system, rather than the exclusions and abstractions of vertical hierarchies.

Piaget's studies with children seem to point in a similar direction. That the girls—even very little girls—already think in a kind of ecological way, more than the boys, who seem to go by rules. But it's hard to know how much of it is cultural and how much genetic. Because the nurturing process is obviously different from the start.

Well, we seem to have a culture that supports different, somewhat complementary, though invidiously compared, gender modes—our own Western yin-yang, with the so-called female mode being consistently devalued. Even though it's been theoretically superseded (and I myself have since written about the insufficiencies of that female-male binary model), Gilligan's book was an important cultural event. She came to write it when tests to gauge levels of maturity in moral thinking—tests that had been designed in trials with all-male Harvard students—continuously resulted in invidious contrasts between the "mature" moral thinking of men and the "immature" thinking of women. I suppose what this amounts to is my desire to prod you a bit more about your penchant for writing decidedly nonstraight narratives, and perhaps for avoiding "ethical" issues. I'm just not convinced by, "I didn't write a more linear, self-enclosed, 'realistic' narrative because I'm inept," as opposed to—

What the reasons might be—why was I inept?

Yes, exactly. There might be a considered, even lived resistance to operating in that sort of structure that has something to do with how you operate in the world and what you value.

Well, discontinuity seems the natural state. It's how I see the world. We come to know anything that has any complexity by glimpses. So it is best to have as many different glimpses from as many different perspectives as possible, rather than trying to develop a linear argument where one thing follows from another.

Which is an artifice anyway—given the messiness of life as lived by anyone in this world.

Both modes are artifices. But, as far as fiction goes, maybe the biggest artifice is the narrative thread—the so-called narrative thread. Which, by the way, is another wonderful aspect of *The Man without Qualities*. Musil starts out by questioning the narrative thread. The first paragraph is a long, detailed list of meteorological data. A long, long paragraph. And at the end of it, he says, "In short, it was a nice summer day in August, 1913." You come to what would be a traditional narrative open-

ing only after you've been given a whole web of information. And this pattern holds for the whole novel. When he gives you narrative line it is in ironical juxtaposition with a grid or web structure. Which either makes Musil, by Gilligan's criterion, an honorary woman or shows that writing is beyond gender distinctions, which is what I tend to think. Writing, at least good writing, would be androgynous, would partake of both male and female modes of thinking.

Yes, I think that too. And I think some of the problems arise if you try to lodge these characteristics in what seem to be the "naturally" corresponding bodies: masculine mode in men only, feminine mode in women only. My feeling is that the healthier ones among us manifest and acknowledge both feminine and masculine elements in our ways of being in the world.

Yes, persons are not archetypes.

And we are not writing in an inherently "phallogocentric" language. Language is woven from feminine and masculine elements.

Even if men dominate the use of language in society, the first encounter with language is usually through the mother. Our feeling about language is at least partly shaped by the female, which makes nonsense of claiming language as the domain of the male archetype exclusively, let alone of identifying the signifier with the phallus.

Yes, our feelings for language are developing from the first moment of audibility—probably in the delivery room, perhaps in the womb. Obviously most of us are coming into contact with the mother's voice, as well as the language rhythms of Mother Goose, at a time when we are accumulating all sorts of associations and resonances that have to do with structures outside of rationalist logics, having to do with very tangible, immediate sorts of experiences. And though, as we "mature," we are systematically trained to ignore them, words are chords, carrying these polyphonic associations and resonances, along with semantic meanings, to our ears and eyes.

And this is maybe what makes literature, or at least poetry, possible. Even thought, Blanchot would say. He postulates that thought needs the "dark" to be stimulated into activity, into finding its own light.

Getting back to the idea of the early acquisition of language being in most circumstances more intimately bound up with the relationship of the child to the mother—not just with a female person, but with the material character of that early interaction—we are gathering all sorts of associations and navigational skills as we're learning language. Words are the attrac-

tors that increasingly draw us into the patterns characteristic of our culture's norms and forms. As Wittgenstein puts it, we're not just learning a vocabulary, we're becoming part of a form of life. As we begin our formal education, we are increasingly asked to put aside a vast store of intuitions that have informed and colored our experience of language—to think with language only in ways that conform to a few closely defined, legitimated and regulated logics. It seems to me that the most valuable service poetry can perform for us estranged, alienated creatures is to awaken in us that store of rich intuitions, the complexity of the conversation between those intuitions and our logics. First off, the poet gets to exercise a fuller self in the act of writing.

Yes, that's why one of my books is called Lawn of the Excluded Middle.

Ah, tell me how you think about what you're doing in that book.

I work with the idea of the empty center as a place of resonance and fertility: the womb, the resonance body of an instrument, or, in logic, the excluded middle. So I code as female what refuses the alternative of true or false and what therefore, according to the rules of logic, doesn't exist. This doesn't mean I reject logic (as if one could!), rather I would like to enlarge, enrich it in exactly the manner you were speaking of. In fact, I use vocabulary from the new physics because it is the discipline that seems to have the most negative capability at this point. It seems to be able to handle the conflicting pictures of classical physics and, say, quantum theory. As A. S. Eddington puts it, we use classical physics on Monday, Wednesday, Friday and quantum theory on Tuesday, Thursday, Saturday.

Lovely! One of the things that's of interest to me in both Hanky and A Form / of Taking / It All, novels by a writer who is primarily a poet, is that both—most dramatically perhaps A Form / of Taking / It All—do allow a more complex entry into language and the way it "really" works in our lives, full of multidirectional and even contradictory vectors, full of layers of experience. For me, much more rewarding than a straight and narrow narrative form. Here's a silly question: When you were writing these books, did you feel like a poet writing a novel, or did writing a novel mean that you had to put something of yourself as poet aside?

I suppose I always feel I'm a poet. And the extent to which I work with metaphor in The Hanky has made this obvious. More basically, although the novel has different requirements, like plot, characters, et cetera, I still feel, whether I work on poetry or a novel, that writing is a dialogue with language. I feel the differences mostly as differences of breath and rhythm. The units are larger in the fiction. In poetry, I have almost a compulsion to great concision.

What do you mean by breath and rhythm? "Breath" can be a sort of loaded, projectile term . . .

It's getting hard to use any word! Well, the engagement with language structures—a dialogue, I would say—is fundamentally shaped by my ear, by the rhythmic units I work in. The rhythm of a paragraph is harder for me than the rhythm of a sentence or line. I think of this as naturally short breath. Otherwise I haven't really questioned why some things go toward prose and some go toward verse. There's been only one case in which a work of mine has gone back and forth between them in different versions, Differences for Four Hands. It ended as a prose poem. It started as an exercise, using Lyn Hejinian's Gesualdo as a syntactic matrix, putting in a different vocabulary and then expanding, playing. I tried to put it into lines, but it didn't seem to work. It is a testimony to the strength of Lyn's prose sentences that I couldn't pull them into verse.

I think of sentences as something you initially hold your breath for. Particularly long German sentences. Like playing a wind instrument where a long phrase or glissando requires taking in an enormous gulp of air and then letting it out slowly, steadily. There's even the technique called "circular breathing."

Yes, but I often have the feeling that I'm panting!

Hyperventilating.

Hyperventilating. Whereas prose needs the deep breath. I don't know if it's a higher anxiety level that makes me feel so short of breath, so panting, the pressure of the white space.

The white space always seems to me to be possibility—open, uncharted territory. Allowing the units of language to breathe more fully, or in a less impacted way—

Emily Dickinson's "Moving on the Dark like Loaded Boats at Night, though there is no Course, there is boundlessness." This wonderful "though" that leaps into another dimension, breathes infinite possibility. But if everything is possible, nothing is. So any start of a poem or a text is extremely anxiety-laden for me. Whereas once there's the smallest little word given, the smallest choice made, I'm in much better shape.

I've always imagined that James Joyce was very anxious about white space, that he experienced it as uncomfortably empty space.

He needed to fill it up.

Yes, to create a plenum—a full, actually overflowing, universe with every potential gap stuffed with more potential meaning. But then in that sheer complexity a new kind of space, the fractal space of indeterminacy, opens up.

In the very extreme, the fullness joins the emptiness. I *want* the white space; it's needed. Clark Coolidge says "to create is to make a pact with nothingness" [in "Notebooks 1976-82" in Michael Palmer's *Code of Signals*]. I want as much of it as possible, because in a way the silence carries the words. But at the same time it is an overwhelming challenge to the words that have to be in dialogue with it.

That's what I'm hearing. That there's a balancing act you're working out between this anxiety of leaving things empty, and yet—

I know you want to talk about the novels, but this gets very much at the *Lawn of Excluded Middle,* which works with the metaphor of the womb as a central emptiness. The empty space necessary for resonance, understanding, fertility, everything. This is where the "law" (of the "excluded middle") turns into "lawn." It's a sort of a structural metaphor behind the whole sequence. It's almost bizarre that they are prose poems, that I didn't work with lines, with the constant facing of the edge where the word meets silence. I seem to have moved the silence from the literal margin to a thematic/ metaphorical middle.

The tension between needing to in some way restrain oneself from making too many marks, too many words, the need to leave things to some degree really empty for, as you say, resonance and possibility, and yet needing also for something to enter into the space for signs of life, this makes me think of what you say in "Alarms and Excursions"—that writing has to do with uncovering possibilities: "My key words would be exploring and maintaining. Exploring a forest not for the timber that might be sold, but to understand it as a world and to keep this world alive." Now to go from the womb to the forest is a stretch, but—

Actually, that is an expansion of a statement by Valéry who very beautifully said, "the poet enters the forest with the express purpose of getting lost." Only then you begin to see. He pits this against the person with a message to deliver, who would try to get *through* the language/forest as quickly as possible and therefore would cut a road which both ignores and destroys much of the forest's life. That has always stuck in my mind.

When I read that in your essay, I wondered about the fact that such a metaphor has to do with exploring a world that already exists, that's already in some way a part of your experience. So you might see it in a new light and work to nourish it, but this is not about "creating or inventing a new world" as the act of fiction is sometimes taken to be.

Yes, but we don't. We don't ever, quite, invent a wholly new world. Language exists already and potentially contains all that can be said in it. I think "the forest of language" is a very good metaphor. It's something we can move around in, there is so much of it. We never completely explore, let alone master it. But we can discover things, make new connections, et cetera. But we don't invent anything ex nihilo.

No, of course not. What we mean by invention or creation is not "out of nothing" but is always no more, and no less, than arranging-composing things in such a way that a relatively new pattern emerges, with a critical difference of some sort. Something that perhaps is connected to critically different processes, changes, that are taking place in the world. This is, after all, what we mean by "contemporary," isn't it?

Yes, as Gertrude Stein puts it [in "Composition as Explanation"]: "Everything is the same except composition and as the composition is different and always going to be different everything is not the same." Always new forms, new structures, new perspectives, new ways of thinking, new ways of putting things together. But all contained within the strange and marvelous structure of language.

Though language itself has changed pretty radically over time, as we see in our etymological dictionaries.

Not "radically." Change of usage, of word-meanings seems on the surface to me. We can still read Old English—albeit with a bit of work. I'm thinking of the "deep" structure of language (though not in Chomsky's technically linguistic sense), even of something like the "central kinship of languages" that Benjamin posits as what makes translation possible. I may have this feeling of language being there beforehand more strongly because I changed my language. Wittgenstein says somewhere that you can't come into language as into a room. But I think, at least for your second language, you can, provided you take certain "steps" of learning. Or into a forest. I walked from one forest into another.

So you walked into the forest of English and got lost?

Very much so! I hope I'll never find my way out.

You wrote, in "Alarms and Excursions," "I don't even have thoughts, I say, I have methods that make language think, take over and me by the hand into sense or offense. Syntax stretched across rules, relations of force. Fluid the dip of the plumb-line, the pull of eyes. What if the mother didn't censor the child's looking, didn't wipe the slate clean? Would the child know from the start that there are no white pages, that we always write over a text already there? No beginnings, all unrepentant middle."

I'm happy that you picked that one out. But if there's the palimpsest then why am I anxious about the white space? It's contradictory. Or is it? Actually, the text already there is, for me, the whole past of the particular language, the whole culture, that is to say, a plenitude *almost* as large, *almost* as unlimited and full of possibilities as emptiness.

Later you say, "A sentence is made by coupling." Which is an interesting metaphor because of course it means connecting, but also something sexual.

Sexual, yes, I mean it to be.

And then "the progeny of the sentence."

Right. I'm casting language itself in the role of the muse. More than muse, even—that it's language itself that takes over and (pro-) creates. And that our work as writers is to learn to prod the language structures within us and without us into becoming active. I have taken this from Edmond Jabès. He sees the writer as mere catalyst. The words have their own affinities: "Light is in these lovers' strength of desire."

If you take that far enough, you have a form of mysticism—that we all are sort of swimming in, navigating through this vital, energetic, inspirited medium . . .

Yes, I would agree to that. Language is the one transcendence that I find available to me. I mean God . . . is God.

Well "God" is part of the language.

Exactly. "It's a word my culture gives me," Jabès said when I asked how he reconciled his atheism with constantly writing about God. And there is a parallel, if we can disregard the difference between a concept and a whole symbolic system: both "God" and language are human inventions, but inventions that are larger than the inventor, that transcend their origin. Rather a mystery—or at least a paradox.

Are you interested in theories of the origin of language?

Not really, but that was a very strong German preoccupation that I grew up with. All the eighteenth-century German thinkers wrote about how language might have come into being.

The "first word."

The first word is like the first principle. It's very much like God. But also trying to get back to something like the essence of humanity, how it could have come about. Kant wrote about it. Herder wrote about it. Wilhelm von Humboldt.

Given the philosophical atmosphere in which you grew up, with ideas of connections between language and a supposed "essence" of what it means to be human, I

wonder if you have any sense of creating the form of your own humanity in your use of language as a writer, how enacting or participating in language in the way you do, with the forms you use, in some way creates and recreates you as a certain kind of human being.

Oh, definitely, definitely, yes.

Could you say something about that?

I agree with your statement. Writing is an existential act. In writing I am created and creating myself through language. But I'm not sure how much farther I can take it.

Well, I think, as an example, of Tina Darragh, who enacts with her language investigations of various sorts. Interesting, it feels awkward to say in the third person, "She's creating herself as Tina Darragh"—as someone who undertakes a questioning, a very specific quest via her writing, while inventing very specific systems that might invite answers but always have an indeterminate quality so that they never entirely close the investigation down. And it's of course the particulars of her use of language, of her constructed procedures, that make all this possible. She gets to generate and shuffle certain texts and vocabularies and come up with certain kinds of surprises that keep the question alive, rather than killing it off with pedantic research. And she has talked about this as being the move she had to make in her work in order not to write sentimental autobiography.

Aha! Yes, this last applies to my case too. I have already told you that I turned to collage in order not to write about my mother. But there's more to it. The method of collage goes a long way toward embodying the way I feel I am in the world. There is an immensity of data around us, and to choose the ones that are relevant and to connect them is my sense of life also. And, again, there is an anxiety of the too much, of wanting it all, of the impossibility of choosing. I'm now thinking again of the page as palimpsest, the anxiety does not only have to do with the boundlessness of the possibilities, but also with what has been censored, what *is* there, hidden underneath.

So, perhaps, one of the things that the explorer in the forest does is make clearings here and there?

Yes. Sounds like we're getting back to the empty center. In growing up, my greatest anxiety was that I was scattered into all the things that I was doing, experiencing, reading—that I had no center, no self. Out of that developed a strong need to be alone, quiet, sitting at a desk. And trying to put words on a piece of paper became an act of centering. The problem was that I thought of the self as something like a "content"—I was still a long ways from accepting the center as empty, the self as a kind of crossroads, force field, a "form," as Creeley calls the mind. In fact, my sense of form has changed in the same direction, from a kind of "container within which" to an intersection, or multiple intersections *around* which. *The Man without Qualities* was no doubt a factor in this change, both for the psychology and the form. Along with Merleau-Ponty and others.

My guess is that those most anxious about the self are those most closely wed to the first-person singular pronoun. The inability to let go of that—

Because it is so uncertain.

Yes, uncertain, and somehow the belief in the "I" as a kind of concentrated force that will bring things back—*a magnet pulling at the past, or a centripetal force that can counter loss.*

Yes, I think that also comes back to your question of Do I create myself as a writer? Given that the page is such an aid to thinking, a great intersection, it's no surprise that the "I" as an intersection of thought, experience, et cetera would as it were "take place" on the page, on paper.

Though you're not someone who uses the "I" as much as many other writers. It is there; you haven't banished it.

It is there. Claude Royet-Journoud is very proud that in the whole book *The Notion of Obstacle,* he never once uses the word "I." I remember asking, Why are you so proud of that? If I remember correctly, he talked about it in terms of a reaction against the surrealists who always were descending into their "I," and down into the subconscious. He wants a kind of objectivity. Which, to me, is also a little questionable. In any case, in writing, I don't have any desire to get rid of the "I." It makes smaller claims than objectivity!

And you never have had that desire?

There is no getting rid of it anyway. Even the scientists admit that the presence of the observer is always part of the data.

I was just wondering if you had ever had a crisis of the "I."

I told you I didn't feel I even *had* an "I." It had to come about through words.

There's an interesting entering of an "I" that I take to be you as narrator-persona, rather than character, in A Form / of Taking / It All. *There are shifts from character to narrator to historical figures entering into motions that characters have begun, a feeling of there being*

forms of movement that could be entered by many different bodies, many different personas. I'm curious about the relation in that book between the character Amy, the narrator, and you.

The narrator is very much an alter ego of mine, a woman who writes. And the narrator's reflections about writing in the third section are very much mine. Whereas the character of Amy is doubly removed in that she is the creation of the narrator who is also present as a character. And she is for me a figure of otherness both as a poet I do not feel close to and as a gay woman. The first germ of this book goes very far back, to a joke Keith and I had in 1970. We were in Paris, both on fellowships, Keith on an "Amy Lowell," I on an "Alexander von Humboldt." We decided we must write a work about their "mystical marriage"!

Were you talking about doing a collaborative work?

Yes, but it quickly became just a joke. Keith never did anything with it, but with me, it stuck. It became an exploration of otherness: the discovery of America, which forced the Europeans to revise their whole image of the world; relativity and quantum theory, which have forced *us* into a revision even more radical, because the old image is not replaced by another image, but by mathematical formulae that defy being pictured; and, on the personal level, the encounter with another person. This is where Amy Lowell comes in, the enormous woman poet with cigar, in love with another woman.

You talk about "Keith and I" at one point.

I had not remembered this. Do I? In the third section probably.

Yes, and I was curious about that sudden eruption of the "I" that seemed to actually be you.

Yes, the boundary between the narrator and me is weak. Still, I'm puzzled that I did this. It is actually Alexander von Humboldt whom I to some extent identify with. We're both part of the enormous invasion of America by Europe, wave after wave of explorers and conquerors. Of course I prefer Humboldt, who comes as explorer, to Cortés and the other conquerors. But the two are not altogether separable. Even I, as an immigrant, come both to explore and conquer. And this involves/questions male-female archetypes because it is a "masculine" activity—the conquering and exploring—whereas the woman is supposed to be the territory. It also makes homosexuality relevant to the book, beyond the biographies of Amy Lowell and von Humboldt. Actually I'm not done with this yet because the Roger Williams book I am working from [*A Key into the Language of America*] again goes at that—Europeans coming and taking over the land of the Indians, putting a very "male" culture in the position of conquered female. So this seems something that obsesses me, that "works" me.

You are in an interesting position personally with all this. The Europeans come. They take over the land of the Indians. They establish a Eurocentric language-culture which you as European come to and must enter and explore and get lost in and which then, with all its American transformations, takes you over. The American language really has to some extent claimed you and can be said to be exploring you, if we think of the way in which language itself has the capacity to draw out patterns.

Yes.

A very interesting, very complex pattern of connections and movements. Since we're talking about these patterns of attraction and interaction, one of the levels that A Form / of Taking / It All *is operating on has to do with the tension between gravity and movement. The book ends with that wonderfully titled poem* "Unpredicted Particles." *When I had finished it I thought about one of the blurb statements on the cover talking about the formulation of quantum theory as being a major thread in the book.*

It's really only in the fourth section.

Yes, but given the directiveness of blurbology, I was looking for it throughout.

In a way this is exactly right. After all, I do fuse the two large-scale discoveries—America and the quantum—by having Columbus discover the new physics, as it were. I fuse Columbus and Heisenberg, as it were. Not that it would need to be Heisenberg, but most of the scientific quotes happen to be from him. Also, formally it is there all through, the paradox of quantum and wave, in the simultaneous presence of fragment and flow. But explicitly only in the last section, in **"Unpredicted Particles."**

You know, I don't feel this book really ends there.

Do you have trouble with the last section, with it being a poem?

That section seems to me something else in a way, something apart from what preceded it. And it may be that I'm not reading it correctly.

You may well be.

Whatever "correctly" means, but I'm curious about how it came to be in that form, just what it's relation—in your process—was to the previous three sections.

Robert Coover liked the book up to **"Unpredicted Particles"** but thought it a copout that I went into verse. I—defensively—chalked this up to his maybe not being comfortable with poems in general! It's true that the first three sections are in prose, but each section is in a different form—stream of consciousness, collage of historical materials, first-person meditation—so that the expectation of continuity is frustrated each time. The change into verse is a more radical move, but not totally unprepared, it seems to me. There is formal otherness with each new section. And that the change is more radical seems to me justified thematically. The new physics doesn't just make us revise our images. There are no more images, period. No more apple falling as in the Newtonian gravity model. Analogy has been replaced by mathematical formulas.

Aren't particle and wave images as well?

Those are still images, which is perhaps why I keep talking about them. But they don't get us very far. When I try to read books on physics—popularizations, mind you—I very quickly hit a point where the images give out, and where I am totally lost. It just occurs to me that this might have been a reason for going into poetry: poetry has so long been identified with images, especially metaphor, analogy, and I have worked so long against this definition that I may subliminally have intended a kind of manifesto: poetry can go on in this brave new world without images! But of course I use images in the poem! I think of it as a kind of summation: beside Columbus and particles, sexuality comes back in with quotes from Musil's story "Tonka." Which also means I allow prose in, both narrative and theoretical, the latter with quotes from both physics and from Todorov's *The Conquest of America.*

I see this book as raising interesting formal questions. There are brackets for this book that are poetic. The title itself is poetry, three lines from Creeley with line-break indicators. Creeley's lines are "mind is a form / of taking / it all." You drop "mind" and present the line without a subject so that it could be read as formal self-reference. I've tended to read it that way and to think that poetry as "a form of taking it all" is quite a statement! That's the initial bracket, and then at the end you yourself move into poetry. So thinking in terms of genre, I've wondered, when we get to page 76, just prior to the section that is clearly poetic, **"Unpredicted Particles,"** *is it that we don't, can't yet have "it all," whatever that might mean? That we have to move to poetic form for all that eludes prose? Are you at that point in some sense moving into an enactment of poetry as a form of taking it all, or perhaps not that at all? Perhaps, quite the contrary! What would "taking it all" mean anyway?*

The book started with the second part, "A Form of Memory." Which is the most disjunctive, the one that juxtaposes the most disparate materials. I thought of this already as an enactment of "taking it all." The interior monologue of the first part was to provide a frame that would allow people to ease into it, to interpret "A Form of Memory" as a fever vision of Amy sick in Mexico, that is, to "normalize" it. But then I decided this was as far as I wanted to go in that direction. The other parts would have to break it open, not try to hold it in.

There's a history of novels that have incorporated other forms, including poems. It's always an interesting formal decision, that sometimes works better than others.

The first time I consciously encountered such a novel was Novalis's *Heinrich von Ofterdingen.* What struck me there was that the poems are not ornament. You couldn't skip over them and get the plot. The poems forward the action almost as much as the prose. The narrative line continues across the genre difference. I find this very interesting. As I do also the novels that incorporate essays, like Hermann Broch's.

In planning this book did you think, "I'll have a section that is poetry"?

No, I did at first not plan beyond "A Form of Memory," which is modeled on a very wonderful book by Konrad Bayer called *The Head of Vitus Bering.*

You mean the form of that section?

Yes. All I knew was I wanted to do something like *The Head of Vitus Bering,* but also different. For example, I take the collage farther than he does in that I often have my shifts within a sentence.

Yes, a motion that I particularly associate with you, in your poetry as well.

Yes, which subverts the linearity a little farther yet. But it was only gradually that I realized this collage would need other things to go with it.

It's clear to me, and I'm sure to other readers, that you have a great sense of latitude in what can enter a book like this, that you're not laboring under strict generic rules.

No, but this is the freest of all my books. I've not done anything else where the expectation gets jolted that often in different directions.

Did this come before or after "Alarms and Excursions"?

Before.

I see some similarities in—

In the structure? Yes, definitely. "Alarms and Excursions" is really the first essay I've written that I'm happy with. My earlier essays are more or less academic articles, you know. I was pleased to break out of that form. And it may have been possible because I had done *A Form / of Taking / It All* before.

And had Hanky *in some way led you to the point where you could do* A Form*?*

Probably. Also to the point where I began to write mostly prose poems.

It's not a given that a writer, having done a particular kind of book, will then stand as if on a threshold and say, What new *adventures does this position me for? Whatever I do next it's not going to be the same thing. In fact, most mainstream novels that are being read by most people are familiar formulas being used over and over again.*

Right. But that gets boring. Creeley quotes Franz Kline as saying, "If I paint what I know, I bore myself. If I paint what you know, I bore you. So I paint what I don't know."

Christine Hume (essay date 2000)

SOURCE: Hume, Christine. Review of *Reluctant Gravities. Chicago Review* 46, no. 2 (2000): 95-8.

[*In the following review of Waldrop's 1999 volume* Reluctant Gravities, *Hume discusses its poetic and philosophical sources and presents it as a continuation of the linguistic project begun in* The Reproduction of Profiles *and* Lawn of the Excluded Middle.]

In **Reluctant Gravities,** the sequel to the post-Wittgensteinian dialogues of **The Reproduction of Profiles** (1987) and **Lawn of Excluded Middle** (1993). Rosmarie Waldrop embodies a search for form and pattern—biological, social, and linguistic—by using a highly structured prosimetrum. Each section of the book collects four prose "conversations" of four paragraphs each followed by an "interlude" of two "songs" that flank a "meditation" of alternating prose and verse fragments. Generally, the prose "conversations" serve as a lively philosophical and narrative frame for the whole, while the verse sections reconstitute some of the prose into a more lyric, emotive, monovocalic register. As its title indicates, laws and facts in this book are "pulled into spasms of interpretation" (45) and subjectivity. **Reluctant Gravities** breaks down the traditional distinctions between poetry and prose showcased in works such as the Baghavad Gita, Boethius's *De consolatione* *philosophiae*, Thomas Traherne's *Centuries of Meditations*, Jean Toomer's *Cane*, and William Carlos Williams's *Spring and All*. Bent on creating "a space between boundary and blur," Waldrop goes beyond setting the languages of poetry and prose in juxtaposition; she subjects them to each other, drawing them into dialogue.

She has said of her own writing, "I am in dialogue . . . not with a prospective reader . . . but with language itself." She is not interested in creating characters or psychological portraits to do so. The "he" and "she" in the text do not represent personalities: rather, they are rhetorical frames for the synaptic space between thoughts. In her intrepid investigations of the interstices between perception and language—especially in the differences between the ways that men and women understand, interact with, and adopt language—Waldrop follows the model of conversation by shifting between speakers. But the intertextual inventiveness here breaks the glassy surface of communication. As in *Reproduction* [*The Reproduction of Profiles*] and *Lawn* [*Lawn of the Excluded Middle*], Waldrop confronts Wittgenstein's work, with *On Certainty* as a template and the *Tractatus* and *Remarks on Colour* as sources from which the central couple's banter rises. *Gravities* [*Reluctant Gravities*] is a virtual echo chamber of Waldrop's reading. For example, "Perhaps we need change to see what's there, she says. And ambiguity, to be aware of seeing. Seven types of apples" (63), sardonically and playfully jabs at William Empson. A famous Keats line becomes "not easeful by half / in love" (19), whereas "the suck of symbol" (11) is a straight quote from Charles Olson. The electric feedback generated by her synthesis of say, John Ashbery, Robert Musil, Heraclitus, and a physics textbook—all in one section—charges the work with uncanny humor and sudden illumination. "Under the rush of phonemes," she plants risible slips in familiar or expected phrases, producing such puns as "the promised hand" (76) and "opposing thumb and upright imposture" (69). As she resists remaining passively in one discursive location, her structures move us with their breath-taking fluency and fluidity.

Reluctant Gravities's philosophy attaches itself to myriad political, linguistic, and scientific speculations by means of a complex system of polysemic and syllogistic relationships that highlight the slippery relation of fact to inference and understanding. For Waldrop, any pursuit of knowledge is an erotic act. Even more so than *Reproduction* and *Lawn,* this new book creates a somatic language, a language of the body and a body of language, in which the tough-minded self and the sensual self attract and naturally—if reluctantly—gravitate toward each other. The sensual ballasts the ethereal, for she "doubt[s] propositions without body heat or shadow" (68). Her language is urgently physical and earth-bound: "But suddenly a word gets down on all fours and sniffs your crotch" (58). Her work makes public and private languages speak to each other by collapsing historic, mythic, evolutionary, and personal time—not in order to show a totality, but rather to expose the necessarily fragmentary and imitative nature of any and all of these paradigms. "I can't distinguish gravity from grace or other distortions of space," (44) she says and elsewhere collapses Newton's apple and the apple in Genesis. The apple is the thing desired and reached after in her garden of gaps. *Gravities* is shot through with a compulsion toward falling, enacting the reader's pleasure and terror in textual lability.

Waldrop uses our comfortable expectations for expository prose to gain our confidence, then spoofs the authority of the logical proposition with an absurd mock causality. By submitting aphorism to false syllogistic reasoning and fact to delightful narrative uncertainty, she exposes the mechanics of self-deception: whereby we use logical language systems in order to relieve our doubts and excuse our mistakes. If, according to Kurt Gödel, logical systems are always and intrinsically incomplete, Waldrop wholeheartedly entangles Continental logic in American materialism. And, like the Platonic dialogues, her writing often foregrounds questions and difficulties. But, as she says, "the riddle need not have a solution, need not be a riddle" (53). At the fulcrum of her logic is the desire to know—in its most intellectual and erotic glory—but also to distrust standard constructions and genealogies of knowledge. Responding to poetry's traditional reliance on the objective correlative, she asks, "But what happens in the brain if we always relate an object to a certain difficulty?" Instead, "the words come to their senses" (37); they resist our "rage for explanation" (45) and enact experience. Waldrop's most contagious joy is goofing on exposition, for "explanations double-lock the strangeness" (30). And though chaos theory, non-Euclidean geometry, physics, and contemporary cosmology provide trajectories for much of the work here, Waldrop's "crow does not fly as the crow flies" (28).

If, as she writes, we "plunge into the January river for the unreachable that is promised" (90), we can expect to collect noise in lieu of transparency: we can expect to be submerged in language without fixed destiny or destination. And we can expect to keep moving until—*Poof*—Waldrop sabotages our desire for closure as a psychological and ideological tool in the final conversation **"On the Millennium"**: "as if adding zeros could create bluer skies and more self-evident truths. As if the universe could big bang again" (96). By then, we realize we have been, as Emily Dickinson says, "Moving on the Dark like Loaded Boats at Night, though there is no Course, there is boundlessness." In Waldrop's sweeping but courseless discourses, she invents another sort of (a sorted) sublime.

David Clippinger (essay date spring/summer 2001)

SOURCE: Clippinger, David. "Between the Gaps, the Silence and the Rubble: Susan Howe, Rosmarie Waldrop, and (Another) Pound Era." *Denver Quarterly* 36, nos. 1/2 (spring/summer 2001): 189-205.

[*In the following essay, Clippinger discusses the poetry of Waldrop and Susan Howe in relation to two key aspects of the work of Ezra Pound—the crucial role of history in his poetry and his use of polyphonic voices.*]

> *I once said, perhaps rightly: The earlier culture will become a heap of rubble and finally a heap of ashes, but spirits will hover over the ashes.*
>
> —Ludwig Wittgenstein, *Culture and Value*

To speak of twentieth-century American poetry and not address the force of Ezra Pound's influence both in terms of poetic technique and ideational content would be irresponsible. Yet, when turning to women's poetry, most discussions completely avoid Pound—unless he is implied indirectly via H. D. and then in the pejorative sense as her "author" and the phallic creator of "H. D. Imagist."[1] Subsequently, Pound's absence from any dialogue concerning women's poetry seems understandable since his writing often embodies phallocentric concepts, which are most evident by his fascist politics. As Charles Bernstein observes,

> Pound's fascist ideology insists on the author's having an extraliterary point of "special knowledge" that creates a phallic order (these are Pound's terms) over the female chaos of conflicting ideological material.
>
> (123)

The female is perceived as a divisive force that must be subsumed by a phallic order that rescues "truth" from chaos. Such a stance openly refutes the possibility of a women's poetry unless it appropriates a masculine order; and from another perspective, Pound is representative of phallocentric logic that feminist theory challenges and deconstructs. Subsequently, a rather formidable ideological chasm would seem to separate Pound and women's poetry. Nevertheless, I would like to question the value of Pound's poetry within literary historical discussions of women's poetry by exploring the affinities and tensions between Pound's poetic technique of polyphonic voices and his emphasis upon history as suitable and desirable ideational material for poetry with the writings of Susan Howe and Rosmarie Waldrop. By doing so, I wish to recontextualize Pound's place within a poetic landscape that has been hewed and reworked over the last twenty-five years by the emergence of postmodern theory (and specifically feminist modes of critique) and poetry that draws upon that theory. Ultimately, this essay sketches an argument for a reconsideration of Pound's place by demonstrating that his poetic technique and the emphasis upon history

suggest affinities with contemporary women's poetry and feminist modes of critique. More importantly, though, those affinities illuminate an aspect of Pound's poetry that is partially effaced by his phallocentric stance and which is sometimes overlooked in critical readings of Pound—namely, the centrality of ethics and the concomitant dimension of love.

Pound's dictum that an epic is a "poem plus history" sparked the emergence of "historically-minded" poets including Charles Reznikoff, William Carlos Williams, and Charles Olson, to name a few. For the most part, the Pound tradition is predominantly perceived as male poets who regard history as the raw material that their poetry transforms into transcendent order. In the words of Michael Bernstein from his *The Tale of the Tribe: Ezra Pound and the Modern Verse Epic,* the power of the "Pound" poem stems from its ability to "crystallize history, to make actual events live again in the minds of future readers" (9). The modernist poetic stance is concomitant with an authority capable of sifting through the rubble of history in order to present and thereby preserve luminous cultural artifacts. In this respect, Pound's *Cantos* gloss the "great ideas" and luminary moments in human history, and many of the poets who follow in the wake of Pound perceive history as an untroubled and untroubling source. The primary assumption is that history is not only knowable, it is an accurate and truthful portrayal of human events and social psychology; as such, it is the standard against which the implicit goodness or evilness of other events can be gauged. The goal for the poet, as Pound writes in Canto LXXXIX, is

> To know the histories
> To know good from evil
> And to know whom to trust.
>
> (604)

Since history is trustworthy, truthful, and a universal standard of measure, it is accurate, complete, and whole. History, regardless of its multiple manifestations as histories, is total, and the poem participates in that totality via its technique of accentuating the various luminous historical texts that are representative of the truth. Yet Pound's earlier cantos and especially Canto XIII offer an alternate perspective upon the relation of writing and history that troubles the conception of history as a definitive source beyond a plurality of vision. The Canto, which employs the voice of Kung (or Confucius), reads:

> And even I can remember
> A day when the historians left blanks in their writings,
> I mean for things they didn't know,
> But that time seems to be passing.
>
> (60)

The historian's rhetorical stance is that out of good conscience and ethical scholarship, a blank is left for another to "fill in." Totality, therefore, is impossible to achieve—at least under the auspices of the singular writer/historian/poet—and can only be gestured towards as textual aporias. Despite the paradigm of historical incompleteness, the trajectory of *The Cantos* as a whole traces a distinctive shift away from an open text (history with blanks) to the closed (a text that is seemingly complete). That is, whereas the open dominates the earlier *Cantos*, it is subsumed in the later works by the image of totality manifest as the proliferation of universal theories of economics, art, literature, politics, and culture. "In the mid-twenties," Rachel Blau DuPlessis explains,

> *The Cantos* modulated from an early concern for re-illuminating moments of full cultural and emotional achievement (moments of renaissance), to a concern which controls the bulk of the poem: making a "totalitarian synthesis" by the didactic insistence upon certain verities.
>
> ("Objectivist Poetics and Political Vision" 131)

Such a shift places under erasure the blanks and the particular poetics of the earlier *Cantos* in favor of a totalitarian program founded upon unwavering truths expounded with a fundamentalist fervor. Such a revisionary stance within Pound's own ideological script could be read chaos within Pound's own work, via his epiphany of totality, is checked by luminous phallocentric order that the poem itself uncovers.

These two stages of Pound's two poetics mirrors Emmanuel Levinas's discussion in *Totality and Infinity* of the two modes of apprehending and comprehending the world—the systemic (totalizing) and the creative (or infinitizing). For Levinas, systemic meaning renders form and closure, but it also brackets off possibility and difference. Creativity, on the other hand, engages in the process of the infinite that allows for an ever evolving sense of difference. The "closed" and the "open" within Pound's lexicon are represented by the distinction between "the" history and historical blanks, and that conflict is, more than likely, the result of the strain between Pound's desire for an ideal world (where art, poetry, and ideas are valued) and his recognition of a flawed human world that negates the possibility of such a world. As Pound remarks in Canto 74,

> I don't know how humanity stands it
>   with a painted paradise at the end of it
>   without a painted paradise at the end of it
>
> (450)

Pound proposes two means of accomplishing an ideal image of a society founded upon culture and the arts—fascist ideology (the closed, limited) on one hand and the poetic (the open) on the other. Those two methods, however, stand in direct contestation with one another and contradict each other.

Ultimately, Pound chooses the "total" over the open as the means of rending the image of the "painted paradise," yet his poetics based upon the palimpsest resists such totality. That is, the technique of incorporating polyphonic voices and valences into a text denies poetic closure by unwinding multiple ideational threads. As Charles Bernstein notes,

> The technology of Pound's textual practice created its own logic of desire, which Pound could not derail without giving up an achievement beyond the comprehension of his small-minded, penurious political accounting system. He was obviously unsatisfied with anything but a completely polyphonic style and as a result did not allow his ideological predilections to completely compromise the scope of his formal innovations. . . . The center could not hold because the formal innovations of openly juxtaposing radically different materials undercut this possibility.
>
> (124-125)

The valorization of ideational totality in Pound's poetics, in other words, is subsumed by the polyphonic technique that usurps phallocentric order. Consequently, aporias within *The Cantos* are not only evident at the ideational level of the poems but such gaps are accentuated further by a poetics founded upon the palimpsest (textual erasure and reconstruction) and, thereby, a polyphonic structure that emphasizes multiplicity if not outright chaos.

Regardless of Pound's revisionary stance towards historical aporias, the combination of history and the poetic technique of "blanks" 'embedded in and enacted by *The Cantos* offers a lens to consider the poetry of Rosmarie Waldrop and Susan Howe in relation to Pound's "tradition." Moreover, the internal tension within Pound's poetry is absolutely central to the understanding of Pound in relation to women's poetry and merits deeper consideration. That is, Waldrop and Howe continue the strain of Pound's poetics based upon silences and blanks—a textual stance that Pound himself seemed to have abandoned—while also transforming those absences into a poetics predicated upon ethical issues. Waldrop and Howe's transformation of Pound's poetic methodology as well as his emphasis upon history offers a lens to re-evaluate Pound. Furthermore, the poetics of blanks not only suggests a realignment of that literary lineage but offers an alternative perspective of Pound that is sometimes overlooked in the desire to champion him as a poet of luminous cultural detail.

History is inextricably woven with the poetic for Howe and Waldrop. Howe remarks that "It would be hard to think of poetry apart from history" (*The Birthmark* 158), yet she argues that the writer's work takes place "in and against" history (*The Birthmark* 158-159), which suggests an antagonism regarding history absent in Pound. Subsequently, the poetry of Howe and Waldrop tends to gravitate toward aporias and silences in cultural history—what Howe refers to in *The Europe of Trusts* as the "absent voices" that have been relegated to the margins—rather than the "major" cultural figures Pound delineates in *ABC of Reading* and *Guide to Kulchur*. By foregrounding absences and silences that challenge textual authority and the conception of a "total" history, the ideological apparatuses that propose a complete history are called into question. Instead of history being the integer of measuring truthfulness, the standard itself as an ideological mechanism that sanctions and codifies history, is placed under careful scrutiny. The ways of knowing and the sanctity of history as a complete, trustworthy compendium are regarded with great skepticism. As opposed to Pound's project to provide a poetic compendium of luminous detail that serves as a "schoolbook for princes" (Bernstein 53), Howe and Waldrop perceive human history as a continuum of written, unwritten, and rewritten cultural battles wherein the "losers" have been erased but within the gaps of those texts glimpses of the lingering trace of ideological battle can be unearthed. By drawing upon marginalized figures that embody the lacuna of history and the aporias that language attempts to mask, the goal for Howe and Waldrop is not to resolve difficulties, find the point of origination or sources that clarifies an issue, or to offer a "new" revisionary history. Neither poet proposes a "corrected" history book or a "new" totalitarian order. Rather, these two poets invoke the absences and silences in order to ruminate upon how such processes impact the act of poetry.

While Susan Howe's poetry as a whole offers a sustained and detailed interrogation into the inter-related matrix of language, subjectivity, and history, "Articulation of Sound Forms in Time" from *Singularities* (1990) suggests a number of intriguing and subtle parallels with Pound that offer a clear perspective of the relationship of blanks to Howe's poetry. In brief, "Articulation of Sound Forms in Time" revolves around the historical figure of Reverend Hope Atherton. In May 1676, Atherton accompanied a group of English Colonial soldiers to an Indian village in the Connecticut River Valley. In what has come to be known as the "Falls Fight Massacre," the soldiers ambushed the village and killed 300 of the inhabitants—most of whom were women and children. The surviving Indians, drawing upon various neighboring tribes, amassed a fighting force that routed the retreating English Army. During a particularly heated battle, Atherton, along with seven or eight soldiers, was separated from the English army. When the Indians captured the soldiers, they were tortured and eventually killed, but when Atherton himself surrendered to the Indians, they ran in fear from him assuming him to be the "Englishman's God." Atherton eventually made his way back to his home in Hatfield, but no one believed his account of his "escape." His community and his church shunned him—characterizing him as an "outsider" who was "beside himself." After documenting his account in his defense, he soon died.

Using this historical setting as the backdrop for the poem, "Articulation of Sound Forms in Time" investigates the chasm between Atherton's account and the publicly sanctioned history that refuted and negated his narrative. The forces behind the sanctioned history that Atherton's narrative challenged and the circumstances of his silencing demonstrate the penetrating reach of social order and its seemingly unbridled cultural control. In brief, the poem presents Atherton's informal excommunication as the explicit tension between Manifest Destiny (the conception of a divinely ordained order and logic) and that which refuses to be contained or which challenges the sanctity of Puritan order. Atherton's account was inconceivable given the logical mindset of the Puritans, and he, therefore, remained outside of the bounds of possibilities. A recurring motif of the poem is the tension between social order as a totalizing form and that which will not succumb to such constraints—the "other" or the infinite. The poem demonstrates the tension that runs rampant throughout the poem in lines such as "Distant coherent rational system" (17), "Parmenides prohibition" (177), and "Knowledge narrowly fixed knowledge" (12), as well as in the use of words such as "empirical," "spatio-temporal," "architect," "confine," and "Euclidean." Lines denoting order and the limiting constraints of phallocentric logic and structure are juxtaposed with lines such as "Chaos cast cold intellect back" (34),[2] "Anarchy into named theory" (32), "Inarticulate true meaning" and "untraceable wandering / the meaning of knowing" (25). The historical backdrop of Hope Atherton and the Falls Fight Massacre catalyze Howe's exploration of what cannot be assimilated within a "rational" system, which, therefore, is marginalized and/or placed under erasure—sometimes in the most violent terms—a point that echoes Levinas in his description in *Totality and Infinity* of the impact of violence and war upon ethics.

> But violence does not consist so much in injuring and annihilating persons as in interrupting their continuity, making them betray not only commitments but their own substance, making them carry out actions that will destroy every possibility for action. Not only modern war but every war employs arms that turn against those who wield them. It establishes an order from which no one can keep his distance; nothing henceforth is exterior. War does not manifest exteriority and the other as other; it destroys the identity of the same.
>
> (21)

Violence imposes an order that eliminates otherness and the possibility of action. Therefore, violence erodes the foundation of humanity and openness. As Howe remarks, "Malice dominates the history of Power and Progress. History is the record of winners. Documents were written by the Masters. But fright is formed by what we see not by what they say" (*Europe* 11). The order that accompanies violence creates a totalizing system where both the people who impose the order and those who are forced to submit to it are imprisoned. Any possibilities that reside beyond those established boundaries are effaced and inaccessible. The multiple (or infinite) is subsumed by an image of totality, and the heteroglossic is forced to yield to a single narrative (historical) thread woven by the victors.

Within Howe's writing, fear and conscripted behavior are also an extension of the cultural engendering of form and totality. Atherton's marginalization is a product of his feminization. "In our culture Hope is a name we give women. Signifying desire, trust, promise, does her name prophetically engender pacification of the feminine?" (*Singularities* 4). Hope becomes subject to the phallocentric desire to limit and contain. As Howe explains, "The issue of editorial control is directly connected to the attempted erasure of antinominalism in our culture. Lawlessness seen as negligence is first feminized and then restricted or banished" (*Birthmark* 3). In this vein, the figure of Atherton is inscribed with a metatextual level of symbolism within the poem itself: "I assume Hope Atherton's excursion for an emblem foreshadowing a Poet's abolished limitations in our demythologized fantasy of Manifest Destiny" (4). The task of the poet is to write against predetermined, prescribed order. Whereas Pound views the poem as the means of salvaging history from silence, Howe perceives the poem as a vehicle to survey the abyss of history in order to "tenderly life from the darkside of history, voices that are anonymous, slighted—inarticulate" (*Europe* 14). The thrust of Howe's poetic is to drive against darkness, the tomb of sanctified history, and to resurrect lost voices such as Hope Atherton's. "If history is a record of survivors," Howe writes, "Poetry shelters other voices" (*Birthmark* 47). The poem embraces the "other" in order to bring "similitude and representation to configurations waiting forever to be spoken" (*Europe* 14). "Articulation of Sound Forms in Time" echoes this task in the lines

> Recollection moves across meaning
> Men shut their doors against setting
>
> Flocks roost before dark
> Coveys nestle and settle
>
> Mediation of a world's vast Memory
>
> Predominance pitched across history
> Collision or Collusion with history

> (33)

The poem attempts to unearth repressed or forgotten history and to write against the silence by focusing upon the "Cancelations, variants, insertions, erasures,

marginal notes, stray marks and blanks" that mark the site of repression and are cultural "memories in disguise" (*Birthmark* 9). Nevertheless, codified cultural memory (history) resists intrusion, which is emphasized in the above passage by the image of the slamming of the door against any "disturbance" that challenges the status quo. The "flock" of "memory" settles and solidifies itself against the threat of the unknown, the darkness of the coming "night" that the covey encloses against.

> Like the covey nestled together the darkness, Reverend Atherton's congregation rejected his written account. "No one believed the Minister's letter. He become a stranger to his community and died soon after the traumatic exposure that has earned his poor mention in a seldom mentioned book"

> (*Singularities* 4).

Society sentences Atherton into the historical position of the "blank." His written account is repressed as subversive. History is, therefore, not luminous details, but a sieve that filters things, people, and texts from the sanctioned history in order to shelter a mass consciousness that is fearful of the "Other." As William Bronk astutely observes, the fear of the "Other" manifests as an imposed human-order:

> Fearful of real freedom or actual religion, [most people] erected the prison of an institution around them and so had the safe and make-believe freedom of the prison yard. . . . But since there was a yard within the prison, the defenders of the institution could constitute themselves defenders of freedom, when they really defended not the space within at all, but the enclosure itself, carrying on in this was a continuously hypocritical and reactionary program, keeping the mind within bounds. Thus, though born free, we undertake as quickly as possible to unburden us of our freedom; we confine ourselves tightly and like liquids, take the shape of the thing that holds us.

> (97)

The poem, for Howe, enters into the abandoned edifice of history in order to investigate how memory collides with established history or collaborates (colludes) the text of history. The poem confronts the abyss of history in order to search out the trace of the real and the ghost of the Other—the people and texts that have been erased in order to maintain the facade of cultural order. Peter Nicholls recognizes the affinities between "official" history and writing/editing in Howe's writing:

> But such traces play havoc with the regulation of our culture, and the pursuit of historical veracity is one with the desire for editorial accuracy, since both seek to extirpate what seems arbitrary, unrelated, directionless.

> (591)

The palimpsest for Howe, therefore, assumes a different tone than that of Pound: whereas Pound seeks to maintain and preserve cultural presence, Howe seeks out the absent and questions the historical and cultural context for the textual disappearance and/or silencing of certain figures.

Rosmarie Waldrop's *A Key into the Language of America* echoes Howe's stance toward poetry and the blank of history and offers another contrapuntal voice to Pound's historical stance. Besides sharing the themes of marginalization, gender, language, and subversive history with "Articulation of Sound Forms in Time," the central figure in Waldrop's poem, Roger Williams, mirrors Hope Atherton in a number of substantial ways. Like Atherton, Williams was a preacher and authored the "original" *A Key into the Language of America,* which was both an English/Narragansett language primer as well as an anthropological and moral "lesson" intended for its Christian Colonial audience. Because that "lesson" stood in direct contestation with the dominant ideology of the Massachusetts Bay Colony, Williams was tried by the Massachusetts General Court in 1635 and, subsequently, banished for his attack upon the economically-centered but religiously ordained principle of "vacuum domicilium, the doctrine that the colonists were entitled to land because the Indians were not making full use of it" (xvii). In short, Williams refused to remain within the bounds of conscripted behavior, established beliefs about the native "savages," and the religiously inspired conception of the moral and intellectual superiority of the colonists to the native tribes. Waldrop's poem emerges out of the friction between these texts and, like Howe's use of Atherton as a figure for the contemporary poet, Waldrop extends Williams' conflict into the socio-hisorical register of the present.

Waldrop's *Key* [*A Key into the Language of America*] revolves around the degree to which Williams and his text have been silenced and repeatedly censored by Puritan ideology because "The mirror Roger Williams held up to the colonists in *A Key into the Language of America* was not welcome" (xix). Williams and the various native tribes that he "championed" threatened the Puritan "divine civil order," and, subsequently, their "silencing" was regarded as a moral and civil imperative. Nevertheless, despite Williams' exile and, censorship, his text is one of the few remaining remnants of a nearly obliterated Narragensett history and language. Williams' text unveils a significant historical blank— the silenced layer of the Narragensett—while simultaneously being a trace of suppression by the same forces that "vanquished" his subject. Since *A Key into the Language of America* critiques the sanctity of the Colonial ideological system, it falls prey to the same victimization as the Narragensett.

Waldrop's poem builds upon Williams' analysis of the Narragansett language and culture as an ideational and structural springboard for her poem. She explains,

> Besides giving me a glimpse of a vanished language and culture, [Williams'] *A Key* has given me the form of this work.
>
> In parallel with Roger Williams' anthropological passages, the initial prose section of each of my chapters tries to get at the clash of Indian and European cultures by a violent collage of phrases from Williams with elements from anywhere in my Western heritage . . .
>
> To reinforce the theme of conquest and gender, every chapter adds a narrative section in italics, in the voice of a young woman, ambivalent about her sex and position among the conquerors.
>
> (xxiii)

Similar to the governing poetic principle of juxtaposition of Howe's work and that of *The Cantos, A Key* layers one repressed voice with others to illuminate the reach of ideologically-motivated silencing across centuries, cultures, and genders—the Narragensett, Williams, and the young woman, who mirrors Waldrop herself.[3] These parallels are emphasized by the question of whether Waldrop, like Williams, is indeed "among the privileged, the "conquerors" since, as a female poet, she is subject to the process of censorship inherent within Western society.

> But am I among them? I am white and educated. I am also a poet and a woman. A poet, in our days, is regarded as rather marginal member of society, whose social usefulness is in doubt. As a woman, I do not figure as conqueror in the shell game of archetypes, but as conquered. A "war bride."
>
> (xix-xx)

The female poet occupies the cultural position of the other as an unnecessary social, cultural, and historical supplement. Not only does the established social hierarchy resist the poet's entirely into "society" (regardless of gender), but as a female poet, the sentence is doubly harsh. The poet becomes a "war bride," whose position is further marginalized. As Waldrop emphasizes in the chapter **"Of Marriage,"** to be married is to be bound, contained, and "stabilized" within a dominant melody: "harmony prestabilized / is turning on its / axe to grind / to halt / to bind / to fault" (48). Marriage maintains the status quo, thereby silencing voices by halting, binding, and finding fault. Social order and protocol, therefore, silences "disruptive" voices before they can speak. As Howe remarks, "If you are a woman, archives hold perpetual ironies. Because the gaps and silence are where you find yourself" (*The Birthmark* 158). The social hierarchical imperative, these poems suggest, imposes limitations upon the feminine either upon women or those who occupy a marginalized cultural position such as a poet.

Subsequently, as a poem battles against the "stabilizing" and "binding" of history, it is always in danger of becoming another absent or silenced voice, especially since a poet's social usefulness is questionable. "Official" history either absorbs everything within its limiting, linear narrative, or discards all that does not fit. A poem, for that matter, often refuses to be contained within a "pattern" or theory, and instead presses into unmarked/unmapped territory, which places it in a dubious and marginal position in relation to "sanctified history." Nevertheless, the task of poetry, art, and other forms of representation is to confront the void of historical narrativizing. As the close of Chapter XXX, **"Of Their Paintings,"** emphasizes,

> thinking develops
> out of the negative
>
> the vacuum abhorred
> by nature
> is fertile (variables
> perspectives, paper money)
>
> refinanced memory
> washes white
>
> (62)

Memory is prey to the status quo, a "financed" history that disposes of any "detritus" that does not fit within a contained and approved narrative. "Orders suggest hierarchy and category," Howe argues, and "[c]ategories and hierarchies suggest property" (*MED* [*My Emily Dickinson*] 13). Power, order, and economics are explicitly interwoven, all of which impact the cultural memory. Established history solidifies itself under a mask of public relations, even as that narrative stands in direct contestation with multiplicity. In a manner that rhymes with the meditation of "Articulation of Sound Forms in Time" upon "a world's vast Memory", Waldrop's poem strives against this "white-washing" of memory by offering a haven for those narratives in danger of being subsumed; it gathers the blanks in an effort to stave off historical erasure and premature closure. It pushes perpetually for openness by refusing to silence the voices that speak in and through the poem.

In this light, Waldrop and Howe enact a poetics that echoes the post-structural feminist critique that interrogates the cultural nexus of writing, memory, and ethics. For example, Helene Cixous' conception of the practice of writing in *Rootprints,* mirrors "Articulation of Sound Forms in Time" and *A Key into the Language of America* in significant ways:

> In writing there is also a function of raising up what is forgotten, what is scorned. Not only great things that have been forgotten—not only women—but the little things that have been scorned, seen as detritus. And which are nonetheless part of our lives.
>
> (98)

Writing discovers the forgotten and brings it back within view. Cixous emphasizes that it is not only women who

are subject to cultural scorn and erasure. And in this vein, Marjorie Perloff observes a similar articulated position in Howe's writing as well.

> Most contemporary feminist poetry takes as emblematic its author's own experience of power relations, her personal struggle with patriarchy, her sense of marginalization, her view of social justice. The[s]e are Howe's subjects as well, but in substituting "impersonal" narrative—a narrative made of collage fragments realigned and recharged—for the more usual lyric "I," Howe is suggesting that the personal is always already political, specifically, that the contemporary Irish-American New England woman who is Susan Howe cannot be understood apart from her history. But history also teaches the poet that, however marginalized women have been in American culture and however much men have been the purveyors of power, those who have suffered the loss of the Word are by no means only women.
>
> (310)

The issue is not only women who have been forgotten, but everyone who has been feminized, silenced, and erased by a cultural hegemony desperate to protect its perception of the world and its property. Poetry, for Howe and Waldrop, seeks to resurrect those blanks the "conscientious" historian left for others to fill and to shelter those "forgotten" voices against the continued scourge of history.

Ultimately, Waldrop and Howe employ a compassionate (and passionate) rhetorical stance that presses towards justice. Their work, in this regard, articulates an ethical stance—or to borrow Joan Retallack's terminology, a "poethics" of how to respond to otherness without succumbing to censorship and silencing. That is, their poetry embraces not a singular but multiple visions, and their poetic technique is democratic as opposed to autocratic. But, even as Howe's and Waldrop's work departs thematically from the overarching sweep of a historical stance that posits the certitude of history, their poetry is not necessarily antithetical to the crux of Pound's poetry which is clearly stated in Pound's translation of *Confucius*: "The proper man is concerned with right action" (267); furthermore, he remarks that the crucial issue is the perpetual goal of focusing upon "a discussion of equity (ethics, justice)" (265). While Waldrop and Howe do not valorize the same ideological concepts and narratives as Pound, Howe and Waldrop's poetics demonstrate how Pound's palimpsest—those partially-effaced and erased texts that the poem re-instates—clears a path for a poethics focused upon aporias, textual gaps, absences, and the forces that generate such gaps. In this regard, they recuperate Pound's poetics as wholly fascist by demonstrating the ethical potential in his poetry and poetics founded upon blanks and spaces, which the later Pound seems to have revoked.

Subsequently, along with the reconsideration of the role of ethics in Pound's poetics, "Articulation of Sound

Forms in Time" and *A Key into the Language of America* represent and revisit the originary tension between the completeness or incompleteness of history in *The Cantos* and Pound's championing of "phallocentric" poetry. Despite Pound's sustained efforts to order the chaotic and render an illuminated manuscript that documents the apex of human civilizations, gaps and absences seep into the pages of *The Cantos* and creates an ideationally and technically open text. As much as he resists the chaotic and deems the feminine as secondary to phallocentric order, his poetics predicated upon openness, the infinite, and the ethical suggests obvious parallels with the critiques of Howe, Waldrop, and other feminist critics. Nevertheless, Pound perceived his inability to render definitive form as a failure, as in Canto CXVI, the final completed canto, the inherent limitations of texts and poets amounts to the acknowledged failure of his envisioned "totality":

> Tho' my errors and wrecks lie about me.
> And I am not a demigod
> I cannot make it cohere
>
> (810)

This confessing of "errors" and the admittance of the lack of a universal "human" narrative marks a return to the earlier emphasis upon blanks as a necessary part of a text. That is, a poet cannot present *the* universal poem. Only a "demigod" can accomplish such a task. Human history is, therefore, subject to a temporal dialectic of addition, accretion, and supplementation. The inability to "make it cohere" and achieve totality prompts the search for another center to anchor the poem—the dual focus upon "historical" splendor (the apex of human accomplishments) and ethics.

> To confess wrong without losing rightness:
> Charity I have had sometimes,
>   I cannot make it flow thru
> A little light, like a rushlight
>   to lead back to splendour.
>
> (811)

The objective is to amplify "rightness" without succumbing to errors and sacrificing "charity." By doing so, the poet gestures to an idealized splendour—where historians (and poets) are accurate, conscientious, and trustworthy and the arts play a central role within the social fabric of a culture. Pound confesses that such an era has long passed, but that does not negate his desire for an idealized state based upon charity, love, and ethics.

Subsequently, Pound concludes *The Cantos* with an emphasis upon ethics and love, which Howe and Waldrop ardently pursue in their poetry. Therefore, when Pound asks in Canto CXVI, "I have brought the great ball of crystal; who can lift it?" clearly Howe and Wal-

drop have risen to the challenge of the ethical crux of Pound's poetics by placing critical weight upon the poem as a vehicle of justice and "rightness." The splendor Pound envisions culminates in the centrality of love and peace, and it is highly ironic that through the aegis of feminist critique, poetry has edged closer to actualizing Pound's ethical stance. Nevertheless, as Pound remarks in his *ABC of Reading*, "the value of old work is constantly affected by the value of the new" (76). Certainly, Pound benefits from a new light—not that of the patriarchal "Pound" tradition, but of the women who recognize the value in the ethical crux of Pound's poetics. In this light, Pound's "splendour" is restored by resurrecting the human in Pound's poetry and by making poetry "flow thru" with the force of compassion and ethics—thereby illuminating that dimension of Pound that honors the open, the infinite, and the human. The poetry of Waldrop and Howe honors the tradition of Pound by drawing upon the love, ethics, and poetic technique that constitutes the heart of Pound's great poem, *The Cantos,* and avoids the "errors and wrecks" by reinstating love and personal history as the catalysts for the poem. Human love regains its primacy at the core of the "historical" poem. As Howe explains, "Love is a trajectory across the hollow of history" (*Birthmark* 99). Or in the famous lines from Canto LXXXI, "What thou lovest well remains I . . . 1 what thou lovs't well is thy true heritage [or "history"]" (Canto LXXXI), love is re-interjected into poetry. Howe and Waldrop reinvoke the "spirit" of Pound's poetic love—the love that interrogates the blanks, listens to the silence, and hovers tenderly over the rubble of the past—that resides at the secret heart of the poem, deep within *The Cantos,* and beyond the control of phallic order.

Notes

1. H. D. is linked (much to her discredit) to Pound because of his creation of "H. D. Imagist" as well as the dubious distinction of once being romantically involved with Pound. Any discussion of Pound's influence upon women's poetry usually follows the marriage trope of Pound and H. D., whereby Pound "creates" his female progenies. This essay tries to duplicate this critical shortcoming.

2. This line is lifted directly from an earlier work of Howe's, "There are Not Leaves Enough to Crown to Cover to Crown to Cover" in *The Europe of Trusts,* the title of which is derived from Wallace Stevens' "United Dames of America," which traces the dialectical flux of how "Masses produce / Each one its paradigm."

3. Williams, with his desire to preserve the slighted/ silenced voices, language, and culture of the Narragensett people, provides a literary proto-type for

Waldrop and Howe. That is, Williams work confronts the abyss of social history and teeters precariously at the edge of that abyss in constant danger of falling in or being pushed while trying to recollect the forgotten.

Works Cited

Bernstein, Charles. *A Poetics.* Cambridge: Harvard UP, 1992.

Bernstein, Michael. *A Tale of the Tribe: Ezra Pound and the Modern Verse Epic.* Princeton: Princeton UP, 1980.

Bronk, William. *Vectors and Smoothable Curves: Collected Essays.* Jersey City: Talisman House, 1997.

Cixous, Helene. *Rootprints: Memory and Life Writing.* Eric Prenowitz, trans. New York: Routledge, 1997.

DuPlessis, Rachel Blau. "Objectivist Poetics and Political Vision: A Study of Oppen and Pound" in *George Oppen: Man and Poet.* Orono: National Poetry Foundation, 1981.

Howe, Susan. *The Birth-mark: Unsettling the Wilderness in American Literary History.* Hanover: Wesleyan UP, 1993.

———. *The Europe of Trusts.* Los Angeles: Sun and Moon, 1990.

———. *My Emily Dickinson.* Berkeley: North Atlantic Books, 1985.

———. *Singularities.* Hanover: Wesleyan UP, 1990.

Levinas, Emmanuel. *Totality and Infinity.* Alphonso Lingis, trans. Pittsburgh: Duquesne UP, 1969.

Nicholls, Peter. "Unsettling the Wilderness: Susan Howe and American History." *Contemporary-Literature* 37.4 (1996): 586-601.

Perloff, Marjorie. *Poetic License: Essays on Modernist and Postmodernist Lyric.* Evanston: Northwestern UP, 1990.

Pound, Ezra. *ABC of Reading.* New York: New Directions, 1960.

———. *The Cantos.* New York: New Directions, 1968.

———. *Confucius.* New York: New Directions, 1969.

———. *Guide to Kulchur.* New York: New Directions, 1970.

Stevens, Wallace. *The Collected Poems.* New York: Vintage Books, 1982.

Waldrop, Rosmarie. *A Key into the Language of America.* New York: New Directions, 1994.

Wittgenstein, Ludwig. *Culture and Value.* Peter Winch, trans. Chicago: U of Chicago P, 1980.

Lynn Keller (essay date summer 2001)

SOURCE: Keller, Lynn. "'Fields of Pattern-Bounded Unpredictability': Recent Palimptexts by Rosmarie Waldrop and Joan Retallack." *Contemporary Literature* 42, no. 2 (summer 2001): 376-412.

[*In the following essay, Keller focuses on Waldrop's technique of using various source texts to demonstrate the ways in which language is always already invested with meaning, and draws parallels to the work of Joan Retallack.*]

Looking back on her development as an experimental poet, Rosmarie Waldrop sees as particularly formative the moment when she recognized the usefulness for her writing of "arbitrary pattern" and of a charged interaction between regulation and deviancy:

> It was an important moment for me when I realized consciously that the encounter of a poem-nucleus with an arbitrary pattern (like a rhyme scheme) would tend to pull the nucleus out of its semantic field in unforeseen directions. The tension always generates great energy, not just for bridging the "gap" between original intention and the pattern, but for pushing the whole poem farther. . . . I'm spelling out what Ashbery and others have called the liberating effect of constraints. But what matters is that *any* constraint, *any* pattern can be generative in this way. It does not need to be one of the traditional forms with their heavy closure effect of regularity and recurrence. . . . [E]xtreme formalism rarely works to my satisfaction. More often I use a pattern (e.g. the grammatical structure of a given text), but *also* let the words push and pull in their own directions. Since I make the rules, I also feel free to break them.

> (Lehman 197)

As her reference to "Ashbery and others" acknowledges, such attitudes are by no means unique to Waldrop. Widespread use of the procedural forms Joseph Conte has identified as a distinctly postmodern poetic genre, for example, demonstrates that an interest in the interaction between imposed arbitrary constraints and generative discoveries has propelled a good deal of exploratory poetry in the closing decades of the twentieth century.

Joan Retallack, who has been influenced by John Cage's "aesthetic paradigm of deterministic randomness," is another experimentalist who sees a potential for liberatory stretch in even quite conventional formal regulations (Retallack, "Poethics" 251). Retallack articulates also the limitations she perceives in conventional formal patterns:

> Any formal structure draws us outside ourselves, beyond our personal and expressive logics. Something as simple as meter, rhyme, and *abab* patterns pulls us in directions which have to do with material structures of the language, not just the ego-expressive interests of

the writer. But these forms do not even begin to explore the infinite possibilities of the complex system that is a natural language and the forms of life that give it vitality.

("Poethics" 262)

Retallack goes on to introduce the Cagean strategies that she believes generate forms more appropriate to the teeming multifariousness of contemporary realities:

Chance operations and indeterminacy pull the work of the composer or writer into exploration of the kinds of events and relationships that are characteristic of richly complex systems—from the simple patterns of bone/stone or *abab* to the increased complexity of language generated by mesostic strings to the turbulent patterns of liquid, smoke, ambient noise, and high degrees of semantic and associative multiplicity.

Sharing Cage's conviction that contemporary artists need to recover the continuity of aesthetic experience with the normal processes of living, and that these processes are wonderfully complex, Retallack believes that the artwork should be, like one's immediate experience, "a complex intersection of intention and nonintention, pattern and surprise" ("Poethics" 255). Although Waldrop is less interested in chance operations per se, what Retallack says helps account also for Waldrop's restlessness with "extreme formalism" and her tendency to complicate her own structures and break her own rules.

Seeking forms that are genuinely consonant with the present and that enable movement into the future, Waldrop and Retallack share with Cage and many other innovative artists an interest in bringing their work into line with current scientific modeling of complex systems. Thus Waldrop links her own repeated complication of dichotomous thinking to the coexistence in modern physics of ostensibly incompatible models; the paradox of the inconsistent yet necessarily coexistent quantum and wave finds expression in her work "in the simultaneous presence of fragment and flow" ("Conversation" 373-74). She also finds in quantum physics a challenge to push poetry beyond its traditional identification with the image and into "this brave new world without images!" (375). Retallack, intrigued by more recent developments in science, has produced, as I will demonstrate, verbal versions of the extremely complex fractal patterns that occur in natural phenomena. More generally, in her approach to poetic form, Retallack pursues the implications especially of chaos theory, whose "butterfly effect" (whereby a butterfly beating its wings in China could dramatically affect the weather in New York several months later) supports her hope that opening literary genres and generating new linguistic formulations might ultimately have significant social ramifications.

Among the social transformations both women hope to foster through their writing is the dissolution of the constraints of inherited gender categories and expecta-

tions. In her essay ":RE:THINKING:LITERARY:FEMINISM:" Retallack has pointed optimistically to the convergence between current scientific thinking and the experimental literary forms associated with the feminine (though heretofore produced primarily by men). Science, which now "recogniz[es] both complexity and the constituting presence of chance in nature," points to the relevance of those experimental literary forms that "Western culture has tended to label feminine (forms characterized by silence, empty and full; multiple, associative, nonhierarchical logics; open and materially contingent processes, etc.)." Happily, this coincidence is occurring just at the moment when women finally have enough social power and cultural standing to attempt in significant numbers those "feminine" forms that push the constructed limits of intelligibility (347). Heterogeneous experimental creations that "engage the dynamics of multiplicity" and generate "a proliferation of possibility beyond invidious dualisms"—perhaps especially those produced by women—may help us move beyond the fundamental Western binary of feminine/masculine, ultimately freeing not just women but all "the complex human" (347) to explore a world of "uncompressible possibility" (366).[1]

Just as Cage developed innovative writing from previously used language of "source texts" by Thoreau, Joyce, Wittgenstein, Marshall McLuhan, Buckminster Fuller, and others, both Waldrop and Retallack draw extensively upon preexistent texts in producing their own experimental work. This reflects a belief common to all three that language is not something one possesses and makes one's own in order to express oneself; language is invariably an already used medium and is to be embraced as such, with no pretensions to originality or ownership. Neither Waldrop nor Retallack "writes through" source texts as Cage does—subjecting them to chance operations to select words that appear in mesostics. Yet as Retallack and Waldrop write over and (collagistically) with texts in Western literary tradition, inherited linguistic formulations figure importantly among the ordering structures with and against which they, like Cage, work. Even where the source texts do not provide a formal structure (as when a new work follows "the grammatical structure of a given text"), their verbal arrangements provide a crucial set of limiting constraints that Waldrop and Retallack deliberately encounter and transform in their writing. As Retallack puts it when describing the challenge of contemporaneity, that we "reinvent ourselves and move on,"

Tradition gives us some, but not all, navigational coordinates. . . . It's common to think of identities and traditions as useful limiting structures, points of departure from the known. But epistemological reality principles, like all others, shrivel without the dicey pleasures of permeability, motion, susceptibility to chance occurrences. Isn't it more fruitful to think of identity and tradition ("IT," always intertwined) in ongoing, transformative conversation with a changing world?

("Silence and the Experimental Feminine" 6)[2]

Such a mobile "transformative conversation" with works that are part of our scribal tradition—a conversation often propelled by the conceptual structures of modern physics—will be my focus in the following consideration of the interplay between design and disorder, form and possibility in selected mid-nineties works by Waldrop and Retallack. Waldrop's *Lawn of Excluded Middle,* in interacting with the orders reflected in and generated by three male-authored texts, demonstrates with particular clarity a feminist revisionary dynamic in what I will shortly identify as palimptexts. Retallack's "Afterrimages" and "Icarus FFFF-Falling" employ alternative modes of palimptextual transformation. The "dicey pleasures" of chance procedures give contemporary meanings to received texts in the former, as fractal manipulation does to the patriarchal codes and systems saturating the sources Retallack brings into play in the latter.

Waldrop calls virtually no attention within *Lawn of Excluded Middle* (1993) to that volume's extensive reliance on prior texts. The only clues lie in the ten terse entries on the volume's final page titled "On *Lawn of Excluded Middle.*" Here the names Wittgenstein and A. S. Eddington appear, but without Waldrop's indicating that she draws directly on their work in constructing her text, much less acknowledging the particular titles she draws from.[3] Presumably, this is not because she wishes to be cagey about her sources, but simply because the unidentified source texts for *Lawn* [*Lawn of Excluded Middle.*] function largely as examples of the way in which the language we employ is inevitably a previously used, sedimented medium—something Waldrop has discussed in terms of palimpsest:

> The blank page is not blank. No text has one single author. Whether we are conscious of it or not, we always write on top of a PALIMPSEST.
>
> This is not a question of linear "influence" and not just of tradition, but of writing as a multiple dialogue with a whole net of previous and concurrent texts, traditions, schooling, the culture and language we breathe and move in, which condition us even while we help to construct them.
>
> Historians speak of "the conditions of occurrence"; Duncan, of the "grand collage." . . .
>
> Many of us have foregrounded this awareness of the palimpsest as a method, using, transforming, "translating" parts of other works.

("Form and Discontent" 61)

The palimpsestic method Waldrop has chosen in *Lawn of Excluded Middle* imposes limits and shape on the ordinary "conditions of occurrence," heightening the

writer's consciousness of the ever-present terms of our dialogue with the given arrangements of language. For those readers who become conscious of her use of prior texts, it foregrounds the palimpsestic nature of language and the multiple authorship of texts, while bringing into focus Waldrop's interest in compositional methods constrained by "reduced choice" or "choice at one remove" ("Rosmarie Waldrop"; "Conversation" 348).

While employing Waldrop's term "palimpsest" for her *method* of writing a "multiple dialogue" with prior texts, I have adopted Michael Davidson's term "palimptext" for the *product* which results. Designating "a writing that displays its formations in other writings . . . an arrested moment in an ongoing process of signifying, scripting, and typing," "palimptext" is "a vehicle for circumventing generic categories and period styles by describing writing in its collaborative, quotidian, and intertextual forms" (9). In identifying Waldrop's and Retallack's works as palimptexts, my intention is to convey a more dynamic, interactive intertextuality (and one less bound to historical recovery) than the fixed chronological layering conventionally associated with palimpsests.

Three texts predominate as palimpsestic resources for *Lawn of Excluded Middle,* each representing a different intellectual discipline.[4] The one that surfaces most extensively is Wittgenstein's *Philosophical Investigations, Part I* (completed in 1945), primarily entries from #422 on. A. S. Eddington's *The Nature of the Physical World* (1929), the published version of his Gifford Lectures of 1927, provides important conceptual material and additional language, though less language than *Philosophical Investigations*. Robert Musil's novella "The Perfecting of a Love" (1911) provides a kind of ghost-plot as well as some of the imagery, atmosphere, and thematic preoccupations, but it is the most elusively present of the three texts that can be glimpsed as strata of soil nourishing Waldrop's *Lawn.*

Waldrop's decision to draw concurrently upon works of fiction, philosophy, and science may be partly explained via a passage from "Alarms & Excursions," near the close of that essay's exploration of the public and political dimensions of poetry:

> So maybe our poems offer a challenge to the ruling grammar, offer some patterns of thinking and perception which might not be bad possibilities to consider. But how many readers does a small press book reach? Even if all 1000 copies of a typical press run get sold, even if they all reach readers how much effect is this book going to have on society? None, I am afraid. I suspect it takes similar patterns appearing in many disciplines at the same time. . . . For instance, many of the characteristics of innovative art which bother people to this day (discontinuity, indeterminacy, acceptance of the unescapable human reference point)

were anticipated in science by the turn of the century. In contrast, the fact that they are still an irritant in art would seem to show that it takes art to make people aware of the challenge to their thinking habits or that the challenge has to come in many areas. It also gives us an inkling of how *slowly* mental habits change.

(61-62)

Via the palimpsest of *Lawn,* Waldrop is unobtrusively drawing attention to similar intellectual developments and perceptual shifts that have occurred in separate disciplines in the modern period, presumably to reinforce the changes in thinking those works enact and examine. The authors, born in 1880 (Musil), 1882 (Eddington), and 1889 (Wittgenstein), represent a single generation and its zeitgeist. All three invested themselves in dramatically new and iconoclastic forms of thought and/or expression—forms that test the limits of language and that remain uncomfortable for many in the supposedly postmodern era.

The net linking these three has some biographical strands.[5] Wittgenstein and Musil, having been trained as scientists (if I may count engineering, which Wittgenstein studied, as a science), might well have taken an interest in work by Eddington, a prominent English physicist and popular lecturer. Musil was among the artists who benefited from Wittgenstein's charity, though scholars think it unlikely that Wittgenstein read any of his fiction.[6] Musil, who abandoned another potential career in philosophy, might have read Wittgenstein. Yet their possible awareness of each other's thinking is not the point here. Waldrop seems to have selected the texts contributing to her palimptext primarily because each one is engaged with some of her own particular preoccupations: they play into her interest in exploring the limits of linguistic picture-making, in interrogating the relationship between mental experience and physical phenomena, and in testing everyday language as a medium for gaining access to physical experience or phenomena, including the experiences of sexuality and sexed embodiment.

To some extent, of course, Waldrop may have developed these preoccupations precisely through her reading of Wittgenstein, Musil, and Eddington. In discussing her first responses to Musil's work (when she read *A Man without Qualities* in the mid-fifties), she went beyond noting that his concept of personal identity "rang true" for her and granted his methodological impact: "I was fascinated by the way the narrative calls itself into question, both thematically and by always pitting a two-dimensional grid of details against the famous 'narrative' thread. This became important for my own method of composition: the tension between clusters (lines or single words) scattered on a page and a temporal sequence" ("Rosmarie Waldrop," *Contemporary Authors* 302-3). One could legitimately speak of

Musil as an influence on Waldrop's work, though such discourse should not obscure the extent to which writings by Musil, Wittgenstein, and Eddington extended ideas that were fundamental to Waldrop's perspective even before she read them. When she speaks of the delight she experienced in finding that a "consent to emptiness" or "negative capability" characterizes modernist physics, it is clear that the field exemplifies a stance she already valued before her encounter with Eddington.[7] Similarly, having long resisted poetry's traditional identification with the image, Waldrop had independently approached (though not entirely arrived at) the challenge modern physics offers when it disconcertingly proposes a model of the world that is not amenable to representation by analogies and images, only by "mathematical formulae that defy being pictured" ("Conversation" 372). Yet even with such caveats in mind, "influence" remains too hierarchical, predictable, and unidirectional a term to capture the dynamic shaping the palimptext; "influence" cannot convey the multiple logics, the kaleidoscopic shifts, the unstable and eccentric commentaries generated by the intertextual conversations in *Lawn of Excluded Middle* or more generally in today's poetic palimptexts. While the writers Waldrop draws on in *Lawn* are certainly her intellectual allies and even her mentors, their texts become opportunities for endlessly dynamic translation and transformation.

The mobility and range of suggestion Waldrop achieves by interweaving and transforming the precedent texts invoked in *Lawn* is evident even in the final page of aphoristic explanations. "On *Lawn of Excluded Middle*" suggests Waldrop's alliance with Wittgenstein in faintly echoing the structure of *Philosophical Investigations*; items that are numerically ordered stand in often disjunctive relation and forgo consistent logical sequence. Waldrop's dismissal of the law of excluded middle (the law of *tertium non datur,* according to which A is B or A is *not B*) in the first entry aligns her more directly with Wittgenstein, since both of them prefer more complex and ambiguous notions of truth and falsity to that "venerable old law of logic." The philosopher's name appears only in entry 7, which identifies his activity with Waldrop's literary practice and locates his philosophical dicta within the spatial frame she has named: "Wittgenstein makes language with its ambiguities the ground of philosophy. His games are played on the Lawn of Excluded Middle." An embrace of ambiguity provides the link to modern physics, introduced in entry 8: "The picture of the world drawn by classical physics conflicts with the picture drawn by quantum theory. As A. S. Eddington says, we use classical physics on Monday, Wednesday, Friday, and quantum theory on Tuesday, Thursday, Saturday."[8] By positioning Eddington as if he were merely someone who has presented the idea memorably ("As . . . Eddington says"), Waldrop emphasizes that her book is based on widely accepted, not eccentric, understandings. Musil's name does not appear, yet his contribution to the palimptext is suggested by item 10: "The gravity of love encompasses ambivalence." Of course, "gravity" signals the limitations of Newtonian physics, which preoccupy Eddington and appear as a recurrent motif in *Lawn.* (Indeed, item 9—"For Newton, the apple has the perplexing habit of falling. In another frame of reference, Newton is buffeted up toward the apple at rest"— echoes Eddington in his chapter "A New Picture of Gravitation.")[9] At the same time, "gravity" in the sense of seriousness is one of the most striking traits of Musil's highly nuanced exploration of the ambivalence of love. "The Perfecting of Love" details the inner experience of a woman bonded to her husband in nearly perfect love as she nonetheless moves with seeming inevitability toward sexual infidelity. Musil's somber tale always acknowledges the gravity of love, even while love's ironic inconsistencies are painfully evident. The same is true of Waldrop's portrayal of the interactions of a heterosexual couple in *Lawn of Excluded Middle.* This page of explanatory remarks, then, more than it identifies sources, invites us to see Waldrop reading and writing her world through a multidimensional conversational process.

Waldrop's process of "making language think" contemporaneously requires correction and supplementation in addition to solidarity and open-ended play. The given linguistic formations exposed in *Lawn*'s palimptext are limits that, when put in place, prove generative in themselves and at the same time invite transgression and transformation. Some of this transformation results from Waldrop's adapting received linguistic patterns to her feminist perspective.[10] Of the three authors most visible in her palimptext, only Musil shares Waldrop's interest in female thought, whose stereotypical illogicality Waldrop dismisses in entry 1, while leaving open the possibility that less linear logics are suited to the feminine mind. And, as one would expect of male intellectuals of the early twentieth century, none of them shares Waldrop's desire to explore the idea, made explicit in entry 3, of "[w]omen and, more particularly, the womb, the empty center of the woman's body, the locus of fertility" as the regrettably "excluded middle." Wittgenstein and Eddington, even if they do play on the lawn of the excluded middle, continue unthinkingly to exclude the female from consciousness, writing as if the experiences of "he" were necessarily those of all humankind. (They write, that is, from a homocentric perspective that is often a source of humor in Eddington's prose, though the alternatives he posits are not gynocentric.) Even Musil, who attempts to write sympathetically from within a complex female perspective, slides into stereotypical notions of female bestiality ("she was seized by a wild urge to throw herself down on this rug and kiss the repulsive traces of all those feet, exciting herself with their smell like a bitch

in heat" [217]) and of a female illogicality that might easily be labeled pathological.

Examining a few sections from *Lawn of Excluded Middle* in which the palimpsest is particularly visible will demonstrate how Waldrop works "at once with and against" these three male-authored texts.[11] It will also reveal how her adoption/disruption/transformation of received linguistic orders makes a space for the nonlinear logics which have been associated with the feminine mind and for the resonant space of the female body that, as simultaneously a fertile plenitude and an empty nothingness, provides a potential ground for new writing.

The three sentences that compose the first prose poem in "Lawn of Excluded Middle" make extensive use of two Wittgenstein entries that appear in close proximity to each other. Here is Waldrop's poem:

> When I say I believe that women have a soul and that its substance contains two carbon rings the picture in the foreground makes it difficult to find its application back where the corridors get lost in ritual sacrifice and hidden bleeding. But the four points of the compass are equal on the lawn of the excluded middle where full maturity of meaning takes time the way you eat a fish, morsel by morsel, off the bone. Something that can be held in the mouth, deeply, like darkness by someone blind or the empty space I place at the center of each poem to allow penetration.
>
> (11)

And here are the Wittgenstein entries:

> 422. What am I believing in when I believe that men have souls? What am I believing in, when I believe that this substance contains two carbon rings? In both cases there is a picture in the foreground, but the sense lies far in the background; that is, the application of the picture is not easy to survey.
>
> (126)

> 424. The picture is *there*; and I do not dispute its *correctness*. But *what* is its application? Think of the picture of blindness as a darkness in the soul or in the head of the blind man.
>
> (126)

Another nearby remark in *Philosophical Investigations* is relevant—its detours related to Waldrop's corridors— though not visible in the palimptext:

> 426. A picture is conjured up which seems to fix the sense *unambiguously*. The actual use, compared with that suggested by the picture, seems like something muddied. . . . In the actual use of expressions we make detours, we go by sideroads. We see the straight highway before us, but of course we cannot use it, because it is permanently closed.
>
> (127)

Wittgenstein is puzzling out the relations among actual language games, the mental images we conjure, and what we would express, and between physical and psychological realities. So is Waldrop, but she has a particular angle, as is evident from her pointed substitution of women for men in Wittgenstein's question about the soul. The differences between her words or sentences and Wittgenstein's also indicate immediately her greater preoccupation with social inequities and stereotypes. Thus the impediments she discerns to what Wittgenstein terms "the application of the picture" have to do with long-established biases in patriarchal culture that have led to the containment and demonization of female fecundity (for example, through virgin sacrifice or quarantine of menstruating women). Inherited assumptions about women, Waldrop implies, make it even more difficult to think clearly about women's souls than men's. With "But" Waldrop proposes a utopian alternative, a nonhierarchical space—the lawn of excluded middle—where the four points of the compass are equal, and where, with patience and an insistently sensual/corporeal attention ("the way you eat a fish, morsel by morsel"), greater understanding and meaning will emerge.

Both Wittgenstein and Waldrop are rejecting the common assumption that the meaning of words derives from shared pictures, believing instead that experiential biases of our mental pictures are encoded in backgrounds we have so naturalized that we no longer see them. To make this point, Wittgenstein offers alternative usages to highlight how words acquire different meanings in different contexts: just as questions of spiritual belief are distinct from scientific ones, the picture of darkness conjured by the word "blindness" is not the same for a theologian considering the soul as it is for a man literally lacking eyesight. Waldrop, however, in a significant countermove, brings these differences into the same frame, as if taking the orderly design Wittgenstein has made by sorting out differences, and inserting it into a kaleidoscope where its elements collapse into more polyvalent forms. In so doing, she unsettles naturalized assumptions as Wittgenstein does but deliberately contributes as he does not to "muddying" dichotomous or contrasting categories.[12] In her prose poem, the scientific description of materiality (two carbon atoms) applies to the woman's soul, and the experience of darkness for "someone blind" as readily exemplifies the "lawn" where "maturity of meaning" develops as does the feminizing empty space she places "at the center" of each poem. Such mergings imply that plenitude (for example, darkness for the blind) and emptiness (for example, the penetrable space) meet on this lawn. Where patriarchy's cultural traditions, including the linguistic sediment that Waldrop inherits, appropriate the procreative power of the female to an androcentric model of intellectual or aesthetic creativity, Waldrop insists that a feminine, womblike space in the artwork

is necessary for meaning to emerge. The discovery of meaning is figured in a "penetration" that, by its association with heterosexual intercourse, suggests the need for both masculine and feminine traits.

As already noted, it is Wittgenstein's practice to consider diverse applications in which words mean differently; #593 reads, "A main cause of philosophical disease—a one-sided diet: one nourishes one's thinking with only one kind of example" (155). Yet his examples never take into account gender difference. In contrast, the effect of differential gender expectations, either projected or internalized, on the constitution and communication of meaning is a recurrent concern in *Lawn*. Here, for example, is section 11 of **"Lawn"**:

> Whenever you're surprised that I should speak your language I am suddenly wearing too many necklaces and breasts, even though feeling does not produce what is felt, and the object of observation is something else again. Not modulating keys, not the splash that makes us take to another element, just my body alarmingly tangible, like furniture that exceeds its function, a shape I cannot get around. The way one suddenly knows the boulder in the road for a boulder, immovable, as if not always there, unmodified by inner hollows or the stray weeds and their dusty green, a solid obstacle with only trompe-l'oeil exits toward the subtler body of light accumulating in the distance.

(21)

In this prose poem the syntactic structures are more tangled, reflecting the knotted self-consciousness that unnerves the speaker. When reminded of how consistently women are seen only as sexualized and decorative bodies, the speaker cannot experience her own use of language as exciting possibility (as modulating musical keys or the splash that accompanies a transition from thin air to buoyant water). Instead, she feels entirely stuck in received expectations, with no access to the deviant or mysterious possibilities of the feminine lawn (inner hollows or stray weeds). This is a moment of backsliding into an outdated but tenacious understanding—specifically that of "the [female] body misunderstood as solid" (20), a belief comparable to classical physics' misconception of atomic solidity that preceded modern revelations of "the void within the atom" (Eddington 1).

Given the speaker's distressing awareness of the male "you"'s assumption that, naturally, women don't speak his language, it's not surprising that the fragment of *Philosophical Investigations* evident in the passage comes from an entry (#596) concerning "the feeling of 'familiarity' and of 'naturalness.'" In it Wittgenstein observes: "not everything which is unfamiliar to us makes an impression of unfamiliarity upon us. Here one has to consider what we call 'unfamiliar.' If a boulder lies on the road, we know it for a boulder, but perhaps not for the one which has always lain there. We recognize a man, say, as a man, but not as an acquaintance" (156). In the gender-conscious context of Waldrop's *Lawn,* a further permutation of unfamiliarity arises; a man may think he recognizes what a woman is, may think he is encountering a being comfortably familiar in its limitations and its (dichotomized) difference from him, but his feeling of familiarity is mistaken *even if*—as seems to be the case here—he is well-acquainted with this particular woman.

Modern physics, breezily invoked in "the object of observation is something else again," reinforces Waldrop's point. What is observed depends on the frame of observation. As Eddington notes, "apparent changes in the length, mass, electric and magnetic fields, period of vibration, etc." of a given object in motion are "merely a change of reckoning introduced in passing from the frame in which the object is at rest to the frame in which the observer is at rest" (62). Similarly, surprising changes in a man's perception of a woman's identity may reflect merely a shift in who is speaking and who is silent. Of particular importance in this context is the uncertainty principle, according to which we can measure the velocity of a particle *or* its position but we cannot accurately measure both, since the two measurements interfere with one another. "The principle of indeterminacy is epistemological," remarks Eddington. "It reminds us once again that the world of physics is a world contemplated from within[,] surveyed by appliances which are part of it and subject to its laws. What the world might be deemed like if probed in some supernatural manner by appliances not furnished by itself we do not profess to know" (225). Waldrop's reference to the object of observation suggests that men or patriarchal culture generally should be similarly humble in their assertions of knowing about women.

Physics, as translated by Eddington, also provides a model that helps the speaker move beyond her sense of being blocked in her use of language or limited by her female body. In the succeeding prose poem, after presenting her anxieties in the past tense—anxieties about how commodified images of women interfere with her communicating what she intended—the speaker proposes an alternative aesthetic that obviates such fears:

> I worried about the gap between expression and intent, afraid the world might see a fluorescent advertisement where I meant to show a face. Sincerity is no help once we admit to the lies we tell on nocturnal occasions, even in the solitude of our own heart, wishcraft slanting the naked figure from need to seduce to fear of possession. Far better to cultivate the gap itself with its high grass for privacy and reference gone astray. Never mind that it is not philosophy, but raw electrons jump-

ing from orbit to orbit to ready the pit for the orchestra, scrap meanings amplifying the succession of green perspectives, moist fissures, spasms on the lips.

> (22)

The lies mentioned here play upon those of Musil's protagonist, Claudine, in "The Perfecting of a Love." Having lied to her would-be seducer one evening by denying that she loves her husband, Claudine recalls the other lie she has told during her married life. It was occasioned by a solitary walk during which she had become aware that chance governs human life, that she might have adjusted herself to another man and "never have known anything of the person that one is today":

> For the first time she had felt her being, down to its very foundations, as something indeterminate, had apprehended this ultimate faceless experience of herself in love as something that destroyed the very root, the absoluteness, of existence and would always have made her into a person that she called herself and who was nevertheless not different from everyone else. And it was as if she must let go, let herself sink back into the drift of things, into the realm of unfulfilled possibilities.

> (215)

Waldrop repeats Claudine's revelation of fundamental indeterminacy, applying it to the realm of poetics: an aesthetics of sincerity (like that which underlies personal expressive lyric) rests on false premises about unique determinate identity.

Palimpsestic use of Musil's novella also contributes to Waldrop's formulation of an accommodating strategy, an acceptance of indeterminacy and disjunction. For immediately before the sexual consummation with which the novella closes, Claudine shrinks at the realization that her lover-to-be is "assuming possession of her," and as she undresses she talks about wishing she could jump back and forth across the invisible line between her and her lover or between sexual fidelity and sexual infidelity (222). Following this lead, Waldrop offers as "far better" than an aesthetics of sincerity a mode of writing (and a form of self-conception) in which something like the jumping Claudine longs for hopelessly may be not only possible but necessary. The behavior of excited electrons seems to be Waldrop's model; according to Niels Bohr's theories as Eddington explains them, "the only possible change of state is the transfer of an electron from one quantum orbit to another. Such a jump must occur whenever light is absorbed or emitted" (191). Glimpsed through the layers of palimpsest, "raw electrons jumping" point to the availability of liberating alternatives to the illusion of determinate, fixed selfhood. Comparable abrupt shifts and ruptures (syntactic, referential, and so on) are enacted in the "[g]ap gardening" (*Lawn* 24) Waldrop performs within individual sentences or poems and across the spaces between poems. She also relies constantly on "scrap meanings" (22), a phrase which, in suggesting discarded material suitable for reprocessing, aptly signals the recycling of language fragments involved in writing palimptext.

In the concluding lines of this poem, Waldrop celebrates what may be gained when one "cultivate[s] the gap itself" (22), referring not just to employment of paratactic techniques but more generally to exploration of the in-between spaces dismissed in orthodox philosophy, aesthetics, or social theory and to cultivation of the fertile green lawn of the excluded middle. The possible benefits, presented here in utopian terms, include expanded awareness of one's environment, greater appreciation of one's body, and enhanced erotic fulfillment in one's relation to the world—the amplified "spasms on the lips" in which, recalling Irigaray, linguistic articulation and (female) orgasm merge.

The examples of palimptext I have discussed all come from the title series. This is not an arbitrary choice, for the palimpsestic character of the volume is far from uniform.[13] *Philosophical Investigations* is most frequently visible in the palimpsest of part 1 (the title series of thirty-one numbered prose poems set one per page);[14] in part 2, the linguistic sediment of modern physics is more evident;[15] while Musil's novella seems most present in the first series in part 2, "The Attraction of the Ground," where the I-you dynamic is most pronounced and love is a particularly central concern. Moreover, the obvious palimpsest is densest in the opening series and diminishes thereafter, as if Waldrop first worked within the constraints of that method and then increasingly transgressed them. (Of course, palimpsest remains no matter what, as a condition of all writing. As Waldrop tells Retallack in their published conversation, "the text already there is, for me, the whole past of the particular language, the whole culture, that is to say, a plenitude *almost* as large, *almost* as unlimited and full of possibilities as emptiness" [368].) Perhaps this gradual movement away from apparent overwriting of other texts signals that Waldrop's working from a particular foundation of words already arranged together is only a temporary heuristic structure in her larger project of generating new verbal combinations. Unhappy with "the way we, clamoring for sense, exclude so many unions of words from the sphere of language" (*Lawn* 38), she finds that the sense made by certain writers who are themselves pushing the limits of meaning provides valuable prompts for generating linguistic unions that even she might otherwise have censored. After a while, the volume's organization suggests, such aids become superfluous.

Whether or not received texts are involved, the process of generating linguistic formulations adequate to current understandings of reality navigates a precarious balance of freedom and restriction. The concluding poem in the volume (the final section in **"Accelerating Frame"**) depicts that balancing act as "translation," in the context of negotiating the revelations of modern physics:

> Finally I came to prefer the risk of falling to the arrogance of solid ground and placed myself on the thin line of translation, balancing precariously between body harnessed to slowness and categories of electric charge whizzing across fields nobody could stand on. Working the charge against my retina into the cognate red of a geranium I wondered if the direction of translation should be into arithmetic or back into my native silence. Or was this a question like right or left, reversible? And could it be resolved on the nonstandard model of androgyny, sharing out the sensitive zones among the contenders? Meanwhile everyday language is using all its vigor to keep the apple in the habit of falling though the curve of the world no longer fits our flat feet and matter's become too porous to place them on.

(79)

Waldrop, who has extensive experience translating from several languages, has explained that she thinks of translation—one of the terms she used in describing the method of palimpsest—as "approximation rather than duplication. A re-giving of form" ("Interview" 36). She has explained that "destruction" and "betrayal" of the original are necessary for a translator to get at the "nucleus of energy" from which she or he can rebuild it. This process of deforming and reforming inherited linguistic arrangements generates a baffling field of possibilities, as is evident from the speaker's proliferating questions about the models and directions she might pursue. Interestingly, the course for which she notes limitations is that of "everyday language," which excludes the new and protects outmoded thought.

Waldrop's apparent distancing of her project from "everyday language" by characterizing it as regressive perhaps invites fine-tuning of Marjorie Perloff's claim that Wittgenstein's legacy for poets like Waldrop is in an "ordinary language poetics." In *Wittgenstein's Ladder*, Perloff has developed the important argument that Wittgenstein's "stringent and severe interrogation of language has provided an opening for the replacement of the 'autonomous,' self-contained, and self-expressive lyric with a more fluid poetic paradigm—a paradigm based on the recognition that the poet's most secret and profound emotions are expressed in a language that has always already belonged to the poet's culture, society, and nation" (22). Yet poets draw on the "language pool" in different ways and, without positing a special language for poetry, may still draw from that reservoir selectively. Waldrop's alignment of "everyday language" with what slows change in mental habits may help us distinguish her from those experimentalists (and Retallack is sometimes among them) who deliberately open poetry to the language games prevalent in consumer and mass culture. The linguistic sediment Waldrop chooses to highlight and alter in her recent palimpsestic writing is language deployed with extreme care by intellectuals consciously pushing at conceptual and expressive frontiers. All three men work from a base in customary language games but extend them to enable fresh exploration and explanation of the universe we inhabit. Waldrop brings to their extraordinary (but gender-biased) interventions into everyday language and to the often not-conventionally-logical understandings they formulate the resources of her female body and (in part) not-conventionally-logical "feminine" mind. Section 23 of **"Lawn of Excluded Middle"** hauntingly describes this use of the body in relation to a "clutter" that surely includes the noise of everyday language:

> It's true, the brain is desperate for an available emptiness to house its clutter, as a tone can only grow from a space of silence, lifted by inaudible echoes as birds are by the air inside their bones. So we reach down, although it cannot save us, to the hollows inside the body, to extend them into so many journeys into the world, so many words shelling the echo of absence onto the dry land.
>
> (33)

Simultaneously reaching back into the ordering structures of exemplary yet provocative male-authored texts and reaching down (and beyond order) into the nothingness of silence and space inside her female body, Waldrop hopes to tap the vigor latent in everyday language for use in a gender-balanced language that is "uncommon" now but need not always be so. The ambiguities of "shelling"—suggesting at once a military bombardment and the release of seed—crucially demonstrate the unsettling combination of destruction and creation necessary to this transformative process.

Violation and destruction of received orders are readily visible in the collage by Joan Retallack that appears on the cover of her 1995 collection *AFTERRIMAGES,* just as they are foregrounded within its pages. The small black-and-white image of the entire collage (a portion of which is enlarged in dusty-rose monochrome on the rest of the cover) presents antique illustrations that have not only been cut into fragments but also eaten away by vigorous hole-punching (see figure). Consequently, the entire collage might be read as a shelled landscape of representations in which Newtonian science (figured by a boy covering one eye and looking with the other through a telescope—the activity that caused Newton to "[suffer] . . . from an after-image of the sun"), traditional notions of masculine heroism ("La Liberté ou la Mort"), Eastern cultures (bits of Chinese and Arabic script), and Western gender roles (the stiff figure of the dairymaid, the more relaxed and empowered figure of the young astronomer whose hand rests on an armillary sphere modeling the solar system) are either being riddled with holes or exploding and bursting into flames.

Yet in neither the cover collage nor the poems themselves does Retallack's vision of a past in pieces emphasize despair or nostalgia, since, as with Waldrop, destruction is closely entwined with creation, and apparent disorder with meaningful order. Here again, earlier texts, readily broken apart and manipulated, are a generative presence. Certainly, however, Retallack's work carries the somber weight of a postwar consciousness; *AFTERRIMAGES* is clearly situated near the end of a century of cataclysmic wars and after the development of atomic weapons with power to destroy all life, all civilization. Read as *AFTER RIM AGES,* the title superimposed on the collage may position the writing as following after some decisive temporal boundary or shift. The postatomic context for *AFTERRIMAGES* is more directly signaled with the epigraph from Manhattan Project physicist Victor Weisskopff, who recalls that because of overlapping radio frequencies between the P.A. system at the Alamogordo blast and a local radio station, the first explosion of an atomic bomb was accompanied by a Tchaikovsky waltz. In addition to presenting an eerily ironic juxtaposition of different uses of human creative powers, this bizarre "accompaniment" of waltz and nuclear explosion positions the two within the same trajectory of human achievement, so that scientists' attainment of a sustained nuclear reaction is a historical afterimage of elegant ballroom choreography.[16] Perhaps at the same time, this epigraph positions twentieth-century mass culture (the radio broadcast) as itself a grotesque afterimage, a projection of Romantic traditions onto a world in which such anachronistic aesthetics are ludicrously and terrifyingly inappropriate. In contrast to the waltz with its regular rhythm, the bomb exists at the limits of human regulation: scientists tap the power of the atom; but once activated, the physical laws governing nuclear fission take over completely.

In her title sequence, Retallack uses chance procedures to adapt the order of earlier texts to the world of the 1990s, tossing thirteen paper clips onto each page of collage palimptext she had composed and then transcribing on the lower half of the page only those letters that appeared wholly within the boundaries of the clips. This compositional practice makes visible the possibility of nuclear annihilation; the lower parts of the pages on which the sparse alphabetic afterimages are scattered might well suggest the little that would remain after a nuclear holocaust. But neat dichotomies of wholeness versus fragmentation, plenitude versus emptiness, or fertility versus sterility are not sustained here any more than they are in the work of John Cage, whose central contribution to Western music—what Retallack terms a "paradigm shift"—is a release from binary divisions, particularly those between noise and music or sound and silence. Hence the fragments of a multilingual literary tradition that palimptextually compose so much of "Afterrimages" are not a string of tortured ironies.

They are precious and intriguing bits of language, elements of possibility whose meanings or potential for meaning are only enhanced by their fragmentariness and mutability.

Retallack's use of Chaucer can demonstrate.[17] In drawing upon Chaucer's texts—very like Waldrop using passages from Wittgenstein, Eddington, or Musil (and, one suspects, in deliberate contrast to T. S. Eliot's invocations of Chaucer in *The Waste Land*)—Retallack enacts a freedom to change—to reinterpret and rewrite—that conveys delighting appreciation, polyvalent possibility, and feminist critique. On the first page of "Afterrimages," where the idea of balance is prominent, she places two lines from *Troilus and Criseyde* that might describe virtuous balance in a woman: *"So reulith hire hir hertes gost withinne, / That though she bende, yeet she stant on roote"* (5). In Chaucer's text, however, this characterization reflects a series of perhaps groundless male projections: Pandarus, addressing Troilus, expresses what he imagines Troilus to be imagining about Criseyde's state in a meeting between them that Pandarus claims will shortly take place. A modern prose translation of the passage runs: "Perhaps you're thinking: 'Although it may be so that Nature would cause her to begin to have a kind of pity on my unhappiness, Disdain says, "No, you'll never overcome me!" The spirit in her heart so rules her inwardly that, although she may bend, she still stands firmly rooted. What use is this to help me?'" (49). Pandarus goes on to assure Troilus that these supposed imaginings are false and that in fact Criseyde is primed to give in to his wooing. Inserted into Retallack's text, the passage is at once a compelling bit of found aural and visual texture; a trace from a foundational text of English literary tradition that offers an unusually complex early portrait of a female character; a demonstration of how thoroughly mediated by ideology and patriarchal projection literary representations of women tend to be; and a showcase for some stereotypical expectations of womanly virtue. An exchange between Retallack and Waldrop in their published conversation sheds light on this last dimension. There, Retallack expresses her discomfort with the term "heart" (357). Waldrop concurs, explaining: "It may be because we are women, and the literary 'domain' of women used to be the emotions, the heart, the sentimental story or poem. We don't want to be defined—limited—this way" (359). Retallack adds: "Yes, there is that. But also more generally, there can be a sense that if you just feel something intensely enough—and this goes back to the unease with sincerity—that somehow it, ipso facto, has value of some kind, including truth value" (359). In its first appearance, then, the selection from Chaucer signals the distance between Retallack's aesthetic and one based primarily on emotional responsiveness, sincerity, or constancy.[18]

Alternate forms of precision invoked on the same page of "Afterrimages," scientific models and dictionary definitions, are perhaps better guarantors of value than intense feeling. But change is a governing principle of palimptext, so that they too are subject to mutation (for example, "specificcrystallineformoftaxonomiccategories"). Intriguingly, the chance operations Retallack performed on the text preserved *"e hir hert"*; the afterrimage of Chaucer's lines might speak to the near indelibility of the linkage of the female and feeling, or it might demonstrate that the experimentalist's transformation permits what is elementally valuable—here, the capability of loving or feeling—to be released from its less desirable associations.

Other fragments from Chaucer that appear in the poem—several from the Man of Law's tale and one especially well-known quotation from the Wife of Bath's prologue—also call attention to the subjugation of women in traditional gender roles: the expectation of virginal purity, marital fidelity, filial piety, uncomplaining endurance of suffering, and so forth. But Retallack's fragmentation, deformation, and recontextualization of these narratives demonstrates that we need no longer repeat these misogynist patterns. Simply appropriating and compressing a received line—"HEEREENDETHTHETALEOFTHE-MANOFLAWE"—yields a proclamation of the end of the tale of man of flaw, whose use of narrative for sadistic multiplication of a woman's sufferings need not be our law.

The cultural baggage associated with Chaucer is only part of the story here. In her manuscript "Silence and the Experimental Feminine," Retallack explains that "artists are artists because they have loved the work of artists before them; they spend their lives in conversation with the dead as well as the living. . . . The present is what we, in the urgency of the unprecedented, with the pressures of rapid-fire transformations all around us, make of the past" (ms. 8-9). Retallack's collage in "Afterrimages" of found pieces in many languages—Old Irish, Old English, Middle English, Latin, standard modern English, demotic English ("YO MAMA"), transcribed sounds ("schwoop"), and punning torquings of all these—is a palimptextual display of resources. As such, it stresses the openness of linguistic evolution and the vitality of evolving vernaculars (of which Chaucer's Middle English was one), as well as the somatic pleasures of seeing and speaking words. Old languages don't die, though we may recognize their vitality most readily in preserved literary texts or in etymological roots (*"she stant on roote"*) like those provided for "thicket." Retallack's lovingly irreverent, often humorous play with palimpsestic remains from these texts, with formulaic phrases, with individual words (as in "Lana: Please machine give piece of chow. / (*thanatoast*)") demonstrates the always available possibility of change. Language is endlessly malleable and resilient. The past is as present here as it was for Eliot, but unlike Eliot, Retallack focuses on using its mongrelized, multilingual remains to provoke something new.

The book's title itself inventively disrupts received arrangements of language, interjecting an extra *r* into the word "afterimages." "What a shock!" Randolph Healy exclaims in an insightful review: "A displaced letter in the middle of an established order. Words became highly unstable, fee/free, a single mutation launching them into an entirely different semantic field. . . . The reader was free to enlarge the scope of the poem in almost any direction by following such leads in whatever way they wish. Freed by just one letter. Her own initial" ("Eighteenth Letter"). The doubling of the *r*, an afterimage of that letter, introduces the word "err" and the concept of erring not only as going wrong and astray but also as the exploratory motion of rambling or straying. The verso side of the title page, printed as if it were a reversed transparency, adds further linguistic mutations, which when unreversed would read: "ALTERRIMAGES / AFTEARTHOUGHTS / AFTER/ORS / AFTERMATH." (The triangular image of that text then appears in afterimage on the next page, containing four epigraphs.) Such transformations generate semantic polyphony with implications at once exciting and sobering; this particular series of linguistic permutations brings to the fore change and alteration, alterity, use of ear and mind, intellectually substantial art or theories of art, alternative prospects, and ores for prospecting, but it also suggests opportunities missed or things considered too late and the unpleasant consequences of what came before.

The top portions of the pages of "Afterrimages," which are palimptextual arrangements of fragments that have meaning for Retallack, acknowledge both the pleasures and the burdens of her position of afterness, especially of literary and linguistic belatedness and of postatomic insecurity. In not using the fragments to shore up old ruins, but instead subjecting her collage text to further decimation and transformation by chance procedures, she deliberately generates a further layer of afterrimage. Doing so involves a complex interaction of design and disorder. As N. Katherine Hayles has observed, the Cagean notion of chance procedures itself involves an oxymoronic combination of randomness and intention, of something which exceeds or escapes our designs on the one hand and a process by which we put our designs into effect on the other. What Cage referred to as "purposeful purposelessness" constitutes, Hayles notes, a "subversive intentionality" (231). These phrases capture the dynamics of Retallack's compositional procedure involving paper clips, a procedure that is subtractive, like the optical process of afterimaging

described at the beginning of the text in "Color Plate 25." But paradoxically, it is with the addition of a chance-generated afterimage that each page gains a kind of symmetrical order, though one in which text is mirrored more by its absence than by its repetition.

The breakdown of words into component letters that results from this "purposeful purposelessness" sometimes makes visible alphabetic patterns one would overlook when processing letter-clumps as words. Such exposure of patterning has an ethical (what Retallack calls "poethical") dimension: as the predominant blank spaces call attention to the framing silence or space within which alphabetic sounds or letters acquire meaning, individual letters or letter combinations become freshly visible and audible. Looking to see where the afterrrimages came from in the text, we attend anew to the top section of each page, and in Retallack's view, "What brings art to life, what makes life—even the most difficult life—worth living, is a quality of sustained attention" ("Silence and the Experimental Feminine" ms. 2).

Even if the afterrimage portions of these pages suggest the deeply frightening, almost unimaginable aftermath of an atomic blast, at the same time these portions of the text carry an extremely positive valence, as prompts-to-attention and (a closely related phenomenon) as examples of "radical explorations into silence—the currently unintelligible—in which our future may make sense" (":RE:THINKING:" 358). Sometimes no letters are preserved and only silence is produced—a silence that we have to attend to since it reverberates with the elimination of particular sounds. At other times, recognizable phrases acquire surprising resonance through chance selection, as already noted with the surprising preservation of *e hir hert* in the first poem. My favorite of these astonishing patterns occurs when a passage containing two parenthetic references to philosophical tradition—

> (see a pre-Socratic on fire in the mind)
>   nice being out here in the sun
>   (or St. Augustine on time)

—yields an invitation to appreciate a pleasing pattern of letters accessible to anyone, not just those familiar with Heraclitus and Augustine:

> (see   i in e
>   in   e in
>   o
>   (7)

The pattern, moreover, seems an affirmation of connectedness, an instruction to appreciate apparently different elements as in fact existing "in" each other.

Another afterrimage where the unintelligible yields the surprising but polyphonically legible is one in which the only marks on the blank space read "s[ ]ent" (21).

This brings to mind a Sapphic fragment, something already alluded to and all but named in the top portion of the preceding page:

```
Saph [. . . . . . . . . . . . . . . . . . .]gment
UU-- - - -- - - - - -UU- -?
(now she shines among Lyd . . . wom. . . .
    . . . . . .)?
```

The pseudo-Sapphic remnant generated by Retallack's chance procedures reminds us that the processes that limited the preservation of Sappho's work (both social and natural) still operate and are likely to shape the literary record we transmit into the future. "S[]ent," moreover, suggests "sent" and "silent" (among other possibilities), both of which speak to the dynamics of chance operations here: text becomes silence and silence is rendered audible, while chance sometimes produces selections so readily meaningful that they appear "sent" by some higher power. Through the application of chance procedures, in Retallack's palimptext, regulation and disorder, determinacy and indeterminacy emerge as virtually indistinguishable.

"Icarus FFFFFalling," the second sequence in Retallack's *AFTERRIMAGES,* continues the bifurcated page format of "Afterrimages," but in this text the symmetry does not result from repeating on the bottom half of the page a chance-generated version of the palimptext that appears above. With thematic impact, Retallack shapes this twentieth-century afterrimage of Icarus's fall to form a picture of progressive diminishment—a falling away in perspective space—and that diminution is generated simply by a progressive reduction in the number of lines. After an eccentric first page, each of the subsequent nineteen pages has either the same number of or fewer lines than the page before, and on each page, the same number of lines appear above and, in afterimage, below the bifurcating line of dots.[19] Above the horizontal midline, the text is single-spaced, and below it is double-spaced (signaling the several realms within which Icarus's tale takes place—air and land, or air and sea? registering the transformative character of any afterimage?). In both halves the right and left margins are justified to generate a rectangular block of text, and since the line-and page-breaks seem arbitrary, the text invites reading as continuous—indeed propulsively driven (or gravitationally propelled)—prose.

The earlier texts recognizable as palimpsestic sources in this poem are versions of the tale of Icarus, most notably Ovid's telling of that tale in *Metamorphoses,* though versions by W. H. Auden, William Carlos Williams, and Muriel Rukeyser also contribute. But the "source texts" here are only a point of departure, as is suggested by Retallack's introductory acknowledgment of assistance from those who moved outward into the public realm to flesh out their understanding of a work of literature:

"Thanks to the students in my August 1987 Language & Thinking workshop at Bard College, who when asked to go out and photograph Icarus falling found him everywhere" (36). Provoked by her students' discoveries, Retallack turns her attention (and ours) to the omnipresence of young men's reenactment of the Icarus story, and to the cultural forces determining that reenactment.

"Icarus FFFFFalling," then, is in one sense grounded in the ordering form of a well-known narrative, one portraying a father who pushes his son to take risks even while warning him to be careful, and a son who discovers the exhilaration of risk-taking, goes too high, and consequently plummets into the sea and drowns. It provides no coherent recounting of that story, but fragments of Ovid's telling, both in Latin and in English, are interspersed throughout Retallack's palimptext, and the opening page would seem to acknowledge Ovid's story as in some way foundational. That page presents a facing-page translation of the beginning of Ovid's narrative, where the English printed on the right is a kind of afterrimage of the Latin on the left, providing what Retallack in "Afterrimages" calls a "delicious asymmetry of sight and sound" (6). Overlaid on (falling through?) the center of the facing-page translation, and partly covering it, is a slightly curved column of disjunctive text whose short lines incorporate Latin, pig-Latin, French, and English. Many of these fragments, besides highlighting linguistic translation and metamorphosis, invoke some kind of up or down motion that we might associate with Icarus's flight and fall—for example, "dark islands up light/appetizers cheese dip" (37). However, as the surprise of that last punning phrase indicates, Ovid's narrative is a pattern from which to spin off—not the text's center, but a complex of relations and interactions launching its numerous divagations.

Perhaps the best figure for describing the complex organization of this palimptext, its way of re-forming old orders for the present, is fractal form. Fractals are "complex symmetrical forms that repeat themselves across every available scale but always with variations that never resolve at any scale into simpler forms" (Hayles 233). In literature, it may not be possible to repeat anything at *every* possible scale, but certainly "Icarus FFFFFalling" has a quality of self-similarity in providing innumerable reenactments of the Icarus pattern at various scales, whether these be social (individual, familial, regional, national, etcetera) or textual (letter, phoneme, word, phrase, clause, sentence, paragraph, page or succession of pages, and story).

From multiple perspectives and on constantly shifting scales, "Icarus FFFFFalling" exposes the ways in which Western society, in its glorification of male athleticism, forces young men to undertake terrible risks, manipulates them into being "ready to die for theher thefamily thetribe therace thenation thelaw the onthemoney big idea" (51). The father's desire to have his son perform his own understanding of masculine freedom has been so thoroughly normalized by social codes that both parties are blinded to the dangers involved:

> father instructs son on rules of flight sky Walker Matt Jack George Ethan Gabe Josh the the fixes strange wings on boys shoulders *laeva parte Samos* not goodbye forever or a suicide note just what's to be expected on every wall on every scrap of paper on every matchbox

(38)

Denaturalizing such expectations, Retallack underscores the price paid for our aspirations: the brilliant flash of light made by the first atomic bomb is rendered an afterrimage—that is, a fractal self-similarity on another scale—not just of other military displays ("Mussolini said a bomb exploding in the desert is like a rose bursting into bloom" [47]) but also of the flash made by Icarus falling ("you see a flash of light you hear a splash" [40]). The father's quest rehearses various socially approved ways adult males attempt to assert control and dominance: "*caelum certe* defacto anon unknown über-object always to prepare them for WARS BLASTS RAYS VECTORS VALENCES PROCLIVITIES TROPISMS developing tastes for horror shut in by land'nsea UNDER SOCIAL CONSTRUCTION" (38). "Icarus FFFFFalling" presents Daedalus's compulsion to return to his homeland as an individualized manifestation of ideologies of nationalism that encourage war and colonial expansion. Thus while at one point he is called "Dead-o-Lust" (overdosed on testosterone, perhaps?), the father's eroticism appears to have no object beyond the expansion of his own powers. This suggestion of onanistic egotism is reinforced by the verbal similarity of *penis* and *pennis,* Latin for the feathers with which the famous inventor constructs the wings that extend his reach. The absence of the mother from Icarus's tale ("where is I's mother not that she or any other . . . could save him now" [43]) and her submission to or complicity in the patriarchal order propelling its events constitute another thematic formation recurring in multiple scales in Retallack's poem. Woman's collusion with the system might be read in the lists of middle-American foods provided for a family reunion, as in the "furtiva lacrimosa mother" who, it seems, doesn't dare even to weep openly for the loss of her son.

Even the initial letter of Icarus's name itself propels the poem toward other enactments of the same structuring dynamics. It provides a link to stories of others whose names begin with *I,* including Isaac (another horrifying example of patriarchy's readiness to sacrifice its sons) and Iphis (whose father ordered her put to death at birth because she was not a boy, but who grew up passing as a boy, and in Ovid's story is ever-so-fortunately transformed into one). The letter *I* as first-person pronoun also highlights cultural obsessions with personal identity: focus on *I,* that "clever one-eyed mechanical monster," makes one particularly susceptible to consumer hype, fostering the need for accoutrements of acceptable gender identity—itself another level of enactment for the fractal pattern of this palimptext.

Because of the fractal structure in which it is manipulated, Ovid's narrative does not function as a containing form; what is most striking in the experience of reading "Icarus FFFFFalling" is the simultaneity of its multiple concerns and reenactments, the startling complexity of its polyphony. Pulsing with verbal energy, tumbling pell-mell without punctuation or transition from the Beatles to the Sex Pistols to Mozart to "Palistrami" (a fast-food version of Palestrina), from Reebok sports equipment to pop art to Mendelian genetics, from Socrates to Freud to an immigrant fresh off the boat entering the land of "Anglo-Terror," from Malcolm X to the X chromosome to Alamogordo, the kaleidoscopic text actively discourages an untangling of its elements. Instead, it propels us into the densest possible din of contemporary culture, which includes past culture as well, where Icarus is perpetually falling. A sample:

> perfect palmer his sweet penisship de scribed on de texticular nite you did not withhold your son from me bless you Abe babe or Malcolm ex-ladies man nights they serve baked beans 'n fries modesta peduncle punch errasty Hells Proverbs live from hell EXTERIOR WASH WAX WAYNE ENTER RIGHT EXIT LEFT THANK YOU HAVE A NICE stamp out fires with Morris dances bird he soar too high he soar on his own wingding laws dis courage to think of other order exorcise the male the sport of archery as
>
> · · · · ·
>
> Zeno's arrows fly in no time

(46)

Rhythmic and highly charged, the "buzzing noise" of this richly varied palimptext doesn't add up to one chorus or settle into one tune—but it has nonetheless the elegant design of an infinitely complex fractal geometry.

Whatever its infinite potentialities might be in disclosing more and more Icarus material, the poem moves toward silence, since Retallack has chosen to replicate in the poem's appearance something like Daedalus's view of Icarus's fall—a progressive disappearance into nothingness. The text dwindles as Icarus would appear to diminish as he fell away. On the last page, there are no words above the dots and only two below: "fall over." These follow from the text on the preceding page, but characteristically the syntax moves in several directions at once, precluding any single understanding even of their syntactic function. Thus even the visual closing off of the text functions as open-ended and ongoing. Backing up, one reads, "just trying on the sadness of the verb to be we hope is not too ffffffallen to [page turn and line of dots] / fall over" (55-56). In one reading, the concluding line announces the end of the young man's fall: it's over. It also suggests he will and is falling over again. Additionally, "fall over" might suggest tripping over obstacles, whether the "sadness of the verb to be" or the glorification of aggressive athleticism. From another perspective, the two words reenact the down and up combination of the first page, since the preposition "over" suggests movement above something, while "fall" denotes descent. Read that way—as at once a downward and upward motion— *falling over* becomes an encompassing figure for the seemingly endless levels on which gender is constantly being constructed and the scales on which its impact is manifest, as so effectively conveyed in the intertextual language of this fractal poem.

For Retallack, as for Waldrop, the challenging quest for alternatives to the "disastrous logics of a purely masculine power" requires what Retallack calls the "experimental feminine." It is because they refuse to exclude the (traditionally feminine) unintelligible, incoherent, illogical, and inconsistent that "feminine" approaches to experimental form are potentially adequate to the necessarily confusing dimensions of the truly contemporary. But unintelligibility, if it is to remain distinct from incomprehensibility, needs some modicum of structure, design, regulation. This is one motivation behind their shared interest in imposing pattern and in using earlier texts to do so. Via skillful and skillfully varied use of palimpsestic layerings from previous texts, Waldrop and Retallack achieve exemplary success in generating "fields of pattern-bounded unpredictability" through which we may, without overwhelming disorientation, orient ourselves anew, "keeping imaginative intelligence active amidst the logical rubble" ("Silence and the Experimental Feminine" ms. 8).

Notes

1. See "Conversation" 359-63 for discussion between Retallack and Waldrop of masculine and feminine modes of writing. Both avoid essentialist identification of masculine and feminine with male and female person; both see language as woven from masculine and feminine elements; and both signal a desire to use their own work to awaken us to the intuitive logics, the "polyphonic associations and resonances" associated with the feminine and (though they don't use this phrase) the Kristevan semiotic.

2. This essay, along with the other essays by Retallack cited here, will be published in *The Poethical*

Wager, forthcoming from the University of California Press in fall 2001.

3. Steven R. Evans's excellent entry on Waldrop in the *Dictionary of Literary Biography* pointed me to her sources, though Evans refers with slight inaccuracy to "a textbook of quantum physics from the 1930s" (295).

4. Discussing the similar construction of *Reproduction of Profiles,* Evans notes that the sources seem at first glance "diametrically opposed," and that "by tracing two cognate structures, the logical (Wittgenstein) and the erotic (Kafka), to their common fulcrum in the subject's desire to know, Waldrop throws a communicating wire between two areas of human endeavor that are often kept at a tidy distance" (294).

5. Biographical similarities may also contribute to Waldrop's attraction to the work of Musil, who is among her favorite authors, and Wittgenstein. For instance, it seems likely that Wittgenstein and Musil, being Austrians who often thought of themselves as Germans or Europeans (Luft 15), experienced something close to Waldrop's expatriate's sense of living between languages and cultures.

6. According to biographer Brian McGuinness, Wittgenstein "hardly knew the names of the writers [Ludwig von] Ficker selected for his benefaction in 1914: Musil with whom he has often been compared he probably never read" (37).

7. Evans sensibly links Waldrop's rejection of "the concept of a full and homogeneous center" and her interest in the "empty middle" to her experience growing up in Germany during World War II, to the fact of the concentration camps and their discrediting of the metaphysical concepts used to legitimate fascism (287).

8. Waldrop's attribution is not quite accurate; Eddington, in making this statement, attributes it originally to Sir William Bragg (*The Nature of the Physical World* 194).

9. Eddington, writing with characteristic humor, explains: "The classical conception of gravitation is based on Newton's account of what happened; but it is time to hear what the apple had to say. The apple with the usual egotism of an observer deemed itself to be at rest; looking down it saw the various terrestrial objects including Newton rushing upwards with accelerated velocity to meet it. Does it invent a mysterious agency or tug to account for their conduct? No; it points out that the cause of their acceleration is quite evident. Newton is being hammered by the molecules of the ground underneath him. . . . Newton had to

postulate a mysterious invisible force pulling the apple down; the apple can point to an evident cause propelling Newton up" (115).

10. The dynamic I am outlining is similar to the one Marjorie Perloff observes: noting that Waldrop in *Reproduction of Profiles* shows a greater interest than the Wittgenstein of *Philosophical Investigations* in "the interactive deployment of these language games, in the way language games are related to gender and power," Perloff asserts, "The quest is to escape the imposition of someone else's logic, even someone as close to her own sensibility as Wittgenstein" (208-9). I would shift the emphasis, to claim that such an escape has been achieved, in a relationship of fruitfully ambivalent intimacy. While Perloff characterizes the poems of *Reproduction* as "Wittgenstein parodies" written from a feminist perspective, Jonathan Monroe's more qualified assertion that Waldrop is in "seriously parodic dialogue with Wittgenstein" seems to me more accurate (133).

11. The phrase "at once with and against" appears in Monroe's excellent essay "Syntextural Investigations" (133) as part of his nuanced analysis of Waldrop's stance toward Wittgenstein in *The Reproduction of Profiles*.

12. In characterizing an "erotics of syntax" in Waldrop's *Profiles*, Monroe calls attention to Waldrop's "staging of binaries for the purpose of undoing them in a provisional union that (happily) dissolves into reassertion of difference and back again" (135).

13. Although its palimpsestic character is not uniform, the volume gains formal unification through the similar construction of its parts—series of brief prose poems written in complete propositional sentences—which in turn reflects their common project. That cohering project (in *Reproduction of Profiles* as well as *Lawn of Excluded Middle*) developed partly in response to Wittgenstein, since Waldrop experienced the extreme closure of his propositional writing as a challenge to her usual practice of open forms and grammatically incomplete units: "I tried to work with this challenge, accept the complete sentence (most of the time) and try to subvert its closure and logic from the inside, by constantly sliding between frames of reference. I especially brought the female body in and set into play the old gender archetypes of logic and mind being 'male,' whereas 'female' designates the illogical: emotion, body, matter. Again, I hope that the constant sliding challenges these categories" ("Thinking of Follows" 613).

14. A list of entries from *Philosophical Investigations* that appear elsewhere in the palimpsest of the title series would include in section 3, #439; section 4, #414; section 5, #435; section 8, #474; section 9, #543; section 13, #546; section 14, #549; section 15, #548; section 16, notes on the page containing entries 548-51; section 20, #618 and #621; section 21, 589; section 22, #435 and #673; section 25, entries 454-57. If I've not overlooked text from individual entries in the final sections of "Lawn," that would mean the series replicates the structure I see in the volume as a whole (introduced below), wherein palimpsestic traces of preexistent texts diminish toward the end.

15. Even the title "The Perplexing Habit of Falling," which refers in part to the misogynist Biblical tale of the Fall and to early conceptions of a flat world sailors might fall off, alludes most directly to Eddington's discussion of the law of gravity and the inadequacy of Newtonian physics. The titles of the three series contained there—"The Attraction of the Ground," "Mass, Momentum, Stress," and "Accelerating Frame"—also refer to physics.

16. I have followed Retallack in adding an extra *r* when referring to the afterrimages constructed in the text; I hope such suggestively distorting repetition (evoking terra, terror, err, and so on) will signal the complex and multiple relations to what came before evident in what comes after.

17. As this essay was going to press, Ann Vickery's *Leaving Lines of Gender*, which contains an excellent discussion of *AFTERRIMAGES*, became available. In an analysis complementary to my own, Vickery considers Retallack's use of fragments from *The Canterbury Tales* in the title sequence (175-76).

18. Of course, this is not to suggest that Retallack devalues emotional responsiveness or unsentimentalized passion—quite the contrary.

19. The numbers of lines per half page are as follows: 11, 10, 9, 9, 8, 8, 7, 7, 7, 5, 5, 4, 3, 3, 3, 3, 2, 1, and on the last page a truncated line of text appears below the dividing line with nothing above.

Works Cited

Chaucer, Geoffrey. *Troilus and Criseyde*. Trans. Barry Windeatt. Oxford: Oxford UP, 1998.

Conte, Joseph. *Unending Design: The Forms of Postmodern Poetry*. Ithaca, NY: Cornell UP, 1991.

Davidson, Michael. *Ghostlier Demarcations: Modern Poetry and the Material Word*. Berkeley: U of California P, 1997.

Eddington, A. S. *The Nature of the Physical World*. New York: Macmillan, 1929.

Evans, Steven R. "Rosmarie Waldrop." *DLB* [*Dictionary of Literary Biography*] Fifth Ser. Vol. 169. Detroit: Gale Research, 1996. 284-96.

Hayles, N. Katherine. "Chance Operations: Cagean Paradox and Contemporary Science." *John Cage: Composed in America*. Ed. Marjorie Perloff and Charles Junkerman. Chicago: U of Chicago P, 1994. 226-41.

Healy, Randolph. "The Eighteenth Letter." Online in *LYNX*. http://www.bath.ac.uk/%7eexxdgdc/lynx/lynx138.html.

Lehman, David, ed. *Ecstatic Occasions, Expedient Forms: 65 Leading Contemporary Poets Select and Comment on Their Poems*. New York: Macmillan, 1987.

Luft, David S. *Robert Musil and the Crisis of European Culture, 1880-1942*. Berkeley: U of California P, 1980.

McGuinness, Brian. *Wittgenstein, a Life: Young Ludwig, 1889-1921*. Berkeley: U of California P, 1988.

Monroe, Jonathan. "Syntextural Investigations." *Diacritics* 26.3-4 (1996): 126-41.

Musil, Robert. "The Perfecting of a Love." 1911. Trans. Eithne Wilkins and Ernst Kaiser. *Selected Writings*. Ed. Burton Pike. New York: Continuum, 1986. 179-222.

Perloff, Marjorie. *Wittgenstein's Ladder: Poetic Language and the Strangeness of the Ordinary*. Chicago: U of Chicago P, 1996.

Retallack, Joan. *AFTERRIMAGES*. Hanover, NH: Wesleyan-UP of New England, 1995.

———. "Poethics of a Complex Realism." *John Cage: Composed in America*. Ed. Marjorie Perloff and Charles Junkerman. Chicago: U of Chicago P, 1994. 242-73.

———. ":RE:THINKING:LITERARY:FEMINISM: (*three essays onto shaky grounds*)." *Feminist Measures: Soundings in Poetry and Theory*. Ed. Lynn Keller and Cristanne Miller. Ann Arbor: U of Michigan P, 1994. 344-77.

———. "Silence and the Experimental Feminine." Unpublished essay, 1999.

Vickery, Ann. *Leaving Lines of Gender: A Feminist Genealogy of Language Writing*. Hanover, NH: Wesleyan-UP of New England, 2000.

Waldrop, Rosmarie. "Alarms & Excursions." *The Politics of Poetic Form: Poetry and Public Policy*. Ed. Charles Bernstein. New York: Roof, 1990. 45-72.

———. "A Conversation with Rosmarie Waldrop." Conducted by Joan Retallack. *Contemporary Literature* 40 (1999): 329-77.

———. "Form and Discontent." *Diacritics* 26.3-4 (1996): 54-62.

———. "An Interview with Rosmarie Waldrop." Conducted by Edward Foster. *Talisman* 6 (1991): 27-39.

———. *Lawn of Excluded Middle*. Providence, RI: Tender Buttons, 1993.

———. "Rosmarie Waldrop." *Contemporary Authors Autobiographical Series*. Vol. 30. Detroit: Gale Research, 1999. 297-314.

———. "Rosmarie Waldrop." *L=A=N=G=U=A=G=E* 1.3 (1978). N. pag.

———. "Thinking of Follows." *Moving Borders: Three Decades of Innovative Writing by Women*. Ed. Mary Margaret Sloan. Jersey City, NJ: Talisman House, 1998. 609-17.

Wittgenstein, Ludwig. *Philosophical Investigations*. 1953. Trans. G. E. M. Anscombe. New York: Macmillan, 1968.

Lynn Keller (essay date 2001)

SOURCE: Keller, Lynn. "'Just one of / the girls:—/ normal in the extreme': Experimentalists-To-Be Starting Out in the 1960s." *differences* 12, no. 2 (2001): 63-9.

[*In the following essay, Keller discusses the development of Waldrop's poetic techniques in relation to her biography and her concerns with respect to the power of language and gender issues.*]

Rosmarie Waldrop's confrontations with the extreme began well before the 1960s. Born in Germany in 1935, she experienced what she called "the first drastic change of [her] world" in the first bombing attack she survived, in February of 1943. The second drastic change, in which language played a central role, occurred in 1945: "'Our leader' turned into 'the criminal,' 'the enemy' into 'Amis,' 'surrender' into 'liberation'" ("Rosmarie Waldrop" *Contemporary Authors* 298). It is no wonder Waldrop brought to even her earliest work a preoccupation with the ways language constructs reality. And no wonder she has often asserted that discontinuity is, for her, a natural state; it is the way she sees the world. Concerns about gender in her work, though evident from the start, are entangled with questions of language and perceptual experience. Thus, her early poem **"And how do your see yourself, Mrs. Waldrop?"**—which is in some ways analogous to Fraser's poem contemplating her legs—acknowledges the "queer" experience of looking down at one's unglamorous body ("bulging / breasts heavy belly dwarfed legs"), but focuses more on the equally strange experience of the way a mirrored reflection calls into question the material substance of the body itself: "the way my body / is empty in its skin" (*Aggressive Ways* [*The Aggressive Ways of The Casual Stranger*] 5). Steve Evans has rightly linked Waldrop's career-long preoccupation with the empty middle to her early confrontation with the historical fact of the concentration camps (287). Clearly, the social and cultural contexts for her work of the sixties overlap only partially with those of Fraser and Howe.

Waldrop emigrated to the U.S. late in 1958, just on the eve of the anthology wars. Coming to the University of Michigan, where her new husband, Keith Waldrop, was a graduate student (she had met Keith in Germany in 1954), she was part of a community of writers that defied the configurations associated with those literary hostilities. For the circle of artists gathered around Keith in Ann Arbor included none other than Donald Hall (of Pack, Simpson, and Hall fame), along with W. D. Snodgrass and X. J. Kennedy, as well as more New American and wildly Dadaist types. Keith and his co-editors James Camp and Don Hope, who produced the magazine *Burning Deck* between 1962 and 1965, were determinedly eclectic. The Waldrops, in their introduction to *A Century in Two Decades: A Burning Deck Anthology,* which came out in 1982, recall that while "[t]he two most widely noted anthologies of the time, both representing the period 1945-1960, contain not a single poet in common . . . *Burning Deck* (the magazine) disregarded this split, printing and reviewing a spread of poets wide enough that on occasion an author would complain of being published in such un-programmatic company" (n. pag.). When Burning Deck press came to life in the early seventies, under the joint editorship of Keith and Rosmarie Waldrop, this nonpartisan eclecticism remained, although the press took particular interest in experimental work.

Experimentalism was a subject on which Rosmarie Waldrop was richly informed, since the doctoral dissertation she completed in 1966 analyzed and categorized the various experimental or rule-breaking strategies with which twentieth-century poets have responded to their dissatisfaction with language. With a few exceptions, the poetry she drew upon for her examples was French and German. Waldrop's poetic models, then, were less predominantly anglophone than was the case for her American-born contemporaries Howe and Fraser. Waldrop's literary interest in the fragment, for instance, came first from the German Romantics and was later reinforced by translating Edmond Jabès. In addition, she occupies a linguistic and national betweenness that neither Howe nor Fraser could share—that of being between German and English. Waldrop has characterized herself as "irredeemably between cultures," a situation that recent work like *A Key Into the Language of America* explores. The title of Waldrop's Random House collection, *The Aggressive Ways of the Casual Stranger,* registers her anxieties about being seen as an

aggressive interloper into English, even though by the mid-sixties she was sufficiently removed from German to have acquired an American accent in her native tongue. Her 1967 chapbook *A Dark Octave* concludes with a poem titled **"Between"** (which appeared also in *Aggressive Ways*) that explores her situation of being "not quite at home on either side of the Atlantic." This homelessness has its compensating benefits in that comfort is exchanged for consciousness: "a home makes you forget / unaware / where you are."[1] In her in-between space, however, figured as the ocean or the liquid of a glass window where she is "touched on all sides," she is "aware" of being nowhere. Perhaps echoing the psalmist who teaches that the meek shall inherit the earth, Waldrop ends by proclaiming the large and varied territory opened to her by her odd, amphibious state: "a creature with gills and lungs / I live in shallow water / but / when it rains / I inherit the land" (*Aggressive Ways* 15-16).

Suggesting a similar benefit in awareness, Waldrop has said that her consciousness of not belonging in any language "saved me the illusion of being master of language. I enter it at a skewed angle, through the fissures, the slight difference. I do not 'use' the language. I interact with it" ("Thinking of Follows" 611). These are the kind of statements we would expect from a linguistically innovative poet. But in the 1960s Waldrop's practice had not caught up with her theory; the experimentalism she studied had yet to find much outlet in her own work. This is particularly true of the poems in the first section of *Aggressive Ways*—many of which appeared in her 1970 collection from Perishable Press, *Spring is a Season And Nothing Else*—that, like Howe's and Fraser's early poems, are representationally focused on women's experience, on gendered identity, and on intimate male-female interaction. In their exploration of topics like depression, menstruation, house cleaning, and insomnia, they suggest the impact of the confessional movement, particularly of Plath and Anne Sexton. Influenced by Creeley as well (and by the labor of handsetting type), Waldrop's poems are considerably more compressed than mainstream confessional work; hers are generally in short, free-verse lines usually broken between syntactic units, although the versions in *Aggressive Ways* are often more pared down than the earlier published versions were.

"Confession to Settle a Curse" is reasonably typical of this early poetry of personal statement: it is a deeply angry poem about damage done by the speaker's mother, who "had to lock / everything that can be locked" and who let her daughter know what trouble it was to be bothered all the time by a girl wanting things (scissors, stationary, a coat) stored in locked containers. The poem ends, "I've been bound / made fast / locked / by the key witch / but a small / winner / I'm not / in turn locking / a child / in my arms" [26-27]. Recalling

Fraser's "lyric vise," the word *locks* appears in connection with a prescribed pattern expected of women within heterosexual partnership—in this case, the expectation of motherhood, which Waldrop's apparently autobiographical speaker refuses.[2]

Where Howe and Fraser came to a more fragmented and disjointed art partly through the experience of being mothers, Waldrop's first experiments with collage poetics were, she said, prompted by a desire to escape her mother's control. Currently a master of what she has termed "gap gardening," Waldrop has testified that she first attempted the disjunctions of collage to "get away from writing poems about my overwhelming mother": "I felt I needed to do something 'objective' that would get me out of myself. I took books off the shelf, selected maybe one word from every page or a phrase from every tenth page, and tried to work these into structures" ("Thinking of Follows" 614). Releasing herself from the constraints of conventional lyric did not in fact liberate Waldrop from her preoccupations with her mother. But by relinquishing the representational imperative she seems to have associated with lyric, she was able to find forms of writing in which her mother would not be a controlling, focal presence.[3] Thus, Waldrop goes on to say of those early collage poems, "But when I looked at them a while later: they were still about my mother. . . . This was a revelation—and a liberation. I realized that subject matter is not something to worry about. Your concerns and obsessions will surface no matter what you do. This frees you to work on the form, which is all one can work on consciously" ("Thinking of Follows" 614-15).

"Working on form" seems to have been what all three of the poets I have been discussing wanted to do more and more after the 1960s—not, ultimately, to escape their obsessions and their political concerns, but to develop them differently. I have proposed that the discomforting and alienating betweennesses fostered by their cultural moment, with its tensions between normalcy and extremity, and their not being at home on either side of a number of divides, made these women feel what Fraser speaks of as "the *necessity* behind the pursuit of innovation" (*Translating* [*Translating The Unspeakable: Poetry and The Innovative Necessity*] 3). Beginning in the early seventies, each demonstrated a compulsion to imagine uses of language "that could take [them] beyond the familiar and the well-digested" (Fraser, *Translating* 3). Having begun as gender-conscious poets whose work was concerned with personal relationships and especially the possibility of male/female communications, each in her own way has maintained that focus—but achieved it often as a trait within form, a process enacted within language itself.[4] Experiences of conflicted, precarious, or undecided social and aesthetic positioning pushed them increasingly to explore the betweennesses in and of language.

Waldrop, when ruminating recently about "collage, the splice of life," perhaps spoke for the female experimentalists of her generation: "It is a way of getting out of myself. Into what? An interaction, a dialog with language, with a whole net of earlier and concurrent texts. Relation. Between" ("Rosmarie Waldrop" *Contemporary Authors* 311).

Notes

1. The developing economy of Waldrop's writing is evident if one compares these lines as they appear in *The Aggressive Ways of the Casual Stranger*—"a home makes you forget / unaware / where you are / unless you'd like / to be some other place"—with their earlier appearance in *A Dark Octave*: "a home makes you forget all others / and you aren't aware of where you are / or if you are it is because you think / you'd like to be some other place."

2. Waldrop's decision not to have children also meant that she could enter fully into an editorial, and sometimes a compositional, partnership with her husband. All three women discussed here married writers; the Waldrops' marriage is the only one that lasted.

3. One might speculate that her orderly mother's legacy is evident in Waldrop's fascination with system and regulation even in her most experimental work, a topic I discuss in "'Nothing, for a woman, is worth trying.'"

4. Waldrop's early preoccupation with communication between men and women is particularly well demonstrated in the thirty-eight-part series that closes *The Aggressive Ways of the Casual Stranger*, "As If We Didn't Have to Talk." Far less conventional than the work in the two preceding sections of the volume, it was written in the early 1970s.

Works Cited

Evans, Steven R. "Rosmarie Waldrop." *Dictionary of Literary Biography 169: American Poets Since World War II*. Detroit: Gale Research, 1996: 284-97.

Fraser, Kathleen. *Translating the Unspeakable: Poetry and the Innovative Necessity*. Tuscaloosa: U of Alabama P, 1999.

Waldrop, Keith, and Rosmarie Waldrop. *A Century in Two Decades: A Burning Deck Anthology*. Providence: Burning Deck, 1982.

Waldrop, Rosmarie. *The Aggressive Ways of the Casual Stranger*. New York: Random, 1972.

———. "A Conversation with Rosmarie Waldrop." Conducted by Joan Retallack. *Contemporary Literature* 40 (1999): 329-77.

————. "Rosmarie Waldrop." *Contemporary Authors Autobiographical Series.* Vol. 30. Detroit: Gale Research, 1999: 297-314.

————. "Thinking of Follows." *Moving Borders: Three Decades of Innovative Writing by Women.* Ed. Mary Margaret Sloan. Jersey City: Talisman, 1997. 609-17.

————. *A Key Into the Language of America.* New York: New Directions, 1994.

————. *Spring Is a Season and Nothing Else.* Mount Horeb: Perishable, 1970.

————. *A Dark Octave.* Durham: Burning Deck, 1967.

Lynn Keller (essay date 2002)

SOURCE: Keller, Lynn. "'Nothing, for a Woman, is Worth Trying': A Key into the Rules of Rosmarie Waldrop's Experimentalism." In *We Who Love to Be Astonished: Experimental Women's Writing and Performance Poetics,* edited by Laura Hinton and Cynthia Hogue, pp. 103-15. Tuscaloosa, Ala.: University of Alabama Press, 2002.

[*In the following essay, Keller explores the theory behind Waldrop's experimental poetry, which the critic describes as a "paradoxical attraction at once to system and to deviancy."*]

Rosmarie Waldrop's early thinking about poetic experimentalism is documented in the doctoral dissertation she wrote in the mid-1960s and published in The Hague (Mouton & Co.) in 1971 with the inquiring title *Against Language?* It is, as the lengthy subtitle announces, a study of *'dissatisfaction with language' as theme and as impulse toward experiments in twentieth century poetry.* Analyzing how twentieth-century poets, mostly from Germany and France, try to change language, this dissertation systematically presents the devices with which western poets break the rules of language use. In the introductory chapter, Waldrop identifies three types of discontent with language, each of which generates particular sorts of experimental techniques.[1] Having established the general technical categories of disruption, negation, and borrowing, and drawing heavily on the structuralist polarities of Roman Jakobson, she devotes the rest of the study to enumerating specific techniques within each of these methods and their subcategories. What I find most striking in *Against Language?* is that it provides such an organized categorization of techniques of linguistic disruption.[2] In doing so, the study reveals a characteristic I see as fundamental to the experimentalist poetics Rosmarie Waldrop would soon begin practicing:[3] a paradoxical attraction at once to system and to deviancy.

In her poetry, this is manifest in continual interplay between a pattern-making tendency to order and arrange on the one hand and an attraction to techniques that foster polyphony, polysemy, disorder, uncertainty, rupture, and indeterminacy on the other. Waldrop herself has acknowledged that she is drawn to rules, and also to their violation, recalling:

> It was an important moment for me when I realized consciously that the encounter of a poem-nucleus with an arbitrary pattern (like a rhyme scheme) would tend to pull the nucleus out of its semantic field in unforeseen directions. The tension always generates great energy, not just for bridging the "gap" between original intention and the pattern, but for pushing the whole poem farther. . . . I'm spelling out what Ashbery and others have called the liberating effects of constraints. But what matters is that *any* constraint, *any* pattern can be generative in this way. . . . [E]xtreme formalism rarely works to my satisfaction. More often I use a pattern (e.g., the grammatical structure of a given text), but *also* let the words push and pull in their own directions. Since I make the rules, I also feel free to break them.[4]

Like much of Waldrop's poetry, her recent volume on which I shall focus, *A Key into the Language of America,* taps into the liberatory powers of arbitrary patterns. These imposed orders operate in energizing tension with a "semantic nucleus" involving issues of nothingness, emptiness, and erasure. These concerns, too, are characteristic, as Waldrop signals by taking as epigraph to her extended autobiographical essay John Cage's statement *"Poetry is having nothing to say and saying it: we possess nothing."*[5] This, then, is the second trait I see as fundamental to her experimentalism: a preoccupation with nothingness and emptiness as in fact substantial, generative realms. In much of her work Waldrop explores the ways in which negativity and absence—nothingness, emptiness, erasure, loss, silence, and related conditions such as error, wounding, exile—generate both meaning and art. The nothingness that proves such a fruitful area of exploration in *A Key into the Language of America* is strongly linked to the feminine and to Waldrop's feminist concerns. This feminist perspective, which I posit as the third element key to her poetics, becomes linked to the others via the stereotype that associates the female or the feminine with emptiness—woman's supposedly empty mind, hollow womb, missing penis, etc.—and via Waldrop's sense that adopting rules and then violating them may help the feminist artist generate social as well as aesthetic alternative forms.

Feminist thought has for many decades informed Waldrop's writing, though—in contrast to the poetry commonly recognized as feminist—generally not via the content or subjects of her work. By the early '70s, she had rejected any focus on subject matter per se, having concluded that "subject matter is not something to worry about. Your concerns and obsessions will surface no matter what you do. This frees you to work on form, which is all one can work on consciously."[6] She extended this attitude to feminist content: "I don't want to write 'about' any issues, not even feminist ones, I prefer exploring the forest to hewing a road, even if the road is in a good direction." But she went on to acknowledge, "my feminist consciousness inevitably gets in (like my other assumptions)."[7]

The formal structures and imposed experimental patterns of her work have proved to be one important means by which her feminist concerns emerge. For instance, Waldrop has observed that the disruptive technique she favored in the mid-'70s—a technique of syntactic doubling whereby the object of one phrase functions also as the subject of the next—had feminist implications:

> . . . my feminist concerns were surfacing in this very grammar. Who could have more interest in subverting a rigid subject-object relation than women, who have been treated as the object par excellence? Instead, these poems propose a grammar (a society?) in which subject and object functions are not fixed but reversible roles, where there is no hierarchy of main and subordinate clauses, but a fluid and constant alternation.[8]

In her work of the 1990s, both the feminist consciousness itself and the formal techniques in which it becomes manifest are more complex. The recent volume to which I now turn my attention suggests a less utopian vision than Waldrop's early modeling of egalitarian societies in grammatical inversions and fluidities. In part because of the increasing number and variety of procedural rules she simultaneously imposes and resists, the feminist "semantic field" of this recent work becomes more densely accountable to historical complexity—to the history of languages, of particular relationships, of genders, and of nations.

Waldrop is open about the "rules" she imposed on herself in composing *A Key into the Language of America* and about the interests that motivated them. Her prose introduction, titled "A Key into a Key," outlines the multifaceted sense of commonality she felt with Roger Williams, the non-conformist colonist who founded the settlement of Providence, now the city in Rhode Island where she lives. These connections led to her modeling her book on the curiously collaged structure of Williams's dictionary of the Narragansett language first published in 1643, and to her adopting his title as her own.

Waldrop emphasizes that Williams's *A Key into the Language of America* was written not only to provide Christian missionaries with the linguistic and cultural data they would need to convert the Indians, but also—or even more—to teach the colonists about their

own failings, since the European settlers often seemed to Williams far less virtuous than those who had only "Nature's teaching." While Williams used the Indians as a "mirror" reflecting back to the English colonists their spiritual shortcomings, Waldrop takes Williams as, in some aspects, a mirror of herself, enabling her to explore her ambivalent relation to colonial conquest and cultural dominance. She explains:

> I live in Roger Williams's territory. I was born in 1935, the year Williams's 300-year banishment officially ended. I was born "on the other side," in Germany. Which was then Nazi Germany. I am not Jewish. I was born on the side of the (then) winners. I was still a child when World War II ended with the defeat of the Nazis. I immigrated to the US, the country of the winners, as a white, educated European who did not find it too difficult to get jobs, an advanced degree, a university position. I can see myself, to some extent, as a parallel to the European settlers/colonists of Roger Williams's time. . . . Like Roger Williams, I am ambivalent about my position among the privileged, the "conquerors."[9]

Where Williams's extraordinary knowledge of Narragansett culture heightened his ambivalence about colonial culture and the colonists' treatment of the Indians, Waldrop's gender, as well as her being a poet, reinforces her identification with the marginalized and oppressed. She continues in "A Key into a Key":

> But am I among them [the conquerors]? I am white and educated. I am also a poet and a woman. A poet, in our days, is regarded as rather a marginal member of society, whose social usefulness is in doubt. As a woman, I do not figure as conqueror in the shell game of archetypes, but as conquered. A "war bride." As a woman, I also have no illusions about the Indian societies. They were far from ideal. . . . In the shell game of archetypes, the conquered (people or land) is always female. . . . I can identify with both sides of the conflict and am ambivalent about each side.

(xix-xx)

In addition to fostering exploration of Waldrop's ambivalence about her ambiguously hegemonic and non-hegemonic position as European immigrant and female poet, Williams's *Key* calls attention to the fertile substance to be found in what the dominant culture takes to be nothing. At several points, Waldrop implies that Williams is to be admired precisely because he sees fullness where others perceive a vacuum: most fundamentally, he "recognized a culture where his compatriots saw only savage otherness" (xiv); additionally, in a tract that the Boston magistrates ordered burned, he argued against the doctrine of *vacuum domicilium*, "the doctrine," Waldrop explains, "that the colonists were entitled to the land because the Indians were not making full use of it" (xvii). Granting that the natives cultivated only a small portion of their land, Williams observed that "they used all of it for hunting and, for this purpose, regularly burned the underbrush" (xvii).

He recognized "that the Indians were making rational and full use of the land" (xviii). Those with more power, however, regarding Williams's views as dangerous, denied that same fullness by feminizing it, redefining it as lack. As Waldrop puts it: "The colonization of America put the very 'male' Indian culture in the position of the conquered female, part of the land that was considered there to be 'taken'" (xx). Using Williams's *Key* as her own means to discover the fullness of apparent voids, Rosmarie Waldrop finds in a language "dead" for almost two centuries and in a "vanished" culture abundant material for poetic exploration of very current concerns (xxi, xxii).

In addition to its thematic usefulness, relating to colonialism and cultural conflict as they intersect with language, nothingness, and the feminine, Roger Williams's *Key* also provides the form of Waldrop's **Key into the Language of America.** Her thirty-two chapters follow the sequence of his exactly, each one adopting the title and including some textual material excerpted from his. Moreover, all Waldrop's chapters follow a pattern suggested by the internal composition of Williams's chapters, each of which, Waldrop notes, moves "through three stages: through phrase lists and anthropological observations . . . to a final moralizing poem" (xvi). Waldrop announces her deliberate attempt to generate something analogous: "In parallel to Roger Williams's anthropological passages, the initial prose section of each of my chapters tries to get at the clash of Indian and European cultures by a violent collage of phrases from Williams with elements from anywhere in my Western heritage" (xxii). Thus, for example, the opening of Waldrop's chapter IV, **"Of Their Numbers,"** juxtaposes stock market crashes and the rights asserted in the colonists' "Declaration of Independence" against the Indians' doomed mathematical savvy, seen through Williams's patronizingly appreciative gaze (my brackets identify material taken essentially verbatim from the parallel chapter in Williams):

> Without the help of Wall Street, [how quick they are in casting up] inalienable [numbers]. We do not have them. [With help of] hybrid [corn instead of Europe's pens or] poisons. Edge of ingenuity, between numb and nimble, forest or frigid wave before it crashes.
>
> (9)

Like Williams's, moreover, each of Waldrop's chapters contains a word list and a final poem. But in addition to mimicking the three stages of his chapters, Waldrop adds a fourth structural element that emphasizes her feminist interests: "To reinforce the theme of conquest and gender," she explains, "every chapter adds a narrative section in italics, in the voice of a young woman, ambivalent about her sex and position among the conquerors" (xxiii).

Waldrop highlights the formal regulation of her work by making her **Key into the Language of America** more visually regular than Williams's text. While Williams's chapters in modern reprint range from two to thirteen pages, all Waldrop's chapters are two pages long and the two pages are near mirror-images of each other. In every case, the title on the first page is followed by, first, a prose passage containing some bold-faced phrases from Williams, and second, a word list centered between the left and right margins with one word per line and anywhere from two to seven words per list.[10] On the verso page, prose again comes first; an italicized prose passage in the voice of a woman whose history in some ways overlaps with Waldrop's is followed by a free verse poem usually a few lines longer than the word list on the preceding page. Compared to, for instance, Susan Howe's experiments with historical documents such as the *Eikon Basilike,* this format is extremely tidy and systematic.

Yet Waldrop's devotion to disruption and disorder is also apparent. The typographic and formal contrasts between parts within the chapters and the white space surrounding each piece in the pattern give the work a richly varied visual texture. Supplementing such rule-determined variety are more arbitrary or rule-breaking irregularities: bold face occurs not just in the opening prose chapter sections as announced in the introduction, but unpredictably in other sections as well. So do Narragansett words with their notably unfamiliar spellings and accent marks. Sometimes word fragments or Narragansett words accompanied by translating phrases substitute for English words in the lists. In one chapter, a numbered series of phrases arranged one per line substitutes for prose in the opening section. The form proves considerably less set than the high degree of regulation presented in the "Key into a Key" might suggest.

Moreover, the language itself—continually shifting in syntactic and interpretive density, in cultural and discursive context—renders each section of every chapter thoroughly unpredictable. Syntax is sometimes grammatical, sometimes not; reference may seem consistent for a bit, and then will change or become unclear; dictions shift as formulations move in and out of familiarity. Linguistic instability becomes a principle of composition even for the word lists; these explore widely varying "language contexts" for words in the chapter titles, contexts which may be aural, etymological, semantic, or inaccessible. Sometimes parts of compound words appear, which may themselves function as autonomous terms or only as suggestive fragments, as in the list, "ogue / agent / er," that appears in the chapter titled **"Of Travell."**

Precisely because the volume is so regular in its structure, such variations are notable and heighten readers' awareness of the multiple strands forming any web of linguistic linkages or of cultural conflict. This complexity does not derive from Williams's *Key*; rather, it distinctively characterizes Waldrop's text. For Williams presents two entirely separate languages, limiting his "language contexts" to those useful for communication between Indians and European settlers; and for him, the cultural clash is mediated by one overriding truth, established by Christianity, according to which the behavior of both cultural groups could be judged. In the complex layerings and violated orderings of Waldrop's text, rectitude is far less accessible. This is the case in part because of the "nothing" left where the ordering structures of Williams's Christianity had been—a space that in America in the 1990s comes to be ambiguously occupied by language itself.

A passage from one of the last chapters in Waldrop's **Key, "Of their Paintings,"** reflexively illuminates some of the complex interactions of rule and disruption, void and pattern, emptiness and fertility that I have been describing. The passage is the chapter's third part, the italicized section in the voice of the young woman:

> *I used iodine to paint my wound, a geometrical design interwoven with collision and conflict. Line securing or towing a boat. A motivation to swell. Or scream in the face of immediate, useless nakedness. In spite of having, without restraint, chosen the wrong role models I have female parts and cultivate outward behavior.*
>
> (62)

The initial sentence announcing that the speaker painted a geometrical pattern with an antiseptic fluid suggests that orderly design promotes the healing of wounds. If we take that design to represent the highly regular structure of Waldrop's book, the sentence might suggest that an orderly reworking of the genocidal history to which Williams's *Key* inadvertently contributed and a reexploration of the language he recorded offer hope for transforming the damage and pain of our nation's history. As Waldrop puts it in her essay "Alarms & Excursions," poetry "can make the culture aware of itself, unveil hidden structures. It questions, resists. Hence it can at least potentially anticipate structures that might lead to social change" (47).

But this intimation of the recuperative powers of art's order is tempered by the geometric design most prominent in Waldrop's **Key,** a visual representation of an act of cultural conquest from the perspective of the conquerors. This bizarrely regular image, which appears cropped on the cover and uncropped on the facing pages between Waldrop's introductory "A Key into A Key" and the text of her **Key,** was created to celebrate a triumph of colonialism (Figure 1). Reproduced from a 1638 publication by a colonial Captain Underhill, it depicts the violent conquest led by him and a Captain Mason of "the Indians' Fort or Palizado in New England." Centered in a stylized orderly landscape of

hills and trees are rings of armed Indians and colonists, broken by symmetrical areas of battle on opposite sides of the circular fort. The pointed towers of the fort along with the peaked roofs of the Indian's houses within appear like teeth in a *vagina dentata* at the moment of bold penetration by the British. This geometric drawing may represent, then, the feminization and the wounding of the Narragansett as well as the masculine proving of the colonists—both key to genocidal destruction.

Particularly the cropped version on the cover also suggests an eye, with the ring of soldiers outlining the iris and the Indian fort comprising the pupil. Read this way, the image perhaps speaks to the ways in which history and historiographic patterns are the products of particular perspectives. History is our invention—in Cage's terms, part of the nothing we possess. *Design* may mean not just an artful ordering but also a plan, particularly a dishonest or selfish one; designs, like deliberate ruptures, may serve admirable or reprehensible ideologies alike. Thus in "Alarms & Excursions" Waldrop notes that despite the changing of the language that was being undertaken by experimental artists in pre-Nazi Germany, "the Nazis had no trouble putting [the German language] to work for their purposes" (47).

In line with this observation, the second sentence in the passage from **"Of their Paintings"** points to the arbitrariness of humanly imposed meanings. For *painter* can as well signify the line tied to a boat as a person who wields a paint-brush. The word "securing" might indicate that, whether rope or pigment, the painter's line (or perhaps the poet's) provides stability and security. But again in complication, the next clause—"*A motivation to swell*"—recalls the earlier "collision and conflict," likely sources of wounds and swellings. The wound, or perhaps the painting of the wound, causes swelling and screaming; which is to say that what is produced at the site of rupture or emptiness is likely to involve suffering, even while it may also promote healing.

In abruptly introducing nakedness at this point—*scream in the face of immediate, useless nakedness*—Waldrop is silently drawing on the parallel chapter of Williams's *Key,* using it to highlight gender issues. In the sermonizing poem that closes his chapter, Williams introduces nakedness as the antithesis of being painted. Here are the first and last quatrains of Williams's three-stanza poem:

> *Truth is a Native, naked Beauty; but*
> *Lying Inventions are but Indian Paints;*
> *Dissembling hearts their Beautie's but a Lye.*
> *Truth is the proper Beauty of Gods Saints.*
>
> *Paints will not bide Christs washing Flames of fire,*
> *Fained Inventions will not bide such stormes:*
> *O that we may prevent him, that betimes,*
> *Repentance Teares may wash of all such Formes.*[11]

For Williams, painting symbolizes deceit, a whorish covering of God's naked and enduring truth. But in Waldrop's text, the ugly "fained inventions" seem to be not so much individually willed sins as the conventions of gender roles. The intertext of Williams's lines emphasizes that these roles are inessential and subject to change, preparing for Waldrop's lines that follow, which underscore a person's ability to choose models and modes of behavior (even if one cannot choose the sexed form of one's body). The speaker's "outward behavior" need not be the deceitful feigning Williams deplores; it might be a self-fashioning necessary to the creation of a functioning subject. If so, this painterly application of "color of thought to lacking object" (a line from the first section of this chapter) is a feminist triumph: woman—conventionally defined by her "lack" of, among other things, a penis—gains visibility.

The poem that follows the italicized passage and concludes Waldrop's chapter asserts the possibility of generating change and of constructing something from what is perceived as nothingness. (The notably direct propositional character of the first part of this passage perhaps reflects Waldrop's attraction to regulated order, while the more polysemous and syntactically ambiguous portions, beginning with the open parenthesis, may manifest her tendency to violate the expectations set up by her own procedures.)

> thinking develops
> out of the negative
>
> the vacuum abhorred
> by nature
> is fertile (variables
> perspectives, paper money)
>
> refinanced memory
> washes white
>
> (62)

The fertility announced so unequivocally here is, like design, ideologically uncommitted; thus, "paper money," if read as an example of what can develop out of nothing, reminds us that value may be assigned without basis in anything beyond convention. When Williams closes his poem with the hope that *"Repentance Teares may wash of all such forms,"* he presumes the revelation of an *essential* truth. Waldrop, who is no essentialist, posits a different kind of hope and a more ambiguous one in her closing, "refinanced memory / washes white." These lines might indicate that reinventing the forms of our thought can erase received ideas, offer a clean start; but they might also suggest that such reinvention can whitewash past misdeeds, or impose the ideology of the dominant white culture. Starting again from the *tabula rasa* of nothing or from the empty space opened by a wound does not insure progress. Waldrop only goes so far as to indicate that such re-creation

opens possibilities for changing the coloring of our perceptions; the designs of our historiographic maps; and our valuing of marginalized genders, art forms, and ethnic or social groups.[12]

Testing the relation between artistic deviance and social change—particularly social change involving gender roles and heterosexual interactions—seems to me a primary undertaking of the sections in which Waldrop uses the italicized voice of the woman. Again, her intellectual exploration is conducted via an engagement with rules—or rather, with a well established set of literary conventions—those of the bildungsroman, which traces a process of change in the (usually male) individual. Waldrop's constant interruption of the girl's biographical narrative by the other sections of her chapters provides an insistent reminder that any individual's history is thoroughly interwoven with the violence of local, national, and global history—something few bildungsromans acknowledge. In addition, by obviously imitating the formulas of the male bildungsroman and then problematizing them for her female speaker, Waldrop calls attention to the distinctive difficulties faced in female development within patriarchal societies. Given that genre conventions are not rigid regulations, revising them for feminist purposes—a procedure widespread among women writers—needs to be distinguished from play with more rule-generated proceduralism.[13] Nonetheless, since Waldrop directly invokes the most set patterns characterizing this genre in order to test and challenge its assumptions, her simultaneous use of and rejection of its patterns deserves attention in the context of Waldrop's relation to ordering systems.

The italicized section of chapter I (**"Salutations"**) begins as the conventional first-person life story is supposed to, by locating the protagonist's birth. Here's the entire passage:

> *I was born in a town on the other side which didn't want me in so many. All streets were long and led. In the center, a single person had no house or friends to allay excessive sorrowe. I, like other girls, forgot my name in the noise of traffic, opening my arms more to measure their extension than to offer embrace.*
>
> (4)

The speaker, like the typical restless hero of the novel of education, is one for whom streets and the journeys they symbolize seem to beckon, *"All streets were long and led."* This formulation suggests, however, that, just as all roads once led to Rome, existing streets direct the traveler only to the imperial center or to some locus of patriarchal power. Moreover, the developmental challenge she faces, shaped partly by her historical moment of noisy urban culture, is specific to her feminine gender: *"I, like other girls, forgot my name in the noise of traffic"* (4). The italicized section of Chapter II is even more explicit in linking the speaker's tale to the formulas of bildungsroman: *"I began my education by walking along the road in search of the heroic"* (6). But the heroic is elusive for her, and in succeeding chapters of Waldrop's *Key,* again and again the unhappy female protagonist seems stuck between two unsatisfactory courses: either trying to pursue this education via the masculine notions of violent heroism that tradition and history legitimize, or remaining within the constraints of approved feminine behavior. *"Sticks and stones and swamps and howling wilderness, or inside a patient garden and ability to behave: intrepid waiting"* (24).

Following the latter course prescribed for the domestic feminine would mean going nowhere. In Chapter 4, the Narragansett term for "one of feminine gender" introduces the speaker's resistance to this deadly order of woman's prescribed passivity, silence, and reliable regularity:

> *Pâwsuck with time to dawdle, to cultivate lucidity and metric structure. Yet did not play by numbers. Too many messengers that do not speak. A bowel movement every day and one war every generation. I feared becoming an object too boring for my bones to hold up, however clumsily.*

> (10)

Clearly, social rules for women must be broken. But not via role-reversal. The solution does not lie in the woman's trying to imitate (European) men, though this is not an easy lesson to learn. Thus, at one point the speaker announces: *"In a mixture of panic and mistaken gender I went West, intending the milky way. Common error"* (28). And again later, *"What was the secret of holsters, nearsighted daring, tools between legs? Who went from coast to coast, but stayed always on top with semicircular canals for balance? My antagonism dissolved into the illusion that I was one of them, consenting to slow harm"* (34). While use of "pâwsuck" here perhaps signals women's oppression within Narragansett society, generally Waldrop's inclusion in her *Key* of material from the eradicated Indian culture foregrounds the harmfulness of masculine patriarchal modes as enacted by Anglo-Europeans. Neither the conventional masculine nor the conventional feminine course is acceptable, and the speaker struggles to locate alternatives.

In the bildungsroman, the hero learns from his errors so as to discover his personal path. If progress is available to Waldrop's female adventurer, it is more qualified and more obviously tied into social institutions and public history. The text provides signals of chronological maturation, but the only clear lesson this woman learns is a bit of Marxist analysis, announced in the chapter

"Concerning their Coyne" (XXIV): *"I learned that my face belonged to a covert system of exchange since the mirror showed me a landscape requiring diffidence, and only in nightmares did I find identity or denouement"* (50). As I read the rest of the passage, she tries to call overt attention to woman's commodity function, perhaps by presenting herself as a prostitute, only to find herself more alienated, particularly from other women who are ludicrously blind to their own participation in this economic system: *"At every street corner, I exaggerated my bad character in hopes of being contradicted, but only caused an epidemic of mothers covering their face while exposing private parts"* (50). Similarly, her sexual experiences with men do not generate obvious progress, countering readers' expectations of the bildungsroman's journey toward fulfilled and socially integrated selfhood. The speaker does seem to develop increased acceptance of her sex and sexuality, and greater ability to distinguish her sex from her gender. But she does not gain confidence she can act on this understanding: *"I did not know if my desire to escape cash-and-carry was strong enough to eliminate the platitudes of gender identity or the crowds under my eyelids. I was stuck in a periodicity I supposedly share with Nature, but tired of making concessions to dogs after bones"* (54).

Waldrops's protagonist ends in a situation much like the one in which she began ("single" in the center of a town in Chapter I, "alone" in the center of a city in Chapter XXXII): *"I found myself alone among the rubble of love. I had finally reached the center of the city. It was deserted, in ruins, as useless as my birth and as permanent a site of murder"* (66). Yet I discern some potentially significant gains here. For from her rule-breaking engagement with the rules of the bildungsroman this woman appears to have developed an historical consciousness. In referring to the ruined city as as permanent a site of murder as her birth, the speaker, born "on the other side" (xix, 4), presents herself as, by racial and national heritage, among the privileged invaders who have survived via the socially legitimized murders necessary to war and colonialism. She has also gained access to a possibly generative nothingness in the rubble and ruins now occupying the spaces of collapsed structures—which might include social conventions like those surrounding gender. Whether these ruins will be used to build something of value remains an open question and a looming responsibility for poet and audience alike.

Notes

1. The first cause of discontent, a consciousness that the absolute, ineffable, and transcendent are not in language and may be hidden by it, leads to techniques of disruption that explore the borders of silence. The second cause, the sense that pure

matter or energy, of which the human unconscious is part, defies formulation, leads to experiments that reject logic and, as in automatic writing, approach the conditions of pure flux. The third cause, a dramatically increased preoccupation with the world of physical things, which in their self-sufficiency are found to elude language, leads to techniques that foreground the strangeness of things and the materiality of the word as thing.

2. Waldrop's 1995 lecture "Form and Discontent" provides a recent example of a similarly systematized categorization of "wild" forms (*Diacritics* 26.3-4 [1996]: 54-62).

3. The first section of Waldrop's first volume, *The Aggressive Ways of the Casual Stranger* (New York: Random House, 1972), suggests that her own poetry in the 1960s was not experimental. It contains personally expressive lyrics concerning the domestic issues confronting a young wife, with titles like "And how do you see yourself, Mrs. Waldrop?" "Cleaning," "Menstruation," and "Insomnia."

4. *Ecstatic Occasions, Expedient Forms: 65 Leading Contemporary Poets Select and Comment on Their Poems,* ed. David Lehman (New York: Macmillan, 1987), 197.

5. "Rosmarie Waldrop," *Contemporary Authors Autobiographical Series,* Volume 30 (Detroit: Gale Research, 1998), 297.

6. Rosmarie Waldrop, "Thinking of Follows," *Moving Borders: Three Decades of Innovative Writing by Women,* ed. Mary Margaret Sloan (Jersey City, New Jersey: Talisman House, 1998), 615.

7. "Alarms & Excursions," *The Politics of Poetic Form: Poetry and Public Policy,* ed. Charles Bernstein (New York: ROOF, 1990), 65.

8. "Rosmarie Waldrop," *Contemporary Authors,* 308.

9. Rosmarie Waldrop, *A Key into the Language of America* (New York: New Directions, 1994), xix. Page numbers for subsequent references to this book will appear parenthetically in the text.

10. Comparison with Williams's book reveals that the phrases in bold are often slight modifications, not exact quotations from his text, and that most chapters contain additional material taken directly from Williams but not signaled in bold.

11. Roger Williams, *A Key into the Language of America,* ed. John J. Teunissen and Evelyn J. Hinz (Detroit: Wayne State University Press, 1973), 241.

12. Waldrop's sense of art's powers and limitations here, as well as the figure of the wound painted in red that figures them, is closely related to the work of Edmond Jabes, which she has translated for many years. An epigraph in *The Book of Questions* reads "Mark the first page of the book with a red marker. For, in the beginning, the wound is invisible" (*From the Book to the Book: An Edmond Jabes Reader,* trans. Rosmarie Waldrop [Hanover, NH: Wesleyan University Press, 1991], 31). Jabes is Jewish and his preoccupation with the wound has partly to do with Jewish history. He writes, "There is nothing at the threshold of the open page, it seems, but this wound of a race born of the book, whose order and disorder are roads of suffering. Nothing but this pain, whose past and whose permanence is also that of writing" (34). Translating the wound into writing, as the iodine painter does in Waldrop's *Key,* "is an act of silence that makes it legible to us in its entirety" (Jabes quoted by Waldrop in "Silence, the Devil, and Jabes," *The Art of Translation,* ed. Rosmarie Waldrop [Boston: Northeastern University Press, 1989]), 230.

13. In *Unending Design: The Forms of Postmodern Poetry* (Ithaca: Cornell University Press, 1991), Joseph M. Conte usefully classifies postmodern extended poetic forms as either serial or procedural. A procedural form follows a system of arbitrary constraints which functions as a generative device.

Matthew Cooperman and Rosmarie Waldrop (interview date 2006)

SOURCE: Cooperman, Matthew, and Rosmarie Waldrop. "Love, Like Sentences: An Interview with Rosmarie Waldrop." In *Denver Quarterly* 40, no. 3 (2006): 35-50.

[*In the following interview, conducted by email over the course of a number of years, Cooperman touches on a variety of theoretical concerns that underlie Waldrop's works of poetry.*]

Poet, translator, and publisher, Rosmarie Waldrop has, over the last forty years, facilitated the literary avant garde in America and abroad with peerless grace. Her lucid sentences and procedural verve are testimony to formal invention in prose poetry, not to mention its contiguity with Modernist practice of collage, fragment, and seriality.

Born in 1935, Waldrop is the author of two novels, seventeen books of original poetry, including the trilogy **The Reproduction of Profiles, Lawn of Excluded Middle,** and **Reluctant Gravities,** the intertext **A Key into the Language of America,** and, most recently, **Blindsight** (New Directions) and **Love, Like Pronouns**

(Omnidawn). A prolific translator, Waldrop has brought over twenty books of poetry and prose into English, most significantly the work of Edmond Jabès, but also Jacques Roubaud and Emmanuel Hoquard in French, and Friedericke Mayröcker, Oskar Pastior, Elke Erbe, and Ernst Jandl in German. For many years she has run Burning Deck Press with her husband, the poet and novelist Keith Waldrop.

This interview began as a conversation at Naropa University in the mid-'90s, continued at the National Poetry Foundation Conference in 2000, and extended into 2004, by letter and email.

[Matthew Cooperman]: In its exploratory postmodernism, your work has navigated the destabilization of the lyric tradition in a vigorously restless manner. I'm particularly moved by how the instability has played out as a feminine and feminist subversion. Yet the stance, or stances, book to book, is never dogmatic. How is the cultural mistrust of the lyric tradition, of the lyric "I," played out as an opportunity for you?

[Rosmarie Waldrop]: "The lyric tradition" is a complex phenomenon. Most basically, there is the connection to music, to song—and it is essential. I think Zukofsky has it right: "upper limit music / lower limit speech." We navigate in the tension between those two poles. I write mostly prose poems, and prose poetry by definition places itself near the lower limit—which we may have to clarify as speech *patterns* rather than simply "speech." Because prose distances the oral. It is a child of the printing press. Even free verse was a step away from the obvious music of the traditional lyric, toward a less obvious music, but the prose poem goes farther toward less immediate, less "memorable" (subtler?) rhythms. The rhythms of syntax. This is not a mistrust, but more a desire to complicate the music.

I think you are more accurate in discussing the "lyric I," which has indeed caused much unease. The French poet Claude Royet-Journoud once told me that his book, *La Notion d'obstacle,* did not contain a single instance of the word "I." He was immensely proud of this.

This made me think. But I found I did not share his attitude. On the simplest level, saying "I" seems more modest and manageable than the claim to objectivity that is inherent in avoiding it.

More importantly, the lyric "I" is a grammatical "I." As the linguist Emile Benveniste says, "'I' refers neither to a 'reality' nor to 'objective' positions in time or space. . . . It can only be defined by the always unique instance of discourse that contains it, hence by referring to its own use." Or as Agamben puts it: it indicates that "language is taking place."

This is why Adorno can claim that, in the best poetry, the first-person expression evolves into the voice of language itself.

This "I," this shifting, unstable, and essentially empty sign is a long way from what it has popularly been connected with in recent years, namely the expression of simple-minded, unquestioned subjectivity and identity. The "mistrust of the lyric" you refer to is, I think, a mistrust of this misappropriation. It overlooks that the confessional kind of verse has really no inherent connection to the lyric. Elizabeth Willis has outlined this beautifully in her essay, "The Arena in the Garden."

Gertrude Stein is right: "one has no identity that is when one is in the act of doing anything." Which we could also take back to Keats: "A Poet . . . has no Identity—he is continually in for—and filling some other Body" and "[the chameleon poet] has no self."

Actually, let me give the full Stein quote from "What are Masterpieces" because "I am because my little dog knows me" is quoted so often without its context:

> The thing one gradually comes to find out is that one has no identity that is when one is in the act of doing anything. Identity is recognition, you know who you are because you and others remember anything about yourself but essentially you are not that when you are doing anything . . . I am I because my little dog knows me, but creatively speaking the little dog knowing that you are you and your recognizing that he knows, that is what destroys creation.

Having, *as poet,* no identity, I am free to use multiple "I"s and multiple perspectives. Prose may facilitate this simply because it allows more maneuvering space, as is evident even in the early prose poems of Baudelaire, Rimbaud, Mallarmé. Wanting multiple "I"s is a big part of my use of collage.

I don't see feminism in opposition to the lyric. The lyric is too connected with Sappho and Emily Dickinson for me.

Still, throughout your work there is this "I" taking measure, observing, speaking from. If it's not identifiable with the author per se, it still maintains a presence as a speaking subject, as a phenomenological and psychological subjectivity. To that end, what is the role of autobiography in your work? It's hardly a dominant feature, but neither is it programmatically written out. How do you envision the critique of transparency as also a critique of autobiographical writing?

I didn't set out with a program to critique transparency or the lyric tradition. It's just that, after uncertain beginnings, when I tried anything, it seemed more interesting to explore language pattern than to chronicle experiences—especially as your experiences feed into what you write in any case. And the only thing that one can work on consciously is form.

In the most basic way, everything is autobiography. I wouldn't have written **The Road Is Everywhere** if I hadn't spent a year with a long commute, that is, spent a lot of time sitting in a car. I might not have reached for Roger Williams's *A Key into the Language of America* if I hadn't come to live in Rhode Island.

But we shouldn't forget a) that reading is part of experience and b) that while our experience, our life, feeds writing it doesn't provide form. This is where work comes in. You have to work at form. And when you work you are nobody. I've just quoted Keats and Gertrude Stein on this. We could add many more.

This impersonality has, I think, to do with the change of the "I-you" relation that takes place in writing. Benveniste once more:

> Language is possible only because each speaker sets himself up as a subject by referring to himself as I in his discourse. . . . Because of this, I posits another person, the one who, being, as he is, completely exterior to "me," becomes my echo to whom I can say you and who says you to me. This polarity of persons is the fundamental condition of language.

But in writing, the "you," the other, is language. And our relation to it is neither identification nor a dialectic. It is more what Blanchot calls a "relation of the third kind," a relation of otherness as such. This must in turn affect the "I," abstract it, make it impersonal (paradoxical as that sounds), turn it inside out.

I love **The Road Is Everywhere or Stop This Body.** *After twenty-five years it's still so fresh in its troping of the road; there's driving in the line, in the visual scan of the horizon; and you wryly explore reading in the various "road signs" on the page. While early in your career, its experiments with structure and typography seem signal of where you will go. Could you talk about that book as a seed of later concerns?*

Except for its use of road signs, **The Road Is Everywhere** continued the formal strategy begun in the sequence **"As If We Didn't Have to Talk"** (in **The Aggressive Ways of the Casual Stranger**). I let the object of one phrase ("an ash") pivot into being the subject of the next, without repeating it:

> just a cigarette frays
> analogies out of
> too frequent a departure
> leaves only an ash
> of memory itches
>   . . . . .

I used the pivotal phrases to push at the sentence boundary, to get a nearly unending flow in tension with constant interruption—grammatical, if you look for complete sentences, and rhythmical, through the short lines. I was delighted with the speed that results.

In retrospect, the pivoting of subject and object function must have come out of feminist preoccupations with male subject versus female object. Instead, I propose a pattern where subject and object are not fixed, but temporary, reversible roles, where there is no hierarchy of main and subordinate clauses, but a fluid and constant alternation.

The road signs also reinforce the dichotomy of flow and interruption: often a road sign is part of the sentence, so there is visual interruption within semantic continuity. W. G. Sebald sometimes uses photographs in this way, e.g., a picture of eyes appearing instead of the word "eyes" in a sentence. But more basically, they function as a quick way to establish the basic situation: car on the road.

But perhaps most crucial for my later concerns, I was pushing metaphor out of the texture into the structure: the traffic signs become the "vehicle" for all the possible circulation systems: breath, blood, sex, language, money . . .

Both the push away from literal metaphor and the tension of flow and fragmentation have stayed with me. The particular tumbling of object into subject I gave up because it allowed no subordinate clauses, no digression. "Main clause highway." It drove me to prose, I think.

The tension between subject and object seems just right. A passage from **"As If We Didn't Have to Talk"** *says it well: "In order not to / disperse / I think each movement of / my hands / turns / the page / the interval has all the rights." It's a lovely statement of writerly unendingness. Could you talk about the rights of the interval?*

The interval, the interstice, the between. Break, gap, fragmentation. This whole cluster is very important to me. **"Between"** is the title of one my earliest poems in English. When I felt still very much between my native Germany and my newly adopted country. Between "not all here / or there / a creature with gills and lungs."

Or, in *The Hanky of Pippin's Daughter*:

> BETWEEN, ALWAYS. Between father and mother. Between memory and conjecture. Between English with a German accent and "For an American your German is excellent."

But it's not just my personal situation between countries and cultures. Our reality is no longer substances, but systems of relations, "no longer things, but what happens BETWEEN things," as Charles Olson paraphrases Whitehead.

In language, it is the space between words that lets us recognize the words as words. And in poetry, it is the interval, the empty space from one line to the next that defines the verse. It sets the rhythm and also makes visible the nothing, the not-said, against which we pit our words. For the fraction of a moment, this void stops everything. It suspends the assurance of statement to reintroduce uncertainty, doubt, potential. It makes visible the possibility of language, of representation, of music.

Blanchot has beautifully written on the interval as a site of possibility by contrasting *"The sky is blue"* with *"Is the sky blue? Yes."*

> The "Yes" does in no way reestablish the simplicity of the plain affirmation. In the question, the blue of the sky has given way to the void. The blue has, however, not dispersed, on the contrary it has risen dramatically to its *possibility,* above its actual being. It unfolds in the intensity of this new space, bluer than it has ever been before.

Then again, maybe this interest in the interval just goes back to one of my childhood delights, Christian Morgenstern's poem, "Der Lattenzaun" [The Picket Fence]:

> Es war einmal ein Lattenzaun
> mit Zwischenraum, hindurchzuschaun.
>
> Ein Architekt, der dieses sah,
> stand eines Abends plötzlich da
>
> und nahm den Zwischenraum heraus
> und baute draus ein grosses Haus.
>
> Der Zaun indessen stand ganz dumm,
> mit Latten ohne was herum.
>
> Ein Anblick grässlich und gemein.
> Drum zog ihn der Senat auch ein.
>
> Der Architekt jedoch entfloh
> Nach Afri-od-Ameriko.

In W. D. Snodgrass's translation:

> There was a picket fence between
> whose boards interstices were seen.
>
> One night an evil architect
> turned up, just when you'd least suspect
>
> and slipped out the interstices;
> he built a spacious house from these.
>
> The fence just stood there faint and quailing
> with nothing on its naked palings.
>
> A most disgraceful, obscene sight;
> the Council banished it, outright.
>
> The architect, though, got away
> To Afri- or Americay.

Is this exploration of the interval also an interest in the series, in serial forms?

I have these contradictory impulses: toward flow and toward interruption, continuity and discontinuity. So the poem series is ideal for me. It's really having it both ways: closure and non-closure. The poem doesn't really stop, but the flow is interrupted by semi-closures, as if one were coming up for air every so often. Again, the breaks allow at least potential for shift of perspective, plurality of voices. Sequence, and even more the "through-composed" book, also allows for shifting between different prosodic forms. I have begun to explore that possibility in **"Unpredicted Particles,"** the final section of *A Form / Of Taking / It All,* and in ***Reluctant Gravities,*** with its verse interludes between the prose poems

Differences for Four Hands *(1984) is an interesting book in this regard. The turn to prose seems a way of working out this interruptive impulse. It's also a kind of reclamation project. The title itself distills the concealment of Clara Schumann. What were the origins of that project?*

My piano teacher early on made me a present of *Robert Schumann's musikalische Haus- und Lebensregeln* [Robert Schumann's musical rules for home and life]. The Schumanns were a presence when I was growing up. The couple was usually idealized as an example of a perfect, harmonious union of artists.

In the early 1980s, when I had just finished my novel, *The Hanky of Pippin's Daughter,* I read a biography of Clara Schumann, which considerably modified that picture. And I read or, rather, reread Lyn Hejinian's *Gesualdo.* The two combined into the project of using the syntax of *Gesualdo* as a pattern for a life of the Schumanns. I actually wanted to work in verse again. But the pull toward prose—whether it came from Lyn Hejinian's piece or from my recent work on the novel—proved stronger.

Perhaps what I'm asking in all this is what is your unit of composition? Since you've written extensively in prose forms, I'd venture to say it is not the line, though perhaps it's the fragment. Is it the "new sentence," as Silliman suggests? Or is it the series, or, more largely, the book?

It has steadily expanded over the years. When I began writing, my unit was the single line or sentence, but it quickly became the whole poem. Now I often start with a single poem—until I see that it has vectors beyond itself, or that several poems are starting to build up into a series. But most of my books were conceived as books from the start. This is no doubt Jabès's influence (and Spicer's), but it may also be a natural consequence of working more on syntactical, metonymic forms. If the metaphor is central the single poem seems an adequate space to work it out. If syntax is central, it tends to push on. Olson's "figure of outward." Also a danger, of course.

I like Roland Barthes's statement that "the structure of the sentence . . . is found again, homologically, in the structure of works. Discourse is not simply an adding together of sentences; it is, itself, one great sentence." It posits a kind of fractal structure. On the other hand, I don't think this bears being pushed very far.

The fact of your companionship with Keith Waldrop, your relationship as business partner, creative collaborator, and wife, comes up in many places in your work—"The Senses Loosely, or the Married Woman" in When They Have Senses; *the accomplice in* The Road Is Everywhere; *"Kind Regard" in* Streets Enough to Welcome Snow; *the extended "you" charted through* The Reproduction of Profiles, Lawn of Excluded Middle, *and* Reluctant Gravities. *Has such an artistic union influenced your sense of poetry as fundamentally dialogic?*

While Keith is the big "you" in my life, the "you" in my poems is always grammatical/rhetorical. It is the complement of the "I" in creating the instance of language. I think of this "you" in my poems as encompassing the whole range from impersonal pronoun to addressing a lover to addressing the reader. I don't think of the examples you cite as referring specifically to Keith and/or my marriage. Especially not the "you" in **Reproduction** and the two other books of the trilogy. This "you" is even more strictly rhetorical. It is, on the one hand, constructed as a male archetype with a logical position on everything. (Keith is far less limited—and far less logical, too!) On the other hand, it is part of the "I"—the other voice in the head, in the argument the "I" carries on with herself ("2 Seelen wohnen, ach, in meiner Brust!"). And then (on the "third hand"!), it can also be seen as addressing the reader, putting him/her in the rational position that's argued with, but also trying to involve him/her.

However, you are no doubt right in that our constant dialogue has shaped my sense of poetry in that direction.

You've collaborated with Keith on a number of projects. As a collection, Well Well Reality *distills the activity over many years. The long progression of parts suggests chapbooks, shifting locations, periods in your marriage. I'm sure the procedures varied by project, perhaps even by poem, but have you had a general way of approaching collaboration? Could you talk about that book as an extended project?*

Well Well Reality is not so much a "distillation" as a simple collection. Yes, each part was a chapbook and had its own formal procedure. (**"Until Volume One"** and **"Since Volume One"** had the same rule: the word "until" (resp. "since") occurs in each poem, and on this word authorship changes. But each of us could begin a poem with either the first or the second half.)

There are only two things I can say in general. a) We don't usually sit down together (let alone lock ourselves in a room as Paz, Roubaud, Sanguinetti, and Tomlinson did for their *Renga*). We hand things back and forth. This works better because our work rhythms are very different. **"Alice ffoster-Fallis"** was an exception. It happened almost totally one night in bed! And b) collaboration is exhilarating. Not being responsible for the whole poem makes for great freedom and playfulness. For instance, when collaborating, Keith and I often play with each other's manner—which we wouldn't allow ourselves to do otherwise.

Our collaboration project is extended in that we almost every fall think we should do one and print it up as a New Year's gift. But most of the time the plan gets lost in the shuffle.

I'm intrigued by your procedures across disciplines as well. What was your process with the visual artist Nelson Howe in Body Image? *Or with Jennifer MacDonald in* Peculiar Motions?

These two books are not "true" collaborations. In both cases, the artist did all the responding. There was no back and forth. Though Jennifer Macdonald's skins were/are extremely exciting to me.

Peculiar Motions *is a suggestive text of concealment and revelation. The veiling of the text's body by means of various skins evokes a kind of reclamation. Could you talk about that book as a feminist poetic?*

I certainly have feminist concerns, and my concerns get into my writing, even inform some of my formal decisions (like the subject-object relation I mentioned). They more often surface thematically: e.g., playing ironically with male and female archetypes in *Reproduction of Profiles,* or with the male gaze in **"Psyche and Eros."**

My work is feminist because I am. (Other things also, I hope.) But I don't know that I have a "feminist poetics."

Though I am intrigued by the attempts at working out a feminist poetics or an *écriture feminine.* I like it very much when Joan Retallack (following Luce Irigaray) makes a case for considering the feminine as the *plural,* as all that conspires against monolithic, monotonal, monolinear *universes*. The female as always "in medias mess." Which posits that the proper task of women writers is not the depiction of "woman's experience" in straight mimetic language, but to enable dynamically developing forms, exploring the medium of language itself for possibilities dormant in it, but discouraged by a dominant linear model, e.g., disjunctive syntax, collage, and juxtaposition, depunctuated grammar, etc. Joan sees these as "feminine" forms that make "texts where the so-called feminine and masculine take migratory, paradoxical, and surprising swerves to the enrichment of both, (n)either, and all that lies between. This is not a vision of androgyny, but of range." (This is from her essay, "Re:Thinking:Literary:Feminism"):

> I like it. But what good does the labeling do? Other than make us women feel good? I also like Carol Gilligan's "web image" as characteristic of women's thinking. But the most striking and sustained web structure I know in literature is Robert Musil's *Man without Qualities*. By this I don't mean to say that the web pattern is a characteristic of male thinking, but that male and female thinking, male and female imagination, cannot be neatly separated, and that especially artists (of both sexes) tend to call into question (or simply not fit) those archetypal differences our cultures try to regiment us into.

Of course, I have to admit that in **Lawn of Excluded Middle** I rather fall in with Retallack/Irigaray by setting the third term excluded by logic in analogy to the womb. But it is one thing to use an analogy in a poem or even a statement, and it is quite another to freeze it into a category. I would think it's more important to move beyond the binaries and archetypes.

In her new book, The Poethical Wager, *Retallack suggests this plurality as extension; that the agency of, say, books, or perhaps pronouns, is enlarged by a consideration of social forces, which necessarily interlink with other communities. Your new book,* **Love, Like Pronouns,** *would seem to agree.*

Retallack's very term, "poethics," combines "inner" and "outer," imagination and the social. I think she is working toward nothing less than a re-shaping of our symbolic structures, thinking, and social processes by trying to ground them in a fluid, inclusive imagination. Fairly utopian at this point, but a great goal—and one that takes the social function of art to sublime heights.

Perhaps another way to say plurality is body. From the early "marriage" body of **The Aggressive Ways of the Casual Stranger** *and* **The Road Is Everywhere,** *to the feminist formulations of the trilogy* **The Reproduction of Profiles, Lawn of Excluded Middle,** *and* **Reluctant Gravities** *to the conflation of colonial and contemporary subjects in* **A Key into the Language of America,** *the body is such an interesting figure in your work. And, of course, there is the text's body in all of the Jabès translations. How is the figure and presence of the body central to your poetry? How has it evolved?*

"Marriage body"? On the biographical level: Growing up I wanted nothing as much as being out of my body. I had internalized my environment's (school, Catholic church) hostility to the body without even knowing it. Only the mind, the "Geist" counted. It was as an adult that I discovered the body *as a value*. Erotic, obviously, but not only. I remember the shock of revelation when I saw Valéry opposing "la vie organique profonde" to "la vie *superficielle* que nous nommons *esprit*." And then this idea popped up everywhere: Spinoza's "mind is just an idea of the body," Merleau-Ponty's stress on the body and the senses. Most recently, Damasio's claim that all thought is "grounded in body-representing neural structures," in *Descartes' Error* (which was to underestimate the role of the body!). And neurophysiological research suggests that the Western tradition of placing thought inside the outer shell of the body is wrong. Skin and brain of the human embryo are both formed from the exoderm, so their difference is not definitive, and the center is maybe at the periphery.

Writing is of course part of that "superficial life we call mind/spirit." And language can be said to kill the body. Hegel, in the *System of 1803-04*: "The first act through which Adam made himself master of the animals was to give them a name, i.e., he annihilated them in their existence (as existing creatures)." The cat stops being simply a cat and becomes also a concept. So trying to get the body back *into language* is a challenge. (Of course there is also the opposite view, that the word brings things into being, and of course both are true.)

More specifically, I need the body-imagery to balance and ground—or challenge—the frequent abstract statements. But it is for me also a thematic parallel and complement to poetry's desire to make words untransparent, corporeal. Writing is the most abstract art of all—not so much because language is less sensuous than paint or music, but because the everyday use of language gets us in the killing habit that Hegel talks about. We immediately replace the word by the concept, and the sentence by its meaning. As soon as we've understood, the words are annulled, forgotten. We not only kill the cat, but the word "cat" too. Hence the poets' desire to make language as material, as untransparent, as unconsumable (Ron Silliman's term) as possible, to make us remember words *as words*, as sounds and shapes. If need be by short-circuiting the sense, or delaying it.

Since I've brought up **The Reproduction of Profiles, Lawn of Excluded Middle,** *and* **Reluctant Gravities,** *could you talk about these books as an extended project? How did it evolve, and specifically, how did the dialogic structures evolve?*

The dialogic structure came out of the sources I was using. One was Kafka's "Description of a Struggle," where two men are talking about a woman. And the other, Wittgenstein's *Tractatus.* I couldn't just quote these propositions without adding a different voice, a different angle.

Then, since the *Tractatus* had sparked so much I went on to use the *Philosophical Investigations,* which through its questions seems closer to dialogue.

A while after **The Reproduction of Profiles** was finished, I found myself going back to it or, rather, I realized that there were things in it that I could develop farther, especially the image/theme of the empty center. This became the germ for **Lawn of Excluded Middle.** It was exciting to have one book push beyond itself into a second. For the third volume it didn't happen this way. There was instead a conscious decision on my part that I needed a third volume that would make the dialogue more complex and more equitable. I wanted two voices that would have equal weight. This meant I had to go from "I-you" to "he-she" because an "I" always has more weight than the "you." The voices are still coded male and female, but this time they both move across the same shared territories, e.g., the scientific vocabulary is not given to one voice exclusively, but shared, etc. But when I had these "conversations" going he says-she says-she says in four solid paragraphs per poem, I felt I needed something to interrupt these blocks periodically, to let air in. So I made interludes with little "songs"— verses that draw on the vocabulary of the conversations and frame a "Meditation" in verse and prose. This is in a neutral voice that could belong to either partner, or neither.

Those three books feel like a love letter to Keith, a study of marriage as a linguistic, conceptual, and physical institution. The "you" is rhetorical, but the address seeks embodiment, and so implicates biography, even as it constructs "selves."

In one way, yes, all my writing is addressed to Keith, and if the trilogy feels like a love letter to Keith, great. But it's not the "you" *in* the texts that addresses Keith, rather the whole text, the whole act of writing is directed toward him. Without Keith Waldrop there would be no American poet called Rosmarie Waldrop.

The postscript "theorems" at the end of **Lawn of Excluded Middle** *offer a provocative recursion: "Wittgenstein makes language with it ambiguities the ground of philosophy. His games are played on the lawn of excluded middle." By your own definition, this play occurs upon, or within, women, the "lawn of excluded middle." This posits language to a certain degree as feminine play, or, if we consider* écriture *feminine, a fertile flow. How does the notion of gender free or construct language for you? Do logic and play, system and rupture, function as gendered polarities?*

It's because Wittgenstein admits ambiguity that I say he plays on this lawn. No, I would not posit language in general as feminine play. Not every use of language qualifies. Also, I would not label all use of ambiguity, playfulness, etc. as feminine. I might not even always call it fruitful!

In **Lawn of Excluded Middle,** I play with the analogy of logic's excluded middle, the empty space between true and false, and the womb. But I wouldn't make it into a dogma. (Though maybe into the hair of the dogma, by using it again sometime!)

It is Wittgenstein's language that was the starting point. He writes so well! Though problems of representation are of great interest to me—of course, as a writer!—and quickly got into the text. Also, beside his concern with language, that he proceeds largely by questions—not so much in the *Tractatus,* but in all the later work. This makes for an openness that set my mind working.

Sure, we can gender the polarities of logic and play, system and rupture. Sure, we can play with the archetypes. They can function as a kind of shorthand and allow quick cuts. But the archetypes are not useful for *explaining* anything. After all, they are fossils, sediments of ways of looking at things. They are not instances of thinking, let alone "truth." I hope that my use of them comes across as ironical.

Are you familiar with Susan Stewart's book Poetry and the Fate of the Senses? *She argues the deceptively simple case that poetry relies on the senses to generate a multiplicity of meanings; that the body is necessarily present prior to any claims of speech-effacement such that its acknowledgement is crucial in any extension of poetry beyond speech. It's an interesting paradox. As she puts it, "[The senses'] capacity for extension, volition and distantiation in the end contributes to freeing us from the very burden of immediacy, of the overwhelming flux of external stimuli, sense experience in general can impose." Would you agree?*

To a large extent. It *is* the "deep organic life" that carries the mind. It is impossible to imagine what consciousness could exist without the immediacy of sense experience, which already Vico said was the condition, the site of the imagination. Even more of our capacity to make and recognize form.

> A poem
> like trying
> to remember, is a movement
> of the whole body.

But it is extremely difficult to separate sense impressions out from language and consciousness. We see what our language teaches us to see. Susan Stewart's wonderful book—what scope!—often slants things toward the senses alone for the sake of her argument when, as in the case of this quote, it seems to me a matter of this "amalgam."

She also claims that the senses are the crucial term for the restoration of poetry's social function, and, even further, provide models for intersubjective experience and community. The reason I press this is because it's one of the things that distinguishes, for me, your experimentalism; it never loses sight of the physical body, whether that's a feminist consciousness, or a physical experience of language in the mouth and brain. The body always seeks communication and community.

I'd say the body, the senses seek experience in general, the "world" in general. The senses are directed outward, as is consciousness, for that matter. Merleau-Ponty has a lovely sentence that I used in a poem: "my sensations seem to belong to a me that has always already sided with the world."

Your section of the autobiography Ceci n'est pas Keith, Ceci n'est pas Rosmarie *opens with an epigraph by Cage: "Poetry is having nothing to say and saying it: we possess nothing." So too, late in* A Key into the Language of America *you say, "thinking develops / out of the negative // the vacuum abhorred / by nature / is fertile." How has that nothingness, or erasure, absence, loss, silence, emptiness been revised as a feminist concern?*

Making it a feminist concern is less a revision than a narrower focus. I have made this narrower interpretation the central conceit in **Lawn of Excluded Middle.** The empty center *par excellence* is the womb—and it is the locus of fertility, of the creation of life.

Susan Howe has addressed your question in a historical sense by going after the erased/suppressed voices of women, what she calls the "unacknowledged undervoices"—from captivity narratives and the silencing of Anne Hutchinson in the Antinomian Controversy to the absence of Emily Dickinson in F. O. Matthiessen's *American Renaissance.* "If you are a woman, archives hold perpetual ironies. Because the gaps and silences are where you find yourself," she says in *The Birthmark.* And: "If history is a record of survivors, Poetry shelters other voices."

Is your interest in systems, in a procedural process that ruptures systems, a form of courting this emptiness? That does seem one of the discoveries of **A Key.**

My great lesson on systems and rupturing them came from Novalis and Friedrich Schlegel who reacted to the philosophical system-mania of their time (Hegel, Fichte) by cultivating fragments *as* fragments. It led to a new epistemology. Both parties aimed at the absolute, but

Novalis and Schlegel realized that a system has no chance, that it's always a reduction, whereas fragments might at least catch glimpses of it—exactly because they admit incompletion. Nietzsche's perspectivism comes out of this too.

In **A Key** I work with the clash of two systems, the native Indian culture and the European culture of the settlers, plus the clash between seventeenth-century and twentieth-century ideas. I hoped that the juxtapositions of fragments from all these areas and the shifting perspectives would lead to a more relativistic and therefore more inclusive picture of humankind.

Andrew Mossin (essay date spring 2007)

SOURCE: Mossin, Andrew. "Networks of the Real in Contemporary Poetry and Poetics: Peter Middleton, Susan Schultz, Rosmarie Waldrop." *Journal of Modern Literature* 30, no. 3 (spring 2007): 143-53.

[*In the following excerpted review of Waldrop's* Dissonance (if you are interested), *a collection of essays and notes on her poetic theories, Mossin focuses on the relationship between form and meaning in Waldrop's writings.*]

A leading publisher with her husband, Keith Waldrop, of small press titles through Burning Deck Books and one of this country's most accomplished poets and translators, Rosmarie Waldrop is a familiar figure on the landscape of American poetries. *Dissonance (if you are interested)* gathers together critical writing, essays, meditations, notes, and talks from 1965 to the present. As her title suggests, Waldrop is interested in the incoherencies, the off-key, off-balance moments of perception and experience as these get relayed in the language and form of poetry. Waldrop's range in this collection is notable, as she covers a huge amount of ground in essays and reviews that are divided into three sections: "Apprenticeship and Affinities," "Translation," and "Poetics." Waldrop's mode throughout is that of patient exegesis, a dance of the intellect that emphasizes the relationships between poet and language, form and history, the "I" of interior expression and the pronominal "we" that forms the basis of sociality.

What sustains Waldrop's inquiry is her alertness to the numinous qualities of poetic form, the mysteries of process that demand closer attention. In this sense, *Dissonance* remains very much a poet's book. One senses in reading the work gathered here—especially the early essays on Paul Valéry and Gottfried Benn, Barbara Guest, Charles Olson, Michael Palmer, and Leslie Scalapino—that Waldrop writes with a firm grasp of each poet's particular essence and wants to track how the language is working, what choices are open to each particular poet at the moment of composition. At the same time, Waldrop conceives of the poetic imagination as inherently philosophical (disruptively so) in its working-through of the relationship between poetic form, language, and our subjective experience of the world around us. Thus, in her essay on Olson, Waldrop starts with "Projective Verse" and "Human Universe" and moves into a discussion of the poems that aims to trace the radicalism of Olson's thinking, its post-humanistic reach. At stake for Waldrop is a further clarification of Olson's notion of "contiguity," of openness and space as these configure poetic practice. As she writes of *The Maximus Poems,* "Nobody, not even Olson, can write entirely without analogies and metaphors. But he can and does put the accent on relation by contiguity . . . *The Maximus Poems* point toward a total inclusiveness that we have found perhaps in some novels and epics but rarely in a sequence of poems" (79).

Some of the most striking commentary in *Dissonance* occurs around the subject of translation, a central figure in this book and in Waldrop's poetic imagination. As a prolific translator of texts from the French and German, including work by Edmond Jabés, Jacques Roubaud, Emmanuel Hocquard, Friederike Mayröcker, Elke Erb, Ernst Jandl, and Oskar Pastior, Waldrop defines the work of the translator in stark terms: "We must wrench apart. We must kill" (146). Waldrop makes clear that there is no sublime transparency, no seamless movement from "original" to translator tongue. Rather, translation involves "envy, usurpation, and pleasure in destruction" (145). Translation

> does not just break apart elements and melt them down to a state of lava still contained in a kettle, but pushes the work out of the boundaries of the said, down into the tectonic stresses and heat of the volcano, into the nucleus of creative energy where the work was conceived, where the author's dialogue with the infinite space of (a different) language took place. Only there can it take place again, as a more complex dialogue with the original and its space as well as with the space of the translator's language. Only there can the translator become "the one saying it again."
>
> (152)

In an image drawn from Walter Benjamin, Waldrop suggests that the ideal translation becomes a kind of "transluciferation," one that "does not cover the original, does not block its light" (154). Lingering over that space between the acquisition of form and mortal decay, Waldrop urges us to look closely at the figure of the "mutilated statue," to appreciate the "ravages that point beyond itself and suggest the lost beauty of the original" (154).

Waldrop's intense interest in "creative destruction" as a figure for her work in translation is amply evident as well in the essays that compose the "Poetics" section of

this book. Blurring the boundaries between genres, mixing poetry and prose, notebook entries, and philosophical inquiry, Waldrop limns the processes that give rise to poetry. Writing in "The Ground Is the Only Figure," a series of notebook entries composed in response to a Danish publisher's projected aim of publishing notebooks by a range of notable international poets, Waldrop explores the generative framework of the "notebook" to raise "the question of what is figure, what is ground, and what is their relation" (215). Entries are composed of textual citation, quotation from other poets, material observation of landscapes, houses, and other sensorial data from her surroundings. Throughout this work, Waldrop employs the personal and expressive registers to mark out the sublime and inchoate trajectory of poetic imagination, and to demonstrate the historical contiguities that shape our inmost perception of language—as basis for all we would, but can't, say:

> Growing up in Germany after the Nazi years, my friends and I clung to the idea that at least the holocaust had been so horrible that nothing like it could happen anywhere. And that we could not distance ourselves from it, that we didn't have the luxury of saying "they."
>
> *We swapped knives to peel off childhood like so many skins.*
>
> (219)

The asperity of this observation aligns with Waldrop's effort here to provide a truthful accounting, testimonial to that which has vanished but continues to exert its pull on the present:

> Small memories surface.
>
> *My first schoolday, September 1941, a cool day. Time did not pass, but was conducted to the brain. I was taught. The Nazi salute, the flute. How firmly entrenched, the ancient theories. Already using paper, pen, and ink. Yes, I said, I'm here.*
>
> *I was six or seven dwarfs, the snow was white, the prince at war. Hitler on the radio, followed by Le'hax. I had learned to ride a bike.*
>
> *All hands in the field. Women and prisoners. War internalized as everything. Grammar aligned according to race. Too bitterly other. Surplus of privation. Polish. Yiddish. Prisoners in the field.*
>
> (219)

What's stunning about these "recollections" is the way they enact the language of memory: stuttering, incomplete, syntactically disrupted, partial to sensory information that is non-narrative in quality. What gets remembered, Waldrop reminds us here, always occurs in a grammar "internalized as everything." The innocence of childhood—"I had learned to ride a bike"—exists simultaneously with "All hands in the field. Women and prisoners." While there's much that one could say about the formal perseverance of this kind of work (and its ties to other experimental prose poetry, notably by Lyn Hejinian and Leslie Scalapino), its authenticity—and authority—rests on its actualization of the intimate register of language. Waldrop's effort feels earned, and labor intensive, as she seeks to uncover what is always already present in language. At the base of the real and the unsaid. In other respects, this is the idiom of the survivor, the cultural exile, the foreigner. Existing "between" (a word that Waldrop tells us appears in one of her earliest poems in English), Waldrop registers the wobbly imperfect of our speech as we seek to confront the "systems of relations" (265) that govern our lives. Which is to say, we recognize ourselves here—if we do—as refugees of the actual, bound to a space of writing and thought that, as Waldrop makes clear, is always a "matter of words" (224).

As with [Susan] Schultz's *A Poetics of Impasse,* Waldrop's book ends with a reflection on 9/11, its meanings if not its Truth. Borrowing the title of her essay from John Cage—"Poetry is having nothing to say and saying it"—Waldrop writes: "'The Truth' is unavailable to us, is not on a human scale. It is by definition too complex to be fully grasped. We have to make do with lowercase truths. In the plural. Because there are many. All partial. All contradicting one another" (275). Citing Andrew Joron, Waldrop asks "how can we turn emergency into emergence?" (276). Her response, not surprisingly, is that we re-focus our attentions on form and re-recognize the ways that poetic language gives us the chance to explore and re-define experience: "We turn to words, not so much to 'express' our experiences as to question, reflect, and above all, make them real" (276). The connection between our work in language— "with its possibilities of lies, of fiction" (276) and the complexity of an event like 9/11 that outstrips our linguistic capabilities is clear. Only through the re-presentation of a world in language can we begin to translate experience—historically traumatic, multi-layered, at the fringe of our expressive abilities—and thereby establish a politically and socially coherent response. Which is to say, we assume our responsibilities as citizens; we "argue, analyze, read, yes, with double attention—especially the statements of our government, examine euphemisms ('collateral damage') and hypocrisies" (276). Waldrop's emphatically political gesture here is a refusal of the fixatives of nationalist ideology and cultural othering that have been endemic to this nation's outlook since the terrorist attacks of 9/11. Again, the terms are decisive, the actual words we use to describe and make concrete what we're doing: like Denise Levertov's call to public action against the Vietnam War 35 years ago—"Not to forget but to remember better" (136)—Waldrop's is a vitally addressed reaffirmation of our cultural and political memory in the face of state-sponsored lies. "We are fighting a 'war' that has not been declared and whose definition, like that of 'terrorist,' can change from one day to the next as it suits President Bush" (275). Insofar as the present failures of the U.S. are failures of public imagination and historical responsibility, they occur in a language of factual—and fateful—eventfulness. In our current political circumstances, having "nothing to say" is not the problem. Rather, as Waldrop suggests, the problem is finding the adequate form in which to say *something.*

Works Cited

Levertov, Denise. "Prologue: An Interim." *Poems 1968-1972.* New York: New Directions, 1987.

Schultz, Susan. *A Poetics of Impasse in Modern and Contemporary American Poetry.* Tuscaloosa: U of Alabama P, 2005.

Waldrop, Rosmarie. *Dissonance (if you are interested).* Tuscaloosa: U of Alabama P, 2005.

Christine Hume and Rosmarie Waldrop (interview date summer 2008)

SOURCE: Hume, Christine, and Rosmarie Waldrop. "A Conversation with Rosmarie Waldrop." *Chicago Review* 53/54, nos. 4-2 (summer 2008): 252-61.

[*In the following interview, Hume and Waldrop discuss a number of biographical and theoretical topics, most notably Waldrop's thoughts on rhythm.*]

The following exchange took place over email between December 2005 and March 2006.

* * *

[*Hume*]: *Growing up in an occupied zone in postwar Germany must have given you a sense of English as a force of occupation and incorporation. When you were ten years old, English really did take over! How do you see this early situation as informing your attitude toward, and attunement to, language?*

[Waldrop]: No doubt all that you mention has had an influence, but I can't pin it down. I have the feeling that as a child I was a kind of sponge—just soaking things up without too much sense of what it was all about. Except of course the two radical changes of my world: in 1943 when my hometown was bombed and 1945 when all—well, a lot of—the values changed! But English at that point was simply part of school and what I knew the American soldiers about town spoke. I've always thought it was the conscious change to English, my coming to the US, that not only made me a translator, but gave me a sense of being "between," and a sense of writing as exploring what "happens between." Between words, sentences, people, cultures. But maybe it all started in 1945.

"Between" is everywhere in your work; for instance, from your autobiography:

> *This became important for my own method of composition: the tension between clusters (lines or single words) scattered on a page and a temporal sequence.*
>
> *To accept the complete sentence (most of the time), but to do my best to subvert it from the inside, by sliding between frames of reference . . .*
>
> *It was a way of getting out of myself. Into what? An interaction, a dialog with language, with a whole net of earlier and concurrent texts. Relation. Between.*
>
> *Using Williams's book [A Key into the Language of America] as a matrix allowed me to work out some of my own ambivalences as an immigrant: a "conqueror" of sorts, and yet irredeemably between cultures.*

The way your speaking voice settled between German and English accents suggests how your literary voice stands against absolutes and totalities, how it lands somewhere between seriousness and irreverence, how it disturbs our settled relation to language.

Yet "between" is such a loaded word in our poetry culture, a word with a double edge. It's as often used to describe an opportunistic, professionalized "on-the-fence" aesthetics and politics as it's used to describe inclusivity. It can signal an inquiry into places that appear uninhabited or empty but might also imply a lack of allegiances and alliances. How do you distinguish your own sense of "between" among these possibilities? As someone "between words, sentences, people, cultures" to what or to whom are your most adamant commitments?

I'm glad you see my voice "between seriousness and irreverence." It's maybe the biggest lesson of Dada that we can—and should—be serious and not serious at the same time. Passionately serious, but at the same time able to take some distance on ourselves—and our art. My sense of between is a sense of relation. One of the first poems I wrote in English is called **"Between"** and places itself in the Atlantic ("not all here / or there"). The water not only separates but also connects the continents. Therefore the poem can end with "But when it rains I inherit the land."

I found it very exciting to discover how ubiquitous the image of the electromagnetic field is in the twentieth century. In the field, everything happens between, relation is everything. Whitehead posits the actual world as built up of "occasions" rather than "things" (which he calls "already abstractions from actual occasions"). Kurt Lewin describes mental states as balances of forces and

vectors. Fenollosa examined the sentence and concluded: "A true noun, an isolated thing, does not exist in nature. Things are only terminal points, or rather the meeting points, of actions, cross-sections cut through actions, snap-shots. Neither can a pure verb, an abstract motion, be possible in nature. . . . Thing and action cannot be separated." W. C. Williams says, "the poem is a field of action." Pound writes, "the thing that matters in art is a sort of energy, a force transfusing, welding and unifying." And of course Olson: "At root (or stump) what is, is no longer THINGS but what happens BETWEEN things, these are the terms of the reality contemporary to us—and the terms of what we are." This is perhaps also behind my changing from single-word or very short lines to prose poems. Not that the words in a line are any less in relation than in a sentence! Or the charge between them any less crucial! So maybe this is balderdash.

"Adamant commitments"—I don't think you want me to blather about the Big Values like honesty, truthfulness, love! In my work, I am committed to a questioning attitude, to precision of language (and thinking, if possible), to poetry as inquiry. But almost anything is subject to being questioned, rethought.

"Between" might, in other hands, be construed as reinforcing an ideology of binaries. To say you are "between" is to live with a mother on one side and a father on the other, or a father and a holy ghost, or a liberal and a conservative, or a past and a future. "Between" implies a bifurcation of the world into inner/outer, subject/object, creative/critical, reading/writing, public/private, known/unknown, literal/figurative—all tidy symmetrical fantasies—false divides—that your work actively investigates and complicates.

*"Between" also very much implies a highly spatial imagination—something you highlight in your own poetics, especially in **"The Ground Is the Only Figure"** and through your primary technique, collage. In such a discursive spatiality there is an affective topography of exclusion, where identity is lost. Yet another way to think of being between is temporally, via rhythm. This is something you don't address explicitly your poetics—though obviously you've had a long and fruitful relationship with music.*

Do you identify with Blake's notion of "contraries" as a force for "progression"? Another way I hear your work is as a dialectic between vulgar (with its various connotations—vernacular, public, coarse, rude, barbaric) and refined. Your sense of humor, your use of a dead-pan register at once parodies and manipulates the usual ways of making sense.

You're right about the binary and how ingrained it is in our thinking. But the really pernicious part of it is that usually one of the pair gets valorized over the other, or even to the exclusion of the other. I think of the "between" more in terms of both/and, as a way of extending the grey-zone between the black and white in the direction of multivalence. "The yes and no in everything."

Of course there's also neither/nor! Where exclusion comes in again. But I don't agree that in the "topography of exclusion . . . identity is lost." I would think it could, on the contrary, lead to a strong identity as other. As you know I think of the law of excluded middle as a "lawn," the empty center as fertile, playground, womb, the "empty" space in a flute or a violin that gives bodies to sound.

And yes, the positive side is that the tension between contraries is, as Blake says "a force for progression," a tension that makes us think harder, makes the poem move, develop. Tension is one of the few ways we can talk about rhythm. As long as you write in a regular meter you can talk about rhythm in terms of the tension between the meter and "normal" speech. In free verse, you can talk in terms of the tension between line and sentence. But in prose poems? I've recently used periods as rhythmic markers rather than (or also as) grammatical markers: "How the words are. Suspended around you." That kind of thing.

I haven't written much about rhythm (or the music of verse) because it is so hard to pin down. The sense of rhythm seems to differ widely from one person to the other. I remember trying to work with Donald Hall at the University of Michigan. He read my lines as if they were prose, very fast. Every time, I had to say: I don't hear it like this, I made the lines short to make them slow. But when I read the lines back to him my way he was not convinced. He was helpful on many other aspects of craft, but I realized I could not pay attention to anything he said about rhythm.

The difficulty of talking about rhythm probably has to do with the fact that it is an aspect of time, which is also hard to talk about. I've just started reading G. J. Whitrow's *The Natural Philosophy of Time*. Whitrow spends a good part of the first section on scientists and philosophers from Archimedes to Helmholtz and Poinsot, who, for this very reason, tried to eliminate issues of time and to reduce science to spatial laws like constancy and uniformity. He quotes Einstein: "It is a characteristic of thought in physics . . . that it endeavours in principle to make do with 'space-like' concepts alone, and strives to express with their aid all relations having the form of laws."

The day your last email came, I received the John Cage issue of Aufgabe *in the mail, which includes your response to a lecture Norman O. Brown gave on Cage. It was also the day Barbara Guest died.*

These Cagian coincidences and congruencies keep resonating. I opened Guest's Forces of Imagination: "The Infancy of Poetics" *says only "The poem begins*

in silence." An uncanny correspondence with Cage's pantheon of silences. Guest and Cage are both riveted to absence. Your "Form and Discontent" places the two side by side: "Barbara Guest: 'The dark identity of the poem.' / John Cage: 'The importance of being perplexed.'" And further down the page, we come back to the topic of rhythm, which reiterates, in Guest's characteristic "invisible magic," something along the lines of what you were saying with the Donald Hall anecdote: "Guest: 'The poem enters its own rhythmical waters.'" The difficulty in talking about death, like rhythm, "probably has to do with the fact that it is an aspect of time." "Our time not calculable by stopwatch or plucked string." I want to ask you about Cage, but I'm more immediately moved by Guest's death and have been wondering what your particular response, as a woman who has made her way in the same male-saturated scene—how might this death be different for you than say the death of Creeley or Mac Low, who own the same immortal dimensions as Guest?

It seems there is no catching up with mourning. Poets don't die. They live in their work. It's the death of the person, the friend, that makes me grieve. But with Barbara Guest, Robert Creeley, and Jackson Mac Low dying in short succession—three poets equally important in their very different ways—I do have the feeling it's the end of a world.

I discovered Barbara with the book *Moscow Mansions* and fell immediately under her spell. I soon after wrote a sequence that uses phrases from her "Byron's Signatories." (It's **"Kind Regards,"** a chapbook from 1975 reprinted in *Streets Enough to Welcome Snow*.) I have gone back to her poems again and again. I've always admired her combination of lightness and passion, her sudden veerings in unsuspected directions. In talking with her too, the sudden whimsy that in no way diminished her passionate commitment to poetry and art. But in the poems, the infallible rhythm, the purity of her line . . . it is a great sadness that we won't get any more of it.

In the index to Dissonance, *there is a small list of Guest pages, in the first of which (12-22) I could not find a reference to Guest. This absence of course made the connections between what you are discussing in those pages—mysticism, abstraction, "similarity disorder," an exploration of the limits of language—and Guest's work all the more potent. Because I kept looking for her where she was not, she was always all the more present. "A turbulent presence." It seems like a game fitting to you both—as you can both be perverse and mischievous.*

How awful, this error in the index, 12-22 should have been 121-22! I hope there are not too many more like this!

You often use at least two dominant rhythmic modes in your work, juxtaposing prose against lineated poetry and lists. In the case of the **"Music Is an Oversimplification of the Situation We're In"**—your tribute to Cage—the prose paragraphs are set against a stream of "key" words, which I imagine as a kind of rhythmic murmur under the "main" text—or as the "extraneous" noise that gets picked up in the "recording" in a manner appropriate to Cage or simply as a visual rhythm. It's like a writing-through of Cage and Brown, a verticality set against a horizontal instinct. How do your choices of rhythm interact with your ideas of literary or generic hybridity?

In **"Music Is an Oversimplification"** I thought of the list less as a rhythm than as a palette, the way some painters, like Tom Phillips, put a strip of colors down one side of the painting. The words are all from Cage's *Silence,* which I worked from (rather than Brown's lecture). Obviously nobody is going to *read* that list (alphabetical!), but it does make a contrasting murmur, as you say, and a visual rhythm.

On the other hand, in I began with the prose "conversations," but felt those blocks of prose were so dense that there needed to be a bit more air from time to time. Hence the "interludes" in verse. Here I really wanted to juxtapose two different rhythms and speeds.

As for hybridity in general: my experience is that heterogeneous elements produce a fruitful kind of tension, one that stretches my ideas in the process of wrestling them together. Of course, not all juxtapositions work, it's a matter of finding those that do.

You say that you fell under Barbara Guest's "spell." That implies a kind of magical incantation, a rhythm of perception just outside conscious apprehension, one that arouses affective response and engorges our senses and our sense of our world. It is a deeply physical experience. Our senses of time and rhythm are cultural; yet rhythm also seems to be an instinct. Do you think there's such a thing as an American rhythm?

I don't think rhythm is an instinct, but I agree that it is physical, based on body rhythms like breath and pulse. In language it also relates to everyday speech rhythms. And here your "American rhythm" comes in. At this point I suspect we still have a "Southern rhythm" different from a "New England rhythm," etc. But radio and TV have begun to level those differences and will probably continue the process to the point where we may indeed get an "American rhythm."

But even while I'm spouting this I get suspicious. We can't really abstract any one of the elements in writing. Remember when Housman was raving about "the furies and surges" of Blake's rhythm in: "Tyger, Tyger, burning bright / In the forest of the night," Pound countered with: "Tiger, Tiger, catch 'em quick / All the little lambs

are sick." In other words: the meaning of the words changes the rhythm. And so we're back with rhythm as cultural. I don't think I can sort it out!

As a result of your editorial advocacy, your translation projects, and your own writing, contemporary American poetry looks and sounds much different than it did thirty years ago. I'd love to hear how you characterize that change. What do you find most exciting about contemporary poetry?

You're obviously in overstatement mode. What I've done is a small part of the change and ferment that seems to have begun with the small press explosion in the Sixties, which has now received new impetus with online publishing. And let's not forget, in between, the Language poets whose radical statements ("nonreferential poetry!") riled even the people who didn't read their poems. Outrage is a ferment too.

I think we've had a great "opening of the field." There are many more poetries getting a hearing/showing than before. And while there is of course much that I find dull, there is lots of energy—and surprise.

I've been reading board books to my ten-month old daughter, and I've noticed that many, many of them have a mirror somewhere, asking "where's the baby?" I'm not sure how long the mirror-in-the-book phenomenon has been around, but I find that my own students often read this way. The tendency of readers to identify themselves in the text, to literally look for oneself in the text (and conversely to look for the author too literally, autobiographically) within the text, is disheartening. Your approach to character often frustrates this impulse and focuses on a hybrid voice, the voice of language, or the "not I." You use pronouns (I-you and he-she in the trilogy and in **Love, Like Pronouns**) grammatically, relationally—and it's often very humorous the way they play with their own rhetoricity.

In the Cage tribute, the lists are asemantic throughlines set contrapuntally against larger blocks of text that adopt the rhetoric of exposition (though not its goals). This poem addresses a subject, but even more, it manufactures an atmosphere. The German philosopher Gernot Böhme locates atmospheres as "in between," straddling environmental qualities and human sensibilities, which provoke a dramatic awareness of transitions and relationships. You've said elsewhere that when you collaborate with your husband Keith, the result is a third voice.

I'm very intrigued by the mirror in the children's books. Looking for oneself and for vicarious experience in a book is, I suspect, the way we all start reading. It takes some sophistication to go beyond it. You are an exceptional reader. I've often gotten my pronouns taken literally and the I-you interpreted strictly as a woman talking to a man.

Do you have any future goals for or projects involving hybrid voices (and by this I don't mean genre, but the ability to collaborate with other writers/texts) and collaboration? How do you want your future or current work to develop these approaches?

I can't imagine working without some counterpoint. And it usually comes from other writing. But I don't have a plan or even a strategy beforehand. Some writers do—Marjorie Welish, for instance. I read around until I come across a text that sets off sparks, and I know I can work with it. Unlike Cage, I'm also not sure "what needs to be done." Though I have a sense of what must be avoided! But then both Cage and Marjorie Welish believe in "progress" in the arts, and I don't. There are too many glorious eccentrics. I'm now winding down a sequence that bounces off a semiotic text about zero, vanishing point, and money. This got very difficult because of the material's level of abstraction and developed into a kind of enactment of my ambivalence about abstraction in writing. But now I feel once again faced by a void. Or, as Jabès called it, I'm entering "the book of torment," the space between projects.

I've been trying to write a prose poem for Barbara. I'll put the current state below.

The Poem Begins in Silence

Barbara Guest, 1920-2006

Where language stops matter begins. Of words. The simple contact with a wooden spoon. I don't easily give up on the uncertainties that might, if only for a moment, alleviate grief. But time is perishable. I believe. A sense of consciousness comes precisely. From the flow of perceptions. Relations of warfare and polka dots. And you cannot twice capture the flash of identity between subject and object.

The poem begins in silence, you wrote, mystery, wild gardens, pitch within the ear, chalk, rivulets, shifting persona, shuffling light.

As long as we've not reached, as in a dream, the fibrous, woody substance of words. We are prisoners. Of narratives in the room. Sprawling to consider an emphasis falls. On reality. Neither thick lids nor vowels inclement can obstruct the transparency of the dragon-

fly's wings. While the brain establishes consciousness through stimuli occurring not more than a twenty-fourth of a second apart. You occupy the lotus position.

The poem is fragile, you wrote, the contour elusive, ropes sway, heavy violets, galactic rhythm, sibilants, solitude edged, upward from the neck, provokes night.

When approaching death we cannot go into the matter of darkness. Viewed on the screen of distance, your shadow rephrased. Forbids the instant disclosure. The necessary night entangled in the folds of preoccupation until the next bold seizure of dawn. It is the connecting between moments—not the moments themselves—that is consciousness. Field broken by low running water, dour sky, the earth in twists moving like the water into the body's memory of self.

The poem is a résumé, you wrote, of impalpable vision, the *clairobscur* of thought, a brown mouse, twilight soup, the figure appears, adoptive day, scorched tongue, the edge, always.

After your death we find matter. For many fine tales about your life. And work. The speculative use of minerals, like beryl, to prevent attachment to words from overflowing. To catch the fraction of a second when the seam of present and future is visible in the flash of the lizard's flight. Loss requires restructuring all of our consciousness, our relation to sunrise. And giving way to the emotions.

The poem draws blood, you wrote, kicks away the ladder, rose marble table, folds of skin, mirrors, fans, nimble wind, multiplied by frost, the rage of night.

FURTHER READING

Criticism

Muratori, Fred. "Ambiguity Isn't What It Used to Be—Or Is It?" *Georgia Review* 52, no. 1 (spring 1998): 142-60.

Review of Waldrop's *Another Language: Selected Poems* that praises the poet's "reverent" approach to the English language, which she learned during the post-World War II American occupation of her native Germany.

William Carlos Williams
1883-1963

American poet, novelist, critic, essayist, short story writer, and autobiographer.

For additional information on Williams's life and career, see *PC,* Volume 7.

INTRODUCTION

A major figure of both modernism and imagism, Williams is known for experimental poetry that challenged traditions regarding form and poetic language. His work is associated with vivid imagery and deals with concrete objects rather than abstract ideas as expressed by his oft-quoted dictum "No ideas but in things." Williams's most critically-acclaimed poem is the five-volume epic *Paterson* (1946-58), but his best known single work is the short piece, "The Red Wheelbarrow," which has been included in countless anthologies and is still taught in high school and college literature classes.

BIOGRAPHICAL INFORMATION

Williams was born on September 17, 1883, in Rutherford, New Jersey, which was at that time a small rural town. His parents were William George Williams, a businessman born in England who retained his British citizenship all his life, and Raquel Hélène Hoheb Williams, born in Puerto Rico and educated in Paris. Williams began his education in the Rutherford public schools, where he remained until 1896; he then attended schools in Geneva, Paris, and finally New York City. In 1902 he was admitted to the University of Pennsylvania Medical School; he graduated with an M. D. in 1906, did an internship in New York, and then studied pediatrics at the University of Leipzig. He returned to Rutherford four years later and began practicing medicine, a career he pursued for more than forty years. In 1912, Williams married Florence (Flossie) Herman, with whom he had three sons: William, Eric, and Paul Herman. Meanwhile, in addition to his medical practice, Williams pursued a second career as a writer, publishing short stories, essays, and novels as well as several volumes of poetry. He also served as a mentor to a number of young poets, among them Charles Olson, Robert Creeley, Denise Levertov, and Allen Ginsberg. In 1948, Williams suffered a heart attack, followed by a series of strokes; he was also treated for depression in 1953. He died on March 4, 1963, at his home in Rutherford and is buried in Lyndhurst, New Jersey.

Among Williams's many awards are the *Dial* Award (1926), the Guarantors Prize from *Poetry* magazine (1931), the Russell Loines Memorial Award for poetry (1948), the National Book Award for poetry (1950), the Bollingen Prize (1952), the Levinson Prize (1954), the Oscar Blumenthal Prize (1955), and the Pulitzer Prize in poetry for *Pictures from Brueghel* (1962). Williams was a member of the American Academy of Arts and Letters, the National Institute of Arts and Letters, the Academy of American Poets, and the Bergen County, New Jersey, Medical Association.

MAJOR WORKS

Williams's work has been associated with both the Imagist movement and the Modernist movement. He rejected the influence of British and European literary culture and was committed to creating a body of poetry that was fresh and distinctly American. Williams's first volume of poetry was the rather conventional *Poems,* privately published in 1909 and very different from his later work. Williams himself disparaged the collection later in his career. In 1913, Williams published *The Tempers* which was followed in 1917 by *Al Que Quiere!* and in 1920 by *Kora in Hell: Improvisations.* These volumes featured the economy of language and American colloquial speech that were to become part of Williams's trademark style. The 1923 volume *Spring and All* is a combination of poetry and prose and contains the frequently anthologized poem "The Red Wheelbarrow," a prime example of the poet's privileging of image. In the 1940s, Williams continued to experiment with form and began using the triadic stanza and the variable foot, both of which he employed in *The Wedge* (1944), a volume containing intense images associated with the social conditions of the war years. *Paterson,* Williams's epic representation of a New Jersey city and of an artist with the same name, is often considered his masterpiece. It consists of five volumes, published individually over a twelve-year period from 1946 to 1958, and features a montage technique similar to that used by artists and filmmakers. Williams's final collection of poetry was *Pictures from Brueghel and Other Poems* (1962), which was awarded the Pulitzer Prize in 1963 shortly after the poet's death.

CRITICAL RECEPTION

Williams's goal of establishing an American poetry free of what he considered the outdated standards and influences of the old world has been studied by a number of critics. Part of that project involved breaking free of the influence of some of the most important poets, both English and American, among his contemporaries. Jeff Webb discusses Williams's attempts to distance himself from other modernist poets, particularly Ezra Pound and T. S. Eliot, and Burton Hatlen has studied Williams's early relationship to Pound, H. D., and Wallace Stevens. Even in some of the early poems, according to Hatlen, "we can see Williams beginning to stake out a distinctive position of his own, clearly different from those of Pound, H. D., or Stevens, although sharing with these other poetic masters a determination to find a new voice appropriate to a new, distinctly 'modern,' world of experience." According to Webb, "what makes American writing distinctively American for Williams is the writer's attempt, on the racial model of the Indian and the Negro, to 'annihilate' the living corpses of past texts by consuming and transforming them according to the 'naturalism' of his or her own race." H. T. Kirby-Smith has studied Williams's attempt to escape from meter, contending that the poet's "compulsive Americanism . . . made him certain that any poetry associated with British or European models, myths, or subjects would turn out to have been trammeled by its meters." Michael Golston (see Further Reading) reports that Williams's theory of measure was derived from his knowledge of science, since the poet claimed "that his 'variable foot' acts as a measure for Einsteinian physics, according to the formula: 'variability' in prosody equals 'relativity' in the time/space continuum."

As committed as Williams was to representing the American experience, he was unable to do so during the Great Depression according to Bob Johnson (see Further Reading), who has examined Williams's poetry and prose written during the 1930s, singling out the "alternately angry and euphoric" poems of *An Early Martyr and Other Poems* (1935). He contends that "Williams was incapable of synthesizing the Depression experience in a persuasive way" and that he "failed to locate the object, the phrase, the fact, or the hermeneutic which would give unity to a riven America" during the Depression years.

Scholars have generally considered Williams's five-volume epic *Paterson* to be his greatest poetic achievement. Alba Newmann believes that *Paterson* enacts many of the themes associated with the French theorists Felix Guattari and Gilles Deleuze. Christopher MacGowan explores one of Williams's recurring themes in *Paterson,* that of achieving a distanced stance from which to assess the community or an event within the community—the distance being either temporal or spatial. According to MacGowan, "Williams articulates a series of gestures toward the community from the distance of this demarcated space" and this occurs in other later poems as well as in the epic. Williams's response to Rutherford (and to Paterson) was "divided" and in turn, the community's response to Williams was also mixed. MacGowan reports that Mrs. Williams claimed her husband's poetry was "misunderstood and parodied" in Rutherford. Ann Mikkelsen (see Further Reading) has analyzed *Paterson* as a pastoral, along with the themes of filth and decay in the poem, and finds that in Williams's poetry, "individuals associated with dirt in modern American society, such as women or people of color, cannot be excised from a national narrative, such as pastoral, without destroying the greater body that is the nation." She concludes that Williams "revises pastoral narratives of both the Old World and the New, in the process forging a distinctively twentieth-century pastoral mode."

Williams's best-known individual piece is "The Red Wheelbarrow," a short poem that still appears in anthologies and the syllabi of high school and college literature classes—indeed, the poem has achieved a certain iconic status and is often people's first (and sometimes only) encounter with Williams's poetry. Mark Long refers to "the indelible image" of the poem, and Bill Mohr also discusses the image of the wheelbarrow as a symbol of spring; however, he contends that "the wheelbarrow in question . . . is much more complex than Williams's critics have acknowledged." Sergio Rizzo also finds the usual interpretation of the poem as an example of imagist and objectivist poetic practices to be less complex than a careful study of the poem, along with the commentary and frameworks Williams provided. Rizzo explores questions of race—based on the fact that the owner of the wheelbarrow was an African-American—and contends that "critics *see through* these frames and, in the process, keep a dark figure in the poem's biographical history . . . at the poem's margins."

Many critics have commented on Williams's influence on younger poets and the care he took in mentoring a number of them, including Denise Levertov, Thom Gunn, and Allen Ginsberg. MacGowan has studied the relationship between Williams and the three poets, noting that they "responded in their own ways" to Williams's influence. Alan Golding discusses the pervasive influence of Williams on later experimental writers, especially the Language writers. Golding reports that "in particular, Williams was crucial to the self-definition of Language poetics as it developed *in opposition to* the workshop lyric." Long suggests that Williams's poetry and poetic theories will potentially continue to influence poets, particularly those interested in ecology, noting that "Williams's acute critique of the view that poetic language offers a less-mediated relation to the world might contribute to expanding the range and power of environmental and ecological reflection in contemporary American poetry."

PRINCIPAL WORKS

Poetry

Poems 1909

The Tempers 1913

Al Que Quiere! 1917

Kora in Hell: Improvisations 1920

Sour Grapes 1921

Go Go 1923

Spring and All 1923

The Cod Head 1932

Collected Poems, 1921-1931 1934

An Early Martyr and Other Poems 1935

Adam & Eve & the City 1936

The Complete Collected Poems, 1906-1938 1938

The Wedge 1944

*Paterson. 5 vols. 1946-58

The Clouds 1948

The Pink Church 1949

Selected Poems 1949

The Collected Later Poems 1950

The Collected Earlier Poems 1951

The Desert Music, and Other Poems 1954

Journey to Love 1955

Pictures from Brueghel and Other Poems 1962

Other Major Works

The Great American Novel (novel) 1923

In the American Grain (essays) 1925

A Voyage to Pagany (novel) 1928

The Knife, and Other Stories (short stories) 1932

A Novelette (novel) 1932

White Mule (novel) 1937

Life on the Passaic River (short stories) 1938

In the Money: White Mule—Part II (novel) 1941

The Build-Up: A Novel (novel) 1952

I Wanted to Write a Poem: The Autobiography of the Works of a Poet (autobiography) 1958

The Farmers' Daughters: The Collected Stories (short stories) 1961

**These works were first collected and published as *Paterson* in 1963.

CRITICISM

Christopher MacGowan (essay date 1997)

SOURCE: MacGowan, Christopher. "'Caresses—Withheld': William Carlos Williams's Dialogue with the Future." In *The Future of Modernism*, edited by Hugh Witemeyer, pp. 119-36. Ann Arbor, Mich.: University of Michigan Press, 1997.

[*In the following essay, MacGowan discusses Williams's relationship to the city of Paterson and his influence on later poets including Denise Levertov and Thom Gunn.*]

Ezra Pound, defining "Dr. Williams' Position" as he saw it in a 1928 essay in the *Dial*, argued that this position was one of an outside observer of America and its culture. A major strength of Williams as a writer, for Pound, was his lack of that "porous" quality characteristic of so many American writers, a quality that brought them to absorb every current faddish idea and fashion. "He starts where an European would start," Pound argues, "if an European were about to write of America." He attributes Williams's ability "to observe national phenomena" from without to Williams's multicultural "ancestral endocrines." Williams observes America from a "secure ingle" as "something interesting *but exterior.*" Such for Pound is Williams's version of modernist exile.[1]

Pound's major interest in his essay is Williams's prose (he finds Williams's attempts to enter the minds of his characters in *A Voyage to Pagany* [1928] not Williams at his best). But his perception that Williams views his world from within the space of a "secure ingle" sums up a central feature of the poetry, particularly when the poetry deals with the local community or a contemporary public event. While this characteristic is lessened in the post-1950s work, which often explores memory or emphasizes the poet's distance from the object world by fore-grounding his physical handicaps, in the earlier poetry this "ingle"—sometimes spatial, sometimes temporal—can be carved out in the midst of a poem or sequence striving fully to engage the community and the pressure of a public moment. This split becomes itself a central theme in **Paterson,** and is one of the recurring meanings of the "divorce" motif that runs through the poem.

From the perspective of his temporal or spatial distance Williams assesses the unrealized significance of a public event within a context larger than its immediate moment or examines the community itself along with an implicit or explicit presentation of its unrealized potential. From the straightforward exhortations to "my townspeople" in **Al Que Quiere!** (1917) to the more complex strategies of later poems, Williams articulates a series of gestures toward the community from the distance of this demarcated space. In poems, many of which emphasize beginnings or locate an alternative space in the imagination expressed through art, Williams's distanced perspective finally looks to a space in the future to redeem the unfulfilled space of the present.

In *Paterson* (Book V of which was once to be titled "The River of Heaven") this future is as much his own as the future of the time and landscape the poem explores, although here and throughout his work the reach is also to a future for the poem itself as unfulfilled space. The strategy amounts to calling for a dialogue with the future from within the pressure of the moment, a call answered by a number of poets in the 1950s and later. The call in *Paterson* is explicitly answered by Allen Ginsberg and built into the narrative of the poem, but two other important later poets, Denise Levertov and Thom Gunn, have also acknowledged looking to Williams's work for strategies to articulate their own guarded responses to their particular communities.

Williams's divided response to Rutherford as a community, and as a representative community, emerges in his 1954 autobiographical essay "Seventy Years Deep," in which he asks, "What does my being a poet mean to the people of Rutherford?" The answer is guarded. "At first it was amusing to them; some were critical, others were unconcerned, and a very few were understanding." Then later in the essay he acknowledges that his "intimate contacts" with the individuals of the town have been the source of much of his writing.[2] In a late interview with Edith Heal, Mrs. Williams was more forthright about this division between intimacy and understanding: "There were no literary connections in Rutherford. I asked him not to read his poetry in Rutherford where he was misunderstood and parodied. I told him to cut it out. . . . 'They don't know what it's about . . . it's insulting to you and me.'"[3]

This division also characterizes the response of the community itself, including the city of Paterson, to Williams and his work, one well illustrated by the material collected over the past forty years by the Rutherford Free Public Library.[4] While the library's collection of over two thousand items (newspapers, magazines, books, photographs, audiovisual material, and general artifacts, largely donated by local townspeople) is a remarkable tribute to the community's response to the poet, the discussion of Williams in the local newspapers preserved in the collection often reveals a somewhat bemused and often patronizing attitude. With what might be an accidental oversight, an early clipping preserved from an unidentified local publication records that the poet has just won the 1926 *Dial* award but identifies the recipient as "William Corlas Williams." The *Bergen Evening Record* of 2 March 1932 records:

"Williams, All But Unknown Here, Seeks to Restore Thought, Life, with Word," while thirty-three years later, now titled the *Record,* the paper headlines a nonevent on the second anniversary of Williams's death with: "Paterson doesn't recall William Carlos Williams." Among the obituaries published two years earlier, one notice in another unidentified local publication records that the head of the Passaic County Historical Society (located in the Lambert Castle of *Paterson* Book III), D. Stanton Hammond, "Disliked Poet's 'Paterson.'" The historian comments: "We had him come speak to the Manuscript Club of Paterson and I told him then I didn't think much of his poem. . . . And Williams told me that was my privilege." The notice continues, reporting the historian's comments: "he didn't bother much with Paterson. 'He flowed more in the New York direction. . . . He got too big for Paterson.'" Another newspaper item describes how a letter sent to Williams with the address "Paterson, New Jersey" was briskly returned "addressee unknown."

Ginsberg, Levertov, and Gunn responded in their own ways to these tensions in Williams's poetry, as they evolved their own particular degrees of engagement with communities warily embraced and potentially hostile. Levertov and Gunn, both working within a non-native culture from early in their careers, and thus particularly sensitive to tensions between the self and surroundings, have, in a number of essays, discussed ideas of community in Williams's work. For Levertov "there is virtually nothing that he wrote that does not—especially within the context of his work as a whole—have social implications";[5] while Gunn, in early and recent essays on Williams, has examined the poems in terms of the relationship they evince between the poet and the external world. This ranges from the "remarkable . . . detachment" of **"The Term"** to the "new ease in his relationship with the external world," suggested by the *Pictures from Brueghel* volume, "poems which twenty years before would merely have implied Williams as onlooker."[6] Ginsberg consistently sees Williams as both "the poet / of the streets" and a visionary. Ginsberg's "Death News," the poem on Williams's death in which the lines just cited appear, has an opening epigraph in which Williams contrasts two separate communities, the group within and the threatening community outside:

> *Visit to W. C. W. circa 1957, poets Kerouac Corso Orlovsky on sofa in living room inquired wise words, stricken Williams pointed thru window curtained on Main Street: "There's a lot of bastards out there!"*[7]

Poem III of *Spring and All* (later titled **"The Farmer"**) is a central poem for both Levertov and Gunn to illustrate Williams's response to community. (The poem also begins Pound's selection of Williams's work in his 1933 *Active Anthology*.) For both Levertov and Gunn the key term in the poem is the artist/farmer's role as "composing /—antagonist." For Gunn the artist/farmer is "the antagonist to disorder," while Levertov develops the point further: "He is an *antagonist*—but to what? To the hostility of the environment, which, however, contains the elements that will nourish his crops." Both readings can be extended to emphasize that the artist/farmer, while actively "pacing," engaged in his immediate world of rain, fields, wind, water, weeds, and orchards, imagines (as do the opening pages of *Spring and All*) a possible "harvest" that could concretely embody what is now only his antagonistic "thought" and that would justify and qualify his current isolation. The space for thought is marked out within the physical world (with no compromise made in the engagement with that world's physicality): it "rolls coldly away / . . . leaving room for thought." The "room for thought" marked out in this poem by the farmer, and by the poet who invents and watches his activity, is the space Williams delineates for himself in poem after poem, the space from which to gain his distanced perspective upon community.[8]

Williams also marks out a potentially communal physical space at the center of the 1930s ten-poem group **"Della Primavera Trasportata al Morale."** Within the sequence's narrative of violence, rootedness, personal despair, and artistic triumph, the sixth poem, **"The House,"** voices an unanswered invitation:

> the whole house
> is waiting—for you
> to walk in it at your pleasure—
> It is yours.

(*CP* [*The Collected Poems of William Carlos Williams*] 1 341)

This sequence (its status *as* a sequence unclear in the 1951 *Collected Earlier Poems* from some confusion of titles in the headnote and intertitle pages) illustrates the way Williams can use the contextualizing potential of the sequence form to extend the themes of an individual poem. Surrounding **"The House"** and emphasizing, by contrast, the emptiness of its and the poet's space is **"The Bird's Companion,"** while following **"The House"** is **"The Sea Elephant,"** describing the physical dislocation of one important source of renewed language:

> —torn
> from the sea.
> (In
>
> a practical voice) They
> ought
> to put it back where
> it came from.

(*CP* 1 342)

As the final poem of the sequence, **"The Botticellian Trees,"** makes clear, the only space that can be filled imaginatively now is the space within Botticelli's frame and the poem that parallels it in the sequence, while the communal possibilities of the space in **"The House"** remain on the level of potential, the poet as displaced within his contemporary world as is the sea elephant; the poet, unlike the birds, is companionless (*CP* 1 340-43).

A similar mapping out of unfulfilled space marking the distance from which the poet observes his community informs **"The Attic Which Is Desire"**: also of 1930. Looking out from

> the unused tent
> of
>
> bare beams
> beyond which
>
> directly wait
> the night
>
> and day—

the poet watches, and incorporates visually into his poem, a space that is filled with language—contrasting with the "unused" communal potential of the attic itself:

```
* * *
* S *
* O *
* D *
* A *
* * *
```

(*CP* 1 325)

In each of these three examples isolation is tempered by the promise that the space from which the poet watches the community might become the space upon which that community could be met. This potential is expressed in terms of imagination ("deep thought"), invitation, and desire—terms also never far from the parallel sexual strategies in Williams's engagement with his world. This marked-out space within a hostile world (the "blank fields," the house, the attic) is contrasted in each case with an imaginative space (the harvest, **"The Botticellian Trees,"** the soda sign) that is filled by the exercise of the imagination as articulated through the poem. But the status of this imagined space remains potential and serves to emphasize through its reach back to the poet's own space the distance and isolation from which he engages his community. The third book of *Paterson*, **"The Library,"** functions in much the same way. Here the poet / Dr. Paterson has retreated to the wrong space from which to try to gauge communal potential and recognizes this error through recalling his discovery—in another space, "the basement"—of a physical embodiment of the "beautiful thing" that throughout Book III is struggling to escape from the library.[9]

Some recent comments by Walter Benn Michaels on identity and representation in Williams's work help further define this multiple function of space in the poetry. Arguing that "the privileging of identity and its transformation into a project" are defining characteristics of American modernism, Michaels notes that in Williams's version "this effort of identity takes the form of a critique of representation where representation seems essential (i.e., in language)",[10] for Williams a poem and a word must first and foremost represent itself, and this imperative is linked to a nativist poetics that must not "copy," that is, engage in representation that is merely copying "reality" (45, 39). Thus, the landscape in the first poem of *Spring and All* is primarily a place of language, with the repetitions of *spring* and *all* in its lines being its foremost "reality" (39). But Michaels points out that for Williams "the effort of imitation [through writing] is redeemed when it's mobilized on behalf of identity" (53). Thus, Poe is most "American" when he isolates himself from his community and clears the ground, "in order [Michaels quotes from Williams's *In the American Grain*] to let the real business of composition *show*" (45).

In Michaels's terms the full potential of the communal ground upon which poet and community could meet, and in turn realize their mutually reinforcing identities, can be illustrated through a "representation," by a "composing/antagonist," of the current fracturing of that potential, without giving up the claim that the poem is rooted in a space prior to meaning. The meaning that finally concerns Williams is one yet to be realized communally and that can only be represented by a space marked out by the imagination, in art, and/or in the future. Williams insists that this representation of what *could be* more clearly serves the community and delineates the artist of integrity's relationship to it than a representation of the local, which he would term merely "realistic."

The perspective upon the city of Paterson that this strategy produces in *Paterson,* as noted earlier, is one of the poem's central themes—the poet's "divorce" from his own culture and the people within it, an indictment charged in the poem's prose, for example, by "E. D." (68) and by "Cress" throughout Book II, and also illustrated in its central narrative. The poem records Dr. Paterson's confused and sometimes desperate search for ways to avoid a full confrontation with community, the prose in particular recording many deaths and various kinds of evasions. Book IV of *Paterson* ends with a somersault, another version of the multiple presence of potential action in space, and Book V with a dance—yet another. In what is apparently the latest manuscript we have of the barely started Book VI, beginning "Lucy had a womb," the fertility of space is illustrated through Lucy's thirteen children, the womb space always central to Williams both as doctor and as poet (240). The poem

itself, despite the motions toward a form of closure at the end of Book IV, is one Williams could never finish, for, as previously noted, part of the space he looks to for an alternative includes his own future—for as long as he could imagine one.

This distanced perspective that Williams makes a central theme in *Paterson* has caused the poem to be criticized as not sufficiently engaged with the city that is its ostensible subject—and not only by the head of the Passaic County Historical Society. Charles Olson saw Williams's focus upon the "substance historical of one city" as making the poem time-bound and his treatment as essentially nostalgic, a "blueberry America," for "Bill, with all respect, don't know fr nothing abt what a city *is*." And this—in Williams's terms, narrow—assumption that the city in this poem is only its immediate urban presence (what for Williams, as noted earlier, would be mere "realism") is also behind Michael Bernstein's complaint in *The Tale of the Tribe* that "the political, historical, and economic reality of Paterson, its existence *as a city,* . . . is curiously missing, a virtual blank at the poem's core." For Bernstein these details of Paterson's urban reality only enter the poem with the inclusion of Allen Ginsberg's two letters in Book IV: "at the last moment, Williams does manage to retrieve his missing context. Fascinatingly, all of the suppressed details do enter the poem once, and in a form that reveals with uncanny precision just what *Paterson* had hitherto failed to confront."[11] But, when the poem is seen in the context of Williams's consistent treatment of community, this inability to confront the city itself is particularly emphasized—rather than the details being "retrieve[d]"—by the inclusion of Ginsberg's prose. The first edition's identification of Ginsberg's letter as from "A. P." (for "a poet," Williams told Ginsberg [*Paterson* 289]) further marks the voice as one with which Dr. Paterson might be able to fuse if the space separating voices, generations, and here too the prose and the poetry could be conflated, as they are in the world of the poem's space.

Ginsberg himself, in "Death News," presents his response to hearing of Williams's death while in Benares, India, as a conflation of spaces upon which the two poets can meet:

> If I pray to his soul in Bardo Thodol
> he may hear the unexpected vibration of foreign
>   mercy.
> Quietly unknown for three weeks; now I saw Passaic
> and Ganges one, consenting his devotion . . .
>   . . . Riding on the old
> rusty Holland submarine on the ground floor
> Paterson Museum instead of a celestial crocodile.

His 1984 poem "Written in My Dream by W. C. Williams," from *White Shroud*, articulates another meeting on the common ground of imagination.

In an essential way community is the raw material of Williams's poems, and the imagined possibilities of communal space that come out of his distanced and critical response to that raw material are his invitation to the community to examine itself and its possibilities. The strategy is parallel to what Williams praised in Juan Gris's painting *The Open Window* in 1923: "the attempt is being made to separate things of the imagination from life, and obviously, by using the forms common to experience so as not to frighten the onlooker away but to invite him." The objects of everyday experience in this painting "are seen to be in some peculiar way—detached" (*CP*1 194, 197).

Apparently, Williams found such detachment difficult to build into his poems that respond specifically to public events or public figures. He often hesitated about publishing these poems and was uncertain about their quality, as if by setting a poem too closely alongside a public event his own distance might be dissolved by an implied degree of participation. These poems often remained unpublished for some years, as one way to gain at least temporal distance, while a number of poems responding to very specific local events remained, as far as Williams's wishes were concerned, unpublished or uncollected—too much, perhaps, still the raw material. Sometimes these poems were literally handed to local citizens. The record of some of these local gestures is in the material now part of the Rutherford Library collection.

The public event of Ford Madox Ford's death spurred the 1939 commemorative poem **"To Ford Madox Ford in Heaven."** Williams's uncertainties regarding the poem, its location of Ford within a particular locale and future, tell something of Williams's relation to his own community and of his doubts about this kind of poem. He wrote to his publisher, James Laughlin: "I like [the poem] but it's really the sort of occasional verse which I somewhat mistrust. The subject makes such demands on a man that he is likely for the moment to forget the poem in the occasion—somewhat topical."[12] Williams wavered in particular on the first stanza. He resisted Louis Zukofsky's suggestion to omit the entire poem from his 1944 collection **The Wedge,** although he apparently accepted every other suggestion of the younger poet. But he did leave out most of the first stanza, an omission that was restored almost twenty years later in the revised edition of **Collected Later Poems** (1963).

The omitted lines answer the question posed by the only line of the first stanza retained in the early version: "Is it any better in Heaven, my friend Ford, / than you found it in Provence?" The first stanza's omitted lines make clear that, for Williams, Ford had seen Provence in terms of the qualities of that "greater world where you now reside" (*CP*2 95-96). The remainder of the poem suggests that Ford's visionary sense of Provence

had made him "homeless" in a physical and geographical sense while still, at the same time, very much a grunting and sweating "gross" part of the actual Provence he moved within and recorded in his writing. Ford is described here in terms resembling Williams's sense of his own distanced participation in his community and of the price paid in isolation for a perception of that community's larger potential.

Yet Williams's concern with the pressure of "the occasion," Ford's death, apparently led him to doubt the efficacy of describing the doubleness of Ford's communal commitment so explicitly in terms of "heaven"—despite the sanction, as David Frail has pointed out, offered by Ford's 1914 poem "On Heaven."[13] Although Williams retained the title, the omission of the lines in the first stanza blurred somewhat the double perspective. But, while the pressures of the occasion gave Williams pause, his strong wish to bring attention to Ford as a writer led him to try (unsuccessfully) to publish the poem where it would receive a wide circulation, in the *New Yorker* (*CP*2 466).

Of other poems concerning public events, **"An Early Martyr,"** on the treatment of social activist John Coffey, waited ten years for revision and publication, and **"Impromptu: The Suckers,"** on Sacco and Vanzetti, waited fourteen years. Both **"An Elegy for D. H. Lawrence"** and **"The Death of See"** (on Harry Crosby) first appeared five years after the deaths of the writers they commemorate and **"To the Ghost of Marjorie Kinnan Rawlings"** after seven years. Williams's tribute to Sibelius, written, like the Ford poem, in the year of the subject's death (1957), became—again as with the earlier work—a poem he continued to hesitate about; in this latter case he still apparently revised the poem after the publication of two previous versions (*CP*2 515-16).

A major exception, however, to this discomfort with poems on public figures and occasions is Williams's elegy to his friend Charles Demuth. Here Williams does not distance himself so much from the event and figure through time as from the event and figure as subject. Demuth is mentioned in the dedication but nowhere else in the poem, which subsumes the remembered painter within an organic presentation of one of his favorite subjects, flowers. Thom Gunn has perceptively articulated the doubleness at work in the poem, the physical and allegorical space of the language: "touch by touch, through qualifications and extensions of the literal, and through a constant attention to the double possibilities in words, an apt description of the physical becomes an apt rendering of the allegorical, and vice versa."[14]

The Rutherford Public Library collection has preserved a number of little-known Williams poems that directly address local events or persons. But Williams himself submitted only two of these poems for publication— **"Peter Kipp to the High School"** from 1921 and **"Early Days of the Construction of Our Library"**;[15] he republished neither poem in any of his collections (and neither poem is recorded in Emily Wallace's *Bibliography*). Another poem, **"The Post Office Clerk and His Daily Duty,"** was written for and given to local resident John Kirk in the late 1930s, according to the *Bergen Evening Record* of 5 December 1953 (the occasion of the 1953 article was Mr. Kirk turning up at a local library reception for the poet and telling the story). The poem, published in David Frail's book *The Early Politics and Poetics of William Carlos Williams* (but without the background story reported by the *Record*), concludes by ascribing to the postal clerk behind his counter the same dual role as community servant and community critic that Williams himself played:

> By practice
> grown familiar
> I size you up
> for what you are
> But ask no questions
> standing there
> What I think
> is my own affair.[16]

Of course, Williams's gesture of writing and donating the poem (after waiting in a line at the post office window, "Dr. Williams left and returned later with a poem," John Kirk reported) is a gesture of sharing "my own affair," but the poem remains an example of what I termed earlier the raw material of community, not a poem that points to future space but, rather, a gesture of the moment. **"Plaint,"** however, another poem in the collection, unpublished to my knowledge, was written for—according to a note added by Professor John Dollar—and presented to two Rutherford parents "on the occasion of their naming their baby daughter Meredith." Often in Williams's work, a new baby represents the physical present and a future promise—and, if a patient of Doctor Williams's, his own delivery of that hope into its double presence.

Two further poems concerned with local matters preserved in the Rutherford Library archives appeared in local newspapers (the source of the clippings unrecorded in both cases). They have never been reprinted and, again, are not recorded in the *Bibliography*. Apparently, Williams was behind the publication of neither poem, each coming into the hands of a local newspaper columnist. Each poem, while clearly not fully developed, ends with its own version of a distinct backing away, a recognition of distance.

"The Old Steps of the Passaic General Hospital," apparently from the 1940s, equates the "bowed head" of the poet, as it runs into a new barrier where he expected

to find entrance, with the figures—"heads often enough / bowed"—of another now "vanished" time, the experience a physical and temporal displacement:

"The Old Steps of the Passaic General Hospital"

> With bowed head, walking toward the old steps
> I ran into a wall. The old steps were gone.
> The new start from another quarter more
> convenient, safer, more protected from
> the north wind and Summer sun, and the old
> that led broadly to the carriage way from
> the open porch above them are no more. There
> chestnut branches leaned at one time and in
> Autumn brown nuts would fall. Vanished now
> with the men who mounted, heads often enough
> bowed, to be led without twist, turn to
> obstruction, discretely, straightaway upward

When the Rev. George Talbott published **"The Old Steps of the Passaic General Hospital"** in his local column, the context he placed the poem in was "the glorious tradition of William Wordsworth." While certainly one possible way of articulating Pound's view that Williams's perspective upon America is as an outsider, Rev. Talbott's gesture of association ("Wordsworth and Williams" is the title of his article) is one of inclusion, despite the poem's ambivalent attitude toward the change. Since Williams is, like Wordsworth, glorifying the "commonplace," Talbott's argument runs, he is a communal poet: "Dr. William Carlos Williams of Rutherford." But Williams is like Wordsworth in a more central way in this poem, setting the new "convenient" entrance against the old, in which heroic figures on missions of mercy battled against the nature whose beauty and force they would further battle inside.

The second poem, **"My Nurses,"** is represented in the Rutherford collection by a clipping dated "August 1946." In May of that year Williams had an unsuccessful hernia operation at the Passaic General Hospital. "While there," the clipping records, "his nurses teased him into writing some verses commemorative of his immobilization in bed."

"My Nurses"

> I can hear the rattle of their skirts
> as I watch their minds
> struggling to maintain the discipline
> —of kindness—put to the test;
> girls, that's all they are
> softening their voices to
> the adult necessity of their lives
> tickling my toes but attentive
> to the need but watching always—not
> only the need but what I might be—
> me, jagged stalagmite in this curious
> cavern of a sick room for their wonder
> Asking, asking and wanting to seem
> not to ask; full of caresses—withheld

The double perspective of the last two lines, from the poet's and the nurses' view, encapsulates, as often in

Williams's work, an unfulfilled sexual promise as part of its articulation of distance and potential.

This "commemorative" poem requested by the nurses found its way into print only through those it addressed. Meanwhile, Williams published **"The Injury"** (*CP*2 161-63) in the *Nation,* a poem that describes the same hospital stay but elaborates upon his feeling of isolation entirely from his own point of view. Once again, though, he came to be ambivalent about a poem centered upon a public event, albeit a personal one. He decided that **"The Injury"** is a "weak" poem (*CP*2 476), and he resisted, unsuccessfully, Randall Jarrell's inclusion of it in the 1949 *Selected Poems.*

Denise Levertov's interest in the "social implications" of Williams's work comes from a poet who, like Ginsberg, is much more comfortable in engaging with public events than is Williams. Levertov argues that Williams's poem **"In Chains"** (1939) is "to me one of the most interesting, and least known, of twentieth-century political poems," but her analysis marks the crucial difference between the two poets' public stances. Williams's poem lays out three ways of resisting "blackguards and murderers" in positions of power ("to bend to their designs, / buck them or be trampled"), all of which are finally rejected for a fourth position: "to avoid / being as they are" and—with another image of potential and of fertility—to

> learn . . .
>   how love
> will rise out of its ashes if
> we water it, tie up the slender
> stem and keep the image of its
> lively flower chiseled upon our minds.
>
>   (*CP*2 65)

For Levertov, that Williams presents one of the three rejected options, to "buck them," in negative terms is "a flaw of logic in the poem." Williams's strategy of resistance, however, is one of patience and sympathy ("love"), out of which could come growth, and not one of resistance merely. Levertov's complaint that Williams fails to define the nature of the resistance implied by "buck them" is answered by the kind of resistance the poem finally posits. Something of the delicate relationship Williams tries to articulate between the poet and "the world" is further illustrated by his revisions to this poem. The poet's degree of implication in a world that the "blackguards and murderers . . . torture" shifts from 1944's distant "to torture it" to the final version's "to torture us" with the revised *Collected Later Poems* of 1963, while the early periodical publication's "we will water [love]" for the final version's "we water" stresses more distinctly the status of the healing action as future potential.[17]

The essay of Levertov's from which these comments come was written in 1972, and it demands of Williams a political voice closer to the position of Levertov herself in the late 1960s and early 1970s than to the stance she had taken ten years earlier, when most influenced by Williams's work. A poem like Levertov's "A Map of the Western Part of the County of Essex in England" (from *The Jacob's Ladder* [1961]) is structured along the lines of Williams's position toward community and posits a duality of space in much the same way. The community here is the new world itself, the writer "less a / stranger here than anywhere else." The possibility of joining that community is explored through a memory of childhood places recorded within the space of a map and is seen as one of finding "ancient / rights of way" that could, through patience and imaginative expression, provide a guide to the problem of "picking up fragments of New World slowly, / not knowing how to put them together nor how to join / image with image." The degree of alienation from her adopted country and culture is heightened by the associations and names from a map representing the space of childhood, adolescence, and imaginative growth. But the map also shows the way, through an acknowledgment of the part of the self that remains tied to it, to connect to and articulate a response to the present: to discover, and write from, that "long stem of connection" Levertov sees as part of Williams's own poetics ("Williams: An Essay," from *Candles in Babylon* [1982]). By contrast, a Vietnam poem such as "Advent 1966" (*Relearning the Alphabet* [1970]), dating from the years of Levertov's comments on Williams's **"In Chains,"** eschews any such alternative space from which to avoid fully engaging with the present culture and its actions. "Advent 1966" rejects any mediation that Southwell's poem on the burning Christ child might offer, or that the imagination might offer ("it is my own eyes do my seeing / . . . what I see is there), and—in an inversion of the strategy of "A Map of the Western Part of . . . Essex . . . ," and other early poems that are closer to Williams's poetics—to refuse to "look elsewhere" for any alternative to, or perspective upon, the present horror; "or if I look" to see only "whole flesh of the still unburned." Similarly, "Ways of Conquest" (from *The Freeing of the Dust* [1975]) is a poem that narrates the fusion of two spaces, rather than their, albeit connected, separation.[18]

With Thom Gunn, Pound's sense of Williams's "position" as that of a transatlantic observer comes full circle. In his comments upon Williams, Gunn has sought to bridge what he sees as a gulf between Williams's achievement and its appreciation in Britain. "He is somebody from whom it is time we started taking lessons" he told the readers of *Encounter* in 1965, and more recently Gunn has argued for the importance of Williams's *Collected Poems, Volume I.* As noted earlier, Gunn has commented upon the doubleness of space in Williams's poem **"The Crimson Cyclamen,"** and in general his comments upon Williams's work might have pleased the Reverend Talbott as well as Pound. He sees Williams as occupying a place both of engagement with his American community and of reaching back for expression of that engagement to some central elements of the English tradition, whether "the seventeenth century" or "the Elizabethan conceit at its best."[19]

But Gunn's most direct attempt to use Williams is in a series of poems reflecting an ambivalent response to a community—his 1966 volume *Positives*. Gunn has said of this book, "I was consciously borrowing what I could from William Carlos Williams, trying as it were to anglicize him." But these poems on an England he had left ten years earlier produced a book all but dismissed in Gunn's *Collected Poems* (1994). "When I returned to San Francisco [after the year that produced *Positives*]," Gunn recalls, "it was with half thoughts of ultimately moving back to London"—although he didn't. Whatever Gunn's intentions in *Positives*, Williams's voice is an appropriate vehicle for the uncertain degree of commitment to the community that lies behind the book: a voice that comes out of a recent past and a potential future in another space, across the Atlantic.[20]

The character of the space from which Williams engages his community and speaks to its future—as well as to the future of poetry—receives different responses from Ginsberg, Levertov, and Gunn. But, whether that space is shaped by the European perspective Gunn describes, the visionary dimension emphasized by Ginsberg, or the connection to origins that concerns Levertov, each poet responds to some degree to Williams's call for a dialogue as part of dealing with his or her own contemporary questions of communal commitment. Williams's call for such a dialogue, along with his reach beyond the pressure of the moment, is what finally lifts his work out of what could have been the limitations of that moment and of his own particular brand of modernism. All three poets recognize that this most sexual of poets, so concerned with touch and contact, was at the same time the poet of "caresses—withheld."

Notes

1. Ezra Pound, "Dr. Williams' Position," *Literary Essays of Ezra Pound* (New York: New Directions, 1968) 391-93.

2. "Seventy Years Deep," *Holiday* 16 (November 1954): 55, 78.

3. "Flossie," *William Carlos Williams Newsletter* 2 (Fall 1976): 10.

4. For a description of this collection, see *William Carlos Williams Review* 20 (Fall 1994): 52-57.

5. Denise Levertov, *The Poet in the World* (New York: New Directions, 1973) 259.

6. Thom Gunn, "Inventing the Completely New Poem," *Times Literary Supplement*, 19-25 February 1988, 180; "A New World: The Poetry of William Carlos Williams," *The Occasions of Poetry* (San Francisco: North Point, 1985) 33.

7. *Collected Poems: 1947-1980* (New York: Harper, 1984) 297.

8. Gunn, *Occasions*, 24; Levertov, "The Ideas in the Things," *New and Selected Essays* (New York: New Directions, 1992) 47; Williams, *The Collected Poems of William Carlos Williams, Volume I: 1909-1939*, ed. A. Walton Litz and Christopher MacGowan (New York: New Directions, 1986) 186. Hereafter cited in the text as *CP*1.

9. *Paterson*, ed. Christopher MacGowan (New York: New Directions, 1992) 125, 101. Further page references will be included in the text.

10. Walter Benn Michaels, "American Modernism and the Poetics of Identity," *Modernism/Modernity* 1 (1994): 53, 49. Further page references will be included in the text.

11. Charles Olson, "Mayan Letters," *Selected Writings*, ed. Robert Creeley (New York: New Directions, 1967) 82-84; Michael Bernstein, *The Tale of the Tribe* (Princeton: Princeton UP, 1980) 209, 212. Williams does not incorporate any notice of his subsequent tours of the city with Ginsberg into the poem; see Michael Schumacher, *Dharma Lion: A Critical Biography of Allen Ginsberg* (New York: St. Martin's, 1992) 143.

12. *The Collected Poems of William Carlos Williams, Volume II: 1939-1962*, ed. Christopher MacGowan (New York: New Directions, 1988) 466. Hereafter cited in the text as *CP*2.

13. David Frail, *The Early Poetics and Politics of William Carlos Williams* (Ann Arbor: UMI, 1987) 85.

14. Gunn, "Inventing the Completely New Poem," 179.

15. For the first poem, see *William Carlos Williams Review* 15 (Spring 1989): 2-3; and *CP*1, 566-67, from the third paper printing (1995). For the second poem, see *William Carlos Williams Review* 18 (Spring 1992): 50-51.

16. Frail, *Early Poetics*, 24.

17. Levertov, *Poet in the World*, 259. Also see Linda A. Kinnahan, *Poetics of the Feminine* (New York: Cambridge UP, 1994), for an argument that Levertov reads Williams in terms of her own move away from an object-oriented poetry to one that emphasizes female and maternal space.

18. *Poems, 1960-1967* (New York: New Directions, 1983) 21-22; *Candles in Babylon* (New York: New Directions, 1982) 59-60; *Poems, 1968-1972* (New York: New Directions, 1987) 124; *The Freeing of the Dust* (New York: New Directions, 1975) 19.

19. *Occasions,* 32-33; "Inventing the Completely New Poem," 179.

20. Gunn, *Occasions,* 191.

Glenn Sheldon (essay date winter and spring/summer 1999)

SOURCE: Sheldon, Glenn. "William Carlos Williams's Babel of Voices in the Long Poem *The Desert Music.*" *CEA Critic* 61, nos. 2-3 (winter and spring/summer 1999): 46-55.

[*In the following essay, Sheldon discusses the autobiographical elements of Williams's 1951 poem* The Desert Music.]

William Carlos Williams had never journeyed into Mexico until after World War II; "Dr. Williams spent two days in 1906 escorting a patient to San Luis Potosí but had not attempted to explore farther, a fact that seems surprising in view of his lifelong interest in Latin American culture" (Gunn 234). In 1950, Williams and his wife Flossie crossed the border "for only an evening while he and his wife visited their old friend Robert McAlmon in El Paso" (Gunn 234). That brief experience, although related flatly in Williams's *The Autobiography,* became the basis for his multivoiced poem *The Desert Music* (1951), which represents a genuine rebirth for his late poetic career. It is the work of a mind whose journey reflects mental distances, not physical distances. Here, we must be clear that Williams is a poet as well as a thinker. His work is greatly influenced by his theorist friend Kenneth Burke, who

> denies the idea of a stable self and posits instead the idea that we are made up of a 'Babel of voices.' . . . Consequently, our action within history is real, though our understanding of that history is at best an imperfect interpretation of an imperfect interpretation.
>
> (Bremen 135)

Williams's *The Desert Music* is indeed a departure for the famous poet, then recovering from a stroke. The poem initiates Williams's "Babel of voices"; it works as an imperfect communication of an imperfect perception of what it means to be a poet (to extend Burke's terms), as well as a self-evaluation of Williams's identity as a poet (or, more accurately, identities—as poet, doctor, Hispanic American, and American).

The Desert Music is recognized by critics as quite new for Williams; indeed, it is frequently called a "cubist self-portrait" (Marzán 258). Additionally, critic Drewey Wayne Gunn praises it as "one of Williams's most important poems" (234). Gunn goes on to state that "attention to detail partly explains why the poem is one of the best written by an American about Mexico" (235), but local color was not ultimately Williams's real concern in the poem. Rather, Mexico became a point of isolation in which he must define the nature of poetic inspiration for himself; William Carlos Williams, the poet, is the poem's central character. The poet reinvents himself in a Mexico made real by his own observations and intuition; this reinvention is the poem *The Desert Music.*

Surprisingly, the poem begins its narrative out of sequence. The poem begins when "—the dance begins" (1), invoking the image of a human embryonic form, apparently asleep on one of the bridges that connect Mexico with the United States. In 1963, critic Cecil Robinson saw the figure as a headless corpse, but every critic since then has insisted that the figure is merely sleeping. In *The Desert Music,* Williams observes that the law would define the form as "nothing / but a corpse, wrapped in a dirty mantle" (39-40); however, this poem is about the law of poetry, not civil laws. For Williams, the figure on the bridge cannot be a dispensable nothing; it is, like everything else to this poet, the substance for a poem.

The reader seems to arrive late at the poem, as if a performance has already begun; this figure on the bridge follows "the insensate music, . . . an agony of self-realization" (43-45). If the form is literally a corpse, its fetal position cannot signify eventual rebirth to Williams. After he evokes the "form," Williams immediately amplifies it:

> Is it alive?
>
>   —neither a head,
> legs nor arms!
>
>   It isn't a sack of rags someone
> has abandoned here   .   torpid against
>
> the flange of the supporting girder   .   ?
>
>   an inhuman shapelessness,
> knees hugged tight up into the belly
>
> Egg-shaped!
>   (8-16; typographical features are Williams's)

Interestingly, Williams introduces the ultimate discovery of the figure with the infinitive of the verb "end":

> . . . . to end about a form
> propped motionless—on the bridge
> between Juárez and El Paso—unrecognizable
> in the semi-dark.
>
>   (1-4)

The figure, like the grammar, is suspended in potentiality. Narrative and sequence yield to the infinitive; they remain static until the poet, as the poem's narrator, chooses to animate such "infinities."

The shapelessness of the figure at first appears "inhuman" to the poem's narrator: "knees hugged tight up into the belly / Egg-shaped!" (15-16). The narrator is, of course, Williams himself, as the poem reveals. "So this is William / Carlos Williams, the poet," states one of his Juárez dinner hosts (272-73). However, the poem is also informed by multiple voices, both exterior and interior to the poet. It is a moment of *heteroglossia*, despite Mikhail Bakhtin's precept of the poet's role as monologist. *The Desert Music* is indeed constructed of many voices, "as many voices as there are in a country" (Bremen 140). Paul Mariani, in his succinctly informative essay titled after the poem, praises the "poem's sharp edges and dissociated voices, its crazy quilt of forms ranging from sprawled prose to tight quatrains to heighten the 'realistic' narrative" (126). Williams is a writer who seeks to reevaluate his life in *The Desert Music.* His brief visit into one of Mexico's northernmost cities becomes a physical "journey developed into explicit spiritual or mental pilgrimages" (Gunn xi), a personal journey toward transmutation.

Williams's mind and body become attuned to "foreign" surroundings; details become sources of knowledge at opportune sites for the poet. Additionally, there is a Whitmanesque cataloguing throughout the poem; in the marketplace, there are

    —paper flowers (*para los santos*)
baked red-clay utensils, daubed
with blue, silverware,
dried peppers, onions, print goods, children's
clothing. . . .

                (93-97)

The two primary "things" in the poem, however, are the bridge and the shapeless figure asleep on the bridge.

The bridge links two "sister" cities historically, as well as literally and culturally; it

    spans a divided city and, symbolically at least, two cultures: Juárez, which, although an image in an English-language poem, Williams makes a point of writing with its accent, and El Paso, which although ostensibly Spanish is now English.

                (Marzán 243)

While many critics point out that this life-affirming poem is partly a response to the despair in T. S. Eliot's *The Waste Land,* it also owes its metastructure to Hart Crane's *The Bridge*: "Williams's bridge across the Rio Grande would answer Crane's vision of hell [in *The Bridge*]" (Mariani 126). The symbol of the Indian/American muse is compacted at "the level of a burlesque queen" in both *The Desert Music* and *The Bridge* (Mariani 126). Williams's bridge, then, makes many links.

The adjectives that describe, or do not describe, the figure on the bridge in *The Desert Music* reveal that it is not quite human. "It isn't a sack of rags" (11), we read, that is "torpid" and "egg-shaped" against "the flange of the supporting girder" (13); yet, according to Sherman Paul, the "Indian asleep on the bridge is never as explicitly defined in the poem as he is in *The Autobiography*" (77). Williams writes in *The Autobiography*: "Juarez [*sic*], across the bridge . . . tequila at five cents a glass, a quail dinner and the Mexicans, the poor Indians—one huddled into a lump against the ironwork of the bridge at night—safe perhaps from both sides, incredibly compressed into a shapeless obstruction—asleep" (388-89). In my opinion, this characterization is not more "explicitly defined" than the sleeping figure I find within the poem.

The figure or shapeless form is introduced at the beginning of *The Desert Music* as a "dance begins," only to "end about a form / propped motionless—on the bridge" (1-2). The poem begins with an em dash, as if in interruption, but we must also look at the lines' movements from left to right. The first line of the poem reveals where the poem will end: "about a form"; the "poem taking shape is therefore an 'interjurisdictional' dance with the embryo/form, who in the middle of the bridge on the international border is reborn in being free from rigid laws" (Marzán 245). Williams's use of relative clauses, sometimes syndetic, reinforces the sense of the poem itself as bridgelike. In short, the shapeless form mirrors some aspect of Williams himself

    on the International Boundary. Where else, interjurisdictional, not to be disturbed?

    How shall we get said what must be said?

    Only the poem.

                (18-21)

In the poem, the figure asleep on the bridge represents several things for Williams: It is his poetic identity, or the source of such inspiration; it is his unborn self, a sort of alter image; it is his dual identity as a Hispanic American, which has been torpid because of his choice to make his American identity primary in his life.

The bridge, then, also functions as a birth canal, the site for birth that fights chaos, the aridity of the desert, and writer's block. According to one critic, "'**The Desert Music**' presents images by means of which the self is apprehended across the abysm of time" (Fisher-Wirth 190-91). The fetal figure on the bridge is a "primal pagan ground[,] . . . the terror of birth" to Williams (Paul 78). However, this is a simplification of a complex moment; the figure embodies the terror of birth, the terror of death, and the terror of a life without poetry.

The Desert Music is fertile with potential for creativity, and it is a stark view of the sense of loss that happens when the poetic self is not fulfilled. This unfulfilled potential is what the aging, ailing poet must face within himself when Williams the narrator confronts the figure on the bridge. The poet awakens to the potential of the desert and to the potentials buried within his Hispanic nature. It is only on foreign soil, no matter how brief the journey, that he begins to confront the Other inside himself.

Within Williams's own Hispanic identity (as half Puerto Rican), he finds a surprising resource for creativity that is foregrounded in this pivotal poem. He fills *The Desert Music* with Mexico's nationalistic colors—red and green: "baked red-clay utensils, . . . dried peppers, onions" (94-95), "pomegranate" (145), and "the aniline / red and green candy" (150-51), as well as the "the virgin of her mind. those unearthly / greens and reds" (227-28). Likely, the "paper flowers *(para los santos)*" (93) are green, white, and red—the colors of Mexico's flag. Near the end of the poem, Williams describes the Mexicans as "Indians who chase the white bastards / through the streets on their Independence Day / and try to kill them" (319-21); the association of the stereotype of the "red-skinned" native is juxtaposed against the white-skinned imperialist (with its subtext of "greenbacks"). Conquest is a major theme of the poem, with its mention of "silverware" (95) and repeated references to a "penny" (120, 294, 295), suggesting the conquest of Mexico for its mineral wealth.

At this point in the poem, Williams calls the Mexicans "Spaniards!" (318) before he clarifies them parenthetically as "mostly / Indians" (318-19). Williams is racist here about the Mexican culture; Mexicans are not simply Spaniards or Indians, a false dichotomy that is not lost on the critic Julio Marzán, who calls the outburst a "passionate tongue-lashing[,] . . . [a] misnomer ['Spaniards,' which Williams] often used to describe Spanish-speakers in his life" (255). These lines of the poem clearly amplify Williams's ambivalence (possibly too soft a word) toward his own Puerto Rican heritage. Although the Puerto Rican culture is not interchangeable on all levels with Mexican culture, the two cultures share certain commonalities through historical and cultural interstices. This portion of the poem is a moment of collision between personal (autobiographical) and stereotypical (North American) social assumptions (Otherization); except for "his father and great Spanish writers and artists, in *The Autobiography* Williams paints Spanish-speakers mockingly, subtly invoking social preconceptions and stereotypes" (Marzán 23). Ironically, Williams is now being looked at for the complexity of his Hispanic and cultural identities by critics who occasionally fail to observe this potent racism.

The Desert Music is a conflated confrontation of Williams's complex cultural citizenship:

Throughout the poem a catalog of antagonistic cultural symbols—Juárez and El Paso, the man-embryo, and the poet-doctor, Mexican popular music and Casals' music, empty gestures and meaningful form, the lying and the genuine, English and Spanish, "us" and "them"—haunt Williams, competing, contradicting each other, transforming him constantly while collectively composing him.

(Marzán 242-43)

Thus, Williams's excursion to El Paso's "sistered" city brings him face to face with oppositional options about his own identity; the bridge is truly the path to the self, possibly the self above chaos (if that is not *the* fiction).

As the poem ends, music and meaning swirl like dust in a dust storm. The inclusion of scored music by Pablo Casals is a deliberate contrast to the overly sentimentalized Mexican music in the restaurant; "the continual banging of the *mariachi* music, put out for the American tourists, assailed the poet's ears" (Robinson 260). This evocation of Casals is highly suggestive of Williams's search for artistic genealogy, for "Casals too was born of a mother from Puerto Rico, the land in which he lived and worked after the Spanish Civil War, and where he died. Being Puerto Rican and his mother's favorite musician, Casals was another Williams alter image and a tributary, the musician always evoked by Williams' reference to the cello" (Marzán 256). There is something important in establishing mental, spiritual, and cultural links between the past and the present.

Everywhere that Williams goes in Juárez, he encounters music:

            the music! the
music! as when Casals struck
and held a deep cello tone
and I am speechless

                        There it sat
in the projecting angle of the bridge flange
as I stood aghast and looked at it—
. . . . The music
guards it, a mucus, a film that surrounds it,
a benumbing ink that stains the
sea of our minds—to hold us off—shed
of a shape close as it can get to no shape,
a music! a projecting music

                        I *am* a poet! I
am. I am. I am a poet, I reaffirmed, ashamed

Now the music volleys through as in
a lonely moment I hear it. Now it is all
about me. The dance! The verb detaches itself
seeking to become articulate

And I could not help thinking
of the wonders of the brain that
hears that music and of our
skill sometimes to record it.

(325-54)

The figure, sighted late in the poem but evoked at the poem's beginning, ultimately brings the music—and the dance—to the foreground. Most tourists crossing this bridge, or recrossing this bridge, might dismiss this figure or, at the least, avoid articulating its presence; however, Williams values the "banal and trivial particulars of American life or landscape and making them universal, or revealing the universalities hidden within them" (Miller 981). In other words, Williams carries his talent for observation to Mexico. The bridge, then, between two sister cities in two separate countries is unified by the universal nature of music and dance.

The poem ends, as promised by Williams, "about a form" (3). This returns us to the poem's beginning; the opening cry of "Wait!" (5) indicates that the poet is at last willing to make contact with the Mexican boys begging for pennies. This moment "represents the poet's first confrontation with the aboriginal American culture that history has overlaid with civilization" (Paul 85). The brief journey to Mexico has exposed Williams to the physicality of culture and history. When the poet finally gives the children pennies, it causes "him to hear the inner music again" (Marzán 254). The act of touching, the daring to touch, initiates the journey to creativity. "Like *Paterson*," writes Mariani, "'**The Desert Music**' provided a narrative thread and a journey. This time it was a journey between worlds, and the poem began literally in a no-man's land" (126). The poem is a departure for Williams because Mexico, not North "America" (read "United States"), provides the poem's physical backdrop as well as the locus for him to define his role as poet. Like the form on the bridge, Williams is both shapeless and shaped by exterior forces.

The Desert Music is not just new; it extends the tapestry of Williams's familiar poetic landscape(s). The poem's "reluctance to separate art and life, in its anti-formalism and in its refusal to intellectualize or ignore certain areas of experience" (Bertens 126), is startlingly representative of almost every aspect of Williams's *oeuvre*. Consistently, he uses "materials, inspiration, aesthetic, personal, and public ends" (Paul 103). Nevertheless, Paul reminds us that Williams's poem is "a demonstration of the furthest reach of [Williams's] art" (103). Such a far reach is distant from Paterson, New Jersey; indeed, the poet Charles Olson believes that *The Desert Music* is Williams's "best work . . . and not *Paterson*" (qtd. in Hallberg 65). In either case, place plays a central role in Williams's literary formation of his aesthetic identity, in his personal personae.

Juárez, a foreign place to Williams, leads unexpectedly to the universal; music and dance (particularly at the site of the Other: Williams's bridge) must inevitably appropriate the poet's role as an American:

> but this, following the insensate music,
> is based on the dance:
>
>   an agony of self-realization
> bound into a whole
> by that which surrounds us
>
>   I cannot escape
>
> I cannot vomit it up
>
> Only the poem!
>
> Only the made poem, the verb calls it
>   into being.
>
>   (43-52)

The "this," presumably, is the poem, which Williams describes as "an agony of self-realization / bound into a whole" (45-46). Williams suggests that his self-realization, here and now, leaves him without sense. The figure exists there in front of him, indifferent to the poet's feelings, central to this poem's core of knowledge. The poem's kinesis, as it opposes stasis, remains an epistemological axiom—a rubric of potentiality. The journey to Williams's knowledge about his own suspended identity spans countries (Americans as poets and/or tourists reifying their own real and false truths), personal crises, and poetic landscapes. Williams, as cultural geographer, recognizes boundary and boundaries. For a poet, there is always a way that being between cultures leaves one disturbed, and undisturbed—and disturbed again—because poetry makes *IT* (everything and nothing) make sense. Williams realizes that his identity (hyper-American) is a way to avoid global investment in cultural re-production, the tourist as genealogical ambassador of fictional Otherness. In Mexico, this poet allows, confronts, and yields to his own conquest of creative word usages—a synecdoche for his life.

Poetry, for Williams, is the "music of survival" (61); poetry, as basic as water, answers thirsts beyond the law, beyond borders, even beyond the physical. The desert music that inspires the dance ends about the motionless form, regressed into the shape of an egg (a fetus), "armless, legless, / headless" (333-34); then, suddenly, comes the revelatory exclamation: "I *am* a poet! I / am. I am. I am a poet . . ." (345-46). The revelation, such as it is, occurs because Mexico suddenly surrounds Williams: "Mexico and the United States, grand operatic symbols of Spanish and English. . . . The Rio Grande (where the United States and Mexico fuse) can be the perfect symbol where this embryo can be born" (Marzán 246). The poem is born. Williams marvels at the shapeless figure, asleep between two countries, for "only to a logical mind does this reluctant primal mass seem undefined or unformed; for Williams it is 'form,' a work of art, a poet" (Marzán 257). Interestingly, Mexico proves to be a source of renewal for this most American of poets. The "brief" journey into Juárez (a city in a foreign country, despite its proximity) evolves into discovery—*The Desert Music* as a complex landscape ("soulscape") of the mature, creative self. Williams's "Babel of voices" allows him to hear discordance as discourse; the silent, shapeless form reminds the poet to listen to all of the desert's music.

Works Cited and Consulted

Ahearn, Barry. *William Carlos Williams and Alterity: The Early Poetry.* Cambridge: Cambridge UP, 1994.

Bertens, Hans. "Postmodern Culture(s)." *Postmodernism and Contemporary Fiction.* Ed. Edmund J. Smyth. London: Batsford, 1991.

Bremen, Brian A. *William Carlos Williams and the Diagnostics of Culture.* New York: Oxford UP, 1993.

Doyle, Charles. *William Carlos Williams and the American Poem.* New York: St. Martin's, 1982.

Fisher-Wirth, Ann W. *William Carlos Williams and Autobiography: The Woods of His Own Nature.* University Park: Pennsylvania State UP, 1989.

Gunn, Drewey Wayne. *American and British Writers in Mexico, 1556-1973.* 1969. Austin: U of Texas P, 1974.

Hallberg, Robert von. *Charles Olson: The Scholar's Act.* Cambridge: Harvard UP, 1978.

Mariani, Paul. "'The Desert Music.'" *Critical Essays on William Carlos Williams.* Ed. Steven Gould Axelrod and Helen Deese. Critical Essays on American Literature. New York: G. K. Hall, 1995. 124-28.

Marzán, Julio. *The Spanish American Roots of William Carlos Williams.* Austin: U of Texas P, 1994.

Miller, J. Hillis. "William Carlos Williams and Wallace Stevens." *Columbia Literary History of the United States.* Ed. Emory Elliott. New York: Columbia UP, 1988. 972-92.

Paul, Sherman. *The Music of Survival: A Biography of a Poem by William Carlos Williams.* Urbana: U of Illinois P, 1968.

Robinson, Cecil. *With the Ears of Strangers: The Mexican in American Literature.* Tucson: U of Arizona P, 1963.

Williams, William Carlos. *The Desert Music. The Collected Poems of William Carlos Williams, Volume II: 1939-1962.* New York: New Directions, 1962. 273-84.

———. *The Autobiography of William Carlos Williams.* New York: Random, 1951.

Jeff Webb (essay date spring 2000)

SOURCE: Webb, Jeff. "William Carlos Williams and the New World." *Arizona Quarterly* 56, no. 1 (spring 2000): 65-88.

[*In the following essay, Webb discusses what it meant for Williams to consider himself an American writer and what it is in Williams's writing that makes him distinctly American.*]

> There was a maggot in them. It was their beliefs.
> Bits of writing have been copied into the book for the taste of it.
>
> William Carlos Williams, *In the American Grain*

THE CORPSES OF DEAD INDIANS

"And America? What the hell do you a bloomin foreigner know about the place?" Ezra Pound asked William Carlos Williams in a letter in 1917. "You . . . a "REAL american."!!? INCONCEIVABLE!!!!" A "REAL american"—Pound cites himself as an example—has "the virus, the bacillus of the land" in his blood; Williams has "spanish blood," and in Pound's view, his poems are therefore "unamerican" (31). "You can idealize the place all you like," Pound wrote three years later, "but you haven't a drop of the cursed blood in you" (38). To Pound's embarrassment, Williams quoted the earlier letter in the 1918 prologue to *Kora in Hell* in order to contest Pound's account of what makes a writer an American writer (*Imaginations* 11). Surely, Williams suggests, Pound's endorsement of the view that T. S. Eliot's "La Figlia che Piange" is "the fine flower of the finest spirit of the United States" illustrates the absurdity of thinking that a poem is American by virtue of the author's "blood" (25). "Imagine an international congress of poets at Paris or Versailles," Williams writes.

> Ezra begins by reading 'La Figlia che Piange.' It would be a pretty pastime to gather into a mental basket the fruits of that reading from the minds of the ten Frenchmen present; their impressions of the sort of United States that very fine flower was picked from.
>
> (26)

Eliot may have the "cursed blood" in him, but "La Figlia che Piange" is not an American poem. In Williams' view, it "CONFORMS" to the antiquated standards of the literary establishment, the final stanza "straining after a rhyme" (25). "It adds to the pleasant outlook from the club window," but for this very reason it is not American (25). The poem is conventional, not new. For Williams, then, writing is American not because its author has American "blood," but because its author refuses to conform. This refusal defines the character of what Williams calls "the New World type," exemplified by "Montezuma or, since he was stoned to death in a parley, Gautemozin who had the city of Mexico leveled over him before he was taken" (24). Here Williams reverses Pound's formulation. Montezuma and Gautemozin are natives of the New World not because the "virus of the land" is in their "blood," but because their blood is in the land—literally: they are buried in stones or rubble. The "New World type" is therefore an identity defined not by "blood" but by the spilling of blood, specifically in resisting assimilation by European culture.

The fact that only dead Indians have achieved this sort of identity, which Williams calls "primal and continuous identity with ground itself, where everything is fixed in darkness," suggests that the identity of the "New World type" consists in burial, in being identical with the land (*American* [*In The American Grain*] 33).[1] Indeed, in Williams' chapter on Samuel de Champlain's discovery of Quebec, identity with the ground is embodied by the "corpses" of "dead Indians" in "their graves" (74). Such identity contrasts with Samuel de Champlain's obsessive duplication of the land in "charts, maps, colored drawings" (72). This contrast is crucial. Champlain's maps misrepresent the land simply because they are representations and not the land itself. For Williams, dead Indians *are* the land, as in his statement, "the New World is Montezuma . . . or Gautemozin" (*Imaginations* 24). Indian corpses neither copy the land nor have the land in their blood. Their relation to the land thus surpasses in "authenticity" (*American* 74) the relation achieved by representation, either in the case of Champlain's note taking or Pound's blood virus, which also reproduces the land. Montezuma's and Gautemozin's relation to the land is authentic because it is not really a relation at all, but an identity. Similarly, their relation to themselves, unmediated by thought, is not a relation either. Indian corpses enjoy an identity with themselves.

"Enjoy" is, of course, not the right word, since this sort of identity obtains only in death. Nevertheless, the corpse is Williams' emblem for an identity that is continuously new because it evades forms of representation inherited from the past. Why, then, an *Indian* corpse? After all, as Williams suggests, identity consists not in "blood" but in the spilling of that "blood," by which he means that a corpse cannot be classified by race. Attributing race to the corpse would distort its identity by linking it to a particular group of people with a shared past, thus defining it not as itself but through social and historical categories. But the corpse, because it cannot think, has no relation to the past and is therefore perfectly present to itself and its surroundings. This presence is its identity. According to Williams' ideal of identity, then, the corpse would have no race. Yet Williams contradicts this ideal in idealizing an *Indian* corpse. An Indian corpse is no longer merely a corpse and thus no longer in identity with the ground or

itself. It *represents* identity, thereby giving identity a particular social and historical form, and therefore *misrepresents* it. This contradiction, however, far from being merely a mistake, in fact structures Williams' entire literary project, since the very representational practice that makes the New World visible through writing, also renders it old, a repetition of the past. Even Williams' phrase, "New World type," embodies the contradiction that the New World, when presented in writing, cannot be new. In being presented as a new type, inhabitants of the New World are already old, conforming to members of the same "type" throughout history.[2] The Indian corpse, then, is ultimately a figure not for identity but for the failure of identity in an America in which race is unavoidable because representation (and therefore classification) is unavoidable.

Despite the paradox involved in Williams' desire to write the literature of the New World, he nevertheless envisions a very different aesthetic than Pound's or Eliot's, both of whom he criticizes as "men content with the connotations of their masters"; their poems are "rehash, repetition" (*Imaginations* 24). At stake for Williams in his quarrel with Pound is the nature of American literature and the nature of the American writer. Representation may be the unavoidable, if regrettable, feature of the former, just as race is of the latter, but this does not mean that Williams agrees with Pound about either writing or national identity. Rather than "cribbing from the Renaissance, the Provence and the modern French" (24) like Pound, and then using "blood" to certify the Americanness of the result, Williams reverses the procedure. Fixing on race as the bare minimum of history that is required for the self to be a self, Williams argues that American writers must not have a particular kind of "blood" but the right relation to their "blood." This relation, which Williams sought to both theorize and manifest in his work of the '20s, ensures that the writing will be new—or, at least as new as writing can be.

For Williams, Marcel Duchamp's ready-mades embody the "truly new" in art (*Imaginations* 8). They also illustrate the paradox of the New World. "Duchamp," Williams explains, "decided that his composition for the day would be the first thing that struck his eye in the first hardware store he should enter. It turned out to be a pickaxe, which he bought and set up in his studio. This was his composition" (10).[3] Here, as the magazine *The Blind Man* said of Duchamp's more famous readymade, the inverted urinal, "an ordinary article of life" is "placed so that its useful significance disappears under the new title and point of view" ("Richard Mutt" 5). Yet Williams would have resisted the magazine's conclusion that Duchamp thereby "created a new thought for the object" (5). He cites with approval Duchamp's opinion that "a stained glass window that had fallen out and lay more or less together on the ground was of far greater interest than the thing conventionally composed *in situ*" (*Imaginations* 8). The window is "truly new" in being accidental; it avoids producing a new thought (it is not exactly a work of art), just as it avoids reproducing any old thoughts (it is no longer a familiar artifact). Ideally, what is "new" about the window, hence "truly new" in art, is the absence of any reproduction, including even the reproduction implicit in "a new thought," which is in a sense already old in being a "thought for that object," in representing it. Thus, Duchamp's pickaxe is new because the representation, the pickaxe, is identical to the object represented, also the pickaxe. The representation, if it can even be called a representation, does not reproduce an independent object because it is that object.

Yet Williams calls the pickaxe a "composition." Is it not, like the window, merely a new thing? Referring to Duchamp's *Fountain*, Arthur C. Danto writes that its "conceptual fulcrum" lies in the "question it poses": "why—referring to itself—should this be artwork when something else exactly *like* this, namely *that*—referring now to the class of unredeemed urinals—are just pieces of industrial plumbing?" (14-15). In order for the *Fountain* to be art, Danto suggests, it must refer to ordinary objects, in this case the "class" of things to which it is usually thought to belong, "unredeemed urinals," and it must establish its difference from them. The *Fountain* created a scandal at the time however, because it did not seem to be referential enough to be considered art. Yet by posing the question about its status as art—hence referring to itself as itself, as Danto notes—the *Fountain* in fact differs from other pieces of "industrial plumbing" which typically do not pose questions. The pickaxe similarly differs from its class; in implicitly asking how it is different from other pickaxes, it is not a pickaxe (or not only a pickaxe) but *this*.

The pickaxe could thus be described as a word that refers to only one thing in the world by being that thing. But to create an identity between word and thing by making the thing into a word obviously requires changing the thing; the thing that refers to itself as *this* in Duchamp's "composition" is different from what "struck his eye in the . . . hardware store." Here the problem with the "truly new" work of art is apparent. The moment the work refers to itself it is different from itself. Consequently, what appeals to Williams about Duchamp's ready-mades—their apparent capacity to represent and also to be what he calls "the thing itself" (*Imaginations* 8)—is not achievable in a work of art. To be "the thing itself" is to be, as Williams says of the corpse's identity with the ground, "fixed in darkness," unrepresentable (*American Grain* 34). The corollary of this point is that even if "a work of art means nothing," it nonetheless means or refers to "itself. Which is of

course *something*" (*Embodiment* [*The Embodiment of Knowledge*] 120). Representation cannot be eliminated; even Duchamp's ready-mades fail to be new.

Similarly, the corpses of dead Indians cannot remain in identity with the ground of the New World. In order to function as symbols of authenticity, the corpses must be lifted from the grave, taken out of identity with what made them authentic in the first place, the land. They are in a sense brought to life.[4] Hence, the Caribs slaughtered by Ponce de Leon are, Williams notes, "the inhabitants of our souls, our murdered souls that lie . . . agh" (*American* 39). "We kill them but their souls dominate us" (40). Not only are they by inhabiting us not fully dead but also we, inhabited by them, are not fully alive. The result is the stench that pervades *In the American Grain,* a stench emanating not only from the corpses of dead Indians lifted from the ground, but also from what has "survived to us from the past" generally. The Puritans, for example, are "stinking all about you." "It is an atrocious thing, a kind of mermaid with a corpse for a tail. Or it remains a bad breath in the room. This THING, strange, inhuman, powerful, is like a relic of some died out tribe whose practices were revolting" (115). Williams says that he wants to "annihilate" this "THING," this living corpse, but even art that means "nothing" still self-referentially means *"something."* In this sense, even Duchamp's minimalism lacks what Williams calls "cleanliness," the capacity to observe the hygiene of burial. "We are moderns," he says, "all lacking in a ground sense of cleanliness" (49).[5]

Williams' own writing, then, is not clean or new. Pound himself pointed this out in a 1920 letter. "Your 'representative american' verse will be that which can be translated in foreign languages" and "will appear new to the french or hun or whatever" (44). Clearly, for Pound, "new" refers to a style of writing and not, as for Williams, to a transcendence of writing altogether. At this point in his career, Williams was ready to revise his account of the "new," but he did not believe that Eliot's work was "new" even by Pound's definition. In his view, Eliot had "rejected America" by copying European models (qtd. Schott 4). Seeking instead to accept America, Williams envisioned "a new form of poetic composition, a form for the future" (*Imaginations* 4). Rather than repeating past texts, his "new form" seeks to transform the living corpse of those texts, "this THING," into words that would ideally have no "aroma" (*American* 115, 223). One possible model for that transformation is Edgar Allan Poe, the first writer of the "New World" to whom Williams devotes a major chapter in *In the American Grain* (216). Poe's writing does not seem referential. In fact, Poe "counsels writers to *borrow nothing* from the scene, but to put all the weight of effort into the writing" (227). Thus, although it is "a *new locality* that in Poe is assertive, it is America" (216), what Poe "wanted was connected with no particular place" (220). This *"new locality"* is the text itself, or as Williams also puts it, "here not there" (74). "Here" does not refer to the "GRAND scene" or "NATURAL landscape" of America (227). Rather, "here" refers literally to "here," to itself, to a locality in the text—*this* locality, the *new locality* (227).[6]

The problem, however, is that "here" is not the New World, because even "here" is a version of there, like Poe's own prematurely buried characters, "in the place of sepulture . . . the quick among the dead," neither alive nor dead, neither here nor there. (Poe 105). Even the new locality of modernist self-referentiality has an aroma. As Williams says, America is a "prolific carcass" (*American Grain* 175). "We die—and rot into the magazines and newspapers—and books by the millions—Books" (109). *In the American Grain* recognizes that books are unfortunately but unavoidably "prolific," even when, minimally, "here" refers to "here." With this recognition, Williams shifts his focus from the ideal of identity to the legacy of its absence. Thus, rather than functioning in death as a symbol for identity, the Indian supplies a model for living with the inevitable presence of the past. For Williams, Indians have an exemplary relation to "the cruel beauty they, the living, inherited from the dead" (34). The figures of their idols "were of extra-human size and composed, significantly, of a paste of seeds and leguminous plants, commonly used for food, ground and mixed together and kneaded with human blood, the whole being consecrated with a bath of blood from the heart of a living victim" (34). For the Indians, the spirit of the past is material and edible, meant to be eaten and transformed by the body into something new. Williams' own project of consumption and bodily transformation is not independent; it requires the example of a racially primitive response to the past because "we," "degraded whites riding our fears to market" (108), are out of touch with racial appetites. The notion of racial descent is thus essential to Williams' literary descent towards the ground of modernist nonrepresentational writing, the materiality of language. It explains how the writer can produce writing that attempts to embody America without representing it, without exhuming corpses. For Williams, it is the racial body that produces the exemplary American book.

THE BURIAL OF THE DEAD

That corpse you planted last year in your garden,
Has it begun to sprout?

Eliot, *The Waste Land*

Williams regarded Eliot's *The Waste Land* (1922) as a "great catastrophe to our letters" (*Autobiography* 146). But, unlike Hart Crane, who envisioned a way "through" Eliot "toward a different goal," (qtd. Altieri, "Eliot's Impact" 191), Williams rejected Eliot's method alto-

gether. This rejection is perhaps most direct in **Spring and All** where, as Walter Benn Michaels has noted, Williams' "deployment of 'ing'" in the book's first poem "takes up quite literally the distinctive participles of *The Waste Land*'s opening lines ('breeding,' 'mixing,' 'stirring')" (75). In *The Waste Land*, these participles suggest spring's movement and change, and thus contradict the desire of the speaker—whose voice, as Michael Levenson notes, seems to issue from the earth (172)—to remain dead.

> April is the cruellest month, breeding
> Lilacs out of the dead land, mixing
> Memory and desire, stirring
> Dull roots with spring rain.
> Winter kept us warm, covering
> Earth in forgetful snow, feeding
> A little life with dried tubers.
>
> (53; I, 1-7)

But here even winter, in "covering / Earth in forgetful snow," and presumably protecting the sanctity of the grave, was "feeding / A little life." It is not, of course, winter itself but winter as metaphor that quickens the corpse.[7] "Forgetful snow," the phrase itself, could in this sense be said to exhume the dead corpse, for in attributing the capacity to forget to something that has no capacity to remember, the phrase animates the corpse. The language of representation is unavoidably alive with unintended meaning. Indeed, in depicting death at all, these lines render familiar what is utterly strange. Animated in this way the corpse is alive, yet its life is merely "a little life"; the poetically resurrected corpse is no more fully alive in language (since its life is a function of the language of the past) than it could be fully dead in language (since its death is imbued by language with properties of life). The "distinctive participles" of Eliot's opening thus enact what has been described as the central problem of *The Waste Land,* the problem of being "neither / living nor dead" (I, 39-40). The participles make actions of life (breeding, mixing, stirring, covering, feeding) all a repetition (in a sense, a memory) of the word, "spring."

The Waste Land, then, this "stony rubbish" (I, 20), is neither a place to bury the dead nor (for this reason) a place to sustain the living.[8] Thus, if Hart Crane's way "through" Eliot was to accept this desolate condition of language—though to a different end—then Williams' way *around* Eliot was to question whether language necessarily reproduces the past or, in terms of the burial of the dead, is intrinsically malodorous. Williams' description of Marianne Moore's aim of presenting "each word . . . crystal clear with no attachments; not even an aroma" is also a description of his own aim. "A word is a word most," he says, "when it is separated out by science, treated with acid to remove the smudges, washed, dried, and placed right side up on a clean surface." This cleaning produces a word that is "scrupulously itself," "smeared" neither "with thinking" nor with "the attachments of thought" (*Imaginations* 318). As Williams puts it in *Spring and All,* the work of art "must be real, not 'realism,' but reality itself" (*Collected Poems* 204). Successful cleaning produces the "cleanliness" of burial since a word "with no attachments" is a thing, no longer referential or representational and, like the corpses of dead Indians, in identity with the ground of the New World. Such a word has no aroma. In this sense, Williams inverts spring. What is new or spring-like about the New World is not life or "lilacs out of the dead land" or "flowers that have an odor of perfume" (318) but the deadness of the dead; in *Spring and All,* spring "shivers" "among the long black trees," and its "celebrant" is the "peaceful, dead young man," the "corpse of a suicide" (*Collected Poems* 180-81).⁹

Williams consistently associates spring with the corpse and the land, for example, in **"Sub Terra,"** a burial poem that introduces Williams' "undertaking," and in **"The Accident"** where the death of Williams' patient is simultaneously the beginning of spring: "It is the end! It is spring" (*Imaginations* 307). In **"The farmer deep in thought,"** from *Spring and All,* the beginning is likewise identical with the end, since "blank fields" and "black orchards" ("leaving room for thought") allow "the artist figure of / the farmer" to have "in his head / the harvest already planted" (*Collected Poems* 186). But Williams links spring with the dead corpse perhaps most conspicuously in *Spring and All* with what he calls "our secret project": "the annihilation of every human creature on the face of the earth." "Then at last will the world be made anew" (179). With this annihilation, the world will be new because when people are corpses, words will in a sense also be corpses, unused for communication and therefore new, not "hung by usage with associations" (*American* 221). Thus, again, Miss Moore's "undertaking": to remove words "bodily from greasy contexts" and put them in, or, as Williams says, "against the ground" (*Imaginations* 317, 318).¹⁰ Spring in the New World is therefore literally "spring," the word buried by the modernist undertaker in the dead land of the page. Williams' project **"By the road to the contagious hospital,"** is to enact "spring" by burying the stinking corpse of spring, or what might be called, in the context of *The Waste Land,* the lilac breeding capacity of language, its metaphoric memory and desire. Thus, as Michaels notes, versions of "spring," "and" and "all"

> . . . are distributed through the opening description of "the waste," "brown with dried weeds, standing and fallen / patches of standing water / the scattering of tall trees / all along the road." "Fallen," "tall," "all," and, elsewhere, "small" and even "hospital" repeat the "reality" of "all," an effect that is even more striking with the repetition of "standing" (which produces both "and" and a version of "spring"), then "scattering" and later

> "upstanding" and "spring" itself. . . . There is an important sense in which what these lines do above all is produce the presence on the page of "and," "all," and "ing."

(75)

However, as Michaels adds in a note, "the point is not that the poem has no meaning but that these elements are foregrounded and yet not part of this meaning" (164 n. 34).

Despite the "presence on the page" of these words, however, "spring" never quite arrives in this poem. For "spring" can arrive only by meaning "spring," by referring to itself as a word, as *this* word, otherwise it would mean spring, the season, associated with blooming flowers and budding trees; however, as soon as it refers to itself or *means* "spring" it cannot *be* "spring," for in referring it is no longer purely material and is no longer buried in the dead land of the page. The moment it arrives is necessarily the moment it disappears. In effect, Williams' dead "waste" cannot avoid turning into a version of *The Waste Land* (in which the dead keep coming to life) because "spring" can only be, as Williams puts it in the poem, "lifeless in appearance," and not actually lifeless (*Collected Poems* 183). It is not possible, then, for the poem's "elements"—"spring," "and," and "all"—to be foregrounded without also being part of the poem's meaning.¹¹ Thus, "spring" merely "approaches" in *Spring and All.* Williams announces that "SPRING, which has been approaching for several pages, is at last here." But not quite here, since the claim that it has "been approaching" undoes previous assertions that it has arrived: "It is spring. THE WORLD IS NEW." Indeed, even after "it is spring," further down the page "SPRING is approaching" (182).

Cleaning the word of its attachments is not possible. So, for instance, Williams asks "what about all this writing?" (in the poem of that title) and answers a few lines later,

> O "Kiki"
> O Miss Margaret Jarvis
> The backhandspring
>
> I: clean
>   clean
>   clean: yes. . New-York
>
> Wrigley's, appendicitis, John Marin:
> skyscraper soup—

(*Collected Poems* 200)

In the specific context of each of the middle lines, the word "clean" is a different word, removed, like "Wrigley's," "appendicitis" and John Marin's skyscrapers from the attachments of thought, from familiar contexts. But Williams does not appear to regard this cleaning as successful, for a few lines later he writes, "Pah! / It is unclean / which is not straight to the mark." Here Williams could, of course, mean that he has failed to depict, as Barry Ahearn says, "the most vivid aspect of his affair with [Miss Margaret] Jarvis, namely the violence of her reaction" adding, "Williams has proven 'unclean' by refusing to be 'straight' and faithful to his memory" (149). But as Williams' editors, A. Walton Litz and Christopher MacGowan, point out in the notes to *The Collected Poems,* these biographical references are, at best, uncertain: Jarvis is possibly Margaret Purvis ("the name 'Purvis' appears in the margin of Thirlwall's annotated copy" of *The Collected Earlier Poems*), and "'Kiki' may have been Margaret Purvis's nickname" (503). Indeed, the conspicuous subjectivity of reference or opacity in the second and third lines—"O 'Kiki' / O Miss Margaret Jarvis"—makes it seem more likely that the "backhandspring" here (Williams' poetic acrobatics, or backhanded way of achieving "spring") leaps away from Ahearn's biographical mark and to the graphical mark itself. The mark might, in other words, be taken quite literally to refer to the material elements of "clean"—to the horizontal arrangement of *c*'s, *l*'s, *e*'s, *a*'s, and *n*'s, an arrangement made particularly noticeable by the columnar repetition of the letters when read vertically as is hard to avoid doing; *c, c, c; l, l, l,* etc.—and, consequently, to the different identity of the word in each line. The instance of the word "clean" that is really clean is the middle instance, the one severed from all attachments. "Clean" in this sense is clean because it is *c, l, e, a, n.*

Why, then, is the writing "not straight to the mark"? For the same reason that "spring" does not arrive in *Spring and All*: because "clean" comes to *mean* "clean" and therefore cannot also *be* "clean." Meaning "clean," it is "unclean," "not straight to the mark." "How easy to slip / into the old mode," Williams remarks early on in *Spring and All.* "How hard to / cling firmly to the advance" (191). As it turns out, though, the old mode is not just "easy"; it is in fact the necessary, and thus the necessarily disabling, condition of the new mode. The new, in other words, will always be a version of the old because it must be old merely to appear new. The burial of the dead will never be entirely successful. And this is why Williams' description of the clean word—"separated out by science, treated with acid to remove the smudges, washed, dried, and placed right side up on a clean surface"—could also be the description of a corpse, perhaps a medical cadaver, readied for dissection.

The word, even as a cadaver, has an "aroma." The cadaver is thus a figure for the failure of Williams' artistic "undertaking," at least as he conceived it in opposition to Eliot's. However, this figure shifts focus from what the word is to how it may be used. As Williams approvingly says of Logan Clendening's *The Hu-*

man Body, "the book presumes knowledge of the body itself as the source of all knowing" (*Imaginations* 360). Williams's own knowledge of the body, gained as a medical student dissecting cadavers, is that the relations between the body and its environment are nonrepresentational. The relations are productive, in the sense that "Water, Salts, Fat, etc." are transformed into the materials of the body (359); "the human body," he says, is "an organism for the conversion of food and air into energy and into tissues" (362). But the relations are not directly reproductive: the body does not copy these nutrients. Instead, in this conversion "it is the body speaking" from "within the hide" (362, 359). The body's nonrepresentational "conversion of food and air" is the knowledge that informs Williams' own knowing, his relation to tradition. For if the word cannot be a thing, even in meaning "nothing but itself," then the figure for the failure to be perfectly local, the cadaver, suggests at least a model for producing words out of an alternative locality, the body. The point here is that the locality, or the Americanness, of a word consists not in what it is but in how it is produced. A word will always be a corpse from the past, but the American writer can be original nevertheless. As Williams puts it, there is a "usable past . . . upon which I feed" (qtd. Wagner 82).

DESCENT

Hernando De Soto's men have trouble disposing of his corpse. First, trying to conceal his death from the Indians, "lest the Indians might venture on an attack when they should learn that he whom they feared was no longer opposed to them," they put the body "secretly in a house, where it remained three days." Then they took it "by night to the gate of the town" and buried it there. But the Indians, having seen De Soto ill and "finding him no longer, suspected the reason; and passing by where he lay, they observed the ground loose and looking about talked among themselves." So Luis de Mososco "ordered the corpse taken up at night, and among the shawls that enshrouded it having cast abundance of sand, it was taken out and committed to the middle of the stream" (*American* 58).

> Down, down, this solitary sperm, down into the liquid, the formless, the insatiable belly of sleep; down among the fishes: there was one called bagre, the third part of which was head, with gills from end to end, and along the sides were great spines, like very sharp awls; there were some in the river that weighed from a hundred to a hundred and fifty pounds. There were some in the shape of a barbel; another like a bream, with the head of a hake, having a color between red and brown. There was likewise a kind called peel-fish, the snout a cubit in length, the upper lip being shaped like a shovel. Others were like a shad. There was one called pereo the Indians sometimes brought, the size of a hog and had rows of teeth above and below.

(58)

Williams had been more explicit about De Soto's fate in *The Great American Novel* (1923): "there at the edge of that mighty river he had seen those little fish who would soon be eating him, he, De Soto the mighty explorer" (*Imaginations* 204). If, in the passage from *In the American Grain,* the fish are not "little," it is perhaps because Williams intends to emphasize the importance of their accomplishment. For until De Soto's corpse is consumed by the fishes, it retains its narrative agency: organizing the men, opposing the Indians. But narrative ceases as the corpse sinks into the "formless"; the writing becomes almost purely descriptive, wandering among unfamiliar names and fantastic shapes. However, the fact that the passage does not merely end as narrative ends—which is to say, as the feeding begins—suggests that Williams has adopted the feeding itself as his aesthetic.

After all, if the passage were organized according to representational or narrative principles, then it would end instead of beginning with De Soto's descent into the "formless," into the unrepresentable New World. The New World is unrepresentable because it is characterized by radical "diversity." According to Williams, Columbus views the New World's "bright green trees" as "branches growing in different ways and all from one trunk; one twig is one form and another is a different shape and so unlike that it is the greatest wonder in the world to see the diversity" (*American* 26). But here "diversity" is not only difference, "one twig is one form and another is a different shape," but also uniqueness, "so unlike." In this sense, Williams' remark in a different context that "the locality is the only universal" (qtd. Tomlinson vii) applies to the New World that Columbus discovers, for if all things are different, as in the New World, then the only characteristic things share is difference. Things are unique. Such is the case of the natives Columbus first encounters: "They paint themselves some black, some white, others red and others of what color they can find. Some paint the faces and others the whole body, some only round the eyes and others only on the nose. They are themselves neither black nor white" (25). Here "the universal" is, apparently, unique skin color.[12] But the fact that Columbus first perceives the natives as "themselves neither black nor white," suggests that—even in this first glimpse—they are already seen in terms of black and white, the organizing binary of American racial discourse, and are, for this reason, *not* themselves.[13] What Williams says of Champlain could apply equally well to Columbus: he carries "his own head about prying curiously into the wilderness" and discovers, consequently, not the wilderness but his own head (73). Thus the irony implicit in the titles of these chapters that assert discovery—"The Discovery of The Indies," "The Founding of Quebec," "The Discovery of Kentucky"—is that in each case the new or unique is not discovered or found so much as the old is reproduced,

substituted for the new. "For the problem of the New World," Williams says, "was an awkward one": "how to replace from the wild land that which . . . the Old World meant" (136).

Williams took pains to begin the chapter on Columbus at the end of the story, with Columbus' return to the "home coast" (7).[14] In doing so he meant to emphasize that the New World was old merely in being discovered. It was "a predestined and bitter fruit existing, perversely before the white flower of its birth"; "no more had Columbus landed" than the "flower" was "ravished" (7). Yet, prior to discovery, the New World was "marked with its own dark life which goes on to an immaculate fulfillment in which we have no part" (7). This suggests that what makes the New World new is not the absence of paint or marks, but the absence of a particular kind of painting or writing, marks that would "replace from the wild land that which . . . the Old World meant." In contrast to Columbus or Champlain, "carrying his own head about," the "souls" of the Caribs "lived in their bodies" (39). The soul of the New World is a kind of writing, the writing produced not by culture but by the body.

If, then, the soul of the New World cannot be reproduced without misrepresentation, its writing can nevertheless be imitated. Indians, for instance, do not replace the New World with old meanings because their bodies transform, rather than merely repeat, textual or objective sources: "they who fought their enemies, ate them" (39); "to this party that village is given to be *eaten!*" (127). The painting or writing that constitutes the New World is thus dictated not mimetically by sources but non-mimetically by the body's own rules of transformation. This is a crucial distinction. It suggests that in a title like *The Embodiment of Knowledge* Williams is referring not only to the form of writing (knowledge embodied in the text) but also and perhaps more importantly to the practice of writing (knowledge in the body).[15] Williams is concerned not with what to write on the page but with how to go about writing it. Moreover, this fundamental shift in orientation from embodied meaning to the body producing meaning explains why the chapter on De Soto does not end as De Soto is consumed by the fishes, or, equivalently, why the chapter on Rasles does not end when Rasles is "swallowed" by "THE INDIAN" (121). The writing cannot representationally follow De Soto as he descends into the "formless," but the chapter continues because Williams substitutes for De Soto's descent a parallel descent: his own, towards "that resistant core of nature" in himself, manifest in his body's transformation of sources (105). Instead of trying to represent nature in the writing, Williams aims to let nature express itself by having "nothing in [his] head" (*Imaginations* 289). Thus, the "dark life" of the New World is "marked" precisely because "we"—that is, our heads, the parts of us that replace the New World with the meaning of the old—"have no part" in that marking.

Yet even if the alliterative play "down among the fishes" (for instance, *b*'s and *r*'s: bagre, barbel, bream) could be regarded as the nonrepresentational work of Williams' body transforming source materials by the dictates of its own "dark life," it turns out that, as Bryce Conrad notes, "the facts as well as the metaphors of De Soto's descent into the river comes verbatim from the Fidalgo" (65).[16] "The report of how De Soto's corpse was wrapped in shawls filled with sand and 'committed to the middle of the stream' to conceal the death from the Indians comes verbatim from the record. Even the catalogue of fish in the river comes verbatim from the record" (65). De Soto's burial may be successful, in other words, but Williams' imitation of the feeding that constitutes that success is not as successful; he fails to imitate the ways of the New World by copying the words of the old. This failure illustrates the difficulty of literary descent. In copying, Williams does not transform his sources but merely consumes them; in his terms, he grows "fatter," like the "degraded whites" he criticizes, "riding their fears to market" in the "unconscious porkyard and oilhole" of America (*American Grain* 109). "Degraded whites" require the example of the Indian, not because they should "write of the Indians" or "hogfill the copied style with a gross rural sap" but because they should write like the Indian in consuming and transforming sources.[17] Williams thus aims to make literary descent possible for over-civilized and neurotic whites by appealing to the notion of racial descent. Imitating the primitivism of the Indian—and, as we shall see, the "Negro"—enables whites to discover within their fat copied corpses a living racial body.

WRITING LIKE AN INDIAN

When we think of the body as the sole source of all our good the return of an attenuated or spent "culture" to that ground can never after be seen as anything but a saving gesture.

Williams, "Water, Salts, Fat, etc."

In the "Discovery of Kentucky," Williams' chapter on Daniel Boone, Boone seeks with "primal lust" to be part of the New World, "to grow close to it, to understand it and to be part of its mysterious movements—like an Indian" (137). Williams emphasizes, however, that Boone does not try "to be an Indian," "though they eagerly sought to adopt him into their tribes." Rather, Boone is *himself* in a new world, Indianlike." Boone is *himself,* that is, because he refuses to copy the Indians. Yet if he is "like" them by virtue of this refusal, then he doesn't copy their refusal to copy (or their actual behavior) so much as he imitates that refusal (or their quality of independence). The difference between copying and imitation is the difference

between writing "in the *style* of Shakespeare" and writing "in the manner of Shakespeare" (*Embodiment* 138). Writing "in the manner of Shakespeare" is to "follow his naturalism to a neglected conclusion—a wholly new literature" (138). Naturalism is not a "form" that can be copied. For example, "Negro music" has "the form it has because of its naturalism, because it is *Negro* music" (138). "To do something similar"—that is, to imitate rather than to copy—"we would have to do something that would be the music of the *whites*." Thus Boone is "Indianlike" precisely because he "stood for his race" (*American* 137).

The Indian provides Boone with an example of how to be himself and is thus "the prototype of it all" (137), the American "root" (116). As Williams explains to Larbaud, his interlocutor in an earlier chapter, "Père Sebastian Rasles," "there was, to the north, another force, equal to the Puritans but of opposite character, the French Jesuits; two parties with the Indians between them, two sources opposite." Larbaud asks if he, Williams, is "brimming . . . with those three things: a puritanical sense of order, a practical mysticism as of the Jesuits, and the sum of those qualities defeated by the savage men of your country by the first two." But Williams insists to Larbaud that he speaks "only of sources," not effects. "I wish only to disentangle the obscurities that oppress me, to track them to the root and to uproot them" (116). For Williams, the Indians, unlike the Puritans and the Jesuits, cannot be uprooted because their "root" is race, not culture. In the Indian, then, is a "basis" (213), an example for how to descend beneath the "the field of unrelated culture" that has been "stuccoed" (212) upon the land. In a later chapter, Williams imagines that Sam Houston, for example, "joined the Cherokee Indians of Western Tennessee" (212) for precisely this reason—to descend beneath culture, to find "the ground, his ground, *the* ground, the only ground that he knows, that which *is* under his feet" (213). Houston "was adopted into the tribe" (214).

But the point for Williams is be "Indianlike." This is why Houston's adoption into the tribe may have been for him a "saving gesture," but is nonetheless a "gesture of despair" (213). Boone refuses adoption; he affirms his own "wild logic" (137). It is precisely this sort of independence that makes Edgar Allan Poe the first writer of the New World. Poe "turned his back" on foreign influences and "faced inland, to originality, with the identical gesture of a Boone" (226). "American literature is anchored" in Poe, then, not because he has, like Eliot in Pound's account, the "cursed blood" or, like Pound himself, "the virus, the bacillus of the land" in his "blood." Instead, Poe, like Boone, could be said to have the right relation to his *own* "blood," or "the sense within him of a locality of his own" (225). Out of this locality Poe produces writing that seems to "fly away from sense" (221). For Williams, then, the distinctively American work of art is nonrepresentational, caused by, but not representing, "our history," "climate," "time of flowering in history" and, most importantly, by "our blood" (*Embodiment* 149-50).

In "Advent of the Slaves" Williams explicitly associates nonrepresentational writing with what he calls the "SOMETHIN" of race (*American* 209). In that chapter, Williams says of "M.," the "most loquacious" of "the colored men and women" he has known, that "language grows in the original from his laughing lips" (210). "His shy crooked smile, weary, slow, topping his svelt figure, his straight, slim six feet of willowy grace, drooping from the shoulders, smiling sleepy eyes." Here the alliteration—"language," "laughing," "lips"; "svelt," "straight, slim," "smiling sleepy eyes"—asserting the primacy of sound over meaning, emphasizes the materiality of the words. But what might be called Williams' material *something*—to cite the idea that to mean "nothing" "is of course *something*"—is here crucially matched by what he calls "SOMETHIN." "When they try to make their race an issue," Williams says, "it is nothing"—"Bert Williams, author of a Russian Ballet, *The Kiss*; that's worse than nothin'." But ". . . saying *nothing*, dancing *nothing*, 'NOBODY,' it is a quality—." Williams presents this racial quality in the following passage:

> "Somewhere the sun am shinin'—for ME. . . ." That's SOMETHIN'. Taking his shoes off; that's SOMETHIN' . . . dancing, singing with the wild abandon of being close, closer, closest together; waggin', wavin', weavin', shakin'; or alone, in a cabin at night, in the stillness, in the moonlight—bein' nothin'—with gravity, with tenderness- they arrive and "walk all over god's heaven."
>
> (209)

Here "SOMETHIN" is the nothing of materiality that as the subject of the poem is *something*; for Williams it is also what makes black dialect, like "Negro music," "*Negro*"—the fact that it has "the form it has because of its naturalism" (*Embodiment* 138). Bert Williams speaks out of what Williams calls a "solidity, a racial irreducible minimum" (*American* 209). In Williams' account, therefore, the nonsense language of minstrelsy—"close, closer, closest together; waggin', wavin', weavin', shakin'"—is produced above all by the race of the speaker. Williams would have to reject Bert Williams' partner's view of minstrelsy—"nothing seemed more absurd," George Walker said, "than to see a colored man making himself ridiculous in order to portray himself" (qtd. Sunquist 291)—and subscribe instead to accounts that made Negro art racial, a function of "birth." As Albert C. Barnes put it, "the Negro is a poet by birth; his art and his life are . . . one" (Barnes 20). By contrast the "white man" is dominated by his mind; "his art and his life are no longer one and the same as they were in primitive man" (20). So even if the

language of minstrelsy is, from Walker's perspective, "ridiculous," from Williams' perspective it is an essential model for how to write, like Poe, from "deep roots" (*American* 213). White American writers are thus able to mean nothing only when they write "like an Indian" or do "something similar" to the "Negro's" "saying *nothing*." The material *"something"* produced by modernist self-reference is specifically American only when it derives from the author's own racial "SOMETHIN." American writing is American, in other words, because its ground is not the modernist ground but, the ground of "our species," the ground of race.

But race is not the ground of the New World. America and the New World, as we have seen, are not identical. Corpses become *Indian* corpses only when they are removed from the ground, represented. What is significant about Williams' writing in the '20s is its imagination of what, on the one hand, the New World is, and what, on the other, it must, as the "prolific carcass" of America, appear to be. If the New World is an "Eden" in which each thing is like another only in being "sufficient to itself and so to be valued" (*Imaginations* 7), then America cannot avoid the postlapsarian condition in which words fail to be the things they represent—a failure that has as its consequence that of the Fall: death. Writing is in this sense always animated by the spirit of the past. But what makes American writing distinctively American for Williams is the writer's attempt, on the racial model of the Indian and the Negro, to "annihilate" the living corpses of past texts by consuming and transforming them according to the "naturalism" of his or her own race. *Something* must be their own SOMETHIN. Of course, identifying the Indian and the Negro as examples of racial primitivism is already evidence of the failure to be new, but it is a failure that is for Williams distinctively American.

Notes

I wish to thank Howard Horwitz for his help with various aspects of this essay.

1. One might say that *In the American Grain* (1925) is Williams' attempt to write a new history of America, "to re-name the things seen, now lost in a chaos of borrowed titles, many of them inappropriate, under which the true character lies hid" (v). The book is encyclopedic, relies heavily on original documents, and covers in roughly chronological order a great variety of historical figures from Red Eric to Abraham Lincoln. This essay concentrates primarily on chapters entitled: "The Discovery of Indies" (on Columbus), "The Destruction of Tenochtitlan" (on Montezuma), "De Soto and the New World," "The Founding of Quebec" (on Samuel de Champlain), "Père Sebastian Rasles," "The Discovery of Kentucky" (on

Daniel Boone), "Jacataua," "Advent of the Slaves," "Descent" (on Sam Houston), and "Edgar Allan Poe."

2. In the period, "type" was the primary term used by social theorists and eugenicists to classify social/racial groups. See Horwitz and Lambroso.

3. Apparently, Williams is remembering Duchamp's snow-shovel, titled "In Advance of a Broken Arm," as a pickaxe (Marling 67).

4. North, citing Williams' remark that "in the heart there are living Indians once slaughtered and defrauded," notes that "the more the Indians are cut down and cut off the more the Indians rise and become the soul of America. The more thoroughly exterminated the tribe, the more effectively does it resolve Williams' paradox because then it becomes a collective of outcasts, a democracy somehow made up of those rejected by the mass" (158).

5. The same phrase—"ground sense"—occurs in Williams' funeral poem "Tract" which begins "I will teach you my townspeople / how to perform a funeral" (Collected Poems 72). On cleanliness see Crawford, chapter 6, where he relates Williams' obsession with cleanliness in his poems to the development of antiseptic and aseptic procedures in medicine at the time (98-99), and argues that transparent reference is what makes the words "clean" for Williams, though he acknowledges that "Williams can desire clean words . . . and the medical profession can hold them up as a scientific ideal, but finally their cleanliness is a mirage" (111-12). On corpses as representations of the scene of writing, see Fried; on the modernist image as corpse, see Tiffany.

6. In arguing that Williams' locality is committed to the "here" of the text itself, not to the "there" of what the text might also represent, I depart from realist interpretations. But see Altieri who notes, "the poetry establishment of his own time [treated Williams] as a minor, somewhat quirky local-color realist"—an interpretation that has recently been reproduced in "more sophisticated academic versions" (Painterly Abstraction 224). For examples see Schott, Introduction to Imaginations xvi; Crawford 28; Duffy 12. For notions that the poetry is devoted not to representing but to being the American locality, see Michaels (76, 164n).

7. Both winter and spring in these lines produce life. The agency here is not winter or spring but metaphor itself. Death here is actual and not a metaphor or figure for a diminished life as many critics of Eliot are inclined to read it; see Frye 141 and Smith 122. One of the causes of metaphorical death is the inability of language, saturated as it is

with old meanings unrelated to the immediate object of representation or to the poet's intention, to depict the actual or the intentional.

8. It should be noted that just as the presumed opposites in "The Burial of the Dead," spring and winter, turn out to have the same metaphoric function (that of quickening the corpse into a kind of "buried" life), so also the desert waste and water turn out to have the same function—a place of death that is not also a place of burial. In "Death by Water," for instance, "Phlebas the Phoenician," though "a fortnight dead," "passed the stages of his age and youth" (Eliot 65). We might say therefore that language in The Waste Land—or, language inasmuch as it is intrinsically metaphorical—has one meaning: that of failed presence or, in Lacanian terms, manque d'être. It is perhaps no coincidence that Lacan's 1953 "Discourse at Rome"—the essay in which Lacan announced his break with the psychoanalytic establishment in France—was filled with references to Eliot's "The Hollow Men" and The Waste Land (Davidson 56).

9. Williams notes that the magazine started by Duchamp and Arensberg, The Blind Man (emblematic for Williams, like Duchamp's other work, of the new in art) was accompanied by the suicide of one of its contributors: "Together with Mina Loy and a few others, Duchamp and Arensberg brought out the paper The Blind Man, to which Robert Carlton Brown, with his vision of suicide by diving from a high window of the Singer building, contributed a few poems" (Imaginations 10).

10. Undertaking occurs also in "Portrait of the Author." There Williams associates spring—"flares of / small fires, white flowers!—Agh,"—with the destruction of the world: "The world is gone, torn into shreds / with this blessing." The author's job is to be an "undertaker" and protect the world (he calls it the "cold world") by destroying the flowers of spring: "What have I left undone / that I should have undertaken?" (Collected Poems 172-73). Flowers, by this reading, are caused by the failure of the literary undertaker to bury the words.

11. Michaels' inclination to regard the material "elements" of the poem as not part of the poem's meaning perhaps stems from the idea that "the material condition of language is meaningless," that, for instance, sounds "become signifiers only when they acquire meanings, and when they lose their meanings they stop being signifiers" (Knapp and Michaels 22, 23). With this idea, Knapp and Michaels are, I believe quite rightly, criticizing what they call Paul De Man's "negative theory" (21), the notion that "sounds are signifiers even before meanings (signifieds) are added to them" (22). De Man, they argue, distinguishes between

language and speech acts, maintaining that "language is primarily a meaningless structure to which meanings are secondarily added" (22). Knapp and Michaels dispute this distinction. They contend that the material condition of language is meaningless not because it is a pure instance of language, as for De Man, but because, without also being a speech act, it is not language at all. For other considerations of Williams' "material-ism," see Rapp 81, Loewensohn xvii, Miller 292.

12. In *Spring and All* locality or uniqueness—for instance, the reader's realization of "what he is at the exact moment that he is"—is also equivalent to a human universal, or, "the human race, yellow, black, brown, red and white, agglutinated into one enormous soul" (*Collected Poems* 178, 179). Agglutination is, however, not amalgamation. Agglutination implies that the whole is composed of fused parts rather than of dissolved parts (amalgamation). Thus Williams' imagination here of the human race as "one enormous soul" is not one that recruits the logic of the familiar account of Americanization—the "melting pot"—to serve the universal. For a critical contemporary account of the "melting pot" idea, see Bourne 248-306.

13. For an account of the binarism implicit in American racial discourse, see Hutchison 244, 228.

14. Conrad notes that Williams used "the reversal of the conventional chronology of historical narra-tive" as a "structural principle" in this chapter.

15. Loewinsohn introduces *The Embodiment of Knowledge* with the example of Bill Russell who, "in every move he made manifested an intel-ligence, both mental and physical" (ix).

16. The Fidalgo is an account of "De Soto's story" by "an anonymous Portuguese, who identifies himself only as a Fidalgo from Elvas" (Conrad 57).

17. I adapt the phrase "writing 'like an Indian'" from Michaels (85).

Works Cited

Ahearn, Barry. *William Carlos Williams and Alterity: The Early Poetry.* Cambridge: Cambridge University Press, 1994.

Altieri, Charles. *Painterly Abstraction in Modernist American Poetry: The Contemporaneity of Modernism.* University Park: The Pennsylvania State University Press, 1989.

———. "Eliot's Impact on Twentieth Century Anglo-American Poetry." *The Cambridge Companion to T. S. Eliot.* Ed. A. David Moody. Cambridge: Cambridge University Press, 1994. 189-209

Barnes, Albert C. "Negro Art and America." *The New Negro.* Ed. Alaine Locke. New York: Atheneum, 1992. 19-25.

Bourne, Randolph. "Transnational America." *Randolph Bourne: The Radical Will, Selected Writings 1911-1918.* Ed. Olaf Hansen. Berkeley: University of California Press:, 1982.

Conrad, Bryce. *Refiguring America: A Study of William Carlos Williams' In The American Grain.* Chicago: University of Illinois Press, 1990.

Crane, Hart. "The Bridge." *The Poems of Hart Crane.* Ed. Marc Simon. New York: Liveright, 1986. 43-108.

Crawford, T. Hugh. *Modernism, Medicine, and William Carlos Williams.* Norman: University of Oklahoma Press, 1993.

Danto, Arthur C. *The Philosophical Disenfranchisement of Art.* New York: Columbia University Press, 1986.

Davidson, Harriet. "The Logic of Desire: The Lacanian Subject of *The Waste Land.*" *The Waste Land.* Eds. Tony Davies and Nigel Wood. Buckingham: Open University Press, 1994. 55-82.

Duffey, Bernard. *A Poetry of Presence: The Writing of William Carlos Williams.* Madison: University of Wisconsin Press, 1986.

Eliot, T. S. "The Waste Land." *Collected Poems 1909-1962.* New York: Harcourt Brace & Company, 1963. 51-76.

Fried, Michael. *Realism, Writing, Disfiguration: On Thomas Eakins and Stephen Crane.* Chicago: The University of Chicago Press, 1987.

Frye, Northrop. "Unreal City." *Critical Essays on T. S. Eliot's* The Waste Land. Eds. Lois A. Cuddy and David H. Hirsch. Boston: G. K. Hall and Co., 1991.

Gates, Henry Louis. "Harlem on our Minds." *Critical Inquiry* 24 (1997): 1-12.

Hutchison, George. "Jean Toomer and American Racial Discourse." *Texas Studies in Literature and Language* 35 (1993): 226-50.

Knapp, Steven and Walter Benn Michaels. "Against Theory." *Against Theory: Literary Studies and the New Pragmatism.* Ed. W. J. T. Mitchell. Chicago: University of Chicago Press, 1985. 11-30.

Lambroso, Cesare. Introduction. *Criminology.* By Arthur MacDonald. New York: Funk and Wagnalls, 1892. ii-iv.

Levenson, Michael. *A Genealogy of Modernism: A Study of English Literary Doctrine 1908-1922.* Cambridge: Cambridge University Press, 1984.

Loewinsohn, Ron. Introduction. *The Embodiment of Knowledge.* By William Carlos Williams. New York: New Directions, 1974. ix-xxv.

Marling, William. *William Carlos William and the Painters, 1901-1923*. Athens: Ohio University Press, 1982.

Michaels, Walter Benn. *Our America: Nativism, Modernism and Pluralism*. Durham: Duke University Press, 1995.

Miller, J. Hillis. *Poets of Reality: Six Twentieth Century Writers*. Cambridge: Belknap-Harvard University Press, 1965.

North, Michael. *The Dialect of Modernism: Race, Language and Twentieth Century Literature*. Oxford: Oxford University Press, 1994.

Poe, Edgar Allen. "Loss of Breath: A Tale A La *Blackwood.*" *The Unabridged Edgar Allen Poe*. Ed. Tam Mossman. Philadelphia: Running Press, 1983.

Pound, Ezra. *Pound-Williams: The Selected Letters of Ezra Pound and William Carlos Williams*. Ed. Hugh Witemeyer. New York: New Directions, 1996.

Rapp, Carl. *William Carlos Williams and Romantic Idealism*. Hanover, NH: University Press of New England, 1984.

"The Richard Mutt Case." *The Blind Man* 2 (May 1917): 5.

Sayre, Henry M. *The Visual Text of William Carlos Williams*. Urbana: University of Illinois Press, 1983.

Smith, Grover T. "Memory and Desire: *The Waste Land.*" *Critical Essays on T. S. Eliot's* The Waste Land. Ed. Lois A. Cuddy and David H. Hirsch. Boston: G. K. Hall and Co., 1991.

Sundquist, Eric. *To Wake The Nations: Race in the Making of American Literature*. Cambridge: Belknap-Harvard University Press, 1993.

Tiffany, Daniel. *Radio Corpse: Imagism and the Cryptaesthetic of Ezra Pound*. Harvard University Press: Cambridge, 1995.

Tomlinson, Charles. Introduction. *William Carlos Williams: Selected Poems*. New York: New Directions, 1985.

Wagner, Linda Wagner. *Interviews With William Carlos Williams: "Speaking Straight Ahead."* New York: New Directions, 1976.

Williams, William Carlos. *In the American Grain*. New York: New Directions, 1925.

————. *The Autobiography of William Carlos Williams*. New York: New Directions, 1951

————. *The Collected Poems of William Carlos Williams: Volume I, 1909-1939*. Eds. A. Walton Litz and Christopher Macgowan. New York: New Directions, 1986.

————. *The Embodiment of Knowledge*. Ed. Ron Loewinsohn. New York: New Directions, 1974.

————. *Imaginations*. Ed. Webster Schott. New York: New Directions, 1971.

H. T. Kirby-Smith (essay date summer 2000)

SOURCE: Kirby-Smith, H. T. "In Search of a Foot." *Southern Review* 36, no. 3 (summer 2000): 648-68.

[*In the following essay, Kirby-Smith offers a detailed account of the attempts of Yvor Winters and Williams to formulate a coherent and positive theory of free verse.*]

In 1917, T. S. Eliot, who had been in London and Paris for several years and had observed the opening salvos of Imagist theory with a more experienced eye than most of the campaigners, published "Reflections on *Vers Libre*" in *The New Statesman*. "When a theory of art passes," stated Eliot, with premature sagacity, "it is usually found that a groat's worth of art has been bought with a million of advertisement. The theory which sold the wares may be quite false, or it may be confused and incapable of elucidation, or it may never have existed." Further on, he adds: "If *vers libre* is a genuine verse-form it will have a positive definition. And I can define it only in negatives: (1) absence of pattern, (2) absence of rhyme, (3) absence of metre. . . . What sort of a line that would be which would not scan at all I cannot say." There follows a discussion of the greatest subtlety and erudition, which he ends by arguing that anything that is verse at all must continue to be an extension of an established meter. He quotes for illustration his favorite Jacobean playwrights, and his claim that John Webster's lines in *The White Devil* "deliberately rupture the bonds of pentameter" is unassailable; but he fails to remark that the same playwright deliberately restores the pentameter. "There is no escape from meter; there is only mastery," wrote Eliot, in the frequently quoted passage. Why not, I would ask, a mastery of escape? And yet what Eliot says is so fundamentally sensible that it seems to me to need only one small step that would admit the possibility of extraline variation, or line substitution—call it what you will—in which the metrical foot would give way to the line as atomic unit or fundamental division.

Eliot's essay remains one of the earliest and best assessments of what occurred in prosody in this century's second decade; it should be read and reread entire, not quoted in snippets. Eliot continued to take exception to the idea that *vers libre* was really possible, and also attacked the prose poem in an article published in *The New Statesman* for May 19, 1917, "The Borderline of Prose." Thirty years later, Eliot had softened considerably on these issues, but at that time he insisted on a hard and fast distinction between prose and poetry, and insisted there must be no discussion of either free verse or prose poetry. Yet only four years later he came around to an admission that long poems could take on qualities of prose and that prose could aspire toward poetry; in *The Chapbook: A Monthly Miscellany* of April 1921, he wrote:

> Poetic content must be either the sort of thing that *is usually,* or the same thing that *ought to be,* expressed in verse. But if you say the latter, the prose poem is ruled out; if you say the former, you have said only that certain things can be said in either prose or verse. I am not disposed to contest either of these conclusions, as they stand, but they do not appear to bring us any nearer to a definition of the prose-poem. I do not assume the identification of poetry with verse; good poetry is obviously something else besides good verse; and good verse may be indifferent poetry.

Here Eliot has raised an issue that might seem to be separate from the question of free verse. Much as we may enjoy "Casey at the Bat" or "The Cremation of Sam McGee," we do not promote them to equal status with *Paradise Lost* or with Keats's great odes. Even Robert Service knew better than that, refusing to call himself anything more than a versifier.

My purpose here is to demonstrate how efforts to construct a more positive and definite system of free-verse scansion (than Eliot's) immediately run into absurdities and self-contradictions that cannot be resolved. The reason is that, unlike Eliot, who recognized that free verse required a substrate of regularity, Yvor Winters and William Carlos Williams aimed at providing the new method with its own self-consistent rationale. In the end they differed radically from Eliot and from each other, Winters attempting an exacting and overspecific notation, and Williams simply asserting the existence of his "variable foot" without providing clear examples of what he meant by it.

A seldom-mentioned fact is that in avant-garde publications of the period 1913-'16, Williams's name appeared almost as often as that of Joyce, Pound, or Eliot. Perhaps because most of his work consisted of short poems, and because his spare and deliberately unliterary style lacked the panache and knowingness of his contemporaries—a display of esoteric learning that T. E. Lawrence found ridiculous in Ezra Pound—Williams appeared at first to be a minor camp-follower of the Imagists. Later on, he barely had time as a full-time physician to write poetry and fiction; a completely articulated theory of prosody was not one of his achievements. Yet theorize he did—sporadically, spontaneously, thoughtlessly, obsessively, and with less self-contradiction than one might allow him, given the distractions of his busy life. His disjointed utterances have spread and sprouted like wild thistle.

Two recurrent obsessions lent Williams's obiter dicta a certain consistency. First, he decided early on that what

Pound would later say in the *Cantos* was correct: "To break the pentameter, that was the first heave." At any time during the next fifty years, he was ready to get out his scalpel and cut away at the diseased tissue of British metrics. In a letter to Kenneth Burke of July 19, 1955, he wrote: "To take a flier, I am completely through with the concept and the practice of blank verse. The counting of the five regular syllables [sic] makes me grind my teeth." But alongside this was the conviction that poetry could not do without order. Structure was essential to everything in the universe. At times Williams seemed willing to learn what he could from earlier prosody; prior to attending a writer's conference at which he knew Allen Tate would be present, he set himself to studying George Saintsbury's three-volume history of English prosody and admired much that he found there. In 1947 he tried to interest W. H. Auden in assembling a seminar of four or five "master poets" to discuss technical problems in the composition of poetry; he proposed for texts *Samson Agonistes,* one or more of Pound's *Cantos,* a poem by André Breton, and—amazingly enough—Eliot's *Four Quartets.* Williams was willing to treat with the enemy if he could learn anything thereby; of R. P. Blackmur he remarked humorously that he disliked him so much that he was anxious to meet him. When it came to his own metrics, however, he insisted that any orderly new prosody would have to emerge from his work rather than serving as a pre-established template, that structure was inherent and not external to the poem. Yet he did not embrace the personalized organicism characteristic of many who consider themselves followers of Williams. In my view, at least, the amalgamation of poet-city-doctor in **Paterson** is an imaginative construct almost as detached from Williams as Joyce's Dublin and Stephen Dedalus are from that artist.

The most important thing Williams took from his early friendship with Pound and his connections with the Imagists was the concept—which fitted well with his medical training—of submitting oneself to the object under investigation and seeing it on its own terms. He felt, along with Ford Madox Ford and Pound, that nineteenth-century metrical practices had falsified the poetry and that America in particular needed to free itself of these constraints. At the same time, he always distrusted Whitman, sensing a formless momentum in his poetry that might help to sweep away older traditions but that had nothing constructive of its own to offer. As Williams said of Carl Sandburg in 1948, "There never has been any positive value in the form or lack of form known as free verse into which Sandburg's verse is cast. That drive for new form seemed to be lacking in Sandburg." As soon as Williams had ceased to imitate Keats, and had abandoned rhyme and accentual-syllabic meter, he began to cast about for something to take its place.

Having rejected meter, his next step was to reject the absence of it; in 1917 he contributed an article, "America, Whitman, and the Art of Poetry," to *Poetry Journal.* Here he argued that free verse was a contradiction in terms and that all verse had to be subject to some sort of control. This became his settled conviction, and his effort to hit on a method of control was a lasting obsession. In 1954, in "On Measure—Statement for Cid Corman," he repeated: "No verse can be free, it must be governed by some measure, but not by the old measure. There Whitman was right but there, at the same time, his leadership failed him. The time was not ready for it. We have to return to some measure but a measure consonant with our time and not a mode so rotten that it stinks." That Williams was also free of Ford's imperfectly articulated concept of the personal cadence—which Williams refers to as "rhythm"—is evident in the first paragraph of the same essay:

> Verse—we'd better not speak of poetry lest we become confused—verse has always been associated in men's minds with "measure," i.e., with mathematics. In scanning any piece of verse, you "count" the syllables. Let's not speak either of rhythm, an aimless sort of thing without precise meaning of any sort. But measure implies something that can be measured. Today verse has lost all measure.

In *William Carlos Williams: A New World Naked,* Paul Mariani, summarizing points from an unpublished essay, "Speech Rhythms," that Williams wrote in 1913, argues that "Williams had already rejected *vers libre* even as other American and English poets were on the point of discovering it." In the essay, Williams compared a poem to the sea, which was "an assembly of tides, waves, and ripples." This he set against an *imposed* metric of iambics. Here we see his interest in discovering "natural" rhythms.

At about the same time, Amy Lowell was also speculating about free verse. Lowell's closest collaborator in the science of prosody was a certain Dr. Patterson, of Columbia University, whom she never tired of quoting and whose experiments at measuring metrical intervals with laboratory apparatus she recounted with girlish rapture. In "The Rhythms of Free Verse" (*The Dial,* January 17, 1918), she said, speaking of Patterson, "The man who could write 'by listening for rhythm in irregular sequences, in the criss-cross lappings of many waves upon the shore, in the syncopating cries of a flock of birds, in the accelerating and retarding quivers of a wind-blown tree, we have found a new form of pleasure,' knows very well what poetry is." Many of Williams's and Lowell's early thoughts about rhythmic possibilities were the same, and it seems likely that he took certain ideas from her. For many young poets, Lowell's was the only theory available in 1915.

Like Pound, Williams felt that Whitman had broken open the iambic line and made room for new measures, but that was only the beginning. What was needed was a new unit based on temporal succession rather than syllable-counting or foot-chopping. Williams failed to realize that English meters had never been anything like as abstract or mechanical as he imagined. His compulsive Americanism—characterized by Tate as a "naive jingoism"—made him certain that any poetry associated with British or European models, myths, or subjects would turn out to have been trammeled by its meters. Even Gerard Manley Hopkins seemed to him "constipated," though he would return to Hopkins more than once in trying to establish the nature of his own "variable foot."

Williams's theorizing about free verse is so impatient, eclectic, and at times capricious—and yet in other ways so consistent—and his manner is so insistent, that it is difficult not to be led around by the nose when discussing him. He rejected accentual-syllabic meter—and he rejected free verse. He admired Whitman—but considered him wrongheaded. He detested the idea of a mechanical meter—yet studied the prosody of Robert Bridges, perhaps the most self-conscious metricist ever to achieve distinction. He considered Pound, and especially Eliot, as turncoats who had sold out to European culture—but when he finally hit on his "triadic" or "step-down" poetic line, he could not resist comparing his discovery to Dante's terza rima.

In his 1948 talk at the University of Washington, "The Poem as a Field of Action," Williams's irritable disaffections are obvious:

> I propose sweeping changes from top to bottom of the poetic structure. I said structure. So now you are beginning to get the drift of my theme. I say we are *through* with the iambic pentameter as presently conceived, at least for dramatic verse; through with the measured quatrain, the staid concatenations of sound in the usual stanza, the sonnet. More has been done than you think about this though not yet been specifically named for what it is. I believe something can be said. Perhaps all that I can do here is to call attention to it: a revolution in the conception of the poetic foot—pointing out the evidence of something that has been going on for a long time. . . . The one thing that the poet has not wanted to change, the one thing he has clung to in his dream—unwilling to let go—the place where the time-lag is still adamant—is structure. Here we are unmoveable. But here is precisely where we come into contact with reality. Reluctant, we waken from our dreams. And what is reality? The only reality that we can know IS MEASURE.

Williams might have written with greater consistency if he had had more leisure for study; his talk winds up with a comment on the sonnet that only a person forgetful of Milton's management of the Petrarchan convention, and Wordsworth's modification of Milton, could make: "[I]t is a form which does not admit of the slightest structural change in its composition." Surely he could have thought of Hopkins. Perhaps he was being consciously reckless, careless of any offense he might offer to stodgy academics, those harmless drudges.

The definitive study of Williams's prosody is Stephen Cushman's *William Carlos Williams and the Measure of Measure.* Williams, by his own admission, had no idea in the 1940s just what he had been doing in his poems. Everything was instinctive, a measurement by ear or by a feeling for what was appropriate or convenient. Visual arrangements played some part, he thought, but the most important need was a "fuller conception of the poetic foot." In the 1950s, Williams gradually homed in on what he took to be a fruitful conception: the "relative," or "variable," foot. This conception combined two concerns that I will identify with free verse: voice and technique. The variable foot was to be a measure, but one in which the poet's own voice could be heard with its natural intonations, though the voice was not allowed full control. Pure personal preference led to chaos, as (according to Williams) had happened with Whitman and Sandburg. A variable or a relative foot, however, could be the technical equivalent in poetry to relativity in physics:

> We have no measure by which to guide ourselves except a purely intuitive one which we feel but do not name. I am not speaking of verse which has long since been frozen into a rigid mold signifying its death, but of verse which shows that it has been touched with some dissatisfaction with its present state. It is all over the page at the mere whim of the man who has composed it. This will not do. Certainly an art which implies a discipline as the poem does, a rule, a measure, will not tolerate it. There is no measure to guide us, no recognizable measure. . . . Relativity gives us the cue. So, again, mathematics come to the rescue of the arts. Measure, an ancient word in poetry, something we have almost forgotten in its literal significance as something measured, becomes related again with the poetic. We have today to do with the poetic, as always, but a *relatively* stable foot, not a rigid one.

Though there are hints of his method somewhat earlier, in segments of **Paterson,** the period 1952-'56 found Williams arranging his newly discovered variable feet in groups of three, which stepped down the page from left to right before returning to the left-hand margin to start over. Here is **"Work in Progress,"** maybe the best-known example of his practice:

          Of asphodel, that greeny flower, the least,
                    that is a simple flower
                              like a buttercup upon its

      branching stem, save
                    that it's green and wooden
                              We've had a long life

      and many things have happened in it.
                    There are flowers also
                              in hell. So today I've come

                    to talk to you about them, among
                              other things, of flowers
                                        that we both love, even

      of this poor colorless
                    thing which no one living
                              prizes but the dead see

      and ask among themselves,
                              What do we remember that was
           shaped
                              as this thing

      is shaped? while their eyes
                    fill
                              with tears. By which

      and by the weak wash of crimson
                    colors it, the rose
                              is predicated

Cushman accurately traces the origins of Williams's notions and the steps by which he settled on them; he also correlates and judges numerous respectable opinions about the variable foot and the triadic, or step-down, line. After dismissing all efforts to discover aural or temporal regularity, he concludes that the effect is mainly visual, a "design that is symmetrically elegant and dignified." If I agree with Cushman on the whole, it is not with any intention of denying that rhythm, cadence, and the urgencies of the speaking voice are essential to Williams's poetry. But his use of the triadic line and his belief in the variable foot were really no more than a rationalization of a far more complex set of rhythmic events. Williams knew he had accomplished something new in prosody, and he felt uncomfortable at his inability to say just what it was. Confronted with Saintsbury, whose history he owned and even attempted to master, Williams could not help but wish for some explanation of his own principles.

Williams apparently felt that each unit of each triad contained only one major accent, and that each unit occupied the same amount of time, and that he had therefore achieved his desired measure. Later, he even considered what he had done overelaborate. But if what Williams left us is to be read as he intended, he ought to have specified which syllable in each unit is to receive greatest emphasis, and how many seconds are to be allowed for each line. Since the first line above is longer than any other, perhaps we could take that as a standard for time; the way I read it, it lasts 5.29 seconds. I have no idea which syllable is most important, but I tend to come down hard on "greeny." The line is in fact a passable iambic pentameter. As originally composed, the poem seems almost to have slipped beyond Williams's control back toward accentual-syllabics; reading Kenneth Burke's letter of November 7, 1955, to Williams, I wonder if the restless rearranging that Williams was known for may not have been a way of systematically defeating regular meter as much as an effort to "get it right." Tate went one step in this direction in his pentameter poem "The Mediterranean," by calculatedly making every line's rhythm different from every other while retaining a governing pentameter. The next step would be conscientiously to make each successive line even more radically unlike its predecessor. But let us listen to Burke:

> The first time I read the "Asphodel" poem, it seemed so completely *dissolving* that I actually began to feel faint. All the little nodules of fight had been melted, turned into a succession of breathings-out (each tercet being in effect one such moment). The most disarming kind of utterance one could imagine. Ironically, however, your "titular" moment is iambic tetrameter:
>
>> Of asphodel, that greeny flower,
>> I come, my sweet, to sing of you!
> What shall we make of that?

What indeed! At any rate, Williams made sure in his revision that the tetrameter disappeared. Returning to the poem's final version, and looking at the shortest line, "fill," I find that it takes me about a half-second to get it out, leaving a five-second pause—if we consider the lines isochronic—long enough, I suppose, for the brimming of an eye.

Recordings of Williams's voice reveal his habit of nervous insistence on certain words; this carries over into his prose in his frequent use of italics for emphasis. To the extent that there is any meter to **"Asphodel,"** it probably consists of a loosely regularized record of his ordinary voice. To say this is tantamount to an admission that there is no meter at all—but it is not to deny Williams a metric; his metric consisted of a continual violation of traditional metrics.

Williams's true gift was to do the unexpected. His imitators mostly fail because expectations of the unexpected have already been aroused; the same thing happened with English landscape gardening toward the end of the eighteenth century when one architect's surprises were copied by others; after the first "ha-ha" (a wall disguised by a depression in the ground beyond it, so called for the expression of surprise it was meant to elicit), the ha-ha was nothing but a ha-ha. Williams, in his impatient, irritable, and sometimes contradictory denunciations and temporary espousals, found nothing satisfactory in any prosody and succeeded in writing poem after poem that simply *was not* like any established mode. He was ornery and contrary by nature, though at the same time large-hearted and full of curiosity and enthusiasm. My explanation is not intended to discredit Williams; what he did required the greatest sensitivity to conventional metrics, if not a detailed

knowledge of their history. His adolescent compositions in the manner of Keats were not wasted effort; they were the groundwork for his variations. Once he departed from iambic pentameter, he was gone forever—unlike, say, Theodore Roethke, who made periodic escapes and returns.

According to Mariani, Williams, either in late 1927 or in January 1928, wrote to Yvor Winters, repeating anew what he had concluded long before, that free verse did not exist and that a new measure was needed. Winters, who believed that personal correspondence was to be discarded as irrelevant, kept no letters, but Williams mentioned this letter in a journal. The date is important, because it coincides with Winters's ceasing to write free verse and his new insistence, through doctrine and example, that adequate judgment of the subject of a poem was only possible employing shades of meaning afforded by the framework of a fixed meter.

Winters had been among the first to offer intelligent and sympathetic assessments of Williams's work, and was for some years almost an imitator. Their later years were marked by expressions of mutual contempt of the sort that aging generals reserve for one another long after a war; Winters himself told me (in 1963), "Poor old Bill Williams; he didn't have a brain in his head." But in 1927 he might have been more receptive to what Williams said, especially if he already suspected that he himself had been on the wrong track. In the preface to *The Early Poems of Yvor Winters* (1966), he wrote, "Early in 1928 I abandoned free verse and returned to traditional meters." He asserts that nothing about his new position at Stanford nor any sort of intellectual or religious conversion effected this change, but that he found he could not hope to emulate the poets he most admired unless he employed regular meters.

According to Winters, his ideas on the scansion of free verse had been worked out while he was at the University of Idaho, which was about 1925-'26, after he had already written most of the poems to which the theory applied. About his change of method in 1928 he insists, "My shift from the methods of these early poems to the methods of my later was not a shift from formlessness to form; it was a shift from certain kinds of form to others." Even at the end of his life, then, Winters remained convinced—or insisted on asserting—that for him free verse had been as orderly as any other and that his poems could be scanned. As he writes in his preface:

> When I say that these poems had form, I refer not only to the possibility that the free verse may be scanned by my method, perhaps with difficulty; I refer to the fact that these poems are rhythmical, not merely from line to line, but in total movement from beginning to end, and that the relations between the meanings of the parts is an element in the rhythm, along with the sound.

Winters here recalls the ideas of Amy Lowell, such as her statement, "It is the sense of perfect balance of flow and rhythm." That sentence occurs in the account of free verse that appeared in the 1916 Imagist collection. Similar phrases crept into discussion in the issues of *Poetry* that Winters read; as a young man he had been given the freedom of Harriet Monroe's offices in Chicago. Winters makes no reference to Lowell in *In Defense of Reason,* and nowhere else have I been able to find in his work more than passing reference to her. But he was certainly aware of her as a personage, if nothing else, describing her to his classes as "a great big woman who smoked great big black cigars," and—as I have said—he certainly followed with close attention all the debates over form and formlessness.

Because Winters was for thirty-five years the most serious defender of conventional metrics during a period (1930-'65) that saw the proliferation of whole schools of formless poetry, he is worth attending to. His arguments provide a hidden agenda for the movement now called by many the New Formalism. Among his best-known contemporaries, Tate was almost alone in treating Winters with polite respect, a tribute Winters did not reciprocate. Nearly everyone was either a disciple or an opponent—and there were many more of the latter. Winters made himself the center of a school the mentality of which bears comparison with the monks of the island of Iona, who kept the true faith secure in one of the more distant reaches of Britain while the Roman empire collapsed and the barbarians took control of its former provinces.

Although from his early twenties Winters read and admired traditional poets such as Bridges and Thomas Hardy, there was a way in which he backed into English and American poetry. Exiled to the American Southwest by tuberculosis, he took the complete files of *Poetry* that Harriet Monroe gave him, and subscribed to the *Little Review* and *Others,* both packed with the latest avant-garde work. In the isolation of mining towns and provincial state universities, he absorbed the most experimental poetry of the century; it was as if an architectural student had put himself to school to Antonio Gaudí or Frank Lloyd Wright without a sufficient acquaintance with Gothic or Palladian styles— something I do not doubt has often happened. When he began to write free verse, he was attempting to be wildly different from something he did not know enough about to differ from, or at least he seems not at first to have realized that his models owed their success precisely to what they were working against. Also, he had not yet worked out the practical consequences of certain romantic doctrines, and had not yet observed the effect of those doctrines on the lives of his contemporaries. It is true that his earliest published poems were in regular meters, but when he took up free verse, it was not so much a reaction against those meters; rather, he seems

to have believed that he was embarked on a voyage of discovery. He was not—in his early twenties—as at home in accentual-syllabics as H. D., e. e. cummings, or even Williams had been in their formalist juvenilia. Winters abandoned free verse as soon as he understood that he did not know what he was doing—or so I would explain it. A number of the formal poems he subsequently composed are stiff, stilted, and spoiled by contentious rhetoric; but I am at one with Hayden Carruth in thinking "To the Holy Spirit" one of the high points of modern poetry, along with "The Marriage." Winters probably took the course that was best for him. He began to perceive some kinds of free verse as evidence of a self-destructive romanticism or spiritual hubris, and this perception coincided with a growing understanding of formal meters and a realization that he had been aiming at variation without having yet taken hold of a sufficiently well-established norm to vary against. Put another way, in his youth he began to imitate H. D., Williams, and others without having been immersed in accentual-syllabic meters to the extent they had, and without feeling the same urgency to escape nineteenth-century metrics. This is not to imply that Winters was deficient in learning; he knew a great deal about the prosodies of the Romance languages, as well as English.

As I shall show, the inconsistency of his "scansion" of free verse is just as irrational as Yeats's explaining human personality in terms of phases of the moon. The best that can be said about Winters's theorizing is that it demonstrates his early and serious attention to some of Williams's best poems, and provides the occasion for him to say penetrating and memorable things about various others', including his own. The essence of free verse is that it cannot be scanned into feet; the effect of Winters's method is to prove that free-verse systems of scansion are intrinsically self-defeating. On the level of the individual line of traditional accentual-syllabic meter, a spondee is a spondee because it *is not* an iamb or a trochee, and the same is true of a pyrrhic. That is, the spondee and the pyrrhic can only be used as substitute feet; they cannot form the basis of a scansion. To talk about the scansion of free verse is as reasonable as it would be to talk about spondaic pentameter, and that is an impossibility. With free verse, the problem is reversed. As Winters says, "[T]he norm is perpetual variation," and the expectation is that each line will be rhythmically different, at least from those in the immediate vicinity. At the same time, there will be an implied counterpointing against the possibility of a recurrent rhythm—or, as Eliot put it, the ghost of a meter will advance menacingly or withdraw. The effect can be experienced but is much too complex to be diagrammed using macron-breve notation. Free verse is free verse precisely because it does not have an identifiable foot and because it does not have a recurrent and namable line. To put it that way will not, however, deter subsequent projectors whose prosodic speculations have something in common with the occupations of those who inhabited Swift's flying island. There will always be those who have squared the circle and those who are prepared to assert the existence of a free-verse foot; the impossibility of saying exactly what it may be adds to the charm of the idea.

Winters apparently saw free verse as a new variant of English accentual meter. In "Section II: General Principles of Meter" (from *The Influence of Meter on Poetic Convention*), he makes an unfortunate connection: ". . . the accentual, or Anglo-Saxon, system, according to which the line possesses a certain number of accents, the remainder of the line not being measured, a system of which free verse is a recent and especially complex subdivision . . ." If what he meant was that free verse is an especially complex form of accentual meter that plays natural accents against the accentual-syllabic compromise, we might see this as a reasonable suggestion. What Winters *did not* mean was that Old English alliterative meter was a form of free verse. One has to read Winters with care and note that he says "a certain number" and not "an equal number." The real error, though, is to try to make free verse a newly established regular metrical system.

Further on, Winters makes a questionable claim for the superiority of accentual meters: "Accent, like quantity, is unlimited in its variations. In practice, the manner of distinguishing between an accented and an unaccented syllable is superior, I believe, to the manner of distinguishing in classical verse between a long syllable and a short." No one knows how the Greeks and Romans read their poetry; Winters takes a schoolmaster's view of quantitative meters as rigidly fixed, "arbitrarily classified by rule."

To my chagrin, since I would prefer to be in agreement with both of them, I find Winters lining up with Douglas Bush on the question of Milton's prosody in *Samson Agonistes,* which many readers, including Eliot, have been willing to see as free verse. Winters is disagreeing with Robert Bridges when he says, "[H]e scans Milton incorrectly, it appears to me . . . and more particularly Milton's later work, which merely represents learned variation to an extreme degree from a perfectly perceptible accentual-syllabic norm, variation expressive of very violent feeling." Milton completely departed from the pentameter line, though the pentameter line made possible that departure. Winters and I may be saying the same thing in different words, and he puts it this way so as to leave himself at liberty to propose a system of free-verse scansion, a system he would not care to apply to Milton because it would not work.

The next point Winters makes, to which I would also take exception, is that the sprung rhythm of Hopkins and the syncopated effect that is produced by writing syllabic meters in English—without regard to the accent—are the same thing. It is very hard to see how to equate syllabics, which tend to suppress natural stress, with sprung rhythm, which tends to exaggerate it. Nevertheless, as one says when reading Ruskin's denunciations of Michelangelo, it stimulates thought to see such a thing argued.

I do not agree with Winters's statement that "Wyatt employs the accentual variety of sprung rhythm." Thomas Wyatt's roughness—however lovely the poem "They Flee from Me"—may have resulted from an uncertainty as to how to fuse accent with syllable count. This was plain to so sensitive a metricist as Auden, among many others. It will not do to compare Wyatt with poets of later centuries who went counter to the norm. Wyatt had no norm except Chaucer, whom it was difficult to read properly; he was in the process of reinventing the norm, not diverging from it. One might say that Wyatt, by aiming first of all to give us a poem, and only secondarily to achieve perfection in meter, introduced to his pentameters an ingratiating awkwardness—something he never did in tetrameters, where he was completely at home. But it is the charm of naiveté, not a stratagem of sophistication: "a sweet disorder in the dress." Pointing out an awkwardness in Wyatt's pentameters (as compared, say, with Philip Sidney's) does not diminish the stature of the best English poet of the early sixteenth century, any more than it would damage Giotto to be compared with Raphael.

Winters had a way of inventing metrical criteria to justify his preferences—as we all do. In praising Barnabe Googe's graceful line, "Fair face show friends when riches do abound," he says: "Here the accentual weight of the first and third places is increased to equal approximately the weight of the second and fourth; we might describe the first two feet as spondaic, except that, as there is no compensatory pair of pyrrhics, two extra accents are introduced into the line, with the result that the accentual measure is abandoned and we have no measure left save the purely syllabic." Implied in this is some strange doctrine that requires every spondee in a line of iambic pentameter to be balanced by a pyrrhic; one would like to stop and inquire what to make, then, of Byron's line "Roll on, thou deep and dark blue ocean, roll!" and of Donne's "For God's sake hold your tongue and let me love." There are moments when Winters's criticism seems as relevant to his poetic practice as Hart Crane's proclivity for dropping typewriters out of high windows was to his.

But his discussion of prosody is serious enough. Close attention to placement of accent in conventional meters turns out to be preparation for the arguments advanced in Section III, "The Scansion of Free Verse." Winters opens, as usual, with seeming lucidity: "The foot which

I have used consists of one heavily accented syllable, an unlimited number of unaccented syllables, and an unlimited number of syllables of secondary accent. This resembles the accentual meter of Hopkins, except that Hopkins employed rhyme." He ought also have added that, however extravagant each foot may be, there are equal numbers of feet in each line of a Hopkins poem, or in corresponding lines of their stanzas, except at the end of his "curtal" sonnets—those in which he cut the sonnet form short.

Winters continues by setting out his method of notation. This consists of marking primary stresses with "double points," which look like quotation marks, and secondary stresses with "a single point," or apostrophe. Initially he does not say whether his own free-verse lines will contain one or two feet. The example that follows contains both—or at least some lines have a single primary stress, while others have two. But wait: "Since a line which is complete metrically may for the sake of emphasis be printed as two lines, I shall place a cross-bar (/) at the end of each complete line." So some lines are really not lines. Let that go, however; let us see if—when we allow the "cross-bar" to terminate a "line"—we see anything symmetrical. And so we do—but only for the first five "lines." In most of the poem a "line" includes two "primary stresses," which may appear (typographically) on two successive lines that are really one line. But when we reach "line 6" (the seventh line), we see only one "primary accent" marked.

Quod Tegit Omnia

       "   "
1 Earth darkens and is beaded /
  "   '   "   '
2 with a sweat of bushes and /
    "   '
3 the bear comes forth:

      "   '
the mind stored with /
  " '   "   '
4 magnificence proceeds into /
  " '   "   '
5 the mystery of Time, now /
 '   '   "
6 certain of its choice of /
  "   '   "   '
7 passion but uncertain of the /
 '   "
8 passion's end.
[query: why two different scansions for "passion"?]

            "
                When /
 '   "   '   "
9 Plato temporizes on the nature /
  "   '   "
10 of the plumage of the soul, the /
 "   '   "   '
11 wind hums in the feathers as /
 '   "   "   '
12 across a cord impeccable in /

  "   '   "   '
13 tautness but of no mind: /
              "
14   Time,
 '   "   '
the sine-pondere, most /
 '   "   "   '
15 imperturbable of elements, /
  "   '   "
16 assumes its own proportions,/
  "   '   "   '
17 silently, of its own properties—/
    "
18 an excellence at which one
    "
  sighs. /
                   "   '
19   Adventurer in
 '   "   '
  living fact, the poet /
  "   '   "
20 mounts into the spring /
 '   "   "
21 upon his tongue the taste of /
  "   '   "   '
22 air becoming body: is /
   '   "   '
23 Embedded in this crystalline /
  "   '   "
24 precipitate of Time. /

The inconsistencies of the method employed here seem obvious, though others may choose to remain convinced by it. Before setting out the scansion of a second poem, Winters clears up one anomaly: "The imperfect lines (unassimilable half-lines) are marked with a single asterisk." So perfect lines contain two primary stresses, though the lines may be printed as two lines, each of which has one primary stress. But sometimes these lines with only one primary stress are really "imperfect." Then we reach the end of the poem, and he reconsiders:

> This poem is marked, as I have said, as if it contained two feet to the line. It is possible, however, to regard the poem as having a one-foot line, in which case the lines marked with the single asterisk and those unmarked are regular, and those marked with the double asterisk are irregular. The two-foot hypothesis involves the smaller number of irregular lines, and it would eliminate for this poem a difficulty in the matter of theory; to wit the question of whether a one-foot line is a practical possibility.

The most charitable way to see this is as a young man's effort to work his way through an insoluble problem—one that perplexed William Carlos Williams all his life. Happily for Winters, the two poems in question, "Quod Tegit Omnia" and "The Bitter Moon," are fine examples of phrase-breaking free verse; he learned from Williams (though without Williams's perfect awareness of his point of departure) how to tweak his reader's rhythmic expectations. The lines contain abrupt breaks and reversals of rhythm that almost, at times, approach a regular meter but then veer away from it. "Quod Tegit Omnia" seems to be playing against some sort of trimeter, while "The Bitter Moon" suggests the possibility of a trisyllabic dimeter. One can easily make of the first line of "Quod Tegit Omnia" an iambic trimeter, with substitutions and a hypermetric syllable or feminine ending:

        /   /   *   *   *   / *
      Earth dark | ens and | is beaded

This may seem to offer scant likelihood of a regular meter, but it is not that far from the rhythm of opening lines in poems whose regularity no one can question, such as Thomas Campion's

        * /   / *   /   / *
      I care | not for | these ladies

or one by A. E. Housman—

        / /   * /   *   /   *
      Ho, ev | eryone | that thirsteth

In Winters's poem, though, the trimeter is promptly obliterated, or at least evaded, returning only two or three times, and then only tentatively, such as:

        * /   * / *   / *
      The mys | tery | of time now

But the poem's last line is—despite his willful marking of it—a perfect iambic trimeter:

        * / *   /   * /
      preci | pitate | of time

To some degree his free verse is contrapuntal to an implied background meter, but sometimes he simply trusts his instincts as a poet and breaks his lines accordingly.

At about this time Winters had come to realize what could ensue from a thoroughgoing application of antirational Emersonian principles; both he and Allen Tate attempted to warn Hart Crane to abandon these self-destructive romantic dogmas—with the consequence that both of them have been blamed for Crane's subsequent suicide. (To understand precisely how Winters explained the tragedy of Crane's life, one must read his essay on that poet.) His fear of the dissolution that romantic doctrine had worked on Crane helps explain his rejection of free verse in which, as he rightly perceived, he was drifting toward an impulsive and irrational metric. Although Winters never did recant his tendentious and inconsistent attempts to impose an orderly scansion on free verse, the fact that after 1930 he composed only in regular accentual-syllabic meters is a sufficiently persuasive rejection of the earlier method. His later achievement is surely on par with,

say, the best of the French Parnassians of the nineteenth century. To some this may seem either exaggerated praise or an ironic dismissal, but I mean it in perfect seriousness. Leconte de Lisle's poem about the elephants remains one of my favorites—as it was for Winters—and his own work displays an equal formal dignity.

The tools for satisfactory analysis of free verse do not exist; even in scansion of accentual-syllabic meters, the idea of "substitution" of a foot is relatively recent, and fruitful new concepts—the implied off-beat and the unrealized beat—are known to few of those who teach poetry or write about it. The limited usefulness of the "foot" concept vanishes in discussion of free verse; here we have "substitution" of entire lines, and the difficulty of accounting for what happens approaches that of the three-body problem in celestial mechanics. If there is a foot in free verse it *is* the entire line. Winters may have been verging on that realization.

Much more successful are his discursive accounts of his practice:

> My own free verse was very often balanced on this particular tight-rope. [By which he means a tension between iambic pentameter and a more irregular accentual meter that runs against it.] During the period in which I was composing it, I was much interested in the possibility of making the stanza and wherever possible the poem a single rhythmic unit, of which the line was a part not sharply separate. This effect I endeavored to achieve by the use of run-over lines, a device I took over from Dr. Williams, Miss Moore, and Hopkins, and by the extreme use of a continuous iambic undercurrent, so arranged that it could not be written successfully as blank verse and that it would smooth over the gap from one line of free verse to the next.

Amy Lowell and others among the Imagists had called for the whole poem, or at least a strophe thereof, to serve as a self-contained unit; Winters's reading in those early discussions is evident here. We also see in Winters's account the idea of the line as the block from which the strophe may be composed, much as the foot in older scansions was a distinguishable part of the line, though subsidiary to it. The "iambic undercurrent" of which Winters speaks, which never can quite be resolved into regular pentameters, seems quite similar to what I mean when I argue that, line by line, a good free-verse poem runs counter to the possibility of some regular meter. James East has suggested the image of a palimpsest, with erasures of visible measures faintly glimpsed behind the bold text that holds our attention. I am not speaking of writings that are the effect of incompetence but rather those by poets so thoroughly at home in various meters that they can extemporize and divagate; good free verse resembles the lost art of eighteenth-century musical improvisation—lost because it could not be recorded. It also resembles jazz.

In the rest of his discussion, Winters applies his concepts and notation to other free-verse poets he admired. His taste seems impeccable, but he does not succeed in schematizing the remarkable effects achieved by Williams, H. D., Marianne Moore, and Richard Aldington. "The free-verse foot is very long, or is likely to be," he says. "No two feet composed of different words can ever have exactly the same values either of accent or of quantity." In that case there is no free-verse foot; the whole idea of the foot is to identify units that are essentially the *same*, not ones that are essentially *different*. What we have in free verse is continual variety, continual evasion of the norm. At the end of this section, Winters admits as much.

> The free-verse poet, however, achieves effects roughly comparable to those of substitution in the old meters in two ways: first by the use of lines of irregular length, a device that he employs much more commonly than does the poet of the old meters and with an effect quite foreign to the effect of too few or of extra feet in the old meters; and, secondly, *since the norm is perpetual variation* [my italics], by the approximate repetition of a foot or of a series of feet.

This idea, put in a different way, appears to be what Amy Lowell arrived at as a result of her collaboration with her scientific friend:

> I quite agree with Dr. Patterson that "*vers libre* is at its best when syncopating experience predominates." In my "Tendencies in Modern American Poetry," I spoke of Richard Aldington's and "H. D.'"s practice of *vers libre* as always following the syncopating experience. These poets arrived at their conclusions quite independently.
>
> ("The Rhythms of Free Verse")

What Winters called the norm of perpetual variation, what Lowell named syncopating experience, and what Eliot referred to as the ghost of some established meter are all ways of describing the same thing: variation in which the entire line constantly plays against rhythmic expectations, not merely the expectation of a succession of iambs but also of consistency in line length. This, I take it, is what Williams meant when he spoke of an "ethereal reversal." Even Whitman's line can be seen as an extravagant exception to the deadening regularity of American iambics, which had always been johnny-come-lately imitations of a previous English style. Williams was quite correct to feel it was high time for a prosodic Declaration of Independence.

Winters, on the other hand, concluded that free verse could not attain the precision of traditional verse because in regular meters "each variation, no matter how slight, is exactly perceptible and as a result can be given exact meaning as an act of moral perception." At this point one must begin to consider what is morality and what is perception; happily, I am under no obligation to explain these matters.

Mark Long (essay date 2002)

SOURCE: Long, Mark. "William Carlos Williams, Ecocriticism, and Contemporary American Nature Poetry." In *Ecopoetry: A Critical Introduction,* edited by J. Scott Bryson, pp. 58-74. Salt Lake City, Utah: University of Utah Press, 2002.

[*In the following essay, Long argues that a careful study of Williams's poetry and his theories concerning the impossibility of a direct connection between poetic language and unmediated reality should be of particular use to contemporary poets interested in exemplifying a new framework for interacting with the environment.*]

> I could not be a poet without the natural world.
>
> —Mary Oliver

> Without the human, how would I ever know nature?
>
> —Ansel Adams

Most readers come to William Carlos Williams by way of a red wheelbarrow. This indelible image has come to stand in for the significance and distinctiveness of Williams's literary project. "So much depends" upon the wheelbarrow, and the qualities sustained in the image—

> glazed with rain
> water
> beside the white
> chickens.[1]

Similarly, generations of readers have come to understand Williams's poetics through the phrase "No ideas but in things," those deceptively simple words found in the opening lines of the book-length poem **Paterson.** The phrase signifies a poetics predicated not on ideas but rather on things, underscoring a poetic project that seeks immediate contact with the world. But so much more depends upon **"The Red Wheelbarrow"** in its unexcerpted place in a twenty-seven-section poetic sequence imbedded within the prose of **"Spring and All."** A survey of critical accounts of Williams's poetics will show a surprisingly consistent acceptance of Williams's romantic quest for immediate contact. It will come as no surprise, then, that studies of the social implications of Williams's project have concluded that Williams's social aim, in the words of one contemporary critic—"to free his readers' imaginations so that they could experience the world with sensual immediacy—is profoundly apolitical, even asocial."[2]

This aim to free the imagination as the prior condition to experiencing the world with sensual immediacy has been instrumental in determining the critical conversation about environmental and ecological poetry.[3] Yet, as John Elder suggests in *Imagining the Earth*, nature poetry, at best, does not simply reflect but shapes our vision of nature. "Poetic form," writes Elder, "secures a plot where the fruitful decay of order and intentions may occur; an unsuspected landscape rises through the traces of a poem's plan."[4] Poetic form is, in this definition, an especially promising site for more than simply renewing awareness—"the fruitful decay of order and intentions" depends on encountering an alternative to our necessarily limited experiential and cognitive frames. A poem is understood here as not merely a site for reflecting on our limits but as a space in which we might learn to construct alternative ways of thinking and acting in the world. Seeking primary, preverbal experience, then, is perhaps a necessary but in no way sufficient end for the environmentally or ecologically inclined poet.

More recent studies of nature poetry develop this connection between the experiential and referential function of literature and the politically and socially inflected rhetoric of poets who explicitly seek to reorient language toward the biocentric laws of nature. Writers such as A. R. Ammons, Wendell Berry, Denise Levertov, W. S. Merwin, Gary Snyder, and Adrienne Rich have now been read as ecological poets whose vision of nature seeks to fashion alternatives to the anthropocentric consciousness of modern high culture.[5] This vision, as expressed by Leonard Scigaj in *Sustainable Poetry,* is informed by a belief "that language is a positive instrument that can promote authentic social and environmental relations between humans and their environment—relations that can lead to emancipatory social change."[6] These ambitions are, of course, part of a more general national and international strain that worked in twentieth-century modernism to change the direction of poetry and art, in the words of Jerome Rothenberg and Pierre Joris, "as a necessary condition for changing the ways in which we think and act as human beings."[7] Ecopoets, more specifically, work from the conviction "that poetry is a part of a struggle to save the wild places—in the world and in the mind—and the view of the poem as a wild thing and of poetry and the poet as endangered species."[8]

Theories of writing and reading poetry that underscore language as a function of *poesis* suggest the inadequacy of the view that language separates us from the world— the idea that all human patterns of thought, schemas, and generalizations are impositions on a preexisting state we call nature. Yet critical statements regarding the purpose of poetry will always risk parochialism or, more precisely, narrowing the purpose of poetry to promoting *authentic* relations between the aesthetic object and its extrapoetic referent. Indeed, the pragmatic rhetoric of promoting nature as it is apart from human culture risks underestimating the problem of representation. Ecocritics, Dana Phillips cautions, share "assumptions about the ontological gulf between culture and nature, and the metaphysics of representation suppos-

edly required to bridge that gulf."[9] And if poetry is "a manifestation of landscape and climate, just as the ecosystem's flora and fauna are," in the words of Elder, then the determinative analogy between a poem and an ecosystem may narrow the role of ecocritics to arbiters of the authentic.[10]

The distinctive modernist project of William Carlos Williams provides an exemplary occasion for reflecting on contemporary American poets with ecological and environmental concerns. Williams can help us to reflect on the ambitious attempts to link a poetics of presence with an ecologically informed project for social change.[11] In fact, Williams may prove to be a significant figure as we explore the assumptions that link the craft of poetry with the crafting of ecological change.[12] Charles Olsen has made the case that a poet's "stance toward reality" is crucial to the structuring of a poem; and a better understanding of Williams's stance toward the world might prove especially relevant to enriching the premises and practices of contemporary ecopoetics. But although the critical consensus regarding Williams's quest for immediacy may appear congruent with ecocriticism, I will underscore precisely Williams's argument *against* the idea that poetry might help us reestablish a more immediate contact with the world. My intent is to suggest how Williams's acute critique of the view that poetic language offers a less-mediated relation to the world might contribute to expanding the range and power of environmental and ecological reflection in contemporary American poetry.

David Walker argues, I think rightly, that "Williams is primarily interested not in the physical world itself, but in the dynamic relationship between the world and the life of the mind as it apprehends and responds to that world."[13] This drama of relation energizes Williams's early poetics. In the opening lines of his 1923 text **"Spring and All,"** for example, Williams concludes that "there is a constant barrier between the reader and his consciousness of immediate contact with the world."[14] This precise formulation does not rule out the reader's immediate contact with the world; at the same time, he cautions, we cannot be conscious of that immediate contact. We need not deny immediate contact because the very possibility of cognizing a relation to the world is predicated on the presence of the world. But Williams's formulation does not obscure the important fact that immediacy is logically equivalent to an absence of relation. Further, it needs to be understood in this context that the relation is not simply between matter and form or the mind and the world. Any attempt to *recover* immediacy (what Williams called "the reality that we feel in ourselves") requires a third term, a representational medium that will nevertheless prove once more to be "a covering over" or, in Williams's stronger terms, another "dangerous lie."[15]

Williams's 1925 book *In the American Grain* further explores the process of mediation required to come to terms with the world. American history has always been mediated by our attempts to know it, despite the fact, Williams adds, that the "productive ground . . . the common thing . . . is anonymous about us" (*IAG* [*In the American Grain*], 213). Yet, Williams insists, historical intelligibility must always involve *re*establishing a "ground" by breaking through dead layers of understanding. To "break through dead layers" the writer must "have the feet of his understanding on the ground, his ground, *the* ground, the only ground that he knows, which is under his feet." This concern with placing "the feet" of one's understanding is to be understood in the fundamental sense of *poesis,* or having to do with the making, building, or constructing of something. For the poet the construction must take place in the structural body of the poem, as a question of language and structure. The revolution, Williams presses, must be in the poem. "There is no poetry of distinction without formal invention, for it is in the intimate form that works of art achieve their exact meaning . . . to give language its highest dignity, its illumination in the environment to which it is native."[16]

Williams returns to this problem of locating one's self in the environment in his 1934 essay "The American Background." Here Williams recounts the psychological condition of the English settlers who had come to the North American continent: *"They found not only that they had left England but that they had arrived somewhere else: at a place whose pressing reality demanded not only a tremendous bodily devotion but as well, the more importunately, great powers of adaptability, a complete reconstruction of their most intimate cultural make-up, to accord with the new conditions. The most hesitated and turned back in their hearts at the first glance."* Strange and difficult, Williams continues, *"the new continent induced a torsion in the spirits of the new settlers, tearing them between the old and the new."* The old was the existing European frame of reference; the new was the very environment that surrounded them. The conjunction of a *"pressing reality"* and the immigrants' lack of *"adaptability"* follows Williams's description of how the settlers of the continent *"saw birds with rusty breasts and called them robins."* (They were thrushes. *"Meanwhile, nostalgically, erroneously, a robin."*) *"Thus, from the start,"* Williams concludes, *"an America of which they could have no inkling drove the settlers upon their past. They retreated for warmth and reassurance to something previously familiar."*[17] But at a cost.

The cost was—and is—a failure to understand that "the new and the real, hard to come at, are synonymous" (*SE* [*Selected Essays*], 143). Here Williams presses us to consider the pedagogical function of our experience in constructing a relation to place. One does not learn

(or does so only partially) by assuming that what one needs are more facts, more information, or a closer, more qualitatively precise relationship to one's surroundings. The problem in American history has been "the success of the unrelated, borrowed, the would-be universal culture which the afterwave has run to or imposed on men to impoverish them, if it has not actually disenfranchised their intelligence" (149). Instead, what one needs is a genuinely new means of representing one's experience of place—a means of rendering the world intelligible. In a 1950 letter to Columbia University professor Henry Wells, Williams explains that a poem is "an attempt, an experiment, a failing experiment, toward assertion with broken means but an assertion, always, of a new and total culture, the lifting of an environment to expression."[18] The imagination works with the "broken means" of language not simply through the difficult and consequential work of recovering experience but by moving from experience to its representation.

The new and the real, one might say, become possible. However, for Williams, "Americans have never recognized themselves. How can they? It is impossible until someone invents original terms. As long as we are content to be called by someone else's terms, we are incapable of being anything but our own dupes" (*IAG,* 226). Such an attempt at placement in the world as a necessary means of self-definition is exemplified in Williams's book-length poem *Paterson.* Williams understands well, with Blake, that the condition of the imagination is loss, and he is similarly dedicated to the productive or constitutive function of imaginative work within these limits. Williams's case is, more simply, that a "poetics of presence" is a flat contradiction in terms. Consider the opening lines of the preface to book 1 of the poem: "Rigor of beauty is the quest. But how will you find beauty when it is locked in the mind past all remonstrance?"[19] The phrase "rigor of beauty" leads to the suggestion that beauty cannot be found. The quest for beauty involves the rigorous task of its demonstration—in this case, in the structural body of the poem. Williams immediately follows his question with a solution. His answer begins as the poem breaks into measured lines of verse:

> To make a start,
> out of particulars
> and make them general, rolling
> up the sum by defective means—
>
> (*P* [*Paterson*], 3)

As Williams elaborates, seeking beauty involves moving from a formal system of measurement to the constituent parts of a system, a movement "from mathematics to particulars" (4). The movement involves a quest into the language of the poem—an incursion rather than an excursion. As *Paterson* begins to exemplify this incursive process we come to experience the movement of the poem as it begins to accomplish what the controlling speaker is seeking to overcome: "the language! / is divorced from their minds, / the language . . . the language!" (12). Williams animates divorce as "the sign of knowledge in our time, / divorce! Divorce!" (17). The question of direction in such a condition is in fact a question. In fact, Williams says, "There is no direction. Whither? I / cannot say. I cannot say" (17). The divorce is also between the idea and the thing, despite the presence of

> the roar of the river
> forever in our ears (arrears)
> inducing sleep and silence, the roar
> of eternal sleep.
>
> (17)

Our estrangement from the language we need to represent the world is compounded, Williams suggests, by the ever-present "mass of detail" (19). The problem is "to interrelate on a new ground," and the difficulty "Divorce (the / language stutters)" (21). The drama of these opening sections of the poem is precisely the struggle with representation, as we are tempted to fall back on an outmoded formula. "A chemistry, corollary / to academic misuse, which the theorem / with accuracy, accurately misses" (36).

Williams identifies a crucial problem in the opening pages of **Paterson.** Poetry always and necessarily must attend to the problem of our separation from speech. Rather than being alienated from the world (we are always already in the world, Williams insists), we have not found our way to the resources of our native tongue. We need to begin, in the words of Gary Snyder, by recognizing how wonderful it is "to be born to be a native speaker, to be truly a native of something."[20] His insight does not suggest poetry as simply the place of sentimental attachments, the place of literal topographies. Rather "the place of poetry," to borrow an apposite formulation from Heather McHugh, "is nothing less than the place of love, for language; the place of shifting ground, for human song; the place of the made, for the moving."[21] We go nowhere when we seek to use poetry to transcend itself—to misuse language as a vehicle for a remedial course in immediacy. Not *so much,* but *everything,* depends on the responding sensibility. In this way we come to understand the content of a poem, in the words of Charles Bernstein, as "more an attitude toward the work or toward language or toward the materials of the poem than some kind of subject that is in any way detachable from the handling of the materials. Content emerges from composition and cannot be detached from it; or, to put it in another way, what is detachable is expendable to the poetic."[22] Otherwise there is no distinctive claim for the poem.

Williams emphasizes poetry as a condition for changing the way we think and act as human beings. He is a poet not a philosopher, yet he is confident that the world lies beyond our conceptualizations of it. And he is adamant that the idea of an external world is in fact necessary to the subsequent internal formation of a relation and the embodiment of the relation in the structural invention we come to know as the poem:

> Without invention nothing is well spaced,
> Unless the mind change, unless
> the stars are new measured, according
> to their relative positions, the
> line will not change, the necessity
> will not matriculate: unless there is
> a new mind there cannot be a new
> line, the old will go on
> repeating itself with recurring
> deadliness:
>
> (50)

Recall T. S. Eliot, who observed that "when I say 'invent' I should use inverted commas, for invention would be irreproachable if it were possible." The problem for the poet is *invention,* a term Williams uses to describe the need to break free from the repetition of the old. The poem continues:

> without invention
> nothing lies under the witch-hazel
> bush, the alder does not grow from among
> the hummocks margining the all
> but spent channel of the old swale,
> the small foot-prints
> of the mice under the overhanging
> tufts of the bunch grass will not
> appear: without invention the line
> will never again take on its ancient
> divisions when the word, a supple word,
> lived in it, crumbled now to chalk.
>
> (50)

For Williams invention begins where we are: with the materials at hand and within the symbolic complex we use to measure our place in the world. The loss of presence is indeed a result of how the already-been-formulated shapes the formulations that follow. The difficult problem is that we are habituated to receiving the presence of the world in the terms of what we already know. Invention thus begins with the recognition that invention is necessary but only with the knowledge that there are always more to the prototypes of experience than we have acquired. Invention, for Williams, begins with the figure of descent into the limited frames of perception and cognition we use to craft our experience. Invention then moves toward the need for a form or structure for that experience. For Williams invention restores both the world and the person using the resources of language and who is in constant struggle with the limits of those resources.

Although Williams may have been sympathetic to the idea that poems might offer us ways into the world, he insists that the problem of literary representation cannot be understood as an exchange between something outside the poem and the poet. Representation is demanding precisely because it requires the poet's imagination. But the imagination must find a way to free itself. If we agree that the imagination is a constructive power, simply freeing the perceptive faculties to imagine possible versions of experience does not account for the more difficult problem of constructing a form in which to make intelligible (and to offer for reflection) the formal dynamics of a particular set of relations. The crucial point is that Williams's poetics look not back at reestablishing a lost connection with the world because, as I have said, we are always already in that world. Rather the problem the poet faces is looking forward to the ways we are able to become present to the possibilities of the phenomenal world where we have been living all along. The poet must discover the dynamic substance of the world by representing it as intelligible in the originary structure of the poem. Williams demands a radical commitment to the distinctive human power of language use and to developing the resources of poetic structures. It follows that the ever-present risk of any poetic theory is to define a priori a vital cultural practice. In advocating the distinctiveness of the poem as a "field of action" Williams challenges us in the permanently transitional space between the already known and the as yet unrealized potential of our lives.

The breathtaking structural movement of Williams's best poems (the field of action is *in* the poem)—and his restless commitment to poetic innovation—offers contemporary environmental and ecological poets an inspiring commitment to poetic innovation. The genre of ecopoetry might find a place for Williams in its historical development by using his work to refine its most common assumptions and foundational beliefs. But in his study of the "sustainable" poem, Scigaj construes a more narrow definition of the distinctiveness of ecopoetry. The ecopoem, in Scigaj's definition, "persistently stresses human cooperation with nature conceived as a dynamic, interrelated series of cyclical feedback systems."[23] The tradition of nature poetry is in this way understood as distinct from the environmental poetry written in an age in which environmental concerns were becoming manifest in the poetic imagination. Thus his argument is historical in that it locates in the poetry of the past thirty years an increasing awareness of ecological crisis. Following up Elder's insights about the tradition of American poets whose work concerns the human relation to nature, Scigaj seeks further to "explore new ways of developing a *theoretical* position" for ecopoetry that would "critique poststructuralist language theory and provide an alternative" (xiii). Scigaj then admonishes, "We need a sustainable

poetry, a poetry that does not allow the degradation of ecosystems through inattention to the referential base of all language. We need a poetry that treats nature as a separate and equal other and includes respect for nature conceived as a series of ecosystems—dynamic and potentially self-regulating cyclic feedback systems" (5).

In the face of environmental crisis, Scigaj concludes, we are no longer able to naturalize these ecosystems "into benign backdrops for human preoccupations or reduce them to nonexistence by an obsessive focus on language in our literary creations."[24] The theoretical framework provided by Scigaj here (which is different from the practice of the poets and poems he discusses) therefore potentially determines the kinds of thinking—the subject matter—that would qualify under the rubric of ecopoetry. If the concept of a sustainable poetry is articulated as attentive to the "referential base" of all human activity, ecopoetry would by design "refer" the reader's perception beyond the printed page. The poem is thus understood by the poet, and by implication the reader, as at once pointing to the world as well as to the possible transparencies of language. The affective power of poetry is, in this view, narrowly construed. Williams addresses the practical limits of such a position regarding the content and the affective domain of language in general and the poetic in particular in "The Poem as a Field of Action," his address to Theodore Roethke's students at the University of Washington in 1948. Williams insists that you "can put it down as a general rule that when a poet, in the broadest sense, begins to devote himself to the *subject matter* of his poems, *genre*, he has come to an end of his poetic means" (*SE*, 288). Williams's exemplary efforts to see poetry as a distinctive form of cultural practice underscore how the ecological poet must not be limited to a subject matter such as the environment or to the ideological shape of a belief such as saving the environment.

It will come as no surprise that among postwar American poets with environmental and ecological concerns, one finds a renewable source of interest in Williams's work. Denise Levertov's 1972 essay "Williams and the Duende," for instance, praises Williams's constant (and consistently changing) attempt to take "up the challenge to deal with his time and place"; and Gary Snyder comments in "The New Wind," an essay from the 1960s, that Williams "has been the largest single influence on the present generation of writers."[25] For poets, singular influence can often be traced to the urgent formal intensity of a single poem—an exceptional poem that lives in its demonstration of a new possibility in the art form. For critics, a poet's significance is often understood in terms of what Harold Bloom has called the revisionary ratios of poetic influence. But a poet such as Williams shapes a tradition more fundamentally than by simply providing exemplary poems or by influencing a single poet or poetic school. Williams creates a singular set of conditions for poetic innovation during the second half of the twentieth century.

Adrienne Rich's recent collections of poems attempt to experience and constitute a series of intelligible relations at the local level to reflect on existing patterns of self-knowledge within a larger sense of the social and political world in the process of unfolding. In her poem "Natural Resources," to take an example, Rich writes,

> My heart is moved by all I cannot save:
> so much has been destroyed
> I have to cast my lot with those
> who age after age, perversely,
> with no extraordinary power,
> reconstitute the world.[26]

Yet my interest is less in thematic concern than in Rich's breathtaking allegiance to her craft in these lines as a pledge to a poetics rooted in what Gary Snyder calls the common ground, our native place, of language. Her commitment to the confusing, disorienting, and painful location in and from which she writes reflects an abiding commitment to integrating the descriptive (personal, reflective) and persuasive (political, oratorical) functions of poetry. In *An Atlas of the Difficult World* Rich shows her readers where she is through a Whitmanesque catalog of failures ("These are the materials") and the necessity of the possibilities of personal and collective redemption ("What does it mean to love my country?"). Drawing inspiration from Muriel Rukeyser's example ("There are roads to take"), Rich admonishes us "to catch if you can your country's moment, begin."[27]

Rich's two essays on placement—"Blood, Bread and Poetry: The Location of the Poet" and "Notes Toward a Politics of Location"—elegantly and forcefully trace "the possible credibility of poetry" through her own personal evolution from a conviction of uniqueness as a young poet to her emerging "untutored and half-conscious rendering of the facts of blood and bread, the social and political forces of my time and place."[28] In her sequences of poems in *An Atlas of the Difficult World* Rich further displays her commitment to the aesthetic I have traced out of Williams. These poems demonstrate how personal and political relationships and territories can be mapped and how, in the words of James Baldwin that she uses as inspiration, "Any real change implies the breakup of the world as one has always known it, the loss of all that gave one an identity, the end of safety" (*BBP* [*Blood, Bread, and Poetry: Selected Prose 1979-1985*], 176). Rich's distinctive commitment of the heart and mind to a poetics that calls into question our best version of self and world suggests a definition of the poetic arts "not as a commodity, not as a luxury, not as a suspect activity, but as a precious resource to be made available to all, one necessity for the rebuilding of a scarred, impoverished,

and still-bleeding country" (*BBP*, 185). The rebuilding is accomplished, for Rich as a poet, with the materials of the poem.

Rich categorically rejects poetry as simply seeking, in the satiric words of E. E. Cummings, to "live suddenly / without thinking."[29] For imagining a state of mindless immediacy must suppose that we can depend on our senses, and intuition, to transport us back to a direct, if not more certain, place in the world. Nostalgia for the world in and of itself misses the fact that the world in and of itself is precisely what we already have. Williams can help us to understand that we can know the world, and we can know it differently; the thing in itself is precisely what we do experience and see. The problem will always be how we will come to an awareness of the thingness of the world we have in common by bringing it into form in a particular way. Everything depends, Williams demonstrates—and I think convincingly—on the relations that are established, as there can be no final categorical distinction between the real and the represented. Our representations, although self-sufficient, are never all-sufficient. There are, however, linguistic representations, always the product of an abductive process of inference, that do not prove "sustainable." As Robert Hass reminds us, metonymy is the characteristic form of the poetic image "because all our seeing is metonymic."[30] Yet the way to most fully experience the sudden moments in our lives is by reflecting on the meaning of their partiality and staying open to possible revisions of the meanings we make.

Williams's commitment to his art is grounded in his abiding faith in humanity. His restless attempts to refine the resources of his language can inspire poets and readers to live beyond their limits by discovering what they do not already know. In this sense Williams's aesthetics is *political*,[31] a term Robert von Halberg defines as making categorical thinking difficult. "Poets who are satisfied with rousing simplifications or confirmations of their audience's views sell short the possibilities of their art."[32] A passionate commitment to the environment is perhaps a necessary risk for a poet who wishes to challenge existing modes of human relation to the world. But Williams demonstrates that without a genuine commitment to language and its domain of human culture, a supposed poetics of presence will slide into its relatively insignificant place, unable to articulate other than its own already known and local point of view. This essay only begins to suggest how Williams's insights into the way language renews itself as a specific form of cultural practice might create a specific set of conditions for overcoming these limited forms of artistic practice, especially in poems that are intentionally addressed to the environment and environmental concerns. Williams suggests the limitations of using poetry to disclose phenomenological presence. To expand, not diminish, the affective range and power of poems requires not the mystical one of knowing the world, of seeking something before making. On the contrary, Williams reminds us that the practice of poetry is a part of the constant development of a cultural reality from the potentiality of experience through particular linguistic acts.

Notes

1. William Carlos Williams, *Imaginations,* ed. Webster Schott (New York: New Directions, 1970), 138.

2. David Frail, *The Early Politics and Poetics of William Carlos Williams* (Ann Arbor: UMI Research Press, 1987), 92.

3. Important critical studies in the American tradition of poetry include John Elder, *Imagining the Earth: Poetry and the Vision of Nature* (Urbana: University of Illinois Press, 1985); Guy Rotella, *Reading and Writing Nature: The Poetry of Robert Frost, Wallace Stevens, Marianne Moore, and Elizabeth Bishop* (Boston: Northeastern University Press, 1991); Terry Gifford, *Green Voices: Understanding Contemporary Nature Poetry* (New York: Manchester University Press, 1995); Gyorgyi Voros, *Notations of the Wild: The Poetry of Wallace Stevens* (Iowa City: University of Iowa Press, 1997). Also see Bernard W. Quetchenbach, *Back from the Far Field: American Nature Poetry in the Late Twentieth Century* (Charlottesville: University Press of Virginia, 2000); Jonathan Bate, *Romantic Ecology: Wordsworth and the Environmental Tradition* (New York: Routledge, 1991). Anthologies that have helped to define the field include Robert Bly, ed., *News of the Universe: Poems of a Twofold Consciousness* (San Francisco: Sierra Club, 1980); Sara Dunn and Alan Scholefield, eds., *Beneath the Wide Wide Heaven: Poetry of the Environment from Antiquity to the Present* (London: Virago, 1991); Robert Pack and Jay Parini, eds., *Poems for a Small Planet: Contemporary American Nature Poetry* (Hanover, N.H.: University Press of New England, 1993); John Daniel, ed., *Wild Song: Poems of the Natural World* (Athens: University of Georgia Press, 1998). Among the dissertations on the subject see David Gilcrest, "Greening the Lyre" (Ph.D. diss., University of Oregon, 1995) and Laird Christensen, "Spirit Astir in the World: Sacred Poetry in the Age of Ecology" (Ph.D. diss., University of Oregon, 1997).

4. Elder, 215. Elder is important as one of the first voices pointing the way toward recent developments in the field of ecocriticism in general and the study of ecopoetry more particularly.

5. See Rotella's historical and intellectual survey of the changes and continuities of American poets'

attitudes toward epistemology, aesthetics, and nature that lead to the poems written in the period between the publication of Robert Frost's first book of poems in 1913 and Elizabeth Bishop's final collection in 1976. Also see *Green Voices,* in which Terry Gifford asks, "What, then, have emerged as the criteria for valuing one 'green language' rather than another?" (143). In his detailed and illuminating exposition Gifford identifies "connection," "commitment," and "responsibility" as the dominant constituents in the nature poetry of Kavanagh, MacLean, Heaney, Hughes, et al. For a comparable attempt to define a set of criteria for valuing ecopoetry, see Gyorgyi Voros's discussion of ecology in the poetry and poetics of Wallace Stevens, in which she describes Stevens's sense of relationships as ecological and defines a list of six familiar aspects of Stevens's work that "readily lend themselves to an ecological reading" (83-86).

6. Leonard Scigaj, *Sustainable Poetry: Four American Ecopoets* (Lexington: University Press of Kentucky, 1999), 33.

7. Pierre Joris and Jerome Rothenberg, eds., *Poems for the Millennium: The University of California Book of Modern and Postmodern Poetry,* vol. 1, *From Fin-de-Siècle to Negritude* (Berkeley: University of California Press, 1995), 2.

8. Pierre Joris and Jerome Rothenberg, eds., *Poems for the Millennium: The University of California Book of Modern and Postmodern Poetry,* vol. 2, *From Postwar to Millennium* (Berkeley: University of California Press, 1998), 12.

9. Dana Phillips, "Ecocriticism, Literary Theory, and the Truth of Ecology," in the special ecocriticism issue of *New Literary History* 30, no. 3 (summer 1999): 575-602. Phillips discusses the antitheoretical spirit of ecocriticism, pointing to examples of ecocritics who "treat literary theory as if it were a noxious weed that must be suppressed before it overwhelms more native and greener forms of speech" (579). He cites Lawrence Buell's seminal book *The Environmental Imagination: Thoreau, Nature Writing, and the Formation of American Culture* (Cambridge: Harvard University Press, 1995), in which Buell asks, "Must literature always lead us away from the physical world, never back to it?" (11). Phillips provides a generative critique of the theoretical assumptions behind Buell's project. Using Buell as a case study, Phillips observes that "the result is not so much a new kind of blessedly untheoretical discourse as it is a discourse propped up here and there by some distinctly shaky theory" (579). Phillips also provides an incisive set of observations regarding Elder's analogy between poem and ecosystem—an

analogy, Phillips argues, that "is faulty on scientific as well as literary grounds" (581). For a brief response by Buell to Phillips, see "The Ecocritical Insurgency," *New Literary History* 30, no. 3 (summer 1999): 703, 711 n. 11.

10. Quoted in Phillips, 581.

11. I take the phrase "poetics of presence" from Charles Altieri, "Denise Levertov and the Limits of the Aesthetics of Presence," in *Enlarging the Temple: New Directions in Poetry during the 1960's* (Lewisburg, Penn.: Bucknell University Press, 1980), 26; repr. in Albert Gelpi, ed., *Denise Levertov: Selected Criticism* (Ann Arbor: University of Michigan Press, 1993). Altieri's exploration of postmodern poetics raises important questions regarding the philosophical adequacy of a poetics of presence. "Considered as metaphysical or religious meditation, the poetry of the sixties seems to me highly sophisticated; it takes into account all the obvious secular objections to traditional religious thought and actually continues and extends the inquiries of philosophers as diverse as Heidegger, Whitehead, and Wittgenstein. This very success, however, makes it disappointing that the poetry fails so miserably in handling social and ethical issues." For a critique of Altieri's assumptions more generally as exemplifying the limits of postmodern language theory, and specifically in reference to the second major period of W. S. Merwin's poetry, beginning with the 1967 book of poems *The Lice,* see Scigaj, 18-28, 176-177. Scigaj sets the project of ecocriticism against poststructuralist language theory, arguing that environmental poetry *must* emphasize its referential ground and "contain an activist dimension to foreground particular acts of environmental degradation and degraded planetary ecosystems" (21, my emphasis). Scigaj argues for the phenomenological approach of Merleau-Ponty as the proper theoretical model to elucidate the value of such poetry. Yet despite Scigaj's trenchant insights regarding Altieri's assumptions, in targeting Altieri's "aestheticism" he effaces the specificity of Altieri's readings he chooses not to cite, such as his treatment of Levertov's struggles to adapt her poetics to the pressing political issues in the Vietnam era.

12. The demand for an ethical extension from the relation of individuals, and the relation of individuals to society, to the relation between individuals in a biotic community that includes human beings is predicated on Aldo Leopold's "land ethic," which provides practitioners in the field of ecocriticism with a "mode of guidance" that "changes the role of *Homo sapiens* from conqueror of the land-community to plain member and citizen of it" (Aldo Leopold, *A Sand County Almanac* [New York: Oxford University Press, 1949], 204). The study of literatures of the environment is significantly informed by the understanding that "current environmental problems are largely of our own making, are, in other words, a by-product of culture" (Cheryl Glotfelty and Harold Fromm, eds., *The Ecocritical Reader: Landmarks in Literary Ecology* [Athens: University of Georgia Press, 1996], xxi). The ethical and cultural implications of ecocriticism therefore demand more than simply a rigorous interdisciplinary study of environmental literatures precisely because the cultural rhetoric of environmentalism is practiced with an urgent and irrepressible desire for personal, political, and economic transformation.

13. David Walker, *The Transparent Lyric: Reading and Meaning in the Poetry of Stevens and Williams* (Princeton: Princeton University Press, 1984), 118.

14. Williams, *Imaginations,* 88.

15. William Carlos Williams, *In the American Grain* (New York: New Directions, 1956), 1 (hereafter cited in text as *IAG*).

16. William Carlos Williams, *The Collected Poems of William Carlos Williams: Vol. 2, 1939-1962,* ed. Christopher MacGowan (New York: New Directions, 1998), 55.

17. William Carlos Williams, *Selected Essays* (New York: New Directions, 1969), 134 (hereafter cited in text as *SE*).

18. William Carlos Williams, *The Selected Letters,* ed. John C. Thirlwall (New York: New Directions, 1957), 286.

19. William Carlos Williams, *Paterson,* rev. ed. (New York: New Directions, 1992), 3 (hereafter cited in text as *P*).

20. Gary Snyder, *No Nature: New and Selected Poems* (New York: Pantheon, 1992), v.

21. Heather McHugh, *Broken English: Poetry and Partiality* (Hanover: Wesleyan University Press, 1993), 1.

22. Charles Bernstein, *A Poetics* (Cambridge: Harvard University Press, 1992), 8.

23. Scigaj, 17.

24. Ibid. At its strongest the field of literature and environment provides formidable theoretical insight into the relation between language and the world. At its weakest the field risks limiting its inquiry by pursuing the desire to imagine a more primary mode of conscious experience. The "loss

of the world"—its immediacy, its presence—leads to the desire to lose the word; and in response to this estrangement from what we call nature, including our own naturalness, we attempt a solution by seeking primary or unmediated experience—a wholly understandable desire, it is important to add, given the overwhelming evidence that such estrangement has led to environmental ignorance and ecological irresponsibility. To expand the theoretical insights of environmental literature and the prospects for the practice of ecological literary criticism requires much more than what Dewey called "eulogistic predicates," those structures of thought that seek nostalgic and sentimental attempts to overcome anthropomorphic versions of experience. Williams provides a means of conceptualizing the problem of nostalgically or sentimentally longing for a lost sense of place in the world. (Rather than the redemptive project Northrop Frye described as the myth of the good old days, when people were closer to nature and got their milk from cows instead of bottles, the fields of environmental literature and ecological literary criticism require the distinctly human power of constructing better versions of human experience.) The critical risk for ecopoetry is isolating a canon of poets that encourages our attempt to transcend the linguistic structure of our conceptual life and thereby take us away from that world we wish to feel, understand, indeed preserve. The determinate power of predication gives language the capacity to construct sustainable relations with a world we wish to know and be responsible citizens of rather than enacting the cyclical historical ritual Milan Kundera has called "man's longing not to be man" (Milan Kundera, *The Unbearable Lightness of Being,* trans. Michael Henry Heim [New York: Harper, 1984], 296). Williams argues, to the contrary, that poetry needs to be more human, which is not to say less natural, because we need not simply to reflect on our actions but the conceptual structures that determine how it is we determine what should be done.

25. Denise Levertov, "Williams and the Duende," in *New and Selected Essays* (New York: New Directions, 1992), 37; Gary Snyder, "The New Wind," in *A Place in Space: Ethics, Aesthetics, and Watersheds: New and Selected Prose* (Washington, D.C.: Counterpoint, 1995), 15.

26. Adrienne Rich, *The Dream of a Common Language* (New York: Norton, 1978), 264. Coincidentally, Scigaj refers to sections of Rich's *Atlas of the Difficult World* as "archetypal" ecopoetry (37).

27. Adrienne Rich, *An Atlas of the Difficult World: Poems 1988-1991* (New York: Norton, 1991), 12.

28. Adrienne Rich, *Blood, Bread, and Poetry: Selected Prose, 1979-1985* (New York: Norton, 1985), 171 (hereafter cited in text as *BBP*).

29. E. E. Cummings, *Complete Poems: 1904-1962* (New York: Liveright, 1991), 159.

30. Robert Hass, *Twentieth Century Pleasures: Prose on Poetry* (New York: Eco, 1984), 290.

31. The political aesthetic is his refusal to separate a concern with poetry and place from an inquiry into the place of poetry. A stronger way of putting this equation would be to subordinate the literal discussion of poetry and place to the place of poetry. For a more detailed treatment of the problem of Williams's political aesthetics, especially in relation to the early experimental writing, see my essay "'no confusion—only difficulties': William Carlos Williams's Poetics of Apposition," *William Carlos Williams Review* 23, no. 2 (fall 1997): 1-27. In a useful overview essay Robert von Halberg discusses the strengths and limits of Rich's and Snyder's political aesthetics in "Poetry, Politics, and Intellectuals," in *The Cambridge History of American Literature,* vol. 8, *Poetry and Criticism, 1940-1995* (New York: Cambridge University Press, 1996), 9-212. See especially 33-39.

32. Halberg, 26.

Burton Hatlen (essay date spring, fall, and winter 2003)

SOURCE: Hatlen, Burton. "From the Transcendental to the Immanent Sublime: The Poetry of William Carlos Williams, 1913-1917." *Paideuma* 32, nos. 1-3 (spring, fall, and winter 2003): 123-55.

[*In the following essay, Hatlen discusses the influence of the poets H. D., Ezra Pound, and Wallace Stevens on Williams during the years 1913-1917, and Williams's ultimate liberation from that influence.*]

Until 1917, William Carlos Williams found his way forward as a poet primarily in dialogue with three other "strong" poets among his contemporaries, Ezra Pound, H. D., and Wallace Stevens. I mark 1917 as a crucial turning point, because in that year Williams moved away from traditional models in the radically experimental **"Improvisations,"** eventually collected as **Kora in Hell.**[1] I emphasize Williams's relationships to other poets in these early years because, although several important critical studies have demonstrated the influence of the visual arts on Williams's early poetry,[2] that influence becomes decisive, I believe, only with **Kora in Hell,** which attempts to adapt Cubist and/or Dadaist methods of fragmentation and collage to the literary text. And I select Pound, H. D., and Stevens as especially important to Williams's development during these years because in the crucial "Prologue" to **Kora in Hell** Williams quotes at length from and argues with letters to him by these three poets.[3] Up to and through the World War I years, I want to argue, all four of the poets I have here grouped together were engaged in working through their relationship with a poetics of the Sublime that had evolved through the nineteenth century, reaching a limit-point, or perhaps a final "decadence," in the poetry of the 1890s. In this essay, I will focus primarily on Williams, but as background I will also sketch in the Sublime engagements of Pound, H. D., and Stevens, all of whom were also during these years, in different ways and at different paces, beginning to move beyond the Romantic Sublime toward a more specifically Modernist Sublime. With respect to Williams specifically, I will here describe his early ventures, conducted primarily in the pages of *The Egoist,* into a poetry of the Archaic Sublime that shows the direct influence of H. D., and a poetry of the Erotic Sublime that looks primarily toward Pound; and I will also propose that with the founding of *Others* he enters into a dialogue with Stevens turning on the question of how the Sublime stands within the natural world. I will then look at some early poems in which Williams begins to find his own distinctive voice, as he explores the poetics of what I shall call the Immanent (or, sometimes, the Everyday) Sublime.

I

I begin by reviewing some familiar biographical information. William Carlos Williams met Ezra Pound in 1903, when both were students at the University of Pennsylvania, and shortly thereafter both aspiring poets met and fell in love with Hilda Doolittle, daughter of a professor of astronomy at the university. In 1908 Pound moved more-or-less permanently to Europe, first to Venice and then to London; and in 1911 Hilda Doolittle also moved to London, where a few years later she married the British poet Richard Aldington. Despite the geographic separation, Pound and Williams corresponded frequently over the next six years, as Pound took upon himself the nurturing of Williams's nascent career as a poet. In 1912, Pound became "Foreign Correspondent" of *Poetry* magazine out of Chicago, and in 1913 he became the literary editor of a London-based magazine, *The New Freewoman,* soon renamed *The Egoist.* Pound invited Williams to send him work for both magazines, which became the first important outlets for Williams's poetry. In 1914 Pound announced the birth of a new poetic movement, *Imagisme,* and assembled a selection of work by members of this movement in *Des Imagistes,* published both as a special issue of Alfred Kreymborg's magazine *The Glebe* and as a book by Boni and Liveright in New York. In later years

Pound said that he founded *Imagisme* primarily to create an audience for the work of Hilda Doolittle, now metamorphosed into H. D., and her husband Aldington (*Letters* 213). But he also found a place in *Des Imagistes* for a poem by Williams, "Postlude," which had been published in 1913 both in *The New Freewoman* and in *Poetry.* In 1914 Aldington and then, after he went off to the war, H. D. succeeded Pound as literary editors of *The Egoist,* and they continued to be hospitable to Williams's work, publishing more than a dozen of his early poems, including **"The Wanderer,"** a poem that is widely regarded as his first major achievement.

Beginning in 1915, however, Williams also began to establish links with a quite different group of writers and artists, grouped loosely around the magazine *Others;* the salon of Walter Arensberg, sometime poet and patron of the visual arts; the New York Dada group, which included Marcel Duchamp, Man Ray, and Francis Picabia; and the art gallery of Alfred Stieglitz, which exhibited the new European artists along with innovative American painters, sculptors, and photographers.[4] In comparison to Pound and H. D., Alfred Kreymborg and Maxwell Bodenheim, both central figures in the *Others* group, have come to seem as, at best, marginal figures. But in this New York milieux Williams did come into contact with two major poets who could serve, in some measure, as a counterweight to the pull of London: Wallace Stevens, also a visitor to Arensberg's salon and a contributor to *Others,* and Marianne Moore, who had known H. D. when they were students at Bryn Mawr, and whose early poems had been appearing alongside Williams's in *The Egoist.* In 1918, Williams tried to sort out his relationships to the London and New York groups in an essay that eventually became the "Prologue to **Kora in Hell.**"[5] In this essay Williams symbolically situates himself in a space somewhere between his old Philadelphia friends, to whom he remains deeply loyal, and a new group of associates who had explicitly rejected the alternative of expatriation, and who thus supported his impulse to affirm an explicitly American identity, over against what he saw as a rejection of America in the work of Pound, H. D., and—this last poet was distinctly NOT an old friend—T. S. Eliot.[6] Pound, H. D. and Stevens all offered Williams models of how poetry might engage the conditions of life in the new century. Williams listened carefully to what all three poets were saying to him, and in his early poetry, up to the **"Improvisations"** of **Kora in Hell,** we can, I believe, observe him seeking a poetic voice of his own, both in dialogue with and in opposition to the voices of these other rising poets. It is this process that I want to trace in this essay.

In their early work, all of the poets that I have here brought together were, I am proposing, working through their relationship to a poetics of the Sublime that had evolved through the nineteenth century, passed through a fundamental transformation in the work of the Pre-Raphaelites (including Swinburne) and their apologists, especially Ruskin and Pater, and then sunk into deliquescence in the poetry of Dowson *et al.* For Pound and his poetic allies, including Williams, the key issue in their efforts to move beyond the poetic idiom of the nineteenth century was never simply stylistic, a purging from poetry of all those "thees," "thous," and "e'res," etc. Rather, Pound, H. D., Stevens, and Williams were all in various ways engaged with fundamental questions about human consciousness and the world it apprehends, and about the role of language in this process; and fore-grounding their relation to the Romantic Sublime offers a convenient way to bring into focus their approach to these questions. In the nineteenth century, the arts had offered themselves as, in effect, an alternative to religion: a way of engaging a transcendent spiritual dimension within human experience, without recourse to the sectarian dogmatism characteristic of all forms of religious orthodoxy. I use the term "Sublime" as a shorthand term to denote the search for a specifically artistic revelation (religion and philosophy had other ways of trying to engage the numinous) of an ineffable dimension of existence beyond the power of the human mind to grasp and control or even to name, so that even the word "God" comes to seem reductive. We might think here of the ways in which the music of Beethoven or Wagner or Mahler reaches toward something that seems to lie beyond sound itself, or the attempts of Turner or Monet to record a light that appears to emerge from somewhere beyond this world. So too, in English and American poetry, Blake, Wordsworth, Shelley, Keats, Byron, and a little later Whitman and Dickinson all established models of a poetics of the Sublime that haunted their successors.

For the artists of the nineteenth century, the experience of the Sublime is an encounter between—as Harold Bloom proposes, quoting Emerson—"I and the Abyss" (255). In his classic 1976 analysis, *The Romantic Sublime,* Thomas Weiskel breaks down this experience into three temporal phases or—the word I will here generally prefer—"moments." "In the first phase," says Weiskel, "the mind is in a determinate relation to the object, and this relation is habitual, more or less unconscious . . . , and harmonious. This is the state of normal perception and comprehension, the syntagmatic linearity of reading or talking a walk or remembering or whatnot" (23). But then, abruptly, "the habitual relation of mind and object breaks down. Surprise or astonishment is the affective correlative, and there is an immediate intuition of a disconcerting disproportion between inner and outer. Either mind or object is suddenly in excess—and then both are, since their relation has become radically indeterminate" (23). But after this moment of radical indeterminacy, "in the third, or reactive, phase of the sublime moment, the mind recovers

the balance of inner and outer by constituting a fresh relation between itself and the object such that the very indeterminacy which erupted in phase two is taken as symbolizing the mind's relation to a transcendent order" (24). Or as Bloom suggests, pointing to Whitman as his example, the "I" recuperates itself through a metaphoric identification with/incorporation of the very Otherness that had threatened to overwhelm it. The end result is an at least quasi-religious experience: in Weiskel's words, "The essential claim of the sublime is that we can make contact with something beyond the human" (3). But for the nineteenth century, what went by the name of "religion" betrayed that transcendental experience by reducing it to a dogmatic formula. The work of art, on the other hand, can honor the experience itself, open us toward the ineffable, without, in Keats's words, "any irritable straining after fact or reason."

But an art that seeks to evoke the experience of the ineffable inevitably has recourse to certain characteristic gestures, which end by becoming one more period style. Painters may seek out settings conducive to the Sublime: ocean vistas, mountain landscapes, etc. Artists in any medium will, as I have already suggested, strain to transcend the formal limits of art, reaching toward silence, emptiness, absence. Or the painter or poet might follow the movements of the eye as it moves up from the mundane details of everyday life immediately before us, toward an abyss opening up beyond the horizon. By the beginning of the twentieth century, the struggle of the nineteenth century arts to break through the limits of artistic form had reached a crisis point, as the various languages that the arts had invented to invoke an ineffable "beyond" (and that *was* the function of those Swinburnian poeticisms, those gorgeous harmonies of Mahler) seemed to become habitual gestures, clichés. The poets of the 1890s cultivated a self-conscious "decadence" in many different ways, but their work is *truly* decadent in its tendency to echo stylistically the great nineteenth-century poets and painters, without the sense of urgency that we see in Blake and Wordsworth, Whitman and Dickinson, and without the faith shared by all these poets that we can, by a supreme act of the imagination, make ourselves spiritually at home on this earth. As the artistic idioms of the nineteenth century became increasingly empty, the poets of the Modernist generation sensed themselves to be living in a moment of spiritual and artistic crisis. It seems increasingly clear that Modernism both breaks with and attempts to recuperate Romanticism,[7] and I believe that we can best understand both what is old and what is new in Modernism by reading the work of poets like Pound and Williams and Stevens and H. D. as attempts to adapt the poetics of the Sublime to a new century, one marked by even more technological acceleration and cultural fragmentation than the nineteenth century had seen, and thus by a steadily deepening spiritual hunger.

In the rest of this paper I will attempt to trace the process by which Williams, in the years from 1913 to 1917, moved from an essentially nineteenth-century Poetics of the Transcendent Sublime to a distinctively twentieth-century Poetics of the Immanent Sublime, within and in part through a dialogue with Pound, H. D. and Stevens.[8] It seems to me important to emphasize that neither during this period nor later did Williams repudiate the Sublime as such.[9] All of his poetry is marked by a sense that the things of this world are numinous, infused with a radiance that he hesitates to call "divine" simply because he is deeply resistant to all forms of religious dogma. In thus giving precedence to the quality of Williams's poetic vision rather than to his technical inventions, I am, in effect, reaffirming J. Hillis Miller's vision of Williams as a "poet of reality" who, after the "disappearance of God" (I am here alluding to the title of Miller's first book) in the late nineteenth century, offered us a new way of standing "barefoot in reality." For I believe that the key issue, for poets and for everyone else, is whether or not we perceive the world given to us by the senses as empty of meaning, so much dead matter evoking only nausea, or as infused with *gloire*, what Hopkins called "inscape"; and I count Williams in this latter company. Furthermore, in this essay I hope to show that the "what" of Williams's poetry is bound up at every moment with the "how": that in rethinking the language of poetry, he was also working his way toward a new vision of the world, one which discovers a sense of the sublime, not in the putatively archaic world of myth, symbol, and natural processes envisioned by H. D., nor in (or at least not solely in) the powerful Beatrice/Vampire figures invoked by Pound, nor in the essentially Wordsworthian natural sublime of Stevens, but in the streets of the city that he walked or drove through on his medical rounds, and in the faces of the patients to whom he ministered.

II

To establish a benchmark for Williams's engagement with and increasing divergence from the models represented by H. D. and Pound, I begin with **"Postlude,"** a poem that H. D. praises extravagantly in the letter quoted by Williams in **Kora in Hell** ("your **Postlude,**" she says, "stands, a Nike, supreme among your poems," an example of "*real* beauty—and real beauty is a rare and sacred thing in this generation" [*SE* [*Selected Essays*] 10][10]) and that Pound too seemed to favor over all of Williams's other poems, including it not only in *Des Imagistes* but in his *Profile* anthology of 1932:

> Now that I have cooled to you
> Let there be gold of tarnished masonry,
> Temples soothed by the sun to ruin
> That sleep utterly.

> Give me hand for the dances,
> Ripples at Philae, in and out,
> And lips, my Lesbian,
> Wall flowers that once were flame.

> Your hair is my Carthage
> And my arms the bow,
> And our words arrows
> To shoot the stars
> Who from that misty sea
> Swarm to destroy us.

> But you there beside me—
> Oh how shall I defy you,
> Who wound me in the night
> With breasts shining
> Like Venus and like Mars?
> The night that is shouting Jason
> When the loud eaves rattle
> As with waves above me
> Blue at the prow of my desire.

> O, prayers in the dark!
> O, incense to Poseidon!
> Calm in Atlantis.

(*CP* [*Collected Poems*] I, 3-4)

It is easy to see why H. D. liked **"Postlude,"** which is so reminiscent of her early poems that we might almost call the poem an exercise in imitation. H. D.'s first published poems, including "Hermes of the Ways" and "Priapus, Keeper of Orchards," had appeared in the January 1913 issue of *Poetry,* inviting us into a quasi-Greek world of temples and seaside gardens, all vibrant with erotic energy. In "Priapus" (28-29), for example, the speaker, overwhelmed with the unbearable "loveliness" of the orchard, falls "prostrate / crying, / you have flayed us / with your blossoms, / spare us the beauty / of fruit-trees." The presiding deity is Priapus, the "rough-hewn / god of the orchard," whom the speaker attempts to appease with gifts of "fallen hazelnuts, / stripped late of their green sheaths, / grapes, red-purple, / their berries / dripping with wine, / pomegranates already broken."[11] "Priapus" carries us from the second moment of the Romantic Sublime, with the speaker overwhelmed, laid "prostrate" by the sheer fecundity of the natural world as personified in Priapus, and into the third moment, in which the speaker recovers her selfhood by offering the presiding deity of the orchard an "offering" of fruits of the earth. For the young H. D., access to such Sublime moments demands a flight from the mundane world of 20th Century Philadelphia or London, into a timeless world of myth and symbol represented for her primarily by ancient Greece—or, later in her life, Egypt; and for this reason I call H. D.'s an "Archaic Sublime." Williams certainly read H. D.'s first poems upon their publication in the January 1913 issue of *Poetry,* and **"Postlude"** followed them hot apace, in the June 1913 issue. Williams's poem echoes H. D.'s first poems in many ways: the vaguely classical ambience, the sense of breathless urgency, the incantatory edge to the rhetoric ("Give me hand for the dances, / Ripples at Philae, in and out"), the syntax that pulls back from common speech to evoke a sense of unworldliness ("Temples soothed by the sun to ruin / That sleep utterly"). More fundamentally, Williams shares with H. D. a sense of the world as pulsing with a barely-controlled sexuality, and both poets seem to experience sexuality as painful, in the "wound" suffered by Williams's speaker, and in the "breaking" of the pomegranates and the oozing forth of all those juices in H. D.'s poems. But there is, of course, an important difference too. Williams's speaker is clearly male, in a state of post-coital calm, all passion spent, while a sense of stifled desire is more characteristic of H. D.'s voice.

There are in **"Postlude"** also strong echoes of Pound's early poems. In the years up to 1913, the Poundian Sublime is also in its way "Archaic," insofar as it is always mediated through history: sometimes of ancient Greece or Rome, but more often, in the early poetry, of Medieval Provence or Renaissance Italy. But I label Pound's an "Erotic Sublime," insofar as it revolves around a cult of the Lady that derives from his Medieval and Renaissance models, and more immediately from Rossetti and other Pre-Raphaelites. In Rossetti's world the Lady plays two roles: the "Blessed Damozel," drawing her lover toward heaven, or the vampire (Sister Helen, Lilith) who seeks to lure men's souls to destruction. In both of her incarnations, the Pre-Raphaelite Lady is a figure of immense power, and the same is true of the ubiquitous Ladies of Pound's early poetry. Many, perhaps most of Pound's pre-Imagist poems purport to be sung in celebration of a Lady, and one collection, *Canzoni,* consists almost entirely of such poems. In Pound the Lady often suffuses the entire environs through which the poet passes. In "Praise of Ysolt," for example, his Lady comes to the poet "As the moon calleth the tides," "as fire upon pinewoods," and finally "as the sun calleth to the seed, / As the spring upon the bough" (*Collected Early Poems* 79-80). As she becomes co-extensive with the cosmos, the Lady becomes for Pound the Other toward whom all his hopes and fear are directed. He claims to desire only to honor and serve her: "And all who read these lines will love her then / Whose laud is all their burthen, and whose praise / Is in my heart forever" (*Collected Early Poems* 63). Yet the same poet who wrote these lines was also capable of declaring, in a notorious passage from canto 29, "the female / Is an element, the female / Is a chaos / An octopus / A biological process" (144). Insofar as the Lady becomes an all-encompassing presence, she is inevitably the object both of desire and fear on the part of the male consciousness. On the one hand, she seems to offer all that the human heart longs for, an ultimate bliss; but at the same time she (or She) threatens to swallow up and annihilate the puny male ego. Thus in the writings of Rossetti and Pound the

second of the three characteristic moments of the Sublime, the sense of a radical disproportion between consciousness and its object, occurs usually in the relationship of a man to a woman, or the poet to his muse; while the third moment may take the form of a direct assertion of phallic sexuality that attempts to impose the male will upon the "chaos" of the woman—or perhaps the writing of a poem that will pursue, symbolically, the same goal.

Commenting on **"Postlude"** in his 1950s conversations with John C. Thirwall, Williams identified the poem as evocative of the "[r]arified atmosphere of the Pre-Raphaelite Brotherhood" (*CP* I, 473), an atmosphere embodied for Williams in the person of his friend Pound. In **"Postlude,"** the woman to whom the poem is addressed is an object of both desire (or at least the memory of desire—"Wall flowers that once were flame") and fear on the part of the speaker: he wants to "defy" her but cannot, and her breasts (truly Other, for they shine "Like Venus and like Mars") "wound" him "in the night." The woman to whom the poem is addressed stands over against the speaker as radically Other, an Abyss that threatens to swallow him up, and thus he seeks to retreat into "Temples soothed by the sun." But instead he finds himself in Philae, the center of Isis-worship in Egypt; and the Great Mother, at once seductively female ("like Venus") and threateningly male ("like Mars"), seems to rule over this poem. However, the fundamental Otherness of Woman is reinforced within the poem by other kinds of Otherness as well. I would point in particular to the image of "the stars / Who from that misty sea / Swarm to destroy us," to the "night that is shouting Jason" (presumable a summons to depart, in quest of the Golden Fleece—or are we hearing the voice of a Medea, summoning her treacherous lover to learn his fate?—in either case the shout seems threatening), and to the "waves" that rise "above me / Blue at the prow of my desire." Woman, the Night, and the Sea—as repeatedly in the history of the poetic Sublime (think, for example, of Whitman's "Out of the Cradle"), all three suggest an inchoate void that threatens to engulf the spark of human consciousness. As in many other poems of the Sublime, however, the ego here also "tropically" regrounds itself upon the abyss, or perhaps incorporates the abyss into itself. Facing the stars that "swarm to destroy us" out of "that misty sea," the poet fends off this threat with the words—presumably—of this poem itself. So too, while the waves rise above his fragile boat, his desire cuts through the waves, carrying him forward. And the androgynous qualities of the Lady also prove useful. The addressee is, indeed, "my Lesbian" (Sappho perhaps, or perhaps H. D. herself—did Williams already know of her bisexuality?), no longer an object of male sexual desire, but by virtue of that fact itself a potential object of identification for the speaker. The poem thus becomes a prayer not only in but also to the dark, incense offered to the god of the sea, and the reward is "calm in Atlantis"—even as we are being swallowed up by the whelming sea, it would appear, we can create within the imagination a place of serenity.

In the years between 1914 and 1917, Williams published in magazines such as *The Egoist* and *Others* and/or in *Al Que Quiere!* several other poems that turn on the image of the Lady as at once infinitely desirable and profoundly threatening.[12] At times the Lady seems to encompass the entire world: in **"At Dawn"** the "war of your great beauty is in all the skies" (*CP* I, 36), and in **"To the Outer World,"** "she" becomes the air itself. In **"A La Lune,"** the Lady shows herself, in time-honored fashion, as the moon, serenely indifferent to "our little journeys endlessly repeated" (*CP* I, 39). More disturbing are the recurrent images of Woman as, in Pound's term, "octopus," an engulfing vortex that threatens to suck in the man and annihilate him. **"Virtue"** (*CP* I, 89), for example, opens with an image of "whirlpools of / orange and purple flame" that threaten to suck the unwary into "the steaming phallus-head / of the mad sun himself." This whirlpool, we then learn, is "the smile of her / the smell of her / the vulgar inviting mouth of her!" But "she" is, it seems, a vacuum, for when we try to see "her," all that happens is "the fixing of an eye / concretely upon emptiness!" And as the poem ends, we discover that we are perhaps in a burlesque house, amid a crowd of men—"cross-eyed men, a boy / with a patch," etc.—watching in awe and horror as the stripper reveals her genitals for their contemplation. Similarly, **"Keller Gegen Dom"** (*CP* I, 91-92) offers an image of a young man hurrying toward a sexual encounter, through a doorway that opens "like some great flower." Within, he finds "a dark vinegar-smelling place / from which trickles / the chuckle of / beginning laughter": we have here, as I read these lines, a nightmare image of the female genitals, as an Abyss that lures in the unwary, and repays the man's devotion only with mocking laughter. *Al Que Quiere!* also includes a group of what can only be called pedophilic poems. In **"The Ogre"** the poet speaks—only in his mind, to be sure—to a "sweet child," telling her, "little girl with well-shaped legs / you cannot touch the thoughts / I put over and under and around you. / This is fortunate for they would / burn you to an ash otherwise" (*CP* I, 95). And in **"Sympathetic Portrait of a Child,"** the poet projects his sexual fantasies onto another little girl, the daughter of a murderer, as he persuades himself that she is flirting with him. Such eroticization of the child suggests a man who is deeply frightened of female sexuality and who sees in the pre-pubescent girl-child a possibility of momentary mastery over one of these dangerous creatures.[13]

III

More interesting than any of these poems, however, is **"March,"** a poem in which Williams engages both the Archaic and the Erotic Sublime, but in ways that suggest a real growth beyond the models provided him by H. D. and Pound. **"March"** was first published in *The Egoist* in 1916, heavily edited by H. D.—it was this poem that elicited the letter from her quoted by Williams in the "Prologue" to *Kora in Hell*.[14] In time-honored Sublime fashion, Williams here confronts an Otherness that threatens to engulf him, but that he also longs to incorporate into himself.[15] The first section of **"March"** offers a striking image of the March wind and sky as a revelation of the Abyss, a vast and inhuman power:

> Winter is long in this climate
> and spring—a matter of a few days
> only,—a flower or two picked
> from mud or from among wet leaves
> or at best against treacherous
> bitterness of wind, and sky shining
> teasingly, then closing in black
> and sudden, with fierce jaws.

(*CP* I, 137)

Only three years after **"Postlude,"** Williams is here in full command of the enjambed line that will become his poetic signature, as we move from the casual, almost conversational opening, through the search for a flower or two amid the mud and wet leaves. Then the eye moves, as so often in the poetry of the Sublime, toward the sky, which first winks "teasingly," and then opens its terrible jaws. Many of the images introduced here will recur throughout the poem. The storm-battered flowers, as often in Williams's poetry, suggest the sexuality of women, while the fierce jaws, which may suggest a great cat, may also be the jaws of a venomous snake as it strikes, and images of snakes will also recur later.

"March," the poet declares at the opening of section two (*CP* I, 137-38), "you remind me of / the pyramids, our pyramids—/ stript of the polished stone / that used to guard them!" The pyramids may seem almost as ancient as Nature itself, and as a human creation they suggest the possibility that the artifacts we create might protect us from the "fierce jaws" of an unmediated Nature. But note that the pyramids become March-like only when stripped of human attempts to beautify them—i.e., the "polished stone / that used to guard them"—and are thereby exposed directly to the weather. A pattern emerges here that will continue throughout the poem: we erect pyramids to ward off the destructive ravages of time and thus hold the abyss at bay, but at the same time we—or at least our poet—want these artifacts to embody within themselves, in a humanized and therefore relatively safe form, the very power that threatens to overwhelm us. An identification with a potentially overwhelming Otherness, a regrounding of the imperiled self upon this very Otherness—these maneuvers are, I have suggested, fundamental to a poetics of the Sublime, and thus I claim **"March"** as a classic instance of such a poetics. In the poem, the pyramids (shortly to be supplanted by monumental Babylonian friezes) represent one type of artifact that both resists and embodies the Abyss. Vast age itself, as Kant notes, may seem to overwhelm us: indeed, Kant himself adduces the pyramids as a principal instance of the Sublime—specifically, what I have here called the Archaic Sublime. But to Williams, they become "our" pyramids in their capacity to endure eons of battering by the weather, and to survive by adapting to the weather. And the second section of **"March"** also introduces us to a second possible way of engaging the Abyss, for March is also, the poet declares, "like Fra Angelico / at Fiesole, painting on plaster!" (How, exactly, Fra Angelico's painting is like March will be revealed to us more fully in section four of the poem, as discussed below.) And Williams then rounds out section two of **"March"** by introducing us to a third instance of a human artifact that will survive the destructive force of those March winds by absorbing their power into itself: namely, Williams's poem, which he hopes will create "the blessedness of warmth" that will enable him to survive the ravages of the March wind, but which will also "have you / in it March."

The third section of **"March"** (*CP* I, 138-39) returns to the Archaic, this time in the form of the friezes that once lined the "sacred way to / Nebuchadnezzar's throne hall," now excavated after "ten thousand dirt years." In the friezes, man confronts Nature, in the form of "lions / standing on their hind legs, / fangs bared"—the image echoes the "fierce jaws" of the March wind and sky, as described in the first section. But the king triumphs over the lions, "his shafts / bristling in their necks!" The fierce energies of the archaic have been, it seems, buried under the tides of history, but now the March winds ("storms from my calendar /—winds that blow back the sand!") have, by "strange craft," "whipt up a black army" of "Natives cursing and digging," who have unearthed an array of "dragons with / upright tails and sacred bulls." Williams's mode of discourse here is uncharacteristically symbolic—both in form and significance the figures of the frieze are reminiscent of Yeats's "rough beast, its hour come round at last," who shakes off the desert sands to announce its return into history. And like Yeats, Williams is both attracted to (the "Natives digging at old walls" are "digging me warmth—digging me sweet loneliness") and frightened by the resurgence of these primal forces. But then in section four (*CP* I, 139-40), Williams offers another, very different image of the Archaic, as he returns to Fra Angelico, at work on a fresco of the Annunciation to Mary, "in a monastery . . . in Fiesole."[16] The Annunciation, as artists from Cimabue to Rossetti have remembered, is both a world-transforming and an inescapably sexual moment, as the word of God, transmitted by a very physical and in

many images seductive angel, enters (usually through the ear) the Virgin, there to become flesh. Williams is impressed by the quiet thoughtfulness of the Virgin in Fra Angelico's painting—"she is intently serious," as she watches the angel, whose eyes hold "the eyes of Mary / as a snake's hold a bird's." We are here once again in the presence of energies that are both primal and sacred. As Williams the pediatrician knew full well, the creation of new life is a process both brutal and mysterious; and these are women's mysteries, which men participate in only by invitation, as onlookers. At the same time, the image of the mesmerizing angel's eyes also suggests how helpless is the Virgin, as she is caught up, willy nilly, in these sacred mysteries. However, Williams also wants us to keep at least one eye on Fra Angelico himself, for is it possible that the artist has, by making this painting, drawn these overwhelming mysteries into himself and made them his own—just as the poet wants to bring the energies of March into his poem?

In the fifth and final section of **"March"** (*CP* I, 140-41), we return to the present and the direct confrontation with the winds of March: "But! Now for the battle! / Now for murder—now for the real thing!" Yet rather than seeing the fierce, devouring jaws of the wind as his enemy, the poet now performs the imaginative leap traditional to a poetics of the Sublime, as he *identifies with* the wind. Specifically, he presents his sexual energies, released by imaginative contact with the Babylonian friezes and the Fra Angelico painting (his own sexuality is now "lean, serious as a virgin"), as roaming through the world like the winds, "snakelike," "seeking flowers—flowers," or simply "one flower / in which to warm myself!" (Dedicated readers of Williams will recognize the ways these lines anticipate the "one man—like a city" and the "Innumerable women, each like a flower" of **Paterson** [7].) The alien winds strike back: "Counter-cutting winds / strike against me / refreshing their fury!" But *all* these winds now seem to be male, and he summons them to "defy" all resistance, with "even more / desperation than ever—being / lean and frozen!" Inspired by the "blue bulls of Babylon," he and his fellow men will all become rapists: "Fling yourselves upon / their empty roses—/ cut savagely!" As the poet incorporates into himself the inhuman Otherness of the March winds, then, he himself becomes violent, inhuman: the woman/flower becomes simply an "empty" vessel, which he will brutally penetrate. And yet, in the last lines of the poem, the speaker also turns again to art as a possible alternative: "But—/ think of the painted monastery / at Fiesole." There is, I think, a recognition here of the dangers of unleashing fully the archaic, primal forces that this poem invokes. The real danger in the experience of the Sublime is that we will be left with a Self so Transcendent that it becomes inhuman, indifferent to the pleasures and pains of ordinary human existence. In very different ways, the poetics of both Pound and H. D. carried them into these dangerous waters. Williams sailed there too, but his last-minute identification with the humble painter of Fiesole/Florence, who himself identified with the humble Virgin in her blue dress, perhaps points toward the possibility that art can affirm rather than negate the human.

IV

In much of his early poetry, I have proposed, Williams was working through some possibilities of the Sublime represented for him by the poetry of Pound and H. D. A few years after he began his dialogue with Pound and H. D., Williams opened a parallel dialogue with Wallace Stevens, conducted in part through personal contact and in part through their work, especially contributions to two American poetry magazines important to both of them in these years, *Poetry* and *Others*. Harold Bloom has, of course, established Stevens as the prototype of the American Sublime, and thus we should not be surprised to discover that Williams's dialogue with Stevens also turns on what to make of the heritage of the Sublime. At issue here, however, is a quite different version of the Sublime than the one that Williams encountered in the writings of his Philadelphia friends. To Stevens the Abyss manifests itself, not primarily in the dizzying depths of the Archaic or in the figure of the enticing but potentially engulfing Lady, but in Nature. In Stevens's early poetry, "The Snow-Man" offers an example of the second "moment" of the Sublime, in which a hitherto complacent self comes face to face with the Abyss. Cultivating a "mind of winter," the poet looks at "the boughs / Of the pine-trees crusted with snow" and "The spruces rough in the distant glitter // Of the January sun," listens to the "misery in the sound of the wind," and experiences a revelation of the "Nothing that is not there and the nothing that is" (8). As an example of the second, recuperative "moment," when the Self takes possession of the Otherness that it confronts, I might adduce another standard anthology piece, "Anecdote of the Jar," in which the imagination, symbolized by a jar, "took dominion everywhere," and made itself the center of the "slovenly wilderness" (60-61). Both "The Snow-Man" and "Anecdote of the Jar" postdate the period I am here discussing and thus could not have influenced the Williams of *Al Que Quiere!*,[17] but Williams almost certainly *did* read another characteristically "Sublime" poem by Stevens, "Valley Candle," published in the December 1917 issue of *Others*, a magazine that Williams was then co-editing:

> My candle burned alone in an immense valley.
> Beams of the huge night converged on it,
> Until the wind blew.
> Then beams of the huge night

> Converged upon its image,
> Until the wind blew.

> (41)

The night is "huge," an Abyss. Consciousness is a tiny candle in the night. As the only point of light within the immense darkness, it can see itself as the "center," the point on which the night converges—until the wind blows, snuffing out the candle. We are left with the imagination, which can reconstruct that point of light, as a mental image now; but again the wind blows, and the light of the imagination too goes out, as night swallows all.

Given the modalities of the Sublime that we see in poems like "The Snow Man" and "Valley Candle," it is not surprising that Stevens was drawn to a short poem by Williams that he read in the December 1916 issue of *Others,* titled **"El Hombre"**:

> It's a strange courage
> you give me ancient star:

> Shine alone in the sunrise
> toward which you lend no part!

> (*CP* I, 76)

This poem enacts, in brief, both moments of the Sublime. First, the speaker perceives the "ancient" star as utterly alone, "Other." Yet at the same time, he identifies with it, resolves to take courage from the star—to, in effect, reground himself within the very Otherness that the star represents. In response to this poem, Stevens wrote "Nuances on a Theme by Williams," first published in the December 1918 issue of *The Little Review* (Edelstein 200). After repeating Williams's lines as quoted above, with a comma inserted after "give me," Stevens elaborates on Williams's theme as follows:

> I
> Shine alone, shine nakedly, shine like bronze
> that reflects neither my face nor any inner part
> of my being, shine like fire, that mirrors nothing.

> II
> Lend no part to any humanity that suffuses
> you in its own light.
> Be no chimera of morning,
> Half-man, half-star.
> Be not an intelligence,
> Like a widow's bird
> Or an old horse.

> (15)

In effect, Stevens takes it upon himself to underscore the Sublime implications of Williams's lines. His commentary warns us away from any impulse that we might feel to treat Williams's star as a metaphor. First, Stevens jettisons Williams's title, **"El Hombre,"** perhaps because it might invite a metaphorical reading: "Real men are self-reliant—they know how to stand alone, like that star, and like me," etc. Second, Williams starts by talking about himself, not about the star. Stevens, in effect, omits the self entirely, except insofar as it is implicitly present in the language of the poem. Instead he emphasizes the utterly alien, inhuman character of the star, which "mirrors nothing" and is indifferent to a humanity that seeks to project its own emotional associations onto it. Has Stevens misread Williams's poem, bending it to his own purposes? No, I don't think so, for the real power of Williams's poem is in the twist of that last line, "toward which you lend no part": this star is, it seems, resolutely indifferent to the small dreams of humankind.

As further evidence that Stevens did not misread **"El Hombre,"** I would point to the frequency with which the Williams of the World War I years echoes the sense of the Void that we have seen in the poetry of Stevens. In **"March,"** we have already seen an example of the ways in which, for Williams as for Stevens, the winds of winter serve as a metaphor for the implacable Otherness of the world we confront. In **"Winter Sunset,"**[18] the winds are momentarily still, but the poem offers us an image of the emptiness of the universe that rivals anything in Stevens:

> Then I raised my head
> and stared out over
> the blue February waste
> to the blue bank of hill
> with stars on it
> in strings and festoons—
> but above that:
> one opaque
> stone of a cloud
> just on the hill
> left and right
> as far as I could see;
> and above that
> a red streak, then
> icy blue sky!
>
> It was a fearful thing,
> to come into a man's heart
> at that time; that stone
> over the little blinking stars
> they'd set there.

> (*CP* I, 69)

As we see repeatedly in the tradition of the nineteenth-century Sublime, the eye here moves steadily upward, toward the sky; and when it finally arrives at the "icy blue sky," the imagination quails: there is nothing to hang onto here. We drop back to that "stone of a cloud," sitting on the horizon; but when that stone "comes into" the speaker's heart—and note that he does draw this Otherness into himself—it sits there like a dead weight, a "fearful thing," for its Presence defines the absolute Absence in that empty sky above. But Williams is not

willing to abandon the theme without a final twist: who, we might ask, is the "they" who "set" the "little blinking stars" on the skyline? The Other is momentarily anthropomorphized, but the overtones are paranoid; this "they" seems no friend to humankind.

As an example of the second moment of the Stevensian or "Natural" Sublime in Williams's poems of the mid-teens, I offer **"Conquest,"** where we see the poet engaged in a recuperation of the Self through an imaginative identification with the Other:

> Hard, chilly colors:
> straw-grey, frost-grey
> the grey of frozen ground:
> and you, O sun,
> close above the horizon!
> It is I holds you—
> half against the sky
> half against a black tree trunk
> icily resplendent!
>
> Lie there, blue city, mine at last—
> rimming the banked blue-grey
> and rise, indescribable smoky-yellow
> into the overpowering white!

> (*CP* I, 90)

Here we get another landscape that demands of us a "mind of winter," but on this occasion the imagination of the poet seizes control: the world, it seems, is a canvas and the painterly eye of the poet firmly pastes the sun against this otherwise bleak landscape. In this act of possession, the city, edging the horizon, becomes "mine at last"; but after the dash in the second stanza, both the landscape and the syntax seem to squirm out of control, for although the poet tells the city to "lie there," nevertheless it also "rises." Words fail the speaker—the color of the city is "indescribable." And as it rises, the city seems to dissolve into the "overpowering white"—of, perhaps, a snowstorm closing in. Does the poet "conquer" this scene? Or does the erasing whiteness overpower both the city and the poet? The resolution of the poem is thus ambiguous—although I think that we can decipher here a powerful struggle between a landscape that opens toward the Abyss and a poetic imagination that seeks to possess both the landscape and the Abyss itself. This struggle, I might add, once again has sexual overtones. This poem is dedicated to "F. W.," presumably Flossie Williams; and as Litz and MacGowan note, in these early poems, "'grey' seems to be associated with Florence Williams" (*CP* I, 489). Thus the struggle to master a landscape composed entirely of tones of grey may be a struggle on the part of the poet to achieve sexual mastery over his wife—a struggle in which, as Marjorie Perloff notes (192 ff), he evidently failed, turning away from Flossie into a life of masturbatory fantasy, interspersed with affairs with other women. In this respect, this landscape poem may circle back to some of the concerns of the "woman as octopus" poems discussed previously.

V

The poems by Williams that I have discussed thus far are—perhaps with the exception of **"March"**—of interest less for any intrinsic merits they may possess than for what they tell us about the poet's relationships with his contemporaries, and about his efforts to come to terms with the English and American poetic heritage. But in at least a few of his early poems, we can see Williams beginning to stake out a distinctive position of his own, clearly different from those of Pound, H. D., or Stevens, although sharing with these other poetic masters a determination to find a new voice appropriate to a new, distinctly "modern," world of experience. The first such poem is **"The Wanderer,"** first published in the March 1914 issue of *The Egoist,* and then substantially revised for publication as the concluding poem of *Al Que Quiere!*[19] The Keatsian overtones of **"The Wanderer"** (Williams told Edith Heal that the poem "is actually a reconstruction from memory of my early Keatsian *Endymion* imitation that I destroyed, burned in a furnace" [*IWWP* [*I Wanted to Write a Poem: The Autobiography of The Works of a Poet*] 25-26]) invite a reading of the poem as a conscious effort to redact the nineteenth-century poetic Sublime for twentieth-century uses.[20] Indeed Carl Rapp has proposed, in language echoing Weiskel's description of the Romantic Sublime, that in **"The Wanderer"** Williams affirms "an essentially romantic conception of his own vocation" (7) by drawing "all things into himself. As the 'all' enters his mind, it becomes his idea, while he, on the other hand, becomes the single, transcendent point of unity— the *logos,* the center, the coherence" (18). However, a second important group of critics reads **"The Wanderer"** in very different terms, seeing it as the poem in which Williams decisively casts off the last vestiges of Romantic subjectivity and gives himself over wholly to a world of "things" in their absolute immediacy. To J. Hillis Miller, for example, in this poem Williams abandon "his private consciousness, that hollow bubble in the midst of the solidity of the world," and as a consequence the poem "celebrates the homecoming which makes his poetry possible" (*Poets of Reality* 287), a homecoming to the world of immediate sensory experience. And James E. B. Breslin agrees with Miller that **"The Wanderer"** breaks with Romanticism in important ways: "if the influence of Keats is resurrected here, it is in order to be purged. . . . In Williams's mythology, we encounter our origins not by ascending a tower or mountain, but by descending to the stream of the present—not by transcendence but by immersion" (23).

I will here pause only briefly over **"The Wanderer,"** which has been the subject of several extended critical discussions.[21] I would note, however, that in centering a long poem on a female muse-figure, Williams is again following in the tradition of Pound and the Pre-Raphaelites before him. But Williams's muse is neither a Blessed Damozel looking benignly down from heaven, nor one of the Ladies, sometimes overpowering but always the radiant focus of erotic desire, that populate Pound's early poetry. Rather she is, as Williams himself said, on one level simply "my grandmother, raised to heroic proportions" (*IWWP* 26); and at various points in the poem she metamorphoses into a seagull, an aging Broadway whore ("Ominous, old, painted—/ With bright lips, and lewd Jew's eyes / Her might strapped in by a corset / To give her age youth" [*CP* I, 110]), a prophetess who can show all time to the poet, and finally a priestess who baptizes the poet in the waters of the "filthy Passaic." This baptism is the climax of the poem, and the sacramental imagery attests that Williams, like his nineteenth-century forebears, continued to see poetry in religious terms, evoking an experience of the Holy within the world. Indeed, **"The Wanderer"** carries a heavy freight of religious allusions. The poem opens with a section titled "Advent," a word that can mean (says my *American Heritage* dictionary) simply "the arrival of something momentous," but that also has strong religious associations: in Christian tradition, the Advent season includes the four Sundays before Christmas. When the Muse first reveals herself, furthermore, she does so as a "great sea-gull" in whom "all the persons of godhead" are manifest—Williams, who intermittently attended a Unitarian church, here reveals himself as a covert Trinitarian. The seagull, moreover, invites the poet to a characteristically Sublime experience in which "the beauty of all the world" is revealed to him, thus "recreating the whole world, / This is the first day of wonders!" (*CP* I, 109). And in the final lines of the poem, we find ourselves participating in a second sacrament, the Eucharist, as the muse tells the river to "Live . . . / Remembering this our son, / In remembrance of me and my sorrow" (*CP* I, 117)—echoing the words of Christ at the Last Supper, "This do in remembrance of me," with Williams himself, as the "son," becoming Christ.

But for the nineteenth-century poet, the vision of the Sublime demanded a movement UP from this world: an ascent of Mt. Snowden (Wordsworth), or a movement of the eyes up from the mundane details of what lies before us toward a light emanating from the Beyond (Turner, and all subsequent painters of the Sublime— see, for example, the American landscapes reproduced in Wilton and Barringer) or perhaps an ascent from the transitory world of the senses, toward the archaic and eternal (this is, I am suggesting, the aspiration of H. D. up to the World War II years, as also of Pound in his early work). In **"The Wanderer,"** however, Williams begins to find a direction that is distinctively his own. "How shall I be a mirror to this modernity?" (*CP* I, 108) the poet asks in the opening section—NOT "how shall I resurrect the world of the antique gods?" And throughout it is specifically a MODERN world that the poet's Muse wants him to engage, plunging him—and us—in turn into the sensual frenzy of the Broadway crowds, a scene that is antithetical both to H. D.'s Archaic Sublime and to the Natural Sublime of Stevens; then carrying us out to New Jersey, first to a visit to Paterson during the 1913 strike and then beyond to the mountains and farms outside the city; and arriving at a moment of climax and resolution in Santiago Grove, a riverside park in Rutherford, New Jersey. For Williams the characteristic pattern of movement, here as in all of his work, is not an ascent toward the Sublime but rather a DESCENT, finally into the depths of the Passaic River.[22] And the climax of the poem, contra Rapp, is not an absorption of the universe into a "single, transcendent point of unity," but rather a rupture and dispersal of the self. In the baptism scene with which the poem climaxes, the river enters the youth and the youth enters the river, and at this moment "I knew all—it became me." Here is, it seems, the climactic moment of the Sublime experience, in which the Abyss without becomes the Abyss within. But at this moment, Williams's Wanderer splits in two: as he stands on the shore, "I saw myself / Being borne off under the water! / I could have shouted out in my agony / At the sight of myself departing / Forever. . . ." (*CP* I, 116). For Williams, then, the moment of Unity remains deeply ambiguous, at best an ideal against which we can test our experiences of this broken world, rather than a condition that we can actually inhabit; and in this respect **"The Wanderer"** opens up some radical new possibilities within the poetics of the Sublime.

While in its theme and stance **"The Wanderer"** may set the direction for Williams's life-work as a writer, the symbolic, even allegorical poetic mode of the poem is not characteristic of his later work. In at least a few of the poems that he wrote before 1917, however, we can see Williams finding, if only intermittently, not only a point of view but also a poetic method that anticipates his mature work. As a fully developed instance of what I call the Immanent or Everyday Sublime, I would point to the second of the three poems in *Al Que Quiere!* titled **"Pastoral,"** which I quote in full:

> When I was younger
> it was plain to me
> I must make something of myself.
> Older now
> I walk back streets
> admiring the houses
> of the very poor:
> roof out of line with sides
> the yards cluttered
> with old chicken wire, ashes,
> furniture gone wrong;
> the fences and outhouses
> built of barrel-staves
> and parts of boxes, all,

> if I am fortunate,
> smeared a bluish green
> that properly weathered
> pleases me best
> of all colors.

>   No one
> will believe this
> of vast import to the nation.

                                                  (*CP* I, 64-65)

Here we remain resolutely on the earth, rather than rising toward a "beyond." Yet in its quiet way, the poet also invites us to see the everyday objects he looks at on his walk as numinous, radiant with a light that glows from within. To achieve this moment of vision, the poem invites us to leave the poet's (and, by implication, our) middle class neighborhood, where our perceptions are numbed by habit, and to go walking with him into the poorer regions of the city; thus the poem begins with a deliberate disruption of habitual perception. In labeling the poem a **"Pastoral,"** Williams invites us to enter a state of *otium*, ease, the traditional posture of the pastoralist. Thus the title not only makes the claim that "this is a poem" and thus about something important; it also claims that this is a certain kind of poem, in which experience is savored for its own sake. We have come here simply to *look* at old chicken wire and barrel-staves, and to see them as worth looking at for their own sakes. For me, the key line is "if I am fortunate": the moment of vision comes to us, not by willfully seeking it out, but by accident—or by divine grace. Both Townley (80) and Breslin complain that there is too much commentary in these early poems; and of **"Pastoral"** specifically, Breslin says that here Williams has sought to "heighten his material" by "closing . . . with an enigmatic, oracular utterance" (52)— with the implication that in due course he would learn to let the things of the world speak for themselves, without any rhetorical overlay. But I would argue not only that Williams had to work his way toward the minimalist poetics of **"Between Walls,"** but that the mild tension between the mundane things here named and the meta-poetic framing is essential to the distinctive effect of **"Pastoral."** By challenging our habitual assumptions both about poems and about slum neighborhoods, Williams demands that we see the everyday *as poetic*—and in the context of a post-Romantic poetics, he is thereby demanding that we see everyday experience as Sublime.

I conclude with a brief discussion of **"January Morning"** (*CP* I, 100-104), another poem published for the first time in *Al Que Quiere!* Roger Gilbert has described **"January Morning"** as "Williams' first fully realized masterpiece in his mature idiom" (3), and I would agree with this judgment. The suite begins with a playing off of America against Europe:

I have discovered that most of
the beauties of travel are due to
the strange hours we keep to see them:

the domes of the Church of
the Paulist Fathers in Weehawken
against a smoky dawn—the heart stirred—
are beautiful as Saint Peters
approached after years of anticipation.

St Peter's here also means the "Sublime in the old sense"—the cathedral was, after all, designed by Michelangelo, whose name is virtually synonymous with the Sublime. But seen at the right moment, against a smoky dawn, Weehawken offers equal sublimities. Liberated to discover the Sublime in the everyday, Williams juxtaposes a series of snapshots of specific urban/ suburban scenes, of people ("—and a semicircle of dirt-colored men / about a fire bursting from an old / ash can"), animals ("—and a young horse with a green bed-quilt / on his withers shaking his head: / bared teeth and nozzle high in the air!"), or inanimate objects ("—and the worn, blue car rails (like the sky!) / gleaming among the cobbles!").

"January Morning" is a breakthrough text for Williams because he here, for the first time, gives himself the freedom to bring together such moments of perception, with no pretense of any logical or thematic connection among them. Each moment is luminous, with a light that issues from the things seen, rather than being projected by the viewer: "—and the sun, dipping into the avenues / streaking the tops of / the irregular red houselets, // and / the gay shadows dropping and dropping." Williams himself becomes an object among other objects: "The young doctor is dancing with happiness / in the sparkling wind, alone / at the prow of the ferry!" And his happiness comes from a sense simply that he is here, inhabiting a purely phenomenal world: "He notices / the curdy barnacles and broken ice crusts / left at the slip's base by the low tide / and thinks of summer and green / shell-crusted ledges among / the emerald eel-grass!" Within this phenomenal world, there is no longer a "high" or a "low," a "here" or a "beyond": "Exquisite brown waves—long / circlets of silver moving over you! / enough with crumbling ice crusts among you! / The sky has come down to you, / lighter than tiny bubbles, face to / face with you!" The images of the world as seen from the prow of the ferry obviously echo Whitman's "Crossing Brooklyn Ferry." But as Gilbert notes, in passages such as the one just quoted, the "self-aggrandizing Whitmanian 'I' has dropped out completely; now sky and water commune directly, 'face to face,' without the poet's active mediation" (9). The end result is "Sublime," if at all, only in one sense: Williams is offering us a radiant world, pulsing with *gloire*. But this Immanent Sublime is also clearly a long step away from the Transcendental Sublime of the Romantics. With Williams, rather, we enter the world of

the Everyday Sublime, where even the souls of the dead stay close to the earth, "—among the little sparrows / behind the shutter."

Notes

1. For the precise dates and for the significance of this shift, see Holsapple.

2. See especially Dijkstra, Tashjian, MacGowan, Schmidt, Diggory, and Halter.

3. But I would acknowledge that distinctly lesser poets such as Kreymborg and Bodenheim were also important to Williams during these years. Furthermore, in the teens and on into the 1920s, Williams also kept one eye on the Chicago school of Sandburg, Lindsay, and Masters, who claimed to represent a forcefully "American" poetics.

4. Dijkstra's chapter on "The New York Avant-Garde" (3-46) offers a richly detailed account of this artistic milieu. See also Tashjian 56-63 and Naumann *passim*. The ways in which various groups of poets and visual artists overlapped during these years is suggested by a well-known 1916 photograph taken in Williams's yard at 9 Ridge Road, showing Williams with, *inter alia*, Alfred Kreymborg and Maxwell Bodenheim, both members of the *Others* group, along with Man Ray, Marcel Duchamp, and Walter Arensberg, a key link between the poets and the painters. The photograph is reproduced in Weaver following 84, in Mariani following 460, and in Naumann 30.

5. Although *Kora* was not published until 1920, in *Selected Essays* Williams prefaces the "Prologue" with the date September 1, 1918, and the essay was published in part under the title "Prologue: The Return of the Sun," in the April 1919 issue of *The Little Review*.

6. Eliot eventually succeeded H. D. as literary editor of *The Egoist*, and neither in that capacity nor later did he show any interest in Williams's work. Williams's animosity toward Eliot certainly stemmed in part from a sense that Pound, and perhaps H. D. as well, had abandoned him to adopt this new favorite.

7. For example, while T. E. Hulme purported to reject Romanticism in favor of a new Classicism, the French sources on which he drew, especially Bergson and Sorel, remain distinctly Romantic.

8. I have or will pursue elsewhere the ways in which Pound, H. D., and Stevens responded to the sense that, by the end of the 19th Century, the traditional vocabulary of the Sublime had become a set of empty habitual gestures, but I have introduced these other poets here because I think that we can understand the way Williams moved beyond the

crisis in nineteenth-century poetic rhetoric only by reading his early poetry as in dialogue with theirs. The lifelong friendship of Pound and Williams, the obvious parallels between their poetic careers, and the emergence of what many observers see as a "Pound/Williams tradition" in the poetry of, for example, Charles Olson and Robert Creeley have prompted a voluminous body of biographical and critical commentary on the relationship of these two poets: see, for example, Riddel's "Decentering the Image" and the essays by Parkinson and Cook cited in my bibliography. With respect to the specific concerns of this essay, the influence of Pound on Williams's early poetry has been fully recognized by Breslin (13-20), although the contrast that he develops between Pound the "esthete" and Williams the "democratic poet" seems to me simplistic. *The William Carlos Williams Review* has devoted a special issue to the relationship of Williams and Stevens (18.2, Fall 1992). J. Hillis Miller has brought together Williams and Stevens on several occasions, writing parallel chapters on the two poets in both *Poets of Reality* and *The Linguistic Moment,* and discussing their similarities and differences in an essay in the *Columbia Literary History of the United States.* In this latter essay, Miller emphasizes how the works of both poets evoke an evanescent, unsayable "it," an absence that is at once a presence. This "it" seems very similar to what I mean by the Sublime. See also the chapter on the relationship of the two poets in Hugh Kenner's *A Homemade World* (50-80), David Walker's *The Transparent Lyric,* and the chapter on Williams (77-91) in Glen MacLeod's *Wallace Stevens and Company.* Williams's relationship with H. D. has received relatively little discussion to date. Barry Ahearn's "Williams and H. D., or Sour Grapes" emphasizes Williams's ambivalent behavior toward H. D., rather than the poetic affinities between the two.

9. I must acknowledge that Williams rarely if ever employs the terminology of the Sublime in speaking of his own work. It seems worth noting, however, that in a letter of May 21, 1909, Pound urged his friend to "read . . . Longinus 'on the Sublime'" (*Pound/Williams Letters* 15). That Williams probably took Pound's advice is suggested by the opening sentence of the "Prologue" to *Kora in Hell*: "The sole precedent I can find for the broken style of my prologue is *Longinus on the Sublime* and that far-fetched" (*SE* 3).

10. Both Burke and Kant, the founding theorists of the modern sublime, make a sharp distinction between the Beautiful and the Sublime, but Pound, H. D., and Williams do not. Generally, as in this quotation from H. D., they use the word "beauty"—and they use it often in their early writ-

ings—to encompass not only the Beautiful in the Burke/Kant sense but also the Sublime.

11. I quote from H. D.'s *Collected Poems.* On its original publication in *Poetry* and then in *Des Imagistes,* each line of the poem begins with a capital letter, and the "you"s and "your"s are "thee"s and "thy"s.

12. Along with publishing poems in *The Egoist,* Williams contributed a two-part response to a serialized book, *Lingual Psychology,* by the editor of the magazine, Dora Marsden. Williams's response draws upon the theories of Otto Weininger, author of *Sex and Character,* to argue for a sharp distinction between male and female mentality: men, Williams suggest, are driven by their nature to pursue abstractions, while women are inescapably rooted in biological processes. Mariani argues that this mode of thinking led Williams, as he increasingly sought to root himself in the concrete physicality of existence, to see woman as "superior" to men (142), but such essentialist thinking can obviously move instead in a very different direction, toward a sense that women seek to pull men down to a purely physical level of existence by enslaving them in what Weininger called a "coitus-cult." See Weaver 17-29 for a full discussion of Weininger's influence on Williams.

13. In "The Fallen Leaf and the Stain of Love: The Displacement of Desire in Williams' Early Love Poetry," Marjorie Perloff has argued at some length that the sexual attitudes expressed in Williams's early poems are deeply twisted, and this brief survey tends to confirm her argument.

14. Williams initially quarreled with her revisions but later accepted them; the excised passages, as printed in the notes to *CP* I, suggest that her critical instincts were sound. Litz and MacGowan tell the full story in *CP* I, 493-95. Williams did not include "March" in *Al Que Quiere!,* although the poem predates the 1917 publication of this book; but he placed the poem second after "The Late Singer," another *Egoist* poem, in *Sour Grapes,* published in 1921.

15. In this ambivalence toward these primal powers, Williams is similar to many other writers of the World War I generation, including not only Pound and H. D. but also, for example, Eliot, Yeats, and Lawrence.

16. In fact, the Fra Angelico fresco is not in Fiesole but in the San Marco monastery in Florence.

17. "Anecdote of the Jar" first appeared in the October 1919 issue of *Poetry.* "The Snow Man" was printed in the October 1921 issue of the same magazine. For these dates see Edelstein 201 and 202.

18. Both "Winter Sunset" and the next poem that I shall discuss, "Conquest," appeared for the first time in *Al Que Quiere!*, published in December 1917. In the absence of magazine publication, it is difficult to determine the order of priority between these poems and Stevens's "Valley Candle," first published in the December 1917 issue of *Others*, almost simultaneously with the publication of Williams's book. (For publication dates of these poems, see Edelstein 198 and Wallace 11.) However, Mariani tells us (128) that when Williams became co-editor of *Others* in July 1916, he immediately asked Stevens for contributions, and it seems plausible that he had "Valley Candle" in hand while he was still writing poems that would go into his book. In any case, the affinities between "Valley Candle" on the one hand and "Winter Sunset" and "Conquest" on the other seem to me sufficiently strong to allow me to speak of a dialogue between the two poets, although I hesitate to speak of the Stevens poem as "influencing" the two Williams poems in question.

19. In revising the poem, Williams added a few lines and cut or tightened several more, and he eliminated dozens of inversions and other "poeticisms," to make the language more resolutely American, but the structure and content remain essentially unchanged. There are sufficient differences between the two versions so that Litz and MacGowan print both in the *Collected Poems 1909-1939*, on pages 27-36 and 108-17 respectively. Williams included "The Wanderer" as the last poem in the 1938 *Complete Collected Poems* and as the first poem in the *Collected Earlier Poems* of 1951; in both instances the placement suggests that Williams saw the poem as central to his *oeuvre*. "The Wanderer" also early achieved a semi-canonical status when Conrad Aiken selected it as the only Williams poem in his Modern Library anthology of *Modern American Poetry*, first published in 1927 and for more than two decades thereafter a chief entry point for readers exploring contemporary American poetry.

20. Norman Finkelstein argues persuasively that the starting point for Williams's poem is specifically Keats's second Hyperion fragment, "The Fall of Hyperion." In the original "Hyperion," Keats had begun to compose a quasi-Miltonic narrative poem about the fallen Titans, their hopes of recovering their lost kingdom, and Apollo's challenge to the last of the regnant Titans, Hyperion; but the fragment breaks off half-way into Canto III, shortly after Apollo is introduced. In recommencing the poem shortly before his death, Keats shifted his emphasis away from the Titans themselves to the questing poet who visits the realm of the Titans, guided by a Virgil-Muse named Moneta; but again the fragment breaks off, this time after only a little more than one canto. The shift from the myth as such to the subjective apprehension of the myth, from the gods to the poetic imagination, is decisive for the subsequent history of Romanticism—and for Williams's poem.

21. See Miller, *Poets of Reality* 287-92, Riddel *passim*, Finkelstein *passim*, Rapp 3-30, Breslin 20-24, Frail 81-95, and Lawson *passim*. Some sentences of my discussion of "The Wanderer" are adapted from my essay on the poem, forthcoming in the *William Carlos Williams Encyclopedia*.

22. The importance of this descent pattern in Williams's work has been stressed not only by Breslin, in his discussion of "The Wanderer," but also by Thomas Whitaker 23-36.

Works Cited

Ahearn, Barry. "Williams and H. D., or Sour Grapes." *Twentieth Century Literature* 35.3 (Fall 1989): 299-309.

Bloom, Harold. *Poetry and Repression: Revisionism from Blake to Stevens.* New Haven, CT: Yale UP, 1976.

Breslin, James E. B. *Williams Carlos Williams: An American Artist.* Chicago: U of Chicago P, 1970.

Cook, Albert. "Projections of Measure: The Continued Synergies of Pound and Williams." *Arizona Quarterly* 45.1 (Summer 1989): 35-61.

Diggory, Terence. *William Carlos Williams and the Ethics of Painting.* Princeton, NJ: Princeton UP, 1991.

Dijkstra, Bram. *Cubism, Stieglitz, and the Early Poetry of William Carlos Williams.* Princeton, NJ: Princeton UP, 1969.

Edelstein, J. M. *Wallace Stevens: A Descriptive Bibliography.* Pittsburgh: Pittsburgh UP, 1973.

Finkelstein, Norman. "Beauty, Truth, and The Wanderer." *William Carlos Williams: Man and Poet.* Ed. Carroll F. Terrell. Orono, ME: National Poetry Foundation, 1983. 233-42.

Frail, David. *The Early Politics and Poetics of William Carlos Williams.* Ann Arbor, MI: UMI Research Press, 1987.

Gilbert, Roger. "'Sunday Morning,' 'January Morning,' and Romantic Tradition." *William Carlos Williams Review* 18.2 (Fall 1992): 2-12.

H. D. (Hilda Doolittle). *Collected Poems 1912-1944.* Ed. Louis L. Martz. New York: New Directions, 1983.

Halter, Peter. *The Revolution in the Visual Arts and the Poetry of William Carlos Williams.* Cambridge, UK: Cambridge UP, 1994.

Holsapple, Bruce. "Williams on Form: *Kora in Hell.*" *William Carlos Williams and the Language of Poetry.* Ed. Burton Hatlen and Demetres Tryphonopoulos. Orono, ME: National Poetry Foundation, 2002. 79-126.

Kenner, Hugh. *A Homemade World: The American Modernist Writers.* New York: William Morrow, 1975.

Lawson, Andrew. "Divisions of Labor: William Carlos Williams's 'The Wanderer' and the Politics of Modernism." *William Carlos Williams Review* 20.1 (Spring 1994): 1-22.

MacGowan, Christopher. *William Carlos Williams's Early Poetry: The Visual Arts Background.* Ann Arbor, MI: UMI Research Press, 1984.

MacLeod, Glen G. *Wallace Stevens and Company. The Harmonium Years 1913-1923.* Ann Arbor, MI: UMI Research Press, 1983.

———, ed. *A Special Issue on Williams and Stevens. William Carlos Williams Review* 18.2 (Fall 1992).

Mariani, Paul. *William Carlos Williams: A New World Naked.* New York: McGraw-Hill, 1981.

Miller, J. Hillis. *The Disappearance of God: Five 19th-Century Writers.* New York: Schocken Books, 1965.

———. *The Linguistic Moment from Wordsworth to Stevens.* Princeton, NJ: Princeton UP, 1985.

———. *Poets of Reality: Six Twentieth Century Writers.* New York: Atheneum, 1969.

———. "William Carlos Williams and Wallace Stevens." *Columbia Literary History of the United States.* Ed. Emory Elliott, et al. New York: Columbia UP, 1988. 972-92.

Naumann, Francis M. *New York Dada 1915-1923.* New York: Harry N. Abrams, 1994.

Parkinson, Thomas. "Pound and Williams." In *Parkinson, Poets, Poems, Movements.* Ann Arbor, MI: UMI Research Press, 1987. 31-47.

Pound, Ezra. *The Cantos of Ezra Pound.* New York: New Directions, 1986.

———. *Collected Early Poems.* Ed. Michael John King. New York: New Directions, 1976.

———. *The Letters of Ezra Pound 1907-1941.* Ed. D. D. Paige. New York: Harcourt, Brace, and World, 1950.

———and William Carlos Williams. *Pound/Williams: Selected Letters of Ezra Pound and Williams Carlos Williams.* Ed. Hugh Witemeyer. New York: New Directions, 1996.

Perloff, Marjorie. "The Fallen Leaf and the Stain of Love: The Displacement of Desire in Williams' Early Love Poetry." *The Rhetoric of Love in the Collected Poems of William Carlos Williams.* Ed. Christina Giorcelli and Maria Anita Stefanelli. Rome: Edizioni Associate, 1993. 189-212.

Rapp, Carl. *William Carlos Williams and Romantic Idealism.* Hanover, NH: Brown UP, 1984.

Riddel, Joseph. "Decentering the Image: The 'Project' of 'American' Poetics?" *Textual Strategies: Perspectives in Post-Structuralist Criticism.* Ed. Josué V. Harari. Ithaca, NY: Cornell UP, 1979. 322-58.

Schmidt, Peter. *William Carlos Williams, the Arts, and Literary Tradition.* Baton Rouge, LA: Louisiana State UP, 1988.

Stevens, Wallace. *Collected Poetry and Prose.* Ed. Frank Kermode and Joan Richardson. New York: The Library of America, 1997.

Tashjian, Dickran. *William Carlos Williams and the American Scene, 1920-1940.* New York: Whitney Museum of American Art and Berkeley: U of California P, 1978.

Townley, Rod. *The Early Poetry of William Carlos Williams.* Ithaca, NY: Cornell UP, 1975.

Walker, David. *The Transparent Lyric: Reading and Meaning in the Poetry of Stevens and Williams.* Princeton, NJ: Princeton UP, 1984.

Wallace, Emily Mitchell. *A Bibliography of William Carlos Williams.* Middletown, CT: Wesleyan UP, 1968.

Weaver, Mike. *William Carlos Williams: The American Background.* Cambridge, UK: Cambridge UP, 1971.

Weiskel, Thomas. *The Romantic Sublime: Studies in the Structure and Psychology of Transcendence.* Baltimore: Johns Hopkins UP, 1976.

Whitaker, Thomas R. *William Carlos Williams.* Revised Edition. Boston: Twayne Publishers, 1989.

Williams, William Carlos. *The Collected Poems.* Vol. 1, 1909-1939. Ed. A. Walton Litz and Christopher MacGowan. New York: New Directions, 1986.

———. *I Wanted to Write a Poem: The Autobiography of the Works of a Poet.* Reported and ed. Edith Heal. New York: New Directions, 1978.

———. *Paterson.* Revised edition prepared by Christopher MacGowan. New York: New Directions, 1992.

———. *Selected Essays.* New York: Random House, 1954.

Wilton, Andrew and Tim Barringer. *American Sublime: Landscape Painting in the United States 1820-1880.* London, UK: Tate Publishing, 2002.

Mitchum Huehls (essay date spring 2004)

SOURCE: Huehls, Mitchum. "Reconceiving Perceiving: William Carlos Williams' World-Making Words of

'Kora in Hell: Improvisations.'" *Paideuma* 33, no. 1 (spring 2004): 57-88.

[*In the following essay, Huehls uses Ludwig Wittgenstein's theories of language to characterize Williams's project in "Kora in Hell" as one of world building and the creation in language of a new "form of life."*]

> "*Truth cannot be out there—cannot exist independently of the human mind—because sentences cannot so exist, or be out there. The world is out there, but descriptions of the world are not. Only descriptions of the world can be true or false. The world on its own—unaided by the describing activities of human beings—cannot.*"
>
> —Richard Rorty, *Contingency, Irony, and Solidarity*

> "*. . . holy the visions holy the hallucinations holy the miracles holy the eyeball . . .*"
>
> —Allen Ginsberg, "Footnote to Howl"

In the "Prologue" to **"Kora in Hell: Improvisations,"** William Carlos Williams claims, "Thus seeing the thing itself without forethought or afterthought but with great intensity of perception, my mother loses her bearings or associates with some disreputable person or translates a dark mood. She is a creature of great imagination" (8). This mode of perception and apprehension that Williams ascribes to his mother constitutes his own poetic project throughout **"Kora in Hell"**; like mother, like son, we might say. Williams interrogates the implications of perceiving phenomena with such an "intensity of perception" that one is disoriented from the sensory realm, and he attempts to create a condition in which the disorientation from the sensory remains commensurable with a valid perception of the object. Williams' way of seeing implies a unique phenomenological and ontological conception of the object being perceived and further necessitates a unique form of language that allows for the sufficient articulation of the thing being perceived.

In **"Kora in Hell,"** Williams provides his readers with much more than Pound's "direct treatment of the thing" or Eliot's "objective correlative" because by the time Williams' apprehension of the thing has been articulated and has reached the reader, the empirically determined, ontological reality of the thing has been left far behind. Although many of Williams' poetic statements often read as if he wants to transcribe the very essence of the thing-in-itself upon the page, the resulting text demonstrates that he actually creates new forms of life through a language that maintains only the loosest ties to the initial phenomena being perceived.[1] Thus when Williams maintains that "the thing that stands eternally in the way of really good writing is always one: the virtual impossibility of lifting to the imagination those things which lie under the direct scrutiny of the senses, close to the nose" (14), he is not lamenting the difficulty of transparently reconstructing phenomena through a cor-respondence theory of language but is instead speaking of the difficulty of transforming one form of life (reality) into another (language) via the imagination. He does not try to represent the objectivity of the thing but to dissolve that ostensible objectivity. Thus, Williams bemoans *mere* sensory apprehension, since "the senses witnessing what is immediately before them in detail see a finality which they cling to in despair, not knowing which way to turn. Thus the so-called natural or scientific array becomes fixed, the walking devil of modern life." The ideal poetry, then, does not transparently represent the thing itself but instead "nicks the solidity of this apparition" of the thing itself to create new forms of life in which things achieve new value and meaning (14).

From Williams' initial claims about the nature of perception, I want to suggest that the engagement of the imagination, perhaps the main character in **"Kora in Hell,"** is tantamount to the author's written mediation of the thing perceived through language. I will consider what happens philosophically and linguistically when an author must move from perception to apprehension to articulation of the thing. A substantial body of criticism, asserting that **"Kora in Hell"** exemplifies Williams' "no ideas but in things" mantra, maintains that the text attempts to capture the metaphysical Truths of Williams' world by stripping his writing of symbolic language in order to privilege objective perception through an objectivized use of language. Stephen Tapscott asserts in *American Beauty,* for instance, that Williams sees "the need for two kinds of objectivity, both toward the world and toward words," and that he therefore attempts "to write poems that can liberate things to be both physical and metaphysical" (126). Tapscott correctly identifies the challenge that Williams confronts in his poetry—that "we simply do not see the world clearly, because corrupt forms of language and outmoded conceptions intervene between us and the world" (128)—but **"Kora in Hell"** shows Williams reveling in and dancing with this challenge instead of futilely trying to conjure the metaphysical thing itself upon the page. Similarly, Bram Dijkstra cites **"The Red Wheelbarrow"** as an emblematic example of how Williams uses language so objectively that "the words are facts, the direct linguistic equivalents to the visual object under scrutiny" (168). Not only are these claims theoretically naïve, but they also rob Williams' writing of its powerful world-making potential.[2] I will argue that **"Kora in Hell"** demonstrates Williams' anxiety over the move from perception to articulation (which must transition through apprehension), and thus struggles with but ultimately avoids the trappings of a meaningless private language. Instead, Williams' text enacts a public language, elides the distinction between poetic and everyday language, attempts to describe instead of explain reality, and achieves its meaning from the contextualized use of language instead of through any essential meaning of words. Such acts of articulation, through an engaged imagination, make **"Kora in Hell"** what Wittgenstein calls a "form of life" that presents solutions to the difficulty of treating and articulating the object by recognizing the contingencies of language.

Before discussing the positive attributes of Williams' use of language in **"Kora in Hell,"** it is first necessary to debunk a common reading of **"Kora"** that tends to imply that much of the text can only be interpreted as a private language since Williams' process of perceiving reality and transcribing it daily into poetic expression is a necessarily private experience. The private language theory is closely related to the philosophical problem of other minds (how can we ever be sure of knowledge beyond solipsism?). Or as Wittgenstein raises the question (and answers in the negative) in *Philosophical Investigations,* "[C]ould we also imagine a language in which a person could write down or give vocal expression to his inner experiences—his feelings, moods, and the rest—for his private use? . . . The individual words of this language are to refer to what can only be known to the person speaking; to his immediate private sensations" (243).[3] Not only is the notion of private language philosophically inaccurate, it is also of limited use in critically approaching a text—leading to vacuous critical commentary like Joseph Slate's take on **"Kora in Hell"**: "What he [Williams] wrote about did not matter at all" (464). Ron Loewinsohn summarizes a lengthy history of similarly vacuous criticism on **"Kora in Hell"** that abandons any attempt to offer meaningful statements about the text and that instead forwards a private language argument to discount **"Kora"** variously as "opacity," "private extempore effusions," "self-indulgence," "self-therapy," and "solipsism" (221).

Of course, Williams himself tacitly endorses such inadequate interpretations when in the prologue to the City Lights edition of **"Kora,"** he says of his text, "What to do with it? It would mean nothing to a casual reader" (29). Williams solved this ostensible quandary by adding the italicized "explanations" beneath each passage to illuminate the prose poetry, but even without those "explanations," we should not vitiate the text and its meanings by treating them as personalized and therefore inaccessible perceptions of Williams' subjective reality. In a study of Pound's and Eliot's self-theorizing, Frederic Hargreaves demonstrates the uselessness of a private language approach to poetry by showing such an argument to be tautologically nonsensical. A subscription to the private language theory allows any critical commentary to be applied equally to any text because all it can assert is that "a poem is good because it conveys private states which cannot be publicly defined" (735). Perhaps even more disturbing, the emphasis on the poet's inner state of mind implies a conception of poetry in which its ability to convey

meaning exists "almost independently of language," so that "poetry conveys experience barely connected with words . . . and the experience, although itself understood, cannot be put into words" (737).[4]

Although Williams struggles throughout **"Kora in Hell"** with the relationship between private experience and language, his text refuses to theorize itself out of existence through an assertion of private language. Hargreaves engages Wittgenstein's discussion of private language to argue against Pound and Eliot that language's "meaning depends upon the role or purpose a word plays in the context of social activity" and that "a word can [never] acquire meaning simply by being connected with a purely inner state of consciousness" (728). To assert that a perception or experience can be articulated in a private language and have it remain in the realm of language is counterintuitive to the function and nature of language. Because such a language would be private and lacking rules and criteria, it would be impossible for it to be spoken by more than one person and so could not be considered a language with significant meaning.[5] Wittgenstein explains that an individual cannot give herself a private meaning of a word for the same reason that one's right hand cannot meaningfully give one's left hand money (*PI* [*Philosophical Investigations*] 268). This solipsistically circular process fails to create significant meaning because it fails to achieve any "criterion of correctness." "One would like to say: whatever is going to seem right to me is right. And that only means that here we can't talk about 'right'" (*PI* 258). This is not to say that language must point to an external, metaphysical truth to legitimate its meaning, but rather that "a great deal of stage-setting in the language is presupposed if the mere act of naming is to make sense" (*PI* 257). This stage-setting is constituted by a common knowledge of the contextualized (within a language-game) use of language that necessarily precludes all language from being private.

If it becomes philosophically impossible to describe **"Kora in Hell"** as an expression of private language, and if the text also resists the fixity of a transparent, objective language, then what happens instead? Wittgenstein reconciles the tension between the private and the objective by allowing for private reference or association in language but not private meaning. He states that "the word 'red' means something known to everyone; and in addition, for each person, it means something known only to him (or perhaps rather: it *refers* to something known only to him)" (*PI* 273, Wittgenstein's emphasis).[6] The alternative, then, is a language whose words are radically open to meaningful signification (although not to the extent that they become meaningless), and this is the world that **"Kora in Hell"** creates. In *Wittgenstein's Ladder,* Marjorie Perloff calls this mode of signification a "fluid poetic paradigm" that replaces the myth of "the 'autonomous,' self-contained, and self-expressive lyric" by recognizing that "the poet's most secret and profound emotions are expressed in a language that has always already belonged to the poet's culture, society, and nation" (22).

In the first sections of **"Kora in Hell,"** Williams presents his own negotiation of the personal and the objective through the image of whistling. Whistling first appears in the third section of chapter I where "the dark canals are whistling, whistling for who will cross to the other side" (32). Although Williams' gloss of the passage claims that the whistles actually come from "an old woman with a girl on her arm, histing and whistling across a deserted canal to some late loiterer trudging aimlessly on beneath the gas lamps," it serves in both instances as a call to motion, a call to the observer to do more than "remain with hands in pocket leaning upon [his] lamppost" (32). The motion entailed in crossing to the other side becomes the first step in leaving behind "the whitest aprons and brightest doorknobs in Christendom" that constitute the autonomous and useless realm of the objective thing in itself. The whistle both maintains the privacy of the perceiving experience and converts it into a meaningful, public (although still created by the whistler), improvisational melody. A few paragraphs later, whistling becomes a way to make a meaningful expression despite the fact that "the tunes changing, changing, darting so many ways" tend to leave the listener "sprawling" or "hip bogged" in his attempts to make meaning. The whistle resists the ascription of a metaphysical foundation to the tune, and instead swirls up a blustery motion of "leaves swarming; curving down the east in their braided jackets" (33) that is perpetually in the process of creating meaning. Perhaps the best example of the whistle as an expression that integrates the private and the public without a static, foundational reference to the thing itself, comes in the final paragraph of chapter II, where the personal whistle actually constitutes nature: "—and I? Must dance with the wind, make my own snow flakes, whistle a contrapuntal melody to my own fugue! Huzza then, this is the dance of the blue moss bank! Huzza then, this is the mazurka of the hollow log! Huzza then, this is the dance of rain in cold trees" (34). The whistle, therefore, becomes a new language that is able to both describe and create reality. In fact, singing and dancing pervade **"Kora in Hell,"** and the extended metaphor is further reinforced by musical notations like *"allegro," "tutti i instrumenti,"* and *"D.C. al Fine"* that Williams incorporates into the text, thereby transforming the poem into a scored piece of music with new meaning making capacities.

Although this middle space of the whistle is able to accommodate the "changing, changing, darting so many ways" of experience while still providing meaningful expression to that experience, the processes of perceiving and apprehending the object and the implications they have for our phenomenological understanding of the object remain vague. In other words, given the constant flux that Williams describes in **"Kora,"** how can the poet ask epistemological questions and legitimate his phenomenological statements about the object without giving in to the apparent incommensurability between perception and articulation? Williams again refers to his mother to provide an example of how to perceive and legitimate observed phenomena: "Whatever is before her is sufficient to itself and so to be valued" (7). Although this might initially read as an ontological statement that gestures toward a metaphysical conception of the thing in itself, such foundationalism is mitigated by the pragmatic empiricism of the process of observing. In claiming that the sufficiency of the object provides its own legitimization of value, Williams conceives a mode of legitimizing meaning in a way that refuses to look toward any external, metaphysical point of reference nor toward some deeper, internal point of essential reference.[7] Instead, Williams presents a circular (yet non-solipsistic) and pragmatic mode of valuation that refuses to search for analogs to the perceived object (be they internal or external). Thus, Williams claims in **"Spring and All"** that the use of the word "like" makes for empty writing and that "What I put down of value will have this value: an escape from crude symbolism, the annihilation of strained associations, complicated ritualistic forms designed to separate the work from 'reality'—such as rhyme, meter as meter and not as the essential of the work, one of its words" (100, 102). Furthermore, in *The Poetics of Indeterminacy* Marjorie Perloff maintains that Williams' disavowal of the analog leads to a poetry in which "the particulars . . . point to nothing *behind* them" (117). Indeed, although Williams does not repudiate figurative language per se, passages like the following allow the things perceived to significate their own value according to their own phenomenological (and not ontological) sufficiency: "Once again the moon in a glassy twilight. The gas jet in the third floor window is turned low, they have not drawn the shade, sends down a flat glare upon the lounge's cotton-Persian cover where the time passes with clumsy carresses [sic]" (**"Kora"** 63). Such figurative yet overtly non-symbolic language provides descriptions that legitimate their meanings without calling on a foundation external or internal to the objects to create value.

But what makes Williams' "sufficiency" any different from essence? The difference corresponds to the distinction between phenomenological and ontological conceptions of the thing being perceived. It is easy to confuse the two, as Burton Hatlen does in an essay comparing the poetics of Williams and Louis Zukofsky. Hatlen claims that Williams' primary poetic task is "to make sure that his words remain absolutely faithful to 'things' in their sensory immediacy" (66), and he associates

Williams' poetry with a correspondence theory of truth that constructs the poet as a *cogito* force hell-bent on controlling reality. Of course, any decent reading of **"Kora in Hell"**'s prologue tells us that Williams believes that "sensory immediacy" leads to "a finality which they [the senses] cling to in despair, not knowing which way to turn" (14). The idea of essence that Hatlen ascribes to Williams' poetics is too fixed and stable; for Williams, the object's sufficiency is a matter of perspective—it is sufficient because it is being perceived in the only way it can, from the perspective of the perceiver. In his study of Wittgenstein's *Tractatus Logico-Philosophicus*, Joachim Schulte states, "And just as I cannot get from my visual field into yours, or confuse my pain with yours, so I cannot describe my world from a standpoint lying outside of it—cannot compare it with fundamentally different possibilities" (63). Reality, then, is tantamount to perspective since we cannot get outside of perspective.[8] Or as Wittgenstein puts it in the *Tractatus,* "solipsism . . . coincides with pure realism" since "[w]hatever we see can be other than it is" and "[w]hatever we can describe at all could be other than it is" (5.64, 5.634).[9] This is an abandonment of the ontological in favor of the perspectivally apprehended phenomenological; or, "The world is all that is the case" (*Tractatus* 1). Accordingly, we can understand Williams' repudiation of the analog simply as a desire to shed the word (and the world) of its former perspectives, those false values that he describes as the "associational or sentimental" (14).

This emptying of symbolic meaning "loosen[s] the attention" that has previously "been held too rigid on the one plane instead of following a more flexible, jagged resort" (14), thereby precluding sufficiency from ever attaining the foundational stagnation of essentialism. **"Kora in Hell"** presents many objects and scenes that resist ontological readings by challenging the definitional criteria that would be required to obtain epistemological certainty of the phenomena. For instance, Williams flounders while attempting to gain a precise knowledge of a hill in the lead question to chapter XX, "Where does this downhill turn up again?"—an attempt that will inevitably fail because his limited perspective makes the sufficiency of the thing his only recourse to obtaining knowledge of the hills (69). Williams raises similar dilemmas when he further questions, "And who'll say what's pious or not pious or how I'll sing praise to God?" (69). Trying dogmatically to define piety by referencing a metaphysical deity or even the *Bible* is like trying to "hold spirit round the arms" or like determining the precise moment that downhill becomes uphill or where "the edge lifted between sunlight and moonlight" can be demarcated (71). Williams proceeds by claiming that any strict enforcement of such definitional criteria (in an attempt to assure assertions of necessity) causes us to be "[d]riven to the wall" just like the gamboling boy who when pushed

"too close" becomes "a devil at the table" or like the spirit that when held too tightly "takes lies for wings, turns poplar leaf and flutters off" (69-70). These rigid attempts to define and confine phenomenal signification ultimately lead to epistemological failure—they are inadequate means of knowing and representing objects and experience. The attempt to gain knowledge of the spirit, for instance, leaves the general populous "pointing at the sky" in a futile act of Augustinian, ostensive knowledge acquisition.

Importantly, the self-valuation of the thing that is sufficient to itself is not tautologically circular but rather has a diachronic aspect to it as well (a wheel rolling forward as opposed to a wheel spinning in place)—a diachronicity achieved through the possibility of constantly shifting perspective. Williams first introduces the option of the diachronic circuit in the second chapter that begins with the rhetorical question, "Why go further?" (32). His question seems to imply that we could adamantly push explanations and justifications of meaning straight ahead, a motion that figures inquiry as a grasping for some higher meaning that might legitimate the object being perceived. Williams realizes, however, that such false points of reference only dogmatically ossify the object so that we "arrive at the perfection of a tiger lily or a china doorknob" (32). Williams indicates that to pursue these empty ends would be to break "the back of a willing phrase [asking language to exceed its capacity of meaningful legitimization]" and instead suggests that we "try to follow the wheel through—approach death at a walk, take in all the scenery" (32). The wheel here becomes a balance between the monomania of the linear and the redundancy of the circular. By adding more than circular motion to the wheel, change and contingency are permitted to slip into attempts to constitute value from experience. In chapter XII, for instance, Williams presents a cycle of peace and agitation that remains permeable to change: "Violence has begotten peace, peace has fluttered away in agitation. A bewildered change has turned among the roots and the Prince's kiss as far at sea as ever." These cycles maintain the self-sufficiency of the objects of experience, but by introducing an element of contingency in their forward revolution, they create the possibility for surprises like the man who "[t]hinking to have brought all to one level . . . finds his foot striking through where he had thought rock to be and stands firm where he had experienced only a bog hitherto" (52). Williams later explains that because we are unable to call on any stable, external reference for the legitimization of meaning, those attempting to derive meaningful value from their experiences must interpret as they go (67).

Although the wheel's diachronic motion disallows the construction of any foundational meaning (we have rolled far from such transparent essentializing), it does facilitate a metonymic mode of meaning-making wherein the object being perceived derives its value from its relative relations to other objects. Lacking a metaphysical center, Williams places objects side by side to create contingent and paratactic instead of absolute meaning.[10] Thomas Joswick describes Williams' technique by calling it a "new syntax of relationships" that "recreate the world not by a repetition of the same, nor by a unification of particulars in a transcendent whole, but by the repetition of the difference and 'cleavage'—the pairing of things and words in alogical and preconceptual relationships" (111). The image of leaves swirled together in a meaningful dance becomes the primary image that Williams engages to represent the contingent creation of value. Each leaf's significance is derived from its relative relation to and motion with the other leaves that participate in the dance. In his explanation of the third section of chapter II Williams maintains, "Thus a poem is tough by no quality it borrows from a logical recital of events nor from the events themselves but solely from that attenuated power which draws perhaps many broken things into a dance giving them a full being" (16-17). Williams argues elsewhere in the prologue that "discover[ing] in things those inimitable particles of dissimilarity to all other things which are the peculiar perfections of the thing in question" is to be preferred to making meaning by analogy or simile (a practice that he considers to be "a pastime of very low order") (18). Consequently, Williams juxtaposes the deaths of "[a] young woman who had excelled at intellectual pursuits" and "a fellow of very gross behavior" to allow each event to provide meaning to the other through their paratactic relation (38). Similarly, Williams celebrates the "exquisite differences never to be resolved" of a Polish Father who "comes at midnight through mid-winter slush to baptize a dying newborn" (43) and asserts that "[t]hat which is known has value only by virtue of the dark . . . by the forces of darkness opposed to it" (74). Williams thus places an emphasis on *how* meaning is made through relationships rather than on *what* meaning is made by the object or event itself.

The contingency that this metonymic mode of meaning making introduces into the empirical perception of the phenomenal object necessitates that the mode of apprehension be as "changing, changing, darting so many ways" as the world that is being apprehended. Consequently, as Jesse Green explains in his essay on **"Kora in Hell,"** Williams in not interested "simply in 'things' but in the relation between thing and idea—that is to say, in the maelstrom of the perceptual or imaginative process itself" (297). Williams' imagination, then, becomes the factor that introduces post-foundational contingency to the process of apprehension. The man who "finds his foot striking through where he had thought rock to be" chooses incorrectly when he decides to ignore "the caress of the imagination" out of fear (52) since without the imagination, his senses can only "see a finality which they cling to in despair" (14). A similar phenomenal dilemma presents itself in chapter XII with the presentation of "[s]omething to grow used to; a stone too big for ox haul, too near for blasting." Williams refuses to be foiled by the obstacle blocking the forward spinning of his wheels, and thus apprehends the obstacle imaginatively in order to offer solutions: "Take the road around it or—scrape away, scrape away . . . Marry a gopher to help you! . . . The whole family take shovels, babies and all!" (53). This mode of imaginative apprehension further removes Williams' poetics from any foundational attachment to a metaphysically centered meaning. Indeed, in the midst of any such weighty center, Williams asserts, "No need to take the thing too seriously" (49), "What a fool ever to be tricked into seriousness" (65), and "hallucination comes to rescue on the brink of seriousness" (66). Jesse Green explains Williams' move into the hallucinatory as an attempt "to take in the instability of what is 'at hand.' And not only at hand, indeed, but *in mind,* for the instability Williams has really come up against here is that of the relation between actual things themselves and what goes on in the mind" (299).

Wittgenstein theorizes the contingency of apprehension by borrowing the famous duck/rabbit picture used in psychology in which it is equally reasonable for an individual to assert that the picture is of a duck or of a rabbit. Wittgenstein claims that each animal constitutes one "aspect" of the overall picture (so although it remains impossible to say whether the picture is a duck or a rabbit, it is meaningful to say that duck and rabbit images are two aspects of the same picture). To see an aspect, however, is not to see an object; seeing an aspect is like saying, "I see a likeness between these two faces" whereas seeing an object is like saying, "I see *this*" (*PI* 193). The necessary contingency that the notion of aspect introduces into the apprehension process creates a situation in which seeing is tantamount to interpreting (Williams' "interpreting as they go" (67)). Furthermore, the process of interpreting an aspect of a picture or object involves the engagement of the imagination. Wittgenstein provides this example: "Here is a game played by children: they say that a chest, for example, is a house; and thereupon it is interpreted as a house in every detail. A piece of fancy is worked into it" (*PI* 206). Reading this example of a child's imagination discovering the various aspects of a chest, it is hard not to be reminded of the similar description in **"Kora in Hell"** when Williams asserts, "My little son's improvisations exceed mine: a round stone to him's a loaf of bread or 'this hen could lay a dozen golden eggs'" (74). It is important to point out here that neither Wittgenstein nor Williams speaks of the imaginative discovery of aspects in a discourse that opposes the ontologically real to the perspectivally imagined. It is useless to ask questions about one thing being more real than another when there is no foundational, external point of reference from which to determine value and when meaning can only be created contingently vis-à-vis the paratactic positioning of the objects being perceived. In other words, "What I can see something *as,* is what it can be a picture of" (*PI* 201). This "*as*-ness" puts us on our way to eliding the distinction between phenomenal and linguistic worlds that will allow us to interpret **"Kora in Hell"** as "form of life."

If phenomena and their apprehension are governed by the contingency of meaning attendant with the crisis of value that occurs when phenomena can only be conceived as sufficient to themselves yet non-essential, then the articulation of that apprehension must be similarly governed by the contingencies of linguistic meaning. Under such conditions, language can only make grammatical as opposed to ontological statements. Thus it is precisely in order to remain open to the possible meanings achieved through such articulation that Williams claims: "It is to loosen the attention, my attention since I occupy part of the field, that I write these improvisations" (14). The loosening accommodates the proliferation of meaning generated by the unstable phenomenal world. The apprehended aspect of the phenomena does not signify any ontologically true meaning but instead signifies an action and use to the phenomena. To speak ontologically is to force language to move toward an exactness that it is necessarily incapable of attaining. Instead, Wittgenstein explains that although "[w]e feel as if we had to *penetrate* phenomena: our investigation . . . is directed not towards phenomena, but . . . towards the *'possibilities'* of phenomena"; "[o]ur investigation is therefore a grammatical one" (*PI* 90). Once apprehended by the imagination, the "possibilities [aspects] of phenomena" obtain their fullest realization through their articulation in language, and this is what constitutes Williams' poetic task in **"Kora in Hell"** (i.e., Williams actualizes the possibilities instead of penetrating the essence of phenomena). The first section of chapter XXVII presents this move from perception to articulation by first posing another difficulty like the stone in the road: "The particular thing . . . dwarfs the imagination, makes logic a butterfly, offers a finality that sends us spinning though space, a fixity the mind could climb forever." Williams then proves such finality and fixity to be susceptible to the contingencies immanent in apprehending phenomena by asserting, "There is no thing that with a twist of the imagination cannot be something else" (81). Significantly, however, the thing does not become something else simply through the twisting of the imagination but only by first writing down and articulating that the thing becomes something else (i.e., this is a linguistic as well as an imaginative process).

Therefore, after perception and imagination, language must enter the equation—there remains no other means of constituting the empirically perceived and imaginatively tinctured world that Williams describes than by casting it into language. Wittgenstein describes the necessity of the move into language in this imaginary conversation (perhaps with a poet?): "But when I imagine something, something certainly *happens*! Well, something happens—and then I make a noise. What for? Presumably in order to tell what happens" (*PI* 363). Without the linguistic turn, Williams' poetic process would be incomplete and impotent. Joswick recognizes the necessity of the linguistic as he explains that "[n]either the flight of the imagination away from the world [apprehension through imagining] . . . nor the poetics of the particular [perceiving of phenomena], should be taken alone as Williams' resolve in **"Kora."** It is the 'pairing' of the two in the 'scribbling,' the actual writing, that is primary for Williams" (111). For instance, despite the fact that Williams seems to be abandoning words for physical experience when he asks, "then how will you expect a fine trickle of words to follow you through the intimacies of this dance without—oh, come let us walk together into the air awhile first," notice that we could not "walk together into the air" without the "fine trickle of words" that constitutes the invitation (34). The possibility of articulation always rescues Williams from any phenomenological or epistemological impasse. When confronted with the unanswerable questions discussed earlier (where does uphill become downhill? where is the edge between moonlight and sunlight?), Williams always turns to the craft of writing. He advises in the third section of chapter XX, for instance, that we need not fret if the articulation does not "cut onyx into a ring to fit a lady's finger"; instead, in the craft of poetry as in the craft of ring-cutting, the purpose and meaning come from the articulation itself. Although this engagement in language is imprecise (only a road made of "brown dirt"), "[f]or all that, one may see his face in a flower along it—even in this light" (70). Although the poetic representation remains inexact and non-essential, an imaginative perception (a "face in a flower") is articulated and is thereby able to achieve significant meaning.

Such significant meaning, however, is not complete or exact meaning. The contingencies and indeterminacies of the phenomena and their apprehension exist precisely because their articulation in language will be necessarily contingent and indeterminate. As Wittgenstein exclaims in *Philosophical Investigations,* "A proposition is a queer thing!" to the extent that the proposition fails to deliver on our assumption of "a pure intermediary between the propositional *signs* and the facts [phenomena]" (94). Instead of assuming transparent mediation between facts and signs, Wittgenstein suggests that we simply see each realm as equivalent to the other: "These concepts: proposition, language, thought, world, stand in line one behind the other, each equivalent to each" (*PI* 96). Williams directly confronts these inadequacies of language throughout **"Kora in Hell,"** but they do not preclude him from using language to express the inadequacies of language or to describe phenomena in prose poem format.

In the first chapter, for instance, Williams confronts the contingency of language as it enacts the discrepancy between the facts of the world and the language of the signs used to articulate those phenomena. In the parenthetical imperative, "Rot dead marigolds—an acre at a time! Gold, are you?," we see Williams realizing the futility of trying to determine an ontological meaning of the phenomenal ("Gold, are you?") from the sign itself ("gold" being embedded in "marigold") (31). The "gold" in "marigold" does not necessarily connote the actuality of the thing and so the word "marigold" must either remain in the realm of the denotative or exist in a realm of indeterminate, connotated meaning. This is just the first of many examples in which Williams is unable to articulate adequately the meanings of his imaginative expressions because of the contingency of language. A few sections later, Williams exclaims, "*Ay dio!* I would say so much were it not for the tunes changing, changing, darting so many ways. One step and the cart's left you sprawling" (33). This openness of meaning disallows any linguistic friction with which Williams can get a toehold on his attempts to articulate his imaginative construal of the phenomenal world. Thus the awareness of the limited power of naming in language that we see in the statement, "Oh call me a lady and think you've caged me. Hell's loose every minute, you hear?" (39). Again, we see that the assignation of a sign to a phenomenon cannot connote a fixed meaning since the "Hell" of contingency constitutes the true nature of language.[11]

Challengingly for Williams, it is a nature that seems to work as a counterforce to the dominant metaphor of **"Kora in Hell,"** the dance. "Dance! Sing! Coil and uncoil! Whip yourselves about! Shout the deliverance! . . . Here is dancing! The mind in tatters. And so the music wistfully takes the lead" (57). If we take this expression of dynamic energy to be the aim of Williams' poetic task, then an earlier passage presents the difficulty of attaining this orgiastic frenzy with a language that constantly impedes the full tattering of the mind. Here it appears that Williams is attempting to dance with a woman, but the words keep getting in the way: "The words of the thing twang and twitter to the gentle rocking of a high-laced boot and the silk above that . . . Reaching far over as if—But always she draws back and comes down upon the word flatfooted. For a moment we—but the boot's costly and the play's not mine. The pace leads off anew. Again the words break it and we both come down flatfooted" (55). The jerky hesitations signified by the dashes and the dancers' inability to move nimbly indicate that the dancers (and

the writers of the dance) fail to take the advice included in the passage: "The trick of the dance is in following now the words, *allegro,* now the contrary beat of the glossy leg" (55). The dance, like the word, cannot be controlled; meaning cannot be dictated and must, instead, follow from the grammar of the word and from the "contrary beat" (as opposed to some essential beat) of phenomena.

Although the above examples demonstrate how the move into language impedes the dance and makes the dancers flatfooted, Williams, realizing that language is simultaneously the best tool at his disposal, is ultimately able to dance anyway by constructing meaning contingently. Williams presents this compromise between the facts and the signs as he describes his ideals of perception and articulation while simultaneously acknowledging the difficulty in attaining such ideals: "The wish would be to see not floating visions of unknown purport but the imaginative qualities of the actual things being perceived accompany their gross vision in a slow dance, interpreting as they go. But inasmuch as this will not always be the case one must dance nevertheless as he can" (67). Williams would certainly agree with Wittgenstein that "We are up against trouble caused by our way of expression" (*The Blue and Brown Books* 48) and that the "notion of the meaning of a word surrounds the working of language with a haze which makes clear vision impossible" (*PI* 5); but by assuming these difficulties as given, Williams "dance[s] nevertheless as he can" and creates what Burton Hatlen calls a "poetics of absence."[12] Such a poetics maintains that "if the seeable is by definition unsayable, then language, rather than giving us Being in its fullness, must reconcile itself to the more difficult task of enacting our endless and endlessly frustrated struggle *toward* Being" (76). This Wittgensteinian understanding of language transforms the phenomena of the world into limit points in order to create meaning. In other words, meaning is defined as the point up to which the thing is articulable. And despite the frenetic nature of the dance, Williams retains an awareness of the role such limits play in the making of meaning. We see this in the third section of chapter XXV in which Williams claims, "A man can shoot his spirit up out of a wooden house, that is, through the roof—the roof's slate—but how far?" and then glosses this proposition by writing, "It is obvious that if in flying an airplane one reached such an altitude that all sense of direction and every intelligible perception of the world were lost there would be nothing left to do but to come down to that point at which eyes regained their power" (79). I wish to highlight three important ways that Williams' text intelligibly represents the dances of his daily reality while acknowledging the radical contingency of that reality, its apprehension, and its articulation (i.e., he writes precisely at that threshold where the eyes regain their power or are about to exceed their power). (1) He employs everyday as opposed to poetic language; (2) he provides descriptions while intentionally avoiding explanations; (3) he derives the meaning of his language from its contextualized use in the text.

Poetic language purports to construct a realm of highly aestheticized and autonomous writing that treats the word as an object in and of itself, entirely removed from its social context and public use. The idea of poeticity, developed by the Russian Formalists, exists in contradistinction to the pragmatic, use-value oriented language of everyday communication. Perloff cites Jakobson's "What is Poetry?" to provide an example of this overdetermined conception of language: "Poeticity is present when the word is felt as a word and not a mere representation of the object being named or an outburst of emotion, when words and their composition, their meaning, their external and inner form, acquire a weight and value of their own instead of referring indifferently to reality" (*Wittgenstein's Ladder* 52). Incredibly enough, several critics have read Williams' writings as pristine examples of this *l'art pour l'art* stance. In comparing Williams' poetics to Stieglitz's aesthetics, for instance, Dijkstra claims that each artist's representation of phenomena, "when emphasized properly and removed as much as possible from an extraneous, contextual environment, can come to represent in their freedom from anecdotal reference, experiences which touch upon the most profound, pre-rational . . . sources of man's action" (145). Dijkstra's portrayal of such an autonomous language may be accurate, but only in an unreal vacuum as his formula is contingent on a decontextualized environment, an oxymoron of the first order. Perloff explains in *Wittgenstein's Ladder* that Wittgenstein handily solves the debate around whether or not there is a distinction between poetic and ordinary language by "demonstrating that (1) there is in fact *no* material difference, but that (2) the *use* to which we put language varies so much that words and sentences become, as it were, unfamiliar when they reappear in a new context" (19-20). Therefore Jakobson's notion of "poeticity" rests on false assumptions of our ability to subjugate the grammar of language to achieve a more refined (and inevitably stagnant) notion of the word.

It becomes more appropriate to say, then, that Williams does not use ordinary language *as opposed to* poetic language, but rather that he simply uses language in all of its contingency and indeterminacy. Eliding the poetic/ordinary distinction grants all language the qualities that were previously reserved for either the poetic or the ordinary. As Perloff explains, "Wittgenstein's *ordinary* is best understood as quite simply *that which is*, the language we do *actually* use when we communicate with one another" (*WL* [*Wittgenstein's Ladder*] 57). Ordinary language, then, can be both denotative and connotative, literal and figurative, anecdotal and aestheticized—it becomes the given. Thus, Wittgenstein

can assert the equivalency of "proposition, language, thought, [and] world" (*PI* 96) and Williams can disavow the symbolic while continuing to engage with the metaphoric. Williams' protestation against the symbolic rests not in a poetic/ordinary language distinction but in a desire to resist language's stagnation. As Craig Owens explains, "[T]he symbol is precisely that part of the whole to which it may be reduced. The symbol does not represent essence, it *is* essence" (1058). It is such reduction of which Williams is wary; consequently, in **"Kora in Hell"** he combines common, everyday language and contexts with the figurative powers of the imagination to create a text that refuses to sit still.

As was mentioned earlier, Williams' description of his mother in the prologue immediately adumbrates the poetic techniques he will employ in **"Kora"**; thus her direct and non-aestheticized discussion of corpses ("They say sometimes people look terrible and they come and make them look fine. They push things into their mouths!" [7-8]) prepares us for Williams' own engagement with the everyday. From Jacob Louslinger in the first chapter to the obstetrician who "cut[s] the baby from its stem. Slop[s] in disinfectant, roar[s] with derision at the insipid blood stench" (66), Williams refuses to euphemize the events or the language that constitute his poetry. The invitation that appears early in **"Kora,"** to "walk together into the air awhile first" (34), is fulfilled later in chapter XI as we follow "On through the vapory heather!," but it is only a "lewd anecdote" that is the impetus to this adventurous chase of life. A few chapters later Williams openly reveals his "everyday" poetics when he describes a poem whose words "spoke of gross matter of the everyday world such as are never much hidden from a quick eye" (56). Although the "lewd anecdotes" and "gross matters" receive direct treatment as they constitute the content of **"Kora,"** they also receive imaginative treatment, but in a way that does not make them any less everyday. This imaginative transformation is explicitly articulated in the third section of chapter XIV: "Bitter words spoken to a child ripple in the morning light! Boredom from a bedroom doorway thrills with anticipation! The complaints of an old man dying piecemeal are starling chirrups. Coughs go singing on springtime paths across a field; corruption picks strawberries" (57). Williams' imaginative treatment of the everyday allows his text to multiply meaning and to demonstrate just how context-specific meaning making is. In another explicit poetic statement, Williams explains,

> That which is heard from the lips of those to whom we are talking in our day's affairs mingles with what we see in the streets and everywhere about us as it mingles also with our imaginations. By this chemistry is fabricated a language of the day which shifts and reveals its meaning as clouds shift and turn in the sky and sometimes send down rain or snow or hail.

(59)

The mutability of the clouds and the open possibility of what form of precipitation they might send to Earth demonstrate the contextually constructed and contingent nature of the meanings contained in **"Kora."** In engaging the language of the everyday, then, Williams takes a pragmatic step away from perceiving and articulating phenomena as metaphysical ontologies and instead finds significant meaning in phenomena through a perspectival (and therefore pragmatic) empiricism.

In addition to employing everyday language, Williams manifests this perspectival empiricism by creating a text of description as opposed to explanation.[13] To attempt to provide an explanation of an event or object is to try vainly to achieve an ontological knowledge as opposed to an empirical knowledge of the phenomenological world. Explanation makes claims to necessary causality, truth and falsehood, and foundational modes of justification. However, if the thing is sufficient to itself in a non-essential way, explanation's attempts to legitimate necessarily the value of the phenomenon will inevitably fail. Wittgenstein deconstructs the distinction between explanation and description in the *Tractatus* where he writes, "Objects can only be *named*. Signs are their representatives. I can only speak *about* them: I cannot *put them into words*. Propositions can only say *how* things are, not *what* they are" (3.221). The distinction that Wittgenstein makes between "how" and "what" is the difference between a phenomenological and an ontological interrogation of the world. The "how" accommodates contingency by focusing on the use and context of the phenomenon whereas the "what" desperately chases after a necessary fixity in which all phenomena have a stable and final place in the world. We again see Wittgenstein emphasizing action and use over ontology when in *Philosophical Investigations* he writes, "Our mistake is to look for an explanation where we ought to look at what happens as a 'protophenomenon.' That is, where we ought to have said: *this language-game is played*" (654). Since the phenomenon is limited by perspective and can only be known to the perceiver, language becomes the only means of access we have to gaining knowledge of the object. Wittgenstein, therefore, also allows us to move beyond the phenomenological vs. ontological distinction into a linguistic vs. ontological distinction. In other words, ultimately the only access we have to phenomena is through the language that we use to understand them. Therefore to focus on the action and use of the phenomenon is actually to highlight the action or use (grammar) of the language itself. "If we construe the grammar of the expression of sensation on the model 'object and designation' the object drops out of consideration as irrelevant" (*PI* 293), since all that remains actually *communicable* is the linguistic designation. The loss of the object and maintenance of the designation is tantamount to a shift from the phenomenological to the linguistic or grammatical realms of understanding.

Similarly, the relationship between the descriptive, expository, above-the-line sections and the interpretive, explanatory, below-the-line sections of **"Kora in Hell"** causes the object, the phenomenal content of the poem that Williams perceives and apprehends, to drop out so that only the imaginative and linguistic remain. What Williams asserts as a poem followed by an interpretation quickly becomes all one poem. As Christopher MacGowan points out, "There is no constant relationship between the two kinds of passage that would permit a conclusive summary" (58). The first section of chapter V enacts this dropping out of the phenomenal realm as the interpretive section claims, "So to accept it [remorse] is to attempt to fit the emotions of a certain state to a preceding state to which they are in no way related" (38-39). This attempt at relating two disparate states of meaning is precisely what the divided format of each section entails (i.e., the passage describes what happens when we attempt to explain or interpret). This statement about interpretation that comes in the interpretation renders the interpretation contingent on its own interpretation of itself. In other words, if the interpretation of a passage tells us that to interpret is to attempt vainly to fit two unrelated states together, then the interpretation deconstructs itself, fails to provide a meaningful interpretation of the first, descriptive passage, and thereby leaves the imaginative and the linguistic as our only recourse to meaning. Williams seems to reach the same conclusion as the passage ends by asserting, "Imagination though it cannot wipe out the sting of remorse can instruct the mind in its proper uses" (39).

And so, the phenomena having fallen out, description in language remains. Wittgenstein sums up our present position by stating, "We must do away with all explanation, and description alone must take its place. And this description gets its light, that is to say its purpose, from the philosophical problems. These are, of course, not empirical [phenomenological] problems [anymore]; they are solved, rather, by looking into the workings of our language" (*PI* 109). Williams' attempts to look "into the workings of our language" are constituted by his conceding of control to the workings of his imagination, and writing descriptively facilitates his investigation. Although there is little to be gained from explanation, the descriptive portrayal of phenomena allows for their recasting in language to provide the impetus to a new world, or to what Wittgenstein would call a new "form of life."[14] We can see this happening in the section in which Williams describes two corpses: "The frontispiece is her portrait and further on—the obituary sermon: she held the school upon her shoulders. Did she. Well—turn in here then:—we found money in the blood and some in the room on the stairs . . . and thirteen empty whiskey bottles" (37). The scenes have been translated into descriptive language without onto-logically aimed explanation, thereby allowing the phenomenal world to be remade into a new form of life. Just as the dead woman and man will journey on to a new form of (after)life, the transformation of the phenomenal into the linguistic accomplishes a similar task because the linguistic, being contingent on the perspectival, will necessarily withhold meaning. Wil-liams, then, seems to realize that description permits the multiplication of meaning and therefore more accurately "portrays" the nature of phenomena and language whereas explanation shuts down possibilities of mean-ing making.

One way that description is able to accentuate the condi-tions of possibility of language is through the necessary forward motion it brings to language. Explanatory language is equivalent to the attempt to make a rule, but rules need prior explanations to justify the present explanation. Thus the extent to which doubt can enter into an explanation is the extent to which we must look anterior to the present explanation to seek its justifica-tion. This infinite regress of possible explanations undermines our ability to find purpose or meaning in explanation whereas a description, which Wittgenstein describes as "a representation of a distribution in space" (*PI* 187), does not seek justification in anterior descrip-tions but in the contextualized use of the language in the present. It is easy to overlook the diverse functions of any given word since all words are created out of the same materials and any given word with multiple func-tions looks and sounds the same as the functions vary. Nevertheless, "the meaning of a word is its use in the language" (*PI* 43) so that "In saying 'When I heard this word, it meant . . . to me' one refers to a *point of time* [occasion] and to a *way of using the word*" (*PI* 175). Deriving meaning from occasion and use demonstrates recognition of the contingency of both language and the phenomena that it attempts to describe. Explanation wants to assert that something had to happen the way it did whereas description acknowledges that there are many other ways that what happened could have hap-pened (*Culture and Value*, 37).

"Kora in Hell" is filled with these instances of contingent openness in which an event could happen in various ways—like when Williams is driving through the country to a woman's house. "Ah there's the house at last, here's April, but—the blinds are down! It's all dark here. Scratch a hurried note. Slip it over the sill. Well, some other time" (37). Not only does the event Williams describes gain its meaning from the condi-tions of the occasion, but the language itself makes dif-ferent meanings depending on what function we give to "April"—month or woman? A passage in chapter X also enacts this variability achieved from the multiple

uses of language. Williams is describing a scene in a house that immediately changes upon the introduction of the *double entendre* which acts as a point of bifurca-tion from which an event and its meanings can move in various directions: "Really there's little more to say than: flowers in a glass basket under the electric glare; the carpet is red, mostly, a hodge-podge of zig-zags that pass for Persian fancies. Risk a *double entendre*. But of a sudden the room's not the same!" (49). Williams demonstrates a poetics of whim that proceeds by "will-o'-the-wisp" and that remains perpetually open to alternate motions and meanings—value is assigned ac-cording to what appears "to be most appropriate to the occasion" (50). Williams introduces this notion of con-textualized use in the opening pages of **"Kora"** as he states, "[H]ere is penny-royal if one knows to use it" (31). We can read this as Williams offering us his prose poem in all its multiple uses just as penny-royal is a type of mint but is also used in herbal medicines to drive away mosquitoes and as an herbal inducer of abor-tions. Williams reiterates this focus on use-value in the next section where he tells us that he "would rather feed pigs in Moonachie and chew calamus root and break crab's claws at an open fire" than possess "a closet full of clothes and good shoes and my-thirty-year's-master's-daughter's two cows for me to care for and a winter room with a fire in it" (31). He would rather live and interact with the fire than simply own it, and the descriptive, contextualized engagement with everyday language and events that Williams pursues throughout **"Kora"** permit him to create a new world in which he can actively "chew calamus root and break crab's claws at an open fire," for "to imagine a language means to imagine a form of life" (*PI* 19).

Having gone from perception to apprehension to articulation, attempting to solve some of the problemat-ics of the treatment and representation of the phenom-enal world, we have come to the brink of a new world, a world constituted by language.[15] If the phenomenal world has always actually been a contingently created linguistic world, then it becomes possible to engage in new world-making projects through our subsumption in language; **"Kora in Hell"** represents one such project. If "[t]*he limits of my language* mean the limits of my world" since "[w]e cannot think what we cannot think; so what we cannot think we cannot *say* either," then the expansion and imaginative re-creation of the limits of language will precipitate the creation of new conditions of possibility for the world (*Tractatus* 5.6, 5.62).[16] Wil-liams' poetry, then, discovers the limits of language and therefore of our knowable reality while simultaneously challenging those limits and constituting new ones. In *On Certainty* Wittgenstein dismisses traditional notions of truth by defining truth simply as the limit of one's present understanding: "80. The truth of my statements is the test of my understanding of these statements. 81. That is to say: if I make certain false statements, it becomes uncertain whether I understand them. . . . 83. The truth of certain empirical propositions belongs to our frame of reference" (12e). Knowledge becomes coterminous with one's capacity to articulate that knowledge which is in turn coterminous with one's frame of reference.

Williams' task of expanding our frame of reference is an explicitly linguistic one. As he states in a gloss hidden in the prologue, "By action itself almost nothing can be imparted" since "[t]he world of actions is a world of stones" (16). Although action, a primary facet of the phenomenal world, does not constitute meaning, language, which does constitute meaning, can create new versions of action. Consequently, Williams does not disavow the usefulness of the active, but he incorporates it into the linguistic by transforming it into a metaphor for language's world making capability. In other words, the actions that constitute the content of **"Kora in Hell"** are not actual actions but are instead metaphors for linguistic action. We see this enacted in a passage already discussed: "Then how will you expect a fine trickle of words to follow you through the intimacies of this dance without—oh, come let us walk together into the air awhile first" (34). Williams seems to be privileging integrated action between humans and nature at the expense of words that can only inadequately perform such tasks; but ironically, the invitation to interact with nature is only possible because of the conditions of possibility of his language. Here, to walk into the air is to venture into a new realm where language has yet to tread but where it will be able to adapt and forge new meaning. "The poet should be forever at the ship's prow" to open new doors and "break with banality" (28). Williams' vision clearly exceeds any merely objective representation of things themselves. In fact, it is such objectivism (moldiness) that **"Kora in Hell"**'s dance attempts to leave behind. Such is the message of passages like, "Yes, reading shows reading. What you read is what they think and what they think is twenty years old or twenty thousand and it's all one to the little girl in the *pissoir.* Likewise to me" (61) and "the bitter tongue of an old woman is eating, eating, eating venomous words with thirty years' mould on them and all shall be eaten back to honeymoon's end" (62).

This moldiness and ossification, however, can be counteracted by the creative act of a poetry that recognizes the contingency and use-value of language. The poetic act, figured as weaving in the passage mentioned above, is able to recreate a world that has been staled by convention, habit, and a loss of perspective. Through language and its mutable limits, Williams is able to "put the flower back into the stem" and "win roses upon dead briars" (62). Elsewhere the obstacles of the phenomenal world are overcome by Williams' imaginative use of language that provides alternative perspectives of the circumstances of existence. In chapter XX, for instance, Williams presents two obstacles, a wall that cannot be climbed and clouds that cannot be grasped. Portraying the occasion in language, however, enacts a "scene shifting that has clipped the clouds' stems and left them to flutter down; heaped them at the feet" so that "you cannot deny you have the clouds to grasp now, *mon ami!*" and "[t]he wall's clipped off too, only its roots are left" (69). These poetic acts of world making mitigate the dilemma that began our investigation and that seems to begin Williams' own investigations of his world—how best to represent the objects of the phenomenal world. In a way, the very act of representing becomes the answer to understanding what happens during the move from perception to articulation (i.e., even perception is an act of articulation). Or, as mentioned in an above footnote, being always already in a realm of articulation, questions of representation become unhelpful and thus drop out of our inquiry.

Although expanding these frames of reference does a greater justice to the nature of language and to our relationship with and understanding of the world, the imaginative shift into the linguistic world performs a necessary violence to the empirical realm of the senses. The imagination is able to swirl the leaves together into a dance of new poetic meaning, but the leaves must first be ripped from their branches.[17] As Joswick points out, "The way to 'beginnings' demands a destructive descent through the forms and structures that bind words to referents in literature" (112). This violent descent provides another valence of meaning to **"Kora in Hell,"** rendering Kora as a contingent mode of aesthetic world-creating that the poet must rescue from the trappings of a hell that adamantly subscribes to a correspondence theory of truth. The loss of this truth is tantamount to the loss of the world: "Rich as are the gifts of the imagination bitterness of world's loss is not replaced thereby." Ultimately, however, the imagination, the ability to articulate the world in contingent language, mitigates the loss to the extent that we cannot even know the loss of the world without the imagination (i.e., language precedes and constitutes our ability to gain knowledge of the world anyway). As Williams claims, "[T]o weigh a difficulty and to turn it aside without being wrecked upon a destructive solution bespeaks an imagination of force sufficient to transcend action. The difficulty has thus been solved by ascent to a higher plane. It is energy of the imagination alone that cannot be laid aside" (18). The phenomenal objects fall out, and all that remains is the imaginative use of language. This point is reiterated later when Williams portrays the violence immanent in imaginative meaning through the image of "All beauty [that] stands upon the edge of the deflowering" (as all trees stand on the edge of de-leafing?). He admits to performing such violence to the sensory world as he states, "I confess I wish my wife younger," but remains unabashed in his violence by responding to those who criticize him for having lewd and unchaste thoughts by quipping, "You'll say this has nothing in it of chastity. Ah well, chastity is a lily of the valley that only a fool would mock" (59).

Having confronted the loss of the world that is entailed by abandoning oneself to a world entirely imaginative and linguistic, Williams is able to create a poetry that is a new "form of life." As he recounts in *Spring and All,* the method to the madness of **"Kora"** was "to let the imagination have its own way to see if it could save itself" (116). Indeed, it seems that the imagination does save itself by proving its ability to constitute a new frame of reference with new and expanded limits of meaning making capability.

What **"Kora in Hell"** finally offers us is a new way of seeing, a form of life radically more linguistic and imaginative than the phenomenal world that it purports to represent. As Wittgenstein remarks in *Philosophical Investigations,* when we "have a new conception and interpret it as seeing a new object," what we have really "discovered is a new way of looking at things. As if [we] had invented a new way of painting; or, again, a new metre, or a new kind of song" (401). Whether or not we can fit the content of our own perception into Williams' new way of seeing is irrelevant—**"Kora"** does not attempt to comment on what we see, but rather on how we can see in new and imaginative ways. Williams' prose poem makes it possible for us to see like the baby in the beginning of chapter XXII whose "[e]yes open" and "[h]ere's a new world" (73). In his study of prose poetry, Stephen Fredman claims that **"Kora in Hell"** presents a wholeness that is not completeness (38). The poem as a form of life, then, constitutes a wholeness that simultaneously acknowledges its incompleteness (the possibility for mistakes and contingencies and other forms of life) while still remaining sufficient to itself. Although this self-sufficiency represents an anti-foundational mode of value formation, that same sufficiency will also lead to **"Kora in Hell"**'s new form of life becoming conventionalized and routine like the form of life that **"Kora"** wants to subvert. This is because the form of life is also and primarily, simply reality; "[w]hat has to be accepted, the given, is—so one could say—*forms of life*" (*PI* 226). And although he sets up **"Kora"**'s new form of life to stagnate into new habits and conventions, Williams approves of the new form of life functioning as the given, as he asserts in *Spring and All* that works of art "must be real, not 'realism' but reality itself" (117). Despite an impending ossification, however, by moving us from one given and assumed reality to another Williams has exposed the scaffolding of our world and proven that, through language, we can imaginatively construct it as we will.

Notes

1. The concept "form of life" comes from Wittgenstein's later philosophy and is given various meanings throughout his writings. Perhaps its most important aspect (and the way I am using it here) refers to the apparent transparency between what we consider reality or life and those linguistic constructions with their arbitrary rules that constitute that reality or life. A language-game is a form of life, but to speak of it as a language-game is to be conscious of its arbitrary constructs whereas to speak of it as a form of life is to imply that we generally act in our language games unself-consciously, as if we were simply living.

2. Roy Miki's book length study of "Kora" entitled *The Prepoetics of William Carlos Williams: Kora in Hell,* manages to avoid the drive towards the metaphysical that seems to motivate many other "Kora" critics. His tendency to ground his argument in Williams' autobiography in order to find correspondences between the crises of his personal life and the crises of language manifest in the poetry, however, leads him to overemphasize the "hermetic" and "private" nature of "Kora" in a way that undermines our ability to ascribe any significant meaning to the language itself.

3. Unless otherwise noted, citations from *Philosophical Investigations* refer to the item number (the first half of Wittgenstein's text is an enumerated list of philosophical thoughts) and not to the page number.

4. The obvious Wittgensteinian rebuttal to these claims might ask, "How is it possible to have knowledge of that which cannot be articulated (either mentally or vocally) in language?" This point will enter into my later discussion of articulating the phenomenal world.

5. One of the integral features of Wittgenstein's notion of the "language-game" is that specific rules of the game provide the participant with criteria of action and meaning making that allow her to make sense of the language. It is only because our language-games function according to such rules that we can assert that something is "right" or "correct."

6. Unless otherwise noted, all italics appearing in quotations are those of the author quoted.

7. To point to either the external or to the internal is to maintain the distinction between the phenomenon and its context. I want to erase that distinction and argue that context is actually all that is available in our attempts at justifying meaning.

8. To avoid implying a causal dependence between reality and perspective, I am careful, here, not to say that reality is *determined* by perspective. To

do so would be to subscribe to a representational-ist understanding of the world that would maintain an ability to look at each thing (reality and perspective) independently. (This is also why arguments for a relativistic reality are inaccurate since to be relative something must be in relation to another thing, and that relation would belie the point that calling reality relative is trying to make.) Richard Rorty splits these hairs well in *Objectivity, Relativism, and Truth* where he explains that "[t]he problem for antirepresentationalists [e.g., Wittgenstein] is to find a way of putting their point which carries no such suggestion [of causal dependence]. Antirepresentationalists need to insist that 'determinacy' is not what is in question—that neither does thought determine reality, nor, in the sense intended by the realist, does reality determine thought" (5). I am attempting to make a similar claim, arguing a coequality or always already-ness of reality and perspective, (later of reality and language) rather than a causality.

9. Like *Philosophical Investigations*, Wittgenstein's *Tractatus Logico-Philosophicus* is a list of philosophical propositions. All citations from the *Tractatus* will list the item number and not the page number.

10. Significantly, this is precisely the model that Saussure provides for understanding how language makes meaning (i.e., "cat" only means "cat" because it does not mean "cot").

11. Describing this as "Hell" provides another, more figurative meaning to the title, "Kora in Hell." We could thus make the claim that the prose poem is about being trapped in a world bereft of adequate tools for meaning making.

12. Hatlen uses this phrase to describe Zukofsky's poetics and ascribes the opposite, the "poetics of presence," to Williams in a deprecating way. Hatlen's theories are interesting, but I believe he misreads Williams' poetry. Consequently, I am applying the term he uses for Zukofsky to Williams despite the fact that Hatlen uses it against Williams.

13. As with the poetic vs. ordinary language distinction, I acknowledge that the dichotomy exists for some critics. I will argue, however, that just as the previous distinction was spurious, Williams and Wittgenstein show this one to be as well.

14. A fuller discussion of the world-making capacity of Williams' poetry and Wittgenstein's notion of "form of life" will conclude the paper.

15. The trajectory that I have followed, from the world of the phenomenal object, through its perception, apprehension, and articulation, has moved us into a linguistic world. Of course, Wittgenstein would argue that we are always already in a linguistic world, and this paper agrees. For the purposes of demonstrating that, however, I have started with the phenomenal because that is where Williams begins despite the fact that "Kora in Hell" is an example of the linguistic world that we always already inhabit. In other words, I started speaking of phenomena so as to prove that all we can really do is *speak* of phenomena.

16. It is important to note that to speak of the world here is not to speak of physical properties but to speak of the meaning we make and the knowledge we obtain of the world. Language does not constitute the physical properties of reality but does constitute our ability to understand and speak about those physical properties. Thus, creating a new world through language would be more accurately described as opening up the conditions of possibility for describing the world which in turn allows us to understand the world in new ways. So to the extent that our linguistic understanding of the world constitutes our world, new modes of understanding create new worlds.

17. The image of the swirling leaves also makes the shift from the phenomenological into the linguistic tantamount to a shift from the organic to the inorganic. Remember, however, that this is not a shift as much as a recognition of the always already linguistic and inorganic.

Works Cited

de Saussure, Ferdinand. "Selections from 'The Course in General Linguistics'." *The Continental Philosophy Reader.* Ed. Richard Kearney and Mara Rainwater. London: Routledge, 1996.

Dijkstra, Bram. *The Hieroglyphics of a New Speech: Cubism, Stieglitz, and the Early Poetry of William Carlos Williams.* Princeton: Princeton UP, 1969.

Fredman, Stephen. *Poet's Prose: The Crisis in American Verse.* Cambridge: Cambridge UP, 1983.

Ginsberg, Allen. *Howl: and other Poems.* San Francisco: City Lights Books, 1959.

Green, Jesse D. "Williams' *Kora in Hell*: The Opening of the Poem as 'Field of Action'." *Contemporary Literature* 13 (1972): 295-314.

Hatlen, Burton. "Zukofsky, Wittgenstein, and the Poetics of Absence." *Sagetrieb* 1.1 (1982): 63-93.

Hargreaves, Frederic K., Jr. "The Concept of Private Meaning in Modern Criticism." *Critical Inquiry* 7 (1981): 727-46.

Joswick, Thomas P. "Beginning with Loss: The Poetics of William Carlos Williams's *Kora in Hell: Improvisations*." *Texas Studies in Literature and Language* 19 (1977): 98-118.

Loewinsohn, Ron. "'Fools have big wombs': William Carlos Williams' *Kora in Hell*." *Essays in Literature* 4.1 (1977): 221-37.

MacGowan, Christopher. *William Carlos Williams's Early Poetry: The Visual Arts Background*. Ann Arbor: UMI Research Press, 1984.

Miki, Roy. *The Prepoetics of William Carlos Williams: Kora in Hell*. Ann Arbor: UMI Research Press, 1983.

Owens, Craig. "From 'The Allegorical Impulse: Towards a Theory of Postmodernism'." *Art in Theory, 1900-1990: An Anthology of Changing Ideas*. Ed. Charles Harrison and Paul Wood. Oxford: Blackwell Publishers, 1992. 1051-60.

Perloff, Marjorie. *The Poetics of Indeterminacy: Rimbaud to Cage*. Chicago: Northwestern UP, 1983.

———. *Wittgenstein's Ladder: Poetic Language and the Strangeness of the Ordinary*. Chicago: The U of Chicago P, 1996.

Rorty, Richard. *Contingency, Irony, and Solidarity*. Cambridge: Cambridge UP, 1989.

———. *Objectivity, Relativism, and Truth*. Cambridge: Cambridge UP, 1991.

Schulte, Joachim. *Wittgenstein: An Introduction*. Trans. William H. Brenner and John F. Holley. Albany: State UP of New York, 1992.

Slate, Joseph Evans. "Kora in Opacity: Williams' *Improvisations*." *Journal of Modern Literature* 1 (1971): 463-76.

Tapscott, Stephen. *American Beauty: William Carlos Williams and the Modernist Whitman*. New York: Columbia UP, 1984.

Williams, William Carlos. "Kora in Hell: Improvisations." *Imaginations*. Ed. Webster Schott. New York: New Directions, 1970.

———. "Spring and All." *Imaginations*. Ed. Webster Schott. New York: New Directions, 1970.

Wittgenstein, Ludwig. *The Blue and the Brown Books*. New York: Harper & Row, 1960.

———. *Culture and Value*. 2nd ed. Ed. G. H. von Wright and Heikki Nyman. Trans. Peter Winch. Chicago: U of Chicago P, 1980.

———. *On Certainty*. Ed. G. E. M. Anscombe and G. H. von Wright. Trans. Denis Paul and G. E. M. Anscombe. New York: Harper & Row, 1969.

———. *Philosophical Investigations*. Trans. G. E. M. Anscombe. New York: MacMillan, 1968.

———. *Tractatus Logico-Philosophicus*. Trans. D. F. Pears and B. F. McGuinness. New Jersey: The Humanities Press, 1974.

Miriam Marty Clark (essay date fall 2004)

SOURCE: Clark, Miriam Marty. "Art and Suffering in Two Late Poems by William Carlos Williams." *Literature and Medicine* 23, no. 2 (fall 2004): 226-40.

[*In the following essay, Clark discusses the themes of suffering and the liberatory power of art in Williams's poetry, focusing on the later poems "To a Dog Injured in the Street" and "The Yellow Flower."*]

> What is the work a cure for? (All works are "medicine." Otherwise, why bother to write them?)
>
> Kenneth Burke to William Carlos Williams, 9 June 1953, *The Humane Particulars, The Collected Letters of William Carlos Williams and Kenneth Burke*

To the end of his life, William Carlos Williams's writing is informed by the erudite touch and the epistemological stance of the doctor.[1] But bodily suffering provokes a complicated response, one that troubles the interface, sometimes incorrectly characterized as seamless, between Williams's two vocations and disrupts the interpenetration of the "inner world of the subject" and the "outer world of things" that J. Hillis Miller sees as both the method and the accomplishment of the poems.[2] My subject in this essay is two poems written in the aftermath of the disabling strokes Williams suffered in 1951 and 1952. I want to look closely at the way these poems, **"To a Dog Injured in the Street"** and **"The Yellow Flower,"** struggle under the burdens of illness and old age to make sense of suffering and to reconcile it with the aims and measures of art. I begin, though, by situating them in an extended consideration of human suffering, ethical responsibility, and poetic will, one strand of the doctor's story as it develops over half a century from early poems like **"Sick African"** (1917)—where the poet stands apart from the patient and his illness as he might stand back in contemplation of a painting—through the morally and aesthetically ambitious poems of his midcareer and finally to the moving poems that follow Williams's own descent into illness.

Suffering in others generates a range of reactions in Williams, from profound compassion to detached curiosity to harsh impatience and cold fury. These responses and the self-scrutiny that attends them— "almost Augustinian" Robert Coles calls it—form one strand of the doctor-poet's story over a long career.[3] A second strand, also very familiar to Williams's readers, is diagnostic. His interpretation of symptoms is broad based and far reaching, beginning in medical knowledge and linguistic attunement but extending to include psychological, economic, and political reasoning, effacing disciplinary boundaries in order to comprehend and address the causes of illness and suffering.

Kenneth Burke, Williams's friend and interlocutor for more than forty years, describes him as a "benignly nosological" poet whose diagnostic skill informs both his medical and his poetic practice.[4] Williams's mind is defined, for Burke, by its power to move between a "professional concern with the body as a suffering or diseased object" and a "natural or poetic"—even a sexual—interest in the body (284). "[H]e could," Burke observes, "both use flowers as an image of lovely womanhood and speak of pathology as a 'flower garden.' The principle made for great mobility, for constant transformations. . . . [H]e proceeded circumstantially, without intellectualistic shortcuts—and with the combined conscientiousness of both disciplines, as man of medicine and medicine man" (282). Burke stresses the continuities the poems establish between inner, private experience and the external world of communication and action. Poetry, like doctoring, is dialogic as stories are told, desires articulated, suffering expressed (however indirectly) on the one side, attention paid, diagnoses ventured, treatment proffered on the other. Words have—in proportion to their diagnostic accuracy—*medicinal* powers to remedy both individual suffering and collective woes.[5] Williams's doctoring is not only humane, as Burke points out, but also comprehensive and deeply imaginative in a world where art, like medicine, has the power to cure.

Indispensable as Burke's way of reading is to an understanding of Williams's poetry, its immediate effect is to naturalize the relationship between the body and language, between what Burke calls "animal" motives—including pain, hunger, and physical danger—and the symbolic operations of art.[6] Burke observes, for instance, that Williams's "stress upon the all-importance of the bodily element accounts also for the many cruel references to subsidence that are scattered through *The Collected Later Poems*" (284). Burke's term "subsidence"—not a euphemism but a way of reading—focuses attention not on the unspeakability of loss and death but on their enmeshment in symbolic systems: dead trees cut for firewood, Burke points out, are linked to fire, signifying "lust at heart"; purgation is paired with promise, rot with life and greening (285).[7]

But even in its subtlest tropes and its most far-reaching constructions of the imagination, Williams's poetry retains a sense of the body and its afflictions as things that cannot be assimilated or fully addressed in art. Suffering commonly enters the poems as interruption. A voice—not the doctor's—interrupts and vies for ownership of the language of distress and pain in poems like **"A Cold Front"** (1944) or **"The Raper from Passenack"** (1935). Or a presence interrupts the progress of a text. **"To Elsie"** (1923) addresses a fifteen-year-old girl removed by the state from her troubled home and sent "to work in / some hard-pressed / house in the suburbs—/ some doctor's family."[8] Seductive as she is disturbing to the speaker of the poem, Elsie *embodies* the debasement of her native community (through isolation, incest, and disease) as well as its lingering, danger-

ous vitality. Her wordless presence halts for a moment the relentless processes of American modernization and the confident advance of William's modernist project in *Spring and All,* where the poem first appears. Elsewhere, too, a face, a gesture, an uttered need, a bitter outpouring mark the nearness and the distress of other people. Such textual interruptions begin in and echo the incessant interruptions that characterize Williams's life as a doctor. "Someday! Someday! we'll be free," he writes to Burke in the fall of 1945, "no babies will be being born, no one will have a cold, no one will have miscarriages—there will be no committee meetings or clinical conferences."[9]

These poetic interruptions go broadly to issues of power—medical, authorial, male—but I want to argue here that they make a more specific challenge to the adequacy of the doctor-poet's diagnostic terms and to the usefulness of both art and medicine as responses to the deepest forms of human suffering. The measures by which Williams attends to them constitute both a verbal strategy and an ethical stance, one of attunement, responsiveness, what Stanley Cavell calls "inhabitation."[10] The poems admit, acknowledge, at times seem to accede altogether to these claims and presences. The rape victim in **"The Raper from Passenack,"** seizes command of the poem, for example, correcting the doctor's bemused sympathy in her own furious and dismayed account of what has happened. She notes bitterly that medicine cannot (in 1935) cure the thing she fears most, syphilis: "I'd rather a million times / have been got pregnant," she tells the doctor. "But it's the foulness of it can't / be cured" (1:386-7, 35-8). But if many poems move like this one to accommodate and give voice to human distress, in other moments (the apostrophe that interrupts the opening section of *Spring and All,* for instance) the very fact of suffering rebukes the imagination and repudiates art's claims to power even as, in much more mundane ways, suffering patients devour the hours and days that might be spent writing.[11]

And so a more difficult third strand in the doctor-poet's story arises where language and art prove inadequate to acute suffering and trauma. Edith Wyschogrod, writing about recent discourses of the body, observes that "the pain and death to which bodies are subject remain an *hors texte,* an unsurpassable negation both inside and outside the field of meaning."[12] This third strand addresses the encounter between the vulnerable body, standing doggedly outside the text and the world-making enterprise of modern language, the work of modern poetry as Williams invents and practices it. In its susceptibility to pain, sickness, aging, and death, the body vexes the poet's will to transform it through language, to attend to it by listening, and to remedy it through art. In its suffering, the body refuses mediation into object, image, discourse, or narrative. "Natural concerns"—Burke's term (284)—do not always merge smoothly into poetic ones; pathology will not, for the patient, become a flower garden.

The poems that are my subject were written within a few months after the second of the devastating strokes Williams suffered in the early 1950s. Even as those living with illnesses like cancer and AIDS have gained a voice in recent literary texts, the survivors of strokes remain mostly silent, as often for bodily reasons (aphasia, paralysis) as for social ones (stigma, misunderstanding).[13] In a poem called "Phone Call to Rutherford," Paul Blackburn recalls a conversation with Williams not long before his death in 1963. Williams discourages a visit from Blackburn, telling him,

        "I have dif-fi   /   culty
                        speaking, I
        cannot count on it, I
        am afraid it would be too em-
                        ba
                        rass-ing
        for me   ."

"Bill, can you still / answer letters?" Blackburn asks. "No." Williams tells him, "my hands / are tongue-tied."[14]

The poems of Williams's final decade, darkened and deepened by illness, seem worthy of close attention in part for his refusal to fall silent in spite of those "tongue-tied" hands and in the face of very substantial physical disabilities. Biographer Paul Mariani has traced the events of Williams's life in the early fifties in some detail, describing the impact of the strokes, the incapacitating depression that followed the second one, the new sense of mortality that suffuses the volumes published during that time, *The Desert Music* and *Journey to Love,* and Williams's fierce determination, despite the insult to "mind and eye and tongue" to continue his work as a poet.[15] My interest here, however, is less in the remarkable and affecting persistence of Williams's powers through suffering than in the force of his engagement, his extended negotiation *in art* of the private trauma of illness.

Cut close to bone and nerve, these poems, **"To a Dog Injured in the Street"** and **"The Yellow Flower,"** measure more fully than any of Williams's earlier work the destructive power of pain. Even as the strokes forced his full retirement from the practice of medicine, they press the question of whether art can cure or ease. "Man alone / is that creature who / cannot escape suffering / by flight," Williams writes in **"For Eleanor and Bill Monahan"** (2:253, 34-7). What, if anything, art holds out against the inescapable is the question that drives these poems.

Elaine Scarry's now classic study, *The Body in Pain,* offers, I want to suggest, some illumination of these texts and helps to explain the forcefulness of their address to suffering and to the threat of erasure represented for Williams by the combination of his strokes and the atomic bomb. I will turn to the poems in more particular ways in just a moment, but I want to begin by marking very briefly some common features. To begin with, both of the poems are situated on the boundary between interior and exterior worlds, observing closely that moment when pain is projected *from* an interior, private space where language is ruined and voice deconstructed by suffering *into* the public, communicative space of the text. If, for the poet, projection comes ultimately to the search for a language and a rhetoric adequate to pain, it begins in the encounter of human vulnerability with the "naturally existing external world" which is immune, inanimate, inhuman, indifferent, "ignorant," Scarry writes, "of the 'hurtability' of human beings."[16] In the "phenomenon of projection," she argues, "part of the work of creating [is] *to deprive the external world of the privilege of being inanimate*" (285, Scarry's italics). The human imagination, she continues, "reconceives the external world, divesting it of its immunity and irresponsibility not by literally putting it in pain or making it animate but by, quite *literally, 'making it' as knowledgeable about human pain as if it were itself animate and in pain*" (288-9, Scarry's italics). The natural images of these late poems, particularly the images of flowers, document this encounter and are transformed through their proximity to suffering; this is not a new strategy for Williams—it goes back at least as far as **"The Widow's Lament in Springtime"** (1921)—but the distribution of pain and privation into natural images takes on new significance and force through these two books.

Second, these poems reverse the process by which real pain is converted into fictions of power. The making of power out of pain is an essential feature of torture and certain kinds of war in Scarry's analysis; in their reversal—the deconstruction of the fictions of power into expressions of pain—Williams's late poems also involve a reversal of what happens thirty years earlier in *Spring and All,* its achievement of aesthetic freedom and modernist power through the repudiation of human suffering. Third, the poems enact the transformation of body into voice by which, in Scarry's analysis, pain is translated into power, for "power," she observes, "is in its fraudulent as in its legitimate forms always based on distance from the body" (46).

"It is myself," Williams writes at the beginning of **"To a Dog Injured in the Street,"**

        not the poor beast lying there
                yelping with pain
        that brings me to myself with a start—
                as at the explosion
                        of a bomb, a bomb that has laid
        all the world waste.

                                (2:255, 1-7)

Throughout this poem Williams projects suffering onto animals—the injured dog, another dog remembered from childhood, a rabbit. This is one way, a striking one, of divesting the external world of its immunity to pain. Vulnerable and without recourse to language, subject to carelessness, misunderstanding, and cruelty, animals provide a vivid metaphor for the human being under conditions of suffering. The fictions of power at stake here—signified by the car, the bomb, the ego, and the unrestrained will—are the same ones at work in earlier Williams, but in these late poems their power is founded on the suffering and losses of others. The accidental injury to a dog that causes the speaker of the poem pain echoes the willfully violent automotive fantasies of Williams's earlier texts—**"The Young Housewife"** (1916) where the woman is compared to a fallen leaf and the leaves are then crushed under the wheels of the speaker's car; the third prose section of **Spring and All,** where the marrow of children is gaily crushed under the wheels of heavy cars; and the uncontrolled car that serves as an image of American culture hurtling forward at the end of **"To Elsie."** The image of the bomb, too, echoes the world-destroying blasts of **Spring and All,** even as it recalls the real bombs of the Second World War. Here the illusion of power cannot be upheld, as it is in **Spring and All,** but disintegrates into inarticulate suffering—a yelp, a start, a near faint. All that can be maintained as the fictions of power retreat and falter is song itself—as the body becomes voice—set against the cries of the dumb beasts. "I can do nothing / but sing about it," Williams writes, "and so I am assuaged / from my pain" (2:255, 8-11).

Williams's return to boyhood in the second half of **"To a Dog Injured in the Street"** furthers the poem's address to powerlessness and pain. The boy's responses are bodily, not verbal; they are intuitive and sexually naïve, far from the medical and aesthetic stances that the adult doctor-poet brings to real world suffering. He kicks away nursing puppies in a mistaken effort to defend his English setter, Norma, from harm. That the dog has a name and "expressive eyes" (line 33) and that she is at some level his *responsibility* suggest her significant place in the domestic and ethical worlds the boy inhabits. He then recalls a second story, in which a hunter eviscerates a dead rabbit by thrusting a knife "up into the animal's private parts" (line 52).

We can trace a path that runs from the dumb animals through the prelinguistic gestures of the young boy and the euphemistic narrative of the older boy, which veils suffering and vulnerability (though not from the boy himself, who "almost fainted" [line 53]), and finally to the poet himself who transforms the cries of a dying dog into song. By its invocation of French Resistance poet René Char, however, the poem invites us to continue beyond this point. As I have already suggested,

Williams's poem takes its lodgings right at the boundary between private acuities and imaginative responses, between mute suffering and the imaginative acts—in this case, singing—that distribute human sentience and make it knowable. "What differentiates men and women from other creatures," Scarry writes,

> is neither the natural acuity of our sentience nor the natural frailty of the organic tissue in which it resides but instead the fact that ours is, to a vastly greater degree than that of any other animal, objectified in language and material objects and is thus fundamentally transformed to be communicable and endlessly sharable.

(255)

Williams's initial depiction of himself and his art verges on the comical. The suffering he sees is not human, after all, and it is not motivated by cruelty, only by a reckless or luckless car; moreover, his song is almost as helpless—and artless—as the dog's yelp. But the poem takes a more serious turn as he reflects on Char's achievement. For Char, suffering does not produce a poetry explicitly concerned with pain but brings him instead,

> to speak only of
> sedgy rivers,
> of daffodils and tulips
> whose roots they water,
> even to the free-flowing river
> that laves the rootlets
> of those sweet-scented flowers
> that people the
> milky
> way.

(2:256, 20-9)

For Scarry, the relationship of pain and imagination takes the shape of an arc, with the created object returning to the *"human site"* (307, Scarry's italics) to remake the makers, restoring what has been lost to pain. "[B]y means of the poem . . ." she writes, taking a verbal artifact as one of her examples, the poet "enters into and in some way alters the alive percipience of other persons" (307). In this arc, reciprocity entails not only a return to and a remaking of the self but an amplitude, created objects exceeding in number and in kind the distributed pain they respond to. A seamstress makes many coats, not all of them in response to an immediate need; a poet writes many poems, most at some distance from anguish and suffering. This abundance and variety—where pain and deprivation are sublimated—fund aesthetic pleasure. In other words, Scarry contends, pain and imagination give rise to beauty.

It is at this farther pitch of imagination that Williams situates Char. Close as Williams's own response lies to miseries, and local ones at that, Char writes with an ample beauty that seems remote from the terrible things he has seen and suffered. In this kind of writing, invention—perhaps Williams's oldest and most powerful virtue—is paired with moral and aesthetic courage. "Rene Char," he writes,

> you are a poet who believes
> in the power of beauty
> to right all wrongs
> I believe it also.
> With invention and courage
> we shall surpass
> the pitiful dumb beasts,
> let all men believe it,
> as you have taught me also
> to believe it.
>
> (2:257, 58-64)

Such writing is not for making new, the noble work of high modernism, but for an empowering transformation of the suffering body into voice. More extraordinary, by Williams's account, than his own projection onto the mute animals and stammering boys, the powerful beauty of Char's poems serves not simply to blot out suffering, as Williams's own songs do, but to restore justice. The fact that the word "believe" appears four times in three sentences gives this statement, the final one of the poem, both a creedal force and an incantatory power even as it extends and is answerable to the religious longings that run through the volumes of the early fifties.

But I want to follow Scarry's provocative argument one step further to argue that "believe" here functions not simply as a declaration of intellectual conviction or aesthetic affiliation but as the activity of "sustained imagining," which she describes as "the intensification of the body and the projection of its attributes outward onto a disembodied referent" (197), a "devoting [of] one's physical interior to something outside itself" (202). Williams's song, though less assured and still lingering at the scene of pain, shares with Char's poetry of free-flowing rivers and sweet-scented daffodils the activity of belief as it turns what has been felt and suffered into words.

The poem that follows this one in *The Desert Music,* "The Yellow Flower," is among Williams's frankest expressions of his late sorrow and of his confidence in the power of art, explored with new intensity in the face of his own suffering. It is equally striking as a meditation on the nature of creating, in Scarry's words, "the relation between body and image, body and belief, body and artifact" (179). Like **"To a Dog Injured in the Street," "The Yellow Flower"** attends closely to the boundary where private acuity becomes shareable as word and text. **"To a Dog Injured in the Street"** implies in its progress from dumb beast to surrealist poet a narrative of increasing expressive capability and ethical responsibility. Williams approaches the subject differently in this poem, depending on a striking series

of liminal metaphors: a window signifying the boundary of interior and exterior; an open mouth marking the boundary between the interior and exterior of the body and representing the human capacity to *project* from the interior into civilization; a receptive eye marking the same boundary as well as the capacity to *receive* and to be remade by images from the exterior; and hands that act as a tool extending the body's sentience and its powers into the world.

The body and its hidden content of human sentience—feelings of sadness, loss, immobility—are constructed in relation to four particular images in this poem. First, there is the image of the yellow flower, which evokes the uninflected, un*imagined* natural world and marks the poem's distance from it: "It is / a mustard flower / and not a mustard flower," he says of it (2:258, 18-20). Second, there is the image of the natural world—again signified by the yellow flower—transformed by human need and inventiveness. The flower is sacrilized, made the subject of worship ("men / sing secretly their hymns / of praise" [2:257, 12-3] to it), invested with supernatural power to transfix and to cure. The language of sacredness, no mere mythic gesture, points to the quality of belief at stake in acts of imagination, that turning of the inside out. Third, there is the image of an artifact, Michelangelo's *Slaves,* which is parallel to the poem as a made thing with power both to express and to address human suffering and at the same time subject to the poem's interrogation of the relation between the body's pain and the work of aesthetic making. Finally, there is the self speaking. This image is refracted into several: the radically deformed physical self mirrored by the window and likened to the crooked flower; the interior content of the self projected into and onto the yellow flower; and the self as maker conveyed in the "as if" comparison to Michelangelo, whose imaginative art is, as I have already noted, like Williams's own.

"What shall I say, because talk I must?" he begins,

> That I have found a cure
> for the sick?
> I have found no cure
> for the sick
> but this crooked flower
> which only to look upon
> all men
> are cured.
>
> (2:257, 1-9)

These opening lines of the poem register weariness and despair. The man of words has no zeal for talk; at the end of his career the doctor has discovered no cures. Later he notes that "my will" has "drained from me" (lines 34-5). The flower he gazes at is "crooked," "obscure," "deformed," "ungainly" (lines 17, 18, 22, 26) in ways that—seen through a glass, as he sees it—mirror the poet's stricken self. As expressions of his own physical suffering, the twisted petals and fleshy leaves both enthrall and torture him, just as his own physical presence had enthralled and thrilled him thirty-five years before in **"Danse Russe,"** where he danced "naked, grotesquely / before my mirror," admiring himself while others in his household slept (1:86-7, 8-9). For a moment in front of the window in which the image of flower stands side by side with his reflection, it is the only thing he can think or speak of.

But if the image tortures him, it also offers a cure; "only to look upon" the flower, he notes, "all men / are cured." The sickness he speaks of is marked by despair and paralysis. "I am sad," he writes, comparing himself to Michelangelo, "as he was sad / in his heroic mood" (2:259, 55-7). If Williams hears in Michelangelo's enduring dissatisfaction with his work an echo of his own sadness and anxiety, he also finds in Michelangelo's *Slaves* a second image for his own stricken, partially paralyzed body in the carved figures that seem to struggle to free themselves from imprisoning blocks of stone. Williams's desolation is audible, but at every point torture and paralysis are linked closely with freedom achieved through art. "I have eyes," he writes,

> that are made to see and if
> they see ruin for myself
> and all that I hold
> dear, they see
> also
> through the eyes
> and through the lips
> and tongue the power
> to free myself
> and speak of it, as
> Michelangelo through his hands
> had the same, if greater,
> power.
>
> (2:259, 60-73)

Art's emancipatory power, fervently embraced in *Spring and All,* confidently advanced in the poetry and prose of the thirties and forties, returns finally to the poet himself to liberate him from enslavement in a damaged body and a despairing spirit. The force and eloquence of these lines bear witness to this liberation, which emerges from crookedness and deformity to free the enthralled and enslaved speaker through a reassertion of art's power, and his own.

The image of the poet with an open mouth—in a stance of belief and imaginative projection—is a striking emblem of this power. The lips and tongue are able to free him by giving voice, becoming voice. But in this culminating moment the poem also seems in danger of folding inward, retreating to the plane geometry of the arc, accepting the artifact as a perfect inversion of pain. Such a danger is implicit in Scarry's argument, as Geoffrey Galt Harpham has pointed out. Harpham notes in particular "the priority of the internal determinants of her thinking, the relation of concept to concept in her system, over the referential matching of descriptions to material facts."[17] He goes on to observe, "So rooted in the 'incontestable reality of the body' and its afflictions, *The Body in Pain* is actually more vitally concerned with language."[18] In this respect Scarry bears some similarity to Burke, whose own stake, as I have already suggested, is linguistic and conceptual; in Burke, suffering is construed as victimage and catharsis, death as mortification and transcendence. Williams, on the other hand, now both doctor and patient, writes through disability and against pain; the body reasserts itself—a troubling remainder—outside the conceptual structure the poem advances. "Which leaves, to account for," Williams writes, "the tortured bodies / of / the slaves themselves" (2:259, 74-7). Bodily pain and bodily enslavement stand as reference points against the powerful linguistic claims of the poem.

The other remainder is the crooked yellow flower, "not a mustard flower at all," Williams writes, "but some unrecognized / and unearthly flower" (2:259, 80-2). Unnamed, unnaturalized, the flower retains its mystery, refusing domestication into human narratives. Throughout Williams's writing flowers are associated with mythic Kore, the female principle and figure of the poet's desire. Kore's story—like the story of pain and imagining—is one of loss and renewal. But for Williams, Kore is an expansive figure, representing beauty, imagination, sexual energy, intellectual force, danger, knowledge, love itself. She is inscribed but never fully contained in the narrative of bodily pain and the humane remedies of art. Even in its tortured state, the flower is a reminder that the amplitude and mystery of the world are not altogether enfolded in human transactions, human artifacts.[19]

And yet Michelangelo's work restores Williams's courage and renews his vocation as a poet, even in the face of death. The flower, he writes at last, is there "for me to naturalize / and acclimate / and choose it for my own" (2:259, 83-5). What follows, though not from this one moment only, is nearly a decade of astonishing late work. "Like Brancusi, like Brueghel," Mariani writes, "he would continue to work at his craft until the last stroke hit or until he became incapable any longer of handling a pencil or wrestling with his new electric typewriter which snarled and spit back at him whenever his left forefinger tried to dance across the keys."[20] If Mariani's account captures the remarkable force of this vocation and its persistence to the end of Williams's life, these poems are among the fullest reckoning of art's powers against the inevitable unmaking of the body.

Notes

1. Burke writes insightfully about Williams as *"tactus eruditus"* in "William Carlos Williams, 1883-1963," 283.

2. Miller, "William Carlos Williams," 288. For Miller this interpenetration implies a stress on language, shifting emphasis from the subject and the circumstance of their utterance. Later, in *The Linguistic Moment,* he describes Williams's poems in this way: "No symbolism, no depth, no reference to a world beyond the world, no pattern of imagery, no dialectical structure, no interaction of subject and object—just description, just the placing of words on the page so the intrinsic virtue of each may best operate" (359).

3. Coles, introduction to *Doctor Stories* by William Carlos Williams, xii.

4. Burke, "William Carlos Williams," 285. Subsequent references are cited parenthetically in the text.

5. The idea of literature as remedy—medicine, corrective, equipment for living—runs through Burke's work from the early 1930s on. It is most straightforwardly advanced in *The Philosophy of Literary Form* but underlies the theories of dramatism and logology that are Burke's most significant contribution to American philosophy and criticism.

6. Burke discusses this idea in the first few pages of chapter 1 of *Language of Symbolic Action,* "Definition of Man," 4-9.

7. Here Burke cites an earlier poem by Williams, "The Wanderer," in *The Collected Poems* 1:110, 96. References are to volume, page, and line. In "What are the Signs of What?" another essay collected in the same volume, Burke offers this comment—instructive in this context—on the relationship of words to the material world. "If the things of nature are, for man, the visible signs of their verbal entitlements," he writes, "then nature gleams secretly with a most fantastic shimmer of words and social relationships. And quite as men's views of the supernatural embody the forms of language and society in recognized ways, so their views of the natural would embody these same forms, however furtively. In this sense things would be the signs of words" (379).

8. Williams, *The Collected Poems,* 1:217, 37-40. Subsequent references to Williams's poetry are drawn from this collection with volume, page, and line number cited parenthetically in the text.

9. Williams to Burke, 14 October 1945, *The Humane Particulars,* 81.

10. Cavell, *The Senses of Walden,* 134. Gerald Bruns uses Cavell's argument and this term instructively in the discussion of modern and contemporary poetry that appears in part 3 of his book *Tragic Thoughts at the End of Philosophy.*

11. In the opening section of *Spring and All,* Williams turns from his project to quote a "noble apostrophe," a strenuous attack advanced by a nameless and perhaps imaginary "they." "'I do not like your poems; . . .'" their complaint begins. "'You seem neither to have suffered nor, in fact, to have felt anything very deeply. There is nothing appealing in what you say but on the contrary the poems are positively repellent. They are heartless, cruel, they make fun of humanity. . . . Are you a pagan? Have you no tolerance for human frailty?'" The passage ends by returning to the question of suffering: "'You have not yet suffered a cruel blow from life. When you have suffered you will write differently.'" Williams is dismissive, interpreting the complaint to say, "'You have robbed me. God, I am naked. What shall I do?'—By it they mean that when I have suffered (provided I have not done so as yet) I too shall run for cover" (1:177).

12. Wyschogrod, "Towards a Postmodern Ethics," 54-5 (Wyschogrod's italics). For Wyschogrod "pantextuality" represents one line of postmodern thinking about the body; "much that was previously interpreted as nature," she observes, "has been newly franchised as text" (54). "Corporeality," on the other hand, understands the body "as a field of significations legible to the astute reader" (54). Wyschogrod is interested in points where these discourses converge and in the ethical challenges implicit in both ways of "reading" the body. She argues that *touch,* which poses difficulties for classical analysis of the senses as for contemporary understanding, works to establish the vulnerability of the body-subject and to extend a "solicitation and a proscription: 'Do not injure me'" (63). For Williams, a sense of the corporeal subject arises from a professional concern with the body and the need to read the body medically. Whether the "erudite touch" that marks Williams's engagement with the world and with other people extends a comparable "restraining order against violence" (63) is an issue worthy of further consideration.

13. Bodily causes are not subject, as social ones might be, to persuasive speech or the power of language. West's *Stroke of Genius* is one recent first-person account of stroke.

14. Blackburn, "Phone Call to Rutherford," lines 4-6, 11-12, and 13-14.

15. Mariani, *William Carlos Williams,* 635. Mariani draws on various accounts, including Williams's own and those of his wife and son, to describe Williams's condition following the strokes. The attacks affected Williams's vision, which made reading difficult or impossible, and his speech, which made his talk slurred and barely audible in public settings. The right side of his body was

partially paralyzed and his right hand became useless for typing—"an injury to my right flipper" he called it in a letter to Fred Miller (9 January 1953, in *William Carlos Williams,* 657). The second stroke led to a major depression for which Williams was hospitalized for eight weeks. Williams called the eight months following the second attack "a living hell" (660). While some of his symptoms improved for a time, repeated small strokes through the late 1950s and early 1960s further weakened and disabled him.

16. Scarry, *The Body in Pain,* 288-9. Subsequent references are cited parenthetically in the text.

17. Harpham, "Elaine Scarry and the Dream of Pain," 211.

18. Ibid., 211.

19. Scarry's argument reckons this not as excess or remainder but as essential to the structure of belief, an outward turn not only from the body but from the human transaction "onto a disembodied referent" (197).

20. Mariani, 724.

Bibliography

Blackburn, Paul. "Phone Call to Rutherford." In *The Cities.* New York: Grove Press, 1967.

Bruns, Gerald. *Tragic Thoughts at the End of Philosophy: Language, Literature, and Ethical Theory.* Evanston, IL: Northwestern University Press, 1999.

Burke, Kenneth. "Definition of Man." In *Language as Symbolic Action: Essays on Life, Literature, and Method,* 3-24. Berkeley: University of California Press, 1966.

———. *The Philosophy of Literary Form: Studies in Symbolic Action.* Berkeley: University of California Press, 1973.

———. "What are the Signs of What? (A Theory of Entitlement)." In *Language as Symbolic Action,* 359-79.

———. "William Carlos Williams, 1883-1963." In *Language as Symbolic Action,* 282-91.

Cavell, Stanley. *The Senses of Walden.* San Francisco: North Point Press, 1981.

Coles, Robert, ed. Introduction to *Doctor Stories* by William Carlos Williams, vii-xvi. New York: New Directions, 1984.

East, James H., ed. *The Humane Particulars, The Collected Letters of William Carlos Williams and Kenneth Burke.* Columbia: University of South Carolina Press, 2003.

Harpham, Geoffrey Galt. "Elaine Scarry and the Dream of Pain." *Salmagundi* 130-1 (2001): 202-34.

Mariani, Paul. *William Carlos Williams.* New York: McGraw-Hill, 1981.

Miller, J. Hillis. "William Carlos Williams." In *Poets of Reality: Six Twentieth-Century Writers,* 285-359. Cambridge, MA: Harvard University Press, 1965.

———. "Williams." In *The Linguistic Moment: From Wordsworth to Stevens,* 349-89. Princeton: Princeton University Press, 1985.

Scarry, Elaine. *The Body in Pain: The Making and Unmaking of the World.* New York: Oxford University Press, 1985.

West, Paul. *A Stroke of Genius: Illness and Self-Discovery.* New York: Viking, 1995.

Williams, William Carlos. *The Collected Poems of William Carlos Williams.* Edited by A. Walton Litz and Christopher Mac Gowan. 2 vols. New York: New Directions, 1986-88.

Wyschogrod, Edith. "Towards a Postmodern Ethics: Corporeality and Alterity." In *The Ethical,* edited by Edith Wyschogrod and Gerald McKenny, 54-65. Oxford: Blackwell, 2003.

Bill Mohr (essay date fall 2004)

SOURCE: Mohr, Bill. "The Wheelbarrow in Question: Ideology and the Radical Pellucidity of William Carlos Williams's Images." *William Carlos Williams Review* 24, no. 2 (fall 2004): 27-39.

[*In the following essay, Mohr argues that the images presented in two of Williams's most anthologized poems—"The Red Wheelbarrow" and "Poem"—are significantly more complicated than many critics have acknowledged.*]

> The image is a seen thing.
> The symbol is a thought thing.
> The symbol, when received by the reader, must be re-
>   thought, understood,
> the image be re-seen, & the emotional impact received
>   from the envisionment is what is sought by the poet.

Stuart Perkoff, Unpublished journal entry, March, 1957[1]

"The Red Wheelbarrow" (*CP* [*The Collected Poems*]1 224) and **"Poem"** ("As the cat / climbed over" *CP*1 352) are perhaps two of William Carlos Williams's most anthologized poems, and even as new areas of social critique and cultural investigation have expanded literature's scope, the familiarity of these poems enables critics to invoke them as immediate points of common reference. Mark Long, for example, begins an essay on the relationship between poetry and the rapidly developing field of ecocriticism, by citing "the indelible image" of **"The Red Wheelbarrow"** as the way that most readers first encounter Williams (58). Pointing to "the qualities sustained in the image" as the ostensible explanation for how this poem has developed an iconic status, Long quotes the last four lines of the poem:

> glazed with rain
> water
>
> beside the white
> chickens

But Long assumes that everyone knows what these qualities are, and in keeping the category singular—"the image"—reaffirms the apparent precision and stability of the poem.[2] Long has considerable company in those who agree that "the image" of these lines is a fixed entity, even as they decry it as puzzling. Cleanth Brooks, for instance, argues against both the form and the content of **"The Red Wheelbarrow"** as arbitrary.

> Reading the poem is like peering at some ordinary object through a pin prick in a piece of cardboard. The fact that the pin prick frames it arbitrarily endows it with a puzzling, and exciting, freshness that seems to hover on the verge of revelation. And that is what the poem is actually about: "so much depends"—but what we do not know.
>
> (173-74)

In equating the poem with a child's self-constructed, disposable toy, Brooks takes a not-so-sly swipe at Williams, and makes it appear as though the contraction of vision provides unimpeded contact with what we are supposed to be looking at. Indeed, critics do tend to react to the poem as though the alleged arbitrariness were a magnifying device placed in front of a tiny hole in cardboard. Carl Dennis describes the image as though Williams were Charles Weston with a telephoto lens.

> [T]he objective second half suggests that value does not come from the symbolic overtones the poet imparts to an object but from our openness to literal context, though this context is accidental (beaded with raindrops and beside white chickens) and momentary (lasting only until the drops evaporate and the chickens move).
>
> (48)

The shift from glazed to beaded as an intrinsic part of the "arbitrary" or "accidental" image seems to have happened faster than a cat's legs going in and out of a flowerpot. The imposition of the word "beaded" as a choice of modifying the description that Williams offers may seem like a logical ekphrasis, but it is a misinterpretation caused by readers being lulled into believing that they recognize what Paul Naylor calls their "'real world' landscapes." The nominative assumptions that we as readers know where we are standing in relation-

ship to the images Williams presents in these poems needs to be questioned again, especially given Williams's published comments about **"The Red Wheelbarrow"** several years after its first appearance in *Go-Go* and *Spring and All*. These comments raise substantial questions not only about the difference between the image that impelled Williams to write the poem and the relatively static picture readers usually derive in response to the poem, but in the case of the wheelbarrow, how that picture is framed.

In the mid-1930s, William Rose Benet's anthology *Fifty Poets* organized itself around the choices made by the poets themselves. Benet provided the introductory commentary, which in Williams's case included the assessment that he was "an original poet of the left wing whose theorizing has frequently hamstrung his inspiration." As requested by Benet, Williams sent along a paragraph in which he explained his choice of why this was one of his favorite poems.

> The wheelbarrow in question stood outside the window of an old negro's house on a back street in the suburb where I live. It was pouring rain and there were white chickens walking about in it. The sight impressed me somehow as about the most important, the most integral that it had ever been my pleasure to gaze upon. And the meter though no more than a fragment succeeds in portraying this pleasure flawlessly, even it succeeds in denoting a certain unquenchable exaltation—in fact I find the poem quite perfect.
>
> (60)

Williams is recounting in prose a combination of the conclusions of his **"Pastoral"** poems: "These things astonish me beyond words," and "No one / Will believe this of vast / import to the nation." The description he provides out of memory is far different than how the poem is read. Where are the raindrops that seem to well up in so many descriptions?

When Williams writes "glazed with rain," he means that on one level literally—glazed with the motion of water, in the same fashion that Shakespeare suggests in the lines that Samuel Johnson cites in his definition of glaze: "Sorrow's eye, glazed with brining tears / Divides one thing entire to many objects" (814). We should note that the predicate in both cases is in the present tense, so that given a choice of making glazed read "being glazed" or "that has been glazed," the former's spontaneity is to be preferred as more consistent. In that single instant of Williams's line, it is the entire scene that is being glazed. It is precisely the motion of the rain that he wishes us to imagine at that moment, a motion that shifts into nominative stillness—what he calls exaltation—and then recedes into the chickens. Hugh Kenner, in his dismayingly snide comments about this poem in *A Homemade World*, suggests that Williams wants us to imagine that the wheelbarrow is glazed, but the chickens aren't, missing the point of what the word "beside" does (57-60). The odd part of this poem is that the object that seems to be the most important is not at the center of the picture. The chickens are at the center of the picture; the wheelbarrow is beside, subordinate yet absolutely essential in its contingency as a symbol of spring. (Williams, we should remember, has been promising in *Spring and All* for several pages that the titular season is on its way. This is rain, and not snow.) Part of the suppleness of Williams's eye and ear is that he has it both ways: the storm is happening, and it is finished. The pre-Socratic thump of essence in water sitting still shouldn't distract us from the motion an instant earlier, a turn that "wheel" implies.

In suggesting that despite its common description, the image is ambiguous, I am also questioning the assumption that nothing else is happening in the poem. The theme of the poem is that being and becoming are almost indistinguishable. If stillness and motion could respectively be said to represent those categories, then the enjambment of "glazed with rain / water" is meant to provide an abrupt pivot of liminality. The descent beckons, as Williams would later write, after which the stark and nominative "water" provides us with a hint of the glow to come. The first noun we encounter is "wheel" and its enjambment is meant to suggest the central theme. Normally, we think of a wheel as turning, but this one isn't. Rain, on the other hand, as the wheel of water, is turning. The wheelbarrow is being glazed, although that wheel does stop, or it will at some point. When it has been stopped long enough, we can assume that a muted parallel or equivalent within the poem will become more visible, if we slow becoming down frame by frame, at least as slowly as those who claim to be able to see beads of water on the barrow. So much of the difference between being and becoming depends on that nanosecond between the wheelbarrow being glazed and the glazed wheelbarrow, a transition as instantaneous as the peck of the chicken, which in the vaporous sliver of time that its beak jolts the damp earth will resemble the wheelbarrow in that it too has three points of contact: two legs, and one object different from the two legs that prefers to be in motion.[3] In a certain sense, the fragment of meter actually extends itself a little further than Williams lets on in his comment. Each couplet has an initial two-stress line followed by a single stress, just as both the wheelbarrow and the chickens could be said to replicate this triad. A wheelbarrow has two main legs and its turning point. Chickens have two legs and the pivots of their beaks. If one were a painter, one would notice this infinitesimally rapid simultaneity of equivalence. Williams wants us to remember that it is keen attention that we must pay to others that constitutes the love measured in the poem's opening.

The word *water* is the concrete counterpart to the second word in the poem, *much,* though water's position in the poem—at a spot that one normally expects the climax of a plot, about three-fourths or four-fifths the way through a story—and the fact that it is not necessary for the vividness of the poem's imagery make it suspect. In a sense, Williams is saying that water can be compared only to itself, and that nothing perhaps but nothingness is dependent on it. But note that nothing is said about raindrops. There is rain, and implied puddles, and chickens, probably bedraggled a bit, but nevertheless getting as bright and shiny from the washing as the wheelbarrow.

Williams's choice of emphasis in a hierarchy of values is also part of the ambiguity of the image. As a doctor often paid only in the goods produced by his patients, he knows all too well how much depends on those chickens. In pointing to the wheelbarrow, an object of labor, he is confronting a problem that seems to be inherent in any aesthetic emerging in the modern period, the discord Emerson says in "Nature" exists between nature and man: "you cannot freely admire a noble landscape if laborers are digging in the field hard by. The poet finds something ridiculous in his delight until he is out of the sight of men" (39). The erasure of the laborer from the poem requires that the owner of the wheelbarrow be eliminated. The rain dissolves that impediment for Williams. He is able to "be secret and exult," as Yeats said in another context, because the rain has temporarily removed any potential worker. This solitude is the link with romanticism that Williams cannot shake himself free of. We know that when Williams was studying to be a doctor, his major poetic model was Keats: "Keats, during the years at medical school, was my God. *Endymion* really woke me up. I copied Keats's style religiously, starting my magnum opus of those days on the pattern of *Endymion*" (A [*The Autobiography of William Carlos Williams*] 53). Throughout his career, Williams is constantly translating and transmuting Keats. "Bright star would I were as steadfast as thou art" becomes the poignant, quivering distant object of Williams's **"El Hombre":** "Shine alone in the sunrise / Toward which you lend no part." In thinking about how brightly this wheelbarrow has radiated all these years, we should not be surprised to find a line in *Endymion*: "oh for some bright essence to lean upon." The imagination may be an autonomous force in *Spring and All,* but its romantic habits are difficult to make completely new. For Williams, the bright wheelbarrow became the secret essence nothing more could be said about, but only pointed to as that which could be leaned and depended upon to remain irreducible to anything else.

The wheelbarrow in question, therefore, is much more complex than Williams's critics have acknowledged. In part, this has happened because Williams's images often play their cards with a poker face, and the bet is not a nickel a hand. It's for the whole casino. In *The Poetics of Indeterminacy*, Marjorie Perloff examines the poems of *Spring and All,* describing their images as "perfectly transparent. . . . They are images without depth, but in the shallow space in which they coexist, they create enormously varied configurations" (131). In arguing that "the referentiality of the images is subordinated to their compositional value" (138), Perloff quotes Viktor Shklovsky as a contemporary of Williams who had similar aims in regards to the plasticity of the imagination: "An image is not a permanent referent for those immutable complexities of life which are revealed through it; its purpose is not to perceive meaning, but to create a special perception of the object" (115). Perloff also points out, however, that "[e]ach lyric embedded in Williams's 'free prose' sustains rival possibilities: it is at once self-reflexive and open-ended" (137). In addition to metonymic clusters that Perloff notices, one of the ways this open-endedness can be understood is that, whatever the degree of referentiality may or may not be, the visibility of the images is not subordinate to anything. The lighting of these poems is not indeterminate. On the contrary, in this collage of prose and poetry, there are few shadows. This is American light, stark, direct, pellucid. The paradox in Williams's poetry is that the stronger the light, the less clear the meaning. His pellucidity has limits, although the objects in his poems seem unaware of the glare he is subjecting them to. The ability of the objects in his images to absorb every available brushstroke of light is in part because Williams insists that "the word must be put down for itself, not as a symbol of nature but a part, cognizant of the whole—aware—civilized" (*CP* 1 189). In developing this poetics, he is still making a place for things and referentiality as "rival possibilities." In *Spring and All,* the rain, the chickens, and the wheelbarrow are all manifestations of his analysis of comparison in the prologue to *Kora*: "the thing in question" that he wants to find "the peculiar perfections of" is always contrasting its "inimitable particles of dissimilarity to all other things" (1 18). If what depends on the things in **"The Red Wheelbarrow"** is elusive, perhaps the pellucidity of these images dissolves these "inimitable particles" and makes the "paint upon canvas" seem of "more importance than the literal appearance of the image depicted" (A 265).

The deceptiveness of Williams's images as arguments about the process of how we remember what we know, and how what we know shapes the instants we remember, consistently challenges our preconceptions of the material that deserves to be considered worthy of becoming an object in a poem. In choosing the apparently anti-poetic, especially the most ordinary increments of daily happenstance, Williams seems to leave many of his poems vulnerable to superficial examination, a situation that Theodor Adorno cautions us about

in *Aesthetic Theory,* "When Williams sabotages the poetic and approximates an empirical report, the actual result is by no means such a report" (123). The meticulousness of Williams's sketching of images is among the antipoetic gestures that subvert the "actual result" of his poem. Williams's **"Poem"** about a cat and flowerpot is equivalent to **"The Red Wheelbarrow"** in its radical pellucidity. Indeed, the literalness of **"Poem"** seems to have forestalled any consideration of its metaphoric strategies. Thom Gunn, for instance, cites **"Poem"** along with **"The Red Wheelbarrow"** as "more purely imagist than any of the original works of the Imagists." In that mode, Gunn argues, the only meaning to be found is not in the words of the poem, but in "the impulse behind the writing of the poem" (24). The problem is that the words of the poems—and the lines themselves—are deceptive in terms of the image depicted; being in motion from the outset of the poem, the cat is even more ambiguous than the wheelbarrow.

Sometimes the oldest strategies provide the best way to reinvestigate the familiar. Sounding a poem out is one way to start, and when the vowels and consonants are played for their effects, the "t" sounds are undeniably very strong, though seemingly without the degree of "puzzling portentousness" that Brooks assigned to the wheelbarrow. *Cat, forefoot, right, jamcloset,* and *flowerpot* seem firmly grounded within the boundaries of denotation. But what about *pit*—is that equivalent in its literalness to *cat* and *flowerpot*? First of all, is that word really needed to describe the action of the poem? No, it's there for another reason: to suggest the idea of the poem. "No ideas but in things," he is always quoted as insisting. The problem is that readers have stopped thinking about his ideas. Unlike *barrow,* though, *pit* cannot be categorized so easily as literal. The word suggests perdition, or at least a zone of abjection where one waits for one's older siblings to decide whether to murder you or to sell you as a slave to a caravan on its way to Pharaoh's markets. Even today's slang carries this nuance, "How are things on your job?" "Oh, it's the pits." A pit is dangerous: the fall is the least of one's problems. Clambering out is the difficult part.

But it is just a flowerpot, and the cat is nimble. In any metaphor, we need to keep things in proportion, starting with the actual movement of the cat. Consider the specificity of how many legs of the cat are in the flowerpot—two: "first the right / forefoot / carefully / then the hind". So if there are two, the cat could be said to be half in and half out of the flowerpot. We know that what we would usually find in this object is also half-in and half-out. The stalk and petals are there for us to savor, while the root system is hidden away. This is just to say that the cat, for an instant, is no longer an animal, but is being compared to a flower blossoming. How long does the beauty of a flower endure, let alone linger? How much power does it have to sustain its presence? It is as evanescent in its improvisation as a cat stepping in and out of a flowerpot. Williams returns to this theme of brevity in another much longer poem later in his life, in which he describes a tousled man performing a pirouette for his invalid mother. The moment seems to overwhelm his mother, but she finally shouts "Bravo!" That exclamation, combined with her clapping, brought the man's spouse hustling out of the kitchen. The poem concludes: "What's going on here? She said. / But the show was over" (*CP* 2 268).[4] The poem is not over, however, since it can be replayed in what James Joyce called "the ear of the mind" with the same delight of jaunty agency until the reader and the themes of these poems are finally experiencing a providential reciprocity.

In questioning to what extent these two well-known poems of Williams are able to stay constrained within Williams's own denial of their imaginative viability, I am primarily interested in the question of how certain we can be of recognizing the meaning of a poem. How do images in a poem function as a means of knowing the world, and what is the relationship of imagination to knowledge? How does subjectivity construct and affect a reader's understanding of the poem's implications for how one should examine every object and idea that sets up camp within modernity, and how does that process enable a reader to break the grip of ideology? Influenced by John Dewey and Alfred North Whitehead, Williams's poems and prose repeatedly emphasized the value of knowing a place, but what is the relationship between "the condition of knowledge," culture and place? What, if anything, is there in the poems we have just looked at that makes, in Charles Bernstein's words, "the consciousness-constituting activity of ideology audible," and how does the poem as "the ear of the mind" enable us to hear the limits of our alertness to what we do not yet know?

In *Writing the Radical Center,* John Beck reminds us that "[i]magination is, for Williams, the interaction of subject and object in space and time, not a transcendent subjectivity that exists for and of itself" (21). Beck goes on to refine the relationship between identity and knowledge by building on J. Hillis Miller's assertion that in Williams "the distinction between subject and object" vanishes.

> By obscuring Williams's anti-dualism as a dissolution of difference, Miller misses the point of why Williams formulated his anti-dualistic position, which is at root politically motivated. Miller makes Williams's use of relativity sound like relativism, which dampens the impact of Williams's insistence that democracy is grounded in the freedom to be where one is, at that moment, free to define that being, the limit of that freedom (and an essential limit) being the recognition and acknowledging of the freedom and equality of every other element within the field to likewise define

itself. . . . Enabling differences to be maintained as mutually interactive and fluid agents, rather than as polarized and divorced opposites, is the core of Williams's poetics and politics, the need to insist upon and to enact this process involving him in the project of positing a workable aesthetic democracy.

(20)

In this sense, therefore, we can see that what "depends on" the red wheelbarrow, the rain, and the chickens is our ability to maintain a simultaneous awareness of both the quiescence and the volatility of these objects as subjects within the singular limits of perception. This renitent formation of knowledge as dependent on place will always be subject to variegated pressures of modern hierarchies, which thrive on tacit dualisms. Williams knows all too well that his propositions to link knowledge, self, and place into an empowering dialogue are up against an insatiable congeries of vested ideological forces that are "certainly antagonistic to this realization of place. It hates it, tears down fences that delineate, is jealous of differences,—distrusts all elevations of the realization of intense place, set a premium on placelessness" (*EK* [*The Embodiment of Knowledge,* Ron Loewinsohn, ed. (1974)] 134). The chiastic intensity of place and knowledge in Williams's paradigm of culture makes the resulting production of imaginative activity less likely to be useful as a potential commodity. What Williams calls the "near side of reality" (*EK* 132) is a self-knowledge that involves the intimate measurement of every "stand-point," in Whitehead's sense of the term, as a means by which individuals can approximate their relationships with others, and thereby challenge, no matter how uneven the resources available to the contesting entities, ideology's massive grip.

The tricky part of "*self*-knowledge," as Terry Eagleton reminds us, is that "To know myself is no longer to be the self that I was a moment before I knew it" (94). Williams invokes this specific problem in terms of being a reader on the first page of *Spring and All*: how does one "know what he is at the exact moment that he is." While of course we can smugly tell each other that Williams could have started knowing what he is by saying where he was when he had his moment of satori with the rain and the chickens, I would suggest that we can hear the consciousness-constituting activity of the imagination and its relation to ideology by considering Bernstein's analysis of the role of poetry in social life:

> Poetry is aversion of conformity in the pursuit of new forms, or can be. By form I mean ways of putting things together, or stripping them apart, I mean ways of accounting for what weighs upon any one of us, or that poetry tosses up into an imaginary air like so many swans flying out of a magician's depthless black hat so that suddenly, like when the sky all at once turns white or purple or day-glo blue, we breathe more deeply.

(1)

If we are to ask what constituted American poetry in the past century, we need to remember that the challenge to conformity raised by modernists such as Williams is essential to recent re-evaluations of twentieth-century American poetry that have focused on restoring poems from the left or radical edges of cultural production. It is heartening to see Lola Ridge appearing in anthologies again after an absence of almost thirty years. And if Edwin Rolfe is finally being read again, can Don Gordon be far behind? The restoration of work by radicals should remind us to stay aware of how radical other work was that may not have called for social revolution. As John Lowney has pointed out, "social change is hardly uniformly affirmed in *Spring and All*" (67). Indeed, one of the few places where any mass movement is represented is at a baseball game in which "the beautiful illusion" that Williams denounces at the beginning of *Spring and All* insidiously permeates a crowd. This lack of a coherent social program, however, should not obscure Williams's aspirations for a more empowering vision of the individual within the contingencies of culture.

"Only the imagination is real," Williams wrote towards the end of his life (*CP*2 334). This is still a dangerous statement. Maybe, in fact, it is more dangerous than ever. The potential and real tyrants of the world are able to exercise their power in proportion to how much time any of us have in any given day to look closely at a flowerpot, and to consider the ambiguity of that which seems familiar. The reality of the imagination includes how much we are willing to stand up for poetry and those who wrote it in the past century. Perhaps we can best honor their work by making our imagination of their work as subversive in as many different ways as they wrote.

Notes

1. Stuart Perkoff (1930-74) was a poet primarily associated with Venice West, a Beat community including poets such as Bruce Boyd and John Thomas that emerged in Venice, California beginning in the mid-1950s. Both Perkoff and Boyd appeared in Donald Allen's *The New American Poetry* (Grove Press, 1960), which is often regarded as the anthology that demonstrated Williams's influence on an entire generation of younger poets. This particular journal entry shows the roots of modernist poetics in romantic aesthetic strategies, in particular Shelley's *Defence of Poetry*: "[Poets'] language is vitally metamorphical; that is, it marks the before unapprehended relations of things and perpetuates their apprehension until the words which represent them become, through time, signs for portions or classes of thoughts instead of pictures of integral thoughts." Whether Perkoff was directly responding to Shelley's argument is

probably impossible to determine. Perkoff only attended college for a few weeks, and although his journals indicate a wide range of reading, from Kafka to Genet to Creeley, one can never be certain how much of the traditional poetics he might have thought about.

> If, by a series of beautiful & true images, images for the most part completely objective, the poet forces the reader to experience that scene imaged—then is that not metaphor? in the sense previously discussed?

>   to experience
> any scene
>   —to really
> & totally experience
> anything—
>   this is
> the holiest moment! & those
> poems
>   (not metaphorless
> but metaphored)
> do bring that abt.

2. "Sharp," "hard," and "exact" seem to be the favorite words used to describe "The Red Wheelbarrow." James Breslin argues out of a deft, but familiar certitude with the poem: "short, jagged lines and long vowels slow down our movement through the poem, breaking off each part of the scene for exact observation. Any symbolic reading of the scene, a possible imposition by the observer, is carefully resisted; its hard, literal, objective reality is insisted upon. . . . [T]he wheelbarrow is red and it has just been rained on, giving it a fresh, 'glazed' appearance" (Axelrod and Deese 104). Lisa Steinman comments that Williams is "probably best known for the sparse, hard-edged use of language found in early poems such as 'The Red Wheelbarrow'" (81). Roy Harvey Pearce's analysis of the poem concedes Williams's "power to collocate such objects into sharply annotated images like these," but Pearce frames Williams's skill within his personal "predicament" of being unable to make objects "relate coherently one to the other," thus resulting in a poem that is "notably sentimental" (339). Thomas Whitaker provides one of the few dissenting indications that something else might be happening in what Breslin calls a "crisp, intense lyric." Whitaker emphasizes the felicitous subtlety of Williams in scoring the images:

> Line units, stress, quantity, echoing sounds—all are adjusted to render the delicate movement of apprehending a "new world." Each quantitatively long holding of surface appearance lifts it into esthetic abstraction ("a red wheel," "glazed with rain," "beside the white"). The descent into short, trochaic rendering of the substance beneath that surface then gives a more inclusive comprehension, which in turn leads to a related surface. Each pattern refreshes without becom-

ing final; and at the central climax, the momentary abstraction becomes a metaphorical transformation, "glazed," which is followed by a more complex descent.

Whitaker stops short, however, of suggesting any thematic implications of the interplay between abstraction and descent.

3. J. Hillis Miller strips Williams's poem of any relationship to the rain whatsoever:

> Williams has an extraordinary ability to pick a single thing out of the multitude existing and focus on it with intense concentration, as if it were the only object in the world, incomparable, unique. . . . The wheelbarrow, in a famous poem, does not stand for anything or mean anything. It is an object in space dissociated from the objects around it, without reference beyond itself. It is what it is. The aim of the poem is to make it stand there for the reader in its separateness, as the words of the poem stand on the page.

(Axelrod and Deese 94-95)

4. While working on this essay, I read Natalie Gerber's provocative and thoughtful essay on Williams's prosody, "Getting the 'Squiggly Tunes Down' on the Page: Williams's Triadic-Line Verse and American Intonation," which calls particular attention to this poem. Gerber and I disagree about the poem's achievement, though I would concede that it is a minor poem by Williams. Nevertheless, it reiterates the theme of these earlier major poems in a way that has not been accredited.

Works Cited

Adorno, Theodor W. *Aesthetic Theory.* Trans. and ed. Robert Hulot-Kentor. Minneapolis: U of Minnesota P, 1997.

Axelrod, Steven Gould and Helen Deese. *Critical Essays on William Carlos Williams.* New York: G. K. Hall, 1995.

Beck, John. *Writing The Radical Center: William Carlos Williams, John Dewey, and American Cultural Politics.* Albany: State U of New York P, 2001.

Benet, William Rose, ed. *Fifty Poets: An American Auto-Anthology.* New York: Duffield and Green, 1933.

Bernstein, Charles. *A Poetics.* Cambridge: Harvard UP, 1992.

Brooks, Cleaneth and Robert Penn Warren. *Understanding Poetry.* New York: Holt, Rinehart, and Winston, 1960.

Dennis, Carl. *Poetry as Persuasion.* Athens: U of Georgia P, 2001

Eagleton, Terry. *Ideology: An Introduction.* London: Verso, 1991.

Emerson, Ralph Waldo. "Nature," Chap. VII, "Spirit." *The Collected Works of R. W. Emerson.* Vol. 1: Nature, Addresses, and Lectures. Ed. Robert E. Spiller. Cambridge: Harvard UP, 1971.

Gerber, Natalie. "Getting the 'Squiggly Tunes Down' on the Page: Williams's Triadic-Line Verse and American Intonation." *Rigor of Beauty.* Ed. Ian Copestake. London: Peter Lang, 2004. 219-51.

Gunn, Thom. *The Occasions of Poetry: Essays in Criticism and Autobiography.* Expanded Edition. Ed. and intro. Clive Wilmer. San Francisco: North Point Press, 1985.

Johnson, Samuel. *Dictionary of the English Language.* Vol. 1. London: Thomas Tegg, 1832.

Kenner, Hugh. *A Homemade World: The American Modernist Writers.* New York: Knopf, 1975; rpt. Baltimore: Johns Hopkins UP, 1989.

Levertov, Denise. *Poems 1960-1967.* New York: New Directions, 1967.

Long, Mark. "William Carlos Williams, Ecocriticism, and Contemporary American Poetry." *Ecopoetry A Critical Introduction.* Ed. J. Scott Bryson. Salt Lake City: U of Utah P, 2002.

Lowney, John. *The American Avant-Garde Tradition: William Carlos Williams, Postmodern Poetry, and the Politics of Cultural Memory.* Lewisburg, PA: Bucknell University Press, 1997.

Perkoff, Stuart. Journals, unpublished. U of California, Special Collections. Stuart Perkoff Collection.

Pearce, Roy Harvey. "Williams and the 'New Mode.'" *The Continuity of American Poetry.* Middletown, CT: Wesleyan UP, 1987

Perloff, Marjorie. *The Poetics of Indeterminacy: Rimbaud to Cage.* Princeton: Princeton UP, 1981.

Shelley, Percy Bysshe. *Shelley's Prose.* Ed. David Lee Clark. Albuquerque: U of New Mexico P, 1954. 278-79.

Steinman, Lisa. *Made in America: Science, Technology, and American Modernist Poets.* New Haven: Yale UP, 1987.

Whitaker, Thomas R. *William Carlos Williams.* Rev. ed. Boston: G. K. Hall, 1989.

Alan Golding (essay date 2004)

SOURCE: Golding, Alan. "'What about all this writing?': Williams and Alternative Poetics." *Textual Practice* 18, no. 2 (2004): 265-82.

[*In the following essay, Golding discusses the pervasive influence of Williams on later poets including Ron Silliman, Bob Perelman, Rachel Blau DuPlessis, Alice Notley, Rae Armantrout, and Lyn Hejinian.*]

To begin, a William Carlos Williams mini-anthology from what one might call the long 1920s:

> —'[W]riting deals with words and words only and . . . all discussions of it deal with single words and their association in groups'; 'the only real in writing is writing itself'.[1]

> —'But can you not see, can you not taste, can you not smell, can you not hear, can you not touch—words? . . . Words, white goldenrod, it is words you are made out of'; 'he objectifies the words as the material of poetry'.[2]

> —'Am I a word? Words, words, words—'.[3]

> —'[James Joyce] has in some measure liberated words, freed them for their proper uses. He has [to] a great measure destroyed what is known as "literature"'.[4]

> —'Liberate the words'; 'FIRST let the words be free'.[5]

> '[T]he imagination of the listener and of the poet are left free to mingle in the dance'; 'the author and reader are liberated to pirouette with the words'.[6]

Linguistic self-reflectiveness; attention to the materiality of written language; the self as constructed in and by language; a cultural politics of oppositionality, and especially opposition to 'Literature'; a Marinetti-like view of words in freedom, allied to the embrace of readerly freedom; the problematics of signification; generic hybridity enacted through various forms of disjunction and parataxis: even in the decade of **'The Red Wheelbarrow'**, these were central attributes of Williams' writing and thinking about writing. They were also the attributes that drew a later generation of experimental writers to Williams, and it is that influence which I want to explore in this essay.

As Hank Lazer argues, recent literary history has given us 'two Dr. Williamses'[7]—the Williams beloved of creative writing programmes, with his emphasis on quotidian detail and speech, and the Williams of the late teens and twenties hybrid texts, the self-consciously avant-gardist Williams who has proven a central figure for the most serious poetic avant-garde of the past three decades, the Language writers. In particular Williams was crucial to the self-definition of Language poetics as it developed *in opposition to* the workshop lyric, since under the sign of the plain-spoken, quotidian Williams this latter mode dominated much of American poetry through the 1970s and 1980s. In contrast to this 'attenuated version of Williams', as Bob Perelman recalls, it was 'the romance of an oceanic, uncontrolled poetry, as in Williams's **"The Yachts"**, or *Spring and All* and *The Descent of Winter*' that constituted part of his appeal to a number of Language writers.[8] Yet Williams' importance for recent experimental poetries, while widely acknowledged, is oddly little discussed in specific terms. Scholarship on Williams in the avant-garde contexts of his own times abounds, but even

otherwise valuable work connecting him to later avant-garde poetics and to particular poets (Linda Kinnahan's *Poetics of the Feminine*, John Lowney's *The American Avant-Garde Tradition*) does little to connect his writing to the broader framework of recent experimental practice.[9] To begin addressing this critical lacuna, I will discuss briefly the 'second' Williams' importance to certain crucial moments of self-definition early in the history of Language writing, examining how his name and work are used and invoked at those moments. I go on to consider his presence in the theoretical, critical and poetic work of some of the movement's practitioners and certain fellow travellers—a range of workers in what Benjamin Friedlander's 'Hecuba Whimsy' calls a 'poetics of the material text'.[10]

The first key moment and text in understanding the nature of Williams' importance to Language writing is the 1970 New Directions publication of *Imaginations,* which brought *Spring and All* complete to a new audience for the first time after decades of unavailability. (The further importance of *Imaginations* was its placement of *Spring and All* in coherent relation to Williams' other hybrid texts of the period, including *Kora in Hell,* **'The Descent of Winter'** and *The Great American Novel*.) Harvey Brown's Frontier Press edition of *Spring and All* also appeared in the same year, and it was in this edition that a number of these poets first encountered that text. As Perelman says in what should be taken as a representative statement, 'for me, the complete version of Williams' *Spring and All,* with the fractured Dada-like prose, came out in 1970, not in 192[3]'.[11] Whereas *The Wedge* (1944) had been more important for the New American poets of the 1950s who constitute one precursor group for Language writing, Ron Silliman asserts in 1981 that 'many young poets today feel that [Williams'] finest work is to be found in *Spring & All* and the other books composed between 1920 and '32'.[12]

The year 1971 brought the first issue of Barrett Watten's *This* magazine, in which Robert Grenier's widely cited essay 'On speech' marks a move away from Williams in Williams' own name. He begins, 'it isn't the spoken any more than the written, now, that's the progression from Williams'.[13] In this formulation, the emergent Language move beyond the speech-based poetics of (in one version) the New Americans and (in another) the contemporary free verse lyric is couched as a 'progression from Williams'. At the same time, however, Grenier invokes Williams to authorize this move, adapting 'his castigation of "the sonnet" and his trope of a tactically extremist rhetoric: *To me, all speeches say the same thing*, or: why not exaggerate, as Williams did, for our time proclaim an abhorrence of "speech" designed as was his castigation of "the sonnet" to rid us, as creators of the world, from reiteration of the past dragged on in formal habit. I HATE

SPEECH'.[14] In other words, as Perelman rightly points out, what is often taken as an inaugural manifesto statement of Language writing rests on a repetition of Williams:

> This repetition of a prior originary act in the name of novelty is similar to Williams's destroying and recreating the world in the opening prose of *Spring and All*: Grenier wanted to join in the creation of an already created world . . . his attack reenacted Williams's attack, with the workshop voice poem the target rather than the genteel sonnet.[15]

The tendency among Language writers to use Williams in their developing arguments against a speech-based poetics is confirmed by remarks such as Silliman's that '[before Jack Spicer] one has to go back to William Carlos Williams' *Spring & All* to find a use of the line break as devoted to nuances of meaning' as distinct from the registration of or imitation of speech.[16] Indeed, Silliman's early essays (from about 1977 to 1985) represent another site where Williams appears as central to the development of Language poetics, a trend culminating in Silliman's titling his germinal 1986 anthology of language writing *In the American Tree* (after the Kit Robinson poem and KPFA radio show of that title).[17] Silliman begins his well-known 1980 essay, 'The new sentence', which theorizes a central concept of one branch of language poetics, with the dramatic and perhaps exaggerated one-sentence paragraph: 'The sole precedent I can find for the new sentence is *Kora in Hell: Improvisations* and that one far-fetched.'[18] This statement, of course, echoes directly Williams' own beginning of the Prologue to *Kora*: 'The sole precedent I can find for the broken style of my prologue is *Longinus on the Sublime* and that one farfetched.'[19] For Silliman, 'the first American prose poet[s] of consequence' are the Williams of *Kora* and the Stein of *Tender Buttons*.[20] He goes on to specify what he finds important for his own practice in *Kora*: 'the sentences allow only the most minimal syllogistic shift to the level of reference, and some . . . permit no such shift whatever.'[21] For Silliman, then, Williams becomes a kind of urtheorist of the sentence, in a way articulated by Stephen Fredman. Fredman in fact discusses *Kora* in terms that he frankly borrows from Silliman on the new sentence. For both Silliman and the Williams of *Kora,* a primary question is 'What is a sentence?' and both address that question via a disjunctive, paratactically organized prose the central unit of which is Silliman's 'new sentence', or what Fredman calls the 'generative sentence'. As an experiment in syntax-based prose prosody, *Kora* anticipates such work of Silliman's as *Ketjak* and *Tjanting,* work in which 'the actual relationship between any of the clauses is always more potential than certain'.[22] Fredman argues, then, that '*Kora in Hell* asks for a reading that pays particular attention to its transitory surface, to the way words and things appear and are linked in the moment of its writing', and a reading

that 'break[s] the normal reading pace [of prose]'[23]— just the kind of reading most appropriate for Silliman's own work, which Fredman addresses briefly later in his book.

In another essay, 'Z-sited path', Silliman engages in a more general discussion of Williams' *influence* on twentieth-century poetics—an influence so pervasive, he argues, that to describe someone's writing as 'Williamsesque' is largely meaningless.[24] Out of this 'universalization' of Williams' influence,[25] Silliman wants to rescue one particular Williams. One acknowledged site of that influence has been the creative writing workshop, and Silliman inveighs—in a characteristically antagonistic early Language moment—against a 'neo-academic verse' in which 'what remains are the surface features of Williams' poetry'.[26] More precisely, what remains are the surface features of one *kind* of Williams poetry—an image-centred concreteness, and the simple vocabulary of everyday speech with those notorious Polish mothers lurking behind it. What has been lost or suppressed in many recent poets' reading of Williams, Silliman argues, is 'the identification of method with content'; the connection between 'this [identification] and a broader social vision'; 'the essential oppositionality of his work'; and 'its challenge to the perceptual limits of the reader', a challenge embodied for Silliman as for other Language writers in *Spring and All.*[27] Part of what Silliman finds important is *Spring and All*'s emphasis on constructedness and defamiliarization, or in Williams' recurrent terms from that text, 'design', 'composition' and 'detachment'. As he puts it in a 1992 interview with Manuel Brito, 'the onrush of capitalist technological development has permanently thrown over the organicist closure of "natural" cycles. That understanding is what makes William Carlos Williams' *Spring & All* the defining poem of the first half of the 20th century, at least for me. I'm including the prose in that text in my definition of that work as a poem'.[28] The construction of *Spring and All* compels Silliman, then, rather than the more widely noted organicism of individual poems such as **'By the road to the contagious hospital'.**

Silliman acknowledges Williams' biographical importance to him openly. At age 16, and attracted by the book's colour, he opened *The Desert Music* in the Albany, CA library, and although he had written nothing yet, the title poem convinced him that he would become a poet—perhaps through its famous assertion 'I *am* a poet! I / am. I am. I am a poet, I reaffirmed, ashamed'.[29] **'The Desert Music'** helped him, he says, in 'thinking through what a person in a text is';[30] this and the older poet's attention to senses of noun, fact, facticity, were what Silliman found central. Later Silliman read the Frontier Press edition of *Spring and All* while writing his first book, *Crow* (1971). Again he was struck by the use of the first person and 'the wonderful sense of detail' in a poem like 'What about all this writing', which became a kind of talismanic text for Silliman (he cites it, for instance, in his 1987 book *Lit*).[31] *Crow* begins with an epigraph from **Spring and All**—'the perfection of new forms as additions to nature'.[32] The 'new forms' of *Crow* consist of thirty-two untitled short (often minimalist) poems in which idiosyncratic line breaks possibly modelled on Williams are used to heighten attention to easily overlooked details of language and to create aural puns, homonyms and multiple possibilities for meaning. Also as in Williams, the line is frequently visual in *Crow*, the poem typically constructed out of a registration of observed fact and a few sounds, themselves registered as facts. Lines such as 'on, o, blocks of wood. on / a lot' combine the visual materiality of the repeated 'o', the different sounds of 'o', and literal detail (a truck up on blocks).[33] Another poem moves by the smallest rearrangements of letters, from 'rain' to 'rain is' to 'raisins' to 'plows in the rain', as its 'chokecherry' recalls Williams' Elsie, 'under some hedge of choke-cherry / or viburnum'.[34]

After *Crow*, Silliman 'wanted to explore the function of the "I", the first person singular' in a way that resulted in what he calls 'my most Williamsesque work', the 1976 'Berkeley'.[35] When one reads the opening lines, this comment seems surprising: 'I thought you might be here / I was alone and it was almost two / I have enjoyed my lunch / I knew right away I made a mistake / I glanced back once / I mean it / I thought so'.[36] How is this list poem 'Williamsesque?' Well, again it depends on what Williams we are talking about. In 'Berkeley', the 'I' and other pronouns and deictics have no stable reference; the 'I' changes line by line, and is clearly not to be associated with the poet, especially when one knows that the text is constructed from a range of unacknowledged literary sources. A procedural text like 'Berkeley' programmatically reinforces the idea of 'I' as a pronoun, a placeholder, and in its investigation of personhood as a language function it recalls the Williams of **Spring and All,** for whom the statement 'nothing / I have done' 'is made up of / nothing / and the diphthong // ae // together with / the first person / singular / indicative / of the auxiliary / verb / to have'.[37]

The idea of the two different Williams, a premise of Silliman's 'Z-sited path', is also articulated explicitly in Charles Bernstein's defence of an oppositional, avant-gardist Williams in his influential 1983 talk, 'The academy in peril: William Carlos Williams meets the MLA'—delivered, Lazer writes, on the same day that Louis Simpson was celebrating the workshop Williams in another room at the convention.[38] At issue for Bernstein, as for Silliman, is the canonization of a particular version of Williams: 'as Williams passes through the narrow and well-guarded gates of official verse culture, it likely will be at the expense of so decontextualizing and neutralizing his work that it will be unrecognizable

on his own terms', which were consistently oppositional.[39] Thus, Bernstein argues, *his* Williams 'may be a token inclusion in a canon that excludes what he stands for . . . heard but not listened to'.[40] Two Williams also feature in another 1983 Bernstein talk/essay, 'Words and pictures', but these two are opposed around what Bernstein calls a 'poetics of optics' or of 'sight' and a 'poetics of vision'.[41] Bernstein critiques in Williams' Imagist/Objectivist work (his example is **'The Lily'**) 'the object-focussed, extratemporal, singled perspective that is, in actuality, a static idealization of the experience of looking'.[42] Later Williams poems such as **'Tribute to the Painters'** and **'Shadows',** however, represent in his view a 'movement . . . decisively away from the static, ahistorical "thing seen"' towards a poetics of vision: 'an engagement of all the senses, and of thought, beyond the readily visible, the statically apparent'.[43] Meanwhile, like Silliman, Bernstein stresses the significance of **Spring and All** 'in the current flowering of paratactic (serially disjunct) prose-format poetry'.[44] For Bernstein as for Silliman—and perhaps not surprisingly, given the shared commitment to breaking down genre boundaries in Williams' work of the 1920s and Language poetics—Williams' disjunct *critical* prose influences later prose *poetry,* even as Bernstein also writes that Williams 'in his imagin[a]tive prose' was one model for the kind of writing encouraged in L=A=N=G=U=A=G=E magazine.[45]

One poetic-critical mixed-genre text that features Williams prominently is Bob Perelman's *The Marginalization of Poetry: Language Writing and Literary History*—one of the most influential genealogies of Language writing, partly for being produced from within the movement itself. In the essay-poem 'An Alphabet of Literary History', Williams appears first in section B:

> Meanwhile, back on the Nowheresville float,
>
> Williams was burning leaves of grass,
> trying to avoid the bitter smoke.
>
> He went inside and searched
> the refrigerator. The plums were gone. The
>
> cold of verbal construction was delicious
> in isolation but the question of
>
> social value remained in abeyance: there
>
> was really nothing to eat.[46]

This complexly intertextual moment finds Williams burning his bridges to Whitman ('burning leaves of grass') in an allusion to his own **'Burning the Christmas Greens'** (one of Williams' many versions of the destruction/creation myth that Grenier repeats in 'On Speech') while he is confronted with the 'question of / social value' deferred, in Perelman's reading, in his own 'This is just to say'. Image (Christmas greens) becomes text (leaves of grass), and the cold of Williams' famous plums becomes 'the cold of verbal construction', in a way that highlights the material textuality of his work. In this passage, then, the two Williams meet and blur—the Williams of the fetishized concrete image, and the Williams of the material found poem, the refrigerator poem that becomes 'art'.

I want to dwell briefly on the implications of this passage because it points to differences among various Language writers' readings of Williams. Just as there is no monolithic 'Williams', there is no monolithic *Language* version of Williams. Barrett Watten writes of 'the "nonaesthetic" observed detail [as] the key to social insight' in Williams and compares the technique to Silliman's (although Watten also suggests that, unlike Silliman, Williams distances himself from the multiplicity of the social contexts that he invokes).[47] Silliman frames the issue similarly when he praises Williams' sense of fact and detail and his ability to connect these formal choices 'to a broader social vision'. Bernstein, however, as I have said, finds the observed detail in Williams static and limited, contrasting it with the 1950s Williams who wrote of 'the tyranny of the image / and how / men / in their designs / have learned / to shatter it'.[48] And for Perelman, 'This is just to say' becomes a site at which to engage critically the political risks of an image-centered poetics, a poem 'delicious / in isolation' like its own plums but where 'the question of / social value remained in abeyance'.

To return to Perelman's 'Alphabet of Literary History': Williams appears most centrally in section P (perhaps for **Paterson,** in which **'The Descent'** first appeared) of the poem, which is modelled structurally and in its diction on **'The Descent',** and begins 'language writing beckons / as modernism beckoned / Critical genealogy is a kind / of art Prose'.[49] In the 'critical genealogy' of this poem, 'Language writing' is the descent to modernism's ascent. But to trace this narrative of only apparent decline is to produce 'art Prose, / a sort of Poetics / even // a Poem'.[50] It is to rewrite lines of genealogy and of poetry (Williams own), and to produce the 'new genres' remarked upon a few lines later in the poem. In taking us from prose to poetics to poem, this section of 'Alphabet' (and the poem as a whole) models a sliding across and between genres that is exactly one of the lessons Perelman and other language poets took from Williams, in this case paradoxically using one of Williams' more generically *un*ambiguous texts to do so.

Finally, Williams reappears crucially at the very end of Perelman's book in the comic prose dream conversation, 'A false account of talking with Frank O'Hara and Roland Barthes in Philadelphia'. A fictionalized O'Hara sees the poet Perelman looking out of the window in the stereotypical gesture of the isolated poet, and writing, as if they were his own, Williams' words from 'The last words of my English grandmother', 'What are those fuzzy things out there . . .'.[51] This moment initiates a brief exchange between 'I' (Perelman) and 'O'Hara' on the distinction between 'quoting' and 'saying', which ends abruptly with Roland Barthes' interpolation that 'You Americans are obsessed with self-fashioned lineage, aren't you?'[52] Williams here becomes the crux in a dizzying spiral of citation that raises serious questions about a speaker's ownership of his/her language. Both O'Hara and Perelman claim to be 'quoting Williams's grandmother', or more precisely quoting Williams quoting her. In Perelman's genre-crossing critical history of language writing, then, one that mixes straightforward literary history, close readings, an insider's narrative of a literary community, essay poems and dream narrative, Williams occupies a privileged place, the final predecessor (outside of O'Hara and Barthes themselves) with whom the book leaves us.

Citation and the ownership of language form the basis of Perelman's discussion of Williams in his 1979 talk 'The first person'. There Perelman quotes passages from the beginning of *The Great American Novel* (where 'words' are really the main character) on which he comments as follows: 'Words are already created and so they've usurped Williams' function as a creator. Their meanings are already there ahead of his impulse to write them down. He can't get out of this impasse; he can't break the words and stay interested, and he can only identify with them mockingly'.[53] Later in the talk he remarks, 'I identify quite a lot with Williams, especially the early Williams and his growls and anger at the amount of prerecording in his head'.[54] This sense of the poet's inevitably belated relationship to language underlies the citational quality central to Perelman's (and much other Language) writing, his habit of torquing relatively familiar moments from earlier texts into quirky, ironic versions of themselves. Williams is one of the writers whom he consistently tweaks in this way. In *Captive Audience* we encounter a version of the well-known formulation from **'Asphodel, That Greeny Flower'**: locked into history and temporality, dulled by the 'trademarked voice' of the news media, people 'sit staring / at the subtext of / their clock radios. People continue / to die miserably from the lack / of news to be found / *there,* too, doctor, / every day, as the display / changes a nine to a ten'.[55] In 'To the Past', Perelman revisits what could be seen as the unconsciously gendered voyeurism of **'The Desert Music'**: 'In some other poem / you wiggle your can / crazily, signifying America / for William Carlos Williams making music // in a gender / desert'.[56] That Perelman alludes to such canonical, easily recognizable passages of Williams is precisely the point: they are an unavoidable part of the overdetermined or 'prerecorded' language that he is given to work with, and writing out of such a sense of language forms part of Perelman's kinship with Williams.

Williams has also figured centrally much earlier in Perelman's career, specifically in his first book *Braille* (1975). *Braille* was 'culled from a year-long series of improvisations, inspired by reading Williams' *Kora in Hell*'[57]—a series written, Williams-fashion, at the rate of one improvisation a day and narrowed down to sixty-one lineated and prose poems for publication. In its interweaving of thirty-two prose and twenty-nine lineated poems, the structure parallels loosely the relationship between improvisation and commentary in *Kora*.[58] Incorporating the reflexive function of Williams' intervening commentaries into its own texts, and covering a wider formal range than *Kora, Braille*, written 1972-73, comprises a series of experiments in different sentence forms and lengths, in prose and in usually stanzaic free verse. The last paragraph of 'Youngstown', for instance, combines the sound play, methodological self-reflectiveness, speed of movement and disrupted syntax or 'brokenness of . . . composition'[59] characteristic of *Kora*:

> When to the sound of mind I bring these words scattering them ahead of me in exact statement bingo! then attitudes jar and what else do you have except an attitude to shine said the anthropocentric sun sing said the line of song say these things and see where they put me get me revealed the crooked cries of bingo the large task.[60]

Here an iambic opening clause and almost obsessive alliteration combine in statements of method ('these words scattering them ahead of me', 'say these things and see where they put me') and purpose ('attitudes jar') also marked by Williams-like exclamation ('bingo!'), phrasal and sentence fragments, and a speed of association created partly *by* these fragments and partly by the absence of punctuation.

Williams' importance for Language and related innovative poetries has not manifested itself solely in a 'gender desert'; that is, it has not been limited to the male practitioners whom I have discussed so far. However, women writers aligning themselves with Williams' more exploratory language practices have at the same time often felt a greater need to negotiate his gender politics. (Without naming Williams, Lyn Hejinian remarks in *My Life* that 'his work was wiser than the horny old doctor he was', though her interest in and commitment to his work is clear from such texts as her review of Paul Mariani's 1981 biography, which I shall discuss below.)[61] Rachel Blau DuPlessis confronts the issue most directly in her semi-autobiographical essay '*Pater-daughter*', which she begins by noting the 'conventional vocabulary of race and gender' even in the 'radical literature' of *Spring and All*.[62] By the year 2004, this has become a widely assimilated observation about male modernists, precisely because of the work on gender narratives in modernism done by DuPlessis and others. But it was significantly less so when DuPlessis originally wrote the essay in 1984 at a key transitional point in her own poetic career, the moment of *(HOW)ever* magazine (founded in 1983) and a point between her revisionist feminist sequence 'from The "History of Poetry"' and 'Writing', the ur-poem for her ongoing serial work *Drafts*. For DuPlessis, as for her Language contemporaries, Williams' 'great moments' occur in the work of 1918 to 1932 (from *Kora in Hell* to '**A Novelette**'), and also in parts of *Paterson*, moments where he 'releases his poem to pass beyond gendered limits into contradictory and swarming meanings' and that she describes in Kristevan terms: 'the writing in motion, a rhythm, a pulse, desire always and desire shifting'.[63] (The further terms in which DuPlessis describes *Paterson*'s importance for her read like a thumbnail description of her own *Drafts*: 'the great confrontative entry into accumulation, discontinuity, fissure, rift'.)[64] Acknowledging that Williams provides the basis for one kind of female poetics, and redeeming parts of his work from its own gender politics, DuPlessis highlights from *Spring and All* 'two statements that certainly invent modern American poetry'—'write down that which happens at that time' and 'to practice skill in recording the force moving'.[65] She uses these statements as a paradigm for reading not just the work of Beverly Dahlen, her immediate subject, but a whole subsequent line of innovative women poets: 'What does it mean when a woman writes down that which happens at that time [a historically devalued kind of women's writing] (thus, say, Bernadette Mayer's *Midwinter Day* [1982]). What, indeed, can it be to follow the force moving, recording it, for what moves, what writes, when the writer is a woman[?]'[66] Indeed Mayer herself remarks to Alice Notley, in a letter written on 27 January 1980 and quoted by Notley, that 'I've always been grateful to [Williams] for resuscitating the prose mixed with poetry form which is a form I like and seems like a good form to be in a hurry in'.[67]

DuPlessis writes of the woman poet's ambivalent imperative to 'both follow [Williams] and leave him' due to the combination of poetic radicalism and gender conservatism.[68] Her own following occurs at various points in her serial work. Her notes on the 1984-85 'Writing', 'a poem written very much under the regime of WCW',[69] cite Williams' '**January Morning**,' and while she does not make the connection explicit, the Williams poem probably offers her a model of serial composition and of a particular kind of 'dailiness'. This suggestion is borne out by DuPlessis' quotation of "**January Morning**" in her 'Draft 23'. In the self-reflective part 14 of this modular twenty-four-part poem, one component of 'these quirky manifestations /

Incidents of a time, spare and concise' is 'the "and" of Williams'.[70] This 'and', preceded by a dash, begins seven parts of the fifteen-part **'January Morning'** and gives that poem its paratactic structure of layered, brief 'incidents of a time'—the structure, in those terms from **Spring and All** that DuPlessis cites, of 'writing down that which happens at that time'. Meeting Williams' beginning in her poem's ending, and with another formal nod in his direction, DuPlessis quotes fragments of **'January Morning'**'s first stanza in her fragmentary final section: '"strange hours" // "we keep" // That is, our lives.'[71]

Even as she celebrates Williams in her 1980 talk 'Doctor Williams' heiresses', Alice Notley records an ambivalence similar to DuPlessis' 'following' and 'leaving': 'There was always you. To love as a poet & to love & hate as a man'.[72] Although Notley's associations with Language writing are tangential, she first delivered 'Doctor Williams' Heiresses' in the series now thought of as one key site of Language writing's West Coast development, the 80 Langton Street series, and it was published by Lyn Hejinian under her Tuumba imprint. The talk begins with a playful genealogical narrative that leads up to the New American poetry and after, and to the more specific assertion that 'the one named Alice Notley fell in love with her grandfather William Carlos Williams'.[73] The voice of Ted Berrigan expounds on the various possibilities that Williams opened up, but Notley is more interested in Williams' value for women writers: 'you could use him to sound entirely new if you were a woman . . . Williams makes you feel that you can say anything, including your own anything'.[74] Notley suggests a view of gender as enablingly performative. In relation to Williams' self-construction as an 'American male', a woman poet can be both a 'female' and a person: 'there's this way to be yourself, a woman, & person that has a lot to do with William Carlos Williams'.[75] In a 1988 interview, she explains:

> Doctor Williams' Heiresses is about that. It's about my being able to relate to him and identify with him out of sexual reversal. I guess my theory was that . . . it was probably easier to be like Williams if you were a woman, because you couldn't be like him because you were a woman—and opposites can be same in spirit, and you could relate to a person like that in this whole opposite way—in a battle of the sexes way.[76]

DuPlessis' commentary in another context suggests how this 'sexual reversal' in a female poet reader can have its roots in an aspect of Williams' work. 'The shifts of gender positionality in the enounced are part of the labile attractions of early Williams' (as in a poem like **'Transitional'**), she argues, and goes on to read Williams in terms of both the range and limits of 'gender mobility' and 'split identification' in his work.[77] **'Transitional'** begins in just such a moment of a male

speaker's 'split identification': 'First he said: / It is the woman in us / That makes us write.'[78] The poem moves further into a gendered doubleness with the speaker's address to his apparently male interlocutor: 'We are not men / Therefore we can speak / And be conscious / (of the two sides)'.[79] Pushing such double identifications further, in 'Dear Dark Continent' Notley breaks down gender integrity in a way that helps clarify her comments on Williams, by breaking down pronominal integrity: 'I'm wife I'm mother I'm / myself and him and I'm myself and him and him // . . . // But I and this he (and he) makes ghosts of / I and all the *hes* there would be, won't be // because by now I am he, we are I, I am we.'[80] This elasticity of gender identification—which in 'Dear Dark Continent' could be read more conservatively as the wife and mother's merging with (male) family—increases dramatically in range, and becomes a central subject of, Notley's 'September's Book'. There 'I' is variously 'a man when I didn't / know it then' and 'the famous crouching / Aphrodite of Rhodes'; later in the poem 'I'm become this boyish-woman boy-woman little girl butch' and have to 'find my dead brother self, sir, yes'.[81] 'Do you think we men want only to be babies and women want to be perfect old men?' the speaker of one section asks; and later, 'which of us is he and she?'[82]

A different form of 'doubleness' underlies Rae Armantrout's attraction to Williams' work. In a 1999 talk, Armantrout speaks of Williams and Dickinson as two of her early literary loves. In particular she cites what she sees as an erotic subtext running through **'The Attic Which Is Desire'**, with its 'narrow, vaginal column of text, transfixed by the ejaculatory soda'.[83] It is this 'doubleness' in Williams (though he is hardly the only source of it) that appeals to a poet who describes her work as 'a poetics of the double-take, the crossroads'; her example of this tendency in her own writing is 'View'.[84] As with Armantrout's own poetry, Williams' doubleness is achieved by compression. From her first undergraduate poetry workshop at San Diego State University in 1967, Armantrout remembers 'reading **"The Attic Which Is Desire"** and being awestruck at the concentration of meaning and feeling Williams had managed to contain in those few words'.[85] She writes of Williams' 'brevity' as part of her earliest positive response to him, and of 'liking his early poem, **"Metric Figure"**, especially'[86]—this encounter occurring through Louis Untermeyer's *Modern American Poetry,* which she was given by her English teacher.[87] Brevity, compression—as Armantrout says in formulating her reading of Williams (and of Dickinson), 'I was drawn to poems that seemed as if they were either going to vanish or explode—to extremes, in other words, radical poetries'.[88]

The more specific linkage of the aesthetically exploratory and the erotic that Armantrout locates in her early reading of Williams likewise appears in her early poetry (and maintains itself through her career), for instance, in an almost programmatic passage of the mixed prose-poetry text 'Vice': 'I understand the masochist. She wants to be jerked free of habit, thrown headlong into strange positions, unmanageable acts.'[89] Here the masochist is also the poet, desiring 'strange [subject] positions' and a violent breaking up of linguistic norms or 'habits' (though also ambivalently lacking in agency—the verbs describing her are passive, befitting the 'masochist'). In a later piece, 'Getting Warm', Bob Perelman finds 'the poet achieving orgasm', while I have read the same poem as moving towards a meta-phorical description of Dickinson.[90] These two readings seem thoroughly incompatible. Combined, however, they would put encrypted sexuality together with a radically innovative female poetics in a way anticipated by Armantrout's earliest encounters with Williams.

In his reading of 'Getting Warm', Perelman hears the poem as 'concentrating on the silences between the cries that are mentioned', and Armantrout's poetics of the double-take does indeed also foreground 'between-ness'—the moments or spaces between words, images, perceptions, stanzas, statements.[91] Armantrout discusses Williams from this point of view in her talk 'Poetic silence'. There she uses Williams as her first example of ways in which a writer 'make[s] room for silence, for the experience of cessation', citing in **'January Morning'** (to which we have also seen DuPlessis responding) Williams' use of ellipsis, deliberate inconsequentiality, and 'end[ing] on a note of irresolution'—tropes characteristic of Armantrout's own poems.[92] In this way, Williams 'manage[s] to empty a moment into which questions then rise . . . to make us feel the weight of silence, and of the world'.[93]

The term that Perelman elsewhere associates with Williams' appeal, however, 'oceanic', has a negative charge for Armantrout, who connects it with Cixous' *écriture féminine* in remarking that '[Cixous'] preferred text had a rather oceanic feel to it: seamless, boundless, transcending binary categories. I imagine this model could inspire some poets working today. I myself don't find it very useful.' Her interviewer, Lyn Hejinian, responds: 'I would go even farther than you and express outright queasiness and even dislike of oceanic tenden-cies, whether they are expressed in poetry or in theoreti-cal writings. They seem the result of very poor observation'.[94] 'Observation', meanwhile, is central to that aspect of Armantrout's poetics rooted in Williams: 'Williams was the first poet I read seriously, and Ron Silliman was my first poet friend, so I guess I did start out in the Pound/Williams . . . Silliman school of poet-ics. By this I mean a notational observation of an "outer" world combined with a keen attunement to the

possibilities of form.'[95] We might recall here Silliman's own emphasis on the importance for him of fact and facticity in Williams.

Armantrout's emphasis on Williams' doubleness can return us, at least tropically, to the idea of the 'two Dr Williamses', which also provides an organizing principle for Hejinian's 1981 review of Paul Mariani's Williams biography.[96] Hejinian critiques Mariani for his inatten-tion to Williams' 'sense of the weight and value of words' and for overemphasizing thematic interpretation: 'It is not in terms of "meaning" that Williams has exerted such a strong and beneficial influence on American letters.'[97] Hejinian argues for the influence of a different Williams, a proponent of 'a poetics in which the word is the concrete perceptible fact and the structure is tantamount to statement', who begins *The Wedge* with the invocation that 'the writing / be of words'.[98] If one function of the academy, as Silliman argues, is the social organization of writing into 'literature',[99] this Williams, the Williams of many recent writers committed to formally exploratory work, stands outside literature, both as defined in High Modernism and as defined in much of the recent poetry scene. This Williams is not the author of **'The Red Wheelbarrow'** or **'Between Walls'** but rather the linguistically self-reflective Williams of the lines cited above: 'nothing / I have done // is made up of / nothing / and the diphthong // ae . . .'[100] It is the Williams who pursued a cultural politics of oppositionality through a poetics of generic hybridity and a materialist attention to language as writ-ten. It is the Williams of the jumpily Dadaist 'What about all this writing', invoked by Silliman in his book *Lit* via the quoted line 'O Miss Margaret Jarvis'.[101] That Silliman should allude to Williams' 'writing' in the context of 'Lit', his term for institutionalized literature and his version of Bernstein's 'official verse culture', speaks exactly to the importance of the older poet for recent experimental writing. Language and other exploratory poetics can be read as the apotheosis of that moment early in *Spring and All* when 'the terms "verac-ity", "actuality", "real", "natural", "sincere", are being discussed at length'.[102] In engaging that discussion, Language writing especially was often accused by its detractors of opacity and incoherence. On these points, I will conclude by citing the 10 November 1917 letter from Ezra Pound that Williams reprints in the prologue to *Kora*. Referring to some of the recently published improvisations, Pound writes: 'I was very glad to see your wholly incoherent unAmerican poems in the L[ittle] R[eview]. . . . The thing that saves your work is opacity, and don't forget it.'[103] Rather than his much-vaunted clarity, it was this opacity, alleged incoherence and disjoining of language from conventional forms of reference and subjectivity that proved foundational for at least one particular group of Williams' later poet readers.

Notes

Thanks to Rachel Blau DuPlessis, for resources and exchanges helpful to the development of this essay.

1. William Carlos Williams, *Imaginations* (New York: New Directions, 1970), p. 145; William Carlos Williams, *The Embodiment of Knowledge,* ed. Ron Loewinsohn (New York: New Directions, 1974), p. 13.

2. Williams, *Imaginations,* p. 159; Williams, *Embodiment,* p. 128.

3. Williams, *Imaginations,* p. 166.

4. Ibid., pp. 16, 169.

5. Ibid., pp. 166, 172.

6. Ibid., pp. 49, 149.

7. Hank Lazer, *Opposing Poetries,* vol. 2, *Readings* (Evanston, IL: Northwestern University Press, 1996), pp. 19-28.

8. Bob Perelman, *The Marginalization of Poetry: Language Writing and Literary History* (Princeton, NJ: Princeton University Press, 1996), pp. 12, 88.

9. Linda Kinnahan, *Poetics of the Feminine: Authority and Tradition in William Carlos Williams, Mina Loy, Denise Levertov, and Kathleen Fraser* (New York: Cambridge University Press, 1994); John Lowney, *The American Avant-Garde Tradition: William Carlos Williams, Postmodern Poetry, and the Politics of Cultural Memory* (Lewisburg, PA: Bucknell University Press, 1997). As one exception to this generalization, see Stephen Fredman, *Poet's Prose: The Crisis in American Verse* (New York: Cambridge University Press, 1983).

10. Benjamin Friedlander, 'A short history of language poetry/according to "Hecuba Whimsy"', *Qui Parle* 12:2 (2001), p. 117.

11. Bob Perelman, 'A conversation with Bob Perelman', interview by Peter Nicholls, *Textual Practice,* 12 (1998), p. 534.

12. Ron Silliman, *The New Sentence* (New York: Roof, 1989), p. 23.

13. Robert Grenier, 'On Speech', in Ron Silliman (ed.), *In the American Tree: Language, Poetry, Realism* (Orono, ME: National Poetry Foundation, 1986), p. 496.

14. Ibid.

15. Perelman, *Marginalization of Poetry,* p. 43.

16. Silliman, *New Sentence,* p. 157.

17. Before its appearance as the prefatory poem in Silliman's anthology, 'In the American Tree' was published in Robinson's *Down and Back* (Berkeley, CA: The Figures, 1978). For a discussion of the poem, see Barrett Watten, *Total Syntax* (Carbondale and Edwardsville: Southern Illinois Press, 1985), pp. 62-4. Watten concludes with the key remark that 'distance, rather than absorption, is the intended effect' (p. 64).

18. Silliman, *New Sentence,* p. 63.

19. Williams, *Imaginations,* p. 6.

20. Silliman, *New Sentence,* p. 83.

21. Ibid., p. 84.

22. Fredman, *Poet's Prose,* p. 50.

23. Ibid., pp. 15-16.

24. Silliman, *New Sentence,* p. 130.

25. Ibid.

26. Ibid., pp. 135-6.

27. Ibid., p. 136.

28. Silliman, interview with Manuel Brito, in Manuel Brito (ed.), *A Suite of Poetic Voices: Interviews with Contemporary American Poets* (Santa Brigida: Kadel Books, 1992), p. 162.

29. William Carlos Williams, *The Collected Poems of William Carlos Williams,* vol. 2, 1939-1962, ed. Christopher MacGowan (New York: New Directions, 1988), p. 284.

30. Ron Silliman, untitled talk on William Carlos Williams, Modernist Studies Association, Kelly Writers House, Philadelphia, 12 October 2000. Sound file available at http://dept.english.upenn.edu/~wh/9poets.html.

31. Silliman, ibid.; Williams, *Imaginations,* pp. 113-15.

32. Ron Silliman, *Crow* (Ithaca, NY: Ithaca House, 1971).

33. Ibid., p. 12.

34. Ibid., p. 2; Williams, *Imaginations,* p. 132.

35. Silliman, untitled talk.

36. Ron Silliman, 'Berkeley', in Michael Lally (ed.), *None of the Above: New Poets of the USA* (Trumansburg, NY: The Crossing Press, 1976), p. 63.

37. Williams, *Imaginations,* p. 104.

38. Lazer, *Opposing Poetries,* vol. 2, p. 25.

39. Charles Bernstein, *Content's Dream: Essays 1975-1984* (Los Angeles, CA: Sun and Moon, 1986), p. 246.

40. Ibid., p. 251.

41. Ibid., pp. 137, 139.

42. Ibid., p. 137.

43. Ibid., pp. 159, 139.

44. Ibid., p. 301.

45. Ibid., p. 450.

46. Perelman, *Marginalization of Poetry*, p. 147.

47. Watten, *Total Syntax*, p. 109.

48. William Carlos Williams, *Pictures From Brueghel and Other Poems* (New York: New Directions, 1962), p. 137.

49. Perelman, *Marginalization of Poetry*, pp. 152-3.

50. Ibid., p. 153.

51. Ibid., p. 164.

52. Ibid., p. 165.

53. Bob Perelman, 'The First Person', *Hills*, 6/7 (spring 1980), p. 148.

54. Ibid., p. 161.

55. Bob Perelman, *Captive Audience* (Great Barrington, MA: The Figures, 1988), pp. 58-9.

56. Bob Perelman, *The Future of Memory* (New York: Roof, 1988), p. 63.

57. Bob Perelman, *Ten to One: Selected Poems* (Hanover, NH: Wesleyan University Press/ University Press of New England, 1999), p. 1.

58. For Perelman's critical commentary not on *Kora* per se but on disjunct prose in Stendhal, Michael Gottlieb and Clark Coolidge, see his essay 'Plotless prose', *Poetics Journal*, 1 (1982), pp. 25-34. It is worth noticing that Williams' genre-bending 'improvisations' do not get discussed as prose poems in two major studies of the genre, Jonathan Monroe's *A Poverty of Objects: The Prose Poem and the Politics of Genre* (Ithaca, NY: Cornell University Press, 1987) and Michel Delville's *The American Prose Poem: Poetic Form and the Boundaries of Genre* (Gainesville: University Press of Florida, 1998).

59. Williams, *Imaginations*, p. 16.

60. Perelman, *Braille* (Ithaca, NY: Ithaca House, 1975), p. 4.

61. Lyn Hejinian, *My Life* (Los Angeles, CA: Sun and Moon, 1986), p. 53. 'Hecuba Whimsy' calls Williams 'a rarely remarked influence' on Hejinian (Friedlander, 'A short history', p. 132).

62. Rachel Blau DuPlessis, *The Pink Guitar: Writing as Feminist Practice* (New York: Routledge, 1990), p. 41.

63. Ibid., p. 59.

64. Ibid., p. 61. DuPlessis' engagement with Williams began with college reading and continued into her unpublished Columbia University dissertation, *The Endless Poem: Paterson of William Carlos Williams and The Pisan Cantos of Ezra Pound*. The work from that dissertation haunts both *The Pink Guitar* and *Drafts*.

65. Ibid., p. 110. Williams' statements occur in *Imaginations*, p. 1.

66. DuPlessis, *The Pink Guitar*, p. 111.

67. Alice Notley, *Doctor Williams' Heiresses* (Willits, CA: Tuumba Press, 1980), n. pag.

68. DuPlessis, *The Pink Guitar*, p. 111.

69. E-mail to the author, 6 December 2000. Quoted with permission.

70. Rachel Blau DuPlessis, *Drafts 1-38, Toll* (Middletown, CT: Wesleyan University Press, 2001), p. 49.

71. DuPlessis, *Drafts*, p. 53.

72. Notley, *Doctor Williams' Heiresses*.

73. Ibid.

74. Ibid.

75. Ibid.

76. Alice Notley, 'Alice Notley (1)', interview with Edward Foster, in Edward Foster (ed.), *Poetry and Poetics in a New Millennium* (Jersey City: Talisman House, 2000), p. 71.

77. Rachel Blau DuPlessis, *Genders, Races and Religious Cultures in Modern American Poetry, 1908-1934* (New York: Cambridge University Press, 2001), pp. 31-4.

78. William Carlos Williams, *The Collected Poems of William Carlos Williams*, vol. 1, *1909-1939*, ed. A. Walton Litz and Christopher MacGowan (New York: New Directions, 1988), p. 40.

79. Ibid.

80. Alice Notley, *Selected Poems of Alice Notley* (Hoboken, NJ: Talisman House, 1993), p. 1.

81. Ibid., pp. 33, 39, 40.

82. Ibid., pp. 42, 44. 'Hecuba Whimsy' sets Notley against the materialist poetics that is the subject of 'her' essay and that I am tracing to Williams (Friedlander, 'A short history', p. 136). However,

these moments of diffused, displaced and often cross-gendered subjectivity in Notley strike me as one point of contact.

83. Rae Armantrout, 'Cheshire poetics', *Fence,* 3:1 (2000), p. 94.

84. Ibid., p. 96. Armantrout discusses this poem in 'Cheshire Poetics', p. 94; it appears in *Extremities* (Berkeley, CA: The Figures, 1978), p. 25.

85. Rae Armantrout, *True* (Berkeley, CA: Atelos, 1998), p. 56.

86. Ibid., p. 36. Williams has two early poems called 'Metric Figure'. 'Metric Figure' ('There is a bird in the poplars—') is the one that appears in the Untermeyer anthology.

87. Ibid., p. 35.

88. Armantrout, 'Cheshire poetics', p. 92.

89. Armantrout, *Extremities,* p. 27.

90. 'Getting Warm' appears in Rae Armantrout, *Necromance* (Los Angeles: Sun and Moon, 1991), p. 43. For Perelman's reading, see Bob Perelman, 'Exactly: the poetry of Rae Armantrout', in Tom Beckett (ed.), *A Wild Salience: The Poetry of Rae Armantrout* (Cleveland, OH: Burning Press, 1999), p. 160; for mine, see Alan Golding, '"Drawings with words": Susan Howe's visual poetics', in Laura Hinton and Cynthia Hogue (eds), *'We Who "Love to Be Astonished"': Experimental Women's Writing and Performance Poetics* (Tuscaloosa: University of Alabama Press, 2002), p. 164.

91. Perelman, 'Exactly', p. 160.

92. Rae Armantrout, 'Poetic silence', in Bob Perelman (ed.), *Writing/Talks* (Carbondale and Edwardsville: Southern Illinois University Press, 1985), pp. 34, 35.

93. Ibid., p. 40.

94. Rae Armantrout, 'An interview with Rae Armantrout', interview with Lyn Hejinian, in Beckett, *A Wild Salience,* p. 17. Again, we do not have a single 'alternative' Williams, as elements of the 'oceanic' are much more important to DuPlessis' reading of him.

95. Ibid., p. 25.

96. Paul Mariani, *William Carlos Williams: A New World Naked* (New York: McGraw-Hill, 1981).

97. Lyn Hejinian, 'An American opener', *Poetics Journal,* 1 (1982), pp. 61, 64.

98. Ibid., p. 64; Williams, *Collected Poems,* vol. 2, p. 55.

99. 'Literature is the social organization of writing' (Silliman, *The New Sentence,* p. 129). See also Silliman's remark that 'the process of public canonization, that which converts the broad horizon of writing into the simplified and hierarchic topography of Literature, capital L, is a disease', in 'Canons and institutions: new hope for the disappeared', in Charles Bernstein (ed.), *The Politics of Poetic Form: Poetry and Public Policy* (New York: Roof, 1990), p. 152.

100. Williams, *Imaginations,* p. 104.

101. Ron Silliman, *Lit* (Elmwood: Potes and Poets, 1987), p. 53.

102. Williams, *Imaginations,* p. 93.

103. Ezra Pound, *The Letters of Ezra Pound 1907-1941,* ed. D. D. Paige (New York: Harcourt, Brace & World, 1950), p. 124.

Ron Callan (essay date 2004)

SOURCE: Callan, Ron. "William Carlos Williams's *An Early Martyr*: The Descent Beckons." In *Rebound: The American Poetry Book,* edited by Michael Hinds and Stephen Matterson, pp. 99-109. Amsterdam: Rodopi, 2004.

[*In the following essay, Callan analyzes* An Early Martyr *as an unappreciated part of the Williams canon and argues that the later revisions of the work detract rather than add to its value.*]

When one thinks of the Williams canon, **Spring and All, In the American Grain, White Mule, The Wedge, Paterson,** and **Pictures from Breughel** come to mind. **An Early Martyr** (1935) seems beyond that pale. It is a book of its time, resonant with issues from the 1930s: the Depression, left-wing politics, and "Objectivism".[1] It also comes close to what is generally accepted as the end of Williams's "early" phase, and a time in which he was having difficulty writing poetry, measuring poems.[2] Also, **An Early Martyr** is not marked by the poet's radical combination of poetry and prose passages.[3] However, both in the manner of its construction and the ways in which Williams used it thereafter, **An Early Martyr** adds considerably to the range of his achievements. My interest here is in the process toward publication, the consequences of the arrangement of the poems, the effect of Williams's recycling of material from earlier publications, and the unravelling of the primacy of the book in its reinvention in later versions. I am influenced in this by Stanley Koehler's work on Williams's "descent" in the 1940s[4] and particularly the notion that "Memory is a kind / of accomplishment".[5] **An Early Martyr** was a new book of poems in 1935 that undermined the simple autonomy of the object.

Published by Alcestis Press, *An Early Martyr* was Williams's (at the time, almost 52 years old) fifth book of poems (excluding his "first" book, *Poems,* which he insisted should not be published again). Williams had waited twelve years for a book of poems after *Spring and All.* The publisher, Ronald Lane Latimer, was, according to Williams, a "strange person", adding that the name was an "an alias, I think".[6] His suspicions were correct. Alan Filreis's study of the pseudonymous Latimer's work with Wallace Stevens reveals Latimer's complexity (even confusion) of name and mind. His first editorial for *Alcestis Quarterly* promoted the poet who tries "to capture and intensify the beauty of things as he sees them" (Stevens and Edith Sitwell are his examples) over the one who uses art as "an instrument of an economic theory" (Auden and Spender).[7] Latimer would later admit:

> I love the idea of bringing out a proletarian . . . poet in a deluxe edition! These lovely incongruities.[8]

Filreis describes Latimer's change of mind as "spectacular".[9] It was this "strange person", an aesthete who discovers the truth of the Communist Party while remaining committed to deluxe publications, who provided Williams with an almost unique opportunity—the publication of a book of poems.

Williams was ill-prepared for the project, as this 1935 letter to Latimer indicates:

> Certainly, I'd like to have a book of verse by the Alcestis Press. I haven't a damned thing to send you for #3 [*Alcestis Quarterly*]—not even a line of a poem. Everything has been snatched out of my hands the moment it's written. I am even starting to write them to order now.
>
> (SL [*The Selected Letters of William Carlos Williams*] 152)

To add to the complexity of the offer, Latimer sought to produce a limited edition on *duca di modena* and all-rag paper. Of the 165 copies, 135 would be for sale at "seven and a half Depression dollars".[10] In context, the complete, unabridged *Ulysses,* published by Random, sold for $3.50.[11] This was in a market where book sales in the U.S. had dipped from 214 million in 1929 to 111 million in 1933.[12] *An Early Martyr* added eight copies to the total for 1935-36.[13] Alcestis Press published two books for Williams (and books for Stevens, Allen Tate and Robert Penn Warren) before Latimer "went broke and quit" (A [*The Autobiography of William Carlos Williams*] 299).

An Early Martyr is dedicated to John Coffey (printed Coffee here and in Williams's *Autobiography*), a political activist, shoplifter, Robin Hood figure, and subject of the title poem. After the dedication, Williams notes, "Many of these poems have been published / in the

magazines—almost all of them".[14] This is not quite accurate. Some of the poems are taken, without substantial changes to the originals, from *Spring and All*: "**The Right of Way**" (Poem XI), "**The Black Winds**" (Poem V), and "**The Farmer**" (Poem III). In addition he made a small but significant change to "**Young Romance**" (Poem IX). "**The Sadness of the Sea**" is a rewritten section from *The Descent of Winter* (1928), and "**The Wind Increases**" was originally published in *Della Primavera Trasportata al Morale,* a sequence published in 1930. Finally, some of his more recent publications in magazines were carefully edited. The most dramatic example of this is "**The Locust Tree in Flower**" where he pared the original down to single-word lines. *An Early Martyr* is not a new book of poems gathered from magazines. In fact, it represents Williams's fascination with the links between past and present expressed some years later: "Yes, most assuredly, I am conscious in everything I write of a usable past, a past as alive in its day as every moment is alive in me."[15]

In this reading, *An Early Martyr* represents another challenge by Williams to the meaning of a book of poems. This is less evident than, for example, in *Spring and All.* However, by the 1930s he was presenting his work as a poet in a more traditional sense—he excluded the prose from *Spring and All* in the 1934 *Complete Collected Poems.* One might speculate that the rapidly developing academic interest in the microtext of the poem (and the canonization of T. S. Eliot's work) was one context for the change in direction. More telling though, as the letter to Kay Boyle indicates, was his concern with the technical aspects of poetry. Continuing to assess the influence of Whitman's work, Williams was keen to establish a measure, not free verse, to reflect his America. This is an important focus for many of his essays throughout the 1930s—the material is words and the work is technical.[16] Certainly the mere asymmetric design of many of the poems and the general range of forms in *An Early Martyr* are testimony to Williams's tireless experimentation. However, it must be remembered that, as John Beck says, "Williams's belief in technique is likewise [comparison is to John Dewey's work] understood as a nonideological means of accurately constructing a response to, and out of, historical contingency".[17] Poetry and history/politics were related elements for him.

Particularly challenging (though hidden from most readers of *An Early Martyr*) was his use of poems from *Spring and All,* his self-plagiarism. In *Spring and All* Williams had attacked, "THE TRADITIONALISTS OF PLAGIARISM", those who insist on the value of tradition and seek to limit the pursuit of the new.[18] Remarkably, he returned to *Spring and All* to plagiarize his own work and make it new. In some cases he makes changes to a poem to create a new poem of sorts; in others, the poems are copies which rely on contexts to establish their new credentials. This may recall Whitman's various editions of *Leaves of Grass*; however, here we do not get another version of *Spring and All*. Williams's book presents a layered textual site requiring careful and progressive excavation. As the poems are reused without any reference to the original, the consequences for readers and critics are quite serious—limited knowledge results in limited responses. His tactics have affected our current (and indeed future) knowledge of the book. A. Walton Litz and Christopher MacGowan unfortunately decided not to reprint some of the "copies" in their definitive *Collected*—they merely refer readers back to *Spring and All* or elsewhere. In this *Collected, An Early Martyr* becomes less a book in its own right and more a number of poems with references to other poems. The editors' decision does not allow easy access to the contexts created by Williams's construction. In 1935 it was a book with full texts and absent contexts; now it is a book with full contexts and absent texts. There are thirty poems in the original publication of *An Early Martyr*. I shall begin by discussing the opening three poems to establish the importance of the arrangement of the poems. Then I will discuss the critical mid-point poems to establish the significance of *Spring and All* and the lingering effect it has on the book as a whole.[19]

II

John Coffey of **"An Early Martyr"** is presented in a five-stanza poem, lightly punctuated to reflect his rebelliousness. He becomes a "factory whistle" shouting "Sense, sense, sense!" against the double-crossing standards of the courts (*CP* [*The Collected Poems of William Carlos Williams*] *1* 378). In doing so, Coffey seizes the signal for industry's control of the masses. Unlike his real-life defeat (he is committed to a mental institution), the young revolutionary infiltrates the system he opposes and uses its voice for his ends. The whistle, originally transformed from a meaningless sound into a symbolic utterance by the factory owners, is remade as a word: "sense". The world is turned upside down and the fool speaks sense; the poet/artist unravels the strait-jacket and frees the madman. The poem is to-the-point and didactic. Robert von Hallberg reads "poles of discourse" into *An Early Martyr* of description and explanation: **"An Early Martyr"** is explanatory, offering "a structure of understanding."[20] This directness also exercises Barry Ahearn who mistakenly decides **"An Early Martyr"** is a "dramatic monologue".[21] Limited as both views are, they reflect the immediacy of the poem, its force of reality.

Theme and form change dramatically in **"Flowers by the Sea"** (*CP1* 378). Hallberg sees this as a shift from didacticism to description.[22] Here the imagination plays upon flowers and the sea in ways that suppress the tendency to narrative in **"An Early Martyr"**. However,

something of the rebellion remains as the absence of full-stops is set against the clear structure of four couplets. The voice is lyrical, precious, and separate from social concerns. The flowers are transformed to be "hardly flowers"; the sea, a "plantlike stem". The relatedness of distinct objects indicates the power of the imagination to transform them—flower can be sea and sea, flower. When set against the immediacy of **"An Early Martyr"**, one could say that this is a satire on poetry that ignores social issues. **"Flowers by the Sea"** performs magic; Coffey lives in the real world where magicians/deviants are incarcerated. Side by side, these poems present a clash of values. However, the emphasis in **"Flowers by the Sea"** is on the energy produced by their interaction—"restlessness" is the result. This is the imaginative thrust which made the "factory whistle" into "sense", which unpicked the lock on social inequalities. To say simply that flower is flower and sea is sea is to say that right is right and wrong is wrong, and, consequently, that challenges to authority are forms of madness. **"Flowers by the Sea"** expresses a paradoxical world, a world which produces shocking and delightful results. Hallberg accounts for this as "poetry which can both see and understand".[23]

His reading of the poem is similar to my own here. However, this interpretation only becomes clear in the third poem, which indicates the level of complexity to which Williams aspires. **"Item"** offers no specific location but shifts us back to a social setting. It deals with the violence perpetrated by a figure or figures of authority which leaves the woman as simply "a note / at the foot of the page" (*CP1* 379). In placing the footnote in the main text, Williams disrupts the normal angle of vision. As significant is that the woman appears as both a realized human figure and as a textual citation. **"Item"** straddles the worlds of the opening poems and acts as a statement of inclusiveness. It points to the social and political power in a mere footnote or lyric poem. It redefines **"An Early Martyr"** by undercutting the realism of Coffey's story. He is reclaimed as text, as a figure of the poem. Wedged between these two poems is the fragile **"Flowers by the Sea"**, now humming with political resonances drawn from the adjacent material. The shifting perspectives within and between the opening three poems point to the interests of the book: to measure text requires context.

However, establishing a consistent line of argument is difficult given the force of each individual experience. As John Beck writes, "Williams cannot bring himself to think of political action in terms of a class struggle, but as a defense of individual liberty".[24] This becomes a vital issue as the contexts intensify and the book reaches midpoint, shared by the fifteenth and sixteenth poems in the collection: **"Solstice"** and **"The Yachts"**. **"Solstice"** records "the shortest day of the year" (*CP1* 388). Williams's 1928 collection, *The Descent of Winter,* had ended on the 18th of December, but here darkness is an optimistic mid-point: "the shortest day of the year // is favourable"—an ending without punctuation to signal an open vista. The vision is fulfilled by the next poem, **"The Yachts"**. As in **"Item"**, story and image combine to explore the clash of two elemental forces in America: paradoxically, individualism takes on individualism. I say this because the yachts are signs of American enterprise and individualism. However, the beaten masses also represent individualism. Here though it is individualism-in-the-making, unrealized, but guaranteed, as Williams saw it, in America as nowhere else in the world: "Then I have been tremendously impressed with the past of the United States. That's deep in my blood. Nothing has displaced one bit of my emotions—the regular 4th of July stuff! [*sic*] that I once felt so strongly."[25]

The yacht races are a metonym for American achievements (American crews were unbeatable in these races for many years). They are also a metonym for its failures, "an indictment of the untouchable brilliance of American capitalism".[26] The *terza rima* of the opening stanza links it to Dante's *Inferno,* to man's epic ambitions and sinfulness.[27] The poet's unwillingness to sustain the *terza rima* beyond the first two stanzas points to the sterility of such gestures:

> Williams dangles the Dantesque pattern before us just long enough to make us wonder whether or not it is really there. Then, having hinted at prosodic ancestry, he abandons the model.[28]

The American form must be looser, more adaptable and less epical, and its immediate success, evident in the glory of the yachts, is greater—more about winning; less about sin. However, the vision shifts when the sea becomes a "sea of faces" (*CP1* 389). The yachts take on a new level of meaning, becoming powerful and anti-democratic forces which "pass over" the beaten masses (*CP1* 389). The poem opens out to include images of a mass slaughter, as the sea "resembles an entanglement of watery bodies" (*CP1* 389), in which Dante's vision of suffering is recalled. The actions of the yachts mirror those of Coffey's judges, those who determine the limited value of footnotes. Here at the point of extreme darkness came the promise of light and hope. The yachts prove to be a false dawn, emerging as symbols of hell not heaven, of fascism not democracy. **"The Yachts"** is the preface to **"Young Romance"** (Poem IX *CP1* 200-2), the first poem taken from *Spring and All.* In its original publication it was prefaced by the following:

> Whitman's proposals are of the same piece with the modern trend toward imaginative understanding of life. The largeness which he interprets as his identity with the least and the greatest about him, his "democracy" represents the vigor of his imaginative life.

> (*CP1* 199)

This promotes much of what **"The Yachts"** almost represented. The poem gives expression to the "least and the greatest"; it points to the "vigor of . . . imaginative life". However, it recalls a sinful world older than American democracy. In *Spring and All,* Whitman urged the young lovers forward; in *An Early Martyr,* the context is more complex—William's recontextualization of the poem ("The Yachts not Whitman) undermines the lovers' hopes. The words may be the same but **"Young Romance"** now draws little comfort from the lovers: he "watched" while she "tore [her] hair" (*CP1* 391).

The changes to **"Young Romance"** point to the limitations of Whitman's vision and the terrible consequences of the powerful yachts. In *Spring and All* we read,

> but I merely
> caress you curiously
>
> fifteen year ago and you still
> go about the city, they say
> patching up sick school children[29]

In 1923, the poet remembers the past but can "caress" in the present. While there is a marked separation of narrator from the woman, he can still bring her to life, still caress her. This is not quite Whitman's assumption, but it is a related level of relationship which emphasizes the power of the poet.

Williams changed the tense to "caressed" in *An Early Martyr.*[30] The change may seem slight, but is important given his removal of the stanza break for the 1938 *Complete Collected*:

> Clean is he alone
> after whom stream
> the broken pieces of the city—
> flying apart at his approaches
>
> but I merely
> caressed you curiously
> fifteen years ago and you still
> go about the city, they say
> patching up sick school children[31]

> (*CP1* 391)

In all versions, Williams is not "[c]lean" nor is he separate from his subject—relationships are limited. The poem records the woman's fifteen-year commitment to her work apart from him. He recognizes the dangers inherent in Whitman's assumptions and he seeks to limit them by recognizing the woman's freedom—he hears of her from second-hand sources ("they say"). However, the change to "caressed", and the later deletion of the paragraph break stress the dislocation of the speaker/poet from the woman/subject. The revisions signal the poet's limited power (he cannot "caress" her now) and the paradoxical freedom inherent in this new poetic vision. The past is in the past and what he recalls are memories. The shift in the later versions is increasingly away from assumptive authority, from transcendence of time, to a celebration of difference. The vigour and optimism of Whitman's vision is retained, but the shift is towards an understanding and expression of necessary circumferences. A new beginning is made in re-measuring memories and poems.

This grounding of the imagination leads Williams to consider transcendental experiences. He writes of Sappho and Shakespeare in **"Hymm to Love Ended"**, of Lawrence in **"An Elegy for D. H. Lawrence"**, of the rituals of chat and time in **"Sunday"**, and of the power of "isms" in **"The Catholic Bells"**. In the main these poems offer a visual order on the page to suggest a relief from the asymmetry to this point. They suggest how individuals succeed beyond an immediate sense of self. They are, however, potentially reactionary in seeking to circumvent the issues raised by the process to date. It is *Spring and All*'s **"The Auto Ride"** which recalls the here-and-now. The perspective returns to ground level as the narrator drives a car. The poem's couplets-as-stanzas point away from grander themes to focus on ordinary people, ending with, "I saw a girl with one leg / over the rail of the balcony" (*CP1* 206). Here the speed of the car produces an abundance of images—individual moments not represented as part of transcendent or ritualized contexts. It was enough, as Williams says immediately after the poem in *Spring and All,* to "write down what happens at the time" (206). In *An Early Martyr,* it is not enough because, in this context, the girl represents a blasphemous priestess on a balcony/pulpit. Her leg becomes a dangling, undefined signifier as the car/congregation speeds past. Once it was enough to record its reality. Now contexts are added which include hymns, masses, and literary history. Against the weight of this past, the blasphemous footnote is redrawn in a textual space which shares ground with those transcendent experiences—following **"The Catholic Bells"**, the lower-case world offers its own solace.

The final movement of the book includes three poems, **"To Be Hungry Is To Be Great"** (*CP1* 400), **"A Poem for Norman Macleod"** (*CP1* 401) and **"You Have Pissed Your Life"** (*CP1* 401-2). The first two mark Williams's confidence in what is available "at the time". Valuable material is found and celebrated—the "yellow grass-onion" which when "well cooked" complements "beer" (**"To Be Hungry"**) and "gum" from the "balsam" which is a cure for "constipation" (**"Norman Macleod"**). Both poems suggest that high culture disregards resources at hand and limits the imagination. A cure is earned by attending to the ordinary: "noble has been / changed to no bull"—European aristocracy gives way to American pragmatism. *An Early Martyr*

moves towards a conclusion of confidence reminiscent of *Spring and All*'s "rich" and local **"Black eyed susan"** (*CP1* 236). However, martyrdom is recalled with the chant, "You have pissed your life" (*CP1* 401-2). This repeated charge connects the poet to John Coffey's "madness". He, who rescued marginalized figures by attention to details, is now himself marginalized, declared less than a footnote. The book closes with memories of its beginning and links the subject of the book with its writer—both suffer the wrong-headed judgement of the powerful; both, in different ways, are marked as martyrs for an apparently lost cause.

However concealed, Williams's use of *Spring and All* in *An Early Martyr* is significant. On one level, the latter is a conventional book of poems. That said, it seems to me that Williams presses on with his work in significant ways. The self-plagiarism reminds us of some of his concerns then and the success it suggested, the awakening in **"Spring and All"**. However, Williams's vision in 1935 has altered and his self-plagiarism indicates his continuous interests as it points to subtle changes. Dealing with the hard facts of Depression America, Williams draws on his own resources as he tests them. In context, his *Spring and All* poems give as they yield—contributing images of survival to the rebels and being recontextualized to show the limitations and adaptability of the earlier vision. Ultimately the presence of *Spring and All* points to Williams's continual challenge to the notions of simple time and space; here he undercuts the microtext of the poem and the autonomy of the book of poems. As in his image of Coffey as the whistle, Williams infiltrates notions of the pure poem to point to ever present contexts—the individual cannot be separated from society.

III

Williams rewrote *An Early Martyr* twice: for the 1938 *Complete Collected* and for his *Collected Earlier Poems* in 1951. The chart in the appendix following this essay indicates the changes he introduced in each case. The first noteworthy change in 1938 is in the order in which **"Item"** and **"The Locust Tree in Flower"** appear. Together now, **"Locust Tree in Flower"** and **"Flowers by the Sea"** "secure that aesthetic orientation with some purely natural subjects".[32] Once, however, this is completed, Williams develops a strong line of community-focused poems. This is emphasized by the deletion of **"The Sadness of the Sea"**. Indeed the tension between the social and the pastoral (almost strophe-antistrophe in the original) is all but removed but for **"Tree and Sky"**. It means that that mid-point crisis which I addressed above is less obvious. More damaging, nine of the twelve poems were removed from the latter half of the book. Williams returned all *Spring and All* poems to the original volume for the *Complete*

Collected. The effect of these changes is to suggest a clear line of development in *An Early Martyr,* emphasized at the end with the exclusion of **"You Have Pissed Your Life"**. The conclusion now rests with a sense of real achievement. The book opens with John Coffey and closes with Norman Macleod, martyr to saviour— however tentative, new nobility is at hand. It represents significantly fewer of the possibilities in the original as the lingering martyrdom is excised.

The publication of *The Collected Earlier Poems* represents another life for *An Early Martyr.* Williams added six poems to the 1938 list to bring the total to twenty-four. He did this by adding five poems which could have been included in the original volume as they were written before 1935 (including the earlier version of **"The Locust Tree in Flower"**); the sixth, **"A Portrait of the Times"**, was written after the original publication. Still the rebel, Williams chose to place the later version of **"The Locust Tree in Flower"** before the earlier one. All additions were placed towards the front of the book and five of them emphasized a pastoral world, superficially promoting the poetic over the political. Robert J. Cirasa describes them as "six, lyrically inconsequential poems".[33] Whatever their value, Williams does not depoliticize the book, but he thoroughly embeds social commentary in the natural cycle evident, for example, in **"Wild Orchard"**:

> one, risen as a tree,
> has turned
> from his repose.[34]

Here the repose gives way to action as the death of winter gives way to spring. It is a romantic, even sentimental, simile. Beginning with an account of a radical socialist, this book charts a patient journey to the vision of a radical poet—it tends to stress poetics over politics. To add to its problematic status, Williams placed *An Early Martyr* before *Al Que Quiere!* in the *Collected Earlier Poems,* suggesting that it was a book written in 1915 or 1916.[35] Why he did this is a very contentious issue. Cirasa offers evidence to suggest that the placement was Williams's error as he was recovering from a recent stroke;[36] Paul Mariani records that Williams's recuperation was "amazingly rapid" and that he had the energy and ability to complete projects;[37] and Litz accepts that the placement was the result of Williams's wish for a "thematic arrangement".[38] In addition, there is no record that Williams objected to the arrangement in *Collected Earlier Poems.*[39]

One could argue that each subsequent edition of *An Early Martyr* added to its depoliticization. Moving it to the relative obscurity of the 1910s certainly suggests this—it is now a World War I book without reference to that war. In addition, the book is set in immediate contexts which are difficult to assess. We move, for

example, from **"A Poem for Norman Macleod"** to the opening lines of **"Sub Terra"** in *Al Que Quierre!*:

> Where shall I find you,
> you my grotesque fellows
> that I seek everywhere
> to make up my band?

(CEP [The Collected Earlier Poems of William Carlos Williams]117)

Certainly a poet seeks an audience in both poems, but the detail, sharp focus, and humour of **"Norman Macleod"** is not matched by the generalized plea from a would-be leader of a band. While a sensitive reader might have noticed the uneven development from book to book within the collection, establishing its significance would have been difficult. In setting these books adjacent to each other, Williams may have established some thematic continuity but on the level of content and form he undoubtedly created confusion. Effectively this undermines the coherence of the collection as a whole as it emphasizes the need for contexts. How one book relates to another becomes an important issue. Is this displacement of *An Early Martyr* similar to his recycling of *Spring and All* poems? Yes is the answer because the new locations undo established meanings. This does not simply apply to books adjacent to *An Early Martyr.* We should note that it now precedes *Spring and All.* Once we know the history of these books, then we have to consider what, for example, **"The Yachts"** brings now to Whitman in *Spring and All* or how we read Williams's attack on plagiarists?

In addition, however much the original *An Early Martyr* has been trimmed, it still remains an indication of left-wing interests. My argument is that the placement has much to do with politics. *The Collected Earlier Poems* was compiled in 1951 by Williams. He was no longer facing the Depression; now it was the Cold War and anti-Communist witch-hunts. As Mariani observes, the McCarthy era was far from over.[40] Williams's direct literary response was expressed in *Tituba's Children* (1950)—his play links Washington politics in the 1940s to the witch trials in Salem in 1692.[41] Williams was clearly keen and unafraid to address Cold War politics. One would imagine that keeping *An Early Martyr* in the 1930s would have added to his credentials as a politically minded poet; placing it as he did seems to neutralize its politics. Given Williams's work on *Tituba's Children,* this is inexplicable unless we accept that Williams moved his proletarian portraits to radicalise an earlier period. He began *The Collected Earlier Poems* with **"The Wanderer"** which includes a sympathetic, if sentimental view, of working-class Paterson. *An Early Martyr* does much to accentuate that representation. In its revised softer tones, this version of *An Early Martyr* almost blends into the period as it unsettles his poetic practices at the time. In doing so it draws attention to itself. Williams realigns his interests in left-wing politics to emphasize that this version was more than a response to the Depression or the Cold War, but was also a significant factor in his development as a poet.

An Early Martyr has had a remarkable publication history. Initially it was a response to crises (Depression to writing) and an opportunity (willing publisher). It is a strange gathering of poems from a variety of sources. In it Williams offers complex views of individual liberty and social justice. In tandem is the relationship between individual poem and book, and between book and book. Superficially he returns to poems as microtexts and away from the poem/prose blend that had excited him (and continued to excite him). In doing so, he offers a book for readers schooled in practical criticism. However, he subverts that gesture by creating an intratextual network in which contexts rival individual poems for our attention. His fascination with American democracy and the relationship between the individual and the masses run parallel to his attention to the ways in which individual poems or groups of poems should be measured. Williams was interested in "rebellion", as he told Marianne Moore in a letter of October 18, 1935 (*SL* 155). Promoting challenging contexts (usable past, memory, adjacency, dislocation) becomes a fundamental part of that rebelliousness as it signals his developments in descent during the 1940s and beyond.

Notes

1. Louis Zukofsky influenced Williams's political and literary interests at the time and Williams had contributed significantly to *An "Objectivist" Anthology*, ed. Louis Zukofsky, New York, 1932. In his article for it, "Recencies", Zukofsky wrote of the "desire for an inclusive object" (15).

2. This is especially evident in his long letter to Kay Boyle, William Carlos Williams, in *The Selected Letters of William Carlos Williams*, ed. John C. Thirlwall, New York, 1957, 129-35. In it he wrote, "Free verse—if it ever existed—is out. Whitman was a magnificent failure" (135). Subsequent references to this book will appear in the text as *SL*.

3. Again the letter to Boyle is instructive.

4. G. Stanley Koehler, *Countries of the Mind: The Poetry of William Carlos Williams*, Lewisburg, PA, 1998, 17.

5. "The Descent", in *The Collected Poems of William Carlos Williams*, ed. Christopher MacGowan, New York, II, 245.

6. William Carlos Williams, *The Autobiography of William Carlos Williams*, New York, 1951, 299. Subsequent references to this book will appear in the text as *A*.

7. Alan Filreis, *Modernism from Right to Left: Wallace Stevens, the Thirties, and Literary Radicalism*, Cambridge, 1994, 124.

8. Ronald Lane Latimer letter to Willard Mass, undated, late 1934, quoted in Filreis, 113.

9. Filreis, 124.

10. Paul Mariani, *William Carlos Williams: A New World Naked*, New York, 1981, 369.

11. Filreis, 128.

12. *Ibid.*, 114.

13. Mariani, 388.

14. William Carlos Williams, *An Early Martyr and Other Poems*, New York, 1935.

15. William Carlos Williams, "The Situation in American Writing: Seven Questions", in *Partisan Review: A Quarterly of Literature and Marxism*, VI/4 (Summer 1939), 41. Interesting in this regard is that Williams produced two *Complete Collected Poems* in the 1930s.

16. See particularly, "A Point for American Criticism", "Marianne Moore", "Kenneth Burke", "The Basis of Faith in Art", and "Against the Weather", in *Selected Essays of William Carlos Williams* (1954), New York, 1969.

17. John Beck, *Writing the Radical Centre: William Carlos Williams and American Cultural Politics*, New York, 2001, 120.

18. *The Collected Poems of William Carlos Williams*, eds A. Walton Litz and Christopher MacGowan, New York, 1986, I, 182 and 185. Subsequent references to this book will appear in the text as *CP1*.

19. I am reading these recycled poems as part of Williams's plan for the book and not as mere padding—a point made by Robert J. Cirasa in his *The Lost Works of William Carlos Williams: The Volumes of Collected Poetry as Lyrical Sequences*, Madison, WI, 1995, 330n.

20. Robert von Hallberg, "The Politics of Description: W. C. Williams in the 'Thirties'", in *ELH*, XLV/1 (Spring 1978), 133-34.

21. Barry Ahearn, *William Carlos Williams and Alterity: The Early Poetry*, Cambridge, 1994, 171-72.

22. von Hallberg, 134.

23. *Ibid.*, 136.

24. Beck, 126.

25. William Carlos Williams, "The Situation in American Writing: Seven Questions", in *Partisan Review: A Quarterly of Literature and Marxism*, VI/4 (Summer 1939), 43.

26. Beck, 128.

27. Williams was to write of Dante's work in 1939 in "Against the Weather" where he is seen as a "dogmatist" who must be "split" (*Selected Essays of William Carlos Williams* [1954], New York, 1969, 207).

28. Stephen Cushman, *William Carlos Williams and the Meaning of Measure*, New Haven, 1985, 85.

29. Williams, *Spring and All*, np, Contact Publishers [41].

30. William Carlos Williams, *An Early Martyr and Other Poems*, New York, 1935, 39.

31. Litz and MacGowan use the 1938 version, "Young Love", for their *Collected*. See William Carlos Williams, *The Complete Collected Poems of William Carlos Williams 1906-1938*, Norfolk, CT, 1938, 113.

32. Cirasa, 240.

33. *Ibid.*, 272.

34. William Carlos Williams, *The Collected Earlier Poems of William Carlos Williams*, New York, 1951, 89.

35. It should be noted that Williams also placed a version of *Della Primavera Trasportata Al Morale* (1930) before *An Early Martyr* in this collection.

36. Cirasa, 269-71.

37. Mariani, 631.

38. A. Walton Litz and Christopher MacGowan, "Editing William Carlos Williams", in *Representing Modernist Texts: Editing as Interpretation*, ed. George Bornstein, Ann Arbor, 1991, 50.

39. Cirasa, 271.

40. Mariani, 591.

41. *Tituba's Children*, in William Carlos Williams, *Many Loves and Other Plays*, New York, 1961, 225-300.

Sergio Rizzo (essay date fall 2005)

SOURCE: Rizzo, Sergio. "Remembering Race: Extra-poetical Contexts and the Racial Other in 'The Red Wheelbarrow.'" *Journal of Modern Literature* 29, no. 1 (fall 2005): 34-54.

[*In the following essay, Rizzo provides an in-depth analysis of the aesthetic and socio-political content of Williams's "The Red Wheelbarrow," focusing on issues of race and gender.*]

Although once at the center of debates about modern poetry, the canonical status of William Carlos Williams' **"The Red Wheelbarrow,"** along with the imagist and objectivist practice it represents, now seems beyond dispute. If anything, the poem runs the risk of becoming, as Denise Levertov described it, one of those "tiresomely familiar and basically unrevealing anthology 'specimens'" (263). By the same token, the tendency to treat the poem as an "anthology specimen" owes something to Williams' efforts to remove it from its original context in *Spring and All.* For despite the intense critical scrutiny the poem has received over the years, very little attention has been paid to what Williams said about it and the different frameworks he provided for it. As if transfixed by its telescopic power, critics *see through* these frames and, in the process, keep a dark figure in the poem's biographical history—Marshall, the red wheelbarrow's African-American owner—at the poem's margins.

To my knowledge, Williams only mentions the owner of the wheelbarrow on two occasions. One is in an article, "Seventy Years Deep," written for *Holiday* magazine (1954) and the other appears in an introduction to the poem in an anthology entitled *Fifty Poets, An American Auto-Anthology* (1933) edited by William Rose Benét.

The article "Seventy Years Deep" is a human-interest story in which Williams presents himself as a poet of the people. The article's subtitle describes him as "A physician who is considered by many to be America's greatest living poet . . . [who] attributes his success to what he has learned from the people of his home town—Rutherford, New Jersey" (54). Stressing his connection to the community, Williams presents himself through what is, for the most part, a sentimental condensation of incidents found in his autobiography. He works to reassure the reader that his two roles as doctor and poet were not in conflict with one another, and in his effort to attribute his success to what he has learned from the people of his hometown, he gives his fullest account of the emotional and personal significance of **"The Red Wheelbarrow"** for him. What he remembers about the poem is that it

> sprang from affection for an old Negro named Marshall. He had been a fisherman, caught porgies off Gloucester. He used to tell me how he had to work in the hold in freezing weather, standing ankle deep in cracked ice packing down the fish. He said he didn't feel cold. He never felt cold in his life until just recently. I liked that man, and his son Milton almost as much. In his back yard I saw the red wheelbarrow surrounded by the white chickens. I suppose my affection for the old man somehow got into the writing.
>
> (78)

Marshall's story helps Williams illustrate that as a doctor he "served all kinds of people" (78)—a fact for which he has every reason to be proud. Beyond that, though, the biographical connection between Marshall and **"The Red Wheelbarrow"** illustrates how Williams' dual roles as doctor and poet "formed a whole" in which his "patients have been food for [his] muse" (55). However, Williams' desire, late in his life, to say that his "affection for the old man somehow got into the writing" suggests his muse had trouble digesting Marshall and the black working-class experience he represents. Undoubtedly, Williams has a genuine affection for this man and sympathy for his plight that "somehow" get into the poem.[1] But the question to ask is how they got there, because the poem, and Williams' lifelong relationship with it, would suggest that every effort was made to erase from the poem not only Marshall but, perhaps more importantly, Williams' feelings for him.

Exposing the emotional roots of **"The Red Wheelbarrow"** is in keeping with the Williams of the fifties. This is a decade of intense personal recollection for him, reflected in the publication of his autobiography (1951), a novel based on his marriage and in-laws, *The Build-Up* (1952), his *Selected Letters* (1957), an autobiographical commentary on his publications, *I Wanted to Write a Poem* (1958), and a memoir of his mother, *Yes, Mrs. Williams* (1959). In addition, his poetry of the fifties reflects his evolution from the spare modernism of his earlier imagist (1910-20s) and objectivist (1930s) phases, through his epic *Paterson I-IV* (1946-51), and culminating in the more personal or even "confessional" voice found in such works as *Asphodel, That Greeny Flower* (1955) and *Paterson V* (1958). Williams' poetic development implies a critique of his earlier modernism, whose anti-aestheticism, it could be argued, only succeeds in replacing one form of aestheticism with another. Moving away from the notion of the poem as an image depicting "'an intellectual and emotional complex in an instant of time'" (Kenner in *Pound* 185), in Ezra Pound's words, or what Louis Zukofsky called a "'strictly objective estimate of all the class forces'" (Von Hallberg 146), or his own notion of the poem as a "machine made of words" (*CP* [*Collected Poems*] II 54), his poetry of the late forties and fifties sought verse forms that could better accommodate history and personal feeling. Likewise, his attempt in the *Holiday* article to locate Marshall in his remembrance of **"The Red Wheelbarrow"** is an effort to reassert feelings and associations circumscribed by the poem's modernist formalism.

When Williams first mentions **"The Red Wheelbarrow"** he reveals that its technique is not far from his remembrance of the poem or Marshall. Despite evidence to the contrary, Williams asserts, "I am not good at remembering what I have written. I just want to get rid of it. I don't recall any particular poem except perhaps the brief, the very brief one, called **'The Red Wheelbarrow'**" (75). As part of his presentation of

himself as a busy doctor-poet writing in between patient visits and making notes at moments of inspiration on prescription pads, he wants to avoid being seen as a "man of letters;" recalling "the brief, the very brief one" helps him do that.[2] Nonetheless, **"The Red Wheelbarrow"** also serves as an example of the "technical mastery" (55) the poet must have in order to grasp the seemingly insignificant details of everyday life and thereby creatively transform them into art. However, perhaps the poem's brevity is itself suspect. On the one hand, its brevity is the mark of the poem's "success," which becomes the trademark of Williams' distinctive synthesis of European imagism with his American place—what Louis Zukofsky, speaking of *Spring and All,* praised as Williams' "exclusion of sentimentalisms, extraneous comparisons, similes, [and] overweening autobiographies of the heart" (141). On the other hand, it marks Williams' failure to identify, at least in any critical fashion, feelings and people associated with the poem until thirty years after its first appearance.

Criticism of Williams for his brevity is not new. In contrast to Zukofsky or Kenneth Burke, who famously praised Williams as "the master of the glimpse" ("First Law" 47), a number of reviewers found fault with his brevity or at least saw it as a point of diminishing return. In Conrad Aiken's review of Williams' **Collected Poems: 1921-31,** he criticizes Williams for a "conscious avoidance of *completeness,* whether of statement or form . . ." (290). In the same year, Babette Deutsch in her review says, "The reliance on the eye, the singling out of the brief moment, however intense, is a limitation upon his words" (130). Randall Jarrell, in his introduction to **Williams Selected Poems,** says: "Williams' imagist-objectivist background and bias have helped his poems by their emphasis on truthfulness, exactness, concrete 'presentation'; but they have harmed the poems by their underemphasis on organization, logic, narrative, generalization—and the poems are so short, often, that there isn't time for much" (xv). By the time of Jarrell's introduction, Williams was already correcting for the "underemphasis" of his "imagist-objectivist background and bias" with his epic project **Paterson,** which Jarrell admired as his "most impressive single piece" (xviii).

We need to look more carefully at Williams' "imagist-objectivist background" and how **"The Red Wheelbarrow"** relates to it. Although easy to classify as an imagist poem, the work it appears in, *Spring and All,* is something else altogether. Published when Williams was forty, *Spring and All* is a threshold work between the "young" imagist Williams of *The Tempers* (1913) and *Al Que Quiere!* (1917) and the "mature" Williams of objectivism and *Paterson.* In its Dadaesque mixing of prose and poetry, here Williams moves beyond the boundaries of his earlier imagism, leading Zukofsky to include *Spring and All* on his list of essential reading in his "An 'Objectivist' Anthology" (1932). However, as Paul Mariani in his biography of Williams points out, "unfortunately almost no one saw Williams' book in the original edition. . . . In effect, *Spring and All* all but disappeared as a cohesive text until its republication nearly ten years after Williams' death" (209). Instead of *Spring and All,* most readers came to understand **"The Red Wheelbarrow"** through the anthologies and first collections of his work that helped to establish his reputation in the thirties—most importantly the *Collected Poems: 1921-31,* published by Carl Rakosi's Objectivist Press, and the *Complete Collected Poems* **(1938),** published by James Laughlin's New Directions Press—which became the standard for the various collections that followed. In the process of re-contextualizing the poem, Williams provides a complex commentary upon it, most of which has been ignored.

One line of commentary can be found in the different titles Williams gives **"The Red Wheelbarrow."** Like all the twenty-seven poems in *Spring and All,* its original title was simply a Roman numeral, **XXII,** establishing its similarity with the other poems published with it. Compare the typographical effect of the Roman numerals with the title given to it in anthologies and the *Collected Poems* where the full capital letters sit atop the tiny poem like an over-sized crown: **THE RED WHEELBARROW.** The title **"XXII"** gives no indication which of the stanzas or which of the poem's elements carries more weight. Not only does the later title destroy the poem's compositional equipoise, its use of the definite article takes "*a* red wheel / barrow" out of the in(de)finite world of the imagination and into the (de)finite world of real wheelbarrows. Or, at least, the poem's title reasserts the kind of referentiality or illusionary realism—what the prose sections of *Spring and All* inveigh against as the "plagiarism after nature" (*CP*I 198)—that influential critics like J. Hillis Miller, Joseph Riddel, and Marjorie Perloff see *Spring and All*'s radical modernism as rejecting.

Four years after the 1934 publication of the *Collected Poems,* the poems from *Spring and All* appeared in the *Complete Collected Poems* with Roman numerals as their only titles. This suggests that in the later collection Williams wanted to return to something more in line with their original presentation in *Spring and All,* where the Roman numerals emphasize the poems' interdependence. This feeling is reinforced by the fact that in the *Complete Collected Poems* the poems are nearly run together, with the Roman numerals making only slight transitions. However, a footnote by A. Walton Litz and Christopher MacGowan in their *The Collected Poems of William Carlos Williams, Volume 1* mentions the fact that in the *Complete Collected Poems* Williams reversed the order of **"The Red Wheelbarrow"** (XXII) with the poem that came before it in *Spring and All,* **"Quietness"** (XXI), so that the "better

poem," as Williams called **"The Red Wheelbarrow,"** would "have the better presentation and not be cut in half by the page" (501). Although *Spring and All*'s sense of discrete poem sequences separated by prose sections is already undermined by stringing the poems together one after the other, the original distinct four-poem sequence of which **"The Red Wheelbarrow"** is a part (XIX-XXII) is further undermined by Williams' concern for the poem's appearance. Even as Williams attempts to restore the poems to something like their original context, he is thinking of them, **"The Red Wheelbarrow"** especially, as separate units. What is paramount is that the "better poem" be preserved as a discreet and autonomous entirety.

By the time of the 1951 publication of *The Collected Earlier Poems,* the last printing of *Spring and All*'s poems supervised by Williams, he settles for a "compromise" which results in the publication of the Roman numerals along with the verbal titles. So, for its 1951 publication, the poem's title becomes **"XXI. The Red Wheelbarrow."** The history of the poem's titling through the collections of 1934, 1938, and 1951 (typo)graphically depicts Williams' own attempt to decide whether the poem was about some*thing* or whether the poem was a thing-in-itself whose primary relationship was with those other verbal "things" found interspersed between the prose sections of *Spring and All.* Williams' indecision is reflected in the criticism about the poem that takes one side or another or tries to reconcile the difference through various dualisms: idea-thing, subject-object, universal-particular, metaphor-metonymy, etc. However, with or without the Roman numerals, the title, **"The Red Wheelbarrow,"** works against the poem's compositional equipoise and its interdependence with the other poems and moves the poem towards the conventional symbolism and referentiality that *Spring and All*'s modernist praxis rejects.

Williams' last published mention of **"The Red Wheelbarrow"** occurs in his discussion of *Spring and All* in his memoir *I Wanted to Write a Poem* (1958). He discusses the poem specifically in terms of the different approaches taken in titling the prose and poetry sections of *Spring and All.* Written when "all the world was going crazy about typographical form," the titling of the prose sections "is really a travesty on the idea" (36). The nonsensical titling of the prose sections or "chapters" that "are numbered all out of order, sometimes with a Roman numeral, sometimes with an Arabic, anything that came in handy" (37) not only pokes fun at the concern for typographical form, it is also in keeping with what the prose has to say: "The prose is a mixture of philosophy and nonsense. It made sense to me, at least to my disturbed mind—because it *was* disturbed at that time—but I doubt it made sense to anyone else" (37). In contrast to the hurly-burly of "philosophy and nonsense" found in the prose, Williams explains:

> But the poems were kept pure—no typographical tricks when they appear—set off from the prose. They are numbered consistently; none had titles though they were to have titles later when they were reprinted in **Collected Poems.** Here, for instance, on page 74 are the eight lines later to be known as **'The Red Wheelbarrow'**—here, without a title, simply a number on a page:
>
> > So much depends
> > upon
> >
> > a red wheel
> > barrow
> >
> > glazed with rain
> > water
> >
> > beside the white
> > chickens
>
> Some of the poems were considered good. **'By the road to the contagious hospital'** has been praised by the conventional boys for its form.
>
> (37)

Although one other poem receives mention, Williams suggests that **"The Red Wheelbarrow"** is the purest of **Spring and All**'s pure products. In discussing the titling of the prose and poetry in **Spring and All,** he only recalls the poem's original numeric title and the later title, **"The Red Wheelbarrow,"** given to it in **Collected Poems** (1934). He doesn't mention his attempts to preserve the numeric title in the **Complete Collected Poems** (1938) or the compromise combination of the two titles in the **Collected Earlier Poems** (1951). In fact, he doesn't seem to see the numeric title at all. He says that as "simply a number on the page" the poem is "without a title." This is consistent with the view that the poetry, unlike the prose, is presented without any "typographical tricks." The significance of the "trickery" involved in giving the poems numbers—especially Roman numerals with their intended or unintended connotations of classicism, Western civilization, and imperialism—disappears from his remembrance of **Spring and All.** By showcasing **"The Red Wheelbarrow"** as an island of serene order, simplicity, consistency and transparency in an otherwise chaotic world of prose, the product of a "disturbed mind," where Roman numerals mix indiscriminately with Arabic ones, Williams helps to separate the poem from its original context. Once again, in his concern for the "pure" poem, he is willing to revise the original and more radical context of **Spring and All.**

As Williams sought different titles for the poem, little or no regard seems to be given to Marshall's role in the poem and even less to the black working-class experience he represents. Nonetheless, in so far as the title, **"The Red Wheelbarrow,"** works to make the poem's "a red wheel / barrow" *the* wheelbarrow upon which so much depends, one could argue the definite article indicates its owner. In a certain way, it does, although the owner is usually read in terms of some abstraction—mankind, primitive man, rural life—not in terms of a historically specific individual.[3] More than Marshall or these other owners, though, what the title's definite article indicates is Williams' ownership or authority, stating in effect: here is *the* red wheelbarrow I discovered and turned into "a red wheel / barrow." As Williams removes the poem from **Spring and All** and finds new contexts for it, he seeks to establish both his authority to speak for it, and, more importantly, its authority to speak for him. At some points in this process the emotional significance of Marshall all but disappears. At other points, however, Williams opens the poem up to the sort of symbolism and sentiment—those "extraneous comparisons, similes, [and] overweening autobiographies of the heart" that Zukofsky praised Williams for avoiding in **Spring and All**—that allow the figure of Marshall to appear.

Just as Williams' *Holiday* article reveals a tension between the African-American source of the poem's inspiration and its technical mastery, a similar tension appears in the introduction Williams writes for the poem in Benét's 1933 anthology, *Fifty Poets, An American Auto Anthology.* Benét's introduction makes it clear what the anthology wants from Williams in the way of "inspiration" and "highly original work" (60). He wants Williams' pure poetry, free of the "left wing" and "theorizing" (60).[4] And, Williams is willing to oblige him. The following is Williams' introduction to the poem in its entirety:

> I am enclosing a favorite short poem of mine for your anthology with the paragraph to accompany it which you ask for. It's a nice idea.
>
> The wheelbarrow in question stood outside the window of an old negro's house on a back street in the suburb where I live. It was pouring rain and there were white chickens walking about in it. The sight impressed me somehow as about the most important, the most integral that it had ever been my pleasure to gaze upon. And the meter though no more than a fragment succeeds in portraying this pleasure flawlessly, even it succeeds in denoting a certain unquenchable exaltation—in fact I find the poem quite perfect.
>
> (60)

Williams' choice of **"The Red Wheelbarrow"** is motivated by more than his desire to put his best foot forward. He probably has the anthology's title, *An American Auto-Anthology,* in mind. He sees **"The Red Wheelbarrow"** as the quintessential expression of himself as an American self, man and place fused into one—much as he does in his recollection of the poem in his *Holiday* article twenty years later. The recognition of racial difference that helps to define this experience as noteworthy is not as personally revealing as the account he gives of it in the *Holiday* article. Here the "old negro's house" is merely part of the "local color." As such it is meant to convey a sentimental feeling to the (white) reader. Otherwise, why mention the race of the owner of the house at all? The introduction emphasizes Williams' ability to derive an "integral" aesthetic feeling of "pleasure" and, even, "a certain unquenchable exaltation" from the humble materials he has to work with. The anonymous owner of the house is out of the picture as is Williams' affection for him. Or, if these elements are there, they are subsumed by Williams' efforts to present a "perfect" poem.

In contrast to the subjective experience Williams presents in *Fifty Poets,* elsewhere he presents the poem as a formal exercise in the objective apprehension of the external world.[5] These two approaches have been extended by the long critical reception the poem enjoys, arguing possible interpretations not only in terms of Williams' poetic practice, but also as part of broader epistemological debates around such dualisms as subject-object, mind-matter, form-content, poetry-prose and metaphor-metonymy. In taking one side or another of an opposing dualism or synthesizing/transcending both, critics have tended to split between those who see the poem's significance as residing in its content (what the poem says or means) versus those who argue its significance is found in its form (what the poem makes or does).

Dissatisfied with thematic and formalist approaches, Allen Dunn, in "Williams' Liberating Need," recognizes that the critics tend to ignore the context(s) Williams' first provides for **"The Red Wheelbarrow"** in *Spring and All*—both the theory of its prose sections and the poetic sequence of which the poem is a part. In his reading of the poem's relationship to the prose sections and its poetic sequence, he argues **"The Red Wheelbarrow"** illustrates the revolutionary force of the imagination engaged in the paradoxical exercise of "a change without a difference" (55). While Dunn's focus on the poem's struggle with society's hierarchical values defining art, reality, and the self is useful, one has to ask in the world of lived experience and social struggle—or "the world of human values" (50) that Dunn says the poem's critics have ignored and that he wants to reconnect the poem with—what would be the value of "a change without a difference"? Furthermore, once we acknowledge the Other political realities informing the poem and its contexts we can appreciate another ideological struggle going on—one that would qualify, although not deny, Williams belief in the power of the imagination.

Following Dunn's lead, I would like to begin with the poem's role in its original four-poem sequence in *Spring and All* (XIX-XXII or **"Horned Purple," "The Sea," "Quietness,"** and **"The Red Wheelbarrow"**).[6] In Dunn's reading of the sequence, he sees **"The Red Wheelbarrow"** as occupying the tail end of a spectrum of erotic intensity beginning with the "Dirty satyrs" of **"Horned Purple"** which is "diffused into the world of ordinary objects" (57) represented by the "lascivious" leaves of **"Quietness"** and, finally, the red wheelbarrow. For Dunn, a vestige of erotic desire remains in **"The Red Wheelbarrow"**; however, he argues, the trace of desire exists only as part of a strategy of imaginative destruction that "alleviates consciousness of the desire which always precedes and exceeds its object," culminating in the paradoxical resolution of "change without out a difference" (58). Dunn quite rightly locates **"The Red Wheelbarrow"** in the context of erotic desire, a context that is largely lost in the poem's recontextualization into anthologies and poetry collections and ignored by most critics. However, once we see how Williams' erotic desire is racialized, one has to be skeptical about any transcendence **"The Red Wheelbarrow"** provides, or any claims for the power of the imagination to alleviate "consciousness of the desire which always precedes and exceeds its object." In fact, these claims are contradicted.

In the explicitly erotic theme of **"Horned Purple,"** the "Dirty satyrs" are identified by their gender and age, "boys of fifteen and seventeen," class, "drivers for grocers or taxidrivers," and race, "white and colored." In their uncouth courting rituals—"vulgarity raised to the last power"—they trespass, breaking off the limbs of lilac bushes to stick them in their caps or over their ears. Their phallic display gives expression to the elemental life forces of spring, which puts them at odds with the community that is defined in terms of property and capitalism. They tear the bushes apart "with a curse for the owner." Then "They stand in doorways / on the business streets with a sneer / on their faces." Outside the business interests that govern the other members of the community, they recover something of a primitive and mythological past as they turn themselves into "Dirty satyrs." The satyr, a creature that blurs the line between the human and the animal, represents and amplifies the group's racial mix of "white and colored." It is not a matter of which half is which, just that Williams imagines racial difference giving access to a primitive sexuality represented by their "dark kisses—rough faces" in the poem's final line.

In **"The Sea"** the primitive boundary crossing begun by the "Dirty satyrs" is radically advanced. Here the human form, "her young body," breaks apart in "the sea of many arms," just as the words of the poem threaten to dissolve into the onomatopoeia of the sea, "ula lu la lu."[7] In the orgiastic coital pull and push of the sea, the energies of Eros and Thanatos are indistinguishable. While the "dark" forces of nature are potentially liberating in **"Horned Purple,"** in **"The Sea"** they threaten to wipe out the most fundamental distinctions between Self and Other: "Underneath the sea where it is dark / there is no edge / so two—." In this last stanza, the "dark" place found beneath the sea echoes the "dark kisses" in the last stanza of **"Horned Purple."** But here the experience of primal energies takes the poet's consciousness to the edge of "no edge," where the distinction between Self and Other *almost* disappears.

In **"Quietness,"** after the climactic near-dissolution of the Self, the poet awakes "one day" to find himself/ herself "in Paradise / a Gipsy." In this quiet post-coital "Paradise" the gender identifications with the aggressive masculinity of **"Horned Purple"** and the passive femininity of **"The Sea"** are transcended in the gender-neutral "Gipsy." A person from nowhere and anywhere, the racial and ethnic ambiguity of a Gypsy, defined in *Webster's* as a "dark Caucasoid," also resolves and neutralizes the threat of racial difference and the dark forces represented by it. In this New World Eden the "Gipsy" doesn't need the leaves to hide his/her nakedness. There is no shame because there is no God (nor anyone else for that matter). Consequently, the "Gipsy" is free to admire ". . . the blandness / of the leaves—/ so many / so lascivious / and still."

It may be without God, but the New World Eden still needs its saints, as Williams makes clear in an earlier prose passage of *Spring and All.* In discussing the need for a modern art that moves beyond the "'beautiful illusion[s]'" of past art, he says that "the great works of the imagination" live ". . . by their power TO ESCAPE ILLUSION and stand between man and nature as saints once stood between man and the sky—their reality in such work, say, as that of Juan Gris" (*CP*I 199). Worthy of Juan Gris or any number of the modernists that have been cited by the critics, **"The Red Wheelbarrow"** is Williams' attempt to translate modernism's new visual "reality" into poetry. In so far as his art has the power to "ESCAPE ILLUSION" Williams sees it standing "between man and nature as saints once stood between man and sky . . ." While the new sainthood is able to question and perhaps escape the "beautiful illusions" of past art, it still has its own illusions, not the least of which are the ways in which these saints define (or fail to define) such concepts as "man and nature." For the modern artists Williams is emulating, their new mode of seeing—for example, the cubist's "mobility and indeterminacy" (129) that Perloff mentions—is heavily indebted to the Euro-centric anthropological and archeological projects of the early twentieth-century and their quest for Primitive Man.[8]

As the finale to its four-poem sequence in *Spring and All,* **"The Red Wheelbarrow"** takes the reader even further in the aesthetic resolution of the dark erotic forces that first emerge in **"Horned Purple."** In the poem preceding **"The Red Wheelbarrow,"** the last trace of these dark forces is the Gypsy who enjoys the quiet contemplation of "lascivious" leaves. In **"The Red Wheelbarrow,"** Williams takes the reader to an even quieter place of visual contemplation where the words on the page become like paint on a silent canvas or objects suspended in mute space. The human figures that people the previous three poems disappear. The Gypsy's contemplation of nature is replaced by a disembodied consciousness concentrating on the man-made wheelbarrow. Focusing on this homely object, Williams hopes to create a modern artifact that transcends the last vestiges of romantic association contained in the persona of the "Gipsy" and the erotic associations contained in the "lascivious" leaves. In the modernist tour de force that concludes the sequence there is little or no room for Marshall; however, what Williams perceives to be his primitive essence does make it into the poem.

Williams has quite a bit to say about primitives in the prose sections preceding the four-poem sequence of **"The Red Wheelbarrow."** Before examining those comments, though, we can look more closely at how the poem might relate to the larger thematic structuring of *Spring and All* in terms of race and gender. In a brilliant reading of *Spring and All*'s final poem, **"The Wildflower"** or **"Black eyed susan,"** Perloff reveals how the "Arab / Indian / dark woman" in all of her "'rich . . . savagery' has been at the core of *Spring and All* from the beginning" (136). On a thematic level **"Wildflower"** is the final expression of a sexual desire for a "dark woman," that Perloff claims is "ubiquitous in Williams' text" (137). The discovery and promise of sexual union with the "dark woman" is what promises redemptive contact for the poetic consciousness trapped within the otherwise colorless landscape of contemporary life. On a metonymic level, **"Wildflower"** is connected to prior poems through the colors of the "Black eyed susan" that represent the "rich . . . savagery" of the "dark woman" in contrast with the "white daisy" that represents the "Crowds" of white "farmers / who live poorly" (*CP*I 236). Perloff sees the coda poem's "white daisy" echoing the "white / chickens" found in **"The Red Wheelbarrow."** As well, she sees the vibrant red of the wheelbarrow as representing the lifeblood of the "dark woman" which connects it to all the other "bleeding reds [that] emerge from the dreary landscape of the **'Interborough Rapid Transit Co.'"** (147) in *Spring and All.*

Concerned to prove that the referentiality of *Spring and All*'s images is "subordinated to their compositional value" (138), Perloff reads the "dark woman" as a Kora motif metonymically linking the other poems. However, more could be done with the metaphorical value of race in *Spring and All.* The first question to ask is how does Williams appreciation for the "rich . . . savagery" of the "dark woman" that finds its way into the poem relate to the absent presence of Marshall's black masculinity? Combined with the thematic and color associations Perloff draws out, perhaps one could see Williams' admiration for the red wheelbarrow's black owner as lifting the poem's technical virtuosity into a whole other realm of social commentary and irony. The comment that "so much depends / upon" the wheelbarrow could be an acknowledgement of the precarious nature of Marshall's life of manual labor. And the vibrant red of the wheelbarrow glazed with rainwater could embody Marshall's blood, sweat and tears, silently condemning "the white / chickens" beside it. However, if these feelings are in the poem, they can only begin to emerge with the discovery of Marshall thirty years later in William's account of the poem in his article for *Holiday*. In the context of *Spring and All,* any sympathy for Marshall is overwhelmed by the more pressing needs of the psycho-sexual forces behind Williams pursuit of an "anti-poetic" modernism.

In its opening pages, *Spring and All* sets itself up as an extended defense of a modern antipoetry. In the voice of an uncomprehending and outraged public, an anonymous critic asks, "Is this what you call poetry? It is the very antithesis of poetry. It is antipoetry" (*CPI* 177). The critic's outrage at "You moderns!" makes clear their art is an affront in terms of content "There is nothing appealing in what you say but on the contrary the poems are positively repellent." With regards to form: "Rhyme you may take away but rhythm! Why there is none in your work whatever" (*CPI* 177). Thirty-five years later in his memoir *I Wanted to Write a Poem,* Williams recalls the opening pages of *Spring and All* with the modern poet's response to the critics as reading like "a manifesto" and "important enough to quote":

> Perhaps this noble apostrophe means something terrible for me. I am not certain, but for the moment I interpret it to say: "You have robbed me. God, I am naked. What shall I do?"—By it they mean that when I have suffered (provided I have not done so as yet) I too shall run for cover; that I too shall seek refuge in fantasy. And mind you, I do not say that I will not. To decorate my age.
>
> (37-38)

The poet's "manifesto" doesn't try to defend itself against the charge of being antipoetic. Indeed, his/her modern antipoetry provides a "naked" truth that others can't handle. Although the poet is careful to admit that in the face of the reality his/her antipoetry reveals he/she too might "run for cover," "seek refuge in fantasy," or "decorate," this response would only be a sign of the artist's failure. However, Williams' commitment to a modern antipoetic "realism" reveals racial and sexual fantasies that provide their own problematic "cover" and "refuge."

Outing Williams as a closet romantic in his famous preface to Williams' first volume of collected poems published in 1934, Wallace Stevens identifies the central dynamic in Williams' poetry as the struggle between "sentimental" and "anti-poetic" impulses.[9] What is important to stress is that both impulses are central to **"The Red Wheelbarrow"** and both are related to gender difference as it plays itself out in sexual activity. As Stevens explains:

> Something of the unreal is necessary to fecundate the real; something of the sentimental is necessary to fecundate the anti-poetic. Williams, by nature, is more of a realist than is commonly true in the case of a poet. One might, at this point, set oneself up as the Linnaeus of aesthetics, assigning a female role to the unused tent in **'The Attic Which Is Desire,'** and a male role to the soda sign; and generally speaking one might run through these pages and point out how often the essential poetry is the result of the conjunction of the unreal and the real, the sentimental and the anti-poetic, the constant interaction of two opposites. This seems to define Williams and his poetry.
>
> (214)

Two noteworthy readings of **"The Red Wheelbarrow"** implicitly using the terms and dynamic Stevens identifies come from Roy Harvey Pearce and Hugh Kenner. Pearce says that "At its worst," the poem's "pathos and sentimentalism" results in "togetherness in a chicken-yard. At its best it is an exercise in the creation of the poetic out of the anti-poetic" (97). With his usual flair for ridicule, Kenner makes the gender dynamics of the poem's "pathos and sentimentalism" more explicit. Illustrating how the poem's form turns its prosaic subject matter into art, he asks the reader to consider the poem's sixteen words as a sentence: "So much depends upon a red wheelbarrow glazed with rainwater beside the white chickens." From this, he concludes, "Try it over, in any voice you like: it is impossible. It could only be the gush of an arty female on a tour of Farmer Brown's barnyard" (*Homemade* 60). Although using the term with trepidation, Stevens at least sees sentiment as a necessary and active force in Williams' poetry. For both Pearce and Kenner, the imposition of masculine form, his anti-poetic modernism, is what saves Williams' poetry from sliding into a feminine sentimentality— "togetherness in a chicken-yard" or "the gush of an arty female."

In his unintentional role as a "Linnaeus of aesthetics," Kenner puts his finger on the soft feminine center of **"The Red Wheelbarrow"**'s muscular modernism that *makes* something (*"il miglior fabbro"*). In the implicit value system of both Williams and Kenner, it is this (masculine) making that turns the (feminine) saying into art. Furthermore, this remaking of a feminine essence into a masculine form occurs on the visual level. Through the use of enjambment Williams cuts and suspends the snake-like sentence expressing feminine sentiment into what Kenner, quoting Stevens, describes as a "'Mobile-like arrangement'" (*Homemade* 59). The silent space of visual non-narrative art helps to stifle the feminine emotion that is simultaneously so central to the poem and so unseemly.

At this level, **"The Red Wheelbarrow"** is caught up in "the sexual politics of enjambmental form" (50) that Sharon Dolin finds in her essay "Enjambment and the Erotics of the Gaze in Williams's Poetry." Although focusing on just three poems from *Spring and All* (XI, **"In passing with my mind,"** XVIII, **"To Elsie,"** and XXVI, **"At the Ball Game"**) we can extend her thesis:

> The phallic gaze, finally, dominates many of the *Spring and All* poems, asserting itself through enjambmental interest in eroticized visual detail. Irigaray (1985) has written that the extreme 'oculocentrism' of our culture privileges the penis because it can be seen; '*Nothing to be seen is equivalent to having no thing. No being and no truth* . . . [V]isual dominance therefore carried out in actual fact' (48, her emphasis). Perhaps the obsession with vision, with fixing the particularity of objects, in Williams's poems is so the I/eye, fearing castration, can reconfirm its phallic dominance through visual dominance.
>
> (50)

Dolin's thesis gives a new meaning to Burke's explanation of Williams' objectivism: "For all of his 'objectivist' accuracy, Williams' details are not in essence descriptions of things but portraits of personalities" ("Williams" 56). And in **"The Red Wheelbarrow,"** the personality that is most vividly portrayed, much more than the wheelbarrow's black owner, is Williams' own.

As a portrait of castration anxiety, however, it is necessary to recognize that the sources provoking the fear of castration in **"The Red Wheelbarrow,"** and hence the fetishistic scopophilia attempting to control that fear, are racialized. Stevens, again, suggests how Williams' anti-poetic is connected to race, or the "primitive,"[10] as well as gender. Although not using the term explicitly, it is easy to read from Stevens' description of Williams' "passion for the anti-poetic":

> His passion for the anti-poetic is a blood passion and not a passion of the inkpot. The anti-poetic is his spirit's cure. He needs it as a naked man needs shelter or as an animal needs salt. To a man with a sentimental side the anti-poetic is that truth, that reality to which all of us are forever fleeing.
>
> (213)

As a "blood passion," the anti-poetic is an assertion of a primitive (masculine) need, like a naked man's need for shelter or an animal's need for salt. For "a man with a sentimental side" confronting contemporary life—"as

one looks out of the window at Rutherford or Passaic, or as one walks the streets of New York" (213)—the anti-poetic is "a source of salvation" (213). Consequently, the feminine gives access to a primitive experience, or as Stevens puts it, "something of the sentimental is necessary to fecundate the anti-poetic," which provides a "truth" and "reality" amidst the shallow and transitory commercial values of modern consumer capitalism.

Understanding how Williams' anti-poetic modernism incorporates mythical dualisms involving both race and gender, we can return to the poem's role in *Spring and All* with a new understanding of the erotic forces it tries to resolve. The trajectory of the erotic forces from **"Horned Purple"** to **"The Red Wheelbarrow"** tries to suggest they have been tamed and can be safely contemplated in the zone of a *"thing made,"* as Kenner calls it, "a zone remote from the world of sayers and sayings" (*Homemade* 60). But the "dark" forces Williams sees as empowering his anti-poetic seem to want to drag the made thing back into the "world of sayers and sayings." One axis along which the primitive tries to speak its silence occurs in the metonymic links Perloff uncovers in the poem's color scheme—the red of the "red wheel / barrow" which links it to the vital blood of the "Arab / Indian / dark woman" in contrast with the "white / chickens" which links them to the ghostly "Crowds" of white "farmers / who live poorly." Through the narrative impulse of *Spring and All*, in its desire to say more rather than show more, the figure of the "dark woman" partially emerges within the framework of **"The Red Wheelbarrow."** A "rich . . . savagery" outside the established economic order restates the conflict found in the opening poem of the sequence, **"Horned Purple,"** with its "white and colored" boys whose phallic display flouts the (primarily white) business interests of the community. Besides suggesting that the initial tensions of the four-poem sequence have not been transcended, her bloody metonymic appearance within the poem suggests her mutilation. Like Philomela, another mythical other, it is a double mutilation, a repetition with a difference. The bloody "castration" of Philomela's mouth works to both silence and make visible her rape, which was motivated by castration anxiety in the first place, the desire to prove phallic dominance through the sexual conquest of (an)other woman outside the boundaries set by the Law of the Father. Likewise, in Williams' desire to express his phallic dominance through sexual contact with the other woman in *Spring and All*, the phallic gaze of his anti-poetic modernism in **"The Red Wheelbarrow"** both works to silence and make visible the native other's historical rape.

The "dark woman" is sister to another distinct set of mutilated beings in the poem who are also cut out by Williams' modernist representation of the primitive forces he admires and fears. In **"Horned Purple,"** for example, the poet identifies with and draws strength from the phallic display of the "Dirty satyrs." However, as the power of their "dark kisses" threaten the poet's ability to distinguish between Self and Other, the phallic gaze that seizes upon the wheelbarrow completes the excising of phallic black masculinity first glimpsed in **"Horned Purple."** Dismembered, the primitive life force that begins the poetic sequence can become a tool or, as Mary Ellen Solt aptly calls the wheelbarrow, "a primitive machine" (26). The ability to turn "primitive peoples" into "primitive machines" was central to the colonial mindset as was the emasculation of the black man. A more sentimental portrait of the wheelbarrow as a symbol of the reification of black (masculine) labor occurs in Williams' acknowledgement of the wheelbarrow's owner as the "old negro" in the *Fifty Poets* anthology and as Marshall in the *Holiday* article. But even the more sentimental recognition of black humanity by whites often requires the castration or asexualization of the black male (Uncle Tom as the classic example). So the castration anxieties the poem's fetishistic scopophilia tries to control are provoked by two distinct primitive forces within the poem—black masculinity and black femininity. In the former, it is a masculinity that must become feminized or castrated, in the latter, femininity is already seen as a "castrated man." Far from allowing the imagination to alleviate "consciousness of the desire which always precedes and exceeds its object" the poem's fetishistic scopohilia marks its "object(s)" as the site of an unspeakable primal scene.

What Williams says about primitives in the prose section "introducing" the four-poem sequence I've been discussing helps illustrate what Williams is trying to achieve in the poems. The notion of primitives comes in when Williams explains the difference between old modes of art, "prose painting, representative work" (*CP*I 220) and the new modes, or the poetry of a "new form dealt with as a reality in itself." While conceding that the old mode will continue, he insists that the "jump from that to Cézanne or back to certain of the primitives is the impossible" (*CP*I 220). Here the new mode is defined as a combination of a sophisticated newness (Cézanne) and, as the preposition "back" suggests, an unsophisticated oldness (the primitives). However, the primitive as concurrent with the present is a point he insists upon in the following paragraph:

> The primitives are not back in some remote age—they are not BEHIND experience. Work which bridges the gap between the rigidities of vulgar experience and the imagination is rare. It is new, immediate—It is so because it is actual, always real. It is experience dynamized into reality.
>
> (*CP* I 220)

It is hard to tell whether these contemporary primitives are primitive peoples who find themselves in a present not entirely their own," or whether the reference is to the artists who make use of primitive subjects and/or forms. This uncertainty might be intentional and speaks to Williams' notion of a fusion or integration of the artist ("the imagination") and his or her subject ("vulgar experience"). Whether it is through unsophisticated primitive peoples or sophisticated use of primitive forms, the primitive gives access to a timeless and universal truth, as the following paragraph suggests: "Time does not move. Only ignorance and stupidity move. Intelligence (force, power) stands still with time and forces change about itself—sifting the world for permanence, in the drift of nonentity" (*CP*I 220). Elsewhere, Williams makes the commonality between primitives and artists in their ability to uncover the universal more explicit: "'The only universal is the local as savages, artists and—to a lesser extent—peasants know'" (Tomlinson vii).

After asserting the timelessness of the primitive, Williams relates the story of Pío Baroja, a class parable with clear autobiographical resonance for Williams. Baroja leaves his medical profession and the "so called intellectual class" (220) to open a bakery in Madrid. Despite his dissatisfaction with the lack of imagination he finds in his middle-class existence, Baroja, like Williams, nonetheless "sees no interest in isolation" (220). Williams' belief in the artist as a social being earns him much deserved praise and respect. However, in rejecting isolation and turning to others as a solution to his class predicament he relies upon a notion of primitive contact that reinforces the assumptions of class privilege he wants to overcome. The moral Williams extracts from Baroja's renunciation of class privilege (and responsibility) is that: "Here it seems to be that a man, starved in imagination, changes his milieu so that his food may be richer—The social class, without the power of expression, lives upon imaginative values" (220). In the middle class artist's quest for richer "food," the "social class" the artist turns to is described in terms of a puzzling paradox—while it "lives upon imaginative values" it lacks the "power of expression." Williams tries to explain further in terms of "primitive types":

> I mean only to emphasize the split that goes down through the abstractions of art to the everyday exercises of the most primitive types.
>
> there is a sharp division—the energizing force of the imagination on one side—and the acquisitive—PROGRESSIVE force of the lump on the other.
>
> (*CP* I 220)

What starts out being a difference in class turns into a more essential difference, a primal difference. In the process of moving from a "social class" to "primitive types" their "imaginative values" disappear. Now he returns to the earlier notion of the prose section where he says there is a "gap" between "vulgar experience" (the primitives) and the "imagination" (the artist) that only rare works of art can bridge. It is only through these paradoxically (un)imaginative primitives that Williams can imagine an escape from the confines of his own class position. This paradoxical view of the (un)imaginative primitive is behind what Williams describes in more abstract terms as the "jump between fact and the imaginative reality" (*CP*I 221) or what Miller in his influential reading celebrated as Williams' imaginative "leap into things."

Williams is using the artist's supposed access to an enduring primitivism to get beyond what he sees as the transitory and superficial divisions of class. Imaginative contact with the primitive or the elemental—and not the dialectics of "class consciousness"—is what provides civilization with true progress. However, the poetic sequence that follows this theorizing paints a vivid portrait of what "the energizing force of the imagination" can do to those it sees as part of the "PROGRESSIVE force of the lump." The "fact" of these essential categories demarcating Self and Other in the prose section isn't deconstructed by the "imaginative reality" of the poems that follow it. From the phallic display of the "Dirty satyrs" to Marshall's wheelbarrow, the black working-class experience is reduced to an essential primitivism. The racial and sexual categories energizing the four poems are kept intact, if not reinforced. As the prose paragraph immediately following the conclusion of **"The Red Wheelbarrow"** says: "The fixed categories into which life is divided must always hold. These things are normal—essential to every activity. But they exist—but not as dead dissections" (*CP*I 224). This succinctly states the "plot" of the four-poem sequence and its conclusion with **"The Red Wheelbarrow."** The distinction of Self and Other threatened by the blurring of racial and gender categories in **"Horned Purple"** and **"The Sea"** is both reaffirmed and stabilized by their aesthetic resolution or objectification within **"Quietness"** and **"The Red Wheelbarrow."** But **"The Red Wheelbarrow"** can't deliver on its promise of a new relationship to things, moving beyond the "dead dissections" of the past, as long as its reliance upon the old relationships between people is not acknowledged.

To his credit, Williams keeps his understanding of race and gender open to revision. Indeed, *Spring and All* can be read as an attempt to move beyond the earlier and cruder theories of race found, for example, in his letter, "A Criticism of Miss Marsden's 'Lingual Psychology'," written for *The Egoist* in 1917.[12] After *Spring and All,* through his poetry and fiction of the thirties he continues to express his concern with sympathetic portraits and characters. His most complex and productive attempt to comprehend racial difference occurs within the liberal inclusiveness of his epic *Paterson.* There are other noteworthy if problematic efforts— *Man Orchid,* for example, an unfinished collaboration

with Fred Miller which was going to be an improvisational novel inspired by black jazz and whose protagonist was based on a white man they mistakenly took for "'a light-skinned negro'" (Mariani 514). A comment Williams makes late in his life in an interview with Walter Sutton suggests such fundamental misunderstandings continued to dog his liberal sympathies. Discussing his dissatisfaction with the beat poets and their self-conscious "primitivism," Williams says: "I've known many primitive people, but they are surprisingly complex when you get to know them. Their primitive natures disappear. They become quiet. We value them as individuals not because of their beat characteristics but because they are capable of becoming more like us" (*Interviews* 56). Perhaps it is a liberal identification complex such as this that explains how the red wheelbarrow's owner (dis)appears from the poem, setting up Marshall's reappearance some thirty years later, as the poet tries to find room for him, and his affection for him, somewhere in the context of his art.

Notes

1. Carl Rapp, based on an account of the poem's occasion attributed to the director of the Rutherford Public Library, considers the possibility that ". . . Williams glimpsed the wheelbarrow during a lull in a medical emergency in which one of his young patients lay between life and death . . ." (*William Carlos Williams and Romantic Idealism.* Hanover and London: Brown UP, 1984: 89).

2. Thomas Whitaker mentions a comment by Williams that the poem was "'written in two minutes'" (*William Carlos Williams.* Boston: Twayne Publishers, 1989: 46).

3. In his elegant reading of the poem, Charles Altieri says, "no poem in English is more spatial and timeless. The objects seem to have no history . . . we become aware by the end that they represent a form of rural life whose essential habits and dependence on natural processes have never really changed" ("Objective Image and Act of Mind in Modern Poetry." *PMLA* 91 [Jan. 1976]: 112). Altieri and other critics who read the poem as representing "rural life" ignore the fact that in the *Fifty Poets* anthology, Williams identifies the "old negro" who owns the wheelbarrow as living in the same suburb as he does. However, the critics' ability to disregard the poem's suburban setting, I would argue, has much to do with Williams' notion of the primitive that informs and surrounds the poem.

4. Many of those on America's left wing would've been surprised to learn that Williams was one of their own. It seems to me Benet makes the mistake of connecting aesthetic radicalism with political radicalism; nonetheless, his comment illustrates

the suspicion with which Williams was regarded by the literary establishment.

5. See, for example, his "A Note on Poetry" that introduces "The Red Wheelbarrow" along with other poems he includes in the *Oxford Anthology of American Poetry* (Eds. William Rose Benet and Norman Holmes Pearson. NY: Oxford UP, 1938: 1313-4), in which he explains his poetic practice in terms of objectivism.

6. All citations of *Spring and All* and the four-poem sequence mentioned above come from A. Walton Litz and Christopher MacGowan's *The Collected Poems of William Carlos Williams, Volume I* (New York: New Directions, 1986: 221-4).

7. The reference to Edgar Allan Poe suggests the poet as alienated artist who drowns or "goes under." Earlier in *Spring and All*, Williams says the following about Poe: "From the time of Poe in the U.S.—the first American poet had to be a man of great separation—with close identity with life. Poe could not have written a word without the violence of expulsive emotion combined with the in-driving force of a crudely repressive environment. Between the two his imagination was forced into being to keep him to that reality, completeness, sense of escape which is felt in his work—his topics. Typically American—accurately, even inevitably set in his time" (*CP* I 198).

8. As early as 1928, anticipating such critics as Perloff and Riddel, Gorham Munson links the poetry of Williams' *Spring and All* to cubism. Unlike Perloff and Riddel, though, he sees the connection not in terms of a shared appreciation for indeterminacy. Instead, he finds a similar sense of "primitivism" in their work, although he seems uninterested in the Euro-centric nature of the term: "[Williams] is attempting to leap straight from contact (sharp perceptions) to the imagination (order in the highest sense) without working through culture (the attempt to grasp reality practically, emotionally and intellectually). Thus to my mind his primitivism is leading him back to sophistication, the sophistication of a Parisian cubist painter" (*William Carlos Williams, The Critical Heritage.* Ed. Charles Doyle. London: Routledge and Kegan Paul, 1980: 104).

9. See Mariani's account of Williams' discomfort with Stevens' introduction, in particular Stevens' reading of his poetry in terms of an antipoetic, which only increased through the years. In fact, despite the clear antipoetic orientation of *Spring and All*, late in his life Williams could say: "'I didn't agree with Stevens that it [the antipoetic] was a conscious means I was using. I have never been satisfied that the anti-poetic had any validity or even existed'" (*A New World* 340).

10. Although once a more common term in discussing Williams' poetry, with such critics as Gorham Munson, Yvor Winters (*Primitivism and Decadence* [NY: Arrow Editions, 1937]), Mary Ellen Solt (William Carlos Williams: Poems in the American Idiom." *Folio* 15 [Winter 1960]: 3-28), Robert Kern ("Williams, Brautigan, and the Poetics of Primitivism." *Chicago Review* 27.1 [1975]: 45-57) and Dickran Tashjian (*Skyscraper Primitives* [Middletown, Conn.: Wesleyan UP, 1975]), the term has disappeared from contemporary scholarship on Williams.

11. Several years after the publication of *Spring and All*, Williams makes another comment in the *Embodiment of Knowledge* (Ed. Ron Loewinsohn. NY: New Directions, 1974) that tries to explain the primitive modernity of certain groups: "People cannot get used to the Jews: it is the persistence of a type out of phase. The Negro is another. In each case it is a phase which happens to coincide but roughly, by accident with the present—somewhat out of line" (51-2).

12. In this attempt by Williams theorize gender he says: "It is well established that primitive man—that is the tribesman—when not busied with women and when free to perform his own will is either hunting, fishing, loafing, or drunk. Man will only work when forced to do so, or when inveigled into it by a woman, or at least by a predominant female psychology" (*The Egoist* 4.7 [Aug. 1917]: 111).

Works Cited

Aiken, Conrad. "The Well Worn Spirit." *The New Republic.* Apr. 18, 1934: 289-91.

Altieri, Charles. "Objective Image and Act of Mind in Modern Poetry." *PMLA* 91 (Jan. 1976): 101-14.

Benét, William Rose. "William Carlos Williams." *Fifty Poets, An American Auto-Anthology.* Ed. William Rose Benét. NY: Duffield and Green, 1933.

Burke, Kenneth. "Heaven's First Law." *William Carlos Williams, A Collection of Critical Essays.* Ed. J. Hillis Miller. Englewood Cliffs, NJ: Prentice-Hall, 1966: 47-50.

———. "William Carlos Williams, 1883-1963." *William Carlos Williams, A Collection of Critical Essays.* Ed. J. Hillis Miller. Englewood Cliffs, NJ: Prentice-Hall, 1966: 50-7.

Deutsch, Babette. "Williams, The Innocent Eye and the Thing-In-Itself." *William Carlos Williams, The Critical Heritage.* Ed. Charles Doyle. London: Routledge and Kegan Paul, 1980.

Dolin, Sharon. "Enjambment and the Erotics of the Gaze in Williams's Poetry." *American Imago* 50.1 (Spring 1993): 29-52.

Dunn, Allen. "Williams's Liberating Need." *Journal of Modern Literature* 16.1 (Summer 1989): 49-59.

Jarrell, Randall. "Introduction." *Selected Poems by William Carlos Williams.* NY: New Directions, 1969.

Kenner, Hugh. *A Homemade World: The American Modernist Writers.* NY: Knopf, 1975.

———. *The Pound Era.* Berkeley: University of California Press, 1971.

Kern, Robert. "Williams, Brautigan, and the Poetics of Primitivism." *Chicago Review* 27.1 (1975): 45-57.

Levertov, Denise. *The Poet in the World.* NY: New Directions, 1973.

Mariani, Paul. William Carlos Williams, A New World Naked. NY: W. W. Norton and Company, 1981.

———. *William Carlos Williams, The Poet and His Critics.* Chicago: American Library Association, 1975.

Miller, J. Hillis. *Poets of Reality, Six Twentieth-Century Writers.* Cambridge, Mass.: Harvard UP, 1965.

Munson, Gorham. Excerpted from *Destinations: A Canvass of American Literature Since 1900* in *William Carlos Williams, The Critical Heritage.* Ed. Charles Doyle. London: Routledge and Kegan Paul, 1980.

Pearce, Roy Harvey. "Williams and the 'New Mode'." *William Carlos Williams, A Collection of Critical Essays.* Ed. J. Hillis Miller. Englewood Cliffs, NJ: Prentice-Hall, 1966.

Perloff, Marjorie. *The Poetics of Indeterminacy: Rimbaud to Cage.* Princeton, NJ: Princeton UP, 1981.

Rapp, Carl. *William Carlos Williams and Romantic Idealism.* Hanover and London: Brown UP, 1984.

Riddel, Joseph N. *The Inverted Bell: Modernism and the Counterpoetics of William Carlos Williams.* Baton Rouge: Louisiana State UP, 1974.

Solt, Mary Ellen. "William Carlos Williams: Poems in the American Idiom." *Folio* 15 (Winter 1960): 3-28.

Stevens, Wallace. "Williams." *Opus Posthumous.* Ed. Milton J. Bates. NY: Random House, 1990: 213-5.

Tashjian, Dickran. *Skyscraper Primitives.* Middletown, Conn.: Wesleyan UP, 1975.

Tomlinson, Charles. "Introduction." *William Carlos Williams, Selected Poems.* NY: New Directions, 1985.

Von Hallberg, Robert. "The Politics of Description: W. C. Williams in the Thirties." *Journal of English History* 45.1 (Spring 1978): 131-51.

Whitaker, Thomas. *William Carlos Williams.* Boston: Twayne Publishers, 1989.

Williams, William Carlos. "A Criticism of Miss Marsden's 'Lingual Psychology'." *The Egoist* 4.7 (Aug. 1917): 110-11.

Peter Verdonk (essay date 2005)

SOURCE: Verdonk, Peter. "Painting, Poetry, Parallelism: Ekphrasis, Stylistics and Cognitive Poetics." *Language and Literature* 14, no. 3 (2005): 231-44.

[*In the following essay, after a general discussion of ekphrasis—the technique of representing a work of visual art in verse—Verdonk presents Williams's "The Dance" as a remarkably accomplished example of the genre.*]

"The Dance"

In Brueghel's great picture, The Kermess,[1]
  the dancers go round, they go round and
  around, the squeal and the blare and the
  tweedle of bagpipes, a bugle and fiddles
  tipping their bellies (round as the thick-
sided glasses whose wash they impound)
  their hips and their bellies off balance
  to turn them. Kicking and rolling about
the Fair Grounds, swinging their butts, those
shanks must be sound to bear up under such
  rollicking measures, prance as they dance
  in Brueghel's great picture, The Kermess.

William Carlos Williams, *Selected Poems* (1985)

EKPHRASIS IN CLASSICAL RHETORIC

Poems describing a work of art, like **'The Dance'** by William Carlos Williams, are traditionally associated with a literary sub-genre called ekphrasis, which is a transliteration of a Greek word meaning 'description'. (The spelling ecphrasis is also current.) However, contrary to what might be expected, the term has its origin not in poetics but in classical rhetoric, the art of persuasion. Here ekphrasis was usually defined as a self-contained description, often of a common topic, which could be inserted at an appropriate place in a piece of oratory so as to enhance its persuasive powers. For this purpose, the teachers of ancient rhetoric required an ekphrasis to be so vivid that it would bring the event or object described before the mind's eye of the listener. To give a typical example, I quote below a brief passage from *Rhetorica ad Herennium (Rhetoric for Herennius)*, an early Latin handbook, written perhaps around 84 BC by an anonymous author, who addressed it to an unidentified Herennius.[2] This is what he has to say on *descriptio,* the Latin equivalent of ekphrasis:

Vivid Description is the name for the figure which contains a clear, lucid, and impressive exposition of the consequences of an act, as follows:

But, men of the jury, if by your votes you free this defendant, immediately, like a lion released from his cage, or some foul beast loosed from his chains, he will slink and prowl about in the forum, sharpening his teeth to attack everyone's property, assaulting every man, friend and enemy, known to him or unknown, now despoiling a good name, now attacking a life, now bringing ruin upon a house and its entire household, shaking the republic from its foundations. Therefore, men of the jury, cast him out from the state, free every one from fear, and finally, think of yourselves. For if you release this creature without punishment, believe me, gentlemen, it is against yourselves that you will have let loose a wild and savage beast.

([Cicero], 1989: IV.xxxix.51)

CROSS-FERTILIZATION BETWEEN RHETORIC AND POETICS

It will not be difficult to see that precisely this type of rhetorical figure of description is a prime candidate for evolving into a literary figure, though without necessarily losing its persuasive features (Cockcroft, 2003: 54). Indeed, there was a lot of cross-fertilization going on between rhetoric and poetics, with the rhetoricians spicing up their oratory with expressive images from poetry, and the poets tapping the rich resources of rhetoric (Verdonk, 1999: 293). For example, in his rhetorical handbook *De Oratore* (*On the Orator*) (55BC), Cicero holds that the orator has three main functions, namely 'the winning over, the instructing and the stirring of men's minds' (1988: II.xxviii.121). In the literary camp, these rhetorical aspirations are echoed in Horace's verse essay *Ars Poetica* (c. 20-23 BC), where the ideal poet is described as having 'blended profit and pleasure, at once delighting and instructing the reader' (1991: 333).

EKPHRASIS AS A LITERARY FIGURE

Now, literary ekphrasis, as it ultimately evolved from rhetoric, can be taken in a wider and a narrower sense. In the wider sense, it is a detailed description of any real or imagined object or scene, or of an abstract idea, mental image or state of emotion. In the more restricted sense, ekphrasis is associated with poetry addressing not only works of visual art, such as paintings, tapestries and sculpture, but also architectural art, and functional artefacts such as goblets, vases, and weaponry like swords, shields and suits of armour. In this case too, all these objects may be real or fictional. At this point, it appears useful to follow Hollander's example in his fine book on ekphrasis, entitled *The Gazer's Spirit: Poems Speaking to Silent Works of Art* (1995), by making a distinction between 'actual' and 'notional' ekphrasis. Actual ekphrastic poems are engaged with particular and identifiable works of art or artefacts, whereas in the case of notional ekphrasis the artistic objects addressed are purely fictional (1995: 4).[3] In antiquity, and long after, notional ekphrasis abounds, and it has become an established convention to regard Homer's description of the making of the legendary shield of Achilles in the *Iliad* as its generic prototype (1974: XVIII.483-608). Homer's masterpiece was emulated several times in later epics, including Virgil's description of Aeneas' shield in *The Aeneid* (Virgil, 1974: VIII.626-731), while in our times it has been transferred to a modern anti-heroic setting by W. H. Auden in his bitter poem 'The

Shield of Achilles' (1966: 294-5). These and many other classical instances of notional ekphrasis also inspired a great many English poets, from Chaucer, Spenser and Shakespeare to the Romantics, with, I think, Keats's 'Ode on a Grecian Urn' as the acme of perfection.[4]

Perhaps unsurprisingly, a bird's eye view of Western art history shows that different periods have different ekphrastic agendas. For instance, it is remarkable that in the 20th century so many poets, both inside and outside Britain, produced such a lot of actual ekphrastic poems addressing real and identifiable paintings, and it is even more remarkable that for some unexplained reason the 16th-century Flemish painter Pieter Brueghel the Elder became their special favourite (Kranz, 1975). His pictures provided an inspiration for poets such as John Berryman, Walter de la Mare, Sylvia Plath, Wislawa Szymborska, William Carlos Williams and, notably, W. H. Auden, who perhaps set this fashion with his justly celebrated ekphrastic poem 'Musée des Beaux Arts', which specifically mentions Pieter Brueghel's *Landscape with the Fall of Icarus* and alludes to a few other pictures by the same artist (Verdonk, 1987). William Carlos Williams, for that matter, wrote no fewer than 10 poems on paintings by Brueghel, which were all collected in his book *Pictures from Brueghel and Other Poems* (1962), for which he was awarded the Pulitzer Prize for Poetry only two months after his death in March 1963. Williams's poem **'The Dance',** which will be discussed later, had been published earlier in *The Wedge* (1944) and was subsequently included in *Selected Poems* (1985).

THE BOND BETWEEN POETRY AND THE VISUAL ARTS

Considering notional and actual ekphrasis in a wider perspective, it appears that in the history of Western art there has traditionally been a strong bond between poetry and the visual arts. Thus, in the opening chapter of his *Poetics,* Aristotle (384-322 BC) yokes the two arts together in the fundamental statement: 'Some artists, whether by theoretical knowledge or by long practice, can represent things by imitating their shapes and colours, and others do so by the use of the voice' (1983: 32). The keywords here are 'represent' and 'imitate', the latter being a translation of the Greek word *mimesis.* Indeed, though using different media, poetry and painting were long regarded as imitative arts, because they both used mimetic representation to depict humans and objects in their relationship to the outside world.

This close affinity between the two arts, which were therefore often designated as the 'sister arts', found its fullest expression in Horace's (65-8 BC) frequently quoted simile *Ut pictura poesis* ('A poem is like a picture'), which occurs in his earlier mentioned verse essay *Ars Poetica* (1991: 361). This Horatian formula had a very long career and profoundly influenced several theories of poetry, as well as the arts in general, until well into the 18th century, when the classical norm that art should be concerned with *mimesis*, i.e. the imitation of 'reality', began to give way to the ideal of romantic emotion and individual expression.

THE RIVALRY BETWEEN WORD AND IMAGE

Though the ideas of classical *mimesis* may belong to the past, those of ekphrasis are, in a general sense, still very much alive, in that they continue to feed our constant and irresistible urge to bring about some kind of productive or creative interplay between word and image (Baker-Smith, 1990: 1002). It is perhaps what 2000 years ago Quintilian had in mind when he coined the catch-phrase 'word-picture' (*verbis depingitur*), and insisted that a speech must appeal not only to the hearing but also to the 'eyes of the mind' (*oculis mentis*) (1986: VIII.III.61-72). As a matter of fact, countless writers of shaped poetry, concrete poetry, comic strips and illustrated advertisements, and of course filmmakers, have satisfied this preoccupation with vision and language. Incidentally, it will be noted that the ekphrastic endeavours of these, what might be called, mixed arts actually produce more or less concrete images, whereas the language of ekphrastic poetry characteristically does not, for if it did, it would have to be called shaped or concrete poetry. Quite the contrary, the language of ekphrastic poetry is expected to call the image to mind, to conjure it up, as it were.[5]

Apart from this prevailing desire for some productive or creative interaction between word and image, there is at the same time a tension and even rivalry between our cognitive abilities of language and vision. For instance, when in classical times the image was used to jazz up the persuasive powers of the orator, it was still the word that remained in control. In contrast, it seems to me that in recent years in many areas of communication, notably in the mass media and multimedia, it is now the image that dominates the word. In point of fact, if ekphrasis is taken in its broadest sense of an attempt to capture the visual in words, the present-day state of affairs in modern communicative rhetoric may well be seen as an inversion of this classical ideal, in that now 'images are given the task . . . of explaining words, rather than the reverse' (Nunberg, 1996: 264).

A BRIEF EXPOSÉ OF COGNITIVE POETICS AS A SPIN-OFF FROM THE COGNITIVE SCIENCES

After the above thumbnail sketch of the cultural history of ekphrasis, and a brief ideological aside, which some people might see as a sign of culture pessimism, I shall make a very short explanatory statement about cognitive poetics, also known as cognitive stylistics.

Given the limited scope of this article, I cannot begin to describe here in detail what cognitive poetics is all about. Therefore, an extremely brief summary must suf-

fice. Cognitive poetics, then, is one of the valuable spin-offs from research into the cognitive sciences in general and cognitive linguistics in particular. It is an interdisciplinary study of how readers process literary texts, or perhaps better still, 'of what happens when a reader reads a literary text' (Stockwell, 2002: 5). Probably the main reason why many students of style find fresh inspiration in cognitive linguistics is that this approach does not regard language as a separate and independent cognitive faculty, as it is assumed to be in Chomskyan linguistics. (Compare, for instance, Steven Pinker's fascinating book *The Language Instinct* published in 1994, which is largely inspired by Chomsky's ideas.) On the contrary, cognitive linguists hold that there is a close interactive and meaningful relationship between our linguistic and other cognitive abilities, which include thinking, experience, imagination, learning, memory, perception, attention, emotion, reasoning and problem-solving. All these abilities enable humans to survive and make sense of the world around them. From this it follows that cognitive linguistics is thoroughly experiential from a physical, social, cultural, ideological and emotive point of view. To put it differently, cognitive linguists seek to explain the formal manifestations of language not only in terms of the non-linguistic cognitive abilities which are their plausible providers, but also in terms of the communicative or discursive functions that such empowered language structures perform (Taylor, 2002: 8-9).[6] Yet another source of inspiration for stylistics and poetics is that cognitive linguistics was (and still is) developed in relation to other cognitive sciences such as cognitive psychology, anthropology, psycholinguistics and artificial intelligence. This interdisciplinary approach has yielded completely new concepts, theories and ideas which will enable students of style and poetics to analyse, describe and rationalize 'the effects of literary texts on the mind of the reader' (Gavins and Steen, 2003: 2). For example, metaphor, metonymy and other figures are no longer seen as an embellishment of language to create a particular stylistic effect, resulting from a process of objective thinking of an independent mind; rather, they are seen as a reflection of how people *construe* their knowledge and experience of the world around them (Lee, 2001: 6-7; Taylor, 2002: 11; my emphasis).[7] Furthermore, cognitive poetics also draws on other cognitive concepts such as schema theory and frames for research into readers' comprehension of texts (Emmott, 1997; Semino, 1997), and the concept of figure and ground to account for readers' response to foregrounding (Emmott, 2002; Stockwell, 2002), and some other theoretical concepts from the cognitive sciences that cannot be discussed here because of lack of space. Therefore, I refer to the following recently published collections of articles: Csábi and Zerkowitz (2002), Gavins and Steen (2003), and Semino and Culpeper (2002). They deal with a wide variety of examples of how cognitive poetics can be fruitfully combined with theories and insights from cognitive linguistics and other cognitive disciplines, showing how the cognitive sciences have given fresh impetus to stylistics and poetics.

COGNITIVE POETICS IN RELATION TO POETICS, STYLISTICS, LINGUISTICS AND DISCOURSE ANALYSIS

As its name implies, cognitive poetics is also closely linked with poetics, both in its classical narrower sense of a systematic theory of poetry and in its modern broader sense of 'science' of literature, which includes literary and cultural theory, literary criticism, literary history and aesthetics. Furthermore, it is essential for an effective application of cognitive poetics to keep drawing on the resources of stylistics, linguistics and, last but not least, discourse analysis so as to assess through verbal analysis the validity of readerly intuitions (Stockwell, 2002: 60). This versatility of approach and open-mindedness are called for because in the humanities there are different forms of rationalization, different kinds of arguments and argumentation, and all have strong theoretical foundations, so that any claim of the cognitive sciences to exclusiveness or to having the best methods would lead to a barren exercise.

THE NATURE OF LITERARY DISCOURSE

I return to my discussion of literary ekphrasis with the important observation that it is in fact concerned with a double representation, namely a verbal representation of a pictorial one (Hamilton, 2003: 216). Now, a representation implies not only that it represents *something* but also that it represents this something *to someone* (Jackendoff, 2002: 19). Therefore, it may be said that an ekphrastic poem embodies a communicative triangle between the artist, the poet's persona and the reader. In other words, it is very much a discourse, which I define as an interpersonal and context-bound act of communication verbalized in a text, and waiting to be inferred from it. Importantly, context is a matter not simply of physical circumstances but also of the ideas, values, beliefs and emotions inside people's heads. In this sense all communication is a meeting of minds, and meaning is achieved to the extent that the contexts of the communicating parties come together. With regard to the meanings of *literary* discourses I hold the view that they are indefinite, undetermined, unstable and indeed often unsettling. So every time readers try to infer a discourse from the same literary text, they are sure to find other meanings, which again and again will refuse to be pinned down (Verdonk, 2002: 22). When I wrote this, I was not questioning the basic assumption in most stylistic work that 'the language of literature' does not stand aloof from 'ordinary language'. In fact, I was only trying to formulate tentatively what it is that makes literary discourse different from other types of social discourse. As Simpson has succinctly phrased it, cognitive poetics appears to provide theoretical strategies that allow stylisticians to address precisely this problem in their work, on the basis of the argument that literature is perhaps better conceptualized as a way of reading than as a way of writing (2004: 39).

A STYLISTIC-CUM-COGNITIVE POETIC READING OF
WILLIAM CARLOS WILLIAMS'S 'THE DANCE'

I will now present a reading of William Carlos Williams's ekphrastic poem **'The Dance',** prompted by a linguistic stylistic analysis. (When I say 'a' reading, I mean of course that it is 'my' reading.) Concurrently with this reading as well as at the end of it, I will suggest what non-linguistic cognitive capacities might be supposed to underlie some of the poem's rhetorical elements or perceived effects, in other words, to what extent they could be rationalized from a cognitive poetic perspective.[8]

When turning my attention to the poem, I am prompted by my real-world experience that all discourse is interpersonal, and therefore I assume instinctively the role of the person being spoken to, and listen to the voice of the speaker in the poem whom I expect to express certain views or sentiments. In poetics this speaker is usually indicated as the poem's 'persona', which is the Latin word for the mask through which the actors in a classical play spoke their lines. Interestingly, the term persona derives from Latin *per-sonare,* which means to 'sound through'. This verb is most appropriate in this case because by means of a series of highly expressive sound patterns the persona attempts to make me almost literally hear the bouncing of the dancers in the Brueghel painting, as well as the din of the music to which they dance. For me these sounds not only are mimetic, in that they add to the poem's lexical meaning by enacting that meaning, but also create meaning by triggering associations between particular sounds and other sensations, memories or images stored in my mind. When saying this, I am well aware that when listening to speech in everyday discourse I tend to disregard the sounds of words and listen only for the meaning. But as a result of social-cultural conditioning and my knowledge of this generic category, I have acquired the cognitive-emotive awareness that in poetic discourse particular individual sounds or patterns of sound tend to reinforce or even add to the poem's lexical sense.

With regard to patterns, I perceive that this poem's discourse makes profitable use of parallelism, that is, it features repetitive patterns on all levels of language organization. It is a well-known fact that humans are invariably charmed by linguistic quirks involving patterned structures of repetition. Most interestingly, cognitive linguists claim that our innate habit to structure things into symmetrical patterns, including patterns of repetition, is in fact a projection of our embodied understanding of symmetry in the world around us. We project this understanding metaphorically on to all our perceptions, actions and imaginings, so as to make sense of the world (Turner, 1991: 91). Not surprisingly, this ingrained disposition is stimulated maximally by symmetric structures in art of various forms such as literature, music, painting, sculpture and architecture. Indeed, embodied experience is a key concept in cognitive linguistics. It claims that meaning, understanding, imagination and rationality originate in and are determined by the patterns of our bodily as well as social and cultural experiences, which is diametrically opposed to the abstract, propositional account of meaning in Western philosophy dissociated from any personal experience (Johnson, 1987; Lakoff, 1987; Lakoff and Johnson, 1980, 1999).

In poetry, sound patterns, which include prosodic effects such as metre and rhythm, rhyme, stanza forms and other sound effects like alliteration, assonance and onomatopoeia, are the staple instances of parallelism on the phonological level. Thus in my reading of the metrical structure of **'The Dance'** the syllable count per line varies from eight to 11 and the number of stresses from three to four. But when rereading it aloud, I hear (and metaphorically feel!) that its metrical ground plan is not drawn line by line, but ranges right across the poem. Almost bodily, I join in on the beat on the first syllable of 'Brueghel' in the first line and then I feel I am being moved rhythmically round and round from line to line in a waltz-like dance in triple time on the fairly regular dactylic beat of óne, twŏ, thrĕe.⁹

My sense of being swept off my feet by these 'rollicking measures' of a dance is intensified by the syntactic pull of the run-on lines, which carry me breathlessly through to the end. Besides, in a great many of these lines the pull is particularly strong because the run-on occurs right in the middle of a syntactic constituent. In other words, in the case of enjambment I get two conflicting prompts: the metrical line-boundary tells me to pause, while the unfinished syntax pulls me into the next line (Verdonk, 2002: 61). This syntactic counterpoint to the poem's metre also comes out in the overall grammatical structure of the poem, which consists of only two sentences, with the result that in my reading I am allowed only one brief pause and this comes right at the moment when the dancers turn. Indeed, everything interacts with everything because even the absence of end-rhyme, which would have marked off the line boundaries, speeds up the wild verse-movement of the poem, and to cap it all, many of the lines end with normally weak-stressed function words such as 'and', 'the', 'about', 'those' and 'such', which spur me on to read ever faster in search of words of fuller meaning.

In doing so, I experience yet another sound pattern. This time it is produced by some strings of alliterative consonantal sounds, of which particularly the frequently repeated bilabial plosive /b/, as in 'blare', 'bagpipes', 'bugle', 'bellies', 'butts' and 'bear up', makes my inner ear aware of the thumping rhythm of the music as well as of the stamping feet of the dancers. By now I think that the poem's sound structure is its most powerful rhetorical device, because the cacophony of this kermess dance is not only magnified even further by some patterns of assonance, as in the repeated 'go round and around', and in 'squeal' and 'tweedle', but there are also the sound associations evoked by the poem's diction, such as the descriptive nouns of the different noises—the already mentioned 'squeal' and 'tweedle' and 'blare'—and the names of the different musical instruments, 'bagpipes', 'bugle' and 'fiddles'. At this point, I realize that the noises are mentioned first and only then the instruments that produce them. The effect of this syntactic order is that I experience almost physically my search for the producers of this ear-splitting pandemonium. For this perceptual experience I refer to my subsequent discussion of the figure-ground principle.

Shifting now to the grammatical level, I become aware of a repetitive pattern of present participles of verbs of motion such as 'tipping', 'kicking', 'rolling' and a few others. I feel that they all converge in sustaining the poem's untiring rhythm because grammatically present participles usually denote continuing action, while here they simultaneously match and reinforce the sense of the motion verbs.

Indeed, it is remarkable that the complexity of the poem's parallelism can still be added to by yet another linguistic element, namely the repeated explicit use of the co-ordinating conjunction 'and', which is traditionally called syndeton from the Greek *syndéton,* meaning 'bound together'. This rhetorical device intensifies for me the listing of all the things to be seen in the painting, and, in terms of vicarious experience, all the things to be 'heard'.

Next I notice how the speaker in the poem's discourse exploits the use of the present tense, as well as of the definite article, to draw me as it were into the scene of the picture. First there is the consistent deictic use of the present tense, conveying the dramatic immediacy of the speaker's eye-witness account of the picture, and suggesting that his present is my present. Psychologically, it is indeed all self-induced suggestion on my part, because the fact of the matter is that I am unable to check the persona's use of the present tense in relation to real time, as I would have been in a face-to-face conversation. However, guided by my social and cognitive experience to relate a discourse to the context of its occurrence, to take the speaker's viewpoint, and to understand how things would look from his or her time and place, I am able to interpret the persona's use of the present tense as a representation of the time as he experienced it, while describing the picture. At this point, I wish to refer to what I said earlier about ekphrasis being a matter of double representation, namely a verbal representation of a pictorial one. In this context I also said that the poem actually embodies a triangular discourse between the painter, the poet's persona and the reader. So the conclusion must be that the painter played the same game with the poet's persona as the latter plays with me, the reader. More specifically, the artist has persuaded the poet's persona to assume a presence in the world of the painting through his pictorial rhetoric. In the same way, the latter (i.e. the poet's persona) has persuaded me to imagine myself as participating in the situation described in the poem through his verbal rhetoric.

This leads me to a consideration of the particular use of the definite article in the poem's discourse, which appears to be yet another rhetorical device to engage me, the reader, in the role of addressee. By pretending that virtually all the things he sees are as 'definite' for me as they are for himself, the persona thrusts me, as it were, into the immediate situational context of looking at the painting. In fact, this use of the definite article is in essence 'deictic', too, because it signals that the persona controls the perspective and decides what information in the discourse is rhetorically assumed to be known to the addressee, and by proxy to me, the reader.

Coming to the last line, it strikes me that it repeats literally the first line. I am tempted to interpret this repetition, which appears to frame or enclose the ekphrastic discourse of the poem, as an iconic representation of the framing of the picture.[10] In terms of cognitive perception, I think that texts can suggest spatiality and boundedness. Therefore, this framing of the poem may have the iconic effect of suggesting similarity between the verbal and the visual representations, which, after all, is likely to be the main objective of ekphrasis. This framing, for that matter, may also allude to the fact that paintings and poems are characteristically self-contained so that we have to make a kind of effort to relate them to a relevant context so as to engage them in a discourse.

This last observation brings to mind the theory of figure-ground organization, which is crucial to cognitive linguistics, in particular to the so-called prominence view of language (Ungerer and Schmid, 1996: xiii). The figure-ground phenomenon, which was first described by the Danish gestalt psychologist Edgar Rubin in 1915, may be defined as our mental faculty to distinguish a perceived object (the figure) from its background (the ground). Usually this distinction is relatively easy, but sometimes it is made difficult as, for

example, in the case of camouflage, which causes the figure to blend with the ground. As is only to be expected, artists, like for instance the Dutch graphic artist M. C. Escher, may make playful use of this visual mode of perception by designing ambiguous prints or pictures in which the figure could be ground, or the other way round. This basic principle is also applied in cognitive linguistics, for example, for the explication of locative relations and clause patterns (Langacker, 1987, 1991; Ungerer and Schmid, 1996 serves as an excellent introduction).

Obviously, Brueghel's picture as a self-contained object, with its frame forming clearly defined edges, conspicuously stands out as a figure against its background, in this case a wall of a museum in Vienna. However, when scanning across the scene in the picture, it will be noticed that our figure-ground organization is in essence flexible. By changing our focus on different details of the scene, we can repeatedly create different figure-ground relations. From this it follows that the figure-ground theory is closely linked to the human attentional system, in that our attention is captured by the figure or, the other way round, we create a figure precisely because we concentrate our attention on it. Thus, it is particularly striking that the poet completely ignores the couple in the foreground, who seem to be dashing across purposefully on a diagonal line, rather than being drawn into the dance. In fact, the poet's attention seems to concentrate on about one-third of the area of the picture, that is, the left foreground and right centre.[11]

Now, this is all about visual perception, but in cognitive linguistics figure-ground alignments also apply to other sensory perceptions (Taylor, 2002: 10). Consider, for example, our auditory ability to pick out a particular note from a piece of background music or a particular voice from a babble of voices. Furthermore, the figure-ground theory also relates to our cognitive ability to mentally structure situations and texts in all sorts of ways, for instance, by selecting or omitting specific circumstances, by describing participants in various degrees of detail, by providing different perspectives, and by creating conspicuous stylistic features or tendencies that stand out as figures against the background of the rest of the text (Taylor, 2002: 11). In point of fact, it may be concluded that, in addition to all the other cognitive motivations I suggested in my analysis, the theory of figure-ground organization provides yet another rational explanation for all the foregrounded patterns of sound, syntax, grammar and diction that captivated my attention when reading this poem, so much so that I really felt drawn into the boisterous world of Brueghel's painting, like Alice who stepped through the looking-glass into Looking-Glass House after many times repeating her favourite phrase 'Let's pretend'.

Notes

I thank the New Directions Publishing Corporation for their permission to quote William Carlos Williams's poem 'The Dance' with the following credit lines:

'The Dance (In Brueghel's)' By William Carlos Williams, from *COLLECTED POEMS: 1939-1962, VOLUME II,* copyright © 1944 by William Carlos Williams. Reprinted by permission of New Directions Publishing Corporation.

Furthermore, I am grateful to Ron Carter and Peter Stockwell of the University of Nottingham and Mick Short of Lancaster University for inviting me to read earlier versions of this article to staff members and graduate students. The ensuing discussions were most inspiring. I also thank Henry Widdowson, Robert Cockeroft and an anonymous reviewer for their useful comments and suggestions.

1. See http://www.khm.at/staticE/page228.html for a reproduction and brief description of Brueghel's picture 'The Kermess', also called 'Peasant Dance', at the Kunsthistorisches Museum in Vienna. In the Low Countries the Kermess used to be a local popular feast day and fair, originally to mark the anniversary of the consecration of the local church; cf. modern Dutch 'kermis' (funfair; AmE. carnival) derived from 'kerk' (church) + 'mis' (mass) via the older forms 'keremisse' and 'kermiss(e)'.

2. For a very long time *Rhetorica ad Herennium* was attributed to Cicero, and his name, though in square brackets, still features on the cover of the English edition in the prestigious Loeb Classical Library. However, in the meantime all recent editors have agreed that this attribution must be erroneous (Kennedy, 1999: 108).

3. Henry Widdowson, who was so kind as to read a draft of this article, questions the usefulness of Hollander's distinction between actual and notional ekphrasis for stylistics. Does it matter, he wonders, whether a poet has the object in sight or in mind? Or whether, if in mind, it is imperfectly recalled, deliberately modified, or even entirely imagined? For even when there are deictic signals in the text that suggest a particular picture, we cannot be sure that this is not a device for creating a vacuum effect to draw the reader in. My response to this query is that when I say that Hollander's distinction between actual and notional ekphrasis might be useful, I am only thinking of ekphrasis from an art-historical point of view. So I entirely agree with him that the distinction is of little use to a stylistic or rhetorical analysis of an ekphrastic poem.

4. Though we know he made a drawing of a particular vase and was impressed by other Greek vases in the British Museum and that he relied on various literary resources, Andrew Motion has argued convincingly that Keats's urn is his own invention (1997: 389-91).

5. For further details on the theory and practice of ekphrasis, see Aisenberg, 1995; Heffernan, 1991, 1994; Lessing, 1984 [1766]; Mitchell, 1980, 1986; Steiner, 1982.

6. Given the vast number of publications on cognitive linguistics, I can only suggest a limited selection for further reading. Useful introductions include Dirven and Verspoor (2004), Lakoff (1987), Lee (2001), Taylor (2002) and Ungerer and Schmid (1996). Suitable for more advanced study are Janssen and Redeker (1999) and Langacker (1999), as are the two seminal books, Langacker (1987) and (1991).

7. The cognitive approach to metaphor, metonymy and other rhetorical figures has grown into an extensive field of research, which has yielded a huge number of publications. A small selection includes Freeman (1993), Gibbs (1994), Gibbs and Steen (1999), Goatly (1997), Kövecses (2002), Lakoff (1987), Lakoff and Johnson (1980), Lakoff and Turner (1989), Panther and Radden (1999), Steen (1994) and (1999), Weber (1995).

8. In doing this exercise, I act on a suggestion made by Peter Stockwell in his inspirational book *Cognitive Poetics* (2002: 7).

9. For this sense of being moved almost bodily as a result of the poem's rhythms, I found support in Raymond Gibbs's plenary paper at the PALA Conference 2001 in Budapest (2002).

10. For further reading on iconicity in language and literature, see the edited volumes of Nänny and Fischer (1999) and Fischer and Nänny (2001) as well as Nänny and Fischer (forthcoming). These two researchers have also developed a highly interesting website on iconicity: http://home.hum.uva.nl/iconicity/

11. For this keen observation I am indebted to Robert Cockroft.

References

Aisenberg, K. (1995) *Ravishing Images: Ekphrasis in the Poetry and Prose of William Wordsworth, W. H. Auden and Philip Larkin.* New York: P. Lang.

Aristotle (1983) *Classical Literary Criticism. Aristotle: On the Art of Poetry. Horace: On the Art of Poetry. Longinus: On the Sublime,* trans. T. S. Dorsch. Harmondsworth: Penguin Books.

Auden, W. H. (1966) *Collected Shorter Poems 1927-1957.* London: Faber and Faber.

Baker-Smith, D. (1990) 'Literature and the Visual Arts', in M. Coyle et al. (eds) *Encyclopedia of Literature and Criticism,* pp. 991-1003. London: Routledge.

Cicero (1988) *De Oratore,* Books I-II, trans. E. W. Sutton and H. Rackham. London: Heinemann.

[Cicero] (1989) *Rhetorica ad Herennium,* trans. H. Caplan. London: Heinemann.

Cockroft, R. (2003) *Rhetorical Affect in Early Modern Writing: Renaissance Passions Reconsidered.* Basingstoke: Palgrave Macmillan.

Csábi, S. and Zerkowitz, J. (eds) (2002) *Textual Secrets: The Message of the Medium.* Budapest: School of English and American Studies, Eötvös Loránd University.

Dirven, R. and Verspoor, M. (2004) *Cognitive Exploration of Language and Linguistics.* Amsterdam: John Benjamins.

Emmott, C. (1997) *Narrative Comprehension.* Oxford: Clarendon Press.

Emmott, C. (2002) 'Responding to Style: Cohesion, Foregrounding and Thematic Interpretation', in M. Louwerse and W. van Peer (eds) *Thematics: Interdisciplinary Studies,* pp. 91-117. Amsterdam: John Benjamins.

Fischer, O. and Nänny, M. (eds) (2001) *The Motivated Sign: Iconicity in Language and Literature,* vol. 2. Amsterdam: John Benjamins.

Freeman, D. C. (1993) 'According to my Bond: *King Lear* and Re-cognition', *Language and Literature* 2(1): 1-18.

Gavins, J. and Steen, G. (eds) (2003) *Cognitive Poetics in Practice.* London: Routledge.

Gibbs, R. W. (1994) *The Poetics of Mind: Figurative Thought, Language, and Understanding.* Cambridge: Cambridge University Press.

Gibbs, R. W. (2002) 'Feeling Moved by Metaphor', in S. Csábi and J. Zerkowitz (eds) *Textual Secrets: The Message of the Medium,* pp. 13-28. Budapest: School of English and American Studies, Eötvös Loránd University.

Gibbs, R. W. and Steen, G. (eds) (1999) *Metaphor in Cognitive Linguistics.* Amsterdam: John Benjamins.

Goatly, A. (1997) *The Language of Metaphors.* London: Routledge.

Hamilton, C. A. (2003) 'Ekphrasis, Repetition and Ezra Pound's "Yeux Glauques"', *Imaginaires* 3: 215-23.

Heffernan, J. (1991) 'Ekphrasis and Representation', *New Literary History* 22(2): 297-316.

Heffernan, J. (1994) *The Museum of Words: The Poetics of Ekphrasis from Homer to Ashbery.* Chicago, IL: University of Chicago Press.

Hollander, J. (1995) *The Gazer's Spirit: Poems Speaking to Silent Works of Art.* Chicago, IL: University of Chicago Press.

Homer (1974) *The Iliad,* trans. E. V. Rieu. Harmondsworth: Penguin Books.

Horace (1991) *Satires, Epistles and Ars Poetica,* trans. H. R. Fairclough. Cambridge, MA: Harvard University Press.

Jackendoff, R. (2002) *Foundations of Language: Brain, Meaning, Grammar, Evolution.* Oxford: Oxford University Press.

Janssen, T. and Redeker, G. (eds) (1999) *Cognitive Linguistics: Foundations, Scope and Methodology.* Berlin: Mouton.

Johnson, M. (1987) *The Body in the Mind: The Bodily Basis of Meaning, Imagination and Reason.* Chicago, IL: University of Chicago Press.

Kennedy, G. A. (1999) *Classical Rhetoric and its Christian and Secular Tradition from Ancient to Modern Times,* 2nd edn. Chapel Hill: University of North Carolina Press.

Kövecses, Z. (2002) *Metaphor.* Oxford: Oxford University Press.

Kranz, G. (1975) *Gedichte auf Bilder: Anthologie und Galerie.* Munich: Deutscher Taschenbuch Verlag.

Lakoff, G. (1987) *Women, Fire, and Dangerous Things: What Categories Reveal about the Mind.* Chicago, IL: University of Chicago Press.

Lakoff, G. and Johnson, M. (1980) *Metaphors We Live By.* Chicago, IL: University of Chicago Press.

Lakoff, G. and Johnson, M. (1999) *Philosophy in the Flesh: The Embodied Mind and its Challenge to Western Thought.* New York: Basic Books.

Lakoff, G. and Turner, M. (1989) *More Than Cool Reason: A Field Guide to Poetic Metaphor.* Chicago, IL: University of Chicago Press.

Langacker, R. W. (1987) *Foundations of Cognitive Grammar*: vol. 1, *Theoretical Prerequisites.* Stanford, CA: Stanford University Press.

Langacker, R. W. (1991) *Foundations of Cognitive Grammar*: vol. 2, *Descriptive Applications.* Stanford, CA: Stanford University Press.

Langacker, R. W. (1999) 'Assessing the Cognitive Linguistic Enterprise', in T. Janssen and G. Redeker (eds) *Cognitive Linguistics: Foundations, Scope and Methodology,* pp. 13-60. Berlin: Mouton.

Lee, D. (2001) *Cognitive Linguistics.* Oxford: Oxford University Press.

Lessing, G. E. (1984 [1766]) *Laocoön,* trans. E. A. McCormick. Baltimore, MD: Johns Hopkins University Press.

Mitchell, W. J. T. (ed.) (1980) *The Language of Images.* Chicago, IL: University of Chicago Press.

Mitchell, W. J. T. (1986) *Iconology: Image, Text, Ideology.* Chicago, IL: University of Chicago Press.

Motion, A. (1997) *Keats.* London: Faber and Faber.

Nänny, M. and Fischer, O. (eds) (1999) *Form Miming Meaning: Iconicity in Language and Literature,* vol. 1. Amsterdam: John Benjamins.

Nänny, M. and Fischer, O. (forthcoming) 'Iconicity in Literary Texts', in K. Brown (ed.) *The Encyclopedia of Language and Linguistics,* 2nd edn. Amsterdam: Elsevier.

Nunberg, G. (ed.) (1996) *The Future of the Book.* Berkeley: University of California Press.

Panther, K. U. and Radden, G. (eds) (1999) *Metonymy in Language and Thought.* Amsterdam: John Benjamins.

Pinker, S. (1994) *The Language Instinct.* London: Penguin Books.

Quintilian (1986) *Institutio Oratoria,* Books VII-IX, trans. H. E. Butler. London: Heinemann (Loeb Classical Library).

Rubin, E. (1921 [1915]) *Visuell Wahrgenommene Figuren,* trans. P. Collett. Copenhagen: Gyldenalske Boghandel.

Semino, E. (1997) *Language and World Creation in Poems and Other Texts.* London: Longman.

Semino, E. and Culpeper, J. (eds) (2002) *Cognitive Stylistics: Language and Cognition in Text Analysis.* Amsterdam and Philadelphia, PA: John Benjamins.

Simpson, P. (2004) *Stylistics: A Resource Book for Students.* London: Routledge.

Steen, G. (1994) *Understanding Metaphor in Literature.* Harlow: Longman.

Steen, G. (1999) 'From Linguistic to Conceptual Metaphor in Five Steps', in R. W. Gibbs and G. Steen (eds) *Metaphor in Cognitive Linguistics,* pp. 57-77. Amsterdam: John Benjamins.

Steiner, W. (1982) *The Colors of Rhetoric.* Chicago, IL: University of Chicago Press.

Stockwell, P. (2002) *Cognitive Poetics.* London: Routledge.

Taylor, J. R. (2002) *Cognitive Grammar.* Oxford: Oxford University Press.

Turner, M. (1991) *Reading Minds: The Study of English in the Age of Cognitive Science.* Princeton, NJ: Princeton University Press.

Ungerer, F. and Schmid, H. J. (1996) *An Introduction to Cognitive Linguistics.* Harlow: Addison Wesley Longman.

Verdonk, P. (1987) '"We Have Art in Order that We May Not Perish from Truth": The Universe of Discourse in Auden's "Musée des Beaux Arts"', *Dutch Quarterly Review of Anglo-American Letters* 17(2): 77-96.

Verdonk, P. (1999) 'The Liberation of the Icon: A Brief Survey from Classical Rhetoric to Cognitive Stylistics', *Journal of Literary Studies* 15(3-4): 291-304.

Verdonk, P. (2002) *Stylistics.* Oxford: Oxford University Press.

Virgil (1974) *The Aeneid,* trans. W. F. Jackson Knight. Harmondsworth: Penguin Books.

Weber, J. J. (1995) 'How Metaphor Leads Susan Rawlings into Suicide: A Cognitive Linguistic Analysis of Doris Lessing's "To Room Nineteen"', in P. Verdonk and J. J. Weber (eds) *Twentieth-century Fiction: From Text to Context,* pp. 32-44. London: Routledge.

Williams, William Carlos (1944) *The Wedge.* Cummington, MA: Cummington Press.

Williams, William Carlos (1962) *Pictures from Brueghel and Other Poems.* New York: New Directions.

Williams, William Carlos (1985) *Selected Poems.* New York: New Directions.

Alba Newmann (essay date spring 2006)

SOURCE: Newmann, Alba. "*Paterson*: Poem as Rhizome." *William Carlos Williams Review* 26, no. 1 (spring 2006): 51-73.

[*In the following essay, Newmann analyzes Williams's* Paterson *as an enactment of many of the linguistic and epistemological themes presented in the 1987 work* A Thousand Plateaus *by French theorists Gilles Deleuze and Felix Guattari.*]

> A book has neither object nor subject; it is made of variously formed matters, and very different dates and speeds. . . . There is no difference between what a book talks about and how it is made. (3)
>
> The rhizome is . . . a map and not a tracing. . . . What distinguishes the map from the tracing is that it is entirely oriented toward an experimentation in contact with the real. (12)
>
> —A Thousand Plateaus, G. Deleuze and F. Guattari

The significance of place, and of the American scene in particular, is one of the features by which William Carlos Williams distinguished his work from that of his expatriate contemporaries. Advocating the poetic value of the American experience and idiom, Williams rejected Eliot's, and even Pound's, classicism and Eurocentrism and grounded his work in the particulars of his native New Jersey. While the setting for a piece like Eliot's "J. Alfred Prufrock" remains ambiguous (are these the smoky, half-deserted streets of St. Louis or London?), Williams's *Paterson* requires that poem and place be one. He asserts, within *Paterson*'s first few pages, that ideas and things are inextricably linked: the ideas of the American city and the American experience must reside within the city-as-thing. *Paterson* cannot exist as some vague semblance of city; it must be made of Paterson itself. As one speaker in Book III says:

> of this, make it of *this*, this
> this, this, this, this.

> (*P* [*Paterson*] 141)

Williams was born and raised in Rutherford, New Jersey, neighboring Paterson; he resided there, practicing medicine, throughout his adult life. Although the first volume of *Paterson* was not published until 1946, as early as 1926 Williams had begun thinking about the city as poetic material. In that year, he wrote a poem called **"Paterson,"** elements of which he would eventually integrate into his long work. He later explained, in a series of interviews, that the scale of the city (neither as large as New York, nor as small as Rutherford), the richness of its history, and the presence of the Passaic River and Falls influenced his choice of locale (*IWWP* [*I Wanted to Write a Poem: The Autobiography of The Works of a Poet*] 72-3).

Many have used Williams's emphasis on the American scene to define his ideal of "contact." And, indeed, in the manifesto written for the first issue of the "little magazine" bearing that name, Williams explains: "For native work in verse, fiction, criticism or whatever is written we mean to maintain a place, insisting on that which we have not found insisted upon before, the essential contact between words and the locality that breeds them, in this case America" (*Contact* 1). This may not, however, adequately express the full extent of what "contact" means for his poetry. As Williams's friend, philosopher Kenneth Burke, points out, "the implications of 'contact' . . . were quite different and went much deeper [than a simple cult of 'Amurricanism']" (*Language* 283). Instead, Burke describes contact in terms of a productive physicality, one that enacts rather than duplicates (283). Because of its proliferative potential, "contact" is realized within a poem not in an act of description or duplication, but in an act of being. As Williams says in Book III of *Paterson*, "Language / is not a vague province" (*P* 110):

> The province of the poem is the world.
> When the sun rises, it rises in the poem

> and when it sets darkness comes down
> and the poem is dark.

> (100)

Williams and Burke share a concern with the translation of physical and conceptual worlds into language—as an enactment, rather than a mirroring of those worlds. In their writings, they each describe a revelatory or transcendental "naming" process which brings words and things into contact with one another. As Brian Bremen discusses in *William Carlos Williams and the Diagnostics of Culture*, this poetic naming represents a condensation of the experiential and the imagined, which is and must always be more than a mimetic process: it must, for Burke, be a "symbolic action," for Williams, a freeing of language and its structures that facilitates discovery on the part of author and reader.

Both men are concerned with the accretions of commonly held beliefs, to which they give various names—"facts," "knowledge," "the symbols of authority"—that can deny "contact" between words, ideas, and things, because they are proscriptive, rather than responsive to and engaged with the world itself. The reified compartmentalization that results from these "ideologies" is representative of the "divorce" that Williams finds all around him, what Bremen describes as "a separation, a dissonance that leads to the most chilling acts . . ." (37). Antithetical to "contact," such rigid orders—systems of separation and hierarchy (the "order, perfect and controlled / on which empires, alas, are built")—are dangerous (*P* 178). They prevent interaction and enactment, that is, the productive synergies of words and things. They allow for an over-reliance on the traditions and authority of the past. And they inhibit empathy and imagination, two fundamental ways in which the poet can make contact with the world.

Because "contact" is so central to Williams's writing, we must look for explanatory models that will help us better understand its functioning, particularly within his longest work, *Paterson*. Such a model cannot resort to a jingoistic explanation of his interest in writing the American scene; nor can it be solely based on the idea of the concrete made textual, or the textual made concrete. To more fully understand the operations of contact, we must take Williams's "empathic imagination" into account, where the interaction of the imagination and the materials of the world makes revelation and discovery possible.

In 1987, Burke wrote to Bremen that perhaps *Paterson* could be read as "a Baedeker": "its very *title* would suggest the totality of his art-as-contact, informing the reader, as *tourist*, of what is going on in *Paterson* as both a place and a poem." Burke's emphasis on the word "title" is suggestive of his concept of "entitlement": that transcendental naming process described above, which creates a "summarizing vessel," into which experiential data is condensed, offering an analogical representation of the many, complex characters which must be connected to constitute the concept or thing being named (*Grammar* 516).[1] For Burke, the book named after the place, the book which contains the place, can be read as a "summarizing vessel" for Williams's greater project of "art-as-contact." The choice of the "guidebook" as vessel resonates with Burke's dual focus on language (or "symbolicity") and action: it is language ("book") and a call to action ("guide").

As a model for understanding *Paterson,* Burke's analogy is both promising and problematic. In its capacity to open unfamiliar territory to the reader, to invite "travel" through Paterson/*Paterson* and contact with unfamiliar terrain, the Baedeker represents *Paterson* well. Williams, as I will discuss below, *was* consciously engaged with the rhetoric of place—the stuff of which guidebooks are made—a focus that contributes significantly to the relevance of Burke's conceit. Accordingly, I begin with a closer examination of the guidebook and its implications as an explanatory model for Williams's poem and its practice of contact. To invoke the Baedeker, however, is to call upon specific cultural and historical positions with regards to the landscape—positions that claim objectivity and dominion.[2] While Burke is celebrating the totality of art-as-contact, his comparison evokes another totality—one that overwrites the complexities and contradictions of a place in service to a readily followed formula, designed to deliver readers from point A to point B, both in terms of their location and their understanding of the place.

The guidebook is a tool of orientation. Whether it presents a linear, descriptive narrative, or a series of compartmentalized data (introduction, history, culture, where to stay, where to eat, etc.), its ability to *enact* the terrain it describes is debatable. In *Spring and All,* Williams expresses his disdain for the "traditionalists of plagiarism" (drawing on a phrase from Poe's critique of Longfellow): those who adhere to convention, rather than emphasizing imagination, innovation, or insight. How easily might the guidebook become one of the "prose paintings" or "copies" that Williams critiques: an exercise in "plagiarism" rather than discovery? We should consider Burke's summarizing vessel more closely, but in doing so, we must ask whether the guidebook is not representative of one of the "older forms" that the poet urges us to destroy, so that the imagination may be free from its ideology of "facts." The trick is to find a model, be it summarizing vessel or otherwise, that will not, as Bremen describes, "solidify into a 'calculus'—a predetermined form in which we fit our discoveries in advance" effectively blocking discovery rather than aiding it (112).

While the Baedeker comparison attends to the text-and-place as one, it cannot represent Williams's efforts to get out from under the thumb of traditional authorities—to "make it new." Nor can the guidebook model account for the richness of Williams's city/man/poem, its intertextuality and layering, its arrivals and departures, both structural and thematic. The subversion of conventions, the rejection of "classical" values and aesthetics, and the transvaluation of the seemingly mundane, or even monstrous, into the celebrated create a text that is as much a tool of disorientation as it is one of orientation—because in disruption and disorientation there is the potential for discovery.

Paterson is not only an invitation or guide, it is an enactment; it is a text that shifts, flows, and falls, that breaks off and starts again, that "somersaults" and escapes. Because of these complexities, and because of Williams's position with regards to poetry's capacity to produce rather than simply duplicate, Burke's notion of the poem as guidebook is, ultimately, unable to explain the poem's practice of contact adequately. Instead, I offer an alternative, connecting *Paterson* with the writings of the French philosopher Gilles Deleuze and his co-author, psychologist Félix Guattari, to suggest a "rhizomic" reading of *Paterson*'s practice of contact.

I. POEM AS GUIDEBOOK

The Baedeker company began publishing guidebooks in Germany during the first third of the nineteenth century, participating in the birth of the guidebook as a genre, an early nineteenth-century phenomenon in both Europe and Britain. As travel became increasingly popular among members of the middle classes, the Baedeker quickly rose to prominence, and by 1856 was a standard accouterment of the traveler in Europe, and even the Middle East (Hinrichsen 8, 14). Initially available in German and then French, the publication of English editions began in 1861, and from that time forward, as Burke's reference suggests, the guidebooks became so ubiquitous that a reference to "a Baedeker" became shorthand for any guide (Eggert 207).

Characteristically, these books contained (as the now more common Fodor's or Frommer's do) information about popular scenic, cultural, and historical sites, as well as accommodations, food, and travel logistics. In Burke's words:

> A town in Italy, say, is famous for its Cathedral, or the number of paintings by one famous artist. The Baedeker informs tourists of these facts. Also it adds notable details about its history over the centuries, possible trips to surrounding areas, inns, restaurants, figures who had been notable citizens, picturesque sights, such as cascades or outlooks, etc.
>
> (Letter to Bremen)

A Baedeker could cover an entire nation, a region, or a single city. Its goal was to facilitate travelers' interactions with the spaces in which they were traveling.

Like a guidebook, Williams's poem aims to introduce the reader/visitor to a specific space—the city of Paterson, New Jersey. The text tells the reader/visitor where to look, focuses our gaze and attention, and reflects information that the author feels will enrich our experience, including details designed to titillate interest and inform. Although the site Williams has chosen to guide us through is not standard tourist fare, like the "city in Italy" to which Burke refers, Paterson has its own scenic highlights, its own claims to historic significance (if not fame). It is not accidental, after all, that Burke mentions "cascades" in his description of the Baedeker: the Passaic Falls are first and foremost among Paterson's scenic offerings. Many episodes in the poem, particularly in Book I, focus on the falls—their appearance, sound, and magnitude, their historic and economic significance.

The park, too, with its view of the town and river valley, is another of the highlights which garners attention in the poem, and serves as the setting for a walking tour. Itineraries for such tours are a common feature of many travel books (Baedeker's included), and *Paterson*'s Section I of Book II, **"Sunday in the Park,"** is particularly evocative of this convention. The section follows the ascent of a pedestrian, climbing through a local park to a cliff and its "picturesque summit," then doubling back again. The summit affords a view of the surrounding landscape and prominent features of the local terrain, both built and natural. Along the way, the poem makes note of local flora—sand-pine, cedar, sumac; it describes the activity of hikers, picnickers, and lovers; and marks the milestones of the climb.

This ascent links the poem to a tradition predating the formal guidebook: the aestheticizing language of late eighteenth- and early-to-mid-nineteenth-century travel accounts, particularly those written in the English Romantic tradition. Often, as Robin Jarvis argues, this tradition was paired with the literature of pedestrianism. Compare, for instance, *Paterson*'s:

> At last he comes to the idlers' favorite
> haunts, the picturesque summit, where
> the blue-stone (rust-red where exposed)
> has been faulted at various levels
> (ferns rife among the stones)
> into rough terraces and partly closed in
> dens of sweet grass, the ground gently sloping
>
> (*P* 56)

with a passage from a 1793 edition of *Descriptive Sketches*:

> Now as we lower trace the river's course,
> The prospect opens, we have left behind

> The lofty rocks and overhanging crags,
> And nothing now doth greet the ravish'd sight
> But graceful slopes and richly planted meads,
> And the smooth surface of the distant sea.
>
> (qtd. in Jarvis 84)

Williams's own description is arguably more lyrical than Miss M. Bowen's (the author of "The Walk," quoted above), but both participate in the "picturesque": "a mixture of masculine ruggedness and unrepressed elemental forces"—the rough and exhilarating faulted stones and crags—and "feminine depths, pleasing variety, and partial concealments"—gentle and soothing dens of sweet grass and graceful slopes (Jarvis 60).

In part, Williams achieves a romanticized affect in the poem by incorporating textual material from actual nineteenth- (and early twentieth-) century accounts. The passages adapted largely verbatim from Charles P. Longwell's *A Little Story of Old Paterson as Told by an Old Man* (1901), offer examples, such as the lines

> Branching trees and ample gardens gave
> the village streets a delightful charm and
> the narrow old-fashioned brick walls added
> a dignity to the shading trees.
>
> (*P* 194)

Although Williams often alters the passages he acquires from outside sources, the florid vocabulary and sensationalist descriptive techniques found in many pieces remain, as is the case with the tale of the Rev. and Mrs. Cumming, taken from John Barber's and Henry Howe's *Historical Collections of the State of New Jersey* (1844):

> On Monday morning, [the Rev. Cumming] went with his beloved companion to show her the falls of the Passaic, and the surrounding beautiful, wild and romantic scenery. . . . Having ascended the flight of stairs (the Hundred Steps) Mr. and Mrs. Cumming walked over the solid ledge to the vicinity of the cataract, charmed with the wonderful prospect, and making various remarks upon the stupendous works of nature around them.
>
> (14)

Similarly, Baedeker guides incorporate commentary from past (and often famous) visitors. So, for instance, in a contemporary Baedeker's *Portugal* we get Lord Byron, in 1809, describing the village of Cintra as

> perhaps in every respect the most delightful in Europe; it contains beauties of every description, natural and artificial. Palaces and gardens rising in the midst of rocks, cataracts, and precipices; convents on stupendous heights—a distant view of the sea and the Tagus.
>
> (78)

And later, quoting from its own edition of 1908:

. . . [Lisbon] in spite of the absence of a mountain background or distinguished buildings, possesses a beauty of its own in the picturesque disposition of its terraces, its view of the wide expanses of the Tagus, and the luxuriant vegetation of its public gardens and parks.

(79)

As Burke points out in his letter, both guidebook and poem include historical anecdotes in order to add color and depth to the scene. As early as page nine, Williams begins to incorporate vignettes from Paterson's past—scenes of life, primarily from the nineteenth century, but some reaching back to the colonial period. Many of these take place in the immediate vicinity of the Falls. A number of the historical passages indicate Paterson's history of tourism, prior to the writing of this "guide" to the city. They also begin to situate Paterson within the broader context of American history: "General" George Washington "rested" in the area, and Hamilton stopped there, too (*P* 10, 12, 70). The history of the Native American populations of the region—and their encounters with European colonists—also plays a significant part in the poem.

Williams had begun thinking about this poem at a time when many American writers were abandoning their native country for Europe. Throughout its composition, he urged a return to American roots, and a recognition of vernacular value. His poem argues that *here* is a place in which men of merit (Washington, Hamilton, Chief Pogatticut) found value: the historical episodes emphasize the cultural relevance of the site and the persistence of its value over time. These depictions also focus on the remarkable in Paterson. *Here* is a site of extraordinary abundance (long an American trope), as seen in the discovery of pearls in local mussels or the catching of enormous fish (9, 11, 34). Here, too, is a site of drama and heroism: the daring deeds of locals, the major events that shaped the city's past and present. Like the core samples brought up by the digging of the artesian well in Book III, Williams's materials are excavated from local sources (139).

In *A Tourist's New England: Travel Fiction 1820-1920*, Dona Brown observes, "Tourism is actually one of the oldest industries in New England—as old as the industrial revolution" (4). Many early visitors came to the region, not to witness its lovely scenery, but because they wanted to examine firsthand the economic, industrial, and social developments underway in the still-young nation. Williams appears similarly interested in those elements of the city's and the nation's development—its experimental and productive nature. According to Brown, factories were a common stop along a New England tourist's path. The subsequent craze for landscape consumption shifted the focus away from the man-made and onto the natural environment; still,

Paterson's industrial history might have played an important role in its early history as tourist destination (4-5). And certainly, it plays an important role in the poem. It was not as a scenic attraction, but as a location for future industry that Hamilton was drawn to the Passaic Falls. The silk mills were, for a time, the region's source of fame and monetary well-being, and they figure repeatedly in the poem. While industrial presence may no longer be a feature praised in many guidebooks, it was a source of power and value for Paterson, and, importantly, for the industrializing nation the city synecdochically represents.

Williams understands the mechanisms at work within the guidebook genre, how sites are invested with value by the author's descriptive and rhetorical choices; and he is able to use some of these conventions to position Paterson similarly—even in commemorating the less familiar, less picturesque elements of the city.[3] At the same time, however, he understands the reification of place that the guidebook genre enforces, with its over-reliance on traditional, middle-class values and aesthetics, its structure, based on "exact hierarch[ies] of importance" and its "severely factual flavour" (Eggert 210); and this makes its conventions ready targets for his more iconoclastic tendencies.

Accordingly, Williams repeatedly manipulates the conventions, complicating and disrupting them. Descriptions of scenery that begin in a typical, travel-guide tone, may take a decidedly sexual turn, like the observation tower which "stands up / prominently / from its pubic grove," or the juxtaposition, on a single page, of the image of "the deep-set valley . . . almost hid / by dense foliage" with the "labia that rive" in childbirth (*P* 53, 192). In creating landscapes that carry sexual charge, the poet may be commenting upon the conversion of place into a site of desire and conquest, where the traveler becomes paramour. Of course, he would not be the first to conflate land and body. If anything, he is taking a trend already present in the language of travel narrative and accentuating it, at the same time disrupting the guidebook's rhetorical claims to a helpful objectivity.

Within the first ten pages of the poem, we realize that Williams is not solely invested in aestheticizing the surrounding landscapes or connecting those landscapes with desire. The Passaic River begins, we are told, in "oozy fields / abandoned to grey beds of dead grass, / black sumac, withered weed-stalks, / mud and thickets cluttered with dead leaves" (7). And, as the poem continues, the poet includes anecdotes from the city's present and past that cast a pall over the local scene; so, for instance, just before children sprinkle flowers in front of Lafayette's feet, a news report describes how a baby girl was murdered by her father and buried under a rock, wrapped in a paper bag (194-5).

Revelations of violence are an intrinsic element of the fabric Williams is creating, as are images of "monstrosity"—the torture of Indian prisoners, the murder of children, the exhumation of a hydro-encephalitic man, "Peter the Dwarf," whose skull has been buried in a separate coffin from his body. This is no strategy for putting visitors at ease with their surroundings. Nor is it one designed to put the "best face forward" for Paterson and its historical residents. It offers a stark contrast to the techniques of the Baedeker, which according to Paul Eggert "pre-digested" experiences for travelers, according to a previously established aesthetic, and confirmed "existing ways of understanding the foreign" (213, 212). As early as 1908 (when E. M. Forster's *A Room with a View*, which comments on the guide, was first published), the Baedeker had gained the reputation of being staid and stodgy, the crutch of the timid or incurious traveler. None of these qualities resonates with the portrait of place Williams is constructing, nor the kind of traveler he wants to entice.

In general, guidebooks are not written by locals or for locals, but rather by "expert" travelers who come, assess, and depart—who maintain a distance between themselves and the spaces through which they pass. Their standards of judging, and the depth to which they are able to penetrate the local scene are determined by their status as outsiders and authorities. The fragments which constitute the poem's epigraph point to a number of recurring concerns within the book, among which are: "a local pride" and "a reply to Greek and Latin with the bare hands" (*P* 2). "Local pride" is an affirmation of value and a source of insight in Paterson itself. Williams explained in a press release, placed before the text by the editor of the 1992 edition, that he chose to write about Paterson because of his "intimate" knowledge of the city (xiii). This local knowledge makes the kind of facile generalizations that streamline a guide unlikely, if even possible.

In Book III, a speaker invites us to "take a ride around, to see what the town looks like" (106). Later, taking a ride is dismissed as removing the visitor too greatly from the environment in which she or he should be immersed. Instead the text urges:

> WALK in the world
> (you can't see anything
> from a car window, still less
> from a plane or from the moon!? Come
> off of it.)

> (211)

To walk offers the opportunity to collect local knowledge—to be in contact with the world as it is, not as it might be seen in passing, or from a great distance. Of course, as I have mentioned, some travel guides do promote pedestrian travel—but only through the "good"

parts of town. In contrast, the excerpted letters of Allen Ginsberg serve as testimony from a local informant and fellow walker about where the true values of Paterson reside:

> . . . I inscribe this missive somewhat in the style of those . . . who recognized one another . . . as fellow citizenly Chinamen of the same province, whose gastanks, junkyards, fens of the alley, millways, funeral parlors, river-visions—aye! the falls itself—are images white-woven in their very beards.

> (172-3)

and later

> I have been walking the streets and discovering the bars—especially around the great Mill and River streets. Do you know this part of Paterson? I have seen so many things—negroes, gypsies, an incoherent bartender in a taproom overhanging the river, filled with gas, ready to explode, the window facing the river painted over so that people can't see in. I wonder if you have seen River Street most of all, because that is really the heart of what is to be seen.

> (193)[4]

While many tourists (and, likely, tour-guide writers) long to get to the "heart of what is to be seen," it is the purview of locals, who have walked the less "scenic" streets, to have both the knowledge of and pride in these places, even (or especially) when the heart of what is to be seen is unexpected.

Williams and Ginsberg share an interest in bringing to light the uncelebrated aspects of Paterson. Their resistance to canonical assertions of value, in favor of a local, "hands on" approach is another iteration of "contact," as well as a possible response on Williams's part to Eliot, Pound, and the expatriate community in general. The "bare hands" with which Williams replies to Greek and Latin (those emblems of canonicity and Eurocentrism) are suggestive of a fisticuffs—showing Greek and Latin a thing or two "with the gloves off"— but the bare hands offer, at the same time, an implication of intimacy unachieved by the icons of authority. Bare hands can actually touch the world. Williams, as a doctor, who, in Burke's words, possessed the "knowing touch"—the ability to "read" and understand his patients and the world through touch—was certainly aware of the power of this form of intimate contact (*Language* 283).

II. POEM AS RHIZOME

Roughly fifty years after Williams published the first volume of *Contact*, Deleuze and Guattari wrote their own manifesto in praise of contact: *A Thousand Plateaus*, the second volume of their larger project *Schizophrenia and Capitalism*. Both men belonged to that generation of French thinkers and activists who, having experienced the events of May 1968, were deeply committed to revealing the mechanisms that establish and maintain authority, and to exploring how individuals can challenge the constructs and categorizations of the world "as we know it" in search of new insights.

In the introduction to *A Thousand Plateaus,* they explain the model of the "rhizome" as an anti-hierarchical means of organizing knowledge and of recognizing intersections and engagements between seemingly disparate ideas and things. Botanically speaking, the rhizome is a branching, often subterranean, asexual means of reproduction (for plants such as the iris, ginger, and bamboo) that has no "center." All segments of the rhizome are fertile: any segment broken off from the rest may serve as a new starting point—a new origin for life. This model of fertile, acentered branching, which can be interrupted without being destroyed, represents the system of connections, or contacts, that Deleuze and Guattari propose in their writings. Unlike its botanical namesake, which is characterized by a uniformity of genetic material, their rhizome has a necessarily heterogeneous composition—it brings all manner of materials into productive contact with one another: "it is made of variously formed matters, and very different dates and speeds" (*Thousand* 3). Their description suggests a preliminary, but interesting, correlation between the composition of **Paterson,** built as it is of variously formed matters (prosaic, poetic, historic, public, personal) and very different dates and speeds, and that of the rhizome.

Deleuze and Guattari contrast the acentered system of communication and proliferation found in the rhizome with the "root/radical" or arboreal system of the "tree," in which knowledge is organized around and branches out of a central "trunk." In the arboreal system, the trunk is understood as the origin, the source of authenticity or authority. Its branches are mere iterations or representations of their own content; they grow out of the trunk, and are completely dependent upon it. They have no vitality of their own, and are isolated from productive contact with other branches. Traditional theories of perception and representation (such as the Platonic) reflect this arboreal model—where "reality" or "truth" is the trunk, and perception, experience, and representation (at even further removes) are weaker echoes of the core.

A number of critics have discussed anti-Platonism in the works of Williams, as well as in those of Deleuze and Guattari.[5] Two principle aspects of this opposition are worth noting here. One is Williams's emphasis on the significance and substance of the real in the world, and our ability to access it. This is the "quality of independent existence, of reality which we feel ourselves" that Williams attributes to nature (**CP** [*The Collected Poems*] 1 207-8). Similarly, in his survey of

Deleuze's philosophy, John Marks discusses Deleuze's attention to the hecceity or "this-ness" of the things of the world, identifying it with a "life" within things, within the "real" (reminding one of the mandate in Book III of **Paterson,** to "make it of *this,* this / this, this, this, this" [*P* 141]) (Marks 38). The second is, as Brian Bremen notes, that Platonic thought demotes our representations of the world to "an imperfect imitation of thought, which is an imperfect imitation of that ideal essence within or behind reality"—an articulation of the arboreal model Deleuze and Guattari criticize (20). Neither they nor Williams accept this "imperfect" echo as the only role of thought or representation. For them, there are always at least two types of representations— ones which echo or mirror (i.e., "plagiarisms," like the branches of the tree), and ones which engage with, which *produce,* such as the poem (a "machine" of words, designed to produce) and the rhizome.

Marks, using Deleuze's and Guattari's own terminology, describes the rhizome as "a multiplicity," which "seeks to move away from the binary subject/object structure of Western thought" producing, instead, a form of "polytonality" (45, 25). A multiplicity is neither one thing nor another—it is the network of relationships between things. As an example, Marks points to Deleuze's writings on Spinoza:

> . . . best considered as a project of free indirect discourse. . . . Deleuze seeks to work with other thinkers and artists so that his own voice and the voice of the author [about whom he is writing] become indistinct. In this way, he institutes a zone of indiscernibility between himself and the authors with whom he works.
>
> (25)

This practice is, again, a rejection of the "arboreal" structure, in which the subject (in this case, Spinoza's writings) would be the trunk, and the historian's or critic's writings mere branches off of this trunk, branches that can never develop the productive synergy that occurs when the boundaries between subject and object are dissolved. This concept of multiplicity and the ways in which it functions resonate with the "mutuality" of identity that Bremen emphasizes in his reading of Williams's poetry, in terms of its revelation of interdependences and a resistance against traditional systems of power and privilege.[6]

In their writings, Williams, Deleuze, and Guattari resist the authoritarian or "scientistic" privileging of a single perspective, a single voice—the self over the other, or the other over the self—the enforced "clarity" which interrupts contact. The blurring of distinctions between the voice of the author and subject describes both the fusing of Paterson as man, poem, and city, and Williams's incorporation and manipulation of passages by other writers throughout his poem. Among the most prominent of these are the "Cress" letters, originally written by Marcia Nardi, as well as correspondence from Dahlberg and Pound, and the Ginsberg letters already noted. It is the practice of multiplicity that leads us to the productive, if sometimes uncomfortable, questions of "who is speaking?" and "for whom?" within these writings.

The Cress letters may be the most problematic of these for readers. Quoted at much greater length than any of the other interpolated texts, their raw vulnerability can suggest misuse, both as unfair divulgence and a co-optation of voice. In *What is Philosophy?*, Deleuze and Guattari respond to similar concerns, but suggest an alternative understanding of the role of such constitutive voices. According to them, each "concept" is made up of multiple elements that do not lose their own identities and are not entirely subsumed or co-opted by their incorporation into the larger concept. Instead, they create "a 'fragmentary whole' . . . made up of components which remain distinct, whilst allowing something to pass between them" (*What is* 16, 20, qtd. in Marks 42). Of course, the "Cress" letters are not the texts exactly as they were written to Williams; but as elements of the rhizome, they maintain a distinct voice of their own, at the same time that they participate in the collective, intersecting voice of the poem. Williams goes further, in his correspondence with Burke, to explain that the poetic act "in full" is composed similarly—of the "conjunction" of the work of the poet and the reader or critic (*Humane* 154). That the rhizome, the multiplicity, and the concept operate similarly is not coincidental, since each, in its way, expresses Deleuze's and Guattari's belief in a productive and revolutionary contact that amounts to more than the sum of its parts, without diminishing the individual elements from which the "whole" is manifested. For the poem, the purpose of incorporating and layering all of the many texts, personal as well as public, is to create resonances—that something which "pass[es] between"—to reveal something not yet witnessed or understood about the individual voices and about Paterson as a whole, to take

> . . . a mass of detail
> to interrelate on a new ground, difficultly;
> an assonance, a homologue
> triple piled
> pulling the disparate together to clarify
> and compress

(P 19)

Like Williams and Burke, Deleuze and Guattari distinguish between "traditional" forms of representation and the more active "interventions" of language in the world. Elaborating upon this distinction, they suggest a contrast between "tracing" and "mapping." The rhizome, they state, is a map and not a tracing. According to them, "what distinguishes the map from the trac-

ing is that it is entirely oriented toward an experimentation in contact with the real" (*Thousand* 12). This map is quite different from the typical atlas or road map with which we are familiar, that is, an object that traces the contours of the terrain it describes and regularly situates the viewer in a position of privilege, looking down from above the fray. Instead, this map "fosters connections between fields [and] . . . is open and connectable in all of its dimensions; it is detachable, reversible, susceptible to constant modification" (12). It is an interactive exploration of an indeterminate number of points of contact: the intersections of heterogeneous materials, often unexpected, always productive.

The plateaus to which the title of Deleuze's and Guattari's work refers are the segments of the rhizomatous map—discrete in so far as they contain a certain "consistency" of their own (which should not be confused with homogeneity—think, instead, of the consistency of a force field made up of waves or particles, or a field of grass composed of many leaves). The definition of plateaus, or planes of consistency, is necessary for the rhizome to describe something other than a system of inscrutable flux or disassociated points. There is a body of content here, and order, but it is not a rigid order. It is always flexible and active; and each plateau is connected to others by experimental connections, by what the authors describe as "lines of flight" (12).

In contrast, a "tracing" is "like a photograph or X-ray that begins by selecting or isolating . . . what it intends to reproduce" (*Thousand* 13). The tracing (unlike the map) "describe[s] a de facto state," and "maintain[s] balance in intersubjective relations" (such as hierarchies, or fixed perspectives). In pursuit of clarity, it "organize[s], stabilize[s], neutralize[s] the multiplicities according to the axes of significance and subjectification belonging to it" (13). According to Deleuze and Guattari, all of "tree logic is a logic of tracing and reproduction" (12). The map, however, "unfolds potential;" it reveals a dense and complex fabric, or "assemblage," that "ceaselessly establishes connections between semiotic chains, organizations of power, and circumstances relative to the arts, sciences, and social struggles" (7).

The interest in bringing "organizations of power, and circumstances relative to the arts, sciences, and social struggles" into contact is certainly in keeping with Williams's own philosophical stance. His articulation of the differences between prose and poetry (particularly in **Spring and All**) parallels the distinction between the tracing and the map. As Bremen relates, prose and poetry "reflect two different 'methods of projection', two 'ways of thinking,' whereby the world is either 'copied' according to some previously existing set of conventions, or alternately, 'made anew,' in Williams's terms, by a new way of seeing" (*CP*1 178-82, 204-10, qtd. in Bremen 16-17). The journalistic tendencies of prose lend themselves to representational tracing, to "plagiarizing" nature; but poetry, according to Williams, exists to create something new—an addition to nature. Within **Paterson,** the incorporation of prose *into* the poetry allows the prosaic textual material to participate in Williams's more powerful and inventive poetic mapping.

The tracing, with its regime of "facts," correlates with the Baedeker's agenda of delivering, in a pocket-sized document, all the "relevant" information about a destination, "according to the axes of significance and subjectification belonging to it." While the guidebook is, no doubt, more complex than a photograph, it creates artificially still surfaces and descriptive units that have closure by hierarchizing and omitting information in service to a linear trajectory. In contrast, *Paterson*-as-map accesses not only surfaces, things seen from a distance, but depths and experiences, crosscurrents and reversals. Its "perspective" is one of immersion—seen from the midst of the flow—the flow of images, time, water. This is one of the reasons the river is such a fundamental figure in the poem. Immersion in the river's waters, an image of contact, offers an antidote to the conceptual "divorce" that so worried Williams. Even the potential divorce (death, separation) brought about by the action of falling, which occurs repeatedly within the poem, may be mitigated by the possibility of falling as water does or falling into water: "Only the thought of the stream comforts him, / its terrifying plunge, inviting marriage" (*P* 82). Even when the product of falling is death, as is the case with the student in Book IV, immersion still produces metamorphosis, invention—a becoming of something that was not (164-5).

The river proves a central vehicle for "contact," as rivulets and ripples join the larger flow, carrying "rumors of separate worlds" to one another (*P* 25). Both the river's movement and the movement of the poem more broadly evoke the "lines of flight," which "evolv[e] by subterranean steps and flows, along river valleys or train tracks . . ." (Deleuze and Guattari, *Thousand* 7).[7] Discussing this movement and the connection between plateaus, Brian Massumi, the translator of *A Thousand Plateaus,* makes a point of explaining that the French term for flight, "fuite," is a term for escape—related to the English "to flee"—but not to our airborne "flight" (xvi). A rhizomic map may be dense or spare, depending on the number of lines of flights it observes, but there is always much that escapes from one plateau and infiltrates the next.

Early on, Williams links the movement of water with the movement of thoughts through the mind:

Jostled as are the waters approaching
the brink, his thoughts

interlace, repel and cut under,
rise rock-thwarted and turn aside
but forever strain forward—or strike
an eddy and whirl, marked by a
leaf or curdy spume, seeming
to forget.

(*P* 7-8)

The linkage between liquidity and thought is relevant to the operation of lines of flight, in that it is the mind with its fluid capacity to imagine that allows us, as cognitive beings, to recognize contact, even when the physical evidence says otherwise:

It is the imagination
which cannot be fathomed.
It is through this hole we escape . . .

(210)

Institutions, of culture or education, teach us to accept "absolute" scales, such as those of rationality or propriety, to fix distances, and to recognize certain categories at the expense of other potential contacts. The flexibility of the mind, however, moving by liquid, subterranean paths, eludes these strictures, allowing for invention and revelation.

Language, too, as thought enacted, becomes a fluid figure—flowing, falling, crashing down within the poem: "The language cascades into / the invisible, beyond and above; the falls / of which it is the visible part" (145). As the episodes focusing on the force of the Falls and effects of the flood suggest, water is not easily contained, it has a power to resist stagnation, to resist the "designs" placed on it (unlike the sun which rises, ignorant, within the same "slot" each day) (4). In Book I, a speaker cautions against the "writing of stale poems," products of "Minds like beds always made up / (more stony than a shore)" (4-5). Such a bed is the course of the river too narrowly defined, a course in which the mind of the poet and the river itself are unwilling to remain:

unwilling to lie in its bed
and sleep, and sleep, sleep
in its dark bed.

(97)

The slipping and blending suggested by the movement of water is also expressed prosodically, in the slippage of sounds and the metamorphoses of words across lines. So for instance, we have the movement of "ribbon" into "robin," on page 18, with the r sound continuing into "Erudite" and then "Erasmus." Or, on the following page, the flow of "white" into "swallows," "flowered," "shallow," and "water" (19). Working within the materiality of the language, Williams recognizes assonance and consonance as forms of contact, ways in which words touch and inform each other, to trigger unexpected associations or harmonies for the reader.

Images shift and slip, as well. In Book III, Section III, a chain of dog-related events links an unspecified present with a Native American past and, further, with a mythical Greek past: a dog is killed for biting a passerby; a dog is killed to accompany the death of a chief; a dog's body is carried by the river down to Acheron. Through these moments, the city of Paterson participates in a pattern connecting the mundane events of its present with a current of events through time and cultures.

And the river is not the only agent of escape. Not all lines of flight are liquid—some walk, or run away. A decision to "leave the path" to walk "across-field" (as a line of flight does) precipitates a rhizomic chain of associations in the mind of the walker. The rapid convolutions of thought make this a difficult sequence to describe, a difficulty prefigured at its opening:

> Walking—
> he leaves the path, finds hard going
> across-field, stubble and matted brambles
> seeming a pasture—but no pasture.
>
> (47)

As the walker moves through "file-sharp grass," "a flight of empurpled wings" startles up from the field, then plunges into cover once again (47). The wings are those of grasshoppers that dodge ahead of the walker as he moves. The figure of the grasshoppers is transformed into "a grasshopper of red basalt," which tumbles from the walker's mind, falling like a stone from an eroding bank under a tropic downpour. The tropical location and the grasshopper are then linked together in the thought of "Chapultepec! grasshopper hill!" (Chapultepec, a mountain outside of Mexico City, means, literally, "grasshopper hill" in the Aztec language.) Echoing the movement of the flying grasshoppers, an imagined trajectory of a stone that has been thrown pairs with the "red basalt" of the mind: "his mind a red stone carved to be / endless flight," becomes, in its final permutation, "Love that is a stone endlessly in flight" (47-9). Flight, in and of itself, becomes a line of flight in this portion of the poem, as does the image of the grasshopper, and the red stone—perhaps seen while on a walk, perhaps conjured from memory. As this series of passages suggests, the poem brings a mass of images, textures, rhythms, ideas, and things into "contact." Some touch by location on the page, others by the repetition of sounds, lines, or images lifted from one source and set down in another. In some cases, like the grasshopper episode, the linkages seem to follow a particular stream of consciousness, perhaps the consciousness of Paterson-as-man. Others happen without obvious human focalization.

Structurally, the poem's interpolations and polyvocality highlight the significance of mingling and heterogeneity, resisting divorce; but this appears figuratively as well, in the "masticated" mud that is dredged up after the flood, in the congeries of flowers in the Cloister's tapestries. It is evoked in scenes of trespass, metamorphosis, and miscegenation. The Ringwood episode in Book I tells of a community of runaways—dispossessed Tuscarora Indians; women, both black and white, who have escaped enslavement; and deserting Hessian soldiers—all of whom have taken to the woods, to create a "bold association," which Williams describes as "strange if not beautiful" (12-13). There is a power implicit in this "strangeness," its disruption of norms, its testaments to the productive potential of heterogeneity, coupled with the movement of escape.

The power of the poet, to invent and to make discoveries, is not always a matter of linking two things or ideas together, of marrying or summing; it is equally important to "estrange" to disrupt expectation and association, looking at dissonance as well as resonance, for

> Dissonance
> (if you are interested)
> leads to discovery
>
> (175)[8]

There are benefits to shaking things up, to "turning the inside out" (140). In **Paterson,** incidents of disruption, particularly the fire, but also the tornado and images of inundation and draining, lead to discovery and reveal fertile potentials. The tornado and the fire impact rigid institutions of society—the church is turned on its foundation, the Library, "sanctuary to our fears" with its "smell of stagnation and death," is purged by flame (98, 101). Fire does more than empty that which it touches, it transforms and releases: "The beauty of fire-blasted sand / that was glass, that was a bottle: unbottled" (118). Williams recognizes the kinship between fire and poetry when he defines the act of writing as "a fire and not only of the blood" (113). Like writing, fire is rhizomic in its potential to leap from page to page, "from house to house, building to building," releasing that which it connects through the association and destruction of conflagration (119). The atomic fire that can "smash the world wide" is at work in the poem and in the city of Paterson: "a city in itself, that complex / atom, always breaking down" (170, 177). **Paterson** testifies to those processes of building up and tearing down that defy containment. This is appropriate to the rhizome, as, according to Deleuze and Guattari,

> It is not a question of this or that place on earth, or of a given moment in history, still less of this or that category of thought. It is a question of a model that is

perpetually in construction or collapsing, and of a process that is perpetually prolonging itself, breaking off and starting up again.

(*Thousand* 20)

At the poem's opening, the poet lays out this project:

> To make a start,
> out of particulars
> and make them general, rolling
> up the sum, by defective means—

(*P* 3)

Initially, the "defective means" seem a statement of failure; but there is a degree to which the inability to make a total sum is not a failure, but a necessary condition—it preserves a means of escape. Even the poet must, at times, acknowledge that things escape from the names that have been placed on them:

> a flower within a flower whose history
> (within the mind) crouching
> among the ferny rocks, laughs at the names
> by which they think to trap it. Escapes!

(22)

Both connection and disruption can be described in terms of escape. And escape is fundamental to understanding the rhizome as a descriptive, but not totalizing, model for contact. *Paterson,* as rhizome, is a text that is never finished, never total; it is "perpetually in construction or collapsing," "perpetually prolonging itself, breaking off and starting up again." Book V extends what was initially defined as a four-book work; and at his death, Williams was working on yet another extension and expansion of the poem. Even within the pieces that are "complete," we see the rejection of a terminal form in the poem's anti-teleological fragmentation and doubling back, suggested by the image of the snake with its tail in its mouth, and the man's emergence from the sea at the poem's end (229-30). The fracturing and joining within the poem, its perpetual movement, and its ability to "resist the final crystallization" make the rhizome/map a powerful figure with which to discuss *Paterson* (*P* 109).

Had Burke left us with a more fully developed explanation of his vision of *Paterson*-as-guidebook, he might have focused, ultimately, on the ways in which Williams "moves in on" or infiltrates and subverts the dominating structures of the guidebook, allowing it to engage differently with the world it represents—a position that would have been in keeping with much of his other writings on the poet's work. In the absence of such information, it is interesting to note that both Burke's summarizing vessel for the poem and the rhizome share mapping connotations. Though it is not entirely surprising that a book linked to a place as intimately as *Paterson* is to its namesake should call

out to be discussed spatially, the idea of movement—of mind, of time, and of place—and the means of documenting this movement are at the heart of Williams's poetic project, and are expressed, in different ways, in the Baedeker and the rhizome. Burke is correct in knowing that Williams is trying to show his readers something about the nature of Paterson, its significance—to put Paterson on the map, and to "show us around"—but Williams does much more, immersing us in it, its complexity, contradictions, and fecundity. As readers, we encounter in *Paterson* not only a document of place, but an explosion of it, a thickening of our understanding of what such a place could mean that corresponds with the thickening of the identity of city and man and text—"triple piled," in Williams's terms. The model of the rhizome is well suited to revealing such a city/man/poem, as Williams knew and expressed it. It allows for an openness, a flux that is critical to understanding *Paterson* not only as a representation, but as a place of rivers, a process, a defiance of authority, and as "an experimentation in contact with the real."

Notes

1. For a further discussion of Burke's summarizing vessel, see Bremen, *WCW and the Diagnostics of Culture,* 32.

2. Both formalist and poststructuralist scholars have made note of the appropriative strain within Williams's writing about place. Critics like Kinereth Meyer have spoken about Williams's writing as an act of possessing, an attempt to possess America—often drawing on Williams's description of his writing process for *In the American Grain* (1925). Certainly, Williams is concerned with questions of appropriation (of land and of language), but there is too much that escapes in *Paterson* for me to believe that its aim, or its effect, is simply to *possess* through poetry. Such readings decline to see in *Paterson* both a "a dispersal and a metamorphosis" as well as a "gathering up" (*P* 2). There is a significant tension, here, however. As Williams began the research necessary for the composition of his poem, he was excited by the wealth of detail he encountered: "I . . . fell in love with my city . . . all the facts I could ask for, details exploited by no one" (*IWWP* 73). His description is enthusiastically appropriative. His excitement at having discovered the "unexploited" terrain of Paterson clearly puts him in the role of exploiter; however, as an act of claiming, it may also be designed to offset the acts of abandonment Williams witnessed among his peers—allowing him to write, in Joel Conarroe's words, a celebratory "anti-exile poem" (21).

3. In doing so, Williams also lays the groundwork for other artists interested in bringing New Jersey

to light, "in all the sordidness of its abused beauty and energy" (Deutsch 101). Most notable among these is Robert Smithson, the conceptual and earthworks artist, who was a patient of Williams's as a child, and who would later write "A Tour of the Monuments of Passaic, New Jersey" (1967) (cf. *Robert Smithson: The Collected Writings*).

4. Despite Williams's investments in resisting authority and those "order[s] perfect and controlled / upon which empires, alas, are built," it is worth noting the Orientalizing, and generally exoticizing, aspect of Ginsburg's rhetoric in these passages, echoing common tropes of Imperial literatures of travel.

5. John Marks, for instance, explains, "Deleuze actively seeks out an alternative tradition from which he can draw support against the line which runs through Plato, Hegel, and Heidegger" (16).

6. See Bremen, chapters 2, 4, and 5, in particular, for their discussion of mutuality.

7. This particular quote comes from a discussion of the operations of language, but because Deleuze and Guattari are describing language as rhizomatous, I do not believe this elision misrepresents their thinking.

8. I would like to note, briefly, the movement of the "i", "n", and "d" sounds as they move through the three lines: Williams's beautiful use of assonance and consonance in a passage that discusses dissonance.

Works Cited

Baedeker's Portugal. Hampshire England: AA Publishing, 1999.

Bremen, Brian. *William Carlos Williams and the Diagnostics of Culture.* New York: Oxford UP, 1993.

Brown, Dona, ed. *A Tourist's New England: Travel Fiction, 1820-1920.* Hanover, NH: UP of New England, 1999.

Burke, Kenneth. *A Grammar of Motives.* Berkeley: U of California P, 1969.

———. *Language as Symbolic Action.* Berkeley: U of California P, 1987.

———. Letter to Brian Bremen. July 21 and 24, 1987. Collection of Brian Bremen. Austin, TX.

Conarroe, Joel. *William Carlos Williams's Paterson: Language and Landscape.* Philadelphia: U of Pennsylvania P, 1970.

Deleuze, Gilles, and Félix Guattari. *A Thousand Plateaus: Capitalism and Schizophrenia.* Trans. Brian Massumi. Minneapolis: U of Minnesota P, 1987.

———. *What is Philosophy?* Trans. Hugh Tomlinson and Graham Burchell. London: Verso, 1994.

Deutsch, Babette. *Poetry in Our Time.* New York: Columbia UP, 1956.

Eggert, Paul. "Discourse versus Authorship: The Baedeker Travel Guide and D. H. Lawrence's *Twilight in Italy.*" In *Texts and Textuality: Textual Instability, Theory, and Interpretation.* Ed. Philip Cohen. New York: Garland, 1997. 207-34.

Hinrichsen, Alex. *Baedeker-Katalog.* Trans. Michael Wild. Bevern, Germany: Ursula Hinrichsen Verlag, 1989.

Jarvis, Robin. *Romantic Writing and Pedestrian Travel.* New York: St. Martin's, 1997.

Marks, John. *Gilles Deleuze: Vitalism and Multiplicity.* London: Pluto, 1998.

Meyer, Kinereth. "Possessing America: William Carlos Williams's *Paterson* and the Poetics of Appropriation." In *Mapping American Culture.* Ed. Wayne Franklin and Michael Steiner. Iowa City: U of Iowa P, 1992. 152-67.

Smithson, Robert. *Robert Smithson: The Collected Writings.* Ed. Jack Flam. Berkeley: U of California P, 1996.

Williams, William Carlos. Untitled Manifesto. *Contact* 1 (December 1920): 1.

———, and Kenneth Burke. *The Humane Particulars: The Collected Letters of William Carlos Williams and Kenneth Burke.* Ed. James H. East. Columbia: U of South Carolina P, 2003.

Jon Chatlos (essay date fall 2006)

SOURCE: Chatlos, Jon. "Automobility and Lyric Poetry: The Mobile Gaze in William Carlos Williams' 'The Right of Way.'" *Journal of Modern Literature* 30, no. 1 (fall 2006): 140-54.

[*In the following essay, Chatlos presents a reading of Williams's "The Right of Way" based on the assumption that the images viewed by the motorist in the poem are continuous rather than separated, and argues that this enacts a "dynamized ekphrasis."*]

William Carlos Williams' **"The Right of Way,"** a lyric poem from the experimental collection *Spring and All* (1923), is about the mobile gaze of a male motorist in the early days of the motorcar.[1] Short though the poem is, it makes a large and complex statement about the interplay of image and word in early twentieth-century America. The poem both richly portrays the visual experience of 1920s automobility (Urry)—the spectacles, stories, subjectivities, and social relations that the motorcar created—and implicitly compares motorcar spectatorship and cinematic spectatorship. Among the implicit similarities between motorcar and movies, the most suggestive is the "editing." Are the images seen by the motorist disjoined into discrete spectacles by a poetics of montage (an "automobility of attractions," to work a variation on Tom Gunning's well-known phrase)? Or are they joined by an eyeline match that produces a coherent narrative about voyeurism and passing? The editing works both ways: it enacts an unresolved ambiguity between spectacle and narrative. Of course Williams renders this ambiguous visual experience not in images but in words. The resulting text is an ekphrasis with a twist: not "the verbal representation of visual representation" (Mitchell 152), but the verbal representation of visual culture.

The poem runs as follows:

> In passing with my mind
> on nothing in the world
>
> but the right of way
> I enjoy on the road by
>
> virtue of the law—(5)
> I saw
>
> an elderly man who
> smiled and looked away
>
> to the north past a house—
> a woman in blue (10)
>
> who was laughing and
> leaning forward to look up
>
> into the man's half
> averted face
>
> and a boy of eight who was (15)
> looking at the middle of
>
> the man's belly
> at a watchchain—
>
> The supreme importance
> of this nameless spectacle (20)
>
> sped me by them
> without a word—
>
> Why bother where I went?
> for I went spinning on the
>
> four wheels of my car (25)
> along the wet road until
>
> I saw a girl with one leg
> over the rail of a balcony

(Williams, *Collected Poems 1* 205-06)

"The Right of Way" does not declare that its motorist is male, but it implies it. How? First, social history sug-

gests it. Driving a motorcar in the early 20th century is a gendered activity: in the 1920s, males drove much more often than did females (Scharff 13). Second, the poem as a system of words intimates it. The motorist is active, seeing, and speaking, while the girl on the balcony is passive, seen, and silent. To the explicit female space of the balcony corresponds the implicit male space of the motorcar. And the motorist arrogates to himself the right to "enjoy" the road as perhaps only a male of the era would. Finally, even if the poem did not provide any clues about the gender of its narrator, I would assume, with Sue Lanser, that he is male: "In the absence of textual information to the contrary, a certain degree zero of narrator identity is presumed" (Lanser 165-66). Williams is male. So is his motorist.

The male motorist is like a cinematic spectator: he is seated, he views screen images, his gaze is mobile, his pleasure is visual, and the sights that he sees are imaginatively edited. But the poem is not just about automobile vision as an analogue for movie vision; it is also about automobile vision as a thing in itself. If the moviegoer is totally immobile in his seat, the motorist is both immobile and moving; unlike the moviegoer, the motorist is at once seated and projected (Virilio 13). If the moviegoer sees images on a screen, the motorist sees images through a screen—the rectangular frame of his windshield or window, which he views off to the side ("right of way"), not frontally. The technology of the screen is not distinctive to the cinema, but extends back to Renaissance painting and forward to computer displays (Manovich 94-95). If the gaze of the moviegoer is mobile, it is "a mobilized virtual gaze" (Friedberg 2), while the gaze of the motorist is a mobilized real gaze. The automobile spectator sees in real time, he composes his own journey, and the images that he views are auratic and unrepeatable. Finally, if the pleasure of the moviegoer is primarily visual, the pleasure of the motorist is somatic as well as visual. Williams' motorist speeds and spins down a wet road, enjoying the thrill and danger of a combined visual/kinesthetic experience. In this sense, we might say that automobility does not aspire to the condition of the movies; rather, the movies aspire to the condition of automobility: embodied spectatorship. Like Hale's Tours and Imax, "cinema 'at the cutting edge'" mimics travel, providing a multiple sensory experience (Lauren Rabinowitz, "More than the Movies" 104).

"The Right of Way" is cinematic not because Williams explicitly compares the motorcar with the movies but because motorcar and movies have a common ground: the larger culture of visual modernity. Jacques Aumont calls this new culture "The Variable Eye, or The Mobilization of the Gaze": 19th- and 20th-century technologies (the *étude*, the panorama, the railroad, the cinema) that combine moving and seeing to create a new modern subject. Jean-Louis Comolli speaks of "machines of the visible," while Mark Sandberg broadens this formulation to "institutions of the visible" (353-54): the kinetoscope and the mutoscope, the moving sidewalk, mobile wax museums, the World's fairs, window shopping, cinema—and automobility. **"The Right of Way"** responds well to the insights of film style and film theory not because the poem is really about cinema but because, along with cinema, it is one practice in a larger culture of the mobile gaze.

The most suggestive cinematic dimension of **"The Right of Way"** is what might be called its editing—the relations between the images that the motorist sees. Are these images connected?

They are not, at least on one strong reading of the poem. On this way of looking, no logic or desire connects the sights of (1) man/woman/boy and (2) the girl on the balcony. We have here a poetic version of film montage: the relationships between images are discontinuous. Williams says this in the poem, he endorses a similar poetics of discontinuity elsewhere in his writings, and critics agree with this interpretation of the poem.

Let us look at the poem more closely to find support for this reading. At the start of the poem we learn that the motorist's mind is on "nothing in the world" as he passes—it is a *tabula rasa,* open to the world and what a mobile gaze will bring him. Or rather his empty mind *is* on one thing: his "right of way" (line 3)—a license to drive (his "right of way"), a freedom not to watch ahead on the thoroughfare ("right of way") but to glimpse sights off to the side ("right of way"). And this right of way he doubly enjoys: he has the privilege to it and he takes pleasure in it. We might call this pleasure deconstructive: the joy of detaching one supremely important sight from the next, and the joy of seeing each hard-edged object in itself.

In this receptive frame of mind the motorist sees a first attraction: the old man, woman, and boy. Despite the fact that the motorcar is moving, what he views is a still-motion tableau with no motion blur. The figures are mute, as if in a silent movie. They smile and look at each other, and their body placement and sightlines suggest a classical triangular composition. What their behavior and group composition mean the driver does not explore: he is aggressively unreflective. But *that* they mean something astonishing is clear: "The supreme importance / of this nameless spectacle / sped me by them / without a word" (lines 19-22).

The driver then spins on, lighthearted, free of past perceptions and conceptions: "Why bother where I went?" (line 23). Having detached his eye and mind from this last image, he sees a new random attraction: the girl on the balcony. This image too is a still-motion tableau. The girl is framed by the balcony, but her leg breaks the horizontal line of the rail. It is difficult to say what the leg over the balcony means. Is the girl displaying herself? Is she climbing over the balcony? If so, why? Is she sitting, poised over the railing? Does she have one leg or two? Is the motorist making a gag? Or is he witnessing a tragedy in the making? He does not know, and he does not bother to surmise.

In summary the motorist drives without reflecting (lines 1-5); then he sees a sight (lines 6-18); then he drives some more without reflecting (lines 19-26); then he sees another sight (lines 27-28). A reader familiar with the tradition of Western lyric expects the opposite: first a report or description of the outside world, then a reflection on it. Williams' speaker refuses to reflect, and then he simply looks again.

The most basic analytic shape of the poem is a simple visual repetition. The driver sees urban bystanders once, and then he sees them again. This visual repetition is enacted verbally by a grammatical repetition: "I saw" is the skeletal independent clause of the first half of the poem (line 6), and "I saw a girl" (line 27) repeats the words and the scopic motif. The poem pares its images to miniature dimensions: a two-shot. The implication is that the second image is not final: the voyage/poem might continue indefinitely. Images seen from the roadster are images of urban modernity: mobile, fleeting, aleatory, discrete. **"The Right of Way"** enacts a kind of discontinuity editing.

Elsewhere in his writings, Williams endorses the theory behind this practice of seeing and writing. In **Kora in Hell** (1920), an early improvisational work, Williams advises readers to see "the thing itself without forethought or afterthought but with great intensity of perception" (**Kora in Hell** 8). In Williams' **"Prologue,"** he depicts his mother, as a flâneuse, acting out an I-see-this-I-see-that aesthetic: as she strolls the streets of Rome, she promenades her eye from sight to sight, disconnecting one image from the next. Her mobilized gaze is an early version of the mobilized gaze of the motorist in **"The Right of Way."** In the *Selected Essays*, Williams offers a similar dictum about mobility and disjunction: poetry "passes without repugnance from thing to thing" (*Selected Essays* 124). And in **Spring and All** Williams calls for a poetry of "separation" and "cleavage" (**Collected Poems I** 188, 194, 198).

Critics of **"The Right of Way"** endorse the idea that the images seen by the motorist are thoroughly and pleasurably discontinuous. Two early critics, Lois Bar-Yaacov and Roy Miki, helpfully place their brief readings within the larger context of Williams' automobile poetry. Bar-Yaacov claims that, for Williams, to drive is to empty the mind and open an innocent eye to the world: "The 'I' is so feckless, so lacking in aim or innerness, that we experience it only as a machine for recording visual experience" (273). Miki adds that the Williams motorist experiences and records his world as a series of visual details in movement, a sequence of discrete, disjoined objects: "The driver in transit passes through a field of many surfaces, his eyes shifting and turning with photographic rapidity, things appearing and disappearing. . . . The eyes inevitably [are] struck, in a way *stung* by particulars that appear in view and as quickly disappear" (114-15). Current critics read the poem in like fashion. Sharon Dolin places her interpretation in the context of psychoanalytic theory: the male motorist's "excessive, eroticized attention to discrete body parts and objects" gives him pleasure but robs him of mastery over the images upon which he gazes (35). And Susan McCabe, in *Cinematic Modernism*, analyzes the poem in the context of the film avant-garde—surrealism.

But the discontinuities of automobility are perhaps more comparable to the discontinuities of the "cinema of attractions"—the period of early cinema, from 1895 to about 1906—than to those of surrealist film. Tom Gunning argues that the cinema of attractions is not a primitive lead-up to the sophisticated storytelling of later fiction film. Rather it is a cinematic system in its own right, standing in dynamic tension with classical continuity cinema. What are the elements of this system? First, it is a medium of spectacular visual display. It presents its spectacle of unusual subject matter, new technique, and magic tricks and gags as if simply to say, "See!" Second, it combines these images not into an integrated narrative but into a montage—a disconnected series of images that create a visual experience much "like a ride on a streetcar." Temporally, it follows a logic of "now you see it, now you don't." Third, it functions to astonish, fascinate, and stimulate its spectator, not to absorb him into a self-contained fictional universe. The spectator of the cinema of attractions is aggressively superficial, joyfully anti-contemplative (Gunning, "Cinema of Attractions" 66, 68; "'Now You See It'" 76, 82).

Eclipsed by continuity cinema in the years after 1906, the cinema of attractions, according to Gunning, does not disappear but "goes underground," resurfacing in the film avant-garde of the 1920s and serving as inspiration for it. Indeed, Gunning borrows the terms "attractions" from the avant-garde filmmaker and theater director Sergei Eisenstein, who himself coined the term in 1923—the same year that Williams published *Spring and All* (Gunning, "Cinema of Attractions" 64, 66).

"The Right of Way" enacts what we might call an automobility of attractions. Each image in the poem is a spectacle unto itself, displayed as if to say to the motorist and reader, "See!" The images follow each other randomly, not causally—like the images seen during "a ride on a streetcar." And the motorist is not contempla-

tive about but astonished by the sights he sees. Even the final image of the "girl with one leg / over the rail of a balcony" follows a logic of attractions. The girl has one leg not because she is an amputee but because one of her legs, hanging over the balcony, comes into the motorist's sight before the other. The gag is then acted out verbally and graphically by a witty enjambment: the first line of the "couplet" reveals the first leg of the girl, as if she has only one leg. The second line reveals and restores the second leg, but only after readers have turned the corner of the enjambment and have had their own leg pulled. Each image in the poem functions as a discrete spectacle or attraction.

Alongside this first reading exists a second: not that the images that the motorist sees have nothing to do with each other, but that they are related to each other; not that the visual experience of the motorist is discontinuous, but that it is continuous. So **"The Right of Way"** can be read not just as about discrete attractions but also as about narrative integration.

On this second reading, the two images that the motorist sees are related by a subtle narrative about voyeurism and passing. To unfold a pun that the poem makes, the structure of the poem is a "watchchain": an eyeline match in which the motorist watches the old man, who watches the girl (and the reader watches the motorist watching). The sightline of the old man speeds the motorist ahead to the girl. The motorist enjoys the sight of the girl—the display—but he is ambivalent about his voyeurism. And so he plays the innocent—he passes.

This second reading is complex and subtle. We need to build a case for it slowly, by pointing out patterns that exist both in the poem and in Williams' work in general. Williams criticism has not addressed this dimension of the poem.

If we examine the composition of the scene of elderly man, woman, and boy, we notice that the first of these figures, the elderly man, is the clear center of attention. In almost painterly fashion, all lines of vision converge upon him: the woman laughs and leans forward "to look up / into the man's half / averted face" (lines 12-14); the boy looks at the man's watchchain. The old man himself, however, looks away from the group, pulling or directing our line of vision from that frame of reference to something outside it. All three figures are looking. But only the man looks away, smiling as he does so. What is the meaning of his double gesture of averted glimpse and smile?

A brief detour through Williams' other writings will put us on track to a suggestive answer. In **"The Young Housewife,"** another automobile poem, the poet-driver steals a series of glimpses of a housewife who regularly "comes to the curb / . . . and stands / shy, uncorseted, tucking in / stray ends of hair." He "bow[s] and pass[es] smiling" (***Collected Poems*** *1* 57). In **"Sympathetic Portrait of a Child,"** "the murderer's little daughter / who is barely ten years old" steals glimpses of the narrator, "smiling excitedly" the while:

> As best she can
> she hides herself
> in the full sunlight
> her cordy legs writhing
> beneath the little flowered dress
> that leaves them bare
> from mid-thigh to ankle—
> Why has she chosen me
> for the knife
> that darts along her smile?

> (***Collected Poems*** *1* 94-95)

And in *The Great American Novel,* the narrator (a poet, doctor, and motorist) secretly observes his own wife as she reads in bed. When she sees through and exposes his spying, a smile of power slips from his lips to hers (*Imaginations* 161).

In all these texts, a smile is a sign that a mystery has been glimpsed. What sort of a mystery? A "thing in itself" or "rare moment" of wonder, certainly; but, more specifically, a "rare moment" charged with sexuality: a young housewife in negligee, an unsettling exchange between a male narrator and a murderer's ten-year-old daughter with legs "bare / from mid-thigh to ankle" (cf. **"Winter Quiet,"** *Collected Poems* *1* 84-85). How has the mystery been glimpsed? Via a stolen glance. The "thing seen"—in this paradigm, most often a female exposed suggestively to view—is evasive, resistant to visual attention that is too frontal or sustained. And the person who is looking and smiling—most often a male—feels he is seeing something that perhaps ought not to be seen, doing something that perhaps ought not to be done. The smile, then, is often charged with elusive connotations of guilt and power, as well as with suggestions of wonder, knowledge, and pleasure.

Given the fact that the female leg is a recurrent example of mystery in Williams, and given the patterned interlinking in Williams of the images of mystery, glimpse, and smile—the smile as a sign that a mystery has been momentarily viewed—it is reasonable to assume that the imagery in **"The Right of Way"** is linked by a similar logic. In **"The Right of Way,"** I propose it is the girl's leg that causes the elderly man to look and smile.

The motorist, of course, does not make this connection explicit. In fact, he seems to deny it: "Why bother where I went?" But on one strong reading, it exists and is central to the organization of the poem, as I hope to show.

Because the elderly man is the center of attention of the woman and boy, the eyes of the motorist gravitate to the elderly man. Because the elderly man looks away, the eyes of the motorist follow the old man's eye direction, from sightline to sight (young girl). An eyeline match thus explains the poem's two-shot structure and compositional energy: in a first shot, we see the man looking, and in a second shot we see what he looks at. The poem ends after two shots not because the mobile gaze might go on forever, but because the male's mobile gaze has lighted on its endpoint. That this eye direction is shared by males is all the more powerful. Laura Mulvey argues this point in "Visual Pleasure and Narrative Cinema": "As the [male] spectator identifies with the main male protagonist, he projects his look on to that of his like, his screen surrogate, so that the power of the male protagonist as he controls events coincides with the active power of the erotic look, both giving a satisfying sense of omnipotence" (20). The identification of male spectator and male protagonist is a lynchpin not only of classical Hollywood film form and ideology but also of poetry based on the mobile gaze—including poetry that presents itself as alternative or avant-garde.

The pun that captures the ambiguity of this eyeline match is the word "watchchain." An eight-year-old boy looks at the elderly man's watchchain, the meaning of which is unexplored by the unsurmising motorist. The watchchain seems to be a warrant for the man's authority (social standing) and perhaps desire (cf. the appetitive word "belly," line 17). See **"Virtue,"** in which "men in vests with gold watch chains" are summoned by a smiling girl with a "vulgar inviting mouth" (***Collected Poems*** *1* 89). In addition, the watchchain is a key play on words—one of several in the poem. The smiling man is a road sign for the motorist, pointing him toward the dangling leg. The motorist watches the man, who watches the girl. **"The Right of Way"** is indeed continuous. Its structure is that of a watchchain.

There is then an interconnection, however tenuous, between the speaker and the images that he encounters from his passing roadster; he is not as disinterested or innocent as he makes himself out to be. A similar sense of secret connection or desire underlines the *Autobiography,* which compares the practices of medicine and poetry:

> My "medicine" was the thing which gained me entrance to these secret gardens of the self. . . . I was permitted by my medical badge to follow the poor, defeated body into those gulfs and grottos.

> (Williams, *Autobiography* 288)

Likewise, later in the *Autobiography*:

> He is half-ashamed to have people suspect him of carrying on a clandestine, a sort of underhand piece of spying on the public at large. . . . His only fear is that the source of his interest, his daily going about among human beings of all sorts, all ages, all conditions will be terminated. That he will be found out.

> (Williams, *Autobiography* 358-59)

Williams' legal "right of way" in the world of driving, like his "medical badge" or license in the world of pediatrics and obstetrics, is an authority which gains him entrance to the "secret gardens of the self," "the source of his . . . daily going about among human beings of all sorts, all ages, all conditions." While driving, the speaker of **"The Right of Way"** anticipates encountering such secrets: his mind is in a state of alert expectancy. His eye is not so much innocent, indiscriminately recording all it passes by, as it is "diagnostic" in the special sense in which the term may be applied to Williams—examining, with a combination of "professional disinterest" and clandestine personal fascination, the mystery that at times briefly exhibits itself.

A "watchchain" structure is not uncommon in Williams. We see it in another automobile poem, **"View of a Lake"** (*Collected Poems I* 380-81), in which stalled motorists view a group of children, while the children, backs turned to the traffic, look yet farther on toward a lake. And we see it in the medical short stories of the 1930s. Indeed, **"The Right of Way"** is like a skeletal doctor's story: an authority figure (motorist with right of way / doctor with medical badge) is directed by a group of interested people (threesome of man, woman, and boy / family of the patient) to a distant but attractive young female calling for attention ("a girl with one leg / over the rail of a balcony" / a stand-offish but erotic female patient in need of "diagnosis" and "cure"). The threesome, led by the protagonist male, is "supremely important" in that it points to the "straight, hard thing" which is the leg.

The puns of the poem continue in the form of the question that the motorist asks after seeing the old man, woman, and boy, but before seeing the girl: "Why bother where I went?" His question is similar to the famous Archie Bunker query analyzed by Paul de Man:

> [A]sked by his wife whether he wants to have his bowling shoes laced over or laced under, Archie Bunker answers with a question: "What's the difference?" Being a reader of sublime simplicity, his wife replies by patiently explaining the difference between lacing over and lacing under, whatever this may be, but provokes only ire. "What's the difference" did not ask for difference but means instead "I don't give a damn what the difference is." The same grammatical pattern engenders two meanings that are mutually exclusive: the literal meaning asks for the concept (difference) whose existence is denied by the figurative meaning.
>
> (de Man 9)

Like Archie Bunker's question, the motorist's "Why bother where I went?" "engenders two meanings that are mutually exclusive." On the one hand, it signals (figuratively and by cliché) that the motorist is jaunty and carefree. I didn't bother where I went. My route was aimless and random. I was open to whatever might come down the road. On the other hand, it signals (literally) quite the opposite attitude: not an aimlessness or randomness of route, but a sense of unalterable destination. Why bother where I went? My route was pre-planned; no digression was possible. A hidden but fixed trajectory—the old man's look—sped me to my destination (the exposed girl). Unlike Archie Bunker's question, the motorist's question is powerfully ambiguous not because husband and wife have opposite interpretations of its meaning but because one man utters a phrase with mutually exclusive meanings. The motorist is both a spectator of sublime simplicity and a passer.

In fact **"The Right of Way"** is built around a pun on passing, complicating its narrative of voyeurism and visibility:

> In passing with my mind
> on nothing in the world
>
> but the right of way
> I enjoy on the road by
>
> virtue of the law—
>
> (lines 1-5)

This phrase captures the antithetical meanings of the poem. On the one hand, "in passing" suggests casualness ("in passing" as in "by the way") and the fleeting passage of time and space—all intimations that the poem is an improvisation about a set of discrete and fleeting visual attractions that appear to a happy-go-lucky motorist. On the other hand, "in passing" suggests that the motorist is not casual—not innocent, but playing the innocent, disguising himself in order to look like what he is not. On this reading, he feigns pleasure in the discontinuity of automobile vision—the lack of connection among the images that he sees. But he finds pleasure in continuity: he follows the directionality of the old man's gaze in order to look up the girl's skirt. And he finds pleasure in the very act of passing, the titillating chance of being outed to his audiences. Passing now is

> a virtuoso tightrope performance, a flirtation with risk by flaunting your disguise in a context in which you know that it will *fool only some people*—an act, in other words, that has built into it the exhilarating possibility of exposure and destruction.
>
> (Peter Rabinowitz 141)

While passing has a long history in the United States, one of its richest eras started with the Plessy v. Ferguson decision (1896) legalizing "separate but equal" and continued through the 1950s: an era coinciding with the birth and rise to prominence of the automobile and of cinema. The same culture that produces a "frenzy of the visible" (Comolli 122) produces classes of subjects in a frenzy to hide their identity from view, pretending to be something that they are not. Of course the driver of **"The Right of Way"** is passing not in order to gain legitimate rights but in order to enjoy his dubious "right" to visual pleasure.

"The Right of Way" thus sustains two rival interpretations. On the one hand, the poem reads as an exercise in radical discontinuity: it is the record of a pair (implicitly, a series) of random roadside images seen by an automobile driver in transit. On the other hand, the poem reads as an account of tenuously interconnected items, a sequence of images linked by the silent logic of a "watchchain." This allegiance to both discontinuity and continuity is typical of Williams' improvisational writings. In a letter to John Riordan, Williams summarizes the matter in this way:

> But my failure to work inside a pattern—a positive sin—is the cause of my virtues. I cannot work inside a pattern because I can't find a pattern that will have me. My whole effort . . . is to find a pattern, large enough, modern enough, flexible enough to include my desires. And if I should find it I'd wither and die.
>
> (Letter to John Riordan)[2]

Mike Weaver discusses Williams' divided allegiance in similar terms: "Williams was strenuously opposed to completion, and to perfection as 'composition.' He was equally opposed to the incompletion of the broken object" (154-55). The distinctiveness of the experimental writings of the 1920s—including **"The Right of Way"**—is that the dimension of incoherence is strongly fore-grounded while the dimension of coherence is troubled or automatized. One important undertaking for Williams criticism today is to recognize the radical practice of discontinuity in the improvisational writings without overlooking the possible presence of pattern. A second important undertaking is to relate this ambivalence in Williams to a set of contemporary debates about early twentieth-century visual culture (Charney, Linda Williams) and visual/verbal relations (Yacobi, Heffernan).

One of these debates focuses on the contested status of ekphrasis. Is **"The Right of Way"** an ekphrastic poem? On a traditional definition of the term—"the verbal representation of visual representation" (Mitchell 152)—it is not. The poem's images—the trio of man/woman/boy and the single girl—are not visual representations but visual objects. Yet if we remember that Williams is an experienced and successful ekphrastic poet, author of **"Portrait of a Lady"** and *Pictures from Brueghel,* and if we remember that the improvisational writings vigorously attack the idea of representation ("plagiarism after nature"—*Collected Poems I* 198), then we might suspect that Williams' position on ekphrasis here is more complex. In **"The Right of Way,"**

the motorcar is not a transportation machine meant to deliver a person to a fixed destination, but a machine of the visible meant to deliver non-stop images of surprise and pleasure. And the motorist passes not to escape notice as an underprivileged member of society but to escape notice as a voyeur. Given this "dynamization" (*Collected Poems I* 219, 220, 235) of traditional meanings, I propose that **"The Right of Way"** is a dynamized ekphrasis.

Tamar Yacobi, in his essay "Pictorial Models and Narrative Ekphrasis," maps out a model of "ekphrastic dynamism" (602) that is useful to this argument. Yacobi claims that while writers use a wide variety of ekphrastic forms, critics neglect many of these forms, privileging the traditional "work-to-work . . . relations between word and image" (603). One neglected form is the "work-to-model" relation, in which a given verbal text refers not to a unique visual work but to many works, a "generalized reference to artistic practice" (628). Thus an individual verbal text by Isak Dinesan will often refer not to an individual text of spatial art but to a general spatial model or theme: "Lacoön [sic], Diana and Acteon, the adoration of the Magi, the Madonna with child, and so on" (627). Williams takes this model a step further. **"The Right of Way"** refers not just to a general artistic practice but to an artistic practice that is also and inextricably social: the mobility of the gaze, the gendering of the gaze as male, the invisibility of the male motorist in his visual (diegetic) world, and the ambiguous work of the male motorist to remain invisible to his readership—his passing. **"The Right of Way"** is a dynamized ekphrasis about the new visual culture of automobility.

Notes

I want to thank Mark Holden and Anthony O. Tyler for helpful comments on an earlier draft of this essay.

1. "The Right of Way" was originally published in the first edition of *Spring and All* (Contact: Dijon, 1923), where it was called poem XI. It reappeared in *An Early Martyr* (1935) under the title "The Auto Ride." In *The Collected Earlier Poems* (1951), Williams gave names to the poems of *Spring and All.* Poem XI is titled "The Right of Way." The critical tradition since the publication of *The Collected Earlier Poems* has referred to the poem as "The Right of Way."

2. William Carlos Williams to John Riordan, 1926, Oct. 13, MSS 7456, etc., Clifton Waller Barrett Library of American Literature, Special Collections, University of Virginia Library. By William Carlos Williams, from PREVIOUSLY UNPUBLISHED MATERIAL, copyright © 2006 by Paul H. Williams and the Estate of William Eric Wil-

Works Cited

Aumont, Jacques. "The Variable Eye, or the Mobilization of the Gaze." Trans. Charles O'Brien and Sally Shafto. *The Image in Dispute: Art and Cinema in the Age of Photography*. Ed. Dudley Andrew. Austin: U of Texas P, 1997. 231-58.

Bar-Yaacov, Lois. "Driving into the 20th Century: A Study of Some William Carlos Williams Poems." *Hebrew University Studies in Literature* 7-8 (1979-80): 261-80.

Charney, Leo, and Vanessa R. Schwartz, ed. *Cinema and the Invention of Modern Life*. Berkeley: U of California P, 1995.

Comolli, Jean-Louis. "Machines of the Visible." *The Cinematic Apparatus*. Ed. Teresa de Lauretis and Stephen Heath. New York: St. Martin's, 1980. 121-42.

DeMan, Paul. *Allegories of Reading: Figural Language in Rousseau, Nietzsche, Rilke, and Proust*. New Haven: Yale UP, 1979.

Dolin, Sharon. "Enjambment and the Erotics of the Gaze in Williams's Poetry." *American Imago* 50.1 (Spring 1993): 29-54.

Friedberg, Anne. *Window Shopping: Cinema and the Postmodern*. Berkeley: U of California P, 1993.

Gunning, Thomas. "The Cinema of Attractions: Early Film, Its Spectator, and the Avant-Garde." *Wide Angle* 8 (1986): 63-70.

———. "'Now You See It, Now You Don't': The Temporality of the Cinema of Attractions." *The Velvet Light Trap* 32 (1993): 71-84.

Heffernan, James A. W. *Museum of Words: The Poetics of Ekphrasis from Homer to Ashbery*. Chicago: U of Chicago P, 1993.

Lanser, Susan Sniader. *The Narrative Act: Point of View in Prose Fiction*. Princeton: Princeton UP, 1981.

Manovich, Lev. *The Language of the New Media*. Cambridge: MIT Press, 2001.

McCabe, Susan. *Cinematic Modernism: Modernist Poetry and Film*. Cambridge: Cambridge UP, 2005.

Miki, Roy. "Driving and Writing." *William Carlos Williams: Man and Poet*. Ed. Carroll F. Terrell. Orono: National Poetry Foundation, U of Maine at Orono, 1983. 111-28.

Mitchell, W. J. T. *Picture Theory*. Chicago: U of Chicago P, 1994.

Mulvey, Laura. "Visual Pleasure and Narrative Cinema." *Visual and Other Pleasures*. Bloomington: Indiana UP, 1989. 14-27.

Rabinowitz, Lauren. "More than the Movies: A History of Somatic Visual Culture through Hale's Tours, IMAX, and Motion Simulation Rides." *Memory Bytes: History, Technology and Digital Culture*. Ed. Lauren Rabinovitz and Abraham Geil. Durham, NC: Duke UP, 2004. 99-125.

Rabinowitz, Peter J., and Michael J. Smith. *Authorizing Readers: Resistance and Respect in the Teaching of Literature*. New York: Teachers College, 1998.

Sandberg, Mark B. "Effigy and Narrative: Looking into the Nineteenth-Century Folk Museum." *Cinema and the Invention of Modern Life*. Ed. Leo Charney and Vanessa R. Schwartz. Berkeley: U of California P, 1995. 320-61.

Scharff, Virginia. *Taking the Wheel: Women and the Coming of the Motor Age*. New York: Free Press, 1991.

Urry, John. "The 'System' of Automobility." *Theory, Culture, and Society* 21.4-5 (2004): 25-39.

Virilio, Paul. "Dromoscopy, or The Ecstasy of Enormities." Trans. Edward R. O'Neill. *Wide Angle* 20.3 (1998): 11-22.

Weaver, Mike. *William Carlos Williams: The American Background*. Cambridge: Cambridge UP, 1971.

Williams, Linda. *Hard Core: Power, Pleasure, and "The Frenzy of the Visible."* Berkeley: U of California P, 1989.

Williams, William Carlos. *The Autobiography of William Carlos Williams*. New York: New Directions, 1967.

———. *The Collected Earlier Poems of Williams Carlos Williams*. New York: New Directions, 1951.

———. *The Collected Poems of William Carlos Williams. Volume I: 1909-1939*. Ed. A. Walton Litz and Christopher MacGowan. New York: New Directions, 1986.

———. *The Great American Novel. Imaginations*. Ed. Webster Schott. New York: New Directions, 1970. 153-227.

———. *Kora in Hell: Improvisations. Imaginations*. Ed. Webster Schott. New York: New Directions, 1970. 1-82.

———. Letter to John Riordan. 13 Oct. 1926. Ms. 7456. Clifton Waller Barrett Library of American Literature. Special Collections. University of Virginia Library.

———. *Pictures from Brueghel and Other Poems*. New York: New Directions, 1962.

————. *Selected Essays of William Carlos Williams.* Ed. John C. Thirlwall. New York: New Directions, 1984.

Yacobi, Tamar. "Pictorial Models and Narrative Ekphrasis." *Poetics Today* 16 (1995): 599-649.

Bob Perelman (essay date 2007)

SOURCE: Perelman, Bob. "Doctor Williams's Position, Updated." In *Contemporary Poetics*, edited by Louis Armand, pp. 67-95. Evanston, Ill.: Northwestern University Press, 2007.

[*In the following essay, Perelman offers a detailed reexamination of Williams's poem, "Asphodel, That Greeny Flower," focusing on issues of authenticity, candor, and the continuing value of the poem.*]

> My heart rouses
>   thinking to bring you news
>   of something
> that concerns you
>   and concerns many men. Look at
>   what passes for the new.
> You will not find it there but in
>   despised poems.
>   It is difficult
> to get the news from poems
>   yet men die miserably every day
>   for lack
> of what is found there.
>   Hear me out
>   for I too am concerned
> and every man
>   who wants to die at peace in his bed
>   besides.
>
>   —William Carlos Williams

TRIVIA

In the early 1950s when William Carlos Williams wrote **"Asphodel, That Greeny Flower,"**[1] poetry had recently been pushed to the unfamiliar precincts of the American front pages by the crescendoing public drama of Ezra Pound: his raving but clearly profascist radio speeches during the war; the aborted treason trial at the war's end; and the long firestorm over his being awarded the Bollingen Prize in 1949. Williams's forced withdrawal from consideration for the position of poetry consultant to the Library of Congress in 1952 had been something of a public event, too, though in this, as with most everything else, he was overshadowed by Pound. One factor contributing to Williams's defeat was his lifelong association with Pound. In **"Asphodel,"** after decades of absorbing, chafing against, and seconding Pound's lessons, Williams offers a correction, more socially nuanced and ethically capacious, to Pound's absolutist "Literature is news that STAYS news."[2] Pound grants

writing (only the best writing, of course) extraordinary powers and brooks no personal, spatial, or temporal obstacle to legibility: it *is,* and it *stays,* news. For Williams, news is equally valuable, but its reception is more specific. The body is the locus of poetry's claimed effects: an embodied reader either gets the news and can die in bed at peace or does not receive the blessing and dies miserably. Williams's claim, unlike Pound's, recognizes failure as one of the structuring possibilities of valid poetry.

Such senses of contingency have mostly fallen away, however, as for many readers the passage has come to stand as a proclamation of poetry's virtues with any possibility of failure omitted. The title for Adrienne Rich's essays, *What Is Found There,* quarries out a positive assertion from lines where Williams only names a lack; more recently, as controversies over Amiri Baraka's "Somebody Blew Up America" and the cancellation of Laura Bush's poetic soiree have again put poetry on the front page,[3] "the news from poems" has become something of a commonplace, a basic justification of poetry or simply a synonym for it. A letter writer to the *New York Times* quotes the lines and then comments, "What people find in poetry is a deeper, more creative and moral way of looking at the world";[4] a review of an anthology of international poetry is entitled "The News from Poetry"—in both cases the difficulties and absence at the heart of Williams's claim have been erased. While its appearances on op-ed pages and the like could in some sense be a vindication for Williams, it is hard to avoid the sense that it is precisely the vagueness of these lines that is latched onto, making them say something like, "Poetry is wonderful, but *they* just don't get it," a sense that reinforces the standoff between individual and community that the passage is addressing in the first place.

I remain intrigued by the confident, oddly blank promise of Williams's claim. I realize how conveniently comforting it can be and, when it is quoted in defense of poetry I don't particularly respect, how it can sound like the stiffest cultural ideology. But I am not willing, finally, to resign myself to writing in a world without such a promise. The lines are a commonsense riddle which both points out the modernist endgame that has pinched poetry into specialist niches and at the same time promises that, in some unspecified way, poetry's social dilemma is capable of being solved.

Williams's current centrality in American poetry is an obvious but nevertheless odd fact of literary history. When his poetry is read closely, there are repeated oddnesses that can't be resolved by appeals to voice, theory, or history. These oddnesses point to what I am interested in here: qualities I call social and poetic candor, terms I will discuss in the final section. For now, I don't want to be misunderstood as intending to sweep away all prior readings. The useful and, at best, inspiring achievements of the poetry are there, as many readers have found; but, as many readers are also undoubtedly aware, Williams's work is full of problematic moments. I have come to see them not simply as blemishes, miscalculations, or carelessness, which, if we like Williams, are to be overlooked or forgiven or, if we don't, serve to prove that he's second-rate. Rather, they are a fundamental part of his writing. This doesn't redeem them. What, in the "Eumaeus" chapter of *Ulysses,* may look at first like terrible writing becomes yet another example of Joyce's mastery: nothing like that happens with Williams. Nor is it a matter of Williams the democratic modernist exemplifying a proletarian agenda and writing unrefined work to yank elite readers down to the real world. For all of its use of everyday language and events around him, Williams's poetry can no more be mistaken for ordinary language than can Dickinson's or Zukofsky's. For all its legibility, it guards its news jealously. **"The Clouds"** contains an apt emblem of this. His initial description of the clouds ends:

> a rank confusion of the imagination still uncured,
> a rule, piebald under the streetlamps, reluctant
> to be torn from its hold.[5]

By writing the word "rule," Williams posits its existence, but he is unable to articulate it, to tear it loose from the imagination; he has no cure (either medically or in the sense of proper aging) for its confusions. The same unresolved struggle is present in his sense of news. The still-prevalent received idea makes the modernist poet the one who knows and who challenges readers to overcome their own ignorance. But Williams's pronouncement "It is difficult to get the news from poems" applies to him as much as to those who die miserably without it: their condition is part of his— and our—difficulty.

When pressed, the sentence itself is quite slippery—an odd thing to say, since the language couldn't be simpler or more direct. It's not hard to place it in poetic history: the stakes are obvious. This is the American idiom that Williams supported in the face of Pound's and Eliot's Euro-historical erudition. But even though "news" and "get" are the most basic American words, they are not simple or clear.

Why is it difficult to get the news from poems? Is it a lack of literary expertise? "People don't get how to read poetry; they read for plot or imagery and don't get what really makes a poem news." Is it a problem of circulation? "It's hard to get the crucial poetry books in local libraries and bookstores." Or, using "get" in its most untranslatable sense, is it that pedantic imaginations, inflexible libidos, and tin ears are impervious to poetic inspiration? "They just don't get it." This last sense makes news quasi-transcendental, something like the "good news" of the Gospel.

Is this the "imprecision" that both Pound and Eliot abhor? Their poetics are distinct from one another, but both supply criteria that Williams's poetry fails to meet. For Pound, poetry had to be clear; for Eliot, it has to embody hieratic power. Though Pound consistently gave Williams himself a ration of praise for his "opacity,"[6] it was not a quality he praised elsewhere. In *ABC of Reading* he admitted logopoeia, "the dance of the intellect among the words,"[7] which allows the words to dance as well, but by midcentury, words had to dance in their prescribed places: the necessity for an unwobbling pivot made the mot juste the only acceptable poetic currency. What we now so often and easily call polysemy was taboo. Eliot's distaste for the contemporary vulgate was spelled out in carefully conventional terms in "Burnt Norton": "Words strain / . . . / Under the tension, slip, slide, perish, / Decay with imprecision." Williams's language is imprecise; "polysemous" is a bit grand to apply to it, though "socially polysemous" is not inaccurate. A paradoxical praise-adjective would be "trivial," in the ancient sense of *tri-via*: where three roads meet. There is tremendous traffic in words there, jammed in contradiction, zealous, lost, wandering, purposeful, mired in the boredom of blockage. It's where we still live.

INSPIRATION: WILLIAMS AND ION

> My heart rouses
>   thinking to bring you news
>   of something
>   that concerns you
>   and concerns many men.

Thinking to bring you my sense of the news from **"Asphodel,"** my heart rouses, but not without qualms. Rouses because I am continually struck by the claim these lines make; familiarity does not flatten it. At times, I can find it inspiring, to use that most suspect word. It is not simply saying that poetry can enrich any life—an easy enough proposition to agree with, especially for those enriched lives already committed to poetry. The claim here intends a wider reach, out beyond any established audience to society at large, and thus it is harder to believe. The news from poems can answer to the sharpest personal and the largest social demands? What kind of answer would that be? Would wars stop, to allow for harmonious lives and happy deathbed scenes on a universal scale?

Like the audience listening to Homer in the *Ion,* is my feeling of inspiration simply a link of contagious excitement, attached to nothing more substantial than what I read to be Williams's feeling of excitement?

Despite being 2,300 years old and despite the fact that the poetry it discusses is oral,[8] the *Ion* offers an interesting frame in which to consider **"Asphodel."** This is not because of the poem's references to the *Iliad.* Such references are either vacuous ("The sea! The sea! / Always / when I think of the sea / there comes to mind / the *Iliad*") or almost comically inappropriate in a poem that, among other things, is meant as an apology for the poet's infidelities ("there comes to mind / the *Iliad* / and Helen's public fault / that bred it").[9] But comparing Williams to the rhapsodist Ion does bring out an interesting implications for both poet and reader.

Coming into dialogue with Socrates, Ion is certain of poetry's emotional power and epistemological plenitude. Its power is undeniable: the evidence is there in his body and the bodies of others: when the poem is pitiful, he weeps, the audience weeps; when it is horrific, his hair stands on end, their hair stands on end. He also believes that his prize-winning recitations of Homer give him access to all the skills and knowledge represented in the poems, until Socrates shows him (and us) that what he considers to be his knowledge is neither his nor knowledge, that his words are shaped "not by art or science . . . but by . . . divine possession."[10] In the *Ion* Plato does not have Socrates spell out the conclusions that are so emphatic in the *Republic,* but they are implicit here: poetry's unwieldy power makes people dangerous; Ion and his audience become emotional automatons following the feelings scripted by the poems; and these scripts sprawl promiscuously across ethical boundaries.[11]

In "**Asphodel**" poetry arrives in much the same way as it does for Ion, despite a different poetic technology: Williams speaks elegiacally of "the words / made solely of air / or less, / that came to me / out of the air / and insisted / on being written down."[12] While there is no Socrates in "**Asphodel**" nor any magnetized audience, there is that initial poetic enthusiasm: "My heart rouses / thinking to bring you news." But what is the news? "News / of something." A cynical reading could parse this as a variant (in the American idiom) of Lear's substanceless fulmination: "I will do such things—/ What they are, yet I know not; but they shall be / The terrors of the earth."[13] Or, in a harsher reading, one could inflect it into a naive version of the "drumroll . . . pratfall" trope that Eliot dramatizes in "Prufrock," where the initial stanza leads up to the portentous "overwhelming question" only to dissolve into light verse: "Oh, do not ask, 'What is it?' / Let us go and make our visit." Such an inflection would read like so: "I bring you [the most crucial] news of [. . . um, well . . .] something."

This is too harsh. But whether one reads it harshly or forgivingly, the news remains unspecified: it fills Williams with enthusiasm, but ultimately he does not know what this news is and cannot translate it out of the medium of his enthusiasm. Possibly the news *is* nothing but his enthusiasm. This lack of specific content can be a virtue since breadth of address seems the point. The news concerns "you"—Williams's wife Flossie—and

"many men," a universality which is then amplified: "every day" men suffer the want of this news; it concerns "every man." However, if poetic news should be construed as purely a function of personal and universal address without its content mattering, what happens next in "**Asphodel**" isn't all that encouraging: just a few lines after announcing that he has crucial news for her, the poet has to beg Flossie to keep listening, "Hear me out," a refrain which is varied throughout the poem. Perhaps she tunes out because the news seems only addressed to a male public ("all men"), with the additional, singular, aggrieved wife singled out privately in hopes of restoring domestic tranquillity.

LOCATION, LOCATION, LOCATION

Thinking to transmit the news from "**Asphodel**" via critical prose written at the beginning of the twenty-first century, I am filled with qualms, which are not helped by my having used, straightaway and without any saving irony or contextual specificity, "inspiring," a word which marks criticism as bellelettristic and poetry as naive cape-wielding. The problem with Williams, to miscite John Ashbery, is there is not enough of a problem. At this point, it's not easy to think of his work as news, especially "**Asphodel**," a late poem where his avant-garde antagonisms have all but evaporated and where the language—sometimes eloquent, sometimes sloppy or banal—is never difficult in a modernist sense.

"**Asphodel**" is not a critically fashionable poem nor a poetically fashionable one. While it is celebrated for the lines I've been discussing, and praised (and sometimes panned) for its depth of sentiment, it is not a particularly modernist poem nor a forward-looking poem in terms of technique. It is obviously the poem of an old man. Old age, memory, and approaching death are predominant subject matter: in Greek myth, asphodel grows next to the Elysian fields. Stylistically, the poem shows what is known as "slackening of the artist's power": it can be prolix, words are repeated carelessly, the rhetoric is clumsy in places. Its many moments when Williams addresses his wife Flossie can be strained and mawkish: "You have forgiven me," the poet asserts at one particularly unconvincing moment.

The poem has its strengths, too, amid these problems. But whatever one's aesthetic verdict, "**Asphodel**" is situated to offer a useful perspective on modernist poetry: Does midcentury mark its conclusion, or, as Marjorie Perloff and I and others have argued, its midpoint? (Midpoint in a noncontinuous historical trajectory, that is.) A major retrospection of Williams's career, the poem can stand out as one of the more visible conclusive points of American modernist poetry. It's less easy to imagine it as a midpoint, since, as I've said, it seems stylistically retrogressive (for example, in its unpainterly, crudely symbolic flower imagery, or its non-ironic allusions from Spenser, using the same phrases that Eliot had, one thought, made permanently ironic thirty years earlier in *The Waste Land*). However, **"Asphodel"**'s odd mix of genre and subject remains quite germane. It is a love poem, aggressively intimate (emotionally, not bodily) and confessional, poetic territory that Williams explored quite a bit before Ginsberg, O'Hara, Lowell, Rich, or Plath. It is an ars poetica written from a personally situated, noninstitutional perspective.

Williams is now a central figure in American poetry history. But the center is a bland place to be, at best. Williams scores points as a modernist, but in terms of critical cachet he's not in the first rank. The basic elements of his poetics are easy to domesticate: the American idiom, "no ideas but in things," "a poem is a machine made of words," the variable foot. That poetry should use the contemporary idiom has long been poetic common sense; "no ideas but in things" can be taken as a slogan gesturing rather abstractly toward the here and now,[14] "a poem is a machine of words" as a slogan aligning the poet with modernity; the variable foot might encode Williams's dynamic intuitions behind his own poetic practice, but the only point on which readers agree is that it's a vague formulation. It does not take much reading outside the critical demonstration-pieces to find that many of Williams's poems don't stay within the confines of any of these notions.

His work is hard to characterize or evaluate. He has become an honored predecessor for an uncomfortably wide range of contemporary poets. Heterogeneous in itself, his work has had unmistakable influence on a contradictory set of heirs, leading to the polemical plainness of Levine and Rich as much as to O'Hara's erotic wit, Ginsberg's prophetic politics, and the textual activism of Language writing. Just about any poem not in regular meter could claim Williams as a precursor.

His work points to the future in contradictory ways. For Charles Bernstein, Williams's poetic iconoclasm remains an unfinished project. Bernstein sees the academy and other gatekeeping institutions allowing only a tamed Williams to circulate: "As Williams passes through the narrow and well-guarded gates of official verse culture, it likely will be at the expense of so de-contextualizing and neutralizing his work that it will be unrecognizable on his own terms . . . official verse culture is no more hospitable to Williams's literary politics now than it was fifty years ago."[15] For Robert Pinsky, it is the democratic Williams who awaits acknowledgment: Williams's "influence has been immense, but his model has yet to be completely realized"; his work aspired to put poetic innovation at the service of cultural legibility: "originality of technique and the ambition to write a poetry of American life, in language based on the American idiom, embodied a single, unified project."[16]

Logically, both positions value the range of Williams's address and the vividness of his language; but when placed in a Bourdieuvian literary field, the poet-critics represent starkly polarized positions: poet laureate versus Language writer, official verse culture versus oppositional poetries.[17] It is striking that it is possible for Williams to be claimed as a central figure by both positions, something that is far less likely in the cases of Stein, Olson, Zukofsky, Riding, or Pound.

Poetic principalities guard their borders fiercely, while at the same time claiming right of unimpeded passage from the poetic sphere to the world at large. Two factors lie behind these contradictory attitudes toward boundaries: one is the current state of the poetic field, which is crowded as never before; the other is the powerful momentum of a modernist legacy. For close to a century we have been living and writing under its dispensation in which the news and the new have been synonymous, both standing for the central value organizing all battles for poetic position. "Make It New" describes the impulse governing significant writing. How to determine what is significant? "Literature is news that STAYS news." In other words, the new is news that stays news. Inside this circle the problem of poetry's social authority is solved: poetic knowledge ceases to be merely specialized; poetry (particular, eccentric) is united with history (universal).

Recent developments have made this tight certainty brittle. Poetry, in its most general sense, has become a social fact to a fairly wide extent. It may not play an authoritative role in the culture—its niche in the entertainment industry is minor, as is its presence in the curriculum at all levels—nevertheless, more people in more situations write, hear, and study more different kinds of poetry than ever before. Innovative poetry is not totally excluded from this modest success. There are now more innovative publications, venues, paper and electronic archives, Listservs and blogs, more reviews of innovative work, more critical articles and books, more slots in syllabi than ever before. To be sure, innovation is still almost always given the cold shoulder when it comes to jobs, awards, grants, and standard anthologies; and senses of embattlement are widespread. But—what is the social objective of the battle? To supplant the mainstream? Doubtful. What, then? To defend the circle where New = News?

Poetic innovation and news have become unspecific, formally and factually. There is little way of determining, strictly from internal evidence, whether a poem is innovative. Few results appearing under the right name in the right place could be excluded: chance procedures; improvisation; collaboration; Steinian meditation involving syntactic fracture, repetition, or rhythmic play; allusive literary collage; antiliterary pastiche; plain denotation à la Reznikoff; highly worked or slack verbal surfaces—the list could go on. As for news, it is becoming more obvious by the minute that it is extraordinarily difficult to separate it from ideology, from propaganda, from weaponry. Both the new and the news have become something like Freud's primal words except that they don't point to some originary condition but to an unfathomable terminus improbably called the present. There are other key words in the **"Asphodel"** passage: "every man," "you," "bed." Here I'll confine myself to that quarrelsome pair—don't call them twins—new and news.

A Fable

When it comes to poetry, the present, the cumbersome obvious present, plays the most uncanny trick on the new.

After some period of coalescence, the new emerges into the present. There must have been some fortunate hours or it wouldn't have emerged at all. But the hours were fortunate and the new does emerge, energetically. Having done so, it fortifies its identity by focusing its aim, which is to progress directly and unambiguously toward the future. It streamlines its modes to get there more quickly and to separate itself from its compromised, conservative, mildewed rivals. After intense stretches of invention, self-presentation, polemic, self-correction, gathering articulation, and further invention all happening more or less simultaneously, a time comes to take stock of how far it has progressed.

Now the present is no nimble magician; there is no sudden revelation from behind a flashing cape. But it happens every time: the new has not reached the future; for all its ferocious velocity, it finds itself stuck fast in the past. Nostalgia becomes an occupational hazard at this point . . .

The New and Its Reproductive Practices

If time is a one-way, irreversible continuum, the past will always resolve into a receding vista of terms denoting periodization: Postlanguage, Language writing, New American poetry, Objectivism, high Modernism, Romanticism. For some, the avant-garde is visible right behind high Modernism; others place it in front; others see it everywhere; still others don't see it at all. Many reproductions of the vista are sold each year; most omit the avant-garde. All versions of the vista ironize vanguard aspirations; iconoclasm always becomes "The New is Dead, Long Live the New!" a salute to the unchanging reign of Continuity.

For those of us temporarily enmeshed in the present, however, things are not so clear. Rather than the steady hand of chronology smoothly adding to the shelves, there's a chronic battle of the books. Behind makeshift barricades, partisans hurl small magazines, chapbooks, Listservs, and blogs like cobblestones against the uncomprehending but irritated enemy; they heap up regressive prizewinning volumes, careers, academies, and entire centuries to feed the bonfires. Powerful currents of comradeship unite the partisans, but they are subject to disruption, with accusations of double-dealing not uncommon. It's not surprising: the enemy has control over a great deal of institutional recognition, so that without the constant support from other members of the group behind the barricade, an individual career can fade rapidly.

The partisans' place in the synchronous literary field is tight and embattled; but their temporal claims are secure and immense. Breathing space in the present may be circumscribed, but the present opens securely onto the future, and the past is under control as well. It can be destroyed, as with the futurists, or shaped by definition and identification: either way it's under control. A list of some representative stances: Stendhal enlists past writers into his partisan fight for an emergent romanticism: "Molière was romantic in 1670, because the court was full of Orontes and the châteaux in the provinces were full of very discontented Alcestes. Actually, ALL GREAT WRITERS WERE THE ROMANTICS OF THEIR DAY."[18] Baudelaire sets up a two-state solution, granting autonomy to both the present and eternity: "By 'modernity' I mean the ephemeral, the fugitive, the contingent, the half of art whose other half is the eternal and the immutable."[19] Zukofsky's capsule poetics in section 6 of "A" unites the past; an observed, multiform present; and the future as he asks for writing that is "objectively perfect / Inextricably the direction of historic and contemporary particulars."[20] The salient aspect of this formula is the assertion of control: the artwork is objectively perfect and coincides exactly with the direction of history. In this regard, Zukofsky is quite like Eliot: "The existing monuments form an ideal order among themselves, which is modified by the introduction of the new (the really new) work of art among them."[21] In asserting his power to enter and to change the past ideal order, Eliot idealizes his own power under the name of the new; Zukofsky's claim of perfection does the same, although the power is put in history's name.

It's awkward to yoke Eliot with Zukofsky or with any partisans of innovation. The strain is evident in the single word "monuments" Eliot uses to designate literary works. This gesture of protoinstitutionalization anticipates his full conversion to exaggerated respectability and assiduous genuflection to the triumphant theological literariness he invented. He never acknowledged the invention nor the triumph, instead acting out a pious self-extinction in the service of tradition: "We shall often find that not only the best, but the most individual parts of his work may be those in which the dead poets, his ancestors, assert their immortality most vigorously. And I do not mean the impressionable period of adolescence, but the period of full maturity."[22] To reach full maturity is also to enlist in the ranks of the dead. As for mere living, that's for "impressionable adolescence."

If Eliot's dead ventriloquizing poets are subtracted, the 1988 quasi manifesto by six Language writers makes a claim on tradition that is structurally similar to Eliot's in one way. For us the avant-garde tradition was as crucial and established a fact as Eliot's tradition. Language writing's emergence was not "an unusual narrative. Developments of such collective activity have characterized the history of the avant-garde" such as "the Black Mountain, San Francisco Renaissance, and New York schools of poetry." In a move that, again, has surprising similarities to Eliot, we assumed a position of normative mature knowledge as we called those who repressed or were ignorant of our tradition parochial: "On analogy with the visual arts, where the 'avant-garde' is felt to be a virtual commonplace, the situation of poetry is as if the entire history of radical modernism . . . had been replaced by a league of suburban landscape painters."[23] Unlike Eliot, we emphasized community: our basic principle was "not the 'self-sufficiency of language' or the 'materiality of the sign' but *the reciprocity of practice implied by a community of writers who read each other's work.*"[24] But it was our community, defined solely by the activity of reading and writing, temporarily free from larger social striations and antagonisms.

The general pattern, where power over history is wielded to solidify an embattled position in the present literary field, is maintained in Steve Evans's recent castigation of the journal *Fence*. The ferocity of the charge of apostasy against the avant-garde is clear from the title, "The Resistible Rise of Fence Enterprises"—change "Fence Enterprises" to "Arturo Ui" and you have the title of Brecht's allegory of Hitler's rise. Evans draws a fiery line between the avant-garde and writing that is merely "linguistically innovative," "indeterminate," or "experimental."[25] The avant-garde is distinguished less by any formal distinctions than its set toward the social and toward history in the present. The avant-garde is "collective and contentious";[26] its core values are "solidarity, integrity and generosity." But without the "imaginative work of connecting [its] expressions back to the social forces, contradictions, and struggles that animate contemporary life," the avant-garde falls into "formalism."[27] For Evans, this is the fate of *Fence,* which supports, in its editor's words, "a distinguished grey area," taking care to "exclude no one . . . in the name of an academic purity, or a preordained set of obscurities." Evans calls this a "facile pluralism," which selectively appropriates "radical poetic techniques, shorn of their contexts and motivating commitments."[28] Borrowing Adorno's description of

compromised atonal composers, Evans predicts that such a "despicable artistic credo" will only produce "a respectably routined neo-academicism"; "self-flattery" that mistakes "linguistic for social structures," it has no future and is merely a "spent poetics . . . the radical imagination has already left . . . behind."[29] Despite Evans's eloquent evocation of outward, synchronic social context as fundamental to the avant-garde, the coup de grâce that defines it and condemns *Fence* is temporal. Because of its desire for social generality, *Fence* is expelled from history.

My section heading promised an account of reproductive practices of the new, but there's been precious little in evidence. If it occurs at all, reproduction takes place not in the secure realm of history but in the embattled social spaces of the present, with the inevitable danger of becoming reproducible, routine doxa, some "respectably routined neo-academicism." Schematically, a pessimistic logician could say: if the new reproduces, it's not new. Existence itself, if continued, is problematic: How can extending across the temporal boundary of the present moment be distinguished from extending across spatial, institutional boundaries that separate a *Fence* magazine from the genuine avant-garde? If the continuous and the contiguous aren't fenced off, they will dissolve the avant-garde community. Controlling extension is basic to avant-garde self-fashioning, thus Spicer's insistence that his books not leave the Bay Area or his comment that poetry means nothing to nonpoets[30] and Olson's valorization of "a nation of nothing but poetry."[31]

The motley, ersatz, Delphic territories of the new encompass the hard-to-read historical demands that are basic to interesting poetry, but it's my sense that a different syntax is needed to direct these demands outward toward the heteronymous present rather than toward the goal of a purely autonomous future. Seen in this light, Williams's poetic messiness is a sign of his continually making contact with the present, where his poems faced dissolution. Mess—not the transgressive waste of Bataille's general economy, but just plain mess—sloppiness, compromise, common sense: these qualities can attend the best of Williams's poems. To be sure, Williams always proclaims a desire for breakthrough, freshness, the word cleaned of all common gunk, but his writing gives evidence of a more interesting lack of rigor. To recall his nemesis Eliot's phrase, it half-enacts a kind of poetic "self-extinction": rather than poetic autonomy, contact with the outside.

But the basic question of value obtrudes here. I don't mean to be valorizing mess, per se. Isn't there a bad infinity of messy, compromised, commonsense, uninteresting poetry? How is value authenticated in poetry?

EXPERTISE, WITNESS, AUTHENTICATION

Intellectual hoaxes dramatize the boundaries of authenticity. Unlike plagiarism and forgeries, which are meant to stay concealed, these hoaxes are constructed to be revealed and then reveal incompetence. It takes an expert to construct a hoax; a hoax targets would-be experts (though others may be fooled); it takes an expert to reveal a hoax. More than a simple lie like a bomb hoax, an intellectual hoax is a guerrilla weapon in a battle of possession of knowledge.

But in poetry, where knowledge and imagination have been fencing for millennia, knowledge and expertise remain elemental Gordian knots. Thus, while there have been poetry hoaxes, at least in some empirical sense, it's an awkward point that the poetry produced in these hoaxes is as legible as any other poetry. In fact, in the case of "Ern Malley," where the poetry was meant to be nonsense, the resulting poems now seem more interesting than the serious poetry of the poets who constructed the hoax.[32] Reading Ern Malley no longer elicits the hoax-cry: "Can you believe someone took this seriously?" A hoax poem is a highly unstable form. There have been hoax poets, but it seems there can't ultimately be hoax poems. Then again, if hoax poetry can't be differentiated from other poetry, doesn't that imply that all poetry is something of a hoax? Sidney's defense of poetry, that the poet "nothing affirms, and therefore never lieth," could easily be cited in support of such a dismissal of poetry's claims to authenticity.

Here I want to consider an interesting recent (1997) example: the Yasusada affair, or hoax, depending on how you want to parse it. It is in marked contrast with two closely contemporaneous events: the debates over the Smithsonian's Enola Gay presentation and Alan Sokal's pseudoscientific essay, "Transgressing the Boundaries: Toward a Transformative Hermeneutics of Quantum Gravity," that hoaxed the editors of *Social Text*.[33] Tapping into widespread anger and angst over perceived postmodern assaults on certainty, the Sokal hoax reverberated through academia and beyond to the op-ed pages of the *New York Times*; Yasusada reached the front page of the Japanese equivalent, *Asahi Shimbun*. But the parallel stops there: the Sokal hoax stayed a hoax while for many critics and poets the Yasusada poems mutated into something at least semiauthentic. In the Smithsonian/Enola Gay wrangles the politics of history was clear, with the strength of different constituencies measurable by what could or couldn't be included in an exhibition marking the fiftieth anniversary of Hiroshima. In contrast, the question of the historical validity of a Yasusada poem dispersed into questions of imaginative sympathy and poetic license.

A basic polemical joke of Sokal's "Transgressing the Boundaries" is that time and space are no longer binding categories: "The key point is that this invariance group [involving the Einstein field equation $G\mu v = 8\pi GT\mu v$] 'acts transitively': . . . any space-time point, if it exists at all, can be transformed into any other. . . . The infinite-dimensional invariance group erodes the distinction between observer and observed; the p of Euclid and the G of Newton, formerly thought to be constant and universal, are now perceived in their ineluctable historicity." Later we learn that "the key property of quantum mechanics is precisely its *nonlocality*."

This is the first half of a polemical pedagogy addressing two groups: a coterie, the targets of the hoax; and general readers. At first, the coterie is the advanced group: they may not be able to make much of $G\mu v = 8\pi GT\mu v$, but they do know that it's interesting when long-accepted constants are shown "in their ineluctable historicity." After the second step—Sokal's revelation that the science was bogus—the general readers have become the advanced group, with the coterie now the remedial class. Common sense has been confirmed: the general reader has already ("always already," as the saying goes) passed the test. The incomprehension provoked by "$G\mu v = 8\pi GT\mu v$" and by the equally strange "ineluctable historicity" is the correct answer. The lesson for the coterie is less pleasant: transgressing the boundaries of your discipline is wrong, using words outside your training is foolish. It is akin to the bitter precept presented to the Poky Little Puppy: if you dig under the fence, you won't get back in time for strawberry shortcake. Time and space, especially social time and social space, are quite real: you belong inside the fence, not outside; dessert occurs uniquely in time and space, so once you miss it, it's gone.

The hoax's teaching stops at this point. It does not teach topology or quantum mechanics, only that these concepts are out of the reach of mere citation. A sphere of specialized knowledge is defended against illegitimate experts, with common sense the ultimate court of appeal. Sokal worked both sides of the expertise boundary: as a physicist, his scientific howlers were real howlers; but getting his nonexpert theory-babble published also scored hoax points. Physics was knowledge, requiring an expert to draw the line between significance and nonsense; but apparently anyone could pretend to write theory.

No experts were dethroned nor were any lines sharply drawn by the ambiguous rhetorical address of the Yasusada affair. To give a quick synopsis of the story: notebooks of a hitherto-unknown and now deceased poet, Araki Yasusada, surfaced in 1996, translated into idiomatic English but containing many indications of Japanese provenance. The work was accompanied by an unusual narrative, provided by the translators: Yasusada was a *hibakusha,* a survivor of the A-bomb at Hiroshima; but his disjunctive poems were unlike those of other survivors. Late in life he had enthusiastically discovered Roland Barthes and Jack Spicer, displaying an appetite for poetic experiment and theory that placed him on the innovative side of the divide between language and self (or text and experience; or defamiliarization and communication). Such tension goes back at least to Mallarmé and Swinburne, but the emergence of the language movement in the 1970s had re-promoted it into a basic polemic structuring the English-speaking poetic field. After almost three decades, the binary still has enough inertia to be self-replicating, having less to do with specific poems or poets than with creating differentiated areas. A critic still needn't have read any Language writing to decry it as theory-driven, mechanistic, antipoetic.[34] But as a *hibakusha* Yasusada had full rights on either side of the divide. His poetry was innovative, but it was also the quintessential "poetry of witness," to use Carolyn Forché's term for work produced by "significant poets who endured conditions of historical and social extremity during the twentieth century."[35] Poems of witness themselves bear "the trace of extremity within them, and . . . are, as such, evidence of what occurred."[36] If Hiroshima wasn't a historical extreme, what was? Yasusada's wife and one daughter were killed instantly, according to the translators' notes; another daughter died from radiation four years later; Yasusada himself died of cancer in 1972.

Mad Daughter and Big-Bang

December 25, 1945*

> Walking in the vegetable patch
> late at night, I was startled to find
> the severed head of my
> mad daughter lying on the ground.
>
> Her eyes were upturned, gazing at me, ecstatic-like
> . . .
>
> (From a distance it had appeared
> to be a stone, haloed with light,
> as if cast there by the Big-Bang).
>
> What on earth are you doing, I said,
> you look ridiculous.
> Some boys buried me here,
> she said sullenly.
>
> Her dark hair, comet-like, trailed behind . . .
>
> Squatting, I pulled the
> turnip up by the root.

> * [*In the aftermath of the bombing, many survivors moved into the foothills of the Chugoku mountains surrounding Hiroshima. This was the case with Yasusada and his daughter.*][37]

The translators' note, its bureaucratic prose undergirding the extremity of Hiroshima, is a crucial frame. Forché's introduction to *Against Forgetting*, her anthol-

ogy of poetry of witness, begins with a similar gesture, quoting "the coroner's report for corpse #12": "Cause of death: shot in the nape. In the back pocket of the trousers a small notebook was found soaked in the fluids of the body and blackened by wet earth. This was cleaned and dried in the sun."[38] The notebook contained the last poems of the Hungarian poet Miklós Radnóti. His death, unlike Yasusada's, was real, but the same rhetorical structure governs both accounts. The poetry of witness involves two witnesses: the prose historian, bureaucrat, attesting to the authenticity of the poet-witness. Read without its note, the Yasusada poem could be a dream, or a small narrative meditation inflected toward surrealism, tinged with astronomical imagery; the note reframes it as tragedy. (In any case, the final line break, "the / turnip," is pure Williams.)

Yasusada's amalgamation of poetic antagonisms was interesting to many, and his poems were accepted by a wider range of magazines than was usually open to one poet. What followed was more interesting: rumors that there was no Yasusada. A consensus soon emerged that the author was Kent Johnson, a contemporary American translator and poet. Wesleyan University Press quickly dropped publication plans; but the results of Yasusada's nonexistence were quite publishable, and within a year Roof Books issued *Doubled Flowering*. This volume gathered the now-pseudographic writing; some initial reaction (for the editor Arthur Vogelsang, it was "essentially a criminal act";[39] for John Solt, translator of Japanese poetry, it was "Japanesed crap"[40]); and an overview by Marjorie Perloff, who showed how careful reading might easily have revealed some of the historical impossibilities involved: there were no scuba divers before World War II; in 1925 there was no Hiroshima University for Yasusada to have attended, and so on.[41]

Ron Silliman's prehoax comments on Yasusada are those of an expert: "There's an elevation in tone . . . that reminds me more of Michael Palmer than Spicer, perhaps because the translators are all Hiroshima poets (one of whom seems to spend half of each year in Sebastopol). . . . These works kept me up last night and probably will again."[42] The contrast with the Sokal hoax is marked: far from having his authority diminished by having placed his detailed poetic knowledge in enthusiastic service of the supposedly Japanese poems, Silliman furnishes a posthoax blurb for *Doubled Flowering* in which he agrees with Perloff: "The 'scandal' of these poems lies not in the problematics of authorship, identity, persona, race or history. . . . This book makes the argument for anti-essentialism. That it has done it so well infuriates folks with a proprietary interest in categories. Thank you, Araki Yasusada!"

In one sense there are no boundaries to transgress here: at least the boundaries of time, place, and identity are fully porous. But within the literary field the boundary separating innovative from noninnovative was monitored carefully. Transgressing the boundaries of identity, narration, and emotional scripting was fully consonant with staying within the territory of innovative poetry.

What has happened to the notion of hoax? The issues of expertise and knowledge, so sharply bounded in the Sokal hoax, are fuzzy here. Knowledge of Japanese poetry, not to mention the experiences of a *hibakusha,* don't seem crucial. Nor are there are simple criteria of contemporary poetic mastery: they can only be judged in poetic context. Gestures an untrained reader might find outrageously incompetent often occur in the work of the sophisticated writers. Two examples from celebrated innovative poets:

The goop / is like mulberry soup

The Great Wall of China is really a thrill
It cleaves through the air like a silver pill

It was built by the hand of man for good or ill
Showing what he can do when he decides not to kill

The fact of authorship, of innovative provenance, is crucial in literary judgment. To one who knows Jack Spicer's work, "goop" sounds its despairing, jokey chord. Ashbery's readers know that the clunkiness of these lines is just another example of his wide formal repertoire. By authenticating Johnson's authorship, Perloff and Silliman grant him a place within the antimainstream arena where judgments such as Solt's "Japanesed crap" are no longer relevant. Either this now is textbook antiessentialism or, viewed as an act of "imaginative sympathy" (which is how Kent Johnson characterized *Doubled Flowering* at a panel, without acknowledging authorship), "Yasusada" becomes a poetic device associated with the tradition (going back at least to Whistler) of American innovative artists not letting lack of knowledge derail their enthusiastic engagement with Asia. Pound's *Cathay* and Noh translations are notable positive results.

Another piece, which I'll now say was written by Johnson, not Yasusada, runs as follows:

[*undated*]*

two daikons

three rice cakes

one [*blotted by crease. eds.*] seaweed packet

4 crane eggs

empress oil chrysanthemum root best rice

Bear yourself with a serious air through the labyrinth of the market. Feign to ignore the [blotted by crease, eds.] spirit medium of plum-coloured lips

American cologne

* [*Despite the curious interjection, this appears to be a shopping list. It was found in one of the notebooks, folded into an origami bird.*][43]

Read inside the innovative frame, the translators' fictional authentication that this page is witness to Hiroshima becomes an authentic poetic element in a context where fragmented poetic utterance and shopping lists are both poetry. Such poetic intention is very clear at the end of the book, as *Doubled Flowering* ends with a slightly modified pastiche of the ending of Spicer's *After Lorca:* The penultimate "Yasusada" piece begins, "Dear Spicer, This is the last letter";[44] the last letter in Spicer's *After Lorca,* "Dear Lorca, This is the last letter."[45] Such literariness makes it easier to hear in this excerpt an echo of Williams's interview with Mike Wallace in book 5 of **Paterson**:

Q: . . . here's part of a poem you yourself have written: . . . "2 partridges / 2 mallard ducks / a Dungeness crab / 24 hours out / of the Pacific / and 2 live-frozen / trout/ from Denmark . . ." Now, that sounds just like a fashionable grocery list!

A: It is a fashionable grocery list.

Q: Well—is it poetry?[46]

POETIC NEWS

It is poetry. Why? Because it's in a poem, and the interviews, letters, and historical documents in **Paterson** are also poetry, as is the asterisk-ringed SODA transfixing **"The Attic Which Is Desire."** No list of poetic innovation can be at all fashionable if it doesn't include the pastiche we find in countless passages in *The Cantos,* just about any line in a Moore poem, Ginsberg's citations of newspapers and radio in "Wichita Vortex Sutra." As Williams says to Mike Wallace, "Poetry can be made out of anything." He cites the musical verve of speech, which lifts it out of the quotidian: "If you treat [it] rhythmically, ignoring the practical sense it forms a jagged pattern. It is, to my mind, poetry." Modernist framing easily incorporates social noise and historical marks. But when poetry moves outside its frame, the result is impropriety if not scandal: from Pound's broadcasts and Bollingen upsets to the recent flaps over Baraka's poem and Laura Bush's poetry tea. A basic reaction of supporters or critics is to put a poetic frame back around the whole mess, which, to simplify, is basically what happened with Pound. It has been a constant strategy for over half a century: the former president of Students for a Democratic Society, Bill Ayres, uses it to defend Baraka: "Spreading myths and printing falsehoods may violate the standards of a decent newspaper, but they are the very stuff of poetry, and that's why no one with an ounce of sense goes to Homer or . . . Bob Dylan for the facts."[47]

But **"Asphodel"** does attempt to incorporate fact, most notably the atomic bomb. However, it does so by reducing it to a rumor of cataclysm, which is then made "poetic" with clumsy, poeticized sleight of hand as Williams splits the actual devastation caused by the bomb into "heat" and "light":

> in an eternity
>   the heat will not overtake the light.
>   That's sure.
> That gelds the bomb,
>   permitting
>   that the mind contain it.
> This is that interval,
>   that sweetest interval,
>   when love will blossom,
> come early, come late
>   and give itself to the lover.
>   Only the imagination is real![48]

Decades earlier, the author of *Spring and All* had warned against such stale metaphors: "Crude symbolism is to associate emotions with natural phenomena such as anger with lightning, flowers with love."[49] One of the myriad descriptions of imagination in *Spring* is apropos:

> Imagination is not to avoid reality, nor is it description nor an evocation of objects or situations, it is to say that poetry does not tamper with the world but moves it—It affirms reality most powerfully and therefore, since reality needs no personal support but exists free from human action, as proven by science in the indestructibility of matter and of force, it creates a new object, play, a dance which is not a mirror up to nature, but—[50]

In **"Asphodel"** the unscriptable force of the bomb flattens this to a brittle assertion: "Only the imagination is real!"

I realize that in criticizing **"Asphodel"** for its handling of the bomb, I'm sliding from poetic to historical news, and thus I could be said to frame the issue in Zhdanovian terms, where the utterly superstructural poem must be judged by how well it matches a prescribed real world. Such show trials are not of the slightest use. But an opposite conclusion where the poem is detached from referential demands employs a similar Zhdanovian binary, separating the spheres instead of forcing them together. Nor will splitting the difference between these two positions find some semireferential middle ground where the structures of news and poetry can be durably reconciled: they're incommensurate.

The news, both external and poetic, in Williams's own poems is often contradictory, garbled, or imaginary— here, for instance, the "sweetest interval" in **"Asphodel"** merely names aesthetic autonomy.

CANDOR

But the social and poetic candor of Williams's writing as a whole remains something to learn from. The word *candor* comes from Allen Ginsberg, who used it increasingly in his last years as a capsule description of his poetics, ethics, and politics—three aspects of what he intended as a unified activity. For him, candor revealed the unfallen body; enacted the healthy, spontaneous mind; and, by extension, would eventually reveal and enact world liberation, political, spiritual, sexual. He wasn't naive about the difficulties involved, but he was optimistic.

Williams's candor is more contradictory, revealing his limited and often problematic social personhood (doctor; husband; philanderer; father; atheist; more or less avant-garde poet, privately enthusiastic, publicly obscure and frustrated), his subject position (male; American; white but non-WASP; heterosexual; middle-class), his place in history (the Model T; the telephone; the typewriter; world wars), and in space (hometown; Nowheresville, New Jersey, but with New York City nearby). A real person is writing: "real" and "person" in all their theoretical clumsiness and shame. But this does not make Williams himself the privileged core of the poetry: knowing the life is not a prerequisite for reading the poems, nor is what the poems reveal the life of the person Williams.

Williams's social candor means simply that his writing never hides any of his social coordinates. These coordinates are not static; they intersect ceaselessly with the positions of many others. Williams's hourly social mobility as a doctor was clearly a benefit here; and the poems present a much more focused and interactive social existence than is the case with Whitman's enthusiastic spectating: "I behold the picturesque giant and love him"—society and nature were equally picturesque for Whitman. Compare Williams:

> Doc, listen—fiftyish, a grimy hand
> pushing back the cap: In gold—
> Volunteers of America
>
> I got
> a woman outside I want to marry, will
> you give her a blood test?[51]

But accuracy of registration is something of an intermittent by-product of Williams's poetic candor.

Again, a contrast with Ginsberg will be useful. Ginsberg's candor meant fidelity to the body at the moment of composition: "first thought, best thought." Since, as another of his slogans has it, "mind is shapely," such discipline would ensure that the poem would be shapely as well. Williams's compositional methods are not completely different, to be sure, since improvisation marks much of his work; but his attention is given primarily to the poem, which neither is an unaltered record of process nor does it preexist as any kind of template or received form. Poetic candor means that

Williams is constantly working on, witnessing, and adjusting the form of the poem as he writes it. Such is the case whether the time of writing is a single period of two minutes between patients or a series of stops and starts over years as with *Paterson.* The results are valuable beyond conventional standards of articulation and coherence or innovative standards of unpredictable language. They are a bit out of focus from either perspective, which is why Williams is so widely acknowledged but not all that deeply respected. His work, even in *Spring and All,* was never purely new. The sheen of newness was always scuffed by the poems' contact with social space. A small poem from the early 1940s, **"Details for Patterson,"** can illustrate. This poem seems to have been cobbled together from Williams's manuscript *Detail and Parody for the Poem Paterson* (1939), where versions of the first two stanzas comprise a poem, and the third and fifth stanzas stand as two separate poems. These pieces, less interesting when separated, combine into an odd whole.

"I just saw two boys." Not a very prepossessing opening. It seems unexceptional to think that the "I" represents the poet. "One of them gets paid for distributing circulars": a scrap of realism; but adding "and he throws it down the sewer," with the singular "it" not matching the plural "circulars," reframes this as a quoted voice, not Williams's. But it won't help to take Williams's suggestion in the Mike Wallace interview and treat this rhythmically, ignoring the practical sense so that it becomes "poetry." This is leaden language which the described action mimes. Printed matter, circulars, are waste. They might be the newsprint Pound so loathes in the Hell Cantos; they might be small press books: print on paper—dreck. But speech is not the answer here; it is certainly not presented as the valorized solution.

The speaker continues with the tiny story: "I said, Are you a Boy Scout? / He said, no. / The other one was." For me the salient feature of this is the glacial clumsiness, capped off with the bizarreness of a received idea decayed into unfamiliarity. "I have implicit faith in / the Boy Scouts."[52]

"If you talk about it / long enough / you'll finally write it—/ If you get by the stage / when nothing / can make you write—If you don't die first." With no transition, this new voice has a querulous urgency, which I take as the poet berating himself. But the boundaries of person are oddly fluid. It wasn't the poet who was talking, but the Boy Scout admirer. But then again it wasn't the Boy Scout admirer who was working up the courage to finally write. I can't keep the speakers of these first two parts completely separate; but the poet's melodramatic consideration of death at the end of the stanza feels like some overblown but not utterly false reaction to the linguistic gloom of the opening stanza. If *those* are your

social materials, do you really want to write? But then again, what better to do with such stuff than to try to make a poem, active and unpredictable, of it?

"I keep those bests that love / has given me / Nothing of them escapes—" Out in Paterson spoken and printed words go down the sewer. In the poet's mind, the gifts of love are held onto tightly, too rightly to permit any retroactive description of them. The next lines continue the passionate tautness, but what are they saying? "I have proved it"—proved what? That none of love's bests have escaped you? Who did you have to prove this to? The voice insists further, "proven once more in your eyes." The vocabulary and tone are self-consistent in the stanza, but the rhetorical, emotional, situational dynamics are as mysterious as anything in Ashbery, at least to me. "Proven once more," as if another emotional test has been passed, but what test? What was the first one? "Your eyes" belong to the beloved, presumably; though they could also be the reader's.[53] In either case, the relation is odd: the lover keeps the ecstasy of love locked tightly away inside and yet asks for confirmation from the beloved.

I don't sense any attempt here to construct a mystery or a Rube Goldberg machine. What is so incommensurate and irresolvable here has to do with candid verbal registration and a kind of free-floating flickering negative capability that's closer to Jameson's cognitive mapping than Keats's beautiful empathy. Here speech, mimetic depiction of banality, internal didactic rant, and stumbling approaches to more illuminated states of mind are all granted equal access to the page.

There is also compositional force making the best of these materials. As the stanzas follow one another, each makes something different and a little more active out of what has come before.

In the last stanza, who says "Go marry!" to whom? Is the poet speaking to himself? "Go marry! your son will have / blue eyes and and still / there'll be no answer / you have not found a cure."

This is one of the ways that Williams insists on the value of what emerges in successive stanzas moment by moment. The poem is made of "historic and contemporary particulars," but they're not "objectively perfect," nor are they moving inextricably in the single proper historical direction. This is not the new in the midst of some mysterious virgin auto-reproduction. It is [underline "is"] a new poem, made out of materials heavy with the inertia of an unredeemed history. It cures nothing. The blue-eyed son is not a poem; nor is the poem some miraculous offspring.

The last lines start with an odd simulacrum of conversation, although the you and the I seem to refer to the same person: "No more have I for that enormous / wedged flower, my mind / miraculously upon / the dead stick of night."

The American idiom? I suppose, but it's stirred around so much that most of this can't be called idiomatic. Williams the materialist, no ideas but in things? With that miraculous, socially wedged flower for a writing mind? Hardly. Then what? If we try to paraphrase what is being said—and paraphrase often remains a usefully heretical act—then the question is: What is the problem for this "I," i.e., Williams? What is he failing to find a cure for?

Apparently, it's his writing mind: "for that enormous / wedged flower, my mind / miraculously upon / the dead stick of night." Having the writing mind be something that needs a cure is admitting a powerfully traumatic defeat.

In a complex twist, however, Williams is admitting defeat precisely when his process of composition—which seems to have stretched intermittently over a period of years—finally reflects a little inspiration.

The motion of the poem is various, unpredictable; and the more closely it's read, the more surprising it is.

Notes

1. William Carlos Williams, "Asphodel, That Greeny Flower," in *The Collected Poems of William Carlos Williams,* 2 vols.; vol. 1, ed. A. Walton Litz and Christopher MacGowan; vol. 2, ed. Christopher MacGowan (New York: New Directions, 1988), 2:318.

2. Ezra Pound, *ABC of Reading* (New York: New Directions, 1960), 29.

3. As I write, the events are familiar to those in the United States, but as the half-life of any public memory is getting shorter and shorter, I include them here. In the fall of 2002, Amiri Baraka's "Somebody Blew Up America" caused a storm when he read it publicly. Among its many pungent polemical thrusts, the item that caused the outcry was the suggestion that the Israeli government had had advance knowledge of the September 11, 2001, terrorist attacks on the United States. The problem, commentators and politicians kept repeating, was not the poem—they all granted Baraka freedom of expression—but that he read it in his capacity as poet laureate of New Jersey: taxpayers mustn't be forced to finance such poems. In the spring of 2003, Laura Bush's poetry afternoon at the White House was canceled due to administration worries over the possibility of the invited poets making leftist political statements. The cancellation created much more publicity, of course, which helped create Web sites, readings, and anthologies of poems protesting the Iraq war.

4. Kate Farrell, letter to the editor, *New York Times,* February 12, 2003, A36; Margo Jefferson, "The News from Poetry," *New York Times Book Review,* May 11, 2003, 27.

5. Williams, "The Clouds," in *Collected Poems,* 2:171.

6. Pound to Williams in 1917: "You thank your bloomin gawd you've got enough Spanish blood to muddy up your mind. . . . The thing that saves your work is *opacity,* and don't you forget it" (*Selected Letters of Ezra Pound and William Carlos Williams,* ed. Hugh Witemeyer [New York: New Directions, 1996], 124). In his 1928 review, "Dr. Williams's Position," *Dial* 85, no. 5 (November 1928): 395-404, Pound describes Williams's work as "opaque, obscure, obfuscated, confused, truncated," qualities which become signs of intellectual honesty given the situation confronting the writer in the United States. While "art" may be "the supreme achievement," Williams's work furnishes "the other satisfactory effect, that of a man hurling himself at an indomitable chaos, and yanking and hauling as much of it as possible into some sort of order (or beauty), aware of it both as chaos and as potential" (*The Selected Letters of William Carlos Williams,* ed. John C. Thirlwall [New York: New Directions, 1957], 394-96).

7. Pound, *ABC of Reading,* 37.

8. It is generally agreed that the Homeric poems coalesced out of oral performance and that by the latter sixth century B.C. they had been transcribed in a form that resembles what we read today. (Details of the transition from oral to written are far from settled.) But although the Homeric poems had existed in written form for over a century by the time Plato wrote the *Ion,* they and other poems functioned orally. "Homer may, for convenience, be taken as the last representative of the purely oral composition. . . . It is certain that all his poet successors were writers. But it is equally certain that they always wrote for recitation and for listeners." Eric Havelock, *Preface to Plato* (Cambridge, Mass.: Harvard University Press, 1982), 46.

9. Williams, "Asphodel," in *Collected Poems,* 2:315.

10. Plato, *Ion,* trans. Lane Cooper, in *Plato: The Collected Dialogues,* ed. Edith Hamilton and Hunting-

POETRY CRITICISM, Vol. 109

WILLIAMS

ton Cairns, Bollingen Series 71 (Princeton, N.J.: Princeton University Press, 1963), 536c.

11. Plato, *Ion,* 222.

12. Williams, "Asphodel," in *Collected Poems,* 2:325.

13. *King Lear,* ed. Jay L. Halio (Cambridge: Cambridge University Press, 1992), act 2, scene 4, lines 273-74.

14. Geoff Ward, *Statutes of Liberty: The New York School of Poets* (London: Palgrave, 1993), 55: "To Williams, the task . . . was to demystify, to purge writing of metaphysics, and celebrate what actually impinges on the senses as the sum total of what is. To enable the reader to see as if for the first time becomes the aim, but Williams failed to see (or did see, and didn't care) that such a recourse to origin, to a primary moment of authentic perception, is nothing if not metaphysical."

15. Charles Bernstein, *Content's Dream* (Los Angeles: Sun and Moon Press, 1986), 247-48: "The Academy in Peril: William Carlos Williams Meets the MLA." This is the first place that Bernstein articulates the influential concept of "official verse culture": "the poetry publishing and reviewing practices" of magazines such as *Parnassus,* the *New Yorker, American Poetry Review,* etc., and academic presses; the hiring practices of university writing and literature programs; "the interlocking accreditation" of judges giving each other awards; and "the self-appointed keepers of the gate who actively put forward biased . . . accounts of American poetry, while claiming, like all disinformation propaganda, to be giving . . . non-partisan views."

16. Robert Pinsky, *Poetry and the World* (Hopewell, N.J.: Ecco Press, 1988), 18-19.

17. For three decades, this boundary has been the site of charged debate. More recently, the rise of identity poetries has established perspectives from which Pinsky and Bernstein would seem quite close: both are white, male, hetero, somewhat Jewish-identified, intellectual spokesmen for poetry. For discussion of "official verse culture," see Bernstein, *Content's Dream,* 247-51.

18. Stendhal, *Racine and Shakespeare,* trans. Guy Daniels (New York: Crowell-Collier Press, 1962), 145.

19. Charles Baudelaire, "The Painter of Modern Life," in *Art in Theory, 1815-1900,* ed. Charles Harrison and Paul Wood with Jason Gaiger (London: Blackwell, 1998), 497.

20. Louis Zukofsky, *"A"* (Berkeley and Los Angeles: University of California Press, 1978), 24.

21. T. S. Eliot, *The Complete Poems and Plays 1909-1950* (New York: Harcourt Brace Jovanovich, 1971), 5.

22. Ibid., 4.

23. Steve Benson, Carla Harryman, Lyn Hejinian, Bob Perelman, Ron Silliman, and Barrett Watten, "Aesthetic Tendency and the Politics of Poetry: A Manifesto," *Social Text* 19/20 (Fall 1988): 261-75.

24. Ibid., 271. Though the piece was printed as "Aesthetic Tendency and the Politics of Poetry: A Manifesto," the magazine's editors added the designation "Manifesto" without consulting us.

25. Steve Evans, "The Resistible Rise of Fence Enterprises," http://third-factory.net/resistible.html, 8.

26. Ibid., 1.

27. Ibid., 8.

28. Ibid., 1-3.

29. Ibid., 6-9.

30. Jack Spicer, *The House That Jack Built: The Collected Lectures of Jack Spicer,* ed. Peter Gizzi (Middletown, Conn.: Wesleyan University Press, 1998), 167.

31. "It is a nation of nothing but poetry . . ." in *The Collected Poems of Charles Olson,* ed. George F. Butterick (Berkeley and Los Angeles: University of California Press, 1987), 562.

32. See Michael Heyward, *The Ern Malley Affair* (London: Faber and Faber, 1993).

33. Alan Sokal, "Transgressing the Boundaries: Toward a Transformative Hermeneutics of Quantum Gravity," in *Fashionable Nonsense: Postmodern Intellectuals' Abuse of Science,* by Alan Sokal and Jean Bricmont (New York: Picador USA, 1998).

34. There are still numerous instances of this opposition. For instance, in an interview with Robert Pinsky in the Winter 2002 issue of *Barrow Street,* Daniela Gioseffi observes, "The language school of poetry seems to be about art for art's sake; and the abstract or action poetry schools, or the New

339

York School, a sort of laid-back observation on the poet's experience" (77; cited in a post from Tom Fink to Ron Silliman's Web log: http://ronsilliman.blogspot.com/2003_02_01_ron silliman_archive.html). The designations may seem quite blurry, but the basic choice between Art and Life remains constant.

35. Carolyn Forché, introduction to *Against Forgetting: Twentieth-Century Poetry of Witness,* ed. Carolyn Forché (New York: Norton, 1993), 29.

36. Ibid., 30.

37. Ariki Yasusada, *Doubled Flowering: From The Notebooks of Ariki Yasusada* (New York: Roof Press, 1997), 11.

38. Forché, *Against Forgetting,* 29.

39. Yasusada, *Doubled Flowering,* 130.

40. Ibid., 131.

41. Marjorie Perloff, "In Search of the Authentic Other: The Poetry of Araki Yasusada," in Yasusada, *Doubled Flowering,* 148-68.

42. Ibid., 149.

43. Yasusada, *Doubled Flowering,* 26.

44. Ibid., 117.

45. Jack Spicer, *The House That Jack Built,* 51.

46. William Carlos Williams, *Paterson,* rev. ed. prepared by Christopher MacGowan (New York: New Directions, 1992), 222.

47. *New York Times,* October 5, 2002, A26.

48. Williams, *Collected Poems,* 2:334.

49. Ibid., 1:188.

50. Ibid., 234-35.

51. Williams, *Paterson,* 103.

52. Williams, *Collected Poems,* 2:24.

53. Elsewhere, Williams does address the reader erotically, with an indeterminate amount of irony: "In the imagination, we are henceforth (so long as you read) locked in a fraternal embrace, the classic caress of author and reader. We are one. Whenever I say 'I' I mean also 'you.' And so, together, as one, we shall begin" (*Collected Poems,* 1:78).

FURTHER READING

Criticism

Coles, Robert. "Dr. William Carlos Williams: Affection, Anger, and their Discontents." *Literary Imagination* 2, no. 1 (winter 2000): 23-30.

> Recounts his own discussions with Williams covering topics including the poet's practice of medicine and the psycho-therapeutic value of the stories of Anton Chekhov.

Crawford, T. Hugh. "Williams and the Bomb: The Great Destroyer or the Magic Bullet?" *William Carlos Williams Review* 25, no. 1 (spring 2005): 27-42.

> Examines the contradictions in Williams's attitude toward the nuclear age.

Dennison, Julie. "Williams and H. D. Figure It Out: Reconceiving the Childbirth Metaphor in 'His' *Paterson,* 'Her' *Trilogy.*" *Paideuma* 33, nos. 2-3 (fall and winter 2004): 223-45.

> Discusses *Paterson* and H. D.'s *Trilogy* as textual challenges to the use of the childbirth metaphor and its association with patriarchal appropriation of procreation as creativity.

Golston, Michael. "Weathered Measures and Measured Weathers: W. C. Williams and the Allegorical Ends of Rhythm." *Textual Practice* 18, no. 2 (2004): 251-64.

> Discusses the ramifications of Williams's efforts to break the link between measure and rhythm—with respect to ideology and to the poet's relationship to developments in contemporary science—and discusses Williams's influence on later postmodern poetry.

Johnson, Bob. "'A Whole Synthesis of His Time': Political Ideology and Cultural Politics in the Writings of William Carlos Williams, 1929-1939." *American Quarterly* 54, no. 2 (June 2002): 179-215.

> Discusses Williams's position with respect to politics and literary culture through the Depression era, with reference to his fiction, criticism, and poetry.

Mikkelsen, Ann. "'The Truth about Us': Pastoral, Pragmatism, and *Paterson.*" *American Literature* 75, no. 3 (September 2003): 601-27.

> Discusses the themes of dirt, foulness, and unblinking realism in the multi-volume poem *Paterson,* and ultimately judges Williams successful in forging a form of pastoral appropriate to the twentieth century and to the New World.

Young, David. "William Carlos Williams Writes 'January Morning.'" In *Six Modernist Moments in Poetry*, pp. 68-90. Iowa City, Iowa: University of Iowa Press, 2006.

Presents a detailed analysis of Williams's 1917 poem, "January Morning," and argues that the writing of the poem should be seen as a key moment in the development of literary modernism.

Additional coverage of Williams's life and career is contained in the following sources published by Gale: *American Writers*; *American Writers Retrospective Supplement*, Vol. 1; *Authors and Artists for Young Adults*, Vol. 46; *Concise Dictionary of American Literary Biography, 1917-1929*; *Contemporary Authors*, Vols. 89-92; *Contemporary Authors New Revision Series*, Vol. 34; *Contemporary Literary Criticism*, Vols. 1, 2, 5, 9, 13, 22, 42, 67; *Dictionary of Literary Biography*, Vols. 4, 16, 54, 86; *Discovering Authors*; *Discovering Authors 3.0*; *Discovering Authors: British*; *Discovering Authors: Canadian Edition*; *Discovering Authors Modules: Most-studied Authors* and *Poets*; *Encyclopedia of World Literature in the 20th Century*, Ed. 3; *Exploring Poetry*; *Literature Resource Center*; *Major 20th-Century Writers*, Ed. 1, 2; *Major 21st-Century Writers* (eBook), 2005; *Modern American Literature*, Ed. 5; *Nonfiction Classics for Students*, Vol. 4; *Poetry Criticism*, Vol. 7; *Poetry for Students*, Vols. 1, 6, 11; *Poets: American and British*; *Reference Guide to American Literature*, Ed. 4; *Reference Guide to Short Fiction*, Ed. 2; *Short Stories for Students*, Vol. 27; *Short Story Criticism*, Vol. 31; *Twayne's United States Authors*; *World Literature Criticism*, Ed. 6; and *World Poets*.

How to Use This Index

> **Calvino, Italo**
> 1923-1985 .... **CLC 5, 8, 11, 22, 33, 39,**
> **73; SSC 3, 48**

list all author entries in the following Gale Literary Criticism series:

AAL = Asian American Literature
BG = The Beat Generation: A Gale Critical Companion
BLC = Black Literature Criticism
BLCS = Black Literature Criticism Supplement
CLC = Contemporary Literary Criticism
CLR = Children's Literature Review
CMLC − Classical and Medieval Literature Criticism
DC = Drama Criticism
FL = Feminism in Literature: A Gale Critical Companion
GL = Gothic Literature: A Gale Critical Companion
HLC = Hispanic Literature Criticism
HLCS = Hispanic Literature Criticism Supplement
HR = Harlem Renaissance: A Gale Critical Companion
LC = Literature Criticism from 1400 to 1800
NCLC = Nineteenth-Century Literature Criticism
NNAL − Native North American Literature
PC = Poetry Criticism
SSC = Short Story Criticism
TCLC = Twentieth-Century Literary Criticism
WLC = World Literature Criticism, 1500 to the Present
WLCS = World Literature Criticism Supplement

The cross-references

> See also CA 85-88, 116; CANR 23, 61;
> DAM NOV; DLB 196; EW 13; MTCW 1, 2;
> RGSF 2; RGWL 2; SFW 4; SSFS 12

list all author entries in the following Gale biographical and literary sources:

AAYA = Authors & Artists for Young Adults
AFAW = African American Writers
AFW = African Writers
AITN = Authors in the News
AMW = American Writers
AMWR = American Writers Retrospective Supplement
AMWS = American Writers Supplement
ANW = American Nature Writers
AW = Ancient Writers
BEST = Bestsellers
BPFB = Beacham's Encyclopedia of Popular Fiction: Biography and Resources
BRW = British Writers
BRWS = British Writers Supplement
BW = Black Writers
BYA = Beacham's Guide to Literature for Young Adults
CA = Contemporary Authors
CAAS = Contemporary Authors Autobiography Series
CABS = Contemporary Authors Bibliographical Series
CAD = Contemporary American Dramatists
CANR = Contemporary Authors New Revision Series
CAP = Contemporary Authors Permanent Series
CBD = Contemporary British Dramatists
CCA = Contemporary Canadian Authors
CD = Contemporary Dramatists
CDALB = Concise Dictionary of American Literary Biography

CDALBS = *Concise Dictionary of American Literary Biography Supplement*

CDBLB = *Concise Dictionary of British Literary Biography*

CMW = *St. James Guide to Crime & Mystery Writers*

CN = *Contemporary Novelists*

CP = *Contemporary Poets*

CPW = *Contemporary Popular Writers*

CSW = *Contemporary Southern Writers*

CWD = *Contemporary Women Dramatists*

CWP = *Contemporary Women Poets*

CWRI = *St. James Guide to Children's Writers*

CWW = *Contemporary World Writers*

DA = *DISCovering Authors*

DA3 = *DISCovering Authors 3.0*

DAB = *DISCovering Authors: British Edition*

DAC = *DISCovering Authors: Canadian Edition*

DAM = *DISCovering Authors: Modules*

   DRAM: *Dramatists Module;* **MST:** *Most-studied Authors Module;*

   MULT: *Multicultural Authors Module;* **NOV:** *Novelists Module;*

   POET: *Poets Module;* **POP:** *Popular Fiction and Genre Authors Module*

DFS = *Drama for Students*

DLB = *Dictionary of Literary Biography*

DLBD = *Dictionary of Literary Biography Documentary Series*

DLBY = *Dictionary of Literary Biography Yearbook*

DNFS = *Literature of Developing Nations for Students*

EFS = *Epics for Students*

EW = *European Writers*

EWL = *Encyclopedia of World Literature in the 20th Century*

EXPN = *Exploring Novels*

EXPP = *Exploring Poetry*

EXPS = *Exploring Short Stories*

FANT = *St. James Guide to Fantasy Writers*

FW = *Feminist Writers*

GFL = *Guide to French Literature,* Beginnings to 1789, 1798 to the Present

GLL = *Gay and Lesbian Literature*

HGG = *St. James Guide to Horror, Ghost & Gothic Writers*

HW = *Hispanic Writers*

IDFW = *International Dictionary of Films and Filmmakers: Writers and Production Artists*

IDTP = *International Dictionary of Theatre: Playwrights*

LAIT = *Literature and Its Times*

LAW = *Latin American Writers*

JRDA = *Junior DISCovering Authors*

MAICYA = *Major Authors and Illustrators for Children and Young Adults*

MAICYAS = *Major Authors and Illustrators for Children and Young Adults Supplement*

MAWW = *Modern American Women Writers*

MJW = *Modern Japanese Writers*

MTCW = *Major 20th-Century Writers*

NCFS = *Nonfiction Classics for Students*

NFS = *Novels for Students*

PAB = *Poets: American and British*

PFS = *Poetry for Students*

RGAL = *Reference Guide to American Literature*

RGEL = *Reference Guide to English Literature*

RGSF = *Reference Guide to Short Fiction*

RGWL = *Reference Guide to World Literature*

RHW = *Twentieth-Century Romance and Historical Writers*

SAAS = *Something about the Author Autobiography Series*

SATA = *Something about the Author*

SFW = *St. James Guide to Science Fiction Writers*

SSFS = *Short Stories for Students*

TCWW = *Twentieth-Century Western Writers*

WLIT = *World Literature and Its Times*

WP = *World Poets*

YABC = *Yesterday's Authors of Books for Children*

YAW = *St. James Guide to Young Adult Writers*

Literary Criticism Series
Cumulative Author Index

20/1631
See Upward, Allen

A/C Cross
See Lawrence, T. E.

A. M.
See Megged, Aharon

A. Uthor
See Breytenbach, Breyten

Aaron, Sidney
See Chayefsky, Paddy

Abasiyanik, Sait Faik 1906-1954 ... **TCLC 23**
See also CA 123, 231

Abbey, Edward 1927-1989 .... **CLC 36, 59; TCLC 160**
See also AAYA 75; AMWS 13; ANW; CA 45-48; 128; CANR 2, 41, 131; DA3; DLB 256, 275; LATS 1:2; MTCW 2; MTFW 2005; TCWW 1, 2

Abbott, Edwin A. 1838-1926 .... **SSC 135; TCLC 139**
See also DLB 178

Abbott, Lee K(ittredge) 1947- .... **CLC 48**
See also CA 124; CANR 51, 101; DLB 130

Abe, Kobo 1924-1993 ...... **CLC 8, 22, 53, 81; SSC 61; TCLC 131**
See also CA 65-68; 140; CANR 24, 60; DAM NOV; DFS 14; DLB 182; EWL 3; MJW; MTCW 1, 2; MTFW 2005; NFS 22; RGWL 3; SFW 4

Abe Kobo
See Abe, Kobo

Abelard, Peter c. 1079-c. 1142 ..... **CMLC 11, 77**
See also DLB 115, 208

Abell, Kjeld 1901-1961 .... **CLC 15**
See also CA 191; 111; DLB 214; EWL 3

Abercrombie, Lascelles
1881-1938 .... **TCLC 141**
See also BRWS 16; CA 112; DLB 19; RGEL 2

Abhavananda
See Crowley, Edward Alexander

Abish, Walter 1931- ... **CLC 22, 246; SSC 44**
See also CA 101; CANR 37, 114, 153; CN 3, 4, 5, 6; DLB 130, 227; MAL 5; RGHL

Abrahams, Peter (Henry) 1919- .... **CLC 4**
See also AFW; BW 1; CA 57-60; CANR 26, 125; CDWLB 3; CN 1, 2, 3, 4, 5, 6; DLB 117, 225; EWL 3; MTCW 1, 2; RGEL 2; WLIT 2

Abrams, M(eyer) H(oward) 1912- ... **CLC 24**
See also CA 57-60; CANR 13, 33; DLB 67

Abse, Dannie 1923- .. **CLC 7, 29, 266; PC 41**
See also CA 53-56; CAAS 1; CANR 4, 46, 74, 124; CBD; CN 1, 2, 3; CP 1, 2, 3, 4, 5, 6, 7; DAB; DAM POET; DLB 27, 245; MTCW 2

Abutsu 1222(?)-1283 .... **CMLC 46**
See also DLB 203

Abutsu-ni
See Abutsu

Achebe, Albert Chinualumogu
See Achebe, Chinua

Achebe, Chinua 1930- .... **BLC 1:1, 2:1; CLC 1, 3, 5, 7, 11, 26, 51, 75, 127, 152, 272, 278; SSC 105; WLC 1**
See also AAYA 15; AFW; BPFB 1; BRWC 2; BW 2, 3; CA 1-4R; CANR 6, 26, 47, 124; CDWLB 3; CLR 20; CN 1, 2, 3, 4, 5, 6, 7; CP 2, 3, 4, 5, 6, 7; CWRI 5; DA; DA3; DAB; DAC; DAM MST, MULT, NOV; DLB 117; DNFS 1; EWL 3; EXPN; EXPS; LAIT 2; LATS 1:2; MAICYA 1, 2; MTCW 1, 2; MTFW 2005; NFS 2, 33; RGEL 2; RGSF 2; SATA 38, 40; SATA-Brief 38; SSFS 3, 13, 30; TWA; WLIT 2; WWE 1

Acker, Kathy 1948-1997 .... **CLC 45, 111; TCLC 191**
See also AMWS 12; CA 117; 122; 162; CANR 55; CN 5, 6; MAL 5

Ackroyd, Peter 1949- .. **CLC 34, 52, 140, 256**
See also BRWS 6; CA 123; 127; CANR 51, 74, 99, 132, 175; CN 4, 5, 6, 7; DLB 155, 231; HGG; INT CA-127; MTCW 2; MTFW 2005; RHW; SATA 153; SUFW 2

Acorn, Milton 1923-1986 .... **CLC 15**
See also CA 103; CCA 1; CP 1, 2, 3, 4; DAC; DLB 53; INT CA-103

Adam de la Halle c. 1250-c.
1285 .... **CMLC 80**

Adamov, Arthur 1908-1970 .... **CLC 4, 25; TCLC 189**
See also CA 17-18; 25-28R; CAP 2; DAM DRAM; DLB 321; EWL 3; GFL 1789 to the Present; MTCW 1; RGWL 2, 3

Adams, Alice 1926-1999 .... **CLC 6, 13, 46; SSC 24**
See also CA 81-84; 179; CANR 26, 53, 75, 88, 136; CN 4, 5, 6; CSW; DLB 234; DLBY 1986; INT CANR-26; MTCW 1, 2; MTFW 2005; SSFS 14, 21

Adams, Andy 1859-1935 .... **TCLC 56**
See also TCWW 1, 2; YABC 1

Adams, (Henry) Brooks
1848-1927 .... **TCLC 80**
See also CA 123; 193

Adams, Douglas 1952-2001 .... **CLC 27, 60**
See also AAYA 4, 33; BEST 89:3; BYA 14; CA 106; 197; CANR 34, 64, 124; CPW; DA3; DAM POP; DLB 261; DLBY 1983; JRDA; MTCW 2; MTFW 2005; NFS 7; SATA 116; SATA-Obit 128; SFW 4

Adams, Douglas Noel
See Adams, Douglas

Adams, Francis 1862-1893 .... **NCLC 33**

Adams, Henry 1838-1918 .... **TCLC 4, 52**
See also AMW; CA 104; 133; CANR 77; DA; DAB; DAC; DAM MST; DLB 12, 47, 189, 284; EWL 3; MAL 5; MTCW 2; NCFS 1; RGAL 4; TUS

Adams, Henry Brooks
See Adams, Henry

Adams, John 1735-1826 .... **NCLC 106**
See also DLB 31, 183

Adams, John Quincy 1767-1848 .. **NCLC 175**
See also DLB 37

Adams, Mary
See Phelps, Elizabeth Stuart

Adams, Richard 1920- .... **CLC 4, 5, 18**
See also AAYA 16; AITN 1, 2; BPFB 1; BYA 5; CA 49-52; CANR 3, 35, 128; CLR 20, 121; CN 4, 5, 6, 7; DAM NOV; DLB 261; FANT; JRDA; LAIT 5; MAICYA 1, 2; MTCW 1, 2; NFS 11; SATA 7, 69; YAW

Adams, Richard George
See Adams, Richard

Adamson, Joy(-Friederike Victoria)
1910-1980 .... **CLC 17**
See also CA 69-72; 93-96; CANR 22; MTCW 1; SATA 11; SATA-Obit 22

Adcock, Fleur 1934- .... **CLC 41**
See also BRWS 12; CA 25-28R, 182; CAAE 182; CAAS 23; CANR 11, 34, 69, 101; CP 1, 2, 3, 4, 5, 6, 7; CWP; DLB 40; FW; WWE 1

Addams, Charles 1912-1988 .... **CLC 30**
See also CA 61-64; 126; CANR 12, 79

Addams, Charles Samuel
See Addams, Charles

Addams, (Laura) Jane 1860-1935 . **TCLC 76**
See also AMWS 1; CA 194; DLB 303; FW

Addison, Joseph 1672-1719 .... **LC 18, 146**
See also BRW 3; CDBLB 1660-1789; DLB 101; RGEL 2; WLIT 3

Adelard of Bath c. 1070-c. 1150 . **CMLC 119**

Adichie, Chimamanda Ngozi
1977- .... **BLC 2:1**
See also AAYA 80; CA 231

Adiga, Aravind 1974- .... **CLC 280**
See also CA 282

Adler, Alfred (F.) 1870-1937 .... **TCLC 61**
See also CA 119; 159

Adler, C(arole) S(chwerdtfeger)
1932- .... **CLC 35**
See also AAYA 4, 41; CA 89-92; CANR 19, 40, 101; CLR 78; JRDA; MAICYA 1, 2; SAAS 15; SATA 26, 63, 102, 126; YAW

Adler, Renata 1938- .... **CLC 8, 31**
See also CA 49-52; CANR 95; CN 4, 5, 6; MTCW 1

Adorno, Theodor W(iesengrund)
1903-1969 .... **TCLC 111**
See also CA 89-92; 25-28R; CANR 89;
DLB 242; EWL 3

Ady, Endre 1877-1919 .... **TCLC 11**
See also CA 107; CDWLB 4; DLB 215;
EW 9; EWL 3

A.E.
See Russell, George William

Aelfric c. 955-c. 1010 .... **CMLC 46**
See also DLB 146

Aelred of Rievaulx 1110-1167 ..... **CMLC 123**

Aeschines c. 390B.C.-c. 320B.C. .... **CMLC 47**
See also DLB 176

Aeschylus 525(?)B.C.-456(?)B.C. .. **CMLC 11,
51, 94; DC 8; WLCS**
See also AW 1; CDWLB 1; DA; DAB;
DAC; DAM DRAM, MST; DFS 5, 10,
26; DLB 176; LMFS 1; RGWL 2, 3;
TWA; WLIT 8

Aesop 620(?)B.C.-560(?)B.C. .... **CMLC 24**
See also CLR 14; MAICYA 1, 2; SATA 64

Affable Hawk
See MacCarthy, Sir (Charles Otto) Desmond

Africa, Ben
See Bosman, Herman Charles

Afrika, Jan
See Breytenbach, Breyten

Afton, Effie
See Harper, Frances Ellen Watkins

Agapida, Fray Antonio
See Irving, Washington

Agar, Emile
See Kacew, Romain

Agee, James 1909-1955 ...... **TCLC 1, 19, 180**
See also AAYA 44; AITN 1; AMW; CA 108;
148; CANR 131; CDALB 1941-1968;
DAM NOV; DLB 2, 26, 152; DLBY
1989; EWL 3; LAIT 3; LATS 1:2; MAL
5; MTCW 2; MTFW 2005; NFS 22;
RGAL 4; TUS

Agee, James Rufus
See Agee, James

A Gentlewoman in New England
See Bradstreet, Anne

A Gentlewoman in Those Parts
See Bradstreet, Anne

Aghill, Gordon
See Silverberg, Robert

Agnon, Shmuel Yosef Halevi
See Agnon, S.Y.

Agnon, S.Y. 1888-1970 .... **CLC 4, 8, 14; SSC
30, 120; TCLC 151**
See also CA 17-18; 25-28R; CANR 60, 102;
CAP 2; DLB 329; EWL 3; MTCW 1, 2;
RGHL; RGSF 2; RGWL 2, 3; WLIT 6

Agrippa von Nettesheim, Henry Cornelius
1486-1535 .... **LC 27**

Aguilera Malta, Demetrio
1909-1981 .... **HLCS 1**
See also CA 111; 124; CANR 87; DAM
MULT, NOV; DLB 145; EWL 3; HW 1;
RGWL 3

Agustini, Delmira 1886-1914 .... **HLCS 1**
See also CA 166; DLB 290; HW 1, 2; LAW

Aherne, Owen
See Cassill, R(onald) V(erlin)

Ai 1947-2010 .... **CLC 4, 14, 69; PC 72**
See also CA 85-88; CAAS 13; CANR 70;
CP 6, 7; DLB 120; PFS 16

Aickman, Robert (Fordyce)
1914-1981 .... **CLC 57**
See also CA 5-8R; CANR 3, 72, 100; DLB
261; HGG; SUFW 1, 2

Aidoo, (Christina) Ama Ata
1942- .... **BLCS; CLC 177**
See also AFW; BRWS 15; BW 1; CA 101;
CANR 62, 144; CD 5, 6; CDWLB 3; CN
6, 7; CWD; CWP; DLB 117; DNFS 1, 2;
EWL 3; FW; WLIT 2

Aiken, Conrad 1889-1973 ... **CLC 1, 3, 5, 10,
52; PC 26; SSC 9**
See also AMW; CA 5-8R; 45-48; CANR 4,
60; CDALB 1929-1941; CN 1; CP 1;
DAM NOV, POET; DLB 9, 45, 102; EWL
3; EXPS; HGG; MAL 5; MTCW 1, 2;
MTFW 2005; PFS 24; RGAL 4; RGSF 2;
SATA 3, 30; SSFS 8; TUS

Aiken, Conrad Potter
See Aiken, Conrad

Aiken, Joan (Delano) 1924-2004 ...... **CLC 35**
See also AAYA 1, 25; CA 9-12R, 182; 223;
CAAE 182; CANR 4, 23, 34, 64, 121;
CLR 1, 19, 90; DLB 161; FANT; HGG;
JRDA; MAICYA 1, 2; MTCW 1; RHW;
SAAS 1; SATA 2, 30, 73; SATA-Essay
109; SATA-Obit 152; SUFW 2; WYA;
YAW

Ainsworth, William Harrison
1805-1882 .... **NCLC 13**
See also DLB 21; HGG; RGEL 2; SATA
24; SUFW 1

Aitmatov, Chingiz 1928-2008 .. **CLC 71; SSC
131**
See also CA 103; CANR 38; CWW 2; DLB
302; EWL 3; MTCW 1; RGSF 2; SATA
56

Aitmatov, Chingiz Torekulovich
See Aitmatov, Chingiz

Ajar, Emile
See Kacew, Romain

Akers, Floyd
See Baum, L. Frank

Akhmadulina, Bella 1937- ... **CLC 53; PC 43**
See also CA 65-68; CWP; CWW 2; DAM
POET; EWL 3

Akhmadulina, Bella Akhatovna
See Akhmadulina, Bella

Akhmatova, Anna 1888-1966 ..... **CLC 11, 25,
64, 126; PC 2, 55**
See also CA 19-20; 25-28R; CANR 35;
CAP 1; DA3; DAM POET; DLB 295; EW
10; EWL 3; FL 1:5; MTCW 1, 2; PFS 18,
27, 32; RGWL 2, 3

Aksakov, Sergei Timofeevich
1791-1859 .... **NCLC 2, 181**
See also DLB 198

Aksenov, Vasilii
See Aksyonov, Vassily

Aksenov, Vasilii Pavlovich
See Aksyonov, Vassily

Aksenov, Vassily
See Aksyonov, Vassily

Akst, Daniel 1956- .... **CLC 109**
See also CA 161; CANR 110

Aksyonov, Vassily 1932-2009 ..... **CLC 22, 37,
101**
See also CA 53-56; CANR 12, 48, 77;
CWW 2; DLB 302; EWL 3

Aksyonov, Vassily Pavlovich
See Aksyonov, Vassily

Akutagawa Ryunosuke 1892-1927 ... **SSC 44;
TCLC 16**
See also CA 117; 154; DLB 180; EWL 3;
MJW; RGSF 2; RGWL 2, 3

Alabaster, William 1568-1640 .... **LC 90**
See also DLB 132; RGEL 2

Alain 1868-1951 .... **TCLC 41**
See also CA 163; EWL 3; GFL 1789 to the
Present

Alain de Lille c. 1116-c. 1203 .... **CMLC 53**
See also DLB 208

Alain-Fournier
See Fournier, Henri-Alban

Al-Amin, Jamil Abdullah 1943- ...... **BLC 1:1**
See also BW 1, 3; CA 112; 125; CANR 82;
DAM MULT

Alanus de Insluis
See Alain de Lille

Alarcon, Pedro Antonio de
1833-1891 .... **NCLC 1, 219; SSC 64**

Alas (y Urena), Leopoldo (Enrique Garcia)
1852-1901 .... **TCLC 29**
See also CA 113; 131; HW 1; RGSF 2

Albee, Edward (III) 1928- ... **CLC 1, 2, 3, 5,
9, 11, 13, 25, 53, 86, 113; DC 11; WLC
1**
See also AAYA 51; AITN 1; AMW; CA
5-8R; CABS 3; CAD; CANR 8, 54, 74,
124; CD 5, 6; CDALB 1941-1968; DA;
DA3; DAB; DAC; DAM DRAM, MST;
DFS 25; DLB 7, 266; EWL 3; INT
CANR-8; LAIT 4; LMFS 2; MAL 5;
MTCW 1, 2; MTFW 2005; RGAL 4; TUS

Albee, Edward Franklin
See Albee, Edward (III)

Alberti, Leon Battista 1404-1472 ...... **LC 173**

Alberti, Rafael 1902-1999 .... **CLC 7**
See also CA 85-88; 185; CANR 81; CWW
2; DLB 108; EWL 3; HW 2; RGWL 2, 3

Alberti Merello, Rafael
See Alberti, Rafael

Albert of Saxony c. 1316-1390 .... **CMLC 110**

Albert the Great 1193(?)-1280 ...... **CMLC 16**
See also DLB 115

Alcaeus c. 620B.C.- .... **CMLC 65**
See also DLB 176

Alcala-Galiano, Juan Valera y
See Valera y Alcala-Galiano, Juan

Alcayaga, Lucila Godoy
See Mistral, Gabriela

Alciato, Andrea 1492-1550 .... **LC 116**

Alcott, Amos Bronson 1799-1888 ... **NCLC 1,
167**
See also DLB 1, 223

Alcott, Louisa May 1832-1888 . **NCLC 6, 58,
83, 218; SSC 27, 98; WLC 1**
See also AAYA 20; AMWS 1; BPFB 1;
BYA 2; CDALB 1865-1917; CLR 1, 38,
109; DA; DA3; DAB; DAC; DAM MST,
NOV; DLB 1, 42, 79, 223, 239, 242;
DLBD 14; FL 1:2; FW; JRDA; LAIT 2;
MAICYA 1, 2; NFS 12; RGAL 4; SATA
100; TUS; WCH; WYA; YABC 1; YAW

Alcuin c. 730-804 .... **CMLC 69**
See also DLB 148

Aldanov, M. A.
See Aldanov, Mark (Alexandrovich)

Aldanov, Mark (Alexandrovich)
1886-1957 .... **TCLC 23**
See also CA 118; 181; DLB 317

Aldhelm c. 639-709 .... **CMLC 90**

Aldington, Richard 1892-1962 .... **CLC 49**
See also CA 85-88; CANR 45; DLB 20, 36,
100, 149; LMFS 2; RGEL 2

Aldiss, Brian W. 1925- .. **CLC 5, 14, 40, 290;
SSC 36**
See also AAYA 42; CA 5-8R, 190; CAAE
190; CAAS 2; CANR 5, 28, 64, 121, 168;
CN 1, 2, 3, 4, 5, 6, 7; DAM NOV; DLB
14, 261, 271; MTCW 1, 2; MTFW 2005;
SATA 34; SCFW 1, 2; SFW 4

Aldiss, Brian Wilson
See Aldiss, Brian W.

Aldrich, Ann
See Meaker, Marijane

Aldrich, Bess Streeter
1881-1954 .... **TCLC 125**
See also CLR 70; TCWW 2

Alegria, Claribel
See Alegria, Claribel

Alegria, Claribel 1924- .... **CLC 75; HLCS 1; PC 26**
See also CA 131; CAAS 15; CANR 66, 94, 134; CWW 2; DAM MULT; DLB 145, 283; EWL 3; HW 1; MTCW 2; MTFW 2005; PFS 21

Alegria, Claribel Joy
See Alegria, Claribel

Alegria, Fernando 1918-2005 .... **CLC 57**
See also CA 9-12R; CANR 5, 32, 72; EWL 3; HW 1, 2

Aleixandre, Vicente 1898-1984 .... **HLCS 1; TCLC 113**
See also CANR 81; DLB 108, 329; EWL 3; HW 2; MTCW 1, 2; RGWL 2, 3

Alekseev, Konstantin Sergeivich
See Stanislavsky, Constantin

Alekseyer, Konstantin Sergeyevich
See Stanislavsky, Constantin

Aleman, Mateo 1547-1615(?) .... **LC 81**

Alencar, Jose de 1829-1877 .... **NCLC 157**
See also DLB 307; LAW; WLIT 1

Alencon, Marguerite d'
See de Navarre, Marguerite

Alepoudelis, Odysseus
See Elytis, Odysseus

Aleshkovsky, Joseph 1929- .... **CLC 44**
See also CA 121; 128; DLB 317

Aleshkovsky, Yuz
See Aleshkovsky, Joseph

Alexander, Barbara
See Ehrenreich, Barbara

Alexander, Lloyd 1924-2007 .... **CLC 35**
See also AAYA 1, 27; BPFB 1; BYA 5, 6, 7, 9, 10, 11; CA 1-4R; 260; CANR 1, 24, 38, 55, 113; CLR 1, 5, 48; CWRI 5; DLB 52; FANT; JRDA; MAICYA 1, 2; MAIC-YAS 1; MTCW 1; SAAS 19; SATA 3, 49, 81, 129, 135; SATA-Obit 182; SUFW; TUS; WYA; YAW

Alexander, Lloyd Chudley
See Alexander, Lloyd

Alexander, Meena 1951- .... **CLC 121**
See also CA 115; CANR 38, 70, 146; CP 5, 6, 7; CWP; DLB 323; FW

Alexander, Rae Pace
See Alexander, Raymond Pace

Alexander, Raymond Pace
1898-1974 .... **SSC 62**
See also CA 97-100; SATA 22; SSFS 4

Alexander, Samuel 1859-1938 .... **TCLC 77**

Alexeiev, Konstantin
See Stanislavsky, Constantin

Alexeyev, Constantin Sergeivich
See Stanislavsky, Constantin

Alexeyev, Konstantin Sergeyevich
See Stanislavsky, Constantin

Alexie, Sherman 1966- .... **CLC 96, 154; NNAL; PC 53; SSC 107**
See also AAYA 28; BYA 15; CA 138; CANR 65, 95, 133, 174; CN 7; DA3; DAM MULT; DLB 175, 206, 278; LATS 1:2; MTCW 2; MTFW 2005; NFS 17, 31; SSFS 18

Alexie, Sherman Joseph, Jr.
See Alexie, Sherman

al-Farabi 870(?)-950 .... **CMLC 58**
See also DLB 115

Alfau, Felipe 1902-1999 .... **CLC 66**
See also CA 137

Alfieri, Vittorio 1749-1803 .... **NCLC 101**
See also EW 4; RGWL 2, 3; WLIT 7

Alfonso X 1221-1284 .... **CMLC 78**

Alfred, Jean Gaston
See Ponge, Francis

Alger, Horatio, Jr. 1832-1899 .... **NCLC 8, 83**
See also CLR 87; DLB 42; LAIT 2; RGAL 4; SATA 16; TUS

Al-Ghazali, Muhammad ibn Muhammad
1058-1111 .... **CMLC 50**
See also DLB 115

Algren, Nelson 1909-1981 ..... **CLC 4, 10, 33; SSC 33**
See also AMWS 9; BPFB 1; CA 13-16R; 103; CANR 20, 61; CDALB 1941-1968; CN 1, 2; DLB 9; DLBY 1981, 1982, 2000; EWL 3; MAL 5; MTCW 1, 2; MTFW 2005; RGAL 4; RGSF 2

al-Hamadhani 967-1007 .... **CMLC 93**
See also WLIT 6

al-Hariri, al-Qasim ibn 'Ali Abu Muhammad al-Basri
1054-1122 .... **CMLC 63**
See also RGWL 3

Ali, Ahmed 1908-1998 .... **CLC 69**
See also CA 25-28R; CANR 15, 34; CN 1, 2, 3, 4, 5; DLB 323; EWL 3

Ali, Tariq 1943- .... **CLC 173**
See also CA 25-28R; CANR 10, 99, 161, 196

Alighieri, Dante
See Dante

al-Kindi, Abu Yusuf Ya'qub ibn Ishaq c.
801-c. 873 .... **CMLC 80**

Allan, John B.
See Westlake, Donald E.

Allan, Sidney
See Hartmann, Sadakichi

Allan, Sydney
See Hartmann, Sadakichi

Allard, Janet CLC 59

Allen, Betsy
See Harrison, Elizabeth (Allen) Cavanna

Allen, Edward 1948- .... **CLC 59**

Allen, Fred 1894-1956 .... **TCLC 87**

Allen, Paula Gunn 1939-2008 . **CLC 84, 202, 280; NNAL**
See also AMWS 4; CA 112; 143; 272; CANR 63, 130; CWP; DA3; DAM MULT; DLB 175; FW; MTCW 2; MTFW 2005; RGAL 4; TCWW 2

Allen, Roland
See Ayckbourn, Alan

Allen, Sarah A.
See Hopkins, Pauline Elizabeth

Allen, Sidney H.
See Hartmann, Sadakichi

Allen, Woody 1935- ..... **CLC 16, 52, 195, 288**
See also AAYA 10, 51; AMWS 15; CA 33-36R; CANR 27, 38, 63, 128, 172; DAM POP; DLB 44; MTCW 1; SSFS 21

Allende, Isabel 1942- ... **CLC 39, 57, 97, 170, 264; HLC 1; SSC 65; WLCS**
See also AAYA 18, 70; CA 125; 130; CANR 51, 74, 129, 165; CDWLB 3; CLR 99; CWW 2; DA3; DAM MULT, NOV; DLB 145; DNFS 1; EWL 3; FL 1:5; FW; HW 1, 2; INT CA-130; LAIT 5; LAWS 1; LMFS 2; MTCW 1, 2; MTFW 2005; NCFS 1; NFS 6, 18, 29; RGSF 2; RGWL 3; SATA 163; SSFS 11, 16; WLIT 1

Alleyn, Ellen
See Rossetti, Christina

Alleyne, Carla D. CLC 65

Allingham, Margery (Louise)
1904-1966 .... **CLC 19**
See also CA 5-8R; 25-28R; CANR 4, 58; CMW 4; DLB 77; MSW; MTCW 1, 2

Allingham, William 1824-1889 ...... **NCLC 25**
See also DLB 35; RGEL 2

Allison, Dorothy E. 1949- . **CLC 78, 153, 290**
See also AAYA 53; CA 140; CANR 66, 107; CN 7; CSW; DA3; DLB 350; FW; MTCW 2; MTFW 2005; NFS 11; RGAL 4

Alloula, Malek CLC 65

Allston, Washington 1779-1843 .... **NCLC 2**
See also DLB 1, 235

Almedingen, E. M.
See Almedingen, Martha Edith von

Almedingen, Martha Edith von
1898-1971 .... **CLC 12**
See also CA 1-4R; CANR 1; SATA 3

Almodovar, Pedro 1949(?)- .... **CLC 114, 229; HLCS 1**
See also CA 133; CANR 72, 151; HW 2

Almqvist, Carl Jonas Love
1793-1866 .... **NCLC 42**

al-Mutanabbi, Ahmad ibn al-Husayn Abu al-Tayyib al-Jufi al-Kindi
915-965 .... **CMLC 66**
See also RGWL 3; WLIT 6

Alonso, Damaso 1898-1990 .... **CLC 14**
See also CA 110; 131; 130; CANR 72; DLB 108; EWL 3; HW 1, 2

Alov
See Gogol, Nikolai

al'Sadaawi, Nawal
See El Saadawi, Nawal

al-Shaykh, Hanan 1945- .... **CLC 218**
See also CA 135; CANR 111; CWW 2; DLB 346; EWL 3; WLIT 6

Al Siddik
See Rolfe, Frederick (William Serafino Austin Lewis Mary)

Alta 1942- .... **CLC 19**
See also CA 57-60

Alter, Robert B. 1935- .... **CLC 34**
See also CA 49-52; CANR 1, 47, 100, 160, 201

Alter, Robert Bernard
See Alter, Robert B.

Alther, Lisa 1944- .... **CLC 7, 41**
See also BPFB 1; CA 65-68; CAAS 30; CANR 12, 30, 51, 180; CN 4, 5, 6, 7; CSW; GLL 2; MTCW 1

Althusser, L.
See Althusser, Louis

Althusser, Louis 1918-1990 .... **CLC 106**
See also CA 131; 132; CANR 102; DLB 242

Altman, Robert 1925-2006 .... **CLC 16, 116, 242**
See also CA 73-76; 254; CANR 43

Alurista
See Urista, Alberto

Alvarez, A. 1929- .... **CLC 5, 13**
See also CA 1-4R; CANR 3, 33, 63, 101, 134; CN 3, 4, 5, 6; CP 1, 2, 3, 4, 5, 6, 7; DLB 14, 40; MTFW 2005

Alvarez, Alejandro Rodriguez
1903-1965 . **CLC 49; DC 32; TCLC 199**
See also CA 131; 93-96; EWL 3; HW 1

Alvarez, Julia 1950- .. **CLC 93, 274; HLCS 1**
See also AAYA 25; AMWS 7; CA 147; CANR 69, 101, 133, 166; DA3; DLB 282; LATS 1:2; LLW; MTCW 2; MTFW 2005; NFS 5, 9; SATA 129; SSFS 27, 31; WLIT 1

Alvaro, Corrado 1896-1956 .... **TCLC 60**
See also CA 163; DLB 264; EWL 3

Amado, Jorge 1912-2001 ... **CLC 13, 40, 106, 232; HLC 1**
See also CA 77-80; 201; CANR 35, 74, 135; CWW 2; DAM MULT, NOV; DLB 113, 307; EWL 3; HW 2; LAW; LAWS 1; MTCW 1, 2; MTFW 2005; RGWL 2, 3; TWA; WLIT 1

Ambler, Eric 1909-1998 .... **CLC 4, 6, 9**
See also BRWS 4; CA 9-12R; 171; CANR 7, 38, 74; CMW 4; CN 1, 2, 3, 4, 5, 6; DLB 77; MSW; MTCW 1, 2; TEA

Ambrose c. 339-c. 397 .... **CMLC 103**

Ambrose, Stephen E. 1936-2002 .... **CLC 145**
See also AAYA 44; CA 1-4R; 209; CANR 3, 43, 57, 83, 105; MTFW 2005; NCFS 2; SATA 40, 138

Antiphon c. 480B.C.-c. 411B.C. .... **CMLC 55**
Antoine, Marc
  See Proust, Marcel
Antoninus, Brother
  See Everson, William
Antonioni, Michelangelo
  1912-2007 .... **CLC 20, 144, 259**
  See also CA 73-76; 262; CANR 45, 77
Antschel, Paul
  See Celan, Paul
Anwar, Chairil 1922-1949 .... **TCLC 22**
  See also CA 121; 219; EWL 3; RGWL 3
Anyidoho, Kofi 1947- .... **BLC 2:1**
  See also BW 3; CA 178; CP 5, 6, 7; DLB
  157; EWL 3
Anzaldua, Gloria (Evanjelina)
  1942-2004 .... **CLC 200; HLCS 1**
  See also CA 175; 227; CSW; CWP; DLB
  122; FW; LLW; RGAL 4; SATA-Obit 154
Apess, William 1798-1839(?) .... **NCLC 73;**
  NNAL
  See also DAM MULT; DLB 175, 243
Apollinaire, Guillaume 1880-1918 .... **PC 7;**
  TCLC 3, 8, 51
  See also CA 104; 152; DAM POET; DLB
  258, 321; EW 9; EWL 3; GFL 1789 to
  the Present; MTCW 2; PFS 24; RGWL 2,
  3; TWA; WP
Apollonius of Rhodes
  See Apollonius Rhodius
Apollonius Rhodius c. 300B.C.-c.
  220B.C. .... **CMLC 28**
  See also AW 1; DLB 176; RGWL 2, 3
Appelfeld, Aharon 1932- ... **CLC 23, 47; SSC**
  42
  See also CA 112; 133; CANR 86, 160;
  CWW 2; DLB 299; EWL 3; RGHL;
  RGSF 2; WLIT 6
Appelfeld, Aron
  See Appelfeld, Aharon
Apple, Max (Isaac) 1941- .... **CLC 9, 33; SSC**
  50
  See also AMWS 17; CA 81-84; CANR 19,
  54; DLB 130
Appleman, Philip (Dean) 1926- .... **CLC 51**
  See also CA 13-16R; CAAS 18; CANR 6,
  29, 56
Appleton, Lawrence
  See Lovecraft, H. P.
Apteryx
  See Eliot, T. S.
Apuleius, (Lucius Madaurensis) c. 125-c.
  164 .... **CMLC 1, 84**
  See also AW 2; CDWLB 1; DLB 211;
  RGWL 2, 3; SUFW; WLIT 8
Aquin, Hubert 1929-1977 .... **CLC 15**
  See also CA 105; DLB 53; EWL 3
Aquinas, Thomas 1224(?)-1274 ...... **CMLC 33**
  See also DLB 115; EW 1; TWA
Aragon, Louis 1897-1982 .... **CLC 3, 22;**
  TCLC 123
  See also CA 69-72; 108; CANR 28, 71;
  DAM NOV, POET; DLB 72, 258; EW 11;
  EWL 3; GFL 1789 to the Present; GLL 2;
  LMFS 2; MTCW 1, 2; RGWL 2, 3
Arany, Janos 1817-1882 .... **NCLC 34**
Aranyos, Kakay 1847-1910
  See Mikszath, Kalman
Aratus of Soli c. 315B.C.-c.
  240B.C. .... **CMLC 64, 114**
  See also DLB 176
Arbuthnot, John 1667-1735 .... **LC 1**
  See also BRWS 16; DLB 101
Archer, Herbert Winslow
  See Mencken, H. L.

Archer, Jeffrey 1940- .... **CLC 28**
  See also AAYA 16; BEST 89:3; BPFB 1;
  CA 77-80; CANR 22, 52, 95, 136; CPW;
  DA3; DAM POP; INT CANR-22; MTFW
  2005
Archer, Jeffrey Howard
  See Archer, Jeffrey
Archer, Jules 1915- .... **CLC 12**
  See also CA 9-12R; CANR 6, 69; SAAS 5;
  SATA 4, 85
Archer, Lee
  See Ellison, Harlan
Archilochus c. 7th cent. B.C.- .... **CMLC 44**
  See also DLB 176
Ard, William
  See Jakes, John
Arden, John 1930- .... **CLC 6, 13, 15**
  See also BRWS 2; CA 13-16R; CAAS 4;
  CANR 31, 65, 67, 124; CBD; CD 5, 6;
  DAM DRAM; DFS 9; DLB 13, 245;
  EWL 3; MTCW 1
Arenas, Reinaldo 1943-1990 .. **CLC 41; HLC**
  1, TCLC 191
  See also CA 124; 128; 133; CANR 73, 106;
  DAM MULT; DLB 145; EWL 3; GLL 2;
  HW 1; LAW; LAWS 1; MTCW 2; MTFW
  2005; RGSF 2; RGWL 3; WLIT 1
Arendt, Hannah 1906-1975 .... **CLC 66, 98;**
  TCLC 193
  See also CA 17-20R; 61-64; CANR 26, 60,
  172; DLB 242; MTCW 1, 2
Aretino, Pietro 1492-1556 .... **LC 12, 165**
  See also RGWL 2, 3
Arghezi, Tudor
  See Theodorescu, Ion N.
Arguedas, Jose Maria 1911-1969 .... **CLC 10,**
  18; HLCS 1; TCLC 147
  See also CA 89-92; CANR 73; DLB 113;
  EWL 3; HW 1; LAW; RGWL 2, 3; WLIT
  1
Argueta, Manlio 1936- .... **CLC 31**
  See also CA 131; CANR 73; CWW 2; DLB
  145; EWL 3; HW 1; RGWL 3
Arias, Ron 1941- .... **HLC 1**
  See also CA 131; CANR 81, 136; DAM
  MULT; DLB 82; HW 1, 2; MTCW 2;
  MTFW 2005
Ariosto, Lodovico
  See Ariosto, Ludovico
Ariosto, Ludovico 1474-1533 ... **LC 6, 87; PC**
  42
  See also EW 2; RGWL 2, 3; WLIT 7
Aristides
  See Epstein, Joseph
Aristides Quintilianus fl. c. 100-fl. c.
  400 .... **CMLC 122**
Aristophanes 450B.C.-385B.C. .... **CMLC 4,**
  51; DC 2; WLCS
  See also AW 1; CDWLB 1; DA; DA3;
  DAB; DAC; DAM DRAM, MST; DFS
  10; DLB 176; LMFS 1; RGWL 2, 3;
  TWA; WLIT 8
Aristotle 384B.C.-322B.C. .... **CMLC 31, 123;**
  WLCS
  See also AW 1; CDWLB 1; DA; DA3;
  DAB; DAC; DAM MST; DLB 176;
  RGWL 2, 3; TWA; WLIT 8
Arlt, Roberto 1900-1942 .. **HLC 1; TCLC 29**
  See also CA 123; 131; CANR 67; DAM
  MULT; DLB 305; EWL 3; HW 1, 2;
  IDTP; LAW
Arlt, Roberto Godofredo Christophersen
  See Arlt, Roberto
Armah, Ayi Kwei 1939- . **BLC 1:1, 2:1; CLC**
  5, 33, 136
  See also AFW; BRWS 10; BW 1; CA 61-
  64; CANR 21, 64; CDWLB 3; CN 1, 2,
  3, 4, 5, 6, 7; DAM MULT, POET; DLB
  117; EWL 3; MTCW 1; WLIT 2

Armatrading, Joan 1950- .... **CLC 17**
  See also CA 114; 186
Armin, Robert 1568(?)-1615(?) .... **LC 120**
Armitage, Frank
  See Carpenter, John
Armstrong, Jeannette (C.) 1948- .... **NNAL**
  See also CA 149; CCA 1; CN 6, 7; DAC;
  DLB 334; SATA 102
Arnauld, Antoine 1612-1694 .... **LC 169**
  See also DLB 268
Arnette, Robert
  See Silverberg, Robert
Arnim, Achim von (Ludwig Joachim von
  Arnim) 1781-1831 .. **NCLC 5, 159; SSC**
  29
  See also DLB 90
Arnim, Bettina von 1785-1859 ...... **NCLC 38,**
  123
  See also DLB 90; RGWL 2, 3
Arnold, Matthew 1822-1888 ..... **NCLC 6, 29,**
  89, 126, 218; PC 5, 94; WLC 1
  See also BRW 5; CDBLB 1832-1890; DA;
  DAB, DAC, DAM MST, POET, DLB 32,
  57; EXPP; PAB; PFS 2; TEA; WP
Arnold, Thomas 1795-1842 .... **NCLC 18**
  See also DLB 55
Arnow, Harriette (Louisa) Simpson
  1908-1986 ...... **CLC 2, 7, 18; TCLC 196**
  See also BPFB 1; CA 9-12R; 118; CANR
  14; CN 2, 3, 4; DLB 6; FW; MTCW 1, 2;
  RHW; SATA 42; SATA-Obit 47
Arouet, Francois-Marie
  See Voltaire
Arp, Hans
  See Arp, Jean
Arp, Jean 1887-1966 .... **CLC 5; TCLC 115**
  See also CA 81-84; 25-28R; CANR 42, 77;
  EW 10
Arrabal
  See Arrabal, Fernando
Arrabal, Fernando 1932- .. **CLC 2, 9, 18, 58;**
  DC 35
  See also CA 9-12R; CANR 15; CWW 2;
  DLB 321; EWL 3; LMFS 2
Arrabal Teran, Fernando
  See Arrabal, Fernando
Arreola, Juan Jose 1918-2001 .... **CLC 147;**
  HLC 1; SSC 38
  See also CA 113; 131; 200; CANR 81;
  CWW 2; DAM MULT; DLB 113; DNFS
  2; EWL 3; HW 1, 2; LAW; RGSF 2
Arrian c. 89(?)-c. 155(?) .... **CMLC 43**
  See also DLB 176
Arrick, Fran
  See Angell, Judie
Arrley, Richmond
  See Delany, Samuel R., Jr.
Artaud, Antonin 1896-1948 ... **DC 14; TCLC**
  3, 36
  See also CA 104; 149; DA3; DAM DRAM;
  DFS 22; DLB 258, 321; EW 11; EWL 3;
  GFL 1789 to the Present; MTCW 2;
  MTFW 2005; RGWL 2, 3
Artaud, Antonin Marie Joseph
  See Artaud, Antonin
Arthur, Ruth M(abel) 1905-1979 ..... **CLC 12**
  See also CA 9-12R; 85-88; CANR 4; CWRI
  5; SATA 7, 26
Artsybashev, Mikhail (Petrovich)
  1878-1927 .... **TCLC 31**
  See also CA 170; DLB 295
Arundel, Honor (Morfydd)
  1919-1973 .... **CLC 17**
  See also CA 21-22; 41-44R; CAP 2; CLR
  35; CWRI 5; SATA 4; SATA-Obit 24
Arzner, Dorothy 1900-1979 .... **CLC 98**
Asch, Sholem 1880-1957 .... **TCLC 3**
  See also CA 105; DLB 333; EWL 3; GLL
  2; RGHL

Babbis, Eleanor
See Friis-Baastad, Babbis Ellinor
Babel, Isaac
See Babel, Isaak (Emmanuilovich)
Babel, Isaak (Emmanuilovich)
1894-1941(?) . **SSC 16, 78; TCLC 2, 13, 171**
See also CA 104; 155; CANR 113; DLB 272; EW 11; EWL 3; MTCW 2; MTFW 2005; RGSF 2; RGWL 2, 3; SSFS 10; TWA
Babits, Mihaly 1883-1941 .... **TCLC 14**
See also CA 114; CDWLB 4; DLB 215; EWL 3
Babur 1483-1530 .... **LC 18**
Babylas
See Ghelderode, Michel de
Baca, Jimmy Santiago 1952- . **HLC 1; PC 41**
See also CA 131; CANR 81, 90, 146; CP 6, 7; DAM MULT; DLB 122; HW 1, 2; LLW; MAL 5
Baca, Jose Santiago
See Baca, Jimmy Santiago
Bacchelli, Riccardo 1891-1985 .... **CLC 19**
See also CA 29-32R; 117; DLB 264; EWL 3
Bacchylides c. 520B.C.-c.
452B.C. .... **CMLC 119**
Bach, Richard 1936- .... **CLC 14**
See also AITN 1; BEST 89:2; BPFB 1; BYA 5; CA 9-12R; CANR 18, 93, 151; CPW; DAM NOV, POP; FANT; MTCW 1; SATA 13
Bach, Richard David
See Bach, Richard
Bache, Benjamin Franklin
1769-1798 .... **LC 74**
See also DLB 43
Bachelard, Gaston 1884-1962 ...... **TCLC 128**
See also CA 97-100; 89-92; DLB 296; GFL 1789 to the Present
Bachman, Richard
See King, Stephen
Bachmann, Ingeborg 1926-1973 ..... **CLC 69; TCLC 192**
See also CA 93-96; 45-48; CANR 69; DLB 85; EWL 3; RGHL; RGWL 2, 3
Bacon, Francis 1561-1626 ..... **LC 18, 32, 131**
See also BRW 1; CDBLB Before 1660; DLB 151, 236, 252; RGEL 2; TEA
Bacon, Roger 1214(?)-1294 ... **CMLC 14, 108**
See also DLB 115
Bacovia, G.
See Bacovia, George
Bacovia, George 1881-1957 .... **TCLC 24**
See Bacovia, George
See also CA 123; 189; CDWLB 4; DLB 220; EWL 3
Badanes, Jerome 1937-1995 .... **CLC 59**
See also CA 234
Bage, Robert 1728-1801 .... **NCLC 182**
See also DLB 39; RGEL 2
Bagehot, Walter 1826-1877 .... **NCLC 10**
See also DLB 55
Bagnold, Enid 1889-1981 .... **CLC 25**
See also AAYA 75; BYA 2; CA 5-8R; 103; CANR 5, 40; CBD; CN 2; CWD; CWRI 5; DAM DRAM; DLB 13, 160, 191, 245; FW; MAICYA 1, 2; RGEL 2; SATA 1, 25
Bagritsky, Eduard
See Dzyubin, Eduard Georgievich
Bagritsky, Edvard
See Dzyubin, Eduard Georgievich
Bagrjana, Elisaveta
See Belcheva, Elisaveta Lyubomirova
Bagryana, Elisaveta
See Belcheva, Elisaveta Lyubomirova

Bailey, Paul 1937- .... **CLC 45**
See also CA 21-24R; CANR 16, 62, 124; CN 1, 2, 3, 4, 5, 6, 7; DLB 14, 271; GLL 2
Baillie, Joanna 1762-1851 ...... **NCLC 71, 151**
See also DLB 93, 344; GL 2; RGEL 2
Bainbridge, Beryl 1934- ...... **CLC 4, 5, 8, 10, 14, 18, 22, 62, 130, 292**
See also BRWS 6; CA 21-24R; CANR 24, 55, 75, 88, 128; CN 2, 3, 4, 5, 6, 7; DAM NOV; DLB 14, 231; EWL 3; MTCW 1, 2; MTFW 2005
Baker, Carlos (Heard)
1909-1987 .... **TCLC 119**
See also CA 5-8R; 122; CANR 3, 63; DLB 103
Baker, Elliott 1922-2007 .... **CLC 8**
See also CA 45-48; 257; CANR 2, 63; CN 1, 2, 3, 4, 5, 6, 7
Baker, Elliott Joseph
See Baker, Elliott
Baker, Jean H.
See Russell, George William
Baker, Nicholson 1957- .... **CLC 61, 165**
See also AMWS 13; CA 135; CANR 63, 120, 138, 190; CN 6; CPW; DA3; DAM POP; DLB 227; MTFW 2005
Baker, Ray Stannard 1870-1946 .... **TCLC 47**
See also CA 118; DLB 345
Baker, Russell 1925- .... **CLC 31**
See also BEST 89:4; CA 57-60; CANR 11, 41, 59, 137; MTCW 1, 2; MTFW 2005
Baker, Russell Wayne
See Baker, Russell
Bakhtin, M.
See Bakhtin, Mikhail Mikhailovich
Bakhtin, M. M.
See Bakhtin, Mikhail Mikhailovich
Bakhtin, Mikhail
See Bakhtin, Mikhail Mikhailovich
Bakhtin, Mikhail Mikhailovich
1895-1975 .... **CLC 83; TCLC 160**
See also CA 128; 113; DLB 242; EWL 3
Bakshi, Ralph 1938(?)- .... **CLC 26**
See also CA 112; 138; IDFW 3
Bakunin, Mikhail (Alexandrovich)
1814-1876 .... **NCLC 25, 58**
See also DLB 277
Bal, Mieke (Maria Gertrudis)
1946- .... **CLC 252**
See also CA 156; CANR 99
Baldwin, James 1924-1987 ...... **BLC 1:1, 2:1; CLC 1, 2, 3, 4, 5, 8, 13, 15, 17, 42, 50, 67, 90, 127; DC 1; SSC 10, 33, 98, 134; TCLC 229; WLC 1**
See also AAYA 4, 34; AFAW 1, 2; AMWR 2; AMWS 1; BPFB 1; BW 1; CA 1-4R; 124; CABS 1; CAD; CANR 3, 24; CDALB 1941-1968; CN 1, 2, 3, 4; CPW; DA; DA3; DAB; DAC; DAM MST, MULT, NOV, POP; DFS 11, 15; DLB 2, 7, 33, 249, 278; DLBY 1987; EWL 3; EXPS; LAIT 5; MAL 5; MTCW 1, 2; MTFW 2005; NCFS 4; NFS 4; RGAL 4; RGSF 2; SATA 9; SATA-Obit 54; SSFS 2, 18; TUS
Baldwin, William c. 1515-1563 .... **LC 113**
See also DLB 132
Bale, John 1495-1563 .... **LC 62**
See also DLB 132; RGEL 2; TEA
Ball, Hugo 1886-1927 .... **TCLC 104**
Ballard, James G.
See Ballard, J.G.
Ballard, James Graham
See Ballard, J.G.

Ballard, J.G. 1930-2009 ..... **CLC 3, 6, 14, 36, 137; SSC 1, 53**
See also AAYA 3, 52; BRWS 5; CA 5-8R; 285; CANR 15, 39, 65, 107, 133, 198; CN 1, 2, 3, 4, 5, 6, 7; DA3; DAM NOV, POP; DLB 14, 207, 261, 319; EWL 3; HGG; MTCW 1, 2; MTFW 2005; NFS 8; RGEL 2; RGSF 2; SATA 93; SATA-Obit 203; SCFW 1, 2; SFW 4
Ballard, Jim G.
See Ballard, J.G.
Balmont, Konstantin (Dmitriyevich)
1867-1943 .... **TCLC 11**
See also CA 109; 155; DLB 295; EWL 3
Baltausis, Vincas 1847-1910
See Mikszath, Kalman
Balzac, Guez de (?)-
See Balzac, Jean-Louis Guez de
Balzac, Honore de 1799-1850 ... **NCLC 5, 35, 53, 153; SSC 5, 59, 102; WLC 1**
See also DA; DA3; DAB; DAC; DAM MST, NOV; DLB 119; EW 5; GFL 1789 to the Present; LMFS 1; NFS 33; RGSF 2; RGWL 2, 3; SSFS 10; SUFW; TWA
Balzac, Jean-Louis Guez de
1597-1654 .... **LC 162**
See also DLB 268; GFL Beginnings to 1789
Bambara, Toni Cade 1939-1995 ..... **BLC 1:1, 2:1; CLC 19, 88; SSC 35, 107; TCLC 116; WLCS**
See also AAYA 5, 49; AFAW 2; AMWS 11; BW 2, 3; BYA 12, 14; CA 29-32R; 150; CANR 24, 49, 81; CDALBS; DA; DA3; DAC; DAM MST, MULT; DLB 38, 218; EXPS; MAL 5; MTCW 1, 2; MTFW 2005; RGAL 4; RGSF 2; SATA 112; SSFS 4, 7, 12, 21
Bamdad, A.
See Shamlu, Ahmad
Bamdad, Alef
See Shamlu, Ahmad
Banat, D. R.
See Bradbury, Ray
Bancroft, Laura
See Baum, L. Frank
Banim, John 1798-1842 .... **NCLC 13**
See also DLB 116, 158, 159; RGEL 2
Banim, Michael 1796-1874 .... **NCLC 13**
See also DLB 158, 159
Banjo, The
See Paterson, A(ndrew) B(arton)
Banks, Iain 1954- .... **CLC 34**
See also BRWS 11; CA 123; 128; CANR 61, 106, 180; DLB 194, 261; EWL 3; HGG; INT CA-128; MTFW 2005; SFW 4
Banks, Iain M.
See Banks, Iain
Banks, Iain Menzies
See Banks, Iain
Banks, Lynne Reid
See Reid Banks, Lynne
Banks, Russell 1940- . **CLC 37, 72, 187; SSC 42**
See also AAYA 45; AMWS 5; CA 65-68; CAAS 15; CANR 19, 52, 73, 118, 195; CN 4, 5, 6, 7; DLB 130, 278; EWL 3; MAL 5; MTCW 2; MTFW 2005; NFS 13
Banks, Russell Earl
See Banks, Russell
Banville, John 1945- .... **CLC 46, 118, 224**
See also CA 117; 128; CANR 104, 150, 176; CN 4, 5, 6, 7; DLB 14, 271, 326; INT CA-128
Banville, Theodore (Faullain) de
1832-1891 .... **NCLC 9**
See also DLB 217; GFL 1789 to the Present

Bastos, Augusto Roa
See Roa Bastos, Augusto

Bataille, Georges 1897-1962 .... **CLC 29; TCLC 155**
See also CA 101; 89-92; EWL 3

Bates, H(erbert) E(rnest) 1905-1974 .... **CLC 46; SSC 10**
See also CA 93-96; 45-48; CANR 34; CN 1; DA3; DAB; DAM POP; DLB 162, 191; EWL 3; EXPS; MTCW 1, 2; RGSF 2; SSFS 7

Bauchart
See Camus, Albert

Baudelaire, Charles 1821-1867 . **NCLC 6, 29, 55, 155; PC 1, 106; SSC 18; WLC 1**
See also DA; DA3; DAB; DAC; DAM MST, POET; DLB 217; EW 7; GFL 1789 to the Present; LMFS 2; PFS 21; RGWL 2, 3; TWA

Baudouin, Marcel
See Peguy, Charles (Pierre)

Baudouin, Pierre
See Peguy, Charles (Pierre)

Baudrillard, Jean 1929-2007 .... **CLC 60**
See also CA 252; 258; DLB 296

Baum, L. Frank 1856-1919 ...... **TCLC 7, 132**
See also AAYA 46; BYA 16; CA 108; 133; CLR 15, 107; CWRI 5; DLB 22; FANT; JRDA; MAICYA 1, 2; MTCW 1, 2; NFS 13; RGAL 4; SATA 18, 100; WCH

Baum, Louis F.
See Baum, L. Frank

Baum, Lyman Frank
See Baum, L. Frank

Baumbach, Jonathan 1933- .... **CLC 6, 23**
See also CA 13-16R; 284; CAAE 284; CAAS 5; CANR 12, 66, 140; CN 3, 4, 5, 6, 7; DLBY 1980; INT CANR-12; MTCW 1

Bausch, Richard 1945- .... **CLC 51**
See also AMWS 7; CA 101; CAAS 14; CANR 43, 61, 87, 164, 200; CN 7; CSW; DLB 130; MAL 5

Bausch, Richard Carl
See Bausch, Richard

Baxter, Charles 1947- .... **CLC 45, 78**
See also AMWS 17; CA 57-60; CANR 40, 64, 104, 133, 188; CPW; DAM POP; DLB 130; MAL 5; MTCW 2; MTFW 2005; TCLE 1:1

Baxter, Charles Morley
See Baxter, Charles

Baxter, George Owen
See Faust, Frederick

Baxter, James K(eir) 1926-1972 .... **CLC 14**
See also CA 77-80; CP 1; EWL 3

Baxter, John
See Hunt, E. Howard

Bayer, Sylvia
See Glassco, John

Bayle, Pierre 1647-1706 .... **LC 126**
See also DLB 268, 313; GFL Beginnings to 1789

Baynton, Barbara 1857-1929 . **TCLC 57, 211**
See also DLB 230; RGSF 2

Beagle, Peter S. 1939- .... **CLC 7, 104**
See also AAYA 47; BPFB 1; BYA 9, 10, 16; CA 9-12R; CANR 4, 51, 73, 110; DA3; DLBY 1980; FANT; INT CANR-4; MTCW 2; MTFW 2005; SATA 60, 130; SUFW 1, 2; YAW

Beagle, Peter Soyer
See Beagle, Peter S.

Bean, Normal
See Burroughs, Edgar Rice

Beard, Charles A(ustin) 1874-1948 .... **TCLC 15**
See also CA 115; 189; DLB 17; SATA 18

Beardsley, Aubrey 1872-1898 .... **NCLC 6**

Beatrice of Nazareth 1200-1268 .. **CMLC 114**

Beattie, Ann 1947- ..... **CLC 8, 13, 18, 40, 63, 146; SSC 11, 130**
See also AMWS 5; BEST 90:2; BPFB 1; CA 81-84; CANR 53, 73, 128; CN 4, 5, 6, 7; CPW; DA3; DAM NOV, POP; DLB 218, 278; DLBY 1982; EWL 3; MAL 5; MTCW 1, 2; MTFW 2005; RGAL 4; RGSF 2; SSFS 9; TUS

Beattie, James 1735-1803 .... **NCLC 25**
See also DLB 109

Beauchamp, Katherine Mansfield
See Mansfield, Katherine

Beaumarchais, Pierre-Augustin Caron de 1732-1799 .... **DC 4; LC 61**
See also DAM DRAM; DFS 14, 16; DLB 313; EW 4; GFL Beginnings to 1789; RGWL 2, 3

Beaumont, Francis 1584(?)-1616 .. **DC 6; LC 33**
See also BRW 2; CDBLB Before 1660; DLB 58; TEA

Beauvoir, Simone de 1908-1986 .... **CLC 1, 2, 4, 8, 14, 31, 44, 50, 71, 124; SSC 35; TCLC 221; WLC 1**
See also BPFB 1; CA 9-12R; 118; CANR 28, 61; DA; DA3; DAB; DAC; DAM MST, NOV; DLB 72; DLBY 1986; EW 12; EWL 3; FL 1:5; FW; GFL 1789 to the Present; LMFS 2; MTCW 1, 2; MTFW 2005; RGSF 2; RGWL 2, 3; TWA

Beauvoir, Simone Lucie Ernestine Marie Bertrand de
See Beauvoir, Simone de

Becker, Carl (Lotus) 1873-1945 ..... **TCLC 63**
See also CA 157; DLB 17

Becker, Jurek 1937-1997 .... **CLC 7, 19**
See also CA 85-88; 157; CANR 60, 117; CWW 2; DLB 75, 299; EWL 3; RGHL

Becker, Walter 1950- .... **CLC 26**

Becket, Thomas a 1118(?)-1170 .... **CMLC 83**

Beckett, Samuel 1906-1989 ... **CLC 1, 2, 3, 4, 6, 9, 10, 11, 14, 18, 29, 57, 59, 83; DC 22; SSC 16, 74; TCLC 145; WLC 1**
See also BRWC 2; BRWR 1; BRWS 1; CA 5-8R; 130; CANR 33, 61; CBD; CDBLB 1945-1960; CN 1, 2, 3, 4; CP 1, 2, 3, 4; DA; DA3; DAB; DAC; DAM DRAM, MST, NOV; DFS 2, 7, 18; DLB 13, 15, 233, 319, 321, 329; DLBY 1990; EWL 3; GFL 1789 to the Present; LATS 1:2; LMFS 2; MTCW 1, 2; MTFW 2005; RGSF 2; RGWL 2, 3; SSFS 15; TEA; WLIT 4

Beckett, Samuel Barclay
See Beckett, Samuel

Beckford, William 1760-1844 .... **NCLC 16, 214**
See also BRW 3; DLB 39, 213; GL 2; HGG; LMFS 1; SUFW

Beckham, Barry (Earl) 1944- .... **BLC 1:1**
See also BW 1; CA 29-32R; CANR 26, 62; CN 1, 2, 3, 4, 5, 6; DAM MULT; DLB 33

Beckman, Gunnel 1910- .... **CLC 26**
See also CA 33-36R; CANR 15, 114; CLR 25; MAICYA 1, 2; SAAS 9; SATA 6

Becque, Henri 1837-1899 .... **DC 21; NCLC 3**
See also DLB 192; GFL 1789 to the Present

Becquer, Gustavo Adolfo 1836-1870 .... **HLCS 1; NCLC 106**
See also DAM MULT

Beddoes, Thomas Lovell 1803-1849 .. **DC 15; NCLC 3, 154**
See also BRWS 11; DLB 96

Bede c. 673-735 .... **CMLC 20**
See also DLB 146; TEA

Bedford, Denton R. 1907-(?) .... **NNAL**

Bedford, Donald F.
See Fearing, Kenneth

Beecher, Catharine Esther 1800-1878 .... **NCLC 30**
See also DLB 1, 243

Beecher, John 1904-1980 .... **CLC 6**
See also AITN 1; CA 5-8R; 105; CANR 8; CP 1, 2, 3

Beer, Johann 1655-1700 .... **LC 5**
See also DLB 168

Beer, Patricia 1924- .... **CLC 58**
See also BRWS 14; CA 61-64; 183; CANR 13, 46; CP 1, 2, 3, 4, 5, 6; CWP; DLB 40; FW

Beerbohm, Max
See Beerbohm, (Henry) Max(imilian)

Beerbohm, (Henry) Max(imilian) 1872-1956 .... **TCLC 1, 24**
See also BRWS 2; CA 104; 154; CANR 79; DLB 34, 100; FANT; MTCW 2

Beer-Hofmann, Richard 1866-1945 .... **TCLC 60**
See also CA 160; DLB 81

Beethoven, Ludwig van 1770(?)-1827 .... **NCLC 227**

Beg, Shemus
See Stephens, James

Begiebing, Robert J(ohn) 1946- .... **CLC 70**
See also CA 122; CANR 40, 88

Begley, Louis 1933- .... **CLC 197**
See also CA 140; CANR 98, 176; DLB 299; RGHL; TCLE 1:1

Behan, Brendan 1923-1964 ...... **CLC 1, 8, 11, 15, 79**
See also BRWS 2; CA 73-76; CANR 33, 121; CBD; CDBLB 1945-1960; DAM DRAM; DFS 7; DLB 13, 233; EWL 3; MTCW 1, 2

Behan, Brendan Francis
See Behan, Brendan

Behn, Aphra 1640(?)-1689 .. **DC 4; LC 1, 30, 42, 135; PC 13, 88; WLC 1**
See also BRWR 3; BRWS 3; DA; DA3; DAB; DAC; DAM DRAM, MST, NOV, POET; DFS 16, 24; DLB 39, 80, 131; FW; TEA; WLIT 3

Behrman, S(amuel) N(athaniel) 1893-1973 .... **CLC 40**
See also CA 13-16; 45-48; CAD; CAP 1; DLB 7, 44; IDFW 3; MAL 5; RGAL 4

Bekederemo, J. P. Clark
See Clark-Bekederemo, J. P.

Belasco, David 1853-1931 .... **TCLC 3**
See also CA 104; 168; DLB 7; MAL 5; RGAL 4

Belben, Rosalind 1941- .... **CLC 280**
See also CA 291

Belben, Rosalind Loveday
See Belben, Rosalind

Belcheva, Elisaveta Lyubomirova 1893-1991 .... **CLC 10**
See also CA 178; CDWLB 4; DLB 147; EWL 3

Beldone, Phil "Cheech"
See Ellison, Harlan

Beleno
See Azuela, Mariano

Belinski, Vissarion Grigoryevich 1811-1848 .... **NCLC 5**
See also DLB 198

Belitt, Ben 1911- .... **CLC 22**
See also CA 13-16R; CAAS 4; CANR 7, 77; CP 1, 2, 3, 4, 5, 6; DLB 5

Belknap, Jeremy 1744-1798 .... **LC 115**
See also DLB 30, 37

Bell, Gertrude (Margaret Lowthian) 1868-1926 .... **TCLC 67**
See also CA 167; CANR 110; DLB 174

Bell, J. Freeman
  See Zangwill, Israel
Bell, James Madison 1826-1902 ..... **BLC 1:1;
  TCLC 43**
  See also BW 1; CA 122; 124; DAM MULT;
  DLB 50
Bell, Madison Smartt 1957- ..... **CLC 41, 102,
  223**
  See also AMWS 10; BPFB 1; CA 111, 183;
  CAAE 183; CANR 28, 54, 73, 134, 176;
  CN 5, 6, 7; CSW; DLB 218, 278; MTCW
  2; MTFW 2005
Bell, Marvin (Hartley) 1937- ...... **CLC 8, 31;
  PC 79**
  See also CA 21-24R; CAAS 14; CANR 59,
  102; CP 1, 2, 3, 4, 5, 6, 7; DAM POET;
  DLB 5; MAL 5; MTCW 1; PFS 25
Bell, W. L. D.
  See Mencken, H. L.
Bellamy, Atwood C.
  See Mencken, H. L.
Bellamy, Edward 1850-1898 ..... **NCLC 4, 86,
  147**
  See also DLB 12; NFS 15; RGAL 4; SFW
  4
Belli, Gioconda 1948- .... **HLCS 1**
  See also CA 152; CANR 143; CWW 2;
  DLB 290; EWL 3; RGWL 3
Bellin, Edward J.
  See Kuttner, Henry
Bello, Andres 1781-1865 .... **NCLC 131**
  See also LAW
Belloc, Hilaire 1870-1953 ... **PC 24; TCLC 7,
  18**
  See also CA 106; 152; CLR 102; CWRI 5;
  DAM POET; DLB 19, 100, 141, 174;
  EWL 3; MTCW 2; MTFW 2005; SATA
  112; WCH; YABC 1
**Belloc, Joseph Hilaire Pierre Sebastien Rene
  Swanton**
  See Belloc, Hilaire
Belloc, Joseph Peter Rene Hilaire
  See Belloc, Hilaire
Belloc, Joseph Pierre Hilaire
  See Belloc, Hilaire
Belloc, M. A.
  See Lowndes, Marie Adelaide (Belloc)
Belloc-Lowndes, Mrs.
  See Lowndes, Marie Adelaide (Belloc)
Bellow, Saul 1915-2005 ...... **CLC 1, 2, 3, 6, 8,
  10, 13, 15, 25, 33, 34, 63, 79, 190, 200;
  SSC 14, 101; WLC 1**
  See also AITN 2; AMW; AMWC 2; AMWR
  2; BEST 89:3; BPFB 1; CA 5-8R; 238;
  CABS 1; CANR 29, 53, 95, 132; CDALB
  1941-1968; CN 1, 2, 3, 4, 5, 6, 7; DA;
  DA3; DAB; DAC; DAM MST, NOV,
  POP; DLB 2, 28, 299, 329; DLBD 3;
  DLBY 1982; EWL 3; MAL 5; MTCW 1,
  2; MTFW 2005; NFS 4, 14, 26, 33; RGAL
  4; RGHL; RGSF 2; SSFS 12, 22; TUS
Belser, Reimond Karel Maria de
  1929- .... **CLC 14**
  See also CA 152
Bely, Andrey
  See Bugayev, Boris Nikolayevich
Belyi, Andrei
  See Bugayev, Boris Nikolayevich
Bembo, Pietro 1470-1547 .... **LC 79**
  See also RGWL 2, 3
Benary, Margot
  See Benary-Isbert, Margot
Benary-Isbert, Margot 1889-1979 .... **CLC 12**
  See also CA 5-8R; 89-92; CANR 4, 72;
  CLR 12; MAICYA 1, 2; SATA 2; SATA-
  Obit 21

Benavente, Jacinto 1866-1954 .... **DC 26;
  HLCS 1; TCLC 3**
  See also CA 106; 131; CANR 81; DAM
  DRAM, MULT; DLB 329; EWL 3; GLL
  2; HW 1, 2; MTCW 1, 2
Benavente y Martinez, Jacinto
  See Benavente, Jacinto
Benchley, Peter 1940-2006 .... **CLC 4, 8**
  See also AAYA 14; AITN 2; BPFB 1; CA
  17-20R; 248; CANR 12, 35, 66, 115;
  CPW; DAM NOV, POP; HGG; MTCW 1,
  2; MTFW 2005; SATA 3, 89, 164
Benchley, Peter Bradford
  See Benchley, Peter
Benchley, Robert (Charles)
  1889-1945 .... **TCLC 1, 55**
  See also CA 105; 153; DLB 11; MAL 5;
  RGAL 4
Benda, Julien 1867-1956 .... **TCLC 60**
  See also CA 120; 154; GFL 1789 to the
  Present
Benedetti, Mario 1920-2009 .... **SSC 135**
  See also CA 152; 286; DAM MULT; DLB
  113; EWL 3; HW 1, 2; LAW
**Benedetti, Mario Orlando Hardy Hamlet
  Brenno**
  See Benedetti, Mario
Benedetti Farrugia, Mario
  See Benedetti, Mario
**Benedetti Farrugia, Mario Orlando Hardy
  Hamlet Brenno**
  See Benedetti, Mario
Benedict, Ruth 1887-1948 .... **TCLC 60**
  See also CA 158; CANR 146; DLB 246
Benedict, Ruth Fulton
  See Benedict, Ruth
Benedikt, Michael 1935- .... **CLC 4, 14**
  See also CA 13-16R; CANR 7; CP 1, 2, 3,
  4, 5, 6, 7; DLB 5
Benet, Juan 1927-1993 .... **CLC 28**
  See also CA 143; EWL 3
Benet, Stephen Vincent 1898-1943 ..... **PC 64;
  SSC 10, 86; TCLC 7**
  See also AMWS 11; CA 104; 152; DA3;
  DAM POET; DLB 4, 48, 102, 249, 284;
  DLBY 1997; EWL 3; HGG; MAL 5;
  MTCW 2; MTFW 2005; RGAL 4; RGSF
  2; SSFS 22, 31; SUFW; WP; YABC 1
Benet, William Rose 1886-1950 ..... **TCLC 28**
  See also CA 118; 152; DAM POET; DLB
  45; RGAL 4
Benford, Gregory 1941- .... **CLC 52**
  See also BPFB 1; CA 69-72, 175, 268;
  CAAE 175, 268; CAAS 27; CANR 12,
  24, 49, 95, 134; CN 7; CSW; DLBY 1982;
  MTFW 2005; SCFW 2; SFW 4
Benford, Gregory Albert
  See Benford, Gregory
Bengtsson, Frans (Gunnar)
  1894-1954 .... **TCLC 48**
  See also CA 170; EWL 3
Benjamin, David
  See Slavitt, David R.
Benjamin, Lois
  See Gould, Lois
Benjamin, Walter 1892-1940 .... **TCLC 39**
  See also CA 164; CANR 181; DLB 242;
  EW 11; EWL 3
Ben Jelloun, Tahar 1944- .... **CLC 180**
  See also CA 135, 162; CANR 100, 166;
  CWW 2; EWL 3; RGWL 3; WLIT 2
Benn, Gottfried 1886-1956 .. **PC 35; TCLC 3**
  See also CA 106; 153; DLB 56; EWL 3;
  RGWL 2, 3
Bennett, Alan 1934- .... **CLC 45, 77, 292**
  See also BRWS 8; CA 103; CANR 35, 55,
  106, 157, 197; CBD; CD 5, 6; DAB;
  DAM MST; DLB 310; MTCW 1, 2;
  MTFW 2005

Bennett, (Enoch) Arnold
  1867-1931 .... **TCLC 5, 20, 197**
  See also BRW 6; CA 106; 155; CDBLB
  1890-1914; DLB 10, 34, 98, 135; EWL 3;
  MTCW 2
Bennett, Elizabeth
  See Mitchell, Margaret
Bennett, George Harold 1930- .... **CLC 5**
  See also BW 1; CA 97-100; CAAS 13;
  CANR 87; DLB 33
Bennett, Gwendolyn B. 1902-1981 .... **HR 1:2**
  See also BW 1; CA 125; DLB 51; WP
Bennett, Hal
  See Bennett, George Harold
Bennett, Jay 1912- .... **CLC 35**
  See also AAYA 10, 73; CA 69-72; CANR
  11, 42, 79; JRDA; SAAS 4; SATA 41, 87;
  SATA-Brief 27; WYA; YAW
Bennett, Louise 1919-2006 .... **BLC 1:1; CLC
  28**
  See also BW 2, 3; CA 151; 252; CDWLB
  3; CP 1, 2, 3, 4, 5, 6, 7; DAM MULT;
  DLB 117; EWL 3
Bennett, Louise Simone
  See Bennett, Louise
Bennett-Coverley, Louise
  See Bennett, Louise
Benoit de Sainte-Maure fl. 12th cent.
  - .... **CMLC 90**
Benson, A. C. 1862-1925 .... **TCLC 123**
  See also DLB 98
Benson, E(dward) F(rederic)
  1867-1940 .... **TCLC 27**
  See also CA 114; 157; DLB 135, 153;
  HGG; SUFW 1
Benson, Jackson J. 1930- .... **CLC 34**
  See also CA 25-28R; DLB 111
Benson, Sally 1900-1972 .... **CLC 17**
  See also CA 19-20; 37-40R; CAP 1; SATA
  1, 35; SATA-Obit 27
Benson, Stella 1892-1933 .... **TCLC 17**
  See also CA 117; 154, 155; DLB 36, 162;
  FANT; TEA
Bentham, Jeremy 1748-1832 .... **NCLC 38**
  See also DLB 107, 158, 252
Bentley, E(dmund) C(lerihew)
  1875-1956 .... **TCLC 12**
  See also CA 108; 232; DLB 70; MSW
Bentley, Eric 1916- .... **CLC 24**
  See also CA 5-8R; CAD; CANR 6, 67;
  CBD; CD 5, 6; INT CANR-6
Bentley, Eric Russell
  See Bentley, Eric
ben Uzair, Salem
  See Horne, Richard Henry Hengist
Beolco, Angelo 1496-1542 .... **LC 139**
Beranger, Pierre Jean de
  1780-1857 .... **NCLC 34**
Berdyaev, Nicolas
  See Berdyaev, Nikolai (Aleksandrovich)
Berdyaev, Nikolai (Aleksandrovich)
  1874-1948 .... **TCLC 67**
  See also CA 120; 157
Berdyayev, Nikolai (Aleksandrovich)
  See Berdyaev, Nikolai (Aleksandrovich)
Berendt, John 1939- .... **CLC 86**
  See also CA 146; CANR 75, 83, 151
Berendt, John Lawrence
  See Berendt, John
Beresford, J(ohn) D(avys)
  1873-1947 .... **TCLC 81**
  See also CA 112; 155; DLB 162, 178, 197;
  SFW 4; SUFW 1
Bergelson, David (Rafailovich)
  1884-1952 .... **TCLC 81**
  See also CA 220; DLB 333; EWL 3
Bergelson, Dovid
  See Bergelson, David (Rafailovich)

Boell, Heinrich Theodor
See Boell, Heinrich
Boerne, Alfred
See Doeblin, Alfred
Boethius c. 480-c. 524 .... **CMLC 15**
See also DLB 115; RGWL 2, 3; WLIT 8
Boff, Leonardo (Genezio Darci)
1938- .... **CLC 70; HLC 1**
See also CA 150; DAM MULT; HW 2
Bogan, Louise 1897-1970 .... **CLC 4, 39, 46, 93; PC 12**
See also AMWS 3; CA 73-76; 25-28R; CANR 33, 82; CP 1; DAM POET; DLB 45, 169; EWL 3; MAL 5; MBL; MTCW 1, 2; PFS 21; RGAL 4
Bogarde, Dirk
See Van Den Bogarde, Derek Jules Gaspard Ulric Niven
Bogat, Shatan
See Kacew, Romain
Bogomolny, Robert L. 1938- .... **SSC 41; TCLC 11**
See also CA 121, 164; DLB 182; EWL 3; MJW; RGSF 2; RGWL 2, 3; TWA
Bogomolny, Robert Lee
See Bogomolny, Robert L.
Bogosian, Eric 1953- .... **CLC 45, 141**
See also CA 138; CAD; CANR 102, 148; CD 5, 6; DLB 341
Bograd, Larry 1953- .... **CLC 35**
See also CA 93-96; CANR 57; SAAS 21; SATA 33, 89; WYA
Bohme, Jakob 1575-1624 .... **LC 178**
See also DLB 164
Boiardo, Matteo Maria 1441-1494 .... **LC 6, 168**
Boileau-Despreaux, Nicolas
1636-1711 .... **LC 3, 164**
See also DLB 268; EW 3; GFL Beginnings to 1789; RGWL 2, 3
Boissard, Maurice
See Leautaud, Paul
Bojer, Johan 1872-1959 .... **TCLC 64**
See also CA 189; EWL 3
Bok, Edward W(illiam)
1863-1930 .... **TCLC 101**
See also CA 217; DLB 91; DLBD 16
Boker, George Henry 1823-1890 . **NCLC 125**
See also RGAL 4
Boland, Eavan 1944- ... **CLC 40, 67, 113; PC 58**
See also BRWS 5; CA 143, 207; CAAE 207; CANR 61, 180; CP 1, 6, 7; CWP; DAM POET; DLB 40; FW; MTCW 2; MTFW 2005; PFS 12, 22, 31
Boland, Eavan Aisling
See Boland, Eavan
Bolingbroke, Viscount
See St. John, Henry
Boll, Heinrich
See Boell, Heinrich
Bolt, Lee
See Faust, Frederick
Bolt, Robert (Oxton) 1924-1995 ...... **CLC 14; TCLC 175**
See also CA 17-20R; 147; CANR 35, 67; CBD; DAM DRAM; DFS 2; DLB 13, 233; EWL 3; LAIT 1; MTCW 1
Bombal, Maria Luisa 1910-1980 .... **HLCS 1; SSC 37**
See also CA 127; CANR 72; EWL 3; HW 1; LAW; RGSF 2
Bombet, Louis-Alexandre-Cesar
See Stendhal
Bomkauf
See Kaufman, Bob (Garnell)
Bonaventura NCLC 35
See also DLB 90

Bonaventure 1217(?)-1274 .... **CMLC 79**
See also DLB 115; LMFS 1
Bond, Edward 1934- .... **CLC 4, 6, 13, 23**
See also AAYA 50; BRWS 1; CA 25-28R; CANR 38, 67, 106; CBD; CD 5, 6; DAM DRAM; DFS 3, 8; DLB 13, 310; EWL 3; MTCW 1
Bonham, Frank 1914-1989 .... **CLC 12**
See also AAYA 1, 70; BYA 1, 3; CA 9-12R; CANR 4, 36; JRDA; MAICYA 1, 2; SAAS 3; SATA 1, 49; SATA-Obit 62; TCWW 1, 2; YAW
Bonnefoy, Yves 1923- . **CLC 9, 15, 58; PC 58**
See also CA 85-88; CANR 33, 75, 97, 136; CWW 2; DAM MST, POET; DLB 258; EWL 3; GFL 1789 to the Present; MTCW 1, 2; MTFW 2005
Bonner, Marita
See Occomy, Marita (Odette) Bonner
Bonnin, Gertrude 1876-1938 .... **NNAL**
See also CA 150; DAM MULT; DLB 175
Bontemps, Arna 1902-1973 ... **BLC 1:1; CLC 1, 18; HR 1:2**
See also BW 1; CA 1-4R; 41-44R; CANR 4, 35; CLR 6; CP 1; CWRI 5; DA3; DAM MULT, NOV, POET; DLB 48, 51; JRDA; MAICYA 1, 2; MAL 5; MTCW 1, 2; PFS 32; SATA 2, 44; SATA-Obit 24; WCH; WP
Bontemps, Arnaud Wendell
See Bontemps, Arna
Boot, William
See Stoppard, Tom
Booth, Irwin
See Hoch, Edward D.
Booth, Martin 1944-2004 .... **CLC 13**
See also CA 93-96, 188; 223; CAAE 188; CAAS 2; CANR 92; CP 1, 2, 3, 4
Booth, Philip 1925-2007 .... **CLC 23**
See also CA 5-8R; 262; CANR 5, 88; CP 1, 2, 3, 4, 5, 6, 7; DLBY 1982
Booth, Philip Edmund
See Booth, Philip
Booth, Wayne C. 1921-2005 .... **CLC 24**
See also CA 1-4R; 244; CAAS 5; CANR 3, 43, 117; DLB 67
Booth, Wayne Clayson
See Booth, Wayne C.
Borchert, Wolfgang 1921-1947 .... **TCLC 5**
See also CA 104; 188; DLB 69, 124; EWL 3
Borel, Petrus 1809-1859 .... **NCLC 41**
See also DLB 119; GFL 1789 to the Present
Borges, Jorge Luis 1899-1986 ... **CLC 1, 2, 3, 4, 6, 8, 9, 10, 13, 19, 44, 48, 83; HLC 1; PC 22, 32; SSC 4, 41, 100; TCLC 109; WLC 1**
See also AAYA 26; BPFB 1; CA 21-24R; CANR 19, 33, 75, 105, 133; CDWLB 3; DA; DA3; DAB; DAC; DAM MST, MULT; DLB 113, 283; DLBY 1986; DNFS 1, 2; EWL 3; HW 1, 2; LAW; LMFS 2; MSW; MTCW 1, 2; MTFW 2005; PFS 27; RGHL; RGSF 2; RGWL 2, 3; SFW 4; SSFS 17; TWA; WLIT 1
Borne, Ludwig 1786-1837 .... **NCLC 193**
See also DLB 90
Borowski, Tadeusz 1922-1951 .... **SSC 48; TCLC 9**
See also CA 106; 154; CDWLB 4; DLB 215; EWL 3; RGHL; RGSF 2; RGWL 3; SSFS 13
Borrow, George (Henry)
1803-1881 .... **NCLC 9**
See also BRWS 12; DLB 21, 55, 166
Bosch (Gavino), Juan 1909-2001 .... **HLCS 1**
See also CA 151; 204; DAM MST, MULT; DLB 145; HW 1, 2

Bosman, Herman Charles
1905-1951 .... **TCLC 49**
See also CA 160; DLB 225; RGSF 2
Bosschere, Jean de 1878(?)-1953 ... **TCLC 19**
See also CA 115; 186
Boswell, James 1740-1795 ... **LC 4, 50; WLC 1**
See also BRW 3; CDBLB 1660-1789; DA; DAB; DAC; DAM MST; DLB 104, 142; TEA; WLIT 3
Boto, Eza
See Beti, Mongo
Bottomley, Gordon 1874-1948 ..... **TCLC 107**
See also CA 120; 192; DLB 10
Bottoms, David 1949- .... **CLC 53**
See also CA 105; CANR 22; CSW; DLB 120; DLBY 1983
Boucicault, Dion 1820-1890 .... **NCLC 41**
See also DLB 344
Boucolon, Maryse
See Conde, Maryse
Bourcicault, Dion
See Boucicault, Dion
Bourdieu, Pierre 1930-2002 .... **CLC 198**
See also CA 130; 204
Bourget, Paul (Charles Joseph)
1852-1935 .... **TCLC 12**
See also CA 107; 196; DLB 123; GFL 1789 to the Present
Bourjaily, Vance (Nye) 1922- .... **CLC 8, 62**
See also CA 1-4R; CAAS 1; CANR 2, 72; CN 1, 2, 3, 4, 5, 6, 7; DLB 2, 143; MAL 5
Bourne, Randolph S(illiman)
1886-1918 .... **TCLC 16**
See also AMW; CA 117; 155; DLB 63; MAL 5
Boursiquot, Dionysius
See Boucicault, Dion
Bova, Ben 1932- .... **CLC 45**
See also AAYA 16; CA 5-8R; CAAS 18; CANR 11, 56, 94, 111, 157; CLR 3, 96; DLBY 1981; INT CANR-11; MAICYA 1, 2; MTCW 1; SATA 6, 68, 133; SFW 4
Bova, Benjamin William
See Bova, Ben
Bowen, Elizabeth 1899-1973 ..... **CLC 1, 3, 6, 11, 15, 22, 118; SSC 3, 28, 66; TCLC 148**
See also BRWS 2; CA 17-18; 41-44R; CANR 35, 105; CAP 2; CDBLB 1945-1960; CN 1; DA3; DAM NOV; DLB 15, 162; EWL 3; EXPS; FW; HGG; MTCW 1, 2; MTFW 2005; NFS 13; RGSF 2; SSFS 5, 22; SUFW 1; TEA; WLIT 4
Bowen, Elizabeth Dorothea Cole
See Bowen, Elizabeth
Bowering, George 1935- .... **CLC 15, 47**
See also CA 21-24R; CAAS 16; CANR 10; CN 7; CP 1, 2, 3, 4, 5, 6, 7; DLB 53
Bowering, Marilyn R(uthe) 1949- .... **CLC 32**
See also CA 101; CANR 49; CP 4, 5, 6, 7; CWP; DLB 334
Bowers, Edgar 1924-2000 .... **CLC 9**
See also CA 5-8R; 188; CANR 24; CP 1, 2, 3, 4, 5, 6, 7; CSW; DLB 5
Bowers, Mrs. J. Milton
See Bierce, Ambrose
Bowie, David
See Jones, David Robert
Bowles, Jane (Sydney) 1917-1973 ..... **CLC 3, 68**
See also CA 19-20; 41-44R; CAP 2; CN 1; EWL 3; MAL 5
Bowles, Jane Auer
See Bowles, Jane (Sydney)

Brown, Dee 1908-2002 .... **CLC 18, 47**
See also AAYA 30; CA 13-16R; 212; CAAS 6; CANR 11, 45, 60, 150; CPW; CSW; DA3; DAM POP; DLBY 1980; LAIT 2; MTCW 1, 2; MTFW 2005; NCFS 5; SATA 5, 110; SATA-Obit 141; TCWW 1, 2

Brown, Dee Alexander
See Brown, Dee

Brown, George
See Wertmueller, Lina

Brown, George Douglas
1869-1902 .... **TCLC 28**
See also CA 162; RGEL 2

Brown, George Mackay 1921-1996 ... **CLC 5, 48, 100**
See also BRWS 6; CA 21-24R; 151; CAAS 6; CANR 12, 37, 67; CN 1, 2, 3, 4, 5, 6; CP 1, 2, 3, 4, 5, 6; DLB 14, 27, 139, 271; MTCW 1; RGSF 2; SATA 35

Brown, James Wlllie
See Komunyakaa, Yusef

Brown, James Wlllie, Jr.
See Komunyakaa, Yusef

Brown, Larry 1951-2004 .... **CLC 73, 289**
See also CA 130; 134; 233; CANR 117, 145; CSW; DLB 234; INT CA-134

Brown, Moses
See Barrett, William (Christopher)

Brown, Rita Mae 1944- .... **CLC 18, 43, 79, 259**
See also BPFB 1; CA 45-48; CANR 2, 11, 35, 62, 95, 138, 183; CN 5, 6, 7; CPW; CSW; DA3; DAM NOV, POP; FW; INT CANR-11; MAL 5; MTCW 1, 2; MTFW 2005; NFS 9; RGAL 4; TUS

Brown, Roderick (Langmere) Haig-
See Haig-Brown, Roderick (Langmere)

Brown, Rosellen 1939- .... **CLC 32, 170**
See also CA 77-80; CAAS 10; CANR 14, 44, 98; CN 6, 7

Brown, Sterling Allen 1901-1989 ...... **BLC 1; CLC 1, 23, 59; HR 1:2; PC 55**
See also AFAW 1, 2; BW 1, 3; CA 85-88; 127; CANR 26; CP 3, 4; DA3; DAM MULT, POET; DLB 48, 51, 63; MAL 5; MTCW 1, 2; MTFW 2005; RGAL 4; WP

Brown, Will
See Ainsworth, William Harrison

Brown, William Hill 1765-1793 .... **LC 93**
See also DLB 37

Brown, William Larry
See Brown, Larry

Brown, William Wells 1815-1884 ... **BLC 1:1; DC 1; NCLC 2, 89**
See also DAM MULT; DLB 3, 50, 183, 248; RGAL 4

Browne, Clyde Jackson
See Browne, Jackson

Browne, Jackson 1948(?)- .... **CLC 21**
See also CA 120

Browne, Sir Thomas 1605-1682 .... **LC 111**
See also BRW 2; DLB 151

Browning, Robert 1812-1889 . **NCLC 19, 79; PC 2, 61, 97; WLCS**
See also BRW 4; BRWC 2; BRWR 3; CD-BLB 1832-1890; CLR 97; DA; DA3; DAB; DAC; DAM MST, POET; DLB 32, 163; EXPP; LATS 1:1; PAB; PFS 1, 15; RGEL 2; TEA; WLIT 4; WP; YABC 1

Browning, Tod 1882-1962 .... **CLC 16**
See also CA 141; 117

Brownmiller, Susan 1935- .... **CLC 159**
See also CA 103; CANR 35, 75, 137; DAM NOV; FW; MTCW 1, 2; MTFW 2005

Brownson, Orestes Augustus
1803-1876 .... **NCLC 50**
See also DLB 1, 59, 73, 243

Bruccoli, Matthew J. 1931-2008 .... **CLC 34**
See also CA 9-12R; 274; CANR 7, 87; DLB 103

Bruccoli, Matthew Joseph
See Bruccoli, Matthew J.

Bruce, Lenny
See Schneider, Leonard Alfred

Bruchac, Joseph 1942- .... **NNAL**
See also AAYA 19; CA 33-36R, 256; CAAE 256; CANR 13, 47, 75, 94, 137, 161, 204; CLR 46; CWRI 5; DAM MULT; DLB 342; JRDA; MAICYA 2; MAICYAS 1; MTCW 2; MTFW 2005; SATA 42, 89, 131, 176; SATA-Essay 176

Bruin, John
See Brutus, Dennis

Brulard, Henri
See Stendhal

Brulls, Christian
See Simenon, Georges

Brunetto Latini c. 1220-1294 .... **CMLC 73**

Brunner, John (Kilian Houston)
1934-1995 .... **CLC 8, 10**
See also CA 1-4R; 149; CAAS 8; CANR 2, 37; CPW; DAM POP; DLB 261; MTCW 1, 2; SCFW 1, 2; SFW 4

Bruno, Giordano 1548-1600 .... **LC 27, 167**
See also RGWL 2, 3

Brutus, Dennis 1924-2009 ..... **BLC 1:1; CLC 43; PC 24**
See also AFW; BW 2, 3; CA 49-52; CAAS 14; CANR 2, 27, 42, 81; CDWLB 3; CP 1, 2, 3, 4, 5, 6, 7; DAM MULT, POET; DLB 117, 225; EWL 3

Bryan, C.D.B. 1936-2009 .... **CLC 29**
See also CA 73-76; CANR 13, 68; DLB 185; INT CANR-13

Bryan, Courtlandt Dixon Barnes
See Bryan, C.D.B.

Bryan, Michael
See Moore, Brian

Bryan, William Jennings
1860-1925 .... **TCLC 99**
See also DLB 303

Bryant, William Cullen 1794-1878 . **NCLC 6, 46; PC 20**
See also AMWS 1; CDALB 1640-1865; DA; DAB; DAC; DAM MST, POET; DLB 3, 43, 59, 189, 250; EXPP; PAB; PFS 30; RGAL 4; TUS

Bryusov, Valery Yakovlevich
1873-1924 .... **TCLC 10**
See also CA 107; 155; EWL 3; SFW 4

Buchan, John 1875-1940 .... **TCLC 41**
See also CA 108; 145; CMW 4; DAB; DAM POP; DLB 34, 70, 156; HGG; MSW; MTCW 2; RGEL 2; RHW; YABC 2

Buchanan, George 1506-1582 .... **LC 4, 179**
See also DLB 132

Buchanan, Robert 1841-1901 .... **TCLC 107**
See also CA 179; DLB 18, 35

Buchheim, Lothar-Guenther
1918-2007 .... **CLC 6**
See also CA 85-88; 257

Buchner, (Karl) Georg 1813-1837 ..... **DC 35; NCLC 26, 146; SSC 131**
See also CDWLB 2; DLB 133; EW 6; RGSF 2; RGWL 2, 3; TWA

Buchwald, Art 1925-2007 .... **CLC 33**
See also AITN 1; CA 5-8R; 256; CANR 21, 67, 107; MTCW 1, 2; SATA 10

Buchwald, Arthur
See Buchwald, Art

Buck, Pearl S. 1892-1973 .... **CLC 7, 11, 18, 127**
See also AAYA 42; AITN 1; AMWS 2; BPFB 1; CA 1-4R; 41-44R; CANR 1, 34; CDALBS; CN 1; DA; DA3; DAB; DAC; DAM MST, NOV; DLB 9, 102, 329; EWL 3; LAIT 3; MAL 5; MTCW 1, 2; MTFW 2005; NFS 25; RGAL 4; RHW; SATA 1, 25; TUS

Buck, Pearl Sydenstricker
See Buck, Pearl S.

Buckler, Ernest 1908-1984 .... **CLC 13**
See also CA 11-12; 114; CAP 1; CCA 1; CN 1, 2, 3; DAC; DAM MST; DLB 68; SATA 47

Buckley, Christopher 1952- .... **CLC 165**
See also CA 139; CANR 119, 180

Buckley, Christopher Taylor
See Buckley, Christopher

Buckley, Vincent (Thomas)
1925-1988 .... **CLC 57**
See also CA 101; CP 1, 2, 3, 4; DLB 289

Buckley, William F., Jr.
See Buckley, William F.

Buckley, William F. 1925-2008 .... **CLC 7, 18, 37**
See also AITN 1; BPFB 1; CA 1-4R; 269; CANR 1, 24, 53, 93, 133, 185; CMW 4; CPW; DA3; DAM POP; DLB 137; DLBY 1980; INT CANR-24; MTCW 1, 2; MTFW 2005; TUS

Buckley, William Frank
See Buckley, William F.

Buckley, William Frank, Jr.
See Buckley, William F.

Buechner, Frederick 1926- ..... **CLC 2, 4, 6, 9**
See also AMWS 12; BPFB 1; CA 13-16R; CANR 11, 39, 64, 114, 138; CN 1, 2, 3, 4, 5, 6, 7; DAM NOV; DLBY 1980; INT CANR-11; MAL 5; MTCW 1, 2; MTFW 2005; TCLE 1:1

Buell, John (Edward) 1927- .... **CLC 10**
See also CA 1-4R; CANR 71; DLB 53

Buero Vallejo, Antonio 1916-2000 ... **CLC 15, 46, 139, 226; DC 18**
See also CA 106; 189; CANR 24, 49, 75; CWW 2; DFS 11; EWL 3; HW 1; MTCW 1, 2

Bufalino, Gesualdo 1920-1996 .... **CLC 74**
See also CA 209; CWW 2; DLB 196

Bugayev, Boris Nikolayevich
1880-1934 .... **PC 11; TCLC 7**
See also CA 104; 165; DLB 295; EW 9; EWL 3; MTCW 2; MTFW 2005; RGWL 2, 3

Bukowski, Charles 1920-1994 ... **CLC 2, 5, 9, 41, 82, 108; PC 18; SSC 45**
See also CA 17-20R; 144; CANR 40, 62, 105, 180; CN 4, 5; CP 1, 2, 3, 4, 5; CPW; DA3; DAM NOV, POET; DLB 5, 130, 169; EWL 3; MAL 5; MTCW 1, 2; MTFW 2005; PFS 28

Bulgakov, Mikhail 1891-1940 .... **SSC 18; TCLC 2, 16, 159**
See also AAYA 74; BPFB 1; CA 105; 152; DAM DRAM, NOV; DLB 272; EWL 3; MTCW 2; MTFW 2005; NFS 8; RGSF 2; RGWL 2, 3; SFW 4; TWA

Bulgakov, Mikhail Afanasevich
See Bulgakov, Mikhail

Bulgya, Alexander Alexandrovich
1901-1956 .... **TCLC 53**
See also CA 117; 181; DLB 272; EWL 3

Bullins, Ed 1935- ...... **BLC 1:1; CLC 1, 5, 7; DC 6**
See also BW 2, 3; CA 49-52; CAAS 16; CAD; CANR 24, 46, 73, 134; CD 5, 6; DAM DRAM, MULT; DLB 7, 38, 249; EWL 3; MAL 5; MTCW 1, 2; MTFW 2005; RGAL 4

Bulosan, Carlos 1911-1956 .... **AAL**
See also CA 216; DLB 312; RGAL 4

Bulwer-Lytton, Edward
1803-1873 .... **NCLC 1, 45**
See also DLB 21; RGEL 2; SATA 23; SFW 4; SUFW 1; TEA

Bulwer-Lytton, Edward George Earle Lytton
See Bulwer-Lytton, Edward

Bunin, Ivan
See Bunin, Ivan Alexeyevich

Bunin, Ivan Alekseevich
See Bunin, Ivan Alexeyevich

Bunin, Ivan Alexeyevich 1870-1953 ... **SSC 5; TCLC 6**
See also CA 104; DLB 317, 329; EWL 3; RGSF 2; RGWL 2, 3; TWA

Bunting, Basil 1900-1985 ...... **CLC 10, 39, 47**
See also BRWS 7; CA 53-56; 115; CANR 7; CP 1, 2, 3, 4; DAM POET; DLB 20; EWL 3; RGEL 2

Bunuel, Luis 1900-1983 ... **CLC 16, 80; HLC 1**
See also CA 101; 110; CANR 32, 77; DAM MULT; HW 1

Bunyan, John 1628-1688 .... **LC 4, 69, 180; WLC 1**
See also BRW 2; BYA 5; CDBLB 1660-1789; CLR 124; DA; DAB; DAC; DAM MST; DLB 39; NFS 32; RGEL 2; TEA; WCH; WLIT 3

Buonarroti, Michelangelo
1568-1646 .... **PC 103**
See also DLB 339

Buravsky, Alexandr CLC 59

Burchill, Julie 1959- .... **CLC 238**
See also CA 135; CANR 115, 116

Burckhardt, Jacob (Christoph)
1818-1897 .... **NCLC 49**
See also EW 6

Burford, Eleanor
See Hibbert, Eleanor Alice Burford

Burgess, Anthony 1917-1993 . **CLC 1, 2, 4, 5, 8, 10, 13, 15, 22, 40, 62, 81, 94**
See also AAYA 25; AITN 1; BRWS 1; CA 1-4R; 143; CANR 2, 46; CDBLB 1960 to Present; CN 1, 2, 3, 4, 5; DA3; DAB; DAC; DAM NOV; DLB 14, 194, 261; DLBY 1998; EWL 3; MTCW 1, 2; MTFW 2005; NFS 15; RGEL 2; RHW; SFW 4; TEA; YAW

Buridan, John c. 1295-c. 1358 ...... **CMLC 97**

Burke, Edmund 1729(?)-1797 .... **LC 7, 36, 146; WLC 1**
See also BRW 3; DA; DA3; DAB; DAC; DAM MST; DLB 104, 252, 336; RGEL 2; TEA

Burke, Kenneth (Duva) 1897-1993 ... **CLC 2, 24**
See also AMW; CA 5-8R; 143; CANR 39, 74, 136; CN 1, 2; CP 1, 2, 3, 4, 5; DLB 45, 63; EWL 3; MAL 5; MTCW 1, 2; MTFW 2005; RGAL 4

Burke, Leda
See Garnett, David

Burke, Ralph
See Silverberg, Robert

Burke, Thomas 1886-1945 .... **TCLC 63**
See also CA 113; 155; CMW 4; DLB 197

Burney, Fanny 1752-1840 .... **NCLC 12, 54, 107**
See also BRWS 3; DLB 39; FL 1:2; NFS 16; RGEL 2; TEA

Burney, Frances
See Burney, Fanny

Burns, Robert 1759-1796 ... **LC 3, 29, 40; PC 6; WLC 1**
See also AAYA 51; BRW 3; CDBLB 1789-1832; DA; DA3; DAB; DAC; DAM MST; POET; DLB 109; EXPP; PAB; RGEL 2; TEA; WP

Burns, Tex
See L'Amour, Louis

Burnshaw, Stanley 1906-2005 ..... **CLC 3, 13, 44**
See also CA 9-12R; 243; CP 1, 2, 3, 4, 5, 6, 7; DLB 48; DLBY 1997

Burr, Anne 1937- .... **CLC 6**
See also CA 25-28R

Burroughs, Augusten 1965- .... **CLC 277**
See also AAYA 73; CA 214; CANR 168

Burroughs, Edgar Rice 1875-1950 . **TCLC 2, 32**
See also AAYA 11; BPFB 1; BYA 4, 9; CA 104; 132; CANR 131; DA3; DAM NOV; DLB 8; FANT; MTCW 1, 2; MTFW 2005; RGAL 4; SATA 41; SCFW 1, 2; SFW 4; TCWW 1, 2; TUS; YAW

Burroughs, William S. 1914-1997 . **CLC 1, 2, 5, 15, 22, 42, 75, 109; TCLC 121; WLC 1**
See also AAYA 60; AITN 2; AMWS 3; BG 1:2; BPFB 1; CA 9-12R; 160; CANR 20, 52, 104; CN 1, 2, 3, 4, 5, 6; CPW; DA; DA3; DAB; DAC; DAM MST, NOV, POP; DLB 2, 8, 16, 152, 237; DLBY 1981, 1997; EWL 3; GLL 1; HGG; LMFS 2; MAL 5; MTCW 1, 2; MTFW 2005; RGAL 4; SFW 4

Burroughs, William Seward
See Burroughs, William S.

Burton, Sir Richard F(rancis)
1821-1890 .... **NCLC 42**
See also DLB 55, 166, 184; SSFS 21

Burton, Robert 1577-1640 .... **LC 74**
See also DLB 151; RGEL 2

Buruma, Ian 1951- .... **CLC 163**
See also CA 128; CANR 65, 141, 195

Bury, Stephen
See Stephenson, Neal

Busch, Frederick 1941-2006 .. **CLC 7, 10, 18, 47, 166**
See also CA 33-36R; 248; CAAS 1; CANR 45, 73, 92, 157; CN 1, 2, 3, 4, 5, 6, 7; DLB 6, 218

Busch, Frederick Matthew
See Busch, Frederick

Bush, Barney (Furman) 1946- .... **NNAL**
See also CA 145

Bush, Ronald 1946- .... **CLC 34**
See also CA 136

Busia, Abena, P. A. 1953- .... **BLC 2:1**

Bustos, Francisco
See Borges, Jorge Luis

Bustos Domecq, Honorio
See Bioy Casares, Adolfo; Borges, Jorge Luis

Butler, Octavia 1947-2006 . **BLC 2:1; BLCS; CLC 38, 121, 230, 240**
See also AAYA 18, 48; AFAW 2; AMWS 13; BPFB 1; BW 2, 3; CA 73-76; 248; CANR 12, 24, 38, 73, 145, 240; CLR 65; CN 7; CPW; DA3; DAM MULT, POP; DLB 33; LATS 1:2; MTCW 1, 2; MTFW 2005; NFS 8, 21, 34; SATA 84; SCFW 2; SFW 4; SSFS 6; TCLE 1:1; YAW

Butler, Octavia E.
See Butler, Octavia

Butler, Octavia Estelle
See Butler, Octavia

Butler, Robert Olen, Jr.
See Butler, Robert Olen

Butler, Robert Olen 1945- .... **CLC 81, 162; SSC 117**
See also AMWS 12; BPFB 1; CA 112; CANR 66, 138, 194; CN 7; CSW; DAM POP; DLB 173, 335; INT CA-112; MAL 5; MTCW 2; MTFW 2005; SSFS 11, 22

Butler, Samuel 1612-1680 .... **LC 16, 43, 173; PC 94**
See also DLB 101, 126; RGEL 2

Butler, Samuel 1835-1902 .... **TCLC 1, 33; WLC 1**
See also BRWS 2; CA 143; CDBLB 1890-1914; DA; DA3; DAB; DAC; DAM MST, NOV; DLB 18, 57, 174; RGEL 2; SFW 4; TEA

Butler, Walter C.
See Faust, Frederick

Butor, Michel (Marie Francois)
1926- .... **CLC 1, 3, 8, 11, 15, 161**
See also CA 9-12R; CANR 33, 66; CWW 2; DLB 83; EW 13; EWL 3; GFL 1789 to the Present; MTCW 1, 2; MTFW 2005

Butts, Mary 1890(?)-1937 ... **SSC 124; TCLC 77**
See also CA 148; DLB 240

Buxton, Ralph
See Silverstein, Alvin; Silverstein, Virginia B.

Buzo, Alex
See Buzo, Alexander (John)

Buzo, Alexander (John) 1944- .... **CLC 61**
See also CA 97-100; CANR 17, 39, 69; CD 5, 6; DLB 289

Buzzati, Dino 1906-1972 .... **CLC 36**
See also CA 160; 33-36R; DLB 177; RGWL 2, 3; SFW 4

Byars, Betsy 1928- .... **CLC 35**
See also AAYA 19; BYA 3; CA 33-36R, 183; CAAE 183; CANR 18, 36, 57, 102, 148; CLR 1, 16, 72; DLB 52; INT CANR-18; JRDA; MAICYA 1, 2; MAICYAS 1; MTCW 1; SAAS 1; SATA 4, 46, 80, 163; SATA-Essay 108; WYA; YAW

Byars, Betsy Cromer
See Byars, Betsy

Byatt, A. S. 1936- .... **CLC 19, 65, 136, 223; SSC 91**
See also BPFB 1; BRWC 2; BRWS 4; CA 13-16R; CANR 13, 33, 50, 75, 96, 133, 205; CN 1, 2, 3, 4, 5, 6; DA3; DAM NOV, POP; DLB 14, 194, 319, 326; EWL 3; MTCW 1, 2; MTFW 2005; RGSF 2; RHW; SSFS 26; TEA

Byatt, Antonia Susan Drabble
See Byatt, A. S.

Byrd, William II 1674-1744 .... **LC 112**
See also DLB 24, 140; RGAL 4

Byrne, David 1952- .... **CLC 26**
See also CA 127

Byrne, John Joseph
See Leonard, Hugh

Byrne, John Keyes
See Leonard, Hugh

Byron, George Gordon
See Lord Byron

Byron, George Gordon Noel
See Lord Byron

Byron, Robert 1905-1941 .... **TCLC 67**
See also CA 160; DLB 195

C. 3. 3.
See Wilde, Oscar

Caballero, Fernan 1796-1877 .... **NCLC 10**

Cabell, Branch
See Cabell, James Branch

Cabell, James Branch 1879-1958 .... **TCLC 6**
See also CA 105; 152; DLB 9, 78; FANT; MAL 5; MTCW 2; RGAL 4; SUFW 1

Cabeza de Vaca, Alvar Nunez
1490-1557(?) .... **LC 61**

Cable, George Washington
1844-1925 .... **SSC 4; TCLC 4**
See also CA 104; 155; DLB 12, 74; DLBD 13; RGAL 4; TUS

FANT; INT CANR-27; MTCW 1, 2;
MTFW 2005; NFS 5; SATA 83, 127;
SCFW 2; SFW 4; SUFW 2; YAW

Cardenal, Ernesto 1925- .... **CLC 31, 161;
HLC 1; PC 22**
See also CA 49-52; CANR 2, 32, 66, 138;
CWW 2; DAM MULT; DLB 290;
EWL 3; HW 1, 2; LAWS 1; MTCW 1, 2;
MTFW 2005; RGWL 2, 3

Cardinal, Marie 1929-2001 .... **CLC 189**
See also CA 177; CWW 2; DLB 83; FW

Cardozo, Benjamin N(athan)
1870-1938 .... **TCLC 65**
See also CA 117; 164

Carducci, Giosue (Alessandro Giuseppe)
1835-1907 .... **PC 46; TCLC 32**
See also CA 163; DLB 329; EW 7; RGWL
2, 3

Carew, Thomas 1595(?)-1640 ..... **LC 13, 159;
PC 29**
See also BRW 2; DLB 126; PAB; RGEL 2

Carey, Ernestine Gilbreth
1908-2006 .... **CLC 17**
See also CA 5-8R; 254; CANR 71; SATA
2; SATA-Obit 177

Carey, Peter 1943- .... **CLC 40, 55, 96, 183;
SSC 133**
See also BRWS 12; CA 123; 127; CANR
53, 76, 117, 157, 185; CN 4, 5, 6, 7; DLB
289, 326; EWL 3; INT CA-127; LNFS 1;
MTCW 1, 2; MTFW 2005; RGSF 2;
SATA 94

Carey, Peter Philip
See Carey, Peter

Carleton, William 1794-1869 ... **NCLC 3, 199**
See also DLB 159; RGEL 2; RGSF 2

Carlisle, Henry (Coffin) 1926- .... **CLC 33**
See also CA 13-16R; CANR 15, 85

Carlsen, Chris
See Holdstock, Robert

Carlson, Ron 1947- .... **CLC 54**
See also CA 105, 189; CAAE 189; CANR
27, 155, 197; DLB 244

Carlson, Ronald F.
See Carlson, Ron

Carlyle, Jane Welsh 1801-1866 ... **NCLC 181**
See also DLB 55

Carlyle, Thomas 1795-1881 ..... **NCLC 22, 70**
See also BRW 4; CDBLB 1789-1832; DA;
DAB; DAC; DAM MST; DLB 55, 144,
254, 338; RGEL 2; TEA

Carman, (William) Bliss 1861-1929 ... **PC 34;
TCLC 7**
See also CA 104; 152; DAC; DLB 92;
RGEL 2

Carnegie, Dale 1888-1955 .... **TCLC 53**
See also CA 218

Caro Mallén de Soto, Ana c. 1590-c.
1650 .... **LC 175**

Carossa, Hans 1878-1956 .... **TCLC 48**
See also CA 170; DLB 66; EWL 3

Carpenter, Don(ald Richard)
1931-1995 .... **CLC 41**
See also CA 45-48; 149; CANR 1, 71

Carpenter, Edward 1844-1929 .... **TCLC 88**
See also BRWS 13; CA 163; GLL 1

Carpenter, John 1948- .... **CLC 161**
See also AAYA 2, 73; CA 134; SATA 58

Carpenter, John Howard
See Carpenter, John

Carpenter, Johnny
See Carpenter, John

Carpentier, Alejo 1904-1980 .. **CLC 8, 11, 38,
110; HLC 1; SSC 35; TCLC 201**
See also CA 65-68; 97-100; CANR 11, 70;
CDWLB 3; DAM MULT; DLB 113; EWL
3; HW 1, 2; LAW; LMFS 2; RGSF 2;
RGWL 2, 3; WLIT 1

Carpentier y Valmont, Alejo
See Carpentier, Alejo

Carr, Caleb 1955- .... **CLC 86**
See also CA 147; CANR 73, 134; DA3;
DLB 350

Carr, Emily 1871-1945 .... **TCLC 32**
See also CA 159; DLB 68; FW; GLL 2

Carr, H. D.
See Crowley, Edward Alexander

Carr, John Dickson 1906-1977 .... **CLC 3**
See also CA 49-52; 69-72; CANR 3, 33,
60; CMW 4; DLB 306; MSW; MTCW 1,
2

Carr, Philippa
See Hibbert, Eleanor Alice Burford

Carr, Virginia Spencer 1929- .... **CLC 34**
See also CA 61-64; CANR 175; DLB 111

Carrere, Emmanuel 1957- .... **CLC 89**
See also CA 200

Carrier, Roch 1937- .... **CLC 13, 78**
See also CA 130; CANR 61, 152; CCA 1;
DAC; DAM MST; DLB 53; SATA 105,
166

Carroll, James Dennis
See Carroll, Jim

Carroll, James P. 1943(?)- .... **CLC 38**
See also CA 81-84; CANR 73, 139; MTCW
2; MTFW 2005

Carroll, Jim 1949-2009 .... **CLC 35, 143**
See also AAYA 17; CA 45-48; 290; CANR
42, 115; NCFS 5

Carroll, Lewis 1832-1898 . **NCLC 2, 53, 139;
PC 18, 74; WLC 1**
See also AAYA 39; BRW 5; BYA 5, 13; CD-
BLB 1832-1890; CLR 18, 108; DA; DA3;
DAB; DAC; DAM MST, NOV, POET;
DLB 18, 163, 178; DLBY 1998; EXPN;
EXPP; FANT; JRDA; LAIT 1; MAICYA
1, 2; NFS 27; PFS 11, 30; RGEL 2; SATA
100; SUFW 1; TEA; WCH; YABC 2

Carroll, Paul Vincent 1900-1968 ...... **CLC 10**
See also CA 9-12R; 25-28R; DLB 10; EWL
3; RGEL 2

Carruth, Hayden 1921-2008 .... **CLC 4, 7, 10,
18, 84, 287; PC 10**
See also AMWS 16; CA 9-12R; 277; CANR
4, 38, 59, 110, 174; CP 1, 2, 3, 4, 5, 6, 7;
DLB 5, 165; INT CANR-4; MTCW 1, 2;
MTFW 2005; PFS 26; SATA 47; SATA-
Obit 197

Carson, Anne 1950- .... **CLC 185; PC 64**
See also AMWS 12; CA 203; CP 7; DLB
193; PFS 18; TCLE 1:1

Carson, Ciaran 1948- .... **CLC 201**
See also BRWS 13; CA 112; 153; CANR
113, 189; CP 6, 7; PFS 26

Carson, Rachel 1907-1964 .... **CLC 71**
See also AAYA 49; AMWS 9; ANW; CA
77-80; CANR 35; DA3; DAM POP; DLB
275; FW; LAIT 4; MAL 5; MTCW 1, 2;
MTFW 2005; NCFS 1; SATA 23

Carson, Rachel Louise
See Carson, Rachel

Cartagena, Teresa de 1425(?)- .... **LC 155**
See also DLB 286

Carter, Angela 1940-1992 ...... **CLC 5, 41, 76;
SSC 13, 85; TCLC 139**
See also BRWS 3; CA 53-56; 136; CANR
12, 36, 61, 106; CN 3, 4, 5; DA3; DLB
14, 207, 261, 319; EXPS; FANT; FW; GL
2; MTCW 1, 2; MTFW 2005; RGSF 2;
SATA 66; SATA-Obit 70; SFW 4; SSFS
4, 12; SUFW 2; WLIT 4

Carter, Angela Olive
See Carter, Angela

Carter, Martin (Wylde) 1927- .... **BLC 2:1**
See also BW 2; CA 102; CANR 42; CD-
WLB 3; CP 1, 2, 3, 4, 5, 6; DLB 117;
EWL 3

Carter, Nick
See Smith, Martin Cruz

Carter, Nick
See Smith, Martin Cruz

Carver, Raymond 1938-1988 ..... **CLC 22, 36,
53, 55, 126; PC 54; SSC 8, 51, 104**
See also AAYA 44; AMWS 3; BPFB 1; CA
33-36R; 126; CANR 17, 34, 61, 103; CN
4; CPW; DA3; DAM NOV; DLB 130;
DLBY 1984, 1988; EWL 3; MAL 5;
MTCW 1, 2; MTFW 2005; PFS 17;
RGAL 4; RGSF 2; SSFS 3, 6, 12, 13, 23;
TCLE 1:1; TCWW 2; TUS

Cary, Elizabeth, Lady Falkland
1585-1639 .... **LC 30, 141**

Cary, (Arthur) Joyce (Lunel)
1888-1957 .... **TCLC 1, 29, 196**
See also BRW 7; CA 104; 164; CDBLB
1914-1945; DLB 15, 100; EWL 3; MTCW
2; RGEL 2; TEA

Casal, Julian del 1863-1893 .... **NCLC 131**
See also DLB 283; LAW

Casanova, Giacomo
See Casanova de Seingalt, Giovanni Jacopo

Casanova, Giovanni Giacomo
See Casanova de Seingalt, Giovanni Jacopo

Casanova de Seingalt, Giovanni Jacopo
1725-1798 .... **LC 13, 151**
See also WLIT 7

Casares, Adolfo Bioy
See Bioy Casares, Adolfo

Casas, Bartolome de las 1474-1566
See Las Casas, Bartolome de

Case, John
See Hougan, Carolyn

Casely-Hayford, J(oseph) E(phraim)
1866-1903 .... **BLC 1:1; TCLC 24**
See also BW 2; CA 123; 152; DAM MULT

Casey, John (Dudley) 1939- .... **CLC 59**
See also BEST 90:2; CA 69-72; CANR 23,
100

Casey, Michael 1947- .... **CLC 2**
See also CA 65-68; CANR 109; CP 2, 3;
DLB 5

Casey, Patrick
See Thurman, Wallace (Henry)

Casey, Warren 1935-1988 .... **CLC 12**
See also CA 101; 127; INT CA-101

Casey, Warren Peter
See Casey, Warren

Casona, Alejandro
See Alvarez, Alejandro Rodriguez

Cassavetes, John 1929-1989 .... **CLC 20**
See also CA 85-88; 127; CANR 82

Cassian, Nina 1924- .... **PC 17**
See also CWP; CWW 2

Cassill, R(onald) V(erlin)
1919-2002 .... **CLC 4, 23**
See also CA 9-12R; 208; CAAS 1; CANR
7, 45; CN 1, 2, 3, 4, 5, 6, 7; DLB 6, 218;
DLBY 2002

Cassiodorus, Flavius Magnus Aurelius c.
490(?)-c. 583(?) .... **CMLC 43, 122**

Cassirer, Ernst 1874-1945 .... **TCLC 61**
See also CA 157

Cassity, (Allen) Turner 1929- .... **CLC 6, 42**
See also CA 17-20R; 223; CAAE 223;
CAAS 8; CANR 11; CSW; DLB 105

Cassius Dio c. 155-c. 229 .... **CMLC 99**
See also DLB 176

Castaneda, Carlos (Cesar Aranha)
1931(?)-1998 .... **CLC 12, 119**
See also CA 25-28R; CANR 32, 66, 105;
DNFS 1; HW 1; MTCW 1

Castedo, Elena 1937- .... **CLC 65**
See also CA 132

Castedo-Ellerman, Elena
See Castedo, Elena

Castellanos, Rosario 1925-1974 .... **CLC 66;**
HLC 1; SSC 39, 68
See also CA 131; 53-56; CANR 58; CD-
WLB 3; DAM MULT; DLB 113, 290;
EWL 3; FW; HW 1; LAW; MTCW 2;
MTFW 2005; RGSF 2; RGWL 2, 3

Castelvetro, Lodovico 1505-1571 .... **LC 12**

Castiglione, Baldassare 1478-1529 ..... **LC 12,**
165
See also EW 2; LMFS 1; RGWL 2, 3;
WLIT 7

Castiglione, Baldesar
See Castiglione, Baldassare

Castillo, Ana 1953- .... **CLC 151, 279**
See also AAYA 42; CA 131; CANR 51, 86,
128, 172; CWP; DLB 122, 227; DNFS 2;
FW; HW 1; LLW; PFS 21

Castillo, Ana Hernandez Del
See Castillo, Ana

Castle, Robert
See Hamilton, Edmond

Castro (Ruz), Fidel 1926(?)- .... **HLC 1**
See also CA 110; 129; CANR 81; DAM
MULT; HW 2

Castro, Guillen de 1569-1631 .... **LC 19**

Castro, Rosalia de 1837-1885 ... **NCLC 3, 78;**
PC 41
See also DAM MULT

Castro Alves, Antonio de
1847-1871 .... **NCLC 205**
See also DLB 307; LAW

Cather, Willa 1873-1947 .... **SSC 2, 50, 114;**
TCLC 1, 11, 31, 99, 132, 152; WLC 1
See also AAYA 24; AMW; AMWC 1;
AMWR 1; BPFB 1; CA 104; 128; CDALB
1865-1917; CLR 98; DA; DA3; DAB;
DAC; DAM MST, NOV; DLB 9, 54, 78,
256; DLBD 1; EWL 3; EXPN; EXPS; FL
1:5; LAIT 3; LATS 1:1; MAL 5; MBL;
MTCW 1, 2; MTFW 2005; NFS 2, 19,
33; RGAL 4; RGSF 2; RHW; SATA 30;
SSFS 2, 7, 16, 27; TCWW 1, 2; TUS

Cather, Willa Sibert
See Cather, Willa

Catherine II
See Catherine the Great

Catherine, Saint 1347-1380 ... **CMLC 27, 116**

Catherine the Great 1729-1796 .... **LC 69**
See also DLB 150

Cato, Marcus Porcius
234B.C.-149B.C. .... **CMLC 21**
See also DLB 211

Cato, Marcus Porcius, the Elder
See Cato, Marcus Porcius

Cato the Elder
See Cato, Marcus Porcius

Catton, (Charles) Bruce 1899-1978 . **CLC 35**
See also AITN 1; CA 5-8R; 81-84; CANR
7, 74; DLB 17; MTCW 2; MTFW 2005;
SATA 2; SATA-Obit 24

Catullus c. 84B.C.-54B.C. .... **CMLC 18**
See also AW 2; CDWLB 1; DLB 211;
RGWL 2, 3; WLIT 8

Cauldwell, Frank
See King, Francis (Henry)

Caunitz, William J. 1933-1996 .... **CLC 34**
See also BEST 89:3; CA 125; 130; 152;
CANR 73; INT CA-130

Causley, Charles (Stanley)
1917-2003 .... **CLC 7**
See also CA 9-12R; 223; CANR 5, 35, 94;
CLR 30; CP 1, 2, 3, 4, 5; CWRI 5; DLB
27; MTCW 1; SATA 3, 66; SATA-Obit
149

Caute, (John) David 1936- .... **CLC 29**
See also CA 1-4R; CAAS 4; CANR 1, 33,
64, 120; CBD; CD 5, 6; CN 1, 2, 3, 4, 5,
6, 7; DAM NOV; DLB 14, 231

Cavafy, C. P.
See Cavafy, Constantine

Cavafy, Constantine 1863-1933 .... **PC 36;**
TCLC 2, 7
See also CA 104; 148; DA3; DAM POET;
EW 8; EWL 3; MTCW 2; PFS 19; RGWL
2, 3; WP

Cavafy, Constantine Peter
See Cavafy, Constantine

Cavalcanti, Guido c. 1250-c.
1300 .... **CMLC 54**
See also RGWL 2, 3; WLIT 7

Cavallo, Evelyn
See Spark, Muriel

Cavanna, Betty
See Harrison, Elizabeth (Allen) Cavanna

Cavanna, Elizabeth
See Harrison, Elizabeth (Allen) Cavanna

Cavanna, Elizabeth Allen
See Harrison, Elizabeth (Allen) Cavanna

Cavendish, Margaret 1623-1673 . **LC 30, 132**
See also DLB 131, 252, 281; RGEL 2

Cavendish, Margaret Lucas
See Cavendish, Margaret

Caxton, William 1421(?)-1491(?) .... **LC 17**
See also DLB 170

Cayer, D. M.
See Duffy, Maureen

Cayrol, Jean 1911-2005 .... **CLC 11**
See also CA 89-92; 236; DLB 83; EWL 3

Cela, Camilo Jose
See Cela, Camilo Jose

Cela, Camilo Jose 1916-2002 .... **CLC 4, 13,**
59, 122; HLC 1; SSC 71
See also BEST 90:2; CA 21-24R; 206;
CAAS 10; CANR 21, 32, 76, 139; CWW
2; DAM MULT; DLB 322; DLBY 1989;
EW 13; EWL 3; HW 1; MTCW 1, 2;
MTFW 2005; RGSF 2; RGWL 2, 3

Celan, Paul 1920-1970 ... **CLC 10, 19, 53, 82;**
PC 10
See also CA 85-88; CANR 33, 61; CDWLB
2; DLB 69; EWL 3; MTCW 1; PFS 21;
RGHL; RGWL 2, 3

Cela y Trulock, Camilo Jose
See Cela, Camilo Jose

Celine, Louis-Ferdinand 1894-1961 .. **CLC 1,**
3, 4, 7, 47, 124
See also CA 85-88; CANR 28; DLB 72;
EW 11; EWL 3; GFL 1789 to the Present;
MTCW 1; RGWL 2, 3

Cellini, Benvenuto 1500-1571 .... **LC 7**
See also WLIT 7

Cendrars, Blaise
See Sauser-Hall, Frederic

Centlivre, Susanna 1669(?)-1723 .... **DC 25;**
LC 65
See also DLB 84; RGEL 2

Cernuda, Luis 1902-1963 ..... **CLC 54; PC 62**
See also CA 131; 89-92; DAM POET; DLB
134; EWL 3; GLL 1; HW 1; RGWL 2, 3

Cernuda y Bidon, Luis
See Cernuda, Luis

Cervantes, Lorna Dee 1954- ..... **HLCS 1; PC**
35
See also CA 131; CANR 80; CP 7; CWP;
DLB 82; EXPP; HW 1; LLW; PFS 30

Cervantes, Miguel de 1547-1616 . **HLCS; LC**
6, 23, 93; SSC 12, 108; WLC 1
See also AAYA 56; BYA 1, 14; DA; DAB;
DAC; DAM MST, NOV; EW 2; LAIT 1;
LATS 1:1; LMFS 1; NFS 8; RGSF 2;
RGWL 2, 3; TWA

Cervantes Saavedra, Miguel de
See Cervantes, Miguel de

Cesaire, Aime
See Cesaire, Aime

Cesaire, Aime 1913-2008 .... **BLC 1:1; CLC**
19, 32, 112, 280; DC 22; PC 25
See also BW 2, 3; CA 65-68; 271; CANR
24, 43, 81; CWW 2; DA3; DAM MULT,
POET; DLB 321; EWL 3; GFL 1789 to
the Present; MTCW 1, 2; MTFW 2005;
WP

Cesaire, Aime Fernand
See Cesaire, Aime

Cesaire, Aime Fernand
See Cesaire, Aime

Chaadaev, Petr Iakovlevich
1794-1856 .... **NCLC 197**
See also DLB 198

Chabon, Michael 1963- ... **CLC 55, 149, 265;**
SSC 59
See also AAYA 45; AMWS 11; CA 139;
CANR 57, 96, 127, 138, 196; DLB 278;
MAL 5; MTFW 2005; NFS 25; SATA 145

Chabrol, Claude 1930- .... **CLC 16**
See also CA 110

Chairil Anwar
See Anwar, Chairil

Challans, Mary
See Renault, Mary

Challis, George
See Faust, Frederick

Chambers, Aidan 1934- .... **CLC 35**
See also AAYA 27; CA 25-28R; CANR 12,
31, 58, 116; CLR 151; JRDA; MAICYA
1, 2; SAAS 12; SATA 1, 69, 108, 171;
WYA; YAW

Chambers, James **CLC 21**
See also CA 124; 199

Chambers, Jessie
See Lawrence, D. H.

Chambers, Robert W(illiam)
1865-1933 .... **SSC 92; TCLC 41**
See also CA 165; DLB 202; HGG; SATA
107; SUFW 1

Chambers, (David) Whittaker
1901-1961 .... **TCLC 129**
See also CA 89-92; DLB 303

Chamisso, Adelbert von
1781-1838 .... **NCLC 82**
See also DLB 90; RGWL 2, 3; SUFW 1

Chamoiseau, Patrick 1953- ..... **CLC 268, 276**
See also CA 162; CANR 88; EWL 3;
RGWL 3

Chance, James T.
See Carpenter, John

Chance, John T.
See Carpenter, John

Chand, Munshi Prem
See Srivastava, Dhanpat Rai

Chand, Prem
See Srivastava, Dhanpat Rai

Chandler, Raymond 1888-1959 .... **SSC 23;**
TCLC 1, 7, 179
See also AAYA 25; AMWC 2; AMWS 4;
BPFB 1; CA 104; 129; CANR 60, 107;
CDALB 1929-1941; CMW 4; DA3; DLB
226, 253; DLBD 6; EWL 3; MAL 5;
MSW; MTCW 1, 2; MTFW 2005; NFS
17; RGAL 4; TUS

Chandler, Raymond Thornton
See Chandler, Raymond

Chang, Diana 1934- .... **AAL**
See also CA 228; CWP; DLB 312; EXPP

Chang, Eileen 1920-1995 .... **AAL; SSC 28;**
TCLC 184
See also CA 166; CANR 168; CWW 2;
DLB 328; EWL 3; RGSF 2

Chang, Jung 1952- .... **CLC 71**
See also CA 142

Chang Ai-Ling
See Chang, Eileen

Channing, William Ellery
1780-1842 .... **NCLC 17**
See also DLB 1, 59, 235; RGAL 4

Chao, Patricia 1955- .... **CLC 119**
See also CA 163; CANR 155

Chaplin, Charles Spencer
1889-1977 .... **CLC 16**
See also AAYA 61; CA 81-84; 73-76; DLB 44

Chaplin, Charlie
See Chaplin, Charles Spencer

Chapman, George 1559(?)-1634 . **DC 19; LC 22, 116; PC 96**
See also BRW 1; DAM DRAM; DLB 62, 121; LMFS 1; RGEL 2

Chapman, Graham 1941-1989 .... **CLC 21**
See also AAYA 7; CA 116; 129; CANR 35, 95

Chapman, John Jay 1862-1933 .... **TCLC 7**
See also AMWS 14; CA 104; 191

Chapman, Lee
See Bradley, Marion Zimmer

Chapman, Walker
See Silverberg, Robert

Chappell, Fred (Davis) 1936- .... **CLC 40, 78, 162; PC 105**
See also CA 5-8R, 198; CAAE 198; CAAS 4; CANR 8, 33, 67, 110; CN 6; CP 6, 7; CSW; DLB 6, 105; HGG

Char, Rene 1907-1988 ..... **CLC 9, 11, 14, 55; PC 56**
See also CA 13-16R; 124; CANR 32; DAM POET; DLB 258; EWL 3; GFL 1789 to the Present; MTCW 1, 2; RGWL 2, 3

Char, Rene-Emile
See Char, Rene

Charby, Jay
See Ellison, Harlan

Chardin, Pierre Teilhard de
See Teilhard de Chardin, (Marie Joseph) Pierre

Chariton fl. 1st cent. (?)- .... **CMLC 49**

Charlemagne 742-814 .... **CMLC 37**

Charles I 1600-1649 .... **LC 13**

Charriere, Isabelle de 1740-1805 .. **NCLC 66**
See also DLB 313

Charron, Pierre 1541-1603 .... **LC 174**
See also GFL Beginnings to 1789

Chartier, Alain c. 1392-1430 .... **LC 94**
See also DLB 208

Chartier, Emile-Auguste
See Alain

Charyn, Jerome 1937- .... **CLC 5, 8, 18**
See also CA 5-8R; CAAS 1; CANR 7, 61, 101, 158, 199; CMW 4; CN 1, 2, 3, 4, 5, 6, 7; DLBY 1983; MTCW 1

Chase, Adam
See Marlowe, Stephen

Chase, Mary (Coyle) 1907-1981 .... **DC 1**
See also CA 77-80; 105; CAD; CWD; DFS 11; DLB 228; SATA 17; SATA-Obit 29

Chase, Mary Ellen 1887-1973 .... **CLC 2; TCLC 124**
See also CA 13-16; 41-44R; CAP 1; SATA 10

Chase, Nicholas
See Hyde, Anthony

Chase-Riboud, Barbara (Dewayne Tosi)
1939- .... **BLC 2:1**
See also BW 2; CA 113; CANR 76; DAM MULT; DLB 33; MTCW 2

Chateaubriand, Francois Rene de
1768-1848 .... **NCLC 3, 134**
See also DLB 119; EW 5; GFL 1789 to the Present; RGWL 2, 3; TWA

Chatelet, Gabrielle-Emilie Du
See du Chatelet, Emilie

Chatterje, Saratchandra -(?)
See Chatterji, Sarat Chandra

Chatterji, Bankim Chandra
1838-1894 .... **NCLC 19**

Chatterji, Sarat Chandra
1876-1936 .... **TCLC 13**
See also CA 109; 186; EWL 3

Chatterton, Thomas 1752-1770 ..... **LC 3, 54; PC 104**
See also DAM POET; DLB 109; RGEL 2

Chatwin, (Charles) Bruce
1940-1989 .... **CLC 28, 57, 59**
See also AAYA 4; BEST 90:1; BRWS 4; CA 85-88; 127; CPW; DAM POP; DLB 194, 204; EWL 3; MTFW 2005

Chaucer, Daniel
See Ford, Ford Madox

Chaucer, Geoffrey 1340(?)-1400 ... **LC 17, 56, 173; PC 19, 58; WLCS**
See also BRW 1; BRWC 1; BRWR 2; CD-BLB Before 1660; DA; DA3; DAB; DAC; DAM MST, POET; DLB 146; LAIT 1; PAB; PFS 14, RGEL 2; TEA; WLIT 3; WP

Chaudhuri, Nirad C(handra)
1897-1999 .... **TCLC 224**
See also CA 128; 183; DLB 323

Chavez, Denise 1948- .... **HLC 1**
See also CA 131; CANR 56, 81, 137; DAM MULT; DLB 122; FW; HW 1, 2; LLW; MAL 5; MTCW 2; MTFW 2005

Chaviaras, Strates 1935- .... **CLC 33**
See also CA 105

Chayefsky, Paddy 1923-1981 .... **CLC 23**
See also CA 9-12R; 104; CAD; CANR 18; DAM DRAM; DFS 26; DLB 23; DLBY 7, 44; RGAL 4

Chayefsky, Sidney
See Chayefsky, Paddy

Chedid, Andree 1920- .... **CLC 47**
See also CA 145; CANR 95; EWL 3

Cheever, John 1912-1982 ..... **CLC 3, 7, 8, 11, 15, 25, 64; SSC 1, 38, 57, 120; WLC 2**
See also AAYA 65; AMWS 1; BPFB 1; CA 5-8R; 106; CABS 1; CANR 5, 27, 76; CDALB 1941-1968; CN 1, 2, 3; CPW; DA; DA3; DAB; DAC; DAM MST, NOV, POP; DLB 2, 102, 227; DLBY 1980, 1982; EWL 3; EXPS; INT CANR-5; MAL 5; MTCW 1, 2; MTFW 2005; RGAL 4; RGSF 2; SSFS 2, 14; TUS

Cheever, Susan 1943- .... **CLC 18, 48**
See also CA 103; CANR 27, 51, 92, 157, 198; DLBY 1982; INT CANR-27

Chekhonte, Antosha
See Chekhov, Anton

Chekhov, Anton 1860-1904 ...... **DC 9; SSC 2, 28, 41, 51, 85, 102; TCLC 3, 10, 31, 55, 96, 163; WLC 2**
See also AAYA 68; BYA 14; CA 104; 124; DA; DA3; DAB; DAC; DAM DRAM, MST; DFS 1, 5, 10, 12, 26; DLB 277; EW 7; EWL 3; EXPS; LAIT 3; LATS 1:1; RGSF 2; RGWL 2, 3; SATA 90; SSFS 5, 13, 14, 26, 29; TWA

Chekhov, Anton Pavlovich
See Chekhov, Anton

Cheney, Lynne V. 1941- .... **CLC 70**
See also CA 89-92; CANR 58, 117, 193; SATA 152

Cheney, Lynne Vincent
See Cheney, Lynne V.

Chenier, Andre-Marie de 1762-1794 . **LC 174**
See also EW 4; GFL Beginnings to 1789; TWA

Chernyshevsky, Nikolai Gavrilovich
See Chernyshevsky, Nikolay Gavrilovich

Chernyshevsky, Nikolay Gavrilovich
1828-1889 .... **NCLC 1**
See also DLB 238

Cherry, Carolyn Janice
See Cherryh, C.J.

Cherryh, C.J. 1942- .... **CLC 35**
See also AAYA 24; BPFB 1; CA 65-68; CANR 10, 147, 179; DLBY 1980; FANT; SATA 93, 172; SCFW 2; YAW

Chesler, Phyllis 1940- .... **CLC 247**
See also CA 49-52; CANR 4, 59, 140, 189; FW

Chesnutt, Charles W(addell)
1858-1932 .... **BLC 1; SSC 7, 54, 139; TCLC 5, 39**
See also AFAW 1, 2; AMWS 14; BW 1, 3; CA 106; 125; CANR 76; DAM MULT; DLB 12, 50, 78; EWL 3; MAL 5; MTCW 1, 2; MTFW 2005; RGAL 4; RGSF 2; SSFS 11, 26

Chester, Alfred 1929(?)-1971 .... **CLC 49**
See also CA 196; 33-36R; DLB 130; MAL 5

Chesterton, G. K. 1874-1936 . **PC 28; SSC 1, 46; TCLC 1, 6, 64**
See also AAYA 57; BRW 6; CA 104; 132; CANR 73, 131; CDBLB 1914-1945; CMW 4; DAM NOV, POET; DLB 10, 19, 34, 70, 98, 149, 178; EWL 3; FANT; MSW; MTCW 1, 2; MTFW 2005; RGEL 2; RGSF 2; SATA 27; SUFW 1

Chesterton, Gilbert Keith
See Chesterton, G. K.

Chettle, Henry 1560-1607(?) .... **LC 112**
See also DLB 136; RGEL 2

Chiang, Pin-chin 1904-1986 .... **CLC 68**
See also CA 118; DLB 328; EWL 3; RGWL 3

Chiang Ping-chih
See Chiang, Pin-chin

Chief Joseph 1840-1904 .... **NNAL**
See also CA 152; DA3; DAM MULT

Chief Seattle 1786(?)-1866 .... **NNAL**
See also DA3; DAM MULT

Ch'ien, Chung-shu 1910-1998 .... **CLC 22**
See also CA 130; CANR 73; CWW 2; DLB 328; MTCW 1, 2

Chikamatsu Monzaemon 1653-1724 ... **LC 66**
See also RGWL 2, 3

Child, Francis James 1825-1896 . **NCLC 173**
See also DLB 1, 64, 235

Child, L. Maria
See Child, Lydia Maria

Child, Lydia Maria 1802-1880 .. **NCLC 6, 73**
See also DLB 1, 74, 243; RGAL 4; SATA 67

Child, Mrs.
See Child, Lydia Maria

Child, Philip 1898-1978 .... **CLC 19, 68**
See also CA 13-14; CAP 1; CP 1; DLB 68; RHW; SATA 47

Childers, (Robert) Erskine
1870-1922 .... **TCLC 65**
See also CA 113; 153; DLB 70

Childress, Alice 1920-1994 .... **BLC 1:1; CLC 12, 15, 86, 96; DC 4; TCLC 116**
See also AAYA 8; BW 2, 3; BYA 2; CA 45-48; 146; CAD; CANR 3, 27, 50, 74; CLR 14; CWD; DA3; DAM DRAM, MULT, NOV; DFS 2, 8, 14, 26; DLB 7, 38, 249; JRDA; LAIT 5; MAICYA 1, 2; MAIC-YAS 1; MAL 5; MTCW 1, 2; MTFW 2005; RGAL 4; SATA 7, 48, 81; TUS; WYA; YAW

Chin, Frank 1940- ..... **AAL; CLC 135; DC 7**
See also CA 33-36R; CAD; CANR 71; CD 5, 6; DAM MULT; DLB 206, 312; LAIT 5; RGAL 4

Chin, Frank Chew, Jr.
See Chin, Frank

Chin, Marilyn 1955- .... **PC 40**
See also CA 129; CANR 70, 113; CWP;
DLB 312; PFS 28

Chin, Marilyn Mei Ling
See Chin, Marilyn

Chislett, (Margaret) Anne 1943- ...... **CLC 34**
See also CA 151

Chitty, Thomas Willes 1926- .... **CLC 6, 11**
See also CA 5-8R; CN 1, 2, 3, 4, 5, 6; EWL
3

Chivers, Thomas Holley
1809-1858 .... **NCLC 49**
See also DLB 3, 248; RGAL 4

Chlamyda, Jehudil
See Gorky, Maxim

Ch'o, Chou
See Shu-Jen, Chou

Choi, Susan 1969- .... **CLC 119**
See also CA 223; CANR 188

Chomette, Rene Lucien 1898-1981 .. **CLC 20**
See also CA 103

Chomsky, Avram Noam
See Chomsky, Noam

Chomsky, Noam 1928- .... **CLC 132**
See also CA 17-20R; CANR 28, 62, 110,
132, 179; DA3; DLB 246; MTCW 1, 2;
MTFW 2005

Chona, Maria 1845(?)-1936 .... **NNAL**
See also CA 144

Chopin, Kate 1851-1904 ...... **SSC 8, 68, 110;
TCLC 127; WLCS**
See also AAYA 33; AMWR 2; BYA 11, 15;
CA 104; 122; CDALB 1865-1917; DA3;
DAB; DAC; DAM MST, NOV; DLB 12,
78; EXPN; EXPS; FL 1:3; FW; LAIT 3;
MAL 5; MBL; NFS 3; RGAL 4; RGSF 2;
SSFS 2, 13, 17, 26; TUS

Chopin, Katherine
See Chopin, Kate

Chretien de Troyes c. 12th cent. - . **CMLC 10**
See also DLB 208; EW 1; RGWL 2, 3;
TWA

Christie
See Ichikawa, Kon

Christie, Agatha 1890-1976 . **CLC 1, 6, 8, 12,
39, 48, 110; DC 39**
See also AAYA 9; AITN 1, 2; BPFB 1;
BRWS 2; CA 17-20R; 61-64; CANR 10,
37, 108; CBD; CDBLB 1914-1945; CMW
4; CN 1, 2; CPW; CWD; DA3; DAB;
DAC; DAM NOV; DFS 2; DLB 13, 77,
245; MSW; MTCW 1, 2; MTFW 2005;
NFS 8, 30, 33; RGEL 2; RHW; SATA 36;
SSFS 31; TEA; YAW

Christie, Agatha Mary Clarissa
See Christie, Agatha

Christie, Ann Philippa
See Pearce, Philippa

Christie, Philippa
See Pearce, Philippa

Christine de Pisan
See Christine de Pizan

Christine de Pizan 1365(?)-1431(?) ...... **LC 9,
130; PC 68**
See also DLB 208; FL 1:1; FW; RGWL 2,
3

Chuang-Tzu c. 369B.C.-c.
286B.C. .... **CMLC 57**

Chubb, Elmer
See Masters, Edgar Lee

Chulkov, Mikhail Dmitrievich
1743-1792 .... **LC 2**
See also DLB 150

Churchill, Caryl 1938- .... **CLC 31, 55, 157;
DC 5**
See also BRWS 4; CA 102; CANR 22, 46,
108; CBD; CD 5, 6; CWD; DFS 25; DLB
13, 310; EWL 3; FW; MTCW 1; RGEL 2

Churchill, Charles 1731-1764 .... **LC 3**
See also DLB 109; RGEL 2

Churchill, Chick
See Churchill, Caryl

Churchill, Sir Winston
1874-1965 .... **TCLC 113**
See also BRW 6; CA 97-100; CDBLB
1890-1914; DA3; DLB 100, 329; DLBD
16; LAIT 4; MTCW 1, 2

Churchill, Sir Winston Leonard Spencer
See Churchill, Sir Winston

Chute, Carolyn 1947- .... **CLC 39**
See also CA 123; CANR 135; CN 7; DLB
350

Ciardi, John (Anthony) 1916-1986 . **CLC 10,
40, 44, 129; PC 69**
See also CA 5-8R; 118; CAAS 2; CANR 5,
33; CLR 19; CP 1, 2, 3, 4; CWRI 5; DAM
POET; DLB 5; DLBY 1986; INT
CANR-5; MAICYA 1, 2; MAL 5; MTCW
1, 2; MTFW 2005; RGAL 4; SAAS 26;
SATA 1, 65; SATA-Obit 46

Cibber, Colley 1671-1757 .... **LC 66**
See also DLB 84; RGEL 2

Cicero, Marcus Tullius
106B.C.-43B.C. .... **CMLC 121**
See also AW 1; CDWLB 1; DLB 211;
RGWL 2, 3; WLIT 8

Cimino, Michael 1943- .... **CLC 16**
See also CA 105

Cioran, E(mil) M. 1911-1995 .... **CLC 64**
See also CA 25-28R; 149; CANR 91; DLB
220; EWL 3

Circus, Anthony
See Hoch, Edward D.

Cisneros, Sandra 1954- .... **CLC 69, 118, 193;
HLC 1; PC 52; SSC 32, 72**
See also AAYA 9, 53; AMWS 7; CA 131;
CANR 64, 118; CLR 123; CN 7; CWP;
DA3; DAM MULT; DLB 122, 152; EWL
3; EXPN; FL 1:5; FW; HW 1; LAIT 5;
LATS 1:2; LLW; MAICYA 2; MAL 5;
MTCW 2; MTFW 2005; NFS 2; PFS 19;
RGAL 4; RGSF 2; SSFS 3, 13, 27; WLIT
1; YAW

Cixous, Helene 1937- .... **CLC 92, 253**
See also CA 126; CANR 55, 123; CWW 2;
DLB 83, 242; EWL 3; FL 1:5; FW; GLL
2; MTCW 1, 2; MTFW 2005; TWA

Clair, Rene
See Chomette, Rene Lucien

Clampitt, Amy 1920-1994 .... **CLC 32; PC 19**
See also AMWS 9; CA 110; 146; CANR
29, 79; CP 4, 5; DLB 105; MAL 5; PFS
27

Clancy, Thomas L., Jr.
See Clancy, Tom

Clancy, Tom 1947- .... **CLC 45, 112**
See also AAYA 9, 51; BEST 89:1, 90:1;
BPFB 1; BYA 10, 11; CA 125; 131;
CANR 62, 105, 132; CMW 4; CPW;
DA3; DAM NOV, POP; DLB 227; INT
CA-131; MTCW 1, 2; MTFW 2005

Clare, John 1793-1864 .. **NCLC 9, 86; PC 23**
See also BRWS 11; DAB; DAM POET;
DLB 55, 96; RGEL 2

Clarin
See Alas (y Urena), Leopoldo (Enrique
Garcia)

Clark, Al C.
See Goines, Donald

Clark, Brian (Robert)
See Clark, (Robert) Brian

Clark, (Robert) Brian 1932- .... **CLC 29**
See also CA 41-44R; CANR 67; CBD; CD
5, 6

Clark, Curt
See Westlake, Donald E.

Clark, Eleanor 1913-1996 .... **CLC 5, 19**
See also CA 9-12R; 151; CANR 41; CN 1,
2, 3, 4, 5, 6; DLB 6

Clark, J. P.
See Clark-Bekederemo, J. P.

Clark, John Pepper
See Clark-Bekederemo, J. P.

Clark, Kenneth (Mackenzie)
1903-1983 .... **TCLC 147**
See also CA 93-96; 109; CANR 36; MTCW
1, 2; MTFW 2005

Clark, M. R.
See Clark, Mavis Thorpe

Clark, Mavis Thorpe 1909-1999 ...... **CLC 12**
See also CA 57-60; CANR 8, 37, 107; CLR
30; CWRI 5; MAICYA 1, 2; SAAS 5;
SATA 8, 74

Clark, Walter Van Tilburg
1909-1971 .... **CLC 28**
See also CA 9-12R; 33-36R; CANR 63,
113; CN 1; DLB 9, 206; LAIT 2; MAL 5;
RGAL 4; SATA 8; TCWW 1, 2

Clark-Bekederemo, J. P. 1935- ...... **BLC 1:1;
CLC 38; DC 5**
See also AAYA 79; AFW; BW 1; CA 65-
68; CANR 16, 72; CD 5, 6; CDWLB 3;
CP 1, 2, 3, 4, 5, 6, 7; DAM DRAM,
MULT; DFS 13; DLB 117; EWL 3;
MTCW 2; MTFW 2005; RGEL 2

Clark-Bekederemo, John Pepper
See Clark-Bekederemo, J. P.

Clark Bekederemo, Johnson Pepper
See Clark-Bekederemo, J. P.

Clarke, Arthur
See Clarke, Arthur C.

Clarke, Arthur C. 1917-2008 .. **CLC 1, 4, 13,
18, 35, 136; SSC 3**
See also AAYA 4, 33; BPFB 1; BYA 13;
CA 1-4R; 270; CANR 2, 28, 55, 74, 130,
196; CLR 119; CN 1, 2, 3, 4, 5, 6, 7;
CPW; DA3; DAM POP; DLB 261; JRDA;
LAIT 5; MAICYA 1, 2; MTCW 1, 2;
MTFW 2005; SATA 13, 70, 115; SATA-
Obit 191; SCFW 1, 2; SFW 4; SSFS 4,
18, 29; TCLE 1:1; YAW

Clarke, Arthur Charles
See Clarke, Arthur C.

Clarke, Austin 1896-1974 .... **CLC 6, 9**
See also BRWS 15; CA 29-32; 49-52; CAP
2; CP 1, 2; DAM POET; DLB 10, 20;
EWL 3; RGEL 2

Clarke, Austin C. 1934- .... **BLC 1:1; CLC 8,
53; SSC 45, 116**
See also BW 1; CA 25-28R; CAAS 16;
CANR 14, 32, 68, 140; CN 1, 2, 3, 4, 5,
6, 7; DAC; DAM MULT; DLB 53, 125;
DNFS 2; MTCW 2; MTFW 2005; RGSF
2

Clarke, Gillian 1937- .... **CLC 61**
See also CA 106; CP 3, 4, 5, 6, 7; CWP;
DLB 40

Clarke, Marcus (Andrew Hislop)
1846-1881 .... **NCLC 19; SSC 94**
See also DLB 230; RGEL 2; RGSF 2

Clarke, Shirley 1925-1997 .... **CLC 16**
See also CA 189

Clash, The
See Headon, (Nicky) Topper; Jones, Mick;
Simonon, Paul; Strummer, Joe

Claudel, Paul (Louis Charles Marie)
1868-1955 .... **TCLC 2, 10**
See also CA 104; 165; DLB 192, 258, 321;
EW 8; EWL 3; GFL 1789 to the Present;
RGWL 2, 3; TWA

Daly, Maureen 1921-2006 .... **CLC 17**
See also AAYA 5, 58; BYA 6; CA 253;
CANR 37, 83, 108; CLR 96; JRDA; MAI-
CYA 1, 2; SAAS 1; SATA 2, 129; SATA-
Obit 176; WYA; YAW

Damas, Leon-Gontran 1912-1978 ... **CLC 84;**
TCLC 204
See also BW 1; CA 125; 73-76; EWL 3

Damocles
See Benedetti, Mario

Dana, Richard Henry Sr.
1787-1879 .... **NCLC 53**

Dangarembga, Tsitsi 1959- .... **BLC 2:1**
See also BW 3; CA 163; NFS 28; WLIT 2

Daniel, Samuel 1562(?)-1619 .... **LC 24, 171**
See also DLB 62; RGEL 2

Daniels, Brett
See Adler, Renata

Dannay, Frederic 1905-1982 .... **CLC 3, 11**
See also BPFB 3; CA 1-4R; 107; CANR 1,
39; CMW 4; DAM POP; DLB 137; MSW;
MTCW 1; RGAL 4

D'Annunzio, Gabriele 1863-1938 ... **TCLC 6,**
40, 215
See also CA 104; 155; EW 8; EWL 3;
RGWL 2, 3; TWA; WLIT 7

Danois, N. le
See Gourmont, Remy(-Marie-Charles) de

Dante 1265-1321 .... **CMLC 3, 18, 39, 70; PC**
21, 108; WLCS
See also DA; DA3; DAB; DAC; DAM
MST, POET; EFS 1; EW 1; LAIT 1;
RGWL 2, 3; TWA; WLIT 7; WP

d'Antibes, Germain
See Simenon, Georges

Danticat, Edwidge 1969- . **BLC 2:1; CLC 94,**
139, 228; SSC 100
See also AAYA 29; CA 152, 192; CAAE
192; CANR 73, 129, 179; CN 7; DLB
350; DNFS 1; EXPS; LATS 1:2; LNFS 3;
MTCW 2; MTFW 2005; NFS 28; SSFS
1, 25; YAW

Danvers, Dennis 1947- .... **CLC 70**

Danziger, Paula 1944-2004 .... **CLC 21**
See also AAYA 4, 36; BYA 6, 7, 14; CA
112; 115; 229; CANR 37, 132; CLR 20;
JRDA; MAICYA 1, 2; MTFW 2005;
SATA 36, 63, 102, 149; SATA-Brief 30;
SATA-Obit 155; WYA; YAW

Da Ponte, Lorenzo 1749-1838 .... **NCLC 50**

d'Aragona, Tullia 1510(?)-1556 .... **LC 121**

Dario, Ruben 1867-1916 .... **HLC 1; PC 15;**
TCLC 4
See also CA 131; CANR 81; DAM MULT;
DLB 290; EWL 3; HW 1, 2; LAW;
MTCW 1, 2; MTFW 2005; RGWL 2, 3

Darko, Amma 1956- .... **BLC 2:1**

Darley, George 1795-1846 .... **NCLC 2**
See also DLB 96; RGEL 2

Darrow, Clarence (Seward)
1857-1938 .... **TCLC 81**
See also CA 164; DLB 303

Darwin, Charles 1809-1882 .... **NCLC 57**
See also BRWS 7; DLB 57, 166; LATS 1:1;
RGEL 2; TEA; WLIT 4

Darwin, Erasmus 1731-1802 .... **NCLC 106**
See also BRWS 16; DLB 93; RGEL 2

Darwish, Mahmoud 1941-2008 .... **PC 86**
See also CA 164; CANR 133; CWW 2;
EWL 3; MTCW 2; MTFW 2005

Darwish, Mahmud -2008
See Darwish, Mahmoud

Daryush, Elizabeth 1887-1977 ...... **CLC 6, 19**
See also CA 49-52; CANR 3, 81; DLB 20

Das, Kamala 1934-2009 ..... **CLC 191; PC 43**
See also CA 101; 287; CANR 27, 59; CP 1,
2, 3, 4, 5, 6, 7; CWP; DLB 323; FW

Dasgupta, Surendranath
1887-1952 .... **TCLC 81**
See also CA 157

Dashwood, Edmee Elizabeth Monica de la
Pasture 1890-1943 .... **TCLC 61**
See also CA 119; 154; DLB 34; RHW

da Silva, Antonio Jose
1705-1739 .... **NCLC 114**

Daudet, (Louis Marie) Alphonse
1840-1897 .... **NCLC 1**
See also DLB 123; GFL 1789 to the Present;
RGSF 2

Daudet, Alphonse Marie Leon
1867-1942 .... **SSC 94**
See also CA 217

d'Aulnoy, Marie-Catherine c.
1650-1705 .... **LC 100**

Daumal, Rene 1908-1944 .... **TCLC 14**
See also CA 114; 247; EWL 3

Davenant, William 1606-1668 .... **LC 13, 166;**
PC 99
See also DLB 58, 126; RGEL 2

Davenport, Guy (Mattison, Jr.)
1927-2005 . **CLC 6, 14, 38, 241; SSC 16**
See also CA 33-36R; 235; CANR 23, 73;
CN 3, 4, 5, 6; CSW; DLB 130

David, Robert
See Nezval, Vitezslav

Davidson, Donald (Grady)
1893-1968 .... **CLC 2, 13, 19**
See also CA 5-8R; 25-28R; CANR 4, 84;
DLB 45

Davidson, Hugh
See Hamilton, Edmond

Davidson, John 1857-1909 .... **TCLC 24**
See also CA 118; 217; DLB 19; RGEL 2

Davidson, Sara 1943- .... **CLC 9**
See also CA 81-84; CANR 44, 68; DLB
185

Davie, Donald (Alfred) 1922-1995 .... **CLC 5,**
8, 10, 31; PC 29
See also BRWS 6; CA 1-4R; 149; CAAS 3;
CANR 1, 44; CP 1, 2, 3, 4, 5, 6; DLB 27;
MTCW 1; RGEL 2

Davie, Elspeth 1918-1995 .... **SSC 52**
See also CA 120; 126; 150; CANR 141;
DLB 139

Davies, Ray(mond Douglas) 1944- ... **CLC 21**
See also CA 116; 146; CANR 92

Davies, Rhys 1901-1978 .... **CLC 23**
See also CA 9-12R; 81-84; CANR 4; CN 1,
2; DLB 139, 191

Davies, Robertson 1913-1995 .. **CLC 2, 7, 13,**
25, 42, 75, 91; WLC 2
See also BEST 89:2; BPFB 1; CA 1, 33-
36R; 150; CANR 17, 42, 103; CN 1, 2, 3,
4, 5, 6; CPW; DA; DA3; DAB; DAC;
DAM MST, NOV, POP; DLB 68; EWL 3;
HGG; INT CANR-17; MTCW 1, 2;
MTFW 2005; RGEL 2; TWA

Davies, Sir John 1569-1626 .... **LC 85**
See also DLB 172

Davies, Walter C.
See Kornbluth, C(yril) M.

Davies, William Henry 1871-1940 ... **TCLC 5**
See also BRWS 11; CA 104; 179; DLB 19,
174; EWL 3; RGEL 2

Davies, William Robertson
See Davies, Robertson

Da Vinci, Leonardo 1452-1519 ..... **LC 12, 57,**
60
See also AAYA 40

Daviot, Gordon
See Mackintosh, Elizabeth

Davis, Angela (Yvonne) 1944- .... **CLC 77**
See also BW 2, 3; CA 57-60; CANR 10,
81; CSW; DA3; DAM MULT; FW

Davis, B. Lynch
See Bioy Casares, Adolfo; Borges, Jorge
Luis

Davis, Frank Marshall 1905-1987 ... **BLC 1:1**
See also BW 2, 3; CA 125; 123; CANR 42,
80; DAM MULT; DLB 51

Davis, Gordon
See Hunt, E. Howard

Davis, H(arold) L(enoir) 1896-1960 . **CLC 49**
See also ANW; CA 178; 89-92; DLB 9,
206; SATA 114; TCWW 1, 2

Davis, Hart
See Poniatowska, Elena

Davis, Natalie Zemon 1928- .... **CLC 204**
See also CA 53-56; CANR 58, 100, 174

Davis, Rebecca Blaine Harding
See Davis, Rebecca Harding

Davis, Rebecca Harding 1831-1910 . **SSC 38,**
109; TCLC 6
See also AMWS 16; CA 104; 179; DLB 74,
239; FW; NFS 14; RGAL 4; SSFS 26;
TUS

Davis, Richard Harding
1864-1916 .... **TCLC 24**
See also CA 114; 179; DLB 12, 23, 78, 79,
189; DLBD 13; RGAL 4

Davison, Frank Dalby 1893-1970 ..... **CLC 15**
See also CA 217; 116; DLB 260

Davison, Lawrence H.
See Lawrence, D. H.

Davison, Peter (Hubert) 1928-2004 . **CLC 28**
See also CA 9-12R; 234; CAAS 4; CANR
3, 43, 84; CP 1, 2, 3, 4, 5, 6, 7; DLB 5

Davys, Mary 1674-1732 .... **LC 1, 46**
See also DLB 39

Dawson, (Guy) Fielding (Lewis)
1930-2002 .... **CLC 6**
See also CA 85-88; 202; CANR 108; DLB
130; DLBY 2002

Day, Clarence (Shepard, Jr.)
1874-1935 .... **TCLC 25**
See also CA 108; 199; DLB 11

Day, John 1574(?)-1640(?) .... **LC 70**
See also DLB 62, 170; RGEL 2

Day, Thomas 1748-1789 .... **LC 1**
See also DLB 39; YABC 1

Day Lewis, C. 1904-1972 .. **CLC 1, 6, 10; PC**
11
See also BRWS 3; CA 13-16; 33-36R;
CANR 34; CAP 1; CN 1; CP 1; CWRI 5;
DAM POET; DLB 77; EWL 3; MSW;
MTCW 1, 2; RGEL 2

Day Lewis, Cecil
See Day Lewis, C.

de Andrade, Carlos Drummond
See Drummond de Andrade, Carlos

de Andrade, Mario 1892(?)-1945 ... **TCLC 43**
See also CA 178; DLB 307; EWL 3; HW 2;
LAW; RGWL 2, 3

Deane, Norman
See Creasey, John

Deane, Seamus (Francis) 1940- ...... **CLC 122**
See also CA 118; CANR 42

de Athayde, Alvaro Coelho
See Pessoa, Fernando

de Beauvoir, Simone
See Beauvoir, Simone de

de Beer, P.
See Bosman, Herman Charles

De Botton, Alain 1969- .... **CLC 203**
See also CA 159; CANR 96, 201

de Brissac, Malcolm
See Dickinson, Peter

de Campos, Alvaro
See Pessoa, Fernando

de Chardin, Pierre Teilhard
See Teilhard de Chardin, (Marie Joseph)
Pierre

Dove, Rita 1952- . **BLC 2:1; BLCS; CLC 50, 81; PC 6**
See also AAYA 46; AMWS 4; BW 2; CA 109; CAAS 19; CANR 27, 42, 68, 76, 97, 132; CDALBS; CP 5, 6, 7; CSW; CWP; DA3; DAM MULT, POET; DLB 120; EWL 3; EXPP; MAL 5; MTCW 2; MTFW 2005; PFS 1, 15; RGAL 4

Dove, Rita Frances
See Dove, Rita

Doveglion
See Villa, Jose Garcia

Dowell, Coleman 1925-1985 .... **CLC 60**
See also CA 25-28R; 117; CANR 10; DLB 130; GLL 2

Downing, Major Jack
See Smith, Seba

Dowson, Ernest (Christopher)
1867-1900 .... **TCLC 4**
See also CA 105; 150; DLB 19, 135; RGEL 2

Doyle, A. Conan
See Doyle, Sir Arthur Conan

Doyle, Sir Arthur Conan
1859-1930 ..... **SSC 12, 83, 95; TCLC 7; WLC 2**
See also AAYA 14; BPFB 1; BRWS 2; BYA 4, 5, 11; CA 104; 122; CANR 131; CD-BLB 1890-1914; CLR 106; CMW 4; DA; DA3; DAB; DAC; DAM MST, NOV; DLB 18, 70, 156, 178; EXPS; HGG; LAIT 2; MSW; MTCW 1, 2; MTFW 2005; NFS 28; RGEL 2; RGSF 2; RHW; SATA 24; SCFW 1, 2; SFW 4; SSFS 2; TEA; WCH; WLIT 4; WYA; YAW

Doyle, Conan
See Doyle, Sir Arthur Conan

Doyle, John
See Graves, Robert

Doyle, Roddy 1958- .... **CLC 81, 178**
See also AAYA 14; BRWS 5; CA 143; CANR 73, 128, 168, 200; CN 6, 7; DA3; DLB 194, 326; MTCW 2; MTFW 2005

Doyle, Sir A. Conan
See Doyle, Sir Arthur Conan

Dr. A
See Asimov, Isaac; Silverstein, Alvin; Silverstein, Virginia B.

Drabble, Margaret 1939- ...... **CLC 2, 3, 5, 8, 10, 22, 53, 129**
See also BRWS 4; CA 13-16R; CANR 18, 35, 63, 112, 131, 174; CDBLB 1960 to Present; CN 1, 2, 3, 4, 5, 6, 7; CPW; DA3; DAB; DAC; DAM MST, NOV, POP; DLB 14, 155, 231; EWL 3; FW; MTCW 1, 2; MTFW 2005; RGEL 2; SATA 48; TEA

Drakulic, Slavenka
See Drakulic, Slavenka

Drakulic, Slavenka 1949- .... **CLC 173**
See also CA 144; CANR 92, 198; DLB 353

Drakulic-Ilic, Slavenka
See Drakulic, Slavenka

Drakulic-Ilic, Slavenka
See Drakulic, Slavenka

Drapier, M. B.
See Swift, Jonathan

Drayham, James
See Mencken, H. L.

Drayton, Michael 1563-1631 . **LC 8, 161; PC 98**
See also DAM POET; DLB 121; RGEL 2

Dreadstone, Carl
See Campbell, Ramsey

Dreiser, Theodore 1871-1945 .... **SSC 30, 114; TCLC 10, 18, 35, 83; WLC 2**
See also AMW; AMWC 2; AMWR 2; BYA 15, 16; CA 106; 132; CDALB 1865-1917; DA; DA3; DAC; DAM MST, NOV; DLB 9, 12, 102, 137; DLBD 1; EWL 3; LAIT 2; LMFS 2; MAL 5; MTCW 1, 2; MTFW 2005; NFS 8, 17; RGAL 4; TUS

Dreiser, Theodore Herman Albert
See Dreiser, Theodore

Drexler, Rosalyn 1926- .... **CLC 2, 6**
See also CA 81-84; CAD; CANR 68, 124; CD 5, 6; CWD; MAL 5

Dreyer, Carl Theodor 1889-1968 ...... **CLC 16**
See also CA 116

Drieu la Rochelle, Pierre
1893-1945 .... **TCLC 21**
See also CA 117; 250; DLB 72; EWL 3; GFL 1789 to the Present

Drieu la Rochelle, Pierre-Eugene 1893-1945
See Drieu la Rochelle, Pierre

Drinkwater, John 1882-1937 .... **TCLC 57**
See also CA 109; 149; DLB 10, 19, 149; RGEL 2

Drop Shot
See Cable, George Washington

Droste-Hulshoff, Annette Freiin von
1797-1848 .... **NCLC 3, 133**
See also CDWLB 2; DLB 133; RGSF 2; RGWL 2, 3

Drummond, Walter
See Silverberg, Robert

Drummond, William Henry
1854-1907 .... **TCLC 25**
See also CA 160; DLB 92

Drummond de Andrade, Carlos
1902-1987 .... **CLC 18; TCLC 139**
See also CA 132; 123; DLB 307; EWL 3; LAW; RGWL 2, 3

Drummond of Hawthornden, William
1585-1649 .... **LC 83**
See also DLB 121, 213; RGEL 2

Drury, Allen (Stuart) 1918-1998 .... **CLC 37**
See also CA 57-60; 170; CANR 18, 52; CN 1, 2, 3, 4, 5, 6; INT CANR-18

Druse, Eleanor
See King, Stephen

Dryden, John 1631-1700 ..... **DC 3; LC 3, 21, 115; PC 25; WLC 2**
See also BRW 2; BRWR 3; CDBLB 1660-1789; DA; DAB; DAC; DAM DRAM, MST, POET; DLB 80, 101, 131; EXPP; IDTP; LMFS 1; RGEL 2; TEA; WLIT 3

du Aime, Albert
See Wharton, William

du Aime, Albert William
See Wharton, William

du Bellay, Joachim 1524-1560 .... **LC 92**
See also DLB 327; GFL Beginnings to 1789; RGWL 2, 3

Duberman, Martin 1930- .... **CLC 8**
See also CA 1-4R; CAD; CANR 2, 63, 137, 174; CD 5, 6

Dubie, Norman (Evans) 1945- .... **CLC 36**
See also CA 69-72; CANR 12, 115; CP 3, 4, 5, 6, 7; DLB 120; PFS 12

Du Bois, W. E. B. 1868-1963 .... **BLC 1:1; CLC 1, 2, 13, 64, 96; HR 1:2; TCLC 169; WLC 2**
See also AAYA 40; AFAW 1, 2; AMWC 1; AMWS 2; BW 1, 3; CA 85-88; CANR 34, 82, 132; CDALB 1865-1917; DA; DA3; DAC; DAM MST, MULT, NOV; DLB 47, 50, 91, 246, 284; EWL 3; EXPP; LAIT 2; LMFS 2; MAL 5; MTCW 1, 2; MTFW 2005; NCFS 1; PFS 13; RGAL 4; SATA 42

Du Bois, William Edward Burghardt
See Du Bois, W. E. B.

Dubus, Andre 1936-1999 ..... **CLC 13, 36, 97; SSC 15, 118**
See also AMWS 7; CA 21-24R; 177; CANR 17; CN 5, 6; CSW; DLB 130; INT CANR-17; RGAL 4; SSFS 10; TCLE 1:1

Duca Minimo
See D'Annunzio, Gabriele

Ducharme, Rejean 1941- .... **CLC 74**
See also CA 165; DLB 60

du Chatelet, Emilie 1706-1749 .... **LC 96**
See also DLB 313

Duchen, Claire CLC 65

Duck, Stephen 1705(?)-1756 .... **PC 89**
See also DLB 95; RGEL 2

Duclos, Charles Pinot- 1704-1772 .... **LC 1**
See also GFL Beginnings to 1789

Ducornet, Erica 1943- .... **CLC 232**
See also CA 37-40R; CANR 14, 34, 54, 82; SATA 7

Ducornet, Rikki
See Ducornet, Erica

Dudek, Louis 1918-2001 .... **CLC 11, 19**
See also CA 45-48; 215; CAAS 14; CANR 1; CP 1, 2, 3, 4, 5, 6, 7; DLB 88

Duerrematt, Friedrich
See Durrenmatt, Friedrich

Duffy, Bruce 1953(?)- .... **CLC 50**
See also CA 172

Duffy, Maureen 1933- .... **CLC 37**
See also CA 25-28R; CANR 33, 68; CBD; CN 1, 2, 3, 4, 5, 6, 7; CP 5, 6, 7; CWD; CWP; DFS 15; DLB 14, 310; FW; MTCW 1

Duffy, Maureen Patricia
See Duffy, Maureen

Du Fu
See Tu Fu

Dugan, Alan 1923-2003 .... **CLC 2, 6**
See also CA 81-84; 220; CANR 119; CP 1, 2, 3, 4, 5, 6, 7; DLB 5; MAL 5; PFS 10

du Gard, Roger Martin
See Martin du Gard, Roger

Duhamel, Georges 1884-1966 .... **CLC 8**
See also CA 81-84; 25-28R; CANR 35; DLB 65; EWL 3; GFL 1789 to the Present; MTCW 1

du Hault, Jean
See Grindel, Eugene

Dujardin, Edouard (Emile Louis)
1861-1949 .... **TCLC 13**
See also CA 109; DLB 123

Duke, Raoul
See Thompson, Hunter S.

Dulles, John Foster 1888-1959 .... **TCLC 72**
See also CA 115; 149

Dumas, Alexandre (pere)
1802-1870 .... **NCLC 11, 71; WLC 2**
See also AAYA 22; BYA 3; CLR 134; DA; DA3; DAB; DAC; DAM MST, NOV; DLB 119, 192; EW 6; GFL 1789 to the Present; LAIT 1, 2; NFS 14, 19; RGWL 2, 3; SATA 18; TWA; WCH

Dumas, Alexandre (fils) 1824-1895 ...... **DC 1; NCLC 9**
See also DLB 192; GFL 1789 to the Present; RGWL 2, 3

Dumas, Claudine
See Malzberg, Barry N(athaniel)

Dumas, Henry L. 1934-1968 . **BLC 2:1; CLC 6, 62; SSC 107**
See also BW 1; CA 85-88; DLB 41; RGAL 4

du Maurier, Daphne 1907-1989 .. **CLC 6, 11, 59; SSC 18, 129; TCLC 209**
See also AAYA 37; BPFB 1; BRWS 3; CA 5-8R; 128; CANR 6, 55; CMW 4; CN 1, 2, 3, 4; CPW; DA3; DAB; DAC; DAM MST, POP; DLB 191; GL 2; HGG; LAIT 3; MSW; MTCW 1, 2; NFS 12; RGEL 2; RGSF 2; RHW; SATA 27; SATA-Obit 60; SSFS 14, 16; TEA

Du Maurier, George 1834-1896 ..... **NCLC 86**
See also DLB 153, 178; RGEL 2

Dunbar, Alice
 See Nelson, Alice Ruth Moore Dunbar
Dunbar, Alice Moore
 See Nelson, Alice Ruth Moore Dunbar
Dunbar, Paul Laurence
 1872-1906 .... **BLC 1:1; PC 5; SSC 8;**
 TCLC 2, 12; WLC 2
 See also AAYA 75; AFAW 1, 2; AMWS 2;
 BW 1, 3; CA 104; 124; CANR 79;
 CDALB 1865-1917; DA; DA3; DAC;
 DAM MST, MULT, POET; DLB 50, 54,
 78; EXPP; MAL 5; PFS 33; RGAL 4;
 SATA 34
Dunbar, William 1460(?)-1520(?) .... **LC 20;**
 PC 67
 See also BRWS 8; DLB 132, 146; RGEL 2
Dunbar-Nelson, Alice
 See Nelson, Alice Ruth Moore Dunbar
Dunbar-Nelson, Alice Moore
 See Nelson, Alice Ruth Moore Dunbar
Duncan, Dora Angela
 See Duncan, Isadora
Duncan, Isadora 1877(?)-1927 .... **TCLC 68**
 See also CA 118; 149
Duncan, Lois 1934- .... **CLC 26**
 See also AAYA 4, 34; BYA 6, 8; CA 1-4R;
 CANR 2, 23, 36, 111; CLR 29, 129;
 JRDA; MAICYA 1, 2; MAICYAS 1;
 MTFW 2005; SAAS 2; SATA 1, 36, 75,
 133, 141; SATA-Essay 141; WYA; YAW
Duncan, Robert 1919-1988 ... **CLC 1, 2, 4, 7,**
 15, 41, 55; PC 2, 75
 See also BG 1:2; CA 9-12R; 124; CANR
 28, 62; CP 1, 2, 3, 4; DAM POET; DLB
 5, 16, 193; EWL 3; MAL 5; MTCW 1, 2;
 MTFW 2005; PFS 13; RGAL 4; WP
Duncan, Sara Jeannette
 1861-1922 .... **TCLC 60**
 See also CA 157; DLB 92
Dunlap, William 1766-1839 .... **NCLC 2**
 See also DLB 30, 37, 59; RGAL 4
Dunn, Douglas (Eaglesham) 1942- .... **CLC 6,**
 40
 See also BRWS 10; CA 45-48; CANR 2,
 33, 126; CP 1, 2, 3, 4, 5, 6, 7; DLB 40;
 MTCW 1
Dunn, Katherine 1945- .... **CLC 71**
 See also CA 33-36R; CANR 72; HGG;
 MTCW 2; MTFW 2005
Dunn, Stephen 1939- .... **CLC 36, 206**
 See also AMWS 11; CA 33-36R; CANR
 12, 48, 53, 105; CP 3, 4, 5, 6, 7; DLB
 105; PFS 21
Dunn, Stephen Elliott
 See Dunn, Stephen
Dunne, Finley Peter 1867-1936 ...... **TCLC 28**
 See also CA 108; 178; DLB 11, 23; RGAL
 4
Dunne, John Gregory 1932-2003 ..... **CLC 28**
 See also CA 25-28R; 222; CANR 14, 50;
 CN 5, 6, 7; DLBY 1980
Dunsany, Lord
 See Dunsany, Edward John Moreton Drax
 Plunkett
Dunsany, Edward John Moreton Drax
 Plunkett 1878-1957 .... **TCLC 2, 59**
 See also CA 104; 148; DLB 10, 77, 153,
 156, 255; FANT; MTCW 2; RGEL 2;
 SFW 4; SUFW 1
Duns Scotus, John 1266(?)-1308 ... **CMLC 59**
 See also DLB 115
Duong, Thu Huong 1947- .... **CLC 273**
 See also CA 152; CANR 106, 166; DLB
 348; NFS 23
Duong Thu Huong
 See Duong, Thu Huong
du Perry, Jean
 See Simenon, Georges

Durang, Christopher 1949- .... **CLC 27, 38**
 See also CA 105; CAD; CANR 50, 76, 130;
 CD 5, 6; MTCW 2; MTFW 2005
Durang, Christopher Ferdinand
 See Durang, Christopher
Duras, Claire de 1777-1832 .... **NCLC 154**
Duras, Marguerite 1914-1996 . **CLC 3, 6, 11,**
 20, 34, 40, 68, 100; SSC 40
 See also BPFB 1; CA 25-28R; 151; CANR
 50; CWW 2; DFS 21; DLB 83, 321; EWL
 3; FL 1:5; GFL 1789 to the Present; IDFW
 4; MTCW 1, 2; RGWL 2, 3; TWA
Durban, (Rosa) Pam 1947- .... **CLC 39**
 See also CA 123; CANR 98; CSW
Durcan, Paul 1944- .... **CLC 43, 70**
 See also CA 134; CANR 123; CP 1, 5, 6, 7;
 DAM POET; EWL 3
d'Urfe, Honore
 See Urfe, Honore d'
Durfey, Thomas 1653-1723 .... **LC 94**
 See also DLB 80; RGEL 2
Durkheim, Emile 1858-1917 .... **TCLC 55**
 See also CA 249
Durrell, Lawrence 1912-1990 .... **CLC 1, 4, 6,**
 8, 13, 27, 41
 See also BPFB 1; BRWR 3; BRWS 1; CA
 9-12R; 132; CANR 40, 77; CDBLB 1945-
 1960; CN 1, 2, 3, 4; CP 1, 2, 3, 4, 5; DAM
 NOV; DLB 15, 27, 204; DLBY 1990;
 EWL 3; MTCW 1, 2; RGEL 2; SFW 4;
 TEA
Durrell, Lawrence George
 See Durrell, Lawrence
Durrenmatt, Friedrich
 See Durrenmatt, Friedrich
Durrenmatt, Friedrich 1921-1990 . **CLC 1, 4,**
 8, 11, 15, 43, 102
 See also CA 17-20R; CANR 33; CDWLB
 2; CMW 4; DAM DRAM; DLB 69, 124;
 EW 13; EWL 3; MTCW 1, 2; RGHL;
 RGWL 2, 3
Dutt, Michael Madhusudan
 1824-1873 .... **NCLC 118**
Dutt, Toru 1856-1877 .... **NCLC 29**
 See also DLB 240
Dwight, Timothy 1752-1817 .... **NCLC 13**
 See also DLB 37; RGAL 4
Dworkin, Andrea 1946-2005 ..... **CLC 43, 123**
 See also CA 77-80; 238; CAAS 21; CANR
 16, 39, 76, 96; FL 1:5; FW; GLL 1; INT
 CANR-16; MTCW 1, 2; MTFW 2005
Dwyer, Deanna
 See Koontz, Dean
Dwyer, K.R.
 See Koontz, Dean
Dybek, Stuart 1942- .... **CLC 114; SSC 55**
 See also CA 97-100; CANR 39; DLB 130;
 SSFS 23
Dye, Richard
 See De Voto, Bernard (Augustine)
Dyer, Geoff 1958- .... **CLC 149**
 See also CA 125; CANR 88
Dyer, George 1755-1841 .... **NCLC 129**
 See also DLB 93
Dylan, Bob 1941- .... **CLC 3, 4, 6, 12, 77; PC**
 37
 See also AMWS 18; CA 41-44R; CANR
 108; CP 1, 2, 3, 4, 5, 6, 7; DLB 16
Dyson, John 1943- .... **CLC 70**
 See also CA 144
Dzyubin, Eduard Georgievich
 1895-1934 .... **TCLC 60**
 See also CA 170; EWL 3
E. V. L.
 See Lucas, E(dward) V(errall)
Eagleton, Terence
 See Eagleton, Terry
Eagleton, Terence Francis
 See Eagleton, Terry

Eagleton, Terry 1943- .... **CLC 63, 132**
 See also CA 57-60; CANR 7, 23, 68, 115,
 198; DLB 242; LMFS 2; MTCW 1, 2;
 MTFW 2005
Early, Jack
 See Scoppettone, Sandra
East, Michael
 See West, Morris L(anglo)
Eastaway, Edward
 See Thomas, (Philip) Edward
Eastlake, William (Derry)
 1917-1997 .... **CLC 8**
 See also CA 5-8R; 158; CAAS 1; CANR 5,
 63; CN 1, 2, 3, 4, 5, 6; DLB 6, 206; INT
 CANR-5; MAL 5; TCWW 1, 2
Eastman, Charles A(lexander)
 1858-1939 .... **NNAL; TCLC 55**
 See also CA 179; CANR 91; DAM MULT;
 DLB 175; YABC 1
Eaton, Edith Maude
 1865-1914 .... **AAL; TCLC 232**
 See also CA 154; DLB 221, 312; FW
Eaton, (Lillie) Winnifred 1875-1954 .... **AAL**
 See also CA 217; DLB 221, 312; RGAL 4
Eberhart, Richard 1904-2005 ...... **CLC 3, 11,**
 19, 56; PC 76
 See also AMW; CA 1-4R; 240; CANR 2,
 125; CDALB 1941-1968; CP 1, 2, 3, 4, 5,
 6, 7; DAM POET; DLB 48; MAL 5;
 MTCW 1; RGAL 4
Eberhart, Richard Ghormley
 See Eberhart, Richard
Eberstadt, Fernanda 1960- .... **CLC 39**
 See also CA 136; CANR 69, 128
Ebner, Margaret c. 1291-1351 ...... **CMLC 98**
Echegaray (y Eizaguirre), Jose (Maria
 Waldo) 1832-1916 .... **HLCS 1; TCLC 4**
 See also CA 104; CANR 32; DLB 329;
 EWL 3; HW 1; MTCW 1
Echeverria, (Jose) Esteban (Antonino)
 1805-1851 .... **NCLC 18**
 See also LAW
Echo
 See Proust, Marcel
Eckert, Allan W. 1931- .... **CLC 17**
 See also AAYA 18; BYA 2; CA 13-16R;
 CANR 14, 45; INT CANR-14; MAICYA
 2; MAICYAS 1; SAAS 21; SATA 29, 91;
 SATA-Brief 27
Eckhart, Meister 1260(?)-1327(?) .. **CMLC 9,**
 80
 See also DLB 115; LMFS 1
Eckmar, F. R.
 See de Hartog, Jan
Eco, Umberto 1932- .... **CLC 28, 60, 142, 248**
 See also BEST 90:1; BPFB 1; CA 77-80;
 CANR 12, 33, 55, 110, 131, 195; CPW;
 CWW 2; DA3; DAM NOV, POP; DLB
 196, 242; EWL 3; MSW; MTCW 1, 2;
 MTFW 2005; NFS 22; RGWL 3; WLIT 7
Eddison, E(ric) R(ucker)
 1882-1945 .... **TCLC 15**
 See also CA 109; 156; DLB 255; FANT;
 SFW 4; SUFW 1
Eddy, Mary (Ann Morse) Baker
 1821-1910 .... **TCLC 71**
 See also CA 113; 174
Edel, (Joseph) Leon 1907-1997 .. **CLC 29, 34**
 See also CA 1-4R; 161; CANR 1, 22, 112;
 DLB 103; INT CANR-22
Eden, Emily 1797-1869 .... **NCLC 10**
Edgar, David 1948- .... **CLC 42**
 See also CA 57-60; CANR 12, 61, 112;
 CBD; CD 5, 6; DAM DRAM; DFS 15;
 DLB 13, 233; MTCW 1
Edgerton, Clyde 1944- .... **CLC 39**
 See also AAYA 17; CA 118; 134; CANR
 64, 125, 195; CN 7; CSW; DLB 278; INT
 CA-134; TCLE 1:1; YAW

CDALB 1941-1968; CN 1, 2, 3, 4, 5;
CSW; DA; DA3; DAB; DAC; DAM MST,
MULT, NOV; DLB 2, 76, 227; DLBY
1994; EWL 3; EXPN; EXPS; LAIT 4;
MAL 5; MTCW 1, 2; MTFW 2005; NCFS
3; NFS 2, 21; RGAL 4; RGSF 2; SSFS 1,
11; YAW

Ellison, Ralph Waldo
See Ellison, Ralph
Ellmann, Lucy 1956- .... CLC 61
See also CA 128; CANR 154
Ellmann, Lucy Elizabeth
See Ellmann, Lucy
Ellmann, Richard (David)
1918-1987 .... CLC 50
See also BEST 89:2; CA 1-4R; 122; CANR
2, 28, 61; DLB 103; DLBY 1987; MTCW
1, 2; MTFW 2005
Ellroy, James 1948- .... CLC 215
See also BEST 90:4; CA 138; CANR 74,
133; CMW 4; CN 6, 7; DA3; DLB 226;
MTCW 2; MTFW 2005
Elman, Richard (Martin)
1934-1997 .... CLC 19
See also CA 17-20R; 163; CAAS 3; CANR
47; TCLE 1:1
Elron
See Hubbard, L. Ron
El Saadawi, Nawal 1931- ...... BLC 2:2; CLC
196, 284
See also AFW; CA 118; CAAS 11; CANR
44, 92; CWW 2; DLB 346; EWL 3; FW;
WLIT 2
El-Shabazz, El-Hajj Malik
See Malcolm X
Eluard, Paul
See Grindel, Eugene
Eluard, Paul
See Grindel, Eugene
Elyot, Thomas 1490(?)-1546 .... LC 11, 139
See also DLB 136; RGEL 2
Elytis, Odysseus 1911-1996 .... CLC 15, 49,
100; PC 21
See also CA 102; 151; CANR 94; CWW 2;
DAM POET; DLB 329; EW 13; EWL 3;
MTCW 1, 2; RGWL 2, 3
Emecheta, Buchi 1944- ... BLC 1:2; CLC 14,
48, 128, 214
See also AAYA 67; AFW; BW 2, 3; CA 81-
84; CANR 27, 81, 126; CDWLB 3; CN
4, 5, 6, 7; CWRI 5; DA3; DAM MULT;
DLB 117; EWL 3; FL 1:5; FW; MTCW
1, 2; MTFW 2005; NFS 12, 14; SATA 66;
WLIT 2
Emecheta, Florence Onye Buchi
See Emecheta, Buchi
Emerson, Mary Moody
1774-1863 .... NCLC 66
Emerson, Ralph Waldo 1803-1882 . NCLC 1,
38, 98; PC 18; WLC 2
See also AAYA 60; AMW; ANW; CDALB
1640-1865; DA; DA3; DAB; DAC; DAM
MST, POET; DLB 1, 59, 73, 183, 223,
270, 351; EXPP; LAIT 2; LMFS 1; NCFS
3; PFS 4, 17, 34; RGAL 4; TUS; WP
Eminem 1972- .... CLC 226
See also CA 245
Eminescu, Mihail 1850-1889 .. NCLC 33, 131
Empedocles 5th cent. B.C.- .... CMLC 50
See also DLB 176
Empson, William 1906-1984 ... CLC 3, 8, 19,
33, 34; PC 104
See also BRWS 2; CA 17-20R; 112; CANR
31, 61; CP 1, 2, 3; DLB 20; EWL 3;
MTCW 1, 2; RGEL 2
Enchi, Fumiko 1905-1986 .... CLC 31
See also CA 129; 121; DLB 182; EWL 3;
FW; MJW

Enchi, Fumiko Ueda
See Enchi, Fumiko
Enchi Fumiko
See Enchi, Fumiko
Ende, Michael (Andreas Helmuth)
1929-1995 .... CLC 31
See also BYA 5; CA 118; 124; 149; CANR
36, 110; CLR 14, 138; DLB 75; MAICYA
1, 2; MAICYAS 1; SATA 61, 130; SATA-
Brief 42; SATA-Obit 86
Endo, Shusaku 1923-1996 ..... CLC 7, 14, 19,
54, 99; SSC 48; TCLC 152
See also CA 29-32R; 153; CANR 21, 54,
131; CWW 2; DA3; DAM NOV; DLB
182; EWL 3; MTCW 1, 2; MTFW 2005;
RGSF 2; RGWL 2, 3
Endo Shusaku
See Endo, Shusaku
Engel, Marian 1933-1985 .... CLC 36; TCLC
137
See also CA 25-28R; CANR 12; CN 2, 3;
DLB 53; FW; INT CANR-12
Engelhardt, Frederick
See Hubbard, L. Ron
Engels, Friedrich 1820-1895 .. NCLC 85, 114
See also DLB 129; LATS 1:1
Enquist, Per Olov 1934- .... CLC 257
See also CA 109; 193; CANR 155; CWW
2; DLB 257; EWL 3
Enright, D(ennis) J(oseph)
1920-2002 .... CLC 4, 8, 31; PC 93
See also CA 1-4R; 211; CANR 1, 42, 83;
CN 1, 2; CP 1, 2, 3, 4, 5, 6, 7; DLB 27;
EWL 3; SATA 25; SATA-Obit 140
Ensler, Eve 1953- .... CLC 212
See also CA 172; CANR 126, 163; DFS 23
Enzensberger, Hans Magnus
1929- .... CLC 43; PC 28
See also CA 116; 119; CANR 103; CWW
2; EWL 3
Ephron, Nora 1941- .... CLC 17, 31
See also AAYA 35; AITN 2; CA 65-68;
CANR 12, 39, 83, 161; DFS 22
Epicurus 341B.C.-270B.C. .... CMLC 21
See also DLB 176
Epinay, Louise d' 1726-1783 .... LC 138
See also DLB 313
Epsilon
See Betjeman, John
Epstein, Daniel Mark 1948- .... CLC 7
See also CA 49-52; CANR 2, 53, 90, 193
Epstein, Jacob 1956- .... CLC 19
See also CA 114
Epstein, Jean 1897-1953 .... TCLC 92
Epstein, Joseph 1937- .... CLC 39, 204
See also AMWS 14; CA 112; 119; CANR
50, 65, 117, 164, 190
Epstein, Leslie 1938- .... CLC 27
See also AMWS 12; CA 73-76, 215; CAAE
215; CAAS 12; CANR 23, 69, 162; DLB
299; RGHL
Equiano, Olaudah 1745(?)-1797 ..... BLC 1:2;
LC 16, 143
See also AFAW 1, 2; CDWLB 3; DAM
MULT; DLB 37, 50; WLIT 2
Erasmus, Desiderius 1469(?)-1536 ..... LC 16,
93
See also DLB 136; EW 2; LMFS 1; RGWL
2, 3; TWA
Erdman, Paul E. 1932-2007 .... CLC 25
See also AITN 1; CA 61-64; 259; CANR
13, 43, 84
Erdman, Paul Emil
See Erdman, Paul E.
Erdrich, Karen Louise
See Erdrich, Louise

Erdrich, Louise 1954- .... CLC 39, 54, 120,
176; NNAL; PC 52; SSC 121
See also AAYA 10, 47; AMWS 4; BEST
89:1; BPFB 1; CA 114; CANR 41, 62,
118, 138, 190; CDALBS; CN 5, 6, 7; CP
6, 7; CPW; CWP; DA3; DAM MULT,
NOV, POP; DLB 152, 175, 206; EWL 3;
EXPP; FL 1:5; LAIT 5; LATS 1:2; MAL
5; MTCW 1, 2; MTFW 2005; NFS 5; PFS
14; RGAL 4; SATA 94, 141; SSFS 14,
22, 30; TCWW 2
Erenburg, Ilya (Grigoryevich)
See Ehrenburg, Ilya (Grigoryevich)
See also DLB 272
Erickson, Stephen Michael
See Erickson, Steve
Erickson, Steve 1950- .... CLC 64
See also CA 129; CANR 60, 68, 136, 195;
MTFW 2005; SFW 4; SUFW 2
Erickson, Walter
See Fast, Howard
Ericson, Walter
See Fast, Howard
Eriksson, Buntel
See Bergman, Ingmar
Eriugena, John Scottus c.
810-877 .... CMLC 65
See also DLB 115
Ernaux, Annie 1940- .... CLC 88, 184
See also CA 147; CANR 93; MTFW 2005;
NCFS 3, 5
Erskine, John 1879-1951 .... TCLC 84
See also CA 112; 159; DLB 9, 102; FANT
Erwin, Will
See Eisner, Will
Eschenbach, Wolfram von
See von Eschenbach, Wolfram
Eseki, Bruno
See Mphahlele, Es'kia
Esekie, Bruno
See Mphahlele, Es'kia
Esenin, S.A.
See Esenin, Sergei
Esenin, Sergei 1895-1925 .... TCLC 4
See also CA 104; EWL 3; RGWL 2, 3
Esenin, Sergei Aleksandrovich
See Esenin, Sergei
Eshleman, Clayton 1935- .... CLC 7
See also CA 33-36R, 212; CAAE 212;
CAAS 6; CANR 93; CP 1, 2, 3, 4, 5, 6,
7; DLB 5
Espada, Martin 1957- .... PC 74
See also CA 159; CANR 80; CP 7; EXPP;
LLW; MAL 5; PFS 13, 16
Espriella, Don Manuel Alvarez
See Southey, Robert
Espriu, Salvador 1913-1985 .... CLC 9
See also CA 154; 115; DLB 134; EWL 3
Espronceda, Jose de 1808-1842 ..... NCLC 39
Esquivel, Laura 1950(?)- ... CLC 141; HLCS
1
See also AAYA 29; CA 143; CANR 68, 113,
161; DA3; DNFS 2; LAIT 3; LMFS 2;
MTCW 2; MTFW 2005; NFS 5; WLIT 1
Esse, James
See Stephens, James
Esterbrook, Tom
See Hubbard, L. Ron
Esterhazy, Peter 1950- .... CLC 251
See also CA 140; CANR 137; CDWLB 4;
CWW 2; DLB 232; EWL 3; RGWL 3
Estleman, Loren D. 1952- .... CLC 48
See also AAYA 27; CA 85-88; CANR 27,
74, 139, 177; CMW 4; CPW; DA3; DAM
NOV, POP; DLB 226; INT CANR-27;
MTCW 1, 2; MTFW 2005; TCWW 1, 2

Etherege, Sir George 1636-1692 . DC 23; LC 78
See also BRW 2; DAM DRAM; DLB 80; PAB; RGEL 2

Euclid 306B.C.-283B.C. .... CMLC 25

Eugenides, Jeffrey 1960- .... CLC 81, 212
See also AAYA 51; CA 144; CANR 120; DLB 350; MTFW 2005; NFS 24

Euripides c. 484B.C.-406B.C. .... CMLC 23, 51; DC 4; WLCS
See also AW 1; CDWLB 1; DA; DA3; DAB; DAC; DAM DRAM, MST; DFS 1, 4, 6, 25, 27; DLB 176; LAIT 1; LMFS 1; RGWL 2, 3; WLIT 8

Eusebius c. 263-c. 339 .... CMLC 103

Evan, Evin
See Faust, Frederick

Evans, Caradoc 1878-1945 ... SSC 43; TCLC 85
See also DLB 162

Evans, Evan
See Faust, Frederick

Evans, Marian
See Eliot, George

Evans, Mary Ann
See Eliot, George

Evarts, Esther
See Benson, Sally

Evelyn, John 1620-1706 .... LC 144
See also BRW 2; RGEL 2

Everett, Percival 1956- .... CLC 57
See Everett, Percival L.
See also AMWS 18; BW 2; CA 129; CANR 94, 134, 179; CN 7; DLB 350; MTFW 2005

Everett, Percival L.
See Everett, Percival
See also CSW

Everson, R(onald) G(ilmour) 1903-1992 .... CLC 27
See also CA 17-20R; CP 1, 2, 3, 4; DLB 88

Everson, William 1912-1994 .... CLC 1, 5, 14
See also BG 1:2; CA 9-12R; 145; CANR 20; CP 1; DLB 5, 16, 212; MTCW 1

Everson, William Oliver
See Everson, William

Evtushenko, Evgenii Aleksandrovich
See Yevtushenko, Yevgenyn

Ewart, Gavin (Buchanan) 1916-1995 .... CLC 13, 46
See also BRWS 7; CA 89-92; 150; CANR 17, 46; CP 1, 2, 3, 4, 5, 6; DLB 40; MTCW 1

Ewers, Hanns Heinz 1871-1943 ..... TCLC 12
See also CA 109; 149

Ewing, Frederick R.
See Sturgeon, Theodore (Hamilton)

Exley, Frederick (Earl) 1929-1992 .... CLC 6, 11
See also AITN 2; BPFB 1; CA 81-84; 138; CANR 117; DLB 143; DLBY 1981

Eynhardt, Guillermo
See Quiroga, Horacio (Sylvestre)

Ezekiel, Nissim (Moses) 1924-2004 .. CLC 61
See also CA 61-64; 223; CP 1, 2, 3, 4, 5, 6, 7; DLB 323; EWL 3

Ezekiel, Tish O'Dowd 1943- .... CLC 34
See also CA 129

Fadeev, Aleksandr Aleksandrovich
See Bulgya, Alexander Alexandrovich

Fadeev, Alexandr Alexandrovich
See Bulgya, Alexander Alexandrovich

Fadeyev, A.
See Bulgya, Alexander Alexandrovich

Fadeyev, Alexander
See Bulgya, Alexander Alexandrovich

Fagen, Donald 1948- .... CLC 26

Fainzil'berg, Il'ia Arnol'dovich
See Fainzilberg, Ilya Arnoldovich

Fainzilberg, Ilya Arnoldovich 1897-1937 .... TCLC 21
See also CA 120; 165; DLB 272; EWL 3

Fair, Ronald L. 1932- .... CLC 18
See also BW 1; CA 69-72; CANR 25; DLB 33

Fairbairn, Roger
See Carr, John Dickson

Fairbairns, Zoe (Ann) 1948- .... CLC 32
See also CA 103; CANR 21, 85; CN 4, 5, 6, 7

Fairfield, Flora
See Alcott, Louisa May

Falco, Gian
See Papini, Giovanni

Falconer, James
See Kirkup, James

Falconer, Kenneth
See Kornbluth, C(yril) M.

Falkland, Samuel
See Heijermans, Herman

Fallaci, Oriana 1930-2006 .... CLC 11, 110
See also CA 77-80; 253; CANR 15, 58, 134; FW; MTCW 1

Faludi, Susan 1959- .... CLC 140
See also CA 138; CANR 126, 194; FW; MTCW 2; MTFW 2005; NCFS 3

Faludy, George 1913- .... CLC 42
See also CA 21-24R

Faludy, Gyoergy
See Faludy, George

Fanon, Frantz 1925-1961 ...... BLC 1:2; CLC 74; TCLC 188
See also BW 1; CA 116; 89-92; DAM MULT; DLB 296; LMFS 2; WLIT 2

Fanshawe, Ann 1625-1680 .... LC 11

Fante, John (Thomas) 1911-1983 .... CLC 60; SSC 65
See also AMWS 11; CA 69-72; 109; CANR 23, 104; DLB 130; DLBY 1983

Far, Sui Sin
See Eaton, Edith Maude

Farah, Nuruddin 1945- .. BLC 1:2, 2:2; CLC 53, 137
See also AFW; BW 2, 3; CA 106; CANR 81, 148; CDWLB 3; CN 4, 5, 6, 7; DAM MULT; DLB 125; EWL 3; WLIT 2

Fardusi
See Ferdowsi, Abu'l Qasem

Fargue, Leon-Paul 1876(?)-1947 .... TCLC 11
See also CA 109; CANR 107; DLB 258; EWL 3

Farigoule, Louis
See Romains, Jules

Farina, Richard 1936(?)-1966 .... CLC 9
See also CA 81-84; 25-28R

Farley, Walter (Lorimer) 1915-1989 .... CLC 17
See also AAYA 58; BYA 14; CA 17-20R; CANR 8, 29, 84; DLB 22; JRDA; MAICYA 1, 2; SATA 2, 43, 132; YAW

Farmer, Philip Jose
See Farmer, Philip Jose

Farmer, Philip Jose 1918-2009 ..... CLC 1, 19
See also AAYA 28; BPFB 1; CA 1-4R; 283; CANR 4, 35, 111; DLB 8; MTCW 1; SATA 93; SATA-Obit 201; SCFW 1, 2; SFW 4

Farmer, Philipe Jos
See Farmer, Philip Jose

Farquhar, George 1677-1707 . DC 38; LC 21
See also BRW 2; DAM DRAM; DLB 84; RGEL 2

Farrell, J(ames) G(ordon) 1935-1979 .... CLC 6
See also CA 73-76; 89-92; CANR 36; CN 1, 2; DLB 14, 271, 326; MTCW 1; RGEL 2; RHW; WLIT 4

Farrell, James T(homas) 1904-1979 . CLC 1, 4, 8, 11, 66; SSC 28; TCLC 228
See also AMW; BPFB 1; CA 5-8R; 89-92; CANR 9, 61; CN 1, 2; DLB 4, 9, 86; DLBD 2; EWL 3; MAL 5; MTCW 1, 2; MTFW 2005; RGAL 4

Farrell, M. J.
See Keane, Mary Nesta

Farrell, Warren (Thomas) 1943- ...... CLC 70
See also CA 146; CANR 120

Farren, Richard J.
See Betjeman, John

Farren, Richard M.
See Betjeman, John

Farrugia, Mario Benedetti
See Bentley, Eric

Farrugia, Mario Orlando Hardy Hamlet Brenno Benedetti
See Benedetti, Mario

Fassbinder, Rainer Werner 1946-1982 .... CLC 20
See also CA 93-96; 106; CANR 31

Fast, Howard 1914-2003 .... CLC 23, 131
See also AAYA 16; BPFB 1; CA 1-4R, 181; 214; CAAE 181; CAAS 18; CANR 1, 33, 54, 75, 98, 140; CMW 4; CN 1, 2, 3, 4, 5, 6, 7; CPW; DAM NOV; DLB 9; INT CANR-33; LATS 1:1; MAL 5; MTCW 2; MTFW 2005; RHW; SATA 7; SATA-Essay 107; TCWW 1, 2; YAW

Faulcon, Robert
See Holdstock, Robert

Faulkner, William 1897-1962 .... CLC 1, 3, 6, 8, 9, 11, 14, 18, 28, 52, 68; SSC 1, 35, 42, 92, 97; TCLC 141; WLC 2
See also AAYA 7; AMW; AMWR 1; BPFB 1; BYA 5, 15; CA 81-84; CANR 33; CDALB 1929-1941; DA; DA3; DAB; DAC; DAM MST, NOV; DLB 9, 11, 44, 102, 316, 330; DLBD 2; DLBY 1986, 1997; EWL 3; EXPN; EXPS; GL 2; LAIT 2; LATS 1:1; LMFS 2; MAL 5; MTCW 1, 2; MTFW 2005; NFS 4, 8, 13, 24, 33; RGAL 4; RGSF 2; SSFS 2, 5, 6, 12, 27; TUS

Faulkner, William Cuthbert
See Faulkner, William

Fauset, Jessie Redmon 1882(?)-1961 ...... BLC 1:2; CLC 19, 54; HR 1:2
See also AFAW 2; BW 1; CA 109; CANR 83; DAM MULT; DLB 51; FW; LMFS 2; MAL 5; MBL

Faust, Frederick 1892-1944 .... TCLC 49
See also BPFB 1; CA 108; 152; CANR 143; DAM POP; DLB 256; TCWW 1, 2; TUS

Faust, Frederick Schiller
See Faust, Frederick

Faust, Irvin 1924- .... CLC 8
See also CA 33-36R; CANR 28, 67; CN 1, 2, 3, 4, 5, 6, 7; DLB 2, 28, 218, 278; DLBY 1980

Fawkes, Guy
See Benchley, Robert (Charles)

Fearing, Kenneth 1902-1961 .... CLC 51
See also CA 93-96; CANR 59; CMW 4; DLB 9; MAL 5; RGAL 4

Fearing, Kenneth Flexner
See Fearing, Kenneth

Fecamps, Elise
See Creasey, John

Fisher, Dorothy (Frances) Canfield
1879-1958 .... **TCLC 87**
See also CA 114; 136; CANR 80; CLR 71;
CWRI 5; DLB 9, 102, 284; MAICYA 1,
2; MAL 5; YABC 1

Fisher, M(ary) F(rances) K(ennedy)
1908-1992 .... **CLC 76, 87**
See also AMWS 17; CA 77-80; 138; CANR
44; MTCW 2

Fisher, Roy 1930- .... **CLC 25**
See also CA 81-84; CAAS 10; CANR 16;
CP 1, 2, 3, 4, 5, 6, 7; DLB 40

Fisher, Rudolph 1897-1934 ...... **BLC 1:2; HR
1:2; SSC 25; TCLC 11**
See also BW 1, 3; CA 107; 124; CANR 80;
DAM MULT; DLB 51, 102

Fisher, Vardis (Alvero) 1895-1968 .... **CLC 7;
TCLC 140**
See also CA 5-8R; 25-28R; CANR 68; DLB
9, 206; MAL 5; RGAL 4; TCWW 1, 2

Fiske, Tarleton
See Bloch, Robert (Albert)

Fitch, Clarke
See Sinclair, Upton

Fitch, John IV
See Cormier, Robert

Fitzgerald, Captain Hugh
See Baum, L. Frank

FitzGerald, Edward 1809-1883 ...... **NCLC 9,
153; PC 79**
See also BRW 4; DLB 32; RGEL 2

Fitzgerald, F. Scott 1896-1940 ...... **SSC 6, 31,
75; TCLC 1, 6, 14, 28, 55, 157; WLC 2**
See also AAYA 24; AITN 1; AMW; AMWC
2; AMWR 1; BPFB 1; CA 110; 123;
CDALB 1917-1929; DA; DA3; DAB;
DAC; DAM MST, NOV; DLB 4, 9, 86,
219, 273; DLBD 1, 15, 16; DLBY 1981,
1996; EWL 3; EXPN; EXPS; LAIT 3;
MAL 5; MTCW 1, 2; MTFW 2005; NFS
2, 19, 20; RGAL 4; RGSF 2; SSFS 4, 15,
21, 25; TUS

Fitzgerald, Francis Scott Key
See Fitzgerald, F. Scott

Fitzgerald, Penelope 1916-2000 . **CLC 19, 51,
61, 143**
See also BRWS 5; CA 85-88; 190; CAAS
10; CANR 56, 86, 131; CN 3, 4, 5, 6, 7;
DLB 14, 194, 326; EWL 3; MTCW 2;
MTFW 2005

Fitzgerald, Robert (Stuart)
1910-1985 .... **CLC 39**
See also CA 1-4R; 114; CANR 1; CP 1, 2,
3, 4; DLBY 1980; MAL 5

FitzGerald, Robert D(avid)
1902-1987 .... **CLC 19**
See also CA 17-20R; CP 1, 2, 3, 4; DLB
260; RGEL 2

Fitzgerald, Zelda (Sayre)
1900-1948 .... **TCLC 52**
See also AMWS 9; CA 117; 126; DLBY
1984

Flanagan, Thomas (James Bonner)
1923-2002 .... **CLC 25, 52**
See also CA 108; 206; CANR 55; CN 3, 4,
5, 6, 7; DLBY 1980; INT CA-108; MTCW
1; RHW; TCLE 1:1

Flashman, Harry Paget
See Fraser, George MacDonald

Flaubert, Gustave 1821-1880 .... **NCLC 2, 10,
19, 62, 66, 135, 179, 185; SSC 11, 60;
WLC 2**
See also DA; DA3; DAB; DAC; DAM
MST, NOV; DLB 119, 301; EW 7; EXPS;
GFL 1789 to the Present; LAIT 2; LMFS
1; NFS 14; RGSF 2; RGWL 2, 3; SSFS
6; TWA

Flavius Josephus
See Josephus, Flavius

Flecker, Herman Elroy
See Flecker, (Herman) James Elroy

Flecker, (Herman) James Elroy
1884-1915 .... **TCLC 43**
See also CA 109; 150; DLB 10, 19; RGEL
2

Fleming, Ian 1908-1964 ... **CLC 3, 30; TCLC
193**
See also AAYA 26; BPFB 1; BRWS 14; CA
5-8R; CANR 59; CDBLB 1945-1960;
CMW 4; CPW; DA3; DAM POP; DLB
87, 201; MSW; MTCW 1, 2; MTFW
2005; RGEL 2; SATA 9; TEA; YAW

Fleming, Ian Lancaster
See Fleming, Ian

Fleming, Thomas 1927- .... **CLC 37**
See also CA 5-8R; CANR 10, 102, 155,
197; INT CANR-10; SATA 8

Fleming, Thomas James
See Fleming, Thomas

Fletcher, John 1579-1625 . **DC 6; LC 33, 151**
See also BRW 2; CDBLB Before 1660;
DLB 58; RGEL 2; TEA

Fletcher, John Gould 1886-1950 .... **TCLC 35**
See also CA 107; 167; DLB 4, 45; LMFS
2; MAL 5; RGAL 4

Fleur, Paul
See Pohl, Frederik

Flieg, Helmut
See Heym, Stefan

Flooglebuckle, Al
See Spiegelman, Art

Flying Officer X
See Bates, H(erbert) E(rnest)

Fo, Dario 1926- .... **CLC 32, 109, 227; DC 10**
See also CA 116; 128; CANR 68, 114, 134,
164; CWW 2; DA3; DAM DRAM; DFS
23; DLB 330; DLBY 1997; EWL 3;
MTCW 1, 2; MTFW 2005; WLIT 7

Foden, Giles 1967- .... **CLC 231**
See also CA 240; DLB 267; NFS 15

Fogarty, Jonathan Titulescu Esq.
See Farrell, James T(homas)

Follett, Ken 1949- .... **CLC 18**
See also AAYA 6, 50; BEST 89:4; BPFB 1;
CA 81-84; CANR 13, 33, 54, 102, 156,
197; CMW 4; CPW; DA3; DAM NOV,
POP; DLB 87; DLBY 1981; INT CANR-
33; LNFS 3; MTCW 1

Follett, Kenneth Martin
See Follett, Ken

Fondane, Benjamin 1898-1944 ..... **TCLC 159**

Fontane, Theodor 1819-1898 . **NCLC 26, 163**
See also CDWLB 2; DLB 129; EW 6;
RGWL 2, 3; TWA

Fonte, Moderata 1555-1592 .... **LC 118**

Fontenelle, Bernard Le Bovier de
1657-1757 .... **LC 140**
See also DLB 268, 313; GFL Beginnings to
1789

Fontenot, Chester CLC 65

Fonvizin, Denis Ivanovich
1744(?)-1792 .... **LC 81**
See also DLB 150; RGWL 2, 3

Foote, Albert Horton
See Foote, Horton

Foote, Horton 1916-2009 .... **CLC 51, 91**
See also AAYA 82; CA 73-76; 284; CAD;
CANR 34, 51, 110; CD 5, 6; CSW; DA3;
DAM DRAM; DFS 20; DLB 26, 266;
EWL 3; INT CANR-34; MTFW 2005

Foote, Mary Hallock 1847-1938 .. **TCLC 108**
See also DLB 186, 188, 202, 221; TCWW
2

Foote, Samuel 1721-1777 .... **LC 106**
See also DLB 89; RGEL 2

Foote, Shelby 1916-2005 .... **CLC 75, 224**
See also AAYA 40; CA 5-8R; 240; CANR
3, 45, 74, 131; CN 1, 2, 3, 4, 5, 6, 7;
CPW; CSW; DA3; DAM NOV, POP;
DLB 2, 17; MAL 5; MTCW 2; MTFW
2005; RHW

Forbes, Cosmo
See Lewton, Val

Forbes, Esther 1891-1967 .... **CLC 12**
See also AAYA 17; BYA 2; CA 13-14; 25-
28R; CAP 1; CLR 27, 147; DLB 22;
JRDA; MAICYA 1, 2; RHW; SATA 2,
100; YAW

Forche, Carolyn 1950- .. **CLC 25, 83, 86; PC
10**
See also CA 109; 117; CANR 50, 74, 138;
CP 4, 5, 6, 7; CWP; DA3; DAM POET;
DLB 5, 193; INT CA-117; MAL 5;
MTCW 2; MTFW 2005; PFS 18; RGAL
4

Forche, Carolyn Louise
See Forche, Carolyn

Ford, Elbur
See Hibbert, Eleanor Alice Burford

Ford, Ford Madox 1873-1939 ... **TCLC 1, 15,
39, 57, 172**
See also BRW 6; CA 104; 132; CANR 74;
CDBLB 1914-1945; DA3; DAM NOV;
DLB 34, 98, 162; EWL 3; MTCW 1, 2;
NFS 28; RGEL 2; RHW; TEA

Ford, Henry 1863-1947 .... **TCLC 73**
See also CA 115; 148

Ford, Jack
See Ford, John

Ford, John 1586-1639 .... **DC 8; LC 68, 153**
See also BRW 2; CDBLB Before 1660;
DA3; DAM DRAM; DFS 7; DLB 58;
IDTP; RGEL 2

Ford, John 1895-1973 .... **CLC 16**
See also AAYA 75; CA 187; 45-48

Ford, Richard 1944- ... **CLC 46, 99, 205, 277**
See also AMWS 5; CA 69-72; CANR 11,
47, 86, 128, 164; CN 5, 6, 7; CSW; DLB
227; EWL 3; MAL 5; MTCW 2; MTFW
2005; NFS 25; RGAL 4; RGSF 2

Ford, Webster
See Masters, Edgar Lee

Foreman, Richard 1937- .... **CLC 50**
See also CA 65-68; CAD; CANR 32, 63,
143; CD 5, 6

Forester, C. S. 1899-1966 ..... **CLC 35; TCLC
152**
See also CA 73-76; 25-28R; CANR 83;
DLB 191; RGEL 2; RHW; SATA 13

Forester, Cecil Scott
See Forester, C. S.

Forez
See Mauriac, Francois (Charles)

Forman, James
See Forman, James D.

Forman, James D. 1932- .... **CLC 21**
See also AAYA 17; CA 9-12R; CANR 4,
19, 42; JRDA; MAICYA 1, 2; SATA 8,
70; YAW

Forman, James Douglas
See Forman, James D.

Forman, Milos 1932- .... **CLC 164**
See also AAYA 63; CA 109

Fornes, Maria Irene 1930- .... **CLC 39, 61,
187; DC 10; HLCS 1**
See also CA 25-28R; CAD; CANR 28, 81;
CD 5, 6; CWD; DFS 25; DLB 7, 341; HW
1, 2; INT CANR-28; LLW; MAL 5;
MTCW 1; RGAL 4

Forrest, Leon (Richard)
1937-1997 .... **BLCS; CLC 4**
See also AFAW 2; BW 2; CA 89-92; 162;
CAAS 7; CANR 25, 52, 87; CN 4, 5, 6;
DLB 33

Forster, E. M. 1879-1970 .. CLC 1, 2, 3, 4, 9,
10, 13, 15, 22, 45, 77; SSC 27, 96;
TCLC 125; WLC 2
    See also AAYA 2, 37; BRW 6; BRWR 2;
    BYA 12; CA 13-14; 25-28R; CANR 45;
    CAP 1; CDBLB 1914-1945; DA; DA3;
    DAB; DAC; DAM MST, NOV; DLB 34,
    98, 162, 178, 195; DLBD 10; EWL 3;
    EXPN; LAIT 3; LMFS 1; MTCW 1, 2;
    MTFW 2005; NCFS 1; NFS 3, 10, 11;
    RGEL 2; RGSF 2; SATA 57; SUFW 1;
    TEA; WLIT 4
Forster, Edward Morgan
    See Forster, E. M.
Forster, John 1812-1876 .... NCLC 11
    See also DLB 144, 184
Forster, Margaret 1938- .... CLC 149
    See also CA 133; CANR 62, 115, 175; CN
    4, 5, 6, 7; DLB 155, 271
Forsyth, Frederick 1938- .... CLC 2, 5, 36
    See also BEST 89:4; CA 85-88; CANR 38,
    62, 115, 137, 183; CMW 4; CN 3, 4, 5, 6,
    7; CPW; DAM NOV, POP; DLB 87;
    MTCW 1, 2; MTFW 2005
Fort, Paul
    See Stockton, Francis Richard
Forten, Charlotte
    See Grimke, Charlotte L. Forten
Forten, Charlotte L. 1837-1914
    See Grimke, Charlotte L. Forten
Fortinbras
    See Grieg, (Johan) Nordahl (Brun)
Foscolo, Ugo 1778-1827 .... NCLC 8, 97
    See also EW 5; WLIT 7
Fosse, Bob 1927-1987 .... CLC 20
    See also AAYA 82; CA 110; 123
Fosse, Robert L.
    See Fosse, Bob
Foster, Hannah Webster
    1758-1840 .... NCLC 99
    See also DLB 37, 200; RGAL 4
Foster, Stephen Collins
    1826-1864 .... NCLC 26
    See also RGAL 4
Foucault, Michel 1926-1984 . CLC 31, 34, 69
    See also CA 105; 113; CANR 34; DLB 242;
    EW 13; EWL 3; GFL 1789 to the Present;
    GLL 1; LMFS 2; MTCW 1, 2; TWA
**Fouque, Friedrich (Heinrich Karl) de la
    Motte** 1777-1843 .... NCLC 2
    See also DLB 90; RGWL 2, 3; SUFW 1
Fourier, Charles 1772-1837 .... NCLC 51
Fournier, Henri-Alban 1886-1914 ... TCLC 6
    See also CA 104; 179; DLB 65; EWL 3;
    GFL 1789 to the Present; RGWL 2, 3
Fournier, Pierre 1916-1997 .... CLC 11
    See also CA 89-92; CANR 16, 40; EWL 3;
    RGHL
Fowles, John 1926-2005 .... CLC 1, 2, 3, 4, 6,
9, 10, 15, 33, 87, 287; SSC 33, 128
    See also BPFB 1; BRWS 1; CA 5-8R; 245;
    CANR 25, 71, 103; CDBLB 1960 to
    Present; CN 1, 2, 3, 4, 5, 6, 7; DA3; DAB;
    DAC; DAM MST; DLB 14, 139, 207;
    EWL 3; HGG; MTCW 1, 2; MTFW 2005;
    NFS 21; RGEL 2; RHW; SATA 22; SATA-
    Obit 171; TEA; WLIT 4
Fowles, John Robert
    See Fowles, John
Fox, Norma Diane
    See Mazer, Norma Fox
Fox, Paula 1923- .... CLC 2, 8, 121
    See also AAYA 3, 37; BYA 3, 8; CA 73-76;
    CANR 20, 36, 62, 105, 200; CLR 1, 44,
    96; DLB 52; JRDA; MAICYA 1, 2;
    MTCW 1; NFS 12; SATA 17, 60, 120,
    167; WYA; YAW
Fox, William Price, Jr.
    See Fox, William Price

Fox, William Price 1926- .... CLC 22
    See also CA 17-20R; CAAS 19; CANR 11,
    142, 189; CSW; DLB 2; DLBY 1981
Foxe, John 1517(?)-1587 .... LC 14, 166
    See also DLB 132
Frame, Janet 1924-2004 ...... CLC 2, 3, 6, 22,
66, 96, 237; SSC 29, 127
    See also CA 1-4R; 224; CANR 2, 36, 76,
    135; CN 1, 2, 3, 4, 5, 6, 7; CP 2, 3, 4;
    CWP; EWL 3; MTCW 1,2; RGEL 2;
    RGSF 2; SATA 119; TWA
France, Anatole 1844-1924 .... TCLC 9
    See also CA 106; 127; DA3; DAM NOV;
    DLB 123, 330; EWL 3; GFL 1789 to the
    Present; MTCW 1, 2; RGWL 2, 3; SUFW
    1; TWA
Francis, Claude .... CLC 50
    See also CA 192
Francis, Dick 1920-2010 . CLC 2, 22, 42, 102
    See also AAYA 5, 21; BEST 89:3; BPFB 1;
    CA 5-8R; CANR 9, 42, 68, 100, 141, 179;
    CDBLB 1960 to Present; CMW 4; CN 2,
    3, 4, 5, 6; DA3; DAM POP; DLB 87; INT
    CANR-9; MSW; MTCW 1, 2; MTFW
    2005
Francis, Paula Marie
    See Allen, Paula Gunn
Francis, Richard Stanley
    See Francis, Dick
Francis, Robert (Churchill)
    1901-1987 .... CLC 15; PC 34
    See also AMWS 9; CA 1-4R; 123; CANR
    1; CP 1, 2, 3, 4; EXPP; PFS 12; TCLE
    1:1
Francis, Lord Jeffrey
    See Jeffrey, Francis
Franco, Veronica 1546-1591 .... LC 171
    See also WLIT 7
Frank, Anne 1929-1945 ... TCLC 17; WLC 2
    See also AAYA 12; BYA 1; CA 113; 133;
    CANR 68; CLR 101; DA; DA3; DAB;
    DAC; DAM MST; LAIT 4; MAICYA 2;
    MAICYAS 1; MTCW 1, 2; MTFW 2005;
    NCFS 5; RGHL; SATA 87; SATA-Brief
    42; WYA; YAW
Frank, Annelies Marie
    See Frank, Anne
Frank, Bruno 1887-1945 .... TCLC 81
    See also CA 189; DLB 118; EWL 3
Frank, Elizabeth 1945- .... CLC 39
    See also CA 121; 126; CANR 78, 150; INT
    CA-126
Frankl, Viktor E(mil) 1905-1997 ...... CLC 93
    See also CA 65-68; 161; RGHL
Franklin, Benjamin
    See Hasek, Jaroslav
Franklin, Benjamin 1706-1790 .. LC 25, 134;
WLCS
    See also AMW; CDALB 1640-1865; DA;
    DA3; DAB; DAC; DAM MST; DLB 24,
    43, 73, 183; LAIT 1; RGAL 4; TUS
Franklin, Madeleine
    See L'Engle, Madeleine
Franklin, Madeleine L'Engle
    See L'Engle, Madeleine
Franklin, Madeleine L'Engle Camp
    See L'Engle, Madeleine
**Franklin, (Stella Maria Sarah) Miles
    (Lampe)** 1879-1954 .... TCLC 7
    See also CA 104; 164; DLB 230; FW;
    MTCW 2; RGEL 2; TWA
Franzen, Jonathan 1959- .... CLC 202
    See also AAYA 65; AMWS 20; CA 129;
    CANR 105, 166
Fraser, Antonia 1932- .... CLC 32, 107
    See also AAYA 57; CA 85-88; CANR 44,
    65, 119, 164; CMW; DLB 276; MTCW 1,
    2; MTFW 2005; SATA-Brief 32

Fraser, George MacDonald
    1925-2008 .... CLC 7
    See also AAYA 48; CA 45-48, 180; 268;
    CAAE 180; CANR 2, 48, 74, 192; DLB
    352; MTCW 2; RHW
Fraser, Sylvia 1935- .... CLC 64
    See also CA 45-48; CANR 1, 16, 60; CCA
    1
Frater Perdurabo
    See Crowley, Edward Alexander
Frayn, Michael 1933- .... CLC 3, 7, 31, 47,
176; DC 27
    See also AAYA 69; BRWC 2; BRWS 7; CA
    5-8R; CANR 30, 69, 114, 133, 166; CBD;
    CD 5, 6; CN 1, 2, 3, 4, 5, 6, 7; DAM
    DRAM, NOV; DFS 22; DLB 13, 14, 194,
    245; FANT; MTCW 1, 2; MTFW 2005;
    SFW 4
Fraze, Candida (Merrill) 1945- .... CLC 50
    See also CA 126
Frazer, Andrew
    See Marlowe, Stephen
Frazer, J(ames) G(eorge)
    1854-1941 .... TCLC 32
    See also BRWS 3; CA 118; NCFS 5
Frazer, Robert Caine
    See Creasey, John
Frazer, Sir James George
    See Frazer, J(ames) G(eorge)
Frazier, Charles 1950- .... CLC 109, 224
    See also AAYA 34; CA 161; CANR 126,
    170; CSW; DLB 292; MTFW 2005; NFS
    25
Frazier, Charles R.
    See Frazier, Charles
Frazier, Charles Robinson
    See Frazier, Charles
Frazier, Ian 1951- .... CLC 46
    See also CA 130; CANR 54, 93, 193
Frederic, Harold 1856-1898 ... NCLC 10, 175
    See also AMW; DLB 12, 23; DLBD 13;
    MAL 5; NFS 22; RGAL 4
Frederick, John
    See Faust, Frederick
Frederick the Great 1712-1786 .... LC 14
Fredro, Aleksander 1793-1876 .... NCLC 8
Freeling, Nicolas 1927-2003 .... CLC 38
    See also CA 49-52; 218; CAAS 12; CANR
    1, 17, 50, 84; CMW 4; CN 1, 2, 3, 4, 5,
    6; DLB 87
Freeman, Douglas Southall
    1886-1953 .... TCLC 11
    See also CA 109; 195; DLB 17; DLBD 17
Freeman, Judith 1946- .... CLC 55
    See also CA 148; CANR 120, 179; DLB
    256
Freeman, Mary E(leanor) Wilkins
    1852-1930 .... SSC 1, 47, 113; TCLC 9
    See also CA 106; 177; DLB 12, 78, 221;
    EXPS; FW; HGG; MBL; RGAL 4; RGSF
    2; SSFS 4, 8, 26; SUFW 1; TUS
Freeman, R(ichard) Austin
    1862-1943 .... TCLC 21
    See also CA 113; CANR 84; CMW 4; DLB
    70
French, Albert 1943- .... CLC 86
    See also BW 3; CA 167
French, Antonia
    See Kureishi, Hanif
French, Marilyn 1929-2009 . CLC 10, 18, 60,
177
    See also BPFB 1; CA 69-72; 286; CANR 3,
    31, 134, 163; CN 5, 6, 7; CPW; DAM
    DRAM, NOV, POP; FL 1:5; FW; INT
    CANR-31; MTCW 1, 2; MTFW 2005
French, Paul
    See Asimov, Isaac

Goldsmith, Oliver 1730(?)-1774 .... **DC 8; LC 2, 48, 122; PC 77; WLC 3**
See also BRW 3; CDBLB 1660-1789; DA; DAB; DAC; DAM DRAM, MST, NOV, POET; DFS 1; DLB 39, 89, 104, 109, 142, 336; IDTP; RGEL 2; SATA 26; TEA; WLIT 3

Goldsmith, Peter
See Priestley, J(ohn) B(oynton)

Goldstein, Rebecca 1950- .... **CLC 239**
See also CA 144; CANR 99, 165; TCLE 1:1

Goldstein, Rebecca Newberger
See Goldstein, Rebecca

Gombrowicz, Witold 1904-1969 .... **CLC 4, 7, 11, 49**
See also CA 19-20; 25-28R; CANR 105; CAP 2; CDWLB 4; DAM DRAM; DLB 215; EW 12; EWL 3; RGWL 2, 3; TWA

Gomez de Avellaneda, Gertrudis 1814-1873 .... **NCLC 111**
See also LAW

Gomez de la Serna, Ramon 1888-1963 .... **CLC 9**
See also CA 153; 116; CANR 79; EWL 3; HW 1, 2

Goncharov, Ivan Alexandrovich 1812-1891 .... **NCLC 1, 63**
See also DLB 238; EW 6; RGWL 2, 3

Goncourt, Edmond de 1822-1896 ... **NCLC 7**
See also DLB 123; EW 7; GFL 1789 to the Present; RGWL 2, 3

Goncourt, Edmond Louis Antoine Huot de
See Goncourt, Edmond de

Goncourt, Jules Alfred Huot de
See Goncourt, Jules de

Goncourt, Jules de 1830-1870 .... **NCLC 7**
See Goncourt, Jules de
See also DLB 123; EW 7; GFL 1789 to the Present; RGWL 2, 3

Gongora (y Argote), Luis de 1561-1627 .... **LC 72**
See also RGWL 2, 3

Gontier, Fernande 19(?)- .... **CLC 50**

Gonzalez Martinez, Enrique
See Gonzalez Martinez, Enrique

Gonzalez Martinez, Enrique 1871-1952 .... **TCLC 72**
See also CA 166; CANR 81; DLB 290; EWL 3; HW 1, 2

Goodison, Lorna 1947- .... **BLC 2:2; PC 36**
See also CA 142; CANR 88, 189; CP 5, 6, 7; CWP; DLB 157; EWL 3; PFS 25

Goodman, Allegra 1967- .... **CLC 241**
See also CA 204; CANR 162, 204; DLB 244, 350

Goodman, Paul 1911-1972 ..... **CLC 1, 2, 4, 7**
See also CA 19-20; 37-40R; CAD; CANR 34; CAP 2; CN 1; DLB 130, 246; MAL 5; MTCW 1; RGAL 4

GoodWeather, Hartley
See King, Thomas

Goodweather, Hartley
See King, Thomas

Googe, Barnabe 1540-1594 .... **LC 94**
See also DLB 132; RGEL 2

Gordimer, Nadine 1923- ...... **CLC 3, 5, 7, 10, 18, 33, 51, 70, 123, 160, 161, 263; SSC 17, 80; WLCS**
See also AAYA 39; AFW; BRWS 2; CA 5-8R; CANR 3, 28, 56, 88, 131, 195; CN 1, 2, 3, 4, 5, 6, 7; DA; DA3; DAB; DAC; DAM MST, NOV; DLB 225, 326, 330; EWL 3; EXPS; INT CANR-28; LATS 1:2; MTCW 1, 2; MTFW 2005; NFS 4; RGEL 2; RGSF 2; SSFS 2, 14, 19, 28, 31; TWA; WLIT 2; YAW

Gordon, Adam Lindsay 1833-1870 .... **NCLC 21**
See also DLB 230

Gordon, Caroline 1895-1981 . **CLC 6, 13, 29, 83; SSC 15**
See also AMW; CA 11-12; 103; CANR 36; CAP 1; CN 1, 2; DLB 4, 9, 102; DLBD 17; DLBY 1981; EWL 3; MAL 5; MTCW 1, 2; MTFW 2005; RGAL 4; RGSF 2

Gordon, Charles William 1860-1937 .... **TCLC 31**
See also CA 109; DLB 92; TCWW 1, 2

Gordon, Mary 1949- .. **CLC 13, 22, 128, 216; SSC 59**
See also AMWS 4; BPFB 2; CA 102; CANR 44, 92, 154, 179; CN 4, 5, 6, 7; DLB 6; DLBY 1981; FW; INT CA-102; MAL 5; MTCW 1

Gordon, Mary Catherine
See Gordon, Mary

Gordon, N. J.
See Bosman, Herman Charles

Gordon, Sol 1923- .... **CLC 26**
See also CA 53-56; CANR 4; SATA 11

Gordone, Charles 1925-1995 .... **BLC 2:2; CLC 1, 4; DC 8**
See also BW 1, 3; CA 93-96; 180; 150; CAAE 180; CAD; CANR 55; DAM DRAM; DLB 7; INT CA-93-96; MTCW 1

Gore, Catherine 1800-1861 .... **NCLC 65**
See also DLB 116, 344; RGEL 2

Gorenko, Anna Andreevna
See Akhmatova, Anna

Gor'kii, Maksim
See Gorky, Maxim

Gorky, Maxim 1868-1936 ..... **SSC 28; TCLC 8; WLC 3**
See also CA 105; 141; CANR 83; DA; DAB; DAC; DAM DRAM, MST, NOV; DFS 9; DLB 295; EW 8; EWL 3; MTCW 2; MTFW 2005; RGSF 2; RGWL 2, 3; TWA

Goryan, Sirak
See Saroyan, William

Gosse, Edmund (William) 1849-1928 .... **TCLC 28**
See also CA 117; DLB 57, 144, 184; RGEL 2

Gotlieb, Phyllis 1926-2009 .... **CLC 18**
See also CA 13-16R; CANR 7, 135; CN 7; CP 1, 2, 3, 4; DLB 88, 251; SFW 4

Gotlieb, Phyllis Fay Bloom
See Gotlieb, Phyllis

Gottesman, S. D.
See Kornbluth, C(yril) M.; Pohl, Frederik

Gottfried von Strassburg fl. c. 1170-1215 .... **CMLC 10, 96**
See also CDWLB 2; DLB 138; EW 1; RGWL 2, 3

Gotthelf, Jeremias 1797-1854 .... **NCLC 117**
See also DLB 133; RGWL 2, 3

Gottschalk, Laura Riding
See Jackson, Laura

Gould, Lois 1932(?)-2002 .... **CLC 4, 10**
See also CA 77-80; 208; CANR 29; MTCW 1

Gould, Stephen Jay 1941-2002 .... **CLC 163**
See also AAYA 26; BEST 90:2; CA 77-80; 205; CANR 10, 27, 56, 75, 125; CPW; INT CANR-27; MTCW 1, 2; MTFW 2005

Gourmont, Remy(-Marie-Charles) de 1858-1915 .... **TCLC 17**
See also CA 109; 150; GFL 1789 to the Present; MTCW 2

Gournay, Marie le Jars de
See de Gournay, Marie le Jars

Govier, Katherine 1948- .... **CLC 51**
See also CA 101; CANR 18, 40, 128; CCA 1

Gower, John c. 1330-1408 .... **LC 76; PC 59**
See also BRW 1; DLB 146; RGEL 2

Goyen, (Charles) William 1915-1983 .... **CLC 5, 8, 14, 40**
See also AITN 2; CA 5-8R; 110; CANR 6, 71; CN 1, 2, 3; DLB 2, 218; DLBY 1983; EWL 3; INT CANR-6; MAL 5

Goytisolo, Juan 1931- .... **CLC 5, 10, 23, 133; HLC 1**
See also CA 85-88; CANR 32, 61, 131, 182; CWW 2; DAM MULT; DLB 322; EWL 3; GLL 2; HW 1, 2; MTCW 1, 2; MTFW 2005

Gozzano, Guido 1883-1916 .... **PC 10**
See also CA 154; DLB 114; EWL 3

Gozzi, (Conte) Carlo 1720-1806 .... **NCLC 23**

Grabbe, Christian Dietrich 1801-1836 .... **NCLC 2**
See also DLB 133; RGWL 2, 3

Grace, Patricia 1937- .... **CLC 56**
See also CA 176; CANR 118; CN 4, 5, 6, 7; EWL 3; RGSF 2

Grace, Patricia Frances
See Grace, Patricia

Gracian, Baltasar 1601-1658 .... **LC 15, 160**

Gracian y Morales, Baltasar
See Gracian, Baltasar

Gracq, Julien 1910-2007 ..... **CLC 11, 48, 259**
See also CA 122; 126; 267; CANR 141; CWW 2; DLB 83; GFL 1789 to the present

Grade, Chaim 1910-1982 .... **CLC 10**
See also CA 93-96; 107; DLB 333; EWL 3; RGHL

Grade, Khayim
See Grade, Chaim

Graduate of Oxford, A
See Ruskin, John

Grafton, Garth
See Duncan, Sara Jeannette

Grafton, Sue 1940- .... **CLC 163**
See also AAYA 11, 49; BEST 90:3; CA 108; CANR 31, 55, 111, 134, 195; CMW 4; CPW; CSW; DA3; DAM POP; DLB 226; FW; MSW; MTFW 2005

Graham, John
See Phillips, David Graham

Graham, Jorie 1950- .... **CLC 48, 118; PC 59**
See also AAYA 67; CA 111; CANR 63, 118, 205; CP 4, 5, 6, 7; CWP; DLB 120; EWL 3; MTFW 2005; PFS 10, 17; TCLE 1:1

Graham, R. B. Cunninghame
See Cunninghame Graham, Robert Bontine

Graham, Robert
See Haldeman, Joe

Graham, Robert Bontine Cunninghame
See Cunninghame Graham, Robert Bontine

Graham, Tom
See Lewis, Sinclair

Graham, W(illiam) S(ydney) 1918-1986 .... **CLC 29**
See also BRWS 7; CA 73-76; 118; CP 1, 2, 3, 4; DLB 20; RGEL 2

Graham, Winston (Mawdsley) 1910-2003 .... **CLC 23**
See also CA 49-52; 218; CANR 2, 22, 45, 66; CMW 4; CN 1, 2, 3, 4, 5, 6, 7; DLB 77; RHW

Grahame, Kenneth 1859-1932 ...... **TCLC 64, 136**
See also BYA 5; CA 108; 136; CANR 80; CLR 5, 135; CWRI 5; DA3; DAB; DLB 34, 141, 178; FANT; MAICYA 1, 2; MTCW 2; NFS 20; RGEL 2; SATA 100; TEA; WCH; YABC 1

Granger, Darius John
See Marlowe, Stephen
Granin, Daniil 1918- .... CLC 59
See also DLB 302
Granovsky, Timofei Nikolaevich
1813-1855 .... NCLC 75
See also DLB 198
Grant, Skeeter
See Spiegelman, Art
Granville-Barker, Harley
1877-1946 .... TCLC 2
See also CA 104; 204; DAM DRAM; DLB
10; RGEL 2
Granzotto, Gianni
See Granzotto, Giovanni Battista
Granzotto, Giovanni Battista
1914-1985 .... CLC 70
See also CA 166
Grasemann, Ruth Barbara
See Rendell, Ruth
Grass, Guenter
See Grass, Gunter
Grass, Gunter 1927- .. CLC 1, 2, 4, 6, 11, 15,
22, 32, 49, 88, 207; WLC 3
See also BPFB 2; CA 13-16R; CANR 20,
75, 93, 133, 174; CDWLB 2; CWW 2;
DA; DA3; DAB; DAC; DAM MST, NOV;
DLB 330; EW 13; EWL 3; MTCW 1, 2;
MTFW 2005; RGHL; RGWL 2, 3; TWA
Grass, Gunter Wilhelm
See Grass, Gunter
Gratton, Thomas
See Hulme, T(homas) E(rnest)
Grau, Shirley Ann 1929- .... CLC 4, 9, 146;
SSC 15
See also CA 89-92; CANR 22, 69; CN 1, 2,
3, 4, 5, 6, 7; CSW; DLB 2, 218; INT CA-
89-92; CANR-22; MTCW 1
Gravel, Fern
See Hall, James Norman
Graver, Elizabeth 1964- .... CLC 70
See also CA 135; CANR 71, 129
Graves, Richard Perceval
1895-1985 .... CLC 44
See also CA 65-68; CANR 9, 26, 51
Graves, Robert 1895-1985 ... CLC 1, 2, 6, 11,
39, 44, 45; PC 6
See also BPFB 2; BRW 7; BYA 4; CA 5-8R;
117; CANR 5, 36; CDBLB 1914-1945;
CN 1, 2, 3; CP 1, 2, 3, 4; DA3; DAB;
DAC; DAM MST, POET; DLB 20, 100,
191; DLBD 18; DLBY 1985; EWL 3;
LATS 1:1; MTCW 1, 2; MTFW 2005;
NCFS 2; NFS 21; RGEL 2; RHW; SATA
45; TEA
Graves, Robert von Ranke
See Graves, Robert
Graves, Valerie
See Bradley, Marion Zimmer
Gray, Alasdair 1934- .... CLC 41, 275
See also BRWS 9; CA 126; CANR 47, 69,
106, 140; CN 4, 5, 6, 7; DLB 194, 261,
319; HGG; INT CA-126; MTCW 1, 2;
MTFW 2005; RGSF 2; SUFW 2
Gray, Amlin 1946- .... CLC 29
See also CA 138
Gray, Francine du Plessix 1930- ..... CLC 22,
153
See also BEST 90:3; CA 61-64; CAAS 2;
CANR 11, 33, 75, 81, 197; DAM NOV;
INT CANR-11; MTCW 1, 2; MTFW 2005
Gray, John (Henry) 1866-1934 ...... TCLC 19
See also CA 119; 162; RGEL 2
Gray, John Lee
See Jakes, John
Gray, Simon 1936-2008 .... CLC 9, 14, 36
See also AITN 1; CA 21-24R; 275; CAAS
3; CANR 32, 69; CBD; CD 5, 6; CN 1, 2,
3; DLB 13; EWL 3; MTCW 1; RGEL 2

Gray, Simon James Holliday
See Gray, Simon
Gray, Spalding 1941-2004 .... CLC 49, 112;
DC 7
See also AAYA 62; CA 128; 225; CAD;
CANR 74, 138; CD 5, 6; CPW; DAM
POP; MTCW 2; MTFW 2005
Gray, Thomas 1716-1771 . LC 4, 40, 178; PC
2, 80; WLC 3
See also BRW 3; CDBLB 1660-1789; DA;
DA3; DAB; DAC; DAM MST; DLB 109;
EXPP; PAB; PFS 9; RGEL 2; TEA; WP
Grayson, David
See Baker, Ray Stannard
Grayson, Richard (A.) 1951- .... CLC 38
See also CA 85-88, 210; CAAE 210; CANR
14, 31, 57; DLB 234
Greeley, Andrew M. 1928- .... CLC 28
See also BPFB 2; CA 5-8R; CAAS 7;
CANR 7, 43, 69, 104, 136, 184; CMW 4;
CPW; DA3; DAM POP; MTCW 1, 2;
MTFW 2005
Green, Anna Katharine
1846-1935 .... TCLC 63
See also CA 112; 159; CMW 4; DLB 202,
221; MSW
Green, Brian
See Card, Orson Scott
Green, Hannah
See Greenberg, Joanne (Goldenberg)
Green, Hannah 1927(?)-1996 .... CLC 3
See also CA 73-76; CANR 59, 93; NFS 10
Green, Henry
See Yorke, Henry Vincent
Green, Julian
See Green, Julien
Green, Julien 1900-1998 .... CLC 3, 11, 77
See also CA 21-24R; 169; CANR 33, 87;
CWW 2; DLB 4, 72; EWL 3; GFL 1789
to the Present; MTCW 2; MTFW 2005
Green, Julien Hartridge
See Green, Julien
Green, Paul (Eliot) 1894-1981 .. CLC 25; DC
37
See also AITN 1; CA 5-8R; 103; CAD;
CANR 3; DAM DRAM; DLB 7, 9, 249;
DLBY 1981; MAL 5; RGAL 4
Greenaway, Peter 1942- .... CLC 159
See also CA 127
Greenberg, Ivan 1908-1973 .... CLC 24
See also CA 85-88; DLB 137; MAL 5
Greenberg, Joanne (Goldenberg)
1932- .... CLC 7, 30
See also AAYA 12, 67; CA 5-8R; CANR
14, 32, 69; CN 6, 7; DLB 335; NFS 23;
SATA 25; YAW
Greenberg, Richard 1959(?)- .... CLC 57
See also CA 138; CAD; CD 5, 6; DFS 24
Greenblatt, Stephen J(ay) 1943- ...... CLC 70
See also CA 49-52; CANR 115; LNFS 1
Greene, Bette 1934- .... CLC 30
See also AAYA 7, 69; BYA 3; CA 53-56;
CANR 4, 146; CLR 2, 140; CWRI 5;
JRDA; LAIT 4; MAICYA 1, 2; NFS 10;
SAAS 16; SATA 8, 102, 161; WYA; YAW
Greene, Gael CLC 8
See also CA 13-16R; CANR 10, 166
Greene, Graham 1904-1991 .. CLC 1, 3, 6, 9,
14, 18, 27, 37, 70, 72, 125; SSC 29, 121;
WLC 3
See also AAYA 61; AITN 2; BPFB 2;
BRWR 2; BRWS 1; BYA 3; CA 13-16R;
133; CANR 35, 61, 131; CBD; CDBLB
1945-1960; CMW 4; CN 1, 2, 3, 4; DA;
DA3; DAB; DAC; DAM MST, NOV;
DLB 13, 15, 77, 100, 162, 201, 204;
DLBY 1991; EWL 3; MSW; MTCW 1, 2;
MTFW 2005; NFS 16, 31; RGEL 2;
SATA 20; SSFS 14; TEA; WLIT 4

Greene, Graham Henry
See Greene, Graham
Greene, Robert 1558-1592 .... LC 41
See also BRWS 8; DLB 62, 167; IDTP;
RGEL 2; TEA
Greer, Germaine 1939- .... CLC 131
See also AITN 1; CA 81-84; CANR 33, 70,
115, 133, 190; FW; MTCW 1, 2; MTFW
2005
Greer, Richard
See Silverberg, Robert
Gregor, Arthur 1923- .... CLC 9
See also CA 25-28R; CAAS 10; CANR 11;
CP 1, 2, 3, 4, 5, 6, 7; SATA 36
Gregor, Lee
See Pohl, Frederik
Gregory, Lady Isabella Augusta (Persse)
1852-1932 .... TCLC 1, 176
See also BRW 6; CA 104; 184; DLB 10;
IDTP; RGEL 2
Gregory, J. Dennis
See Williams, John A(lfred)
Gregory of Nazianzus, St.
329-389 .... CMLC 82
Gregory of Nyssa c. 335-c. 394 ... CMLC 118
Gregory of Rimini 1300(?)-1358 . CMLC 109
See also DLB 115
Grekova, I.
See Ventsel, Elena Sergeevna
Grekova, Irina
See Ventsel, Elena Sergeevna
Grendon, Stephen
See Derleth, August (William)
Grenville, Kate 1950- .... CLC 61
See also CA 118; CANR 53, 93, 156; CN
7; DLB 325
Grenville, Pelham
See Wodehouse, P. G.
Greve, Felix Paul (Berthold Friedrich)
1879-1948 .... TCLC 4
See also CA 104; 141; 175; CANR 79;
DAC; DAM MST; DLB 92; RGEL 2;
TCWW 1, 2
Greville, Fulke 1554-1628 .... LC 79
See also BRWS 11; DLB 62, 172; RGEL 2
Grey, Lady Jane 1537-1554 .... LC 93
See also DLB 132
Grey, Zane 1872-1939 .... TCLC 6
See also BPFB 2; CA 104; 132; DA3; DAM
POP; DLB 9, 212; MTCW 1, 2; MTFW
2005; RGAL 4; TCWW 1, 2; TUS
Griboedov, Aleksandr Sergeevich
1795(?)-1829 .... NCLC 129
See also DLB 205; RGWL 2, 3
Grieg, (Johan) Nordahl (Brun)
1902-1943 .... TCLC 10
See also CA 107; 189; EWL 3
Grieve, C. M. 1892-1978 ... CLC 2, 4, 11, 19,
63; PC 9
See also BRWS 12; CA 5-8R; 85-88; CANR
33, 107; CDBLB 1945-1960; CP 1, 2;
DAM POET; DLB 20; EWL 3; MTCW 1;
RGEL 2
Grieve, Christopher Murray
See Grieve, C. M.
Griffin, Gerald 1803-1840 .... NCLC 7
See also DLB 159; RGEL 2
Griffin, John Howard 1920-1980 ..... CLC 68
See also AITN 1; CA 1-4R; 101; CANR 2
Griffin, Peter 1942- .... CLC 39
See also CA 136
Griffith, David Lewelyn Wark
See Griffith, D.W.
Griffith, D.W. 1875(?)-1948 .... TCLC 68
See also AAYA 78; CA 119; 150; CANR 80
Griffith, Lawrence
See Griffith, D.W.

Author Index

Griffiths, Trevor 1935- .... **CLC 13, 52**
　See also CA 97-100; CANR 45; CBD; CD
　5, 6; DLB 13, 245
Griggs, Sutton (Elbert)
　1872-1930 .... **TCLC 77**
　See also CA 123; 186; DLB 50
Grigson, Geoffrey (Edward Harvey)
　1905-1985 .... **CLC 7, 39**
　See also CA 25-28R; 118; CANR 20, 33;
　CP 1, 2, 3, 4; DLB 27; MTCW 1, 2
Grile, Dod
　See Bierce, Ambrose
Grillparzer, Franz 1791-1872 .... **DC 14;**
　NCLC 1, 102; SSC 37
　See also CDWLB 2; DLB 133; EW 5;
　RGWL 2, 3; TWA
Grimble, Reverend Charles James
　See Eliot, T. S.
Grimke, Angelina Emily Weld
　See Grimke, Angelina Weld
Grimke, Angelina Weld 1880-1958 ... **DC 38;**
　HR 1:2
　See also BW 1; CA 124; DAM POET; DLB
　50, 54; FW
Grimke, Charlotte L. Forten
　1837(?)-1914 .... **BLC 1:2; TCLC 16**
　See also BW 1; CA 117; 124; DAM MULT,
　POET; DLB 50, 239
Grimke, Charlotte Lottie Forten
　See Grimke, Charlotte L. Forten
Grimm, Jacob Ludwig Karl
　1785-1863 .... **NCLC 3, 77; SSC 36, 88**
　See also CLR 112; DLB 90; MAICYA 1, 2;
　RGSF 2; RGWL 2, 3; SATA 22; WCH
Grimm, Wilhelm Karl 1786-1859 .. **NCLC 3,**
　77; SSC 36
　See also CDWLB 2; CLR 112; DLB 90;
　MAICYA 1, 2; RGSF 2; RGWL 2, 3;
　SATA 22; WCH
Grimm and Grim
　See Grimm, Jacob Ludwig Karl; Grimm,
　Wilhelm Karl
Grimm Brothers
　See Grimm, Jacob Ludwig Karl; Grimm,
　Wilhelm Karl
Grimmelshausen, Hans Jakob Christoffel
　von
　See Grimmelshausen, Johann Jakob Christ-
　offel von
Grimmelshausen, Johann Jakob Christoffel
　von 1621-1676 .... **LC 6**
　See also CDWLB 2; DLB 168; RGWL 2, 3
Grindel, Eugene 1895-1952 .... **PC 38; TCLC**
　7, 41
　See also CA 104; 193; EWL 3; GFL 1789
　to the Present; LMFS 2; RGWL 2, 3
Grisham, John 1955- .... **CLC 84, 273**
　See also AAYA 14, 47; BPFB 2; CA 138;
　CANR 47, 69, 114, 133; CMW 4; CN 6,
　7; CPW; CSW; DA3; DAM POP; LNFS
　1; MSW; MTCW 2; MTFW 2005
Grosseteste, Robert 1175(?)-1253 . **CMLC 62**
　See also DLB 115
Grossman, David 1954- .... **CLC 67, 231**
　See also CA 138; CANR 114, 175; CWW
　2; DLB 299; EWL 3; RGHL; WLIT 6
Grossman, Vasilii Semenovich
　See Grossman, Vasily (Semenovich)
Grossman, Vasily (Semenovich)
　1905-1964 .... **CLC 41**
　See also CA 124; 130; DLB 272; MTCW 1;
　RGHL
Grove, Frederick Philip
　See Greve, Felix Paul (Berthold Friedrich)
Grubb
　See Crumb, R.

Grumbach, Doris 1918- .... **CLC 13, 22, 64**
　See also CA 5-8R; CAAS 2; CANR 9, 42,
　70, 127; CN 6, 7; INT CANR-9; MTCW
　2; MTFW 2005
Grundtvig, Nikolai Frederik Severin
　1783-1872 .... **NCLC 1, 158**
　See also DLB 300
Grunge
　See Crumb, R.
Grunwald, Lisa 1959- .... **CLC 44**
　See also CA 120; CANR 148
Gryphius, Andreas 1616-1664 .... **LC 89**
　See also CDWLB 2; DLB 164; RGWL 2, 3
Guare, John 1938- .... **CLC 8, 14, 29, 67; DC**
　20
　See also CA 73-76; CAD; CANR 21, 69,
　118; CD 5, 6; DAM DRAM; DFS 8, 13;
　DLB 7, 249; EWL 3; MAL 5; MTCW 1,
　2; RGAL 4
Guarini, Battista 1538-1612 .... **LC 102**
　See also DLB 339
Gubar, Susan 1944- .... **CLC 145**
　See also CA 108; CANR 45, 70, 139, 179;
　FW; MTCW 1; RGAL 4
Gubar, Susan David
　See Gubar, Susan
Gudjonsson, Halldor Kiljan
　1902-1998 .... **CLC 25**
　See also CA 103; 164; CWW 2; DLB 293,
　331; EW 12; EWL 3; RGWL 2, 3
Guedes, Vincente
　See Pessoa, Fernando
Guenter, Erich
　See Eich, Gunter
Guest, Barbara 1920-2006 ... **CLC 34; PC 55**
　See also BG 1:2; CA 25-28R; 248; CANR
　11, 44, 84; CP 1, 2, 3, 4, 5, 6, 7; CWP;
　DLB 5, 193
Guest, Edgar A(lbert) 1881-1959 ... **TCLC 95**
　See also CA 112; 168
Guest, Judith 1936- .... **CLC 8, 30**
　See also AAYA 7, 66; CA 77-80; CANR
　15, 75, 138; DA3; DAM NOV, POP;
　EXPN; INT CANR-15; LAIT 5; MTCW
　1, 2; MTFW 2005; NFS 1, 33
Guest, Judith Ann
　See Guest, Judith
Guevara, Che
　See Guevara (Serna), Ernesto
Guevara (Serna), Ernesto
　1928-1967 .... **CLC 87; HLC 1**
　See also CA 127; 111; CANR 56; DAM
　MULT; HW 1
Guicciardini, Francesco 1483-1540 ..... **LC 49**
Guido delle Colonne c. 1215-c.
　1290 .... **CMLC 90**
Guild, Nicholas M. 1944- .... **CLC 33**
　See also CA 93-96
Guillemin, Jacques
　See Sartre, Jean-Paul
Guillen, Jorge 1893-1984 . **CLC 11; HLCS 1;**
　PC 35; TCLC 233
　See also CA 89-92; 112; DAM MULT,
　POET; DLB 108; EWL 3; HW 1; RGWL
　2, 3
Guillen, Nicolas 1902-1989 ... **BLC 1:2; CLC**
　48, 79; HLC 1; PC 23
　See also BW 2; CA 116; 125; 129; CANR
　84; DAM MST, MULT, POET; DLB 283;
　EWL 3; HW 1; LAW; RGWL 2, 3; WP
Guillen, Nicolas Cristobal
　See Guillen, Nicolas
Guillen y Alvarez, Jorge
　See Guillen, Jorge
Guillevic, (Eugene) 1907-1997 .... **CLC 33**
　See also CA 93-96; CWW 2
Guillois
　See Desnos, Robert

Guillois, Valentin
　See Desnos, Robert
Guimaraes Rosa, Joao 1908-1967 ... **CLC 23;**
　HLCS 1
　See also CA 175; 89-92; DLB 113, 307;
　EWL 3; LAW; RGSF 2; RGWL 2, 3;
　WLIT 1
Guiney, Louise Imogen
　1861-1920 .... **TCLC 41**
　See also CA 160; DLB 54; RGAL 4
Guinizelli, Guido c. 1230-1276 ...... **CMLC 49**
　See also WLIT 7
Guinizzelli, Guido
　See Guinizelli, Guido
Guiraldes, Ricardo (Guillermo)
　1886-1927 .... **TCLC 39**
　See also CA 131; EWL 3; HW 1; LAW;
　MTCW 1
Guma, Alex La
　See La Guma, Alex
Gumilev, Nikolai (Stepanovich)
　1886-1921 .... **TCLC 60**
　See also CA 165; DLB 295; EWL 3
Gumilyov, Nikolay Stepanovich
　See Gumilev, Nikolai (Stepanovich)
Gump, P. Q.
　See Card, Orson Scott
Gunesekera, Romesh 1954- .... **CLC 91**
　See also BRWS 10; CA 159; CANR 140,
　172; CN 6, 7; DLB 267, 323
Gunn, Bill
　See Gunn, William Harrison
Gunn, Thom 1929-2004 ..... **CLC 3, 6, 18, 32,**
　81; PC 26
　See also BRWR 3; BRWS 4; CA 17-20R;
　227; CANR 9, 33, 116; CDBLB 1960 to
　Present; CP 1, 2, 3, 4, 5, 6, 7; DAM
　POET; DLB 27; INT CANR-33; MTCW
　1; PFS 9; RGEL 2
Gunn, William Harrison
　1934(?)-1989 .... **CLC 5**
　See also AITN 1; BW 1, 3; CA 13-16R;
　128; CANR 12, 25, 76; DLB 38
Gunn Allen, Paula
　See Allen, Paula Gunn
Gunnars, Kristjana 1948- .... **CLC 69**
　See also CA 113; CCA 1; CP 6, 7; CWP;
　DLB 60
Gunter, Erich
　See Eich, Gunter
Gurdjieff, G(eorgei) I(vanovich)
　1877(?)-1949 .... **TCLC 71**
　See also CA 157
Gurganus, Allan 1947- .... **CLC 70**
　See also BEST 90:1; CA 135; CANR 114;
　CN 6, 7; CPW; CSW; DAM POP; DLB
　350; GLL 1
Gurney, A. R.
　See Gurney, A(lbert) R(amsdell), Jr.
Gurney, A(lbert) R(amsdell), Jr.
　1930- .... **CLC 32, 50, 54**
　See also AMWS 5; CA 77-80; CAD; CANR
　32, 64, 121; CD 5, 6; DAM DRAM; DLB
　266; EWL 3
Gurney, Ivor (Bertie) 1890-1937 ... **TCLC 33**
　See also BRW 6; CA 167; DLBY 2002;
　PAB; RGEL 2
Gurney, Peter
　See Gurney, A(lbert) R(amsdell), Jr.
Guro, Elena (Genrikhovna)
　1877-1913 .... **TCLC 56**
　See also DLB 295
Gustafson, James M(oody) 1925- ... **CLC 100**
　See also CA 25-28R; CANR 37
Gustafson, Ralph (Barker)
　1909-1995 .... **CLC 36**
　See also CA 21-24R; CANR 8, 45, 84; CP
　1, 2, 3, 4, 5, 6; DLB 88; RGEL 2

Hasek, Jaroslav 1883-1923 ... **SSC 69; TCLC 4**
See also CA 104; 129; CDWLB 4; DLB 215; EW 9; EWL 3; MTCW 1, 2; RGSF 2; RGWL 2, 3

Hasek, Jaroslav Matej Frantisek
See Hasek, Jaroslav

Hass, Robert 1941- ...... **CLC 18, 39, 99, 287; PC 16**
See also AMWS 6; CA 111; CANR 30, 50, 71, 187; CP 3, 4, 5, 6, 7; DLB 105, 206; EWL 3; MAL 5; MTFW 2005; RGAL 4; SATA 94; TCLE 1:1

Hassler, Jon 1933-2008 .... **CLC 263**
See also CA 73-76; 270; CANR 21, 80, 161; CN 6, 7; INT CANR-21; SATA 19; SATA-Obit 191

Hassler, Jon Francis
See Hassler, Jon

Hastings, Hudson
See Kuttner, Henry

Hastings, Selina CLC 44
See also CA 257

Hastings, Selina Shirley
See Hastings, Selina

Hastings, Victor
See Disch, Thomas M.

Hathorne, John 1641-1717 .... **LC 38**

Hatteras, Amelia
See Mencken, H. L.

Hatteras, Owen
See Mencken, H. L.; Nathan, George Jean

Hauff, Wilhelm 1802-1827 .... **NCLC 185**
See also DLB 90; SUFW 1

Hauptmann, Gerhart 1862-1946 .... **DC 34; SSC 37; TCLC 4**
See also CA 104; 153; CDWLB 2; DAM DRAM; DLB 66, 118, 330; EW 8; EWL 3; RGSF 2; RGWL 2, 3; TWA

Hauptmann, Gerhart Johann Robert
See Hauptmann, Gerhart

Havel, Vaclav 1936- ..... **CLC 25, 58, 65, 123; DC 6**
See also CA 104; CANR 36, 63, 124, 175; CDWLB 4; CWW 2; DA3; DAM DRAM; DFS 10; DLB 232; EWL 3; LMFS 2; MTCW 1, 2; MTFW 2005; RGWL 3

Haviaras, Stratis
See Chaviaras, Strates

Hawes, Stephen 1475(?)-1529(?) .... **LC 17**
See also DLB 132; RGEL 2

Hawkes, John 1925-1998 .. **CLC 1, 2, 3, 4, 7, 9, 14, 15, 27, 49**
See also BPFB 2; CA 1-4R; 167; CANR 2, 47, 64; CN 1, 2, 3, 4, 5, 6; DLB 2, 7, 227; DLBY 1980, 1998; EWL 3; MAL 5; MTCW 1, 2; MTFW 2005; RGAL 4

Hawking, S. W.
See Hawking, Stephen W.

Hawking, Stephen W. 1942- ..... **CLC 63, 105**
See also AAYA 13; BEST 89:1; CA 126; 129; CANR 48, 115; CPW; DA3; MTFW 2; MTFW 2005

Hawking, Stephen William
See Hawking, Stephen W.

Hawkins, Anthony Hope
See Hope, Anthony

Hawthorne, Julian 1846-1934 .... **TCLC 25**
See also CA 165; HGG

Hawthorne, Nathaniel 1804-1864 ... **NCLC 2, 10, 17, 23, 39, 79, 95, 158, 171, 191, 226; SSC 3, 29, 39, 89, 130; WLC 3**
See also AAYA 18; AMW; AMWC 1; AMWR 1; BPFB 2; BYA 3; CDALB 1640-1865; CLR 103; DA; DA3; DAB; DAC; DAM MST, NOV; DLB 1, 74, 183,

223, 269; EXPN; EXPS; GL 2; HGG; LAIT 1; NFS 1, 20; RGAL 4; RGSF 2; SSFS 1, 7, 11, 15, 30; SUFW 1; TUS; WCH; YABC 2

Hawthorne, Sophia Peabody 1809-1871 .... **NCLC 150**
See also DLB 183, 239

Haxton, Josephine Ayres
See Douglas, Ellen

Hayaseca y Eizaguirre, Jorge
See Echegaray (y Eizaguirre), Jose (Maria Waldo)

Hayashi, Fumiko 1904-1951 .... **TCLC 27**
See also CA 161; DLB 180; EWL 3

Hayashi Fumiko
See Hayashi, Fumiko

Haycraft, Anna 1932-2005 .... **CLC 40**
See also CA 122; 237; CANR 90, 141; CN 4, 5, 6; DLB 194; MTCW 2; MTFW 2005

Haycraft, Anna Margaret
See Haycraft, Anna

Hayden, Robert
See Hayden, Robert Earl

Hayden, Robert E.
See Hayden, Robert Earl

Hayden, Robert Earl 1913-1980 .... **BLC 1:2; CLC 5, 9, 14, 37; PC 6**
See also AFAW 1, 2; AMWS 2; BW 1, 3; CA 69-72; 97-100; CABS 2; CANR 24, 75, 82; CDALB 1941-1968; CP 1, 2, 3; DA; DAC; DAM MST, MULT, POET; DLB 5, 76; EWL 3; EXPP; MAL 5; MTCW 1, 2; PFS 1, 31; RGAL 4; SATA 19; SATA-Obit 26; WP

Haydon, Benjamin Robert 1786-1846 .... **NCLC 146**
See also DLB 110

Hayek, F(riedrich) A(ugust von) 1899-1992 .... **TCLC 109**
See also CA 93-96; 137; CANR 20; MTCW 1, 2

Hayford, J(oseph) E(phraim) Casely
See Casely-Hayford, J(oseph) E(phraim)

Hayman, Ronald 1932- .... **CLC 44**
See also CA 25-28R; CANR 18, 50, 88; CD 5, 6; DLB 155

Hayne, Paul Hamilton 1830-1886 . **NCLC 94**
See also DLB 3, 64, 79, 248; RGAL 4

Hays, Mary 1760-1843 .... **NCLC 114**
See also DLB 142, 158; RGEL 2

Haywood, Eliza (Fowler) 1693(?)-1756 .... **LC 1, 44, 177**
See also BRWS 12; DLB 39; RGEL 2

Hazlitt, William 1778-1830 ...... **NCLC 29, 82**
See also BRW 4; DLB 110, 158; RGEL 2; TEA

Hazzard, Shirley 1931- .... **CLC 18, 218**
See also CA 9-12R; CANR 4, 70, 127; CN 1, 2, 3, 4, 5, 6, 7; DLB 289; DLBY 1982; MTCW 1

Head, Bessie 1937-1986 . **BLC 1:2, 2:2; CLC 25, 67; SSC 52**
See also AFW; BW 2, 3; CA 29-32R; 119; CANR 25, 82; CDWLB 3; CN 1, 2, 3, 4; DA3; DAM MULT; DLB 117, 225; EWL 3; EXPS; FL 1:6; FW; MTCW 1, 2; MTFW 2005; NFS 31; RGSF 2; SSFS 5, 13, 30; WLIT 2; WWE 1

Headley, Elizabeth
See Harrison, Elizabeth (Allen) Cavanna

Headon, (Nicky) Topper 1956(?)- ..... **CLC 30**

Heaney, Seamus 1939- . **CLC 5, 7, 14, 25, 37, 74, 91, 171, 225; PC 18, 100; WLCS**
See also AAYA 61; BRWR 1; BRWS 2; CA 85-88; CANR 25, 48, 75, 91, 128, 184; CDBLB 1960 to Present; CP 1, 2, 3, 4, 5, 6, 7; DA3; DAB; DAM POET; DLB 40,

330; DLBY 1995; EWL 3; EXPP; MTCW 1, 2; MTFW 2005; PAB; PFS 2, 5, 8, 17, 30; RGEL 2; TEA; WLIT 4

Heaney, Seamus Justin
See Heaney, Seamus

Hearn, Lafcadio 1850-1904 .... **TCLC 9**
See also AAYA 79; CA 105; 166; DLB 12, 78, 189; HGG; MAL 5; RGAL 4

Hearn, Patricio Lafcadio Tessima Carlos
See Hearn, Lafcadio

Hearne, Samuel 1745-1792 .... **LC 95**
See also DLB 99

Hearne, Vicki 1946-2001 .... **CLC 56**
See also CA 139; 201

Hearon, Shelby 1931- .... **CLC 63**
See also AITN 2; AMWS 8; CA 25-28R; CAAS 11; CANR 18, 48, 103, 146; CSW

Heat-Moon, William Least 1939- ..... **CLC 29**
See also AAYA 9, 66; ANW; CA 115; 119; CANR 47, 89; CPW; INT CA-119

Hebbel, Friedrich 1813-1863 . **DC 21; NCLC 43**
See also CDWLB 2; DAM DRAM; DLB 129; EW 6; RGWL 2, 3

Hebert, Anne 1916-2000 . **CLC 4, 13, 29, 246**
See also CA 85-88; 187; CANR 69, 126; CCA 1; CWP; CWW 2; DA3; DAC; DAM MST, POET; DLB 68; EWL 3; GFL 1789 to the Present; MTCW 1, 2; MTFW 2005; PFS 20

Hecht, Anthony (Evan) 1923-2004 .... **CLC 8, 13, 19; PC 70**
See also AMWS 10; CA 9-12R; 232; CANR 6, 108; CP 1, 2, 3, 4, 5, 6, 7; DAM POET; DLB 5, 169; EWL 3; PFS 6; WP

Hecht, Ben 1894-1964 ..... **CLC 8; TCLC 101**
See also CA 85-88; DFS 9; DLB 7, 9, 25, 26, 28, 86; FANT; IDFW 3, 4; RGAL 4

Hedayat, Sadeq 1903-1951 . **SSC 131; TCLC 21**
See also CA 120; EWL 3; RGSF 2

Hegel, Georg Wilhelm Friedrich 1770-1831 .... **NCLC 46, 151**
See also DLB 90; TWA

Heidegger, Martin 1889-1976 .... **CLC 24**
See also CA 81-84; 65-68; CANR 34; DLB 296; MTCW 1, 2; MTFW 2005

Heidenstam, (Carl Gustaf) Verner von 1859-1940 .... **TCLC 5**
See also CA 104; DLB 330

Heidi Louise
See Erdrich, Louise

Heifner, Jack 1946- .... **CLC 11**
See also CA 105; CANR 47

Heijermans, Herman 1864-1924 .... **TCLC 24**
See also CA 123; EWL 3

Heilbrun, Carolyn G. 1926-2003 ..... **CLC 25, 173**
See also BPFB 1; CA 45-48; 220; CANR 1, 28, 58, 94; CMW; CPW; DLB 306; FW; MSW

Heilbrun, Carolyn Gold
See Heilbrun, Carolyn G.

Hein, Christoph 1944- .... **CLC 154**
See also CA 158; CANR 108; CDWLB 2; CWW 2; DLB 124

Heine, Heinrich 1797-1856 .... **NCLC 4, 54, 147; PC 25**
See also CDWLB 2; DLB 90; EW 5; RGWL 2, 3; TWA

Heinemann, Larry 1944- .... **CLC 50**
See also CA 110; CAAS 21; CANR 31, 81, 156; DLBD 9; INT CANR-31

Heinemann, Larry Curtiss
See Heinemann, Larry

Heiney, Donald (William) 1921-1993 . **CLC 9**
See also CA 1-4R; 142; CANR 3, 58; FANT

Heyen, William 1940- .... CLC 13, 18
See also CA 33-36R, 220; CAAE 220;
CAAS 9; CANR 98, 188; CP 3, 4, 5, 6, 7;
DLB 5; RGHL

Heyerdahl, Thor 1914-2002 .... CLC 26
See also CA 5-8R; 207; CANR 5, 22, 66,
73; LAIT 4; MTCW 1, 2; MTFW 2005;
SATA 2, 52

Heym, Georg (Theodor Franz Arthur)
1887-1912 .... TCLC 9
See also CA 106; 181

Heym, Stefan 1913-2001 .... CLC 41
See also CA 9-12R; 203; CANR 4; CWW
2; DLB 69; EWL 3

Heyse, Paul (Johann Ludwig von)
1830-1914 .... TCLC 8
See also CA 104; 209; DLB 129, 330

Heyward, (Edwin) DuBose
1885-1940 .... HR 1:2; TCLC 59
See also CA 108; 157; DLB 7, 9, 45, 249;
MAL 5; SATA 21

Heywood, John 1497(?)-1580(?) .... LC 65
See also DLB 136; RGEL 2

Heywood, Thomas 1573(?)-1641 . DC 29; LC
111
See also DAM DRAM; DLB 62; LMFS 1;
RGEL 2; TEA

Hiaasen, Carl 1953- .... CLC 238
See also CA 105; CANR 22, 45, 65, 113,
133, 168; CMW 4; CPW; CSW; DA3;
DLB 292; LNFS 2, 3; MTCW 2; MTFW
2005; SATA 208

Hibbert, Eleanor Alice Burford
1906-1993 .... CLC 7
See also BEST 90:4; BPFB 2; CA 17-20R;
140; CANR 9, 28, 59; CMW 4; CPW;
DAM POP; MTCW 2; MTFW 2005;
RHW; SATA 2; SATA-Obit 74

Hichens, Robert (Smythe)
1864-1950 .... TCLC 64
See also CA 162; DLB 153; HGG; RHW;
SUFW

Higgins, Aidan 1927- .... SSC 68
See also CA 9-12R; CANR 70, 115, 148;
CN 1, 2, 3, 4, 5, 6, 7; DLB 14

Higgins, George V(incent)
1939-1999 .... CLC 4, 7, 10, 18
See also BPFB 2; CA 77-80; 186; CAAS 5;
CANR 17, 51, 89, 96; CMW 4; CN 2, 3,
4, 5, 6; DLB 2; DLBY 1981, 1998; INT
CANR-17; MSW; MTCW 1

Higginson, Thomas Wentworth
1823-1911 .... TCLC 36
See also CA 162; DLB 1, 64, 243

Higgonet, Margaret CLC 65

Highet, Helen
See MacInnes, Helen (Clark)

Highsmith, Mary Patricia
See Highsmith, Patricia

Highsmith, Patricia 1921-1995 ...... CLC 2, 4,
14, 42, 102
See also AAYA 48; BRWS 5; CA 1-4R; 147;
CANR 1, 20, 48, 62, 108; CMW 4; CN 1,
2, 3, 4, 5; CPW; DA3; DAM NOV, POP;
DLB 306; GLL 1; MSW; MTCW 1, 2;
MTFW 2005; NFS 27; SSFS 25

Highwater, Jamake (Mamake)
1942(?)-2001 .... CLC 12
See also AAYA 7, 69; BPFB 2; BYA 4; CA
65-68; 199; CAAS 7; CANR 10, 34, 84;
CLR 17; CWRI 5; DLB 52; DLBY 1985;
JRDA; MAICYA 1, 2; SATA 32, 69;
SATA-Brief 30

Highway, Tomson 1951- ..... CLC 92; DC 33;
NNAL
See also CA 151; CANR 75; CCA 1; CD 5,
6; CN 7; DAC; DAM MULT; DFS 2;
DLB 334; MTCW 2

Hijuelos, Oscar 1951- .... CLC 65; HLC 1
See also AAYA 25; AMWS 8; BEST 90:1;
CA 123; CANR 50, 75, 125, 205; CPW;
DA3; DAM MULT, POP; DLB 145; HW
1, 2; LLW; MAL 5; MTCW 2; MTFW
2005; NFS 17; RGAL 4; WLIT 1

Hikmet, Nazim 1902-1963 .... CLC 40
See also CA 141; 93-96; EWL 3; WLIT 6

Hildegard von Bingen
1098-1179 .... CMLC 20, 118
See also DLB 148

Hildesheimer, Wolfgang 1916-1991 .. CLC 49
See also CA 101; 135; DLB 69, 124; EWL
3; RGHL

Hill, Aaron 1685-1750 .... LC 148
See also DLB 84; RGEL 2

Hill, Geoffrey 1932- .... CLC 5, 8, 18, 45, 251
See also BRWR 3; BRWS 5; CA 81-84;
CANR 21, 89; CDBLB 1960 to Present;
CP 1, 2, 3, 4, 5, 6, 7; DAM POET; DLB
40; EWL 3; MTCW 1; RGEL 2; RGHL

Hill, George Roy 1921-2002 .... CLC 26
See also CA 110; 122; 213

Hill, John
See Koontz, Dean

Hill, Susan 1942- .... CLC 4, 113
See also BRWS 14; CA 33-36R; CANR 29,
69, 129, 172, 201; CN 2, 3, 4, 5, 6, 7;
DAB; DAM MST, NOV; DLB 14, 139;
HGG; MTCW 1; RHW; SATA 183

Hill, Susan Elizabeth
See Hill, Susan

Hillard, Asa G. III CLC 70

Hillerman, Anthony Grove
See Hillerman, Tony

Hillerman, Tony 1925-2008 ...... CLC 62, 170
See also AAYA 40; BEST 89:1; BPFB 2;
CA 29-32R; 278; CANR 21, 42, 65, 97,
134; CMW 4; CPW; DA3; DAM POP;
DLB 206, 306; MAL 5; MSW; MTCW 2;
MTFW 2005; RGAL 4; SATA 6; SATA-
Obit 198; TCWW 2; YAW

Hillesum, Etty 1914-1943 .... TCLC 49
See also CA 137; RGHL

Hilliard, Noel (Harvey) 1929-1996 ... CLC 15
See also CA 9-12R; CANR 7, 69; CN 1, 2,
3, 4, 5, 6

Hillis, Rick 1956- .... CLC 66
See also CA 134

Hilton, James 1900-1954 .... TCLC 21
See also AAYA 76; CA 108; 169; DLB 34,
77; FANT; SATA 34

Hilton, Walter (?)-1396 .... CMLC 58
See also DLB 146; RGEL 2

Himes, Chester (Bomar)
1909-1984 .... BLC 1:2; CLC 2, 4, 7, 18,
58, 108; TCLC 139
See also AFAW 2; AMWS 16; BPFB 2; BW
2; CA 25-28R; 114; CANR 22, 89; CMW
4; CN 1, 2, 3; DAM MULT; DLB 2, 76,
143, 226; EWL 3; MAL 5; MSW; MTCW
1, 2; MTFW 2005; RGAL 4

Himmelfarb, Gertrude 1922- .... CLC 202
See also CA 49-52; CANR 28, 66, 102, 166

Hinde, Thomas
See Chitty, Thomas Willes

Hine, (William) Daryl 1936- .... CLC 15
See also CA 1-4R; CAAS 15; CANR 1, 20;
CP 1, 2, 3, 4, 5, 6, 7; DLB 60

Hinkson, Katharine Tynan
See Tynan, Katharine

Hinojosa, Rolando 1929- .... HLC 1
See also CA 131; CAAS 16; CANR 62;
DAM MULT; DLB 82; EWL 3; HW 1, 2;
LLW; MTCW 2; MTFW 2005; RGAL 4

Hinton, S. E. 1950- .... CLC 30, 111
See also AAYA 2, 33; BPFB 2; BYA 2, 3;
CA 81-84; CANR 32, 62, 92, 133;
CDALBS; CLR 3, 23; CPW; DA; DA3;

DAB; DAC; DAM MST, NOV; JRDA;
LAIT 5; MAICYA 1, 2; MTCW 1, 2;
MTFW 2005; NFS 5, 9, 15, 16; SATA 19,
58, 115, 160; WYA; YAW

Hinton, Susan Eloise
See Hinton, S. E.

Hippius, Zinaida
See Gippius, Zinaida

Hiraoka, Kimitake 1925-1970 ... CLC 2, 4, 6,
9, 27; DC 1; SSC 4; TCLC 161; WLC
4
See also AAYA 50; BPFB 2; CA 97-100;
29-32R; DA3; DAM DRAM; DLB 182;
EWL 3; GLL 1; MJW; MTCW 1, 2;
RGSF 2; RGWL 2, 3; SSFS 5, 12

Hirsch, E.D., Jr. 1928- .... CLC 79
See also CA 25-28R; CANR 27, 51, 146,
181; DLB 67; INT CANR-27; MTCW 1

Hirsch, Edward 1950- .... CLC 31, 50
See also CA 104; CANR 20, 42, 102, 167;
CP 6, 7; DLB 120; PFS 22

Hirsch, Eric Donald, Jr.
See Hirsch, E.D., Jr.

Hitchcock, Alfred (Joseph)
1899-1980 .... CLC 16
See also AAYA 22; CA 159; 97-100; SATA
27; SATA-Obit 24

Hitchens, Christopher 1949- .... CLC 157
See also CA 152; CANR 89, 155, 191

Hitchens, Christopher Eric
See Hitchens, Christopher

Hitler, Adolf 1889-1945 .... TCLC 53
See also CA 117; 147

Hoagland, Edward (Morley) 1932- .. CLC 28
See also ANW; CA 1-4R; CANR 2, 31, 57,
107; CN 1, 2, 3, 4, 5, 6, 7; DLB 6; SATA
51; TCWW 2

Hoban, Russell 1925- .... CLC 7, 25
See also BPFB 2; CA 5-8R; CANR 23, 37,
66, 114, 138; CLR 3, 69, 139; CN 4, 5,
7; CWRI 5; DAM NOV; DLB 52; FANT;
MAICYA 1, 2; MTCW 1, 2; MTFW 2005;
SATA 1, 40, 78, 136; SFW 4; SUFW 2;
TCLE 1:1

Hobbes, Thomas 1588-1679 .... LC 36, 142
See also DLB 151, 252, 281; RGEL 2

Hobbs, Perry
See Blackmur, R(ichard) P(almer)

Hobson, Laura Z(ametkin)
1900-1986 .... CLC 7, 25
See also BPFB 2; CA 17-20R; 118; CANR
55; CN 1, 2, 3, 4; DLB 28; SATA 52

Hoccleve, Thomas c. 1368-c. 1437 ...... LC 75
See also DLB 146; RGEL 2

Hoch, Edward D. 1930-2008 .... SSC 119
See also CA 29-32R; CANR 11, 27, 51, 97;
CMW 4; DLB 306; SFW 4

Hoch, Edward Dentinger
See Hoch, Edward D.

Hochhuth, Rolf 1931- .... CLC 4, 11, 18
See also CA 5-8R; CANR 33, 75, 136;
CWW 2; DAM DRAM; DLB 124; EWL
3; MTCW 1, 2; MTFW 2005; RGHL

Hochman, Sandra 1936- .... CLC 3, 8
See also CA 5-8R; CP 1, 2, 3, 4, 5; DLB 5

Hochwaelder, Fritz 1911-1986 .... CLC 36
See also CA 29-32R; 120; CANR 42; DAM
DRAM; EWL 3; MTCW 1; RGWL 2, 3

Hochwalder, Fritz
See Hochwaelder, Fritz

Hocking, Mary (Eunice) 1921- .... CLC 13
See also CA 101; CANR 18, 40

Hodge, Merle 1944- .... BLC 2:2
See also EWL 3

Hodgins, Jack 1938- .... CLC 23; SSC 132
See also CA 93-96; CN 4, 5, 6, 7; DLB 60

Hulme, Keri 1947- .... **CLC 39, 130**
See also CA 125; CANR 69; CN 4, 5, 6, 7;
CP 6, 7; CWP; DLB 326; EWL 3; FW;
INT CA-125; NFS 24
Hulme, T(homas) E(rnest)
1883-1917 .... **TCLC 21**
See also BRWS 6; CA 117; 203; DLB 19
Humboldt, Alexander von
1769-1859 .... **NCLC 170**
See also DLB 90
Humboldt, Wilhelm von
1767-1835 .... **NCLC 134**
See also DLB 90
Hume, David 1711-1776 .. **LC 7, 56, 156, 157**
See also BRWS 3; DLB 104, 252, 336;
LMFS 1; TEA
Humphrey, William 1924-1997 .... **CLC 45**
See also AMWS 9; CA 77-80; 160; CANR
68; CN 1, 2, 3, 4, 5, 6; CSW; DLB 6, 212,
234, 278; TCWW 1, 2
Humphreys, Emyr Owen 1919- .... **CLC 47**
See also CA 5-8R; CANR 3, 24; CN 1, 2,
3, 4, 5, 6, 7; DLB 15
Humphreys, Josephine 1945- ..... **CLC 34, 57**
See also CA 121; 127; CANR 97; CSW;
DLB 292; INT CA-127
Huneker, James Gibbons
1860-1921 .... **TCLC 65**
See also CA 193; DLB 71; RGAL 4
Hungerford, Hesba Fay
See Brinsmead, H(esba) F(ay)
Hungerford, Pixie
See Brinsmead, H(esba) F(ay)
Hunt, E. Howard 1918-2007 .... **CLC 3**
See also AITN 1; CA 45-48; 256; CANR 2,
47, 103, 160; CMW 4
Hunt, Everette Howard, Jr.
See Hunt, E. Howard
Hunt, Francesca
See Holland, Isabelle (Christian)
Hunt, Howard
See Hunt, E. Howard
Hunt, Kyle
See Creasey, John
Hunt, (James Henry) Leigh
1784-1859 .... **NCLC 1, 70; PC 73**
See also DAM POET; DLB 96, 110, 144;
RGEL 2; TEA
Hunt, Marsha 1946- .... **CLC 70**
See also BW 2, 3; CA 143; CANR 79
Hunt, Violet 1866(?)-1942 .... **TCLC 53**
See also CA 184; DLB 162, 197
Hunter, E. Waldo
See Sturgeon, Theodore (Hamilton)
Hunter, Evan 1926-2005 .... **CLC 11, 31**
See also AAYA 39; BPFB 2; CA 5-8R; 241;
CANR 5, 38, 62, 97, 149; CMW 4; CN 1,
2, 3, 4, 5, 6, 7; CPW; DAM POP; DLB
306; DLBY 1982; INT CANR-5; MSW;
MTCW 1; SATA 25; SATA-Obit 167;
SFW 4
Hunter, Kristin
See Lattany, Kristin Hunter
Hunter, Mary
See Austin, Mary Hunter
Hunter, Mollie 1922- .... **CLC 21**
See also AAYA 13, 71; BYA 6; CANR 37,
78; CLR 25; DLB 161; JRDA; MAICYA
1, 2; SAAS 7; SATA 2, 54, 106, 139;
SATA-Essay 139; WYA; YAW
Hunter, Robert (?)-1734 .... **LC 7**
Hurston, Zora Neale 1891-1960 ..... **BLC 1:2;
CLC 7, 30, 61; DC 12; HR 1:2; SSC 4,
80; TCLC 121, 131; WLCS**
See also AAYA 15, 71; AFAW 1, 2; AMWS
6; BW 1, 3; BYA 12; CA 85-88; CANR
61; CDALBS; DA; DA3; DAC; DAM
MST, MULT, NOV; DFS 6; DLB 51, 86;
EWL 3; EXPN; EXPS; FL 1:6; FW; LAIT

3; LATS 1:1; LMFS 2; MAL 5; MBL;
MTCW 1, 2; MTFW 2005; NFS 3; RGAL
4; RGSF 2; SSFS 1, 6, 11, 19, 21; TUS;
YAW
Husserl, E. G.
See Husserl, Edmund (Gustav Albrecht)
Husserl, Edmund (Gustav Albrecht)
1859-1938 .... **TCLC 100**
See also CA 116; 133; DLB 296
Huston, John (Marcellus)
1906-1987 .... **CLC 20**
See also CA 73-76; 123; CANR 34; DLB
26
Hustvedt, Siri 1955- .... **CLC 76**
See also CA 137; CANR 149, 191
Hutcheson, Francis 1694-1746 .... **LC 157**
See also DLB 252
Hutchinson, Lucy 1620-1675 .... **LC 149**
Hutten, Ulrich von 1488-1523 .... **LC 16**
See also DLB 179
Huxley, Aldous 1894-1963 . **CLC 1, 3, 4, 5, 8,
11, 18, 35, 79; SSC 39; WLC 3**
See also AAYA 11; BPFB 2; BRW 7; CA
85-88; CANR 44, 99; CDBLB 1914-1945;
CLR 151; DA; DA3; DAB; DAC; DAM
MST, NOV; DLB 36, 100, 162, 195, 255;
EWL 3; EXPN; LAIT 5; LMFS 2; MTCW
1, 2; MTFW 2005; NFS 6; RGEL 2;
SATA 63; SCFW 1, 2; SFW 4; TEA; YAW
Huxley, Aldous Leonard
See Huxley, Aldous
Huxley, T(homas) H(enry)
1825-1895 .... **NCLC 67**
See also DLB 57; TEA
Huygens, Constantijn 1596-1687 .... **LC 114**
See also RGWL 2, 3
Huysmans, Joris-Karl 1848-1907 ... **TCLC 7,
69, 212**
See also CA 104; 165; DLB 123; EW 7;
GFL 1789 to the Present; LMFS 2; RGWL
2, 3
Hwang, David Henry 1957- .... **CLC 55, 196;
DC 4, 23**
See also CA 127; 132; CAD; CANR 76,
124; CD 5, 6; DA3; DAM DRAM; DFS
11, 18; DLB 212, 228, 312; INT CA-132;
MAL 5; MTCW 2; MTFW 2005; RGAL
4
Hyatt, Daniel
See James, Daniel (Lewis)
Hyde, Anthony 1946- .... **CLC 42**
See also CA 136; CCA 1
Hyde, Margaret O. 1917- .... **CLC 21**
See also CA 1-4R; CANR 1, 36, 137, 181;
CLR 23; JRDA; MAICYA 1, 2; SAAS 8;
SATA 1, 42, 76, 139
Hyde, Margaret Oldroyd
See Hyde, Margaret O.
Hynes, James 1956(?)- .... **CLC 65**
See also CA 164; CANR 105
Hypatia c. 370-415 .... **CMLC 35**
Ian, Janis 1951- .... **CLC 21**
See also CA 105; 187
Ibanez, Vicente Blasco
See Blasco Ibanez, Vicente
Ibarbourou, Juana de
1895(?)-1979 .... **HLCS 2**
See also DLB 290; HW 1; LAW
Ibarguengoitia, Jorge 1928-1983 ..... **CLC 37;
TCLC 148**
See also CA 124; 113; EWL 3; HW 1
Ibn Arabi 1165-1240 .... **CMLC 105**
Ibn Battuta, Abu Abdalla
1304-1368(?) .... **CMLC 57**
See also WLIT 2

Ibn Hazm 994-1064 .... **CMLC 64**
Ibn Zaydun 1003-1070 .... **CMLC 89**
Ibsen, Henrik 1828-1906 .... **DC 2, 30; TCLC
2, 8, 16, 37, 52; WLC 3**
See also AAYA 46; CA 104; 141; DA; DA3;
DAB; DAC; DAM DRAM, MST; DFS 1,
6, 8, 10, 11, 15, 16, 25; DLB 354; EW 7;
LAIT 2; LATS 1:1; MTFW 2005; RGWL
2, 3
Ibsen, Henrik Johan
See Ibsen, Henrik
Ibuse, Masuji 1898-1993 .... **CLC 22**
See also CA 127; 141; CWW 2; DLB 180;
EWL 3; MJW; RGWL 3
Ibuse Masuji
See Ibuse, Masuji
Ichikawa, Kon 1915-2008 .... **CLC 20**
See also CA 121; 269
Ichiyo, Higuchi 1872-1896 .... **NCLC 49**
See also MJW
Idle, Eric 1943- .... **CLC 21**
See also CA 116; CANR 35, 91, 148; DLB
352
Idris, Yusuf 1927-1991 ... **SSC 74; TCLC 232**
See also AFW; DLB 346; EWL 3; RGSF 2,
3; RGWL 3; WLIT 2
Ignatieff, Michael 1947- .... **CLC 236**
See also CA 144; CANR 88, 156; CN 6, 7;
DLB 267
Ignatieff, Michael Grant
See Ignatieff, Michael
Ignatow, David 1914-1997 .... **CLC 4, 7, 14,
40; PC 34**
See also CA 9-12R; 162; CAAS 3; CANR
31, 57, 96; CP 1, 2, 3, 4, 5, 6; DLB 5;
EWL 3; MAL 5
Ignotus
See Strachey, (Giles) Lytton
Ihimaera, Witi (Tame) 1944- .... **CLC 46**
See also CA 77-80; CANR 130; CN 2, 3, 4,
5, 6, 7; RGSF 2; SATA 148
Il'f, Il'ia
See Fainzilberg, Ilya Arnoldovich
Ilf, Ilya
See Fainzilberg, Ilya Arnoldovich
Illyes, Gyula 1902-1983 .... **PC 16**
See also CA 114; 109; CDWLB 4; DLB
215; EWL 3; RGWL 2, 3
Imalayen, Fatima-Zohra
See Djebar, Assia
Immermann, Karl (Lebrecht)
1796-1840 .... **NCLC 4, 49**
See also DLB 133
Ince, Thomas H. 1882-1924 .... **TCLC 89**
See also IDFW 3, 4
Inchbald, Elizabeth 1753-1821 ...... **NCLC 62**
See also BRWS 15; DLB 39, 89; RGEL 2
Inclan, Ramon del Valle
See Valle-Inclan, Ramon del
Incogniteau, Jean-Louis
See Kerouac, Jack
Infante, Guillermo Cabrera
See Cabrera Infante, G.
Ingalls, Rachel 1940- .... **CLC 42**
See also CA 123; 127; CANR 154
Ingalls, Rachel Holmes
See Ingalls, Rachel
Ingamells, Reginald Charles
See Ingamells, Rex
Ingamells, Rex 1913-1955 .... **TCLC 35**
See also CA 167; DLB 260
Inge, William (Motter) 1913-1973 ..... **CLC 1,
8, 19; DC 37**
See also CA 9-12R; CAD; CDALB 1941-
1968; DA3; DAM DRAM; DFS 1, 3, 5,
8; DLB 7, 249; EWL 3; MAL 5; MTCW
1, 2; MTFW 2005; RGAL 4; TUS

CUMULATIVE AUTHOR INDEX

Ingelow, Jean 1820-1897 .... **NCLC 39, 107**
See also DLB 35, 163; FANT; SATA 33
Ingram, Willis J.
See Harris, Mark
Innaurato, Albert (F.) 1948(?)- ... **CLC 21, 60**
See also CA 115; 122; CAD; CANR 78;
CD 5, 6; INT CA-122
Innes, Michael
See Stewart, J(ohn) I(nnes) M(ackintosh)
Innis, Harold Adams 1894-1952 .... **TCLC 77**
See also CA 181; DLB 88
Insluis, Alanus de
See Alain de Lille
Iola
See Wells-Barnett, Ida B(ell)
Ionesco, Eugene 1909-1994 ... **CLC 1, 4, 6, 9, 11, 15, 41, 86; DC 12; TCLC 232; WLC 3**
See also CA 9-12R; 144; CANR 55, 132;
CWW 2; DA; DA3; DAB; DAC; DAM
DRAM, MST; DFS 4, 9, 25; DLB 321;
EW 13; EWL 3; GFL 1789 to the Present;
LMFS 2; MTCW 1, 2; MTFW 2005;
RGWL 2, 3; SATA 7; SATA-Obit 79;
TWA
Iqbal, Muhammad 1877-1938 .... **TCLC 28**
See also CA 215; EWL 3
Ireland, Patrick
See O'Doherty, Brian
Irenaeus St. 130- .... **CMLC 42**
Irigaray, Luce 1930- .... **CLC 164**
See also CA 154; CANR 121; FW
Irish, William
See Hopley-Woolrich, Cornell George
Irland, David
See Green, Julien
Iron, Ralph
See Schreiner, Olive
Irving, John 1942- . **CLC 13, 23, 38, 112, 175**
See also AAYA 8, 62; AMWS 6; BEST
89:3; BPFB 2; CA 25-28R; CANR 28, 73,
112, 133; CN 3, 4, 5, 6, 7; CPW; DA3;
DAM NOV, POP; DLB 6, 278; DLBY
1982; EWL 3; MAL 5; MTCW 1, 2;
MTFW 2005; NFS 12, 14; RGAL 4; TUS
Irving, John Winslow
See Irving, John
Irving, Washington 1783-1859 . **NCLC 2, 19, 95; SSC 2, 37, 104; WLC 3**
See also AAYA 56; AMW; CDALB 1640-
1865; CLR 97; DA; DA3; DAB; DAC;
DAM MST; DLB 3, 11, 30, 59, 73, 74,
183, 186, 250, 254; EXPS; GL 2; LAIT
1; RGAL 4; RGSF 2; SSFS 1, 8, 16;
SUFW 1; TUS; WCH; YABC 2
Irwin, P. K.
See Page, P.K.
Isaacs, Jorge Ricardo 1837-1895 ... **NCLC 70**
See also LAW
Isaacs, Susan 1943- .... **CLC 32**
See also BEST 89:1; BPFB 2; CA 89-92;
CANR 20, 41, 65, 112, 134, 165; CPW;
DA3; DAM POP; INT CANR-20; MTCW
1, 2; MTFW 2005
Isherwood, Christopher 1904-1986 ... **CLC 1, 9, 11, 14, 44; SSC 56; TCLC 227**
See also AMWS 14; BRW 7; CA 13-16R;
117; CANR 35, 97, 133; CN 1, 2, 3; DA3;
DAM DRAM, NOV; DLB 15, 195; DLBY
1986; EWL 3; IDTP; MTCW 1, 2; MTFW
2005; RGAL 4; RGEL 2; TUS; WLIT 4
Isherwood, Christopher William Bradshaw
See Isherwood, Christopher
Ishiguro, Kazuo 1954- . **CLC 27, 56, 59, 110, 219**
See also AAYA 58; BEST 90:2; BPFB 2;
BRWR 3; BRWS 4; CA 120; CANR 49,
95, 133; CN 5, 6, 7; DA3; DAM NOV;
DLB 194, 326; EWL 3; MTCW 1, 2;
MTFW 2005; NFS 13; WLIT 4; WWE 1

Ishikawa, Hakuhin
See Ishikawa, Takuboku
Ishikawa, Takuboku 1886(?)-1912 ..... **PC 10; TCLC 15**
See Ishikawa Takuboku
See also CA 113; 153; DAM POET
Isidore of Seville c. 560-636 .... **CMLC 101**
Iskander, Fazil (Abdulovich) 1929- .. **CLC 47**
See also CA 102; DLB 302; EWL 3
Iskander, Fazil' Abdulevich
See Iskander, Fazil (Abdulovich)
Isler, Alan (David) 1934- .... **CLC 91**
See also CA 156; CANR 105
Ivan IV 1530-1584 .... **LC 17**
Ivanov, V.I.
See Ivanov, Vyacheslav
Ivanov, Vyacheslav 1866-1949 .... **TCLC 33**
See also CA 122; EWL 3
Ivanov, Vyacheslav Ivanovich
See Ivanov, Vyacheslav
Ivask, Ivar Vidrik 1927-1992 .... **CLC 14**
See also CA 37-40R; 139; CANR 24
Ives, Morgan
See Bradley, Marion Zimmer
Izumi Shikibu c. 973-c. 1034 .... **CMLC 33**
J. R. S.
See Gogarty, Oliver St. John
Jabran, Kahlil
See Gibran, Kahlil
Jabran, Khalil
See Gibran, Kahlil
Jaccottet, Philippe 1925- .... **PC 98**
See also CA 116; 129; CWW 2; GFL 1789
to the Present
Jackson, Daniel
See Wingrove, David
Jackson, Helen Hunt 1830-1885 .... **NCLC 90**
See also DLB 42, 47, 186, 189; RGAL 4
Jackson, Jesse 1908-1983 .... **CLC 12**
See also BW 1; CA 25-28R; 109; CANR
27; CLR 28; CWRI 5; MAICYA 1, 2;
SATA 2, 29; SATA-Obit 48
Jackson, Laura 1901-1991 . **CLC 3, 7; PC 44**
See also CA 65-68; 135; CANR 28, 89; CP
1, 2, 3, 4, 5; DLB 48; RGAL 4
Jackson, Laura Riding
See Jackson, Laura
Jackson, Sam
See Trumbo, Dalton
Jackson, Sara
See Wingrove, David
Jackson, Shirley 1919-1965 . **CLC 11, 60, 87; SSC 9, 39; TCLC 187; WLC 3**
See also AAYA 9; AMWS 9; BPFB 2; CA
1-4R; 25-28R; CANR 4, 52; CDALB
1941-1968; DA; DA3; DAC; DAM MST;
DLB 6, 234; EXPS; HGG; LAIT 4; MAL
5; MTCW 2; MTFW 2005; RGAL 4;
RGSF 2; SATA 2; SSFS 1, 27, 30; SUFW
1, 2
Jacob, (Cyprien-)Max 1876-1944 .... **TCLC 6**
See also CA 104; 193; DLB 258; EWL 3;
GFL 1789 to the Present; GLL 2; RGWL
2, 3
Jacobs, Harriet A. 1813(?)-1897 ... **NCLC 67, 162**
See also AFAW 1, 2; DLB 239; FL 1:3; FW;
LAIT 2; RGAL 4
Jacobs, Harriet Ann
See Jacobs, Harriet A.
Jacobs, Jim 1942- .... **CLC 12**
See also CA 97-100; INT CA-97-100
Jacobs, W(illiam) W(ymark)
1863-1943 .... **SSC 73; TCLC 22**
See also CA 121; 167; DLB 135; EXPS;
HGG; RGEL 2; RGSF 2; SSFS 2; SUFW
1

Jacobsen, Jens Peter 1847-1885 .... **NCLC 34**
Jacobsen, Josephine (Winder)
1908-2003 .... **CLC 48, 102; PC 62**
See also CA 33-36R; 218; CAAS 18; CANR
23, 48; CCA 1; CP 2, 3, 4, 5, 6, 7; DLB
244; PFS 23; TCLE 1:1
Jacobson, Dan 1929- ...... **CLC 4, 14; SSC 91**
See also AFW; CA 1-4R; CANR 2, 25, 66,
170; CN 1, 2, 3, 4, 5, 6, 7; DLB 14, 207,
225, 319; EWL 3; MTCW 1; RGSF 2
Jacopone da Todi 1236-1306 .... **CMLC 95**
Jacqueline
See Carpentier, Alejo
Jacques de Vitry c. 1160-1240 ...... **CMLC 63**
See also DLB 208
Jagger, Michael Philip
See Jagger, Mick
Jagger, Mick 1943- .... **CLC 17**
See also CA 239
Jahiz, al- c. 780-c. 869 .... **CMLC 25**
See also DLB 311
Jakes, John 1932- .... **CLC 29**
See also AAYA 32; BEST 89:4; BPFB 2;
CA 57-60, 214; CAAE 214; CANR 10,
43, 66, 111, 142, 171; CPW; CSW; DA3;
DAM NOV, POP; DLB 278; DLBY 1983;
FANT; INT CANR-10; MTCW 1, 2;
MTFW 2005; RHW; SATA 62; SFW 4;
TCWW 1, 2
Jakes, John William
See Jakes, John
James I 1394-1437 .... **LC 20**
See also RGEL 2
James, Alice 1848-1892 .... **NCLC 206**
See also DLB 221
James, Andrew
See Kirkup, James
James, C(yril) L(ionel) R(obert)
1901-1989 .... **BLCS; CLC 33**
See also BW 2; CA 117; 125; 128; CANR
62; CN 1, 2, 3, 4; DLB 125; MTCW 1
James, Daniel (Lewis) 1911-1988 ..... **CLC 33**
See also CA 174; 125; DLB 122
James, Dynely
See Mayne, William (James Carter)
James, Henry Sr. 1811-1882 .... **NCLC 53**
James, Henry 1843-1916 .... **SSC 8, 32, 47, 108; TCLC 2, 11, 24, 40, 47, 64, 171; WLC 3**
See also AMW; AMWC 1; AMWR 1; BPFB
2; BRW 6; CA 104; 132; CDALB 1865-
1917; DA; DA3; DAB; DAC; DAM MST,
NOV; DLB 12, 71, 74, 189; DLBD 13;
EWL 3; EXPS; GL 2; HGG; LAIT 2;
MAL 5; MTCW 1, 2; MTFW 2005; NFS
12, 16, 19, 32; RGAL 4; RGEL 2; RGSF
2; SSFS 9; SUFW 1; TUS
James, M. R.
See James, Montague
James, Mary
See Meaker, Marijane
James, Montague 1862-1936 ...... **SSC 16, 93; TCLC 6**
See also CA 104; 203; DLB 156, 201;
HGG; RGEL 2; RGSF 2; SUFW 1
James, Montague Rhodes
See James, Montague
James, P. D. 1920- .... **CLC 18, 46, 122, 226**
See also BEST 90:2; BPFB 2; BRWS 4;
CA 21-24R; CANR 17, 43, 65, 112, 201;
CDBLB 1960 to Present; CMW 4; CN 4,
5, 6, 7; CPW; DA3; DAM POP; DLB 87,
276; DLBD 17; MSW; MTCW 1, 2;
MTFW 2005; TEA
James, Philip
See Moorcock, Michael
James, Samuel
See Stephens, James

Author Index

Author Index

Khodasevich, Vladislav Felitsianovich
See Khodasevich, Vladislav
Kidd, Sue Monk 1948- .... **CLC 267**
See also AAYA 72; CA 202; LNFS 1;
MTFW 2005; NFS 27
Kielland, Alexander Lange
1849-1906 .... **TCLC 5**
See also CA 104; DLB 354
Kiely, Benedict 1919-2007 . **CLC 23, 43; SSC
58**
See also CA 1-4R; 257; CANR 2, 84; CN
1, 2, 3, 4, 5, 6, 7; DLB 15, 319; TCLE
1:1
Kienzle, William X. 1928-2001 .... **CLC 25**
See also CA 93-96; 203; CAAS 1; CANR
9, 31, 59, 111; CMW 4; DA3; DAM POP;
INT CANR-31; MSW; MTCW 1, 2;
MTFW 2005
Kierkegaard, Soren 1813-1855 ..... **NCLC 34,
78, 125**
See also DLB 300; EW 6; LMFS 2; RGWL
3; TWA
Kieslowski, Krzysztof 1941-1996 .... **CLC 120**
See also CA 147; 151
Killens, John Oliver 1916-1987 ...... **BLC 2:2;
CLC 10**
See also BW 2; CA 77-80; 123; CAAS 2;
CANR 26; CN 1, 2, 3, 4; DLB 33; EWL
3
Killigrew, Anne 1660-1685 .... **LC 4, 73**
See also DLB 131
Killigrew, Thomas 1612-1683 .... **LC 57**
See also DLB 58; RGEL 2
Kim
See Simenon, Georges
Kincaid, Jamaica 1949- . **BLC 1:2, 2:2; CLC
43, 68, 137, 234; SSC 72**
See also AAYA 13, 56; AFAW 2; AMWS 7;
BRWS 7; BW 2, 3; CA 125; CANR 47,
59, 95, 133; CDALBS; CDWLB 3; CLR
63; CN 4, 5, 6, 7; DA3; DAM MULT,
NOV; DLB 157, 227; DNFS 1; EWL 3;
EXPS; FW; LATS 1:2; LMFS 2; MAL 5;
MTCW 2; MTFW 2005; NCFS 1; NFS 3;
SSFS 5, 7; TUS; WWE 1; YAW
King, Francis (Henry) 1923- .... **CLC 8, 53,
145**
See also CA 1-4R; CANR 1, 33, 86; CN 1,
2, 3, 4, 5, 6, 7; DAM NOV; DLB 15, 139;
MTCW 1
King, Kennedy
See Brown, George Douglas
King, Martin Luther, Jr.
1929-1968 ... **BLC 1:2; CLC 83; WLCS**
See also BW 2, 3; CA 25-28; CANR 27,
44; CAP 2; DA; DA3; DAB; DAC; DAM
MST, MULT; LAIT 5; LATS 1:2; MTCW
1, 2; MTFW 2005; SATA 14
King, Stephen 1947- .... **CLC 12, 26, 37, 61,
113, 228, 244; SSC 17, 55**
See also AAYA 1, 17, 82; AMWS 5; BEST
90:1; BPFB 2; CA 61-64; CANR 1, 30,
52, 76, 119, 134, 168; CLR 124; CN 7;
CPW; DA3; DAM NOV, POP; DLB 143,
350; DLBY 1980; HGG; JRDA; LAIT 5;
LNFS 1; MTCW 1, 2; MTFW 2005;
RGAL 4; SATA 9, 55, 161; SSFS 30;
SUFW 1, 2; WYAS 1; YAW
King, Stephen Edwin
See King, Stephen
King, Steve
See King, Stephen
King, Thomas 1943- .... **CLC 89, 171, 276;
NNAL**
See also CA 144; CANR 95, 175; CCA 1;
CN 6, 7; DAC; DAM MULT; DLB 175,
334; SATA 96
King, Thomas Hunt
See King, Thomas

Kingman, Lee
See Natti, Lee
Kingsley, Charles 1819-1875 .... **NCLC 35**
See also BRWS 16; CLR 77; DLB 21, 32,
163, 178, 190; FANT; MAICYA 2; MAI-
CYAS 1; RGEL 2; WCH; YABC 2
Kingsley, Henry 1830-1876 .... **NCLC 107**
See also DLB 21, 230; RGEL 2
Kingsley, Sidney 1906-1995 .... **CLC 44**
See also CA 85-88; 147; CAD; DFS 14, 19;
DLB 7; MAL 5; RGAL 4
Kingsolver, Barbara 1955- .... **CLC 55, 81,
130, 216, 269**
See also AAYA 15; AMWS 7; CA 129; 134;
CANR 60, 96, 133, 179; CDALBS; CN
7; CPW; CSW; DA3; DAM POP; DLB
206; INT CA-134; LAIT 5; MTCW 2;
MTFW 2005; NFS 5, 10, 12, 24; RGAL
4; TCLE 1:1
Kingston, Maxine Hong 1940- .... **AAL; CLC
12, 19, 58, 121, 271; SSC 136; WLCS**
See also AAYA 8, 55; AMWS 5; BPFB 2;
CA 69-72; CANR 13, 38, 74, 87, 128;
CDALBS; CN 6, 7; DA3; DAM MULT,
NOV; DLB 173, 212, 312; DLBY 1980;
EWL 3; FL 1:6; FW; INT CANR-13;
LAIT 5; MAL 5; MBL; MTCW 1, 2;
MTFW 2005; NFS 6; RGAL 4; SATA 53;
SSFS 3; TCWW 2
Kingston, Maxine Ting Ting Hong
See Kingston, Maxine Hong
Kinnell, Galway 1927- ..... **CLC 1, 2, 3, 5, 13,
29, 129; PC 26**
See also AMWS 3; CA 9-12R; CANR 10,
34, 66, 116, 138, 175; CP 1, 2, 3, 4, 5, 6,
7; DLB 5, 342; DLBY 1987; EWL 3; INT
CANR-34; MAL 5; MTCW 1, 2; MTFW
2005; PAB; PFS 9, 26, 35; RGAL 4;
TCLE 1:1; WP
Kinsella, Thomas 1928- .... **CLC 4, 19, 138,
274; PC 69**
See also BRWS 5; CA 17-20R; CANR 15,
122; CP 1, 2, 3, 4, 5, 6, 7; DLB 27; EWL
3; MTCW 1, 2; MTFW 2005; RGEL 2;
TEA
Kinsella, W.P. 1935- .... **CLC 27, 43, 166**
See also·AAYA 7, 60; BPFB 2; CA 97-100,
222; CAAE 222; CAAS 7; CANR 21, 35,
66, 75, 129; CN 4, 5, 6, 7; CPW; DAC;
DAM NOV, POP; FANT; INT CANR-21;
LAIT 5; MTCW 1, 2; MTFW 2005; NFS
15; RGSF 2; SSFS 30
Kinsey, Alfred C(harles)
1894-1956 .... **TCLC 91**
See also CA 115; 170; MTCW 2
Kipling, Joseph Rudyard
See Kipling, Rudyard
Kipling, Rudyard 1865-1936 . **PC 3, 91; SSC
5, 54, 110; TCLC 8, 17, 167; WLC 3**
See also AAYA 32; BRW 6; BRWC 1, 2;
BRWR 3; BYA 4; CA 105; 120; CANR
33; CDBLB 1890-1914; CLR 39, 65;
CWRI 5; DA; DA3; DAB; DAC; DAM
MST, POET; DLB 19, 34, 141, 156, 330;
EWL 3; EXPS; FANT; LAIT 3; LMFS 1;
MAICYA 1, 2; MTCW 1, 2; MTFW 2005;
NFS 21; PFS 22; RGEL 2; RGSF 2; SATA
100; SFW 4; SSFS 8, 21, 22; SUFW 1;
TEA; WCH; WLIT 4; YABC 2
Kircher, Athanasius 1602-1680 .... **LC 121**
See also DLB 164
Kirk, Russell (Amos) 1918-1994 .. **TCLC 119**
See also AITN 1; CA 1-4R; 145; CAAS 9;
CANR 1, 20, 60; HGG; INT CANR-20;
MTCW 1, 2
Kirkham, Dinah
See Card, Orson Scott
Kirkland, Caroline M. 1801-1864 . **NCLC 85**
See also DLB 3, 73, 74, 250, 254; DLBD
13

Kirkup, James 1918-2009 .... **CLC 1**
See also CA 1-4R; CAAS 4; CANR 2; CP
1, 2, 3, 4, 5, 6, 7; DLB 27; SATA 12
Kirkwood, James 1930(?)-1989 .... **CLC 9**
See also AITN 2; CA 1-4R; 128; CANR 6,
40; GLL 2
Kirsch, Sarah 1935- .... **CLC 176**
See also CA 178; CWW 2; DLB 75; EWL
3
Kirshner, Sidney
See Kingsley, Sidney
Kis, Danilo 1935-1989 .... **CLC 57**
See also CA 109; 118; 129; CANR 61; CD-
WLB 4; DLB 181; EWL 3; MTCW 1;
RGSF 2; RGWL 2, 3
Kissinger, Henry A(lfred) 1923- ..... **CLC 137**
See also CA 1-4R; CANR 2, 33, 66, 109;
MTCW 1
Kittel, Frederick August
See Wilson, August
Kivi, Aleksis 1834-1872 .... **NCLC 30**
Kizer, Carolyn 1925- ..... **CLC 15, 39, 80; PC
66**
See also CA 65-68; CAAS 5; CANR 24,
70, 134; CP 1, 2, 3, 4, 5, 6, 7; CWP; DAM
POET; DLB 5, 169; EWL 3; MAL 5;
MTCW 2; MTFW 2005; PFS 18; TCLE
1:1
Klabund 1890-1928 .... **TCLC 44**
See also CA 162; DLB 66
Klappert, Peter 1942- .... **CLC 57**
See also CA 33-36R; CSW; DLB 5
Klausner, Amos
See Oz, Amos
Klein, A. M. 1909-1972 .... **CLC 19**
See also CA 101; 37-40R; CP 1; DAB;
DAC; DAM MST; DLB 68; EWL 3;
RGEL 2; RGHL
Klein, Abraham Moses
See Klein, A. M.
Klein, Joe
See Klein, Joseph
Klein, Joseph 1946- .... **CLC 154**
See also CA 85-88; CANR 55, 164
Klein, Norma 1938-1989 .... **CLC 30**
See also AAYA 2, 35; BPFB 2; BYA 6, 7,
8; CA 41-44R; 128; CANR 15, 37; CLR
2, 19; INT CANR-15; JRDA; MAICYA
1, 2; SAAS 1; SATA 7, 57; WYA; YAW
Klein, T.E.D. 1947- .... **CLC 34**
See also CA 119; CANR 44, 75, 167; HGG
Klein, Theodore Eibon Donald
See Klein, T.E.D.
Kleist, Heinrich von 1777-1811 .... **DC 29;
NCLC 2, 37, 222; SSC 22**
See also CDWLB 2; DAM DRAM; DLB
90; EW 5; RGSF 2; RGWL 2, 3
Klima, Ivan 1931- .... **CLC 56, 172**
See also CA 25-28R; CANR 17, 50, 91;
CDWLB 4; CWW 2; DAM NOV; DLB
232; EWL 3; RGWL 3
Klimentev, Andrei Platonovich
See Klimentov, Andrei Platonovich
Klimentov, Andrei Platonovich
1899-1951 .... **SSC 42; TCLC 14**
See also CA 108; 232; DLB 272; EWL 3
Klinger, Friedrich Maximilian von
1752-1831 .... **NCLC 1**
See also DLB 94
Klingsor the Magician
See Hartmann, Sadakichi
Klopstock, Friedrich Gottlieb
1724-1803 .... **NCLC 11, 225**
See also DLB 97; EW 4; RGWL 2, 3
Kluge, Alexander 1932- .... **SSC 61**
See also CA 81-84; CANR 163; DLB 75
Knapp, Caroline 1959-2002 .... **CLC 99**
See also CA 154; 207

Landon, Letitia Elizabeth
1802-1838 .... NCLC 15
See also DLB 96
Landor, Walter Savage
1775-1864 .... NCLC 14
See also BRW 4; DLB 93, 107; RGEL 2
Landwirth, Heinz
See Lind, Jakov
Lane, Patrick 1939- .... CLC 25
See also CA 97-100; CANR 54; CP 3, 4, 5,
6, 7; DAM POET; DLB 53; INT CA-97-
100
Lane, Rose Wilder 1887-1968 ...... TCLC 177
See also CA 102; CANR 63; SATA 29;
SATA-Brief 28; TCWW 2
Lang, Andrew 1844-1912 .... TCLC 16
See also CA 114; 137; CANR 85; CLR 101;
DLB 98, 141, 184; FANT; MAICYA 1, 2;
RGEL 2; SATA 16; WCH
Lang, Fritz 1890-1976 .... CLC 20, 103
See also AAYA 65; CA 77-80; 69-72;
CANR 30
Lange, John
See Crichton, Michael
Langer, Elinor 1939- .... CLC 34
See also CA 121
Langland, William 1332(?)-1400(?) .... LC 19,
120
See also BRW 1; DA; DAB; DAC; DAM
MST, POET; DLB 146; RGEL 2; TEA;
WLIT 3
Langstaff, Launcelot
See Irving, Washington
Lanier, Sidney 1842-1881 . NCLC 6, 118; PC
50
See also AMWS 1; DAM POET; DLB 64;
DLBD 13; EXPP; MAICYA 1; PFS 14;
RGAL 4; SATA 18
Lanyer, Aemilia 1569-1645 .... LC 10, 30, 83;
PC 60
See also DLB 121
Lao Tzu c. 6th cent. B.C.-3rd cent.
B.C. .... CMLC 7
Lao-Tzu
See Lao Tzu
Lapine, James (Elliot) 1949- .... CLC 39
See also CA 123; 130; CANR 54, 128; DFS
25; DLB 341; INT CA-130
La Ramee, Pierre de 1515(?)-1572 .... LC 174
See also DLB 327
Larbaud, Valery (Nicolas)
1881-1957 .... TCLC 9
See also CA 106; 152; EWL 3; GFL 1789
to the Present
Larcom, Lucy 1824-1893 .... NCLC 179
See also AMWS 13; DLB 221, 243
Lardner, Ring 1885-1933 .... SSC 32, 118;
TCLC 2, 14
See also AMW; BPFB 2; CA 104; 131;
CDALB 1917-1929; DLB 11, 25, 86, 171;
DLBD 16; MAL 5; MTCW 1, 2; MTFW
2005; RGAL 4; RGSF 2; TUS
Lardner, Ring W., Jr.
See Lardner, Ring
Lardner, Ringold Wilmer
See Lardner, Ring
Laredo, Betty
See Codrescu, Andrei
Larkin, Maia
See Wojciechowska, Maia (Teresa)
Larkin, Philip 1922-1985 .... CLC 3, 5, 8, 9,
13, 18, 33, 39, 64; PC 21
See also BRWR 3; BRWS 1; CA 5-8R; 117;
CANR 24, 62; CDBLB 1960 to Present;
CP 1, 2, 3, 4; DA3; DAB; DAM MST,
POET; DLB 27; EWL 3; MTCW 1, 2;
MTFW 2005; PFS 3, 4, 12; RGEL 2
Larkin, Philip Arthur
See Larkin, Philip

La Roche, Sophie von
1730-1807 .... NCLC 121
See also DLB 94
La Rochefoucauld, Francois
1613-1680 .... LC 108, 172
See also DLB 268; EW 3; GFL Beginnings
to 1789; RGWL 2, 3
**Larra (y Sanchez de Castro), Mariano Jose
de** 1809-1837 .... NCLC 17, 130
Larsen, Eric 1941- .... CLC 55
See also CA 132
Larsen, Nella 1893(?)-1963 ... BLC 1:2; CLC
37; HR 1:3; TCLC 200
See also AFAW 1, 2; AMWS 18; BW 1;
CA 125; CANR 83; DAM MULT; DLB
51; FW; LATS 1:1; LMFS 2
Larson, Charles R(aymond) 1938- ... CLC 31
See also CA 53-56; CANR 4, 121
Larson, Jonathan 1960-1996 .... CLC 99
See also AAYA 28; CA 156; DFS 23;
MTFW 2005
La Sale, Antoine de c. 1386-1460(?) . LC 104
See also DLB 208
Lasarus, B. B.
See Breytenbach, Breyten
Las Casas, Bartolome de
1474-1566 .... HLCS; LC 31
See also DLB 318; LAW; WLIT 1
Lasch, Christopher 1932-1994 .... CLC 102
See also CA 73-76; 144; CANR 25, 118;
DLB 246; MTCW 1, 2; MTFW 2005
Lasker-Schueler, Else 1869-1945 ... TCLC 57
See also CA 183; DLB 66, 124; EWL 3
Lasker-Schuler, Else
See Lasker-Schueler, Else
Laski, Harold J(oseph) 1893-1950 . TCLC 79
See also CA 188
Latham, Jean Lee 1902-1995 .... CLC 12
See also AITN 1; BYA 1; CA 5-8R; CANR
7, 84; CLR 50; MAICYA 1, 2; SATA 2,
68; YAW
Latham, Mavis
See Clark, Mavis Thorpe
Lathen, Emma
See Hennissart, Martha
Lathrop, Francis
See Leiber, Fritz (Reuter, Jr.)
Lattany, Kristin
See Lattany, Kristin Hunter
Lattany, Kristin Elaine Eggleston Hunter
See Lattany, Kristin Hunter
Lattany, Kristin Hunter 1931- .... CLC 35
See also AITN 1; BW 1; BYA 3; CA 13-
16R; CANR 13, 108; CLR 3; CN 1, 2, 3,
4, 5, 6; DLB 33; INT CANR-13; MAI-
CYA 1, 2; SAAS 10; SATA 12, 132; YAW
Lattimore, Richmond (Alexander)
1906-1984 .... CLC 3
See also CA 1-4R; 112; CANR 1; CP 1, 2,
3; MAL 5
Laughlin, James 1914-1997 .... CLC 49
See also CA 21-24R; 162; CAAS 22; CANR
9, 47; CP 1, 2, 3, 4, 5, 6; DLB 48; DLBY
1996, 1997
Laurence, Jean Margaret Wemyss
See Laurence, Margaret
Laurence, Margaret 1926-1987 ..... CLC 3, 6,
13, 50, 62; SSC 7
See also BYA 13; CA 5-8R; 121; CANR
33; CN 1, 2, 3, 4; DAC; DAM MST; DLB
53; EWL 3; FW; MTCW 1, 2; MTFW
2005; NFS 11; RGEL 2; RGSF 2; SATA-
Obit 50; TCWW 2
Laurent, Antoine 1952- .... CLC 50
Lauscher, Hermann
See Hesse, Hermann

Lautreamont 1846-1870 .... NCLC 12, 194;
SSC 14
See also DLB 217; GFL 1789 to the Present;
RGWL 2, 3
Lautreamont, Isidore Lucien Ducasse
See Lautreamont
Lavater, Johann Kaspar
1741-1801 .... NCLC 142
See also DLB 97
Laverty, Donald
See Blish, James
Lavin, Mary 1912-1996 . CLC 4, 18, 99; SSC
4, 67, 137
See also CA 9-12R; 151; CANR 33; CN 1,
2, 3, 4, 5, 6; DLB 15, 319; FW; MTCW
1; RGEL 2; RGSF 2; SSFS 23
Lavond, Paul Dennis
See Kornbluth, C(yril) M.; Pohl, Frederik
Lawes, Henry 1596-1662 .... LC 113
See also DLB 126
Lawler, Ray
See Lawler, Raymond Evenor
Lawler, Raymond Evenor 1922- .... CLC 58
See also CA 103; CD 5, 6; DLB 289; RGEL
2
Lawrence, D. H. 1885-1930 ... PC 54; SSC 4,
19, 73; TCLC 2, 9, 16, 33, 48, 61, 93;
WLC 3
See also BPFB 2; BRW 7; BRWR 2; CA
104; 121; CANR 131; CDBLB 1914-
1945; DA; DA3; DAB; DAC; DAM MST,
NOV, POET; DLB 10, 19, 36, 98, 162,
195; EWL 3; EXPP; EXPS; GLL 1; LAIT
2, 3; MTCW 1, 2; MTFW 2005; NFS 18,
26; PFS 6; RGEL 2; RGSF 2; SSFS 2, 6;
TEA; WLIT 4; WP
Lawrence, David Herbert Richards
See Lawrence, D. H.
Lawrence, T. E. 1888-1935 ..... TCLC 18, 204
See also BRWS 2; CA 115; 167; DLB 195
Lawrence, Thomas Edward
See Lawrence, T. E.
Lawrence of Arabia
See Lawrence, T. E.
Lawson, Henry (Archibald Hertzberg)
1867-1922 .... SSC 18; TCLC 27
See also CA 120; 181; DLB 230; RGEL 2;
RGSF 2
Lawton, Dennis
See Faust, Frederick
Laxness, Halldor (Kiljan)
See Gudjonsson, Halldor Kiljan
Layamon fl. c. 1200- .... CMLC 10, 105
See also DLB 146; RGEL 2
Laye, Camara 1928-1980 .. BLC 1:2; CLC 4,
38
See also AFW; BW 1; CA 85-88; 97-100;
CANR 25; DAM MULT; EWL 3; MTCW
1, 2; WLIT 2
Layton, Irving 1912-2006 ..... CLC 2, 15, 164
See also CA 1-4R; 247; CANR 2, 33, 43,
66, 129; CP 1, 2, 3, 4, 5, 6, 7; DAC; DAM
MST, POET; DLB 88; EWL 3; MTCW 1,
2; PFS 12; RGEL 2
Layton, Irving Peter
See Layton, Irving
Lazarus, Emma 1849-1887 ...... NCLC 8, 109
Lazarus, Felix
See Cable, George Washington
Lazarus, Henry
See Slavitt, David R.
Lea, Joan
See Neufeld, John (Arthur)
Leacock, Stephen (Butler)
1869-1944 .... SSC 39; TCLC 2
See also CA 104; 141; CANR 80; DAC;
DAM MST; DLB 92; EWL 3; MTCW 2;
MTFW 2005; RGEL 2; RGSF 2

Lead, Jane Ward 1623-1704 .... **LC 72**
See also DLB 131

Leapor, Mary 1722-1746 .... **LC 80; PC 85**
See also DLB 109

Lear, Edward 1812-1888 ..... **NCLC 3; PC 65**
See also AAYA 48; BRW 5; CLR 1, 75;
DLB 32, 163, 166; MAICYA 1, 2; RGEL
2; SATA 18, 100; WCH; WP

Lear, Norman (Milton) 1922- .... **CLC 12**
See also CA 73-76

Least Heat-Moon, William
See Heat-Moon, William Least

Leautaud, Paul 1872-1956 .... **TCLC 83**
See also CA 203; DLB 65; GFL 1789 to the
Present

Leavis, F(rank) R(aymond)
1895-1978 .... **CLC 24**
See also BRW 7; CA 21-24R; 77-80; CANR
44; DLB 242; EWL 3; MTCW 1, 2;
RGEL 2

Leavitt, David 1961- .... **CLC 34**
See also CA 116; 122, CANR 50, 62, 101,
134, 177; CPW; DA3; DAM POP; DLB
130, 350; GLL 1; INT CA-122; MAL 5;
MTCW 2; MTFW 2005

Leblanc, Maurice (Marie Emile)
1864-1941 .... **TCLC 49**
See also CA 110; CMW 4

Lebowitz, Fran(ces Ann) 1951(?)- ... **CLC 11,
36**
See also CA 81-84; CANR 14, 60, 70; INT
CANR-14; MTCW 1

Lebrecht, Peter
See Tieck, (Johann) Ludwig

le Cagat, Benat
See Whitaker, Rod

le Carre, John
See le Carre, John

le Carre, John 1931- .... **CLC 9, 15**
See also AAYA 42; BEST 89:4; BPFB 2;
BRWR 3; BRWS 2; CA 5-8R; CANR 13,
33, 59, 107, 132, 172; CDBLB 1960 to
Present; CMW 4; CN 1, 2, 3, 4, 5, 6, 7;
CPW; DA3; DAM POP; DLB 87; EWL
3; MSW; MTCW 1, 2; MTFW 2005;
RGEL 2; TEA

Le Clezio, J. M.G. 1940- . **CLC 31, 155, 280;
SSC 122**
See also CA 116; 128; CANR 147; CWW
2; DLB 83; EWL 3; GFL 1789 to the
Present; RGSF 2

Le Clezio, Jean Marie Gustave
See Le Clezio, J. M.G.

Leconte de Lisle, Charles-Marie-Rene
1818-1894 .... **NCLC 29**
See also DLB 217; EW 6; GFL 1789 to the
Present

Le Coq, Monsieur
See Simenon, Georges

Leduc, Violette 1907-1972 .... **CLC 22**
See also CA 13-14; 33-36R; CANR 69;
CAP 1; EWL 3; GFL 1789 to the Present;
GLL 1

Ledwidge, Francis 1887(?)-1917 .... **TCLC 23**
See also CA 123; 203; DLB 20

Lee, Andrea 1953- .... **BLC 1:2; CLC 36**
See also BW 1, 3; CA 125; CANR 82, 190;
DAM MULT

Lee, Andrew
See Auchincloss, Louis

Lee, Chang-rae 1965- .... **CLC 91, 268, 274**
See also CA 148; CANR 89; CN 7; DLB
312; LATS 1:2

Lee, Don L.
See Madhubuti, Haki R.

Lee, George W(ashington)
1894-1976 .... **BLC 1:2; CLC 52**
See also BW 1; CA 125; CANR 83; DAM
MULT; DLB 51

Lee, Harper 1926- ... **CLC 12, 60, 194; WLC
4**
See also AAYA 13; AMWS 8; BPFB 2;
BYA 3; CA 13-16R; CANR 51, 128;
CDALB 1941-1968; CSW; DA; DA3;
DAB; DAC; DAM MST, NOV; DLB 6;
EXPN; LAIT 3; MAL 5; MTCW 1, 2;
MTFW 2005; NFS 2, 32; SATA 11; WYA;
YAW

Lee, Helen Elaine 1959(?)- .... **CLC 86**
See also CA 148

Lee, John CLC 70

Lee, Julian
See Latham, Jean Lee

Lee, Larry
See Lee, Lawrence

Lee, Laurie 1914-1997 .... **CLC 90**
See also CA 77-80; 158; CANR 33, 73; CP
1, 2, 3, 4, 5, 6; CPW; DAB; DAM POP;
DLB 27; MTCW 1; RGEL 2

Lee, Lawrence 1941-1990 .... **CLC 34**
See also CA 131; CANR 43

Lee, Li-Young 1957- .... **CLC 164; PC 24**
See also AMWS 15; CA 153; CANR 118;
CP 6, 7; DLB 165, 312; LMFS 2; PFS 11,
15, 17

Lee, Manfred B. 1905-1971 .... **CLC 11**
See also CA 1-4R; 29-32R; CANR 2, 150;
CMW 4; DLB 137

Lee, Manfred Bennington
See Lee, Manfred B.

Lee, Nathaniel 1645(?)-1692 .... **LC 103**
See also DLB 80; RGEL 2

Lee, Nelle Harper
See Lee, Harper

Lee, Shelton Jackson
See Lee, Spike

Lee, Sophia 1750-1824 .... **NCLC 191**
See also DLB 39

Lee, Spike 1957(?)- ..... **BLCS; CLC 105, 281**
See also AAYA 4, 29; BW 2, 3; CA 125;
CANR 42, 164; DAM MULT

Lee, Stan 1922- .... **CLC 17**
See also AAYA 5, 49; CA 108; 111; CANR
129; INT CA-111; MTFW 2005

Lee, Tanith 1947- .... **CLC 46**
See also AAYA 15; CA 37-40R; CANR 53,
102, 145, 170; DLB 261; FANT; SATA 8,
88, 134, 185; SFW 4; SUFW 1, 2; YAW

Lee, Vernon
See Paget, Violet

Lee, William
See Burroughs, William S.

Lee, Willy
See Burroughs, William S.

Lee-Hamilton, Eugene (Jacob)
1845-1907 .... **TCLC 22**
See also CA 117; 234

Leet, Judith 1935- .... **CLC 11**
See also CA 187

Le Fanu, Joseph Sheridan
1814-1873 .... **NCLC 9, 58; SSC 14, 84**
See also CMW 4; DA3; DAM POP; DLB
21, 70, 159, 178; GL 3; HGG; RGEL 2;
RGSF 2; SUFW 1

Leffland, Ella 1931- .... **CLC 19**
See also CA 29-32R; CANR 35, 78, 82;
DLBY 1984; INT CANR-35; SATA 65;
SSFS 24

Leger, Alexis
See Leger, Alexis Saint-Leger

Leger, Alexis Saint-Leger
1887-1975 .... **CLC 4, 11, 46; PC 23**
See also CA 13-16R; 61-64; CANR 43;
DAM POET; DLB 258, 331; EW 10;
EWL 3; GFL 1789 to the Present; MTCW
1; RGWL 2, 3

**Leger, Marie-Rene Auguste Alexis
Saint-Leger**
See Leger, Alexis Saint-Leger

Leger, Saintleger
See Leger, Alexis Saint-Leger

Le Guin, Ursula K. 1929- ...... **CLC 8, 13, 22,
45, 71, 136; SSC 12, 69**
See also AAYA 9, 27; AITN 1; BPFB 2;
BYA 5, 8, 11, 14; CA 21-24R; CANR 9,
32, 52, 74, 132, 192; CDALB 1968-1988;
CLR 3, 28, 91; CN 2, 3, 4, 5, 6, 7; CPW;
DA3; DAB; DAC; DAM MST, POP;
DLB 8, 52, 256, 275; EXPS; FANT; FW;
INT CANR-32; JRDA; LAIT 5; MAICYA
1, 2; MAL 5; MTCW 1, 2; MTFW 2005;
NFS 6, 9; SATA 4, 52, 99, 149, 194;
SCFW 1, 2; SFW 4; SSFS 2; SUFW 1, 2;
WYA; YAW

Le Guin, Ursula Kroeber
See Le Guin, Ursula K.

Lehmann, Rosamond (Nina)
1901-1990 .... **CLC 5**
See also CA 77-80; 131; CANR 8, 73; CN
1, 2, 3, 4; DLB 15; MTCW 2; RGEL 2;
RHW

Leiber, Fritz (Reuter, Jr.)
1910-1992 .... **CLC 25**
See also AAYA 65; BPFB 2; CA 45-48; 139;
CANR 2, 40, 86; CN 2, 3, 4, 5; DLB 8;
FANT; HGG; MTCW 1, 2; MTFW 2005;
SATA 45; SATA-Obit 73; SCFW 1, 2;
SFW 4; SUFW 1, 2

Leibniz, Gottfried Wilhelm von
1646-1716 .... **LC 35**
See also DLB 168

Leino, Eino
See Lonnbohm, Armas Eino Leopold

Leiris, Michel (Julien) 1901-1990 ..... **CLC 61**
See also CA 119; 128; 132; EWL 3; GFL
1789 to the Present

Leithauser, Brad 1953- .... **CLC 27**
See also CA 107; CANR 27, 81, 171; CP 5,
6, 7; DLB 120, 282

le Jars de Gournay, Marie
See de Gournay, Marie le Jars

Lelchuk, Alan 1938- .... **CLC 5**
See also CA 45-48; CAAS 20; CANR 1,
70, 152; CN 3, 4, 5, 6, 7

Lem, Stanislaw 1921-2006 ..... **CLC 8, 15, 40,
149**
See also AAYA 75; CA 105; 249; CAAS 1;
CANR 32; CWW 2; MTCW 1; SCFW 1,
2; SFW 4

Lemann, Nancy (Elise) 1956- .... **CLC 39**
See also CA 118; 136; CANR 121

Lemonnier, (Antoine Louis) Camille
1844-1913 .... **TCLC 22**
See also CA 121

Lenau, Nikolaus 1802-1850 .... **NCLC 16**

L'Engle, Madeleine 1918-2007 .... **CLC 12**
See also AAYA 28; AITN 2; BPFB 2; BYA
2, 4, 5, 7; CA 1-4R; 264; CANR 3, 21,
39, 66, 107; CLR 1, 14, 57; CPW; CWRI
5; DA3; DAM POP; DLB 52; JRDA;
MAICYA 1, 2; MTCW 1, 2; MTFW 2005;
NFS 32; SAAS 15; SATA 1, 27, 75, 128;
SATA-Obit 186; SFW 4; WYA; YAW

L'Engle, Madeleine Camp Franklin
See L'Engle, Madeleine

Lengyel, Jozsef 1896-1975 .... **CLC 7**
See also CA 85-88; 57-60; CANR 71;
RGSF 2

Lenin 1870-1924 .... **TCLC 67**
See also CA 121; 168

Lenin, N.
See Lenin

Lenin, Nikolai
See Lenin

Lewisohn, Ludwig 1883-1955 .... **TCLC 19**
  See also CA 107; 203; DLB 4, 9, 28, 102;
    MAL 5
Lewton, Val 1904-1951 .... **TCLC 76**
  See also CA 199; IDFW 3, 4
Leyner, Mark 1956- .... **CLC 92**
  See also CA 110; CANR 28, 53; DA3; DLB
    292; MTCW 2; MTFW 2005
Leyton, E.K.
  See Campbell, Ramsey
Lezama Lima, Jose 1910-1976 .... **CLC 4, 10,**
    101; HLCS 2
  See also CA 77-80; CANR 71; DAM
    MULT; DLB 113, 283; EWL 3; HW 1, 2;
    LAW; RGWL 2, 3
L'Heureux, John (Clarke) 1934- ...... **CLC 52**
  See also CA 13-16R; CANR 23, 45, 88; CP
    1, 2, 3, 4; DLB 244
Li, Fei-kan
  See Jin, Ba
Li Ch'ing-chao 1081(?)-1141(?) .... **CMLC 71**
Lichtenberg, Georg Christoph
    1742-1799 .... **LC 162**
  See also DLB 94
Liddell, C. H.
  See Kuttner, Henry
Lie, Jonas (Lauritz Idemil)
    1833-1908(?) .... **TCLC 5**
  See also CA 115
Lieber, Joel 1937-1971 .... **CLC 6**
  See also CA 73-76; 29-32R
Lieber, Stanley Martin
  See Lee, Stan
Lieberman, Laurence (James)
    1935- .... **CLC 4, 36**
  See also CA 17-20R; CANR 8, 36, 89; CP
    1, 2, 3, 4, 5, 6, 7
Lieh Tzu fl. 7th cent. B.C.-5th cent.
    B.C. .... **CMLC 27**
Lieksman, Anders
  See Haavikko, Paavo Juhani
Lifton, Robert Jay 1926- .... **CLC 67**
  See also CA 17-20R; CANR 27, 78, 161;
    INT CANR-27; SATA 66
Lightfoot, Gordon 1938- .... **CLC 26**
  See also CA 109; 242
Lightfoot, Gordon Meredith
  See Lightfoot, Gordon
Lightman, Alan P. 1948- .... **CLC 81**
  See also CA 141; CANR 63, 105, 138, 178;
    MTFW 2005; NFS 29
Lightman, Alan Paige
  See Lightman, Alan P.
Ligotti, Thomas 1953- .... **CLC 44; SSC 16**
  See also CA 123; CANR 49, 135; HGG;
    SUFW 2
Ligotti, Thomas Robert
  See Ligotti, Thomas
Li Ho 791-817 .... **PC 13**
Li Ju-chen c. 1763-c. 1830 .... **NCLC 137**
Liking, Werewere 1950- .... **BLC 2:2**
  See also CA 293; EWL 3
Lilar, Francoise
  See Mallet-Joris, Francoise
Liliencron, Detlev
  See Liliencron, Detlev von
Liliencron, Detlev von 1844-1909 .. **TCLC 18**
  See also CA 117
Liliencron, Friedrich Adolf Axel Detlev von
  See Liliencron, Detlev
Liliencron, Friedrich Detlev von
  See Liliencron, Detlev
Lille, Alain de
  See Alain de Lille
Lillo, George 1691-1739 .... **LC 131**
  See also DLB 84; RGEL 2

Lilly, William 1602-1681 .... **LC 27**
Lima, Jose Lezama
  See Lezama Lima, Jose
Lima Barreto, Afonso Henrique de
    1881-1922 .... **TCLC 23**
  See also CA 117; 181; DLB 307; LAW
Lima Barreto, Afonso Henriques de
  See Lima Barreto, Afonso Henrique de
Limonov, Eduard
  See Limonov, Edward
Limonov, Edward 1944- .... **CLC 67**
  See also CA 137; DLB 317
Lin, Frank
  See Atherton, Gertrude (Franklin Horn)
Lin, Yutang 1895-1976 .... **TCLC 149**
  See also CA 45-48; 65-68; CANR 2; RGAL
    4
Lincoln, Abraham 1809-1865 .... **NCLC 18,**
    201
  See also LAIT 2
Lincoln, Geoffrey
  See Mortimer, John
Lind, Jakov 1927-2007 ... **CLC 1, 2, 4, 27, 82**
  See also CA 9-12R; 257; CAAS 4; CANR
    7; DLB 299; EWL 3; RGHL
Lindbergh, Anne Morrow
    1906-2001 .... **CLC 82**
  See also BPFB 2; CA 17-20R; 193; CANR
    16, 73; DAM NOV; MTCW 1, 2; MTFW
    2005; SATA 33; SATA-Obit 125; TUS
Lindbergh, Anne Spencer Morrow
  See Lindbergh, Anne Morrow
Lindholm, Anna Margaret
  See Haycraft, Anna
Lindsay, David 1878(?)-1945 .... **TCLC 15**
  See also CA 113; 187; DLB 255; FANT;
    SFW 4; SUFW 1
Lindsay, Nicholas Vachel
  See Lindsay, Vachel
Lindsay, Vachel 1879-1931 ..... **PC 23; TCLC**
    17; WLC 4
  See also AMWS 1; CA 114; 135; CANR
    79; CDALB 1865-1917; DA; DA3; DAC;
    DAM MST, POET; DLB 54; EWL 3;
    EXPP; MAL 5; RGAL 4; SATA 40; WP
Linke-Poot
  See Doeblin, Alfred
Linney, Romulus 1930- .... **CLC 51**
  See also CA 1-4R; CAD; CANR 40, 44,
    79; CD 5, 6; CSW; RGAL 4
Linton, Eliza Lynn 1822-1898 .... **NCLC 41**
  See also DLB 18
Li Po 701-763 .... **CMLC 2, 86; PC 29**
  See also PFS 20; WP
Lippard, George 1822-1854 .... **NCLC 198**
  See also DLB 202
Lipsius, Justus 1547-1606 .... **LC 16**
Lipsyte, Robert 1938- .... **CLC 21**
  See also AAYA 7, 45; CA 17-20R; CANR
    8, 57, 146, 189; CLR 23, 76; DA; DAC;
    DAM MST, NOV; JRDA; LAIT 5; MAI-
    CYA 1, 2; SATA 5, 68, 113, 161, 198;
    WYA; YAW
Lipsyte, Robert Michael
  See Lipsyte, Robert
Lish, Gordon 1934- .... **CLC 45; SSC 18**
  See also CA 113; 117; CANR 79, 151; DLB
    130; INT CA-117
Lish, Gordon Jay
  See Lish, Gordon
Lispector, Clarice 1925(?)-1977 .... **CLC 43;**
    HLCS 2; SSC 34, 96
  See also CA 139; 116; CANR 71; CDWLB
    3; DLB 113, 307; DNFS 1; EWL 3; FW;
    HW 2; LAW; RGSF 2; RGWL 2, 3; WLIT
    1

Liszt, Franz 1811-1886 .... **NCLC 199**
Littell, Robert 1935(?)- .... **CLC 42**
  See also CA 109; 112; CANR 64, 115, 162;
    CMW 4
Little, Malcolm
  See Malcolm X
Littlewit, Humphrey Gent.
  See Lovecraft, H. P.
Litwos
  See Sienkiewicz, Henryk (Adam Alexander
    Pius)
Liu, E. 1857-1909 .... **TCLC 15**
  See also CA 115; 190; DLB 328
Lively, Penelope 1933- .... **CLC 32, 50**
  See also BPFB 2; CA 41-44R; CANR 29,
    67, 79, 131, 172; CLR 7; CN 5, 6, 7;
    CWRI 5; DAM NOV; DLB 14, 161, 207,
    326; FANT; JRDA; MAICYA 1, 2;
    MTCW 1, 2; MTFW 2005; SATA 7, 60,
    101, 164; TEA
Lively, Penelope Margaret
  See Lively, Penelope
Livesay, Dorothy (Kathleen)
    1909-1996 .... **CLC 4, 15, 79**
  See also AITN 2; CA 25-28R; CAAS 8;
    CANR 36, 67; CP 1, 2, 3, 4, 5; DAC;
    DAM MST, POET; DLB 68; FW; MTCW
    1; RGEL 2; TWA
Livius Andronicus c. 284B.C.-c.
    204B.C. .... **CMLC 102**
Livy c. 59B.C.-c. 12 .... **CMLC 11**
  See also AW 2; CDWLB 1; DLB 211;
    RGWL 2, 3; WLIT 8
Li Yaotang
  See Jin, Ba
Lizardi, Jose Joaquin Fernandez de
    1776-1827 .... **NCLC 30**
  See also LAW
Llewellyn, Richard
  See Llewellyn Lloyd, Richard Dafydd Viv-
    ian
Llewellyn Lloyd, Richard Dafydd Vivian
    1906-1983 .... **CLC 7, 80**
  See also CA 53-56; 111; CANR 7, 71; DLB
    15; NFS 30; SATA 11; SATA-Obit 37
Llosa, Jorge Mario Pedro Vargas
  See Vargas Llosa, Mario
Llosa, Mario Vargas
  See Vargas Llosa, Mario
Lloyd, Manda
  See Mander, (Mary) Jane
Lloyd Webber, Andrew 1948- .... **CLC 21**
  See also AAYA 1, 38; CA 116; 149; DAM
    DRAM; DFS 7; SATA 56
Llull, Ramon c. 1235-c. 1316 .... **CMLC 12,**
    114
Lobb, Ebenezer
  See Upward, Allen
Lochhead, Liz 1947- .... **CLC 286**
  See also CA 81-84; CANR 79; CBD; CD 5,
    6; CP 2, 3, 4, 5, 6, 7; CWD; CWP; DLB
    310
Locke, Alain Leroy 1885-1954 .... **BLCS; HR**
    1:3; TCLC 43
  See also AMWS 14; BW 1, 3; CA 106; 124;
    CANR 79; DLB 51; LMFS 2; MAL 5;
    RGAL 4
Locke, John 1632-1704 .... **LC 7, 35, 135**
  See also DLB 31, 101, 213, 252; RGEL 2;
    WLIT 3
Locke-Elliott, Sumner
  See Elliott, Sumner Locke
Lockhart, John Gibson 1794-1854 .. **NCLC 6**
  See also DLB 110, 116, 144
Lockridge, Ross (Franklin), Jr.
    1914-1948 .... **TCLC 111**
  See also CA 108; 145; CANR 79; DLB 143;
    DLBY 1980; MAL 5; RGAL 4; RHW

Lockwood, Robert
  See Johnson, Robert
Lodge, David 1935- .... **CLC 36, 141**
  See also BEST 90:1; BRWS 4; CA 17-20R;
  CANR 19, 53, 92, 139, 197; CN 1, 2, 3,
  4, 5, 6, 7; CPW; DAM POP; DLB 14,
  194; EWL 3; INT CANR-19; MTCW 1,
  2; MTFW 2005
Lodge, David John
  See Lodge, David
Lodge, Thomas 1558-1625 .... **LC 41**
  See also DLB 172; RGEL 2
Loewinsohn, Ron(ald William)
  1937- .... **CLC 52**
  See also CA 25-28R; CANR 71; CP 1, 2, 3,
  4
Logan, Jake
  See Smith, Martin Cruz
Logan, John (Burton) 1923-1987 .... **CLC 5**
  See also CA 77-80; 124; CANR 45; CP 1,
  2, 3, 4; DLB 5
Lo-Johansson, (Karl) Ivar
  1901-1990 .... **TCLC 216**
  See also CA 102; 131; CANR 20, 79, 137;
  DLB 259; EWL 3; RGWL 2, 3
Lo Kuan-chung 1330(?)-1400(?) .... **LC 12**
Lomax, Pearl
  See Cleage, Pearl
Lomax, Pearl Cleage
  See Cleage, Pearl
Lombard, Nap
  See Johnson, Pamela Hansford
Lombard, Peter 1100(?)-1160(?) ... **CMLC 72**
Lombino, Salvatore
  See Hunter, Evan
London, Jack 1876-1916 .... **SSC 4, 49, 133;**
  TCLC 9, 15, 39; WLC 4
  See also AAYA 13, 75; AITN 2; AMW;
  BPFB 2; BYA 4, 13; CA 110; 119; CANR
  73; CDALB 1865-1917; CLR 108; DA;
  DA3; DAB; DAC; DAM MST, NOV;
  DLB 8, 12, 78, 212; EWL 3; EXPS;
  JRDA; LAIT 3; MAICYA 1, 2,; MAL 5;
  MTCW 1, 2; MTFW 2005; NFS 8, 19;
  RGAL 4; RGSF 2; SATA 18; SFW 4;
  SSFS 7; TCWW 1, 2; TUS; WYA; YAW
London, John Griffith
  See London, Jack
Long, Emmett
  See Leonard, Elmore
Longbaugh, Harry
  See Goldman, William
Longfellow, Henry Wadsworth
  1807-1882 .... **NCLC 2, 45, 101, 103; PC**
  30; WLCS
  See also AMW; AMWR 2; CDALB 1640-
  1865; CLR 99; DA; DA3; DAB; DAC;
  DAM MST, POET; DLB 1, 59, 235;
  EXPP; PAB; PFS 2, 7, 17, 31; RGAL 4;
  SATA 19; TUS; WP
Longinus c. 1st cent. - .... **CMLC 27**
  See also AW 2; DLB 176
Longley, Michael 1939- .... **CLC 29**
  See also BRWS 8; CA 102; CP 1, 2, 3, 4, 5,
  6, 7; DLB 40
Longstreet, Augustus Baldwin
  1790-1870 .... **NCLC 159**
  See also DLB 3, 11, 74, 248; RGAL 4
Longus fl. c. 2nd cent. - .... **CMLC 7**
Longway, A. Hugh
  See Lang, Andrew
Lonnbohm, Armas Eino Leopold
  See Lonnbohm, Armas Eino Leopold
Lonnbohm, Armas Eino Leopold
  1878-1926 .... **TCLC 24**
  See also CA 123; EWL 3
Lonnrot, Elias 1802-1884 .... **NCLC 53**
  See also EFS 1
Lonsdale, Roger CLC 65

Lopate, Phillip 1943- .... **CLC 29**
  See also CA 97-100; CANR 88, 157, 196;
  DLBY 1980; INT CA-97-100
Lopez, Barry 1945- .... **CLC 70**
  See also AAYA 9, 63; ANW; CA 65-68;
  CANR 7, 23, 47, 68, 92; DLB 256, 275,
  335; INT CANR-7, CANR-23; MTCW 1;
  RGAL 4; SATA 67
Lopez, Barry Holstun
  See Lopez, Barry
Lopez de Mendoza, Inigo
  See Santillana, Inigo Lopez de Mendoza,
  Marques de
Lopez Portillo (y Pacheco), Jose
  1920-2004 .... **CLC 46**
  See also CA 129; 224; HW 1
Lopez y Fuentes, Gregorio
  1897(?)-1966 .... **CLC 32**
  See also CA 131; EWL 3; HW 1
Lorca, Federico Garcia
  See Garcia Lorca, Federico
Lord, Audre
  See Lorde, Audre
Lord, Bette Bao 1938- .... **AAL; CLC 23**
  See also BEST 90:3; BPFB 2; CA 107;
  CANR 41, 79; CLR 151; INT CA-107;
  SATA 58
Lord Auch
  See Bataille, Georges
Lord Brooke
  See Greville, Fulke
Lord Byron 1788-1824 .... **DC 24; NCLC 2,**
  12, 109, 149; PC 16, 95; WLC 1
  See also AAYA 64; BRW 4; BRWC 2; CD-
  BLB 1789-1832; DA; DA3; DAB; DAC;
  DAM MST, POET; DLB 96, 110; EXPP;
  LMFS 1; PAB; PFS 1, 14, 29, 35; RGEL
  2; TEA; WLIT 3; WP
Lord Dunsany
  See Dunsany, Edward John Moreton Drax
  Plunkett
Lorde, Audre 1934-1992 .... **BLC 1:2, 2:2;**
  CLC 18, 71; PC 12; TCLC 173
  See also AFAW 1, 2; BW 1, 3; CA 25-28R;
  142; CANR 16, 26, 46, 82; CP 2, 3, 4, 5;
  DA3; DAM MULT, POET; DLB 41; EWL
  3; FW; GLL 1; MAL 5; MTCW 1, 2;
  MTFW 2005; PFS 16, 32; RGAL 4
Lorde, Audre Geraldine
  See Lorde, Audre
Lord Houghton
  See Milnes, Richard Monckton
Lord Jeffrey
  See Jeffrey, Francis
Loreaux, Nichol CLC 65
Lorenzo, Heberto Padilla
  See Padilla (Lorenzo), Heberto
Loris
  See Hofmannsthal, Hugo von
Loti, Pierre
  See Viaud, Julien
Lottie
  See Grimke, Charlotte L. Forten
Lou, Henri
  See Andreas-Salome, Lou
Louie, David Wong 1954- .... **CLC 70**
  See also CA 139; CANR 120
Louis, Adrian C. NNAL
  See also CA 223
Louis, Father M.
  See Merton, Thomas
Louise, Heidi
  See Erdrich, Louise
Lovecraft, H. P. 1890-1937 .... **SSC 3, 52;**
  TCLC 4, 22
  See also AAYA 14; BPFB 2; CA 104; 133;
  CANR 106; DA3; DAM POP; HGG;
  MTCW 1, 2; MTFW 2005; RGAL 4;
  SCFW 1, 2; SFW 4; SUFW

Lovecraft, Howard Phillips
  See Lovecraft, H. P.
Lovelace, Earl 1935- .... **CLC 51**
  See also BW 2; CA 77-80; CANR 41, 72,
  114; CD 5, 6; CDWLB 3; CN 1, 2, 3, 4,
  5, 6, 7; DLB 125; EWL 3; MTCW 1
Lovelace, Richard 1618-1658 ..... **LC 24, 158;**
  PC 69
  See also BRW 2; DLB 131; EXPP; PAB;
  PFS 32, 34; RGEL 2
Low, Penelope Margaret
  See Lively, Penelope
Lowe, Pardee 1904- .... **AAL**
Lowell, Amy 1874-1925 ... **PC 13; TCLC 1, 8**
  See also AAYA 57; AMW; CA 104; 151;
  DAM POET; DLB 54, 140; EWL 3;
  EXPP; LMFS 2; MAL 5; MBL; MTCW
  2; MTFW 2005; PFS 30; RGAL 4; TUS
Lowell, James Russell 1819-1891 ... **NCLC 2,**
  90
  See also AMWS 1; CDALB 1640-1865;
  DLB 1, 11, 64, 79, 189, 235; RGAL 4
Lowell, Robert 1917-1977 . **CLC 1, 2, 3, 4, 5,**
  8, 9, 11, 15, 37, 124; PC 3; WLC 4
  See also AMW; AMWC 2; AMWR 2; CA
  9-12R; 73-76; CABS 2; CAD; CANR 26,
  60; CDALBS; CP 1, 2; DA; DA3; DAB;
  DAC; DAM MST, NOV; DLB 5, 169;
  EWL 3; MAL 5; MTCW 1, 2; MTFW
  2005; PAB; PFS 6, 7; RGAL 4; WP
Lowell, Robert Trail Spence, Jr.
  See Lowell, Robert
Lowenthal, Michael 1969- .... **CLC 119**
  See also CA 150; CANR 115, 164
Lowenthal, Michael Francis
  See Lowenthal, Michael
Lowndes, Marie Adelaide (Belloc)
  1868-1947 .... **TCLC 12**
  See also CA 107; CMW 4; DLB 70; RHW
Lowry, (Clarence) Malcolm
  1909-1957 .... **SSC 31; TCLC 6, 40**
  See also BPFB 2; BRWS 3; CA 105; 131;
  CANR 62, 105; CDBLB 1945-1960; DLB
  15; EWL 3; MTCW 1, 2; MTFW 2005;
  RGEL 2
Lowry, Mina Gertrude 1882-1966 .. **CLC 28;**
  PC 16
  See also CA 113; DAM POET; DLB 4, 54;
  PFS 20
Lowry, Sam
  See Soderbergh, Steven
Loxsmith, John
  See Brunner, John (Kilian Houston)
Loy, Mina
  See Lowry, Mina Gertrude
Loyson-Bridet
  See Schwob, Marcel (Mayer Andre)
Lucan 39-65 .... **CMLC 33, 112**
  See also AW 2; DLB 211; EFS 2; RGWL 2,
  3
Lucas, Craig 1951- .... **CLC 64**
  See also CA 137; CAD; CANR 71, 109,
  142; CD 5, 6; GLL 2; MTFW 2005
Lucas, E(dward) V(errall)
  1868-1938 .... **TCLC 73**
  See also CA 176; DLB 98, 149, 153; SATA
  20
Lucas, George 1944- .... **CLC 16, 252**
  See also AAYA 1, 23; CA 77-80; CANR
  30; SATA 56
Lucas, Hans
  See Godard, Jean-Luc
Lucas, Victoria
  See Plath, Sylvia
Lucian c. 125-c. 180 .... **CMLC 32**
  See also AW 2; DLB 176; RGWL 2, 3
Lucilius c. 180B.C.-102B.C. .... **CMLC 82**
  See also DLB 211

Lucretius c. 94B.C.-c. 49B.C. .... **CMLC 48**
See also AW 2; CDWLB 1; DLB 211; EFS
2; RGWL 2, 3; WLIT 8

Ludlam, Charles 1943-1987 .... **CLC 46, 50**
See also CA 85-88; 122; CAD; CANR 72,
86; DLB 266

Ludlum, Robert 1927-2001 .... **CLC 22, 43**
See also AAYA 10, 59; BEST 89:1, 90:3;
BPFB 2; CA 33-36R; 195; CANR 25, 41,
68, 105, 131; CMW 4; CPW; DA3; DAM
NOV, POP; DLBY 1982; MSW; MTCW
1, 2; MTFW 2005

Ludwig, Ken 1950- .... **CLC 60**
See also CA 195; CAD; CD 6

Ludwig, Otto 1813-1865 .... **NCLC 4**
See also DLB 129

Lugones, Leopoldo 1874-1938 .... **HLCS 2;**
TCLC 15
See also CA 116; 131; CANR 104; DLB
283; EWL 3; HW 1; LAW

Lu Hsun
See Shu-Jen, Chou

Lukacs, George
See Lukacs, Gyorgy

Lukacs, Gyorgy 1885-1971 .... **CLC 24**
See also CA 101; 29-32R; CANR 62; CD-
WLB 4; DLB 215, 242; EW 10; EWL 3;
MTCW 1, 2

Lukacs, Gyorgy Szegeny von
See Lukacs, Gyorgy

Luke, Peter (Ambrose Cyprian)
1919-1995 .... **CLC 38**
See also CA 81-84; 147; CANR 72; CBD;
CD 5, 6; DLB 13

Lunar, Dennis
See Mungo, Raymond

Lurie, Alison 1926- ..... **CLC 4, 5, 18, 39, 175**
See also BPFB 2; CA 1-4R; CANR 2, 17,
50, 88; CN 1, 2, 3, 4, 5, 6, 7; DLB 2, 350;
MAL 5; MTCW 1; NFS 24; SATA 46,
112; TCLE 1:1

Lustig, Arnost 1926- .... **CLC 56**
See also AAYA 3; CA 69-72; CANR 47,
102; CWW 2; DLB 232, 299; EWL 3;
RGHL; SATA 56

Luther, Martin 1483-1546 .... **LC 9, 37, 150**
See also CDWLB 2; DLB 179; EW 2;
RGWL 2, 3

Luxemburg, Rosa 1870(?)-1919 ..... **TCLC 63**
See also CA 118

Luzi, Mario (Egidio Vincenzo)
1914-2005 .... **CLC 13**
See also CA 61-64; 236; CANR 9, 70;
CWW 2; DLB 128; EWL 3

L'vov, Arkady **CLC 59**

Lydgate, John c. 1370-1450(?) ..... **LC 81, 175**
See also BRW 1; DLB 146; RGEL 2

Lyly, John 1554(?)-1606 .... **DC 7; LC 41**
See also BRW 1; DAM DRAM; DLB 62,
167; RGEL 2

L'Ymagier
See Gourmont, Remy(-Marie-Charles) de

Lynch, B. Suarez
See Borges, Jorge Luis

Lynch, David 1946- .... **CLC 66, 162**
See also AAYA 55; CA 124; 129; CANR
111

Lynch, David Keith
See Lynch, David

Lynch, James
See Andreyev, Leonid

Lyndsay, Sir David 1485-1555 .... **LC 20**
See also RGEL 2

Lynn, Kenneth S(chuyler)
1923-2001 .... **CLC 50**
See also CA 1-4R; 196; CANR 3, 27, 65

Lynx
See West, Rebecca

Lyons, Marcus
See Blish, James

Lyotard, Jean-Francois
1924-1998 .... **TCLC 103**
See also DLB 242; EWL 3

Lyre, Pinchbeck
See Sassoon, Siegfried

Lytle, Andrew (Nelson) 1902-1995 ... **CLC 22**
See also CA 9-12R; 150; CANR 70; CN 1,
2, 3, 4, 5, 6; CSW; DLB 6; DLBY 1995;
RGAL 4; RHW

Lyttelton, George 1709-1773 .... **LC 10**
See also RGEL 2

Lytton of Knebworth, Baron
See Bulwer-Lytton, Edward

Maalouf, Amin 1949- .... **CLC 248**
See also CA 212; CANR 194; DLB 346

Maas, Peter 1929-2001 .... **CLC 29**
See also CA 93-96; 201; INT CA-93-96;
MTCW 2; MTFW 2005

Mac A'Ghobhainn, Iain
See Smith, Iain Crichton

Macaulay, Catherine 1731-1791 .... **LC 64**
See also DLB 104, 336

Macaulay, (Emilie) Rose
1881(?)-1958 .... **TCLC 7, 44**
See also CA 104; DLB 36; EWL 3; RGEL
2; RHW

Macaulay, Thomas Babington
1800-1859 .... **NCLC 42**
See also BRW 4; CDBLB 1832-1890; DLB
32, 55; RGEL 2

MacBeth, George (Mann)
1932-1992 .... **CLC 2, 5, 9**
See also CA 25-28R; 136; CANR 61, 66;
CP 1, 2, 3, 4, 5; DLB 40; MTCW 1; PFS
8; SATA 4; SATA-Obit 70

MacCaig, Norman (Alexander)
1910-1996 .... **CLC 36**
See also BRWS 6; CA 9-12R; CANR 3, 34;
CP 1, 2, 3, 4, 5, 6; DAB; DAM POET;
DLB 27; EWL 3; RGEL 2

MacCarthy, Sir (Charles Otto) Desmond
1877-1952 .... **TCLC 36**
See also CA 167

MacDiarmid, Hugh
See Grieve, C. M.

MacDonald, Anson
See Heinlein, Robert A.

Macdonald, Cynthia 1928- .... **CLC 13, 19**
See also CA 49-52; CANR 4, 44, 146; DLB
105

MacDonald, George 1824-1905 .... **TCLC 9,**
113, 207
See also AAYA 57; BYA 5; CA 106; 137;
CANR 80; CLR 67; DLB 18, 163, 178;
FANT; MAICYA 1, 2; RGEL 2; SATA 33,
100; SFW 4; SUFW; WCH

Macdonald, John
See Millar, Kenneth

MacDonald, John D. 1916-1986 .. **CLC 3, 27,**
44
See also BPFB 2; CA 1-4R; 121; CANR 1,
19, 60; CMW 4; CPW; DAM NOV, POP;
DLB 8, 306; DLBY 1986; MSW; MTCW
1, 2; MTFW 2005; SFW 4

Macdonald, John Ross
See Millar, Kenneth

Macdonald, Ross
See Millar, Kenneth

MacDonald Fraser, George
See Fraser, George MacDonald

MacDougal, John
See Blish, James

MacDowell, John
See Parks, Tim

MacEwen, Gwendolyn (Margaret)
1941-1987 .... **CLC 13, 55**
See also CA 9-12R; 124; CANR 7, 22; CP
1, 2, 3, 4; DLB 53, 251; SATA 50; SATA-
Obit 55

MacGreevy, Thomas 1893-1967 .... **PC 82**
See also CA 262

Macha, Karel Hynek 1810-1846 .... **NCLC 46**

Machado (y Ruiz), Antonio
1875-1939 .... **TCLC 3**
See also CA 104; 174; DLB 108; EW 9;
EWL 3; HW 2; PFS 23; RGWL 2, 3

Machado de Assis, Joaquim Maria
1839-1908 . **BLC 1:2; HLCS 2; SSC 24,**
118; TCLC 10
See also CA 107; 153; CANR 91; DLB 307;
LAW; RGSF 2; RGWL 2, 3; TWA; WLIT
1

Machaut, Guillaume de c.
1300-1377 .... **CMLC 64**
See also DLB 208

Machen, Arthur **SSC 20; TCLC 4**
See Jones, Arthur Llewellyn
See also CA 179; DLB 156, 178; RGEL 2

Machen, Arthur Llewelyn Jones
See Jones, Arthur Llewellyn

Machiavelli, Niccolo 1469-1527 ... **DC 16; LC**
8, 36, 140; WLCS
See also AAYA 58; DA; DAB; DAC; DAM
MST; EW 2; LAIT 1; LMFS 1; NFS 9;
RGWL 2, 3; TWA; WLIT 7

MacInnes, Colin 1914-1976 .... **CLC 4, 23**
See also CA 69-72; 65-68; CANR 21; CN
1, 2; DLB 14; MTCW 1, 2; RGEL 2;
RHW

MacInnes, Helen (Clark)
1907-1985 .... **CLC 27, 39**
See also BPFB 2; CA 1-4R; 117; CANR 1,
28, 58; CMW 4; CN 1, 2; CPW; DAM
POP; DLB 87; MSW; MTCW 1, 2;
MTFW 2005; SATA 22; SATA-Obit 44

Mackay, Mary 1855-1924 .... **TCLC 51**
See also CA 118; 177; DLB 34, 156; FANT;
RGEL 2; RHW; SUFW 1

Mackay, Shena 1944- .... **CLC 195**
See also CA 104; CANR 88, 139; DLB 231,
319; MTFW 2005

Mackenzie, Compton (Edward Montague)
1883-1972 .... **CLC 18; TCLC 116**
See also CA 21-22; 37-40R; CAP 2; CN 1;
DLB 34, 100; RGEL 2

Mackenzie, Henry 1745-1831 .... **NCLC 41**
See also DLB 39; RGEL 2

Mackey, Nathaniel 1947- ...... **BLC 2:3; PC 49**
See also CA 153; CANR 114; CP 6, 7; DLB
169

Mackey, Nathaniel Ernest
See Mackey, Nathaniel

MacKinnon, Catharine
See MacKinnon, Catharine A.

MacKinnon, Catharine A. 1946- .... **CLC 181**
See also CA 128; 132; CANR 73, 140, 189;
FW; MTCW 2; MTFW 2005

Mackintosh, Elizabeth
1896(?)-1952 .... **TCLC 14**
See also CA 110; CMW 4; DLB 10, 77;
MSW

Macklin, Charles 1699-1797 .... **LC 132**
See also DLB 89; RGEL 2

MacLaren, James
See Grieve, C. M.

MacLaverty, Bernard 1942- ..... **CLC 31, 243**
See also CA 116; 118; CANR 43, 88, 168;
CN 5, 6, 7; DLB 267; INT CA-118; RGSF
2

Malzberg, Barry N(athaniel) 1939- ... **CLC 7**
See also CA 61-64; CAAS 4; CANR 16;
CMW 4; DLB 8; SFW 4

Mamet, David 1947- .. **CLC 9, 15, 34, 46, 91,
166; DC 4, 24**
See also AAYA 3, 60; AMWS 14; CA 81-
84; CABS 3; CAD; CANR 15, 41, 67, 72,
129, 172; CD 5, 6; DA3; DAM DRAM;
DFS 2, 3, 6, 12, 15; DLB 7; EWL 3;
IDFW 4; MAL 5; MTCW 1, 2; MTFW
2005; RGAL 4

Mamet, David Alan
See Mamet, David

Mamoulian, Rouben (Zachary)
1897-1987 .... **CLC 16**
See also CA 25-28R; 124; CANR 85

Mandelshtam, Osip
See Mandelstam, Osip
See also DLB 295

Mandelstam, Osip 1891(?)-1943(?) .... **PC 14;
TCLC 2, 6, 225**
See Mandelshtam, Osip
See also CA 104; 150; EW 10; EWL 3;
MTCW 2; RGWL 2, 3; TWA

Mandelstam, Osip Emilievich
See Mandelstam, Osip

Mander, (Mary) Jane 1877-1949 ... **TCLC 31**
See also CA 162; RGEL 2

Mandeville, Bernard 1670-1733 .... **LC 82**
See also DLB 101

Mandeville, Sir John fl. 1350- ...... **CMLC 19**
See also DLB 146

Mandiargues, Andre Pieyre de
See Pieyre de Mandiargues, Andre

Mandrake, Ethel Belle
See Thurman, Wallace (Henry)

Mangan, James Clarence
1803-1849 .... **NCLC 27**
See also BRWS 13; RGEL 2

Maniere, J. E.
See Giraudoux, Jean

Mankell, Henning 1948- .... **CLC 292**
See also CA 187; CANR 163, 200

Mankiewicz, Herman (Jacob)
1897-1953 .... **TCLC 85**
See also CA 120; 169; DLB 26; IDFW 3, 4

Manley, (Mary) Delariviere
1672(?)-1724 .... **LC 1, 42**
See also DLB 39, 80; RGEL 2

Mann, Abel
See Creasey, John

Mann, Emily 1952- .... **DC 7**
See also CA 130; CAD; CANR 55; CD 5,
6; CWD; DLB 266

Mann, (Luiz) Heinrich 1871-1950 ... **TCLC 9**
See also CA 106; 164, 181; DLB 66, 118;
EW 8; EWL 3; RGWL 2, 3

Mann, Paul Thomas
See Mann, Thomas

Mann, Thomas 1875-1955 ...... **SSC 5, 80, 82;
TCLC 2, 8, 14, 21, 35, 44, 60, 168, 236;
WLC 4**
See also BPFB 2; CA 104; 128; CANR 133;
CDWLB 2; DA; DA3; DAB; DAC; DAM
MST, NOV; DLB 66, 331; EW 9; EWL 3;
GLL 1; LATS 1:1; LMFS 1; MTCW 1, 2;
MTFW 2005; NFS 17; RGSF 2; RGWL
2, 3; SSFS 4, 9; TWA

Mannheim, Karl 1893-1947 .... **TCLC 65**
See also CA 204

Manning, David
See Faust, Frederick

Manning, Frederic 1882-1935 .... **TCLC 25**
See also CA 124; 216; DLB 260

Manning, Olivia 1915-1980 .... **CLC 5, 19**
See also CA 5-8R; 101; CANR 29; CN 1,
2; EWL 3; FW; MTCW 1; RGEL 2

Mannyng, Robert c. 1264-c.
1340 .... **CMLC 83**
See also DLB 146

Mano, D. Keith 1942- .... **CLC 2, 10**
See also CA 25-28R; CAAS 6; CANR 26,
57; DLB 6

Mansfield, Katherine 1888-1923 ..**SSC 9, 23,
38, 81; TCLC 2, 8, 39, 164; WLC 4**
See also BPFB 2; BRW 7; CA 104; 134;
DA; DA3; DAB; DAC; DAM MST; DLB
162; EWL 3; EXPS; FW; GLL 1; MTCW
2; RGEL 2; RGSF 2; SSFS 2, 8, 10, 11,
29; TEA; WWE 1

Mansfield, Kathleen
See Mansfield, Katherine

Manso, Peter 1940- .... **CLC 39**
See also CA 29-32R; CANR 44, 156

Mantecon, Juan Jimenez
See Jimenez, Juan Ramon

Mantel, Hilary 1952- .... **CLC 144**
See also CA 125; CANR 54, 101, 161; CN
5, 6, 7; DLB 271; RHW

Mantel, Hilary Mary
See Mantel, Hilary

Manton, Peter
See Creasey, John

Man Without a Spleen, A
See Chekhov, Anton

Manzano, Juan Franciso
1797(?)-1854 .... **NCLC 155**

Manzoni, Alessandro 1785-1873 ... **NCLC 29,
98**
See also EW 5; RGWL 2, 3; TWA; WLIT 7

Map, Walter 1140-1209 .... **CMLC 32**

Mapu, Abraham (ben Jekutiel)
1808-1867 .... **NCLC 18**

Mara, Sally
See Queneau, Raymond

Maracle, Lee 1950- .... **NNAL**
See also CA 149

Marat, Jean Paul 1743-1793 .... **LC 10**

Marcel, Gabriel Honore 1889-1973 . **CLC 15**
See also CA 102; 45-48; EWL 3; MTCW 1,
2

March, William
See Campbell, William Edward March

Marchbanks, Samuel
See Davies, Robertson

Marchi, Giacomo
See Bassani, Giorgio

Marcus Aurelius
See Aurelius, Marcus

Marcuse, Herbert 1898-1979 .... **TCLC 207**
See also CA 188; 89-92; DLB 242

Marguerite
See de Navarre, Marguerite

Marguerite d'Angouleme
See de Navarre, Marguerite

Marguerite de Navarre
See de Navarre, Marguerite

Margulies, Donald 1954- .... **CLC 76**
See also AAYA 57; CA 200; CD 6; DFS 13;
DLB 228

Marias, Javier 1951- .... **CLC 239**
See also CA 167; CANR 109, 139; DLB
322; HW 2; MTFW 2005

Marie de France c. 12th cent. - ...... **CMLC 8,
111; PC 22**
See also DLB 208; FW; RGWL 2, 3

Marie de l'Incarnation 1599-1672 ..... **LC 10,
168**

Marier, Captain Victor
See Griffith, D.W.

Mariner, Scott
See Pohl, Frederik

Marinetti, Filippo Tommaso
1876-1944 .... **TCLC 10**
See also CA 107; DLB 114, 264; EW 9;
EWL 3; WLIT 7

Marivaux, Pierre Carlet de Chamblain de
1688-1763 .... **DC 7; LC 4, 123**
See also DLB 314; GFL Beginnings to
1789; RGWL 2, 3; TWA

Markandaya, Kamala 1924-2004 ...... **CLC 8,
38, 290**
See also BYA 13; CA 77-80; 227; CN 1, 2,
3, 4, 5, 6, 7; DLB 323; EWL 3; MTFW
2005; NFS 13

Markfield, Wallace (Arthur)
1926-2002 .... **CLC 8**
See also CA 69-72; 208; CAAS 3; CN 1, 2,
3, 4, 5, 6, 7; DLB 2, 28; DLBY 2002

Markham, Edwin 1852-1940 .... **TCLC 47**
See also CA 160; DLB 54, 186; MAL 5;
RGAL 4

Markham, Robert
See Amis, Kingsley

Marks, J.
See Highwater, Jamake (Mamake)

Marks-Highwater, J.
See Highwater, Jamake (Mamake)

Markson, David M. 1927- .... **CLC 67**
See also AMWS 17; CA 49-52; CANR 1,
91, 158; CN 5, 6

Markson, David Merrill
See Markson, David M.

Marlatt, Daphne (Buckle) 1942- .... **CLC 168**
See also CA 25-28R; CANR 17, 39; CN 6,
7; CP 4, 5, 6, 7; CWP; DLB 60; FW

Marley, Bob
See Marley, Robert Nesta

Marley, Robert Nesta 1945-1981 ...... **CLC 17**
See also CA 107; 103

Marlowe, Christopher 1564-1593 . **DC 1; LC
22, 47, 117; PC 57; WLC 4**
See also BRW 1; BRWR 1; CDBLB Before
1660; DA; DA3; DAB; DAC; DAM
DRAM, MST; DFS 1, 5, 13, 21; DLB 62;
EXPP; LMFS 1; PFS 22; RGEL 2; TEA;
WLIT 3

Marlowe, Stephen 1928-2008 .... **CLC 70**
See also CA 13-16R; 269; CANR 6, 55;
CMW 4; SFW 4

Marmion, Shakerley 1603-1639 .... **LC 89**
See also DLB 58; RGEL 2

Marmontel, Jean-Francois 1723-1799 .. **LC 2**
See also DLB 314

Maron, Monika 1941- .... **CLC 165**
See also CA 201

Marot, Clement c. 1496-1544 .... **LC 133**
See also DLB 327; GFL Beginnings to 1789

Marquand, John P(hillips)
1893-1960 .... **CLC 2, 10**
See also AMW; BPFB 2; CA 85-88; CANR
73; CMW 4; DLB 9, 102; EWL 3; MAL
5; MTCW 2; RGAL 4

Marques, Rene 1919-1979 .. **CLC 96; HLC 2**
See also CA 97-100; 85-88; CANR 78;
DAM MULT; DLB 305; EWL 3; HW 1,
2; LAW; RGSF 2

Marquez, Gabriel Garcia
See Garcia Marquez, Gabriel

Marquez, Gabriel Garcia
See Garcia Marquez, Gabriel

Marquis, Don(ald Robert Perry)
1878-1937 .... **TCLC 7**
See also CA 104; 166; DLB 11, 25; MAL
5; RGAL 4

Marquis de Sade
See Sade, Donatien Alphonse Francois

Marric, J. J.
See Creasey, John

Marryat, Frederick 1792-1848 .... **NCLC 3**
See also DLB 21, 163; RGEL 2; WCH

Marsden, James
See Creasey, John
Marsh, Edith Ngaio
See Marsh, Ngaio
Marsh, Edward 1872-1953 .... **TCLC 99**
Marsh, Ngaio 1895-1982 .... **CLC 7, 53**
See also CA 9-12R; CANR 6, 58; CMW 4;
CN 1, 2, 3; CPW; DAM POP; DLB 77;
MSW; MTCW 1, 2; RGEL 2; TEA
Marshall, Alan
See Westlake, Donald E.
Marshall, Allen
See Westlake, Donald E.
Marshall, Garry 1934- .... **CLC 17**
See also AAYA 3; CA 111; SATA 60
Marshall, Paule 1929- .... **BLC 1:3, 2:3; CLC
27, 72, 253; SSC 3**
See also AFAW 1, 2; AMWS 11; BPFB 2;
BW 2, 3; CA 77-80; CANR 25, 73, 129;
CN 1, 2, 3, 4, 5, 6, 7; DA3; DAM MULT;
DLB 33, 157, 227; EWL 3; LATS 1:2;
MAL 5; MTCW 1, 2; MTFW 2005;
RGAL 4; SSFS 15
Marshallik
See Zangwill, Israel
Marsilius of Inghen c.
1340-1396 .... **CMLC 106**
Marsten, Richard
See Hunter, Evan
Marston, John 1576-1634 ...... **DC 37; LC 33,
172**
See also BRW 2; DAM DRAM; DLB 58,
172; RGEL 2
Martel, Yann 1963- .... **CLC 192**
See also AAYA 67; CA 146; CANR 114;
DLB 326, 334; LNFS 2; MTFW 2005;
NFS 27
Martens, Adolphe-Adhemar
See Ghelderode, Michel de
Martha, Henry
See Harris, Mark
Marti, Jose 1853-1895 ..... **HLC 2; NCLC 63;
PC 76**
See also DAM MULT; DLB 290; HW 2;
LAW; RGWL 2, 3; WLIT 1
Martial c. 40-c. 104 .... **CMLC 35; PC 10**
See also AW 2; CDWLB 1; DLB 211;
RGWL 2, 3
Martin, Ken
See Hubbard, L. Ron
Martin, Richard
See Creasey, John
Martin, Steve 1945- .... **CLC 30, 217**
See also AAYA 53; CA 97-100; CANR 30,
100, 140, 195; DFS 19; MTCW 1; MTFW
2005
Martin, Valerie 1948- .... **CLC 89**
See also BEST 90:2; CA 85-88; CANR 49,
89, 165, 200
Martin, Violet Florence 1862-1915 .. **SSC 56;
TCLC 51**
Martin, Webber
See Silverberg, Robert
Martindale, Patrick Victor
See White, Patrick
Martin du Gard, Roger
1881-1958 .... **TCLC 24**
See also CA 118; CANR 94; DLB 65, 331;
EWL 3; GFL 1789 to the Present; RGWL
2, 3
Martineau, Harriet 1802-1876 ...... **NCLC 26,
137**
See also BRWS 15; DLB 21, 55, 159, 163,
166, 190; FW; RGEL 2; YABC 2
Martines, Julia
See O'Faolain, Julia
Martinez, Enrique Gonzalez
See Gonzalez Martinez, Enrique

Martinez, Jacinto Benavente y
See Benavente, Jacinto
Martinez de la Rosa, Francisco de Paula
1787-1862 .... **NCLC 102**
See also TWA
Martinez Ruiz, Jose 1873-1967 .... **CLC 11**
See also CA 93-96; DLB 322; EW 3; EWL
3; HW 1
Martinez Sierra, Gregorio
See Martinez Sierra, Maria
Martinez Sierra, Gregorio
1881-1947 .... **TCLC 6**
See also CA 115; EWL 3
Martinez Sierra, Maria 1874-1974 .. **TCLC 6**
See also CA 250; 115; EWL 3
Martinsen, Martin
See Follett, Ken
Martinson, Harry (Edmund)
1904-1978 .... **CLC 14**
See also CA 77-80; CANR 34, 130; DLB
259, 331; EWL 3
Marti y Perez, Jose Julian
See Marti, Jose
Martyn, Edward 1859-1923 .... **TCLC 131**
See also CA 179; DLB 10; RGEL 2
Marut, Ret
See Traven, B.
Marut, Robert
See Traven, B.
Marvell, Andrew 1621-1678 ... **LC 4, 43, 179;
PC 10, 86; WLC 4**
See also BRW 2; BRWR 2; CDBLB 1660-
1789; DA; DAB; DAC; DAM MST,
POET; DLB 131; EXPP; PFS 5; RGEL 2;
TEA; WP
Marx, Karl 1818-1883 .... **NCLC 17, 114**
See also DLB 129; LATS 1:1; TWA
Marx, Karl Heinrich
See Marx, Karl
Masaoka, Shiki -1902
See Masaoka, Tsunenori
Masaoka, Tsunenori 1867-1902 ..... **TCLC 18**
See also CA 117; 191; EWL 3; RGWL 3;
TWA
Masaoka Shiki
See Masaoka, Tsunenori
Masefield, John (Edward)
1878-1967 .... **CLC 11, 47; PC 78**
See also CA 19-20; 25-28R; CANR 33;
CAP 2; CDBLB 1890-1914; DAM POET;
DLB 10, 19, 153, 160; EWL 3; EXPP;
FANT; MTCW 1, 2; PFS 5; RGEL 2;
SATA 19
Maso, Carole 1955(?)- .... **CLC 44**
See also CA 170; CANR 148; CN 7; GLL
2; RGAL 4
Mason, Bobbie Ann 1940- ... **CLC 28, 43, 82,
154; SSC 4, 101**
See also AAYA 5, 42; AMWS 8; BPFB 2;
CA 53-56; CANR 11, 31, 58, 83, 125,
169; CDALBS; CN 5, 6, 7; CSW; DA3;
DLB 173; DLBY 1987; EWL 3; EXPS;
INT CANR-31; MAL 5; MTCW 1, 2;
MTFW 2005; NFS 4; RGAL 4; RGSF 2;
SSFS 3, 8, 20; TCLE 1:2; YAW
Mason, Ernst
See Pohl, Frederik
Mason, Hunni B.
See Sternheim, (William Adolf) Carl
Mason, Lee W.
See Malzberg, Barry N(athaniel)
Mason, Nick 1945- .... **CLC 35**
Mason, Tally
See Derleth, August (William)
Mass, Anna CLC 59
Mass, William
See Gibson, William
Massinger, Philip 1583-1640 .. **DC 39; LC 70**
See also BRWS 11; DLB 58; RGEL 2

Master Lao
See Lao Tzu
Masters, Edgar Lee 1868-1950 ...... **PC 1, 36;
TCLC 2, 25; WLCS**
See also AMWS 1; CA 104; 133; CDALB
1865-1917; DA; DAC; DAM MST,
POET; DLB 54; EWL 3; EXPP; MAL 5;
MTCW 1, 2; MTFW 2005; RGAL 4;
TUS; WP
Masters, Hilary 1928- .... **CLC 48**
See also CA 25-28R; 217; CAAE 217;
CANR 13, 47, 97, 171; CN 6, 7; DLB
244
Masters, Hilary Thomas
See Masters, Hilary
Mastrosimone, William 1947- .... **CLC 36**
See also CA 186; CAD; CD 5, 6
Mathe, Albert
See Camus, Albert
Mather, Cotton 1663-1728 .... **LC 38**
See also AMWS 2; CDALB 1640-1865;
DLB 24, 30, 140; RGAL 4; TUS
Mather, Increase 1639-1723 .... **LC 38, 161**
See also DLB 24
Mathers, Marshall
See Eminem
Mathers, Marshall Bruce
See Eminem
Matheson, Richard 1926- .... **CLC 37, 267**
See also AAYA 31; CA 97-100; CANR 88,
99; DLB 8, 44; HGG; INT CA-97-100;
SCFW 1, 2; SFW 4; SUFW 2
Matheson, Richard Burton
See Matheson, Richard
Mathews, Harry 1930- .... **CLC 6, 52**
See also CA 21-24R; CAAS 6; CANR 18,
40, 98, 160; CN 5, 6, 7
Mathews, John Joseph 1894-1979 .. **CLC 84;
NNAL**
See also CA 19-20; 142; CANR 45; CAP 2;
DAM MULT; DLB 175; TCWW 1, 2
Mathias, Roland 1915-2007 .... **CLC 45**
See also CA 97-100; 263; CANR 19, 41;
CP 1, 2, 3, 4, 5, 6, 7; DLB 27
Mathias, Roland Glyn
See Mathias, Roland
Matsuo Basho 1644(?)-1694 ...... **LC 62; PC 3**
See also DAM POET; PFS 2, 7, 18; RGWL
2, 3; WP
Mattheson, Rodney
See Creasey, John
Matthew, James
See Barrie, J. M.
Matthew of Vendome c. 1130-c.
1200 .... **CMLC 99**
See also DLB 208
Matthews, (James) Brander
1852-1929 .... **TCLC 95**
See also CA 181; DLB 71, 78; DLBD 13
Matthews, Greg 1949- .... **CLC 45**
See also CA 135
Matthews, William (Procter III)
1942-1997 .... **CLC 40**
See also AMWS 9; CA 29-32R; 162; CAAS
18; CANR 12, 57; CP 2, 3, 4, 5, 6; DLB
5
Matthias, John (Edward) 1941- .... **CLC 9**
See also CA 33-36R; CANR 56; CP 4, 5, 6,
7
Matthiessen, F(rancis) O(tto)
1902-1950 .... **TCLC 100**
See also CA 185; DLB 63; MAL 5
Matthiessen, Peter 1927- ... **CLC 5, 7, 11, 32,
64, 245**
See also AAYA 6, 40; AMWS 5; ANW;
BEST 90:4; BPFB 2; CA 9-12R; CANR
21, 50, 73, 100, 138; CN 1, 2, 3, 4, 5, 6,
7; DA3; DAM NOV; DLB 6, 173, 275;
MAL 5; MTCW 1, 2; MTFW 2005; SATA
27

Author Index

266; EWL 3; LAIT 1, 4; LATS 1:2; MAL
5; MTCW 1, 2; MTFW 2005; RGAL 4;
RGHL; TUS; WYAS 1

Miller, Frank 1957- .... **CLC 278**
See also AAYA 45; CA 224

Miller, Henry (Valentine)
1891-1980 .... **CLC 1, 2, 4, 9, 14, 43, 84;
TCLC 213; WLC 4**
See also AMW; BPFB 2; CA 9-12R; 97-
100; CANR 33, 64; CDALB 1929-1941;
CN 1, 2; DA; DA3; DAB; DAC; DAM
MST, NOV; DLB 4, 9; DLBY 1980; EWL
3; MAL 5; MTCW 1, 2; MTFW 2005;
RGAL 4; TUS

Miller, Hugh 1802-1856 .... **NCLC 143**
See also DLB 190

Miller, Jason 1939(?)-2001 .... **CLC 2**
See also AITN 1; CA 73-76; 197; CAD;
CANR 130; DFS 12; DLB 7

Miller, Sue 1943- .... **CLC 44**
See also AMWS 12; BEST 90:3; CA 139;
CANR 59, 91, 128, 194; DA3; DAM
POP; DLB 143

Miller, Walter M(ichael, Jr.)
1923-1996 .... **CLC 4, 30**
See also BPFB 2; CA 85-88; CANR 108;
DLB 8; SCFW 1, 2; SFW 4

Millett, Kate 1934- .... **CLC 67**
See also AITN 1; CA 73-76; CANR 32, 53,
76, 110; DA3; DLB 246; FW; GLL 1;
MTCW 1, 2; MTFW 2005

Millhauser, Steven 1943- ... **CLC 21, 54, 109;
SSC 57**
See also AAYA 76; CA 110; 111; CANR
63, 114, 133, 189; CN 6, 7; DA3; DLB 2,
350; FANT; INT CA-111; MAL 5; MTCW
2; MTFW 2005

Millhauser, Steven Lewis
See Millhauser, Steven

Millin, Sarah Gertrude 1889-1968 ... **CLC 49**
See also CA 102; 93-96; DLB 225; EWL 3

Milne, A. A. 1882-1956 .... **TCLC 6, 88**
See also BRWS 5; CA 104; 133; CLR 1,
26, 108; CMW 4; CWRI 5; DA3; DAB;
DAC; DAM MST; DLB 10, 77, 100, 160,
352; FANT; MAICYA 1, 2; MTCW 1, 2;
MTFW 2005; RGEL 2; SATA 100; WCH;
YABC 1

Milne, Alan Alexander
See Milne, A. A.

Milner, Ron(ald) 1938-2004 .. **BLC 1:3; CLC
56**
See also AITN 1; BW 1; CA 73-76; 230;
CAD; CANR 24, 81; CD 5, 6; DAM
MULT; DLB 38; MAL 5; MTCW 1

Milnes, Richard Monckton
1809-1885 .... **NCLC 61**
See also DLB 32, 184

Milosz, Czeslaw 1911-2004 .... **CLC 5, 11, 22,
31, 56, 82, 253; PC 8; WLCS**
See also AAYA 62; CA 81-84; 230; CANR
23, 51, 91, 126; CDWLB 4; CWW 2;
DA3; DAM MST, POET; DLB 215, 331;
EW 13; EWL 3; MTCW 1, 2; MTFW
2005; PFS 16, 29, 35; RGHL; RGWL 2,
3

Milton, John 1608-1674 ..... **LC 9, 43, 92; PC
19, 29; WLC 4**
See also AAYA 65; BRW 2; BRWR 2; CD-
BLB 1660-1789; DA; DA3; DAB; DAC;
DAM MST, POET; DLB 131, 151, 281;
EFS 1; EXPP; LAIT 1; PAB; PFS 3, 17;
RGEL 2; TEA; WLIT 3; WP

Min, Anchee 1957- .... **CLC 86, 291**
See also CA 146; CANR 94, 137; MTFW
2005

Minehaha, Cornelius
See Wedekind, Frank

Miner, Valerie 1947- .... **CLC 40**
See also CA 97-100; CANR 59, 177; FW;
GLL 2

Minimo, Duca
See D'Annunzio, Gabriele

Minot, Susan (Anderson) 1956- ...... **CLC 44,
159**
See also AMWS 6; CA 134; CANR 118;
CN 6, 7

Minus, Ed 1938- .... **CLC 39**
See also CA 185

Mirabai 1498(?)-1550(?) .... **LC 143; PC 48**
See also PFS 24

Miranda, Javier
See Bioy Casares, Adolfo

Mirbeau, Octave 1848-1917 .... **TCLC 55**
See also CA 216; DLB 123, 192; GFL 1789
to the Present

Mirikitani, Janice 1942- .... **AAL**
See also CA 211; DLB 312; RGAL 4

Mirk, John (?)-c. 1414 .... **LC 105**
See also DLB 146

Miro (Ferrer), Gabriel (Francisco Victor)
1879-1930 .... **TCLC 5**
See also CA 104; 185; DLB 322; EWL 3

Misharin, Alexandr **CLC 59**

Mishima, Yukio
See Hiraoka, Kimitake

Mishima Yukio
See Hiraoka, Kimitake

Miss C. L. F.
See Grimke, Charlotte L. Forten

Mister X
See Hoch, Edward D.

Mistral, Frederic 1830-1914 .... **TCLC 51**
See also CA 122; 213; DLB 331; GFL 1789
to the Present

Mistral, Gabriela 1899-1957 .... **HLC 2; PC
32; TCLC 2**
See also BW 2; CA 104; 131; CANR 81;
DAM MULT; DLB 283, 331; DNFS;
EWL 3; HW 1, 2; LAW; MTCW 1, 2;
MTFW 2005; RGWL 2, 3; WP

Mistry, Rohinton 1952- ... **CLC 71, 196, 281;
SSC 73**
See also BRWS 10; CA 141; CANR 86,
114; CCA 1; CN 6, 7; DAC; DLB 334;
SSFS 6

Mitchell, Clyde
See Ellison, Harlan; Silverberg, Robert

Mitchell, Emerson Blackhorse Barney
1945- .... **NNAL**
See also CA 45-48

Mitchell, James Leslie 1901-1935 ˙... **TCLC 4**
See also BRWS 14; CA 104; 188; DLB 15;
RGEL 2

Mitchell, Joni 1943- .... **CLC 12**
See also CA 112; CCA 1

Mitchell, Joseph (Quincy)
1908-1996 .... **CLC 98**
See also CA 77-80; 152; CANR 69; CN 1,
2, 3, 4, 5, 6; CSW; DLB 185; DLBY 1996

Mitchell, Margaret 1900-1949 .... **TCLC 11,
170**
See also AAYA 23; BPFB 2; BYA 1; CA
109; 125; CANR 55, 94; CDALBS; DA3;
DAM NOV, POP; DLB 9; LAIT 2; MAL
5; MTCW 1, 2; MTFW 2005; NFS 9;
RGAL 4; RHW; TUS; WYAS 1; YAW

Mitchell, Margaret Munnerlyn
See Mitchell, Margaret

Mitchell, Peggy
See Mitchell, Margaret

Mitchell, S(ilas) Weir 1829-1914 .... **TCLC 36**
See also CA 165; DLB 202; RGAL 4

Mitchell, W(illiam) O(rmond)
1914-1998 .... **CLC 25**
See also CA 77-80; 165; CANR 15, 43; CN
1, 2, 3, 4, 5, 6; DAC; DAM MST; DLB
88; TCLE 1:2

Mitchell, William (Lendrum)
1879-1936 .... **TCLC 81**
See also CA 213

Mitford, Mary Russell 1787-1855 ... **NCLC 4**
See also DLB 110, 116; RGEL 2

Mitford, Nancy 1904-1973 .... **CLC 44**
See also BRWS 10; CA 9-12R; CN 1; DLB
191; RGEL 2

Miyamoto, (Chujo) Yuriko
1899-1951 .... **TCLC 37**
See also CA 170, 174; DLB 180

Miyamoto Yuriko
See Miyamoto, (Chujo) Yuriko

Miyazawa, Kenji 1896-1933 .... **TCLC 76**
See also CA 157; EWL 3; RGWL 3

Miyazawa Kenji
See Miyazawa, Kenji

Mizoguchi, Kenji 1898-1956 .... **TCLC 72**
See also CA 167

Mo, Timothy (Peter) 1950- .... **CLC 46, 134**
See also CA 117; CANR 128; CN 5, 6, 7;
DLB 194; MTCW 1; WLIT 4; WWE 1

Mo, Yan
See Yan, Mo

Moberg, Carl Arthur
See Moberg, Vilhelm

Moberg, Vilhelm 1898-1973 .... **TCLC 224**
See also CA 97-100; 45-48; CANR 135;
DLB 259; EW 11; EWL 3

Modarressi, Taghi (M.) 1931-1997 ... **CLC 44**
See also CA 121; 134; INT CA-134

Modiano, Patrick (Jean) 1945- .... **CLC 18,
218**
See also CA 85-88; CANR 17, 40, 115;
CWW 2; DLB 83, 299; EWL 3; RGHL

Mofolo, Thomas 1875(?)-1948 .... **BLC 1:3;
TCLC 22**
See also AFW; CA 121; 153; CANR 83;
DAM MULT; DLB 225; EWL 3; MTCW
2; MTFW 2005; WLIT 2

Mofolo, Thomas Mokopu
See Mofolo, Thomas

Mohr, Nicholasa 1938- .... **CLC 12; HLC 2**
See also AAYA 8, 46; CA 49-52; CANR 1,
32, 64; CLR 22; DAM MULT; DLB 145;
HW 1, 2; JRDA; LAIT 5; LLW; MAICYA
2; MAICYAS 1; RGAL 4; SAAS 8; SATA
8, 97; SATA-Essay 113; WYA; YAW

Moi, Toril 1953- .... **CLC 172**
See also CA 154; CANR 102; FW

Mojtabai, A(nn) G(race) 1938- ..... **CLC 5, 9,
15, 29**
See also CA 85-88; CANR 88

Moliere 1622-1673 ..... **DC 13; LC 10, 28, 64,
125, 127; WLC 4**
See also DA; DA3; DAB; DAC; DAM
DRAM, MST; DFS 13, 18, 20; DLB 268;
EW 3; GFL Beginnings to 1789; LATS
1:1; RGWL 2, 3; TWA

Molin, Charles
See Mayne, William (James Carter)

Molina, Antonio Munoz 1956- .... **CLC 289**
See also DLB 322

Molnar, Ferenc 1878-1952 .... **TCLC 20**
See also CA 109; 153; CANR 83; CDWLB
4; DAM DRAM; DLB 215; EWL 3;
RGWL 2, 3

Momaday, N. Scott 1934- ...... **CLC 2, 19, 85,
95, 160; NNAL; PC 25; WLCS**
See also AAYA 11, 64; AMWS 4; ANW;
BPFB 2; BYA 12; CA 25-28R; CANR 14,
34, 68, 134; CDALBS; CN 2, 3, 4, 5, 6,
7; CPW; DA; DA3; DAB; DAC; DAM
MST, MULT, NOV, POP; DLB 143, 175,

Munro, Hector H.
See Saki

Munro, Hector Hugh
See Saki

Murakami, Haruki 1949- .... **CLC 150, 274**
See also CA 165; CANR 102, 146; CWW 2; DLB 182; EWL 3; LNFS 2; MJW; RGWL 3; SFW 4; SSFS 23

Murakami Haruki
See Murakami, Haruki

Murasaki, Lady
See Murasaki Shikibu

Murasaki Shikibu 978(?)-1026(?) .. **CMLC 1, 79**
See also EFS 2; LATS 1:1; RGWL 2, 3

Murdoch, Iris 1919-1999 .. **CLC 1, 2, 3, 4, 6, 8, 11, 15, 22, 31, 51; TCLC 171**
See also BRWS 1; CA 13-16R; 179; CANR 8, 43, 68, 103, 142; CBD; CDBLB 1960 to Present; CN 1, 2, 3, 4, 5, 6; CWD; DA3; DAB; DAC; DAM MST, NOV; DLB 14, 194, 233, 326; EWL 3; INT CANR-8; MTCW 1, 2; MTFW 2005; NFS 18; RGEL 2; TCLE 1:2; TEA; WLIT 4

Murdoch, Jean Iris
See Murdoch, Iris

Murfree, Mary Noailles 1850-1922 .. **SSC 22; TCLC 135**
See also CA 122; 176; DLB 12, 74; RGAL 4

Murglie
See Murnau, F.W.

Murnau, Friedrich Wilhelm
See Murnau, F.W.

Murnau, F.W. 1888-1931 .... **TCLC 53**
See also CA 112

Murphy, Richard 1927- .... **CLC 41**
See also BRWS 5; CA 29-32R; CP 1, 2, 3, 4, 5, 6, 7; DLB 40; EWL 3

Murphy, Sylvia 1937- .... **CLC 34**
See also CA 121

Murphy, Thomas 1935- .... **CLC 51**
See also CA 101; DLB 310

Murphy, Thomas Bernard
See Murphy, Thomas

Murphy, Tom
See Murphy, Thomas

Murray, Albert 1916- .... **BLC 2:3; CLC 73**
See also BW 2; CA 49-52; CANR 26, 52, 78, 160; CN 7; CSW; DLB 38; MTFW 2005

Murray, Albert L.
See Murray, Albert

Murray, Diane Lain Johnson
See Johnson, Diane

Murray, James Augustus Henry 1837-1915 .... **TCLC 117**

Murray, Judith Sargent 1751-1820 .... **NCLC 63**
See also DLB 37, 200

Murray, Les 1938- .... **CLC 40**
See also BRWS 7; CA 21-24R; CANR 11, 27, 56, 103, 199; CP 1, 2, 3, 4, 5, 6, 7; DAM POET; DLB 289; DLBY 2001; EWL 3; RGEL 2

Murray, Leslie Allan
See Murray, Les

Murry, J. Middleton
See Murry, John Middleton

Murry, John Middleton 1889-1957 .... **TCLC 16**
See also CA 118; 217; DLB 149

Musgrave, Susan 1951- .... **CLC 13, 54**
See also CA 69-72; CANR 45, 84, 181; CCA 1; CP 2, 3, 4, 5, 6, 7; CWP

Musil, Robert (Edler von) 1880-1942 ... **SSC 18; TCLC 12, 68, 213**
See also CA 109; CANR 55, 84; CDWLB 2; DLB 81, 124; EW 9; EWL 3; MTCW 2; RGSF 2; RGWL 2, 3

Muske, Carol
See Muske-Dukes, Carol

Muske, Carol Anne
See Muske-Dukes, Carol

Muske-Dukes, Carol 1945- .... **CLC 90**
See also CA 65-68, 203; CAAE 203; CANR 32, 70, 181; CWP; PFS 24

Muske-Dukes, Carol Ann
See Muske-Dukes, Carol

Muske-Dukes, Carol Anne
See Muske-Dukes, Carol

Musset, Alfred de 1810-1857 . **DC 27; NCLC 7, 150**
See also DLB 192, 217; EW 6; GFL 1789 to the Present; RGWL 2, 3; TWA

Musset, Louis Charles Alfred de
See Musset, Alfred de

Mussolini, Benito (Amilcare Andrea) 1883-1945 .... **TCLC 96**
See also CA 116

Mutanabbi, Al-
See al-Mutanabbi, Ahmad ibn al-Husayn Abu al-Tayyib al-Jufi al-Kindi

Mutis, Alvaro 1923- .... **CLC 283**
See also CA 149; CANR 118; DLB 283; EWL 3; HW 1; LAWS 1

My Brother's Brother
See Chekhov, Anton

Myers, L(eopold) H(amilton) 1881-1944 .... **TCLC 59**
See also CA 157; DLB 15; EWL 3; RGEL 2

Myers, Walter Dean 1937- ...... **BLC 1:3, 2:3; CLC 35**
See also AAYA 4, 23; BW 2; BYA 6, 8, 11; CA 33-36R; CANR 20, 42, 67, 108, 184; CLR 4, 16, 35, 110; DAM MULT, NOV; DLB 33; INT CANR-20; JRDA; LAIT 5; LNFS 1; MAICYA 1, 2; MAICYAS 1; MTCW 2; MTFW 2005; NFS 30, 33; SAAS 2; SATA 41, 71, 109, 157, 193; SATA-Brief 27; SSFS 31; WYA; YAW

Myers, Walter M.
See Myers, Walter Dean

Myles, Symon
See Follett, Ken

Nabokov, Vladimir 1899-1977 ... **CLC 1, 2, 3, 6, 8, 11, 15, 23, 44, 46, 64; SSC 11, 86; TCLC 108, 189; WLC 4**
See also AAYA 45; AMW; AMWC 1; AMWR 1; BPFB 2; CA 5-8R; 69-72; CANR 20, 102; CDALB 1941-1968; CN 1, 2; CP 2; DA; DA3; DAB; DAC; DAM MST, NOV; DLB 2, 244, 278, 317; DLBD 3; DLBY 1980, 1991; EWL 3; EXPS; LATS 1:2; MAL 5; MTCW 1, 2; MTFW 2005; NCFS 4; NFS 9; RGAL 4; RGSF 2; SSFS 6, 15; TUS

Nabokov, Vladimir Vladimirovich
See Nabokov, Vladimir

Naevius c. 265B.C.-201B.C. .... **CMLC 37**
See also DLB 211

Nagai, Kafu 1879-1959 .... **TCLC 51**
See also CA 117; 276; DLB 180; EWL 3; MJW

Nagai, Sokichi
See Nagai, Kafu

Nagai Kafu
See Nagai, Kafu

na gCopaleen, Myles
See O Nuallain, Brian

na Gopaleen, Myles
See O Nuallain, Brian

Nagy, Laszlo 1925-1978 .... **CLC 7**
See also CA 129; 112

Naidu, Sarojini 1879-1949 .... **TCLC 80**
See also EWL 3; RGEL 2

Naipaul, Shiva 1945-1985 .... **CLC 32, 39; TCLC 153**
See also CA 110; 112; 116; CANR 33; CN 2, 3; DA3; DAM NOV; DLB 157; DLBY 1985; EWL 3; MTCW 1, 2; MTFW 2005

Naipaul, Shivadhar Srinivasa
See Naipaul, Shiva

Naipaul, V. S. 1932- . **CLC 4, 7, 9, 13, 18, 37, 105, 199; SSC 38, 121**
See also BPFB 2; BRWS 1; CA 1-4R; CANR 1, 33, 51, 91, 126, 191; CDBLB 1960 to Present; CDWLB 3; CN 1, 2, 3, 4, 5, 6, 7; DA3; DAB; DAC; DAM MST, NOV; DLB 125, 204, 207, 326, 331; DLBY 1985, 2001; EWL 3; LATS 1:2; MTCW 1, 2; MTFW 2005; RGEL 2; RGSF 2; SSFS 29; TWA; WLIT 4; WWE 1

Naipaul, Vidiadhar Surajprasad
See Naipaul, V. S.

Nair, Kamala
See Das, Kamala

Nakos, Lilika 1903-1989 .... **CLC 29**
See also CA 217

Nalapat, Kamala
See Das, Kamala

Napoleon
See Yamamoto, Hisaye

Narayan, R. K. 1906-2001 ..... **CLC 7, 28, 47, 121, 211; SSC 25**
See also BPFB 2; CA 81-84; 196; CANR 33, 61, 112; CN 1, 2, 3, 4, 5, 6; DA3; DAM NOV; DLB 323; DNFS 1; EWL 3; MTCW 1, 2; MTFW 2005; RGEL 2; RGSF 2; SATA 62; SSFS 5, 29; WWE 1

Narayan, Rasipuram Krishnaswami
See Narayan, R. K.

Nash, Frediric Ogden
See Nash, Ogden

Nash, Ogden 1902-1971 ...... **CLC 23; PC 21; TCLC 109**
See also CA 13-14; 29-32R; CANR 34, 61, 185; CAP 1; CP 1; DAM POET; DLB 11; MAICYA 1, 2; MAL 5; MTCW 1, 2; PFS 31; RGAL 4; SATA 2, 46; WP

Nashe, Thomas 1567-1601(?) . **LC 41, 89; PC 82**
See also DLB 167; RGEL 2

Nathan, Daniel
See Dannay, Frederic

Nathan, George Jean 1882-1958 .... **TCLC 18**
See also CA 114; 169; DLB 137; MAL 5

Natsume, Kinnosuke
See Natsume, Soseki

Natsume, Soseki 1867-1916 .... **TCLC 2, 10**
See also CA 104; 195; DLB 180; EWL 3; MJW; RGWL 2, 3; TWA

Natsume Soseki
See Natsume, Soseki

Natti, Lee 1919- .... **CLC 17**
See also CA 5-8R; CANR 2; CWRI 5; SAAS 3; SATA 1, 67

Natti, Mary Lee
See Natti, Lee

Navarre, Marguerite de
See de Navarre, Marguerite

Naylor, Gloria 1950- . **BLC 1:3; CLC 28, 52, 156, 261; WLCS**
See also AAYA 6, 39; AFAW 1, 2; AMWS 8; BW 2, 3; CA 107; CANR 27, 51, 74, 130; CN 4, 5, 6, 7; CPW; DA; DA3; DAC; DAM MST, MULT, NOV, POP; DLB 173; EWL 3; FW; MAL 5; MTCW 1, 2; MTFW 2005; NFS 4, 7; RGAL 4; TCLE 1:2; TUS

Osborne, Lawrence 1958- .... **CLC 50**
  See also CA 189; CANR 152
Osbourne, Lloyd 1868-1947 .... **TCLC 93**
Osceola
  See Blixen, Karen
Osgood, Frances Sargent
  1811-1850 .... **NCLC 141**
  See also DLB 250
Oshima, Nagisa 1932- .... **CLC 20**
  See also CA 116; 121; CANR 78
Oskison, John Milton
  1874-1947 .... **NNAL; TCLC 35**
  See also CA 144; CANR 84; DAM MULT;
  DLB 175
Ossoli, Sarah Margaret
  See Fuller, Margaret
Ossoli, Sarah Margaret Fuller
  See Fuller, Margaret
Ostriker, Alicia 1937- .... **CLC 132**
  See also CA 25-28R; CAAS 24; CANR 10,
  30, 62, 99, 167; CWP; DLB 120; EXPP;
  PFS 19, 26
Ostriker, Alicia Suskin
  See Ostriker, Alicia
Ostrovsky, Aleksandr Nikolaevich
  See Ostrovsky, Alexander
Ostrovsky, Alexander 1823-1886 .. **NCLC 30,**
  57
  See also DLB 277
Osundare, Niyi 1947- .... **BLC 2:3**
  See also AFW; BW 3; CA 176; CDWLB 3;
  CP 7; DLB 157
Otero, Blas de 1916-1979 .... **CLC 11**
  See also CA 89-92; DLB 134; EWL 3
O'Trigger, Sir Lucius
  See Horne, Richard Henry Hengist
Otto, Rudolf 1869-1937 .... **TCLC 85**
Otto, Whitney 1955- .... **CLC 70**
  See also CA 140; CANR 120
Otway, Thomas 1652-1685 .. **DC 24; LC 106,**
  170
  See also DAM DRAM; DLB 80; RGEL 2
Ouida
  See De La Ramee, Marie Louise
Ouologuem, Yambo 1940- .... **CLC 146**
  See also CA 111; 176
Ousmane, Sembene 1923-2007 .... **BLC 1:3,**
  2:3; CLC 66
  See also AFW; BW 1, 3; CA 117; 125; 261;
  CANR 81; CWW 2; EWL 3; MTCW 1;
  WLIT 2
Ovid 43B.C.-17 .... **CMLC 7, 108; PC 2**
  See also AW 2; CDWLB 1; DA3; DAM
  POET; DLB 211; PFS 22; RGWL 2, 3;
  WLIT 8; WP
Owen, Hugh
  See Faust, Frederick
Owen, Wilfred (Edward Salter)
  1893-1918 ..... **PC 19, 102; TCLC 5, 27;**
  WLC 4
  See also BRW 6; CA 104; 141; CDBLB
  1914-1945; DA; DAB; DAC; DAM MST;
  POET; DLB 20; EWL 3; EXPP; MTCW
  2; MTFW 2005; PFS 10; RGEL 2; WLIT
  4
Owens, Louis (Dean) 1948-2002 .... **NNAL**
  See also CA 137; 179; 207; CAAE 179;
  CAAS 24; CANR 71
Owens, Rochelle 1936- .... **CLC 8**
  See also CA 17-20R; CAAS 2; CAD;
  CANR 39; CD 5, 6; CP 1, 2, 3, 4, 5, 6, 7;
  CWD; CWP
Oz, Amos 1939- ...... **CLC 5, 8, 11, 27, 33, 54;**
  SSC 66
  See also CA 53-56; CANR 27, 47, 65, 113,
  138, 175; CWW 2; DAM NOV; EWL 3;
  MTCW 1, 2; MTFW 2005; RGHL; RGSF
  2; RGWL 3; WLIT 6

Ozick, Cynthia 1928- . **CLC 3, 7, 28, 62, 155,**
  262; SSC 15, 60, 123
  See also AMWS 5; BEST 90:1; CA 17-20R;
  CANR 23, 58, 116, 160, 187; CN 3, 4, 5,
  6, 7; CPW; DA3; DAM NOV, POP; DLB
  28, 152, 299; DLBY 1982; EWL 3; EXPS;
  INT CANR-23; MAL 5; MTCW 1, 2;
  MTFW 2005; RGAL 4; RGHL; RGSF 2;
  SSFS 3, 12, 22
Ozu, Yasujiro 1903-1963 .... **CLC 16**
  See also CA 112
Pabst, G. W. 1885-1967 .... **TCLC 127**
Pacheco, C.
  See Pessoa, Fernando
Pacheco, Jose Emilio 1939- .... **HLC 2**
  See also CA 111; 131; CANR 65; CWW 2;
  DAM MULT; DLB 290; EWL 3; HW 1,
  2; RGSF 2
Pa Chin
  See Jin, Ba
Pack, Robert 1929- .... **CLC 13**
  See also CA 1-4R; CANR 3, 44, 82; CP 1,
  2, 3, 4, 5, 6, 7; DLB 5; SATA 118
Packer, Vin
  See Meaker, Marijane
Padgett, Lewis
  See Kuttner, Henry
Padilla (Lorenzo), Heberto
  1932-2000 .... **CLC 38**
  See also AITN 1; CA 123; 131; 189; CWW
  2; EWL 3; HW 1
Paerdurabo, Frater
  See Crowley, Edward Alexander
Page, James Patrick 1944- .... **CLC 12**
  See also CA 204
Page, Jimmy 1944-
  See Page, James Patrick
Page, Louise 1955- .... **CLC 40**
  See also CA 140; CANR 76; CBD; CD 5,
  6; CWD; DLB 233
Page, Patricia Kathleen
  See Page, P.K.
Page, P.K. 1916-2010 .... **CLC 7, 18; PC 12**
  See also CA 53-56; CANR 4, 22, 65; CCA
  1; CP 1, 2, 3, 4, 5, 6, 7; DAC; DAM MST;
  DLB 68; MTCW 1; RGEL 2
Page, Stanton
  See Fuller, Henry Blake
Page, Thomas Nelson 1853-1922 .... **SSC 23**
  See also CA 118; 177; DLB 12, 78; DLBD
  13; RGAL 4
Pagels, Elaine
  See Pagels, Elaine Hiesey
Pagels, Elaine Hiesey 1943- .... **CLC 104**
  See also CA 45-48; CANR 2, 24, 51, 151;
  FW; NCFS 4
Paget, Violet 1856-1935 .. **SSC 33, 98; TCLC**
  5
  See also CA 104; 166; DLB 57, 153, 156,
  174, 178; GLL 1; HGG; SUFW 1
Paget-Lowe, Henry
  See Lovecraft, H. P.
Paglia, Camille 1947- .... **CLC 68**
  See also CA 140; CANR 72, 139; CPW;
  FW; GLL 2; MTCW 2; MTFW 2005
Pagnol, Marcel (Paul)
  1895-1974 .... **TCLC 208**
  See also CA 128; 49-52; DLB 321; EWL 3;
  GFL 1789 to the Present; MTCW 1;
  RGWL 2, 3
Paige, Richard
  See Koontz, Dean
Paine, Thomas 1737-1809 .... **NCLC 62**
  See also AMWS 1; CDALB 1640-1865;
  DLB 31, 43, 73, 158; LAIT 1; RGAL 4;
  RGEL 2; TUS
Pakenham, Antonia
  See Fraser, Antonia

Palamas, Costis
  See Palamas, Kostes
Palamas, Kostes 1859-1943 .... **TCLC 5**
  See also CA 105; 190; EWL 3; RGWL 2, 3
Palamas, Kostis
  See Palamas, Kostes
Palazzeschi, Aldo 1885-1974 .... **CLC 11**
  See also CA 89-92; 53-56; DLB 114, 264;
  EWL 3
Pales Matos, Luis 1898-1959 .... **HLCS 2**
  See Pales Matos, Luis
  See also DLB 290; HW 1; LAW
Paley, Grace 1922-2007 ... **CLC 4, 6, 37, 140,**
  272; SSC 8
  See also AMWS 6; CA 25-28R; 263; CANR
  13, 46, 74, 118; CN 2, 3, 4, 5, 6, 7; CPW;
  DA3; DAM POP; DLB 28, 218; EWL 3;
  EXPS; FW; INT CANR-13; MAL 5;
  MBL; MTCW 1, 2; MTFW 2005; RGAL
  4; RGSF 2; SSFS 3, 20, 27
Paley, Grace Goodside
  See Paley, Grace
Palin, Michael 1943- .... **CLC 21**
  See also CA 107; CANR 35, 109, 179; DLB
  352; SATA 67
Palin, Michael Edward
  See Palin, Michael
Palliser, Charles 1947- .... **CLC 65**
  See also CA 136; CANR 76; CN 5, 6, 7
Palma, Ricardo 1833-1919 .... **TCLC 29**
  See also CA 168; LAW
Pamuk, Orhan 1952- .... **CLC 185, 288**
  See also AAYA 82; CA 142; CANR 75, 127,
  172; CWW 2; NFS 27; WLIT 6
Pancake, Breece Dexter 1952-1979 . **CLC 29;**
  SSC 61
  See also CA 123; 109; DLB 130
Pancake, Breece D'J
  See Pancake, Breece Dexter
Panchenko, Nikolai CLC 59
Pankhurst, Emmeline (Goulden)
  1858-1928 .... **TCLC 100**
  See also CA 116; FW
Panko, Rudy
  See Gogol, Nikolai
Papadiamantis, Alexandros
  1851-1911 .... **TCLC 29**
  See also CA 168; EWL 3
Papadiamantopoulos, Johannes
  1856-1910 .... **TCLC 18**
  See also CA 117; 242; GFL 1789 to the
  Present
Papadiamantopoulos, Yannis
  See Papadiamantopoulos, Johannes
Papini, Giovanni 1881-1956 .... **TCLC 22**
  See also CA 121; 180; DLB 264
Paracelsus 1493-1541 .... **LC 14**
  See also DLB 179
Parasol, Peter
  See Stevens, Wallace
Pardo Bazan, Emilia 1851-1921 .... **SSC 30;**
  TCLC 189
  See also EWL 3; FW; RGSF 2; RGWL 2, 3
Paredes, Americo 1915-1999 .... **PC 83**
  See also CA 37-40R; 179; DLB 209; EXPP;
  HW 1
Pareto, Vilfredo 1848-1923 .... **TCLC 69**
  See also CA 175
Paretsky, Sara 1947- .... **CLC 135**
  See also AAYA 30; BEST 90:3; CA 125;
  129; CANR 59, 95, 184; CMW 4; CPW;
  DA3; DAM POP; DLB 306; INT CA-129;
  MSW; RGAL 4
Paretsky, Sara N.
  See Paretsky, Sara
Parfenie, Maria
  See Codrescu, Andrei

Plumly, Stanley 1939- .... **CLC 33**
    See also CA 108; 110; CANR 97, 185; CP
    3, 4, 5, 6, 7; DLB 5, 193; INT CA-110

Plumly, Stanley Ross
    See Plumly, Stanley

Plumpe, Friedrich Wilhelm
    See Murnau, F.W.

Plutarch c. 46-c. 120 .... **CMLC 60**
    See also AW 2; CDWLB 1; DLB 176;
    RGWL 2, 3; TWA; WLIT 8

Po Chu-i 772-846 .... **CMLC 24**

Podhoretz, Norman 1930- .... **CLC 189**
    See also AMWS 8; CA 9-12R; CANR 7,
    78, 135, 179

Poe, Edgar Allan 1809-1849 ..... **NCLC 1, 16,
    55, 78, 94, 97, 117, 211; PC 1, 54; SSC
    1, 22, 34, 35, 54, 88, 111; WLC 4**
    See also AAYA 14; AMW; AMWC 1;
    AMWR 2; BPFB 3; BYA 5, 11; CDALB
    1640-1865; CMW 4; DA; DA3; DAB;
    DAC; DAM MST, POET; DLB 3, 59, 73,
    74, 248, 254; EXPP; EXPS; GL 3; HGG;
    LAIT 2; LATS 1:1; LMFS 1; MSW; PAB;
    PFS 1, 3, 9; RGAL 4; RGSF 2; SATA 23;
    SCFW 1, 2; SFW 4; SSFS 2, 4, 7, 8, 16,
    26, 29; SUFW; TUS; WP; WYA

Poet of Titchfield Street, The
    See Pound, Ezra

Poggio Bracciolini, Gian Francesco
    1380-1459 .... **LC 125**

Pohl, Frederik 1919- .... **CLC 18; SSC 25**
    See also AAYA 24; CA 61-64, 188; CAAE
    188; CAAS 1; CANR 11, 37, 81, 140; CN
    1, 2, 3, 4, 5, 6; DLB 8; INT CANR-11;
    MTCW 1, 2; MTFW 2005; SATA 24;
    SCFW 1, 2; SFW 4

Poirier, Louis
    See Gracq, Julien

Poitier, Sidney 1927- .... **CLC 26**
    See also AAYA 60; BW 1; CA 117; CANR
    94

Pokagon, Simon 1830-1899 .... **NNAL**
    See also DAM MULT

Polanski, Roman 1933- .... **CLC 16, 178**
    See also CA 77-80

Poliakoff, Stephen 1952- .... **CLC 38**
    See also CA 106; CANR 116; CBD; CD 5,
    6; DLB 13

Police, The
    See Copeland, Stewart; Sting; Summers,
    Andy

Polidori, John William
    1795-1821 .... **NCLC 51; SSC 97**
    See also DLB 116; HGG

Poliziano, Angelo 1454-1494 .... **LC 120**
    See also WLIT 7

Pollitt, Katha 1949- .... **CLC 28, 122**
    See also CA 120; 122; CANR 66, 108, 164,
    200; MTCW 1, 2; MTFW 2005

Pollock, (Mary) Sharon 1936- .... **CLC 50**
    See also CA 141; CANR 132; CD 5; CWD;
    DAC; DAM DRAM, MST; DFS 3; DLB
    60; FW

Pollock, Sharon 1936- .... **DC 20**
    See also CD 6

Polo, Marco 1254-1324 .... **CMLC 15**
    See also WLIT 7

Polonsky, Abraham (Lincoln)
    1910-1999 .... **CLC 92**
    See also CA 104; 187; DLB 26; INT CA-
    104

Polybius c. 200B.C.-c. 118B.C. ...... **CMLC 17**
    See also AW 1; DLB 176; RGWL 2, 3

Pomerance, Bernard 1940- .... **CLC 13**
    See also CA 101; CAD; CANR 49, 134;
    CD 5, 6; DAM DRAM; DFS 9; LAIT 2

Ponge, Francis 1899-1988 ..... **CLC 6, 18; PC
    107**
    See also CA 85-88; 126; CANR 40, 86;
    DAM POET; DLBY 2002; EWL 3; GFL
    1789 to the Present; RGWL 2, 3

Poniatowska, Elena 1932- . **CLC 140; HLC 2**
    See also CA 101; CANR 32, 66, 107, 156;
    CDWLB 3; CWW 2; DAM MULT; DLB
    113; EWL 3; HW 1, 2; LAWS 1; WLIT 1

Pontoppidan, Henrik 1857-1943 .... **TCLC 29**
    See also CA 170; DLB 300, 331

Ponty, Maurice Merleau
    See Merleau-Ponty, Maurice

Poole, (Jane Penelope) Josephine
    See Helyar, Jane Penelope Josephine

Poole, Josephine
    See Helyar, Jane Penelope Josephine

Popa, Vasko 1922-1991 . **CLC 19; TCLC 167**
    See also CA 112; 148; CDWLB 4; DLB
    181; EWL 3; RGWL 2, 3

Pope, Alexander 1688-1744 ...... **LC 3, 58, 60,
    64, 164; PC 26; WLC 5**
    See also BRW 3; BRWC 1; BRWR 1; CD-
    BLB 1660-1789; DA; DA3; DAB; DAC;
    DAM MST, POET; DLB 95, 101, 213;
    EXPP; PAB; PFS 12; RGEL 2; WLIT 3;
    WP

Popov, Evgenii Anatol'evich
    See Popov, Yevgeny

Popov, Yevgeny CLC 59
    See also DLB 285

Poquelin, Jean-Baptiste
    See Moliere

Porete, Marguerite (?)-1310 .... **CMLC 73**
    See also DLB 208

Porphyry c. 233-c. 305 .... **CMLC 71**

Porter, Connie (Rose) 1959(?)- .... **CLC 70**
    See also AAYA 65; BW 2, 3; CA 142;
    CANR 90, 109; SATA 81, 129

Porter, Gene Stratton
    See Stratton-Porter, Gene

Porter, Geneva Grace
    See Stratton-Porter, Gene

Porter, Katherine Anne 1890-1980 ... **CLC 1,
    3, 7, 10, 13, 15, 27, 101; SSC 4, 31, 43,
    108; TCLC 233**
    See also AAYA 42; AITN 2; AMW; BPFB
    3; CA 1-4R; 101; CANR 1, 65; CDALBS;
    CN 1, 2; DA; DA3; DAB; DAC; DAM
    MST, NOV; DLB 4, 9, 102; DLBD 12;
    DLBY 1980; EWL 3; EXPS; LAIT 3;
    MAL 5; MBL; MTCW 1, 2; MTFW 2005;
    NFS 14; RGAL 4; RGSF 2; SATA 39;
    SATA-Obit 23; SSFS 1, 8, 11, 16, 23;
    TCWW 2; TUS

Porter, Peter (Neville Frederick)
    1929- .... **CLC 5, 13, 33**
    See also CA 85-88; CP 1, 2, 3, 4, 5, 6, 7;
    DLB 40, 289; WWE 1

Porter, R. E.
    See Hoch, Edward D.

Porter, William Sydney
    See Henry, O.

Portillo (y Pacheco), Jose Lopez
    See Lopez Portillo (y Pacheco), Jose

Portillo Trambley, Estela
    1927-1998 .... **HLC 2; TCLC 163**
    See also CA 77-80; CANR 32; DAM
    MULT; DLB 209; HW 1; RGAL 4

Posey, Alexander (Lawrence)
    1873-1908 .... **NNAL**
    See also CA 144; CANR 80; DAM MULT;
    DLB 175

Posse, Abel CLC 70, 273
    See also CA 252

Post, Melville Davisson
    1869-1930 .... **TCLC 39**
    See also CA 110; 202; CMW 4

Postman, Neil 1931(?)-2003 .... **CLC 244**
    See also CA 102; 221

Potok, Chaim 1929-2002 ... **CLC 2, 7, 14, 26,
    112**
    See also AAYA 15, 50; AITN 1, 2; BPFB 3;
    BYA 1; CA 17-20R; 208; CANR 19, 35,
    64, 98; CLR 92; CN 4, 5, 6; DA3; DAM
    NOV; DLB 28, 152; EXPN; INT CANR-
    19; LAIT 4; MTCW 1, 2; MTFW 2005;
    NFS 4, 34; RGHL; SATA 33, 106; SATA-
    Obit 134; TUS; YAW

Potok, Herbert Harold
    See Potok, Chaim

Potok, Herman Harold
    See Potok, Chaim

Potter, Dennis (Christopher George)
    1935-1994 .... **CLC 58, 86, 123**
    See also BRWS 10; CA 107; 145; CANR
    33, 61; CBD; DLB 233; MTCW 1

Pound, Ezra 1885-1972 . **CLC 1, 2, 3, 4, 5, 7,
    10, 13, 18, 34, 48, 50, 112; PC 4, 95;
    WLC 5**
    See also AAYA 47; AMW; AMWR 1; CA
    5-8R; 37-40R; CANR 40; CDALB 1917-
    1929; CP 1; DA; DA3; DAB; DAC; DAM
    MST, POET; DLB 4, 45, 63; DLBD 15;
    EFS 2; EWL 3; EXPP; LMFS 2; MAL 5;
    MTCW 1, 2; MTFW 2005; PAB; PFS 2,
    8, 16; RGAL 4; TUS; WP

Pound, Ezra Weston Loomis
    See Pound, Ezra

Povod, Reinaldo 1959-1994 .... **CLC 44**
    See also CA 136; 146; CANR 83

Powell, Adam Clayton, Jr.
    1908-1972 .... **BLC 1:3; CLC 89**
    See also BW 1, 3; CA 102; 33-36R; CANR
    86; DAM MULT; DLB 345

Powell, Anthony 1905-2000 ... **CLC 1, 3, 7, 9,
    10, 31**
    See also BRW 7; CA 1-4R; 189; CANR 1,
    32, 62, 107; CDBLB 1945-1960; CN 1, 2,
    3, 4, 5, 6; DLB 15; EWL 3; MTCW 1, 2;
    MTFW 2005; RGEL 2; TEA

Powell, Dawn 1896(?)-1965 .... **CLC 66**
    See also CA 5-8R; CANR 121; DLBY 1997

Powell, Padgett 1952- .... **CLC 34**
    See also CA 126; CANR 63, 101; CSW;
    DLB 234; DLBY 01; SSFS 25

Power, Susan 1961- .... **CLC 91**
    See also BYA 14; CA 160; CANR 135; NFS
    11

Powers, J(ames) F(arl) 1917-1999 ..... **CLC 1,
    4, 8, 57; SSC 4**
    See also CA 1-4R; 181; CANR 2, 61; CN
    1, 2, 3, 4, 5, 6; DLB 130; MTCW 1;
    RGAL 4; RGSF 2

Powers, John
    See Powers, John R.

Powers, John R. 1945- .... **CLC 66**
    See also CA 69-72

Powers, Richard 1957- .... **CLC 93, 292**
    See also AMWS 9; BPFB 3; CA 148;
    CANR 80, 180; CN 6, 7; DLB 350;
    MTFW 2005; TCLE 1:2

Powers, Richard S.
    See Powers, Richard

Pownall, David 1938- .... **CLC 10**
    See also CA 89-92, 180; CAAS 18; CANR
    49, 101; CBD; CD 5, 6; CN 4, 5, 6, 7;
    DLB 14

Powys, John Cowper 1872-1963 ... **CLC 7, 9,
    15, 46, 125**
    See also CA 85-88; CANR 106; DLB 15,
    255; EWL 3; FANT; MTCW 1, 2; MTFW
    2005; RGEL 2; SUFW

Powys, T(heodore) F(rancis)
    1875-1953 .... **TCLC 9**
    See also BRWS 8; CA 106; 189; DLB 36,
    162; EWL 3; FANT; RGEL 2; SUFW

Randall, Robert
See Silverberg, Robert
Ranger, Ken
See Creasey, John
Rank, Otto 1884-1939 .... **TCLC 115**
Rankin, Ian 1960- .... **CLC 257**
See also BRWS 10; CA 148; CANR 81,
137, 171; DLB 267; MTFW 2005
Rankin, Ian James
See Rankin, Ian
Ransom, John Crowe 1888-1974 .. **CLC 2, 4,
5, 11, 24; PC 61**
See also AMW; CA 5-8R; 49-52; CANR 6,
34; CDALBS; CP 1, 2; DA3; DAM POET;
DLB 45, 63; EWL 3; EXPP; MAL 5;
MTCW 1, 2; MTFW 2005; RGAL 4; TUS
Rao, Raja 1908-2006 . **CLC 25, 56, 255; SSC
99**
See also CA 73-76; 252; CANR 51; CN 1,
2, 3, 4, 5, 6; DAM NOV; DLB 323; EWL
3; MTCW 1, 2; MTFW 2005; RGEL 2;
RGSF 2
Raphael, Frederic (Michael) 1931- ... **CLC 2,
14**
See also CA 1-4R; CANR 1, 86; CN 1, 2,
3, 4, 5, 6, 7; DLB 14, 319; TCLE 1:2
Raphael, Lev 1954- .... **CLC 232**
See also CA 134; CANR 72, 145; GLL 1
Ratcliffe, James P.
See Mencken, H. L.
Rathbone, Julian 1935-2008 .... **CLC 41**
See also CA 101; 269; CANR 34, 73, 152
Rathbone, Julian Christopher
See Rathbone, Julian
Rattigan, Terence 1911-1977 . **CLC 7; DC 18**
See also BRWS 7; CA 85-88; 73-76; CBD;
CDBLB 1945-1960; DAM DRAM; DFS
8; DLB 13; IDFW 3, 4; MTCW 1, 2;
MTFW 2005; RGEL 2
Rattigan, Terence Mervyn
See Rattigan, Terence
Ratushinskaya, Irina 1954- .... **CLC 54**
See also CA 129; CANR 68; CWW 2
Raven, Simon (Arthur Noel)
1927-2001 .... **CLC 14**
See also CA 81-84; 197; CANR 86; CN 1,
2, 3, 4, 5, 6; DLB 271
Ravenna, Michael
See Welty, Eudora
Rawley, Callman 1903-2004 .... **CLC 47**
See also CA 21-24R; 228; CAAS 5; CANR
12, 32, 91; CP 1, 2, 3, 4, 5, 6, 7; DLB
193
Rawlings, Marjorie Kinnan
1896-1953 .... **TCLC 4**
See also AAYA 20; AMWS 10; ANW;
BPFB 3; BYA 3; CA 104; 137; CANR 74;
CLR 63; DLB 9, 22, 102; DLBD 17;
JRDA; MAICYA 1, 2; MAL 5; MTCW 2;
MTFW 2005; RGAL 4; SATA 100; WCH;
YABC 1; YAW
Raworth, Thomas Moore 1938- .... **PC 107**
See also CA 29-32R; CAAS 11; CANR 46;
CP 1, 2, 3, 4, 5, 7; DLB 40
Raworth, Tom
See Raworth, Thomas Moore
Ray, Satyajit 1921-1992 .... **CLC 16, 76**
See also CA 114; 137; DAM MULT
Read, Herbert Edward 1893-1968 ..... **CLC 4**
See also BRW 6; CA 85-88; 25-28R; DLB
20, 149; EWL 3; PAB; RGEL 2
Read, Piers Paul 1941- .... **CLC 4, 10, 25**
See also CA 21-24R; CANR 38, 86, 150;
CN 2, 3, 4, 5, 6, 7; DLB 14; SATA 21
Reade, Charles 1814-1884 .... **NCLC 2, 74**
See also DLB 21; RGEL 2
Reade, Hamish
See Gray, Simon

Reading, Peter 1946- .... **CLC 47**
See also BRWS 8; CA 103; CANR 46, 96;
CP 5, 6, 7; DLB 40
Reaney, James 1926-2008 .... **CLC 13**
See also CA 41-44R; CAAS 15; CANR 42;
CD 5, 6; CP 1, 2, 3, 4, 5, 6, 7; DAC;
DAM MST; DLB 68; RGEL 2; SATA 43
Reaney, James Crerar
See Reaney, James
Rebreanu, Liviu 1885-1944 .... **TCLC 28**
See also CA 165; DLB 220; EWL 3
Rechy, John 1934- ..... **CLC 1, 7, 14, 18, 107;
HLC 2**
See also CA 5-8R, 195; CAAE 195; CAAS
4; CANR 6, 32, 64, 152, 188; CN 1, 2, 3,
4, 5, 6, 7; DAM MULT; DLB 122, 278;
DLBY 1982; HW 1, 2; INT CANR-6;
LLW; MAL 5; RGAL 4
Rechy, John Francisco
See Rechy, John
Redcam, Tom 1870-1933 .... **TCLC 25**
Reddin, Keith 1956- .... **CLC 67**
See also CAD; CD 6
Redgrove, Peter (William)
1932-2003 .... **CLC 6, 41**
See also BRWS 6; CA 1-4R; 217; CANR 3,
39, 77; CP 1, 2, 3, 4, 5, 6, 7; DLB 40;
TCLE 1:2
Redmon, Anne
See Nightingale, Anne Redmon
Reed, Eliot
See Ambler, Eric
Reed, Ishmael 1938- . **BLC 1:3; CLC 2, 3, 5,
6, 13, 32, 60, 174; PC 68**
See also AFAW 1, 2; AMWS 10; BPFB 3;
BW 2, 3; CA 21-24R; CANR 25, 48, 74,
128, 195; CN 1, 2, 3, 4, 5, 6, 7; CP 1, 2,
3, 4, 5, 6, 7; CSW; DA3; DAM MULT;
DLB 2, 5, 33, 169, 227; DLBD 8; EWL
3; LMFS 2; MAL 5; MSW; MTCW 1, 2;
MTFW 2005; PFS 6; RGAL 4; TCWW 2
Reed, Ishmael Scott
See Reed, Ishmael
Reed, John (Silas) 1887-1920 .... **TCLC 9**
See also CA 106; 195; MAL 5; TUS
Reed, Lou
See Firbank, Louis
Reese, Lizette Woodworth
1856-1935 .... **PC 29; TCLC 181**
See also CA 180; DLB 54
Reeve, Clara 1729-1807 .... **NCLC 19**
See also DLB 39; RGEL 2
Reich, Wilhelm 1897-1957 .... **TCLC 57**
See also CA 199
Reid, Christopher 1949- .... **CLC 33**
See also CA 140; CANR 89; CP 4, 5, 6, 7;
DLB 40; EWL 3
Reid, Christopher John
See Reid, Christopher
Reid, Desmond
See Moorcock, Michael
Reid Banks, Lynne 1929- .... **CLC 23**
See also AAYA 6; BYA 7; CA 1-4R; CANR
6, 22, 38, 87; CLR 24, 86; CN 4, 5, 6;
JRDA; MAICYA 1, 2; SATA 22, 75, 111,
165; YAW
Reilly, William K.
See Creasey, John
Reiner, Max
See Caldwell, (Janet Miriam) Taylor
(Holland)
Reis, Ricardo
See Pessoa, Fernando
Reizenstein, Elmer Leopold
See Rice, Elmer (Leopold)
Remark, Erich Paul
See Remarque, Erich Maria

Remarque, Erich Maria 1898-1970 . **CLC 21**
See also AAYA 27; BPFB 3; CA 77-80; 29-
32R; CDWLB 2; DA; DA3; DAB; DAC;
DAM MST, NOV; DLB 56; EWL 3;
EXPN; LAIT 3; MTCW 1, 2; MTFW
2005; NFS 4; RGHL; RGWL 2, 3
Remington, Frederic S(ackrider)
1861-1909 .... **TCLC 89**
See also CA 108; 169; DLB 12, 186, 188;
SATA 41; TCWW 2
Remizov, A.
See Remizov, Aleksei (Mikhailovich)
Remizov, A. M.
See Remizov, Aleksei (Mikhailovich)
Remizov, Aleksei (Mikhailovich)
1877-1957 .... **TCLC 27**
See also CA 125; 133; DLB 295; EWL 3
Remizov, Alexey Mikhaylovich
See Remizov, Aleksei (Mikhailovich)
Renan, Joseph Ernest 1823-1892 . **NCLC 26,
145**
See also GFL 1789 to the Present
Renard, Jules(-Pierre) 1864-1910 .. **TCLC 17**
See also CA 117; 202; GFL 1789 to the
Present
Renart, Jean fl. 13th cent. - .... **CMLC 83**
Renault, Mary 1905-1983 .... **CLC 3, 11, 17**
See also BPFB 3; BYA 2; CA 81-84; 111;
CANR 74; CN 1, 2, 3; DA3; DLBY 1983;
EWL 3; GLL 1; LAIT 1; MTCW 2;
MTFW 2005; RGEL 2; RHW; SATA 23;
SATA-Obit 36; TEA
Rendell, Ruth
See Rendell, Ruth
Rendell, Ruth 1930- .... **CLC 28, 48, 50**
See also BEST 90:4; BPFB 3; BRWS 9;
CA 109; CANR 32, 52, 74, 127, 162, 190;
CN 5, 6, 7; CPW; DAM POP; DLB 87,
276; INT CANR-32; MSW; MTCW 1, 2;
MTFW 2005
Rendell, Ruth Barbara
See Rendell, Ruth
Renoir, Jean 1894-1979 .... **CLC 20**
See also CA 129; 85-88
Rensie, Willis
See Eisner, Will
Resnais, Alain 1922- .... **CLC 16**
Revard, Carter 1931- .... **NNAL**
See also CA 144; CANR 81, 153; PFS 5
Reverdy, Pierre 1889-1960 .... **CLC 53**
See also CA 97-100; 89-92; DLB 258; EWL
3; GFL 1789 to the Present
Reverend Mandju
See Su, Chien
Rexroth, Kenneth 1905-1982 .... **CLC 1, 2, 6,
11, 22, 49, 112; PC 20, 95**
See also BG 1:3; CA 5-8R; 107; CANR 14,
34, 63; CDALB 1941-1968; CP 1, 2, 3;
DAM POET; DLB 16, 48, 165, 212;
DLBY 1982; EWL 3; INT CANR-14;
MAL 5; MTCW 1, 2; MTFW 2005;
RGAL 4
Reyes, Alfonso 1889-1959 .... **HLCS 2; TCLC
33**
See also CA 131; EWL 3; HW 1; LAW
Reyes y Basoalto, Ricardo Eliecer Neftali
See Neruda, Pablo
Reymont, Wladyslaw (Stanislaw)
1868(?)-1925 .... **TCLC 5**
See also CA 104; DLB 332; EWL 3
Reynolds, John Hamilton
1794-1852 .... **NCLC 146**
See also DLB 96
Reynolds, Jonathan 1942- .... **CLC 6, 38**
See also CA 65-68; CANR 28, 176
Reynolds, Joshua 1723-1792 .... **LC 15**
See also DLB 104

Reynolds, Michael S(hane)
1937-2000 .... **CLC 44**
See also CA 65-68; 189; CANR 9, 89, 97

Reza, Yasmina 1959- .... **DC 34**
See also AAYA 69; CA 171; CANR 145;
DFS 19; DLB 321

Reznikoff, Charles 1894-1976 .... **CLC 9**
See also AMWS 14; CA 33-36; 61-64; CAP
2; CP 1, 2; DLB 28, 45; RGHL; WP

Rezzori, Gregor von
See Rezzori d'Arezzo, Gregor von

Rezzori d'Arezzo, Gregor von
1914-1998 .... **CLC 25**
See also CA 122; 136; 167

Rhine, Richard
See Silverstein, Alvin; Silverstein, Virginia
B.

Rhodes, Eugene Manlove
1869-1934 .... **TCLC 53**
See also CA 198; DLB 256; TCWW 1, 2

R'hoone, Lord
See Balzac, Honore de

Rhys, Jean 1890-1979 .... **CLC 2, 4, 6, 14, 19,
51, 124; SSC 21, 76**
See also BRWS 2; CA 25-28R; 85-88;
CANR 35, 62; CDBLB 1945-1960; CD-
WLB 3; CN 1, 2; DA3; DAM NOV; DLB
36, 117, 162; DNFS 2; EWL 3; LATS 1:1;
MTCW 1, 2; MTFW 2005; NFS 19;
RGEL 2; RGSF 2; RHW; TEA; WWE 1

Ribeiro, Darcy 1922-1997 .... **CLC 34**
See also CA 33-36R; 156; EWL 3

Ribeiro, Joao Ubaldo (Osorio Pimentel)
1941- .... **CLC 10, 67**
See also CA 81-84; CWW 2; EWL 3

Ribman, Ronald (Burt) 1932- .... **CLC 7**
See also CA 21-24R; CAD; CANR 46, 80;
CD 5, 6

Ricci, Nino 1959- .... **CLC 70**
See also CA 137; CANR 130; CCA 1

Ricci, Nino Pio
See Ricci, Nino

Rice, Anne 1941- .... **CLC 41, 128**
See also AAYA 9, 53; AMWS 7; BEST
89:2; BPFB 3; CA 65-68; CANR 12, 36,
53, 74, 100, 133, 190; CN 6, 7; CPW;
CSW; DA3; DAM POP; DLB 292; GL 3;
GLL 2; HGG; MTCW 2; MTFW 2005;
SUFW 2; YAW

Rice, Elmer (Leopold) 1892-1967 ...... **CLC 7,
49; TCLC 221**
See also CA 21-22; 25-28R; CAP 2; DAM
DRAM; DFS 12; DLB 4, 7; EWL 3;
IDTP; MAL 5; MTCW 1, 2; RGAL 4

Rice, Tim 1944- .... **CLC 21**
See also CA 103; CANR 46; DFS 7

Rice, Timothy Miles Bindon
See Rice, Tim

Rich, Adrienne 1929- ..... **CLC 3, 6, 7, 11, 18,
36, 73, 76, 125; PC 5**
See also AAYA 69; AMWR 2; AMWS 1;
CA 9-12R; CANR 20, 53, 74, 128, 199;
CDALBS; CP 1, 2, 3, 4, 5, 6, 7; CSW;
CWP; DA3; DAM POET; DLB 5, 67;
EWL 3; EXPP; FL 1:6; FW; MAL 5;
MBL; MTCW 1, 2; MTFW 2005; PAB;
PFS 15, 29; RGAL 4; RGHL; WP

Rich, Adrienne Cecile
See Rich, Adrienne

Rich, Barbara
See Graves, Robert

Rich, Robert
See Trumbo, Dalton

Richard, Keith
See Richards, Keith

Richards, David Adams 1950- .... **CLC 59**
See also CA 93-96; CANR 60, 110, 156;
CN 7; DAC; DLB 53; TCLE 1:2

Richards, I(vor) A(rmstrong)
1893-1979 .... **CLC 14, 24**
See also BRWS 2; CA 41-44R; 89-92;
CANR 34, 74; CP 1, 2; DLB 27; EWL 3;
MTCW 2; RGEL 2

Richards, Keith 1943- .... **CLC 17**
See also CA 107; CANR 77

Richardson, Anne
See Roiphe, Anne

Richardson, Dorothy Miller
1873-1957 .... **TCLC 3, 203**
See also BRWS 13; CA 104; 192; DLB 36;
EWL 3; FW; RGEL 2

Richardson, Ethel Florence Lindesay
1870-1946 .... **TCLC 4**
See also CA 105; 190; DLB 197, 230; EWL
3; RGEL 2; RGSF 2; RHW

Richardson, Henrietta
See Richardson, Ethel Florence Lindesay

Richardson, Henry Handel
See Richardson, Ethel Florence Lindesay

Richardson, John 1796-1852 .... **NCLC 55**
See also CCA 1; DAC; DLB 99

Richardson, Samuel 1689-1761 ...... **LC 1, 44,
138; WLC 5**
See also BRW 3; CDBLB 1660-1789; DA;
DAB; DAC; DAM MST, NOV; DLB 39;
RGEL 2; TEA; WLIT 3

Richardson, Willis 1889-1977 .... **HR 1:3**
See also BW 1; CA 124; DLB 51; SATA 60

**Richardson Robertson, Ethel Florence
Lindesay**
See Richardson, Ethel Florence Lindesay

Richler, Mordecai 1931-2001 .... **CLC 3, 5, 9,
13, 18, 46, 70, 185, 271**
See also AITN 1; CA 65-68; 201; CANR
31, 62, 111; CCA 1; CLR 17; CN 1, 2, 3,
4, 5, 7; CWRI 5; DAC; DAM MST, NOV;
DLB 53; EWL 3; MAICYA 1, 2; MTCW
1, 2; MTFW 2005; RGAL 2; RGHL;
SATA 44, 98; SATA-Brief 27; TWA

Richter, Conrad (Michael)
1890-1968 .... **CLC 30**
See also AAYA 21; AMWS 18; BYA 2; CA
5-8R; 25-28R; CANR 23; DLB 9, 212;
LAIT 1; MAL 5; MTCW 1, 2; MTFW
2005; RGAL 4; SATA 3; TCWW 1, 2;
TUS; YAW

Ricostranza, Tom
See Ellis, Trey

Riddell, Charlotte 1832-1906 .... **TCLC 40**
See also CA 165; DLB 156; HGG; SUFW

Riddell, Mrs. J. H.
See Riddell, Charlotte

Ridge, John Rollin 1827-1867 ...... **NCLC 82;
NNAL**
See also CA 144; DAM MULT; DLB 175

Ridgeway, Jason
See Marlowe, Stephen

Ridgway, Keith 1965- .... **CLC 119**
See also CA 172; CANR 144

Riding, Laura
See Jackson, Laura

Riefenstahl, Berta Helene Amalia
1902-2003 .... **CLC 16, 190**
See also CA 108; 220

Riefenstahl, Leni
See Riefenstahl, Berta Helene Amalia

Riffe, Ernest
See Bergman, Ingmar

Riffe, Ernest Ingmar
See Bergman, Ingmar

Riggs, (Rolla) Lynn
1899-1954 .... **NNAL; TCLC 56**
See also CA 144; DAM MULT; DLB 175

Riis, Jacob A(ugust) 1849-1914 ..... **TCLC 80**
See also CA 113; 168; DLB 23

Rikki
See Ducornet, Erica

Riley, James Whitcomb 1849-1916 .... **PC 48;
TCLC 51**
See also CA 118; 137; DAM POET; MAI-
CYA 1, 2; RGAL 4; SATA 17

Riley, Tex
See Creasey, John

Rilke, Rainer Maria 1875-1926 .... **PC 2;
TCLC 1, 6, 19, 195**
See also CA 104; 132; CANR 62, 99; CD-
WLB 2; DA3; DAM POET; DLB 81; EW
9; EWL 3; MTCW 1, 2; MTFW 2005;
PFS 19, 27; RGWL 2, 3; TWA; WP

Rimbaud, Arthur 1854-1891 ...... **NCLC 4, 35,
82, 227; PC 3, 57; WLC 5**
See also DA; DA3; DAB; DAC; DAM
MST, POET; DLB 217; EW 7; GFL 1789
to the Present; LMFS 2; PFS 28; RGWL
2, 3; TWA; WP

Rimbaud, Jean Nicholas Arthur
See Rimbaud, Arthur

Rinehart, Mary Roberts
1876-1958 .... **TCLC 52**
See also BPFB 3; CA 108; 166; RGAL 4;
RHW

Ringmaster, The
See Mencken, H. L.

Ringwood, Gwen(dolyn Margaret) Pharis
1910-1984 .... **CLC 48**
See also CA 148; 112; DLB 88

Rio, Michel 1945(?)- .... **CLC 43**
See also CA 201

Rios, Alberto 1952- .... **PC 57**
See also AAYA 66; AMWS 4; CA 113;
CANR 34, 79, 137; CP 6, 7; DLB 122;
HW 2; MTFW 2005; PFS 11

Rios, Alberto Alvaro
See Rios, Alberto

Ritsos, Giannes
See Ritsos, Yannis

Ritsos, Yannis 1909-1990 .... **CLC 6, 13, 31**
See also CA 77-80; 133; CANR 39, 61; EW
12; EWL 3; MTCW 1; RGWL 2, 3

Ritter, Erika 1948(?)- .... **CLC 52**
See also CD 5, 6; CWD

Rivera, Jose Eustasio 1889-1928 ... **TCLC 35**
See also CA 162; EWL 3; HW 1, 2; LAW

Rivera, Tomas 1935-1984 .... **HLCS 2**
See also CA 49-52; CANR 32; DLB 82;
HW 1; LLW; RGAL 4; SSFS 15; TCWW
2; WLIT 1

Rivers, Conrad Kent 1933-1968 .... **CLC 1**
See also BW 1; CA 85-88; DLB 41

Rivers, Elfrida
See Bradley, Marion Zimmer

Riverside, John
See Heinlein, Robert A.

Rizal, Jose 1861-1896 .... **NCLC 27**
See also DLB 348

Roa Bastos, Augusto 1917-2005 ...... **CLC 45;
HLC 2**
See also CA 131; 238; CWW 2; DAM
MULT; DLB 113; EWL 3; HW 1; LAW;
RGSF 2; WLIT 1

Roa Bastos, Augusto Jose Antonio
See Roa Bastos, Augusto

Robbe-Grillet, Alain 1922-2008 ..... **CLC 1, 2,
4, 6, 8, 10, 14, 43, 128, 287**
See also BPFB 3; CA 9-12R; 269; CANR
33, 65, 115; CWW 2; DLB 83; EW 13;
EWL 3; GFL 1789 to the Present; IDFW
3, 4; MTCW 1, 2; MTFW 2005; RGWL
2, 3; SSFS 15

Robbins, Harold 1916-1997 .... **CLC 5**
See also BPFB 3; CA 73-76; 162; CANR
26, 54, 112, 156; DA3; DAM NOV;
MTCW 1, 2

Russell, William Martin 1947- .... **CLC 60**
    See also CA 164; CANR 107; CBD; CD 5,
    6; DLB 233
Russell, Willy
    See Russell, William Martin
Russo, Richard 1949- .... **CLC 181**
    See also AMWS 12; CA 127; 133; CANR
    87, 114, 194; NFS 25
Rutebeuf fl. c. 1249-1277 .... **CMLC 104**
    See also DLB 208
Rutherford, Mark
    See White, William Hale
Ruysbroeck, Jan van 1293-1381 ... **CMLC 85**
Ruyslinck, Ward
    See Belser, Reimond Karel Maria de
Ryan, Cornelius (John) 1920-1974 ..... **CLC 7**
    See also CA 69-72; 53-56; CANR 38
Ryan, Michael 1946- .... **CLC 65**
    See also CA 49-52; CANR 109, 203; DLBY
    1982
Ryan, Tim
    See Dent, Lester
Rybakov, Anatoli (Naumovich)
    1911-1998 .... **CLC 23, 53**
    See also CA 126; 135; 172; DLB 302;
    RGHL; SATA 79; SATA-Obit 108
Rybakov, Anatolii (Naumovich)
    See Rybakov, Anatoli (Naumovich)
Ryder, Jonathan
    See Ludlum, Robert
Ryga, George 1932-1987 .... **CLC 14**
    See also CA 101; 124; CANR 43, 90; CCA
    1; DAC; DAM MST; DLB 60
Rymer, Thomas 1643(?)-1713 .... **LC 132**
    See also DLB 101, 336
S. H.
    See Hartmann, Sadakichi
S. L. C.
    See Twain, Mark
S. S.
    See Sassoon, Siegfried
Sa'adawi, al- Nawal
    See El Saadawi, Nawal
Saadawi, Nawal El
    See El Saadawi, Nawal
Saadiah Gaon 882-942 .... **CMLC 97**
Saba, Umberto 1883-1957 .... **TCLC 33**
    See also CA 144; CANR 79; DLB 114;
    EWL 3; RGWL 2, 3
Sabatini, Rafael 1875-1950 .... **TCLC 47**
    See also BPFB 3; CA 162; RHW
Sabato, Ernesto 1911- .. **CLC 10, 23; HLC 2**
    See also CA 97-100; CANR 32, 65; CD-
    WLB 3; CWW 2; DAM MULT; DLB 145;
    EWL 3; HW 1, 2; LAW; MTCW 1, 2;
    MTFW 2005
Sa-Carneiro, Mario de 1890-1916 . **TCLC 83**
    See also DLB 287; EWL 3
Sacastru, Martin
    See Bioy Casares, Adolfo
Sacher-Masoch, Leopold von
    1836(?)-1895 .... **NCLC 31**
Sachs, Hans 1494-1576 .... **LC 95**
    See also CDWLB 2; DLB 179; RGWL 2, 3
Sachs, Marilyn 1927- .... **CLC 35**
    See also AAYA 2; BYA 6; CA 17-20R;
    CANR 13, 47, 150; CLR 2; JRDA; MAI-
    CYA 1, 2; SAAS 2; SATA 3, 68, 164;
    SATA-Essay 110; WYA; YAW
Sachs, Marilyn Stickle
    See Sachs, Marilyn
Sachs, Nelly 1891-1970 .. **CLC 14, 98; PC 78**
    See also CA 17-18; 25-28R; CANR 87;
    CAP 2; DLB 332; EWL 3; MTCW 2;
    MTFW 2005; PFS 20; RGHL; RGWL 2,
    3

Sackler, Howard (Oliver)
    1929-1982 .... **CLC 14**
    See also CA 61-64; 108; CAD; CANR 30;
    DFS 15; DLB 7
Sacks, Oliver 1933- .... **CLC 67, 202**
    See also CA 53-56; CANR 28, 50, 76, 146,
    187; CPW; DA3; INT CANR-28; MTCW
    1, 2; MTFW 2005
Sacks, Oliver Wolf
    See Sacks, Oliver
Sackville, Thomas 1536-1608 .... **LC 98**
    See also DAM DRAM; DLB 62, 132;
    RGEL 2
Sadakichi
    See Hartmann, Sadakichi
Sa'dawi, Nawal al-
    See El Saadawi, Nawal
Sade, Donatien Alphonse Francois
    1740-1814 .... **NCLC 3, 47**
    See also DLB 314; EW 4; GFL Beginnings
    to 1789; RGWL 2, 3
Sade, Marquis de
    See Sade, Donatien Alphonse Francois
Sadoff, Ira 1945- .... **CLC 9**
    See also CA 53-56; CANR 5, 21, 109; DLB
    120
Saetone
    See Camus, Albert
Safire, William 1929-2009 .... **CLC 10**
    See also CA 17-20R; 290; CANR 31, 54,
    91, 148
Safire, William L.
    See Safire, William
Safire, William Lewis
    See Safire, William
Sagan, Carl 1934-1996 .... **CLC 30, 112**
    See also AAYA 2, 62; CA 25-28R; 155;
    CANR 11, 36, 74; CPW; DA3; MTCW 1,
    2; MTFW 2005; SATA 58; SATA-Obit 94
Sagan, Francoise
    See Quoirez, Francoise
Sahgal, Nayantara (Pandit) 1927- .... **CLC 41**
    See also CA 9-12R; CANR 11, 88; CN 1,
    2, 3, 4, 5, 6, 7; DLB 323
Said, Edward W. 1935-2003 .... **CLC 123**
    See also CA 21-24R; 220; CANR 45, 74,
    107, 131; DLB 67, 346; MTCW 2; MTFW
    2005
Saikaku, Ihara 1642-1693 .... **LC 141**
    See also RGWL 3
Saikaku Ihara
    See Saikaku, Ihara
Saint, H(arry) F. 1941- .... **CLC 50**
    See also CA 127
St. Aubin de Teran, Lisa 1953- .... **CLC 36**
    See also CA 118; 126; CN 6, 7; INT CA-
    126
Saint Birgitta of Sweden c.
    1303-1373 .... **CMLC 24**
St. E. A. of M. and S
    See Crowley, Edward Alexander
Sainte-Beuve, Charles Augustin
    1804-1869 .... **NCLC 5; PC 110**
    See also DLB 217; EW 6; GFL 1789 to the
    Present
Saint-Exupery, Antoine de
    1900-1944 .... **TCLC 2, 56, 169; WLC**
    See also AAYA 63; BPFB 3; BYA 3; CA
    108; 132; CLR 10, 142; DA3; DAM
    NOV; DLB 72; EW 12; EWL 3; GFL
    1789 to the Present; LAIT 3; MAICYA 1,
    2; MTCW 1, 2; MTFW 2005; NFS 30;
    RGWL 2, 3; SATA 20; TWA
**Saint-Exupery, Antoine Jean Baptiste Marie
    Roger de**
    See Saint-Exupery, Antoine de
St. John, David
    See Hunt, E. Howard

St. John, Henry 1678-1751 .... **LC 178**
    See also DLB 101, 336
St. John, J. Hector
    See Crevecoeur, J. Hector St. John de
Saint-John Perse
    See Leger, Alexis Saint-Leger
Saintsbury, George (Edward Bateman)
    1845-1933 .... **TCLC 31**
    See also CA 160; DLB 57, 149
Sait Faik
    See Abasiyanik, Sait Faik
Saki 1870-1916 .... **SSC 12, 115; TCLC 3;
    WLC 5**
    See also AAYA 56; BRWS 6; BYA 11; CA
    104; 130; CANR 104; CDBLB 1890-
    1914; DA; DA3; DAB; DAC; DAM MST,
    NOV; DLB 34, 162; EXPS; LAIT 2;
    MTCW 1, 2; MTFW 2005; RGEL 2;
    SSFS 1, 15; SUFW
Sala, George Augustus 1828-1895 . **NCLC 46**
Saladin 1138-1193 .... **CMLC 38**
Salama, Hannu 1936- .... **CLC 18**
    See also CA 244; EWL 3
Salamanca, J(ack) R(ichard) 1922- .. **CLC 4,
    15**
    See also CA 25-28R, 193; CAAE 193
Salas, Floyd Francis 1931- .... **HLC 2**
    See also CA 119; CAAS 27; CANR 44, 75,
    93; DAM MULT; DLB 82; HW 1, 2;
    MTCW 2; MTFW 2005
Sale, J. Kirkpatrick
    See Sale, Kirkpatrick
Sale, John Kirkpatrick
    See Sale, Kirkpatrick
Sale, Kirkpatrick 1937- .... **CLC 68**
    See also CA 13-16R; CANR 10, 147
Salinas, Luis Omar 1937- ... **CLC 90; HLC 2**
    See also AMWS 13; CA 131; CANR 81,
    153; DAM MULT; DLB 82; HW 1, 2
Salinas (y Serrano), Pedro
    1891(?)-1951 .... **TCLC 17, 212**
    See also CA 117; DLB 134; EWL 3
Salinger, J.D. 1919-2010 ...... **CLC 1, 3, 8, 12,
    55, 56, 138, 243; SSC 2, 28, 65; WLC 5**
    See also AAYA 2, 36; AMW; AMWC 1;
    BPFB 3; CA 5-8R; CANR 39, 129;
    CDALB 1941-1968; CLR 18; CN 1, 2, 3,
    4, 5, 6, 7; CPW 1; DA; DA3; DAB; DAC;
    DAM MST, NOV, POP; DLB 2, 102, 173;
    EWL 3; EXPN; LAIT 4; MAICYA 1, 2;
    MAL 5; MTCW 1, 2; MTFW 2005; NFS
    1, 30; RGAL 4; RGSF 2; SATA 67; SSFS
    17; TUS; WYA; YAW
Salinger, Jerome David
    See Salinger, J.D.
Salisbury, John
    See Caute, (John) David
Sallust c. 86B.C.-35B.C. .... **CMLC 68**
    See also AW 2; CDWLB 1; DLB 211;
    RGWL 2, 3
Salter, James 1925- .... **CLC 7, 52, 59, 275;
    SSC 58**
    See also AMWS 9; CA 73-76; CANR 107,
    160; DLB 130; SSFS 25
Saltus, Edgar (Everton) 1855-1921 . **TCLC 8**
    See also CA 105; DLB 202; RGAL 4
Saltykov, Mikhail Evgrafovich
    1826-1889 .... **NCLC 16**
    See also DLB 238:
Saltykov-Shchedrin, N.
    See Saltykov, Mikhail Evgrafovich
Samarakis, Andonis
    See Samarakis, Antonis
Samarakis, Antonis 1919-2003 .... **CLC 5**
    See also CA 25-28R; 224; CAAS 16; CANR
    36; EWL 3
Samigli, E.
    See Schmitz, Aron Hector

Scudery, Madeleine de 1607-1701 .. **LC 2, 58**
  See also DLB 268; GFL Beginnings to 1789
Scum
  See Crumb, R.
Scumbag, Little Bobby
  See Crumb, R.
Seabrook, John
  See Hubbard, L. Ron
Seacole, Mary Jane Grant
  1805-1881 .... **NCLC 147**
  See also DLB 166
Sealy, I(rwin) Allan 1951- .... **CLC 55**
  See also CA 136; CN 6, 7
Search, Alexander
  See Pessoa, Fernando
Seare, Nicholas
  See Whitaker, Rod
Sebald, W(infried) G(eorg)
  1944-2001 .... **CLC 194**
  See also BRWS 8; CA 159; 202; CANR 98;
  MTFW 2005; RGHL
Sebastian, Lee
  See Silverberg, Robert
Sebastian Owl
  See Thompson, Hunter S.
Sebestyen, Igen
  See Sebestyen, Ouida
Sebestyen, Ouida 1924- .... **CLC 30**
  See also AAYA 8; BYA 7; CA 107; CANR
  40, 114; CLR 17; JRDA; MAICYA 1, 2;
  SAAS 10; SATA 39, 140; WYA; YAW
Sebold, Alice 1963- .... **CLC 193**
  See also AAYA 56; CA 203; CANR 181;
  LNFS 1; MTFW 2005
Second Duke of Buckingham
  See Villiers, George
Secundus, H. Scriblerus
  See Fielding, Henry
Sedges, John
  See Buck, Pearl S.
Sedgwick, Catharine Maria
  1789-1867 .... **NCLC 19, 98**
  See also DLB 1, 74, 183, 239, 243, 254; FL
  1:3; RGAL 4
Sedley, Sir Charles 1639-1701 .... **LC 168**
  See also BRW 2; DLB 131; RGEL 2
Sedulius Scottus 9th cent. -c. 874 .. **CMLC 86**
Seebohm, Victoria
  See Glendinning, Victoria
Seelye, John (Douglas) 1931- .... **CLC 7**
  See also CA 97-100; CANR 70; INT CA-
  97-100; TCWW 1, 2
Seferiades, Giorgos Stylianou
  See Seferis, George
Seferis, George 1900-1971 .... **CLC 5, 11;**
  TCLC 213
  See also CA 5-8R; 33-36R; CANR 5, 36;
  DLB 332; EW 12; EWL 3; MTCW 1;
  RGWL 2, 3
Segal, Erich 1937-2010 .... **CLC 3, 10**
  See also BEST 89:1; BPFB 3; CA 25-28R;
  CANR 20, 36, 65, 113; CPW; DAM POP;
  DLBY 1986; INT CANR-20; MTCW 1
Segal, Erich Wolf
  See Segal, Erich
Seger, Bob 1945- .... **CLC 35**
Seghers
  See Radvanyi, Netty
Seghers, Anna
  See Radvanyi, Netty
Seidel, Frederick 1936- .... **CLC 18**
  See also CA 13-16R; CANR 8, 99, 180; CP
  1, 2, 3, 4, 5, 6, 7; DLBY 1984
Seidel, Frederick Lewis
  See Seidel, Frederick

Seifert, Jaroslav 1901-1986 . **CLC 34, 44, 93;**
  PC 47
  See also CA 127; CDWLB 4; DLB 215,
  332; EWL 3; MTCW 1, 2
Sei Shonagon c. 966-1017(?) ..... **CMLC 6, 89**
Sejour, Victor 1817-1874 .... **DC 10**
  See also DLB 50
Sejour Marcou et Ferrand, Juan Victor
  See Sejour, Victor
Selby, Hubert, Jr. 1928-2004 ..... **CLC 1, 2, 4,**
  8; SSC 20
  See also CA 13-16R; 226; CANR 33, 85;
  CN 1, 2, 3, 4, 5, 6, 7; DLB 2, 227; MAL
  5
Self, Will 1961- .... **CLC 282**
  See also BRWS 5; CA 143; CANR 83, 126,
  171, 201; CN 6, 7; DLB 207
Self, William
  See Self, Will
Self, William Woodward
  See Self, Will
Selzer, Richard 1928- .... **CLC 74**
  See also CA 65-68; CANR 14, 106, 204
Sembene, Ousmane
  See Ousmane, Sembene
Senancour, Etienne Pivert de
  1770-1846 .... **NCLC 16**
  See also DLB 119; GFL 1789 to the Present
Sender, Ramon (Jose) 1902-1982 ...... **CLC 8;**
  HLC 2; TCLC 136
  See also CA 5-8R; 105; CANR 8; DAM
  MULT; DLB 322; EWL 3; HW 1; MTCW
  1; RGWL 2, 3
Seneca, Lucius Annaeus c. 4B.C.-c.
  65 .... **CMLC 6, 107; DC 5**
  See also AW 2; CDWLB 1; DAM DRAM;
  DLB 211; RGWL 2, 3; TWA; WLIT 8
Seneca the Younger
  See Seneca, Lucius Annaeus
Senghor, Leopold Sedar
  1906-2001 .. **BLC 1:3; CLC 54, 130; PC
  25**
  See also AFW; BW 2; CA 116; 125; 203;
  CANR 47, 74, 134; CWW 2; DAM
  MULT, POET; DNFS 2; EWL 3; GFL
  1789 to the Present; MTCW 1, 2; MTFW
  2005; TWA
Senior, Olive (Marjorie) 1941- .... **SSC 78**
  See also BW 3; CA 154; CANR 86, 126;
  CN 6; CP 6, 7; CWP; DLB 157; EWL 3;
  RGSF 2
Senna, Danzy 1970- .... **CLC 119**
  See also CA 169; CANR 130, 184
Sepheriades, Georgios
  See Seferis, George
Serling, (Edward) Rod(man)
  1924-1975 .... **CLC 30**
  See also AAYA 14; AITN 1; CA 162; 57-
  60; DLB 26; SFW 4
Serna, Ramon Gomez de la
  See Gomez de la Serna, Ramon
Serpieres
  See Guillevic, (Eugene)
Service, Robert
  See Service, Robert W.
Service, Robert W. 1874(?)-1958 .... **PC 70;**
  TCLC 15; WLC 5
  See also BYA 4; CA 115; 140; CANR 84;
  DA; DAB; DAC; DAM MST, POET;
  DLB 92; PFS 10; RGEL 2; SATA 20
Service, Robert William
  See Service, Robert W.
Servius c. 370-c. 431 .... **CMLC 120**
Seth, Vikram 1952- .... **CLC 43, 90, 277**
  See also BRWS 10; CA 121; 127; CANR
  50, 74, 131; CN 6, 7; CP 5, 6, 7; DA3;
  DAM MULT; DLB 120, 271, 282, 323;
  EWL 3; INT CA-127; MTCW 2; MTFW
  2005; WWE 1

Setien, Miguel Delibes
  See Delibes Setien, Miguel
Seton, Cynthia Propper 1926-1982 .. **CLC 27**
  See also CA 5-8R; 108; CANR 7
Seton, Ernest (Evan) Thompson
  1860-1946 .... **TCLC 31**
  See also ANW; BYA 3; CA 109; 204; CLR
  59; DLB 92; DLBD 13; JRDA; SATA 18
Seton-Thompson, Ernest
  See Seton, Ernest (Evan) Thompson
Settle, Mary Lee 1918-2005 .... **CLC 19, 61,
  273**
  See also BPFB 3; CA 89-92; 243; CAAS 1;
  CANR 44, 87, 126, 182; CN 6, 7; CSW;
  DLB 6; INT CA-89-92
Seuphor, Michel
  See Arp, Jean
Sevigne, Marie (de Rabutin-Chantal)
  1626-1696 .... **LC 11, 144**
  See also DLB 268; GFL Beginnings to
  1789; TWA
Sevigne, Marie de Rabutin Chantal
  See Sevigne, Marie (de Rabutin-Chantal)
Sewall, Samuel 1652-1730 .... **LC 38**
  See also DLB 24; RGAL 4
Sexton, Anne 1928-1974 .. **CLC 2, 4, 6, 8, 10,
  15, 53, 123; PC 2, 79; WLC 5**
  See also AMWS 2; CA 1-4R; 53-56; CABS
  2; CANR 3, 36; CDALB 1941-1968; CP
  1, 2; DA; DA3; DAB; DAC; DAM MST,
  POET; DLB 5, 169; EWL 3; EXPP; FL
  1:6; FW; MAL 5; MBL; MTCW 1, 2;
  MTFW 2005; PAB; PFS 4, 14, 30; RGAL
  4; RGHL; SATA 10; TUS
Sexton, Anne Harvey
  See Sexton, Anne
Shaara, Jeff 1952- .... **CLC 119**
  See also AAYA 70; CA 163; CANR 109,
  172; CN 7; MTFW 2005
Shaara, Michael 1929-1988 .... **CLC 15**
  See also AAYA 71; AITN 1; BPFB 3; CA
  102; 125; CANR 52, 85; DAM POP;
  DLBY 1983; MTFW 2005; NFS 26
Shackleton, C.C.
  See Aldiss, Brian W.
Shacochis, Bob
  See Shacochis, Robert G.
Shacochis, Robert G. 1951- .... **CLC 39**
  See also CA 119; 124; CANR 100; INT CA-
  124
Shadwell, Thomas 1641(?)-1692 .... **LC 114**
  See also DLB 80; IDTP; RGEL 2
Shaffer, Anthony 1926-2001 .... **CLC 19**
  See also CA 110; 116; 200; CBD; CD 5, 6;
  DAM DRAM; DFS 13; DLB 13
Shaffer, Anthony Joshua
  See Shaffer, Anthony
Shaffer, Peter 1926- ... **CLC 5, 14, 18, 37, 60,
  291; DC 7**
  See also BRWS 1; CA 25-28R; CANR 25,
  47, 74, 118; CBD; CD 5, 6; CDBLB 1960
  to Present; DA3; DAB; DAM DRAM,
  MST; DFS 5, 13; DLB 13, 233; EWL 3;
  MTCW 1, 2; MTFW 2005; RGEL 2; TEA
Shakespeare, William 1564-1616 . **PC 84, 89,
  98, 101; WLC 5**
  See also AAYA 35; BRW 1; BRWR 3; CD-
  BLB Before 1660; DA; DA3; DAB;
  DAC; DAM DRAM, MST, POET; DFS
  20, 21; DLB 62, 172, 263; EXPP; LAIT
  1; LATS 1:1; LMFS 1; PAB; PFS 1, 2, 3,
  4, 5, 8, 9, 35; RGEL 2; TEA; WLIT 3;
  WP; WS; WYA
Shakey, Bernard
  See Young, Neil
Shalamov, Varlam (Tikhonovich)
  1907-1982 .... **CLC 18**
  See also CA 129; 105; DLB 302; RGSF 2

Shamloo, Ahmad
See Shamlu, Ahmad
Shamlou, Ahmad
See Shamlu, Ahmad
Shamlu, Ahmad 1925-2000 .... **CLC 10**
See also CA 216; CWW 2
Shammas, Anton 1951- .... **CLC 55**
See also CA 199; DLB 346
Shandling, Arline
See Berriault, Gina
Shange, Ntozake 1948- .. **BLC 1:3, 2:3; CLC 8, 25, 38, 74, 126; DC 3**
See also AAYA 9, 66; AFAW 1, 2; BW 2; CA 85-88; CABS 3; CAD; CANR 27, 48, 74, 131; CD 5, 6; CP 5, 6, 7; CWD; CWP; DA3; DAM DRAM, MULT; DFS 2, 11; DLB 38, 249; FW; LAIT 4, 5; MAL 5; MTCW 1, 2; MTFW 2005; NFS 11; RGAL 4; SATA 157; YAW
Shanley, John Patrick 1950- .... **CLC 75**
See also AAYA 74; AMWS 14; CA 128; 133; CAD; CANR 83, 154; CD 5, 6; DFS 23
Shapcott, Thomas W(illiam) 1935- .. **CLC 38**
See also CA 69-72; CANR 49, 83, 103; CP 1, 2, 3, 4, 5, 6, 7; DLB 289
Shapiro, Jane 1942- .... **CLC 76**
See also CA 196
Shapiro, Karl 1913-2000 ... **CLC 4, 8, 15, 53; PC 25**
See also AMWS 2; CA 1-4R; 188; CAAS 6; CANR 1, 36, 66; CP 1, 2, 3, 4, 5, 6; DLB 48; EWL 3; EXPP; MAL 5; MTCW 1, 2; MTFW 2005; PFS 3; RGAL 4
Sharp, William 1855-1905 .... **TCLC 39**
See also CA 160; DLB 156; RGEL 2; SUFW
Sharpe, Thomas Ridley 1928- .... **CLC 36**
See also CA 114; 122; CANR 85; CN 4, 5, 6, 7; DLB 14, 231; INT CA-122
Sharpe, Tom
See Sharpe, Thomas Ridley
Shatrov, Mikhail CLC 59
Shaw, Bernard
See Shaw, George Bernard
Shaw, G. Bernard
See Shaw, George Bernard
Shaw, George Bernard 1856-1950 ..... **DC 23; TCLC 3, 9, 21, 45, 205; WLC 5**
See also AAYA 61; BRW 6; BRWC 1; BRWR 2; CA 104; 128; CDBLB 1914-1945; DA; DA3; DAB; DAC; DAM DRAM, MST; DFS 1, 3, 6, 11, 19, 22; DLB 10, 57, 190, 332; EWL 3; LAIT 3; LATS 1:1; MTCW 1, 2; MTFW 2005; RGEL 2; TEA; WLIT 4
Shaw, Henry Wheeler 1818-1885 .. **NCLC 15**
See also DLB 11; RGAL 4
Shaw, Irwin 1913-1984 .... **CLC 7, 23, 34**
See also AITN 1; BPFB 3; CA 13-16R; 112; CANR 21; CDALB 1941-1968; CN 1, 2, 3; CPW; DAM DRAM, POP; DLB 6, 102; DLBY 1984; MAL 5; MTCW 1, 21; MTFW 2005
Shaw, Robert (Archibald) 1927-1978 .... **CLC 5**
See also AITN 1; CA 1-4R; 81-84; CANR 4; CN 1, 2; DLB 13, 14
Shaw, T. E.
See Lawrence, T. E.
Shawn, Wallace 1943- .... **CLC 41**
See also CA 112; CAD; CD 5, 6; DLB 266
Shaykh, al- Hanan
See al-Shaykh, Hanan
Shchedrin, N.
See Saltykov, Mikhail Evgrafovich
Shea, Lisa 1953- .... **CLC 86**
See also CA 147

Sheed, Wilfrid 1930- .... **CLC 2, 4, 10, 53**
See also CA 65-68; CANR 30, 66, 181; CN 1, 2, 3, 4, 5, 6, 7; DLB 6; MAL 5; MTCW 1, 2; MTFW 2005
Sheed, Wilfrid John Joseph
See Sheed, Wilfrid
Sheehy, Gail 1937- .... **CLC 171**
See also CA 49-52; CANR 1, 33, 55, 92; CPW; MTCW 1
Sheldon, Alice Hastings Bradley 1915(?)-1987 .... **CLC 48, 50**
See also CA 108; 122; CANR 34; DLB 8; INT CA-108; MTCW 1; SCFW 1, 2; SFW 4
Sheldon, John
See Bloch, Robert (Albert)
Sheldon, Raccoona
See Sheldon, Alice Hastings Bradley
Shelley, Mary
See Shelley, Mary Wollstonecraft
Shelley, Mary Wollstonecraft 1797-1851 .... **NCLC 14, 59, 103, 170; SSC 92; WLC 5**
See also AAYA 20; BPFB 3; BRW 3; BRWC 2; BRWR 3; BRWS 3; BYA 5; CDBLB 1789-1832; CLR 133; DA; DA3; DAB; DAC; DAM MST, NOV; DLB 110, 116, 159, 178; EXPN; FL 1:3; GL 3; HGG; LAIT 1; LMFS 1, 2; NFS 1; RGEL 2; SATA 29; SCFW 1, 2; SFW 4; TEA; WLIT 3
Shelley, Percy Bysshe 1792-1822 .. **NCLC 18, 93, 143, 175; PC 14, 67; WLC 5**
See also AAYA 61; BRW 4; BRWR 1; CDBLB 1789-1832; DA; DA3; DAB; DAC; DAM MST, POET; DLB 96, 110, 158; EXPP; LMFS 1; PAB; PFS 2, 27, 32; RGEL 2; TEA; WLIT 3; WP
Shepard, James R.
See Shepard, Jim
Shepard, Jim 1956- .... **CLC 36**
See also AAYA 73; CA 137; CANR 59, 104, 160, 199; SATA 90, 164
Shepard, Lucius 1947- .... **CLC 34**
See also CA 128; 141; CANR 81, 124, 178; HGG; SCFW 2; SFW 4; SUFW 2
Shepard, Sam 1943- .... **CLC 4, 6, 17, 34, 41, 44, 169; DC 5**
See also AAYA 1, 58; AMWS 3; CA 69-72; CABS 3; CAD; CANR 22, 120, 140; CD 5, 6; DA3; DAM DRAM; DFS 3, 6, 7, 14; DLB 7, 212, 341; EWL 3; IDFW 3, 4; MAL 5; MTCW 1, 2; MTFW 2005; RGAL 4
Shepherd, Jean (Parker) 1921-1999 .... **TCLC 177**
See also AAYA 69; AITN 2; CA 77-80; 187
Shepherd, Michael
See Ludlum, Robert
Sherburne, Zoa (Lillian Morin) 1912-1995 .... **CLC 30**
See also AAYA 13; CA 1-4R; 176; CANR 3, 37; MAICYA 1, 2; SAAS 18; SATA 3; YAW
Sheridan, Frances 1724-1766 .... **LC 7**
See also DLB 39, 84
Sheridan, Richard Brinsley 1751-1816 . **DC 1; NCLC 5, 91; WLC 5**
See also BRW 3; CDBLB 1660-1789; DA; DAB; DAC; DAM DRAM, MST; DFS 15; DLB 89; WLIT 3
Sherman, Jonathan Marc 1968- .... **CLC 55**
See also CA 230
Sherman, Martin 1941(?)- .... **CLC 19**
See also CA 116; 123; CAD; CANR 86; CD 5, 6; DFS 20; DLB 228; GLL 1; IDTP; RGHL
Sherwin, Judith Johnson
See Johnson, Judith

Sherwood, Frances 1940- .... **CLC 81**
See also CA 146, 220; CAAE 220; CANR 158
Sherwood, Robert E(mmet) 1896-1955 .... **DC 36; TCLC 3**
See also CA 104; 153; CANR 86; DAM DRAM; DFS 11, 15, 17; DLB 7, 26, 249; IDFW 3, 4; MAL 5; RGAL 4
Shestov, Lev 1866-1938 .... **TCLC 56**
Shevchenko, Taras 1814-1861 .... **NCLC 54**
Shiel, M. P. 1865-1947 .... **TCLC 8**
See also CA 106; 160; DLB 153; HGG; MTCW 2; MTFW 2005; SCFW 1, 2; SFW 4; SUFW
Shiel, Matthew Phipps
See Shiel, M. P.
Shields, Carol 1935-2003 . **CLC 91, 113, 193; SSC 126**
See also AMWS 7; CA 81-84; 218; CANR 51, 74, 98, 133; CCA 1; CN 6, 7; CPW; DA3; DAC; DLB 334, 350; MTCW 2; MTFW 2005; NFS 23
Shields, David 1956- .... **CLC 97**
See also CA 124; CANR 48, 99, 112, 157
Shields, David Jonathan
See Shields, David
Shiga, Naoya 1883-1971 .... **CLC 33; SSC 23; TCLC 172**
See also CA 101; 33-36R; DLB 180; EWL 3; MJW; RGWL 3
Shiga Naoya
See Shiga, Naoya
Shilts, Randy 1951-1994 .... **CLC 85**
See also AAYA 19; CA 115; 127; 144; CANR 45; DA3; GLL 1; INT CA-127; MTCW 2; MTFW 2005
Shimazaki, Haruki 1872-1943 .... **TCLC 5**
See also CA 105; 134; CANR 84; DLB 180; EWL 3; MJW; RGWL 3
Shimazaki Toson
See Shimazaki, Haruki
Shirley, James 1596-1666 .... **DC 25; LC 96**
See also DLB 58; RGEL 2
Shirley Hastings, Selina
See Hastings, Selina
Sholem Aleykhem
See Rabinovitch, Sholem
Sholokhov, Mikhail 1905-1984 ..... **CLC 7, 15**
See also CA 101; 112; DLB 272, 332; EWL 3; MTCW 1, 2; MTFW 2005; RGWL 2, 3; SATA-Obit 36
Sholokhov, Mikhail Aleksandrovich
See Sholokhov, Mikhail
Sholom Aleichem 1859-1916
See Rabinovitch, Sholem
Shone, Patric
See Hanley, James
Showalter, Elaine 1941- .... **CLC 169**
See also CA 57-60; CANR 58, 106; DLB 67; FW; GLL 2
Shreve, Susan
See Shreve, Susan Richards
Shreve, Susan Richards 1939- .... **CLC 23**
See also CA 49-52; CAAS 5; CANR 5, 38, 69, 100, 159, 199; MAICYA 1, 2; SATA 46, 95, 152; SATA-Brief 41
Shue, Larry 1946-1985 .... **CLC 52**
See also CA 145; 117; DAM DRAM; DFS 7
Shu-Jen, Chou 1881-1936 . **SSC 20; TCLC 3**
See also CA 104; EWL 3
Shulman, Alix Kates 1932- .... **CLC 2, 10**
See also CA 29-32R; CANR 43, 199; FW; SATA 7
Shuster, Joe 1914-1992 .... **CLC 21**
See also AAYA 50

Shute, Nevil 1899-1960 .... **CLC 30**
See also BPFB 3; CA 102; 93-96; CANR
85; DLB 255; MTCW 2; NFS 9; RHW 4;
SFW 4

Shuttle, Penelope (Diane) 1947- .... **CLC 7**
See also CA 93-96; CANR 39, 84, 92, 108;
CP 3, 4, 5, 6, 7; CWP; DLB 14, 40

Shvarts, Elena 1948- .... **PC 50**
See also CA 147

Sidhwa, Bapsi 1939-
See Sidhwa, Bapsy (N.)

Sidhwa, Bapsy (N.) 1938- .... **CLC 168**
See also CA 108; CANR 25, 57; CN 6, 7;
DLB 323; FW

Sidney, Mary 1561-1621 .... **LC 19, 39**
See also DLB 167

Sidney, Sir Philip 1554-1586 .... **LC 19, 39,
131; PC 32**
See also BRW 1; BRWR 2; CDBLB Before
1660; DA; DA3; DAB; DAC; DAM MST,
POET; DLB 167; EXPP; PAB; PFS 30;
RGEL 2; TEA; WP

Sidney Herbert, Mary
See Sidney, Mary

Siegel, Jerome 1914-1996 .... **CLC 21**
See also AAYA 50; CA 116; 169; 151

Siegel, Jerry
See Siegel, Jerome

Sienkiewicz, Henryk (Adam Alexander Pius)
1846-1916 .... **TCLC 3**
See also CA 104; 134; CANR 84; DLB 332;
EWL 3; RGSF 2; RGWL 2, 3

Sierra, Gregorio Martinez
See Martinez Sierra, Gregorio

Sierra, Maria de la O'LeJarraga Martinez
See Martinez Sierra, Maria

Sigal, Clancy 1926- .... **CLC 7**
See also CA 1-4R; CANR 85, 184; CN 1,
2, 3, 4, 5, 6, 7

Siger of Brabant 1240(?)-1284(?) . **CMLC 69**
See also DLB 115

Sigourney, Lydia H.
See Sigourney, Lydia Howard
See also DLB 73, 183

Sigourney, Lydia Howard
1791-1865 .... **NCLC 21, 87**
See Sigourney, Lydia H.
See also DLB 1, 42, 239, 243

Sigourney, Lydia Howard Huntley
See Sigourney, Lydia Howard

Sigourney, Lydia Huntley
See Sigourney, Lydia Howard

Siguenza y Gongora, Carlos de
1645-1700 .... **HLCS 2; LC 8**
See also LAW

Sigurjonsson, Johann
See Sigurjonsson, Johann

Sigurjonsson, Johann 1880-1919 ... **TCLC 27**
See also CA 170; DLB 293; EWL 3

Sikelianos, Angelos 1884-1951 .... **PC 29;
TCLC 39**
See also EWL 3; RGWL 2, 3

Silkin, Jon 1930-1997 .... **CLC 2, 6, 43**
See also CA 5-8R; CAAS 5; CANR 89; CP
1, 2, 3, 4, 5, 6; DLB 27

Silko, Leslie 1948- ...... **CLC 23, 74, 114, 211;
NNAL; SSC 37, 66; WLCS**
See also AAYA 14; AMWS 4; ANW; BYA
12; CA 115; 122; CANR 45, 65, 118; CN
4, 5, 6, 7; CP 4, 5, 6, 7; CPW 1; CWP;
DA; DA3; DAC; DAM MST, MULT,
POP; DLB 143, 175, 256; EWL 3;
EXPP; EXPS; LAIT 4; MAL 5; MTCW
2; MTFW 2005; NFS 4; PFS 9, 16; RGAL
4; RGSF 2; SSFS 4, 8, 10, 11; TCWW 1,
2

Silko, Leslie Marmon
See Silko, Leslie

Sillanpaa, Frans Eemil 1888-1964 ... **CLC 19**
See also CA 129; 93-96; DLB 332; EWL 3;
MTCW 1

Sillitoe, Alan 1928- .. **CLC 1, 3, 6, 10, 19, 57,
148**
See also AITN 1; BRWS 5; CA 9-12R, 191;
CAAE 191; CAAS 2; CANR 8, 26, 55,
139; CDBLB 1960 to Present; CN 1, 2, 3,
4, 5, 6; CP 1, 2, 3, 4, 5; DLB 14, 139;
EWL 3; MTCW 1, 2; MTFW 2005; RGEL
2; RGSF 2; SATA 61

Silone, Ignazio 1900-1978 .... **CLC 4**
See also CA 25-28; 81-84; CANR 34; CAP
2; DLB 264; EW 12; EWL 3; MTCW 1;
RGSF 2; RGWL 2, 3

Silone, Ignazione
See Silone, Ignazio

Siluriensis, Leolinus
See Jones, Arthur Llewellyn

Silver, Joan Micklin 1935- .... **CLC 20**
See also CA 114; 121; INT CA-121

Silver, Nicholas
See Faust, Frederick

Silverberg, Robert 1935- .... **CLC 7, 140**
See also AAYA 24; BPFB 3; BYA 7, 9; CA
1-4R, 186; CAAE 186; CAAS 3; CANR
1, 20, 36, 85, 140, 175; CLR 59; CN 6, 7;
CPW; DAM POP; DLB 8; INT CANR-
20; MAICYA 1, 2; MTCW 1, 2; MTFW
2005; SATA 13, 91; SATA-Essay 104;
SCFW 1, 2; SFW 4; SUFW 2

Silverstein, Alvin 1933- .... **CLC 17**
See also CA 49-52; CANR 2; CLR 25;
JRDA; MAICYA 1, 2; SATA 8, 69, 124

Silverstein, Shel 1932-1999 .... **PC 49**
See also AAYA 40; BW 3; CA 107; 179;
CANR 47, 74, 81; CLR 5, 96; CWRI 5;
JRDA; MAICYA 1, 2; MTCW 2; MTFW
2005; SATA 33, 92; SATA-Brief 27;
SATA-Obit 116

Silverstein, Sheldon Allan
See Silverstein, Shel

Silverstein, Virginia B. 1937- .... **CLC 17**
See also CA 49-52; CANR 2; CLR 25;
JRDA; MAICYA 1, 2; SATA 8, 69, 124

Silverstein, Virginia Barbara Opshelor
See Silverstein, Virginia B.

Sim, Georges
See Simenon, Georges

Simak, Clifford D(onald) 1904-1988 . **CLC 1,
55**
See also CA 1-4R; 125; CANR 1, 35; DLB
8; MTCW 1; SATA-Obit 56; SCFW 1, 2;
SFW 4

Simenon, Georges 1903-1989 .... **CLC 1, 2, 3,
8, 18, 47**
See also BPFB 3; CA 85-88; 129; CANR
35; CMW 4; DA3; DAM POP; DLB 72;
DLBY 1989; EW 12; EWL 3; GFL 1789
to the Present; MSW; MTCW 1, 2; MTFW
2005; RGWL 2, 3

Simenon, Georges Jacques Christian
See Simenon, Georges

Simic, Charles 1938- .... **CLC 6, 9, 22, 49, 68,
130, 256; PC 69**
See also AAYA 78; AMWS 8; CA 29-32R;
CAAS 4; CANR 12, 33, 52, 61, 96, 140;
CP 2, 3, 4, 5, 6, 7; DA3; DAM POET;
DLB 105; MAL 5; MTCW 2; MTFW
2005; PFS 7, 33; RGAL 4; WP

Simmel, Georg 1858-1918 .... **TCLC 64**
See also CA 157; DLB 296

Simmons, Charles (Paul) 1924- .... **CLC 57**
See also CA 89-92; INT CA-89-92

Simmons, Dan 1948- .... **CLC 44**
See also AAYA 16, 54; CA 138; CANR 53,
81, 126, 174, 204; CPW; DAM POP;
HGG; SUFW 2

Simmons, James (Stewart Alexander)
1933- .... **CLC 43**
See also CA 105; CAAS 21; CP 1, 2, 3, 4,
5, 6, 7; DLB 40

Simmons, Richard
See Simmons, Dan

Simms, William Gilmore
1806-1870 .... **NCLC 3**
See also DLB 3, 30, 59, 73, 248, 254;
RGAL 4

Simon, Carly 1945- .... **CLC 26**
See also CA 105

Simon, Claude 1913-2005 ... **CLC 4, 9, 15, 39**
See also CA 89-92; 241; CANR 33, 117;
CWW 2; DAM NOV; DLB 83, 332; EW
13; EWL 3; GFL 1789 to the Present;
MTCW 1

Simon, Claude Eugene Henri
See Simon, Claude

Simon, Claude Henri Eugene
See Simon, Claude

Simon, Marvin Neil
See Simon, Neil

Simon, Myles
See Follett, Ken

Simon, Neil 1927- .... **CLC 6, 11, 31, 39, 70,
233; DC 14**
See also AAYA 32; AITN 1; AMWS 4; CA
21-24R; CAD; CANR 26, 54, 87, 126;
CD 5, 6; DA3; DAM DRAM; DFS 2, 6,
12, 18, 24, 27; DLB 7, 266; LAIT 4; MAL
5; MTCW 1, 2; MTFW 2005; RGAL 4;
TUS

Simon, Paul 1941(?)- .... **CLC 17**
See also CA 116; 153; CANR 152

Simon, Paul Frederick
See Simon, Paul

Simonon, Paul 1956(?)- .... **CLC 30**

Simonson, Rick CLC 70

Simpson, Harriette
See Arnow, Harriette (Louisa) Simpson

Simpson, Louis 1923- ... **CLC 4, 7, 9, 32, 149**
See also AMWS 9; CA 1-4R; CAAS 4;
CANR 1, 61, 140; CP 1, 2, 3, 4, 5, 6, 7;
DAM POET; DLB 5; MAL 5; MTCW 1,
2; MTFW 2005; PFS 7, 11, 14; RGAL 4

Simpson, Mona 1957- .... **CLC 44, 146**
See also CA 122; 135; CANR 68, 103; CN
6, 7; EWL 3

Simpson, Mona Elizabeth
See Simpson, Mona

Simpson, N(orman) F(rederick)
1919- .... **CLC 29**
See also CA 13-16R; CBD; DLB 13; RGEL
2

Sinclair, Andrew (Annandale) 1935- . **CLC 2,
14**
See also CA 9-12R; CAAS 5; CANR 14,
38, 91; CN 1, 2, 3, 4, 5, 6, 7; DLB 14;
FANT; MTCW 1

Sinclair, Emil
See Hesse, Hermann

Sinclair, Iain 1943- .... **CLC 76**
See also BRWS 14; CA 132; CANR 81,
157; CP 5, 6, 7; HGG

Sinclair, Iain MacGregor
See Sinclair, Iain

Sinclair, Irene
See Griffith, D.W.

Sinclair, Julian
See Sinclair, May

Sinclair, Mary Amelia St. Clair (?)-
See Sinclair, May

Sinclair, May 1865-1946 .... **TCLC 3, 11**
See also CA 104; 166; DLB 36, 135; EWL
3; HGG; RGEL 2; RHW; SUFW

Sinclair, Roy
See Griffith, D.W.

Sinclair, Upton 1878-1968 ...... **CLC 1, 11, 15, 63; TCLC 160; WLC 5**
See also AAYA 63; AMWS 5; BPFB 3; BYA 2; CA 5-8R; 25-28R; CANR 7; CDALB 1929-1941; DA; DA3; DAB; DAC; DAM MST, NOV; DLB 9; EWL 3; INT CANR-7; LAIT 3; MAL 5; MTCW 1, 2; MTFW 2005; NFS 6; RGAL 4; SATA 9; TUS; YAW

Sinclair, Upton Beall
See Sinclair, Upton

Singe, (Edmund) J(ohn) M(illington) 1871-1909 .... **WLC**

Singer, Isaac
See Singer, Isaac Bashevis

Singer, Isaac Bashevis 1904-1991 .. **CLC 1, 3, 6, 9, 11, 15, 23, 38, 69, 111; SSC 3, 53, 80; WLC 5**
See also AAYA 32; AITN 1, 2; AMW; AMWR 2; BPFB 3; BYA 1, 4; CA 1-4R; 134; CANR 1, 39, 106; CDALB 1941-1968; CLR 1; CN 1, 2, 3, 4; CWRI 5; DA; DA3; DAB; DAC; DAM MST, NOV; DLB 6, 28, 52, 278, 332, 333; DLBY 1991; EWL 3; EXPS; HGG; JRDA; LAIT 3; MAICYA 1, 2; MAL 5; MTCW 1, 2; MTFW 2005; RGAL 4; RGHL; RGSF 2; SATA 3, 27; SATA-Obit 68; SSFS 2, 12, 16, 27, 30; TUS; TWA

Singer, Israel Joshua 1893-1944 .... **TCLC 33**
See also CA 169; DLB 333; EWL 3

Singh, Khushwant 1915- .... **CLC 11**
See also CA 9-12R; CAAS 9; CANR 6, 84; CN 1, 2, 3, 4, 5, 6, 7; DLB 323; EWL 3; RGEL 2

Singleton, Ann
See Benedict, Ruth

Singleton, John 1968(?)- .... **CLC 156**
See also AAYA 50; BW 2, 3; CA 138; CANR 67, 82; DAM MULT

Siniavskii, Andrei
See Sinyavsky, Andrei (Donatevich)

Sinibaldi, Fosco
See Kacew, Romain

Sinjohn, John
See Galsworthy, John

Sinyavsky, Andrei (Donatevich) 1925-1997 .... **CLC 8**
See also CA 85-88; 159; CWW 2; EWL 3; RGSF 2

Sinyavsky, Andrey Donatovich
See Sinyavsky, Andrei (Donatevich)

Sirin, V.
See Nabokov, Vladimir

Sissman, L(ouis) E(dward) 1928-1976 .... **CLC 9, 18**
See also CA 21-24R; 65-68; CANR 13; CP 2; DLB 5

Sisson, C(harles) H(ubert) 1914-2003 .... **CLC 8**
See also BRWS 11; CA 1-4R; 220; CAAS 3; CANR 3, 48, 84; CP 1, 2, 3, 4, 5, 6, 7; DLB 27

Sitting Bull 1831(?)-1890 .... **NNAL**
See also DA3; DAM MULT

Sitwell, Dame Edith 1887-1964 ..... **CLC 2, 9, 67; PC 3**
See also BRW 7; CA 9-12R; CANR 35; CDBLB 1945-1960; DAM POET; DLB 20; EWL 3; MTCW 1, 2; MTFW 2005; RGEL 2; TEA

Siwaarmill, H. P.
See Sharp, William

Sjoewall, Maj 1935- .... **CLC 7**
See also BPFB 3; CA 65-68; CANR 73; CMW 4; MSW

Sjowall, Maj
See Sjoewall, Maj

Skelton, John 1460(?)-1529 ..... **LC 71; PC 25**
See also BRW 1; DLB 136; RGEL 2

Skelton, Robin 1925-1997 .... **CLC 13**
See also AITN 2; CA 5-8R; 160; CAAS 5; CANR 28, 89; CCA 1; CP 1, 2, 3, 4, 5, 6; DLB 27, 53

Skolimowski, Jerzy 1938- .... **CLC 20**
See also CA 128

Skram, Amalie (Bertha) 1846-1905 .... **TCLC 25**
See also CA 165; DLB 354

Skvorecky, Josef 1924- . **CLC 15, 39, 69, 152**
See also CA 61-64; CAAS 1; CANR 10, 34, 63, 108; CDWLB 4; CWW 2; DA3; DAC; DAM NOV; DLB 232; EWL 3; MTCW 1, 2; MTFW 2005

Skvorecky, Josef Vaclav
See Skvorecky, Josef

Slade, Bernard 1930-
See Newbound, Bernard Slade

Slaughter, Carolyn 1946- .... **CLC 56**
See also CA 85-88; CANR 85, 169; CN 5, 6, 7

Slaughter, Frank G(ill) 1908-2001 ... **CLC 29**
See also AITN 2; CA 5-8R; 197; CANR 5, 85; INT CANR-5; RHW

Slavitt, David R. 1935- .... **CLC 5, 14**
See also CA 21-24R; CAAS 3; CANR 41, 83, 166; CN 1, 2; CP 1, 2, 3, 4, 5, 6, 7; DLB 5, 6

Slavitt, David Rytman
See Slavitt, David R.

Slesinger, Tess 1905-1945 .... **TCLC 10**
See also CA 107; 199; DLB 102

Slessor, Kenneth 1901-1971 .... **CLC 14**
See also CA 102; 89-92; DLB 260; RGEL 2

Slowacki, Juliusz 1809-1849 .... **NCLC 15**
See also RGWL 3

Smart, Christopher 1722-1771 .... **LC 3, 134; PC 13**
See also DAM POET; DLB 109; RGEL 2

Smart, Elizabeth 1913-1986 .... **CLC 54; TCLC 231**
See also CA 81-84; 118; CN 4; DLB 88

Smiley, Jane 1949- ...... **CLC 53, 76, 144, 236**
See also AAYA 66; AMWS 6; BPFB 3; CA 104; CANR 30, 50, 74, 96, 158, 196; CN 6, 7; CPW 1; DA3; DAM POP; DLB 227, 234; EWL 3; INT CANR-30; MAL 5; MTCW 2005; NFS 32; SSFS 19

Smiley, Jane Graves
See Smiley, Jane

Smith, A(rthur) J(ames) M(arshall) 1902-1980 .... **CLC 15**
See also CA 1-4R; 102; CANR 4; CP 1, 2, 3; DAC; DLB 88; RGEL 2

Smith, Adam 1723(?)-1790 .... **LC 36**
See also DLB 104, 252, 336; RGEL 2

Smith, Alexander 1829-1867 .... **NCLC 59**
See also DLB 32, 55

Smith, Alexander McCall 1948- ..... **CLC 268**
See also CA 215; CANR 154, 196; SATA 73, 179

Smith, Anna Deavere 1950- ...... **CLC 86, 241**
See also CA 133; CANR 103; CD 5, 6; DFS 2, 22; DLB 341

Smith, Betty (Wehner) 1904-1972 .... **CLC 19**
See also AAYA 72; BPFB 3; BYA 3; CA 5-8R; 33-36R; DLBY 1982; LAIT 3; NFS 31; RGAL 4; SATA 6

Smith, Charlotte (Turner) 1749-1806 .... **NCLC 23, 115; PC 104**
See also DLB 39, 109; RGEL 2; TEA

Smith, Clark Ashton 1893-1961 .... **CLC 43**
See also AAYA 76; CA 143; CANR 81; FANT; HGG; MTCW 2; SCFW 1, 2; SFW 4; SUFW

Smith, Dave
See Smith, David (Jeddie)

Smith, David (Jeddie) 1942- .... **CLC 22, 42**
See also CA 49-52; CAAS 7; CANR 1, 59, 120; CP 3, 4, 5, 6, 7; CSW; DAM POET; DLB 5

Smith, Iain Crichton 1928-1998 .... **CLC 64**
See also BRWS 9; CA 21-24R; 171; CN 1, 2, 3, 4, 5, 6; CP 1, 2, 3, 4, 5, 6; DLB 40, 139, 319, 352; RGSF 2

Smith, John 1580(?)-1631 .... **LC 9**
See also DLB 24, 30; TUS

Smith, Johnston
See Crane, Stephen

Smith, Joseph, Jr. 1805-1844 .... **NCLC 53**

Smith, Kevin 1970- .... **CLC 223**
See also AAYA 37; CA 166; CANR 131, 201

Smith, Lee 1944- .... **CLC 25, 73, 258**
See also CA 114; 119; CANR 46, 118, 173; CN 7; CSW; DLB 143; DLBY 1983; EWL 3; INT CA-119; RGAL 4

Smith, Martin
See Smith, Martin Cruz

Smith, Martin Cruz 1942- .. **CLC 25; NNAL**
See also BEST 89:4; BPFB 3; CA 85-88; CANR 6, 23, 43, 65, 119, 184; CMW 4; CPW; DAM MULT, POP; HGG; INT CANR-23; MTCW 2; MTFW 2005; RGAL 4

Smith, Patti 1946- .... **CLC 12**
See also CA 93-96; CANR 63, 168

Smith, Pauline (Urmson) 1882-1959 .... **TCLC 25**
See also DLB 225; EWL 3

Smith, R. Alexander McCall
See Smith, Alexander McCall

Smith, Rosamond
See Oates, Joyce Carol

Smith, Seba 1792-1868 .... **NCLC 187**
See also DLB 1, 11, 243

Smith, Sheila Kaye
See Kaye-Smith, Sheila

Smith, Stevie 1902-1971 .... **CLC 3, 8, 25, 44; PC 12**
See also BRWR 3; BRWS 2; CA 17-18; 29-32R; CANR 35; CAP 2; CP 1; DAM POET; DLB 20; EWL 3; MTCW 1, 2; PAB; PFS 3; RGEL 2; TEA

Smith, Wilbur 1933- .... **CLC 33**
See also CA 13-16R; CANR 7, 46, 66, 134, 180; CPW; MTCW 1, 2; MTFW 2005

Smith, Wilbur Addison
See Smith, Wilbur

Smith, William Jay 1918- .... **CLC 6**
See also AMWS 13; CA 5-8R; CANR 44, 106; CP 1, 2, 3, 4, 5, 6, 7; CSW; CWRI 5; DLB 5; MAICYA 1, 2; SAAS 22; SATA 2, 68, 154; SATA-Essay 154; TCLE 1:2

Smith, Woodrow Wilson
See Kuttner, Henry

Smith, Zadie 1975- .... **CLC 158**
See also AAYA 50; CA 193; CANR 204; DLB 347; MTFW 2005

Smolenskin, Peretz 1842-1885 .... **NCLC 30**

Smollett, Tobias (George) 1721-1771 ... **LC 2, 46**
See also BRW 3; CDBLB 1660-1789; DLB 39, 104; RGEL 2; TEA

Snodgrass, Quentin Curtius
See Twain, Mark

Snodgrass, Thomas Jefferson
See Twain, Mark

Snodgrass, W. D. 1926-2009 .... **CLC 2, 6, 10, 18, 68; PC 74**
    See also AMWS 6; CA 1-4R; 282; CANR 6, 36, 65, 85, 185; CP 1, 2, 3, 4, 5, 6, 7; DAM POET; DLB 5; MAL 5; MTCW 1, 2; MTFW 2005; PFS 29; RGAL 4; TCLE 1:2

Snodgrass, W. de Witt
    See Snodgrass, W. D.

Snodgrass, William de Witt
    See Snodgrass, W. D.

Snodgrass, William De Witt
    See Snodgrass, W. D.

Snorri Sturluson 1179-1241 .... **CMLC 56**
    See also RGWL 2, 3

Snow, C(harles) P(ercy) 1905-1980 ... **CLC 1, 4, 6, 9, 13, 19**
    See also BRW 7; CA 5-8R; 101; CANR 28; CDBLB 1945-1960; CN 1, 2; DAM NOV; DLB 15, 77; DLBD 17; EWL 3; MTCW 1, 2; MTFW 2005; RGEL 2; TEA

Snow, Frances Compton
    See Adams, Henry

Snyder, Gary 1930- . **CLC 1, 2, 5, 9, 32, 120; PC 21**
    See also AAYA 72; AMWS 8; ANW; BG 1:3; CA 17-20R; CANR 30, 60, 125; CP 1, 2, 3, 4, 5, 6, 7; DA3; DAM POET; DLB 5, 16, 165, 212, 237, 275, 342; EWL 3; MAL 5; MTCW 2; MTFW 2005; PFS 9, 19; RGAL 4; WP

Snyder, Gary Sherman
    See Snyder, Gary

Snyder, Zilpha Keatley 1927- .... **CLC 17**
    See also AAYA 15; BYA 1; CA 9-12R; 252; CAAE 252; CANR 38, 202; CLR 31, 121; JRDA; MAICYA 1, 2; SAAS 2; SATA 1, 28, 75, 110, 163; SATA-Essay 112, 163; YAW

Soares, Bernardo
    See Pessoa, Fernando

Sobh, A.
    See Shamlu, Ahmad

Sobh, Alef
    See Shamlu, Ahmad

Sobol, Joshua 1939- .... **CLC 60**
    See also CA 200; CWW 2; RGHL

Sobol, Yehoshua 1939-
    See Sobol, Joshua

Socrates 470B.C.-399B.C. .... **CMLC 27**

Soderberg, Hjalmar 1869-1941 ...... **TCLC 39**
    See also DLB 259; EWL 3; RGSF 2

Soderbergh, Steven 1963- .... **CLC 154**
    See also AAYA 43; CA 243

Soderbergh, Steven Andrew
    See Soderbergh, Steven

Sodergran, Edith 1892-1923 .... **TCLC 31**
    See also CA 202; DLB 259; EW 11; EWL 3; RGWL 2, 3

Soedergran, Edith Irene
    See Sodergran, Edith

Softly, Edgar
    See Lovecraft, H. P.

Softly, Edward
    See Lovecraft, H. P.

Sokolov, Alexander V. 1943- .... **CLC 59**
    See also CA 73-76; CWW 2; DLB 285; EWL 3; RGWL 2, 3

Sokolov, Alexander Vsevolodovich
    See Sokolov, Alexander V.

Sokolov, Raymond 1941- .... **CLC 7**
    See also CA 85-88

Sokolov, Sasha
    See Sokolov, Alexander V.

Solo, Jay
    See Ellison, Harlan

Sologub, Fedor
    See Teternikov, Fyodor Kuzmich

Sologub, Feodor
    See Teternikov, Fyodor Kuzmich

Sologub, Fyodor
    See Teternikov, Fyodor Kuzmich

Solomons, Ikey Esquir
    See Thackeray, William Makepeace

Solomos, Dionysios 1798-1857 .... **NCLC 15**

Solwoska, Mara
    See French, Marilyn

Solzhenitsyn, Aleksandr 1918-2008 ... **CLC 1, 2, 4, 7, 9, 10, 18, 26, 34, 78, 134, 235; SSC 32, 105; WLC 5**
    See also AAYA 49; AITN 1; BPFB 3; CA 69-72; CANR 40, 65, 116; CWW 2; DA; DA3; DAB; DAC; DAM MST, NOV; DLB 302, 332; EW 13; EWL 3; EXPS; LAIT 4; MTCW 1, 2; MTFW 2005; NFS 6; RGSF 2; RGWL 2, 3; SSFS 9; TWA

Solzhenitsyn, Aleksandr I.
    See Solzhenitsyn, Aleksandr

Solzhenitsyn, Aleksandr Isayevich
    See Solzhenitsyn, Aleksandr

Somers, Jane
    See Lessing, Doris

Somerville, Edith Oenone 1858-1949 .... **SSC 56; TCLC 51**
    See also CA 196; DLB 135; RGEL 2; RGSF 2

Somerville & Ross
    See Martin, Violet Florence; Somerville, Edith Oenone

Sommer, Scott 1951- .... **CLC 25**
    See also CA 106

Sommers, Christina Hoff 1950- ...... **CLC 197**
    See also CA 153; CANR 95

Sondheim, Stephen 1930- .. **CLC 30, 39, 147; DC 22**
    See also AAYA 11, 66; CA 103; CANR 47, 67, 125; DAM DRAM; DFS 25, 27; LAIT 4

Sondheim, Stephen Joshua
    See Sondheim, Stephen

Sone, Monica 1919- .... **AAL**
    See also DLB 312

Song, Cathy 1955- .... **AAL; PC 21**
    See also CA 154; CANR 118; CWP; DLB 169, 312; EXPP; FW; PFS 5

Sontag, Susan 1933-2004 ... **CLC 1, 2, 10, 13, 31, 105, 195, 277**
    See also AMWS 3; CA 17-20R; 234; CANR 25, 51, 74, 97, 184; CN 1, 2, 3, 4, 5, 6, 7; CPW; DA3; DAM POP; DLB 2, 67; EWL 3; MAL 5; MBL; MTCW 1, 2; MTFW 2005; RGAL 4; RHW; SSFS 10

Sophocles 496(?)B.C.-406(?)B.C. .... **CMLC 2, 47, 51, 86; DC 1; WLCS**
    See also AW 1; CDWLB 1; DA; DA3; DAB; DAC; DAM DRAM, MST; DFS 1, 4, 8, 24; DLB 176; LAIT 1; LATS 1:1; LMFS 1; RGWL 2, 3; TWA; WLIT 8

Sordello 1189-1269 .... **CMLC 15**

Sorel, Georges 1847-1922 .... **TCLC 91**
    See also CA 118; 188

Sorel, Julia
    See Drexler, Rosalyn

Sorokin, Vladimir CLC 59
    See also CA 258; DLB 285

Sorokin, Vladimir Georgievich
    See Sorokin, Vladimir

Sorrentino, Gilbert 1929-2006 .... **CLC 3, 7, 14, 22, 40, 247**
    See also CA 77-80; 250; CANR 14, 33, 115, 157; CN 3, 4, 5, 6, 7; CP 1, 2, 3, 4, 5, 6, 7; DLB 5, 173; DLBY 1980; INT CANR-14

Soseki
    See Natsume, Soseki

Soto, Gary 1952- ... **CLC 32, 80; HLC 2; PC 28**
    See also AAYA 10, 37; BYA 11; CA 119; 125; CANR 50, 74, 107, 157; CLR 38; CP 4, 5, 6, 7; DAM MULT; DFS 26; DLB 82; EWL 3; EXPP; HW 1, 2; INT CA-125; JRDA; LLW; MAICYA 1; MAIC-YAS 1; MAL 5; MTCW 2; MTFW 2005; PFS 7, 30; RGAL 4; SATA 80, 120, 174; WYA; YAW

Soupault, Philippe 1897-1990 .... **CLC 68**
    See also CA 116; 147; 131; EWL 3; GFL 1789 to the Present; LMFS 2

Souster, (Holmes) Raymond 1921- .... **CLC 5, 14**
    See also CA 13-16R; CAAS 14; CANR 13, 29, 53; CP 1, 2, 3, 4, 5, 6, 7; DA3; DAC; DAM POET; DLB 88; RGEL 2; SATA 63

Southern, Terry 1924(?)-1995 .... **CLC 7**
    See also AMWS 11; BPFB 3; CA 1-4R; 150; CANR 1, 55, 107; CN 1, 2, 3, 4, 5, 6; DLB 2; IDFW 3, 4

Southerne, Thomas 1660-1746 .... **LC 99**
    See also DLB 80; RGEL 2

Southey, Robert 1774-1843 .... **NCLC 8, 97**
    See also BRW 4; DLB 93, 107, 142; RGEL 2; SATA 54

Southwell, Robert 1561(?)-1595 .... **LC 108**
    See also DLB 167; RGEL 2; TEA

Southworth, Emma Dorothy Eliza Nevitte 1819-1899 .... **NCLC 26**
    See also DLB 239

Souza, Ernest
    See Scott, Evelyn

Soyinka, Wole 1934- .. **BLC 1:3, 2:3; CLC 3, 5, 14, 36, 44, 179; DC 2; WLC 5**
    See also AFW; BW 2, 3; CA 13-16R; CANR 27, 39, 82, 136; CD 5, 6; CDWLB 3; CN 6, 7; CP 1, 2, 3, 4, 5, 6 ,7; DA; DA3; DAB; DAC; DAM DRAM, MST, MULT; DFS 10, 26; DLB 125, 332; EWL 3; MTCW 1, 2; MTFW 2005; PFS 27; RGEL 2; TWA; WLIT 2; WWE 1

Spackman, W(illiam) M(ode) 1905-1990 .... **CLC 46**
    See also CA 81-84; 132

Spacks, Barry (Bernard) 1931- .... **CLC 14**
    See also CA 154; CANR 33, 109; CP 3, 4, 5, 6, 7; DLB 105

Spanidou, Irini 1946- .... **CLC 44**
    See also CA 185; CANR 179

Spark, Muriel 1918-2006 .... **CLC 2, 3, 5, 8, 13, 18, 40, 94, 242; PC 72; SSC 10, 115**
    See also BRWS 1; CA 5-8R; 251; CANR 12, 36, 76, 89, 131; CDBLB 1945-1960; CN 1, 2, 3, 4, 5, 6, 7; CP 1, 2, 3, 4, 5, 6, 7; DA3; DAB; DAC; DAM MST, NOV; DLB 15, 139; EWL 3; FW; INT CANR-12; LAIT 4; MTCW 1, 2; MTFW 2005; NFS 22; RGEL 2; SSFS 28; TEA; WLIT 4; YAW

Spark, Muriel Sarah
    See Spark, Muriel

Spaulding, Douglas
    See Bradbury, Ray

Spaulding, Leonard
    See Bradbury, Ray

Speght, Rachel 1597-c. 1630 .... **LC 97**
    See also DLB 126

Spence, J. A. D.
    See Eliot, T. S.

Spencer, Anne 1882-1975 ...... **HR 1:3; PC 77**
    See also BW 2; CA 161; DLB 51, 54

Spencer, Elizabeth 1921- .... **CLC 22; SSC 57**
    See also CA 13-16R; CANR 32, 65, 87; CN 1, 2, 3, 4, 5, 6, 7; CSW; DLB 6, 218; EWL 3; MTCW 1; RGAL 4; SATA 14

Spencer, Leonard G.
    See Silverberg, Robert

Steiner, Rudolf 1861-1925 .... **TCLC 13**
See also CA 107

Stendhal 1783-1842 .... **NCLC 23, 46, 178; SSC 27; WLC 5**
See also DA; DA3; DAB; DAC; DAM MST, NOV; DLB 119; EW 5; GFL 1789 to the Present; RGWL 2, 3; TWA

Stephen, Adeline Virginia
See Woolf, Virginia

Stephen, Sir Leslie 1832-1904 .... **TCLC 23**
See also BRW 5; CA 123; DLB 57, 144, 190

Stephen, Sir Leslie
See Stephen, Sir Leslie

Stephen, Virginia
See Woolf, Virginia

Stephens, James 1882(?)-1950 .... **SSC 50; TCLC 4**
See also CA 104; 192; DLB 19, 153, 162; EWL 3; FANT; RGEL 2; SUFW

Stephens, Reed
See Donaldson, Stephen R.

Stephenson, Neal 1959- .... **CLC 220**
See also AAYA 38; CA 122; CANR 88, 138, 195; CN 7; MTFW 2005; SFW 4

Steptoe, Lydia
See Barnes, Djuna

Sterchi, Beat 1949- .... **CLC 65**
See also CA 203

Sterling, Brett
See Bradbury, Ray; Hamilton, Edmond

Sterling, Bruce 1954- .... **CLC 72**
See also AAYA 78; CA 119; CANR 44, 135, 184; CN 7; MTFW 2005; SCFW 2; SFW 4

Sterling, George 1869-1926 .... **TCLC 20**
See also CA 117; 165; DLB 54

Stern, Gerald 1925- .... **CLC 40, 100**
See also AMWS 9; CA 81-84; CANR 28, 94; CP 3, 4, 5, 6, 7; DLB 105; PFS 26; RGAL 4

Stern, Richard (Gustave) 1928- ... **CLC 4, 39**
See also CA 1-4R; CANR 1, 25, 52, 120; CN 1, 2, 3, 4, 5, 6, 7; DLB 218; DLBY 1987; INT CANR-25

Sternberg, Josef von 1894-1969 .... **CLC 20**
See also CA 81-84

Sterne, Laurence 1713-1768 .. **LC 2, 48, 156; WLC 5**
See also BRW 3; BRWC 1; CDBLB 1660-1789; DA; DAB; DAC; DAM MST, NOV; DLB 39; RGEL 2; TEA

Sternheim, (William Adolf) Carl 1878-1942 .... **TCLC 8, 223**
See also CA 105; 193; DLB 56, 118; EWL 3; IDTP; RGWL 2, 3

Stetson, Charlotte Perkins
See Gilman, Charlotte Perkins

Stevens, Margaret Dean
See Aldrich, Bess Streeter

Stevens, Mark 1951- .... **CLC 34**
See also CA 122

Stevens, R. L.
See Hoch, Edward D.

Stevens, Wallace 1879-1955 .... **PC 6, 110; TCLC 3, 12, 45; WLC 5**
See also AMW; AMWR 1; CA 104; 124; CANR 181; CDALB 1929-1941; DA; DA3; DAB; DAC; DAM MST, POET; DLB 54, 342; EWL 3; EXPP; MAL 5; MTCW 1, 2; PAB; PFS 13, 16, 35; RGAL 4; TUS; WP

Stevenson, Anne (Katharine) 1933- .. **CLC 7, 33**
See also BRWS 6; CA 17-20R; CAAS 9; CANR 9, 33, 123; CP 3, 4, 5, 6, 7; CWP; DLB 40; MTCW 1; RHW

Stevenson, Robert Louis
1850-1894 ...... **NCLC 5, 14, 63, 193; PC 84; SSC 11, 51, 126; WLC 5**
See also AAYA 24; BPFB 3; BRW 5; BRWC 1; BRWR 1; BYA 1, 2, 4, 13; CD-BLB 1890-1914; CLR 10, 11, 107; DA; DA3; DAB; DAC; DAM MST, NOV; DLB 18, 57, 141, 156, 174; DLBD 13; GL 3; HGG; JRDA; LAIT 1, 3; MAICYA 1, 2; NFS 11, 20, 33; RGEL 2; RGSF 2; SATA 100; SUFW; TEA; WCH; WLIT 4; WYA; YABC 2; YAW

Stevenson, Robert Louis Balfour
See Stevenson, Robert Louis

Stewart, J(ohn) I(nnes) M(ackintosh)
1906-1994 .... **CLC 7, 14, 32**
See also CA 85-88; 147; CAAS 3; CANR 47; CMW 4; CN 1, 2, 3, 4, 5; DLB 276; MSW; MTCW 1, 2

Stewart, Mary (Florence Elinor)
1916- .... **CLC 7, 35, 117**
See also AAYA 29, 73; BPFB 3; CA 1-4R; CANR 1, 59, 130; CMW 4; CPW; DAB; FANT; RHW; SATA 12; YAW

Stewart, Mary Rainbow
See Stewart, Mary (Florence Elinor)

Stewart, Will
See Williamson, John Stewart

Stifle, June
See Campbell, Maria

Stifter, Adalbert 1805-1868 ... **NCLC 41, 198; SSC 28**
See also CDWLB 2; DLB 133; RGSF 2; RGWL 2, 3

Still, James 1906-2001 .... **CLC 49**
See also CA 65-68; 195; CAAS 17; CANR 10, 26; CSW; DLB 9; DLBY 01; SATA 29; SATA-Obit 127

Sting 1951- .... **CLC 26**
See also CA 167

Stirling, Arthur
See Sinclair, Upton

Stitt, Milan 1941-2009 .... **CLC 29**
See also CA 69-72; 284

Stitt, Milan William
See Stitt, Milan

Stockton, Francis Richard
1834-1902 .... **TCLC 47**
See also AAYA 68; BYA 4, 13; CA 108; 137; DLB 42, 74; DLBD 13; EXPS; MAI-CYA 1, 2; SATA 44; SATA-Brief 32; SFW 4; SSFS 3; SUFW; WCH

Stockton, Frank R.
See Stockton, Francis Richard

Stoddard, Charles
See Kuttner, Henry

Stoker, Abraham
See Stoker, Bram

Stoker, Bram 1847-1912 ... **SSC 62; TCLC 8, 144; WLC 6**
See also AAYA 23; BPFB 3; BRWS 3; BYA 5; CA 105; 150; CDBLB 1890-1914; DA; DA3; DAB; DAC; DAM MST, NOV; DLB 304; GL 3; HGG; LATS 1:1; MTFW 2005; NFS 18; RGEL 2; SATA 29; SUFW; TEA; WLIT 4

Stolz, Mary 1920-2006 .... **CLC 12**
See also AAYA 8, 73; AITN 1; CA 5-8R; 255; CANR 13, 41, 112; JRDA; MAICYA 1, 2; SAAS 3; SATA 10, 71, 133; SATA-Obit 180; YAW

Stolz, Mary Slattery
See Stolz, Mary

Stone, Irving 1903-1989 .... **CLC 7**
See also AITN 1; BPFB 3; CA 1-4R; 129; CAAS 3; CANR 1, 23; CN 1, 2, 3, 4; CPW; DA3; DAM POP; INT CANR-23; MTCW 1, 2; MTFW 2005; RHW; SATA 3; SATA-Obit 64

Stone, Oliver 1946- .... **CLC 73**
See also AAYA 15, 64; CA 110; CANR 55, 125

Stone, Oliver William
See Stone, Oliver

Stone, Robert 1937- .... **CLC 5, 23, 42, 175**
See also AMWS 5; BPFB 3; CA 85-88; CANR 23, 66, 95, 173; CN 4, 5, 6, 7; DLB 152; EWL 3; INT CANR-23; MAL 5; MTCW 1; MTFW 2005

Stone, Robert Anthony
See Stone, Robert

Stone, Ruth 1915- .... **PC 53**
See also CA 45-48; CANR 2, 91; CP 5, 6, 7; CSW; DLB 105; PFS 19

Stone, Zachary
See Follett, Ken

Stoppard, Tom 1937- ... **CLC 1, 3, 4, 5, 8, 15, 29, 34, 63, 91; DC 6, 30; WLC 6**
See also AAYA 63; BRWC 1; BRWR 2; BRWS 1; CA 81-84; CANR 39, 67, 125; CBD; CD 5, 6; CDBLB 1960 to Present; DA; DA3; DAB; DAC; DAM DRAM, MST; DFS 2, 5, 8, 11, 13, 16; DLB 13, 233; DLBY 1985; EWL 3; LATS 1:2; LNFS 3; MTCW 1, 2; MTFW 2005; RGEL 2; TEA; WLIT 4

Storey, David (Malcolm) 1933- . **CLC 2, 4, 5, 8**
See also BRWS 1; CA 81-84; CANR 36; CBD; CD 5, 6; CN 1, 2, 3, 4, 5, 6; DAM DRAM; DLB 13, 14, 207, 245, 326; EWL 3; MTCW 1; RGEL 2

Storm, Hyemeyohsts 1935- ... **CLC 3; NNAL**
See also CA 81-84; CANR 45; DAM MULT

Storm, (Hans) Theodor (Woldsen)
1817-1888 ... **NCLC 1, 195; SSC 27, 106**
See also CDWLB 2; DLB 129; EW; RGSF 2; RGWL 2, 3

Storni, Alfonsina 1892-1938 . **HLC 2; PC 33; TCLC 5**
See also CA 104; 131; DAM MULT; DLB 283; HW 1; LAW

Stoughton, William 1631-1701 .... **LC 38**
See also DLB 24

Stout, Rex (Todhunter) 1886-1975 ..... **CLC 3**
See also AAYA 79; AITN 2; BPFB 3; CA 61-64; CANR 71; CMW 4; CN 2; DLB 306; MSW; RGAL 4

Stow, (Julian) Randolph 1935- ... **CLC 23, 48**
See also CA 13-16R; CANR 33; CN 1, 2, 3, 4, 5, 6, 7; CP 1, 2, 3, 4; DLB 260; MTCW 1; RGEL 2

Stowe, Harriet Beecher 1811-1896 . **NCLC 3, 50, 133, 195; WLC 6**
See also AAYA 53; AMWS 1; CDALB 1865-1917; CLR 131; DA; DA3; DAB; DAC; DAM MST, NOV; DLB 1, 12, 42, 74, 189, 239, 243; EXPN; FL 1:3; JRDA; LAIT 2; MAICYA 1, 2; NFS 6; RGAL 4; TUS; YABC 1

Stowe, Harriet Elizabeth Beecher
See Stowe, Harriet Beecher

Strabo c. 63B.C.-c. 21 .... **CMLC 37, 121**
See also DLB 176

Strachey, (Giles) Lytton
1880-1932 .... **TCLC 12**
See also BRWS 2; CA 110; 178; DLB 149; DLBD 10; EWL 3; MTCW 2; NCFS 4

Stramm, August 1874-1915 .... **PC 50**
See also CA 195; EWL 3

Strand, Mark 1934- .. **CLC 6, 18, 41, 71; PC 63**
See also AMWS 4; CA 21-24R; CANR 40, 65, 100; CP 1, 2, 3, 4, 5, 6, 7; DAM POET; DLB 5; EWL 3; MAL 5; PAB; PFS 9, 18; RGAL 4; SATA 41; TCLE 1:2

Swenson, May 1919-1989 ...... **CLC 4, 14, 61, 106; PC 14**
See also AMWS 4; CA 5-8R; 130; CANR 36, 61, 131; CP 1, 2, 3, 4; DA; DAB; DAC; DAM MST, POET; DLB 5; EXPP; GLL 2; MAL 5; MTCW 1, 2; MTFW 2005; PFS 16, 30; SATA 15; WP

Swift, Augustus
See Lovecraft, H. P.

Swift, Graham 1949- .... **CLC 41, 88, 233**
See also BRWC 2; BRWS 5; CA 117; 122; CANR 46, 71, 128, 181; CN 4, 5, 6, 7; DLB 194, 326; MTCW 2; MTFW 2005; NFS 18; RGSF 2

Swift, Jonathan 1667-1745 ..... **LC 1, 42, 101; PC 9; WLC 6**
See also AAYA 41; BRW 3; BRWC 1; BRWR 1; BYA 5, 14; CDBLB 1660-1789; CLR 53; DA; DA3; DAB; DAC; DAM MST, NOV, POET; DLB 39, 95, 101; EXPN; LAIT 1; NFS 6; PFS 27; RGEL 2; SATA 19; TEA; WCH; WLIT 3

Swinburne, Algernon Charles 1837-1909 ... **PC 24; TCLC 8, 36; WLC 6**
See also BRW 5; CA 105; 140; CDBLB 1832-1890; DA; DA3; DAB; DAC; DAM MST, POET; DLB 35, 57; PAB; RGEL 2; TEA

Swinfen, Ann CLC 34
See also CA 202

Swinnerton, Frank (Arthur) 1884-1982 .... **CLC 31**
See also CA 202; 108; CN 1, 2, 3; DLB 34

Swinnerton, Frank Arthur 1884-1982 .... **CLC 31**
See also CA 108; DLB 34

Swithen, John
See King, Stephen

Sylvia
See Ashton-Warner, Sylvia (Constance)

Symmes, Robert Edward
See Duncan, Robert

Symonds, John Addington 1840-1893 .... **NCLC 34**
See also BRWS 14; DLB 57, 144

Symons, Arthur 1865-1945 .... **TCLC 11**
See also BRWS 14; CA 107; 189; DLB 19, 57, 149; RGEL 2

Symons, Julian (Gustave) 1912-1994 .... **CLC 2, 14, 32**
See also CA 49-52; 147; CAAS 3; CANR 3, 33, 59; CMW 4; CN 1, 2, 3, 4, 5; CP 1, 3, 4; DLB 87, 155; DLBY 1992; MSW; MTCW 1

Synge, Edmund John Millington
See Synge, John Millington

Synge, J. M.
See Synge, John Millington

Synge, John Millington 1871-1909 ...... **DC 2; TCLC 6, 37**
See also BRW 6; BRWR 1; CA 104; 141; CDBLB 1890-1914; DAM DRAM; DFS 18; DLB 10, 19; EWL 3; RGEL 2; TEA; WLIT 4

Syruc, J.
See Milosz, Czeslaw

Szirtes, George 1948- .... **CLC 46; PC 51**
See also CA 109; CANR 27, 61, 117; CP 4, 5, 6, 7

Szymborska, Wislawa 1923- ... **CLC 99, 190; PC 44**
See also AAYA 76; CA 154; CANR 91, 133, 181; CDWLB 4; CWP; CWW 2; DA3; DLB 232, 332; DLBY 1996; EWL 3; MTCW 2; MTFW 2005; PFS 15, 27, 31, 34; RGHL; RGWL 3

T. O., Nik
See Annensky, Innokenty (Fyodorovich)

Tabori, George 1914-2007 .... **CLC 19**
See also CA 49-52; 262; CANR 4, 69; CBD; CD 5, 6; DLB 245; RGHL

Tacitus c. 55-c. 117 .... **CMLC 56**
See also AW 2; CDWLB 1; DLB 211; RGWL 2, 3; WLIT 8

Tadjo, Veronique 1955- .... **BLC 2:3**
See also EWL 3

Tagore, Rabindranath 1861-1941 .... **PC 8; SSC 48; TCLC 3, 53**
See also CA 104; 120; DA3; DAM DRAM, POET; DFS 26; DLB 323, 332; EWL 3; MTCW 1, 2; MTFW 2005; PFS 18; RGEL 2; RGSF 2; RGWL 2, 3; TWA

Taine, Hippolyte Adolphe 1828-1893 .... **NCLC 15**
See also EW 7; GFL 1789 to the Present

Talayesva, Don C. 1890-(?) .... **NNAL**

Talese, Gay 1932- .... **CLC 37, 232**
See also AITN 1; AMWS 17; CA 1-4R; CANR 9, 58, 137, 177; DLB 185; INT CANR-9; MTCW 1, 2; MTFW 2005

Tallent, Elizabeth 1954- .... **CLC 45**
See also CA 117; CANR 72; DLB 130

Tallmountain, Mary 1918-1997 .... **NNAL**
See also CA 146; 161; DLB 193

Tally, Ted 1952- .... **CLC 42**
See also CA 120; 124; CAD; CANR 125; CD 5, 6; INT CA-124

Talvik, Heiti 1904-1947 .... **TCLC 87**
See also EWL 3

Tamayo y Baus, Manuel 1829-1898 .... **NCLC 1**

Tammsaare, A(nton) H(ansen) 1878-1940 .... **TCLC 27**
See also CA 164; CDWLB 4; DLB 220; EWL 3

Tam'si, Tchicaya U
See Tchicaya, Gerald Felix

Tan, Amy 1952- ..... **AAL; CLC 59, 120, 151, 257**
See also AAYA 9, 48; AMWS 10; BEST 89:3; BPFB 3; CA 136; CANR 54, 105, 132; CDALBS; CN 6, 7; CPW 1; DA3; DAM MULT, NOV, POP; DLB 173, 312; EXPN; FL 1:6; FW; LAIT 3, 5; MAL 5; MTCW 2; MTFW 2005; NFS 1, 13, 16, 31; RGAL 4; SATA 75; SSFS 9; YAW

Tan, Amy Ruth
See Tan, Amy

Tandem, Carl Felix
See Spitteler, Carl

Tandem, Felix
See Spitteler, Carl

Tania B.
See Blixen, Karen

Tanizaki, Jun'ichiro 1886-1965 ... **CLC 8, 14, 28; SSC 21**
See also CA 93-96; 25-28R; DLB 180; EWL 3; MJW; MTCW 2; MTFW 2005; RGSF 2; RGWL 2

Tanizaki Jun'ichiro
See Tanizaki, Jun'ichiro

Tannen, Deborah 1945- .... **CLC 206**
See also CA 118; CANR 95

Tannen, Deborah Frances
See Tannen, Deborah

Tanner, William
See Amis, Kingsley

Tante, Dilly
See Kunitz, Stanley

Tao Lao
See Storni, Alfonsina

Tapahonso, Luci 1953- .... **NNAL; PC 65**
See also CA 145; CANR 72, 127; DLB 175

Tarantino, Quentin 1963- .... **CLC 125, 230**
See also AAYA 58; CA 171; CANR 125

Tarantino, Quentin Jerome
See Tarantino, Quentin

Tarassoff, Lev
See Troyat, Henri

Tarbell, Ida 1857-1944 .... **TCLC 40**
See also CA 122; 181; DLB 47

Tarbell, Ida Minerva
See Tarbell, Ida

Tarchetti, Ugo 1839(?)-1869 .... **SSC 119**

Tardieu d'Esclavelles, Louise-Florence-Petronille
See Epinay, Louise d'

Tarkington, (Newton) Booth 1869-1946 .... **TCLC 9**
See also BPFB 3; BYA 3; CA 110; 143; CWRI 5; DLB 9, 102; MAL 5; MTCW 2; NFS 34; RGAL 4; SATA 17

Tarkovskii, Andrei Arsen'evich
See Tarkovsky, Andrei (Arsenyevich)

Tarkovsky, Andrei (Arsenyevich) 1932-1986 .... **CLC 75**
See also CA 127

Tartt, Donna 1964(?)- .... **CLC 76**
See also AAYA 56; CA 142; CANR 135; LNFS 2; MTFW 2005

Tasso, Torquato 1544-1595 .... **LC 5, 94**
See also EFS 2; EW 2; RGWL 2, 3; WLIT 7

Tate, (John Orley) Allen 1899-1979 .. **CLC 2, 4, 6, 9, 11, 14, 24; PC 50**
See also AMW; CA 5-8R; 85-88; CANR 32, 108; CN 1, 2; CP 1, 2; DLB 4, 45, 63; DLBD 17; EWL 3; MAL 5; MTCW 1, 2; MTFW 2005; RGAL 4; RHW

Tate, Ellalice
See Hibbert, Eleanor Alice Burford

Tate, James (Vincent) 1943- ..... **CLC 2, 6, 25**
See also CA 21-24R; CANR 29, 57, 114; CP 1, 2, 3, 4, 5, 6, 7; DLB 5, 169; EWL 3; PFS 10, 15; RGAL 4; WP

Tate, Nahum 1652(?)-1715 .... **LC 109**
See also DLB 80; RGEL 2

Tauler, Johannes c. 1300-1361 ...... **CMLC 37**
See also DLB 179; LMFS 1

Tavel, Ronald 1936-2009 .... **CLC 6**
See also CA 21-24R; 284; CAD; CANR 33; CD 5, 6

Taviani, Paolo 1931- .... **CLC 70**
See also CA 153

Taylor, Bayard 1825-1878 .... **NCLC 89**
See also DLB 3, 189, 250, 254; RGAL 4

Taylor, C(ecil) P(hilip) 1929-1981 .... **CLC 27**
See also CA 25-28R; 105; CANR 47; CBD

Taylor, Edward 1642(?)-1729 ..... **LC 11, 163; PC 63**
See also AMW; DA; DAB; DAC; DAM MST, POET; DLB 24; EXPP; PFS 31; RGAL 4; TUS

Taylor, Eleanor Ross 1920- .... **CLC 5**
See also CA 81-84; CANR 70

Taylor, Elizabeth 1912-1975 .... **CLC 2, 4, 29; SSC 100**
See also CA 13-16R; CANR 9, 70; CN 1, 2; DLB 139; MTCW 1; RGEL 2; SATA 13

Taylor, Frederick Winslow 1856-1915 .... **TCLC 76**
See also CA 188

Taylor, Henry 1942- .... **CLC 44**
See also CA 33-36R; CAAS 7; CANR 31, 178; CP 6, 7; DLB 5; PFS 10

Taylor, Henry Splawn
See Taylor, Henry

Taylor, Kamala
See Markandaya, Kamala

Taylor, Mildred D. 1943- .... **CLC 21**
See also AAYA 10, 47; BW 1; BYA 3, 8; CA 85-88; CANR 25, 115, 136; CLR 9, 59, 90, 144; CSW; DLB 52; JRDA; LAIT 3; MAICYA 1, 2; MTFW 2005; SAAS 5; SATA 135; WYA; YAW

Tournimparte, Alessandra
See Ginzburg, Natalia
Towers, Ivar
See Kornbluth, C(yril) M.
Towne, Robert (Burton) 1936(?)- ..... **CLC 87**
See also CA 108; DLB 44; IDFW 3, 4
Townsend, Sue 1946- .... **CLC 61**
See also AAYA 28; CA 119; 127; CANR
65, 107, 202; CBD; CD 5, 6; CPW; CWD;
DAB; DAC; DAM MST; DLB 271, 352;
INT CA-127; SATA 55, 93; SATA-Brief
48; YAW
Townsend, Susan Lilian
See Townsend, Sue
Townshend, Pete
See Townshend, Peter
Townshend, Peter 1945- .... **CLC 17, 42**
See also CA 107
Townshend, Peter Dennis Blandford
See Townshend, Peter
Tozzi, Federigo 1883-1920 .... **TCLC 31**
See also CA 160; CANR 110; DLB 264;
EWL 3; WLIT 7
Trafford, F. G.
See Riddell, Charlotte
Traherne, Thomas 1637(?)-1674 .. **LC 99; PC 70**
See also BRW 2; BRWS 11; DLB 131;
PAB; RGEL 2
Traill, Catharine Parr 1802-1899 .. **NCLC 31**
See also DLB 99
Trakl, Georg 1887-1914 .... **PC 20; TCLC 5**
See also CA 104; 165; EW 10; EWL 3;
LMFS 2; MTCW 2; RGWL 2, 3
Trambley, Estela Portillo
See Portillo Trambley, Estela
Tranquilli, Secondino
See Silone, Ignazio
Transtroemer, Tomas Gosta
See Transtromer, Tomas
Transtromer, Tomas 1931- .... **CLC 52, 65**
See also CA 117; 129; CAAS 17; CANR
115, 172; CWW 2; DAM POET; DLB
257; EWL 3; PFS 21
Transtromer, Tomas Goesta
See Transtromer, Tomas
Transtromer, Tomas Gosta
See Transtromer, Tomas
Transtromer, Tomas Gosta
See Transtromer, Tomas
Traven, B. 1882(?)-1969 .... **CLC 8, 11**
See also CA 19-20; 25-28R; CAP 2; DLB
9, 56; EWL 3; MTCW 1; RGAL 4
Trediakovsky, Vasilii Kirillovich
1703-1769 .... **LC 68**
See also DLB 150
Treitel, Jonathan 1959- .... **CLC 70**
See also CA 210; DLB 267
Trelawny, Edward John
1792-1881 .... **NCLC 85**
See also DLB 110, 116, 144
Tremain, Rose 1943- .... **CLC 42**
See also CA 97-100; CANR 44, 95, 186;
CN 4, 5, 6, 7; DLB 14, 271; RGSF 2;
RHW
Tremblay, Michel 1942- .... **CLC 29, 102, 225**
See also CA 116; 128; CCA 1; CWW 2;
DAC; DAM MST; DLB 60; EWL 3; GLL
1; MTCW 1, 2; MTFW 2005
Trevanian
See Whitaker, Rod
Trevisa, John c. 1342-c. 1402 .... **LC 139**
See also BRWS 9; DLB 146
Trevor, Frances
See Teasdale, Sara
Trevor, Glen
See Hilton, James

Trevor, William 1928- ... **CLC 1, 2, 3, 4, 5, 6, 7; SSC 21, 58**
See also BRWS 4; CA 9-12R; CANR 4, 37,
55, 76, 102, 139, 195; CBD; CD 5, 6;
DAM NOV; DLB 14, 139; EWL 3; INT
CANR-37; LATS 1:2; MTCW 1, 2;
MTFW 2005; RGEL 2; RGSF 2; SSFS
10; TCLE 1:2; TEA
Triana, Jose 1931(?)- .... **DC 39**
See also CA 131; DLB 305; EWL 3; HW 1;
LAW
Trifonov, Iurii (Valentinovich)
See Trifonov, Yuri (Valentinovich)
Trifonov, Yuri (Valentinovich)
1925-1981 .... **CLC 45**
See also CA 126; 103; DLB 302; EWL 3;
MTCW 1; RGWL 2, 3
Trifonov, Yury Valentinovich
See Trifonov, Yuri (Valentinovich)
Trilling, Diana (Rubin) 1905-1996 . **CLC 129**
See also CA 5-8R; 154; CANR 10, 46; INT
CANR-10; MTCW 1, 2
Trilling, Lionel 1905-1975 ..... **CLC 9, 11, 24; SSC 75**
See also AMWS 3; CA 9-12R; 61-64;
CANR 10, 105; CN 1, 2; DLB 28, 63;
EWL 3; INT CANR-10; MAL 5; MTCW
1, 2; RGAL 4; TUS
Trimball, W. H.
See Mencken, H. L.
Tristan
See Gomez de la Serna, Ramon
Tristram
See Housman, A. E.
Trogdon, William
See Heat-Moon, William Least
Trogdon, William Lewis
See Heat-Moon, William Least
Trogdon, William Lewis
See Heat-Moon, William Least
Trollope, Anthony 1815-1882 .... **NCLC 6, 33, 101, 215; SSC 28, 133; WLC 6**
See also BRW 5; CDBLB 1832-1890; DA;
DA3; DAB; DAC; DAM MST, NOV;
DLB 21, 57, 159; RGEL 2; RGSF 2;
SATA 22
Trollope, Frances 1779-1863 .... **NCLC 30**
See also DLB 21, 166
Trollope, Joanna 1943- .... **CLC 186**
See also CA 101; CANR 58, 95, 149, 191;
CN 7; CPW; DLB 207; RHW
Trotsky, Leon 1879-1940 .... **TCLC 22**
See also CA 118; 167
Trotter, Catharine 1679-1749 .... **LC 8, 165**
See also BRWS 16; DLB 84, 252
Trotter, Wilfred 1872-1939 .... **TCLC 97**
Troupe, Quincy 1943- .... **BLC 2:3**
See also BW 2; CA 113; 124; CANR 43,
90, 126; DLB 41
Trout, Kilgore
See Farmer, Philip Jose
Trow, George William Swift
See Trow, George W.S.
Trow, George W.S. 1943-2006 .... **CLC 52**
See also CA 126; 255; CANR 91
Troyat, Henri 1911-2007 .... **CLC 23**
See also CA 45-48; 258; CANR 2, 33, 67,
117; GFL 1789 to the Present; MTCW 1
Trudeau, Garretson Beekman
See Trudeau, G.B.
Trudeau, Garry
See Trudeau, G.B.
Trudeau, Garry B.
See Trudeau, G.B.
Trudeau, G.B. 1948- .... **CLC 12**
See also AAYA 10, 60; AITN 2; CA 81-84;
CANR 31; SATA 35, 168
Truffaut, Francois 1932-1984 ... **CLC 20, 101**
See also CA 81-84; 113; CANR 34

Trumbo, Dalton 1905-1976 .... **CLC 19**
See also CA 21-24R; 69-72; CANR 10; CN
1, 2; DLB 26; IDFW 3, 4; YAW
Trumbull, John 1750-1831 .... **NCLC 30**
See also DLB 31; RGAL 4
Trundlett, Helen B.
See Eliot, T. S.
Truth, Sojourner 1797(?)-1883 ...... **NCLC 94**
See also DLB 239; FW; LAIT 2
Tryon, Thomas 1926-1991 .... **CLC 3, 11**
See also AITN 1; BPFB 3; CA 29-32R; 135;
CANR 32, 77; CPW; DA3; DAM POP;
HGG; MTCW 1
Tryon, Tom
See Tryon, Thomas
Ts'ao Hsueh-ch'in 1715(?)-1763 .... **LC 1**
Tsurayuki Ed. fl. 10th cent. - .... **PC 73**
Tsvetaeva, Marina 1892-1941 . **PC 14; TCLC 7, 35**
See also CA 104; 128; CANR 73; DLB 295;
EW 11; MTCW 1, 2; PFS 29; RGWL 2, 3
Tsvetaeva Efron, Marina Ivanovna
See Tsvetaeva, Marina
Tuck, Lily 1938- .... **CLC 70**
See also AAYA 74; CA 139; CANR 90, 192
Tuckerman, Frederick Goddard
1821-1873 .... **PC 85**
See also DLB 243; RGAL 4
Tu Fu 712-770 .... **PC 9**
See also DAM MULT; PFS 32; RGWL 2,
3; TWA; WP
Tulsidas, Gosvami 1532(?)-1623 .... **LC 158**
See also RGWL 2, 3
Tunis, John R(oberts) 1889-1975 ..... **CLC 12**
See also BYA 1; CA 61-64; CANR 62; DLB
22, 171; JRDA; MAICYA 1, 2; SATA 37;
SATA-Brief 30; YAW
Tuohy, Frank
See Tuohy, John Francis
Tuohy, John Francis 1925- .... **CLC 37**
See also CA 5-8R; 178; CANR 3, 47; CN
1, 2, 3, 4, 5, 6, 7; DLB 14, 139
Turco, Lewis 1934- .... **CLC 11, 63**
See also CA 13-16R; CAAS 22; CANR 24,
51, 185; CP 1, 2, 3, 4, 5, 6, 7; DLBY
1984; TCLE 1:2
Turco, Lewis Putnam
See Turco, Lewis
Turgenev, Ivan 1818-1883 . **DC 7; NCLC 21, 37, 122; SSC 7, 57; WLC 6**
See also AAYA 58; DA; DAB; DAC; DAM
MST, NOV; DFS 6; DLB 238, 284; EW
6; LATS 1:1; NFS 16; RGSF 2; RGWL 2,
3; TWA
Turgenev, Ivan Sergeevich
See Turgenev, Ivan
Turgot, Anne-Robert-Jacques
1727-1781 .... **LC 26**
See also DLB 314
Turner, Frederick 1943- .... **CLC 48**
See also CA 73-76, 227; CAAE 227; CAAS
10; CANR 12, 30, 56; DLB 40, 282
Turton, James
See Crace, Jim
Tutu, Desmond M(pilo) 1931- .... **BLC 1:3; CLC 80**
See also BW 1, 3; CA 125; CANR 67, 81;
DAM MULT
Tutuola, Amos 1920-1997 .... **BLC 1:3, 2:3; CLC 5, 14, 29; TCLC 188**
See also AAYA 76; AFW; BW 2, 3; CA
9-12R; 159; CANR 27, 66; CDWLB 3;
CN 1, 2, 3, 4, 5, 6; DA3; DAM MULT;
DLB 125; DNFS 2; EWL 3; MTCW 1, 2;
MTFW 2005; RGEL 2; WLIT 2

Twain, Mark 1835-1910 ... **SSC 6, 26, 34, 87, 119; TCLC 6, 12, 19, 36, 48, 59, 161, 185; WLC 6**
See also AAYA 20; AMW; AMWC 1; BPFB 3; BYA 2, 3, 11, 14; CA 104; 135; CDALB 1865-1917; CLR 58, 60, 66; DA; DA3; DAB; DAC; DAM MST, NOV; DLB 12, 23, 64, 74, 186, 189, 11, 343; EXPN; EXPS; JRDA; LAIT 2; LMFS 1; MAICYA 1, 2; MAL 5; NCFS 4; NFS 1, 6; RGAL 4; RGSF 2; SATA 100; SFW 4; SSFS 1, 7, 16, 21, 27; SUFW; TUS; WCH; WYA; YABC 2; YAW

Twohill, Maggie
See Angell, Judie

Tyler, Anne 1941- . **CLC 7, 11, 18, 28, 44, 59, 103, 205, 265**
See also AAYA 18, 60; AMWS 4; BEST 89:1; BPFB 3; BYA 12; CA 9-12R; CANR 11, 33, 53, 109, 132, 168; CDALBS; CN 1, 2, 3, 4, 5, 6, 7; CPW; CSW; DAM NOV, POP; DLB 6, 143; DLBY 1982; EWL 3; EXPN; LATS 1:2; MAL 5; MBL; MTCW 1, 2; MTFW 2005; NFS 2, 7, 10; RGAL 4; SATA 7, 90, 173; SSFS 1, 31; TCLE 1:2; TUS; YAW

Tyler, Royall 1757-1826 .... **NCLC 3**
See also DLB 37; RGAL 4

Tynan, Katharine 1861-1931 ... **TCLC 3, 217**
See also CA 104; 167; DLB 153, 240; FW

Tyndale, William c. 1484-1536 .... **LC 103**
See also DLB 132

Tyutchev, Fyodor 1803-1873 .... **NCLC 34**

Tzara, Tristan 1896-1963 .... **CLC 47; PC 27; TCLC 168**
See also CA 153; 89-92; DAM POET; EWL 3; MTCW 2

Uc de Saint Circ c. 1190B.C.-13th cent.
B.C. .... **CMLC 102**

Uchida, Yoshiko 1921-1992 .... **AAL**
See also AAYA 16; BYA 2, 3; CA 13-16R; 139; CANR 6, 22, 47, 61; CDALBS; CLR 6, 56; CWRI 5; DLB 312; JRDA; MAICYA 1, 2; MTCW 1, 2; MTFW 2005; NFS 26; SAAS 1; SATA 1, 53; SATA-Obit 72; SSFS 31

Udall, Nicholas 1504-1556 .... **LC 84**
See also DLB 62; RGEL 2

Ueda Akinari 1734-1809 .... **NCLC 131**

Uhry, Alfred 1936- .... **CLC 55; DC 28**
See also CA 127; 133; CAD; CANR 112; CD 5, 6; CSW; DA3; DAM DRAM, POP; DFS 11, 15; INT CA-133; MTFW 2005

Ulf, Haerved
See Strindberg, August

Ulf, Harved
See Strindberg, August

Ulibarri, Sabine R(eyes)
1919-2003 .... **CLC 83; HLCS 2**
See also CA 131; 214; CANR 81; DAM MULT; DLB 82; HW 1, 2; RGSF 2

Ulyanov, V. I.
See Lenin

Ulyanov, Vladimir Ilyich
See Lenin

Ulyanov-Lenin
See Lenin

Unamuno, Miguel de 1864-1936 .... **HLC 2; SSC 11, 69; TCLC 2, 9, 148, 237**
See also CA 104; 131; CANR 81; DAM MULT, NOV; DLB 108, 322; EW 8; EWL 3; HW 1, 2; MTCW 1, 2; MTFW 2005; RGSF 2; RGWL 2, 3; SSFS 20; TWA

Unamuno y Jugo, Miguel de
See Unamuno, Miguel de

Uncle Shelby
See Silverstein, Shel

Undercliffe, Errol
See Campbell, Ramsey

Underwood, Miles
See Glassco, John

Undset, Sigrid 1882-1949 .... **TCLC 3, 197; WLC 6**
See also AAYA 77; CA 104; 129; DA; DA3; DAB; DAC; DAM MST, NOV; DLB 293, 332; EW 9; EWL 3; FW; MTCW 1, 2; MTFW 2005; RGWL 2, 3

Ungaretti, Giuseppe 1888-1970 ... **CLC 7, 11, 15; PC 57; TCLC 200**
See also CA 19-20; 25-28R; CAP 2; DLB 114; EW 10; EWL 3; PFS 20; RGWL 2, 3; WLIT 7

Unger, Douglas 1952- .... **CLC 34**
See also CA 130; CANR 94, 155

Unsworth, Barry 1930- .... **CLC 76, 127**
See also BRWS 7; CA 25-28R; CANR 30, 54, 125, 171, 202; CN 6, 7; DLB 194, 326

Unsworth, Barry Forster
See Unsworth, Barry

Updike, John 1932-2009 .... **CLC 1, 2, 3, 5, 7, 9, 13, 15, 23, 34, 43, 70, 139, 214, 278; PC 90; SSC 13, 27, 103; WLC 6**
See also AAYA 36; AMW; AMWC 1; AMWR 1; BPFB 3; BYA 12; CA 1-4R; 282; CABS 1; CANR 4, 33, 51, 94, 133, 197; CDALB 1968-1988; CN 1, 2, 3, 4, 5, 6, 7; CP 1, 2, 3, 4, 5, 6, 7; CPW 1; DA; DA3; DAB; DAC; DAM MST, NOV, POET, POP; DLB 2, 5, 143, 218, 227; DLBD 3; DLBY 1980, 1982, 1997; EWL 3; EXPP; HGG; MAL 5; MTCW 1, 2; MTFW 2005; NFS 12, 24; RGAL 4; RGSF 2; SSFS 3, 19; TUS

Updike, John Hoyer
See Updike, John

Upshaw, Margaret Mitchell
See Mitchell, Margaret

Upton, Mark
See Sanders, Lawrence

Upward, Allen 1863-1926 .... **TCLC 85**
See also CA 117; 187; DLB 36

Urdang, Constance (Henriette)
1922-1996 .... **CLC 47**
See also CA 21-24R; CANR 9, 24; CP 1, 2, 3, 4, 5, 6; CWP

Urfe, Honore d' 1567(?)-1625 .... **LC 132**
See also DLB 268; GFL Beginnings to 1789; RGWL 2, 3

Uriel, Henry
See Faust, Frederick

Uris, Leon 1924-2003 .... **CLC 7, 32**
See also AITN 1, 2; AMWS 20; BEST 89:2; BPFB 3; CA 1-4R; 217; CANR 1, 40, 65, 123; CN 1, 2, 3, 4, 5, 6; CPW 1; DA3; DAM NOV, POP; MTCW 1, 2; MTFW 2005; RGHL; SATA 49; SATA-Obit 146

Urista, Alberto 1947- .... **HLCS 1; PC 34**
See also CA 45-48R; CANR 2, 32; DLB 82; HW 1; LLW

Urista Heredia, Alberto Baltazar
See Urista, Alberto

Urmuz
See Codrescu, Andrei

Urquhart, Guy
See McAlmon, Robert (Menzies)

Urquhart, Jane 1949- .... **CLC 90, 242**
See also CA 113; CANR 32, 68, 116, 157; CCA 1; DAC; DLB 334

Usigli, Rodolfo 1905-1979 .... **HLCS 1**
See also CA 131; DLB 305; EWL 3; HW 1; LAW

Usk, Thomas (?)-1388 .... **CMLC 76**
See also DLB 146

Ustinov, Peter (Alexander)
1921-2004 .... **CLC 1**
See also AITN 1; CA 13-16R; 225; CANR 25, 51; CBD; CD 5, 6; DLB 13; MTCW 2

U Tam'si, Gerald Felix Tchicaya
See Tchicaya, Gerald Felix

U Tam'si, Tchicaya
See Tchicaya, Gerald Felix

Vachss, Andrew 1942- .... **CLC 106**
See also CA 118, 214; CAAE 214; CANR 44, 95, 153, 197; CMW 4

Vachss, Andrew H.
See Vachss, Andrew

Vachss, Andrew Henry
See Vachss, Andrew

Vaculik, Ludvik 1926- .... **CLC 7**
See also CA 53-56; CANR 72; CWW 2; DLB 232; EWL 3

Vaihinger, Hans 1852-1933 .... **TCLC 71**
See also CA 116; 166

Valdez, Luis (Miguel) 1940 ..... **CLC 84; DC 10; HLC 2**
See also CA 101; CAD; CANR 32, 81; CD 5, 6; DAM MULT; DFS 5; DLB 122; EWL 3; HW 1; LAIT 4; LLW

Valenzuela, Luisa 1938- ...... **CLC 31, 104; HLCS 2; SSC 14, 82**
See also CA 101; CANR 32, 65, 123; CDWLB 3; CWW 2; DAM MULT; DLB 113; EWL 3; FW; HW 1, 2; LAW; RGSF 2; RGWL 3; SSFS 29

Valera y Alcala-Galiano, Juan
1824-1905 .... **TCLC 10**
See also CA 106

Valerius Maximus CMLC 64
See also DLB 211

Valery, Ambroise Paul Toussaint Jules
See Valery, Paul

Valery, Paul 1871-1945 ... **PC 9; TCLC 4, 15, 231**
See also CA 104; 122; DA3; DAM POET; DLB 258; EW 8; EWL 3; GFL 1789 to the Present; MTCW 1, 2; MTFW 2005; RGWL 2, 3; TWA

Valle-Inclan, Ramon del 1866-1936 .. **HLC 2; TCLC 5, 228**
See also CA 106; 153; CANR 80; DAM MULT; DLB 134, 322; EW 8; EWL 3; HW 2; RGSF 2; RGWL 2, 3

Valle-Inclan, Ramon Maria del
See Valle-Inclan, Ramon del

Vallejo, Antonio Buero
See Buero Vallejo, Antonio

Vallejo, Cesar 1892-1938 ... **HLC 2; TCLC 3, 56**
See also CA 105; 153; DAM MULT; DLB 290; EWL 3; HW 1; LAW; PFS 26; RGWL 2, 3

Vallejo, Cesar Abraham
See Vallejo, Cesar

Valles, Jules 1832-1885 .... **NCLC 71**
See also DLB 123; GFL 1789 to the Present

Vallette, Marguerite Eymery
1860-1953 .... **TCLC 67**
See also CA 182; DLB 123, 192; EWL 3

Valle Y Pena, Ramon del
See Valle-Inclan, Ramon del

Van Ash, Cay 1918-1994 .... **CLC 34**
See also CA 220

Vanbrugh, Sir John 1664-1726 .... **LC 21**
See also BRW 2; DAM DRAM; DLB 80; IDTP; RGEL 2

Van Campen, Karl
See Campbell, John W(ood, Jr.)

Vance, Gerald
See Silverberg, Robert

Watkins, Paul 1964- .... **CLC 55**
See also CA 132; CANR 62, 98
Watkins, Vernon Phillips
1906-1967 .... **CLC 43**
See also CA 9-10; 25-28R; CAP 1; DLB
20; EWL 3; RGEL 2
Watson, Irving S.
See Mencken, H. L.
Watson, John H.
See Farmer, Philip Jose
Watson, Richard F.
See Silverberg, Robert
Watson, Sheila 1909-1998 .... **SSC 128**
See also AITN 2; CA 155; CCA 1; DAC;
DLB 60
Watts, Ephraim
See Horne, Richard Henry Hengist
Watts, Isaac 1674-1748 .... **LC 98**
See also DLB 95; RGEL 2; SATA 52
Waugh, Auberon (Alexander)
1939-2001 .... **CLC 7**
See also CA 45-48; 192; CANR 6, 22, 92;
CN 1, 2, 3; DLB 14, 194
Waugh, Evelyn 1903-1966 ... **CLC 1, 3, 8, 13,
19, 27, 44, 107; SSC 41; TCLC 229;
WLC 6**
See also AAYA 78; BPFB 3; BRW 7; CA
85-88; 25-28R; CANR 22; CDBLB 1914-
1945; DA; DA3; DAB; DAC; DAM MST,
NOV, POP; DLB 15, 162, 195, 352; EWL
3; MTCW 1, 2; MTFW 2005; NFS 13,
17, 34; RGEL 2; RGSF 2; TEA; WLIT 4
Waugh, Evelyn Arthur St. John
See Waugh, Evelyn
Waugh, Harriet 1944- .... **CLC 6**
See also CA 85-88; CANR 22
Ways, C.R.
See Blount, Roy, Jr.
Waystaff, Simon
See Swift, Jonathan
Webb, Beatrice 1858-1943 .... **TCLC 22**
See also CA 117; 162; DLB 190; FW
Webb, Beatrice Martha Potter
See Webb, Beatrice
Webb, Charles 1939- .... **CLC 7**
See also CA 25-28R; CANR 114, 188
Webb, Charles Richard
See Webb, Charles
Webb, Frank J. NCLC 143
See also DLB 50
Webb, James, Jr.
See Webb, James
Webb, James 1946- .... **CLC 22**
See also CA 81-84; CANR 156
Webb, James H.
See Webb, James
Webb, James Henry
See Webb, James
Webb, Mary Gladys (Meredith)
1881-1927 .... **TCLC 24**
See also CA 182; 123; DLB 34; FW; RGEL
2
Webb, Mrs. Sidney
See Webb, Beatrice
Webb, Phyllis 1927- .... **CLC 18**
See also CA 104; CANR 23; CCA 1; CP 1,
2, 3, 4, 5, 6, 7; CWP; DLB 53
Webb, Sidney 1859-1947 .... **TCLC 22**
See also CA 117; 163; DLB 190
Webb, Sidney James
See Webb, Sidney
Webber, Andrew Lloyd
See Lloyd Webber, Andrew
Weber, Lenora Mattingly
1895-1971 .... **CLC 12**
See also CA 19-20; 29-32R; CAP 1; SATA
2; SATA-Obit 26

Weber, Max 1864-1920 .... **TCLC 69**
See also CA 109; 189; DLB 296
Webster, John 1580(?)-1634(?) ...... **DC 2; LC
33, 84, 124; WLC 6**
See also BRW 2; CDBLB Before 1660; DA;
DAB; DAC; DAM DRAM, MST; DFS
17, 19; DLB 58; IDTP; RGEL 2; WLIT 3
Webster, Noah 1758-1843 .... **NCLC 30**
See also DLB 1, 37, 42, 43, 73, 243
Wedekind, Benjamin Franklin
See Wedekind, Frank
Wedekind, Frank 1864-1918 .... **TCLC 7**
See also CA 104; 153; CANR 121, 122;
CDWLB 2; DAM DRAM; DLB 118; EW
8; EWL 3; LMFS 2; RGWL 2, 3
Wehr, Demaris CLC 65
Weidman, Jerome 1913-1998 .... **CLC 7**
See also AITN 2; CA 1-4R; 171; CAD;
CANR 1; CD 1, 2, 3, 4, 5; DLB 28
Weil, Simone 1909-1943 .... **TCLC 23**
See also CA 117; 159; EW 12; EWL 3; FW;
GFL 1789 to the Present; MTCW 2
Weil, Simone Adolphine
See Weil, Simone
Weininger, Otto 1880-1903 .... **TCLC 84**
Weinstein, Nathan
See West, Nathanael
Weinstein, Nathan von Wallenstein
See West, Nathanael
Weir, Peter (Lindsay) 1944- .... **CLC 20**
See also CA 113; 123
Weiss, Peter (Ulrich) 1916-1982 .. **CLC 3, 15,
51; DC 36; TCLC 152**
See also CA 45-48; 106; CANR 3; DAM
DRAM; DFS 3; DLB 69, 124; EWL 3;
RGHL; RGWL 2, 3
Weiss, Theodore (Russell)
1916-2003 .... **CLC 3, 8, 14**
See also CA 9-12R; 189; 216; CAAE 189;
CAAS 2; CANR 46, 94; CP 1, 2, 3, 4, 5,
6, 7; DLB 5; TCLE 1:2
Welch, (Maurice) Denton
1915-1948 .... **TCLC 22**
See also BRWS 8; CA 121; 148; RGEL 2
Welch, James 1940-2003 .... **CLC 6, 14, 52,
249; NNAL; PC 62**
See also CA 85-88; 219; CANR 42, 66, 107;
CN 5, 6, 7; CP 2, 3, 4, 5, 6, 7; CPW;
DAM MULT, POP; DLB 175, 256; LATS
1:1; NFS 23; RGAL 4; TCWW 1, 2
Welch, James Phillip
See Welch, James
Weld, Angelina Grimke
See Grimke, Angelina Weld
Weldon, Fay 1931- . **CLC 6, 9, 11, 19, 36, 59,
122**
See also BRWS 4; CA 21-24R; CANR 16,
46, 63, 97, 137; CDBLB 1960 to Present;
CN 3, 4, 5, 6, 7; CPW; DAM POP; DLB
14, 194, 319; EWL 3; FW; HGG; INT
CANR-16; MTCW 1, 2; MTFW 2005;
RGEL 2; RGSF 2
Wellek, Rene 1903-1995 .... **CLC 28**
See also CA 5-8R; 150; CAAS 7; CANR 8;
DLB 63; EWL 3; INT CANR-8
Weller, Michael 1942- .... **CLC 10, 53**
See also CA 85-88; CAD; CD 5, 6
Weller, Paul 1958- .... **CLC 26**
Wellershoff, Dieter 1925- .... **CLC 46**
See also CA 89-92; CANR 16, 37
Welles, (George) Orson 1915-1985 .. **CLC 20,
80**
See also AAYA 40; CA 93-96; 117
Wellman, John McDowell 1945- ...... **CLC 65**
See also CA 166; CAD; CD 5, 6; RGAL 4
Wellman, Mac
See Wellman, John McDowell; Wellman,
John McDowell

Wellman, Manly Wade 1903-1986 ... **CLC 49**
See also CA 1-4R; 118; CANR 6, 16, 44;
FANT; SATA 6; SATA-Obit 47; SFW 4;
SUFW
Wells, Carolyn 1869(?)-1942 .... **TCLC 35**
See also CA 113; 185; CMW 4; DLB 11
Wells, H. G. 1866-1946 . **SSC 6, 70; TCLC 6,
12, 19, 133; WLC 6**
See also AAYA 18; BPFB 3; BRW 6; CA
110; 121; CDBLB 1914-1945; CLR 64,
133; DA; DA3; DAB; DAC; DAM MST,
NOV; DLB 34, 70, 156, 178; EWL 3;
EXPS; HGG; LAIT 3; LMFS 2; MTCW
1, 2; MTFW 2005; NFS 17, 20; RGEL 2;
RGSF 2; SATA 20; SCFW 1, 2; SFW 4;
SSFS 3; SUFW; TEA; WCH; WLIT 4;
YAW
Wells, Herbert George
See Wells, H. G.
Wells, Rosemary 1943- .... **CLC 12**
See also AAYA 13; BYA 7, 8; CA 85-88;
CANR 48, 120, 179; CLR 16, 69; CWRI
5; MAICYA 1, 2; SAAS 1; SATA 18, 69,
114, 156, 207; YAW
Wells-Barnett, Ida B(ell)
1862-1931 .... **TCLC 125**
See also CA 182; DLB 23, 221
Welsh, Irvine 1958- .... **CLC 144, 276**
See also CA 173; CANR 146, 196; CN 7;
DLB 271
Welty, Eudora 1909-2001 .... **CLC 1, 2, 5, 14,
22, 33, 105, 220; SSC 1, 27, 51, 111;
WLC 6**
See also AAYA 48; AMW; AMWR 1; BPFB
3; CA 9-12R; 199; CABS 1; CANR 32,
65, 128; CDALB 1941-1968; CN 1, 2, 3,
4, 5, 6, 7; CSW; DA; DA3; DAB; DAC;
DAM MST, NOV; DFS 26; DLB 2, 102,
143; DLBD 12; DLBY 1987, 2001; EWL
3; EXPS; HGG; LAIT 3; MAL 5; MBL;
MTCW 1, 2; MTFW 2005; NFS 13, 15;
RGAL 4; RGSF 2; RHW; SSFS 2, 10, 26;
TUS
Welty, Eudora Alice
See Welty, Eudora
Wen I-to 1899-1946 .... **TCLC 28**
See also EWL 3
Wentworth, Robert
See Hamilton, Edmond
Werfel, Franz (Viktor) 1890-1945 .... **PC 101;
TCLC 8**
See also CA 104; 161; DLB 81, 124; EWL
3; RGWL 2, 3
Wergeland, Henrik Arnold
1808-1845 .... **NCLC 5**
See also DLB 354
Werner, Friedrich Ludwig Zacharias
1768-1823 .... **NCLC 189**
See also DLB 94
Werner, Zacharias
See Werner, Friedrich Ludwig Zacharias
Wersba, Barbara 1932- .... **CLC 30**
See also AAYA 2, 30; BYA 6, 12, 13; CA
29-32R, 182; CAAE 182; CANR 16, 38;
CLR 3, 78; DLB 52; JRDA; MAICYA 1,
2; SAAS 2; SATA 1, 58; SATA-Essay 103;
WYA; YAW
Wertmueller, Lina 1928- .... **CLC 16**
See also CA 97-100; CANR 39, 78
Wescott, Glenway 1901-1987 .. **CLC 13; SSC
35**
See also CA 13-16R; 121; CANR 23, 70;
CN 1, 2, 3, 4; DLB 4, 9, 102; MAL 5;
RGAL 4
Wesker, Arnold 1932- .... **CLC 3, 5, 42**
See also CA 1-4R; CAAS 7; CANR 1, 33;
CBD; CD 5, 6; CDBLB 1960 to Present;
DAB; DAM DRAM; DLB 13, 310, 319;
EWL 3; MTCW 1; RGEL 2; TEA

Wesley, Charles 1707-1788 .... **LC 128**
  See also DLB 95; RGEL 2

Wesley, John 1703-1791 .... **LC 88**
  See also DLB 104

Wesley, Richard (Errol) 1945- .... **CLC 7**
  See also BW 1; CA 57-60; CAD; CANR
  27; CD 5, 6; DLB 38

Wessel, Johan Herman 1742-1785 .... **LC 7**
  See also DLB 300

West, Anthony (Panther)
  1914-1987 .... **CLC 50**
  See also CA 45-48; 124; CANR 3, 19; CN
  1, 2, 3, 4; DLB 15

West, C. P.
  See Wodehouse, P. G.

West, Cornel 1953- .... **BLCS; CLC 134**
  See also CA 144; CANR 91, 159; DLB 246

West, Cornel Ronald
  See West, Cornel

West, Delno C(loyde), Jr. 1936- .... **CLC 70**
  See also CA 57-60

West, Dorothy 1907-1998 ...... **HR 1:3; TCLC
108**
  See also AMWS 18; BW 2; CA 143; 169;
  DLB 76

West, Edwin
  See Westlake, Donald E.

West, (Mary) Jessamyn 1902-1984 ... **CLC 7,
17**
  See also CA 9-12R; 112; CANR 27; CN 1,
  2, 3; DLB 6; DLBY 1984; MTCW 1, 2;
  RGAL 4; RHW; SATA-Obit 37; TCWW
  2; TUS; YAW

West, Morris L(anglo) 1916-1999 ..... **CLC 6,
33**
  See also BPFB 3; CA 5-8R; 187; CANR
  24, 49, 64; CN 1, 2, 3, 4, 5, 6; CPW; DLB
  289; MTCW 1, 2; MTFW 2005

West, Nathanael 1903-1940 ...... **SSC 16, 116;
TCLC 1, 14, 44, 235**
  See also AAYA 77; AMW; AMWR 2; BPFB
  3; CA 104; 125; CDALB 1929-1941;
  DA3; DLB 4, 9, 28; EWL 3; MAL 5;
  MTCW 1, 2; MTFW 2005; NFS 16;
  RGAL 4; TUS

West, Owen
  See Koontz, Dean

West, Paul 1930- .... **CLC 7, 14, 96, 226**
  See also CA 13-16R; CAAS 7; CANR 22,
  53, 76, 89, 136, 205; CN 1, 2, 3, 4, 5, 6,
  7; DLB 14; INT CANR-22; MTCW 2;
  MTFW 2005

West, Rebecca 1892-1983 ... **CLC 7, 9, 31, 50**
  See also BPFB 3; BRWS 3; CA 5-8R; 109;
  CANR 19; CN 1, 2, 3; DLB 36; DLBY
  1983; EWL 3; FW; MTCW 1, 2; MTFW
  2005; NCFS 4; RGEL 2; TEA

Westall, Robert (Atkinson)
  1929-1993 .... **CLC 17**
  See also AAYA 12; BYA 2, 6, 7, 8, 9, 15;
  CA 69-72; 141; CANR 18, 68; CLR 13;
  FANT; JRDA; MAICYA 1, 2; MAICYAS
  1; SAAS 2; SATA 23, 69; SATA-Obit 75;
  WYA; YAW

Westermarck, Edward 1862-1939 . **TCLC 87**

Westlake, Donald E. 1933-2008 ... **CLC 7, 33**
  See also BPFB 3; CA 17-20R; 280; CAAS
  13; CANR 16, 44, 65, 94, 137, 192; CMW
  4; CPW; DAM POP; INT CANR-16;
  MSW; MTCW 2; MTFW 2005

Westlake, Donald E. Edmund
  See Westlake, Donald E.

Westlake, Donald Edwin
  See Westlake, Donald E.

Westlake, Donald Edwin Edmund
  See Westlake, Donald E.

Westmacott, Mary
  See Christie, Agatha

Weston, Allen
  See Norton, Andre

Wetcheek, J. L.
  See Feuchtwanger, Lion

Wetering, Janwillem van de
  See van de Wetering, Janwillem

Wetherald, Agnes Ethelwyn
  1857-1940 .... **TCLC 81**
  See also CA 202; DLB 99

Wetherell, Elizabeth
  See Warner, Susan (Bogert)

Whale, James 1889-1957 .... **TCLC 63**
  See also AAYA 75

Whalen, Philip (Glenn) 1923-2002 .... **CLC 6,
29**
  See also BG 1:3; CA 9-12R; 209; CANR 5,
  39; CP 1, 2, 3, 4, 5, 6, 7; DLB 16; WP

Wharton, Edith 1862-1937 ... **SSC 6, 84, 120;
TCLC 3, 9, 27, 53, 129, 149; WLC 6**
  See also AAYA 25; AMW; AMWC 2;
  AMWR 1; BPFB 3; CA 104; 132; CDALB
  1865-1917; CLR 136; DA; DA3; DAB;
  DAC; DAM MST, NOV; DLB 4, 9, 12,
  78, 189; DLBD 13; EWL 3; EXPS; FL
  1:6; GL 3; HGG; LAIT 2, 3; LATS 1:1;
  MAL 5; MBL; MTCW 1, 2; MTFW 2005;
  NFS 5, 11, 15, 20; RGAL 4; RGSF 2;
  RHW; SSFS 6, 7; SUFW; TUS

Wharton, Edith Newbold Jones
  See Wharton, Edith

Wharton, James
  See Mencken, H. L.

Wharton, William 1925-2008 ..... **CLC 18, 37**
  See also CA 93-96; 278; CN 4, 5, 6, 7;
  DLBY 1980; INT CA-93-96

Wheatley, Phillis 1753(?)-1784 .... **BLC 1:3;
LC 3, 50; PC 3; WLC 6**
  See also AFAW 1, 2; AMWS 20; CDALB
  1640-1865; DA; DA3; DAC; DAM MST,
  MULT, POET; DLB 31, 50; EXPP; FL
  1:1; PFS 13, 29; RGAL 4

Wheatley Peters, Phillis
  See Wheatley, Phillis

Wheelock, John Hall 1886-1978 .... **CLC 14**
  See also CA 13-16R; 77-80; CANR 14; CP
  1, 2; DLB 45; MAL 5

Whim-Wham
  See Curnow, (Thomas) Allen (Monro)

Whisp, Kennilworthy
  See Rowling, J.K.

Whitaker, Rod 1931-2005 .... **CLC 29**
  See also CA 29-32R; 246; CANR 45, 153;
  CMW 4

Whitaker, Rodney
  See Whitaker, Rod

Whitaker, Rodney William
  See Whitaker, Rod

White, Babington
  See Braddon, Mary Elizabeth

White, E. B. 1899-1985 .... **CLC 10, 34, 39**
  See also AAYA 62; AITN 2; AMWS 1; CA
  13-16R; 116; CANR 16, 37; CDALBS;
  CLR 1, 21, 107; CPW; DA3; DAM POP;
  DLB 11, 22; EWL 3; FANT; MAICYA 1,
  2; MAL 5; MTCW 1, 2; MTFW 2005;
  NCFS 5; RGAL 4; SATA 2, 29, 100;
  SATA-Obit 44; TUS

White, Edmund 1940- .... **CLC 27, 110**
  See also AAYA 7; CA 45-48; CANR 3, 19,
  36, 62, 107, 133, 172; CN 5, 6, 7; DA3;
  DAM POP; DLB 227; MTCW 1, 2;
  MTFW 2005

White, Edmund Valentine III
  See White, Edmund

White, Elwyn Brooks
  See White, E. B.

White, Hayden V. 1928- .... **CLC 148**
  See also CA 128; CANR 135; DLB 246

White, Patrick 1912-1990 . **CLC 3, 4, 5, 7, 9,
18, 65, 69; SSC 39; TCLC 176**
  See also BRWS 1; CA 81-84; 132; CANR
  43; CN 1, 2, 3, 4; DLB 260, 332; EWL 3;
  MTCW 1; RGEL 2; RGSF 2; RHW;
  TWA; WWE 1

White, Patrick Victor Martindale
  See White, Patrick

White, Phyllis Dorothy James
  See James, P. D.

White, T(erence) H(anbury)
  1906-1964 .... **CLC 30**
  See also AAYA 22; BPFB 3; BYA 4, 5; CA
  73-76; CANR 37; CLR 139; DLB 160;
  FANT; JRDA; LAIT 1; MAICYA 1, 2;
  NFS 30; RGEL 2; SATA 12; SUFW 1;
  YAW

White, Terence de Vere 1912-1994 ... **CLC 49**
  See also CA 49-52; 145; CANR 3

White, Walter
  See White, Walter F(rancis)

White, Walter F(rancis)
  1893-1955 ..... **BLC 1:3; HR 1:3; TCLC
15**
  See also BW 1; CA 115; 124; DAM MULT;
  DLB 51

White, William Hale 1831-1913 ..... **TCLC 25**
  See also CA 121; 189; DLB 18; RGEL 2

Whitehead, Alfred North
  1861-1947 .... **TCLC 97**
  See also CA 117; 165; DLB 100, 262

Whitehead, Colson 1969- ...... **BLC 2:3; CLC
232**
  See also CA 202; CANR 162

Whitehead, E(dward) A(nthony)
  1933- .... **CLC 5**
  See also CA 65-68; CANR 58, 118; CBD;
  CD 5, 6; DLB 310

Whitehead, Ted
  See Whitehead, E(dward) A(nthony)

Whiteman, Roberta J. Hill 1947- ...... **NNAL**
  See also CA 146

Whitemore, Hugh (John) 1936- .... **CLC 37**
  See also CA 132; CANR 77; CBD; CD 5,
  6; INT CA-132

Whitman, Sarah Helen (Power)
  1803-1878 .... **NCLC 19**
  See also DLB 1, 243

Whitman, Walt 1819-1892 .. **NCLC 4, 31, 81,
205; PC 3, 91; WLC 6**
  See also AAYA 42; AMW; AMWR 1;
  CDALB 1640-1865; DA; DA3; DAB;
  DAC; DAM MST, POET; DLB 3, 64,
  224, 250; EXPP; LAIT 2; LMFS 1; PAB;
  PFS 2, 3, 13, 22, 31; RGAL 4; SATA 20;
  TUS; WP; WYAS 1

Whitman, Walter
  See Whitman, Walt

Whitney, Isabella fl. 1565-fl. 1575 ..... **LC 130**
  See also DLB 136

Whitney, Phyllis A. 1903-2008 .... **CLC 42**
  See also AAYA 36; AITN 2; BEST 90:3;
  CA 1-4R; 269; CANR 3, 25, 38, 60; CLR
  59; CMW 4; CPW; DA3; DAM POP;
  JRDA; MAICYA 1, 2; MTCW 2; RHW;
  SATA 1, 30; SATA-Obit 189; YAW

Whitney, Phyllis Ayame
  See Whitney, Phyllis A.

Whittemore, (Edward) Reed, Jr.
  1919- .... **CLC 4**
  See also CA 9-12R; 219; CAAE 219; CAAS
  8; CANR 4, 119; CP 1, 2, 3, 4, 5, 6, 7;
  DLB 5; MAL 5

Whittier, John Greenleaf
  1807-1892 .... **NCLC 8, 59; PC 93**
  See also AMWS 1; DLB 1, 243; RGAL 4

Whittlebot, Hernia
  See Coward, Noel

Wicker, Thomas Grey
See Wicker, Tom

Wicker, Tom 1926- .... **CLC 7**
See also CA 65-68; CANR 21, 46, 141, 179

Wickham, Anna 1883-1947 .... **PC 110**
See also DLB 240

Wicomb, Zoe 1948- .... **BLC 2:3**
See also CA 127; CANR 106, 167; DLB 225

Wideman, John Edgar 1941- .. **BLC 1:3, 2:3; CLC 5, 34, 36, 67, 122; SSC 62**
See also AFAW 1, 2; AMWS 10; BPFB 4; BW 2, 3; CA 85-88; CANR 14, 42, 67, 109, 140, 187; CN 4, 5, 6, 7; DAM MULT; DLB 33, 143; MAL 5; MTCW 2; MTFW 2005; RGAL 4; RGSF 2; SSFS 6, 12, 24; TCLE 1:2

Wiebe, Rudy 1934- . **CLC 6, 11, 14, 138, 263**
See also CA 37-40R; CANR 42, 67, 123, 202; CN 1, 2, 3, 4, 5, 6, 7; DAC; DAM MST; DLB 60; RHW; SATA 156

Wiebe, Rudy Henry
See Wiebe, Rudy

Wieland, Christoph Martin 1733-1813 .... **NCLC 17, 177**
See also DLB 97; EW 4; LMFS 1; RGWL 2, 3

Wiene, Robert 1881-1938 .... **TCLC 56**

Wieners, John 1934- .... **CLC 7**
See also BG 1:3; CA 13-16R; CP 1, 2, 3, 4, 5, 6, 7; DLB 16; WP

Wiesel, Elie 1928- ...... **CLC 3, 5, 11, 37, 165; WLCS**
See also AAYA 7, 54; AITN 1; CA 5-8R; CAAS 4; CANR 8, 40, 65, 125; CDALBS; CWW 2; DA; DA3; DAB; DAC; DAM MST, NOV; DLB 83, 299; DLBY 1987; EWL 3; INT CANR-8; LAIT 4; MTCW 1, 2; MTFW 2005; NCFS 4; NFS 4; RGHL; RGWL 3; SATA 56; YAW

Wiesel, Eliezer
See Wiesel, Elie

Wiggins, Marianne 1947- .... **CLC 57**
See also AAYA 70; BEST 89:3; CA 130; CANR 60, 139, 180; CN 7; DLB 335

Wigglesworth, Michael 1631-1705 .... **LC 106**
See also DLB 24; RGAL 4

Wiggs, Susan **CLC 70**
See also CA 201; CANR 173

Wight, James Alfred
See Herriot, James

Wilbur, Richard 1921- .. **CLC 3, 6, 9, 14, 53, 110; PC 51**
See also AAYA 72; AMWS 3; CA 1-4R; CABS 2; CANR 2, 29, 76, 93, 139; CDALBS; CP 1, 2, 3, 4, 5, 6, 7; DA; DAB; DAC; DAM MST, POET; DLB 5, 169; EWL 3; EXPP; INT CANR-29; MAL 5; MTCW 1, 2; MTFW 2005; PAB; PFS 11, 12, 16, 29; RGAL 4; SATA 9, 108; WP

Wilbur, Richard Purdy
See Wilbur, Richard

Wild, Peter 1940- .... **CLC 14**
See also CA 37-40R; CP 1, 2, 3, 4, 5, 6, 7; DLB 5

Wilde, Oscar 1854(?)-1900 ... **DC 17; SSC 11, 77; TCLC 1, 8, 23, 41, 175; WLC 6**
See also AAYA 49; BRW 5; BRWC 1, 2; BRWR 2; BYA 15; CA 104; 119; CANR 112; CDBLB 1890-1914; CLR 114; DA; DA3; DAB; DAC; DAM DRAM, MST, NOV; DFS 4, 8, 9, 21; DLB 10, 19, 34, 57, 141, 156, 190, 344; EXPS; FANT; GL 3; LATS 1:1; NFS 20; RGEL 2; RGSF 2; SATA 24; SSFS 7; SUFW; TEA; WCH; WLIT 4

Wilde, Oscar Fingal O'Flahertie Willis
See Wilde, Oscar

Wilder, Billy
See Wilder, Samuel

Wilder, Samuel 1906-2002 .... **CLC 20**
See also AAYA 66; CA 89-92; 205; DLB 26

Wilder, Stephen
See Marlowe, Stephen

Wilder, Thornton 1897-1975 ..... **CLC 1, 5, 6, 10, 15, 35, 82; DC 1, 24; WLC 6**
See also AAYA 29; AITN 2; AMW; CA 13-16R; 61-64; CAD; CANR 40, 132; CDALBS; CN 1, 2; DA; DA3; DAB; DAC; DAM DRAM, MST, NOV; DFS 1, 4, 16; DLB 4, 7, 9, 228; DLBY 1997; EWL 3; LAIT 3; MAL 5; MTCW 1, 2; MTFW 2005; NFS 24; RGAL 4; RHW; WYAS 1

Wilder, Thornton Niven
See Wilder, Thornton

Wilding, Michael 1942- ...... **CLC 73; SSC 50**
See also CA 104; CANR 24, 49, 106; CN 4, 5, 6, 7; DLB 325; RGSF 2

Wiley, Richard 1944- .... **CLC 44**
See also CA 121; 129; CANR 71

Wilhelm, Kate
See Wilhelm, Katie

Wilhelm, Katie 1928- .... **CLC 7**
See also AAYA 20; BYA 16; CA 37-40R; CAAS 5; CANR 17, 36, 60, 94; DLB 8; INT CANR-17; MTCW 1; SCFW 2; SFW 4

Wilhelm, Katie Gertrude
See Wilhelm, Katie

Wilkins, Mary
See Freeman, Mary E(leanor) Wilkins

Willard, Nancy 1936- .... **CLC 7, 37**
See also BYA 5; CA 89-92; CANR 10, 39, 68, 107, 152, 186; CLR 5; CP 2, 3, 4, 5; CWP; CWRI 5; DLB 5, 52; FANT; MAICYA 1, 2; MTCW 1; SATA 37, 71, 127, 191; SATA-Brief 30; SUFW 2; TCLE 1:2

William of Malmesbury c. 1090B.C.-c. 1140B.C. .... **CMLC 57**

William of Moerbeke c. 1215-c. 1286 .... **CMLC 91**

William of Ockham 1290-1349 ..... **CMLC 32**

Williams, Ben Ames 1889-1953 ..... **TCLC 89**
See also CA 183; DLB 102

Williams, Charles
See Collier, James Lincoln

Williams, Charles 1886-1945 ..... **TCLC 1, 11**
See also BRWS 9; CA 104; 163; DLB 100, 153, 255; FANT; RGEL 2; SUFW 1

Williams, Charles Walter Stansby
See Williams, Charles

Williams, C.K. 1936- .... **CLC 33, 56, 148**
See also CA 37-40R; CAAS 26; CANR 57, 106; CP 1, 2, 3, 4, 5, 6, 7; DAM POET; DLB 5; MAL 5

Williams, Ella Gwendolen Rees
See Rhys, Jean

Williams, Emlyn 1905-1987 .... **CLC 15**
See also CA 104; 123; CANR 36; DAM DRAM; DLB 10, 77; IDTP; MTCW 1

Williams, George Emlyn
See Williams, Emlyn

Williams, Hank 1923-1953 .... **TCLC 81**
See Williams, Hiram King
See also CA 188

Williams, Helen Maria 1761-1827 .... **NCLC 135**
See also DLB 158

Williams, Hiram King 1923-1953
See Williams, Hank

Williams, Hugo (Mordaunt) 1942- ... **CLC 42**
See also CA 17-20R; CANR 45, 119; CP 1, 2, 3, 4, 5, 6, 7; DLB 40

Williams, J. Walker
See Wodehouse, P. G.

Williams, John A(lfred) 1925- .... **BLC 1:3; CLC 5, 13**
See also AFAW 2; BW 2, 3; CA 53-56; 195; CAAE 195; CAAS 3; CANR 6, 26, 51, 118; CN 1, 2, 3, 4, 5, 6, 7; CSW; DAM MULT; DLB 2, 33; EWL 3; INT CANR-6; MAL 5; RGAL 4; SFW 4

Williams, Jonathan 1929-2008 .... **CLC 13**
See also CA 9-12R; 270; CAAS 12; CANR 8, 108; CP 1, 2, 3, 4, 5, 6, 7; DLB 5

Williams, Jonathan Chamberlain
See Williams, Jonathan

Williams, Joy 1944- .... **CLC 31**
See also CA 41-44R; CANR 22, 48, 97, 168; DLB 335; SSFS 25

Williams, Norman 1952- .... **CLC 39**
See also CA 118

Williams, Roger 1603(?)-1683 .... **LC 129**
See also DLB 24

Williams, Sherley Anne 1944-1999 .... **BLC 1:3; CLC 89**
See also AFAW 2; BW 2, 3; CA 73-76; 185; CANR 25, 82; DAM MULT, POET; DLB 41; INT CANR-25; SATA 78; SATA-Obit 116

Williams, Shirley
See Williams, Sherley Anne

Williams, Tennessee 1911-1983 . **CLC 1, 2, 5, 7, 8, 11, 15, 19, 30, 39, 45, 71, 111; DC 4; SSC 81; WLC 6**
See also AAYA 31; AITN 1, 2; AMW; AMWC 1; CA 5-8R; 108; CABS 3; CAD; CANR 31, 132, 174; CDALB 1941-1968; CN 1, 2, 3; DA; DA3; DAB; DAC; DAM DRAM, MST; DFS 17; DLB 7, 341; DLBD 4; DLBY 1983; EWL 3; GLL 1; LAIT 4; LATS 1:2; MAL 5; MTCW 1, 2; MTFW 2005; RGAL 4; TUS

Williams, Thomas (Alonzo) 1926-1990 .... **CLC 14**
See also CA 1-4R; 132; CANR 2

Williams, Thomas Lanier
See Williams, Tennessee

Williams, William C.
See Williams, William Carlos

Williams, William Carlos 1883-1963 .... **CLC 1, 2, 5, 9, 13, 22, 42, 67; PC 7, 109; SSC 31; WLC 6**
See also AAYA 46; AMW; AMWR 1; CA 89-92; CANR 34; CDALB 1917-1929; DA; DA3; DAB; DAC; DAM MST, POET; DLB 4, 16, 54, 86; EWL 3; EXPP; MAL 5; MTCW 1, 2; MTFW 2005; NCFS 4; PAB; PFS 1, 6, 11, 34; RGAL 4; RGSF 2; SSFS 27; TUS; WP

Williamson, David (Keith) 1942- ..... **CLC 56**
See also CA 103; CANR 41; CD 5, 6; DLB 289

Williamson, Jack
See Williamson, John Stewart

Williamson, John Stewart 1908-2006 .... **CLC 29**
See also AAYA 76; CA 17-20R; 255; CAAS 8; CANR 23, 70, 153; DLB 8; SCFW 1, 2; SFW 4

Willie, Frederick
See Lovecraft, H. P.

Willingham, Calder (Baynard, Jr.) 1922-1995 .... **CLC 5, 51**
See also CA 5-8R; 147; CANR 3; CN 1, 2, 3, 4, 5; CSW; DLB 2, 44; IDFW 3, 4; MTCW 1

Willis, Charles
See Clarke, Arthur C.

Willis, Nathaniel Parker 1806-1867 .... **NCLC 194**
See also DLB 3, 59, 73, 74, 183, 250; DLBD 13; RGAL 4

Willy
See Colette

PC Cumulative Nationality Index

Nationality Index

PC -109 Title Index